Updated AP® Edition

EDITION 4

Gateways to Democracy

AN INTRODUCTION TO AMERICAN GOVERNMENT

JOHN G. **GEER**
VANDERBILT UNIVERSITY

RICHARD **HERRERA**
ARIZONA STATE UNIVERSITY

WENDY J. **SCHILLER**
BROWN UNIVERSITY

JEFFREY A. **SEGAL**
STONY BROOK UNIVERSITY

Australia • Brazil • Mexico • Singapore • United Kingdom • United States

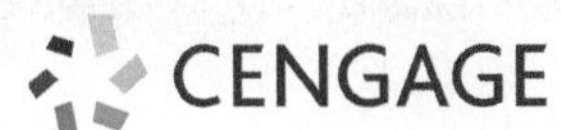

***Gateways to Democracy: An Introduction to American Government,* 4th Edition, Updated AP® Edition**
John G. Geer, Richard Herrera, Wendy J. Schiller, Jeffrey A. Segal

Product Manager: Brad Pothoff

Product Manager, Advanced & Elective Products Program: Jeff Werle

Product Assistant: Emma Collins

Senior Content Developer, Advanced & Elective Products Program: Caitlin Ghegan

Senior Product Marketing Manager: David Lagrange

Senior Content Project Manager: Andrea Wagner

Manufacturing Planner: Julio Esperas

IP Analyst: Alexandra Ricciardi

IP Project Manager: Betsy Hathaway

Production Service: MPS Limited

Compositor: MPS Limited

Art Director: Cate Barr

Text Designer: Diane Beasley

Cover Designer: Sarah Cole

Student Edition:
ISBN: 978-1-337-09800-7

Cengage
20 Channel Center Street
Boston, MA 02210
USA

Cengage is a leading provider of customized learning solutions with employees residing in nearly 40 different countries and sales in more than 125 countries around the world. Find your local representative at **www.cengage.com.**

Cengage products are represented in Canada by **Nelson Education, Ltd.**

To learn more about Cengage platforms and services, visit **www.cengage.com.**

Printed in the United States of America
Print Number: 01 Print Year: 2018

Brief Contents

CHAPTER 1 Gateways to American Democracy 2
CHAPTER 2 The Constitution 26
CHAPTER 3 Federalism 62
CHAPTER 4 Civil Liberties 96
CHAPTER 5 Civil Rights 134
CHAPTER 6 Public Opinion 176
CHAPTER 7 The News and Social Media 212
CHAPTER 8 Interest Groups 248
CHAPTER 9 Political Parties 284
CHAPTER 10 Elections and Campaigns 320
CHAPTER 11 Voting and Participation 356
CHAPTER 12 Congress 396
CHAPTER 13 The Presidency 438
CHAPTER 14 The Bureaucracy 480
CHAPTER 15 The Judiciary 514
CHAPTER 16 Economic, Domestic, and Foreign Policy 554

APPENDIX A The Declaration of Independence 598
APPENDIX B The Constitution of the United States 602
APPENDIX C *Federalist Papers* 10 and 51 618
APPENDIX D Electoral Maps, 2000–2016 626

Contents

Letter to the Teacher xi
Letter to the Student xiii
Resources for Teachers xiv
Acknowledgments xvi
Reviewers xvii
About the Authors xviii
Correlation of *Gateways to Democracy* Updated 4th edition to the AP® U.S. Government and Politics Curriculum Framework xix

CHAPTER 1 Gateways to American Democracy 2

1.1 Gateways: Evaluating the American Political System 4

1.2 Democracy and the American Constitutional System 6

Liberty and Order 6
The Constitution as Gatekeeper 7

1.3 American Political Culture 11

1.4 Responsiveness and Equality: Does American Democracy Work? 13

1.5 The Demands of Democratic Government 17

Self-Interest and Civic Interest 17
Politics and the Public Sphere 19

Your Gateway to American Democracy 23

CHAPTER 2 The Constitution 26

2.1 Before the Constitution 28

The British Constitution 28
Toward Independence 28
The Declaration of Independence 31
The Articles of Confederation 32

2.2 The Constitutional Convention 33

The Delegates 33
Large Versus Small States 34
Nation Versus State 35
North Versus South 36
Gates Against Popular Influence 37
The Ratification Process 39

2.3 Government Under the Constitution 40

The Structure of Government 40
The Amendment Process 43
The Partition of Power 45

2.4 The Ratification Debates 48

Federalists and Antifederalists 48
Consolidation of Federal Authority 48
The Scope of Executive Authority 49
The Scope of Legislative Authority 49
The Lack of a Bill of Rights 50

2.5 The Responsive Constitution 51

The Bill of Rights 51
The Civil War Amendments 52
Amendments That Expand Public Participation 53
Constitutional Interpretation 53
Future Amendments 53
Institutional Changes 55

The Constitution and Democracy 58

CHAPTER 3 Federalism 62

3.1 Why Federalism? 64

Why Unify? 64
Confederal, Unitary, and Federal Systems 65

3.2 Constitutional Framework 66

Grants of Power 67
Limits on Power 68
Groundwork for Relationships 69

3.3 The Changing Nature of American Federalism 73

Nationalization in the Founding Generation (Approximately 1789–1832) 74
The Revolt Against National Authority: Nullification, Slavery, and the Civil War (Approximately 1832–1865) 75
Dual Federalism (Approximately 1865–1932) 78
Cooperative Federalism: The New Deal and Civil Rights (Approximately 1932–1969) 78
The New Federalism (Approximately 1969–1993) 80
Summing Up: Were the Antifederalists Correct? 83

3.4 State and Local Governments 83

State Executive Branches 85
State Legislative Branches 87
State Judicial Branches 87

Local Governments 89
Direct Democracy 91
Federalism and Democracy 92

CHAPTER 4 Civil Liberties 96

4.1 What Are Civil Liberties? 98
Civil Liberties and Civil Rights 98
Balancing Liberty and Order 99
Constitutional Rights 99
The Bill of Rights and the States 99
4.2 Civil Liberties in Times of Crisis 102
From Revolution to Civil War 102
The World Wars 103
The Cold War and Vietnam 104
The War on Terror 105
Civil Liberties and American Values 106
4.3 The First Amendment and Freedom of Expression 106
Freedom of Speech 106
Freedom of the Press 114
The Right of Association 116
4.4 Religious Freedom 116
Free Exercise 117
The Establishment of Religion 118
4.5 The Right to Keep and Bear Arms 120
4.6 Criminal Procedure 121
Investigations 121
Trial Procedures 123
Verdict, Punishment, and Appeal 124
4.7 The Right to Privacy 126
Birth Control and Abortion 126
Homosexual Behavior 129
The Right to Die 129
Student Housing 129
Civil Liberties and Democracy 129

CHAPTER 5 Civil Rights 134

5.1 What Are Civil Rights? 136
Civil Rights and Civil Liberties 136
The Constitution and Civil Rights 136
5.2 Legal Restrictions on Civil Rights 137
Slavery 138
Restrictions on Citizenship 139
Racial Segregation and Discrimination 142
Ethnic Segregation and Discrimination 143
Women's Suffrage 144
Continued Gender Discrimination 146
5.3 The Expansion of Equal Protection 149
State Action 149
Judicial Review 149
5.4 The End of Legal Restrictions on Civil Rights 150
Dismantling Public Discrimination Based on Race 151
Dismantling Private Discrimination Based on Race 152
Dismantling Voting Barriers Based on Race 155
Dismantling Public Discrimination Based on Ethnicity 157
Dismantling Voting Barriers Based on Ethnicity 158
Dismantling Private Discrimination Based on Ethnicity 161
Dismantling Discrimination Based on Gender 162
5.5 Frontiers in Civil Rights 165
Sexual Orientation, Same-Sex Marriage, and Transgender Rights 166
Disability Rights 168
Racial and Religious Profiling 169
Voting Rights for Felons 170
Undocumented Immigrants 171
Civil Rights and Democracy 172

CHAPTER 6 Public Opinion 176

6.1 The Power of Public Opinion 178
The Power of Presidential Approval 178
What Is Public Opinion? 179
The Public's Support of Government 180
6.2 Public Opinion Polls 182
Gauging Public Opinion in the Past 182
Scientific Polling and the Growth of Survey Research 183
Types of Polls 184
Error in Polls 186
6.3 What Drives Public Opinion? 188
Social and Political Environment 188
Generational Effects 189
Self-Interest and Rationality 190
Elites 191
6.4 The Shape of Public Opinion 193
Partisanship 194
Ideology 195
Is the Public Informed? 196
Is the Public Polarized? 198
6.5 Group Differences 202
Socioeconomic Status 202
Age 202
Religion 203

Gender 203
Race and Ethnicity 204
Education 207
Public Opinion and Democracy 208

CHAPTER 7 The News and Social Media 212

7.1 Political News 214
What Are the Mass Media? 214
Functions of the News 214
7.2 The Law and the Free Press 216
7.3 The History of the Press in America 219
The Colonial Era, 1620 to 1750 219
The Founding Era, 1750 to 1790 221
The Partisan Era, 1790 to 1900 222
The Professional Era, 1900 to 1950 223
The Television Era, 1950 to 2000 224
7.4 Mass Media in the Twenty-First Century 226
The Changing Media Environment 226
The Decline of Newspapers 227
The Durability of Radio 228
The Transformation of TV News 230
Infotainment 231
Blogs 231
Social Networking 232
The News Media and Latinos 234
The News Media and Millennials 235
7.5 The Impact of the News Media on the Public 236
The Propaganda Model 236
The Minimal Effects Model 237
The Not-So-Minimal Effects Model 237
7.6 Evaluating the News Media 239
Are the Media Biased? 239
Quality of Information 241
Implications of the Internet 243
The Era of Media Choice 243
The News, Social Media, and Democracy 244

CHAPTER 8 Interest Groups 248

8.1 Interest Groups and Politics 250
What Are Interest Groups? 250
The Right to Assemble and to Petition 250
The History of Interest Groups 252
8.2 Types of Interest Groups 254
Economic Interest Groups 254
Ideological and Issue-Oriented Groups 257
Foreign Policy and International Groups 258
8.3 What Interest Groups Do 259
Inform 259
Lobby 260
Campaign Activities 265
8.4 The Impact of Interest Groups on Democratic Processes 269
Natural Balance or Disproportionate Power 269
Self-Service or Public Service 271
Open or Closed Routes of Influence 273
8.5 Characteristics of Successful Interest Groups 276
Leadership Accountability 276
Membership Stability 277
Financial Stability 279
Influence in the Public Sphere 279
Interest Groups and Democracy 280

CHAPTER 9 Political Parties 284

9.1 The Role of Political Parties in American Democracy 286
What Are Political Parties? 286
What Political Parties Do 287
The Party Nomination Process 289
9.2 The Dynamics of Early Party Development 295
Political Factions: Federalist Versus Antifederalist 295
Thomas Jefferson, Andrew Jackson, and the Emergence of the Democratic Party 296
The Antislavery Movement and the Formation of the Republican Party 297
Party Loyalty and Patronage 298
Reform and the Erosion of Party Control 299
9.3 The Effects of a Two-Party System 300
Limited Political Choice 300
The Structural Limits 301
The Role of Third Parties 302
The Tea Party 304
Party Control of Presidential Nominations 305
Obstacles to Third Parties and Independents 305
Challenges to Party Power from Interest Groups 307
9.4 Party Alignment and Ideology 308
The Parties After the Civil War 308
The New Deal and the Role of Ideology in Party Politics 309
Civil Rights, the Great Society, and Nixon's Southern Strategy 310

The Reagan Revolution and Conservative Party Politics 313
The Modern Partisan Landscape 314
Political Parties and Democracy 316

CHAPTER 10 Elections and Campaigns 320

10.1 The Constitutional Requirements for Elections 322
Presidential Elections 322
Congressional Elections 327
Other Elections 329
10.2 Presidential Campaigns 330
Evolution of the Modern Campaign 330
The Decision to Run and the Invisible Primary 331
Caucuses and Primaries 333
The National Convention 335
Presidential Debates 335
10.3 Issues in Presidential Campaigns 336
Fundraising and Money 336
Swing Voters and States 338
Microtargeting 339
Campaign Issues 340
Negativity 341
Polls and Prediction Models 342
10.4 Congressional Campaigns 343
The Decision to Run and the Primaries 343
The Fall Campaign 345
10.5 Issues in Congressional Campaigns 346
Fundraising and Money 346
The Role of Political Parties 347
Incumbency Advantage 347
Relative Lack of Interest 349
Elections, Campaigns, and Democracy 352

CHAPTER 11 Voting and Participation 356

11.1 The Practice and Theory of Voting 358
The Constitution and Voting 358
Competing Views of Participation 358
11.2 The History of Voting in America 359
Expansion of Voting, 1790s to 1870 360
The Road to Women's Suffrage, 1848 to 1920 361
Denial of African American Suffrage, 1870 to 1965 362
The Civil Rights Movement and African American Voting, 1950s and 1960s 365
The Latino Vote 366
The Vote for 18-Year-Olds, 1971 370
11.3 Who Votes? 370
Turnout 370
The Demographics of Turnout 371
11.4 Why Citizens Vote 374
Economic Model of Voting 374
Psychological Model of Voting 375
Institutional Model of Voting 376
Is Voting in Your Genes? 377
Weather 378
11.5 Assessing Turnout 378
Is Turnout Low? 378
Do Turnout Rates Create Inequality? 381
11.6 Voting Laws and Regulations 382
Reforms to Voting Laws in the 1890s 382
The National Voter Registration Act 383
New Forms of Voting 384
11.7 Participation Beyond Voting 386
Involvement in Political Campaigns 386
Protest Politics 387
E-Participation 391
Voting, Participation, and Democracy 392

CHAPTER 12 Congress 396

12.1 Congress as the Legislative Branch 398
Representation and Bicameralism 398
Constitutional Differences Between the House and Senate 399
12.2 The Powers of Congress 405
Taxation and Appropriation 405
War Powers 405
Regulation of Commerce 406
Appointments and Treaties 406
Impeachment and Removal from Office 406
Lawmaking 408
Authorization of Courts 408
Oversight 409
12.3 The Organization of Congress 410
The Role of Political Parties 410
The House of Representatives 411
The Senate 414
The Committee System 415
Advocacy Caucuses 418
12.4 The Lawmaking Process 419
The Procedural Rules of the House and Senate 419
Legislative Proposals 423

Committee Action 423
Floor Action and the Vote 424
Conference Committee 425
The Budget Process and Reconciliation 425
Presidential Signature or Veto, and the Veto Override 428

12.5 The Member of Congress at Work 429
Offices and Staff 429
Legislative Responsibilities 430
Communication with Constituents 431
The Next Election 432

Congress and Democracy 434

CHAPTER 13 The Presidency 438

13.1 Presidential Qualifications 440
Constitutional Eligibility and Presidential Succession 440
Background and Experience 442
Expansion of the Presidency 443

13.2 Presidential Power: Constitutional Grants and Limits 445
Commander in Chief 446
Power to Pardon 447
Treaties and Recognition of Foreign Nations 447
Executive and Judicial Nominations 449
Veto and the Veto Override 450
Other Powers 452
Congress's Ultimate Check on the Executive: Impeachment 452

13.3 The Growth of Executive Influence 454
Presidential Directives and Signing Statements 455
Power to Persuade 457
Agenda Setting 459

13.4 The President in Wartime 461
Power Struggles Between the President and Congress 461
Power Struggles Between the President and the Judiciary 465

13.5 Organization of the Modern White House 467
The Executive Office of the President 468
The Office of the Vice President 468
The Office of the First Lady 469

13.6 Presidential Greatness 470
Roosevelt: The New Deal and World War II 470
Johnson: The Great Society and Vietnam 472
Reagan: The Reagan Revolution and the End of the Cold War 473

The Presidency and Democracy 476

CHAPTER 14 The Bureaucracy 480

14.1 The American Bureaucracy 482
What Is the Bureaucracy? 482
Constitutional Foundations 483
Structure of the Bureaucracy 484

14.2 Core Components of the Bureaucracy 488
Mission 489
Hierarchical Decision-Making Process 489
Expertise 489
Bureaucratic Culture 490

14.3 Historical Evolution of the Bureaucracy 492
Expansion of Executive Branch Departments 492
Growth of Regulatory Agencies and Other Organizations 493
From Patronage to the Civil Service 495
Career Civil Service 497
Political Appointees 497
Diversity in the Federal Bureaucracy 499
Private-Sector Contract Workers 501
Bureaucrats and Politics 502

14.4 Accountability and Responsiveness in the Bureaucracy 503
Roles of the Legislative and Judicial Branches 504
Efficiency and Transparency 505
Whistleblowing 508
Bureaucratic Failure 508

The Bureaucracy and Democracy 510

CHAPTER 15 The Judiciary 514

15.1 The Role and Powers of the Judiciary 516
English Legal Traditions 516
Constitutional Grants of Power 517

15.2 State and Lower Federal Courts 518
State Courts in the Federal Judicial System 518
District Courts 519
Courts of Appeals 524

15.3 The Supreme Court 525
Granting Review 526
Oral Arguments 527
The Decision 528

15.4 Judicial Decision Making 529
Judicial Restraint: The Legal Approach 531
Judicial Activism: The Extralegal Approach 532

Restraint and Activism in Judicial Decision Making 534
The Impact of Court Rulings 534

15.5 The Appointment Process for Federal Judges and Justices 537

District Courts 537
Courts of Appeals 538
The Supreme Court 541
Demographic Diversity on the Court 544

15.6 Historical Trends in Supreme Court Rulings 545

Expansion of National Power Under the Marshall Court 546
Limits on National Power, 1830s to 1930s 546
Strengthened National Power, 1930s to the Present 547

The Judiciary and Democracy 549

CHAPTER 16 Economic, Domestic, and Foreign Policy 554

16.1 Public Policy Under a Constitutional System 556

The Process of Policy Making 556
The Regulatory Process 558
Blocking Implementation 560
State Governments and Public Policy 560

16.2 Domestic Policy 561

Entitlement Programs, Income Security, and Health Care 562
The Affordable Care Act (ACA) 565
Immigration Policy 566
Energy, Environmental Policy, and Climate Change 570

16.3 Economic Policy 574

Intervention in the Economy 574
Fiscal Policy 575
Monetary Policy 577
Trade Policy 578

16.4 Foreign Policy 584

International Relations and U.S. Foreign Policy Goals 584
Foreign Policy Tools 587

Public Policy and Democracy 593

Appendix

A **The Declaration of Independence 598**
B **The Constitution of the United States 602**
C ***Federalist Papers* 10 and 51 618**
D **Electoral Maps, 2000–2016 626**

Glossary 628
Endnotes 639
Index 673

Features of the AP® Edition

AP® Learning Objectives

CON – 4.A Explain how the president can implement a policy agenda.

CON – 4.B Explain how the president's agenda can create tension and frequent confrontations with Congress.

CON – 4.C Explain how presidents have interpreted and justified their use of formal and informal powers.

CON – 4.D Explain how co has changed th with the nation other branches

PMI – 2.D Explain how the executive branc carry out their r with the goals c

Performance Tasks

Upon the completion of this chapter, you must be able to do

- Explain how the president can use formal and informal power to achieve the ... power, single rather t

Learning about American government can be your first step through the gateway of democracy. Each chapter of *Gateways to Democracy* is built to maximize efficient studying and help you get the most out of your course in American government. These study materials are just part of the guidance for learning what *Gateways to Democracy* provides. Study aids start on the first page of every chapter with **AP® Learning Objectives** and **Performance Tasks** sections, noting which learning objectives and essential details from the curriculum framework apply to that chapter.

Throughout the chapter, margin statements – called **Essential Knowledge** – point out applicable AP® Essential Knowledge statements from the curriculum framework, on the text page in which they are being discussed to allow for deeper discussion of these important AP® concepts.

Essential Knowledge

With the Civil Rights Act of 1964, Congress sought to enforce school integration, which was required under the Fourteenth Amendment. Furthermore, by exercising its power under the commerce clause, Congress sought to end other forms of discriminatory practices such as discrimination in places of employment.

ence (SCLC) led demonstrations i of downtown businesses. The poli cattle prods. Police arrested hundr questioned why King, an outsider, "Letter from Birmingham Jail": "I a violence, King insisted that peacef The negotiations took place and e lunch counters and hire more blac of the KKK exploded a bomb at a l you

Public Policy Connections

1. How does public opinion impact elected officials? Should it?
2. How should the political system respond to immediate demands from citizens who desire more jobs and economic development when those demands might conflict with the need to provide future generations with a clean environment?

Political Science Reasoning

Question 1

Practice 1, Practice 4

What GAO Found U.S. Department of Education (Education) grant staff did not consistently document in the official grant files key required monitoring activities, according to GAO's review of a nongeneralizable sample of 75 discretionary grants. As a result, about $21 million in discretionary grant funds lacked correct documentation of grantee performance in the official grant files GAO reviewed. Specifically, compared to Education's requirements for these files, almost all—69 of 75—were incomplete in terms of certain key documents (that is, grant award notifications, post-award conference re...

Within the *Public Policy* feature of each chapter, **Public Policy Connections** boxes ask you to use political science skills & practices from the curriculum framework to consider how you would deal with various policy issues in current society.

End of chapter **Political Science Reasoning** sections help you apply AP® skills and practices from the curriculum framework as you answer questions using various stimulus material including graphs, tables, text excerpts and images, similar to those found on the AP® exam.

Focus on AP® Success sections which conclude each chapter, help you pull together the applicable AP® concepts and skills being discussed by more deeply understanding how learning objectives and key concepts connect and how to make correlations to themes between chapters.

Focus on AP® Success

1 Gateways to American Democracy

Must Know: Key Concepts

- Participatory Democracy
- Pluralist Democracy
- Elite Democracy
- Federalists
- Limited Government
- Natural Rights
- Popular Sovereignty
- Republicanism
- Social Contract

Thinking Politically

Argumentation

One of the most fundamental decision...

Letter to the Teacher

Dear Introduction to American Government Teacher:

As teachers and scholars of American government, we have come together to write a textbook that engages students in both the process and the policy outcomes of U.S. government. We present an updated lens through which we can examine the theoretical and structural foundations of American democracy and the resulting political process that demands an active and informed citizenry. To help students understand American democracy and see how they can be involved in their government, we peel back the layers of the political system to expose its inner workings and to examine how competing interests can both facilitate and block the people's will. In doing so, we use the conceptual framework of gateways. We contend that there are gates—formal and informal—that present obstacles to participation and empowerment. But there are also gateways that give students a chance to influence the process and to overcome the obstacles. The gateways framework helps students conceptualize participation and civic engagement—even democracy itself. Our book is both realistic and optimistic, contending that the American system can be open to the influence of students and responsive to their hopes and dreams—if they have information about how the system works. But we avoid cheerleading by also pointing out the many gates that undermine the workings of government. Although the size and complexity of the American constitutional system is daunting, it is imperative to prepare for the demands of democratic citizenship. This has never been truer than today, when we have a rapidly changing demographic balance within our population. Today groups that were formerly underrepresented in American politics and society, such as second- and third-generation Latinos, are a powerful force in our government. It is our hope that this textbook can awaken students and motivate them not only to learn about politics but to also participate actively throughout every stage of their lives.

In keeping with the theme of gates and gateways in American politics, we also open each chapter with a **vignette** that tells the story of an individual who has successfully navigated his or her own way in politics. The important role of the vignette for the teacher is to show the students how people like them have made a difference in American political and social life; our vignette subjects vary by historical era, career choice, gender, race, ethnicity, and party affiliation. We also include landmark **Supreme Court cases** related to every chapter's subject to show students the continuous and vital role it plays in both upholding and knocking down gates to policy implementation and political participation. We include **policy features** in each chapter to illustrate how the chapter's core content operates on a real-time, real-life basis. We also have an **Election 2016 feature** in each chapter. To prepare students to evaluate the vast amounts of data present in today's political discourse, we include a **Political Analytics feature** in each chapter, which asks students to look closely at visual representations of data and to think critically about what they see.

New to This Edition

- A dedicated focus on diversity and participation that reflects the changing demographic infrastructure in America today
- Expanded information about the Tea Party, Donald Trump's presidential campaign, and factions in the Republican Party
- Coverage of Hillary Clinton's quest to become the first female U.S. president
- An expanded section on protest politics, including the Black Lives Matter movement
- Discussion of how the Supreme Court has changed and may lean differently after Justice Antonin Scalia's passing
- New information about recent Supreme Court cases and their ramifications, such as *Obergefell v. Hodges* (2015) and same-sex marriage

- New opening chapter vignettes featuring Oregon Governor Kate Brown, author Ta-Nehisi Coates, Utah Representative Mia Love, former President Barack Obama, Los Angeles City Administrative Officer Miguel Santana, and Iowa pollster J. Ann Selzer
- Explanatory text to accompany all figures to help students interpret data

MindTap

As a teacher, **MindTap** is here to simplify your workload, organize and immediately grade your students' assignments, and allow you to customize your course as you see fit. Through deep-seated integration with your Learning Management System, grades are easily exported, and analytics are pulled with the click of a button. MindTap provides you with a platform to easily add in current events videos and RSS feeds from national or local news sources. Looking to include more currency in the course? Add in our KnowNow American Government Blog link for weekly updated news coverage and pedagogy.

Teaching American government remains a vitally important but constantly challenging task for all of us. We know that there are many books to choose from to use in your course. We believe that *Gateways to Democracy* has an innovative approach in reaching and engaging students across a range of backgrounds and enables teachers to more easily achieve their pedagogical goals in American government courses. We have seen it work for our students, and we know it will work for yours.

Sincerely,

John G. Geer, john.g.geer@vanderbilt.edu
Richard Herrera, Richard.Herrera@asu.edu
Wendy J. Schiller, Wendy_Schiller@Brown.edu
Jeffrey A. Segal, jeffrey.segal@stonybrook.edu

Letter to the Student

Dear Student:

Our book begins with a simple question: How does anyone exert political influence in a country of more than 325 million people? Students in American government classrooms across the country are grappling with this question as they develop an appreciation of their role in American public life. In our own classrooms, students ask us: What is my responsibility? Can I make a difference? Does my participation matter? How can I get my opinions represented? These are gateway questions that probe the opportunities and limits on citizen involvement in a democracy. For that reason, we not only provide you with essential information about the American political system but also show you how to become a **more powerful advocate for yourself** within that system. It is not enough to know what you want your government and society to be—you must learn how to make it happen. This course shows you how people from all walks of life have opened gates to influence public policy, and it shows you the relevance of government in your life. It is our hope that this information motivates you not only to learn about politics but also to participate actively throughout every stage of your life.

In keeping with the theme of gates and gateways in American politics, we open each chapter with a vignette that tells the story of someone who has successfully navigated his or her way in politics. These are people like you who have different gender, ethnic, racial, and partisan backgrounds and who have made a difference in American political and social life. We also include other features focusing on the Supreme Court, public policy, the 2016 election, and data analysis that show you how politics plays out in the United States. All of these special features are designed to relate specifically to you—the student—to give you a blueprint with which to navigate the political system. What makes *Gateways to Democracy* different?

- Streamlined learning objectives and outcomes help you better understand the material and prepare for the graded assignments in the course. We have key terms and guide questions throughout each chapter.
- A focus on diversity reflects the changing demographic infrastructure in America, especially among young people, by providing new coverage of the politics and issues affecting all Americans in every chapter.
- Updated accounts are included of people who are changing American politics today.
- Current policy case studies are included on issues such as voter ID laws, fracking, drone warfare, and government surveillance of citizens' communications.

As a student, the benefits of using MindTap with this material are endless. With automatically graded practice quizzes and activities, an easily navigated learning path, and an interactive eBook, you will be able to test yourself inside and outside the classroom with ease. The accessibility of current events coupled with interactive media makes the content fun and engaging. On your computer, phone, or tablet, MindTap is there when you need it, giving you easy access to flashcards, quizzes, readings, and assignments.

As teachers, our main goal both in this book and in the classroom is to empower you as active participants in American democracy. We know that you balance a lot of competing demands for your time, from other classes, to work, to family responsibilities. This book provides you with the core information you need to succeed in your American government classes, and just as important, to knock open the gates that may stand in your way to achieve your goals within the political system.

Sincerely,

John G. Geer, john.g.geer@vanderbilt.edu
Richard Herrera, Richard.Herrera@asu.edu
Wendy J. Schiller, Wendy_Schiller@Brown.edu
Jeffrey A. Segal, jeffrey.segal@stonybrook.edu

Resources for Teachers

Access your Gateways to Democracy, 4e, resources via
www.cengage.com/login.

Log in using your Cengage Learning single sign-on user name and password, or create a new instructor account by clicking on "New Faculty User" and following the instructions.

Gateways to Democracy, 4e—Text Only Edition

ISBN: 978-1-337-09773-4

This copy of the book does not come bundled with MindTap.

MindTap®

MindTap for *Gateways to Democracy, 4e*

Instant Access Code: 978-1-337-69056-0

MindTap for American Government is a fully online, personalized learning experience built upon Cengage Learning content. MindTap combines student learning tools—readings, multimedia, activities, and assessments—into a singular Learning Path that guides students through their course. Through a wealth of activities written to learning outcomes, it provides students with ample opportunities to check themselves for understanding, while also providing teachers and students alike with a clear way to measure and assess student progress. Teachers can use MindTap as a turnkey solution or customize it by adding YouTube videos, RSS feeds, or their own documents directly within the eBook or within each chapter's learning path. The product can be used fully online with its interactive eBook for *Gateways to Democracy* or in conjunction with the printed text.

Instructor Companion Website for *Gateways to Democracy*, 4e

This Instructor Companion website is an all-in-one multimedia online resource for class preparation, presentation, and testing. Accessible through Cengage.com/login with your faculty account, you will find available for download: book-specific Microsoft® PowerPoint® presentations, a test bank compatible with multiple Learning Management Systems, an AP® Teacher's Resource Guide, and Microsoft® PowerPoint® Image Slides.

The test bank, offered in Blackboard, Moodle, Desire2Learn, Canvas, and Angel formats, contains AP® style multiple-choice and free-response questions. Import the test bank into your Learning Management System to edit and manage questions, as well as to create tests.

The AP® Teacher's Resource Guide will help teachers navigate the redesigned AP® course. In each chapter this manual points out applicable AP® disciplinary practices and reasoning skills, big ideas, learning objectives and essential knowledge details from the concept outline. It also provides chapter summaries, and suggested activities and discussion topics for teaching to the AP® U.S. Government and Politics course.

The Microsoft® PowerPoint® presentations are ready-to-use visual outlines of each chapter. These presentations are easily customized for your lectures and offered along with chapter-specific Microsoft® PowerPoint® Image Slides and JPEG Image Libraries. Access the Instructor Companion Website at www.cengage.com/login.

AP® U.S. Government and Politics Cognero for *Gateways to Democracy*, 4e

ISBN: 978-1-337-78985-1

Cengage Learning Testing Powered by Cognero is a flexible, online system that allows you to author, edit, and manage test bank content from multiple Cengage Learning solutions, create multiple test versions in an instant, and deliver tests from your Learning Management System, your classroom, or wherever you want. Written by Eugene Chase, Edmond North High School, Edmond, Oklahoma, this Cognero testing contains 3 full practice exams, reflective of the redesigned AP® U.S. Government and Politics exam. Each of these practice exams contains 55 multiple-choice questions and 4 free-response questions and answer explanations all in AP® format.

Acknowledgments

Writing the fourth edition of an introductory textbook requires a dedicated and professional publishing team. We were extremely fortunate to continue to work with a number of excellent people at Cengage Learning, including Carolyn Merrill, who has since moved on to other adventures. Carolyn was a rock-steady foundation, and her choice of Paula Dohnal as our development editor was outstanding. Paula has guided us through a comprehensive revision of the book to focus more on the vital role that traditionally underrepresented groups, such as Latinos, play in knocking down the gates that stand in the way of participation. Edward Dionne and Cathy Brooks have been vigilant managers of the copyedit process, and Jen Simmons has been terrific in updating our photos and images. We also want to thank the entire sales force at Cengage Learning for their tireless efforts to promote *Gateways to Democracy*.

Our gratitude goes to all of those who worked on the various supplements offered with this text, especially the test bank and Instructor's Manual author, Adam Newmark from Appalachian State University.

By definition, an American government textbook is a sweeping endeavor, and it would not be possible to succeed without our reviewers. They provided truly constructive input throughout the review and revision process. We list their names on the following page, and we are grateful to them for their contributions to this material's development.

Each of us would also like to thank the individuals who supported us throughout the project.

JOHN G. GEER: I would like to thank Carrie Roush and Marc Trussler for their help with revising this textbook. Special mention goes to Drew Engelhardt and Maggie Deichert for their timely efforts in pulling together new material for this fourth edition. As each edition goes into print, my debt to Jeff, Rick, and Wendy only grows. They are tremendous co-authors and even better friends. I am so lucky to work with them on this project. My deepest and most heartfelt appreciation goes to Beth Prichard Geer. Beth makes every part of my life better and supports me in all endeavors. It is a true joy to have a partner on life's amazing journey. For that, I will be forever grateful.

RICHARD HERRERA: I appreciate the opportunity to expand my contributions to *Gateways*. The author team has been wonderfully supportive and helpful to me as I continue to learn the craft of writing and revising a textbook. John, Wendy, and Jeff are an exciting and thoughtful group of scholars with whom to work. The creative process that produced this edition has been a wonderful experience. Their support and suggestions, along with Paula Dohnal's, have been essential to honing my ideas and contributions. I would also like to thank Marian Norris for her support, patience, and encouragement throughout this adventure.

WENDY J. SCHILLER: I would also like to express my appreciation for the opportunity to work with John, Jeff, and Rick—each excellent scholars and colleagues. I would also like to thank my husband, Robert Kalunian, who provides an endless supply of patience, support, and perspective.

JEFFREY A. SEGAL: I thank my co-authors, John, Wendy and Rick, for once again making the endeavor of the new edition a totally enjoyable experience and Paula Dohnal for her fresh look at the materials. Justine D'Elia provided expert research assistance for the two previous editions, for this edition, I thank Alan Champlin for the same. My professional colleagues, both at Stony Brook and beyond, have cheerfully answered innumerable queries from me. I appreciate their assistance.

Reviewers

We would like to thank the instructors who have contributed their valuable feedback through reviews of the third edition in preparation for this fourth edition:

Jennifer Clark, University of Houston
Louis DeSipio, University of California, Irvine
Bond Faulwell, Johnson County Community College
Jason MacDonald, West Virginia University
Elizabeth McNamara, University of North Carolina, Greensboro
Todd Myers, Grossmont College
William Parent, San Jacinto College Central Campus
Dave Price, Santa Fe College
Scot Schraufnagel, Northern Illinois University

About the Authors

JOHN G. **GEER**

(PhD, Princeton University) is Vice Provost for Academic and Strategic Affairs, the Gertrude Conaway Vanderbilt Professor of Political Science, and co-directs the Vanderbilt Poll. Geer has published widely, including *In Defense of Negativity*, which won the Goldsmith Prize from the Shorenstein Center at Harvard University. Geer has been a visiting scholar at Harvard University and Princeton University. Geer teaches Introduction to American Politics, as well as specialty courses on elections and campaigns. His teaching has drawn much note, winning numerous teaching awards at both Arizona State University and Vanderbilt University. Geer is a frequent commentator in the press, with appearances on all the major networks (e.g., Fox News, CBS Evening News, CNN), and he has been quoted in newspapers ranging from *The New York Times* to *The Washington Post* to the *LA Times*. He has done interviews for major international outlets as well, such as BBC and Al Jazeera.

RICHARD **HERRERA**

(PhD, University of California Santa Barbara) is Associate Professor of Political Science and Associate Director for the School of Politics and Global Studies at Arizona State University. He directs the ASU Capital Scholars Washington, DC, Summer Internship program for ASU and coordinates the ASU-McCain Institute for International Leadership Internship Program. He has contributed articles to the *American Political Science Review*, *Journal of Politics*, *Legislative Studies Quarterly*, and *State Politics and Policy Quarterly*. His current research interests are focused on U.S. governors, their ideology, policy agendas, and representative functions. He teaches courses in American Politics, American Political Parties, and American Politics and Film.

WENDY J. **SCHILLER**

(PhD, University of Rochester) is a Professor of Political Science, International and Public Affairs at Brown University (Twitter acct @profwschiller). She was legislative assistant for Senator Daniel P. Moynihan, a federal lobbyist for Governor Mario M. Cuomo, a Guest Scholar and PhD Fellow at the Brookings Institution, and a post-doctoral fellow at Princeton University. She has published *Electing the Senate: Indirect Democracy Before the Seventeenth Amendment* (2015) with Charles Stewart III, *The Contemporary Congress* (2003, 2005, 2015) with Burdett Loomis, and *Partners and Rivals: Representation in U.S. Senate Delegations* (2000). She teaches courses on a wide range of American politics topics, including Introduction to the American Political Process, The American Presidency, Congress and Public Policy, Parties and Interest Groups, and The Philosophy of the American Founding. Professor Schiller is a political analyst for local and national media outlets, including Bloomberg Radio, NPR, and WJAR10, the local NBC affiliate in Providence.

JEFFREY A. **SEGAL**

(PhD, Michigan State University) is SUNY Distinguished Professor and Chair of the Political Science Department at Stony Brook University. He has served as Senior Visiting Research Scholar at Princeton University and held a Guggenheim Fellowship. Segal is best known, with Harold Spaeth, as the leading proponent of the attitudinal model of Supreme Court decision making. Segal has twice won the Wadsworth Award for a book (with Spaeth) or article 10 years or older with lasting influence on law and courts. He has also won the C. Herman Pritchett Award (again with Spaeth) for best book on law and courts. His work on the influence of strategic factors on Supreme Court decision making won the Franklin Burdette Award from APSA. With Lee Epstein, Kevin Quinn, and Andrew Martin, he won Green Bag's award for exemplary legal writing. He has also won a national award sponsored by the American Bar Association for innovative teaching and instructional methods and materials in law and courts.

Correlation of *Gateways to Democracy* Updated 4th edition to the AP® U.S. Government and Politics Curriculum Framework

Unit 1: Foundations of American Democracy

Enduring Understandings	Learning Objectives	Chapter and Page References
LOR-1: A balance between governmental power and individual rights has been a hallmark of American political development.	LOR-1.A: Explain how democratic ideals are reflected in the Declaration of Independence and the U.S. Constitution.	Ch. 1: 5–7, 9, 13–17, Ch. 2: 35–41
Big Idea: *Liberty and Order*	LOR-1.B: Explain how models of representative democracy are visible in major institutions, policies, events, or debates in the U.S.	Ch. 1: 12–13, Ch. 2: 52, Ch. 3: 98, Ch. 7: 274, Ch. 12: 404
CON-1: The Constitution emerged from the debate about the weaknesses in the Articles of Confederation as a blueprint for limited government.	CON-1.A: Explain how Federalist and Anti-Federalist views on central government and democracy are reflected in U.S. foundational documents.	Ch. 2: 52–55, Ch. 3: 97–98, Ch. 4: 103, Ch. 6: 2002
Big Idea: *Constitutionalism*	CON-1.B: Explain the relationship between key provisions of the Articles of Confederation and the debate over granting the federal government greater power formerly reserved to the states.	Ch. 2: 36–37, Ch. 3: 68–70
	CON-1.C: Explain the ongoing impact of political negotiation and compromise at the Constitutional Convention on the development of the constitutional system.	Ch. 2: 30–64, Ch. 3: 70–87
PMI-1: The Constitution created a competitive policy-making process to ensure the people's will is represented and that freedom is preserved.	PMI-1.A: Explain the constitutional principles of separation of powers and checks and balances.	Ch. 2: 49–51, Ch. 12: 409–410, Ch. 13: 449–451, 454, 456–458, Ch. 15: 538–539, 541–548
Big Idea: *Competing Policy-Making Interests*	PMI-1.B: Explain the implications of separation of powers and checks and balances for the U.S. political system.	Ch. 2: 50–51, Ch. 12: 410, 412, Ch. 13: 450, 454, 456, Ch. 15: 554
CON-2: Federalism reflects the dynamic distribution of power between national and state governments.	CON-2.A: Explain how societal needs affect the constitutional allocation of power between national and state governments.	Ch. 2: 53–54, Ch. 3: 71–76, 82–87, Ch. 16: 565–569
Big Idea: *Constitutionalism*	CON-2.B: Explain how the appropriate balance of power between national and state governments has been interpreted differently over time.	Ch. 3: 77–87, Ch. 4 103–105, Ch. 15: 146–150
	CON-2.C: Explain how the distribution of powers among three federal branches and between national and state governments impacts policymaking.	Ch. 2: 49–50, Ch. 3: 82–85, Ch. 16: 565–569

Unit 2: Interactions Among Branches of Government

Enduring Understandings	Learning Objectives	Chapter and Page References
CON-3: The republican ideal in the U.S. is manifested in the structure and operation of the legislative branch.	CON-3.A: Describe the different structures, powers, and functions of each house of Congress.	Ch. 2: 38–39, Ch. 12: 423–426, 428, 431–432, Ch. 16: 579–582
Big Idea: *Constitutionalism*	CON-3.B: Explain how the structure, powers, and functions of both houses of Congress affect the policy-making process.	Ch. 12: 402–436, Ch. 16: 566–568
	CON-3.C: Explain how congressional behavior is influenced by election processes, partisanship, and divided government.	Ch. 12: 408, 428–429, 436–439, Ch. 13: 455, 459, Ch. 14: 507
CON-4: The presidency has been enhanced beyond its expressed constitutional powers.	CON-4.A: Explain how the president can implement a policy agenda.	Ch. 13: 449–456, 459–461, Ch. 16: 588–591
Big Idea: *Constitutionalism*	CON-4.B: Explain how the president's agenda can create tension and frequent confrontations with Congress.	Ch. 2: 45, Ch. 12: 410, Ch. 13: 453–455, 459–460, 465–468
	CON-4.C: Explain how presidents have interpreted and justified their use of formal and informal powers.	Ch. 13: 445, 447–449, 460, 480–481
	CON-4.D: Explain how communication technology has changed the president's relationship with the national constituency and the other branches.	Ch. 7: 226–228, 229, Ch. 13: 461–463
CON-5: The design of the judicial branch protects the Supreme Court's independence as a branch of government, and the emergence and use of judicial review remains a powerful judicial practice.	CON-5.A: Explain the principle of judicial review and how it checks the power of other institutions and state governments.	Ch. 2: 47, 48, 50, Ch. 15: 522, 534, 550
Big Idea: *Constitutionalism*	CON-5.B: Explain how the exercise of judicial review in conjunction with life-tenure can lead to controversy about the legitimacy of the Supreme Court's power.	Ch. 15: 520, 533–538, 541–545, 553–554
	CON-5.C: Explain how other branches in the government can limit the Supreme Court's power.	Ch. 12: 412–413, Ch. 13: 469, 471, Ch. 15: 537
PMI-2: The federal bureaucracy is a powerful institution implementing federal policies with sometimes questionable accountability.	PMI-2.A: Explain how the bureaucracy carries out the responsibilities of the federal government.	Ch. 8: 277, Ch. 14, 498–503,
Big Idea: *Competing Policy-Making Interests*	PMI-2.B: Explain how the federal bureaucracy uses delegated discretionary authority for rule making and implementation.	Ch. 14: 496–498, 510
	PMI-2.C: Explain how Congress uses its oversight power in its relationship with the executive branch.	Ch. 12: 413–414, Ch. 14: 499, 508–509
	PMI-2.D: Explain how the president ensures that executive branch agencies and departments carry out their responsibilities in concert with the goals of the administration.	Ch. 13: 453–454, 463–464, Ch. 14: 486
	PMI-2.E: Explain the extent to which governmental branches can hold the bureaucracy accountable given the competing interests of Congress, the president, and the federal courts.	Ch. 12: 413–414, Ch. 13: 453–454, Ch. 14: 486, 508–509

Unit 3: Civil Liberties and Civil Rights

Enduring Understandings	Learning Objectives	Chapter and Page References
LOR-2: Provisions of the U.S. Constitution's Bill of Rights are continually being interpreted to balance the power of government and the civil liberties of individuals. Big Idea: *Liberty and Order*	LOR-2.A: Explain how the U.S. Constitution protects individual liberties and rights.	Ch. 2: 54–55, Ch. 4: 103–110, Ch. 7: 220–223, Ch. 15: 551–552
	LOR-2.B: Describe the rights protected in the Bill of Rights.	Ch. 4: 110–133
	LOR-2.C: Explain the extent to which the Supreme Court's interpretation of the First and Second Amendments reflects a commitment to individual liberty.	Ch. 4: 110–125
	LOR-2.D: Explain how the Supreme Court has attempted to balance claims of individual freedom with laws and enforcement procedures that promote public order and safety.	Ch. 4: 125–129
LOR-3: Protections of the Bill of Rights have been selectively incorporated by way of the Fourteenth Amendment's due process clause to prevent state infringement on basic liberties. Big Idea: *Liberty and Order*	LOR-3.A: Explain the implications of the doctrine of selective incorporation.	Ch. 4: 105, 112, 127, 129
	LOR-3.B: Explain the extent to which states are limited by the due process clause from infringing upon individual rights.	Ch. 4: 103–110, 127–130, 132–133
PRD-1: The Fourteenth Amendment's equal protection clause as well as other constitutional provisions have often been used to support the advancement of equality. Big Idea: *Civic Participation in a Representative Democracy*	PRD-1.A: Explain how constitutional provisions have supported and motivated social movements.	Ch. 5: 140, 146–151, 154–155, 170–172, Ch. 8: 261
PMI-3: Public policy promoting civil rights is influenced by citizen-state interactions and constitutional interpretation over time. Big Idea: *Competing Policy-Making Interests*	PMI-3.A: Explain how the government has responded to social movements.	Ch. 5: 157, 159–169, Ch. 8: 274–275
CON-6: The Supreme Court's interpretation of the U.S. Constitution is influenced by the composition of the Court and citizen-state interactions. At times, it has restricted minority rights and, at others, protected them. Big Idea: *Constitutionalism*	CON-6.A: Explain how the Supreme Court has at times allowed the restriction of the civil rights of minority groups and at other times has protected those rights.	Ch. 5; 147–148, 158

Unit 4: American Political Ideologies and Beliefs

Enduring Understandings	Learning Objectives	Chapter and Page References
MPA-1: Citizen beliefs about government are shaped by the intersection of demographics, political culture, and dynamic social change. Big Idea: *Methods of Political Analysis*	MPA-1.A: Explain the relationship between core beliefs of U.S. citizens and attitudes about the role of government.	Ch. 1: 11–16
	MPA-1.B: Explain how cultural factors influence political attitudes and socialization.	Ch. 6: 192–195
MPA-2: Public opinion is measured through scientific polling, and the results of public opinion polls influence public policies and institutions. Big Idea: *Methods of Political Analysis*	MPA-2.A: Describe the elements of a scientific poll.	Ch. 6: 186–192
	MPA-2.B: Explain the quality and credibility of claims based on public opinion data.	Ch. 6: 204–205, 212, Ch. 7: 346–347
PMI-4: Widely held political ideologies shape the policy debates and choices in American policies. Big Idea: *Competing Policy-Making Interests*	PMI-4.A: Explain how ideologies of the two major parties shape policy debates.	Ch. 6: 199, 202–203, Ch. 9: 312–320
	PMI-4.B: Explain how U.S. political culture (e.g., values, attitudes, and beliefs) influences the formation, goals, and implementation of public policy over time.	Ch. 1: 13–17, Ch. 6: 212
	PMI-4.C: Describe different political ideologies regarding the role of government in regulating the marketplace.	Ch. 1: 11–12, Ch. 6: 199
	PMI-4.D: Explain how political ideologies vary on the role of the government's role in regulating the marketplace.	Ch. 1: 11–12, Ch. 6: 199
	PMI-4.E: Explain how political ideologies vary on the role of the government in addressing social issues.	Ch. 1: 11–12, Ch. 6: 199
	PMI-4.F: Explain how different ideologies impact policy on social issues.	Ch. 1: 11–12, Ch. 6: 199

Unit 5: Political Participation

Enduring Understandings	Learning Objectives	Chapter and Page References
MPA-3: Factors associated with political ideology, efficacy, structural barriers, and demographics influence the nature and degree of political participation. Big Idea: *Methods of Political Analysis*	MPA-3.A: Describe the voting rights protections in the Constitution and in legislation.	Ch. 5: 148–150, 162–163, Ch. 11: 369–371
	MPA-3.B: Describe different models of voting behavior.	Ch. 11: 378–381
	MPA-3.C: Explain the roles that individual choice and state laws play in voter turnout in elections.	Ch. 6: 200–201, Ch. 11: 379–384
PMI-5: Political parties, interest groups, and social movements provide opportunities for participation and influence how people relate to government and policy-makers. Big Idea: *Competing Policy-Making Interests*	PMI-5.A: Describe linkage institutions.	Ch. 7: 218–220, Ch. 8: 263–265, Ch. 9: 297–293, Ch. 10: 329, 331
	PMI-5.B: Explain the function and impact of political parties on the electorate and government.	Ch. 9: 291–293, Ch. 10: 336, 321, Ch. 12: 414–415, 419–420
	PMI-5.C: Explain why and how political parties change and adapt.	Ch. 9: 292, 313–314, 316–320, Ch. 10: 340–342,
	PMI-5.D: Explain how structural barriers impact third-party and independent-candidate success.	Ch. 9: 301–302, 305–308, Ch. 10: 328–329
	PMI-5.E: Explain the benefits and potential problems of interest-group influence on elections and policy making.	Ch. 8: 254–273, 277–278, Ch. 12: 420–421, 427–428
	PMI-5.F: Explain how variation in types and resources of interest groups affects their ability to influence elections and policy making.	Ch. 8: 279, 280–283
	PMI-5.G: Explain how various political actors influence public policy outcomes.	Ch. 5: 149, 154–167, Ch. 8: 258–265, Ch. 9: 314–320
PRD-2: The impact of federal policies on campaigning and electoral rules continues to be contested by both sides of the political spectrum. Big Idea: *Civic Participation in a Representative Democracy*	PRD-2.A: Explain how the different processes work in a U.S. presidential election.	Ch. 1: 41, Ch. 9: 296–298, Ch. 10: 326–331, Ch. 13: 444
	PRD-2.B: Explain how the Electoral College impacts democratic participation.	Ch. 10: 326–331
	PRD-2.C: Explain how the different processes work in U.S. congressional elections.	Ch. 10: 331–333, 347, 351–352
	PRD-2.D: Explain how campaign organizations and strategies affect the election process.	Ch. 7: 236–238, Ch. 9: 334–338, Ch. 11 394–396
	PRD-2.E: Explain how the organization, finance, and strategies of national political campaigns affect the election process.	Ch. 8: 269–273, Ch. 9: 298, Ch. 10: 342, 352, Ch. 11: 396
PRD-3: The various forms of media provide citizens with political information and influence the ways in which they participate politically. Big Idea: *Civic Participation in a Representative Democracy*	PRD-3.A: Describe the media's role as a linkage institution.	Ch. 6: 187–188, 190, Ch. 7: 218–220, 248–249
	PRD-3.B: Explain how increasingly diverse choices of media and communication outlets influence political institutions and behavior.	Ch. 7: 237, 243–247

1 Gateways to American Democracy

AP® Learning Objectives

LOR – 1.A Explain how democratic ideals are reflected in the Declaration of Independence and the U.S. Constitution.

LOR – 1.B Explain how models of representative democracy are visible in major institutions, policies, events, or debates in the U.S.

Performance Tasks

Upon the completion of this chapter, you must be able to do the following:

- Explain the differences between the various views of U.S. representative democracy: participatory, pluralist, elite.
- Citing specific examples, explain how these views have manifested themselves in U.S. politics and foundational documents.
- Explain the policy implication of each of these views of representative democracy (participatory, pluralist, elite).
- Explain how the Constitution and Declaration of Independence manifest the ideas of: natural rights, popular sovereignty, republicanism, and social contract.

Sandra Baker/Alamy

"*Change will not come if we wait for some other person, or if we wait for some other time. We are the ones we've been waiting for. We are the change that we seek.*"[1]

BARACK OBAMA
Columbia College

Steve Liss/The LIFE Images Collection/Getty Images

It is an American story. Barack Obama was not born into wealth or privilege, yet he secured fame and success. There are not many countries where it is possible for someone of humble origins to rise to the pinnacle of power and influence in the world. But in America it is possible because of the many gateways open to citizens.

Obama's life was not just one of modest beginnings but one defined by diversity—an ever-increasing aspect of American life in the twenty-first century. Obama is multiracial, with a white mother and a black father. He spent his formative years in Indonesia following the divorce of his parents and his mother's remarriage. At age 10, Obama went to live with his grandparents in Hawaii, where he experienced many different cultures.

Obama faced his share of hardships growing up. Not having his father around was difficult, and the moves he made to Indonesia and Hawaii were inevitably unsettling. But his family focused on securing him a good education, which was part of the motivation for his moving back to the United States in the early 1970s.

In 1979, Obama enrolled at Occidental College in Los Angeles. During this time he became active in student organizations opposing South Africa's practice of apartheid—his first effort at using a gateway to influence public policy. After his sophomore year, Obama transferred to Columbia University in New York, completing a bachelor's degree in political science. His interest in politics and the pursuit of gateways of influence continued. After graduating, Obama moved to Chicago to work as a community organizer in Chicago's largely poor and black South Side.

Eventually, Obama enrolled in Harvard Law School, where he became the first African American president of the Harvard Law Review. This recognition drew national media attention and a contract from Random House to write a book about race relations, ultimately titled *Dreams from My Father: A Story of Race and Inheritance*. This memoir touched on themes of race and racial identity. It was also during Obama's stint at Harvard that he met Michelle Robinson, a Chicago South Side native and fellow lawyer who worked for the firm where he completed a summer internship. They married in 1992 and decided to live in Chicago to raise their family.

Obama immersed himself in the African American community in Chicago. He directed the Illinois Vote Project, which increased black turnout in the 1992 election and registered hundreds of thousands of people to vote. Obama continued to pursue the gateway offered by elections. In 1996, Obama ran for and won an Illinois state senate seat, representing the 13th District of Illinois.

During his time as a state senator, Obama worked with both Republicans and Democrats. He helped to pass substantial amounts of legislation on issues ranging from health care and welfare reform to a bipartisan effort to monitor racial profiling in police activity.

Obama decided to run for U.S. Congress against Chicago alderman and incumbent congressman Bobby Rush in the 2000 Democratic primary. But Obama was not nearly as well known as Rush, and he lost by 30 percentage points in the Democratic primary. It was stinging defeat, yet it did not deter Obama. Four years later, he ran for an even bigger prize—the U.S. Senate. This time the well-known and potentially well-financed Democrats chose not to run, making it possible for him to win the primary. Obama's luck continued when the GOP nominee, Jack Ryan, faced a scandal involving his ex-wife and sex clubs, forcing him out of the race. That development opened wide a gate for Obama to win the Senate seat.

As he ran for Senate in 2004, he continued to gain national attention, so much so that he was invited to deliver the keynote address at the 2004 Democratic National Convention. On this huge stage, he gave an inspirational speech that propelled him to the top ranks of possible presidential candidates in 2008. He made the most of that opportunity, running a successful campaign that beat the formidable Hillary Clinton in the primary and then went on to defeat the Republican nominee and war hero, Senator John McCain.

Holding aside one's personal beliefs about President Obama, his story is compelling, speaking directly to how the U.S. political system can work. You can be born into modest circumstances and yet, with grit, determination, and resilience, have a chance to do great things. Not everyone will become president, but everyone can make a real difference by getting involved just as Obama did. Obama's career is proof that the steps you take as a student to be involved in your community can take you places you cannot even imagine right now. The key is to start by walking through one of the many gateways of American politics.

1.1 Gateways: Evaluating the American Political System

Identify the successes we have achieved and the obstacles we face in establishing a "more perfect union"

This text, *Gateways to Democracy*, explains how citizen involvement has expanded American democracy and how each of you can also influence the political system. We call the avenues of influence "gateways." This text serves as a handbook for democratic citizenship by peeling back the layers of American government to reveal the ways you can get involved and to explain the reasons you should do so. The American political system is complicated, large, and sometimes frustrating. As the term *gateways* implies, there are also *gates*—obstacles to influence, institutional controls that limit access, and powerful interests that seem to block the people's will. We describe these as well because to be a productive and influential member of American society, you need to understand how the hurdles and portals of American politics work.

Through citizen involvement, American democracy has achieved many successes:

- Our institutions are amazingly stable.
- The government has weathered many severe crises, yet it has peaceful transitions of power.
- Citizens are able to protest those policies they oppose.
- Americans enjoy substantial freedom.
- American society has offered a gateway to millions of immigrants.
- Americans exhibit more commitment to civic duty than do citizens in nearly all other major democracies.[2]
- Americans show more tolerance of different political views than do citizens in other major democracies.[3]
- Americans' support of marriage equality has surged over the past few years, underscoring a broadening commitment to civil rights.

These successes do not mean that there are not problems:

- Government does not always respond to public opinion.
- Racial tensions persist across the country.
- There is growing poverty in the country.[4]
- The public's trust in the institutions of government has never been so low.[5]
- The rate of turnout in elections is among the lowest of the major democracies.
- Distrust of some religious minorities, such as Muslims and Mormons, remains.[6]
- America has sought at times to erect gates to keep certain groups out.
- Political polarization is on the rise.[7]
- The U.S. national debt in 2016 is approaching $20 trillion.[8]

To solve these and other problems and achieve the "more perfect Union" promised in the Constitution, the nation's citizens must be vigilant and engaged. We have framed our text with the goal of demonstrating the demands and rewards of democratic citizenship. As we explore the American political system, we place special emphasis on the multiple and varied connections among citizenship, participation, institutions, and public policy. Our focus is on the following gateway questions:

- How can you get yourself and your opinions represented in government?
- How can you make government more responsive, and responsible, to citizens?
- How can you make American democracy better?

Jim West/Age fotostock/Superstock

IMAGE 1.1 The current generation of college students is very interested in giving back to the community, as shown in this picture of a Habitat for Humanity project.

The laws that regulate the American economy, social issues, and even political participation are examples of **public policy**—the actions by government to achieve a goal. In the arena of public policy, we determine who gets what, when, and how, and with what result. In each chapter of this book, we will examine a major public policy issue related to the topic. You will find that the public policy process is often divided into five stages:

1. Identifying the problem
2. Placing the problem on the agenda of policy makers
3. Formulating a solution
4. Enacting and implementing the solution
5. Evaluating the effectiveness of the solution.

These stages combine to form an ideal model of the process; however, this process does not always unfold so neatly. You will also find that individuals, organizations, and political institutions all work together to determine public policies: Congress, the president, the executive branch agency that deals with the issue, the courts, political parties, interest groups, and interested citizens. In each chapter, you will learn about an important public policy, analyze who the stakeholders are and how the policy is formed, evaluate the policy, and, finally, construct your own solution (see Public Policy and Gateways to Democracy).

Linda Moon/Shutterstock.com

IMAGE 1.2 The United States has great wealth, but far too many citizens face poverty and homelessness.

1.2 Democracy and the American Constitutional System

Analyze how the constitutional system balances liberty and order

Today democracy is presumed to be a good form of government, and most would say it is the best form. Democracy is the type of government to which many nations aspire, but it has not always been true. Only in the past two centuries—partly through the example of the United States—has democracy gained favor. Let us sketch some of the fundamental aspects of American democracy.

Liberty and Order

Literally and most simply, **democracy** is rule by the people, or **self-government**. In a democracy, the citizens hold political authority, and they develop the means to govern themselves. In practice, that means rule by the majority, and in the years before American independence, **majority rule** had little appeal. In 1644 John Cotton, a leading clergyman of the colonial period, declared democracy "the meanest and worst of all forms of government."[9] Even after American independence, Edmund Burke, a British political philosopher and politician, wrote that a "perfect democracy is . . . the most shameless thing in the world."[10] At the time democracy was associated with mob rule, and mobs were large, fanatical, ignorant, and dangerous. If the mob ruled, the people would suffer. There would be no **liberty** or safety; there would be no **order**. Eighteenth-century mobs destroyed private property, burned effigies of leaders they detested, tarred and feathered their enemies, and threatened people who disagreed with them. In fact, such events occurred in the protests against British rule in the American colonies, and they were fresh in the minds of those who wrote the Declaration of Independence and the Constitution.

John Adams, a signer of the Declaration of Independence and later the nation's second president (1797–1801), was not a champion of this kind of democracy. "Democracy," he wrote, "is more bloody than either aristocracy or monarchy. Remember, democracy never lasts long. It soon wastes, exhausts, and murders itself. There is never a democracy that did not commit suicide."[11] Adams knew about mobs and their effects firsthand. As a young lawyer before the Revolution, he agreed to defend British soldiers who had been charged with murder for firing on protesters in the streets of Boston. The soldiers' cause was unpopular, for the people of Boston detested the British military presence. But Adams believed that, following British law, the soldiers had a right to counsel (a lawyer to defend them) and to a fair trial. In later years, he considered his defense of these British soldiers "one of the best pieces of service I ever rendered my country."[12]

Why? In defending the soldiers, Adams was standing up for the **rule of law**, the principle that could prevent mob rule and keep a political or popular majority under control so it could not trample on **minority rights**. An ancient British legal principle, the rule of law holds that all people are equal before the law, all are subject to the law, and no one is above it. Adams and the others who wrote America's founding documents believed in a **constitutional system** in which the people set up and agree on the basic rules and procedures that will govern them. A constitutional system is a government of laws, not of men. Without a constitution and rule of law, an unchecked majority could act to promote the welfare of some over the welfare of others, and society would be torn apart.

The American constitutional system, therefore, serves to protect both liberty and order. The Constitution sets up a governmental structure with built-in constraints on power (gates) and multiple points of access to power (gateways). It also has a built-in means for altering the basic rules and procedures of governance through amendments. As you might expect, the procedure for passing amendments comes with its own set of gates and gateways.

The Granger Collection, NYC

IMAGE 1.3 Paul Revere printed this famous engraving of the Boston Massacre in 1770. Emphasizing the shedding of innocent blood—five colonists died—it rallied Bostonians to resist British tyranny. Evidence at the trial of the soldiers indicated that they were provoked by the mob with taunts, clubs, and stones. Lawyer John Adams argued for the defense.

The Constitution as Gatekeeper

"If men were angels," wrote James Madison, a leading author of the Constitution and later the nation's fourth president (1809–17), "no government would be necessary. . . . In framing a government which is to be administered by men over men," he continued, "the great difficulty lies in this: You must first enable the government to control the governed; and in the next place oblige it to control itself" (see *Federalist* 51 in the Appendix). Madison and the other **Framers** of the Constitution recognized that the government they were designing had to be strong enough to rule but not strong enough to take away the people's rights. In other words, the Constitution had to serve as a gatekeeper, both allowing and limiting access to power at the same time.

> ***Essential Knowledge***
> According to the social contract theory people agree to live under a government in order to protect their natural rights. If a government fails to do this, the people owe no further allegiance to the government.

James Madison, Thomas Jefferson, John Adams, and the other **Founders** had read many of the great political theorists. They drew, for example, on the ideas of the British political philosophers Thomas Hobbes and John Locke in perceiving the relationship between government and the governed as a **social contract**. If people lived in what these philosophers called a state of nature, without the rule of law, conflict would be unending, and the strong would destroy the weak. To secure order and safety, individuals come together to form a government and agree to live by its rules. In return, the government agrees to protect life, liberty, and property. Life, liberty, and property, said Locke, are **natural (unalienable) rights**—rights so fundamental that government cannot take them away.

> ***Essential Knowledge***
> Natural right, the idea that people have certain rights that cannot be taken away is an essential concept in U.S. politics.

PUBLIC POLICY AND GATEWAYS TO DEMOCRACY

The Gap Between Minimum Wage and Living Wage

The first federal minimum wage requirement was signed into law by President Franklin Delano Roosevelt in 1938 as part of the Fair Labor Standards Act; it set the minimum wage at 25 cents per hour and established a 44-hour workweek. States could mandate pay levels above the federal minimum wage, but they could not go below it. While he was lobbying Congress and the public on behalf of the bill, President Roosevelt said that the United States should give "all our able-bodied working men and women a fair day's pay for a fair day's work."[13] Others have also argued that individuals, families, and communities must be able to earn a living wage in order to rise above the poverty level, which would in turn give them more time and energy to participate in the democratic process.

Today the federal minimum wage is set at $7.25, although more than twenty states require employers to pay more than that wage.[14] Still, even at that wage, working full time leaves these workers still well below what is

TABLE 1.1 Minimum Wage vs. Living Wage by State

State	Wage Gap	Living Wage (1 adult)	Minimum Wage	State	Wage Gap	Living Wage (1 adult)	Minimum Wage
HI	**$6.49**	$13.74	$7.25	MS	**$2.70**	$9.95	$7.25
MD	**$5.82**	$13.07	$7.25	CO	**$2.69**	$10.69	$8.00
DC	**$5.34**	$14.84	$9.50	IA	**$2.68**	$9.93	$7.25
VA	**$5.11**	$12.36	$7.25	WY	**$2.68**	$9.93	$7.25
NY	**$4.75**	$12.75	$8.00	MN	**$2.65**	$10.65	$8.00
MA	**$4.60**	$12.60	$8.00	WV	**$2.65**	$9.90	$7.25
NJ	**$4.26**	$12.51	$8.25	NM	**$2.63**	$10.13	$7.50
NH	**$4.18**	$11.43	$7.25	AZ	**$2.57**	$10.47	$7.90
DE	**$3.93**	$11.68	$7.75	KS	**$2.57**	$9.82	$7.25
GA	**$3.44**	$10.69	$7.25	ND	**$2.54**	$9.79	$7.25
AK	**$3.42**	$11.17	$7.75	IN	**$2.49**	$9.74	$7.25
CA	**$3.34**	$12.34	$9.00	KY	**$2.46**	$9.71	$7.25
NC	**$3.28**	$10.53	$7.25	NV	**$2.41**	$10.66	$8.25
CT	**$3.27**	$11.97	$8.70	VT	**$2.40**	$11.13	$8.73
SC	**$3.24**	$10.49	$7.25	ID	**$2.34**	$9.59	$7.25
LA	**$3.22**	$10.47	$7.25	AR	**$2.31**	$9.56	$7.25
PA	**$3.15**	$10.40	$7.25	OK	**$2.24**	$9.49	$7.25
ME	**$3.11**	$10.61	$7.50	NE	$2.23	$9.48	$7.25
UT	**$3.04**	$10.29	$7.25	SD	$2.23	$9.48	$7.25
FL	**$3.01**	$10.94	$7.93	MO	$2.14	$9.64	$7.50
RI	**$3.01**	$11.01	$8.00	MI	$1.83	$9.98	$8.15
TN	**$3.01**	$10.26	$7.25	MT	$1.82	$9.72	$7.90
TX	**$2.95**	$10.20	$7.25	OR	$1.58	$10.68	$9.10
AL	**$2.92**	$10.17	$7.25	OH	$1.44	$9.39	$7.95
WI	**$2.88**	$10.13	$7.25	WA	$1.02	$10.34	$9.32
IL	**$2.83**	$11.08	$8.25				

Source: Amy K. Glasmeier, "Living Wage Calculator," Massachusetts Institute of Technology. Accessed February 25, 2016, at http://livingwage.mit.edu.

called a "living wage." In other words, many workers are well below the poverty level. Table 1.1 shows the gap between the minimum wage in that state and the "living wage." In all fifty states, the formal minimum wage is below a wage that would allow these workers to climb out of poverty. In cases like the state of Washington, the gap is about $1 (which is still about $2,000 a year). In Virginia, the gap is $5.11, which yields an income difference of just over $10,000. These kinds of data underscore why there have been numerous calls for increasing the minimum wage. The case becomes even more compelling when you consider these data are only addressing workers as supporting themselves. If they are supporting a family, the gap grows considerably.

Even with the data from Table 1.1, there are reasons not to raise the minimum wage. The central argument of opponents of raising the minimum wage is that most of these jobs are located in small businesses that cannot afford to pay the higher wages. Employers may not hire more workers at a higher rate, and they may even fire existing workers, in order to keep their businesses profitable. Those who oppose raising the minimum wage also argue that open trade policies have given an unfair advantage to foreign manufacturers that can hire workers at very low wages, and so produce and sell goods for less.

It is difficult, however, to assess the impact of raising the minimum wage on job growth or trade imbalances because there are so many other factors that affect the economy. For example, the last raise in the federal minimum wage occurred in 2009 in the midst of a major recession caused by a crash in the housing market. How many jobs were lost due to the recession, and how many resulted from the hike in the minimum wage? It is possible that the increased minimum wage contributed to a decline in jobs, but it is also possible that the increase had no effect at all in the larger context of an economic downturn. Economists and other experts have not reached a consensus on this question.

In making a policy choice, you must judge what President Franklin Roosevelt called a "fair day's pay for a fair day's work." In the context of the American democracy, the minimum wage debate raises fundamental questions about the government's role in guaranteeing equality of economic opportunity.

Public Policy Connections

1. If the Articles of Confederation were still in effect today, who would be responsible for setting a minimum wage? What would be the implication for the national economy?
2. Should states be allowed to set a higher minimum wage than what is established by the federal government? What are the economic implications when one state's minimum wage is significantly higher than another's?

But these ideas about government as a social contract were untested theories when Madison and others began to write the Constitution. There were no working examples in other nations. The only model for self-government was ancient Athens, where the people had governed themselves in a **direct democracy**. In Athens, citizens met together to debate and to vote. That was possible because only property-owning males were citizens, and they were few in number and had similar interests and concerns.[15]

But the new United States was nothing like the old city-state of Athens. It was an alliance of thirteen states—former colonies—with nearly 4 million people spread across some 360,000 square miles. Direct democracy was impractical for such a large and diverse country, so those who wrote the Constitution created a **representative democracy** in which the people elect representatives who govern in their name. Some observers, including the Framers, call this arrangement a **republic**, a form of government in which power derives from the citizens, but their representatives make policy and govern according to existing law.

Essential Knowledge
Republicanism or representative democracy is foundational to the U.S. political system

Could a republic work? No one knew, certainly not the Framers. The government they instituted was an experiment, and they developed their own theories about how it would work. Madison, for example, rejected the conventional view that a democracy had to be small and homogeneous so as to minimize conflict. He argued that size and diversity were assets because competing interests in a large country would balance and control—or check—one another and prevent abuse of power. Madison called these competing interests **factions**, and he believed that the most enduring source of faction was "the various and unequal distribution of property. Those who hold, and those who are without property, have ever formed distinct interests in society," he wrote. "Those who are creditors, and those who are debtors, fall under a like discrimination. A landed interest, a manufacturing interest, a mercantile interest, a monied interest, with many lesser interests, grow up of necessity in civilized nations, and divide them into different classes, actuated by different sentiments and views" (see *Federalist* 10 in the Appendix).

Essential Knowledge

In *Federalist* 10, Madison argues that a large republic with divided power is the ideal way to deal with the problems associated with factions.

In a pure democracy, where the people ruled directly, Madison expected that passions would outweigh judgments about the common good. Each individual would look out for himself, for his self-interest, and not necessarily for the interests of society as a whole, which is what we might call **civic interest**. In a republic, however, the people's representatives would of necessity have a broader view. Moreover, they would, Madison assumed, come from the better educated, a natural elite. The larger the republic, the larger the districts from which the representatives would be chosen, and thus the more likely that they would be civic-minded leaders of the highest quality. More important, in a large republic, it would be less likely that any one faction could form a majority. In a small seaside republic, for example, it would be possible for fishing interests to form a majority that could pass laws to the detriment of nonfishing interests. In another small republic, a religious sect could form a majority. But in a large and diverse republic, such narrow-minded majorities would not be possible. Interests would balance each other out, and selfish interests would actually be checked by majority rule.

Balance, control, order—these values were as important to the Framers as liberty. So while the Constitution vested political authority in the people, it also set up a governing system designed to prevent any set of individuals, any political majority, or even the government itself from becoming too powerful. The Framers purposely set up barriers and gates that blocked the excesses associated with mob rule.

Consequently, although the ultimate power lies with the people, the Constitution divides power both horizontally and vertically. Within the federal government, power is channeled into three different branches—the **legislative branch** (Congress), which makes the laws; the **executive branch** (the president and the government departments, or bureaucracy), which executes the laws; and the **judicial branch** (the Supreme Court and the federal courts), which interprets the laws (see Figure 1.1). This horizontal division of power is referred to as the **separation of powers**. To minimize the chance that one branch will become so strong that it can abuse its power and harm the citizenry, each branch has some power over the other two in a system known as **checks and balances**. The Constitution also divides power vertically, into layers, between the national government and the state governments. This arrangement is known as **federalism**. In a further division of powers, state governments create local governments.

The American constitutional system thus simultaneously provides gateways for access and gates that limit access. The people govern themselves, but they do so indirectly and

Legislative Branch

Makes the laws

Executive Branch

Executes the laws

Judicial Branch

Interprets the laws

FIGURE 1.1 The Three Branches of Government

Within the federal government, power is divided into three separate branches.

through a system that disperses power among many competing interests. This textbook explores both the gateways and the gates that channel and block the influence of citizens.

1.3 American Political Culture

Describe the political values and ideologies Americans share

As an experiment, the American republic has been open to change in the course of the nation's history. Despite their theorizing, the Framers could not have anticipated exactly how it would develop. Madison was right, however, about the enduring influence of factions. The people quickly divided themselves into competing interests and shortly into competing **political parties**, groups organized to win elections. The process by which competing interests determine who gets what, when, and how is what we call **politics**.[16]

Madison was right, too, about the sources of division, which are often centered in the unequal distribution of property and competing ideas about how far government should go to reduce inequality. Public opinion about such matters is sometimes described as falling on a scale that ranges from left to right, and when people have a fairly consistent set of views over a range of policy choices, they are said to have a **political ideology**—that is, a coherent way of thinking about government—a philosophy, so to speak. In contrast, **party identification**, or partisanship, is a psychological attachment to a particular party. This attachment is related to political ideology, but it is more personal than philosophical.

A person's ideology can be a strong clue as to what he or she thinks about politics. On the left end of the scale are **liberals** who favor government efforts to increase equality, including higher rates of taxes on the wealthy than on the poor and greater provision of social benefits, such as health care, unemployment insurance, and welfare payments to support those in need. **Conservatives**, on the right, believe that lower taxes will prompt greater economic growth that will ultimately benefit everyone, including the poor. Thus, liberals support a large and active government that will regulate the economy, while conservatives

Essential Knowledge

The idea of limited government, that the government is not all powerful, is an essential concept in U.S. politics.

LEFT (LIBERAL):
Greater faith in a large and active government to promote equality.
RIGHT (CONSERVATIVE):
Greater preference for a small and limited government to encourage economic growth.

FIGURE 1.2 American Political Ideology

Political ideology has been described in many ways. In one popular version, political thought is plotted on a continuum from left (liberal) to right (conservative).

Essential Knowledge

American political culture has been influenced by many factors including globalization. Globalization, and the technological changes that accompany it, have exposed Americans to a variety of new ideas.

fear that such a government will suppress individual liberty and create a dependency that actually harms those it aims to help. Figure 1.2 captures this ideological dimension.

The left–right division is not just about economics, however. For social issues, liberals generally favor less government interference, while conservatives favor rules that will uphold traditional moral values. Conservatives are, therefore, more likely to oppose abortion and same-sex marriage, while liberals are more likely to favor a woman's right to make decisions over reproductive matters as well as the right of same-sex couples to wed.

Although terms such as *conservative* and *liberal* are often used to label American political attitudes, it is often more complicated because of the mix of economic and social issues. In addition, Americans are often not ideologically consistent in their orientation to politics. They are likely to take positions on various issues, leaning left on some and right on others. In fact, most Americans are **moderates**, not seeing themselves as ideologically extreme. A sizable number of Americans also describe themselves as **libertarians**, believing that government should not interfere in either economic matters or social matters. Others take a **populist** perspective, opposing concentrated wealth and adhering to traditional moral values.

These ideological frameworks start to crystallize when people are in their early twenties, especially as they start to learn more about politics and come across competing perspectives. College can be an especially formative period when people start to forge their ideological lenses.

Despite the diversity of American **political culture**, we generally favor **individualism** over communal approaches to property and poverty, especially in comparison to the industrialized democracies of Europe and elsewhere in the world. The United States spends less on government programs to help less-well-off people than many other countries, and it has historically refrained from assuming control of business enterprises, such as railroads and banks, except in times of crisis. The United States tends to favor **capitalism**, an economic system in which business enterprises and key industries are privately owned, as opposed to **socialism**, in which they are owned by government. Yet, to prevent the worst abuses of capitalism, which can arise as businesses pursue profit to the detriment of citizens, Congress has passed laws that regulate privately owned businesses and industries. For example, government monitors banks and financial markets, ensures airline safety, and protects workers from injury on the job.

These regulations tend to moderate vast inequalities in wealth as well. Though prizing individualism, American political culture also has a long-standing tradition of **egalitarianism**. Americans rejected kings in the Revolution and titles of nobility in the Constitution. They also rejected British inheritance laws, which gave virtually all property to the eldest male. With estates divided more equally, and with a vast frontier that allowed land ownership to spread broadly, property in the United States was never as concentrated in the hands of a few as it had been in Europe. This greater equality, in turn, produced a political culture that values each individual's ability to achieve wealth and social status through hard work, not inheritance, and supports a free enterprise economic system, within limits. These observations were first made by Alexis de Tocqueville, one of the many Europeans who traveled to the United States in the nineteenth century to investigate the American experiment. His *Democracy in America* (1835) is a classic study of American institutions and culture. It remains insightful today for its thoughtful observations of American politics and character.

De Tocqueville was impressed by the extent to which individual Americans participated in political life. In a republic, policy making should reflect the will of the people expressed through their elected representatives and interest groups. Madison envisioned that the people's representatives managing the policy-making process would be an elite—well-educated people of "merit." But if the people divide into different classes, as Madison also envisioned, there is a danger to democracy if the people's representatives are an elite who represent only their own interests and not civic-minded leaders who consider the common good. In the 1950s, the sociologist C. Wright Mills in fact wrote about a narrow **power elite** made up of leaders from corporations, government, and the military who controlled the gates and gateways to power. But in the 1960s, the political scientist Robert Dahl took issue with Mills and argued that policy making has a more **pluralist** basis, with authority held by different groups in different areas. In this view, coal companies, as stakeholders, have a large say in coal policy, and farmers, as stakeholders, have a large say in farm policy, rather than a single power elite controlling both policy areas. While it is true, for example, that the coal industry pursues its interests vigorously, so do other industries. Elected representatives seek to balance these various interests even as they seek to do what is best for their constituents. The fact that no one group has a monopoly on power suggests that a more **majoritarian** policy-making process is in the making, in which those with a numerical majority hold the authority.

Essential Knowledge

There are various forms that representative democracies can take: participatory, pluralist, or elite.

Essential Knowledge

A participatory democracy is one in which mostly all segments of society participate in political life.

An elite democracy is one in which an elected "elite" make decisions for the society.

A pluralist democracy recognizes that there are different groups, or "interests" in a society.

Essential Knowledge

American politics displays examples of all three of these models of democracy (participatory, elite, and pluralist).

1.4 Responsiveness and Equality: Does American Democracy Work?

Evaluate American democracy in terms of responsiveness and equality

Does American democracy work? That is a question we will be asking in every chapter of this text, and we invite you to start working on an answer. As citizens, you have both a right and a responsibility to judge the government because it is *your* government.

To guide your thinking, we focus on two basic themes, **responsiveness** and **equality**. Is government responsive to the needs of its citizens? Do all citizens have an equal chance to make their voices heard? We ask you to keep these themes in mind as you learn about the U.S. political system. To give you a basis for making a judgment, we inform you of the findings of political scientists who have been asking and answering these questions for decades. Throughout this text, we present the latest data that speak to these broad issues. It is important to remember that we are not offering our opinions about government; instead, we are putting forward the most important evidence and theories, from a variety of perspectives, over the past fifty or so years. It is up to you to consider them and form your own conclusions.

One way to begin to evaluate American democracy, and to appreciate it, is to look briefly at alternative models of government. In a **monarchy**, an **autocracy**, and an **oligarchy**, a single person or a small elite rules society. Such systems are by definition undemocratic. Rulers in these systems have little reason or need to be responsive to the people. They hold most of the power and are not generally accountable to those they rule. They may try to satisfy the people with programs that meet basic needs for food and safety, but they do so to ensure control. These rulers have a low regard for the opinions of the people and do not want them to be engaged in public life. In these systems, the rulers are excessively wealthy, and the people are likely to be impoverished. To maintain order, the rulers typically rely on a strong army or a secret police force to keep the people in line through fear and intimidation. Rulers in such systems are overthrown when dissatisfaction rises to a level at which citizens are willing to risk their lives in open revolt, as they did in the Ukraine in 2014, or when the army or police conspire to replace one ruler with another.

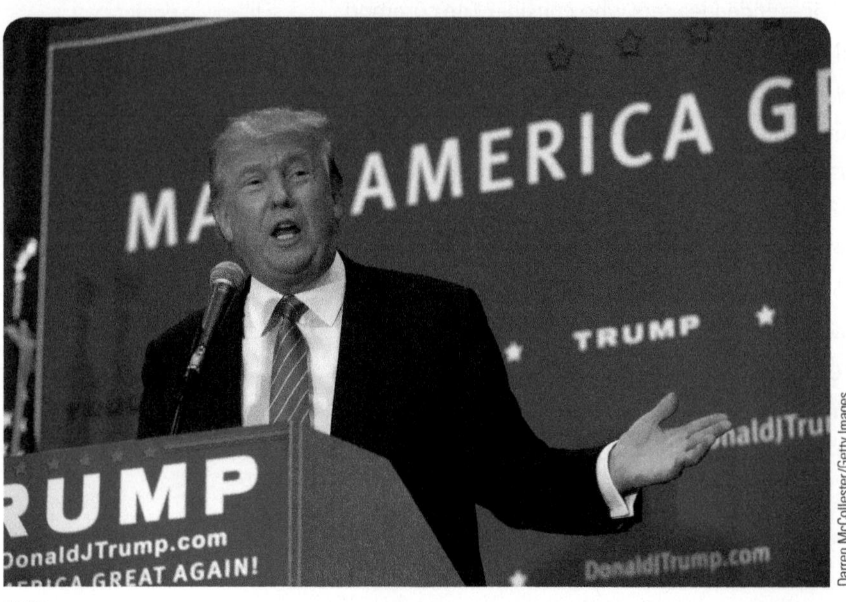

Darren McCollester/Getty Images

IMAGE 1.4 During the 2016 U.S. presidential campaign season, President Trump's rhetoric rocked the political world and activated many previously disengaged voters.

In contrast, a democracy asks its citizens to be actively engaged in their own governance, for the benefit of all. As the preamble to the U.S. Constitution states, the people create government (agree to a social contract) to "establish Justice, insure domestic Tranquility, provide for the common defence, promote the general Welfare, and secure the Blessings of Liberty to ourselves and our Posterity." The American system of government fundamentally provides protection from foreign enemies and from internal disorder; it also strives to meet the common needs of all citizens.

To promote the general welfare, the government develops public policy, as we have seen. Through incentives, it can alter the actions of individuals that lead collectively to bad outcomes. Consider the following example. If everyone drives to work, pollution increases and more resources are consumed. If a few people then decide to take the bus, those decisions, while admirable, do not yield a cleaner environment or save many resources. But if government incentives, such as a tax on cars, encourage many people to take the bus, the result is a cleaner environment and saving of resources.

The government often has a stake in pursuing what economists call **public goods**, goods from which everyone benefits. The core idea is that no one can be excluded. We all get the benefits of clean air, even if we have been driving cars and not taking buses. The fact that people cannot, by definition, be denied access to public goods creates disincentives for people to contribute to their provision. Government can require people to contribute to public goods through taxation. This is a primary justification for government. **Private goods**, by contrast, can be extended to some individuals and denied to others. When a government awards a contract to build a new library, the firm that wins the contract gets private goods (that is, money) from the government. The firms that lost the bid are denied that chance.

Who determines what goods, whether private or public, the government should provide, at what levels, and how to pay for them? These are core public policy problems. There are competing interests at every point in determining who gets what, when, and how. Politics is the process by which the people determine how government will respond. And it is in evaluating the basic fairness of government's response, and the basic equality of the people's general welfare that is thus secured, that we see whether American democracy is working.

Representative democracy succeeds when there is constant interaction between the people and the government. Government must be responsive to the needs and opinions of the people, and the public must find ways to hold government accountable. Government officials who are unresponsive to the people need to be removed from office. Elections provide the most common way to remove elected officials and are the primary mechanism for forging responsiveness. But unelected officials are also responsive to the public. The president appoints Supreme Court justices, with the advice and consent of the Senate, and those justices generally issue judgments that are consistent with public opinion. The bureaucrats who are hired to work in government departments carry out laws that the people's representatives have passed and the president has signed. In addition, work in government is always subject to review and investigation by other branches of government, by the media, and by citizen watchdog groups.

Perhaps complicating the government's requirement to be responsive is the changing nature of policy demands made by its citizens. In 2014, a majority of kindergartners were minorities—the first time in American history.[17] In 12 or so years, those kindergartners will be of voting age, helping to redefine the American electorate. Figure 1.3 confirms this observation. By 2045, whites will no longer represent a majority of the voting population.[18] To be sure, non-whites share many issues that are of concern to white Americans, such as a strong economy. But even so, this change will alter American politics in fundamental ways. People with different racial and ethnic backgrounds may hold views about the role of government and about specific policies that may be different than other groups.

For a government to respond fairly to citizens, all citizens must have an opportunity to participate in it. Each citizen must have a chance to have his or her voice heard, either by voting or by participating in the political process and public life. These ideas form the basis of **political equality**. If citizens are not treated equally, with the same degree of fairness, then the foundation of democratic government is weakened. Simply put, democracy requires political equality, and political equality requires democracy.

Essential Knowledge

The Declaration of Independence, written by Thomas Jefferson, is based on the social contract theory of government.

The notion of equality was enshrined in the Declaration of Independence: "We hold these truths to be self-evident: That all men are created equal; that they are endowed by their Creator with certain unalienable rights; that among these are life, liberty, and the pursuit of

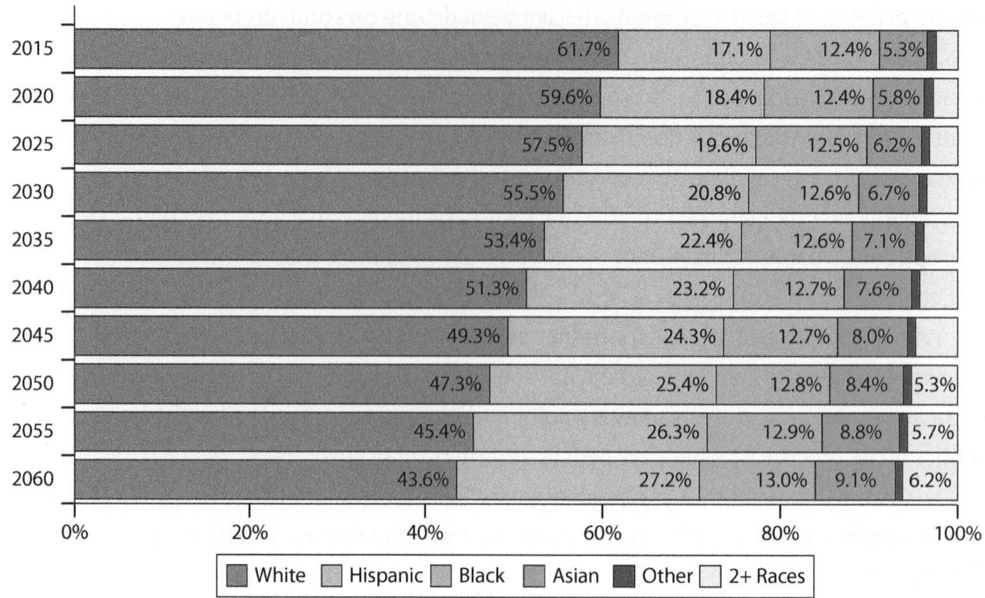

FIGURE 1.3 Increasing Minority Population in the United States

The growing Latino and Asian populations will likely make the United States a minority-majority country within three decades.

Source: U.S. Census Bureau, 2014 National Population Projections: Summary Tables, accessed March 17, 2016, http://www.census.gov/population/projections/data/national/2014/summarytables.html.

happiness." But this ringing statement did not announce an enforceable right, and government under the Constitution has in the course of the nation's history involved profound inequalities, most notably permitting slavery and a severe restriction of the civil rights of the African American minority for nearly two centuries. The American constitutional system was nearly a century and a half old before it guaranteed women the right to vote. Other racial and ethnic minorities have had to challenge the system to secure their rights, and, as the next chapters demonstrate, civil rights are still evolving. One way to evaluate American democracy is to evaluate the degree to which political equality has been achieved.

There are other aspects of equality. **Equality of opportunity** is one aspect—the expectation that citizens will be treated equally before the law and have an equal opportunity to participate in government. Does equality of opportunity also mean that citizens have an equal opportunity to participate in the economy (to get a job, to get rich) and in social life (to join a club, to eat at a restaurant)? And what about **equality of outcome**, the expectation that incomes will level out or that standards of living will be roughly the same for all citizens? In the United States, equality of outcome, or results, might entail the proportional representation of groups that have experienced discrimination in the past; that is, for full equality of outcome in Congress or on corporate boards, the number of African Americans would have to be equal to their proportion in the overall population, about 13 percent. What can, or should, government do to ensure equality of opportunity, or equality of outcome? These questions are hotly contested (see Supreme Court Cases: *Plyler v. Doe*), especially efforts to forge equality of outcome. We return to these issues in the final section of this introductory chapter.

Essential Knowledge

Americans look at core values, such as equality, differently. This impacts how citizens view their relationship with the government.

One way to think further about equality is to contrast American democracy with European democracies, which, as we have seen, have more communal approaches to property and poverty than does the United States and spend more on social programs. European democratic socialism, particularly as it exists in Scandinavian countries, limits extreme wealth through tax policies, and the result is greater income equality than in the United States. But the political culture of these nations does not prize individualism as highly as does the political culture of the United States, and the equality of results valued in democratic-socialist systems is nothing like American egalitarianism, which prizes individual effort and rejects Europe's rigid class divisions and inherited titles and wealth.

If the Declaration of Independence announced equality as a natural right of humankind, then the American democratic experiment has taken a long time to work out what that equality means. In 2015, the Supreme Court made marriage equality the law of the land, extending the right to marry to same-sex couples.[19] Just a few years earlier, the election of Barack Obama as president in 2008 was another significant achievement for American racial equality. Many observers thought it would be decades before the country elected an African American president.[20] That view reflected the long history of discrimination in this country. But Obama's swearing in as president, not just once but twice, sent an undeniable signal about equality in America.

In 2016, Hillary Clinton broke more barriers by becoming the first woman to be nominated for president by a major party. And many others will follow, whether they be Latino, gay, disabled, or Muslim. We challenge you to join these twenty-first-century pioneers. This text will give you the information you need to understand the way American government works and to recognize the gates and the gateways. We also invite you to think critically about American democracy, to engage in a class-wide and nationwide conversation about how well it is working, to offer ideas for making it work better, to influence the decision makers who make public policy, and even to become one of them.

1.5 The Demands of Democratic Government

List the responsibilities of individuals in a democracy

American democracy is not a spectator sport. It does not mean choosing sides and rooting for your team from the sidelines or from the comfort of your living room. It requires more than being a passive fan; you need to get into the game. But politics is more than a game. It shapes your life on a day-to-day basis. As a result, you have both rights and responsibilities. While the specific reasons to be involved in public life may vary, the need to participate does not.

> ***Essential Knowledge***
> A theme in American politics is the need to balance individual liberty with the need for society to be stable and secure. This sets the stage for conflicting views on the role of government and differing policy preferences.

Self-Interest and Civic Interest

The first reason to be involved is **self-interest**. You want government to serve your needs. Those needs, of course, range widely, depending on your stage of life, personal circumstances, and values. Some individuals prefer that the government stay out of people's lives as much as possible, and others prefer governmental assistance for the causes they hold dear. As a student, you may want the government to invest more in higher education and job creation; as a parent, you may want more aid for child care and school construction; as

SUPREME COURT CASES

Plyler v. Doe (1982)

QUESTION: Does the equal protection clause prohibit states from charging children of undocumented workers tuition in order to attend public school?

ORAL ARGUMENT: December 1, 1981 (listen at http://www.oyez.org/cases/1980-1989/1981/1981_80_1538)

DECISION: June 15, 1982 (read at http://caselaw.lp.findlaw.com/cgi-bin/getcase.pl?court=us&vol=457&invol=202)

OUTCOME: Texas violates the equal protection clause when it charges tuition to public school students who cannot prove U.S. citizenship (5–4).

In response to the increasing costs of educating children who were not citizens of the United States, Texas passed a law in 1975 stating that it would not reimburse local school districts for any of those costs. The law also relieved local school districts of any obligation to educate such children.

The parents of certain unnamed Mexican American schoolchildren who were denied access to the Tyler Independent School District filed suit. They claimed that the law deprived their children of the equal protection of the law as guaranteed by one of the clauses of the Fourteenth Amendment to the Constitution.

The Supreme Court ruled with the parents, noting first that while the subjects filing the lawsuit were not citizens of the United States, the Fourteenth Amendment prohibits states from denying the equal protection of the law to all "persons" under its jurisdiction, a term that does not distinguish between citizens and aliens. In reaching this part of the decision, the Court relied on a speech by Congressman John Bingham, one of the authors of the Fourteenth Amendment: "Is it not essential to the unity of the Government and the unity of the people that all persons, whether citizens or strangers, within this land, shall have equal protection in every State in this Union in the rights of life and liberty and property?"

The Supreme Court's equal protection decisions set different standards of review depending on the group being discriminated against in the law. The toughest standard, "strict scrutiny," applies to laws that discriminate on account of race or discriminate against aliens who are legally in the country. The parents bringing the suit admitted that they could not establish that the children were in the country legally. This distinction meant that the Court would only apply its lowest standard of review, "minimal scrutiny." Under strict scrutiny, Texas would have to show that it had a vital or "compelling interest" in passing the law, a difficult hurdle to pass. However, under minimal scrutiny, Texas only had to show a rational justification for the law.

Texas argued that it had a rational justification for the law, protecting the state's budget. It argued that without such a rule, undocumented workers would flood Texas, and the state's citizens would be required to pay more in taxes to educate them.

A majority of justices rejected that argument. They noted that the law places a lifetime hardship on the children, that undocumented workers come to Texas for a variety of reasons, and that prohibiting the employment of undocumented workers would be far more effective in protecting Texas's budget than denying education to their children.

A public education is a gateway for individuals to a higher-paying job, a fuller life, and a more active role in the democratic system. Providing equal access to education is one of the central ways we ensure equality of opportunity in the United States.

Thinking Critically

1. Can you identify reasons unrelated to prejudice that would lead Texas to want to deny education funds to the students in this case?
2. Should the Supreme Court treat cases involving legal immigrants (strict scrutiny) differently from cases involving undocumented residents (minimal scrutiny)?

a working person, you may view job security as the most important government responsibility. Whatever way you define your self-interest, by getting involved you send signals to elected officials, and if enough people agree with you, the government will likely act.

The second reason, what we called earlier *civic interest*, is more complex. The idea is that people get involved in the process because they want to be part of the voluntary organizations that make up the **civil society** that enables communities to flourish. They want to help others, improve their neighborhoods, and create an even better nation. Groups of interested people can accomplish things that individuals acting alone cannot. Sometimes these activities supplement governmental action; for example, neighborhood watch groups keep communities safe, and soup kitchens feed the hungry. Sometimes the activities aim at getting more out of government—more funding for roads or for new sports arenas, for example. By working together, people can encourage greater responsiveness from government. In so doing, they are better able to communicate their needs to a government that, in turn, becomes more responsive.

As gains in civic interest lead to broader public involvement, they also advance equality. In a democracy, the power of individual acts can be amplified, as Obama's actions demonstrate. Sometimes this amplification takes place through the courts; lawsuits arising from an alleged injustice experienced by one person can result in broad rulings that affect a great many. There are spillover effects to activism that can benefit everyone. Several examples come from the civil rights movement, in which students and others successfully sought to desegregate lunch counters, interstate buses, and local schools.[21]

Today's students are more likely to be civic-minded than college students in previous generations. If you were born between 1982 and 2003, you are part of the generation that social science researchers have identified as the **Millennials**. In reaction to the idealistic and ideological baby boomer generation born between 1946 and 1964, and the more cynical Generation X born between 1964 and 1982, Millennials are more likely to be optimistic and practical, and to identify as political independents. They tend to hold more liberal social views and are more likely religiously unaffiliated.[22]

Participation in the public sphere serves the larger civic interest. Voting is the most obvious political act. In addition, people express their views and ideas to public officials by volunteering in political campaigns, attending rallies, writing letters, and organizing meetings. E-mail, websites, blogs, social networking, text messages, and uploading of videos on YouTube offer additional means of joining the debate about politics and having an influence on government. Those who control the levers of power need to know your views so they can respond. With all the new technologies, the interface between people and politicians is now easier than ever.

Politics and the Public Sphere

Your generation has the power to shape the future in which you will live. Will America continue to be a land of opportunity? The following three issues represent some of the important concerns that you and the nation face. Working on these problems is reason enough to take part in the nation's civic life.

Educational Opportunity. Because you are attending college, education policy affects you every day and is important to your future. Education has long been considered both a fundamental component of democratic society and a stepping-stone to economic advancement. But what does it take to get a college degree, and who should bear the burden?

These are important questions because the cost of a college education continues to rise. Private colleges are increasingly expensive, and during times of economic decline, as state and local governments have faced budget cuts, public institutions of higher learning have also raised tuition (see Figure 1.4). The consequence of these increases is that students are taking on more and more debt to pay for these higher costs. This debt imposes a greater financial burden on you and begins to hurt just when you may also be thinking about having a family and buying a house.

If an educated public is necessary to democracy, and if the entire nation benefits from the contributions of college-educated individuals, does the federal government have an obligation to promote educational opportunity? Congress has decided it does and authorizes the Department of Education to spend some $32 billion annually to fund financial aid for higher education, including Pell Grants, work-study programs, and supplemental education opportunity grants. In response to deficit concerns, however, Pell Grants in general have been decreasing—from $41 billion in 2012 to $29 billion in 2015.[23]

College affordability is a concern of all college students and deserves to be a concern for the nation generally. Yet Americans do not hear much discussion about education in the news media; even President Obama's proposal to make community college free did not garner much attention. In the election of 2016, several candidates such as Bernie Sanders made college costs a major issue, but it still typically garners only less than 2 percent of coverage by television, cable, websites, and radio stations.[24] Does the lack of media attention

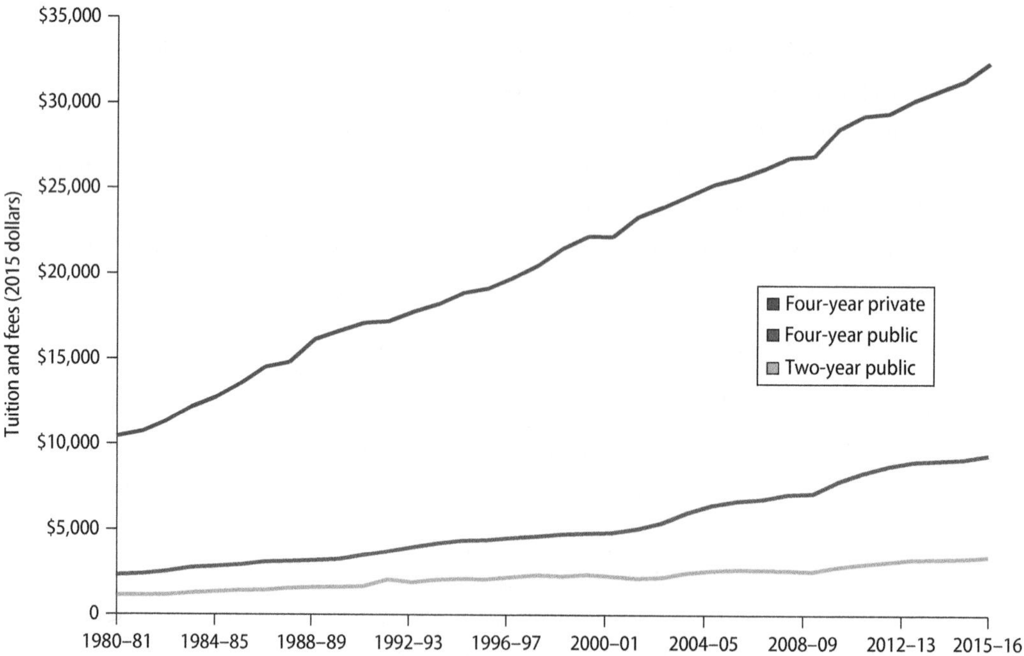

Note: The amounts shown are the list or published tuition and fees, not what students actually pay. Most undergraduates receive grant aid. The amounts shown are "sticker price" and do not account for grant aid. The College Board estimates them by weighting published tuition and fees by full-time undergraduate enrollment. They are deflated using the Consumer Price Index.

FIGURE 1.4 College Costs, 1980–2016

College costs have been increasing at a steady rate over the four decades, drawing the interest of policy makers over the past few years.

Source: College Board compilation of average tuition and fee charges, accessed March 17, 2016, http://trends.collegeboard.org/college-pricing/figures-tables/published-prices-national.

pose a barrier to getting educational opportunity on the policy agenda? What can you do to make government responsive to concerns about education? Education policy is examined in more detail in Chapter 3, Federalism.

Economic Opportunity. Educational opportunity is linked to economic opportunity because the more education you have, the more you are likely to earn. And the differences over the course of a lifetime can be millions of dollars in personal income (see Figure 1.5). But with the economic problems of late, will you be able to find a good job after graduation? In recent years college graduates have not fared as well as they have in the past. This should change as the economy improves.

Having a population of educated citizens who have good-paying jobs and who make a contribution to society is surely good for the entire nation. But does the government have an obligation to create economic opportunity? Should it intervene in business and the marketplace to equalize opportunity or to preserve competition, or should government allow the economy to be shaped by market forces? Throughout this book, we examine the role of government in the economy by taking a hard look at its obligations as well as at federal and state budgets, deficit spending, the national debt, and tax policy. These concerns are currently at the top of the policy agenda because in recent years, the federal government has run historically high deficits (has spent more than it receives in revenue) that have produced a huge jump in the national debt. Just twenty years ago, the national debt was about $5 trillion. In 2016, the national debt was more than $19 trillion, and it is projected to grow to $20 trillion in 2017—a more than three-fold increase.

Paying off this debt will take generations; your great-grandchildren might very well still be paying for it when they reach adulthood. For you, now, the size of this debt means that the federal government has less funding and limited flexibility for investing in programs that might create economic opportunity, such as education, job training, and infrastructure projects. How the government pays off this debt affects you, too, especially changes in the tax system that may alter your future income and job prospects. Thus the

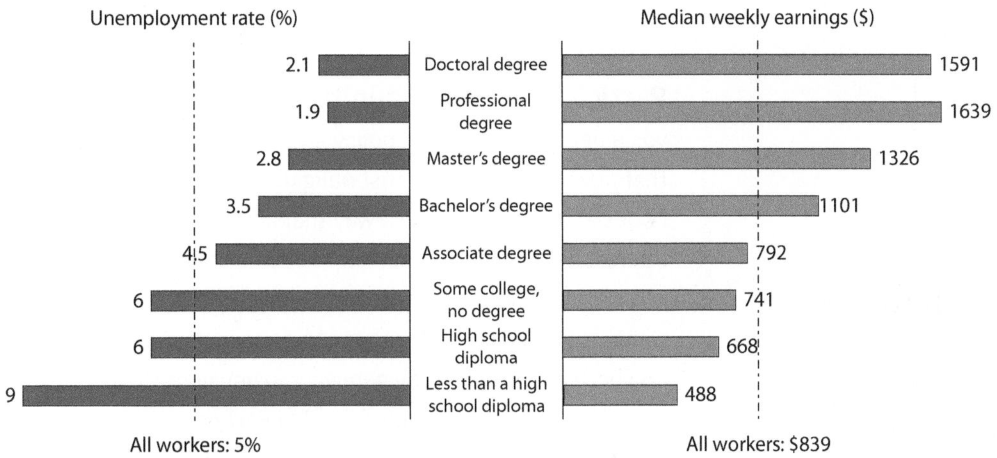

FIGURE 1.5 Earnings and Unemployment Rates by Educational Attainment

The benefits of a college education are clear: You can expect to earn about twice as much per week with a college degree than with only a high school degree.

Source: U.S. Department of Labor, Bureau of Labor Statistics. Employment Projections, accessed March 17, 2016, http://www.bls.gov/emp/ep_table_001.htm.

ELECTION 2016

A Changing and Frustrated Electorate

ALL ELECTIONS PRESENT candidates and parties with the challenge of gauging voters' preferences across a variety of issues. The 2016 election was no exception as Donald Trump and Hillary Clinton used focus groups and surveys to try to get a handle on what voters were looking for in their new president and how best to reach the hearts and minds of the voters. The 2016 election presented candidates with a more complicated picture of the American electorate, and this will be true to an even greater extent in future national elections. This is because the demographics of the United States are shifting, and with those shifts come more complicated sets of policy demands from voters. (See Figure 1.3 and the discussion in Section 1.4.)

These changes in the electorate also are fueling changes in the thinking of white Americans. One manifestation of that is the anger registered by this part of the electorate (see also Figure 1.6). There are notable partisan differences, with Republican white voters angrier than their Democratic counterparts, but the trends among both partisan groups are very much the same. In other words, these voters may have different amounts of anger, but they seem to be reacting to the same events in the same way.[26]

Candidates, therefore, must not only find ways to navigate the changing demographics of American politics, but they must also adapt to changes in the thinking within these key groups. Playing to anger requires a very different set of skills than responding to environmental policy—as Donald Trump so clearly showed. Trump did not mince words. He attacked the establishment relentlessly during his successful quest for the presidency, including members of the news media, special interests in Washington, the Democrats, and even leaders of his own party. By making these wide-ranging and often personal attacks, he gave voice to this anger, which he rode all the way to the White House.

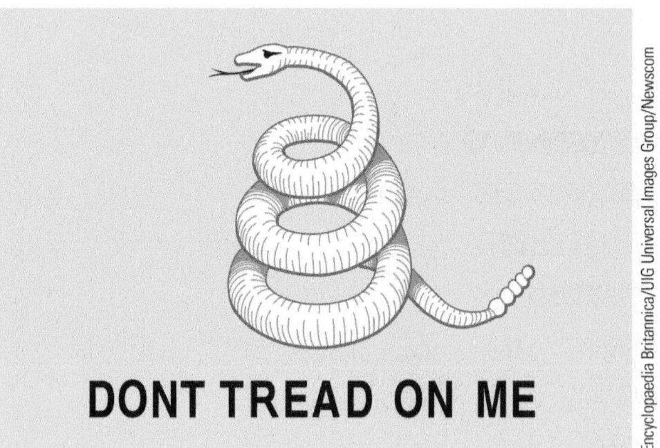

Encyclopaedia Britannica/UIG Universal Images Group/Newscom

IMAGE 1.5 The "Don't Tread on Me" slogan adopted by the Tea Party movement has a long association with resistance and protest. The movement adopted its central symbol, the snake, to represent the colonies in the era of the American Revolution.

federal budget and its ability to expand economic opportunity will directly affect your quality of life and standard of living in both the short run and the long run.

Participation Opportunity. How can you make your voice heard on education policy and economic policy issues that matter to you? Your first obligation is to learn about the issues and then to vote in a way that advances both your self-interest and your civic interest. You can also make your voice heard by joining groups that advocate your position. The U.S. Constitution guarantees rights of free speech and assembly, and both are fundamental gateways in any democracy.

In 2009, citizens formed the Tea Party movement to express their opinions that the government was not being responsive to their interests. The Tea Party movement grew out of localized groups of citizens who believed that the federal government has become too big, too expensive, and too intrusive. In the first set of elections after they formed, members of the Tea Party aligned themselves with

Republicans. In the years since, there has been friction between the Tea Party and more establishment Republicans, but it remains a powerful force at the grassroots level. That friction was never clearer than in the 2016 battle for the Republican presidential nomination, when businessman Donald Trump and Senator Ted Cruz focused on their anti-establishment credentials in the race against establishment favorites Senator Marco Rubio and former Governor Jeb Bush.

Regardless of your opinions about the Tea Party movement, it exemplifies the value of participation and the value of free expression of opinion in American democracy. This movement altered the political landscape by shifting the policy agenda and the direction of public discourse. As individuals and groups make their voices heard with energy and commitment, they fulfill a vital role in democratic government.

Your Gateway to American Democracy

James Madison, a key member of the Founding Fathers, offers an important final thought: "Knowledge will forever govern ignorance; and a people who mean to be their own governors, must arm themselves with the power which knowledge gives."[25] To govern yourself, you will need to understand your government, to be informed about issues you care about, to participate in politics, and to be engaged in the nation's civic life. As Madison and all those who wrote the nation's founding documents understood, an engaged public is the best check on excesses of power that threaten fair and just government. If the people do not meet the demands of democratic citizenship, if they do not fulfill their responsibilities, they will lose the freedoms they cherish.

We have written this text to give you the information you need to understand your government—its gates and gateways. We hope it will also push you to evaluate whether government is working for you and for all the nation's citizens. How democratic are we? How can we be better? One thing is certain: We will not be better unless you are involved. The only way to make American democracy more responsive and more equal is by participating.

We, therefore, invite you—actually, we urge you—to enter the gateways to democracy. These gateways are open to you as an American. They empower you, as a citizen, to play an important role in American civic life, and they enable you to experience the amazing arena of American politics. We look forward to sharing the journey with you.

JOHN G. MABANGLO/EPA/Newscom

IMAGE 1.6 The Black Lives Matter movement set an important tone on many campuses about the need to foster a greater commitment to inclusion, equity, and diversity.

POLITICAL ANALYTICS

Voters Express Anger at Politics as Usual

IN 2016, WHITE VOTERS from both political parties expressed anger at the political system. That anger began years prior to the 2016 election campaign and peaked when the federal government shut down in December 2013. Though white Republican voters express higher levels of dissatisfaction, white Democrats share their discontent, with almost 30 percent of them angry in December 2015. Their frustration is aimed at Washington, D.C.

Bernie Sanders and Donald Trump tapped into that anger in their presidential campaigns, arguing that the political system is broken and that they had answers. More than half of Trump's supporters and 30 percent of Sanders' backers expressed the anger shown in the graphic. Sanders' message that Wall Street has too much power in politics resonated with younger white voters and liberals. Trump's campaign promise to "Make America Great Again" was well received, especially among white voters with lower incomes and education.

Examine the trends in white voters' expressed anger at the U.S. political system.

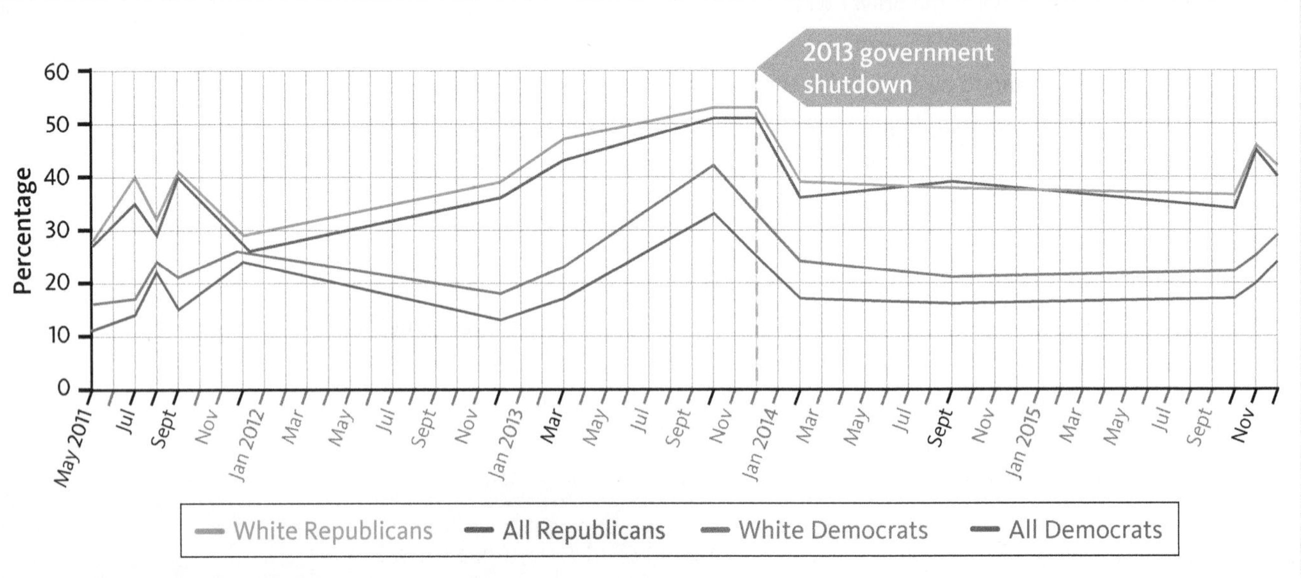

FIGURE 1.6 Anger Among White Voters, 2010–2015

Source: John Leland, "Bernie Sanders and Donald Trump Voters Share Anger, but Direct it Differently," *New York Times*, January 30, 2016. http://www.nytimes.com/2016/01/31/us/bernie-sanders-and-donald-trump-voters-share-anger-but-direct-it-differently.html. Data before September 2014 are taken from Roper's iPoll database. Other data taken from reported toplines at http://www.scribd.com/doc/239977251/Sep14b-Obama-Politics-a-M, http://www.scribd.com/doc/287367315/10-27-15-Republican-Party-toplines, http://www.scribd.com/doc/289515400/Nov-2015-CBS-News-NYT-poll-toplines, and https://www.scribd.com/doc/292971936/CBS-NYT-Poll-Donald-Trump-leads-strong-on-terrorism-economy.

Thinking Critically

1. Why do you think more white Republican voters than white Democratic voters expressed anger at the U.S. political system?
2. How successfully do you think the each party's candidate in the 2016 presidential election channeled that anger into the campaign?

Political Science Reasoning

Question 1

Practice 1, Practice 4

Americans have varying opinions on the role of the government in the life of the nation. Some Americans desire an activist government that would redistribute wealth to help eliminate poverty. Others would use governmental power to protect public virtue. Still others would reject both of these views and call upon the government to engage in only a small range of activities.

Examine the quotes below.

Speaker 1

As for this country, I stand or fall by my refusal to accept as a necessary condition of our future a permanent army of unemployed. On the contrary, we must make it a national principle that we will not tolerate a large army of unemployed, that we will arrange our national economy to end our present unemployment as soon as we can and then to take wise measures against its return. I do not want to think that it is the destiny of any American to remain permanently on relief rolls.[1]

Speaker 2

In this present crisis, government is not the solution to our problem; government is the problem. From time to time we've been tempted to believe that society has become too complex to be managed by self-rule, that government by an elite group is superior to government for, by, and of the people. Well, if no one among us is capable of governing himself, then who among us has the capacity to govern someone else? All of us together, in and out of government, must bear the burden. The solutions we seek must be equitable, with no one group singled out to pay a higher price.[2]

1. What is the view of each speaker as to the role of government in society?
2. What constitutional provisions (including the Bill of Rights) could be used by each speaker to advance his position?
3. Which speaker's point of view comes closest to your point of view regarding the role of government in society?

---

[1]Franklin D. Roosevelt, Fireside Chat, September 30, 1934.
[2]Ronald Reagan, Inaugural Address, January 20, 1981.

Focus on AP® Success

1 Gateways to American Democracy

Must Know: Key Concepts

- Participatory Democracy
- Pluralist Democracy
- Elite Democracy
- Federalists
- Limited Government
- Natural Rights
- Popular Sovereignty
- Republicanism
- Social Contract

Thinking Politically

Argumentation

One of the most fundamental decisions that a political system has to make is how to balance liberty and order. In the United States this has recently played out in the debates that surround the Second Amendment (right to bear arms) and the Fourth Amendment (search and seizure). When the Supreme Court is interpreting these amendments, which value, liberty or order, should receive precedence? To score well on the AP exam you will need a thesis, supporting evidence, and a well-organized essay.

Concept Application

Provide examples of how the Constitution reflects participatory democracy, pluralist democracy, and elite democracy.

Concept Application

Explain how the Constitution both facilitates and restricts citizen involvement in the political process.

Understanding Learning Objectives with Key Concepts

LOR – 1.A Explain how democratic ideals are reflected in the Declaration of Independence and the U.S. Constitution.

- The government of the United States is based on several key ideas. Among these are:
  - Limited government – This is the idea that the government is not all powerful. It is bound by its own laws. In the United States, the principle limits placed upon the national government can be found in the Constitution both in terms of restrictions on governmental action and the structure of government created by that document. For example, both the original texts of the Constitution and the Bill of Rights prohibit the national government from doing things like passing an ex post facto law or establishing an official religion. The governmental power is also limited because it is split between the national and state governments and at the national level is split between three branches.
- Natural rights – The founders believed that certain rights are granted by God. This is significant because if rights such as life, liberty, and property are granted by the government, then the government may take those things away. The theory of natural rights holds that while these important rights are not granted by government, it is the job of the government to protect them.
- Popular sovereignty – This theory holds that the people have the right to rule themselves.
- Republicanism – Republicanism is the idea that government should be based on elected representatives who rule on behalf of the people and are accountable to them during periodic elections.

- Social contract – The social contract theory holds that governmental power is derived from the people. The government can exercise power only so long as it maintains the support of the people. People retain the right to change their form of government as necessary.

LOR – 1.B Explain how models of representative democracy are visible in major institutions, policies, events, or debates in the U.S.

- There are several forms of representative democracy:
  - Participatory democracy – A participatory is based on a fairly broad level of participation in political life. Under this type of democracy, most all positions are elected and citizens frequently use the right to vote on policy through mechanisms such as referendums.
  - Pluralist democracy – A pluralist democracy recognizes the role that groups play in American political life. These groups are commonly referred to as interests or, in Madisonian terms, factions. In the pluralist model, public policy becomes the product of the conflict and compromise among the various groups concerned with a given policy.
  - Elite democracy – An elite democracy is a political system in which there are elements of democracy present. However, in this system the preferences of the elite are far more likely to be translated into public policy. Further, this system tends to minimize participation and civil society.
- The U.S. Constitution contains elements of the above forms of democracy. This creates an inherent tension regarding the degree to which and the manner in which citizens can participate in political decisions. This tension is born in the essays relating to the adoption of the Constitution such as *Federalist* 10 and Brutus 1.

Making Connections

Many of the concepts presented in this chapter are more fully illustrated in subsequent chapters. For example, the concepts of checks and balances and separation of powers are elaborated upon in Chapter 2.

Many of the philosophical debates that surrounded the making of the Constitution can still be seen in how the Court interprets the Bill of Rights. Essentially, when the Court does this it is establishing the legitimate boundaries of governmental action. As you study Chapter 4, Civil Liberties, refer back to this chapter to connect the values that undergird the Bill of Rights with the decisions made by the Court.

The Constitution reflects a desire for political equality. However, at the time of the adoption of the Constitution women, African Americans, and Native Americans were in a position of political inferiority. The chapters on civil rights and interest groups will illustrate how these groups have struggled to achieve equality.

This chapter deals with American political culture. You will see in Chapter 6, Public Opinion how that culture is transmitted to new generations through the process of political socialization.

Going Deeper: *Federalist* 10

The debate for the ratification of the constitution produced a series of essays called the *Federalist Papers*. In these essays Hamilton, Madison, and Jay outline the features of the new constitution and advocate for its adoption.

In *Federalist* 10, Madison deals specifically with factions, or what would be known today as interest groups. Madison set forth that a large republic is more likely to mitigate the negative impact of factions than are the individual states.

> *Among the numerous advantages promised by a well constructed Union, none deserves to be more accurately developed than its tendency to break and control the violence*

of faction. The friend of popular governments never finds himself so much alarmed for their character and fate, as when he contemplates their propensity to this dangerous vice.

Madison then states that there are two ways to deal with factions. The first method is to eliminate them and the second method is to control their effects.

There are again two methods of removing the causes of faction: the one, by destroying the liberty which is essential to its existence; the other, by giving to every citizen the same opinions, the same passions, and the same interests.

It could never be more truly said than of the first remedy, that it was worse than the disease. Liberty is to faction what air is to fire, an aliment without which it instantly expires...

The second expedient is as impracticable as the first would be unwise. As long as the reason of man continues fallible, and he is at liberty to exercise it, different opinions will be formed.

Therefore, since factions cannot be eliminated, the best course of action is to deal with the effects of factions. He asserts that a national government made up of elected representatives can do this and govern better than state governments. This is because it would be far easier for a local faction to control a state government than it would be for them to dominate a national representative government. Further, since the national government would represent a great range of interests, factions would naturally be pitted one against the other. This is because it is more likely a faction could gain a majority within smaller governments, but in a large republic the great diversity of thought should result in no single faction gaining enough power to rule without considering the interests of other groups.

2 The Constitution

AP® Learning Objectives

LOR – 1.A Explain how democratic ideals are reflected in the Declaration of Independence and the U.S. Constitution.

CON – 1.A Explain how Federalist and Anti Federalist views on central government and democracy are reflected in U.S. Foundational Documents.

CON – 1.B Explain the relationship between key provisions of the Articles of Confederation and the debate over granting the federal government greater power formerly reserved to the states.

CON – 1.C Explain the ongoing impact of political negotiation and compromise at the Constitutional Convention on the development of the constitutional system.

PMI – 1.A Explain the constitutional principles of separation of powers and checks and balances.

PMI – 1.B Explain the implications of separation of powers and checks and balances for the U.S. political system.

CON – 2.C Explain how the distribution of power among three federal branches and between national and state government impact policy making.

Performance Tasks

Upon the completion of this chapter, you must be able to do the following:

- Explain and provide examples of major principles of the Constitution and Declaration of Independence.
- Explain how the Constitution was designed to address the defects of the Articles of Confederation and how it is based on major compromises.

Blanscape/Shutterstock.com

"In New York, in Washington, they don't understand our problems. They don't know about the 3 million Mexicans who live in the Southwest. Let us pray to God that we triumph, that the nation's Supreme Court agrees with us."

GUS GARCIA
University of Texas at Austin

Library of Congress Prints and Photographs Division (LC-USZ62-137627)

Gus Garcia, high school valedictorian and star of the debate team at the University of Texas at Austin, grew up observing the social and legal discrimination against Latinos in Texas. It was the 1940s. Like Thurgood Marshall, the famed civil rights attorney and the first African American on the Supreme Court, Garcia wanted to fight for the rights of his people. Garcia followed his undergraduate years at the University of Texas with law school there. After serving in the Judge Advocate General Corps in the military, Garcia returned to Texas where he worked as legal counsel for the League of United Latin American Citizens (LULAC) and helped create the American GI Forum, a veterans group for Latinos, in 1948.

He also ran for the Board of Education in San Antonio, Texas, in 1948, joining forces with a local African American businessman. Their white opponents took out an ad in the local paper on the day before the election declaring, "It is your duty to keep racial and sectional strife out of your schools by electing experienced people who can work together in harmony. . . . Among the other candidates is a Negro undertaker [and] an active member of LULAC"[1] (i.e., Garcia). Garcia won the election, becoming the first Latino to serve on the San Antonio School Board.

In 1948, Garcia won a federal district (trial) court case on behalf of Minerva Delgado and others seeking to deny the state of Texas the authority to segregate Latino public school students as a violation of the Fourteenth Amendment, which guarantees equal protection of the law.[2] This decision, without recognition from higher courts, was largely ignored within the state of Texas. Thurgood Marshall, though, requested access to the *Delgado* case file from the attorneys in that case as part of his battle against racial discrimination.[3] Yet Garcia continued the struggle for Latino civil rights.

In 1952 Garcia began work on the case of *Hernandez v. Texas*.[4] The case would arguably become the most important constitutional decision by the Supreme Court regarding the Latino community in the United States.

Changes to the meaning of the Constitution can come about in two ways. First, there are constitutional amendments, twenty-seven of which have been enacted since 1791. Constitutional interpretation by the Supreme Court provides a second, and far more frequently used, gateway to updating the meaning of the Constitution.

The *Hernandez* case involved the murder conviction of Pedro Hernandez by an all-white jury in Texas. It was the first time that the Supreme Court dealt with a case involving issues related to Latinos as well as the first time a Latino attorney had argued before the Supreme Court. Texas argued that the equal protection clause applied only to African Americans, not other ethnic groups. Garcia, alternatively, argued that within Texas, Mexican Americans were treated as "a class apart" from the white community and should receive the protections of the equal protection clause of the Fourteenth Amendment. The fact that Latinos still had separate schools and bathrooms, and did not sit on juries, convinced a unanimous Supreme Court that "the constitutional guarantee of equal protection of the laws is not directed solely against discrimination between whites and Negroes."[5] The justices were convinced that under the social and legal system in Texas, Mexican Americans were treated as "a separate class"[6] and as such deserved full constitutional protection from the equal protection clause, and that Texas denied Hernandez that protection by excluding Latinos from serving on juries. The Court, which had already heard but not yet decided the *Brown v. Board of Education* case, was interested enough in Garcia's argument that it gave him unscheduled extra time during oral argument, an extremely rare gesture. The Supreme Court reversed the conviction of Hernandez. That reversal allowed Texas to retry Hernandez by a jury that did not exclude Latinos. Hernandez was found guilty again.

Nevertheless, Gus Garcia's legal victory led to a fundamental change in how the U.S. Constitution is interpreted with regard to discrimination against Latinos, granting them legal security under the equal protection clause of the Fourteenth Amendment. Garcia used the constitutional system of the United States to create new rights for the Latino community. Moreover, just two weeks after the *Hernandez* decision, the Supreme Court struck down segregated schools in *Brown v. Board of Education*, a case in which Garcia had been a supporter.

In this chapter, we examine the governing documents prior to the Constitution, particularly the Articles of Confederation and its deficiencies. We also track the debates at the Constitutional Convention and afterward, as the people of the United States decided whether to ratify the new Constitution. They did ratify it, but almost immediately they amended it. After we examine the structure and philosophy behind the new Constitution, we consider its responsiveness, through both amendment and less formal procedures, to changing times.

**The information from this vignette comes from the Salinas article cited in the first footnote as well as* A Class Apart: A Mexican American Civil Rights Story, *PBS Home Video, 2009, from which we pulled the opening quote.*

2.1 Before the Constitution

Assess what drove the colonists to seek independence

From the beginning, Great Britain accorded the American colonists, as British subjects, a certain amount of self-rule. When the colonists perceived that Parliament and the king were blocking their participation in government, they moved toward independence from Britain. They established a new national government under documents that included state constitutions and a national Articles of Confederation. In this section, we trace that process.

The British Constitution

constitution: *Document or set of documents that establish the basic rules and procedures for how a society shall be governed.*

A **constitution** is the fundamental law undergirding the structure of government. In a modern democracy, a constitution sets forth the basic rules and procedures for how the people shall be governed, including the powers and structure of the government, as well as the rights retained by the people.

Unlike many constitutions today, the British constitution is not a single document but rather a series of documents. Beginning with the Magna Carta in 1215, the British constitution defined the rights of the people and Parliament and limited the powers of the king. Following the so-called Glorious Revolution of 1688–89, Parliament asserted the power to suspend the law, to levy taxes, and to maintain a standing army. By the eighteenth century, British subjects believed that the British constitution guaranteed them certain rights, including the right not to be taxed without their consent and the right to be tried by a jury of their peers.

Toward Independence

The American colonists believed they had all the rights of British subjects. Thus they objected when, following the French and Indian War (1754–63), Great Britain tried to recoup some of the costs of defending the colonies by imposing regulations and taxes on them. The Sugar Act of 1764 set forth a long list of items that could be exported only to Great Britain, limiting competition for the colonists' goods. The Stamp Act of 1765 established a tax on virtually all forms of paper used by the colonists. Although Britain had previously levied import and export taxes on the colonies, this was the first direct tax by Britain on the colonists on products made and sold in America.

The colonists reacted angrily, forming trade associations to boycott, or refuse to buy, British goods. They also published pamphlets denouncing the loss of liberty. Led by Patrick Henry, they challenged not just the taxes themselves, but Parliament's authority to pass such measures. "Give me liberty," proclaimed Henry before the Virginia House of Burgesses, "or give me death." Soon enough, riots broke out against Stamp Act collectors, making enforcement impossible.

Britain repealed the Stamp Act in 1766 but replaced it with the Townshend Acts, which imposed new taxes on imports. The colonists mobilized against these new import taxes. Led

North Wind Picture Archives/Alamy

IMAGE 2.1 American Colonists protest the British Stamp Act.

by Samuel Adams, the Massachusetts legislature issued a letter declaring the Townshend Acts unconstitutional because they violated the principle of "no taxation without representation." The colonists thus began to insist that they had the right to participate in the political decisions that affected them.

The British had a more limited view of both participation and representation. At the time, only about one in six British adult males had the right to vote for Parliament, whereas two-thirds of free American adult males could vote for their colonial representatives.[7] Moreover, while most British cities did have representation in Parliament, some—just like the colonies—did not. Rather, representation in Parliament was based on historical population centers, so large new cities such as Manchester and Birmingham sent no representatives to Parliament, while the town of Dunwich continued to send a representative even though storms and erosion had swept it into the North Sea centuries earlier.

The British justified their lack of representation by claiming that all English citizens were represented by all members of Parliament, who purportedly acted in the common good. As political thinker and politician Edmund Burke wrote, "Parliament is a *deliberative* assembly of *one* nation, with *one* interest, that of the whole."[8] The colonists, however, rejected this view.

Aggrieved by taxation without representation, the colonists continued to resist the Townshend Acts through boycotts of taxed goods. Britain responded by dissolving the Massachusetts legislature and seizing a ship belonging to John Hancock, one of the leaders of the resistance. Britain also sent troops to quell the resistance, but the presence of soldiers during peacetime aggravated tensions. British soldiers fired on a threatening crowd in 1770, killing five colonists and wounding six others in what became known as the Boston Massacre. With boycotts of British goods costing Britain far more than the taxes raised,

TABLE 2.1 Events Leading to the Revolution

Year	Event	Description
1764	Sugar Act	Required colonists to export certain items only to Britain
1765	Stamp Act	Imposed taxes on almost all paper products; boycotts and riots followed
1766	Townshend Act	Imposed new taxes on imports; led to rallying cry "no taxation without representation"
1770	Boston Massacre	Five colonists killed by British soldiers; led Parliament to repeal all Townshend Act taxes except for tea tax
1773	Boston Tea Party	Colonists dumped taxed tea into Boston Harbor
1774	Coercive Act	Restricted political freedoms in Massachusetts
1774	Quartering Act	Required colonists to house British soldiers in their homes
1774	First Continental Congress	Rejected reconciliation with Britain and sent grievances to King George III
1775	Second Continental Congress	Acted as the national government of states, 1775–81; approved Declaration of Independence and appointed George Washington as commander of the army

Parliament rescinded all of the Townshend Act taxes except the one on tea. In 1773 Parliament granted the East India Company the exclusive right to sell tea to the colonies, and the company then granted local monopolies in the colonies. Angered by both the tax and the monopoly, colonists once again took action. Disguised as Indians, they dumped a shipload of tea into Boston Harbor (see Table 2.1).

In 1774 Britain responded to the Boston Tea Party with the Coercive Acts, which, among other things, gave the royal governor the right to select the upper house of the Massachusetts legislature. The Coercive Acts also denied Massachusetts the right to try British officials charged with capital offenses. Further legislation, the Quartering Act, required colonists to house British soldiers in their private homes, even during times of peace.[9] These acts convinced many colonists that their liberty was at stake and that rebellion and independence were the only alternatives to British tyranny.

In an attempt to present a more united front about colonial grievances, Benjamin Franklin proposed a congress, or assembly of representatives. The First Continental Congress, with delegates chosen by the colonial legislatures, met in Philadelphia in 1774. It rejected a reconciliation plan with England and instead sent King George III a list of grievances. It also adopted a very successful compact among the colonies not to import any English goods. Finally, it agreed to meet again as the Second Continental Congress in May 1775. This Second Continental Congress acted as the common government of the states between 1775 and 1781.

In April 1775, following skirmishes with British troops in Lexington and Concord, outside of Boston, the Second Continental Congress named George Washington commander of a new Continental Army. In 1776, with hostilities under way, Thomas Paine penned his influential pamphlet *Common Sense*, which called for independence from Britain. "There is something very absurd, in supposing a continent to be perpetually governed by an island," he argued.[10] *Common Sense* was the most widely distributed pamphlet of its time, and it helped convince many Americans that independence was the only way they could secure their right to self-government.

The Declaration of Independence

In June 1776, the Continental Congress debated an independence resolution but postponed a vote until July. Meanwhile, it instructed Thomas Jefferson and others to draft a **Declaration of Independence**. Congress approved the Declaration of Independence on July 4. Jefferson's Declaration relied in part on the writings of John Locke in asserting that people had certain natural (or unalienable) rights that government could not take away, including the right to life and liberty (see Chapter 1, Gateways to American Democracy). For Locke's reference to property, Jefferson substituted "the pursuit of happiness."

Essential Knowledge

Drafted by Jefferson, Adams, and Franklin, the Declaration of Independence states that political power flows from the consent of the governed, and establishes popular sovereignty as a core value of American political life.

Declaration of Independence: *The 1776 document declaring American independence from Great Britain and calling for equality, human rights, and citizen participation.*

The Declaration that Jefferson penned was a radical document. It established the right of the people to alter or abolish governments that do not meet the needs of the people; it declared the colonies independent from Britain; and it contained a stirring call for equality, human rights, and public participation in government that, although not legally enforceable at the time, has inspired generations of Americans seeking to make these ideas a reality.

> *We hold these truths to be self-evident: That all men are created equal; that they are endowed by their Creator with certain unalienable rights; that among these are life, liberty, and the pursuit of happiness; that, to secure these rights, governments are instituted among men, deriving their just powers from the consent of the governed; that whenever any form of government becomes destructive of these ends, it is the right of the people to alter or to abolish it, and to institute new government, laying its foundation on such principles, and organizing its powers in such form, as to them shall seem most likely to effect their safety and happiness.*

The Declaration went on to list grievances against King George III, including suspending popularly elected colonial legislatures, imposing taxes without representation, and conducting trials without juries. It then declared the united colonies to be thirteen "free and independent states." (The full text of the Declaration of Independence is in the Appendix.)

Even before the Declaration, the Continental Congress advised the colonies to adopt new constitutions "under the authority of the people." Reacting against the limitation on rights imposed by the British monarch and by royal governors in the colonies, these new state constitutions severely limited executive power but set few limits on legislative authority. At the same time, Americans made little effort to establish a national political authority, as most Americans considered themselves primarily citizens of the states in which they lived. Nevertheless, the Continental Congress needed legal

Francis G. Mayer/ Fine Art/Corbis

IMAGE 2.2 Members of the Second Continental Congress voted to approve the Declaration of Independence on July 4, 1776, though only John Hancock, president of the Congress, signed it that day.

authority for its actions, and, in 1777, its members proposed a governing document called the **Articles of Confederation**.

Articles of Confederation: *Initial governing authority of the United States, 1781–88.*

The Articles of Confederation

The Articles required unanimous consent of the states for adoption, which did not occur until 1781, just a few months before American victory in the Revolutionary War. They formally established "the United States of America," in contrast to the Declaration, which was a pronouncement of "Thirteen United States of America." According to the Declaration, each of the thirteen independent states had the authority to do all "acts and things which independent states may of right do," such as waging war, establishing alliances, and concluding peace. These were thirteen independent states united in a war of independence. With the Articles, the states became one nation with centralized control over making war and foreign affairs. But due to the belief that Great Britain had violated fundamental liberties, the Articles emphasized freedom from national authority at the expense of order. Thus the states retained all powers not expressly granted to Congress under the Articles.

Moreover, those expressly granted powers were extremely limited. Congress had full authority over foreign, military, and Indian affairs. It could decide boundary and other disputes between the states, coin money, and establish post offices. But Congress did not have the authority to regulate commerce or, indeed, any authority to operate directly over citizens of the United States. For example, Congress could not tax citizens or products (such as imports) directly; it could only request (but not demand) revenues from the states.

In addition to limiting powers, the Articles made governing difficult. Each state had one vote in Congress, with the consent of nine of the thirteen required for most important matters, including borrowing and spending money. Amending the Articles required the unanimous consent of the states. In 1781 tiny Rhode Island, blocking an amendment that would have set a 5 percent tax on imports, denied the whole nation desperately needed revenue. Moreover, the Articles established no judicial branch, with the minor exception that Congress could establish judicial panels on an ad hoc basis to hear appeals involving disputes between states and to hear cases involving crimes on the high seas. There was no separate executive branch, but Congress had the authority to establish an executive committee along with a rotating president who would manage the general affairs of the United States when Congress was not in session.[11]

Essential Knowledge

The Articles of Confederation had several defects, including no central military authority sufficient to suppress rebellion such as Shays' Rebellion and insufficient power to lay and collect taxes.

These deficiencies led to predictable problems. With insufficient funds, the nation's debts went unpaid, hampering its credit. Even obligations to pay salaries owed to the Revolutionary War troops went unfulfilled. Without a centralized authority to regulate commerce, states taxed imports from other states, stunting economic growth. Lack of military power allowed Spain to block commercial access to the Mississippi River. Barbary pirates off the shores of Tripoli captured American ships and held their crews for ransom.

While the government of the United States suffered from too little authority, James Madison, Thomas Jefferson, and others came to believe that the governments of the states possessed too much authority. Popularly elected legislatures with virtually no checks on their authority passed laws rescinding private debts and creating trade barriers against other states. They also began taking over both judicial and executive functions. As Jefferson declared, this aggregation of power was no more acceptable if done by a plural legislature than if done by a unitary executive: "173 despots would surely be as oppressive as one."

Though the legislature was chosen by the people, "An *elective despotism* was not the government we fought for."[12]

With the United States in desperate financial straits, James Madison proposed a convention of states to consider granting the national government the power to tax and to regulate trade. Only five states showed up at this 1786 Annapolis Convention, preventing it from accomplishing much.

As the Annapolis Convention took place, word spread of a revolt in western Massachusetts that made the weakness of the national government all too clear. Revolutionary War hero Daniel Shays and several thousand distressed farmers forced courts to close and threatened federal arsenals. Not until February 1787 did Massachusetts put down Shays's Rebellion. The revolt helped convince the states that, on top of the Articles' other problems, the document provided for too much freedom and not enough order. The Annapolis Convention thus issued an invitation to all thirteen states to meet in Philadelphia in May 1787 to consider revising the Articles of Confederation. This time only Rhode Island declined the invitation.

Bettmann/Corbis

IMAGE 2.3 Daniel Shays led a protest movement of debt-ridden farmers facing foreclosures on their homes and farms. Demanding lower taxes and the issuance of paper money, they engaged in mob violence to force the Massachusetts courts to close.

2.2 The Constitutional Convention

Identify the major compromises at the Constitutional Convention

The delegates who met in Philadelphia were charged with amending the Articles of Confederation so that the national government could work more effectively. Almost immediately, however, they moved beyond that charge and began debating a brand-new constitution. To complete that newly proposed constitution, the delegates needed to reach compromises between large and small states over representation, between northern and southern states over issues related to slavery, and between those who favored a strong national government and those who favored strong state governments. The document they created, which was then sent to the states for ratification, is, with subsequent amendments, the same Constitution we live by today. (The full text of the Constitution of the United States is in the Appendix.)

The Delegates

Constitutional Convention: *Meeting in 1787 at which twelve states intended to revise the Articles of Confederation but ended up proposing an entirely new Constitution.*

The fifty-five delegates to the **Constitutional Convention** of 1787 represented large (Virginia) and small (Delaware) states. They represented states in the south with large slave populations (South Carolina, 43 percent of total population), states in the north with small slave populations (Connecticut, 1 percent of population), but only one state (Massachusetts) with no

FOUNDERS

FRAMERS

John Jay (1745–1829) of New York was a delegate to the First Continental Congress and president of the Second, though he was not present when the Declaration of Independence was signed. He was U.S. minister to Spain from 1780 to 1782 and a negotiator of the peace treaty with Britain in 1783. He was an author of the *Federalist Papers* and the first chief justice of the Supreme Court.

John Adams (1735–1826) of Massachusetts was a delegate to the First and Second Continental Congresses and, with his cousin Samuel, a Signer of the Declaration of Independence. He was a diplomat to France in 1778–79, a negotiator of the peace treaty with Britain in 1783, and U.S. minister to Britain in 1785–88. He was vice president under George Washington and president from 1797 to 1801.

Thomas Jefferson (1743–1826) of Virginia was a delegate to the Second Continental Congress and drafted the Declaration of Independence. He was U.S. minister to France in 1785–89, vice president under John Adams, and president from 1801 to 1809.

Benjamin Franklin (1706–90) was born in Boston but moved to Philadelphia. He was a delegate to the Second Continental Congress and helped draft the Declaration of Independence. He was a diplomat to France in 1776–85 and a negotiator of the peace treaty with Britain in 1783. He was a member of the Constitutional Convention.

James Madison (1751–1836) of Virginia was a delegate to the Second Continental Congress. He was an influential member of the Constitutional Convention and an author of the *Federalist Papers*, and he was instrumental in drafting the Bill of Rights. He was president from 1809 to 1817.

George Washington (1732–99) of Virginia was a delegate to the First and Second Continental Congresses and was commander of the Continental Army. He presided over the Constitutional Convention and was president from 1789 to 1797.

Alexander Hamilton (1755–1804) was born in the West Indies but attended college in New York, and served on General Washington's staff during the Revolution. At the Constitutional Convention, he advocated a strong central government. He was an author of the *Federalist Papers* and the first secretary of the treasury.

FIGURE 2.1 Founders of the United States and Framers of the Constitution

The Founders were the leaders of the American Revolution and the new United States. The Framers were those who wrote the Constitution. All Framers were Founders, but not all Founders were Framers. Only some of the Founders were Signers, the people who signed the Declaration of Independence.

Essential Knowledge

The Constitutional Convention was presided over by Washington. The document itself was drafted by Madison, Hamilton, and other members of the "Grand Committee."

slaves.[13] Not all the delegates were rich, but none were poor. All were white, and all were male. Most were in their thirties or forties, and a majority had legal training.[14] Not surprisingly, the delegates' behavior at the Convention substantially reflected their interests and the statewide interests they represented.[15] The delegates included prominent men, such as James Madison, who would draft much of the Constitution (see Figure 2.1).

The Convention's rules granted each state one vote, regardless of the size of the state or the number of delegates it sent. To secure the assent of all states represented at the Convention, compromises had to be reached that would satisfy the various interests represented there. To keep the gateways to compromise open, the delegates voted to keep their deliberations secret until they completed their work. This decision also created a gate that limited popular influence.

Large Versus Small States

Upon the opening of the Philadelphia Convention in May 1787, Edmund Randolph of Virginia presented the delegates with James Madison's radical proposal for a new government. Known as the Virginia Plan, Madison's proposal included a strong central government that could operate directly on the citizens of the United States without the states acting as intermediaries. The legislative branch would consist of two chambers: a lower chamber elected by the people and an upper chamber elected by the lower chamber. Each chamber would have representation proportional to the populations of the states: the larger the population, the more representatives a state would have. The legislature would have general authority to pass laws that would "promote the harmony" of the United States and could veto laws passed by the states. The Virginia Plan proposed a national executive and a national judiciary, both chosen by the legislature. A council of revision, composed of the executive and judicial members, would have final approval over all legislative acts.

Madison's proposals astonished many of the delegates from the smaller states and some from the larger states as well. To counter the Virginia Plan, on June 15 William Patterson of New Jersey presented the Convention with the New Jersey Plan, which strengthened the Articles by providing Congress with the authority to regulate commerce and to directly tax imports and paper items. It also proposed a national executive chosen by the legislature and a national judiciary chosen by the executive.[16] Each state would retain equal representation in Congress.

The choice between proportional or equal representation generated enormous controversy. Madison insisted that proportional representation for both chambers was the only fair system, and the small states insisted that they would walk out if they lost their equal vote. Roger Sherman of Connecticut proposed what became known as the **Connecticut Compromise**. The makeup of the lower chamber, the House of Representatives, would be proportional to population, but the upper chamber, the Senate, would represent each state equally.

Connecticut Compromise: *Compromise on legislative representation whereby the lower chamber is based on population, and the upper chamber provides equal representation to the states.*

Nation Versus State

While the question of representation threatened the Convention, there was substantial agreement over the role of the national government. The delegates rejected the New Jersey Plan, which would have continued government under the Articles.

The delegates also did not approve the Virginia Plan in full, but the plan substantially influenced the proposed Constitution. Under the new Constitution, the government had the authority to operate directly on the citizens of the United States. Congress was not granted general legislative power, but rather **enumerated powers**—that is, a list of powers it could employ. Among its enumerated powers were the authority to tax to provide for the general welfare; to regulate commerce among the states and with foreign nations; to borrow money; to declare war, raise armies, and maintain a navy; and to make all laws "necessary and proper for carrying into Execution the foregoing Powers." The tax and commerce powers were among those missing from the Articles.

enumerated powers: *Powers expressly granted to Congress by the Constitution.*

Congress did not receive the authority to veto state laws, but the Constitution declared that national law would be supreme over state law, bound state judges to that decision, and created a national judiciary that would help ensure such rulings. Moreover, the Convention set explicit limits on state authority, prohibiting the states from carrying on foreign relations, coining money, and infringing on certain rights. Finally, the Convention approved a national executive (that is, the president) who could serve as a unifying force throughout the land. Table 2.2 presents the components of the Virginia Plan, the New Jersey Plan, and the proposed Constitution.

Essential Knowledge

The Constitution is often referred to as a "collection of compromises." The Connecticut Compromise, commonly known as "the great compromise," was a compromise between the Virginia and New Jersey Plans. Other similar compromises included the three-fifths, commerce, and slave trade compromises.

TABLE 2.2 The Virginia and New Jersey Plans Compared to the Constitution

Issue	Virginia Plan	New Jersey Plan	Constitution
Operation	Directly on people	Through the states	Directly on people
Legislative structure	Bicameral and proportional	Unicameral and equal	Bicameral, with lower chamber proportional and upper chamber equal
Legislative authority	General: power to promote the harmony of the United States	Strict enumerated powers of the Articles of Confederation, plus power to regulate commerce and limited power to tax	Broad enumerated powers
Check on legislative authority	Council of revision	None	Presidential veto, with possibility of a two-thirds override
Executive	Unitary national executive chosen by legislature	Plural national executive chosen by legislature	Unitary national executive chosen by Electoral College
Judiciary	National judiciary chosen by legislature	National judiciary chosen by executive	National judiciary chosen by president with advice and consent of Senate

North Versus South

Resolving the question of nation versus state proved less difficult than resolving the question of representation. More difficult still were questions related to slavery. Although slavery existed in every state except Massachusetts, the overwhelming majority of slaves, nearly 95 percent, were in the southern states, from Maryland to Georgia.[17] As Madison put it, "The States were divided into different interests not by their difference of size, but principally from their having or not having slaves."[18] Not all northern delegates at the Convention opposed slavery, but those who were abolitionists, including Benjamin Franklin, wanted an immediate ban on importing slaves from Africa, prohibitions against the expansion of slavery into the western territories, and the adoption of a plan for the gradual freeing of slaves. Delegates from Georgia and South Carolina, whose states would never accept the Constitution on these terms, wanted guaranteed protections for slavery and the slave trade and no restrictions on slavery in the territories. To secure a Constitution, compromises were necessary.

Many supporters of slavery recognized the horrors of the foreign slave trade, and by 1779 all states except North Carolina, South Carolina, and Georgia had banned it. Leaving the authority to regulate the foreign slave trade to Congress would inevitably have resulted in its being banned everywhere and probably would have kept those three states from joining the union. Thus, a slave trade compromise prohibited Congress from stopping the slave trade until 1808.

three-fifths compromise: *Compromise over slavery at the Constitutional Convention that granted states extra representation in the House of Representatives based on their number of slaves at the ratio of three-fifths.*

A second compromise involved how slaves should be counted when calculating population for purposes of representation. Madison's Virginia Plan based representation on the number of free inhabitants of each state, whereas the southernmost slave states wanted slaves to be fully counted for purposes of representation. Delegates from the northern states, on the other hand, argued that slave states, which by definition denied the humanity of slaves, should not benefit by receiving extra representation based on the number of slaves that they had. Under the Articles, taxes requested of the states were based on the population of each state, with five slaves counting as three people. The Convention agreed to use this three-fifths formula not just for representation but also for whatever direct or population taxes the national government might choose to levy. This **three-fifths compromise** had a significant impact on representation in the House of Representatives,[19] as Figure 2.2 demonstrates.

A third compromise involved slavery in the western territories, and it came not from the Convention but from the government under the Articles, which passed the Northwest Ordinance in July 1787. This ordinance, which established the means for governing the western lands north of the Ohio River (eventually the states of Ohio, Indiana, Illinois, Michigan, and Wisconsin, and parts of Minnesota), prohibited slavery in this territory but also provided that fugitive slaves who escaped to the territory would be returned to their owners. The Constitution incorporated these provisions. With the precedent of prohibiting slavery in the Northwest Territory established in the Northwest Ordinance, the Convention gave Congress the right to regulate the territories of the United States without mentioning whether slavery could be allowed or prohibited.

Essential Knowledge

The Constitution reflects the tension between participatory democracy and indirect participation of the pluralist and elitist models of democracy.

Gates Against Popular Influence

Compared to the British constitutional system, the 1787 Constitution provided direct and indirect gateways for popular involvement (see Figure 2.2). Nevertheless, the Framers did not trust the people to have complete control over choosing the government. In two important ways—the election of the president and the election of the Senate—the Constitution limited popular control.

Originally, state legislatures selected U.S. senators. The Framers feared that a Congress elected directly by the people would be too responsive to the popular will. The indirect election of senators was thus intended to serve as a check on the popular will. In 1913, the Seventeenth Amendment granted the people the right to elect senators directly.

Another gate against the people's participation was the election of the president through the **Electoral College**. Rather than directly electing the president through a popular vote, the Constitution established an Electoral College, in which electors actually choose the president. Each state receives a number of electors equal to its number of representatives plus senators, and each state legislature chooses the manner for selecting the electors from its state—by popular vote, legislative selection, or some other mechanism. State legislatures used to select electors. Today, each state legislature allows the people of the state to choose that state's electors, but in the early days of the **republic**, many state legislatures kept that right for themselves. Yet, the Electoral College remains in effect as a gate against direct popular control.

Electoral College: *The presidential electors, selected to represent the votes of their respective states, who meet every four years to cast the electoral votes for president and vice president.*

republic: *Form of government in which power derives from citizens, but public officials make policy and govern according to existing law.*

Popularly elected state legislatures often passed unjust and confusing laws. What Madison called "a spirit of *locality*" often superseded the common interest, allowing single-chamber legislatures to yield to sudden and violent passions that swept the nation.[20] Others shared Madison's fear. To make the point, George Washington used an analogy. "Why

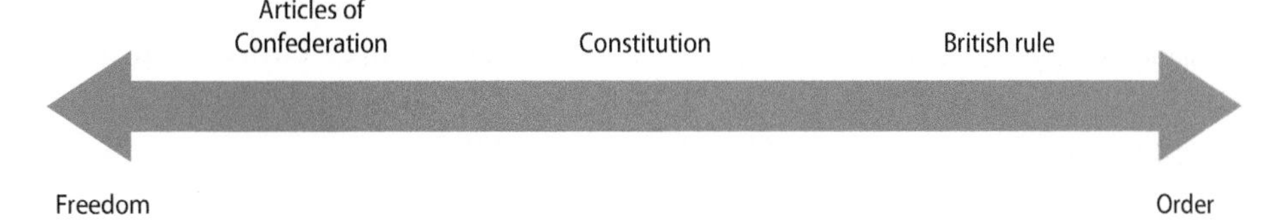

FIGURE 2.2 Relative Balance of Freedom and Order

This figure shows how the Constitution remedied various flaws from the Articles of Confederation. While the Articles lasted only four years, the Constitution has endured for over two hundred years.

POLITICAL ANALYTICS

Impact of the Three-Fifths Compromise

THE THREE-FIFTHS COMPROMISE REACHED at the Constitutional Convention had consequences for how states were represented in the House of Representatives. But how did it actually work after the first census? More than 675,000 slaves lived in the United States in 1790, spread across all of the original states except Massachusetts. More than 90 percent of all slaves lived in the five southern states (Georgia, Maryland, North Carolina, South Carolina, and Virginia).

Figure 2.3 shows how the number of slaves in each of the states translated into "persons" as a result of the three-fifths compromise. The southern states rose in population by close to 400,000 people as a result of the compromise; thus, they had more representation in the House of Representatives than if slaves had not been counted as persons at all. Note the percentage increase in population the states gained by counting each slave as three-fifths of a person rather than not at all. If slaves had been counted as full persons instead, the southern states' population would have grown by more than 600,000 people.

Examine the graph. Notice the total number of citizens and slaves in the United States at the start of the republic as well as where most slaves lived.

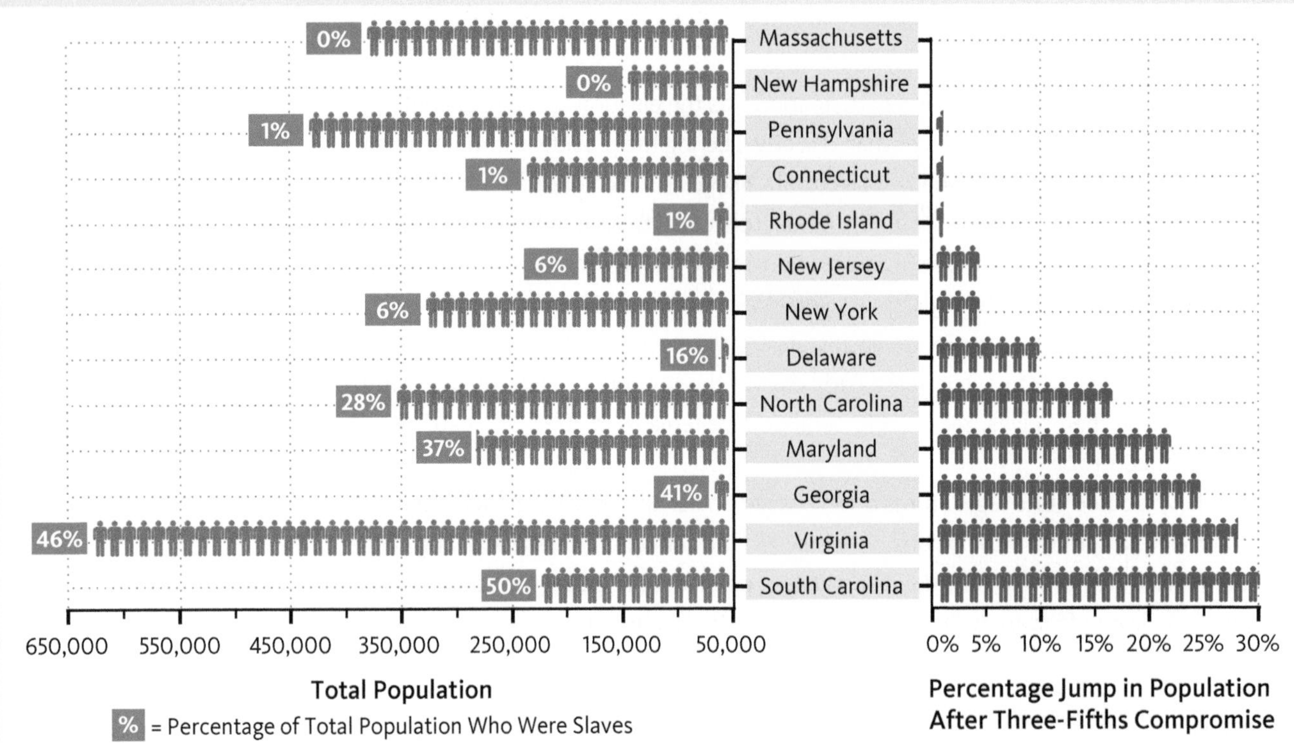

FIGURE 2.3 Citizen and Slave Populations in the Original Thirteen States, 1790

Sources: U.S. Census Bureau, Historical Statistics of the United States, Colonial Times to 1970. Chapter XIV Statistics of Slave, http://www2.census.gov/prod2/decennial/documents/00165897ch14.pdf; U.S. Census, Census of Population and Housing, 1790, http://www.census.gov/prod/www/decennial.html. Accessed March 7, 2016.

Thinking Critically

1. Keeping in mind that the Constitution called for one representative per 30,000 in population, if the three-fifths compromise had not been reached, and slaves had not been counted at all as persons, how would the states have been affected in the House of Representatives?
2. Were the states in the North and South affected by the three-fifths compromise in the same way? Did one group of states benefit more than the other?

do you pour that coffee into your saucer," he asked Thomas Jefferson. "To cool it," replied Jefferson. "Even so," said Washington, "we pour legislation into the senatorial saucer to cool it."[21] The indirect election of senators was thus intended to serve as a check on the popular will. In 1913 the Seventeenth Amendment granted the people the right to elect senators directly.

The Ratification Process

With agreements reached on representation in Congress, federal or national power, and slavery, the delegates made a few final decisions. First, despite the urging of George Mason of Virginia, the delegates chose not to include a **Bill of Rights**—a listing of rights retained by the people that Congress did not have the authority to take away, such as freedom of speech and freedom of religion. Because Congress had enumerated powers only, and because the authority to regulate speech, religion, and other freedoms was not among the powers granted to Congress, delegates believed there was no need to prohibit Congress from abridging such rights.

Bill of Rights: *First ten amendments to the Constitution, which provide basic political rights.*

Second, the delegates needed a method for ratifying, or granting final approval of, the Constitution. Fortunately, the states had already established a precedent for ratifying constitutions in state conventions, rather than through state legislatures.

Similarly, the delegates at the Constitutional Convention chose to send the proposed Constitution to the states for approval via special ratifying conventions to be chosen by the people. The Constitution would take effect among those states approving it when nine of the thirteen states ratified it. The Articles had required that all state legislatures approve a proposed amendment for it to pass, but the Constitutional Convention sought approval from a higher authority: the people of the United States. This process for ratification followed the statement in the Declaration of Independence that "it is the right of the people . . . to institute new government." Hence, the Constitution's preamble establishes the Constitution in the name of "We the People of the United States."

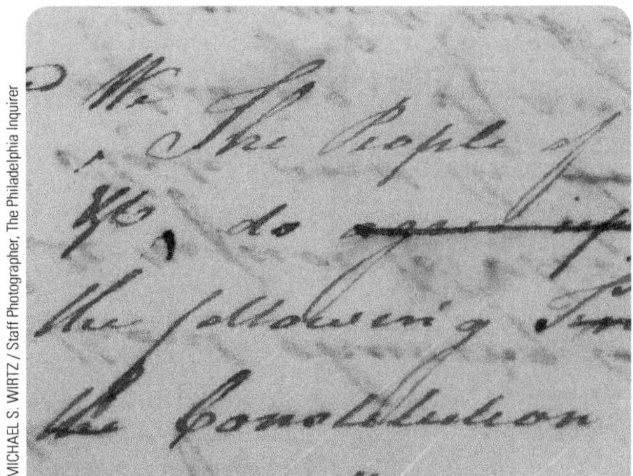

MICHAEL S. WIRTZ / Staff Photographer, The Philadelphia Inquirer

IMAGE 2.4 This draft of the Constitution, written by Pennsylvania delegate James Wilson, was rediscovered in 2010 in Wilson's papers in Philadelphia. At the start of the Constitutional Convention, the delegates adopted a rule of secrecy that has limited access to their thoughts and daily deliberations ever since. Researchers are still uncovering the history of the Convention.

TABLE 2.3 Deficiencies of the Articles of Confederation and Constitutional Remedies

Deficiency in the Articles of Confederation	Remedy in the Constitution
Legislative branch could not regulate commerce	Congress can regulate commerce "among the states"
Legislative branch could only request taxes from states	Congress can directly raise taxes from individuals
Approval of nine of thirteen states needed for passage of major legislation	Approval of a majority of both legislative chambers needed for passage of all legislation; a two-thirds majority needed to override presidential vetoes
No permanent executive branch	A "President of the United States"
No permanent judicial branch	A Supreme Court plus other inferior courts that Congress can establish
Unanimity for constitutional amendments	Approval of two-thirds of each chamber plus three-fourths of the states
Few limits on state authority, mostly over foreign affairs	States limited in foreign affairs, plus could not suppress certain rights through bills of attainder, *ex post facto* laws, and so on

In September 1787, with these final steps taken, delegates to the Constitutional Convention believed they had produced a constitution that remedied the deficiencies of the Articles (see Table 2.3), and they voted on the final document. Some of the delegates had left by September, but thirty-nine signed the document, with only three refusing to do so. Crucially, given Convention rules, a majority of the delegates from each of the states voted yes.

2.3 Government Under the Constitution

Explain how the structure of the Constitution protects liberty

The final document sent to the states for ratification laid out a structure of democratic government and proposed mechanisms whereby the Constitution could be amended. It also reflected the Framers' attempt to establish a government powerful enough to ensure public order yet contain enough gateways to guarantee individual liberty.

The Structure of Government

The Constitution established three branches of government: the legislative, the executive, and the judicial.

The Legislative Branch. The legislative branch, as explained in Chapter 1, makes the laws. The Constitution established a bicameral Congress, consisting of two chambers. The lower chamber, the House of Representatives, is proportioned by population (until the Thirteenth Amendment, the slave population was added to the free population according to the three-fifths formula described previously). Members of the House are elected for two-year terms directly by the people, with voting eligibility determined by each state. Representatives have to be at least 25 years old, residents of the state they serve, and U.S. citizens for at least the previous seven years.

The upper chamber, the Senate, consists of two senators from each state, regardless of size. Designed to serve as a check on the popular will, as well as a remnant of states' rights in the Articles, which would be expressed in the House of Representatives, state legislatures chose senators until 1913 when the Seventeenth Amendment granted the people of each state the exclusive right to do so.[22] A six-year term also serves to limit responsiveness to popular whims, and an age minimum of 30 presumably provides more mature and levelheaded thinking. Senators also have to be residents of the state in which they serve and U.S. citizens for nine years or more.

Bills to levy taxes have to originate in the House, but other bills may originate in either chamber. To become law, a bill has to pass each chamber in identical form and is then presented to the president for his signature. If the president signs the bill, it becomes law, but if he disapproves, he can **veto** the bill. Congress can then override the veto by a two-thirds majority in each chamber.

veto: *Authority of the president to block legislation passed by Congress. Congress can override a veto by a two-thirds majority in each chamber.*

Article I, Section 8, of the Constitution limits Congress's authority to an eighteen-paragraph list, or enumeration, of certain powers. The first paragraph grants Congress the authority "to Collect Taxes . . . to pay the Debts and provide for the common Defence and general Welfare of the United States." Paragraphs 2 through 17 grant additional powers such as borrowing and coining money, regulating commerce, and raising an army. Then paragraph 18 grants Congress the authority to pass all laws "necessary and proper for carrying into Execution the foregoing Powers."

Additionally, the Constitution gives the House the authority to impeach—to bring charges against—the president and other federal officials. The Senate has the sole authority to try cases of impeachment, with a two-thirds vote required for removal from office. The Senate also has the sole authority to ratify treaties, which also require a two-thirds vote, and to confirm executive and judicial branch appointments by majority vote.

The Executive Branch. The executive branch of government consists of a unitary president, chosen for a four-year term by an Electoral College. The Electoral College itself is chosen in a manner set by the legislature of each state. Eventually, every state gave the people the power to vote for its electors (as discussed earlier). A president must be at least 35 years of age, a resident of the United States for the previous fourteen years, and either a natural-born citizen of the United States or a citizen of the United States at the time of the adoption of the Constitution.

As far as legislative and executive powers go, because the Framers believed that the legislative branch would naturally be stronger than the executive branch, they did not feel the need to enumerate the executive powers as they did the legislative powers. Recall that Congress does not have a general legislative authority, but only those legislative powers granted under the Constitution. In contrast, the Constitution provides the president with a general grant of "the executive Power" plus certain specific powers, including the right to veto legislation and grant pardons. The president also is commander in chief of the

ELECTION 2016

Eligibility to Run for President

UNLIKE ISSUES SUCH AS THE DEFENSE budget, welfare, or student loans, the Constitution is rarely an issue in presidential elections. But it became an issue in the 2016 Republican nomination campaign when the front-runner, New York businessman and reality television star Donald Trump, accused one of his competitors for the Republican nomination, the Canadian-born Texas Senator Ted Cruz, of not being a natural-born citizen and thus being ineligible to be president. The Framers of the Constitution, worried that presidents of the newly formed United States of America might have loyalties to other countries, required that the president be a "natural born Citizen or a citizen of the United States, at the time of the Adoption of this Constitution." Additionally, the person must be at least thirty-five years old and a resident of the United for at least fourteen years.

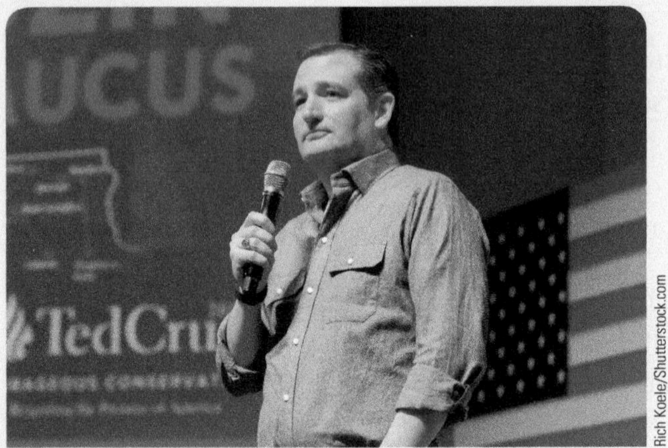

IMAGE 2.5 Texas Senator Ted Cruz sought the Republican presidential nomination in 2016 despite having been born in Canada.

Cruz, though not born in the United States, was a U.S. citizen at birth, as his mother was born in Delaware, and Congress by legislation has declared a person born abroad who has a U.S. citizen for one parent to have been born a U.S. citizen. The controversy disappeared when Trump defeated Cruz for the Republican nomination.

The Constitution does not define what a "natural born citizen" is and the Supreme Court has not rendered a decision on this, so two different views have formed. One is that citizens are either born in the United States, and thus natural born, or born elsewhere and thus naturalized. According to this stricter view, someone such as Ted Cruz was naturalized by statute and is thus ineligible to serve as president.[23]

Many others, though, believe that as Cruz was born a citizen, he is a "natural born citizen." Perhaps the strongest argument for this position is that a 1790 naturalization statute declared that the children of U.S. citizens born outside the United States "shall be considered as natural born citizens."[24] Presumably, the members of the first Congress knew fairly well what the term "natural born" in the brand-new Constitution meant.

A list of recent presidential candidates who were not born in the United States includes Barry Goldwater, the 1964 Republican nominee for president, who was born in Phoenix before Arizona became a state; George Romney, an unsuccessful contender for the 1968 Republican nomination, who was born in Mexico but whose parents were U.S. citizens; and John McCain, the 2008 Republican nominee, who was born in the Panama Canal Zone before the zone was legally regarded as a U.S. Territory.[25]

armed forces. With the advice and consent of the Senate, the president makes treaties and appoints ambassadors, judges, and other public officials. The president leads the executive branch of government, being charged with taking care that the laws are faithfully executed.

The Judicial Branch. The Constitution vests the judicial authority of the United States in one Supreme Court and other inferior courts that Congress might choose to establish. The president appoints judges with the advice and consent of the Senate. They serve "during good Behaviour," which, short of impeachment, means a life term.

The Constitution extends the authority of the federal courts to hear cases involving certain classes of parties to a suit—cases involving the United States, ambassadors, and other public ministers; suits between two or more states or citizens from different states—and certain classes of cases, most notably cases arising under the Constitution, laws, and treaties of the United States. In the historic case *Marbury v. Madison* (1803), the Supreme Court took this authority to hear cases arising under the Constitution of the United States to establish the power of **judicial review**, the authority of the Court to strike down any law passed by Congress when the Court believes the law violates the Constitution (see Supreme Court Cases: *Marbury v. Madison*).[26]

judicial review: *Authority of courts to declare laws passed by Congress and acts of the executive branch to be unconstitutional.*

The Amendment Process

The Constitution provides two paths for changing the Constitution via **amendment**. The first path requires a two-thirds vote in each chamber of Congress, followed by the approval of three-fourths of the states. That statewide approval can be attained either through the state legislatures or through state ratifying conventions, as directed by Congress. The second path allows two-thirds of the states to request a national constitutional convention that could propose amendments that would go into effect when approved by three-fourths of the states (see Figure 2.4). Again, this approval could be obtained through state legislatures or through state ratifying conventions. Additionally, the Constitution prohibits amendments that would deny any state an equal vote in the

amendment: *Formal process of changing the Constitution.*

Essential Knowledge

The framers realized the the Constitution, while a significant improvement over the Articles, was not perfect and would need to be changed with time. The Constitution provides a means that a self-governing people can use to change their fundamental laws.

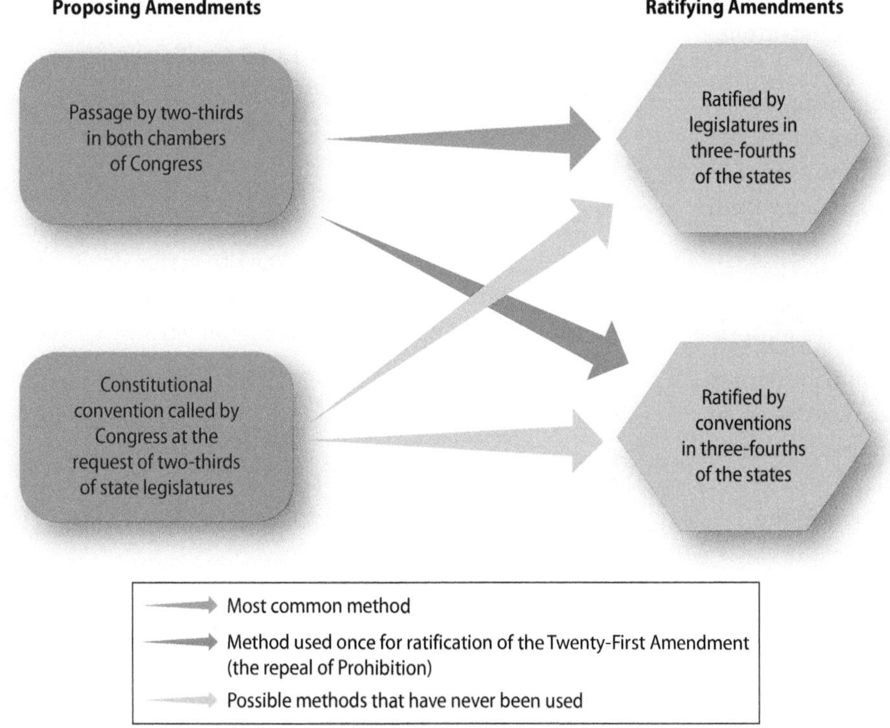

FIGURE 2.4 Amending the Constitution

An amendment can be proposed by two-thirds of each chamber of Congress or by a constitutional convention called by two-thirds of state legislatures. Either way, ratification requires three-quarters of the states to approve the amendment. Why do you think the methods indicated by the blue arrows have never been used?

SUPREME COURT CASES

Marbury v. Madison (1803)

QUESTION: Does Congress have the authority to expand the Supreme Court's original jurisdiction beyond that granted by the Constitution?

ORAL ARGUMENT: February 10, 1803

DECISION: February 23, 1803 (read at http://www.law.cornell.edu/supremecourt/text/5/137)

OUTCOME: No, thus establishing the power of judicial review (4–0)

It is hard to imagine a more momentous decision resulting from what the historian John A. Garraty called, this "trivial squabble over a few petty political plums."* In the closing days of President John Adams's administration, the Federalist Adams nominated William Marbury to the position of justice of the peace for the District of Columbia, and the Federalist Senate confirmed the nomination. But in the hectic final hours of Adams's administration, Secretary of State John Marshall neglected to deliver the commission. When Democratic-Republican Thomas Jefferson became president, his new secretary of state, James Madison, refused to deliver the commission, thus keeping Marbury from assuming his office.

Marbury filed suit at the Supreme Court, believing that the Judiciary Act of 1789 expanded the Court's original jurisdiction to give the Court the authority to hear cases involving writs of *mandamus* (orders to government officials to undertake specific acts) as an original matter—that is, as a trial, and not just as an appeal.

The Supreme Court declared that because the Constitution precisely specified which types of cases the Supreme Court could hear as an original matter, the section of the Judiciary Act that expanded the Court's original jurisdiction conflicted with the Constitution. Moreover, if a law conflicts with the Constitution, either the law is supreme over the Constitution, or the Constitution is supreme over the law. The Court ruled that it must be the case that the Constitution is supreme over the law. Finally, the Court declared that the judiciary would decide such issues. "It is emphatically the province and duty of the judicial department to say what the law is," wrote John Marshall, who in the closing days of the Adams administration had been nominated and confirmed as chief justice of the United States. The Supreme Court would not order Madison to deliver the commission to Marbury. Marbury presumably had the right to get the commission from a different court but never sought to do so. Instead, he returned to his highly successful banking career.

The Court in *Marbury* granted itself the momentous authority of judicial review, the power to strike down laws passed by Congress and state legislatures on the grounds that those laws violate the Constitution. Although the Court did not frequently use this power in the early days of the republic, citizens filing lawsuits would later use it to get the Court to strike down, among other things, segregated schools (*Brown v. Board of Education,* 1954), anti-abortion statutes (*Roe v. Wade,* 1973), and prohibitions on same-sex marriages (*Obergefell v. Hodges*, 2015).

Thinking Critically

1. How does judicial review provide a gateway to participation in the political system?
2. Why is it the judiciary's job to determine whether a law is unconstitutional?

*"The Case of the Missing Commissions," in John A. Garraty, ed., *Quarrels That Have Shaped the Constitution* (New York: Harper and Row, 1964), 13

Senate or any amendment that would have allowed a banning of the foreign slave trade before 1808.

Both paths for amending the Constitution are complex and difficult, which has kept the Constitution from being modified over popular but short-lived issues. Recently, these have included proposed amendments that would require a balanced federal budget, allow the federal or state governments to prosecute those who burn the American flag, and prohibit states from recognizing same-sex marriages. In 1917 Congress proposed and in 1919 the states ratified the temporarily popular Prohibition amendment (the Eighteenth Amendment), which banned the manufacture, sale, and transportation of alcohol, only to have it repealed in 1933 (the Twenty-First Amendment) in the face of massive civil disobedience.

The states have never called a constitutional convention to amend the 1787 Constitution, but Senator Marco Rubio, a contender for the 2016 Republican nomination, has called for a constitutional convention that would limit the size of the national government.[27] It is not clear, though, that a convention called for a particular purpose could be limited to that purpose. Recall that the 1787 Constitutional Convention was originally called merely to amend the Articles of Confederation. Over the years many politicians have called for such conventions without success. Congress, though, has sent thirty-three proposed amendments to the states for ratification. Other than the Twenty-First Amendment (the repeal of Prohibition), which Congress sent to state ratifying conventions, all other proposed amendments went directly to the state legislatures. Of the thirty-three amendments that Congress proposed, twenty-seven have received the required assent of three-fourths of the states. These include the Bill of Rights (the First through the Tenth Amendments), which passed within two years of the adoption of the Constitution, and three Civil War amendments (the Thirteenth through the Fifteenth Amendments) that abolished slavery and attempted to protect the rights of former slaves. We further discuss these and other amendments to the Constitution later in this chapter.

federalism: *System of government in which sovereignty is constitutionally divided between national and state governments.*

Essential Knowledge

Federalist 51 explains Madison's views on how governmental power should be divided. Madison writes that the division of power among the branches of government helps check and control abuses by majorities.

The Partition of Power

In attempting to explain and justify the constitutional structure, James Madison wrote of "the necessary partition of power among the several departments as laid down in the constitution" (see *Federalist* 51 in the Appendix). He acknowledged that elections serve as the primary means of ensuring that the government is responsive to the wishes of the people. If it is not, the people can vote for a new government. Under the Constitution, the people have direct authority to elect the House of Representatives. But to prevent the majority from imposing oppressive laws on the minority, the rest of the government was chosen indirectly, as we have seen.

Lest the people not be sufficient to keep government under control, however, the Constitution had built in "auxiliary precautions," as Madison called them, to make sure government could not concentrate power. Thus, **federalism** splits power between nation and state, **separation of powers** divides the powers that remained with the national government among the three branches of government, and **checks and balances** give each branch some authority over the powers of the other branches. Even after all this, the Constitution places additional limits on both federal and state powers.

separation of powers: *Government structure in which authority is divided among branches (executive, legislative, and judicial), with each holding separate and independent powers and areas of responsibility.*

checks and balances: *Government structure that authorizes each branch of government (executive, legislative, and judicial) to share powers with the other branches, thereby holding some scrutiny of and control over the other branches.*

Federalism. The first means of preventing a concentration of power was to divide authority between the national and state governments. Rather than provide Congress with a general power to legislate in the national interest, the Constitution granted Congress enumerated powers. All powers not granted to Congress remained with the states. This division of power is made explicit in the Tenth Amendment to the Constitution: "The powers not delegated to the United States by the Constitution, nor prohibited by it to the States, are reserved to the States respectively, or to the people."

Essential Knowledge
The separation of powers allows for multiple points of access by citizens to policy makers.

Separation of Powers. Madison believed that "the accumulation of all powers, legislative, executive, and judiciary, in the same hands, whether of one, a few, or many, and whether hereditary, self-appointed, or elective, may justly be pronounced the very definition of tyranny."[28] Thus, after dividing power between the national and state governments, the Constitution separates those powers that it grants to the national government among the three branches. Under the Constitution, all legislative powers granted belong to Congress, the executive power vests in the president of the United States, and the judicial authority resides in a Supreme Court, plus any lower courts Congress might choose to establish. Moreover, because the "legislative authority . . . necessarily, predominates" in a republican government (*Federalist* 51), legislative power was further separated into two distinct chambers, a House and a Senate, each with different manners of election and terms of office.

Essential Knowledge
The powers allocated to the various branches of government are not absolute. Each branch was given power to check the others.

Checks and Balances. Under the Constitution, balance among the branches was achieved by giving each one some authority to counteract, or check, the authority of the other two (see Figure 2.5). Thus the president has the authority to propose legislation to Congress and to veto bills passed by Congress; Congress can override that veto by a two-thirds majority of each chamber. The president has the authority to pardon people convicted of crimes. The president also nominates federal judges, subject to the advice and consent of the Senate. The Senate also advises and consents to high-ranking executive branch appointments, such as ambassadors and cabinet officials. The House can impeach executive and judicial appointees, and the Senate can convict and remove impeached officials from office by a two-thirds majority. Congress, subject to presidential veto, has the authority to establish lower courts and set their jurisdiction (decide what cases they can hear). It also has the authority to set the Supreme Court's appellate jurisdiction. The appellate jurisdiction is the Supreme Court's authority to hear cases on appeal from lower courts and is the heart of the Supreme Court's judicial power. Congress has this authority over the courts; the courts, on the other hand, can decide the constitutionality of laws passed by Congress. While the Constitution does not explicitly grant this power of judicial review to courts, judicial review has been largely unchallenged since announced by the Supreme Court in *Marbury v. Madison*. The courts also have the authority to review the legality of actions taken by executive branch officials.

Essential Knowledge
Impeachment is an example of checks and balances. The impeachment process allows the Congress to remove members of both the executive and judicial branches.

Limits on Powers. The delegation of powers to Congress, and the reservation of all remaining powers to the states, would have given states the same authority to pass oppressive laws that they had under the Articles. To prevent that, the Constitution limits state authority in several ways. First, it makes federal law supreme over state law. Second,

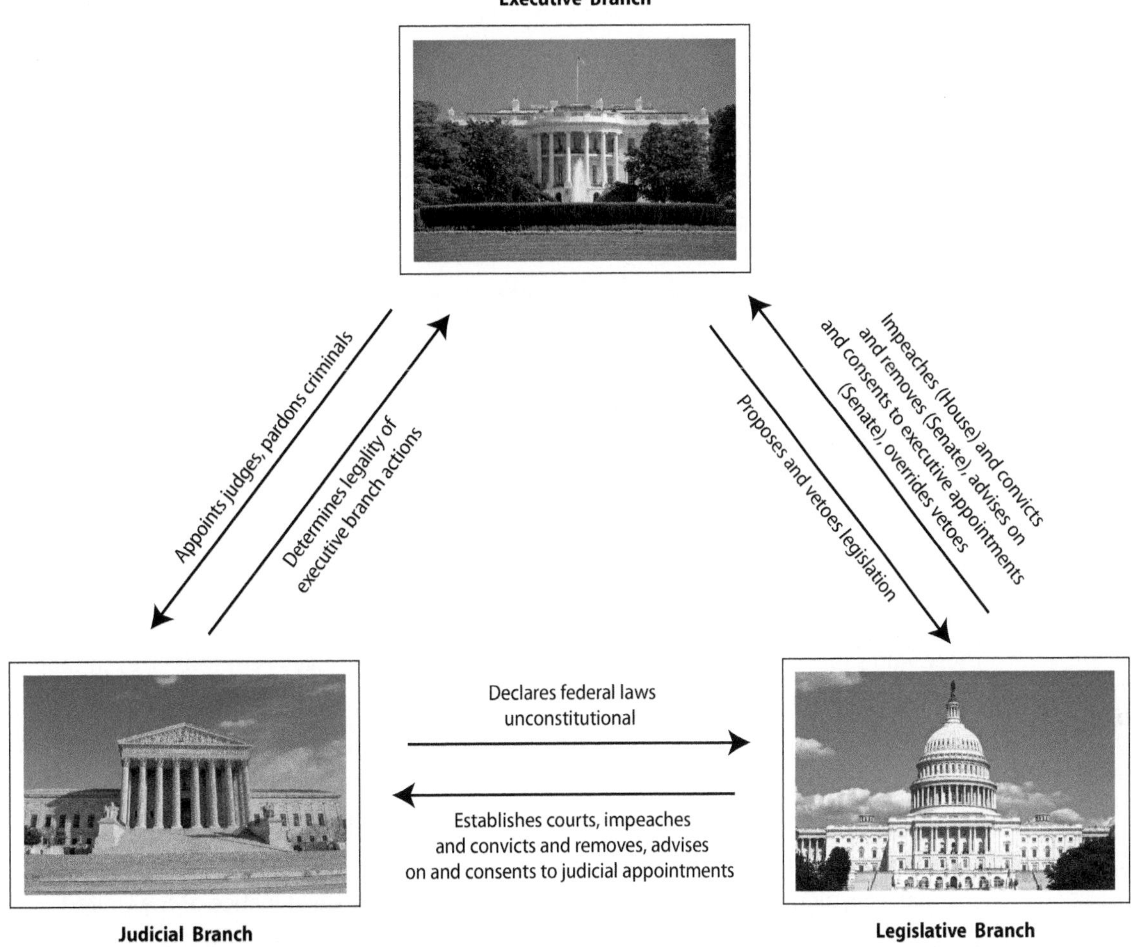

FIGURE 2.5 Checks and Balances

The Constitution provides each branch of government with a partial control over the workings of the other two branches.

it guarantees that the states establish a republican form of government. Third, the Constitution sets limits on the sort of legislation states can pass. They also cannot pass bills of attainder (legislative acts declaring people guilty of crimes) or prosecute individuals under *ex post facto* laws, which make behavior illegal after individuals have engaged in it. In a provision indicative of American egalitarianism, the Constitution denies states the power to grant titles of nobility. While not embracing the notion of equality announced in the Declaration of Independence, the Framers did make it clear that they rejected the British system of inherited social status. The Constitution also prohibits states from passing laws that would allow individuals to disregard the obligation of contracts, such as laws negating debts.

The Constitution also expressly limits the authority of Congress. Like the states, Congress can pass neither bills of attainder nor *ex post facto* laws. It also cannot suspend the writ of *habeas corpus*—a guarantee that incarcerated people can go before a judge to have the legality of their confinement determined—except in cases of invasion or rebellion.

2.4 The Ratification Debates

Analyze why the Antifederalists opposed the Constitution

With the proposed Constitution to be accepted or rejected by the people of the various states, the state ratification debates largely ignored the question of representation that led to the Connecticut Compromise and the three-fifths compromise. Instead, most of the debate concerned the extent of national power under the Constitution, with many expressing fears about the consolidation of federal authority over the states, the scope of executive and legislative power, and the lack of a bill of rights.

Federalists and Antifederalists

Federalists: *Initially, those who supported the Constitution during the ratification period; later, the name of the political party established by supporters of Alexander Hamilton.*

Antifederalists: *Those who opposed the new proposed Constitution during the ratification period.*

By the time the state ratifying conventions started meeting, two distinct camps had formed. Those who supported the Constitution cleverly named themselves **Federalists**, even though they were really more nationalist than federalist. ("Federal," according to Madison, meant "a Confederacy of sovereign states,"[29] which better described the Articles of Confederation, or even the New Jersey Plan, than the new Constitution.) Those who opposed the Constitution, whose leaders included the outspoken Revolutionary leader Patrick Henry of Virginia, became known as the **Antifederalists**.

Madison, along with John Jay, who later became the first chief justice of the United States, and Alexander Hamilton, who later founded the Federalist Party and served as the first secretary of the treasury, wrote eighty-five essays, today known as the *Federalist Papers*, that attempted to convince the citizens of New York to ratify the Constitution. They wrote anonymously under the pen name "Publius," taken from an early leader in the ancient Roman Republic. Madison's essays, especially, are still read today as a leading source for understanding the Constitution. We quoted from them earlier in this chapter and in Chapter 1, and two of the most famous essays, numbers 10 and 51, are in the Appendix. The Antifederalists published their attacks under anonymous pen names as well, most notably "Brutus"—another leader of the ancient Roman Republic—and "Old Whig," named after the English political party that opposed the monarchy.

Consolidation of Federal Authority

Essential Knowledge

The opposition to a new centralized government was stated in Brutus 1, which argued that small, decentralized republics had many benefits, whereas a large central government would endanger individual liberty and the power of the states.

The Antifederalists found much to disapprove of in the proposed Constitution. They argued that the Constitutional Convention had violated the Articles by moving beyond mere amendment and proposing a new government, one that did not require the unanimous consent of the states. They worried that because sovereignty, the ultimate lawmaking authority, could not be split, and because national law was supreme over state law, a national government under the Constitution would inevitably consolidate its authority over the state governments.

The Federalists answered both of these charges by claiming that sovereignty rested not in the legislature, as had typically been believed, but in the people, as the preamble to the

Constitution suggested. Therefore the people could propose any new form of government they wished. And if the people were sovereign, they could split their grant of lawmaking authority between the national and state governments as they saw fit.

The Scope of Executive Authority

Other concerns centered on the scope of executive authority. With no term limits on the executive in the original Constitution, the Antifederalists feared that the president would turn into a monarch, and of the worst type—an elected one. George Mason, who was one of three delegates not to sign the proposed Constitution, also worried that "the President of the United States has the unrestrained Power of granting Pardon," which could be used to instigate crimes and then cover them up by pardoning his criminal partners. Alexander Hamilton responded in *Federalist* 69 with an explanation of the limits on the executive: elections, whereby the president could be voted out of office; impeachment, whereby the president could be removed from office for "high crimes and misdemeanors"; and the limited veto power, which could be overridden. The president of the United States, Hamilton concluded, was much closer in power to the governor of New York than to the king of England.

The Scope of Legislative Authority

Two provisions in Article I, Section 8, of the Constitution, which specified the powers of Congress, particularly alarmed the Antifederalists: the **general welfare clause** and the **necessary and proper clause**. Section 8 of the Constitution begins by stating that "Congress shall have Power to lay and Collect Taxes . . . to . . . provide for the . . . general Welfare of the United States." It concludes by stating that Congress has the power "to make all Laws which shall be necessary and proper for carrying into Execution the foregoing Powers." Antifederalist Brutus contended that "the legislature under this constitution may pass any law which they may think proper."[30] Brutus further wrote that the necessary and proper clause, labeled "the sweeping clause" by the Antifederalists, granted the government "absolute and uncontroulable power, legislative, executive and judicial."[31] James Monroe, who would later serve as the fifth president (1817–25), told the Virginia ratifying convention that the sweeping clause gave Congress "a general power . . . to make all laws that will enable them to carry their powers into effect. There are no limits pointed out. They are not restrained or controlled from making any law, however oppressive in its operation, which they may think necessary to carry their powers into effect."[32]

general welfare clause: *Gives Congress the power to tax to provide for the general welfare (Article I, Section 8).*

necessary and proper clause: *Gives Congress the power to pass all laws necessary and proper to the powers enumerated in Article I, Section 8.*

Madison responded in *Federalist* 41 that the power to tax "to provide for the general Welfare" was not a general grant of power to tax for any purpose whatsoever but, rather, a power to tax for the enumerated powers that followed. "Nothing is more natural nor common than first to use a general phrase, and then to explain and qualify it by a recital of particulars."[33] To Madison, Article I, Section 8, granted the right to tax to provide for the general welfare and then listed various other powers that defined the full scope of the general welfare clause.

Similarly, the Federalists argued that the necessary and proper clause was not a general grant of authority to pass all laws that were necessary and proper, but rather, as the clause explicitly stated, the authority to pass all laws that were "necessary and proper for carrying into Execution the foregoing [that is, previously listed] Powers." Thus, if a law is necessary and proper for borrowing money, or raising an army, or establishing a post office, Congress may pass such a law, for those powers are among the "foregoing Powers" granted Congress. This explicit restriction of the necessary and proper clause to the other powers was absent, however, in the general welfare clause. To Madison, the restriction was obviously implied; to the Antifederalists, it was a threat to limited government.

Nevertheless, to clarify that the Constitution did not provide general powers to Congress, the Federalists agreed to an amendment to the Constitution declaring that "The powers not delegated to the United States by the Constitution, nor prohibited by it to the States, are reserved to the States respectively, or to the people." Interestingly, the amendment parallels a similar provision from the Articles that declared that the states retained all powers not "expressly delegated" to the national government. By limiting congressional authority to those powers delegated to it, rather than the stricter standard of those powers expressly delegated to it, the Constitution creates a somewhat greater authority for **implied powers**.

implied powers: *Powers not expressly granted to Congress but added through the necessary and proper clause.*

The Lack of a Bill of Rights

The most serious charge against the Constitution was that it did not contain a bill of rights. Patrick Henry, who had famously proclaimed "Give me liberty or give me death" in 1765, told the Virginia ratifying convention in 1788 that if the state gives up its powers "without a bill of rights, you will exhibit the most absurd thing to mankind that ever the world saw—[state] government that has abandoned all its powers—the powers of direct taxation, the sword, and the purse. You have disposed of them to Congress, without a bill of rights—without check, limitation, or control."[34]

In contrast, the Federalists argued that a bill of rights was not necessary because Congress had only those powers granted by the Constitution. If Congress was not granted the authority to, say, abridge freedom of the press, it was unnecessary to say that Congress could not abridge freedom of the press. The Federalists, specifically Alexander Hamilton in *Federalist* 84, went further to claim that a bill of rights could be dangerous because listing some rights but not others could imply that the rights not listed could be abridged.

Library of Congress Prints and Photographs Division Washington, D.C.[LC-DIG-ppmsca-17522]

IMAGE 2.6 1787 engraving depicting the conflict between the Federalists and Antifederalists in Connecticut. The Federalists are portrayed as representing trading interests while the Antifederalists are shown as favoring farming interests.

Consider two documents. The first one states that Congress has the right to regulate commerce between the states, to tax to provide for the general welfare, and to raise armies. Under this document, does Congress have the right to abridge the right to assemble? The Federalist answer was no, because Congress has enumerated powers only, and the right to limit freedom of assembly is not one of them. The Antifederalist answer was yes because the power was not prohibited.

Now consider a second document that states that Congress has the right to regulate commerce between the states, to tax to provide for the general welfare, and to raise armies. In addition, it states that Congress may not abridge freedom of the press. May Congress abridge the right to assemble? The Federalists argued that the potential for Congress to regulate the right to assemble is greater in the second document than in the first. That is, in the second case, Congress could say "we are prohibited from abridging freedom of the press, but we are not prohibited from abridging the right to assemble, so we are allowed to do that." By listing certain rights, the Constitution could be interpreted as allowing Congress to limit those freedoms not listed.

It is hard to imagine people concluding from the Federalist argument that rights would be safer without a bill of rights. Not only is this a complicated argument, but combining the necessary and proper clause with the broad powers granted Congress under the Constitution—such as regulating interstate commerce and taxing to provide for the general welfare—probably means that Congress could have found ways to pass laws abridging freedom of assembly, freedom of speech, and other freedoms. The Federalists eventually gave in to the Antifederalist argument, agreeing that amending the Constitution to provide a bill of rights would be among the first items of business under a newly ratified Constitution. To prevent the listing of certain rights to create an assumption that Congress could abridge other rights not listed, the Bill of Rights included the Ninth Amendment: "The enumeration in the Constitution, of certain rights, shall not be construed to deny or disparage others retained by the people."

Despite the Antifederalist arguments about excessive national power, the lack of a bill of rights, and a too-powerful executive, states began ratifying the new Constitution. By June 1788, ten states had ratified, one more than needed to establish the new Constitution. Yet some states delayed. North Carolina and Rhode Island did not ratify until after George Washington was elected president.

2.5 The Responsive Constitution

Illustrate how the Constitution has stayed responsive to changing needs

The government the Framers devised has lasted more than two hundred years. As in 1787, it still has three branches of government, Congress still consists of two chambers, and the Electoral College still chooses the president. But other parts of the U.S. constitutional system have changed substantially, some to fix flaws and some to respond to new circumstances and developing ideas about the nature of equality. Some of these changes, such as the Bill of Rights, came through the formal amendment process. Others were the result of changing interpretation by the Supreme Court about what the Constitution means. Still others are what some call "extraconstitutional." That is, they affect the way the constitutional system operates even though the Constitution itself has not been amended to reflect them. Most prominent is the development of political parties (see Chapter 9, Political Parties).

The Bill of Rights

As part of the fight over ratification, the Federalists agreed that they would propose a Bill of Rights after the new Constitution was ratified, and some state ratifying conventions forwarded proposals for specific amendments. The states then ratified ten of the amendments in 1791 as a Bill of Rights that became part of the Constitution. Many of these amendments stated rights that had been guaranteed under British law or had been abridged by the British during the decade before the Revolution, causing the Americans to demand independence.

The First Amendment guarantees major political rights, including freedom of speech, press, and assembly, and the free exercise of religion. It also prohibits establishing a national religion or, more precisely, any law "respecting an establishment of religion." The Second Amendment protects the right to bear arms; the Third Amendment prohibits the quartering of soldiers in one's home in times of peace. The Fourth, Fifth, Sixth, and Eighth Amendments protect rights relating to criminal procedure, including the right at trial to the assistance of an attorney and the right to a trial by jury (Sixth). The Seventh Amendment protects the right to a trial by jury in civil cases over $20. The criminal procedure amendments also prohibit unreasonable searches and seizures (Fourth); compulsory self-incrimination (Fifth); double jeopardy, or being tried a second time for a crime after one is found not guilty (Fifth); and cruel or unusual punishments (Eighth). The Fifth Amendment also prohibits deprivations of life, liberty, or property without due process of law, and it prohibits the government from seizing private property for a public use without fair or "just" compensation. We examine the meanings of these amendments in Chapter 4, Civil Liberties.

The Civil War Amendments

Following the Civil War, Congress proposed and the states ratified three amendments. The Thirteenth Amendment (1865) prohibits slavery. The Fourteenth Amendment (1868), aimed at protecting the newly emancipated slaves, makes all people born in the United States citizens of the United States. It also prohibits states from denying anyone due process of law,

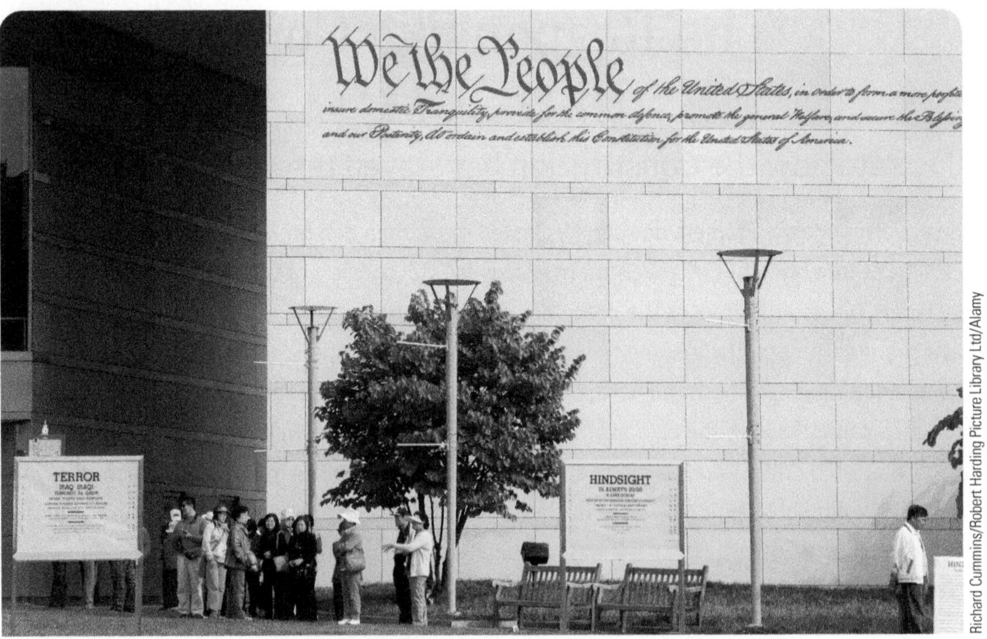

Richard Cummins/Robert Harding Picture Library Ltd/Alamy

IMAGE 2.7 After more than two hundred years, Americans love the Constitution and are interested in learning about it. The original is in a sealed case at the National Archives in Washington, D.C., but visitors to the National Constitution Center in Philadelphia, shown here, enjoy exhibits that tell the story of the Constitution and its contemporary relevance.

the equal protection of the law, as demonstrated in *Plyler v. Doe* (see Chapter 1, Gateways to American Democracy) and the privileges or immunities of citizens of the United States. The Fifteenth Amendment (1870) prohibits states from denying anyone the right to vote on account of race or prior status as a slave. All three amendments give Congress the authority to enforce the measures by appropriate legislation, thus adding to Congress's enumerated powers. These amendments radically changed the structure of the federal government by giving the national government authority over internal matters of the states. We deal with these civil rights more extensively in Chapter 5, Civil Rights.

Amendments That Expand Public Participation

Other amendments have extended the gateways to public participation in government by giving the people the right to vote for their senators directly (Seventeenth, 1913), guaranteeing women the right to vote (Nineteenth, 1920), allowing residents of the District of Columbia to vote in presidential elections (Twenty-Third, 1961), prohibiting states from setting poll taxes as a requirement of voting in federal elections (Twenty-Fourth, 1964), and guaranteeing the right to vote for those age 18 or older (Twenty-Sixth, 1971). For a summary of all the amendments, see Figure 2.6.

Constitutional Interpretation

The Constitution has also changed through interpretation by the Supreme Court (see Public Policy and the Constitution: The Death Penalty). Following the explicit establishment of judicial review in *Marbury v. Madison,* the Court has exercised the authority to determine what the Constitution means. Under that authority, the powers of Congress have grown enormously. During the Great Depression of the 1930s, the Court began to interpret Congress's power to tax to provide for the general welfare as extending beyond the enumerated powers. Rather, in line with the interpretation of the general welfare clause that the Antifederalists feared, the Court now holds that Congress can tax and spend for virtually any purpose that is not expressly prohibited.

Additionally, Congress's authority to regulate commerce between the states is now so grand that it covers virtually all commercial activity, including wheat grown by a farmer for consumption by livestock on that farmer's land because of the effect that all similarly situated wheat could have on national grain markets.[35] But in 2012, the Supreme Court held that the commerce clause did not give Congress the right to mandate that individuals purchase health insurance, upholding that requirement under the taxing part of the general welfare clause.[36]

The growth of national authority confirms that the Antifederalists were correct to insist on a Bill of Rights. Although Congress has not been granted the explicit right to abridge freedom of speech or freedom of the press, it would have the authority to do so under current readings of the commerce, taxing, and various other clauses, were it not for the Bill of Rights.

Future Amendments

Many of the formal changes in the Constitution since the Bill of Rights have centered on greater direct participation: direct voting for senators; no poll taxes; no

Color Code:	Criminal procedure	Participation	Equality	Structure	Miscellaneous

Amendment	Year	Description
First	1791	Prohibits abridging freedoms of religion, speech, press, assembly, and petition
Second	1791	Prohibits abridging the right to bear arms
Third	1791	Prohibits involuntary quartering of soldiers in one's home during peacetime
Fourth	1791	Prohibits unreasonable searches and seizures
Fifth	1791	Affirms the right to indictment by a grand jury and the right to due process; protects against double jeopardy, self-incrimination, and taking of property without just compensation
Sixth	1791	Affirms rights to speedy and public trial, to confront witnesses, and to counsel
Seventh	1791	Affirms right to jury trials in civil suits over $20
Eighth	1791	Prohibits excessive bail, excessive fines, and cruel and unusual punishments
Ninth	1791	Declares that the enumeration of certain rights does not limit other rights retained by the people
Tenth	1791	Reserves the powers not granted to the national government to the states or to the people
Eleventh	1798	Prevents citizens from one state from suing another state in federal court
Twelfth	1804	Requires that electors cast separate votes for president and vice president and specifies requirements for vice presidential candidates
Thirteenth	1865	Prohibits slavery in the United States
Fourteenth	1868	Makes all persons born in the United States citizens of the United States and prohibits states from denying persons within its jurisdiction the privileges or immunities of citizens, the due process of law, and equal protection of the laws; apportionment by whole persons
Fifteenth	1870	Prohibits states from denying the right to vote on account of race
Sixteenth	1913	Grants Congress the power to tax income derived from any source
Seventeenth	1913	Gives the people (instead of state legislatures) the right to choose U.S. senators directly
Eighteenth	1919	Prohibits the manufacture, sale, or transportation of intoxicating liquors
Nineteenth	1920	Guarantees women the right to vote
Twentieth	1933	Declares that the presidential term begins on January 20 (instead of March 4)
Twenty-First	1933	Repeals the Eighteenth Amendment
Twenty-Second	1951	Limits presidents to two terms
Twenty-Third	1961	Grants Electoral College votes to residents of the District of Columbia
Twenty-Fourth	1964	Prohibits poll taxes
Twenty-Fifth	1967	Specifies replacement of the vice president and establishes the position of acting president during a president's disability
Twenty-Sixth	1971	Guarantees 18-year-olds the right to vote
Twenty-Seventh	1992	Sets limits on congressional pay raises

FIGURE 2.6 Amendments to the Constitution

Following the specific protections of the first eight amendments to the Constitution, many subsequent amendments have corrected structural problems in the operation of government. Others have expanded participation and equality.

abridgments of rights to vote on account of race, sex, or age so long as one is 18; and no exclusion of residents of the District of Columbia from voting for president. District residents do not have representation in Congress, however, because the Constitution declares that "The House of Representatives shall be composed of Members chosen every second Year by the People of the several States," and the District of Columbia is not a state. District residents are always hopeful that a constitutional amendment will give them representation. As they overwhelmingly vote for Democrats, the Democratic Party supports such an amendment, but Republicans oppose it. It is unlikely that three-quarters of the states would approve, given the partisan consequences of such a change.

Members of Congress introduced seventy-four proposed constitutional amendments during the 113th Congress (2013–15). Twenty of these proposed changes related to the Supreme Court's 2010 decision *Citizens United v. Federal Election Commission*, which gave corporations the same rights as individuals to make independent campaign expenditures for or against political candidates (see Chapter 8, Interest Groups, for more on the *Citizens United* case and Chapter 10, Elections and Campaigns, for more on campaign financing). A dozen of the proposed amendments would require term limits for members of Congress, nine would require a balanced budget, and five would prohibit taxation as a mechanism of forcing people to purchase health insurance, as in the Affordable Care Act. The rest were distributed over a wide variety of topics.[37] Not one of the proposed amendments received a vote in either chamber.

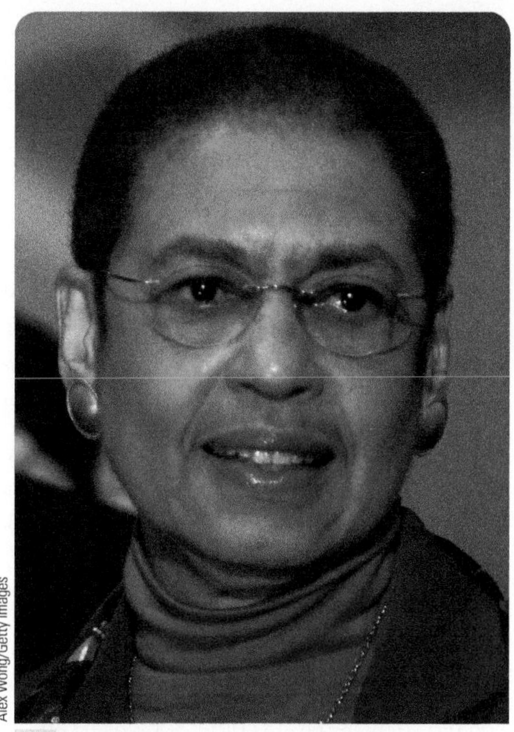

Alex Wong/Getty Images

IMAGE 2.8 Eleanor Holmes Norton is now in her fourteenth term as a nonvoting delegate to Congress from the District of Columbia. The Constitution gives Congress authority over the District of Columbia, and residents were not able to vote for president until 1961. The position Norton holds as a nonvoting delegate was made permanent only in 1971.

Institutional Changes

Not all changes to the Constitution occur via amendment or interpretation. Fundamental changes to the U.S. constitutional system have occurred through the establishment of new institutions, most notably **political parties**. They began to emerge during Washington's first term as president. When Secretary of the Treasury Alexander Hamilton pushed for aggressive use of the necessary and proper clause to allow the national government to regulate the economy, James Madison and Thomas Jefferson rose in opposition (see Chapter 9, Political Parties). These early divisions between political elites laid the groundwork for the emergence of the first set of opposing political parties.

political parties: *Broad coalitions of interests organized to win elections in order to enact a commonly supported set of public policies.*

The rise of political parties has meant that the president and vice president run as members of a political party, not as individuals. In Congress, representatives and senators organize themselves by parties, with members of the majority party having most of the power. The struggle that James Madison envisioned between the different branches of government, with Congress and the president checking each other, really exists only when the president and the majority party in Congress represent different parties—a situation known as divided government. When Congress and the president are of the same party, checks by Congress are curtailed. Members of the president's party in

PUBLIC POLICY AND THE CONSTITUTION

The Death Penalty

The Constitution contains some degree of ambiguity about the death penalty. In several places, it seems to allow capital punishment. The Fourteenth Amendment's due process clause says that states may not deprive people of life, liberty, or property without due process of law, thus suggesting that life, liberty, and property may be taken so long as the states follow due process. Similarly, the Fifth Amendment declares that no person shall be held for a capital crime without indictment by a grand jury. In contrast, the Eighth Amendment prohibits "cruel and unusual" punishments.

Before 1972, most states allowed capital punishment and did so by declaring crimes for which capital punishment could be imposed (usually murder, but sometimes also rape) and then leaving it up to the jury to decide whether capital punishment should be inflicted in a specific case. In 1972, the Supreme Court put a temporary halt to capital punishment, declaring that the process of complete jury discretion was cruel and unusual in that it led to an arbitrary and unequal imposition of the death penalty.[38] According to one justice in this sharply divided case, who received the death penalty and who did not was as arbitrary as who gets hit by lightning. (Figure 2.7 shows the fluctuations in the number of executions per year.)

Various states responded to this decision by requiring juries to follow certain guidelines before imposing the death penalty. In 1976, the Supreme Court ruled 7–2 that the death penalty with such guidelines did not constitute cruel and unusual punishment under the Constitution.[39] Currently, thirty-one states permit capital punishment.[40] In 2016, the Supreme Court struck down Florida's capital punishment system, where the judge and not the jury had the final word on whether the defendant shall be put to death.[41] Given strong public approval for the death penalty—nearly 2–1 in an October 2015 Gallup poll[42]—Congress allows it for certain federal crimes, including terrorist acts that result in death, murder for hire, kidnappings that result in murder, and murder related to the smuggling of aliens.[43] Dzhokhar Tsarnaev, one of the Boston Marathon bombers, was sentenced to death on May 15, 2015, making him the first person sentenced to death by the federal government since the terrorist attacks on September 11, 2001.[44]

Although the Supreme Court has attempted to limit the unequal application of the death penalty, one clear finding from studies is the effect of the race of the victim: Juries are far more likely to impose the death penalty

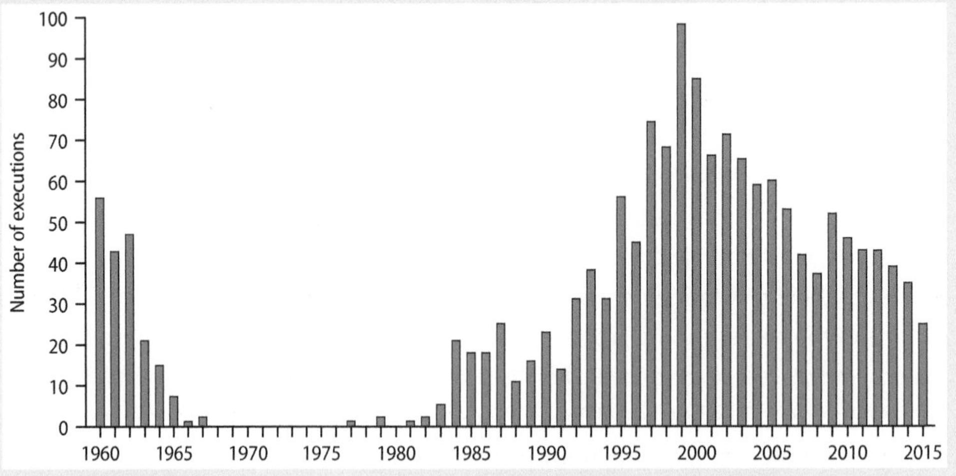

FIGURE 2.7 Annual Executions in the United States, 1960–2015

The number of executions each year dropped significantly in the years before the Supreme Court's temporary halt of capital punishment in 1972, but public support for capital punishment remained high. After the Court reinstituted capital punishment in 1976, the number of executions rose. The number later dipped, as DNA evidence revealing that some death row inmates had been wrongly convicted made the public wary about the death penalty.

Source: Annual Executions, 1960–2015. Death Penalty Information Center, 2016.

when the victim is white than when the victim is black.[45] The Supreme Court has ruled that, even if this were the case overall, someone challenging a death sentence based on such statistics would have to prove that the jury intentionally discriminated in his or her particular case.[46]

The Supreme Court has put limits on who can be sentenced to death. Offenders who were under the age of 18 when their crimes were committed and those convicted of rape, even the rape of a child, cannot receive the death penalty.[47]

Some states have begun to limit their own use of this punishment. The Innocence Project, a group dedicated to reversing convictions of people who were innocent, reports 337 death penalty cases in which DNA testing demonstrated that the wrong person was convicted of the crime.[48] This finding has led many states to reduce the number of death penalty sentences. It has also led many, but not all, states to allow convicted criminals access to DNA evidence, though the Supreme Court does not require them to do so.[49] Illinois was the first state to suspend the use of the death penalty because the evidence in several death penalty cases was shown to be insufficient in establishing guilt, and the newest scientific methods using DNA exonerated several death row inmates.

In considering how well policy making works in the constitutional system, it is worth noting the inconsistent use of the death penalty across states. If two individuals commit the same crime in different states, one might be put to death and the other might be allowed to live. Should states have their own policies on capital punishment, or should the federal government impose a uniform policy on them? The inconsistent use of the death penalty raises questions about equality under the constitutional system and serves as one of the most important examples of the unintended consequences of constitutional design.

Public Policy Connections

1. Evaluate the impact of the death penalty on society. Does the death penalty contribute to lower rates of criminal activity? If so, does the cost of the death penalty (lengthy appeals, etc.) outweigh the benefits? If it does not, does it serve as a way for society to seek just resolution to a heinous criminal action?
2. Should there be a national standard for the death penalty? If yes, what does this do to the reserved powers of the states? If not, why should the location of the crime impact the severity of the penalty imposed?

Congress are more likely to be loyal to the president than they are to their own branch of government.[50]

Political parties also allow for greater responsiveness of politicians to the national welfare. In the early pre-party days of the United States, a representative had little incentive to care about national conditions. A voter could decide whether he (virtually all voters were male then) liked or disliked the job that his representative was doing for his district and could vote accordingly, but he had little way of knowing whether the representative was responsible for the state of the nation. With political parties, however, voters can hold a representative of the party in power accountable not just for the job that the representative is doing for the district but also for the job that the government is doing for the nation. Thus the representatives of the people are more likely to be responsive to the interests of the people.

The Constitution and Democracy

Essential Knowledge

The Constitution, even with its amendments, does not address all controversies in American society. Issues such as the war on terror and electronic surveillance continue to spark debate.

Government under the 1787 Constitution would today be considered severely lacking in both democracy and equality. The government allowed some of the people, mostly white males with property, to choose one chamber of the legislative branch of their government but did not grant the people a direct vote for the other chamber of the legislature or for the chief executive. And a government that allowed slavery would today be a pariah, an outcast, among the nations of the world.

Moreover, in 1787, states regulated the right to vote. Slaves were not allowed to vote, but states differed as to whether women, free blacks, and men without property could vote. In 1790, Georgia, South Carolina, and Virginia prohibited free blacks from voting. South Carolina required voters to believe in God, heaven, and hell. Only New Jersey granted women the right to vote, a right that lasted until 1807. Every state except Vermont required some form of tax payment for voter eligibility.[51]

Yet, compared to the despots and monarchs who had long ruled other countries, the government of 1787 allowed for a remarkable degree of participation by the common person. By giving voters a direct say in their state legislatures and at least indirect influence in all branches of the national government, the 1787 Constitution was a striking break with the past, even if it did not live up to the Declaration's statement that "all men are created equal."

Today participation is much more widespread than in 1787. Although the Electoral College continues to play its role every four years, each state allows the people to choose their electors. In addition, amendments to the Constitution have widened the gateways to democracy. Due to the Seventeenth Amendment, the people today directly choose their senators, making that body directly responsive to public wishes. Moreover, voting equality is guaranteed in various ways: Poll taxes are illegal (Twenty-Fourth Amendment), and voting rights, which are now guaranteed to those 18 years old and older (Twenty-Sixth Amendment), may not be abridged due to race (Fifteenth Amendment) or sex (Nineteenth Amendment).

Although the 1787 Constitution allowed the national government to exercise direct control over the citizenry, the tiny size of the national government left the people with far more control over their daily lives than they have today. But it is also the case that today the people have more control over the government. In addition to new constitutional gateways, opportunities for participation are greater than ever, with the Internet relaying information virtually instantly. It is much easier for representatives to be responsive to their constituents' desires when they can easily learn what their constituents believe, and constituents can readily learn what their representatives have done.

Political Science Reasoning

Question 1

Practice 1, Practice 4

The founders of the United States stated what they thought the purposes of government were in two important documents: the Declaration of Independence and the Constitution of the United States.

Compare the two documents below.

> We hold these truths to be self-evident, that all men are created equal, that they are endowed by their creator with certain unalienable rights, that among these are life, liberty and the pursuit of happiness.—That to secure these rights, governments are instituted among men, deriving their just powers from the consent of the governed, —that whenever any form of government becomes destructive of these ends, it is the right of the people to alter or to abolish it, and to institute new government, laying its foundation on such principles and organizing its powers in such form, as to them shall seem most likely to effect their safety and happiness.[1]
>
> We the people of the United States, in order to form a more perfect union, establish justice, insure domestic tranquility, provide for the common defence, promote the general welfare, and secure the blessings of liberty to ourselves and our posterity, do ordain and establish this Constitution for the United States of America.[2]

1. In what ways do these two documents advance similar principles? In what ways do they differ in principles? According to each document, what is the source of political power?
2. To what extent does the United States achieve the ideals set forth in these two documents?

Question 2

Practice 1, Practice 4

Periodically, political systems change their governing documents. In the case of the United Kingdom, this can with can be done with an act of Parliament. In the many of the states in the United States, this would require a vote of the people. Both the articles of confederation and the Constitution provided for their amendment.

Examine the two documents below.

> **Document 1**
>
> Every State shall abide by the determinations of the United States, in Congress assembled, on all questions which by this confederation are submitted to them. And the Articles of this confederation shall be inviolably observed by every state, and the union shall be perpetual; nor shall any alteration at any time hereafter

[1]Declaration of Independence, 1776.
[2]Constitution of the United States of America, 1789.

be made in any of them, unless such alteration be agreed to in a Congress of the United States, and be afterward confirmed by the legislatures of every State.[3]

Document 2

Congress, whenever two-thirds of both houses shall deem it necessary, shall propose amendments to this Constitution, or, on the application of the legislatures of two-thirds of the several States, shall call a convention for proposing amendments, which, in either case, shall be valid to all intents and purposes, as part of this Constitution, when ratified by the Legislatures of three-fourths of the several States, or by conventions in three-fourths thereof, as the one or the other mode of ratification may be proposed by Congress; provided that no amendment which may be made prior to the year one thousand eight hundred and eight shall in any manner affect the first and fourth clauses in the ninth section of the first article; and that no State, without its consent, shall be deprived of its equal suffrage in the Senate.[4]

1. In both documents, who can propose amendments and who can ratify them?
2. Which document makes it easier for amendments to be proposed?
3. Which document makes it easier for amendments to be ratified?
4. Which document is more likely to produce a policy result aligned with the wishes of the majority of the population?

[3]Articles of Confederation, 1781.
[4]Constitution of the United States of America, 1789.

Focus on AP® Success

2 The Constitution

Must Know: Key Concepts

- Federalists
- Antifederalists
- Declaration of Independence
- Factions
- *Federalist Papers*
- "Antifederalist Papers"
- Republic
- Shays' Rebellion
- Great Compromise
- Electoral College
- Three-Fifths Compromise
- Commerce and Slave Trade Compromise
- Amendment Process
- Articles of Confederation
- Virginia Plan
- New Jersey Plan
- Social Contract Theory
- Federalism

Thinking Politically

Concept Application

There can be some confusion regarding the terms "democracy" and "republic." Much of the confusion raised is because of the changing definitions of the terms. As the founders used the terms, a republic was a political system where governmental authority was vested in elected officials that were held accountable at periodic elections. In such a system citizens exercise political authority indirectly. This was based on their understanding of the Roman Republic. The founders used the term democracy to refer to a political system where citizens exercise direct decision-making authority such as in a New England town meeting or the government of ancient Athens. In those examples, citizens voted directly on policy. As the terms are used by political scientists today, a democracy is any system in which citizens exercise decision making authority either directly or indirectly. As such, it is correct to say that the Constitution was based on democratic principles. However, it is important to note that the Constitution does not provide for any form of direct democracy as can be found in many state constitutions today. What does this lack of direct democracy reveal about framers' view of human nature?

Understanding Learning Objectives with Key Concepts

LOR – 1.A Explain how democratic ideals are reflected in the Declaration of Independence and the U.S. Constitution.

- The Declaration of Independence provides for popular sovereignty (i.e., the right of the people to rule themselves) in the second paragraph. In this paragraph, Jefferson relies upon John Locke's social contract theory: "...Governments are instituted among Men, deriving their just powers from the consent of the governed..."

CON – 1.A. Explain how Federalist and Antifederalist views on central government and democracy are reflected in U.S. foundational documents.

- With the drafting of the Constitution, a national debate began about its ratification. Those who supported ratification were known as Federalists, and those who were against ratification were known as Antifederalists. Among the more prominent Federalists were Hamilton, Madison, and Jay. They authored a series of essays, the *Federalist Papers*, explaining the functioning of the proposed Constitution and advocating for its adoption. In *Federalist* No. 10, Madison argued that the Constitution will mitigate the "mischiefs of faction" because in a large republic it is more difficult for one faction to dominate. Further, the impact of factions is minimized by federalism and checks and balances.

- An opposition point of view is expressed in "Brutus 1." In this essay, the author expresses concern that the new, more powerful central government is more of a threat to individual liberty than are states that currently hold the bulk of political power. These state governments are more easily controlled by local citizens than would be the national government established by the Constitution. The author states, "when the people once part with power, they can seldom or never resume it again but by force."

CON – 1.B Explain the relationship between key provisions of the Articles of Confederation and the debate over granting the federal government greater power formerly reserved to the states.

- There were several deficiencies in the Articles of Confederation. Some of these problems were illustrated by the following events:
  - Shays' Rebellion illustrated the need for a more centralized military as a means to maintain domestic order.
  - Under the Articles of Confederation, the Congress would determine how much of a financial contribution each state would make to the national government. However, the Articles of Confederation lacked any enforcement power to collect those contributions. Many states failed to pay their contribution, which resulted in increased national debt.

CON – 1.C Explain the ongoing impact of political negotiation and compromise at the Constitutional Convention on the development of the constitutional system.

- Among the many compromises of the Constitutional Convention are the following:
  - Great (Connecticut) Compromise. This is a compromise between the Virginia and New Jersey Plans. This compromise created a bicameral legislature where states are represented equally in one house (Senate) and represented based on population in the other (House of Representatives).
  - The Electoral College represents the Framers' beliefs that popular will should be recognized but checked. For the election of the president and vice president, states received electors equal to the numbers of senators plus representatives. Electors are selected in a manner determined by state legislatures.
  - The three-fifths compromise provided that slaves would count as three-fifths of a person for purposes of both taxation and representation. This satisfied both the North (who wanted the South to pay a greater share in taxes) and the South (who wanted to have a greater share of representation).
  - The Commerce and Slave Trade Compromise allows the national government to regulate commerce (as desired by the northern states) while prohibiting the

national government from banning the importation of slaves for 20 years (as desired by the southern states).

- The Constitution also allows for its own formal amendment. This is a two-part process: proposal and ratification. Constitutional amendments can be proposed by a two-thirds vote in both houses of Congress or by a national convention called by two-thirds of the states. Ratification requires the approval of three-quarters of state legislatures or three-quarters of special ratification conventions in each state.

PMI – 1.A Explain the constitutional principles of separation of powers and checks and balances.

- The Constitution provides for limited government in several ways. First is separation of powers. This provides that law making, law executing, and law interpreting functions are divided into separate institutions. Second is the system of checks and balances. This is a system whereby one branch can "check" or counteract the action of another branch.

- In *Federalist* 51, Madison explains how this system will prevent tyranny of the majority.

PMI – 1.B Explain the implications of separation of powers and checks and balances for the U.S. political system.

- Both separation of powers and checks and balances provide for multiple points of access to the policy making process. Some groups might be better situated to pursue legislative action. Other groups might be more inclined to pursue litigation.

- The system of checks and balances allows officials who abuse their power to be removed through impeachment and a removal process. The Constitution also authorizes the Senate to bar a person from further political office if he or she is convicted of the charges presented in the impeachment.

CON – 2.C Explain how the distribution of powers among three federal branches and between national and state governments impacts policy making.

- Policy making is complicated by the fact that decision-making authority is divided between three branches of government at the national level and between the national and state governments. This can potentially lead to gridlock.

Making Connections

Many of the constitutional principles such as federalism and checks and balances are better illustrated in other chapters. As you read the chapters on policy-making institutions, pay particular attention to the interaction between Congress and the president.

Madison regarded factions as undesirable. However, he realized that factions are "sewn in the nature of man." What Madison regarded as factions are today called political parties and interest groups. These political actors are an important part of the U.S. political system. Political parties are particularly important with regard to elections and the organizational structure of Congress. Interest groups can impact elections and policy making primarily in the Congress and bureaucracy.

Going Deeper: Separation of Powers versus Parliamentary Government

The Constitution of the United States provides for both separation of powers and checks and balances. The system as envisioned by Madison is laid out in *Federalist* 51. In this essay, he states that the purpose of this system is to prevent the establishment of a system that abuses the rights of citizens.

He states:

> *In order to lay a due foundation for that separate and distinct exercise of the different powers of government, which to a certain extent is admitted on all hands to be essential to the preservation of liberty, it is evident that each department should have a will of its own; and consequently should be so constituted that the members of each should have as little agency as possible in the appointment of the members of the others.*

However, this system was designed before the emergence of real political parties. By design, political parties impact the functioning of government. Since 1969, the United States has had more years of divided government, government where at least one house of Congress is of the opposite party as the president, than united government. This can contribute to gridlock, where little substantive legislation occurs. However, democratic systems do not have to be organized this way. Many modern democracies are parliamentary. In countries such as the United Kingdom, Japan, Canada, and Australia, the executive is selected by the legislature. The person selected is usually the leader of the largest party or largest coalition in the parliament. As such, there is really never divided government. The majority party or majority coalition can then implement the policies that they have promised the voters. In fact, a similar system is used in many cities in the United States. In these cities, the city council (the legislative branch) selects the city manger (the executive) with the mayor playing a largely ceremonial role.

3 Federalism

AP® Learning Objectives

CON – 1.C Explain the ongoing impact of political negotiation and compromise at the Constitutional Convention on the development of the constitutional system.

CON – 2.A Explain how societal need affect the constitution allocation of power between the national and state governments.

CON – 2.B Explain how the appropriate balance of power between national and state governments has been interpreted differently over time.

CON – 2.C Explain how the distribution of powers among three federal branches and between national and state governments impacts policy making.

Performance Tasks

Upon the completion of this chapter, you must be able to do the following:

- Citing specific examples, explain how the U.S. Constitution divides power between the national government and the states.
- Explain how this division complicates policymaking for both the national and state governments.
- Citing relevant Supreme Court decisions and legislation, explain how the division of power between the national government and the states has changed over time.

Stephen Finn/Alamy

"What gets me up in the morning and has for the last 24 years is that I can be a voice for those that don't have one ... I realized I could make a difference, I could be their voice, I could fight for them.... There's no better place to fight for working families than the governor's chair."[1]

KATE BROWN
University of Colorado at Boulder

AP Images/Don Ryan

When Kate Brown took her oath of office as governor in February 2015, she became Oregon's second and the nation's thirty-sixth female governor in American history. She also became the first openly bisexual governor in the United States. While her sexuality may have presented a gate to her political ambitions, it proved to be nothing more than a headline.

Brown made her sexual identity public as the result of a news story in the *Oregonian*, the most prominent newspaper in Oregon.[2] As a result of that "outing," she talked about the process of coming out to her legislative colleagues: "Representative Bill Markham, who is over 70 years old, extremely conservative, and a legislator for more than 20 years comes to join me. Over lunch he looks up to say, 'Read in the *Oregonian* a few months ago you were bisexual. Guess that means I still have a chance?!'"[3] It is clear that her colleagues judged and valued her legislative professionalism more than her sexual identity. She joins an increasing number of high-level elected officials across the nation who identify as gay or bisexual. In January 2016, there were six members of Congress and one U.S. senator, for example, who so identified.[4]

After earning her bachelor's degree from the University of Colorado at Boulder in 1981 in environmental studies and women's studies, Brown pursued a law degree at Lewis and Clark Law School in Portland. She practiced family and juvenile law and began working with two nonprofits: the Juvenile Rights Project and the Oregon Women's Health and Wellness Alliance.

Brown began her political career when she was appointed to the Oregon state House of Representatives in 1991. The following year, she won her first election to that seat by a mere seven votes. After serving for six years in the Oregon House, she successfully ran for the state Senate and, in 2008, became the state's first woman to serve as senate majority leader.

In her seventeen years in the Oregon legislature, Brown led the effort to pass Oregon's Family and Medical Leave Act. This legislation made Oregon one of the first states to allow parents to stay home with their sick children without jeopardizing their jobs. She was instrumental in advancing Oregon as the first state to require insurance companies to cover preventive health screenings for women. She also helped to pass the Oregon Equality Act prohibiting discrimination in employment and housing on the basis of sexual orientation and was involved in securing Oregon's Family Fairness Act, which legally recognizes committed same-sex relationships as domestic partnerships.[5]

In 2009, Brown was elected Oregon's secretary of state. Oregon does not have a lieutenant governor, who might serve as the sort of state-level vice president. Instead, if there is a vacancy in the Governor's office, the secretary of state ascends to that office. In 2015, Governor John Kitzhaber (D) resigned amidst a political scandal, and Brown became governor. As governor for less than a year, Brown has been ambitious in her policy priorities of education, economy, equity, and safety preparedness on Oregon school and college campuses.[6] She has proposed a gradual rise of the minimum wage to $13.25.

In some ways, Brown's political career has been a matter of being in the right place at the right time. She has been appointed to office twice. Another way to see these events is that Brown pursued gateways when they opened. She was in a position to be appointed to her first elected office as a result of her activities as an attorney and involvement in community organizations. Voting and campaign activities are the most obvious gateways to participating in civic life, but charitable organizations and nonprofits also offer opportunities to get involved. Brown's education put her in a position to walk through gateways, much like many video games have levels that, once achieved, open new portals. Brown's story is one of finding her passions and being ready to accept opportunities as they arise.

She ran successfully for election in 2016, securing the office in her own right with 51 percent of the vote. She will serve for two more years as Governor of Oregon, the remainder of her predecessor's term, and will be eligible for a full four-year term in 2018.

3.1 Why Federalism?

Explain why the Framers chose a federal system

The delegates to the 1787 Constitutional Convention in Philadelphia recognized that the system of government established by the Articles of Confederation was failing. Congress did not have the authority to regulate commerce or to raise money by taxing citizens or imports; it could only request revenues from the states. Thus, the nation's debts went unpaid, and its credit was sinking. Moreover, trade barriers erected by states against other states impeded commerce. Something had to be done. If the delegates were not able to fix the problems caused by the Articles, James Madison and others feared that the union could disintegrate.[7]

IMAGE 3.1 Benjamin Franklin published this political cartoon in his *Pennsylvania Gazette* on May 9, 1754, shortly after hostilities began in the French and Indian War. The earliest depiction of the need for union among Britain's American colonies, it shows New England as one segment and leaves out Delaware and Georgia altogether. Later, during the Revolution, it was a powerful symbol of American unity.

Why Unify?

Federalism presupposes some form of union, so the answer to the question "why federalism?" first requires an answer to the question "why unify?"

The primary answer to the unification question is that some form of union allows smaller political entities to pool their resources to fight a common enemy. The colonists could not have won the Revolutionary War if they had not banded together to fight the British. Benjamin Franklin published his famous "Join, or Die" cartoon to represent the need for the colonists to stick together in military battles in the French and Indian War (1754–63).[8] By the late 1760s, though, the cartoon had come to symbolize the need for united action against British rule. After the Revolution, common threats remained not only from England but also from France and various American Indian tribes.

Beyond military necessity, many colonists considered themselves to be part of a common nation with Americans in the other states. A nation is said to exist when people in a country have a sense of common identity due to a common origin, history, or ancestry, all of which the colonists shared. This sense of common identity made some form of union not only a military necessity but also a political advantage. The American people, however, also had strong loyalties to their states, an attachment that would have made eliminating states politically impossible. How strong the national government would be was the subject of heated debate at the Constitutional Convention.

Confederal, Unitary, and Federal Systems

A **confederal system** had existed under the Articles of Confederation. In a confederal system, independent states grant powers to a national government to rule for the common good in certain limited areas such as defense. The independent states that make up the confederation usually have an equal vote, and the confederation might require unanimous consent or other supermajorities (for example, two-thirds or three-quarters) to pass legislation. The confederal organization usually acts through the states that constitute it rather than acting directly on the citizens of those states.

confederal system: *System of government in which ultimate authority rests with the regional (for example, state) governments.*

But the Framers who met in Philadelphia in 1787 were not inclined to continue the confederal system. A majority of the delegates believed that the New Jersey Plan, which would have strengthened the national government but still granted each state one vote and still required a supermajority to pass most important issues, did not go far enough. They knew that the United States needed a stronger national government.

If a confederal system gives hardly any power to the national government, a **unitary system** of government gives it virtually every power. State or regional governments might still exist under a unitary system, but their powers and, in fact, their very existence are entirely up to the national government. The authority of a state or regional government in a pure unitary system is similar to the relationship between a state government today and the cities and counties that exist under the state's jurisdiction. Counties can make local decisions, but they exist only because their state established them, and a county has only the authority the state grants to it.

unitary system: *System of government in which ultimate authority rests with the national government.*

A confederal system was too weak for the United States, and an overly strong central government would pose its own set of problems. The Framers particularly feared that too much power in any government could lead to tyranny. Freedom would be better guaranteed by dividing governmental powers, rather than by concentrating them in a central government.

The Framers thus established a new system of government, **federalism**. A federal system, like that of the United States, mixes features of confederal and unitary governments. The Constitution created one legislative chamber chosen by the people and based on population, and another chosen by the states and based on equal representation. Within the states' areas of authority—those areas not granted to the national government—their decisions are final and cannot be overturned by the national government. Moreover, the existence of states in a federal system does not depend on the national government; rather, the states derive their authority directly from the people. Nevertheless, within areas of authority granted to the national government, or areas of authority shared by the states and the national government, the national government reigns supreme. Political scientist William Riker defines federalism as a system of government in which there exists "a government of the federation [that is, a national government] and a set of governments of the member units [that is, the states] in which both kinds of governments rule over the same territory and people, and each kind has the authority to make some decisions independently of the other" (see Figure 3.1).[9]

federalism: *System of government in which sovereignty is constitutionally divided between national and state governments.*

A federal system not only reduces the risks of tyranny; it promotes self-government. While any representative democracy involves **self-government**, or government by the people, self-government is enhanced when the decisions that affect the citizens' lives are

self-government: *Rule by the people.*

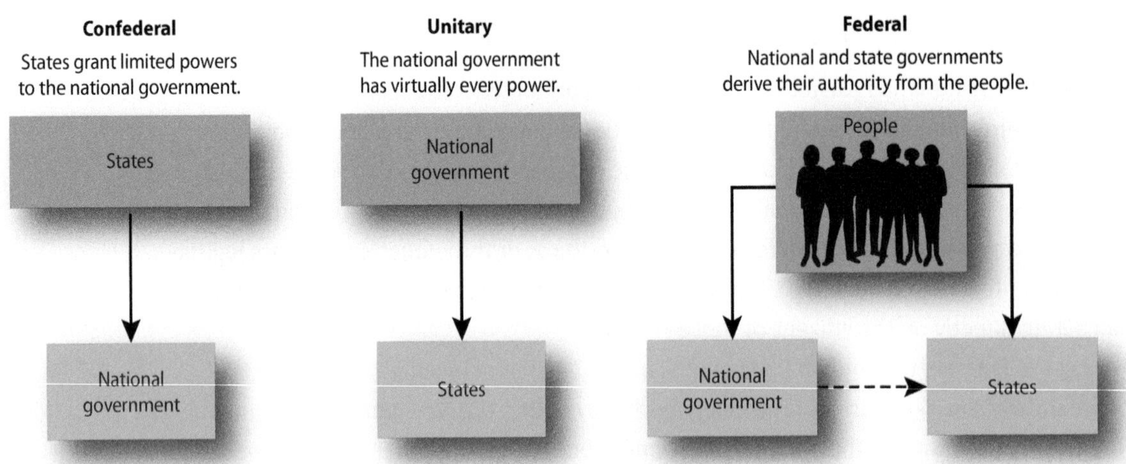

FIGURE 3.1 Confederal, Unitary, and Federal Systems of Government

Political authority is derived from different sources in these three forms of government. In the U.S. federal system, the people provide political authority to the states and the national government.

made by representatives who are local, closer to them, and more similar to them, rather than by representatives who live far away and are dissimilar. Thus self-government is enhanced when people in Massachusetts, to the extent possible, make rules for the people who live in Massachusetts, while people in Texas make rules for the people who live in Texas.

The Framers' choice of a federal system of government was innovative because virtually all of the world's governments at the time were either unitary or confederal. Madison's original Virginia Plan did not propose a pure unitary system—Congress could not eliminate the states. However, by giving Congress a complete veto over laws passed by the states and by granting Congress the general authority to pass laws that would promote "the harmony" of the United States,[10] it would have moved the United States in that direction. The American system was an experiment, and its evolution has been shaped by the tensions, even conflicts, inherent in a system in which power is both divided and shared. Since 1787, about two dozen other nations have ordered themselves as federal systems.

3.2 Constitutional Framework

Summarize how the Constitution institutes the federal system

Essential Knowledge

The fact that the United States is a federation complicates national policymaking.

The Constitution lays the framework of the U.S. federal system in a variety of ways. First, the Constitution grants specified powers to the national government, reserving all remaining powers to the states or the people. Second, the Constitution sets limits on both the powers granted to the federal government and the powers reserved to the states. Third, the Constitution lays out the relationships among the several states as well as between the states and the federal government.

Grants of Power

The Constitution lists the grants of power to Congress in Article I, Section 8. These **enumerated powers** include several powers that could only lie in a national government: raising armies, declaring war, and establishing rules for citizenship. The enumerated powers also grant powers that the central government under the Articles of Confederation did not have, including the power to tax to provide for the general welfare, to borrow money, and to regulate interstate and foreign commerce. To the list of powers in Article I, Section 8, the Framers added one final power that would substantially strengthen the national government: the power to make all laws that are "necessary and proper" for carrying out the enumerated powers.

enumerated powers: *Powers expressly granted to Congress by the Constitution.*

Essential Knowledge

The grants of power to national, delegated, and state governments require negotiation between the levels of government.

The **necessary and proper clause** does not grant Congress the authority to pass any law that it desires. Rather, the clause requires that the law be necessary and proper to one of the listed powers, such as collecting taxes or regulating commerce.

necessary and proper clause: *Gives Congress the power to pass all laws necessary and proper to the powers enumerated in Article I, Section 8.*

The original Constitution does not list the powers of the state governments, as the states retained all powers that were not prohibited by the Constitution. But to ease the concerns of the Antifederalists who wanted this relationship spelled out in the Constitution, the Tenth Amendment declares that "the powers not delegated to the United States by the Constitution, nor prohibited by it to the States, are reserved to the States respectively, or to the people" (see Figure 3.2 for the amendments that pertain to federalism). The **reserve powers** of the states, sometimes referred to as the police powers, include powers to protect the safety, health, and welfare of their citizens, although the federal government now regulates many of these activities. However, marriage and divorce laws, insurance regulations, and professional licensing (of teachers and electricians, for example) remain almost exclusively within state authority, though subject to national requirements that states provide due process and equal protection. States have authority to define and prosecute

reserve powers: *Powers retained by the states under the Constitution.*

Essential Knowledge

The Constitution solved the problems of the Articles of Confederation including: lack of the ability of the central government to maintain domestic order and lack of adequate power to lay and collect taxes.

Color Code: Criminal procedure | Participation | Equality | Structure | Miscellaneous

Amendment	Year	Description
Fifth	1791	Affirms the right to indictment by a grand jury and right to due process; protects against double jeopardy, self-incrimination, and taking of property without just compensation
Tenth	1791	Reserves the powers not granted to the national government to the states or to the people
Eleventh	1798	Prevents citizens from one state from suing another state in federal court
Thirteenth	1865	Prohibits slavery in the United States
Fourteenth	1868	Makes all persons born in the United States citizens of the United States and prohibits states from denying persons within its jurisdiction the privileges or immunities of citizens, the due process of law, and equal protection of the laws; apportionment by whole persons
Fifteenth	1870	Prohibits states from denying the right to vote on account of race
Sixteenth	1913	Grants Congress the power to tax income derived from any source
Seventeenth	1913	Gives the people (instead of state legislatures) the right to choose U.S. senators directly

FIGURE 3.2 Constitutional Amendments That Pertain to Federalism

These amendments to the Constitution specifically affect federalism in the United States. For example, the Thirteenth Amendment abolished slavery in all states, taking away individual states' ability to decide whether slavery would be allowed in their borders.

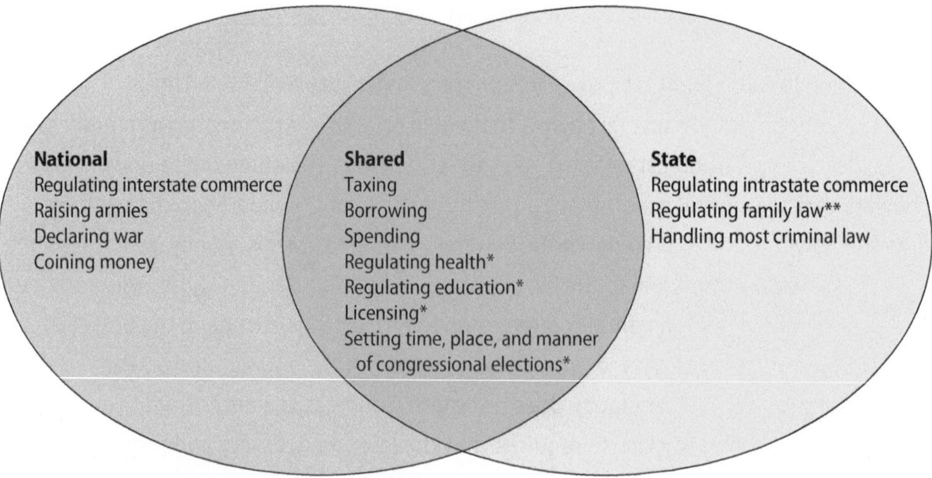

*These were once reserved powers of the states, but the growth of federal authority means that they are now regulated by both.
**Federal courts have eliminated the right of states to prohibit same-sex marriages. See later in this chapter as well as Chapter 5.

FIGURE 3.3 Examples of National, State, and Shared Powers

State governments and the national government exercise political power in several areas, and in some areas, the two levels of government overlap in their authority. For example, both the national and state governments have the power to tax.

most crimes, but the federal government may do so too, with the most prominent examples including federal laws relating to guns, drugs, bank robbery, and terrorism.

concurrent powers: *Powers held by both the national and state governments in a federal system.*

Many powers belong to both the state and national governments. These **concurrent powers** include taxing, borrowing and spending money, making and enforcing laws, establishing court systems, and regulating elections. Many areas that were once exclusively within state authority, such as health care, education (see Public Policy and Federalism: Public Education), and occupational licensing, are now regulated by both the state and the federal governments (see Figure 3.3).

Limits on Power

The Constitution grants only specified powers to the national government, but even those powers are limited. The Constitution prohibits Congress from suspending the writ of *habeas corpus*, the right of individuals who have been arrested and jailed to go before a judge who determines whether their imprisonment is legal. The Constitution also bars the passage of any law that declares an individual guilty of a crime (a bill of attainder) and any law that makes an act illegal after the fact (an *ex post facto* law).

Following concerns expressed by Antifederalists during the state ratification debates that the proposed Constitution granted the national government too much power, one of the first orders of business for the First Congress was a proposed bill of rights. The first ten amendments to the Constitution created associational freedoms (speech, press, assembly, and religion) that Congress could not abridge; limited the authority of governmental prosecutions against alleged criminals by restricting searches and seizures and guaranteeing the right to counsel and to public trials; and protected certain additional rights, including the right to bear arms and the right to jury trials in civil suits over $20 (see Chapter 4, Civil Liberties, for more details on these rights). The Bill of Rights originally applied only to the national government, not to the states.

The Constitution contains its own set of limits on the state governments. Like the national government, states cannot pass bills of attainder or *ex post facto* laws or create titles of nobility. Moreover, states cannot coin money or enter into treaties or alliances with foreign nations. The Constitution also limits the authority of states to tax imports and exports.

The guarantee clause of the Constitution (Article IV, Section 4) guarantees that states shall have a "Republican Form of Government," meaning that a state cannot establish a pure **direct democracy** (although New England towns sometimes run along these lines), a monarchy, or a dictatorship (here the term *republican* has nothing to do with the Republican Party but refers to representative democracy). In *Federalist* 39, Madison defined a republican form of government as one that "derives all its powers directly or indirectly from the great body of the people; and is administered by persons holding their offices during pleasure, for a limited period, or during good behavior."[11] That is, as long as the people who run the government are selected directly (as in the House of Representatives) or indirectly (as in the Electoral College) by the people, and those officeholders either have limited terms of office (as do the president and members of Congress) or can be removed for not meeting the standards of "good behavior" (as in the judiciary), the government can be considered republican.

direct democracy: *Form of democracy in which political power is exercised directly by citizens.*

The Fourteenth (1868) and Fifteenth (1870) Amendments limit state authority further. The Fourteenth Amendment prohibits the states from denying "any person" due process of law and the equal protection of the laws, and the Fifteenth Amendment prohibits states from denying voting rights on account of race, color, or previous condition of servitude (that is, slavery). The Supreme Court later used the due process clause of the Fourteenth Amendment to require the states to follow most of the provisions of the Bill of Rights (see Chapter 4). Thus states must protect the same liberties as the federal government does, resulting in a nationalizing of the country's most basic rights. Both the Supreme Court and Congress have used the Fifteenth Amendment to protect equal voting rights in the states and the equal protection clause of the Fourteenth Amendment to protect other civil rights (see Chapter 5, Civil Rights).

Groundwork for Relationships

In the U.S. federal system, where both the states and the federal governments have the final say over different matters, the Constitution specifies the powers of the national government and restrictions on the powers of both the national and the state governments. In addition, it lays the groundwork for the relationship between the national government and the state governments and for relationships among the state governments.

Ross Franklin/AP Images

IMAGE 3.2 Sheriff Joe Arpaio of Maricopa County, Arizona, is a strident opponent of illegal immigration. Self-proclaimed as "America's Toughest Sheriff," he was denied a seventh term by voters, bringing an end to his twenty-four years as sheriff.

PUBLIC POLICY AND FEDERALISM

Public Education

Despite the fact that federally elected politicians talk frequently about the importance of education, the federal government itself funds about 10 percent of all elementary and secondary education spending.[12] The primary reason for this minimal funding is the federal structure. With education among the reserved powers left to the states, state and local governments developed the responsibility for educating the populace. Originally, states set education policy that local communities then implemented through locally elected school boards.[13] Depending on the state, local school boards had differing amounts of power to establish the curriculum, support extracurricular activities, hire and fire teachers, negotiate salaries for school district employees, and set standards for graduation. Over time, funding for elementary and secondary education became based on local property taxes, with some additional assistance from state governments. Just as the overall wealth of local communities and states varies, so does the amount of funding available for education.

The federal government has intervened in public education for two main reasons: to overcome the denial of equality of educational opportunity by the states and to improve the quality of education. The Supreme Court has struck down segregated schools for black students in *Brown v. The Board of Education*[14] and for Mexican Americans in *Cisneros v. Corpus Christi*[15]; however, despite these legal restrictions on segregation, many African American and Latino students continue to attend schools that are predominantly minority, as shown by Figure 3.4.

Today the federal government has numerous programs to provide equal access to education across income level, race, and level of disability. These programs are under the jurisdiction of a variety of agencies. For example, the Department of Health and Human Services (HHS) oversees the Head Start and Early Head Start programs for low-income children, while the Department of Education has programs for homeless children, remedial education programs for disadvantaged children, and programs for children with disabilities under the Individuals with Disabilities Education Act.

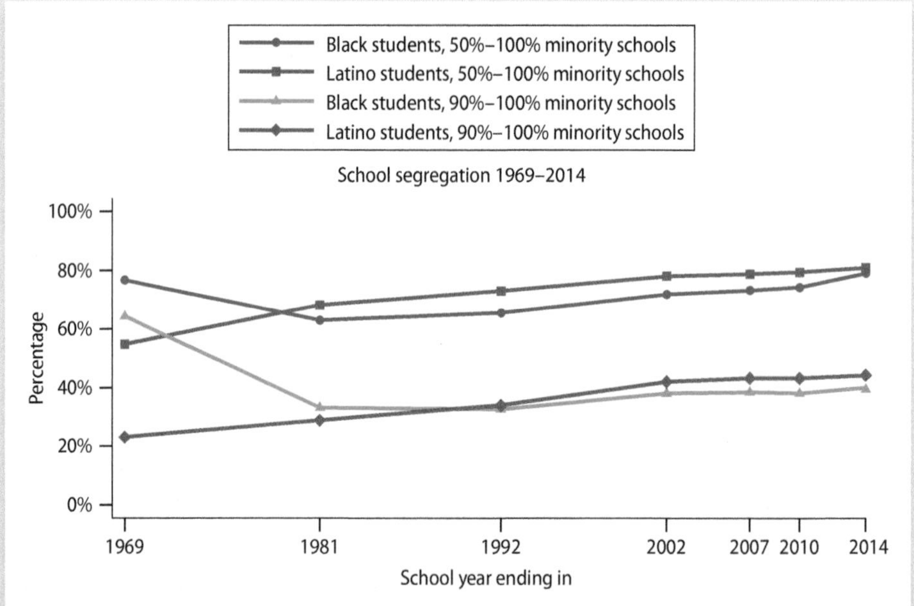

FIGURE 3.4 Percent of African American and Latino Students Attending Highly Segregated Schools, 1969–2014

The percent of African American students attending highly segregated schools (greater than 90 percent minority) dropped sharply between 1969 and 1981 but has slowly risen since then. The percent of Latino students attending highly segregated schools has been increasing as well. That number is now greater for Latino students than for African American students.

Source: Adapted from Gary Orfield, John Kucsera, and Genevieve Siegel-Hawley, "E Pluribus Separation," 2012, The Civil Rights Project and U.S. Department of Education, Common Core of Data, Public Elementary/Secondary School Universe Survey Data 2013–2014, http://civilrightsproject.ucla.edu/research/k-12-education/integration-and-diversity/mlk-national/e-pluribus...separation-deepening-double-segregation-for-more-students/orfield_epluribus_revised_omplete_2012.pdf and https://nces.ed.gov/ccd/pub_overview.asp.

The federal government has also intervened to improve the quality of education. Congress originally played almost no role in public school (K–12) education, but its role increased after World War II. In 1958, it passed the National Defense Education Act, which provided grant money for increased math and science education in elementary and secondary schools. In 1965, Congress passed the Elementary and Secondary Education Act and the Higher Education Act. Each of these programs widened the gateway of access to quality education by increasing federal responsibility to fund specific programs ranging from remedial reading and writing for elementary school children to subsidized loan programs for students in college and graduate school.

Presidents have also initiated educational programs. No Child Left Behind, former President George W. Bush's effort in this area, tried to impose stricter performance and accountability standards for education. Former President Barack Obama, while seeking to set higher standards for the No Child Left Behind program, in 2012 granted partial or full waivers to thirty-three states to give them more flexibility in achieving goals.[16] His administration also supported the "common core," a controversial program that ties some federal spending to states that move toward a national curriculum and greater use of student testing.

States were persuaded into adopting these common standards as part of Obama's Race to the Top initiative, which allowed states to apply for extra federal funds for education provided that they agreed to adopt these standards. Forty-six states and the District of Columbia applied to compete for the federal funds under the Race to the Top program.[17] The total budget for the program, continuing through 2016, is $4 billion established as part of the American Recovery and Reinvestment Act of 2009.[18]

Despite the stronger federal role, however, education under a federal system still permits inequality by allowing a vast disparity in how much money states and local communities choose to spend on it.

Public Policy Connections

1. Public education is a reserved power of the states. However, the federal government's role increased significantly from middle of the twentieth century to the early part of the twenty-first century. Is it appropriate for the federal government to "force" states to adopt a particular set of curriculum standards? Explain.
2. Has the federal government's involvement in public education served to improve the quality of public education or stifle creative policy-making on the part of state governments?

Relationships Between the Nation and the States. The Constitution regulates the relationship between the national government and the states through three main clauses: the supremacy clause, the Tenth Amendment, and the sovereign immunity provision of the Eleventh Amendment. The **supremacy clause** (Article VI) makes the Constitution of the United States, plus all laws and treaties made under the Constitution, supreme over state law. Thus, if federal law conflicts with state law, the federal law (assuming it is within the powers of Congress) is supreme. Moreover, because state and federal courts might differ about whether state law and federal law actually conflict in a particular case, the ultimate decision rests with the U.S. Supreme Court.[19]

supremacy clause: *Makes federal law supreme over state laws (Article VI).*

The supremacy clause also allows for the preemption of state laws. If Congress and the states both seek to regulate an area of concurrent authority, such as pollution control or the minimum wage, the supremacy clause requires states to meet national standards if national standards are higher than state standards. Thus, if a state sets an $8 per hour minimum wage, but Congress sets a $10 minimum wage, businesses in the state must abide by the higher national standard, as we saw in Chapter 1, Gateways to American Democracy. On the other hand, states are usually able to set higher standards than the national government does. So if Congress sets a minimum wage of $9 per hour, but a state sets a minimum wage of $11, businesses in the state must pay the higher state rate. There are two exceptions. First, Congress can declare that it has preempted state legislation in that area, meaning only Congress can legislate on the topic. For example, Congress preempted state regulation of warnings on cigarette packages, prohibiting the states from adding their own warnings. Second, even if Congress has not explicitly declared that it has preempted state activity, the Supreme Court can rule that Congress's regulation is so thorough that Congress must have intended to "occupy the field," thus disallowing state regulations. The Supreme Court struck down state regulations of Communist activities under this exception. More recently, in response to illegal immigration into the United States, Arizona and various other states have passed their own laws to deal with the problems, such as the right of local police officers to request documentation of those suspected of being in the United States illegally as well as harsh punishment for employers who hire undocumented workers. In 2012, the Supreme Court declared that federal law preempted most of the provisions of the Arizona law but did allow Arizona to confirm people's immigration status while enforcing other laws.

As noted earlier, the Tenth Amendment states that all powers not delegated to the national government under the Constitution are reserved to the states or to the people. The Articles of Confederation had a similar clause, but it included the word *expressly* before the word *delegated*. Because the Tenth Amendment omits the word *expressly*, the implication is that the national government retains the sort of **implied powers** granted by the necessary and proper clause.

implied powers: *Powers not expressly granted to Congress but added through the necessary and proper clause.*

If the government illegally harms an individual or seizes a person's property, that person might be inclined to sue the government. The doctrine of sovereign immunity, however, means that a government cannot be sued without its permission. For example, a state might choose to allow suits against it for racial discrimination but might choose to prohibit suits based on the hours or wages of state employees. In a federal system with both state and federal courts, however, a state can prevent suits against itself in its own courts simply by passing a law preventing such suits. It cannot necessarily prevent lawsuits against it in federal court. Thus, in 1793, the Supreme Court allowed the lawsuit of a South Carolina man against the state of Georgia.[20] Following this decision, Congress proposed and the states quickly ratified the Eleventh Amendment, which prohibits federal courts from hearing suits against a state by citizens of another state. The Eleventh Amendment is not absolute: Congress can allow suits based on provisions in constitutional amendments passed after the Eleventh, such as the due process and equal protection clauses of the Fourteenth Amendment.

Relationships Among the States. One of the many problems of governance under the Articles of Confederation was that the states could establish trade barriers against one another, thus limiting economic growth. Therefore, in the **commerce clause** (Article I, Section 8), the Constitution established Congress's exclusive authority to regulate commerce among the states. Thus states may not establish trade barriers against goods from other states. A state may tax goods from other states equal to the amount that it taxes goods produced in its own state, but it cannot charge extra taxes on goods that are made out of state. Congress cannot establish trade barriers in interstate commerce either because Article I, Section 9, prohibits Congress from taxing exports from any state.

commerce clause: *Gives Congress the power to regulate commerce with foreign nations, with Indian tribes, and among the various states (Article I, Section 8).*

The Constitution also requires agreements between two or more states to receive the approval of Congress. States that share rivers, lakes, or other natural resources frequently make agreements over the use of their shared resources so that no one state overuses or overpollutes those resources.[21]

Drew Angerer/Bloomberg/Getty Images

IMAGE 3.3 The Supreme Court ruled in *Obergefell v. Hodges* (2015) that same-sex marriages are legal. Supporters of this decision celebrated the ruling by overlaying a rainbow, a symbol of LGBTQ rights, over pictures of federal buildings such as the White House and the Supreme Court.

Article IV of the Constitution establishes additional rules that guide relationships among the states. The full faith and credit clause generally requires states to accept court decisions made in other states. What happens in Vegas does not necessarily stay in Vegas, as couples who are married (or divorced) there are married (or divorced) throughout the United States. This seemingly simple constitutional rule is now controversial, as some states have recognized same-sex marriages as valid. Under the full faith and credit clause, same-sex marriage performed in Massachusetts would presumably be valid throughout the nation. But the clause allows Congress to create exceptions. Congress passed and President William Jefferson (Bill) Clinton (1993–2001) signed one such exception into law with the Defense of Marriage Act (1996), which relieves the federal government and the states of the obligation of accepting the validity of same-sex marriages performed in other states. President Barack Obama, however, believing the law unconstitutional, in 2011 ordered the Justice Department not to defend it. In 2013, the Supreme Court declared that the provision of the Act that prevented the federal government from recognizing same-sex marriages legally performed in other states was unconstitutional.[22] Moreover, the Supreme Court ruled in 2015 that states must allow same-sex couples to marry. See Chapter 6, Supreme Court Cases: *Obergefell v. Hodges.*

Through its privileges and immunities clause, Article IV also requires states to treat people from other states as equal to their own residents. Thus a state may not limit the right to practice law to residents, nor may it require people to live in the state for a set amount of time to receive welfare benefits. The courts, however, have allowed certain exceptions to this constitutional guarantee, the most notable being the higher tuition that out-of-state residents pay at state universities.

3.3 The Changing Nature of American Federalism

Outline how U.S. federalism has changed over time

The ratification of the Constitution pitted the state-centered Antifederalists against the nation-centered Federalists, and pro-state and pro-nation interests have contested the relative balance between the two ever since. Because a federal system presupposes separate states with guaranteed rights, tension between the layers of government is built-in and inevitable. People who believe in relatively more national power contend that the national government does not derive its powers from the states, but from the people. They cite as evidence the statement in the Preamble that the Constitution was established by "We, the People of the United States." Others believe in greater state power, a view that considers the national government to be an agreement by thirteen independent states (the original colonies) to delegate certain limited powers that they had held to a national government. Those patriots would have preferred the Constitution begin, "We, the States . . ."[23]

From the origins of a two-party system during George Washington's presidency (1789–97) through the expansion of national authority over health care under Barack Obama, politicians and citizens have fought over the proper role of the national and state governments. Different eras show a dominance of one view over the other, but even when one side dominates, the other side pushes back. The nation began with a period of nationalization that lasted until around 1835, followed by the movement toward secession and civil war. Following the Civil War, the states and the federal government had clearly separate powers. In the era following the Great Depression and the election of Franklin Delano Roosevelt (1933–45) in 1932, national power grew enormously, only to retreat slightly following the election of Richard M. Nixon (1969–74) in 1968. Throughout these eras, as we shall see, a recurring substantive theme in the federalism debate has involved racial equality. Americans might have sincere preferences about the relative authority of the national and the state governments, but politicians can also use federalism arguments to mask substantive concerns. For example, while Republicans in recent years have generally supported state authority more often than Democrats, Democrats will support state authority when states support liberal policies, such as medical marijuana, or now in Colorado and Washington, marijuana decriminalization, and Republicans will be particularly supportive of state authority when it supports policies favored by conservatives, such as tighter regulations on immigrants.[24]

Nationalization in the Founding Generation (Approximately 1789–1832)

George Washington did not run as the candidate of any political party in 1789 and 1792, and his administration had no organized opposition. Within his administration, however, divisions over the extent of the authority of the national government split Secretary of the Treasury Alexander Hamilton and his allies from Secretary of State Thomas Jefferson and his allies. Hamilton favored a nation-centered federalism. He sought expansive federal power, and in 1790 proposed that Congress establish the National Bank of the United States under a broad reading of the necessary and proper clause. Jefferson, who favored a state-centered federalism, unsuccessfully opposed the bank, which Congress created with a twenty-year charter. Jefferson's allies, however, were able to limit Hamilton's plan to promote manufacturing through subsidies to producers and taxes on imports. The split between Hamilton and Jefferson over federal authority and other issues led to the development of the first party system in the United States, with the pro-national Hamiltonians labeling themselves the Federalist Party, and the Jeffersonian supporters of **states' rights** labeling themselves the Democratic-Republicans (see Chapter 9, Political Parties).

states' rights: *View that states have strong independent authority to resist federal rules under the Constitution.*

In 1798, when the Federalist administration of John Adams (1797–1801) passed the Sedition Act (see Chapter 4), making criticism of the government illegal, Jefferson wrote a resolution adopted by the Kentucky legislature that declared the act void, claiming that states could decide for themselves which national laws to obey. James Madison authored a similar resolution that the Virginia legislature passed. Known as the Virginia and Kentucky Resolutions, these acts argued for **nullification**, the right of states to nullify, or reject, national laws that went beyond the powers granted in the Constitution. Although the Virginia and Kentucky Resolutions met with little approval outside their home states, the doctrine of nullification has reappeared when pro-state forces have questioned national authority, with the most notable example being the run-up to the Civil War. Efforts at nullification have continued with the Arizona House of Representatives' approval of a bill reaffirming the state's ability to refuse cooperation with the federal government when it deems appropriate to do so.[25]

nullification: *Right of states to invalidate acts of Congress they believe to be illegal.*

The debate over national authority to establish a bank resurfaced after the first National Bank charter expired, and Congress chartered a Second National Bank. The Supreme Court resolved this issue in ***McCulloch v. Maryland*** (1819) in an opinion written by Federalist Chief Justice John Marshall.[26] Marshall stated that Congress had the explicit authority to coin money and collect taxes and declared that the creation of a bank helped reach those goals. Thus creating a bank was an implied power that fell within the scope of authority granted by the necessary and proper clause (see Supreme Court Cases: *McCulloch v. Maryland*).

McCulloch v. Maryland: *1819 Supreme Court decision upholding the right of Congress to create a bank.*

Essential Knowledge

Supreme Court decisions impact the balance of power between the national government and the states. In *McCullough v. Maryland*, the Court allowed for a "loose" interpretation of the elastic clause. The elastic clause provides for what are known as implied powers. Furthermore, the Court asserted that the state of Maryland cannot tax the National Bank because of the supreme clause.

Five years later, the Court, in another opinion by Marshall, established a broad construction, or interpretation, of Congress's enumerated power to regulate interstate commerce. In *Gibbons v. Ogden* (1824), the Court ruled that Congress's authority to regulate commerce among the states gave it, rather than the states, the authority to manage the licensing of steamboats traveling between New York and New Jersey. Marshall further declared that the authority of Congress to regulate commerce between the states did not begin or end at state boundaries but necessarily included commercial activities interior to each state.[27] Between the decisions in *McCulloch* and *Gibbons*, the Supreme Court under Marshall supported the Federalist Party position of a strong national government with expansive powers.

The Revolt Against National Authority: Nullification, Slavery, and the Civil War (Approximately 1832–1865)

As Marshall's Supreme Court pushed the United States in a national direction, the precedent set by the Virginia and Kentucky Resolutions led some states to claim the right to disregard national laws that they believed were unconstitutional or merely unwise. Several New England states threatened to ignore the Embargo Act of 1807, and, in 1828, Vice President John C. Calhoun insisted on South Carolina's right to nullify a federal tariff. As the union was merely a compact among the states, Calhoun argued, dissenting states even had the right to **secede**. Against such claims, Senator Daniel Webster insisted that the union was not a compact of states, but a compact among the people of the United States. President Andrew Jackson (1829–37) reinforced Webster's argument in offering this toast: "Our Union. It must be preserved." Whereupon Calhoun rose to counter Jackson: "The Union, next to our liberty, most dear."[28]

secede: *To formally withdraw from a nation-state.*

Although disagreements over federal tariff rates proved an insufficient instigation to secede, federal authority to regulate slavery eventually led to secession. Slavery

SUPREME COURT CASES

McCulloch v. Maryland (1819)

QUESTION: May the federal government establish a bank? If so, does a state have the right to tax that bank?

ORAL ARGUMENT: February 22, 1819

DECISION: March 6, 1819 (read at http://www.law.cornell.edu/supremecourt/text/17/316)

OUTCOME: Yes, the bank is constitutional, and no, Maryland may not tax it (6–0).

Following the decision of Congress to establish the Second National Bank, the state of Maryland imposed a tax on the Maryland branch. The bank manager, James McCulloch, refused to pay the tax, and Maryland brought suit. The Maryland Supreme Court ruled that the bank was unconstitutional because the Constitution does not grant Congress the specific authority to create a bank. McCulloch appealed to the Supreme Court.

Attorney Daniel Webster, who had served in the House and would later serve in the Senate and as secretary of state, represented McCulloch before the Supreme Court. Among the most famed litigators of his day, Webster also represented the nationalist position before the Supreme Court in a District of Columbia lottery case and a New York steamboat case.*

The Supreme Court's decision, written by Chief Justice John Marshall, began by accepting the nation-centered view of the Constitution's founding: Rather than a compact of states, the government established by the Constitution "proceeds directly from the people; is 'ordained and established,' in the name of the people."

Regarding the power to establish a bank, Marshall noted that while the Constitution makes no reference to a bank, it does provide for coining and borrowing money, paying government debts, and levying taxes. It also allows Congress to pass all laws that are "necessary and proper" to any of the enumerated powers. Declaring that "necessary and proper" does not mean "absolutely necessary," Marshall read the necessary and proper clause to mean "ordinary and appropriate."

In explaining the scope of the necessary and proper clause, Marshall declared, "Let the end be legitimate, let it be within the scope of the Constitution, and all means which are appropriate, which are plainly adapted to that end, which are not prohibited, but consist with the letter and spirit of the Constitution, are constitutional." Thus, creating a bank was an appropriate means of legitimate ends: regulating money and collecting taxes.

As for state taxation of the bank, Marshall based his response on the supremacy clause, observing that "the power to tax involves the power to destroy." Because states cannot destroy creations of the federal government, neither can they tax them.

The *McCulloch* decision created a broad scope for implied powers under the Constitution—powers that are not explicitly in the Constitution but are related to powers that are. Without this broad set of implied powers, Congress could not establish criminal laws for most offenses, investigate executive wrongdoing, provide student loans, establish administrative agencies, or conduct many of the other activities it routinely engages in today.

Thinking Critically

1. If Congress does not have the express authority to establish a national bank, by what authority may it do so?
2. What is the harm to federalism if a state can tax a national bank?

* *Gibbons v. Ogden*, 22 U.S. 1 (1824).

concessions at the Constitutional Convention included the **fugitive slave clause** of Article IV, requiring states to return runaway slaves. Congress passed a Fugitive Slave Law in 1793 that established procedures for the return of slaves. In 1850, as part of the last compromise over slavery, Congress strengthened the national authority over runaways by actually forcing states to aid in their return. The act prohibited jury trials for alleged runaway slaves and paid the newly hired commissioners who heard the cases $10 if they ruled for the slave owner but only $5 if they ruled for the alleged slave.

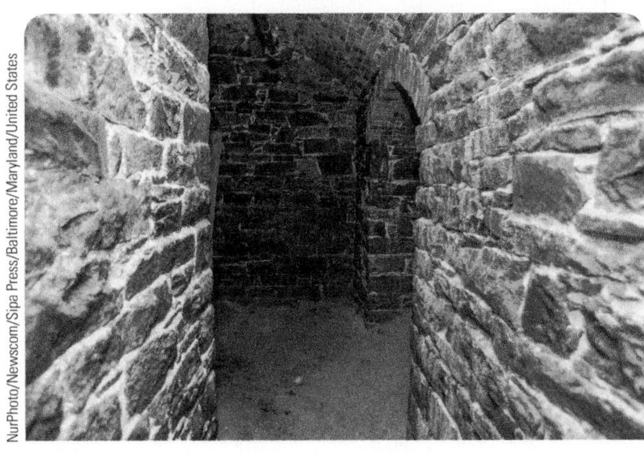

NurPhoto/Newscom/Sipa Press/Baltimore/Maryland/United States

IMAGE 3.4 The Underground Railroad provided assistance to former slaves escaping to freedom. This photo shows hidden passages that existed within houses that served as "stops" on the Underground Railroad.

fugitive slave clause: *Required states to return runaway slaves; negated by the Thirteenth Amendment (Article IV, Section 2)*

Because nothing in the Constitution suggested that Congress had the power to limit slavery in the states, the most heated contests over congressional authority to regulate slavery involved the territories. This debate split abolitionists who wanted to ban slavery in the territories, states' rights supporters such as John C. Calhoun who thought that slave owners had the right to take their slaves into any territory, and those who favored compromises that would allow slavery in some territories but not in others. In 1857, the Supreme Court sided with the states' rights supporters, declaring in *Dred Scott v. Sandford* that Congress had no authority to regulate slavery in the territories (see Chapter 5).[29]

When Abraham Lincoln (1861–65), who favored federal efforts to prohibit slavery in the territories, won the presidential election of 1860, South Carolina seceded. Virtually every grievance listed by South Carolina involved slavery.[30] Other southern states followed, with most noting the question of slavery,[31] and they soon established their own constitution.

During the Civil War, Lincoln used his power as commander in chief to issue the Emancipation Proclamation, which prohibited slavery in states under rebellion, as slave labor was an asset to the Confederate army. Slaves in some of these states were not emancipated until ratification of the Thirteenth Amendment, which prohibited slavery throughout the nation as of December 18, 1865.

The Congresses that followed the Civil War tried to exert federal power over the states to promote equality between freedmen and whites, but President Andrew Johnson (1865–69) vetoed a civil rights bill, claiming it represented a trend toward "centralization and the concentration of all legislative power in the National Government."[32] The bill granted former slaves the rights to make contracts; sue; give evidence; and inherit, purchase, lease, and convey real and personal property. In 1866, Congress passed it over Johnson's veto. But as part of the effort to ensure that all such laws would be constitutional, Congress proposed and the states ratified the Fourteenth Amendment (1868) and the Fifteenth Amendment (1870). These greatly expanded the authority of the national government over the states. The Fourteenth Amendment requires states to provide each person due process of law (see Chapter 4) and the equal protection of the laws (see Chapter 5). The Fifteenth Amendment prevents states from abridging the right to vote on account of race. Like the Thirteenth Amendment, the Fourteenth and Fifteenth Amendments granted Congress the authority to enforce their provisions by appropriate legislation, thus adding to Congress's enumerated powers.

FIGURE 3.5 Dual Federalism and Cooperative Federalism

Dual federalism has been likened to a layer cake (left), and cooperative federalism has been likened to a marble cake (right).

Source: LAITS, University of Texas College of Liberal Arts, © Cengage Learning

In 1883, however, the Supreme Court decided in the *Civil Rights Cases* to keep Congress's powers within the words of the amendments: Congress could prevent states from denying people equality, but it could not prevent private businesses or individuals from doing so, for example, by refusing to hire former slaves or to serve them at inns or restaurants. The Court thus invalidated Congress's Civil Rights Act of 1875, which had prohibited this type of private discrimination. This era, covering the period before and after the Civil War, saw the defeat of the most strident (secessionist) state-centered views, but with the Supreme Court's interpretation of the Civil War amendments, state authority remained strong.

Dual Federalism (Approximately 1865–1932)

dual federalism: *Doctrine holding that state governments and the federal government have almost completely separate functions.*

Although the supporters of state-centered federalism lost the Civil War, the viewpoint of a national government with limited powers did not disappear. A new viewpoint, **dual federalism**, recognized that while the national government was supreme in some spheres, the state governments remained supreme in others, with layers of authority separate from one another; political scientists later compared this arrangement to a "layer cake"[33] (see Figure 3.5). Thus the national government would be supreme over issues such as foreign affairs and interstate commerce, and the states would be supreme in matters concerning intrastate commerce and police powers.

This period of dual federalism left the national government and the states supreme in their respective spheres but granted Congress only a very narrow sphere. Regulations of manufacturing and mining remained under the control of the states, even if the goods later crossed state lines and entered interstate commerce. But a countertrend was emerging. In 1913, Congress passed and the states ratified the Sixteenth Amendment, which granted Congress the power to tax income from whatever source derived, giving the national government access to millions (and later billions and even trillions) of dollars in revenue. The increase in federal authority over areas once left to the states was aided that same year by the ratification of the Seventeenth Amendment, which took the selection of U.S. senators out of the hands of state legislatures and required that they be directly elected by the people of each state. Before 1914, state legislatures hoped senators would be responsive to the needs of the states, but with direct elections, senators had to be responsive to the needs of the people.[34]

Cooperative Federalism: The New Deal and Civil Rights (Approximately 1932–1969)

With the onset of the Great Depression following the stock market crash of 1929, the people wanted national action to aid the economy, and the nation-centered federalism signaled by the Sixteenth and Seventeenth Amendments strengthened considerably the ability of the national government to be responsive to those wishes. In 1932, voters elected Franklin Roosevelt as president. During his campaign, Roosevelt had promised a "New Deal" to Americans who had lost their jobs, their homes, and their savings. Following Roosevelt's inauguration, Congress passed a series of laws designed to lift the ailing economy.

Despite vast support from Congress and the American people for his New Deal policies, Roosevelt saw the Supreme Court strike down one law after another that were designed to lift the ailing economy, often by 5–4 or 6–3 votes. In response, Roosevelt proposed in 1937 to increase the number of justices on the Supreme Court. He would then be able to pack the Court with his own appointees. This controversial **Court-packing plan** met with fierce opposition in Congress. The Supreme Court, however, made passage of the plan unnecessary, for shortly after Roosevelt's proposal, the Court reversed itself and started accepting the broad authority of Congress to regulate the economy.

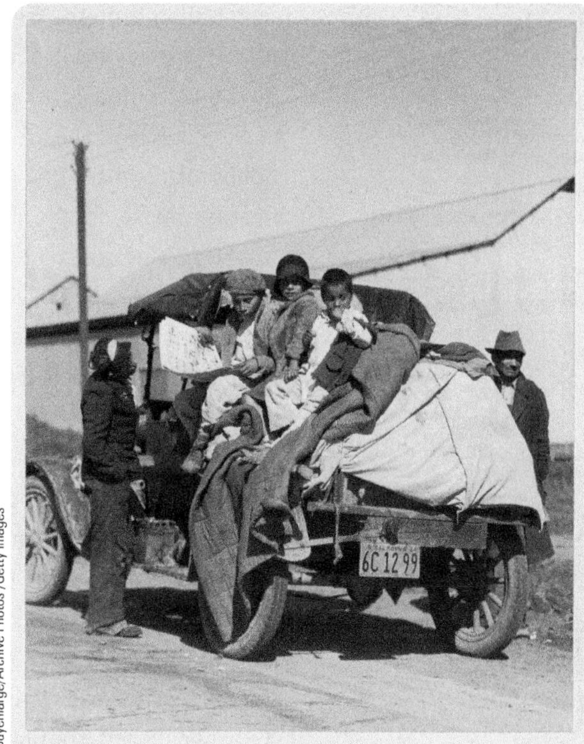

Buyenlarge/Archive Photos /Getty Images

IMAGE 3.5 Migrant Latino farmworkers heading to California to escape the Dust Bowl during the Great Depression.

On taxing and spending, the Court accepted the view that virtually any taxing or spending plan that Congress believed supported the general welfare would be acceptable. Today, for example, although Congress has no direct authority to set drinking ages, it effectively does so by denying federal highway funds to states that set the drinking age under 21; for a variety of reasons, including low voting rates by younger Americans, no states do.

Court-packing plan: *President Franklin Roosevelt's proposal to add new justices to the Supreme Court so that the Court would uphold his policies.*

On commerce, the Court began by accepting the regulation of a giant steel company with operations throughout the United States as an appropriate regulation of interstate commerce.[35] Congress could also use the commerce clause to regulate employment conditions, said the Court, rejecting the Tenth Amendment as a limit on federal power.[36] The Court's definition of what constituted interstate commerce grew to include anything that affected interstate commerce, whether over several states or confined to one state. According to the Court, this included wheat grown on a farm that was consumed on that farm, due to the effect that such wheat and all the similarly used wheat grown by other farmers would have on the market.[37] With federal intervention in manufacturing, farming, and other areas traditionally governed by the states, Roosevelt's nation-centered federalism was said by political scientists to more closely resemble a "marble cake," with specific powers under both national and state authority, than the layer-cake structure of dual federalism.[38]

Essential Knowledge

The Tenth Amendment protects the reserved powers of the states.

State-centered federalism gained some traction in opposition to the push toward equality and civil rights. Following President Harry S. Truman's (1945–53) expressed support for national protections of civil rights, southern segregationists formed the States' Rights Democratic Party and ran South Carolina Governor Strom Thurmond for president in 1948. Then, in *Brown v. Board of Education*, decided in 1954, the Supreme Court struck down school segregation, which had been legally mandated or permitted in twenty states plus the District of Columbia. This Supreme Court decision helped put the federal government at the forefront of the fight for equality. In response to this decision, seven states passed "interposition resolutions" that asserted the right to nullify the Supreme Court decision. Such resolutions have no legal validity.

Essential Knowledge

One of the primary ways in which the states and the national government interact is through grants, both categorical and block. Previously the national government engaged in revenue sharing with state and local governments. The national government can also mandate that state and local governments engage in specific actions as a condition of receiving a grant.

Nation-centered federalism continued to dominate dual federalism through World War II and beyond. President Lyndon Baines Johnson's (1963–69) Great Society program expanded national authority even further, with federal aid to public schools—traditionally a state duty—and health care coverage to the poor (Medicaid) and elderly (Medicare). The Johnson administration gave money to the states for its programs through categorical grants—money for the states to use on priorities set by the national government.

The Johnson administration also expanded national power to ensure greater equality, pushing for passage of the Civil Rights Act (1964), which prohibited job discrimination and segregation in public accommodations, and the Voting Rights Act (1965), which regulated voting rules that had largely been left to the states since the adoption of the Constitution (see Chapter 5).

The New Federalism (Approximately 1969– 1993)

In one of the last challenges to integration, segregationist Governor George Wallace of Alabama ran for president in 1968. His party, the American Independent Party, condemned what it considered to be the unconstitutional use of federal power to desegregate schools and enforce voting rights.[39] Wallace received more than 9 million votes and won the electoral votes of five states. Although Wallace ultimately lost the race, the strength of his campaign signaled a degree of wariness among voters about the powers of the national government. Other politicians, starting with Richard Nixon, the winner of the 1968 election, responded to these concerns.[40]

Presidents, Congress, and the New Federalism. The Nixon administration began the trend, labeled New Federalism, of shifting powers back to the states.[41] The Nixon administration began a general revenue-sharing program that gave the states greater leeway about how the funds from the national government could be spent. The main idea behind Nixon's federalism was that states could more efficiently spend governmental resources than the enormous federal bureaucracy could.

Republican President Ronald Reagan (1981–89) sought to reduce the power of government in general and, as an avid supporter of the New Federalism, of the federal government in particular. In his first inaugural address, he declared, "Government is not the solution to our problem; government is the problem."[42] He thus cut back on categorical grants, replacing them with fewer, more flexible block grants, which set fewer restrictions on how the money could be spent. He also eliminated federal aid to state and local governments (see Figure 3.6).

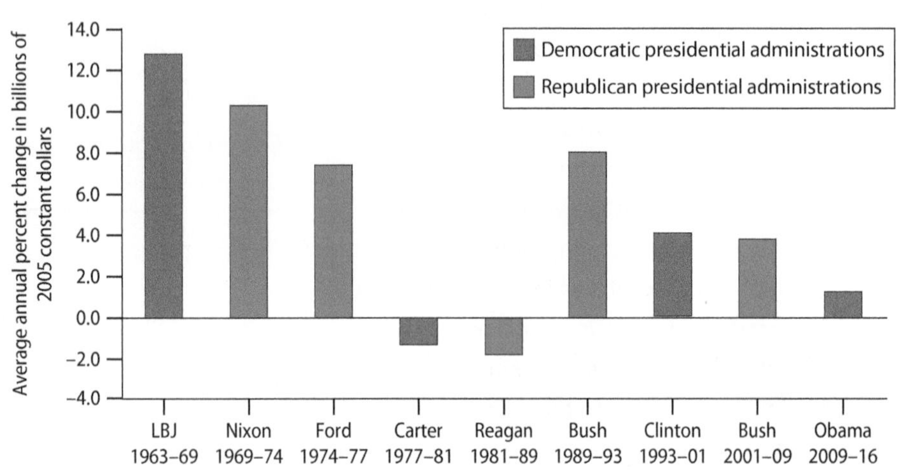

FIGURE 3.6 Annual Percent Change in Federal Aid to State and Local Governments, in Constant Dollars

The amount of federal aid to the states has varied during different presidential administrations. Since Lyndon Johnson's administration, the amount of federal aid to the states has declined dramatically.

Source: Derived by the authors from "Summary Comparison of Total Outlays for Grants to State and Local Governments: 1940–2020 (in Current Dollars, as Percentages of Total Outlays, as Percentages of GDP, and in Constant (FY 2009) Dollars)," accessed January 22, 2016, https://www.whitehouse.gov/omb/budget/historicals.

Nevertheless, Reagan did sign the National Minimum Drinking Age Act, which withheld a percentage of federal highway funds from states that did not increase their drinking age to 21.

Essential Knowledge

The power of the national government relative to the power of the states is still a source of controversy, particularly in the areas of education policy and national security in the post-9/11 world.

The Modern Era (1993–Present). President Bill Clinton did not have strong views on federalism, but one of his early proposals was a plan for national health insurance for all Americans, traditionally an area that had been left to private parties, such as businesses and individuals, and to the states. Opposition to Clinton's plan led both to the plan's defeat and a Republican platform in the 1994 congressional elections called the Contract with America, which included limits on the powers of the federal government. Voters that year chose Republican majorities in both the House and the Senate.

Following the Republican victories, Clinton shifted gears and worked with the Republicans on a devolution of power from the national government to the states, declaring that "The era of big government is over."[43] During the Clinton administration, Congress moved to shift the balance of power toward the states in two important ways. First, it limited unfunded mandates—legal requirements Congress imposes on the states (for example, to provide clean air, disability access, or health benefits to poor people under Medicaid) without supplying the resources to accomplish those activities. Second, Clinton and Congress overhauled the federal welfare system, ending the federal guarantee of welfare to poor families with children, leaving final say on welfare spending with the states.

Although Republicans have typically supported state authority over that of the national government since the New Deal, President George W. Bush (2001–09) oversaw an administration that strengthened national authority, sometimes at the expense of the states.[44] His most prominent actions in this regard included the No Child Left Behind Act (2002), which increased federal involvement in public education, and his prescription drug plan for Medicare, which increased federal involvement in health care.[45] The Bush administration went to court along with the auto industry in an attempt to preempt California's fuel economy and emission standards for cars, which were stricter than national standards.

Following the terrorist attacks of September 11, 2001, Congress and the Bush administration expanded national power in various ways, including the establishment of national standards for driver's licenses and new powers to monitor electronic communications.

On the other hand, the Obama administration has endorsed state-centered federalism, at least where the policies support Democratic Party positions: support for permitting states to set higher standards than the federal government's on fuel economy and tailpipe emissions and a reversal of the Bush administration's crackdown on state medical marijuana programs.[46] The Obama administration chose not to use

Carmen Taylor/AP Images

IMAGE 3.6 When terrorists hijacked planes and crashed them into the World Trade Center Towers in New York City on September 11, 2001, most Americans said their lives changed forever. As with all national crises, following the terrorist attacks, the national government took a greater share of power because only the national government can protect against foreign adversaries. On October 26, 2001, President George W. Bush signed the USA PATRIOT Act, which granted the federal government increased powers over financial transactions, immigration, and domestic criminal activity.

federal authority to prosecute people in Alaska, Colorado, Oregon, and Washington who legally, under the state laws thereof, use marijuana for recreational or medical purposes. In supporting national policies, President Obama reminded Americans of the historical relationship between federalism and the oppression of minority rights in the United States.

The Supreme Court and the New Federalism. By nominating William Rehnquist to be chief justice in 1986, Reagan hoped to move the Court toward state-centered federalism. He was not disappointed. As an associate justice (1972–86), Rehnquist had pressed, often alone on the Court, for what the Supreme Court once labeled "Our Federalism."[47] As chief justice (1986–2005), he further advanced New Federalism, now aided by a Republican bloc that grew to include seven justices. The Rehnquist Court put together pro-state majorities in decisions involving interstate commerce and sovereign immunity.

Concerning interstate commerce, for the first time since 1937, the Court rejected national laws as beyond Congress's authority to regulate under the commerce clause. In one case, the Court struck down congressional legislation banning the possession of guns near schools, declaring that the possession of a gun near a school is not an economic activity.[48] Similarly, the Court rejected a central provision of the Violence Against Women Act, which gave victims of gender-based violence the right to sue their attackers in federal court. A Virginia Tech student who had allegedly been raped by members of the football team sued her attacker and Virginia Tech, a state university, in federal court after the state chose not to bring criminal charges. The Court rejected congressional findings on the effect of such violence on commerce, and it ruled that the section of the act that allowed the lawsuits was beyond Congress's authority either under the commerce clause or under its authority to enforce the equal protection of the laws under the Fourteenth Amendment.

Essential Knowledge

In the case of *United States v. Lopez*, the Court restrained federal power by narrowing the meaning of the commerce clause.

Although these decisions stand in contrast to the decidedly pro-national decisions of the Court since the New Deal, most questions of federal authority still are decided in favor of the national government. The Court allowed Congress to condition highway funds on states having a drinking age of 21, as the small amount of funds at risk (5 percent) made the condition a "pressure" to comply and not a "compulsion."[49] And while it did not allow Congress to take away all federal Medicaid dollars for states rejecting the growth in Medicaid under the Affordable Care Act, it did allow Congress to keep states that rejected the expansion from receiving any new Medicaid money under the Act.[50] Indeed, the Supreme Court continues to uphold Congress's authority to regulate commercial activity. Like politicians, the justices' support for federalism is often dependent on the issue involved.

And while the Roberts Court (2005–present) did not uphold the health care law on commerce grounds, it did uphold the law through the taxing clause, thus allowing the further nationalization of health care policy in the United States.[51]

Federal Aid to States in New Federalism. As we have seen, many state policies involve issues in which the national government does not get involved, whereas in other areas, such as welfare policies, federal mandates and incentives push the states to do what the federal government wants. Federal aid to the states is influenced by a large number of factors, including equal representation in the Senate.[52] The fact that small states have the same number of senators as large states means that small states receive a disproportionate amount of federal aid. For example, in 2012, Wyoming and Alaska received the most aid per capita.[53] These states and eighteen more get more antiterrorism aid per capita than does New York, a frequent terrorist target.[54]

As the president is particularly responsive to the people and party who elected him, it is hardly surprising that states that heavily supported the incumbent president in the previous election, and states whose governors are of the same party as the president, get more federal aid than other states. In addition, recent research suggests that incumbent presidents may selectively direct increased spending toward electorally important swing states in an effort to improve their chances of reelection.[55]

Summing Up: Were the Antifederalists Correct?

The people of the United States ratified the Constitution over the protests of Antifederalists, who claimed that the Constitution gave virtually unlimited powers to the national government. Nevertheless, until the New Deal, either because of congressional inaction or Supreme Court reaction when Congress did act, the powers exercised by the national government were clearly limited. Today, however, due to the popular belief in the need to regulate a complex economy, the historical role that states' rights advocates have played in supporting slavery and segregation, and the Supreme Court's interpretation of the Constitution, Congress has vast powers. The fact that Congress can spend money on virtually anything as long as it is not specifically prohibited by the Constitution, and that the "necessary and proper clause" means "ordinary and appropriate" leads to the conclusion that as far as the powers of the national government are concerned, the Antifederalists were correct: The federal government's powers have few limits. But as the 1994 and perhaps the 2014 elections demonstrate, if the people believe that the national government has too much power, they can—as we have seen—vote for candidates who want to limit that power. In 2015, 60 percent of Americans reported that they thought the federal government had too much power (see Figure 3.7). In the 2016 elections, voters were asked to choose between candidates of two parties with very different views about the balance of the nation–state relationship. Thus in the U.S. federal system, the voters get to decide on that balance.

Essential Knowledge

The Fourteenth Amendment granted citizenship to "all persons born or naturalized in the United States," which included former slaves recently freed.

Essential Knowledge

The interpretation of various clauses, such as the commerce clause and necessary and proper clause, as well as the Tenth and Fourteenth Amendments in the Constitution, can dramatically impact the power of the national government. As such, they are still debated today.

3.4 State and Local Governments

Compare and contrast national and state governments

The Constitution requires that the states maintain a republican form of government, and all have done so by patterning their structure after the national government, with separate legislative, judicial, and executive branches. With the exception of procedures that allow citizens to place proposed laws directly on the ballot, state governments look remarkably similar to the federal government. Local governments, however, use a greater range of organizational options.

POLITICAL ANALYTICS

Antifederalism in Today's Electorate

DURING THE DEBATE OVER THE ADOPTION of the U.S. Constitution, Antifederalists expressed concerns about political power being shifted from the states to the federal government. They feared that the federal government would grow too strong at the expense of state power. This graph shows that in recent years, Americans are increasingly expressing similar concerns. Nearly two-thirds of Americans believe that the federal government has too much power, whereas very few Americans in the past decade or so believed the federal government has too little power.

These views may be expressed in other ways. As discussed in this chapter, states' rights advocates have resurrected nullification efforts in Arizona. More extreme incidents have occurred, such as the January 2016 armed occupation of the Malheur National Wildlife Refuge in Oregon. Antigovernment activists led by Ammon Bundy occupied the facility for more than one month, and one activist died in the conflict. These are extreme examples, but the views presented in this graph may be fueling some of the anger discussed in Chapter 1.

The following graph shows answers to the question, "Do you think the federal government has too much power, has about the right amount of power, or has too little power?" Examine the graph for changes and trends in Americans' views about the power wielded by the federal government.

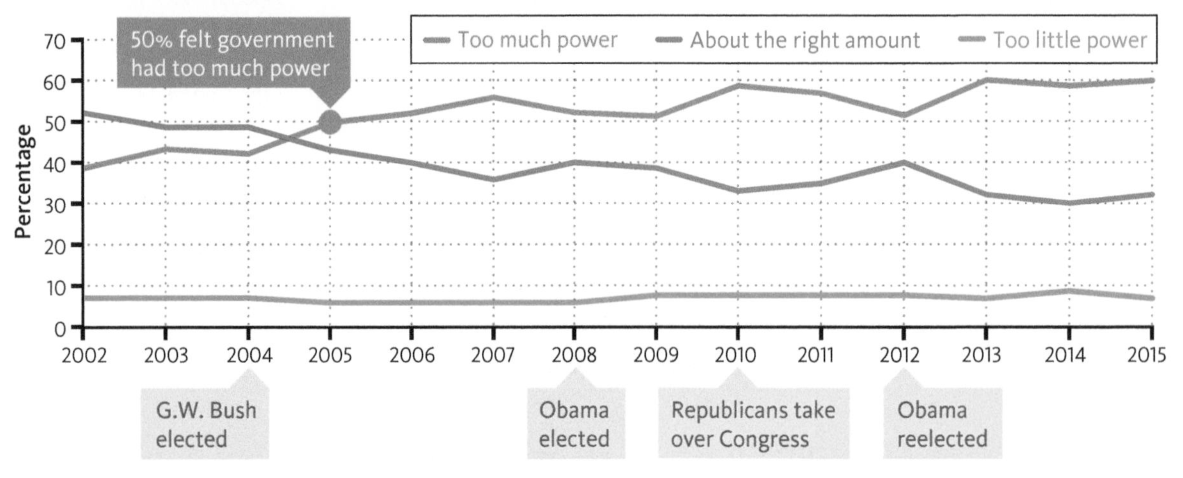

FIGURE 3.7 Changing Views on the Power of the U.S. Government

Source: Gallup Politics, "Public Remains Wary of Federal Government's Power," Jim Norman, October 9, 2015, accessed March 4, 2016, http://www.gallup.com/poll/186065/public-remains-wary-federal-government-power.aspx.

Thinking Critically

1. Do these data support Antifederalist concerns about the growing power of the federal government? Are Americans in 2016 expressing the same concerns as the Antifederalists did in the 1780s?
2. Do you think the views shown in Figure 3.7 are connected to those shown in the Political Analytics feature in Chapter 1 regarding the growth of anger about the political system among some Americans?

State Executive Branches

All fifty states choose the head of the executive branch by direct election. Most states have four-year gubernatorial terms, limit their governors to two consecutive terms, and provide for succession by the lieutenant governor. Figure 3.8 presents the states that use different rules.

The governors of all fifty states have the authority to veto laws subject to override by the state legislatures. Most states further grant their governors a line-item veto, the ability to veto certain parts of a spending bill without vetoing the entire bill. The president does not have this power, so when Congress passes spending bills, it usually does so by combining tens of thousands of separate spending items in an omnibus bill. The president's choice is to sign the entire bill or to veto it; he cannot veto only the appropriations he disfavors. Governors in forty-four states do have that authority, however, giving them a much stronger tool to determine spending than the president.

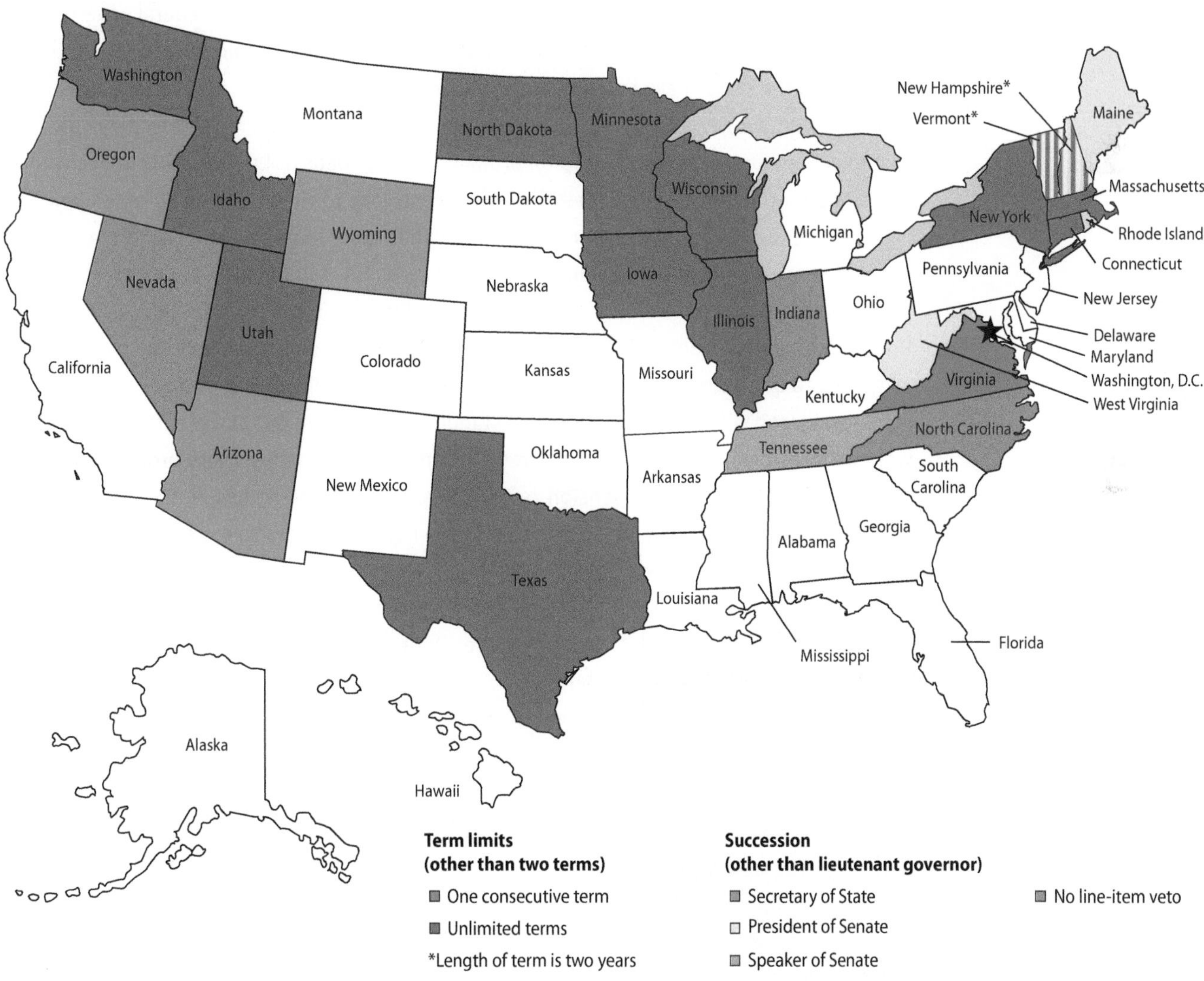

FIGURE 3.8 Exceptions to Typical Gubernatorial Authority

States structure their executive branches in varying ways. Texas, for example, is different from most southern and southwestern states because it has no term limits for governors.

Source: © Cengage Learning; data from Council of State Governments, *The Book of the States*, 2013.

Of those forty-four states, twenty-six allow governors to veto not just appropriations but also language in appropriations bills.[56] Wisconsin's veto authority, known as the "Frankenstein" veto, allows the governor to create entirely new language by crossing out words and numbers throughout a bill, leaving behind new language that could radically change the meaning of the law. For example, when the state created a five-person Minority Business Development Board that gave other officials the authority to appoint three of the five members, the governor vetoed some words so that he assumed the authority to appoint all five members.

In addition to the line-item veto, some states grant governors special budgetary authority to limit spending. West Virginia's constitution does not allow the legislature to increase spending on any item over the amount proposed by the governor. New York's governor has sole authority over the language in spending bills. The legislature can increase or decrease the amounts, but it cannot add provisions excluded from the governor's budget, nor can it change formulas for distributing aid contained in spending bills.[57]

Every state except Vermont requires a balanced budget. Unlike the federal government, which can borrow money to pay for spending programs, typically popular spending increases in the states have to be matched by typically unpopular tax increases. Even states with balanced budget requirements can accumulate long-term liabilities. They may, for example, issue bonds to finance capital projects such as roads or bridges. Alternatively, they may underfund future pensions that they will have to pay to their public employees. According to a recent estimate, the unfunded pension liabilities of state and local governments are now between $2 trillion and $3 trillion.[58] Unlike the federal government, state and municipal governments cannot inflate their currency by printing more money. Vallejo, California; Pritchard, Alabama; Central Falls, Rhode Island; and, most recently, Detroit, Michigan have all gone into bankruptcy, in part due to unfunded pension obligations.[59] Some of these cities have reemerged with more solid financial standing than before but at a great cost to public workers' pensions, which were cut as a result of those bankruptcies. More broadly, some states are now trying to pass pension-reform laws, as Rhode Island has, that limit annual cost-of-living increases and raise contributions by new employees to increase the funds available to pay future pensions.

Eddie Moore/ZUMA Press/Newscom

IMAGE 3.7 Governor Susana Martinez of New Mexico is one of five women elected to the top statewide executive office. Governor Martinez was first elected in 2010 and reelected in 2014.

The Twenty-Second Amendment (ratified in 1947) limits the president of the United States to two terms in office. Similarly, thirty-five states limit governors to two terms, Virginia limits governors to one consecutive term, and fourteen states allow unlimited terms.

The Changing Face of U.S. Governors. Since the start of the republic, white males have been the primary occupants of governors' mansions. The first woman elected governor who was not a wife or widow of a former governor did not win office until 1975.[60] Since 2000, however, women have begun to seek and win the highest state-level executive political office. Since then, twenty-three women have served or are currently serving as U.S. governors.

There is a clear path, or political career ladder, followed by most women who run for and win gubernatorial elections. They tend to have served in state legislatures and in other statewide offices, such as lieutenant governor or secretary of state.[61] Holding an elected office is often seen as a positive trait for candidates because it shows voters they are able to win office and understand the job of an elected official.[62] In 2016, there were five female governors, Mary Fallin (R-OK), Nikki Haley (R-SC), Susana Martinez (R-NM), Gina Raimondo (D-RI), and Kate Brown (D-OR), who was introduced at the opening of this chapter. All but Martinez served in their state legislatures or in another statewide office (but she had been a district attorney). As the Election 2016 section in this chapter shows, the prospects for future women governors depend somewhat on how well potential candidates fare in seeking those lower-level offices. And even when they are finished being governor, these women seek other elected offices. In New Hampshire, for example, Governor Maggie Hassan was in her final term in office and chose to run for U.S. Senator in 2016. In a very tight race, Governor Hassan defeated incumbent Senator Kelly Ayotte by fewer than 700 votes, becoming New Hampshire's newest senator.

State Legislative Branches

On the legislative side, forty-nine of the fifty states have bicameral (two-chamber) legislative branches; Nebraska has only a single chamber. Nebraska also has nonpartisan elections, meaning that candidates for election are not listed under a party banner. Most states have four-year terms for their upper chambers and two-year terms for their lower chambers. Some examples are Arizona and Georgia, which have two-year senate terms instead of four-year ones, and North Dakota and Maryland, which have four-year lower chamber terms rather than two-year ones.

State Judicial Branches

The greatest differences between the national and the state governments appear at the judicial level. Federal judges are nominated by the president and confirmed by the Senate. States have various procedures for selecting judges: Nearly half use an appointment process for judges on their highest court, while the rest use elections (see Figure 3.9). For states that use appointments, most grant the governor the right to make appointments (usually with the consent of the state senate).

While federal judges serve during good behavior, which essentially means life terms, only Rhode Island does that at the state level, with Massachusetts and New Hampshire judges serving until age 70. In the rest of the states, judges have set terms. For example, in the widely copied **Missouri Plan** for selecting judges, also known as the merit plan, a board of experts recommends candidates to the governor, who selects judges from the list. The selected judges are then subject to retention elections. When a judge's term expires, voters get to vote yes or no on retaining the judge. Although judges overwhelmingly win retention elections, being unresponsive to voter preferences on important issues can cost them their seats. Such was the case in November 2010 when Iowa voters rejected the retention of the three Iowa supreme court justices who were part of the unanimous court decision in 2009 blocking the ban on same-sex marriage in Iowa. In

Missouri Plan: *Process for selecting state judges whereby the original nomination is by appointment, and subsequent retention is by a retention election.*

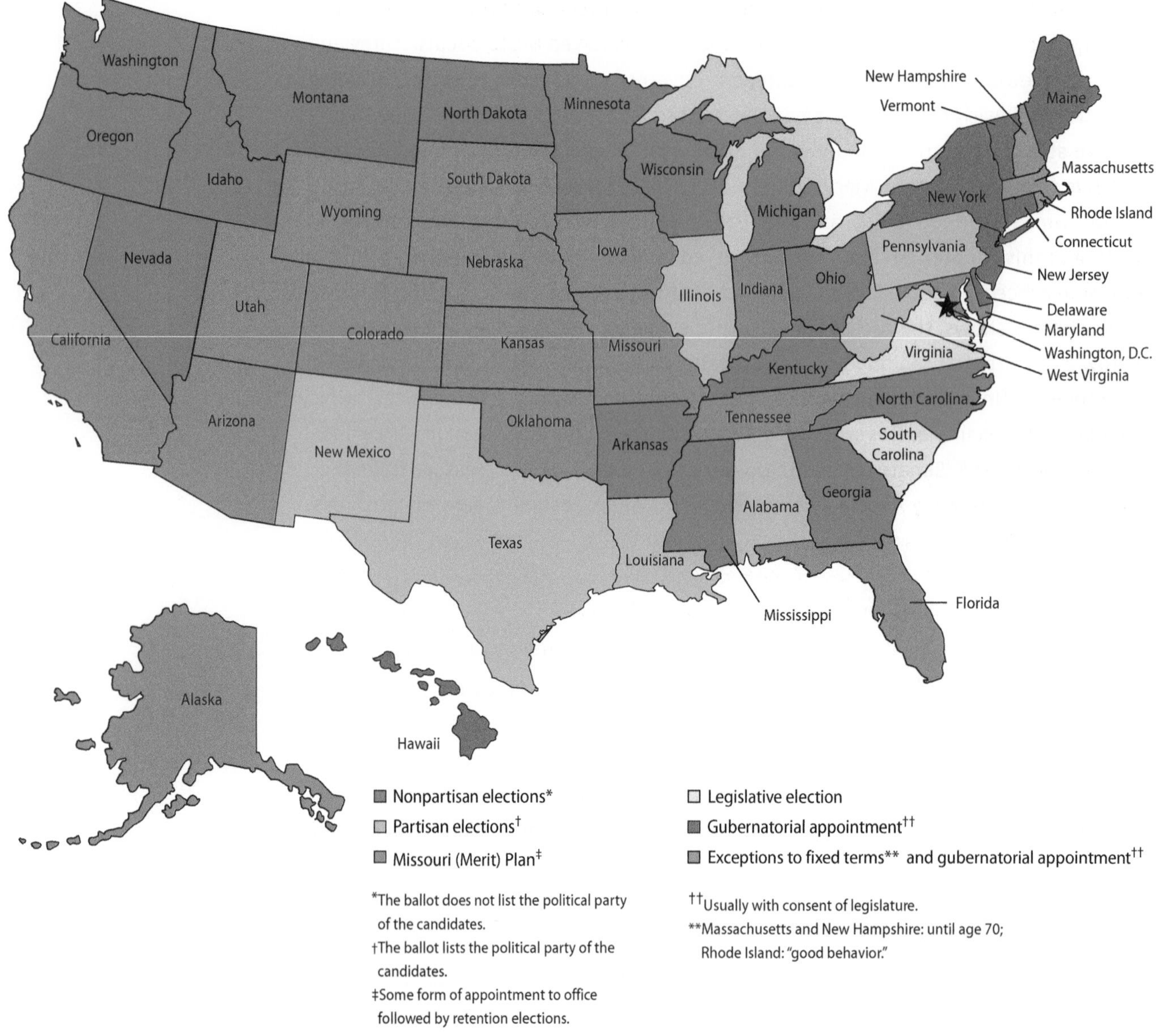

FIGURE 3.9 Judicial Selection to State Supreme Courts

States choose judges to serve on their Supreme Courts in a variety of ways. While most states use the Missouri Plan process, many, like Nevada, also hold nonpartisan elections to select state Supreme Court judges.

Source: © Cengage Learning; data from American Judicature Society, "Methods of Judicial Selection," 2014.

2013, two incumbent supreme court judges in Pennsylvania overcame a serious challenge by conservative groups to their retention in 2013 as a result of their votes to strike down the state's voter identification law. And in 2014, voters in New Mexico ousted Judge Sheri A. Raphaelson after the nonpartisan New Mexico Judicial Performance Evaluation Commission issued a "Do Not Retain" recommendation.[63]

Election of state judges obviously means election campaigns. States have tried to prohibit judicial candidates from making campaign promises about how they would rule if certain issues came before them in court; the parties in such cases have a right to come before judges who have not committed to ruling a certain way before the trial or appeal has even started. The Supreme Court, however, ruled that the First Amendment's right to freedom of speech protects the right of judicial candidates, including their right to discuss their views on relevant issues.[64]

Judicial campaigns also mean campaign contributions, and these are most likely to come from people who might have business before the judges in question. In Texas, for example, where the state supreme court, like the U.S. Supreme Court, chooses whether to hear cases appealed to it, people who contributed to the campaigns of the justices of the supreme court were nine times more likely to have their cases heard than people who did not.[65] This situation arguably violates the common view of how the judiciary should run. This type of "pay to play" gives substantial advantages to those who have money.

In West Virginia, the president of a coal company appealing a $50 million jury verdict spent $3 million to defeat an incumbent West Virginia supreme court justice and elect a challenger who would be friendlier to the company. After the newly elected justice joined a 3–2 majority overturning the award, the U.S. Supreme Court declared that the state court justice could not rightfully participate in the case, given the risk of bias.[66] Generally, state courts can conduct their affairs free of federal court interference unless a federal law, a treaty, or the U.S. Constitution is under consideration. The broad terms in the Constitution and the broad scope of congressional lawmaking mean, however, that the Supreme Court often has the ability to review state court decisions.

Local Governments

Local governments are far more diverse in function and design than state governments. First, there can be several different layers of local governments, with residents regulated by villages, cities, and towns or townships at the most local level and by counties above that. Some local governments run all local services, including police, schools, and sanitation. Many states, however, delegate specialized activities to special jurisdiction governments, such as school boards, water districts, fire districts, library districts, and sewer districts. The United States contains more than 38,000 special jurisdiction governments plus another 13,000 school boards. Overall, there are over 90,000 governmental units in the United States,[67] providing hundreds of thousands of citizens a ready gateway for citizen involvement in public affairs.

Second, local governments, unlike state governments, do not necessarily consist of three separate branches. One reason is that criminal and civil trials are usually handled in state courts, leaving little need for a local community to have its own judicial branch. Many local governments have elected leaders of the executive branch—mayors for villages and cities, county executives for counties, and supervisors for townships—but many use a city-manager system in which the legislative branch appoints a professional administrator to run the executive branch.

The most distinctive form of local government in the United States is the New England town meeting, in which the adult population of the town meets at least once a year to adopt the budget and vote on any legislation being considered. While this gateway to civic involvement is open to all, only about 20 percent of eligible citizens show up at such meetings; as many as 70 percent show up in the smallest towns, but as few as 10 percent attend

ELECTION 2016

Beyond the Presidential Race

MOST OF THE ATTENTION on the 2016 election was on the presidential race between Hillary Clinton and Donald Trump, and rightfully so. But as you have read in this chapter, there are many political offices that were on the 2016 ballot. All 435 seats in the U.S. House of Representatives were up for election. Thirty-four U.S. Senate seats were contested.[68] Across the fifty states, twelve held gubernatorial elections and eighty-six of the ninety-nine state legislative chambers (House/Assembly and Senate) held elections in 2016, resulting in over five thousand seats being filled.[69] And numerous city councils, school boards, and other jurisdictions also held elections.

Those elections have a tremendous impact on the political landscape of the states, local communities, and national-level offices. The state legislative and gubernatorial results of those races will have an effect on the policy priorities of those states in areas such as public university funding, taxes, and social issues such as access to abortions. Moreover, the partisan makeup of state legislatures and governor's offices may affect when and how they cooperate with the Donald Trump administration. As we saw during the Obama administration, some states were hesitant to participate fully in the Affordable Care Act provisions regarding Medicaid expansion.

The Trump administration will have the benefit of working with Republican majorities in both houses of Congress. Senate Republicans retain 51 seats as a result of the 2016 election, and House Republicans hold 239, exceeding the 218 necessary to remain in the majority. At the state level, Republicans captured two additional governor's offices, increasing the number of Republican governors to 33, while Democrats held 16, and one, Alaska, is held by an Independent. Control of state legislatures changed as well. Republicans now control both chambers in 32 states, up from 30 prior to the election. Democrats control both chambers in 13 states, and 4 states split control, while the remaining legislature, Nebraska, is nonpartisan.

In the longer term, these races have importance for the "political career ladders" they create for upcoming elected officials. Members of Congress, governors, and presidents usually have their political start at lower-level offices such as state legislatures. These offices often are the training grounds for politicians who then may use those experiences as stepping-stones to higher office. These offices may be gateways for new generations of elected officials. The results of those elections are therefore important as they provide a glimpse into the future. There is some evidence, however, that women and candidates of color may find it difficult to break through to these lower offices, which may mean that there may be gates in their way.[70] Table 3.1 shows that the vast majority of state legislators are white men. Thus, the potential pool of candidates with experience for higher office may be more limited for women and racial and ethnic minorities because of prior barriers to entry into the political arena.

TABLE 3.1 Demographics of State Legislators, 2015

Group	Number	% of All State Legislators
Female	1,791	24
Male	5,597	76
African American	639	9
Asian American	125	2
Latino	296	4
White	6,328	86

Source: Derived from The New American Leaders Project, "States of Inclusion," http://www.newamericanleaders.org/states_of_inclusion_2016_report.html.

in the larger ones.[71] This form of direct democracy eliminates concerns about whether the policies pursued by the town legislators are responsive to the wishes of the people; the legislators are the people. But it can work only in small towns.

Sandy Macys/Alamy

IMAGE 3.8 The New England town meeting is a fixture in some small towns in the northeastern United States. Residents come together to discuss important local issues and vote directly on resolutions. It is an example of direct democracy in action since there are no representatives who make these decision for the residents.

Direct Democracy

New England town meetings are not the only direct gateways to democracy in American federalism; recall, initiative, and referendum are other examples (see Figure 3.10). Recall is allowed in eighteen states, and it enables citizens who gather enough petition signatures to force a special vote to remove state or local elected officials before their terms expire. Such was the case in Arizona when voters recalled State Senator Russell Pearce, the author of SB 1070, anti-immigration legislation.[72] Wisconsin voters in 2012 reconsidered the tenure of Governor Scott Walker, who had supported legislation that severely curtailed the collective bargaining rights of public employees. Walker won.

Initiative is a process that allows citizens who collect the required number of petition signatures to place proposed laws directly on the ballot for the state's citizens to vote on. Referendum allows legislatures to put certain issues on the ballot for citizen approval and requires legislatures to seek citizen approval for certain actions. Depending on the state, these actions could be proposals to borrow money, increase taxes, or approve constitutional amendments. All fifty states require referenda on some issues. Only twenty-four states allow initiatives.[73] Both procedures enable well-organized citizens to bypass the elected representatives in their state. The U.S. Constitution, in setting specific terms for senators, representatives, and presidents, prohibits recall of federal officials, and in granting all legislative powers to Congress, it similarly prohibits initiative and referendum at the national level.

The number and importance of initiatives have grown in more recent years. In 2008, California voters passed Proposition 8, which banned same-sex marriages in the state. The Supreme Court later upheld a lower court decision striking down that initiative and restoring the right to same-sex marriage in California.[74] Since then and the *Obergefell v. Hodges* (2015) Supreme Court decision, all fifty states allow same-sex marriage (see Chapter 5). In 2014, voters in Alaska, Oregon, and Washington, D.C. approved initiatives legalizing recreational use of marijuana, while voters in Alaska ($9.75), Arkansas ($8.50), Illinois ($10.00), Massachusetts ($11.00), Nebraska ($9.00), and South Dakota ($8.50) approved increases in the minimum wage above the federal rate of $7.25 to the amounts in parentheses.[75] In 2015, however, Ohio voters rejected an initiative to legalize marijuana.[76]

Direct democracy is not without its critics. As are other aspects of American government, initiatives are heavily influenced by money. Although socialists and populists originally pushed for direct democracy to expand the influence of ordinary citizens, the cost of gathering enough signatures to get on the ballot means that initiatives are limited largely to those with great financial resources. For example, almost $4 million was spent in the successful fight to legalize marijuana in Colorado, with 80 percent spent by pro-legalization groups. One group supporting legalization raised almost $1.3 million, while the largest opponent raised $433,000.[77] In the past decade, total spending on state ballot measures was over $4.5 billion.[78]

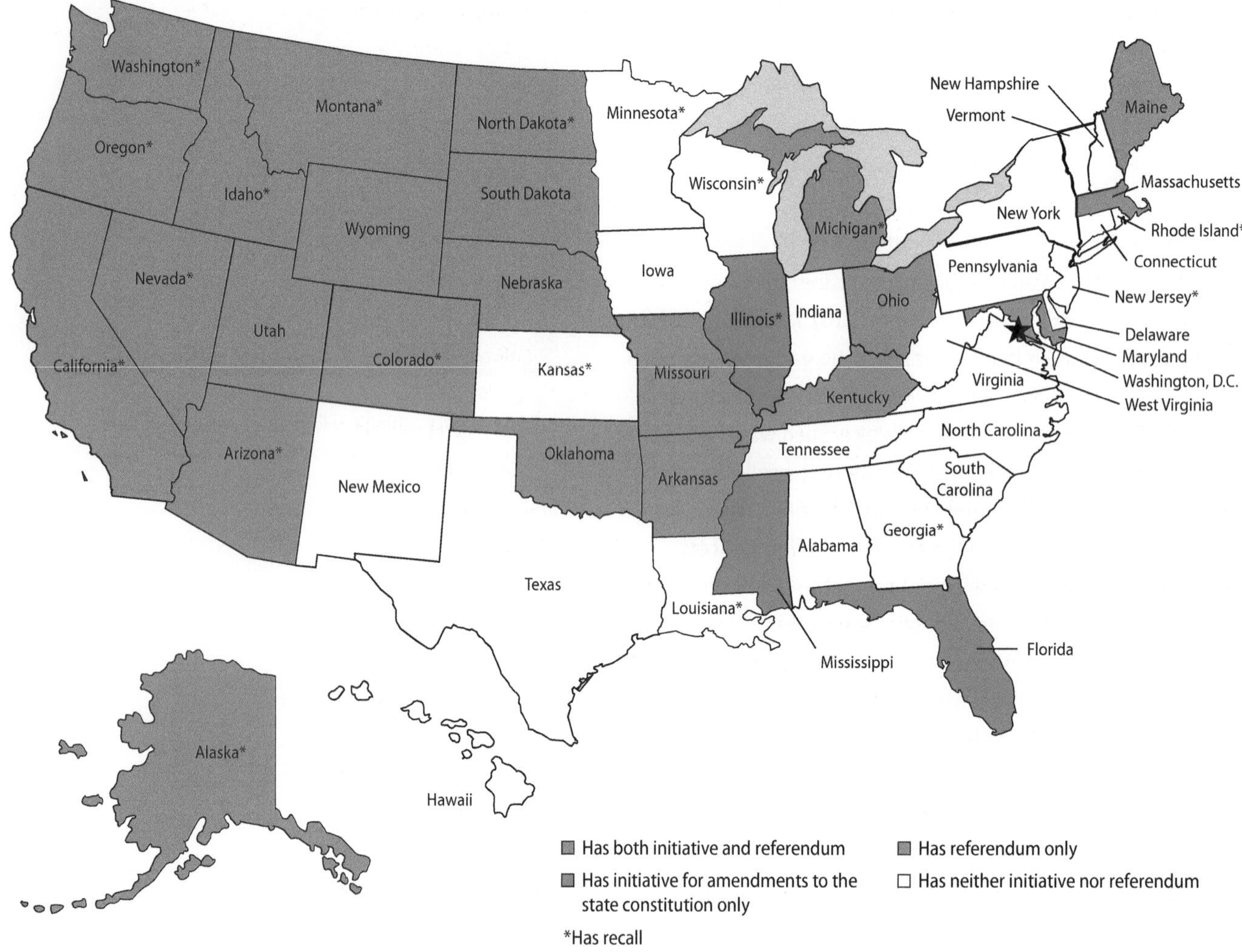

FIGURE 3.10 States That Allow Recall, Initiative, and Referendum

This map shows which states have provisions for direct democracy. Most western states allow for referendum and initiative as means of enacting laws by popular election.

Source: © Cengage Learning; data from Council of State Governments, *The Book of the States*, 2013.

Federalism and Democracy

A federal system has more gateways than a confederal or unitary system. In confederal systems, citizens can influence their local governments, but there is little value in influencing the national government given its limited scope. Alternatively, in unitary systems, the national level has a lot of authority, but citizens cannot work their way through more localized structures to influence it. Federal systems create multiple gateways. However, they also make it less clear who is responsible if policies are not well run. If health care falters, for example, is that the fault of the national government or the state government?

Essential Knowledge

In a federal system policy making is not concentrated in a single level of government. This allows citizens to have multiple points of access to the policy-making process.

Under a unitary system, there is little doubt about who is responsible if a policy fails. A unitary system also means that diverse state laws are replaced with one set of laws on issues such as medical marijuana, gay marriage, divorce, and gun control. Given that Americans have different views on these issues, the strength of a federal system is that it allows people in, say, Arizona, to live under laws created by other people in Arizona, rather than by people throughout the United States. Citizens in states with conservative majorities can obtain conservative government by electing conservative representatives, and citizens in states with liberal majorities can elect liberal representatives.

A unitary system also increases so-called conformity costs by increasing the number of people who disagree with the policies of the government. Conformity costs are not financial; they represent the dissatisfaction that people feel when they live under laws they do not like. Consider medical marijuana, for example. Under a unitary system, the nation would have a single set of medical marijuana laws. Either medical marijuana supporters or opponents would not get their way, regardless of local public opinion. With federalism, each state gets to choose for itself whether to allow the use of medical marijuana. Federalism does not eliminate conformity costs, but it does lower them. Overall, federalism allows the people who live in the most conservative states to have local rules that favor conservative values, and those who live in the most liberal states to choose local rules that favor liberal values. These citizens can also obtain results they desire through direct governing procedures, such as the initiative and referendum. Although initiative procedures presumably provide for greater democratic responsiveness than does filtering preferences through elected representatives, initiatives may be too responsive to citizen desires. Madison, although not referring to the initiative itself, feared direct democracy, believing that citizens were prone to factions that would put self-interest over the best interests of society. Thus, Madison and the Framers preferred a large-scale republic over local democracies, fearful that local majorities would infringe upon the rights of local minorities (see *Federalist* 10 in the Appendix).

One disadvantage of federalism in the United States has been that people opposed to equality for blacks have used arguments about states' rights to protect slavery and limit civil rights. Alternatively, the nation-centric view of federalism has been used to create a more equal society for minorities subject to discrimination.

Overall, though, federalism enhances democracy by enabling more people to live under laws that are made locally, rather than forcing everyone in the nation to live under all of the same rules. State experiments with direct democracy procedures such as the initiative and referendum give citizens a gateway to influence that they do not have with the national government.

Political Science Reasoning

Question 1

Practice 1, Practice 4

In a federal system, there is a division of power between the national government and regional governments (referred to as "states" in the United States). This division necessitates that at each level there be a complete set of policy-making institutions (legislature, executive, judiciary) that would deal with policy at its level. This division also requires that each level have its own Constitution and accompanying Bill of Rights.

Read the documents below.

> The judicial power of the United States is to be vested in a Supreme Court, and in such inferior courts as Congress may from time to time ordain and establish. The powers of these courts are very extensive; their jurisdiction comprehends all civil causes, except such as arise between citizens of the same state; and it extends to all cases in law and equity arising under the constitution. One inferior court must be established, I presume, in each state, at least, with the necessary executive officers appendant thereto. It is easy to see, that in the common course of things, these courts will eclipse the dignity, and take away from the respectability, of the state courts. These courts will be, in themselves, totally independent of the states, deriving their authority from the United States, and receiving from them fixed salaries; and in the course of human events it is to be expected, that they will swallow up all the powers of the courts in the respective states.[1]

> *Gitlow v. New York* (1925)

> For present purposes we may and do assume that freedom of speech and of the press—which are protected by the First Amendment from abridgment by Congress—are among the fundamental personal rights and "liberties" protected by the due process clause of the Fourteenth Amendment from impairment by the State.

1. What claim is being made in Brutus 1?
2. How does the Supreme Court rule in the case of *Gitlow v. New York*? What are the implications of the Supreme Court's decision?
3. After the decision in *Gitlow v. New York*, what are the implications for the ability of the states to define fundamental liberties within their borders?
4. Was the claim in Brutus 1 correct?

Question 2

Practice 1, Practice 4

On January 8, 2002, President George W. Bush signed the No Child Left Behind Act. This bill was a major increase in the involvement of the federal government in American public education.

> **Read the following excerpt from President Bush's speech made on that day.**
>
> [W]e owe the children of America a good education. And today begins a new era, a new time in public education in our country. As of this hour, America's schools will be on a new path of reform, and a new path of results.
>
> Our schools will have higher expectations. We believe every child can learn. Our schools will have greater resources to help meet those goals. Parents will have more information about the schools, and more say in how their children are

[1]Brutus 1, 1787.

educated. From this day forward, all students will have a better chance to learn, to excel, and to live out their dreams . . .

First principle is accountability. Every school has a job to do. And that's to teach the basics and teach them well. If we want to make sure no child is left behind, every child must learn to read. And every child must learn to add and subtract. So in return for federal dollars, we are asking states to design accountability systems to show parents and teachers whether or not children can read and write and add and subtract in grades three through eight.

The fundamental principle of this bill is that every child can learn, we expect every child to learn, and you must show us whether or not every child is learning. I read a quote one time from a young lady in New York. She said, "I don't ever remember taking an exam. They just kept passing me along. I ended up dropping out in the 7th grade. I basically felt nobody cared."

The story of children being just shuffled through the system is one of the saddest stories of America. Let's just move them through. It's so much easier to move a child through than trying to figure out how to solve a child's problems. The first step to making sure that a child is not shuffled through is to test that child as to whether or not he or she can read and write, or add and subtract . . .

[T]his bill's second principle is, is that we trust parents to make the right decisions for their children. Any school that doesn't perform, any school that cannot catch up and do its job, a parent will have these options—a better public school, a tutor, or a charter school. We do not want children trapped in schools that will not change and will not teach.

The third principle of this bill is that we have got to trust the local folks on how to achieve standards, to meet the standards. In Washington, there's some smart people there, but the people who care most about the children in Hamilton are the citizens of Hamilton. The people who care most about the children in this school are the teachers and parents and school board members. And therefore, schools not only have the responsibility to improve, they now have the freedom to improve . . .[2]

1. What are the reasons given by President Bush for this legislation?
2. Refer to the Constitution. Identify a constitutional clause that allows the national government to make education policy. What provisions have been used? Which clause would suggest that education policy is *not* under federal jurisdiction?
3. Is it appropriate for the federal government to play such a role in public education? Develop an essay that either defends or refutes the national government's authority to govern public education. Be sure to articulate a thesis and support your argument using relevant evidence, and provide an articulation and rebuttal of opposing perspectives.

[2]George W. Bush, Speech: No Child Left Behind, January 8, 2002.

Focus on AP® Success

3 Federalism

Must Know: Key Concepts

- Confederation
- Federation
- Marble Cake Federalism
- Layer Cake Federalism
- Exclusive Power or Delegated Power
- Enumerated Power
- Reserved Power
- Block Grants
- Categorical Grants
- Revenue Sharing
- Commerce Clause
- Necessary and Proper Clause or Elastic Clause
- Concurrent Power
- Mandates
- *McCulloch v. Maryland*
- *United States v. Lopez*

Thinking Politically

Argumentation

The power of the national government has increased substantially since the ratification of the Constitution. This is due in part to several provisions in the Constitution such as the commerce clause, necessary and proper clause, and the due process clause of the Fourteenth Amendment. Which of these clauses has caused the greatest increase in the power of the national government?

Understanding Learning Objectives with Key Concepts

CON – 1.C Explain the ongoing impact of political negotiation and compromise at the Constitutional Convention on the development of the constitutional system.

- Many political debates today revolve around what should be the roles of the national and state governments. Prior to the 1930s, the United States practiced a rather strict division of governmental power between the national government and the states known as layer cake federalism, also known as dual federalism. From the 1930s forward there has been a substantive amount of mixing of state and national power. This is known as marble cake federalism, or cooperative federalism. There have also been times of growth of national power such as during war or other crises.

- Many observers have criticized the rise of governmental power related to electronic surveillance and data collection. After 9/11 Congress passed the Patriot Act, which, among other things, made it easier to monitor and track phone, email, and other Internet activity including "meta data." These provisions were modified somewhat with the passage of the USA Freedom Act. This legislation remains controversial today.

- Public education is a power that is reserved to the states. However, the national government is able to make education policy by the use of block and categorical grants. States are often required to agree to certain policy stipulations issued by the national government as a condition of receiving the grants.

CON – 2.A Explain how societal needs affect the constitutional allocation of power between the national and state governments.

- The exclusive powers of the national government are commonly referred to as delegated powers and are provided for in the Constitution. Those powers that are explicitly stated are referred to as expressed powers. These expressed powers can be broadly categorized as: power to set monetary policy, power to set fiscal policy, power to regulate commerce, power to set defense policy, and power to set foreign policy. Powers that are reasonably inferred from the expressed powers are known as implied powers. For example, the ability to create a national back is implied from the enumerate powers of laying and collecting taxes and paying debts. Powers that are retained by the states are known as reserved powers Reserved powers are protected by the Tenth Amendment. For example, the ability to lay and collect taxes. Powers that are shared between the national and state governments are known as concurrent powers. The precise boundaries of these powers are not set and are subject to debate. Depending upon the interpretation of the commerce clause, the ability of the national government to regulate interstate commerce can conflict with the reserved power of the states to regulate intrastate commerce.

- The national and state governments interact with each other for policy making. In addition to states raising their own revenue through internal taxation, they receive grants from the national government. Block grants are grants for a general purpose. Categorical grants are grants for a specific purpose with little to no discretion by the state or local government receiving the grant. The national government can also mandate that states adopt certain policies as a condition of receiving a grant or to come into compliance with a national policy (school desegregation, for example). The fact that governmental policy making is divided between states and the national government is complicated. In many instances, the national government cannot simply pass a law based on its own power granted to it by the Constitution. For example, major social policies of the national government usually require states to be in agreement because that policy area is part of the reserved powers of the states. This agreement is frequently secured through the use of grants. Previously, the national government distributed funds to state and local governments through a program known as revenue sharing. This program did not require states to adopt any specific policy. The program was abolished in 1986.

CON – 2.B Explain how the appropriate balance of power between national and state governments has been interpreted differently over time.

- Federalism in the United States is impacted by the Court's interpretation of several important provisions in the Constitution: Tenth Amendment (which creates the reserved powers), Fourteenth Amendment (which includes the due process clause and the equal protection clause), and the necessary and proper clause (which creates the implied powers). The balance of power between the national and state government shifts over time. This has been caused in part by several Supreme Court cases:

  - In the case of *McCulloch v. Maryland*, the Supreme Court dealt with two constitutional issues: the meaning of the necessary and proper clause (also known and the elastic clause) and the supremacy clause. The decision of the Court allows a broad interpretation of the necessary and proper clause, which has had the effect of increasing the power of the national government.

  - In the case of *United States v. Lopez*, the Court interpreted the commerce clause rather narrowly. This is the first time that the Court has put restrictions on the commerce clause since the 1930s.

CON – 2.C Explain how the distribution of powers among three federal branches and between national and state governments impacts policy making.

- The fact that policy making is divided between two levels of government (national and state) allows citizens to have multiple points of access to this process.

- Policy making is complicated by the fact that decision-making authority is divided between three branches of government at the national level and between the national and state governments. This can potentially lead to gridlock.

Making Connections

When studying the chapters on civil rights and civil liberties, consider how the Fourteenth Amendment's due process clause and equal protection clause have shifted power from state governments to the national government.

Going Deeper: Commerce Clause

The commerce clause of the Constitution gives the national government the power to regulate interstate commerce. The Court's interpretation of what constitutes commerce has evolved over time such that today virtually all business activity is covered by the commerce clause. Indeed, it is only by using the commerce clause that Congress can prohibit many of the discriminatory practices outlined in the Civil Rights Act of 1965.

From the time of the New Deal, the Court has interpreted the commerce clause in a manner that allows Congress to pass laws that regulated activities that only remotely related to commerce. The Gun-Free School Zones Act of 1990 was one such law. The constitutionality of this was challenged in the case of *United States v. Lopez* (1995).

The national government argued that because the position of firearms in schools tends to lead to violent crimes which in turn have a negative impact on the economy, they can be prohibited. The Court rejected this argument and overturned the law. This was the first time since the 1930s that the Court rejected the national government's use of the commerce clause as a justification for the passage of legislation.

4 Civil Liberties

AP® Learning Objectives

LOR – 2.A Explain how the U.S. Constitution protects individual liberties and rights

LOR – 2.B Describe the rights protected in the Bill of Rights.

LOR – 2.C Explain the extent to which the Supreme Court's interpretation of the First and Second Amendments reflects a commitment to individual liberty.

LOR – 2.D Explain how the Supreme Court has attempted to balance the claims of individual freedom with laws and enforcement procedures that promote public order and safety.

LOR – 3.A Explain the implications of the doctrine of selective incorporation.

LOR – 3.B Explain the extent to which states are limited by the due process clause from infringing upon individual rights.

Performance Tasks

Upon the completion of this chapter, you must be able to do the following:

- Citing specific constitutional amendments and Supreme Court decisions, explain how the Court attempts to balance individual liberty with social order with particular reference to freedom of expression, rights of criminal defendants, and the right to privacy.
- Explain how the Supreme Court has utilized the Fourteenth Amendment's due process clause to expand the power of the national government, allowing it to regulate the states in the area of civil liberties.

"My greatest regret is that rather than believing in myself, I allowed someone else's opinion to postpone my dreams."

R. STEPHANIE GOOD
Stony Brook University, Stony Brook, New York

Courtesy of Stephanie Good

R. Stephanie Good started her college career later in life than many people, waiting until she was in her mid-thirties before enrolling first at Nassau Community College on Long Island in New York and then at nearby Stony Brook University. She graduated from both schools with highest honors, but she was as well known for her political activism as she was for her academic excellence. During her college years, she campaigned for public officials, demonstrated on behalf of environmental issues, and got arrested at Stony Brook as part of a "tent-city" protest over housing for graduate students. Committed to the idea that justice is served only when citizens take action on their own behalf, she went on to law school, earning a law degree at Hofstra University and, ten years later, a master's degree in law.

While practicing law, Good started writing. Her first book, *Law School 101,* presents survival techniques for law school and life as an attorney. Her next two books (both coauthored) uncovered corruption in notorious criminal proceedings. *Aruba: The Tragic Untold Story of Natalee Holloway and Corruption in Paradise*, a *New York Times* best seller, recounts the disappearance and presumed murder of a high school student on a school graduation trip. *A Rush to Injustice* tells the story of the Duke University lacrosse case, in which a reelection-seeking prosecutor maliciously filed felony sexual assault charges against college students whom he knew were innocent.

Good's commitment to protection of the innocent was also personal. When she was in law school, she learned that one of her sons had been subjected to inappropriate solicitations by an instructor at their local church. After she went public about this violation, other families revealed inappropriate touching by the instructor. Yet the judicial system did not then consider the matter to be serious, and the instructor received only a fifteen-day sentence. Years later, when Good thought the instructor might be seeking out her son again, she decided to go online to try to find boys who also received unwarranted attention from the instructor, creating a fictitious 13-year-old girl with the AOL handle "teen2hot4u." That handle attracted interest from adult men interested in sex with an underage girl. Good then contacted the Federal Bureau of Investigation (FBI), which asked her to continue to play out her undercover role. Agents schooled Good on how to avoid violating the rights of the people with whom she communicated because although they may have been intent on breaking laws regarding the molestation of children, their rights as citizens also had to be protected, including their right to fair legal proceedings and their right to be considered legally innocent until proven guilty. First, she could not initiate conversations with anyone. Second, she could not be the first person to mention sex. And third, she could not be the first person to suggest a meeting. Despite these restrictions, teen2hot4u attracted the attention of hundreds of men, more than twenty of whom tried to arrange a sexual meeting, got arrested, and then, with Good's testimony, were convicted and sentenced to prison. Good's efforts protected hundreds of young children. She recounted the story in her fourth book, *Exposed: The Harrowing Story of a Mother's Undercover Work with the FBI to Save Children from Internet Sex Predators*. Congressman Tim Bishop (D-NY) awarded Good a certificate of commendation for her work.

Because of her background in criminal investigations, Good taught political science at Stony Brook University, where her real-life experiences have helped make her a tremendously effective and knowledgeable instructor. In both 2012 and 2013, she won the Political Science Department's undergraduate teaching award. When asked why she did not go to college right after high school, she replied that during her teen years, she struggled with family problems, and her guidance counselor told her that she was "not college material."

In a democracy, criminal investigations must be conducted in a way that protects both the victims and society and those who are accused of crimes. Reprehensible crimes, such as sexual abuse of children, test people's willingness to recognize the rights of the accused. Yet without standard and fair criminal proceedings, citizens would be subjected to arbitrary arrest and possibly punishment, as the Duke lacrosse case shows. The tensions surrounding freedom and fair treatment in a democracy extend beyond criminal procedure. Disagreements about politics, particularly during wartime, also test people's willingness to tolerate differences in opinion. Even in peacetime, the tension between liberty, the desire to say or do what one wants, and order, the need for rules necessary for society to function, divide society. Americans want their homes to be secure against police intrusions, but they also want the police to be able to find evidence of crimes committed by others. They want freedom to follow their personal religious beliefs, but they do not want illegal practices to be allowed just because one religion might endorse them. In this chapter, we examine the balance and tension between liberty and order, with particular attention to the liberties guaranteed in the U.S. Constitution.

4.1 What Are Civil Liberties?

Identify what civil liberties are

Essential Knowledge

While the original text of the Constitution contains some rudimentary protections for civil liberties, most protections can be found in the Bill of Rights.

civil liberties: *Those rights, such as freedom of speech and religion, that are so fundamental that they are outside the authority of government to regulate.*

Bill of Rights: *First ten amendments to the Constitution, which provide basic political rights.*

natural (unalienable) rights: *Rights that every individual has and that government cannot legitimately take away.*

Essential Knowledge

Civil liberties protect individual citizens against arbitrary government action. Civil liberties include the right to private property, free speech, and unjust arrest. This is different from civil rights where there are guarantees that various groups will be treated equally in the society. For example men and women must be treated equally. Racial minorities must be treated the same as the rest of the population.

In 1787, the most powerful argument of the Antifederalists against the proposed constitution was that it did not protect fundamental liberties. The Antifederalist declared that these liberties, including the rights of conscience and the right of accused criminals to hear the charges against them, needed to be explicitly stated.[1] As we saw in Chapter 2, The Constitution, the Federalists eventually agreed and, to secure ratification of the Constitution, promised to amend it immediately.

Civil Liberties and Civil Rights

The **civil liberties** that were then written into the Constitution as the first ten amendments, or **Bill of Rights**, were freedoms that Americans held to be so fundamental that government may not legitimately take them away. This placed into law some of the **natural (unalienable) rights** that Thomas Jefferson wrote about in the Declaration of Independence. These include, among others, freedom of speech and religious belief. Supreme Court Justice Robert Jackson wrote in a 1943 case striking down a mandatory flag salute for school children that the government has no authority whatsoever over what we say or think: "If there is any fixed star in our constitutional constellation, it is that no official, high or petty, can prescribe what shall be orthodox in politics, nationalism, religion, or other matters of opinion or force citizens to confess by word or act their faith therein."[2] Civil *liberties* are outside government's authority to regulate, whereas civil *rights* are rights that government is obliged to protect (see Figure 4.1). These are based on the expectation of equality under the law and relate to the duties of citizenship and to opportunities for full participation in civic life. Civil rights are the subject of the next chapter.

FIGURE 4.1 Distinction Between Civil Liberties and Civil Rights

Civil liberties provide a gate or barrier that protects people against interference by the government in fundamental liberties, such as freedom of speech or religion. Civil rights often require active involvement of the government in opening gateways to full civic participation by all, regardless of race, gender, or religion.

Balancing Liberty and Order

The protection of civil liberties requires a governmental system designed to do so. James Madison argued in *Federalist* 10 (see the Appendix) that a representative democracy will be able to keep a minority from violating the rights of others but may not be able to hold back a majority. Thus if a majority wishes to infringe on rights, it often falls to the judiciary, which is not designed to be responsive to public desires, to protect those rights.[3] In this way, the system of separation of powers and of checks and balances would help ensure the rights of all.

While maximizing individual liberty might seem like a great idea, complete liberty could lead to a breakdown of order. As Supreme Court Justice Oliver Wendell Holmes wrote in a World War I speech case, freedom of speech does not mean that an individual has the right to falsely shout "fire!" in a crowded theater and cause a panic.[4] Nor can liberty completely protect people from police investigations when criminal activity is suspected. Too much freedom can lead to anarchy, a state in which everyone does as he or she chooses without regard to others. Alternatively, too much order can lead to tyranny, a state in which the people are not free to make decisions about the private aspects of their lives. Protecting civil liberties thus requires a balance between individual liberty and public order.

Essential Knowledge

In its decisions, the Supreme Court must constantly weigh the competing values to individual liberty and the compelling state interest to provide security. This has been particularly controversial in the areas of electronic surveillance and the regulation of firearms.

The freedom obtained through civil liberties can conflict not only with order but also with equality. In fact, civil liberties and civil rights sometimes conflict with each other. For example, civil rights laws that forbid businesses to refuse to serve customers because of their race limit freedom of association and infringe on property rights. Efforts at colleges to create an equal environment for all students have led to speech codes that restrict what students can say on campus. Society must decide how to strike such balances, and often that decision is a difficult one. In the case of businesses serving all customers, the nation, through its elected representatives in Congress, decided that the restriction on liberty was well worth the gain in equality. In the case of campus speech codes, students have successfully pressured many universities to rescind speech codes, and where the universities have kept the codes, students have used the gateway of the judicial system to bring lawsuits against their schools. The courts have consistently ruled that speech codes at state Universities violate the First Amendment.

Constitutional Rights

The main sources of civil liberties are the Constitution and the Bill of Rights. The articles of the Constitution protect the right to a **writ of *habeas corpus***, the right of individuals to be brought before a judge to have the legality of their imprisonment determined. It also prohibits *ex post facto* laws, which make an act a crime after the act is committed, and bills of attainder, legislative acts that declare individuals guilty of a crime. The Constitution also guarantees the right to a trial by jury.

writ of *habeas corpus*: *Right of individuals who have been arrested and jailed to go before a judge, who determines whether their detention is legal.*

The Bill of Rights, ratified in 1791, protects additional rights, such as freedom of expression, the right to keep and bear arms, and criminal procedure (see Figure 4.2). We will examine each in detail later in the chapter.

The Bill of Rights and the States

As originally written, the Bill of Rights limited the activities of the national government, not the state governments. Only at the end of the nineteenth century did the Supreme Court slowly begin to apply, or **incorporate**, the provisions of the Bill of Rights to the states.

incorporate: *To apply provisions of the Bill of Rights to the states.*

Color Code: Criminal procedure Participation Equality Structure Miscellaneous

First	1791	Prohibits abridging freedoms of religion, speech, press, assembly, and petition
Second	1791	Prohibits abridging the right to bear arms
Third	1791	Prohibits the involuntary quartering of soldiers in a person's home during peacetime
Fourth	1791	Prohibits unreasonable searches and seizures
Fifth	1791	Affirms the right to indictment by a grand jury and right to due process; protects against double jeopardy, self-incrimination, and taking of property without just compensation
Sixth	1791	Affirms rights to speedy and public trial, to confront witnesses, and to counsel
Seventh	1791	Affirms right to jury trials in civil suits over $20
Eighth	1791	Prohibits excessive bail, excessive fines, and cruel and unusual punishments
Ninth	1791	Declares that the enumeration of certain rights does not limit other rights retained by the people
Tenth	1791	Reserves the powers not granted to the national government to the states or to the people
Fourteenth	1868	Makes all persons born in the United States citizens of the United States and prohibits states from denying persons within its jurisdiction the privileges or immunities of citizens, the due process of law, and equal protection of the laws; apportionment by whole persons

FIGURE 4.2 Constitutional Amendments that Pertain to Civil Liberties

A majority of the early amendments to the Constitution protect civil liberties.

The First Amendment is explicit about its application to the national government as it forbids certain actions by Congress. But other amendments are not explicitly tied to the national government. Thus the Fifth Amendment prohibits taking private property without just compensation. Was this a protection of citizens only against actions by the federal government or against their state governments as well?

The original answer, given by the Supreme Court in *Barron v. Baltimore* (1833), was that the Bill of Rights applied to the national government only. Under the *Barron* decision, state governments could, without violating the Constitution, abridge freedom of speech, the press, and religion, conduct unreasonable searches and seizures, and more. State constitutions might protect such rights, but often they did not. During World War I, one citizen of Minnesota was convicted and sentenced to prison for stating that the war was a plot to protect Wall Street investments, another for stating that America needed to be made more democratic.[5] And in 1920, when a Montana farmer spoke ill of the American flag and refused to kiss it, he was sentenced to ten to twenty years of hard labor for violating a state law that prohibited bringing the flag into disrepute.[6]

The Fourteenth Amendment (1868), which adds several restrictions on what the states can do, became a vehicle for the applications of the Bill of Rights to the states. One section declares, "No State shall make or enforce any law which shall abridge the privileges or immunities of citizens of the United States; nor shall any State deprive any person of life, liberty, or property, without due process of law." Some of those who wrote this amendment stated that one of its purposes was to overturn the *Barron v. Baltimore* decision and make the entire Bill of Rights applicable to the states.[7]

The Supreme Court never agreed with this position, known as total incorporation. But beginning in 1897, it slowly began to use the protection of "life, liberty, or property" in the Fourteenth Amendment's due process clause to incorporate some of the provisions of the Bill of Rights as binding on the states. In the 1897 case, the Court used this clause to hold that states could not deprive a railroad of its property without just compensation, a right similarly protected by the Fifth Amendment.[8] In 1925, the Court assumed that the protection of liberty in the due process clause prevented states from restricting freedom of speech, a right similarly protected by the First Amendment.[9] By 1937, the Court had settled on a process of **selective incorporation**, using the due process clause to bind the states to those provisions of the Bill of Rights that it deems to be fundamental rights.[10] This process helps equalize the protection of rights across the United States.

Essential Knowledge

In *Gitlow v. United States*, the Supreme Court established that portions of the Bill of Rights could be made applicable to states. *Gitlow* allowed for selective incorporation. Incorporation is not total. It happens case by case overtime. Still today, portions of the Bill of Rights have not been made applicable to the states.

Today, almost all of the provisions of the First, Second, Fourth, Fifth, Sixth, and Eighth Amendments have been incorporated, with the exception of grand jury indictment and excessive fines (see Table 4.1). Thus, states can indict people, or bring them up on charges, through the decision of judges, though charges in federal courts need the approval of a grand jury, a special jury whose sole duty is to determine whether an individual should be put on trial. The Third Amendment's protection against the quartering of soldiers in one's home during peacetime, a practice that angered the colonists, has not been incorporated but is not likely to be used today. Nor are states required, as the Seventh Amendment commands, to provide jury trials in civil suits over $20.

selective incorporation: *Doctrine used by the Supreme Court to make those provisions of the Bill of Rights that are fundamental rights binding on the states.*

Once incorporated, the Court needs to determine whether that right has been violated. Generally speaking, rather than rule on each case purely on its own, the Court adopts a test to guide its decision and applies the test to the case at hand to determine whether a particular limitation of rights is acceptable. For the political rights in the Bill of Rights, such as freedom of speech, the Court most commonly uses variations of the **compelling interest test**. Under the compelling interest test, the federal government or a state can limit rights

compelling interest test: *Standard frequently used by the Supreme Court in civil liberties cases to determine whether a state has a compelling interest for infringing on a right and whether the law is narrowly drawn to meet that interest.*

TABLE 4.1 Incorporated and Not Incorporated Provisions of the First Through Eighth Amendments

Amendment	Provisions Incorporated	Provisions Not Incorporated
First	Religion, speech, press, assembly, petition	
Second	Keep and bear arms	
Third		Quarter soldiers
Fourth	No unreasonable searches and seizures	
Fifth	Double jeopardy, self-incrimination, due process, taking of property without just compensation	Grand jury indictment
Sixth	Speedy and public trial, right to confront witnesses, right to counsel	
Seventh		Jury trials in civil suits over $20
Eighth	Cruel and unusual punishments, excessive bail	Excessive fines

Source: © Cengage Learning

only if the Supreme Court decides that (1) the government has a compelling interest in passing the law (for example, the law is necessary for the functioning of government) and (2) the law is narrowly drawn to meet that interest. For example, the government might have a compelling interest in banning speech that might incite religious wars, but such a law would have to be narrowly drawn so as not to prevent religious speech that merely calls for struggle against oppression. However, even with such a precise definition, individuals have fought over what constitutes a compelling interest throughout American history.

4.2 Civil Liberties in Times of Crisis

Explain why civil liberties are limited in times of crisis

Attempts to limit civil liberties are more frequent in wartime or when other threats arise as a result of the government's increased concern for order and citizens' increased concerns about security. This pattern has existed from the earliest days of the republic. It continued during the Civil War; the two world wars; and the Cold War; and following the terrorist attacks of September 11, 2001; the San Bernardino, California, murders; and the attacks in Paris in late 2015. Republican presidential nominee Donald Trump proposed excluding Muslims from the United States following the Paris and San Bernardino attacks. Popular support for civil liberties usually rebounds after the crisis ends, though the terrorism crisis shows no signs of ending.

From Revolution to Civil War

In the aftermath of the 1789 French Revolution, while Britain and France were at war, the United States engaged in a limited and undeclared war with France over trade issues. In 1798, as part of the war effort, the Federalist-dominated Congress passed the Sedition Act, which, among other things, made it illegal to "write, print, utter, or publish" any "false, scandalous, and malicious writing" about the federal government, either house of Congress, or the president. The Federalist administration of John Adams (1797–1801) used the act to try opposition (Democratic-Republican) officeholders and newspaper owners, and lower courts upheld the act against claims that the convictions violated the freedoms of speech and press as guaranteed by the First Amendment. When Thomas Jefferson (1801–09) and the Democratic-Republicans took power following the election of 1800, they pardoned those convicted under the act, which had by then expired, and refunded the fines they had paid.

During the Civil War, President Abraham Lincoln (1861–65) suspended the writ of *habeas corpus*, thus allowing southern sympathizers in border states—slave states located between the North and South that did not secede from the Union—to be tried by military tribunals rather than by civilian courts. Military tribunals contain fewer procedural safeguards for defendants than do criminal trials, with a two-thirds vote rather than unanimity required for conviction, lesser standards of evidence, and no *habeas corpus* protections. Given the threat the Civil War posed to the United States, Lincoln thought that a restriction on *habeas corpus* was justified. He famously asked, "Are all the laws but one to go unexecuted and the Government itself go to pieces lest that one be violated?"[11] Because the authority to suspend *habeas corpus* presumably rests with Congress, Congress subsequently affirmed Lincoln's order. Later, Lambdin Milligan, a civilian, was accused of aiding the Confederacy and was sentenced to hang by a military tribunal in Indiana. Because civilian courts were operating in Indiana, the Supreme Court declared in 1866 (after the war and the threat of secession ended) that the government had no authority to deprive Milligan of his right to a trial by jury.[12]

In 1868, the Supreme Court prepared to hear the appeal of journalist William McCardle, a former Confederate soldier who had been convicted of writing "incendiary and libelous articles" about the war. The pro-Union Congress, angry about the *Milligan* decision and concerned about the *McCardle* case, removed the Supreme Court's appellate jurisdiction over *habeas* petitions. As the Constitution explicitly grants Congress the authority to regulate the Court's appellate jurisdiction, the Court, backing away from a confrontation with Congress, dismissed McCardle's appeal.[13]

The World Wars

During World War I, Congress passed the Espionage Act of 1917, which made it a crime to obstruct military recruiting, and amendments known as the Sedition Act of 1918, which banned "disloyal, profane, scurrilous or abusive language" about the Constitution or the government of the United States, as well as speech that interfered with the war effort. Subsequently, juries convicted antiwar activist Charles Schenck, for circulating a flyer to draftees that compared the draft to the involuntary servitude prohibited by the Thirteenth Amendment, and Socialist Party presidential candidate Eugene V. Debs, for giving a speech criticizing the war. The Supreme Court upheld both convictions, noting that greater restrictions on speech could be allowed in wartime.[14] The Court also upheld the conviction of Jacob Abrams, an anarchist and immigrant from Russia who had dropped leaflets in Yiddish and English from his New York City tenement calling for a strike to protest sending American troops into Russia.[15] Russia, engulfed by the Communist revolution, had withdrawn from the war, and the United States had sent troops to aid anti-Communist forces. In a forceful dissent, Justice Oliver Wendell Holmes, who had written the opinion of the Court in the *Schenck* and *Debs* cases, voted this time to overturn the conviction, arguing that the First Amendment protected the **marketplace of ideas**. Under this concept, the government should not restrict the expression of ideas because the people are capable of accepting good ideas and rejecting bad ones.

Essential Knowledge

In the case of *Schenck v. United States*, the Court allowed speech that presents a "clear and present danger" to be prohibited. This is an example of how the Court attempts to strike a balance between liberty and order.

marketplace of ideas: *Idea that the government should not restrict the expression of ideas because the people are capable of accepting good ideas and rejecting bad ones.*

After the war, Congress repealed the Sedition Act, and President Warren G. Harding (1921–23) pardoned Debs. The government also released Abrams from prison but deported him to Russia. Fears that Communism would spread to the United States had led to a crackdown on socialists, Communists, and other radicals. This Red Scare peaked after radicals exploded eight bombs, including one at the house of U.S. Attorney General A. Mitchell Palmer. Following the bombings, the government arrested thousands of Americans, some merely for their speech or associations.[16] Given the atmosphere of fear, the *Washington Post* declared, "There is no time to waste on hairsplitting over infringement of liberty."[17] But when Palmer's warning that radicals would attempt to overthrow the government on May 1, 1920, proved incorrect, the scare began to subside. In no subsequent wars has the government restricted speech as it did with the Sedition Acts of 1798 and 1918.

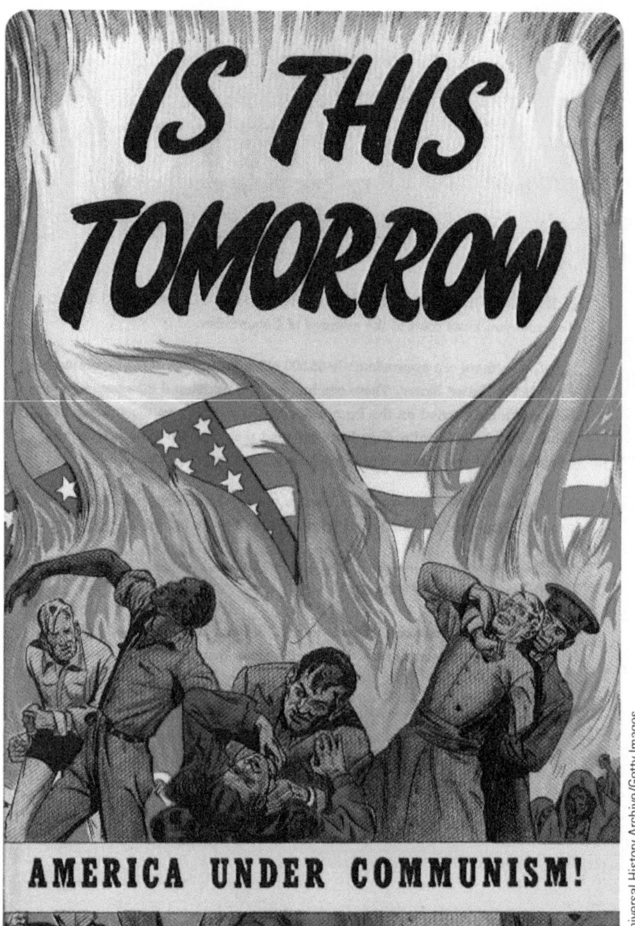

Universal History Archive/Getty Images

IMAGE 4.1 Anti-Communist propoganda from the first Red Scare.

The Cold War and Vietnam

The fear of Communism that had led to a suppression of civil liberties following World War I recurred after World War II. As the Soviet Union forcibly installed Communist dictatorships throughout Eastern Europe, Americans worried that Communism would spread further. Though the United States never fought the Soviet Union directly during this period, frosty relations led to the so-called Cold War.

With allegations, convictions, and at least one confession that Communist spies in the United States gave the Soviets secrets about how to build atomic bombs,[18] Senator Joseph McCarthy (R-WI) began indiscriminately accusing Americans of being "card-carrying" members of Communist organizations or being sympathetic "fellow travelers" of such groups. The McCarthy era was similar to the Red Scare in its agitated suspicion that opposition to the government was Communist-inspired. Congress banned the Communist Party and membership therein and held hearings investigating the political views and personal associations of individual citizens. Hollywood studios began blacklisting screenwriters with left-wing sympathies, while state governments and school districts fired teachers and other state workers suspected of having such beliefs. The Supreme Court originally set strict limits on these investigations,[19] but, following the introduction of several bills that would have limited its authority, the Court backed down and accepted them.[20]

During the McCarthy era, the government imprisoned hundreds of individuals for their political views, and thousands more lost their jobs.[21] McCarthy himself began losing support before his movement did. During the televised 1954 hearings over alleged Communist infiltration of the Army, Americans witnessed the recklessness with which McCarthy attacked people's reputations. Edward R. Murrow, host of the TV program *See It Now*, produced a special show on McCarthy using McCarthy's own speeches to demonstrate the extent to which he had been dishonest in his charges. The public reacted overwhelmingly favorably to Murrow's broadcast. A free press—in this case, television—allowed the marketplace of ideas to flourish and led to McCarthy's downfall. In December 1954, the Senate voted 67–22 to censure McCarthy.

But suspicion of people who criticized the government rose again during the Vietnam War. In the mid-1960s COINTELPRO, the counterintelligence program of the FBI, infiltrated and disrupted groups that expressed opposition to mainline American policies, including antiwar, civil rights, left-wing, and white supremacy groups. Later, a Senate investigation by Frank Church (D-ID) into the legality of COINTELPRO revealed that the FBI's activities had included illegal wiretapping, inciting violence, and encouraging Internal Revenue Service audits of suspects. The FBI had targeted even nonviolent antiwar organizations because of a potential for violence and nonviolent citizens who opposed the war because "they gave 'aid and comfort' to violent demonstrators by lending respectability to their cause."[22] Congress reacted by putting restrictions on surveillance of political organizations, including limits on the sharing of information between the Central Intelligence Agency (CIA) and the FBI.

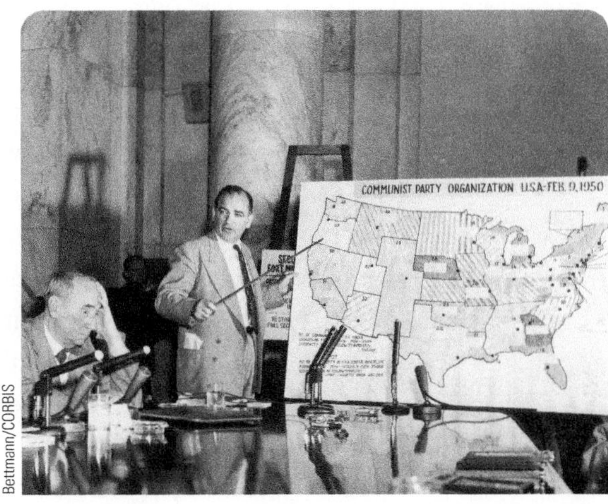

Bettmann/CORBIS

IMAGE 4.2 The name of Senator Joseph McCarthy has been attached to an era noted for fear of Communism and the use of fear tactics to suppress freedom of speech and belief. Here, during the 1954 Army-McCarthy hearings, he testifies on Communist Party organizations in the United States with the aid of a huge map. His dishonesty and abusive treatment of witnesses during these hearings turned both the Senate and the public against him.

The War on Terror

After 9/11, Congress passed the USA PATRIOT Act, which overturned many of the COINTELPRO reforms, blamed by some for intelligence failures prior to the attacks. The act allowed greater sharing of intelligence information and enhancement of law enforcement's ability to tap telephone and e-mail communications. It also regulated financial transactions with overseas entities and eased the process of deporting immigrants suspected of terrorist activities. Beyond the act, President George W. Bush (2001–09) claimed the right, as commander in chief, to detain alleged enemy combatants indefinitely, whether U.S. citizens or foreign nationals. Thus Bush declared Jose Padilla, an American allegedly involved in a plan to detonate a radioactive bomb in the United States, an "enemy combatant" and transferred him from civilian to military authority, where he would have few, if any, procedural rights. The government kept Padilla in complete isolation for more than three and a half years. Unique among those declared enemy combatants, Padilla had not been captured on the field of battle but on American soil, and, having been born in Brooklyn, he was an American citizen.

When the Supreme Court ruled that noncitizens could not be held indefinitely as enemy combatants, it became clear that the government could not hold Padilla either. So, the Justice Department removed Padilla from military custody and charged him under federal criminal law with providing material support to terrorist organizations. The government did not charge him with attempting to detonate a radioactive bomb in the United States or with conspiring to commit terrorist acts in the United States, suggesting that the original claims against him might not have held up in a court of law. His trial in Miami, with the full set of constitutional rights, required that Padilla be represented by counsel, that he be allowed to cross-examine witnesses, and that the government prove its case beyond a reasonable doubt. The government proved its case, and a jury quickly determined that Padilla was guilty. The judge then sentenced him to seventeen years in prison; the sentence was increased to twenty-one years by an appeals court judge.[23]

Although fewer rights exist for enemy combatants who are not U.S. citizens,[24] the Supreme Court has ruled that Congress must authorize hearings to determine the legality of the detention of even foreign enemy combatants. Such hearings must be consistent with the 1949 Geneva Conventions, an international treaty that protects the rights of prisoners of war.[25]

Beyond the enemy combatant cases, President Bush and President Obama have ordered warrantless wiretapping of conversations and interception of e-mail between American citizens and suspected foreign terrorists; normally, wiretapping requires a warrant signed by a judge or magistrate backed by probable cause that a crime is being committed. (See Public Policy and Civil Liberties: National Security Surveillance p. 114).

Beyond surveillance, President Obama ordered the execution via an overseas drone airstrike of Anwar al Awlaki, a U.S. citizen who allegedly had supported al-Qaeda, the group behind the 9/11 attacks, and who had encouraged a variety of terrorist acts against the United States. Attorney General Eric Holder laid out the criteria by which the president could order the execution of a U.S. citizen, stating that "due process and judicial process are not one and the same particularly when it comes to national security."[26] The executive branch, with the most direct responsibility over national security, is more likely to support restrictions on civil liberties during times of crisis than is either the legislative or judicial branch. In 2014, a U.S. Court of Appeals panel ordered the Obama administration to release redacted versions of the documents it used to justify killing Awlaki.[27]

Civil Liberties and American Values

As these examples have demonstrated, in times of crisis, Congress and the president limit civil liberties to secure order, often with public support. The courts, however, being less responsive to public pressure, can push back against these efforts. Thus, the courts forced the government to try Padilla in civilian courts. The courts have also blocked efforts to censor newspapers even when the government has believed that the publication of certain reports would benefit wartime enemies. Nevertheless, in wartime or other times of crisis, concerns about order are at their highest, and protections for civil liberties by national and state governments typically decline. Following the emergency, a political culture that favors freedom means that public support for civil liberties, as well as the government's protections of those liberties, generally rebounds.

4.3 The First Amendment and Freedom of Expression

Distinguish what rights of expression the First Amendment protects

The civil liberties most at risk during times of crisis are those protected by the First Amendment—freedom of speech, freedom of the press, and freedom of association. In this section, we examine each of these freedoms of expression individually. Their scope has expanded over time, despite occasional ratcheting back during wartime.

Freedom of Speech

Essential Knowledge

There is no unlimited right to free speech. The Court allows the restriction of speech that is defamatory or obscene.

While the First Amendment declares that "Congress shall make no law . . . abridging the freedom of speech," the Court has never taken the phrase "no law" literally. Prohibitions on speech once included blasphemy (inappropriate references to God) and defamation (speaking ill of others). States have since rescinded such laws, either legislatively or judicially. Today the Court allows limits on advocacy of unlawful activities, the use of fighting words, hate speech, and symbolic speech. The Court also allows the sort of limits imposed by time, place, and manner regulations, such as prohibitions on protests near public schools when they are in session.

Advocacy of Unlawful Activities. When Justice Holmes wrote, in the opinion in the case of Charles Schenck, that free speech does not mean that a person can falsely shout "fire!" in a theater, he went on to explain that words spoken in wartime may have a different impact than they would in peacetime. "The question in every case," he continued, "is whether the words used are used in such circumstances and are of such a nature as to create a clear and present danger that they will bring about the substantive evils that Congress has a right to prevent." From this statement, the Court adopted the **clear and present danger test**. The Court shifted standards in subsequent decades, at one point allowing states to limit speech that merely had a tendency to cause unlawful acts. But in 1969, the Court moved back toward a stricter protection of civil liberties, ruling that speech cannot be banned unless it leads to "imminent lawless action."[28]

clear and present danger test: *First Amendment test that requires the state to prove there is a high likelihood that the speech in question would lead to a danger that Congress has a right to prevent.*

Fighting Words and Hate Speech. Besides speech that imminently incites unlawful activities, the Supreme Court also allows restrictions on the basis of the fighting words doctrine. "Fighting words" are phrases that might lead the individual to whom they are directed to respond with a punch. Today, hateful racial epithets are the leading examples of fighting words, but when the Supreme Court first developed the doctrine, many milder types of words offended people. Thus, in 1942, the Court used the fighting words doctrine to uphold the conviction of a defendant for calling a town marshal a "God-damned racketeer" and a "damned Fascist."[29]

Related to fighting words is hate speech, which attacks or demeans a group rather than a particular individual. Over the past thirty years, as we noted earlier, more than 350 public colleges and universities have attempted to provide equal, nonhostile educational environments through speech codes that tell students what they are and are not allowed to say.[30] For example, the University of Wisconsin prohibited speech that created "an intimidating, hostile, or demeaning environment for education [or] university-related work."[31] The University of Connecticut's speech code banned "inappropriately directed laughter" and purposefully excluding people from conversations.[32] Tufts University established three separate free speech zones: public areas, where speech could not be prohibited; classrooms and libraries, where derogatory and demeaning speech could be punished; and dorms, where the university placed the strictest restrictions on speech. Whereas students at many universities accepted speech codes, students at Tufts debated the issue, held public forums about freedom of speech, and physically marked off "free speech" from "non–free speech" zones.[33] Under this pressure, Tufts, a private university not legally bound by the Bill of Rights, rescinded the code.

The University of Michigan's speech code prohibited any speech that "stigmatizes or victimizes individuals or groups on the basis of race, ethnicity, religion, sex, sexual orientation, creed, national origin, ancestry, age, marital status, handicap, or Vietnam-era veteran status." In addition to the regulations, the university created guidelines that gave examples of prohibited conduct. The examples included stating in class that women are not as good as men in a particular field, not inviting someone to a party

David McNew/Getty Images News/Getty Images

IMAGE 4.3 California State University, Long Beach, posts a sign designating its free-speech zone, now officially renamed the "Speaker's Platform."

because she is a lesbian, excluding someone from a study group because of race or sex, displaying a Confederate flag, telling jokes about gays or lesbians, laughing at jokes about people who stutter, and commenting in a derogatory way about a particular person's physical appearance.[34]

A graduate student in psychology, concerned that Michigan's code would prevent class discussions of theories that claimed the existence of biological differences between sexes and races, brought suit against the code in federal court. The court struck down the code as violating the First Amendment.[35] Two years later, a federal court struck down the University of Wisconsin's speech code.[36] Thus, the courts have made it clear that while state universities may encourage the goal of equality, they cannot do so by limiting First Amendment rights. Note that the First Amendment applies to these schools because they are state universities. The Bill of Rights limits the national government and, through the selective incorporation doctrine, also limits state governments and thus state universities. Private colleges, though subject to certain federal regulations, are not subject to the Bill of Rights.

The movement to restrict speech on college campuses has moved from public spaces and dorms into the classroom. So-called trigger warnings originally developed among women's rights activists to alert women who may have had traumatic experiences such as physical or sexual violence in their past that an online posting might contain material that could trigger a traumatic memory. Given the rate at which undergraduate students have suffered from these assaults, it is inevitable that any moderate-sized class will have such victims. The idea of trigger warnings in class is to give students warning that readings or classroom lectures might contain such material. For example, the student senate at the University of California at Santa Barbara has resolved that trigger warnings be added to course syllabi to alert students to days in which classroom materials "might trigger feelings of emotional or physical distress." Oberlin College has issued official "trigger warning guidelines" that advised faculty to remove triggering materials from their courses entirely if not directly related to the course's learning goals.[37] Trigger warnings have grown substantially in recent years.[38]

Though students at Tufts fought against the university's speech codes, more typically college students have supported restrictions on campus speech. At Yale University, after a 2015 directive from the Intercultural Affairs Committee urged students to be culturally sensitive in their choices of Halloween costumes, lecturer Erika Christakis sent out an e-mail supportive of the right of students to be "a little bit inappropriate or provocative or, yes, offensive." Following widespread student protests, Christakis resigned her position.[39]

Williams College in Massachusetts created an "Uncomfortable Learning" speaker series to get students to challenge their own beliefs. The students disinvited antifeminist author Suzanne Venker from this series. In the words of *The Williams Record*, "Venkers' views are

SUPREME COURT CASES

Snyder v. Phelps (2011)

QUESTION: May antimilitary and antigay protesters be sued for the distress they caused to the father of a Marine killed in action in Iraq when they picketed at the Marine's funeral?

ORAL ARGUMENT: October 6, 2010 (listen at http://www.oyez.org/cases/2010-2019/2010/2010_09_751)

DECISION: March 2, 2011 (read at http://www.law.cornell.edu/supct/html/09-751.ZS.html)

OUTCOME: The protesters are protected by the First Amendment because they are speaking out on a question of public concern.

For more than twenty years, the congregation of the Westboro Baptist Church in Topeka, Kansas, has picketed the funerals of members of the U.S. military. The church does so to show its opposition to homosexuality and the army's toleration thereof since the establishment of the "Don't Ask, Don't Tell" policy during the Clinton administration. Their pickets infamously declare that "God hates f* [pejorative for homosexuals]" and "Thank God for Dead Soldiers." These pickets at the funeral of Matthew Snyder aggravated his father, who sued the church, the minister (Fred Phelps, now deceased), and several of Phelps's daughters for intentional infliction of emotional distress. A jury awarded Snyder nearly $11 million in damages. When the U.S. Court of Appeals overturned the verdict, Snyder appealed to the Supreme Court.

The Supreme Court ruled 8–1 in favor of the protesters, declaring that the church's views on homosexuality in the military were a matter of public concern, and as such, it did not matter how crudely those concerns were expressed. They compared this intentional infliction of emotional distress to an earlier case upholding a suit dealing with an individual's credit report, which was purely a private matter. Nor did the Court find that the Westboro protests involved "fighting words," which the Court has ruled to be beyond the protections of the First Amendment. Justice Samuel Alito, in dissent, argued that the First Amendment does not give the church the right to brutalize Matthew's father while he is burying his only son. In an earlier speech case, the Court ruled that the function of the First Amendment is to "invite dispute." The boundary between "inviting dispute," which is protected, and "fighting words," which are not, is not always clear.

Thinking Critically

1. Do you believe that the Westboro Church's position on homosexuals and the military is a question of public concern? Explain.
2. Do you believe that the Westboro Church's protests at the funeral constituted "fighting words"? Explain.

---

wrong, offensive and unacceptable. . . . The College should not allow speech that challenges fundamental human rights and devalues people."[40]

The Supreme Court has not reviewed any of the college speech codes, but it has heard other cases related to hate speech. In one case, the Court ruled cross burning, a terrorist tactic historically used by the white supremacist Ku Klux Klan to intimidate African Americans, to be a form of hate speech that could be banned.[41] On the other hand, the Court did not consider picketers at the funerals of U.S. soldiers to be engaged in hate speech, despite their inflammatory signs against homosexuals (see Supreme Court Cases: *Snyder v. Phelps*).

PUBLIC POLICY AND CIVIL LIBERTIES

National Security Surveillance

As President Obama has noted, protection against terrorist threats requires some restrictions on liberty and privacy. Though many people think of the Central Intelligence Agency (CIA) as the main intelligence agency in the United States, it is the National Security Agency (NSA) that conducts virtually all of the security-related electronic surveillance for the government, such as listening to phone calls and reading e-mails. In 1978, Congress passed the Foreign Intelligence Surveillance Act (FISA). The act established secret FISA courts to determine whether the United States could authorize the NSA to conduct national security wiretaps within the United States. The judges on that court are all appointed by the chief justice of the United States from among the U.S. District Courts, without confirmation by the Senate. Prior to the 9/11 attacks in 2001, the FISA courts had never denied a government request for electronic surveillance (see Figure 4.3).[42]

Just six weeks after the 9/11 attacks on the United States, Congress overwhelmingly passed the USA PATRIOT Act. The act expanded the surveillance capabilities of the United States in several ways: It granted the NSA new authority to monitor e-mail, and it allowed a single warrant to cover all phones that a suspect might use.[43] President Bush ordered warrantless wiretapping (by the NSA) of conversations and interception of e-mail between American citizens and suspected foreign terrorists. Congress did endorse aspects of the president's plan after the *New York Times* published stories about the then-secret program. The program expired, but the Obama administration moved—on national security grounds—to block a lawsuit over the wiretapping brought by an Islamic charity alleged to be involved in terrorist activities.[44] In 2012, a Ninth Circuit Court of Appeals panel overturned a district court ruling that the program was illegal and blocked damages claimed by the Al-Haramain Islamic Foundation.[45]

Then in 2013, Edward Snowden, a former employee of the NSA, stole and leaked tens of thousands of documents that he had access to. Those documents revealed that the NSA kept track of every phone call made in the United States, regardless of whether there was any evidence of suspicious activity. These records tracked who called whom and when, but they did not record conversations. The NSA believed that such records could help it uncover information to aid in preventing terrorist attacks.

Many Americans were outraged at what they felt to be a violation of their right to privacy. Yet the 1979 Supreme Court case *Smith v. Maryland* seemed to uphold the constitutionality of the government's warrantless use of "pen registers," devices that kept track of who called whom when without recording the conversations. The fact that the Court upheld the use of pen registers suggests that the NSA program is constitutional.[46] President Obama additionally defended the program by stating, "You can't have 100% security and then

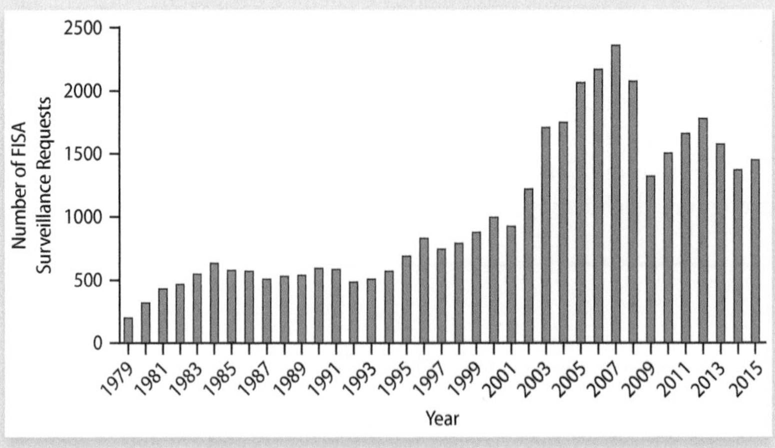

FIGURE 4.3 Annual Number of FISA Surveillance Requests

Note: There were four rejected surveillance applications in 2003, one in 2006, four in 2007, one in 2008, one in 2009, one in 2013, and one in 2015. In all other years, no surveillance applications were rejected.

Source: Adapted from the source material here: http://epic.org/privacy/wiretap/stats/fisa_stats.html

have 100% privacy and zero inconvenience. You know, we're going to have to make some choices as a society."[47]

Nevertheless, a lower court judge ruled that the ability of the government to obtain these records *en masse* made the violation far more serious than the individual record keeping from the 1979 case.[48] President Obama called for an end to the NSA's bulk collection of data in March 2014.[49] Despite President Obama's call to end the data collection, a lower court judge ruled that the NSA's bulk data collection program may be unconstitutional.[50]

The NSA has also filed individualized surveillance requests. Between 2002 and 2013, the court rejected only twelve of nearly twenty-one thousand surveillance applications, about 0.06 percent.[51] Part of the reason for this is that the objects of the surveillance obviously do not get to provide evidence to counter the government's position. The director of the Administrative Office of the U.S. Courts has proposed a special advocate to promote the public's privacy interests in any particular case.[52] The American Civil Liberties Union (ACLU) filed suit against the NSA, but federal courts ruled that without evidence proving they were wiretapped, they didn't have standing to sue.

Following the 9/11 attacks, public opinion shifted strongly toward governmental efforts to increase security, even at the expense of liberty and privacy. Following the San Bernardino murders by a husband/wife team who supported the terrorist group ISIS, the FBI sought access to the encrypted iPhone that had been in possession of the husband. Though the city of San Bernardino owned the phone and the husband had died in a shootout after the attacks, Apple CEO Timothy Cook refused to assist, citing an invasion of users' privacy. The conflict ended when private parties broke the code. If these programs keep future attacks from occurring, they may be very effective at keeping the freedom–order equation in balance.

ymgerman/Shutterstock.com

IMAGE 4.4 Under some iPhone privacy settings, after ten unsuccessful attempts at entering the passcode, the phone deletes everything on it. The FBI, fearful that San Bernardino shooter Syed Rizwan Farook used such settings, asked Apple to create software that would prevent that from happening. Apple refused to do so, but private parties cracked the encryption for the FBI.

Public Policy Connections

1. In the eighteenth century, Benjamin Franklin was quoted as saying "Those who would give up essential Liberty, to purchase a little temporary Safety, deserve neither Liberty nor Safety." Is privacy an essential liberty? If so, does Franklin's quote still hold true today? If not, how would Franklin regard the federal government's mass collection of electronic data?
2. What obligations do tech companies have to law enforcement? Should they voluntarily comply with requests from law enforcement for electronic data on their customers, or should they require law enforcement to obtain a search warrant?

Symbolic Speech. In the 1960s, the Des Moines school district suspended students Mary Beth Tinker, her brother John, and a third student when they wore black armbands to protest the Vietnam War. The students voiced no opinions while wearing these armbands, and no disruptions in their schools occurred. The Iowa Civil Liberties Union, an interest group that supports civil rights and liberties, brought suit against the school board, claiming

Essential Knowledge

Tinker v. Des Moines Independence Continuity School District is an example of how the Supreme Court has interpreted the First Amendment to protect symbolic speech.

ELECTION 2016

Extension of the USA PATRIOT Act

HOW IMPORTANT ARE CIVIL LIBERTIES in presidential elections? Usually not very, though in the election of 1800, Thomas Jefferson defeated John Adams in part due to the Alien and Sedition Acts that Adams signed into law. The 2016 election took place in the long shadow of the 9/11 terrorist attacks. In May 2011, President Obama signed a four-year extension of three expiring provisions of the USA PATRIOT Act: roving wiretaps that followed persons rather than phones, searches of business records, and the extended definition of "agents of a foreign power" to include non-U.S. persons who engage in international terrorism without being a member of any particular terrorist group.[53] The extension of the act then expired on June 1, 2015. The following day, Congress passed the USA Freedom Act, which restored most of the provisions of the PATRIOT Act with a notable exception: the NSA could no longer collect mass data on whom people call; instead, the data would be held by the phone companies and the NSA could obtain the information with judicial consent.

The main contenders for the Republican and Democratic nominations took varied views on these provisions. Not surprisingly, Senator Rand Paul (R-KY), who leans in a strongly libertarian direction (see Chapter 1 for a definition of "libertarian"), opposed any extension of the act. In fact, he led a temporary, one-person battle against consideration of the measure (see Chapter 12, Congress, for a discussion of how senators can delay consideration of bills). Senator Ted Cruz (R-TX), a more traditional conservative, surprisingly opposed extension of the PATRIOT Act but cosponsored the Freedom Act. Republican Presidential nominee Donald Trump urged at least a temporary exclusion of foreign Muslims from the United States. All other Republicans, including Trump, supported the PATRIOT Act provisions.

On the Democratic side, Senator Bernie Sanders of Vermont opposed both the PATRIOT Act and the milder Freedom Act. Former Secretary of State Hillary Rodham Clinton supported only the Freedom Act.[54] Republican presidential nominee Donald Trump, under heavy criticism, replaced his call for an exclusion of Muslims with a call for "extreme vetting" of refugees from Syria or other countries where terrorism has been rampant.

---

that students are equal to other Americans and retain the freedom of speech rights granted by the First Amendment. The Supreme Court agreed.[55] In this instance, the armbands were considered **symbolic speech**, like other nonverbal activities that convey a political message, such as saluting the flag, burning the flag, or burning draft cards—the latter two actions also undertaken by anti–Vietnam War protesters. Alternatively, in another case, employees of a local sheriff's office "liked" the Facebook page of the person running for office against the sheriff. The sheriff fired the employees, who argued that their First Amendment rights had been violated. The court has ruled that "liking" a Facebook page is too shallow an expressive act to count as constitutionally protected speech.[56]

symbolic speech: *Actions, such as burning the flag, that convey a political message without spoken words.*

The Court has allowed prohibitions on the burning of draft cards because Congress has a **content-neutral** justification for requiring draft-eligible citizens to be in possession of their draft cards. That is, draft cards are essential to the smooth running of the draft,[57] and prohibiting their destruction is not intended to suppress the views of those who burn them. The Court once ruled that states also have a neutral justification for limiting protests near health care facilities that conduct abortions, even if most of the protesters are advocating

content-neutral: *Free speech doctrine that allows certain types of regulation of speech, as long as the restriction does not favor one side or another of a controversy.*

pro-life positions.[58] But in 2014 the Court reached a unanimous decision striking down a Massachusetts law limiting protests at facilities where abortions are performed.[59] The Court has also overturned laws that require saluting the flag, as such laws do intend to instill a political viewpoint.[60] Similarly, the Court has overturned laws prohibiting flag burning, as such laws are not content-neutral: They are based almost entirely on opposition to the idea being delivered by flag burning.[61] (Of course, flag burners can be arrested on charges that would apply to anyone who starts a fire in public.)

Bettmann/Corbis

IMAGE 4.5 Mary Beth and John Tinker were teenagers in 1965 when they wore black armbands to school to protest the Vietnam War, and they were suspended. Arguing that students have free speech rights, the Iowa Civil Liberties Union sued the school district on their behalf and appealed the suspension in a series of cases that were finally appealed to the Supreme Court. In 1969, the Court ruled in the Tinkers' favor, stating: "It can hardly be argued that either students or teachers shed their constitutional rights to freedom of speech or expression at the schoolhouse gate."

On the other hand, the content-neutral rule, like most constitutional rules, is not absolute. Some messages can be regulated solely because of opposition to the message, as when the Supreme Court upheld a student's suspension for unfurling a banner at a parade that declared "Bong Hits 4 Jesus" because of the banner's promotion of drug use.[62] It is easy for the Court to formulate simple rules, such as a prohibition on content-based regulations, but harder for the Court to apply those rules consistently in the unusual cases that come before it.

Moreover, states have more authority in controlling their own speech than the speech of its residents. In 2015, the Court ruled that Texas did not have to be content-neutral when deciding which license plate designs to accept—in this case, rejecting a design featuring the Sons of Confederate Veterans that included the Confederate battle flag.[63] In North Carolina, a district court judge rejected the state's attempt to put the antiabortion slogan "choose life" on its license plate without a pro-choice alternative as an unconstitutional form of viewpoint discrimination.[64]

Essential Knowledge

The Court permits reasonable restrictions on freedom of expression that relate to time, place, and manner. These restrictions must be "content neutral."

Time, Place, and Manner Regulations. The fact that the First Amendment protects freedom of speech does not mean there is a right to speak wherever one wants, whenever one wants. Regulations of the time, place, and manner of speech, such as when or where protests may take place, are generally valid as long as they are neutral or equal—that is, they do not favor one side or another of a controversy. Thus states can prohibit protests near school grounds that interfere with school activities as there is no indication that such bans favor one side of any controversy over any other side.[65] Alternatively, the American Nazi Party, with backing from the pro–free speech ACLU, won the right to protest in the heavily Jewish Chicago suburb of Skokie because the main reason that Skokie sought to block the march was opposition to the Nazis' views.[66] Many also feared that the

Pat Canova/Alamy

IMAGE 4.6 Florida license plate expressing the state's pro-life (anti-abortion) position. The Supreme Court has upheld such speech by states.

march would serve as a severe psychological trigger for the many Holocaust survivors who lived in Skokie.

Freedom of the Press

Thomas Jefferson, among other Founders, thought freedom of the press crucial to a free society because the press keeps the public informed about the government's activities. When the Bill of Rights was written, "the press" meant newspapers; today the term covers not only the large companies that own television and radio stations but also individually run blogs and Internet sites that anyone can create. While freedom of the press once belonged to those who owned one, today it belongs to everyone.

Like freedom of speech, however, freedom of the press is not absolute. In extraordinarily extreme cases, the government can censor items before they are published. This practice is known as **prior restraint**. In other situations, the government can punish people after the fact for what they publish.

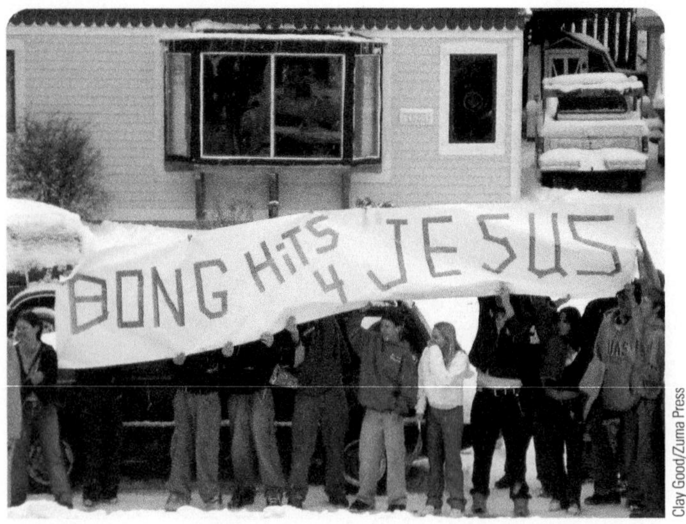

Clay Good/Zuma Press

IMAGE 4.7 In 2002, high school student Joseph Frederick unfurled this banner while his class watched the Olympic Torch relay pass through Juneau, Alaska. When the principal suspended Frederick for the banner's message about drugs, Frederick sued, saying that his free speech rights had been violated. The court of appeals, relying on the *Tinker* case, reversed the suspension, but in 2007, the Supreme Court upheld it, saying a student's free speech rights did not extend to the promotion of illegal drugs.

prior restraint: *Government restrictions on freedom of the press that prevent material from being published.*

Essential Knowledge

In the case of *New York Times v. United States*, the Court protected the freedom of the press by prohibiting most instances of prior restraint.

Prior Restraint. Following English law, freedom of the press in the colonies and in the early years of the United States meant freedom from prior censorship;[67] today, an extraordinary burden of proof of imminent harm is needed before the courts will shut down a newspaper before a story is printed. Even when the *New York Times* began publishing excerpts from a top-secret Pentagon analysis of U.S. involvement in the Vietnam War, the courts refused to stop the presses. The story of this case, *New York Times v. United States* (1971),[68] is told in more detail in Chapter 7, The News and Social Media. One case in which the courts said that the government had met the extraordinary burden standard involved the publication of instructions on how to build a hydrogen bomb,[69] but generally, court approval of censorship by prior restraint has been so difficult to achieve that the federal government has not sought it since the 1970s. Thus, even as many major newspapers published information leaked by Edward Snowden that the United States considered to be highly classified, the government did not attempt to prevent the news media from publishing it, although it did indict Edward Snowden.

First Amendment law protects the Internet and blogs from government censorship in much the same way that it protects newspapers, but the technology of the Internet makes censorship far more difficult. This was the lesson learned by a federal judge who tried to censor Julian Assange's WikiLeaks website,[70] which publishes confidential documents from government, business, and religious organizations. Though the judge ordered the Wikileaks.org domain name disabled, WikiLeaks already had mirror sites set up all over the world. Facing a barrage of criticism from bloggers and mainstream media groups, and given the ineffectiveness of his original decision, the judge reversed himself. But while many people may support the right of WikiLeaks to publish allegations of money laundering by a Swiss bank, as in this case, what happens when WikiLeaks publishes, as it has, a diagram of the first atomic bomb or secret documents about the war in Afghanistan?[71] Such cases show the difficulty of balancing freedom of the press versus censorship in a dangerous world.

Subsequent Punishment. In certain instances, the government can engage in subsequent punishment, fining, and/or imprisoning writers and publishers after the fact for what they publish. Examples here include penalties for libel and for publishing obscenity, incitement to acts of violence, and secret military information.

The standards for convicting in a case of libel—the publishing of false and damaging statements about another person—vary according to whether that person is a public figure. The Supreme Court has made it harder for public figures than for ordinary individuals to sue for libel because public figures have access to the media and can more readily defend themselves without lawsuits. For public figures to sue, the materials must be false and damaging, and the writer or publisher must have acted with actual malice—that is, with knowledge that the material was false or with reckless disregard of whether it was true or false. Further, satire is largely exempt from libel laws. Such was in the case in *Hustler Magazine's* spoof on the "first time" for the Reverend Jerry Falwell, the founder of the conservative Christian group the Moral Majority.[72] For private figures to sue for libel, the material must be false and damaging, and there must be some degree of negligence, but the actual malice test does not apply.

Before development of the World Wide Web, only those who published printed materials could libel someone, but even then, the damage would largely be limited to those who subscribed to the publication. With the Internet, anyone can libel anyone else, and the whole world can see it. At Yale University, for example, anonymous contributors to a popular law school message board wrote derogatory comments about several female law students, including fabricated statements about their mental capacity and sexual activities. Because anyone, including potential employers, can see such statements, the potential for harm is enormous.[73] Given the anonymous nature of the posts, identifying and prosecuting the source of the statements can be difficult, if not impossible. Because freedom of speech is a fundamental right, there is no easy solution to protecting privacy in the Internet age.

The term *seditious libel* refers to the criticizing of government officials, regardless of whether the criticism is true, false, or just a matter of opinion. During the colonial era, the 1735 New York trial and acquittal of John Peter Zenger established that seditious libel is not a reason for punishment, although, as we have seen, Congress twice made sedition a crime during wartime.

Today, the government can seek subsequent punishment against individuals who publish military secrets or obscene materials. Pornographic material is not necessarily obscene, and pornography that falls short of the legal definition of obscenity receives First Amendment protection. Specifically, for materials to be obscene, they must pass all three parts of what has become known as the ***Miller* test**: (1) to the average person, applying contemporary community standards as established by the relevant state, the work, taken as a whole (not just isolated passages), appeals to the prurient (sexual) interest; (2) the work depicts in an offensive way sexual conduct specifically defined by the state law; and (3) the work lacks serious literary, artistic, political, or scientific value (SLAPS).[74]

***Miller* test:** *Supreme Court test for determining whether material is obscene.*

Under the *Miller* test, only "hard-core" materials could be banned.[75] The government has much greater leeway to prohibit "kiddie porn" that uses actual children[76] but not "virtual child pornography," which uses computer-simulated children.[77] Nor can the government's desire to protect children from indecent materials on the Internet be used as a justification for prohibiting online pornography that does not reach the level of obscenity.[78] Similarly, the state may not ban the purchase of violent video games by minors.[79] The *Miller* test reversed a trend toward greater protection of pornography that the liberal Warren Court (1954–69) had instituted and opposed the general trend of greater rights of the press to publish without fear of prosecution by the state. According to a 2010 decision, under the *Miller* test, states may not ban fetish videos that, in the case at hand, showed women in high heels crushing the skulls of puppies.[80]

The Right of Association

The First Amendment's protections include the right of the people to peaceably assemble. This includes the right to hold public protests that meet time, place, and manner regulations, and it was crucial to the success of the civil rights and women's suffrage movements (see Chapter 5, Civil Rights).

In the United States, the right of association also includes the right to associate with whom one wants, as well as the right not to associate with those with whom one does not want to associate. As we observed earlier, here a civil liberty can conflict with a civil right, as when a restaurant owner might choose, for example, not to serve people of a certain race. This dilemma was resolved by the Civil Rights Act and subsequent court challenges in the 1960s so far as businesses that serve the public are concerned (see Chapter 5). But if a private group's expressed beliefs reject association with people of certain groups, such as Boy Scouts rejecting homosexuals and the Ku Klux Klan rejecting blacks and Jews, the group has a right of association that overrides state laws banning discrimination.

If a group discriminates for no apparent purpose, however, state laws can limit the right of association. Thus the Court declared that Minnesota has the right to prevent the Jaycees from discriminating against women because the presence of women does not violate any of the expressive interests of the Jaycees.[81] On the other hand, New Jersey's law prohibiting private groups from discriminating against homosexuals did not override the Boy Scouts' stated belief that homosexuality is inconsistent with the group's values. The Court thus allowed the Scouts to prohibit homosexuals from being members.[82] (Due to increasing public support for the rights of homosexuals, the Scouts have since backed off this practice.[83])

4.4 Religious Freedom

Determine what religious freedoms the First Amendment protects

The First Amendment sets forth two distinct protections about religion. Congress, and now the states, generally may not prevent people from practicing their religious beliefs. They also cannot pass laws that establish an official religion or even favor one religion over another.

Free Exercise

Many of the first settlers in the American colonies came because of restrictions on their religious beliefs in England, where the Anglican Church was established as the official religion. When these settlers arrived, they did not establish general freedom of religion but, rather, freedom for their religion. In 1635, for example, the Massachusetts Puritans banished Roger Williams for his disagreements with the church. Williams established a colony in what would become Rhode Island that was the first to grant religious "liberty of conscience." Other colonies followed. Maryland's Toleration Act (1649) guaranteed freedom of worship to all Christians, including Catholics, who often faced persecution in Protestant Europe. British colonists in Flushing, New Amsterdam (now Queens, New York), fought for the religious freedom of others, protesting Dutch Governor Peter Stuyvesant's persecution of Quakers. The Flushing Remonstrance (1657), a historic demand for religious freedom, called on the governor to let "every man stand or fall to his own Master."[84]

Essential Knowledge

The degree to which government can regulate and practice religion continues to be a source of conversation and controversy. There is conflict between upholding the establishment clause—whereby no singular religion can be preferred—and allowing the free exercise of religion in a nation where there is a clear religious majority.

Victories for religious freedom, though significant, were rare in the colonial period. In 1786, however, the Virginia General Assembly passed Thomas Jefferson's Statute for Religious Freedom, which declared freedom of religious conscience to be a natural right of mankind that governments could not restrict. Five years later, this right was affirmed in the **free exercise clause** of the Bill of Rights. Like all the provisions of the Bill of Rights, however, it originally protected individuals only against the national government, and at the time only two states—Virginia and Rhode Island—had unqualified religious freedom. Maryland demanded belief in Christianity; Delaware and North Carolina required belief in the divinity of the Bible; Pennsylvania and South Carolina required belief in the divinity of the Bible plus heaven and hell; and Connecticut, Maryland, Massachusetts, New Hampshire, and South Carolina limited civil office to Christians or Protestants.[85] So ingrained was state authority to regulate religion that when James Madison proposed an amendment that would have limited such authority, Congress rejected it.[86] Today, however, with the incorporation of the Bill of Rights, the right of individuals to the free exercise of religion is also outside of state authority to regulate.

free exercise clause: *First Amendment clause protecting the free exercise of religion.*

Under the First Amendment, the government cannot criminalize an individual's private religious beliefs. Nor can the government ban specific religious activities, including student-run publications,[87] just because they are based on religious beliefs. For example, the Supreme Court struck down a ban on religious-based animal sacrifices because killing animals for other reasons was not prohibited.[88] But not all religious-based activities are protected, and states are generally free to pass laws that restrict religious practices as long as such laws have a **valid secular (nonreligious) purpose**. For example, states can ban polygamy, even though marriage with multiple wives is still a central belief in some religions.[89] The state court of Utah, however, in response to a case brought by the family featured on the television show *Sister Wives*, has recently ruled that the ban on cohabitation is an unconstitutional violation of religious freedom. Thus while the state may continue to prevent a man from having multiple marriage licenses, it cannot prevent a man from living with multiple women.[90]

valid secular purpose: *Supreme Court test that allows states to ban activities that infringe on religious practices as long as the state has a nonreligious rationale for prohibiting the behavior.*

Under the free exercise clause, the Supreme Court will not allow inquiries into the sincerity of someone's religious beliefs or even into what constitutes a religion. This has

IMAGE 4.8 Rally by pro-choice advocates against state laws that would limit the ability of clinics that provide abortions to stay open.

led Satanists, people who worship the Devil, to request Satanist prayers at the start of Phoenix city council meetings. The Council has chosen to start its meetings with a moment of silence rather than include Satanic prayers at the beginning of meetings.[91]

In the 1960s, the Court ruled that states must have a compelling interest before they can abridge people's religious practices, even if the law restricting the practice has a valid secular purpose. Thus even though the government has a valid secular purpose in conducting a military draft, members of religious groups that oppose warfare, such as Quakers, may be exempt. In the case of former boxing champion Muhammad Ali, a Muslim, who argued that he could only fight wars declared by Allah or the Prophet, the Court overturned a conviction for draft evasion.[92]

Essential Knowledge

In the case of *Wisconsin v. Yoder*, the Court ruled the laws that unduly burden a religious group are not permitted. For example, Amish children are exempt from compulsorily education laws after eighth grade due to the unique nature of their religion.

One case that demonstrates the contest between the branches of government over what constitutes free exercise concerns the use of the hallucinogenic drug peyote in religious rituals. In 1990, when two Native American drug counselors who used peyote were fired from their jobs and denied unemployment compensation, the Supreme Court used the valid secular purpose test to uphold Oregon's decision to deny this compensation.[93] Members of Congress overwhelmingly disapproved, however, and passed legislation, the Religious Freedom Restoration Act (RFRA), stating that the Supreme Court must use the compelling interest test in deciding free exercise cases. The Supreme Court responded by declaring part of RFRA unconstitutional, repeating the statement from *Marbury v. Madison* that the province of the judicial branch is "to say what the law is."[94] Congress does have the authority, however, to declare the religious use of peyote to be legal, and it has done so. Moreover, Congress has decided that its own laws must have a compelling interest before they can limit religious freedom.

Generally, states need only have a valid secular purpose to pass laws that also happen to restrict religious practices. On the other hand, the Supreme Court has established a "ministerial exception" that frees religious organizations from having to abide by federal antidiscrimination laws—in this case, the Americans with Disabilities Act—when choosing their ministers. The Court here used the free exercise clause to limit the scope of an otherwise valid act of Congress.[95]

The Establishment of Religion

establishment clause: *First Amendment clause prohibiting governmental establishment of religion.*

The **establishment clause** of the First Amendment prevents Congress from recognizing one church as the nation's official church, as Britain had done with the Anglican (Episcopal) Church. Originally, states were free to establish state religions if they chose to, and when the Constitution was adopted, nearly half the states had done so.[96] The antiestablishment movement began in Virginia, where between 1784 and 1785,

James Madison fought tax assessments used to support Christian religious teachers, and Thomas Jefferson secured passage of the Disestablishment Bill in 1786, which ended Virginia's official establishment of the Anglican Church. In an 1802 letter to the Baptists of Danbury, Connecticut, Jefferson called for a "wall of separation" between church and state. The Supreme Court adopted that phrase in 1947 but declared that using taxpayer funds to provide public transportation to parochial schools did not breach the wall.[97]

The establishment clause literally prohibits not just the establishment of religion but also any law "respecting an establishment of religion." The Supreme Court has taken this phrase to mean that steps by the government favoring one religion over another, or even religion over no religion, cannot be taken, even if those steps fall far short of an official establishment of religion.

The Supreme Court's test for determining whether laws violate the establishment clause is known as the ***Lemon* test**, named after a litigant in a 1971 case.[98] Under this test, a challenged law must be shown to have a secular (nonreligious) legislative purpose and a primary effect that neither advances nor inhibits religion. The law must also avoid an excessive entanglement between church and state, such as a strict monitoring of church activities. Using these standards, the Supreme Court has banned organized school prayers and devotional Bible readings.[99] The Bible can be read as part of a comparative religion course, however, and students may pray silently. The Supreme Court has also used this test to strike down laws that prohibited the teaching of evolution[100] as well as laws granting equal time for creation science—the position that scientific evidence supports the biblical view of creation—if evolution is taught.[101] A district court judge in Pennsylvania ruled that "intelligent design"—a view that claims that the world is too complex to have resulted from evolution and that there must have been a purposeful designer of the universe (that is, God)—was nothing more than creation science with a new name.[102] Whether doctrines are called creation science or intelligent design, courts have ruled that they are religious doctrines that cannot constitutionally be taught as part of the science curricula in public schools. Nevertheless, state legislatures, presumably in an attempt to be responsive to their constituents, continue to approve creation science curricula. Tennessee and Louisiana explicitly allow creationist instruction, Texas and Arkansas have publicly funded charter schools that teach creationism, and ten other states fund private schools that teach creationism.[103]

***Lemon* test:** *Test for determining whether aid to religion violates the establishment clause.*

Essential Knowledge

In the case of *Engle v. Vitale*, the Supreme Court ruled that school sponsored and teacher-led prayer violated the establishment clause. However, students may voluntarily pray in school.

It is often difficult to understand why some activities violate the establishment clause and others do not. Separationists believe, with Jefferson, that there should be a strict wall between church and state. Accommodationists, on the other hand, believe that as long as the state does not favor one religion over another, it can generally pass laws that support religion. The Supreme Court's decisions on these grounds have been mixed, with conservative justices typically supporting the accommodationist position and liberal justices typically supporting the separationist view (see Chapter 15, The Judiciary, on ideology and the Supreme Court). The end result has been confusion: The Court allows short religious prayers by clergy at high school graduation ceremonies as long as students are not compelled to participate,[104] but not by students at high school football games.[105] States may provide textbooks for secular subjects in parochial schools,[106] but not instructional aids such as charts and maps.[107]

4.5 The Right to Keep and Bear Arms

Outline how the "right to bear arms" has been interpreted

Essential Knowledge

The Supreme Court's decisions on Second Amendment cases rest upon its desire to protect individual liberty.

While many if not most Americans agree about the fundamental aims of the various First Amendment rights, no such agreement exists about the fundamental aims of the Second Amendment. The amendment declares, "A well regulated Militia, being necessary to the security of a free State, the right of the people to keep and bear Arms, shall not be infringed." Supporters of gun rights view the amendment as providing an individual right to keep and bear arms, while opponents view the "well regulated Militia" clause as limiting this right to those in organized militias.

At the time of the amendment's passage, the term *militia* meant all free, able-bodied adult males, who could be called on to protect their states or communities from external military threats. The Founders favored citizen militias, which could be called on in moments of crisis, over standing armies, which could pose a threat to liberty.

AP Images/Haraz N. Ghanbari

IMAGE 4.9 Otis McDonald, a plaintiff in *McDonald v. Chicago*, joined the suit against Chicago's handgun law because he wanted to have a handgun at home to protect himself from gangs. On June 18, 2010, the Supreme Court ruled that the Constitution incorporated the Second Amendment, declaring that states could not ban private possession of guns for self-defense.

Not until the 1934 National Firearms Act did the federal government attempt to regulate gun ownership. In 1939, the Supreme Court upheld a conviction under the act for possession of a sawed-off shotgun against a Second Amendment challenge, unanimously ruling that because such weapons had never been used by any militia, they did not receive Second Amendment protection. The Court sidestepped the question about whether there was an individual right to bear arms.

The Supreme Court finally decided that issue in 2008, ruling that there is an individual right to possess a gun, at least for self-defense in one's home.[108] The case involved a law prohibiting the private possession of firearms by the District of Columbia, which is a "federal enclave" and, for constitutional purposes, thus considered part of the federal government rather than a state. The Court's 5–4 decision split along ideological lines, with the five most conservative justices, including the late Justice Antonin Scalia, supporting an individual right to keep and bear arms for self-defense, indicating that the right can be regulated but not denied. The four most liberal justices dissented, arguing that the "well regulated Militia clause" limits whatever right of gun ownership exists to military purposes. Without Scalia, the Court became split 4–4 on the issue. Justice Scalia's position should prevail, though, given President Donald Trump's support for Second Amendment rights.

The conclusion that the Second Amendment protects an individual right to bear arms does not answer the question of whether that amendment is also binding on the states. The

Supreme Court answered that question in 2010, declaring in a 5–4 vote that the right is incorporated.[109] Again, Justice Scalia provided the crucial fifth vote for the individual-right position.

In December 2012, a crazed gunman murdered twenty children and six adults at Sandy Hook Elementary School in Newtown, Connecticut. President Obama and many Democrats called for stricter gun control in the wake of the shooting. On the other side, the National Rifle Association (NRA), a powerful pro-gun interest group (see Chapter 8, Interest Groups), at first kept quiet about the attack, but eventually called for arming teachers and loosening gun control laws as a response.[110] By any objective measure, the NRA won this debate. Though armed teachers are not common, Congress failed to enact President Obama's requests for tighter criminal background checks, to reinstate a ban on assault weapons that had lapsed, or to limit the number of rounds that ammunition magazines could hold.

At the state level, in the years since Sandy Hook, ninety-nine bills tightening access to guns passed while eighty-eight bills easing access passed.[111] New York, one of the few states to tighten gun control following the Newtown tragedy, expanded a ban on assault rifles, limited the number of bullets that could be held in a gun magazine to seven, and made it harder for people suffering from mental illness to obtain weapons. A federal judge later upheld the constitutionality of most of these provisions.[112] Alternatively, in 2014, Georgia's governor signed a bill that allows citizens who have concealed carry permits to bring guns into bars, churches, school zones, government buildings, and certain parts of airports.[113] Texans may now carry concealed handguns on public college campuses and may openly carry handguns throughout almost all other places.[114]

Essential Knowledge

In the case of *McDonald v. Chicago*, the Supreme Court incorporated the Second Amendment, forbidding states to infringe upon the right to possess firearms.

4.6 Criminal Procedure

Describe what protections the Bill of Rights provides to those accused of crimes

Provisions in the Fourth, Fifth, Sixth, and Eighth Amendments contain the heart of the protections afforded people against arbitrary police and law enforcement tactics. They protect the manner in which the police conduct investigations, the procedures used at trial, and the punishments that may be given following conviction. The liberal Warren Court greatly expanded the rights of accused criminals, but since then, more conservative courts have trimmed those rights.

Essential Knowledge

The Court has attempted to strike a balance between liberty and order in its interpretation of several amendments that relate to criminal justice.

Investigations

The major limits on investigating crimes involve the authority to search for physical evidence and the warnings that must be given before questioning a suspect. The police also cannot entrap people into committing crimes they would not otherwise commit, which is why R. Stephanie Good, in her role as "teen2hot4u," could never be the first person to bring up the subject of potential sexual activity.

Searches and Seizures. The English practice of issuing writs of assistance, general warrants that allow searches of any person or place with no expiration until the death of the king, was among the causes that led to the American Revolution. Thus, the Fourth

Amendment prohibits unreasonable searches and seizures. Although the amendment does not specify what makes a search unreasonable, it does specify that warrants must be backed by probable cause, "particularly describing the place to be searched and the persons or things to be seized."

The Supreme Court has never interpreted the amendment to require warrants for all searches or seizures. If the police see illegal goods in plain view, they may seize them without a warrant. Similarly, if they observe a crime, they do not have to get a warrant before they arrest the individual. The Supreme Court has also established a broad right to search the person and the area within his or her control following an arrest and incident to it. This right now permits the police to conduct strip searches of arrestees entering the general population of a jail, even for the most minor violations, such as driving without a seat belt.[115] The police, though, may not search the contents of a cell phone confiscated incident to a lawful arrest due to the enormous amount of private information contained on cell phones.[116]

expectation of privacy test: *Supreme Court test for whether Fourth Amendment protections apply.*

The areas over which individuals have Fourth Amendment protections are those in which there is an **expectation of privacy**. According to the Supreme Court, there are no Fourth Amendment rights in areas over which there is no expectation of privacy, such as discarded garbage, someone else's home, a hotel room once one has checked out, or an international border. The Supreme Court has not ruled on the issue, but several state supreme courts have upheld the right of schools to search lockers used by students because students have a diminished expectation of privacy over their lockers. While students at public universities do have an expectation of privacy in their college dorm rooms, many schools require them to waive their Fourth Amendment rights when they sign their dorm contracts. (Like the First Amendment, the Fourth Amendment does not limit private parties, such as private universities.) More generally, people waive their Fourth Amendment rights whenever they grant permission for the police to search, as long as the police request is not coercive.[117]

As for biological searches, police may require Breathalyzer tests of people suspected of drunk driving, but blood tests require a warrant.[118] On the other hand, the Court recently upheld Maryland's requirement that all persons charged with certain crimes submit DNA samples for the state's database.[119] The DNA samples remain with the state even if the state later drops the charges or the person is found not guilty.

For areas over which there is an expectation of privacy, the degree of Fourth Amendment protection depends on the level of that expectation, as determined by the Supreme Court. For example, the Court has ruled that individuals have the highest expectation of privacy in their homes, nearly as much in their places of business, but substantially less in their cars.[120] There is no expectation of privacy if what is exposed is in plain view, even if, like a marijuana patch on private property, it requires a low-flying plane to view it.[121] There is no expectation of privacy over smells, allowing police to use drug-sniffing dogs to establish probable cause. Drug-sniffing dogs, however, may not enter the porch outside a home in order to sniff for illegal drugs.[122] There is, however, an expectation of privacy over the thermal (heat) signals given off by homes, thus prohibiting the police from using heat monitors to establish probable cause for indoor marijuana growing.[123]

Searches of homes almost always require a warrant (and thus probable cause). Searches of businesses usually do, but the Court allows warrantless searches of businesses that are subject to health, safety, or administrative regulations, such as restaurants, construction sites, and banks. For example, a restaurant kitchen suspected of health violations may be searched without a warrant. The police may establish, without probable cause, roadblocks to stop all cars on a road to check for licenses and registration or for drunk drivers. They may, of course, pull over any car for an observed violation, and they may search the car incident to arrest if they choose to arrest the person for that violation.[124] They may also pull over a person based on an anonymous tip.[125] The Court has ruled that police require a warrant to physically place a GPS transmitter on a car to trace a person's movements, as placing the transmitter on the car requires a physical trespass.[126] The Court explicitly left open the constitutionality of relying on cell phone towers to provide the same information, as such information does not involve a physical intrusion by the police. The Court also allows drug testing without probable cause in "special needs" cases, such as student athletes and people applying for jobs at the U.S. Customs Office, but not of politicians seeking elective office.[127]

Essential Knowledge

Pretrial rights of the accused and the prohibition of unreasonable searches and seizures are intended to ensure that citizen liberties are not eclipsed by the need for social order and security.

If the police conduct a search that is later found to be in violation of the Fourth Amendment, the **exclusionary rule** holds that the evidence cannot be used in trial. Originally established by the Supreme Court in 1914, the doctrine was made binding on state and local governments, where most law enforcement takes place, by means of selective incorporation in *Mapp v. Ohio* (1961).[128] Defenders support the rule, which is not explicitly in the Constitution, as the only means of making sure that the police follow the Fourth Amendment. Police will have less incentive to violate the Fourth Amendment if they know that the evidence from illegal searches cannot be used in court. Critics complain that excluding such evidence allows guilty people to go free simply because the police made a mistake.[129] The Supreme Court has backtracked a bit on the rule, establishing a good faith exception, which allows evidence to be used if the police obtain a warrant but the warrant is later found to lack probable cause.[130] There is also an "inevitable discovery" exception, which allows illegally obtained evidence to be used if the court finds that the evidence would have been discovered even without the illegal search.[131]

exclusionary rule: *Supreme Court rule declaring that evidence found in violation of the Fourth Amendment cannot be used at trial.*

Essential Knowledge

The exclusionary rule prohibits illegally obtained evidence from being used in a criminal prosecution. In a series of cases, including *Mapp*, this rule was applied to the states via "selective incorporation."

Interrogations. The Fifth Amendment protects the right against self-incrimination, being forced to give testimony against oneself during criminal investigations or at criminal trials. The Supreme Court originally interpreted the self-incrimination clause to prohibit coerced confessions because they are inherently unreliable. But in the famous 1966 decision *Miranda v. Arizona*, the Court declared that the right against self-incrimination would be protected regardless of whether there was any evidence of coercion.[132] Rather, prior to police interrogation of subjects who are in custody, the subjects must be told that (1) they have the right to remain silent, (2) anything they say may be used against them, and (3) they have the right to an attorney, free if they cannot afford one. Police strenuously objected to these requirements at first, fearing that they would drastically curtail legitimate confessions. But in 2000, the Court upheld the *Miranda* decision, noting that its requirements had become so embedded in routine police practice that they had become part of the national culture.[133]

Essential Knowledge

In the landmark decision *Miranda v. Arizona*, the Supreme Court sought to protect the rights of criminal defendants to due process. It also ruled there are "public safety" exceptions to the Miranda Rule, requiring the accused to be informed of their Fifth and Sixth Amendment rights.

Trial Procedures

The trial protections of the Bill of Rights include the right to indictment by a grand jury (Fifth Amendment), the right to counsel and an impartial jury (both Sixth Amendment), and

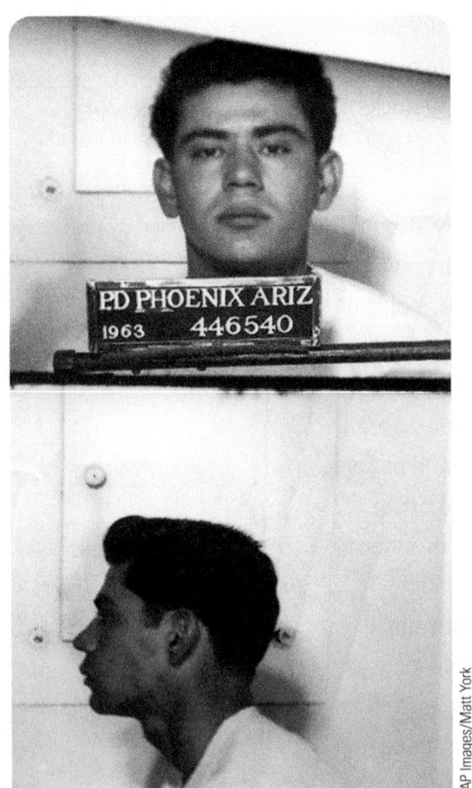

AP Images/Matt York

IMAGE 4.10 Booking photo of Ernesto Miranda. His case led the Warren Court to require police to give arrested suspects "Miranda warnings."

the right against self-incrimination (Fifth Amendment), which, as noted, applies to trials as well as investigations. The Fifth Amendment also contains a general right to due process of law.

To prevent the government from bringing people to trial without sufficient cause, the Fifth Amendment requires indictment by a grand jury, which indicts by majority vote. This right has not been incorporated so it applies to the federal government only, which prosecutes only a small percentage of total criminal cases, as criminal law is mostly under the authority of the states.

The Sixth Amendment's right to counsel originally meant that defendants could have an attorney represent them if they could afford one. In *Powell v. Alabama* (1932), a case involving undoubtedly false allegations of rape filed against several black youths, the Supreme Court ruled that, in death penalty cases where the defendants were ignorant, illiterate, or the like, the government must provide an attorney if defendants cannot afford one.[134] In 1963, the Court recognized in the landmark *Gideon v. Wainwright* case how crucial counsel is in even simple felony cases.[135] Today, the rule applies to any case in which a defendant could receive as little as one day of jail time.[136]

The Sixth Amendment also guarantees the right to a trial by an impartial jury. Originally, a jury trial meant twelve people deciding unanimously, but the Court now allows juries as small as six people, and twelve-person juries need not decide unanimously.[137] The *impartial* part of the clause grants the defense and prosecutor unlimited rights to challenge potential jurors for cause. Examples include knowing other people in the case, having been a victim of a similar crime, and not having an open mind on the issue. These challenges must be approved by the trial judge. State rules also grant prosecutors and defense counsel a limited number of peremptory challenges, or challenges without cause. The substantive limit on peremptory challenges is that neither side may use the potential juror's race or gender as a reason for the challenge.[138]

Essential Knowledge

In the case of *Gideon v. Wainwright*, the Supreme Court ruled that states must provide legal representation to poor persons accused of felonies.

The application of the self-incrimination clause to trials means that defendants cannot be compelled to be witnesses against themselves. That is, they have an absolute right not to testify, and the prosecution cannot even make note to the jury that the defendant chose not to testify.

Verdict, Punishment, and Appeal

At the end of a trial, the jury must decide whether to convict or acquit the defendant. Following conviction, the judge imposes a sentence, unless it is a death penalty case, in which case the jury decides. Convicted defendants may usually appeal their convictions to a higher court.

Double Jeopardy. If the jury acquits the defendant, the double jeopardy clause prevents the person from being tried again for the same offense. But if the jury cannot reach a verdict, the government can retry the defendant. Also, if the defendant is found guilty at trial but the conviction is overturned on appeal, the defendant may be tried again. The

Supreme Court does allow a defendant to be tried separately for the same offense by the state government and the federal government, even if the defendant was found not guilty at the state or federal trial that was held first. Because most crimes are either state offenses or federal offenses, this form of double jeopardy does not often occur.

The main exception concerns a trial for the federal crime of violating someone's civil rights, which is occasionally prosecuted after a state acquittal on the specific offense (such as murder or assault). For example, in 2012, George Zimmerman, an armed neighborhood watch coordinator, shot 17-year-old African American Trayvon Martin while Martin was walking through Zimmerman's gated community. Zimmerman approached Martin, a scuffle ensued in which Zimmerman suffered mild head injuries, and Zimmerman fatally shot Martin. Zimmerman was charged with murder but was acquitted based on Florida's Stand Your Ground Law, which does not require people in Florida to retreat in the face of a threat. Many people called for then-U.S. Attorney General Eric Holder to prosecute Zimmerman for violating Martin's civil rights. A federal investigation into the incident found insufficient evidence to indict Zimmerman.[139]

The federal government plans to try Dylann Roof, the self-professed racist who allegedly murdered nine African Americans at the Emanuel African Church in Charleston, South Carolina, in 2015 on federal "hate crime" charges. The trial will follow his state trial for murder.[140]

Essential Knowledge

The Eighth Amendment's prohibitions against "cruel and unusual punishment" have been interpreted through a series of cases. The standards that have developed are also applicable to the states through selective incorporation.

Sentencing. Following a guilty verdict, the judge determines the sentence, except in death penalty cases, where the jury makes the determination. Sentences must not violate the Eighth Amendment's prohibition on cruel and unusual punishment. The concern of the Framers undoubtedly grew out of English punishments that included torture.[141] The phrase itself, however, is highly ambiguous, leaving courts with a fair amount of discretion about whether punishments are unconstitutional.

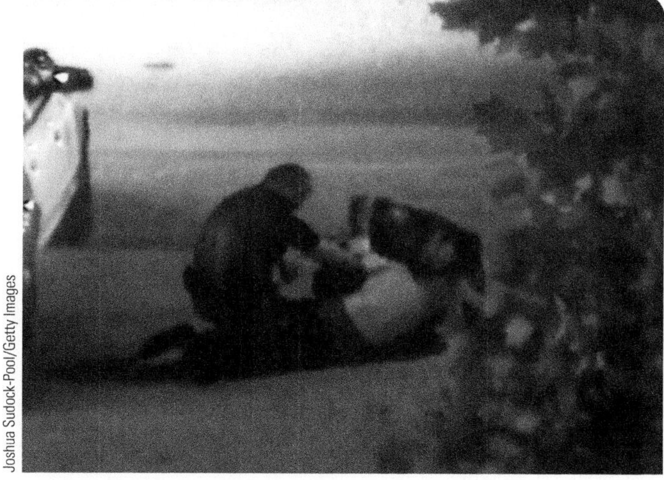

Joshua Sudock-Pool/Getty Images

IMAGE 4.11 Two California police officers shown here beating a mentally ill homeless person, Kelly Thomas. After the officers were found not guilty of murder, Thomas's father filed civil charges against the officers. The suit settled for $4.9 million.

As for the length of the sentence imposed, the Supreme Court grants great leeway to the states. In 1980, the Court upheld the sentencing to a life term with the possibility of parole of a defendant who had committed his third felony. The first felony was fraudulent use of a credit card for an $80 purchase, the second a forged check for $28.36, and the third accepting payment of $120.75 to fix an air conditioner that he never fixed.[142] As the defendant found out, the Supreme Court rarely finds constitutional violation in the length of a sentence.

On the death penalty, however, the Supreme Court ruled in 1972 that the complete discretion given to juries as to which people are convicted of capital crimes was so arbitrary as to constitute cruel and unusual punishment.[143] Then, in 1976, the Court ruled mandatory death sentences to be unconstitutional but allowed states to impose the death penalty provided they give jurors specific guidelines to consider, such as the brutality of the crime or whether the crime was murder for hire.[144] (See Chapter 2 for more on the death penalty.)

Appeals. Convicted criminals do not have a right to appeal a trial court conviction unless a federal constitutional right has been violated. How states handle violations of state constitutional rights are largely up to the states, even if evidence is later found that the convicted criminal is factually innocent. Although the continued imprisonment or execution of a factually innocent person might appear to be a quintessential case violating due process, the Supreme Court has ruled that people convicted of crimes before DNA testing became available do not have a constitutional right to such evidence, which in many cases could definitively prove their innocence or guilt.[145] Indeed, there is no constitutional right for a factually innocent person not to be executed for a capital crime after a jury has concluded that the person is legally guilty, even if new evidence creates strong doubts as to guilt.[146]

4.7 The Right to Privacy

Assess what constitutes the right to privacy

Although a number of constitutional provisions bear on privacy, such as search and seizure, self-incrimination, and First Amendment freedoms, none explicitly grants a general right to privacy. Nevertheless, the Ninth Amendment demands that the listing of certain rights, such as speech and religion, should not be understood as invalidating rights not listed. Since 1965, the Supreme Court has used the Ninth Amendment, the due process clause of the Fourteenth Amendment, and other privacy-related amendments to establish a general right to privacy. Subsequently the Court has faced decisions about whether to expand this privacy right to include abortion, homosexual behavior, and the right to die.

Birth Control and Abortion

In 1873, Anthony Comstock, a crusader for traditional morality, lobbied Congress to pass a law prohibiting the transportation in interstate commerce of both pornography and birth control. Many states, including Connecticut, passed their own Comstock Laws, which prohibited the use of birth control, even by married couples. In 1961, Estelle Griswold, executive director of the Planned Parenthood League of Connecticut, opened a birth control clinic in order to get arrested or fined so that she could challenge the constitutionality of the law. Her $100 fine, upheld by the Connecticut Supreme Court, allowed her to appeal to the U.S. Supreme Court. In *Griswold v. Connecticut* (1965), the Court voided what one justice called "an uncommonly silly law."[147] The case established a **right to privacy** (see Figure 4.4), and the Court soon expanded this decision to cover the right of unmarried people to use birth control.[148] Birth control as a political issue was then dormant until 2012, when the secretary of health and human services interpreted the Patient Protection and Affordable Care Act requirement that insurance plans cover birth control under the category of preventive medicine. The Catholic Church, which believes using birth control goes against church teachings, protested the application of these rules to cover employee health insurance at Church-affiliated schools and hospitals. The Obama administration then revised its policies

right to privacy: *Constitutional right inferred by the Court that has been used to protect unlisted rights such as sexual privacy and reproductive rights, plus the right to end life-sustaining medical treatment.*

No Soldier shall, in time of peace be quartered in any house, without the consent of the Owner. ...
Third Amendment
Congress shall make no law ... abridging ... the right of the people peaceably to assemble. ...
First Amendment
The right of the people to be secure in their persons, houses, papers, and effects, against unreasonable searches and seizures, shall not be violated. ...
Fourth Amendment
The enumeration in the Constitution, of certain rights, shall not be construed to deny or disparage others retained by the people.
Ninth Amendment
No person ... shall be compelled in any criminal case to be a witness against himself. ...
Fifth Amendment
... nor shall any State deprive any person of life, liberty, or property, without due process of law. ...
Fourteenth Amendment (section 1)
In 1965, in *Griswold v. Connecticut*, the Supreme Court overturned a Connecticut law that made it a crime for any person, including married couples, to use birth control. This landmark case drew on guarantees in the First, Third, Fourth, Fifth, Ninth, and Fourteenth Amendments to establish a general right to privacy. These guarantees are the right of association, the prohibition against quartering soldiers, the protection against unreasonable searches, the protection against self-incrimination, the rights retained by the people, and the due process of law. Justice William O. Douglas, who wrote the opinion, explained the justification with reference to "penumbras," or "zones": "Specific guarantees in the Bill of Rights have penumbras formed by emanations from those guarantees that help give them life and substance." He also stated the justification more bluntly: "Would we allow the police to search the sacred precincts of marital bedrooms for the tell-tale signs of the use of contraceptives? The very idea is repulsive."

FIGURE 4.4 The Right to Privacy

The Supreme Court established a general right to privacy from various specific privacy-related rights in the First, Third, Fourth, Fifth, Ninth, and Fourteenth Amendments.

to mandate that the insurance companies themselves cover the cost of birth control rather than the Church, or any other organization that objects to the use of birth control as part of its fundamental teachings.

Even more controversial than the question of birth control is the question of abortion. Before the middle of the nineteenth century, most states followed the English practice of making abortion illegal only after "quickening"—that is, noticeable movement by the fetus, usually around the sixteenth to eighteenth week of pregnancy. By the end of the nineteenth century, most states had eliminated the quickening distinction, making abortion illegal throughout pregnancy. By the 1950s, every state but Alabama had banned abortion except to save the life of the mother; Alabama's broader exception included preserving the mother's health.

Following a substantial increase in birth defects caused by the sedative thalidomide (1957–61) and a German measles epidemic (1962–65), deaths from illegal abortion, and the

Essential Knowledge
In the *Roe v. Wade* decision, the Court attempts to strike a balance between a woman's right to privacy and a compelling state interest.

resurgence of the women's rights movement, interest groups such as the National Association for the Reform of Abortion Laws (NARAL) organized for the loosening of antiabortion laws. Between 1967 and 1969, ten states passed laws allowing abortion if there were a "substantial risk" that the child would be born with a "grave physical or mental defect" or that continuing the pregnancy would "gravely impair the physical or mental health of the mother" and in cases of rape or incest.[149] In 1970, three states legalized previability abortions, those performed before the sixth month of pregnancy, when the fetus could not survive on its own.

Roe v. Wade: *1973 Supreme Court case extending the right to privacy to abortion.*

Then, in 1973, the Supreme Court decided ***Roe v. Wade***, which established a national right to abortion.[150] Using the compelling interest test, the Court declared that states had a compelling interest in preventing abortion in the third trimester, when the fetus could live on its own, and a compelling interest in regulating abortion during the second trimester to protect the health of the woman seeking the procedure. The state had no interest in regulating or preventing abortion in the first trimester. The Court's ruling took the issue out of state politics, where it had been located, and situated it in national politics, where it has become a perennial controversy, with presidential candidates regularly vowing to nominate Supreme Court justices who would either uphold or strike down *Roe v. Wade*. Since that time, states have sought to regulate and limit the procedure, and in the past twenty years, abortion rates have slowly declined.

Following years of debate about *Roe v. Wade*, the Court reconsidered the decision in 1992.[151] That decision upheld the basic right to abortion established in *Roe v. Wade* but replaced the compelling interest/trimester framework, declaring that states could regulate abortion prior to viability as long as those regulations did not constitute an undue burden on a woman's right to terminate her pregnancy. According to the Court, spousal notification constitutes an undue burden, but requiring doctors to provide the woman with information about the risks of abortion and a twenty-four-hour waiting period does not. Parental consent for minors is not an undue burden as long as the minor has an option of seeking a judge's approval if she cannot obtain a parent's consent.

Perhaps the most controversial abortion procedures are those conducted late in a pregnancy. The Supreme Court struck down Nebraska's ban of these "partial-birth" abortions in 2000 in a 5–4 decision because the state law did not contain an exception for the woman's health.[152] Congress responded with national legislation banning partial-birth abortions, and the Court upheld the statute by a 5–4 vote in 2007.[153] The difference was the replacement of Justice Sandra Day O'Connor, who voted to strike the statute in 2000, by Justice Samuel Alito, who voted to uphold the statute in 2007.

Abortion remains a salient issue in national politics, with the Supreme Court's role front and center. While the Supreme Court continues to enforce the *Roe v. Wade* decisions, state legislatures have been very active in attempting to limit access to abortion. In 2015, seventeen states enacted fifty-seven abortion restrictions. Some of these involve mandatory waiting periods (three new states for a total of twenty-seven) of up to seventy-two hours (North Carolina and Oklahoma), regulations banning the use of telemedicine for the administration of abortion drugs (four new states for a total of nineteen), and bans on abortions at twenty weeks post-fertilization (West Virginia and Wisconsin); five states (Arkansas, Indiana, Ohio, Oklahoma, and Tennessee) introduced or expanded targeted regulation of abortion provider (TRAP) laws (which are similar to Texas laws struck down by the

Supreme Court).[154] Forty-three states prohibit late term abortions, typically after viability of the fetus.[155]

The continued importance of abortion at the national level (see Chapter 15) is evidenced at confirmation hearings for Supreme Court nominees. At these hearings senators ask more questions about *Roe v. Wade* than about any other case.[156]

Homosexual Behavior

As of 1961, every state had laws prohibiting sodomy, and these laws were broad enough to cover virtually all sexual conduct between people of the same sex. In the next decades, some states decriminalized sodomy, and by 1986, twenty-four states continued to outlaw sodomy between consenting adults. Georgia, one of the states that continued such laws, authorized twenty-four years of imprisonment for a single act of consensual sexual behavior that fell under its sodomy laws. In a case challenging this law, the Supreme Court declared that the right to privacy did not cover homosexual behavior.[157] At the time, more than 80 percent of Americans thought that homosexual behavior was "always" or "almost always" wrong.[158] But by 2003, with the percentage of Americans with this belief down more than 20 percentage points, the Supreme Court reversed itself, declaring in ***Lawrence v. Texas*** that "the liberty protected by the Constitution allows homosexual persons the right to choose to enter upon relationships in the confines of their homes and their own private lives"[159] (see Chapter 5 for the Court's decision on same-sex marriage).

Lawrence v. Texas: *2003 Supreme Court case extending the right to privacy to homosexual behavior.*

The Right to Die

As part of the right to privacy, the Supreme Court has held that that people who make their wishes clearly known have a constitutional right to terminate life-sustaining care, such as artificial feeding or insertion of breathing tubes.[160] This right does not, however, include the right to assisted suicide, when physicians or family members provide ill people with pills or other means of ending life.[161]

Student Housing

The Supreme Court rejected the use of the right to privacy to strike down laws that ban more than two unrelated unmarried people from living together in the same house or apartment. Instead, it declared that states have a legitimate interest in passing land use legislation.[162]

Civil Liberties and Democracy

At the beginning of the chapter, we quoted Justice Robert Jackson opinion from the flag salute case that no government official can declare what shall be required in terms of basic beliefs and values. But what if elected officials do so anyway? Jackson responded that it was then the courts' job to protect such rights: "The very purpose of a Bill of Rights was to withdraw certain subjects from . . . political controversy, to place them beyond the reach of majorities and officials and to establish them as legal principles to be applied by the courts. One's . . . fundamental rights may not be submitted to vote; they depend on the outcome of no elections."[163]

POLITICAL ANALYTICS

Tolerance of Unpopular Ideas

TOLERANCE OF THE RIGHTS of others with whom we disagree is a core value of the United States. Allowing freedom of speech to occur contributes to lively political discussion and can, in the best of cases, elevate everyone's understanding of different points of view. Americans have a fairly high level of tolerance when it comes to allowing others to exercise freedom of speech. As Figure 4.5 shows, the willingness of Americans to allow Communists and atheists to give speeches has generally increased over the past sixty years. Tolerance toward racists has decreased slightly, but still, the majority of those surveyed thought racists should be allowed to speak publicly about their views.

A marketplace of ideas suggests that when multiple viewpoints and ideas are expressed, people will be able to consider those ideas and adopt those they support—rather than being exposed to only a narrow range of perspectives. Colleges and universities can serve as such a marketplace of ideas because students from different backgrounds and from all around the world can gather to express their views about politics and society. In the process, they may reinforce their own views or reconsider their perspectives in light of those held by others.

In Figure 4.5, examine the willingness of the Americans surveyed to allow disfavored groups to give speeches.

FIGURE 4.5 Percentage of Americans Who Support Allowing Speeches by Members of Disfavored Groups, 1982–2014

Source: General Social Survey, various years.

Thinking Critically

1. Is tolerance of the views held by others with whom we disagree important for maintaining the balance between order and liberty? Are today's colleges and universities marketplaces of ideas?
2. The rhetoric in the 2016 presidential primary campaign contained what some would call racist overtones. Do you think voters should tolerate such rhetoric by political leaders?

Judicial decisions do not exist in a vacuum. Over the long run, if the Court is unresponsive to the people, new presidents will appoint new judges who better represent the people's preferences.[164] And while the Supreme Court is not accountable to the electorate in the same way that Congress and the president are, Congress and the president do have ways to try to hold the Court accountable. For example, in 1937, President Franklin Roosevelt threatened to pack the Court as a result of its decisions on economic policy. In the 1950s, Congress threatened to take away the Court's authority to hear certain types of cases in the wake of its decisions on congressional investigations of Communists. In recent years, members of Congress have threatened to impeach justices over Court decisions with which they disagreed.

These attempts failed—the older ones largely because the Court proved responsive to the threats and backed away from its original positions. This outcome suggests that one way or another, the Court cannot stand alone in protecting civil liberties if popular support is not behind it. One of the difficulties in protecting civil liberties in a democracy is that although it is easy to feel sympathy for teenagers who wear black armbands to protest war, most litigants whose cases set precedents that protect all of the nation's freedoms are not as wholesome, and the causes they espouse may be racist, sexist, or violent.[165]

Unlimited liberties can also harm social order, particularly in times of crisis. Note, however, that in the period following 9/11, Congress made no attempt to criminalize antiwar speech, as it had during World War I; there was little public demand for such restrictions, as tolerance of opposing viewpoints among Americans has increased dramatically over the years. **Political tolerance**, the willingness of people to put up with ideas with which they disagree, is essential to both the marketplace of ideas and democratic stability.[166]

political tolerance: *Willingness of people to put up with ideas with which they disagree.*

Consider the willingness of Americans to allow members of disliked groups to give speeches in their community. With the exception of racists, this willingness has increased (see Figure 4.5). If the people are tolerant, elected politicians will be tolerant also.

Similarly, the appointment process furthers responsiveness. Although critics have attacked the Supreme Court for establishing a right to privacy that is not explicitly in the Constitution, this decision remains highly popular, with 98 percent of Americans considering the right essential or important.[167] In 1986, when Supreme Court nominee Robert Bork stated that he rejected the validity of this right, the Senate rejected his appointment. But if the public loses its concern over civil liberties, sooner or later, the Supreme Court will as well.

Political Science Reasoning

Question 1

Practice 1, Practice 2

Barron v. Baltimore (1833)

The question thus presented is, we think, of great importance, but not of much difficulty. The Constitution was ordained and established by the people of the United States for themselves, for their own government, and not for the government of the individual States. Each State established a constitution for itself, and in that constitution provided such limitations and restrictions on the powers of its particular government as its judgment dictated. The people of the United States framed such a government for the United States as they supposed best adapted to their situation and best calculated to promote their interests. The powers they conferred on this government were to be exercised by itself, and the limitations on power, if expressed in general terms, are naturally, and we think necessarily, applicable to the government created by the instrument. They are limitations of power granted in the instrument itself, not of distinct governments framed by different persons and for different purposes.

If these propositions be correct, the fifth amendment must be understood as restraining the power of the general government, not as applicable to the States. In their several constitutions, they have imposed such restrictions on their respective governments, as their own wisdom suggested, such as they deemed most proper for themselves. It is a subject on which they judge exclusively, and with which others interfere no further than they are supposed to have a common interest.

Gitlow v. New York (1925)

For present purposes we may and do assume that freedom of speech and of the press—which are protected by the First Amendment from abridgment by Congress—are among the fundamental personal rights and "liberties" protected by the due process clause of the Fourteenth Amendment from impairment by the States. We do not regard the incidental statement in *Prudential Ins. Co. v. Cheek*, . . . that the Fourteenth Amendment imposes no restrictions on the States concerning freedom of speech, as determinative of this question.

It is a fundamental principle, long established, that the freedom of speech and of the press which is secured by the Constitution, does not confer an absolute right to speak or publish, without responsibility, whatever one may choose, or an unrestricted and unbridled license that gives immunity for every possible use of language and prevents the punishment of those who abuse this freedom . . . Reasonably limited, it was said by Story in the passage cited, this freedom is an inestimable privilege in a free government; without such limitation, it might become the scourge of the republic.

1. Identify and explain the reasoning used in each of the above Supreme Court decisions.
   - **a.** The question at the heart of *Barron v. Baltimore* is whether or not the Fifth Amendment ought to apply to the states. What is the Court's answer, and what is their reasoning?
   - **b.** The question at the heart of *Gitlow v. New York* is whether or not the First Amendment ought to apply to the states. What is the Court's answer, and what is their reasoning?

2. How do the above decisions represent a change in power of the national government? What has changed between these two decisions? Identify and explain one major implication of this transformation in the role of the Court and the Constitution.

Question 2

Practice 1, Practice 2

Citizens United v. Federal Election Commission (2010)

Before the Bipartisan Campaign Reform Act of 2002 (BCRA), federal law prohibited—and still does prohibit—corporations and unions from using general treasury funds to make direct contributions to candidates or independent expenditures that expressly advocate the election or defeat of a candidate, through any form of media, in connection with certain qualified federal elections . . .

The law before us is an outright ban, backed by criminal sanctions. Section 441b makes it a felony for all corporations—including nonprofit advocacy corporations—either to expressly advocate the election or defeat of candidates or to broadcast electioneering communications within 30 days of a primary election and 60 days of a general election. Thus, the following acts would all be felonies under §441b: The Sierra Club runs an ad, within the crucial phase of 60 days before the general election, that exhorts the public to disapprove of a Congressman who favors logging in national forests; the National Rifle Association publishes a book urging the public to vote for the challenger because the incumbent U. S. Senator supports a handgun ban; and the American Civil Liberties Union creates a website telling the public to vote for a Presidential candidate in light of that candidate's defense of free speech. These prohibitions are classic examples of censorship . . .

We find no basis for the proposition that, in the context of political speech, the government may impose restrictions on certain disfavored speakers. Both history and logic lead us to this conclusion...

This protection has been extended by explicit holdings to the context of political speech . . . Under the rationale of these precedents, political speech does not lose First Amendment protection "simply because its source is a corporation."

1. What is the reasoning used in the Supreme Court's *Citizens United v. Federal Election Commission* decision?
2. What are the electoral implications of the decision?

Focus on AP® Success

4 Civil Liberties

Must Know: Key Concepts

- Selective Incorporation
- Establishment Clause
- Free Exercise Clause
- Fourteenth Amendment Due Process Clause
- *Engel v. Vitale*
- *Wisconsin v. Yorker*
- *Tinker v. Des Moines Independent Community School District*
- *New York Times Co. v. United States*
- *Schenck v. United States*
- *Gideon v. Wainwright*
- *Roe v. Wade*
- *McDonald v. Chicago*
- *Miranda v. Arizona* – "Miranda Rule"
- Prior Restraint
- Public Safety Exception
- Defamation
- Obscenity

Thinking Politically

SCOTUS Application

The cases listed in the Key Concepts are "mandatory" for the AP exam. After reading the chapter and outside research for each case, you should be able to: identify the constitutional provision in question and summarize (including legal reasoning) the opinion of the Court (majority opinion) as well as the opinions of the dissenting justices and concurring justices. You should be able to compare the opinion of the Court with any dissenting opinions in the case as well as with majority opinions in similar cases. You should also be able to summarize the political and social impact of these cases.

Argumentation

The First Amendment states that "Congress shall make no law ... abridging the freedom of speech, or the press..." However, the Supreme Court has ruled that these are not absolute rights. There are always limits to expression including speech. Review the Court's decisions in *Schenck v. United States*. Does the Court strike the correct balance between individual liberty and social order? For evidence, consider the limitations placed on expression (such as speech) in other democratic societies.

Concept Application

The role of religion in public life has been a source of controversy in recent decades. This is particularly true with regard to government displays of religiosity (i.e., nativity scenes in the town square and public school prayer). The First Amendment contains two clauses that deal with religion. They are the establishment clause, which prohibits governmentally sanctioned religious activity, and the free exercise clause, which prohibits the government from unduly interfering in the practice of religion. The government can give grants to non-profit charitable organizations. If those organizations are religious, this might constitute an establishment of religion thus violating the First Amendment. If those organizations are automatically excluded from applying for grants, that might constitute a form of discrimination based solely on religion, again violating the First Amendment. How should the Supreme Court balance the sometimes competing values espoused by the establishment clause and the free exercise clause?

Understanding Learning Objectives with Key Concepts

LOR – 2.A Explain how the U.S. Constitution protects individual liberties and rights.

- The first ten amendments to the U.S. Constitution are known as the Bill of Rights. These amendments serve as the mainstay for the liberties and rights of people.
- The term "civil liberties" refers to the protections that individuals have against arbitrary and capricious government action. This is different than "civil rights," which refers the requirement for equal treatment.
- Portions of the Bill of Rights have been applied by the Supreme Court to the states. The process of interpretation and application is ongoing.

LOR – 2.B Describe the rights protected in the Bill of Rights.

- The Bill of Rights sets forth the rights and liberties of individuals. It protects things such as religious liberty, freedom of speech, and the right to due process.

LOR – 2.C Explain the extent to which the Supreme Court's interpretation of the First and Second Amendments reflects a commitment to individual liberty.

- There are no absolute rights in the Bill of Rights other than, perhaps, the right of freedom of belief. This does not mean the right to act upon those beliefs. As such, one of the tasks of the Supreme Court is to determine the boundaries of those rights.
- The rights found in the Constitution, including the Bill of Rights, must be interpreted in a broader societal context. The Court's job is to balance the rights of the majority with the minority and the desire for individual freedom with social order.
- The Supreme Court's decision in *Engel v. Vitale* illustrates the Court's belief that the government should be limited in its ability to prescribe religious activities in public schools. This interpretation is based on the establishment clause.
- The Court's decision in *Wisconsin v. Yoder* acts as an example of how it sought to balance the legitimate state interest of an educated citizenry with a competing value of religious liberty. In this decision, the Court held that the laws that required members of the Amish faith to attend school beyond eighth grade were a violation of the free exercise clause and as such were unconstitutional.
- The Court recognizes that the First Amendment protects symbolic speech. An example of this is the Court's decision in the case of *Tinker v. Des Moines Independent Community School District***.** In this case the court ruled that students have a right to free speech in school.
- The Court attempts to balance individual liberty with social order by permitting certain restrictions to First Amendment freedoms such as "time, place and manner" rules on peaceable assembly and prohibitions on obscenity. In *Schenck v. United States*, the Court permitted restrictions on speech that presents "a clear and present danger."
- The Court states that the Constitution contains at "heavy presumption against prior restraint." As such, it is very difficult for the government to censor the press even in cases of national security. A leading case in this area is *New York Times v. United States* (1971).
- The Supreme Court has interpreted the Second Amendment's right to keep and bear arms in the light of its commitment to individual liberty. This is illustrated by *McDonald v. Chicago* (2010).

LOR – 2.D Explain how the Supreme Court has attempted to balance the claims of individual freedom with laws and enforcement procedures that promote public order and safety.

- As the Court has interpreted the Eighth Amendment's prohibition of "cruel and unusual" punishment, it has permitted the death penalty while limiting its scope and insisting on procedural safeguards.
- There is ongoing debate on the government's regulation of firearms in light of the Second Amendment and the government's bulk collection of electronic data out of respect for Fourth Amendment protections.

LOR – 3.A Explain the implications of the doctrine of selective incorporation.

- Originally, the Bill of Rights only restricted the national government and not the states. The due process clause of the Fourteenth Amendment has been used to incorporate (make applicable to the states) most all of the protections of the Bill of Rights. This is exemplified in many cases such as *Gitlow v. New York*, which held that the First Amendment applies to the states. However, states may impose restrictions on speech that present a threat to public safety.

- In the case of *McDonald v. Chicago*, the Court again demonstrated its commitment to individual liberty by incorporating the Second Amendment's right to keep and bear arms, making it applicable to the states.

LOR – 3.B Explain the extent to which states are limited by the due process clause from infringing upon individual rights.

- The Miranda Rule, derived from the case of *Miranda v. Arizona*, is an example of how the Court attempts to balance individual liberty with social order. The Court's decision requires that a person must be advised of his or her rights upon entry into the criminal justice system. However, the Court permits limited exceptions to this rule in unusual circumstances where public safety demands it.
- The Sixth Amendment, as stated and interpreted by the Supreme Court, requires that individuals have rights to legal counsel, speedy and public trial, and a fair and impartial jury.
- Also protected are unreasonable searches and seizures including warrantless collection of certain cell phone data as well as limitations on the collection and use of telecommunications metadata.
- The Court's decision in *Gideon v. Wainwright* required the state to pay for legal counsel in felony cases if the defendant could not afford it.
- Additionally, the Court has applied the exclusionary rule to the states. That rule prohibits evidence in court if it was obtained in violation of the Fourth Amendment.
- The court has interpreted the Ninth Amendment (applicable to the states through the Fourteenth Amendment's due process clause) as protecting a right to privacy including a woman's right to an abortion (*Roe v. Wade*). This was based, in part, on a right to privacy implied by the language of the Third, Fourth, and Fifth Amendments.

Making Connections

- Review how the Constitution provides for the selection of members of the judiciary in Chapters 2 and 15. The fact that judges are not elected tends to give them more latitude in making some unpopular decisions that might be necessary to protect civil liberties.
- Selective incorporation shifts power to the national government by creating a national standard for the protection of civil liberties. This standard is determined by the Supreme Court.

Going Deeper: First Amendment Freedoms

Engle v. Vitale (1962)

Until the 1960s, many states (including New York) had school sponsored, teacher-led prayer.

New York's voluntary, teacher-led prayer was "Almighty God, we acknowledge our dependence upon Thee, and we beg Thy blessings upon us, our parents, our teachers and our country. Amen"

This practice is challenged in the case of *Engel v. Vitale* (1962).

In this decision the court prohibits the practice stating:

> *The history of governmentally established religion, both in England and in this country, showed that whenever government had allied itself with one particular form of religion, the inevitable result had been that it had incurred the hatred, disrespect and even contempt of those who held contrary beliefs.*

Many found the decision objectionable. This decision, in part, begins the culture war that impacts politics today.

Wisconsin v. Yoder (1972)

State governments have a legitimate interest in an educated citizenry. However, some contend the compulsory school attendance laws may violate parents' and students' religious beliefs.

In particular, the Amish believed that education beyond eighth grade undermined their traditional way of life, which is an essential part of their religious beliefs.

In the case of *Wisconsin v. Yoder* (1972), the Court attempted to balance the interests of the state with the religious rights of the Amish.

Prohibiting the application of the law to the Amish, the court states:

> *Aided by a history of three centuries as an identifiable religious sect and a long history as a successful and self-sufficient segment of American society, the Amish in this case have convincingly demonstrated the sincerity of their religious beliefs, the interrelationship of belief with their mode of life, the vital role that belief and daily conduct play in the continued survival of Old Order Amish communities and their religious organization, and the hazards presented by the State's enforcement of a statute generally valid to others.*

5 Civil Rights

AP® Learning Objectives

PRD – 1.A Explain how constitutional provisions have supported and motivated social movements.

PMI – 3.A Explain how the government has responded to social movements.

CON – 6.A Explain how the Supreme Court has at times allowed the restriction of civil rights of minority groups and at other times has protected those rights.

Performance Tasks

Upon the completion of this chapter, you must be able to do the following:

- Using specific documents and examples, explain how values enshrined in the U.S. Constitution have motivated various groups to struggle for equality.
- Citing specific constitutional provisions, explain how the U.S. government has responded to the demands made by various groups for equality under the law.
- Citing specific cases and legislation, explain how the U.S. Congress and the U.S. Supreme Court have both ignored and responded to demands for equality under the law.

Don Smetzer/Alamy

*"I need everyone to stop pretending that nothing is wrong."**

ERIKA ANDIOLA
Arizona State University

Win McNamee/Getty Images News/Getty Images

Escaping domestic violence, Erika Andiola's mother came to the United States from Mexico without documentation with Erika and two of Erika's siblings when Erika was only 11. Erika originally received a scholarship to attend Arizona State University, but a new Arizona law prohibited undocumented students from receiving scholarships, so the scholarship was rescinded. Even though her undocumented status made it difficult to find employment, Erika worked to pay for tuition, studied, and graduated from Arizona State in 2009 with a B.A. in psychology. Erika then went to work for Congresswoman Kyrsten Sinema (see the opening vignette in Chapter 10, Elections and Campaigns). She also began lobbying to support President Obama's proposed DREAM Act, which would have granted permanent residency to undocumented immigrants if they arrived in the United States before they turned 16, received an honorable discharge from the military, or completed at least two years toward a college degree. While the bill passed the House in 2010, it never received the supermajority necessary to end the filibuster against it in the Senate. In 2012, however, President Obama directed Immigration and Customs Enforcement (ICE) to stop deporting undocumented students who met DREAM Act standards.

Despite the president's order, in 2013, agents from ICE broke into the Andiola family house, arresting Erika's mother and brother. Erika organized a huge protest against the arrests, and they were released the following day. As Marielena Hincapié, executive director of the National Immigration Law Center, put it, "Not all immigrant families have the benefit of Erika to mobilize the whole country overnight." Erika used the gateway of grassroots activism to get the government to use its discretion not to deport her family. Due to the massive support she received from around the country, her efforts succeeded.

In 2014, Andiola began a hunger strike at ICE headquarters in Phoenix, Arizona. One week later, Phoenix police arrested her, a move that could have led to her deportation but, perhaps due to her status as an activist for undocumented Americans, they did not. She launched #not1more in an attempt to get President Obama, who has deported more undocumented residents than any other president, to end deportations. She also began a hunger strike at the White House.

Andiola remains optimistic about the future. When asked by the *New York Times* where her activism is leading, the woman who originally went to college to become a psychologist replied, "I haven't been able to think that far. At this point, I just want to be able to pass immigration reform. I want to be able to keep my mom here, and we'll see where life takes me from there."[1]

In 2016, Andiola joined Bernie Sanders's presidential campaign as national press secretary for Latino outreach. In accepting the position, she declared, "For us, what matters is really again, making sure Bernie gets introduced to a lot more Latinos. . . . Obviously he's not as known as Secretary Clinton."[2]

In this chapter, we look at the idea of equality, how it has changed, and how the federal government's enforcement of it has changed as well. We examine how grassroots racial, ethnic, and gender-based movements pressured the courts to protect civil rights and how Congress enforced court rulings with legislation. As with civil liberties (see Chapter 4, Civil Liberties), however, finding the right balance of rights for minority groups frequently divides members of society from one another, and divides democratically responsive legislatures from lifetime-appointed judges.

*The webcam video in which this quote appears—filmed after Andiola's mother and brother were arrested by immigration police—is widely available online, including at https://www.youtube.com/watch?v=nMPWhn8HEJk.

5.1 What Are Civil Rights?

Define civil rights

Although the Declaration of Independence declared that "All men are created equal," the Constitution originally had little to say about equality, at least as the concept is understood today. Even the debate over the ratification of the Constitution had little to do with equality. It was much more about how much power to invest in the federal government. Today, however, equality is a hallowed principle of American political culture, but the notion and the reality evolved slowly over two centuries.

Civil Rights and Civil Liberties

civil rights: *Set of rights centered around the concept of equal treatment that government is obliged to protect.*

Civil rights are rights related to the duties of citizenship and the gateways for participation in civic life that the government is obliged to protect. These rights are based on the expectation of equality under the law. The most important is the right to vote. In contrast to civil liberties (see Chapter 4), Americans have struggled hard to gain civil rights.

Civil rights also differ from civil liberties in that while government is the only authority that can suppress liberties—for example, by suppressing freedom of speech or forbidding a certain religious belief—both government and private entities, such as individuals or businesses, have the capacity to engage in discrimination by treating people unequally.

public discrimination: *Discrimination by national, state, or local governments.*

private discrimination: *Discrimination by private individuals or businesses.*

The government can therefore take three different roles when it comes to civil rights. It can engage in state-sponsored or **public discrimination** by actively discriminating against people. It can treat people equally but permit **private discrimination** by allowing individuals or businesses to discriminate. Finally, it can try, as the U.S. government has since the 1960s, to treat people equally and to prevent individuals or businesses from discriminating. Thus it falls to government to protect individuals against unequal treatment and to citizens to ensure that the government itself is not discriminating against individuals or groups. In a democracy, the majority rules, but the gateways for minorities must also be kept open.

The Constitution and Civil Rights

Despite the statement on equality in the Declaration of Independence, the role of the government with regard to ensuring equality was not written into the Constitution, and the United States has a bleak history on civil rights. The Founders were not much concerned with equality as it is understood today. Many of them owned slaves, and they did not see a contradiction between doing so and the Declaration's statement on equality. The Constitution gave the states authority over voting, and most states restricted the right to vote to free males with a certain amount of property. Slaves could not vote, and in a few states, even free African Americans could not vote—neither could women (except in New Jersey) or Native Americans.[3] During the nation's first century and even thereafter, state laws and the national government actively discriminated against people on the basis of race, gender, and ethnic background.

Following the Civil War, the Thirteenth Amendment ended slavery, and the Fourteenth Amendment forbade states to deny any person "the equal protection of the laws." Nevertheless, the equality of African Americans was not thereby guaranteed. Some of the members of Congress who wrote the Fourteenth Amendment believed that equality was limited to "the right to go and come; the right to enforce contracts; the right to convey his property; the right to buy property" and little more.[4] The courts agreed, and the federal government made little effort to ensure equal treatment during the nation's second century.

Meanwhile, women won the right to vote (1920), but not the right to full participation in public life. Native Americans born on reservations became citizens (1924), but not until the civil rights and women's movements of the 1950s and 1960s did legal discrimination against African Americans, women, and ethnic minorities end. Today, the government actively aims to treat individuals and groups as equals before the law and to use its authority to prevent state and local governments, and individuals and businesses, from discriminating.

In the past half-century, the meaning of "all men are created equal" has been expanded to include women and all people subject to the jurisdiction of the United States. Yet Americans still debate the meaning of *equality*. Should, or can, the government ensure **equality of opportunity** for all people? Should, or can, it engineer **equality of outcome**? That is, is it enough for society to provide equality of opportunity by prohibiting discrimination? What if that still leaves members of groups that have historically been discriminated against, such as women and minorities, with fewer advanced degrees and lower incomes? As it has throughout the course of the nation's history, the meaning of equality continues to evolve.

equality of opportunity: *Expectation that citizens may not be discriminated against on account of race, gender, or national background and that every citizen should have an equal chance to succeed in life.*

equality of outcome: *Expectation that equality is achieved if results are comparable for all citizens regardless of race, gender, or national background or that such groups are proportionally represented in measures of success in life.*

In the next sections, we see how, as the idea of equality expanded, the federal government moved from actively treating different groups unequally under the law, to asserting equality under the law but doing little to protect it, to actively enforcing it.

5.2 Legal Restrictions on Civil Rights

Explain how the federal and state governments suppressed civil rights

Slavery split the United States from the founding of the nation through the Civil War. After the Civil War, the Constitution prohibited slavery. It also prohibited the states from denying equality, but many states continued to discriminate. Both Congress and the Supreme Court had the authority to enforce equality, but neither took action. Women, African Americans, and ethnic minorities suffered under unequal laws, with denial of the right to vote and laws that limited their full participation in labor markets, professions, and public life. Discriminatory laws also affected Asians, prohibiting those who were not born in the United States from becoming citizens and later preventing them from immigrating to the United States altogether.

Library of Congress Prints and Photographs Division[LC-USZC4-6204]

IMAGE 5.1 An anti–slave trade etching from 1792.

Slavery

Slavery came to the colonies in 1619 when a Virginian purchased Africans from a Dutch shipper. Colonial Africans originally were servants, largely indistinct from indentured servants of other races who bound themselves to service for a limited number of years in return for free passage to Britain's American colonies. But African slavery soon became established in colonial law. In 1664, Maryland passed legislation declaring that all "Negroes or other slaves hereafter imported . . . shall serve for life."[5] The law also made slaves of the children of slaves.

The compromises made at the Constitutional Convention allowed the United States to form, but they also allowed slavery to grow and spread. By 1808, when Congress banned the further importation of slaves from Africa, the slave population had reached 1 million, and it continued growing through natural increase thereafter. With neither slave nor free forces dominant politically, Congress continued to compromise. The Missouri Compromise (1820) banned slavery in the territories north of the southern border of Missouri, thus keeping most of the vast lands of the Louisiana Purchase free. The Compromise of 1850 allowed territories captured in the Mexican War to decide for themselves whether to be free or slave. The Kansas-Nebraska Act (1854) undid the Missouri Compromise by allowing each territory to vote on whether to allow slavery. The Supreme Court further extended the reach of slavery in ***Dred Scott v. Sandford*** (1857).[6]

***Dred Scott v. Sandford*:** *The 1857 Supreme Court decision declaring that blacks could not be citizens and Congress could not ban slavery in the territories.*

Dred Scott, a slave who had moved with his master from the slave state of Missouri to the free Wisconsin Territory and then back to Missouri, sued in federal court for his freedom based on his extended stay in free territory. The Supreme Court's decision in the case, written by Chief Justice Roger Taney, a former slave owner, declared (1) that no black—slave or free—could be an American citizen, and thus that no black could sue in a federal court; (2) that blacks were "beings of an inferior order" who had "no rights which the white man was bound to respect"; (3) that the Declaration of Independence's statement that "all men are created equal" did not include men of African heritage; (4) that Congress's authority to "make all needful Rules and Regulations respecting the Territory . . . [of] the United States" did not include the right to prohibit slavery in those territories; and (5) that slaves were the property of their owners, so freeing Scott would violate his owner's Fifth Amendment right not to be deprived of his property without due process of law. With this decision, the regulation of slavery in the territories was removed from the national authority of Congress and placed in the hands of local authorities in the territories.

The 1860 election of Abraham Lincoln (1861–65), who opposed the extension of slavery, prompted southern states to secede from the union. During the ensuing Civil War, Lincoln issued the Emancipation Proclamation, which made slavery illegal in those states in rebellion as of January 1, 1863. The Proclamation did not pertain to border states that retained slavery but remained in the Union. Slavery was finally ended in the United States following Union victory and ratification of the Thirteenth Amendment in 1865 (see Figure 5.1).

Color Code: Criminal procedure Participation Equality

Amendment	Year	Provision
Thirteenth	1865	Prohibits slavery in the United States
Fourteenth	1868	Makes all persons born in the United States citizens of the United States and prohibits states from denying persons within its jurisdiction the privileges or immunities of citizens, the due process of law, and equal protection of the laws; apportionment by whole persons
Fifteenth	1870	Prohibits states from denying the right to vote on account of race
Nineteenth	1920	Guarantees women the right to vote
Twenty-Fourth	1964	Prohibits poll taxes

FIGURE 5.1 Constitutional Amendments That Pertain to Civil Rights

Since 1865, increasing equality and participation has been an important theme in Constitutional amendments.

Restrictions on Citizenship

The Constitution was not explicit on birthright citizenship, but the clause requiring that presidents be natural-born citizens seemingly implies that people born in the United States are citizens.[7] Yet on the basis of ethnic background, some groups were denied the status of **citizenship** and the privileges it entailed, such as property rights and the protection of civil liberties.

citizenship: *Full-fledged membership in a nation.*

The Constitution explicitly allows people not born in the United States to become citizens through naturalization by granting Congress the authority "to establish a uniform rule of naturalization." Congress's first such law, the Naturalization Act of 1790, restricted citizenship to "free white persons" who had lived in the United States for two years, swore allegiance to the United States, and had "good character." Though restrictive on race, the act allowed Catholics, Jews, and other "free white persons" to become naturalized citizens, rights that most European nations did not allow. The act also declared people born overseas to parents who were U.S. citizens to be natural-born citizens. Congress first allowed non-whites to become naturalized citizens in 1870, when it extended naturalization to "persons of African descent."

Native Americans. In 1823, the Supreme Court declared that Native Americans were merely inhabitants, "an inferior race of people, without the privileges of citizens."[8] The legislative policy of the United States toward Native Americans included forcible removal from various territories under the Indian Removal Act of 1830 and the creation of land reserved for them (reservations) starting with the Indian Appropriations Act in 1851. The Fourteenth Amendment's citizenship clause did not remedy this situation: The Court ruled in 1884 that the clause did not provide citizenship to Native Americans born on reservations because reservations are not fully under the jurisdiction of the United States.[9] Not until the Indian Citizenship Act of 1924 did Congress provide natural-born citizenship to Native Americans born on reservations.

Latinos. Latinos in the Southwestern United States arrived prior to American settlers. They lived in areas from Texas to California, and Tejanos, the term for people of Mexican descent living in Texas, fought alongside other Texans in battles against the Mexican Army. Perhaps due to the close affiliation with Mexico, many Tejanos, Californios, and other Latinos lost their properties after the Treaty of Guadalupe Hidalgo, which ended the Mexican-American War and resulted in Mexico ceding to the United States what is now California, Nevada, New Mexico, Arizona, Utah, Texas, Wyoming, and Colorado. After the United States annexed Texas, Anglos forcibly expelled many Tejanos. Those who remained, though formally granted citizenship, were often faced with "second-class" status with few recognized rights.[10]

The history of the treatment of Latinos by the U.S. government is a mixed one. In the late 1920s and early 1930s, approximately 2 million people of Mexican descent were deported to Mexico due to economic and political pressures stemming from the Great Depression. Roughly 60 percent of those expelled during what became known as the Mexican Repatriation were U.S. citizens. "Federal, state, and local governments working together involuntarily removed many U.S. citizens of Mexican ancestry, many of whom were born in the United States. These citizens cannot be said to have been 'repatriated' to their native land."[11] As a result of the Mexican Repatriation, the nation lost roughly one-third of its Mexican population. A similar program took place in the 1950s under the offensive name "Operation Wetback,"[12] and similar "roundups" have occurred as recently as 1997.[13] In 2005, the California Assembly passed the "Apology Act for the 1930s Mexican Repatriation Program" in recognition of the coerced removal of legal residents of Mexican descent.

The Mexican Repatriation delayed for decades the full emergence of the Latino community as a political, economic, and social force in the United States.[14] Civil rights enjoyed by Latinos today were not always recognized as such, nor are they guaranteed to be so in the future. As Latinos continue to be the fastest-growing ethnic group in the United States, it is clear there have been many gates to political participation placed before them, which are discussed more in depth in Chapter 11, Voting and Participation.

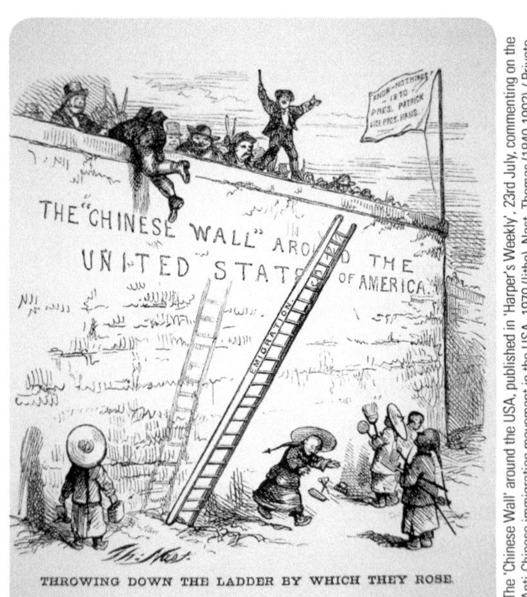

IMAGE 5.2 Drawing of a wall depicting the exclusion of Chinese immigrants from the United States.

The 'Chinese Wall' around the USA, published in 'Harper's Weekly', 23rd July, commenting on the Anti-Chinese immigration movement in the USA, 1970 (litho), Nast, Thomas (1840-1902) / Private Collection / Peter Newark Pictures / The Bridgeman Art Library

Asian Americans. Even after Congress allowed "persons of African descent" to become naturalized citizens in 1870, Asians still could not become naturalized citizens. Often states enacted discriminatory legislation to bar Asians from benefiting from opportunities granted to other residents. California's 1879 constitution prohibited Chinese from voting and from employment in state and local government. In 1913, California prohibited Japanese immigrants from purchasing farmland.[15]

Indeed, fear of Chinese immigrants led to an 1882 prohibition on the immigration of Chinese to America. That ban was the first significant restriction on immigration to the United States. Congress extended this ban to all Asians in 1921. The ban stayed in effect until 1943, when Congress allowed an annual quota of 105 immigrants from China, a World War II ally. The 1943 act also allowed Chinese to become naturalized citizens but did not allow other Asians to do so. Congress ended this restriction on Asian naturalization in 1952 but kept strict limits on the number of Asian immigrants until 1965.

Beyond the setbacks of the anti-Asian immigration policies, President Franklin Delano Roosevelt (1933–45), following the Japanese attack on Pearl Harbor, issued an executive order for the evacuation of all 110,000 people of Japanese ancestry who resided west of the Rocky Mountains—whether citizen (most of them) or not—and their placement in relocation camps. Congress ratified the president's order, and in 1944 the Supreme Court endorsed it in *Korematsu v. United States,* ruling that the authority for relocation was within the war power of the United States.[16]

Although the government justified the program on the grounds of military necessity rather than racial animosity, it did not attempt wholesale roundups of German Americans despite the existence of the German American Bund, a pro-Nazi association with about twenty thousand members before the war. That the government even rounded up Japanese American children from orphanages suggests that racial animosity was more important than security concerns.[17] The program remained in effect through the war years, although the government filed no charges of disloyalty or subversion against any person of Japanese ancestry. Many Japanese Americans valiantly served the United States in segregated military units during the war.

Immigration Limits. Congress used immigration laws to keep out ethnic groups as well as anyone considered undesirable, including "idiots," insane people, paupers, felons, polygamists, anarchists, and people coming for "immoral purposes."[18] Immigration officials used the morality clauses to keep homosexuals from entering the country until 1979.[19] During the last several presidential elections, Democrats have consistently favored increasing immigration to the United States along with a "path to citizenship." On the Republican side nominees have taken both sides of the issue. The 2000 and 2004 Republican nominee, George W. Bush, favored increased immigration, as did 2008 Republican nominee John McCain. In 2012, Republican nominee Mitt Romney suggested that strict conditions for undocumented residents in the United States would lead to "self deportation." In 2016, Republican presidential nominee Donald Trump proposed building a wall between Mexico and the United States as well as prohibiting Muslims from entering the United States.

In the early twentieth century, immigration soared, only to drop back during World War I. After the war, the Ku Klux Klan (KKK) resurfaced, now targeting immigrants, Catholics, and Jews as well as blacks. With nearly 5 million members and chapters throughout the country, the KKK joined others with less violent supremacist beliefs to pressure Congress to limit immigration.[20] The Immigration Act of 1924 established quotas for ethnic groups based on the proportion of Americans from each nationality resident in 1890, thereby severely limiting the number of whites considered to be of "lower race"—that is, those from southern and eastern Europe,[21] who constituted a huge proportion of immigrants from the 1890s on. This also reduced the number of Jewish immigrants eligible to enter during the critical years before World War II and the Holocaust. Under the act, the quota for Italy, for example, dropped more than 90 percent[22] from the percentage allowed in the Immigration Act of 1921, which also established quotas but based them on the proportion of each nationality resident in 1910.

In 1952, President Harry S. Truman (1945–53), claiming that such quotas were un-American, vetoed a bill that continued the national quota system, but Congress overrode his veto. With the Immigration and Nationality Act of 1965, Congress rescinded the quota system and the especially severe restrictions on Asian immigration. Today, to apply for citizenship, one must have had legal permanent residence for five years, or three years if married to a U.S. citizen. Applicants also must be of good moral character and must be able to pass a test on questions such as "who elects the president?"

Racial Segregation and Discrimination

The end of slavery did not make former slaves equal citizens. Immediately after the war, southern states wrote new constitutions that severely limited the civil and political rights of the freedmen. These so-called black codes prevented them from voting, owning land, and leaving their plantations. Congress responded with the Civil Rights Act of 1866, which guaranteed the right of freedmen to make contracts, sue in court if those contracts were violated, and own property. Congress also established military rule over the former Confederate states, which would end in a state when it passed a new state constitution that guaranteed black suffrage and when it ratified the Fourteenth Amendment. With former Confederates barred from voting, blacks constituted a majority of the electorate in several states, and more than six hundred freedmen served in state legislatures during **Reconstruction**, as this era was called.

Reconstruction: *The period from 1865 to 1877 in which the former Confederate states gained readmission to the Union and the federal government passed laws to help the emancipated slaves.*

The Fourteenth Amendment (1868), in addition to guaranteeing that no state shall deny any person due process of law (see Chapter 4), prohibits states from denying any person the **equal protection** of the law. It also makes all people born in the United States citizens of the United States, overturning the Supreme Court's ruling in the *Dred Scott* case that blacks could not be U.S. citizens. In an attempt to prevent states from rescinding the right of black suffrage, the Fifteenth Amendment (1870) declared that the right to vote could not be abridged on account of race.

equal protection clause: *Prevents states from denying any person the equal protection of the laws (Fourteenth Amendment).*

Opponents of freedmen rights turned to violence. In 1866, Confederate veterans formed the Ku Klux Klan (KKK), a terrorist organization aimed at restoring white supremacy. In 1873, white supremacists massacred more than a hundred blacks in Colfax, Louisiana, as part of an ongoing election dispute. The federal government brought charges against three of the perpetrators, but the Supreme Court reversed their conviction, arguing that the Fourteenth Amendment gave Congress the authority to act only against states that violated civil rights (public discrimination), not against individuals who did so (private discrimination).[23]

Reconstruction ended with a deal over the 1876 election. A close and contested race between Republican Rutherford B. Hayes and Democrat Samuel Tilden was resolved when southern Democrats in Congress agreed to allow Hayes to become president in return for the withdrawal of federal troops from the South. Freed from military rule, white supremacist groups such as the KKK embarked on a campaign of lynching and other forms of terrorism against blacks.

State governments were not responsive to the victims because, despite the Fifteenth Amendment, southern politicians established a set of rules that kept blacks from voting. **Poll taxes** limited the voting of poor blacks (as well as of poor whites). The white primary took advantage of the fact that, with the Republican Party negatively associated with Lincoln and the Civil War, the Democratic Party completely dominated southern politics. Therefore, whoever won the local Democratic primary for an office was sure to win in the general election. Excluding blacks from voting in Democratic primaries meant that blacks had no effective vote at all. Even so, states used literacy tests to disqualify voters. These involved reading and interpreting difficult passages. To avoid disqualifying white voters as well, grandfather

poll taxes: *Tax on voting; prohibited by the Twenty-Fourth Amendment (1964).*

clauses gave exemptions to men whose grandfathers had been eligible to vote. The men who received these exemptions were, of course, always white (see Chapter 11 for further discussion of these techniques and an example of a literacy test).

South Carolina Dept. of Archives and History

South Carolina Dept. of Archives and History

IMAGES 5.3 AND 5.4 In segregated school systems, the schools for black children and the schools for white children were almost never equal. These insurance photographs show Liberty Hill Colored School and Summerton Graded School in Clarendon County, South Carolina, in 1948. They were used as evidence in *Briggs v. Elliott*, one of the school segregation cases decided with *Brown v. Board of Education* (1954).

These legal strategies effectively disenfranchised black men. In addition, state and local **Jim Crow laws** enforced segregation of whites and blacks in all public places. When a New Orleans civil rights organization challenged a Louisiana law requiring segregated railway cars by having Homer Plessy, who was one-eighth black, sit in the whites-only car, the Supreme Court upheld the segregation.[24] *Plessy v. Ferguson* (1896) established the **separate-but-equal doctrine**, which held that states could segregate the races without violating the equal protection clause of the Fourteenth Amendment as long as the separate facilities were equal.[25] Southern states segregated schools, libraries, and other public institutions and required the segregation of restaurants, inns, and other places of public accommodation. The facilities were almost never equal. African Americans in northern states often experienced discrimination in hiring, housing, hotels, and restaurants, though segregation was not enforced by law. African Americans could serve in the military but generally in segregated units under white officers. During the late nineteenth and early twentieth centuries, discrimination was state-sponsored in the South; elsewhere in the nation, people engaged in private discrimination without challenge.

Jim Crow laws: *Southern laws that established strict segregation of the races and gave their name to the segregation era.*

separate-but-equal doctrine: *Supreme Court doctrine that upheld segregation as long as there were equivalent facilities for blacks.*

Ethnic Segregation and Discrimination

Latinos and other ethnic groups experienced many of the same discriminatory practices as did African Americans. The separate-but-equal doctrine of *Plessy v. Ferguson* (1896) applied to Hispanics and other minorities. White voters instituted segregation in the South and the West. Phoenix, Arizona, ran separate schools for blacks, Native Americans, and Mexicans.[26] California ran separate schools for Asians as well as Mexicans,[27] while Texas kept Mexican Americans in separate classrooms.[28] In areas of the Southwestern United States, Latinos were required to sit in the back of buses, sit in movie theater balconies, and attend separate public schools. The end of segregation practices aimed at African Americans did not necessarily end them for Latinos (see Table 5.1).

Essential Knowledge

The *Plessy* decision is an example of when the United States did not uphold the rights of minorities. It was later overturned by the *Brown* decision (1954) and the Civil Rights Act of 1964.

TABLE 5.1 Timeline of Civil Rights and Latinos

Year	Event
1912	New Mexico enters the union as an officially bilingual state, with voting in both Spanish and English, as well as bilingual education.
1917	The U.S. Congress passes the Jones Act, granting citizenship to Puerto Ricans.
1921	*Orden Hijos de América* (Order of the Sons of America) organizes Mexican American workers to raise awareness of civil rights issues and fight for fair wages, education, and housing.
1928	Octaviano Larrazolo (R-NM) becomes the first Latino U.S. senator.
1929	The League of United Latin American Citizens (LULAC) organizes against discrimination and segregation and promotes education among Latinos. It remains the largest and longest-lasting Latino civil rights group in the country.
1948	The American G.I. Forum forms in Texas to combat discrimination and improve the status of Latinos; branches eventually form in twenty-three states.
1954	*Hernandez v. Texas* strikes down discrimination based on class and ethnic distinctions.
1965	Congress passes the Voting Rights Act.
1965	Cesar Chavez and Dolores Huerta found the United Farm Workers association. It becomes the largest and most important farm worker union in the nation. Huerta becomes the first woman to lead such a union. The Grape Boycott becomes one of the most significant social justice movements for farm workers in the United States.
1966	*Katzenbach v. Morgan* allows Congress to prohibit English proficiency voting requirements for Puerto Ricans in New York.
1968	The Mexican American Legal Defense and Education Fund (MALDEF) is established, becoming the first legal fund to pursue protection of the civil rights of Mexican Americans. The Puerto Rican Legal Defense and Education Fund is founded in 1972.
1970	*Cisneros v. Corpus Christi Independent School District* extends the *Brown* decision to Latinos.
1973	*White v. Regester* calls for the creation of single-member election districts to prevent the dilution of Latino and African American voting strength.
1974	The first major Latino voter registration organization, the Southwest Voter Registration Education Project (SVREP) launches, registering more than 2 million Latino voters in the first twenty years.
1975	Congress votes to expand the Voting Rights Act to require language assistance at the polls and that election materials be available in multiple languages.
1982	*Plyler v. Doe* extends Fourteenth Amendment equal protection to children of undocumented workers.
1994	*Johnson v. DeGrandy* establishes the importance of proportionality as part of the totality of circumstances that must be considered in the redistricting process in this case from Florida involving Cuban Americans.
2001	The DREAM Act first introduced in Congress.
2009	Sonia Sotomayor becomes first Latino Supreme Court Justice.
2013	*Shelby v. Holder* strikes down original formulas from the Voting Rights Act of 1965 that trigger requirements for states and local governments to obtain preclearance for changes to their election laws.

Source: Derived from "Latino Civil Rights Timeline, 1903 to 2006" in Teaching Tolerance, Southern Poverty Law Center, http://www.tolerance.org /latino-civil-rights-timeline.

Women's Suffrage

By law and by custom, women were also excluded from public life from the earliest days of the nation. In 1776, Abigail Adams had urged her husband, John Adams, to "remember the ladies" in drafting the nation's founding documents. In language similar to that later used by Jefferson in the Declaration, she warned, "if particular care and attention is not paid to the ladies, we are determined to foment a rebellion, and will not hold ourselves bound by any laws in which we have no voice or representation."[29] Nevertheless, neither the Declaration nor the Constitution made any provision for women's rights. Rather, the states continued the English policy of coverture, which granted married women no rights independent of their husbands. They could not own property, keep their own wages, or sign contracts. As for voting, each state set its own rules. In 1789, only New Jersey allowed women the right to vote (provided the women met the state's property requirements), a right the people of the state rescinded via referendum in 1807.[30]

In 1848 leaders of the **women's suffrage movement** met in Seneca Falls, New York, to organize for the right to vote. They prepared a "Declaration of Sentiments" that used the language of the Declaration of Independence to assert that "all men and women are created equal," but few results came from this meeting. Then, in 1869, Susan B. Anthony and Elizabeth Cady Stanton formed the National Woman Suffrage Association (NWSA), which lobbied for the right of women to vote and unsuccessfully opposed the Fifteenth Amendment unless it was changed to include women's suffrage. With the NWSA focused on gaining national suffrage through constitutional amendment, an alternative organization, the American Woman Suffrage Association (AWSA), formed to press for state-by-state suffrage rights.

women's suffrage movement: *Movement to grant women the right to vote.*

In 1872, a Missouri voting registrar prohibited suffragist Virginia Minor from registering to vote. Minor sued, arguing that the privileges of citizenship, as guaranteed by the Fourteenth Amendment, include the right to vote. The Supreme Court ruled, however, that citizenship does not imply a right to vote.[31]

That same year the Court ruled that the right to practice law was not a privilege or immunity guaranteed by the Fourteenth Amendment, allowing Illinois to keep law a male-only profession. Representing common views at the time, one justice wrote, "The paramount destiny and mission of women are to fulfill the noble and benign offices of wife and mother. This is the law of the Creator."[32] States passed various types of so-called protective legislation that limited the jobs women could work at and/or the number of hours they could work. These laws had the express purpose of protecting women because of their status as wives and mothers, but their main impact was to act as a gate that put women at a disadvantage in the employment market.[33]

Although women's rights advocates typically opposed protective legislation, they focused their attention on the right to vote. With the courts rejecting a gateway to voting through the Fourteenth Amendment, suffragists focused on the legislative arena. Anthony presented the 1887 Congress with ten thousand petition signatures demanding women's suffrage. In 1894, suffragists presented the New York legislature with six hundred thousand signatures. The suffragist movement, though, was not universally admired; many people opposed voting equality for women because it threatened their notions of appropriate gender roles. In 1913, a mob attacked a suffrage parade in Washington, D.C., and suffragist protests outside the White House in 1917 led to hundreds of arrests.

While state control of voting gave southern states the power to disenfranchise blacks, it also gave western states the power to experiment with women's suffrage. The territory of Wyoming granted women's suffrage in 1869 and continued it upon statehood in 1890. Males in Colorado voted for women's suffrage in 1893. Utah granted women the right to vote in 1895. In 1913, Illinois granted women the right to vote for president but not for other national offices. In 1916, the people of Montana elected the first woman to serve in the U.S.

Library of Congress Prints and Photographs Division [LC-USZ62-31799]

IMAGE 5.5 During World War I, members of the National Woman's Party picketed the White House. Wearing banners announcing their colleges, they challenged President Woodrow Wilson to bring home the concern for liberty that he expressed for Europe. More than 150 women were arrested, and about 100 were sentenced to federal prisons, where some went on hunger strikes and were force-fed.

House of Representatives, Jeannette Rankin (see Figure 5.2).

Suffragist amendments failed numerous times in Congress before receiving the necessary two-thirds vote in both chambers in 1919.[34] By August 1920, with effective lobbying by suffragist groups, three-quarters of the states ratified the Nineteenth Amendment, guaranteeing women the right to vote in the November 1920 presidential election (see Chapter 11, Voting and Participation).

Continued Gender Discrimination

Nevertheless, public law and private attitudes constituted gates that blocked women from full participation in the nation's public life. Radical feminists pushed for an equal rights amendment, which would have overturned protective legislation and other laws that treated men and women differently. Although introduced in Congress in 1923 and every year thereafter, it was not taken seriously. Even in 1945, only a minority of white males nationally thought that women should be able to take jobs outside the home.[35]

Not surprisingly, the federal and state governments were responsive to these sorts of views. As late as 1972, eleven states continued to enforce coverture laws.[36] Louisiana, for example, gave a husband, "as 'head and master' of property jointly owned with his wife," the complete right to dispose of such property without his wife's consent.[37] Teachers were commonly forced to retire if they got married.[38] Outside of coverture laws, Social Security provided survivors' benefits for children if their working fathers died but not if their working mothers died. It similarly provided unemployment benefits to children of unemployed fathers but not to children of unemployed mothers. Males in the military received benefits for their dependents that females in the military did not receive. Idaho gave preferences to men over women in determining who would administer a dead relative's estate. Utah required parents to support sons until age 21 but daughters only until age 18. A woman could not work as a bartender in Michigan unless she was the wife or daughter of the bar's owner.[39]

Because women were treated differently than men under the law, many laws also discriminated against men. Colorado allowed females to drink beer at age 18; males had to wait until they turned 21. California, like many states, made it a crime for males of any age to have sexual relations with females under the age of 18 but had no corresponding penalty for females having sexual relations with underage males. Alabama,

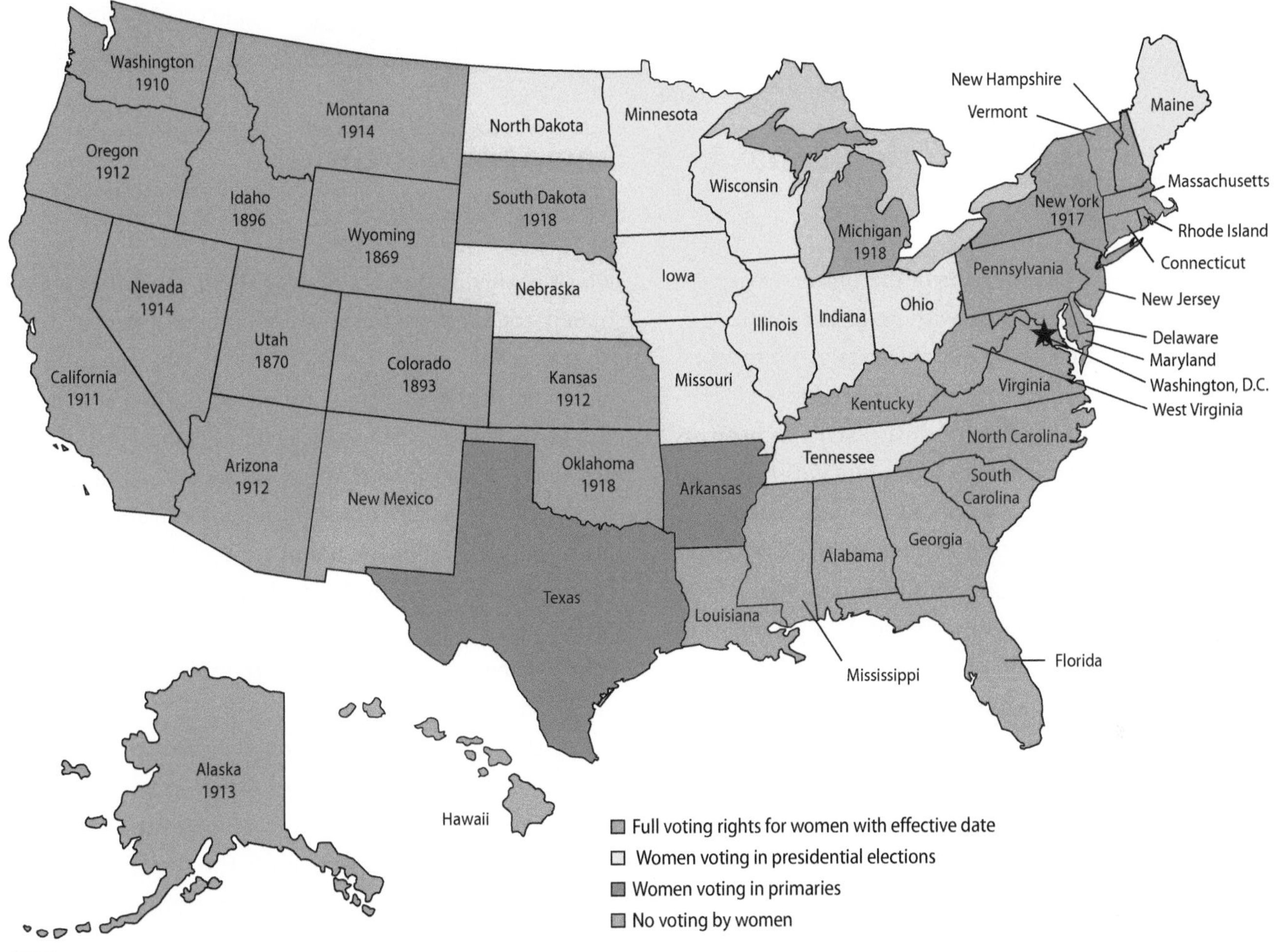

FIGURE 5.2 Women's Suffrage Before 1920

Because states control voting laws, women's suffrage advocates campaigned at the state level, and, before the Nineteenth Amendment was ratified in 1920, women could vote in some elections in most states. The Nineteenth Amendment superseded state law, stating that the right to vote could not be denied or abridged by the United States, or by any state, on account of sex.

Source: Data from Mary Beth Norton et al., *A People and a Nation: A History of the United States*, 8th ed. (Boston: Houghton Mifflin, 2008), 608.

like many states, imposed alimony obligations on men only. New York allowed unwed mothers, but not unwed fathers, to block the adoption of their children. Florida provided property tax relief to widows but not to widowers. Even today, only males have to register for the military draft.[40] Many of these laws were based on an implicit assumption that women, viewed as the weaker sex, needed special protection by the government.[41] As late as 1961, the Supreme Court exempted women from jury duty because they were "the center of home and family life."[42] Hillary Clinton, who in 2008 became the first female to win a presidential primary, became the first female to win a major party presidential nomination in 2016, and received more popular votes in the 2016 election than President Trump.

ELECTION 2016

Voting Behavior of Demographic Groups

THE BATTLE FOR CIVIL rights in the United States has had many consequences, with perhaps the most important ones concerning more diverse electorates brought about by expansions of voting-rights protections. Because the Democratic Party has been at the forefront of these changes, nonwhite voters have been an ever-increasing part of the Democratic Party's constituency. Not since Lyndon Johnson in 1964 has a Democrat received a majority of the white vote. In fact, the contest for the Democratic presidential nomination between former Secretary of State Hillary Clinton and Vermont Senator Bernie Sanders was largely decided by nonwhite voters, who in state after state supported Clinton over Sanders by substantial margins. Secretary Clinton started the campaign with substantial advantages in name recognition and campaign donations over Senator Sanders. Sanders, who labels himself a "democratic socialist," called for an economic "revolution" that would reverse the growing inequality trend in the United States, where the top 1 percent receive an ever-increasing share of the nation's income. Senator Sanders nearly upset Secretary Clinton in Iowa, which is 92 percent white; he won the New Hampshire primary, where 94 percent of the residents are white.[43] After that, though, the campaign shifted to more diverse states such as Nevada (28 percent Latino)[44] and the southern states of Super Tuesday with their large African American populations. Clinton won 45 percent[45] of the Latino vote in Nevada[46] and about 80 percent of the African American vote on Super Tuesday.[47] In South Carolina, she won the vote of senior African Americans by a whopping 96–3 margin.[48] After that, despite Sanders's narrow victory in Michigan, which is only 21 percent African American.[49] the threat of Senator Sanders taking the nomination largely disappeared.

Minorities are a small proportion of the Republican constituency, so despite Donald Trump's insults to Mexicans, Muslims, and African Americans,[50] he rather easily won his party's nomination. While Trump's two major opponents for the nomination, Senators Ted Cruz (R-TX) and Marco Rubio (R-FL), have parents from Cuba, Trump nevertheless won the Latino vote in Nevada; the total number of Latino voters in the state was very small.[51]

In the 2016 general election, African Americans made up 12 percent and Latinos made up 11 percent of the electorate, compared with 13 percent and 10 percent in 2012, respectively.[52] The slight decline in African American voters is not surprising given the enthusiasm from President Obama's reelection campaign. The increase in Latino voting since 2012 is probably a result of their increased percentage of the population, the anti-Mexican rhetoric of Republican nominee Donald Trump, and get-out-the-vote programs by various Latino groups, including the nation's largest Spanish-language television network, Univision.[53] The 2016 *New York Times* exit poll showed that Latinos voted for Democratic nominee and Secretary of State Hillary Rodham Clinton by a 65–29 margin. Alternatively, whites voted for Trump by a 58–37 margin. As whites were 70 percent of the electorate, they were able to win. Future Republicans are going to have to nominate candidates who can find support among the ever-growing Latino population, as President George W. Bush did.

5.3 The Expansion of Equal Protection

Assess how equal protection has expanded

Today, Congress, constitutional amendments, and court decisions have put an end to the public discrimination documented in previous sections, and no clause has been as powerful in this effort as the equal protection clause of the Fourteenth Amendment, which prohibits states from denying any person the equal protection of the law. The amendment gives Congress the authority to enforce its provisions by appropriate legislation, adding to Congress's enumerated powers by allowing the passage of laws that prevent states from discriminating. Additionally, the Supreme Court, through the power of judicial review, retains the authority to strike state laws that violate equal protection. During the first half of the twentieth century, the meaning of equality changed for many Americans, and they organized to press the federal government into playing a crucial role to fight both public and private discrimination. This section examines gradual expansion of equal protection prior to the civil rights movement.

State Action

Shortly after the passage of the Fourteenth Amendment, Congress tried to ban private discrimination at inns, public conveyances, theaters, and other public places. The Supreme Court rejected congressional authority to do so in the *Civil Rights Cases* (1883), ruling that the Fourteenth Amendment prohibited public discrimination by the states only, not private discrimination by businesses or individuals. From the 1880s until the 1940s, the federal government remained passive with regard to discrimination, allowing states and locales to require segregation of the races and permitting public and private institutions to make their own rules regarding it.

In 1948, however, the Court ruled that private discrimination can be prohibited if it involves significant **state action**. The case involved housing. A group of homeowners signed a contract pledging never to sell their homes to blacks, but one of the homeowners did so. The neighbors sued to prevent the new owners from taking possession of the house, and the state supreme court ruled in favor of the neighbors. The U.S. Supreme Court reversed the state supreme court, ruling that judicial enforcement of the discriminatory private contract constitutes state action and thus is prohibited by the Fourteenth Amendment.[54]

state action: *Action by a state, as opposed to a private person, that constitutes discrimination and therefore is an equal protection violation.*

Judicial Review

While the state-action doctrine allowed the Supreme Court to prohibit limited types of private discrimination, the equal protection clause of the Fourteenth Amendment is better suited to fighting public discrimination. In the next two decades, the Supreme Court actively applied the equal protection clause of the Fourteenth Amendment to do so. Congress also has the authority to enforce the equal protection clause, but democratically elected legislatures and executives are not necessarily designed to be responsive to minority groups, for they are chosen by a majority of voters. Thus civil rights organizations such as

TABLE 5.2 Supreme Court Scrutiny in Equal Protection Cases

Claim of Discrimination	Standard of Review	Test
Unprotected category	Lowest	Rational basis to achieve a legitimate governmental objective
Sex	Heightened	Exceedingly persuasive justification; use of sex as a governmental category must be substantially related to important governmental objectives
Race, ethnicity, religion, and legally admitted aliens	Strict	Most rigid scrutiny; use of race as a governmental category must be precisely tailored to meet a compelling governmental interest

the National Association for the Advancement of Colored People (NAACP) and the League of United Latin American Citizens (LULAC) turned to the judiciary, whose members are not elected and so do not directly depend on majority support, for assistance in establishing legal equality.

As with civil liberties issues, for which the Court uses the standard of compelling interest (see Chapter 4), in civil rights cases, the Court has constructed tests to determine whether laws violate the equal protection clause. Depending upon the group whose right has been violated, the Court sets different standards of how closely it will scrutinize the law alleged to violate equal protection. There are at least three levels. The Court reserves the toughest standard of review, strict scrutiny, for laws alleged to discriminate on account of race, ethnicity, religion, or status as a legally admitted alien. It uses mid-level, or heightened, scrutiny for laws that discriminate on account of sex and the lowest level of scrutiny, rational basis, for general claims of discrimination (see Table 5.2).

5.4 The End of Legal Restrictions on Civil Rights

Identify the groups at the forefront of the civil rights movement

The events that brought about the government's shift from enforcing discrimination to protecting against it did not begin with the government. It began with pressure from groups who were discriminated against that mobilized on their own behalf. This gateway of public pressure generally involves the use of civil liberties such as freedom of speech and of assembly to engage in protests and other activities aside from voting because minority groups, by definition, do not have the numbers to change policies through the ballot box alone.

The African American soldiers and sailors who fought for freedom in World War II often returned uneasily to their hometowns, particularly in the South, where segregation remained the law. This led to vocal demands for civil rights at home. Additionally, the difficult but ultimately successful integration of Major League Baseball by African American Jackie Robinson in 1947 showed that even the most segregated of American institutions could survive and even thrive following integration.

The three largest legal barriers African Americans faced in the post–World War II era were state-sponsored segregation of supposedly separate-but-equal public facilities, such as schools and buses; the legal right of private businesses not to serve customers or hire people on account of race; and effective prohibitions on the right to vote, such as discriminatorily enforced literacy tests. These gates blocking full civic participation existed throughout the United States but were most prevalent in the former slave states. After we trace the African American struggle for equal rights, we turn to the the Latino movement and then the women's movement, which likewise pressured the government to dismantle ethnic and gender-based discrimination.

Carl Iwasaki/Time Life Pictures/Getty Images

IMAGE 5.6 In 1950, when Linda Brown was entering third grade, her father Oliver Brown tried to enroll her in the Sumner School. The 10-year-old had been going to Monroe School, walking between train tracks and along streets without sidewalks to get there. Although it was closer, Sumner was for white students, and when Oliver Brown was told Linda could not attend, he took his case to the NAACP. Here the family stands in front of their home; Linda is on the left.

Dismantling Public Discrimination Based on Race

Among the most consequential forms of segregation from the Jim Crow era was the mandatory separation of schools for whites and blacks. Beginning in 1935, the NAACP's Legal Defense Fund embarked on a legal campaign—led by Thurgood Marshall—to dismantle the system of separate-but-equal schools in southern and border states that were always separate but rarely equal. After a series of cases in which the Supreme Court struck down specific segregated schools because they were not equal,[55] the Court ruled more generally in ***Brown v. Board of Education*** (1954) that separate schools were inherently unequal, even if the facilities were essentially similar (see Supreme Court Cases: *Brown v. Board of Education*). Segregation in schools violated the equal protection clause of the Fourteenth Amendment. The Fourteenth Amendment only requires that states provide equal protection of the laws, but on the same day as the *Brown* decision, the Supreme Court used the due process clause of the Fifth Amendment to prohibit the national government from denying equal protection.[56]

Brown v. Board of Education: *The 1954 Supreme Court decision striking down segregated schools.*

As historic as the *Brown* decision was, the case by itself did little to desegregate southern schools. Part of the problem was that the Court allowed local circumstances to influence the rate of integration, ambiguously requiring that local districts desegregate "with all deliberate speed."[57] Further, southern segregationists launched a massive resistance to the *Brown* decision. This campaign included "The Southern Manifesto," a document signed by 101 southern members of Congress deploring the *Brown* decision; the denial of state funds to any integrated school; and tuition grants for white students to attend segregated private schools. In addition, unruly segregationist mobs threatened black students seeking to integrate previously white schools. While neither the Supreme Court nor the Dwight D. Eisenhower administration (1953–61) could prevent every school disruption by segregationist mobs, both intervened in Little Rock, Arkansas. Eisenhower federalized the Arkansas National Guard and sent in the 101st Airborne to protect the black students seeking to integrate Central High School, while the Supreme Court, declaring that it had the final say on what the Constitution means, rejected the threat of violence as a justification for delaying integration (see Chapter 13, The Presidency, and Chapter 15, The Judiciary, for more on the Little Rock case).[58]

Essential Knowledge

In the *Brown* decision, the Supreme Court ruled that "Separate educational facilities are inherently unequal." This was a landmark interpretation of the Fourteenth Amendment's equal protection clause.

In 1963, segregationist Governor George Wallace of Alabama famously "stood at the schoolhouse door" to prevent two black students from registering at the University of Alabama. He stepped aside only when President John F. Kennedy (1961–63) sent troops to enforce integration.

Essential Knowledge

Many districts have used cross town busing as a way to integrate schools. The Court has permitted this intra-district busing. However, it never required inter-district busing, busing between school districts.

Nevertheless, with few blacks able to vote, there was little need for southern politicians or school board officials to be responsive to their concerns. Only when the federal government took action did states respond. After Congress cut off federal aid to segregated schools in 1964, many districts began to integrate.[59] The rate of integration increased further in the late 1960s when the Supreme Court ended the "all deliberate speed" era and required an immediate end to segregated schools, thus pushing open the gateways to greater equality.[60]

Outside of schools, civil rights activists fought segregation in public facilities. The first grassroots action to receive nationwide attention was a bus boycott in Montgomery, Alabama. On December 1, 1955, police arrested Rosa Parks, a 42-year-old black seamstress and an active member of the NAACP, for refusing to give her seat to a white person. In response, the black community, led by a 26-year-old Baptist minister, Martin Luther King Jr., launched a boycott of city buses. Blacks walked, bicycled, and shared rides to avoid using the Montgomery bus system. Although the city arrested boycotters, and violent segregationist terrorists firebombed King's home, the boycotters held firm for more than a year. The Supreme Court then declared Montgomery's segregated bus system unconstitutional.[61] A new ordinance allowing blacks to sit anywhere on any bus ended the boycott. King became one of the national leaders of the emerging civil rights movement and Rosa Parks its first heroine.

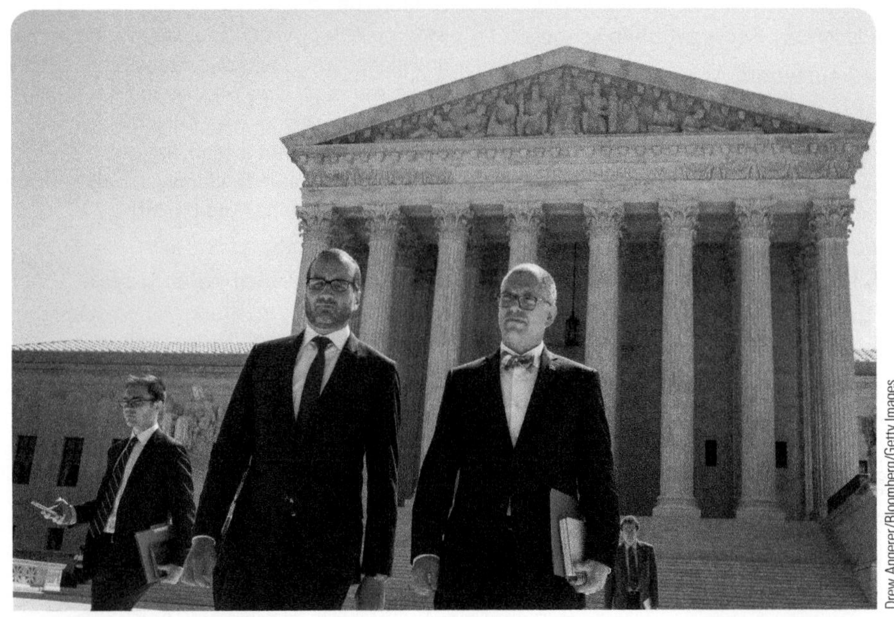

Drew Angerer/Bloomberg/Getty Images

IMAGE 5.7 James "Jim" Obergefell, the named plaintiff in the *Obergefell v. Hodges* case, right, and Chad Griffin, president of the Human Rights Campaign, center, exit the U.S. Supreme Court in Washington, D.C., on Monday, June 22, 2015. The Supreme Court ruled 5–4 that states violate the equal protection clause when they prohibit same-sex marriages.

With the *Brown* precedent in hand, the Supreme Court struck down state-mandated segregation not only in public transportation but also in other public facilities, such as beaches and city auditoriums. Given the massive opposition to the *Brown* decision, however, the Court refused to hear the appeal by a black woman sentenced to prison for the "crime" of marrying a white man.[62] As one justice reportedly said when the Court rejected another interracial marriage case, "One bombshell at a time is enough."[63] Not until 1967 in *Loving v. Virginia* did the Court strike down miscegenation, finding no compelling interest in a law that prohibited interracial marriage.[64]

Dismantling Private Discrimination Based on Race

The decisions of businesses about whether to serve customers or hire workers on account of their race (or sex) were largely beyond judicial authority because the Fourteenth Amendment's equal protection clause only prevents states from discriminating; it does not bar private discrimination. Thus, if a restaurant chose not to serve blacks or an

SUPREME COURT CASES

Hernandez v. Texas (1954)
Brown v. Board of Education (1954)

QUESTIONS: *Hernandez:* Does the equal protection clause allow Texas to exclude Mexican Americans from juries? *Brown:* Can states provide segregated schools for black and white school children?

ORAL ARGUMENT:
Hernandez: January 11, 1954 Brown: December 7–9, 1953

DECISION:
Hernandez: May 3, 1954 (read at http://laws.findlaw.com/us/347/475.html)
Brown: May 17, 1954 (read at http://laws.findlaw.com/us/347/483.html)

OUTCOME:
Hernandez: No. The equal protection clause protects Mexican Americans (9–0).
Brown: No. Separate educational facilities are inherently unequal (9–0).

As noted in Chapter 2, The Constitution, Texas systematically excluded Mexican Americans from the murder trial of Pete Hernandez. Famed attorney and activist Gus Garcia told the Supreme Court that while the intent of the equal protection clause was to prevent racial discrimination against former slaves and their descendants, Texas treated Mexican Americans as a "class apart," and they therefore should be shielded against discriminatory laws by the equal protection clause. The Court agreed.

Two weeks later, the Supreme Court decided the *Brown* case. When Linda Brown was in third grade, her father, with the help of the NAACP, brought a suit against the Topeka school board for refusing to allow her to attend the local school that white children in their neighborhood attended.

In *Plessy v. Ferguson* (1896), the Supreme Court had ruled that the equal protection clause of the Fourteenth Amendment did not prohibit the states from establishing separate-but-equal facilities for whites and blacks. The Court did not really begin to look at whether the facilities were equal or not until 1938, when it held that Missouri's paying for blacks to go to law school out of state was not the same as providing facilities within the state that were equal to its white law school.* A pair of 1950 cases declared, first, that admitting a black to an all-white school but forcing him to sit in a separate row and dine at a separate table was unconstitutional,† and second, that the equality of separate schools had to be compared on both objective factors that could be measured, such as the number of faculty members, and subjective factors that could not be measured, such as the reputation of the faculty.‡

The *Brown* case came to the Supreme Court with similar desegregation cases from South Carolina, Virginia, Delaware, and Washington, D.C. Thurgood Marshall, who was in charge of legal strategy for the NAACP and would later become the first African American to serve on the Supreme Court, argued the *Brown* case. He readily admitted that the schools in Linda Brown's case were roughly equal in objective characteristics but argued that segregation in and of itself denied black students the equal protection of the laws by creating a feeling of inferiority among them.

The Supreme Court's preliminary vote following the arguments showed a majority favoring striking down segregation, with two or three dissenters. Chief Justice Earl Warren, however, thought that a decision that was bound to be met with resistance in the South should be unanimous if at all possible. Following several months of bargaining and persuasion, he eventually got every member of the Court to agree that the Court should strike down school segregation.

**Missouri ex rel. Gaines v. Canada*, 305 U.S. 337 (1938).
† *McLaurin v. Oklahoma*, 339 U.S. 637 (1950).
‡ *Sweatt v. Painter*, 339 U.S. 629 (1950).

Thinking Critically

1. Can separate schools ever be equal?
2. Why were the courts more likely to be responsive to the problems of segregation than the legislature would be?

employer chose not to hire them, there was little a court could do unless Congress passed legislation forbidding such actions. The effort to dismantle private discrimination thus took two tracks: protests to pressure businesses into serving blacks, and lobbying to pressure Congress into passing legislation that would make private discrimination in commercial matters illegal.

The grassroots protests began when four African American freshmen at North Carolina Agricultural and Technical College in Greensboro sat down at the whites-only counter at Woolworth's, asked for coffee, and refused to leave when they were not served. Within weeks, the sit-ins spread to dozens of other cities. One protest leader, Diane Nash, along with other young participants in the sit-ins, formed the Student Nonviolent Coordinating Committee (SNCC), which along with the Congress of Racial Equality (CORE) served as the more activist "younger brothers" of the NAACP.

Essential Knowledge

King's "Letter from Birmingham Jail" is an eloquent statement about the quest for equality provided for in the Fourteenth Amendment's equal protection clause.

In 1961, CORE organized freedom rides, trips on interstate buses into the segregated South, where the integrated buses were legal under federal law even though they violated local segregation rules. Mobs attacked the buses—firebombing one of them—and beat the riders. Under pressure from the federal government, including protection of the riders by federal marshals, the states eventually agreed not to interfere with interstate travelers.[65]

Essential Knowledge

With the Civil Rights Act of 1964, Congress sought to enforce school integration, which was required under the Fourteenth Amendment. Furthermore, by exercising its power under the commerce clause, Congress sought to end other forms of discriminatory practices such as discrimination in places of employment.

In the spring of 1963, Martin Luther King Jr.'s Southern Christian Leadership Conference (SCLC) led demonstrations in Birmingham, Alabama, to bring about the integration of downtown businesses. The police met demonstrators with fire hoses, police dogs, and cattle prods. Police arrested hundreds of protesters, including King. When white clergymen questioned why King, an outsider, had come to Birmingham, King answered in his famous "Letter from Birmingham Jail": "I am in Birmingham because injustice is here."[66] Rejecting violence, King insisted that peaceful civil disobedience was the only gateway to negotiation. The negotiations took place and ended with Birmingham businesses agreeing to integrate lunch counters and hire more blacks. Nevertheless, or perhaps because of this, members of the KKK exploded a bomb at a local black church on a Sunday morning, murdering four young girls.

Essential Knowledge

Affirmative action programs are designed to ameliorate the impact of past discriminatory practices. These programs do take race into account. They are controversial. Some judges insist that the Constitution be color blind. Other judges believe that only policies that harm minority groups are prohibited.

Earlier that summer, King had led two hundred thousand protesters at the March on Washington for Jobs and Freedom. Though the march grew out of historic employment discrimination against African Americans, it is now remembered mostly as a march for civil rights. It was there that King delivered his historic "I Have a Dream" speech, in which he declared that one day the United States would live up to the national creed declared by Thomas Jefferson in the Declaration of Independence: "We hold these truths to be self-evident: that all men are created equal." He also added a line that opponents of affirmative action have frequently used (or misused) to suggest that King would have been opposed to such plans, speaking of the day when his children "will not be judged by the color of their skin but by the content of their character."[67]

Civil Rights Act: *Prohibits discrimination in employment, education, and places of public accommodation (1964).*

President Kennedy proposed a civil rights bill that would have banned discrimination in public accommodations, such as restaurants and hotels. Five days after Kennedy's assassination in November 1963, President Lyndon B. Johnson (1963–69) told Congress that nothing could better honor Kennedy than passage of this bill. The next year, Congress passed the **Civil Rights Act**, which significantly strengthened Kennedy's original bill by also prohibiting employment discrimination on account of "race, color, religion, sex, or national origin."

Because the Fourteenth Amendment's equal protection clause applies only to state-sponsored discrimination, the Supreme Court upheld Congress's authority to ban private discrimination under the interstate commerce clause. Given the Court's broad interpretation of interstate commerce (see Chapter 3, Federalism), the Court ruled that even small inns and restaurants had to abide by the act.[68]

In 1971, the Supreme Court interpreted the Civil Rights Act to limit job qualification requirements that had a disparate impact on whites and blacks.[69] For example, if more whites receive high school diplomas than blacks, requiring a high school diploma for a job would be more harmful to blacks than to whites. A business seeking to establish job requirements that have a disparate impact would have to prove that the requirement is necessary to the job. In the late 1970s and through the 1980s, a more conservative Supreme Court reached a series of decisions that restricted civil rights protections—for example, making disparate impact more difficult to prove and ruling that discrimination against pregnant women was not a form of sex discrimination under the Civil Rights Act.[70] Passing new laws, Congress overturned these Court decisions plus several others, thus demonstrating widespread support for the continued protection of civil rights. The new rules, for example, make it easier to find that job tests have a disparate impact but leave it to the courts to determine whether disparate impact, by taking race into account, conflicts with the equal treatment obligation of the Civil Rights Act.[71]

Dismantling Voting Barriers Based on Race

As noted previously, the end of Reconstruction left black men in the South with a constitutional right to vote but a hostile social and legal environment that made it extremely difficult for them to do so. The Supreme Court pushed things along, striking down grandfather clauses (1915) and white primaries (1944), the latter in a suit filed by the NAACP.[72] Congress and the states pushed things along further, outlawing poll taxes with the Twenty-Fourth Amendment (1964). Martin Luther King Jr. identified four gates that kept blacks from voting: white terrorist control of local governments and sheriffs' departments; arrests on trumped-up charges of those seeking to vote; the discretion given to registrars, where "the latitude for discrimination is almost endless"; and the arbitrary nature of literacy tests.[73]

During the summer of 1964, voting rights supporters from around the country, many of them college students, moved south to help with voter registration drives. Klansmen murdered three of the volunteers in Philadelphia, Mississippi, that June. In March 1965, King organized a voting rights march from Selma to Montgomery, Alabama. With national news media on hand, Alabama police, under the authority of Governor George Wallace, beat the marchers with whips, nightsticks, and cattle prods. Selma natives murdered two more voting rights activists.

Essential Knowledge

Congress passed the Voting Rights Act of 1965 under its power to implement the Fifteenth Amendment. The act prohibited most discriminatory practices in voting.

A week later, President Johnson addressed a joint session of Congress, calling for passage of the strictest possible voting rights legislation. Congress responded by passing the **Voting Rights Act (VRA)** in August 1965. The act limited literacy, interpretation, and other such tests for voting. It required states with low voter registration levels, essentially seven southern states plus Alaska, to receive preclearance from the Justice Department for any changes to its voting laws. It also established new criminal penalties for those who sought to keep people from voting on account of race. The law was an enormous success. By 2008, blacks and whites voted at essentially the same rate nationwide[74] and at slightly higher rates in some southern states.[75] In 2012, blacks had a higher turnout rate than whites.[76]

Voting Rights Act: *Gives the federal government the power to prevent discrimination in voting rights (1965).*

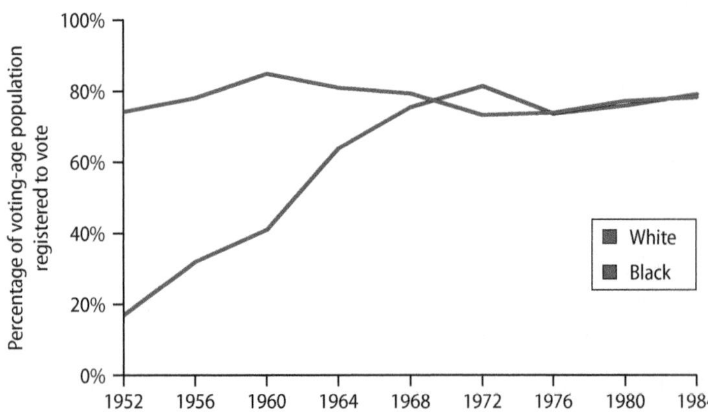

FIGURE 5.3 White and Black Southern Voter Registration, 1952–1984

Dramatic increases in black voter registration preceded passage of the Voting Rights Act in 1965, but substantial equality between whites and blacks did not occur until after its passage.

Source: Data from Harold W. Stanley, *Voter Mobilization and the Politics of Race* (New York: Praeger, 1987), Appendix A.

In 2013, however, the Supreme Court voted 5–4 in *Shelby County v. Holder* to strike down the 1965 formula that established which jurisdictions needed to obtain preclearance.[77] Until Congress passes a new formula, no jurisdictions need to obtain preclearance. This decision may depress future black turnout as states like Texas move to pass voter identification laws that were previously blocked under the VRA by the Justice Department[78] (see Figure 5.3).

While the Civil Rights Act and the VRA ended most forms of legal discrimination in the United States, much discrimination "under the color of law" (i.e., by public officials) still exists. The **Black Lives Matter** movement grew out of a series of incidents between typically young male African Americans and the police officers charged with protecting them. It began after the acquittal of neighborhood watch coordinator George Zimmerman for the killing of Trayvon Martin in 2012 in Sanford, Florida.[79] The movement grew in prominence following several high-profile killings of African Americans, including the following:

Black Lives Matter: *Movement that grew out of the perceived discounting of black lives by police and juries.*

- Oscar Grant by BART transit officers (2009)
- Michael Brown in Ferguson, Missouri (2014)
- Eric Garner (2014), who died from a chokehold by police in New York City after failing to refrain from selling untaxed cigarettes
- 12-year-old Tamir Rice (2014), shot in Cleveland, Ohio, while in possession of a toy gun that lacked the orange band that designates toy guns
- Laquan McDonald (2014), who, while in possession of a knife, was yards away from the Chicago police when they shot him sixteen times
- Freddie Gray (2015), who died from injuries suffered in the back of a police van in Baltimore, Maryland
- Sandra Bland (2015), who died in police custody following an arrest for failing to signal a lane change; she was then taken into custody following her refusal to put out her cigarette after being asked to by the arresting officer
- Walter Scott (2015), shot in the back while unarmed and running away from police.

Needless to say the degree of official blame in each of these cases varies, but the Black Lives Matter movement has become a powerful force in American politics, disrupting speeches by 2016 Democratic presidential candidates Hillary Clinton[80] and Bernie Sanders,[81] as well as 2016 Republican presidential candidate Donald Trump.[82]

In response to these tragedies, police in Baltimore cut back on more aggressive policing, with a sharp spike in homicides.[83] The New York City Council is considering a series of bills that will decriminalize so-called quality-of-life offenses such as the illegal cigarette sales that led to Eric Garner's death.[84] In Chicago, citizens have called on Mayor Rahm Emanuel to resign over the fact that the city held on to the video that showed the shooting death of Laquan McDonald for over a year. Emanuel is calling for changes in how police officers are trained.[85]

Dismantling Public Discrimination Based on Ethnicity

Similar to African Americans, Latinos began the struggle for civil rights in the court system through interest groups such as the American G.I. Forum, LULAC, and later the Mexican American Legal Defense and Education Fund (MALDEF). One of the first steps Latinos took toward securing civil rights was to be recognized as a protected class of people under the Fourteenth Amendment. As we have seen, the attorneys in *Hernandez v. Texas* argued that Hispanics were a class of individuals entitled to the same due process guarantees as were African Americans and other racial groups.[86] The court agreed and also ruled that Mexican Americans could not be systematically excluded from juries, a key gateway of citizenship.

In 1970, the Supreme Court extended the *Brown* ruling to apply to Latinos and other minority groups in *Cisneros v. Corpus Christi Independent School District*.[87] Because Mexican Americans were considered white, the Corpus Christi Independent School District created two sets of schools: one set for African American and Latino children and the other for "All-White" (non-Latino) children. In that way, they circumvented the desegregation ruling of *Brown*. Attorney James de Anda, supported by the MALDEF, argued that the separate schools system was unconstitutional because Mexican Americans were a separate and distinct group from whites. The Supreme Court recognized Latinos as a distinct ethnic minority group that had been subject to discriminatory practices.[88] Latino American school children were no longer subject to separate but equal educational facilities. In *Plyler v. Doe* (1982), described in Chapter 1, Gateways to American Democracy, the court expanded protections further, deciding that the children of undocumented workers were entitled to free public education in Texas.[89]

Equal opportunities in education for Latinos also involved the funding systems in local school districts. In many areas, public schools are funded through property taxes. As a result, within the same metropolitan area, there may be large disparities in funding for public schools. Some districts may include geographical areas in which property values are significantly lower than others. As a result, the educational facilities and materials may be less in those areas than in affluent neighborhoods. In the early 1970s, parents of children in San Antonio claimed that such a disparity was a violation of the equal protection clause in the Fourteenth Amendment. The Supreme Court in *San Antonio Independent School District v. Rodriguez* (1973) determined that education was not a fundamental right deserving of such protections and that the funding mechanisms of the school district were constitutional.[90] Advocates for school financing reform continued their efforts in state courts with some success.[91] The Texas legislature has since made limited progress in its attempts to reform the funding disparities in public education as mandated by state courts. So, in some ways, there are now gateways to education for children of all races and ethnicities. In other ways, educational gateways are only partially open and remain unequal.

Public education is a major gateway to participation in civic life. Its denial constitutes a gate that prevents equality. Yet other gates in lesser yet still important areas also existed. Public swimming pools, buses, and water fountains, for example, were segregated. In the early 1950s, sometimes there was no "equal" facility available to Latinos. Latino elected officials helped lead the effort to break down these and other types of barriers to citizenship. Prominent among them is Henry B. Gonzalez, the first Mexican American to be elected to the San Antonio City Council. One of his first victories was opening public facilities such as swimming pools to all residents. When he served in the Texas Senate, he filibustered a series of bills aimed at circumventing the *Brown* case. He held the floor for a record twenty-two hours and defeated all but two of the bills. He later served as Congressman from the 20th District in Texas, now occupied by Joaquín Castro (see the opening vignette in Chapter 12, Congress).[92]

Dismantling Voting Barriers Based on Ethnicity

Just as segregation was not limited to African Americans, voting laws created gates blocking Latinos' ability to exercise the right to vote. Poll taxes influenced Mexican Americans in the Southwest, for whom the cost to vote was a greater burden than for white voters. And while the Jim Crow version of literacy tests often involved tests of obscure political and historical facts for first-time voters, such as African Americans in the South, literacy requirements influenced Latinos differently. New York, for example, required "new" voters (i.e., Puerto Ricans) to provide evidence of English-language proficiency as a requisite for voter registration. In 1966, however, the Supreme Court ruled in *Katzenbach v. Morgan* (see Supreme Court Cases, Chapter 11) and *Cardona v. Power* that provisions of the 1966 Voting Rights Act (VRA) prevented New York from imposing English-language requirements for voting.[93] In 1970, the VRA was amended to eliminate all literacy tests, and, in 1975, Congress further amended the VRA to protect language minorities. As a result of those and subsequent amendments to the VRA, states and other political units, such as counties or cities, must provide voting information, assistance, and ballots in the minority language if more than 5 percent of the citizens of voting age in the jurisdiction are of a language minority or their number exceeds ten thousand.[94]

Bill Clark/CQ-Roll Call Group/Getty Images

IMAGE 5.8 Pedro Pierluisi is the nonvoting House of Representatives delegate from Puerto Rico. The Constitution limits representation in the House to "States," so while Puerto Rico and the District of Columbia have delegates in Congress, neither can vote.

Language requirements were only one type of gate. Other, less obvious gates to participation blocked Latino voters. The manner by which elections are structured may also create gates to meaningful participation. In Dallas County and Bexar County in Texas, for example, elections had been conducted on an at-large basis, meaning that candidates ran in multi-member districts. Ethnic minorities could not garner a high enough percentage of the vote to elect Latino or other representatives who embodied their interests. This form of election is still common in many jurisdictions and is not necessarily a violation of voting rights.

In 1973, however, the Supreme Court ruled in *White v. Regester* that the VRA prohibited electoral plans that may effectively dilute the voting strength of minorities, in this case Latinos.[95] The multi-member district elections in those jurisdictions were being used as a means to minimize the voting strength of Hispanic (in San Antonio) and African American (in Dallas) citizens. Such plans limited the effective participation of those groups to elect candidates of their choice. The Supreme Court mandated that single-member districts be used. As a result of this decision, groups such as MALDEF, Communities Organized for Public Service (COPS), and Southwest Voter Registration and Education Project (SVREP) and their leaders organized to change the way many local elections were structured (see below). Evidence shows that the impact of election practices was dramatic. After the switch to single-member districts in 1977, the San Antonio city elected five Mexican Americans to the city council as well as one African American candidate. For the first time in the city's history, a majority of the city council was composed of minorities.[96]

The effects of the increased representation of Hispanics in San Antonio were not just symbolic. Most of the newly elected members came from geographical areas of the city that had previously experienced little or no representation on the council. The new city council had members from every area of the city. Policies adopted by the council changed, and new priorities in city services were devoted to previously underserved areas of the city.[97]

It was MALDEF that brought *White v. Regester* and many other cases forward. In the 1970s, MALDEF undertook ninety-three federal and state cases in Texas alone: 76 percent of the cases involved desegregation, and 14 percent were cases about voting and other political rights.[98] That is one reason why MALDEF has come to be known as the "law firm of the Latino community."

Another driving force behind the *White v. Regester* case that opened a gateway for the election of Hispanics from the local level to Congress is Communities Organized for Public Service (COPS). COPS exemplifies how church- and neighborhood-based organizations can open gateways for minority groups. COPS organized in San Antonio's West Side, a densely populated and poor area of the city and home to mostly Mexican American residents. Those neighborhoods were largely without sidewalks and curbs. Led by Ernesto Cortés, COPS advocated for increased services to the city's previously unrepresented areas. Streets in those areas began to be paved, homes no longer flooded when it rained due to the curbs, and school children walked to school on sidewalks. They began to hold "accountability nights" where city councilpersons were held accountable for keeping their promises. In the process, they empowered Hispanic residents to participate in the political process, opening a gateway.

One of many organizations aiding in the election of Latinos is the Southwest Voter Registration Education Project (SVREP), whose mission is "to empower Latinos and other minorities by increasing their participation in the American democratic process."[99] SVREP does more than register voters; it also organizes training for future Latino leaders through the Latino Academy. The motto of SVREP is "*Su Voto Es Su Voz*" ("Your Vote Is Your Voice"). The joining of that motto of the United Farm Workers (UFW), "*¡Si, Se Puede!*" ("Yes, We Can!"), which Barack Obama borrowed in his successful 2008 presidential campaign, may inspire new generations of Latinos seeking the expansion of civil rights for Latinos.

There have been other practices and limits to the gateways to participation for Latinos, including voter identification laws. And the Supreme Court has indicated that electoral plans such as majority-minority districts (i.e., electoral districts in which a majority of the population is composed of minorities) need not maximize the voting strength of minority communities (e.g., Cuban Americans in *Johnson v. DeGrandy*).[100] See Chapter 11 for a discussion of the impact of the VRA and Supreme Court decisions on Latino voter turnout.

POLITICAL ANALYTICS

State-by-State Voter Identification Requirements

ARTICLE 1 OF THE U.S. CONSTITUTION gives the states responsibility for setting the time, place, and manner of elections while also reserving for Congress the power to intervene where it deems necessary. As you have read, Congress did intervene in 1965 with the Voting Rights Act. States, however, have largely been given leeway in determining the requirements their citizens must meet to vote. One requirement that some states have enacted, especially since 2010, is voter identification. Some states require voters to provide a government-issued form of identification in order to vote.

Figure 5.4 shows how states differ in the requirements voters must satisfy. In this case, *strict identification requirements* means that voters without acceptable identification, as determined by each state, may vote on a provisional ballot and may need to take additional steps after Election Day for it to be counted. *Non-strict identification requirements* means that at least

Strict ID | Non-Strict ID | No ID Required | Photo Required | Preclearance Previously Required

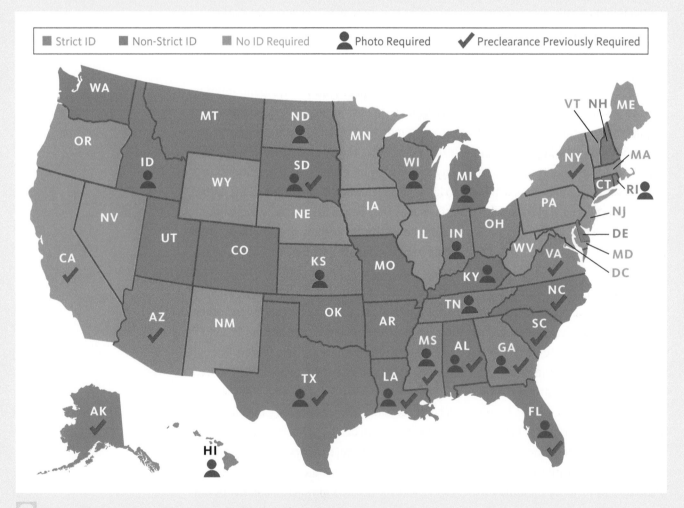

FIGURE 5.4 Voter Identification Laws by State, 2016

some voters without acceptable identification have an option to cast a ballot that will be counted without further action on their part.[101] In addition, most states in the strict category require photo identification.

Figure 5.4 also shows which states were under the VRA provision that required states to get preclearance before enacting such voter identification requirements, prior to the *Shelby County v. Holder* (2013) Supreme Court decision.

Sources: National Conference of State Legislatures. August 22, 2016. *Voter Identification Requirements, Voter Laws.* http://www.ncsl.org/research/elections-and-campaigns/voter-id.aspx; U.S. Department of Justice, Civil Rights Division, *Jurisdictions Previously Covered by Section 5.* https://www.justice.gov/crt/jurisdictions-previously-covered-section-5.

In Figure 5.4, examine the variety of voter identification requirements that exist among the states and notice which states have the strictest requirements.

Thinking Critically

1. Do requirements for voting such as photo identification place an unreasonable burden on voters?
2. Should the requirements for voting be uniform across the states?

Dismantling Private Discrimination Based on Ethnicity

Like women, Latinos have faced an uphill battle in the workplace. Deprived of their lands following Texas's break with Mexico, deported during the Great Depression and other periods, Latinos have long filled the demand for unskilled labor, particularly in the field of agriculture. As a result, perhaps the best known of civil rights efforts among Latinos is in the agriculture industry. Cesar Chavez and Dolores Huerta organized the United Farm Workers (UFW) union to secure safe working conditions and increased wages for laborers. Formed in 1962, the UFW continues to work to improve conditions for agriculture workers. When the UFW began, farm workers earned less than one dollar per hour. The first task of Chavez and Huerta was to organize the workers so that they could bargain collectively with growers. Once formed, they called for boycotts of fruit and vegetables as well as strikes against growers in order to gain the right to bargain collectively. The UFW counts among its successes bargaining agreements that required growers to provide rest periods for workers, toilets in fields, clean drinking water, and protections against dangerous pesticides.[102] The UFW increased the collective voice of Latinos in the agriculture industry and fought for basic human and civil rights.

The UFW also registered Latinos to vote and encouraged them to become active politically. The success of the UFW and other Latino organizations in ending segregation and discrimination continues as it does for other groups. For Latinos, efforts continue to provide adequate funding for education, expand educational opportunities to DREAMers, and prevent the efforts by some to limit political participation (see the discussion of voter identification laws in Chapter 11).[103] As with any social movement, leadership and organization are vital to the success of groups seeking equal protection and due process. As noted at the beginning of this section, much of the impetus for change begins with pressure from groups. As Chavez said, "Those who attack our union often say, 'It's not really a union. It's something else: A social movement. A civil rights movement. It's something dangerous. . . .' [T]he UFW has always been something more than a union—although it's never been dangerous if you believe in the Bill of Rights."[104]

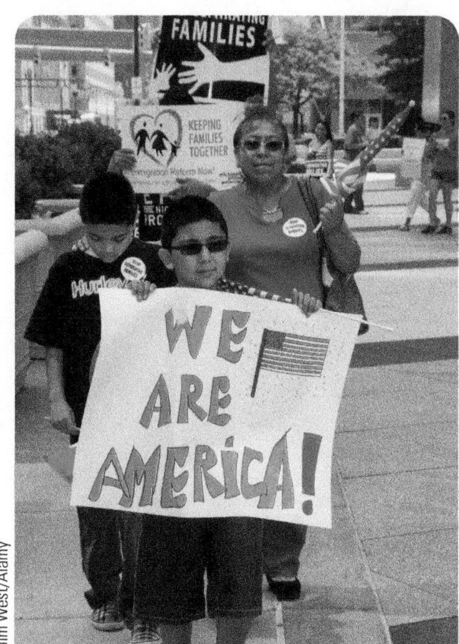

Jim West/Alamy

IMAGE 5.9 Young undocumented immigrants protesting outside the Federal Building in Detroit, Michigan.

As Latinos continue to be the fastest-growing ethnic group in the United States, it is clear that many gates to political participation have been placed before them. Latinos are slowly becoming a political force in the United States (see Chapter 11). Civil rights enjoyed by Latinos today were not always recognized as such, nor are they guaranteed to be so in the future. Elected officials such as Senator Marco Rubio (R-FL), Senator Ted Cruz (R-TX), and Republican Governor Susana Martínez from New Mexico, as well as emerging leaders such as Julian Castro, a Democrat who was the mayor of San Antonio and served as the Secretary of Housing and Urban Development, will have an increasing role in the nature of those rights. And emerging generations of Latinos such as Erika Andiola, leader of the Arizona DREAM Coalition, are poised to continue working to secure those rights, including volunteering to work for candidates running for office.[105]

Essential Knowledge

The National Organization for Women (NOW) seeks to end discriminatory practices based on sex. The organization was formed before the cases of *Reed v. Reed* and *Craig v. Boren*, in which the Supreme Court interpreted the Fourteenth Amendment's equal protection clause to cover sex as well as race.

Dismantling Discrimination Based on Gender

The success of the civil rights movement inspired other groups, most notably women, to put pressure on the political system to obtain equal rights under the law. Women active in the civil rights movement easily shifted the movement's strategies to promoting rights for women, particularly after the publication of Betty Friedan's *The Feminine Mystique* (1963), a book considered by many to have launched the modern American feminist movement. Based on a survey Friedan sent to her Smith College classmates in advance of their fifteenth reunion, the book broadcast the dissatisfaction that many American women felt in their roles as wives and mothers. About the same time, the Kennedy administration's President's Commission on the Status of Women, charged with making recommendations for overcoming sex discrimination, urged passage of the **Equal Pay Act**. Passed by Congress in 1963, the act prohibits employers from paying different wages for the same job on account of sex. Although the act did not prohibit discrimination in the hiring of male and female workers, that prohibition came with the Civil Rights Act of 1964. See Public Policy and Civil Rights: Workplace Equality.

Equal Pay Act: *Prohibits different pay for males and females for the same work (1963).*

Bettmann/Corbis

IMAGE 5.10 In 1960, when Columbia law student Ruth Bader Ginsburg applied for a Supreme Court clerkship, Justice Felix Frankfurter chose not to interview her. Ginsburg went on to a distinguished career as a professor of law and chief litigator for the American Civil Liberties Union, eventually arguing cases before the Court, which she joined in 1993 as the second female associate justice. She is pictured here in 1977.

Following passage of the Civil Rights Act, Friedan helped found the National Organization for Women (NOW), which advocated for women's rights through education and litigation. NOW protested airline policies that forced flight attendants (then known as stewardesses) to retire at marriage or age 32 and help-wanted ads that listed jobs by gender, as well as protective legislation. NOW also supported abortion rights and the proposed Equal Rights Amendment (ERA), which would have prohibited the federal government and the states from discriminating on account of sex.

In 1972, the American Civil Liberties Union (ACLU) established the Women's Rights Project, which worked to eliminate discriminatory laws. The first project director, future Supreme Court Justice Ruth Bader Ginsburg, developed a litigation strategy for ending gender-based discrimination. Prior to Ginsburg's work, the Court had rejected equal protection claims for women. Ginsburg first persuaded the Court to strike laws based on the rational-basis standard and then got the Court to approve a heightened-scrutiny standard. This is a step below the strict scrutiny used in cases discriminating on account of race, but the standard is tough enough that the Court usually strikes laws that discriminate according to sex.

Meanwhile, the ERA, passed by Congress and sent to the states for ratification in 1972, began to falter. An anti-ERA movement led by political activist

Phyllis Schlafly reversed the momentum by arguing that the amendment would remove special privileges women enjoyed with regard to protective legislation, Social Security benefits, and exemption from the draft. Ironically, another argument against the ERA was that it was unnecessary because the Supreme Court was striking down most laws that discriminated on account of sex. Despite an extension of the deadline to 1982, the ERA ultimately fell three states short of the three-quarters majority needed to pass an amendment (see Figure 5.5).

By the 1980s, the civil rights era was over, and the nation had taken a conservative turn. But like African Americans, whose office-holding and participation in civic life generally increased after passage of the VRA, women were increasingly taking public roles. In 1984, two years after the ERA failed, only 17 percent of Americans thought that the United States was ready to elect a woman president. In 2008, the Democratic presidential primary campaign of New York Senator Hillary Clinton and the Republican nomination of Alaska Governor Sarah Palin for vice president were evidence that the nation was ready. In 2016, the campaign of former Secretary of State Hillary Clinton demonstrated that the Democratic Party was ready to nominate a woman for the top of the ticket, and while she did not win the Electoral College, a plurality of Americans were ready to elect her to be president.

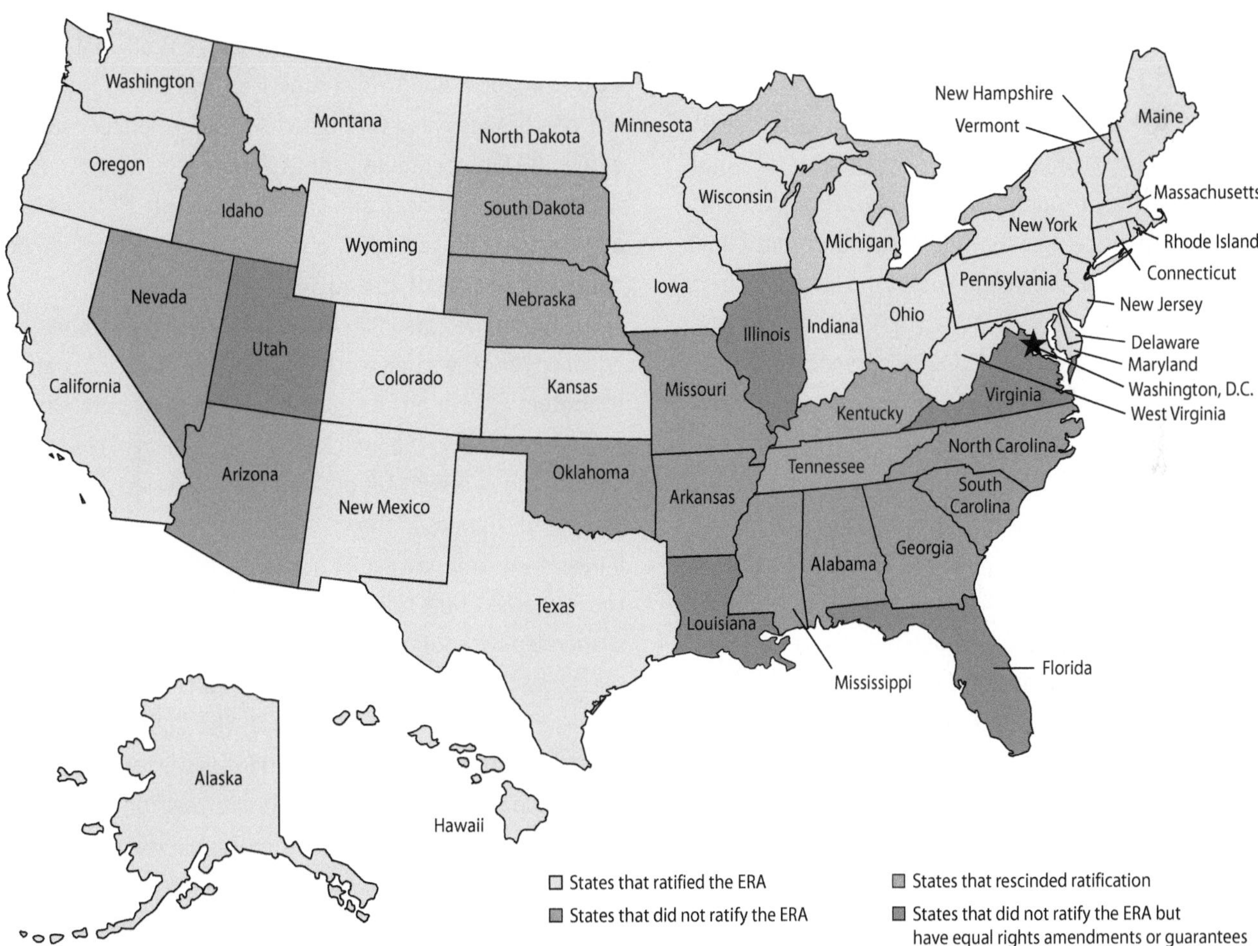

FIGURE 5.5 States Approving the Equal Rights Amendment

Passed by Congress in 1972 and sent to the states for ratification, the Equal Rights Amendment got a quick start and then faltered as opposition materialized and grew. In 1979, Congress extended the deadline for ratification to 1982, but in 1982, the amendment expired. Thirty-five states (of the thirty-eight needed) had voted to ratify it, and five states had voted to rescind ratification.

Source: Data from http://www.equalrightsamendment.org.

PUBLIC POLICY AND CIVIL RIGHTS

Workplace Equality

Although national legislation and constitutional amendments define civil rights policy, and the Supreme Court interprets such laws—deciding whether they are constitutional and, if so, what they mean—the day-to-day protection of civil rights now falls to two separate executive branch agencies. One is the Civil Rights Division of the Department of Justice, with sections on educational opportunity, employment, housing, voting, and disability rights. The other is the Equal Employment Opportunity Commission (EEOC), which protects against sexual harassment in the workplace and promotes gender equity.

The EEOC is an independent agency with commissioners selected for five-year fixed terms. Unlike the heads of government departments, EEOC commissioners cannot be removed by the president. They are thus thought to be shielded from political pressures, but fixed terms also limit responsiveness to the president, who is the chief executive of the United States.

Congress established the EEOC as part of the Civil Rights Act of 1964. The original EEOC could receive and investigate complaints of discrimination on the basis of race, sex, religion, and national origin (Congress later added age and disability status). As one of the compromises that allowed the act to pass, the EEOC originally had no enforcement power. Rather, it could refer to the Justice Department any case in which there were patterns or practices of discrimination. In 1972, Congress provided the commission with the right to file lawsuits against companies that discriminate.

Although Congress passed the basic law declaring discrimination based on race or sex to be illegal, the EEOC established the guidelines that prohibited discrimination against hiring married women, pregnant women, and mothers. The commission also allowed companies that had previously engaged in discriminatory practices to establish affirmative action plans with quotas for hiring and promoting women and minorities.

From a policy standpoint, the underlying principle of equal pay is that two people who are employed in the same job and do the same quality of work should be paid the same wage. Achieving gender equality in the workplace means that there are no barriers to advancement or hiring based on gender and that gender plays no role in how employees are treated and compensated. Unfortunately, true pay equity has not been achieved in the American workplace. Though the census statistics below do not control for the type of job worked, data from 2015 show that women earned only 82.5 percent of what men earned in 2014. For African American and Latino women, this percentage was a bit higher: African American women earned 89.9 percent and Latinas earned 89.0 percent of what African American and Latino men made.[106] Additionally, the gap falls to slightly above 89.9 percent for women between the ages of 25 and 34.[107]

Though the Equal Pay Act is supposed to guarantee equal pay for the same work, and the Civil Rights Act aims to protect against any form of employment discrimination on account of sex, the judicial branch has also played a pivotal role. A recent set of Supreme Court decisions has prompted changes in the laws governing discrimination, harassment, and pay equity in the workplace. In one case, the Supreme Court ruled in favor of a woman who was suspended without pay for more than a month and was reassigned to a less desirable position after she claimed sex discrimination in the workplace. The Court decided that an indefinite suspension without pay is retaliation that would reasonably deter any employee from making a discrimination complaint, and, therefore, it was illegal.[108]

But the Court's 2007 ruling in *Ledbetter v. Goodyear Tire and Rubber Co.* had the greatest impact on public policy.[109] In 1998, Lilly Ledbetter filed a complaint with the EEOC that she had consistently received poor job performance evaluations because of her gender and that over the nineteen years she had worked at the Goodyear Tire plant, her pay had fallen well below her male colleagues who did the same type of job. Her employer countered that, even if that had been true in the past, she did not file her complaint within the 180 days required by the Civil Rights Act. The Court ruled in favor of Goodyear, stating that Ledbetter's claims alleging sex discrimination were time-barred because the discriminatory decisions relating to pay had been made more than 180 days prior to the day she filed the charge with the EEOC. In her dissent, Justice Ruth Bader Ginsburg wrote that the effect of this ruling would allow "any annual pay decision not contested immediately (within 180 days) . . . [to become] grandfathered, a fait accompli beyond the province of Title VII ever to repair."[110] Basically, a company could pay a woman less on the basis of gender, and as long as she did not contest the discriminatory wage within 180 days, the discriminatory wage could not be challenged in federal court.

In 2009, Congress reversed the Court's ruling by passing the Lilly Ledbetter Fair Pay Act, which was the first act that President Obama signed into law. The act restarts the clock each time an employee receives a paycheck that has been compromised by discriminatory practices.[111] Many equal pay advocates think that this new law will be helpful but not nearly helpful enough to close the salary gap between men and women. Indeed, early reports suggest that some individual women have been able to sue who would not have been able to do so before the act but that these individual suits have done little to close the gender pay gap.[112]

In 2014, President Obama moved to increase equality through the Paycheck Fairness Act, which would revise remedies for paycheck inequality, increase enforcement activity against unequal pay, and limit exceptions to rules against sex discrimination in wages.[113] With every Republican voting against it, the Senate failed to obtain the sixty votes needed to cut off debate.[114] With this legislative stalemate, President Obama issued two executive orders to accomplish what he could on his own. First, federal contractors could not punish workers for discussing their wages among one another. He also required federal contractors to file data with the federal government showing how they pay employees by race and by sex.[115] The bill was reintroduced into the House in March 2015, but, by November 2016, had not moved past the subcommittee stage.[116]

Public Policy Connections

1. Should the government require employers to develop a pay scale that standardizes employee pay, or should employers be free to account for market forces and individual qualifications with regard to pay?
2. Should the government take steps to require that employers equalize the pay between traditionally male jobs and traditionally female jobs?

5.5 Frontiers in Civil Rights

Describe the new battles for civil rights

Many of the civil rights battles against legal discrimination have been won: Governments cannot discriminate on account of race or sex, and businesses cannot discriminate in hiring employees or serving customers. But the expanded notion of equality promoted by the civil rights and women's rights movements inspired other groups, such as homosexuals and the disabled, to demand full access to equality. At the same time, as the fight over the ERA made clear, the extension of rights for some may involve a loss of privileges for others, and sometimes rights clash. Congress and the courts have sought to define the meaning and limits of rights as new areas of conflict emerge over such issues as racial and religious profiling, the voting rights of felons, and the civil rights of undocumented immigrants. Whatever the new issues, however, the trend in the United States has been for a broader meaning of equality and greater support for civil rights.

Sexual Orientation, Same-Sex Marriage, and Transgender Rights

Stonewall riots: *Street protest in 1969 by gay patrons against a police raid of a gay bar in New York; the protest is credited with launching the gay rights movement.*

The movement to protect the rights of homosexuals first received widespread public attention in 1969 when a police raid on the Stonewall Inn, a gay bar in New York City, turned into a riot by the bar's patrons and gay rights supporters living in the area. The **Stonewall riots** became the signature event of a growing gay rights movement. Activists soon formed the Gay Liberation Front, which established branch organizations around the world. By the 1990s, the movement had expanded into a broader LGBT movement that sought to protect the rights of lesbians, gays, bisexuals, and transgendered persons. Given the historical importance of the Stonewall Inn, many supporters of the LGBT community met there following the June 2016 mass shooting at an LGBT nightclub in Orlando, Florida, to hold a vigil for the wounded survivors.

At the time of the Stonewall riots, all states banned sodomy, which would include virtually all sexual activity between same-sex couples.[117] In the following years, several states decriminalized homosexual activity, but as noted in Chapter 4, the Supreme Court ruled in 1986 that homosexual activity was not a fundamental right, so states could still keep homosexuality illegal if they so choose. Colorado went further, passing an amendment to its state constitution that prohibited the state, or any city or town in the state, from passing laws that granted civil rights protections on account of sexual orientation. The Supreme Court struck this law in 1996, claiming that it was born of dislike toward gays.[118] Then, in *Lawrence v. Texas* (2003), the Supreme Court reversed the 1986 decision and declared that states could not prohibit sexual activity between people of the same sex (see Supreme Court Cases for Chapter 6, Public Opinion).[119]

Although a current majority of Americans are accepting of homosexual partnerships,[120] issues related to homosexual rights have historically been fraught with conflict. Under President Bill Clinton (1993–2001), Congress enacted a "don't ask, don't tell" policy for the military. Prior to the implementation of this policy, simply having homosexual tendencies, without any evidence of homosexual activities, was sufficient grounds for discharge. Under the policy, sexual orientation alone was not a ground for discharge, but lesbians, gays, and bisexuals were discharged for engaging in homosexual relationships or for discussing their sexual orientation. Barack Obama opposed the "don't ask, don't tell" policy and in 2010 signed a bill repealing it. The military now directs that same-sex spouses of U.S. soldiers receive the same benefits that opposite-sex spouses receive.[121] Nevertheless, when soldiers are stationed overseas, certain spousal rights, including passports, visas, and housing allowances, may be limited, depending on the host country.[122]

When the Hawaii Supreme Court ruled in 1993 that, under the state constitution, Hawaii would have to show a compelling interest in its prohibition of same-sex marriages, opponents feared that same-sex marriages performed in Hawaii would have legal recognition throughout the United States. In 1996, Congress passed and President Clinton signed the Defense of Marriage Act (DOMA), which defines marriage, for the purpose of federal law, as between a man and a woman. The act did not prohibit same-sex marriage, but it declared that neither the individual states nor the United States have to recognize same-sex marriages legally performed in other states. In *United States v. Windsor*, the Supreme Court declared that the section of DOMA that limited spousal recognition under federal law to a man and a woman was unconstitutional.[123] The decision dealt only with federal recognition of same-sex marriage and said nothing about state bans on the practice.

Brennan Linsley/AP Images

IMAGE 5.11 The owner of the Masterpiece Cakeshop in Lakewood, Colorado, claimed that making a wedding cake for a same-sex couple violated his Christian beliefs. The Colorado courts ruled against him, stating that no one should be turned away from a public business because of whom they love.

In 2015, the Supreme Court agreed to hear a case regarding state bans on same-sex marriage. The case, *Obergefell v. Hodges*, was a consolidation of cases originating from Michigan, Kentucky, Ohio, and Tennessee. There were two primary questions the Court had to consider: Could states ban same-sex marriages, and did they have to recognize same-sex marriages performed legally out of state? In a 5–4 decision, the Court ruled that bans on same-sex marriage violated the equal protection clause of the Fourteenth Amendment. By handing down the decision in *Obergefell*, the Supreme Court made same-sex marriages legal in all fifty states and required that they be recognized equally under the law.[124]

National public opinion remains mixed on the matter of same-sex marriage, which, given the current makeup of the Supreme Court, remains the law of the land (see Figure 5.6). While a substantial majority of Americans favor allowing same-sex marriage,[125] the major political parties are divided on the issue: Democrats are typically more supportive of same-sex marriage than Republicans are. Because support for same-sex marriage is much greater among younger Americans than among older Americans, public support for same-sex marriage will almost certainly increase over time.

As support for same-sex marriage grows, LGBT activists have started pressing for the rights of transgender individuals. In February 2016, the city of Charlotte, North Carolina, enacted a local ordinance allowing transgender people to use bathroom facilities that match their gender identities. In March, the North Carolina legislature passed HB2, a law

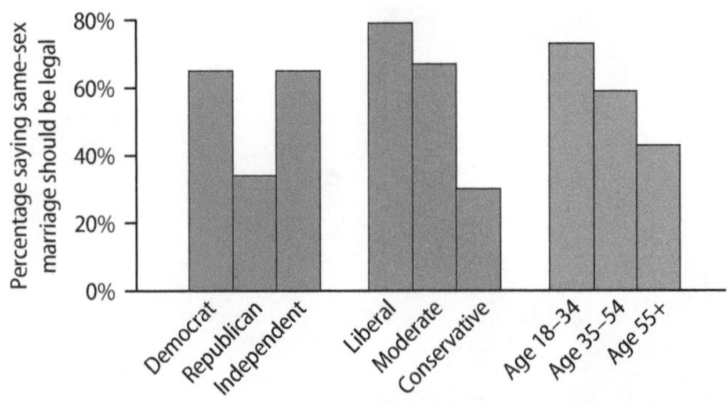

FIGURE 5.6 Views on Same-Sex Marriage, 2015

Younger voters support same-sex marriage at substantially higher rates than do older voters.

Source: http://www.people-press.org/2015/06/08/same-sex-marriage-detailed-tables/, date June 8, 2015; accessed February 22, 2016.

that prohibited cities from expanding on North Carolina's own antidiscrimination laws, which protect race, religion, national origin, handicap status, or biological sex. Thus, laws in cities such as Charlotte, Chapel Hill, Durham, and Raleigh that extended protections to sexual orientation or gender identity were void.[126] In response to the law, businesses General Electric and Hewlett Packard decided to boycott the state. So did musicians Ringo Starr, Bruce Springsteen, and Maroon 5.[127]

On May 2, 2016, the EEOC declared that "denying an employee equal access to a common restroom according to the employee's gender identity is sex discrimination," which is prohibited by Title VII of the Civil Rights Act.[128] Less than two weeks later, a joint directive to public schools by the Department of Justice and the Department of Education declared that such schools must allow transgender students to use the bathroom of their choice. This controversial move set off a barrage of criticism: The governor of North Carolina sued the Justice Department; Texas Lieutenant Governor Dan Patrick told school superintendents not to abide by the rules. On the other hand, House Democratic leader Nancy Pelosi tweeted support for the rules.[129] As President Trump supports these rules, they are likely to remain in place, as will the disagreement over this newest controversy in civil rights.

Disability Rights

Advocates for the rights of the disabled, encouraged by the civil rights, women's rights, and other movements, successfully lobbied for the Rehabilitation Act of 1973, which prohibits discrimination against disabled individuals by any federal agency or by any private program or activity that receives federal funds. The landmark Americans with Disabilities Act (ADA) passed in 1990 goes further, requiring public and private employers to make "reasonable accommodations" to known physical and mental limitations of employees with disabilities and, if possible, to modify performance standards to accommodate an employee's disability.

To comply with the act, public transportation authorities have made buses and trains accessible to people in wheelchairs. Public accommodations, such as restaurants, hotels, movie theaters, and doctors' offices, must also meet ADA accessibility standards, within reason, removing barriers from existing structures. Related legislation, the Individuals with Disabilities Education Act (IDEA; 1990, updated 2004), requires states to provide free public education to all children with disabilities in the least-restrictive environment appropriate to their particular needs.

Congress does not provide a full list of disabilities covered under the ADA but rather covers any disability that "substantially limits a major life activity." Thus, a trucking company need not make accommodations for a driver who can see clearly out of only one eye because the disability does not substantially limit a major life activity. On the other hand, the ADA does protect people who have HIV or AIDS. It even protects people with severe drug and alcohol problems, provided the drug use in question is not illegal.[130]

Many organized interests support the rights of the disabled. While prejudice against people of different races, religions, sexual orientation, and country of origin might lead

IMAGES 5.12 AND 5.13 Disability-rights groups have advocated moving from the current accessibility sign (left) to the newer one (right), which is much more dynamic.

tuulijumala/Shutterstock.com

The Accessible Icon Project

responsive representatives to oppose the rights of minorities, there are few if any votes to be had by lobbying against the rights of the disabled. Nevertheless, when at the end of 2011 the Department of Labor proposed new rules that would push employers toward a goal of having 7 percent of their employees be people with disabilities, business groups opposed the rules, claiming they would be costly to implement.[131]

Racial and Religious Profiling

Profiling—the use by police of racial, ethnic, or religious characteristics in determining whom to investigate for particular kinds of crimes—is controversial because it entails unequal treatment under the law. For example, along the I-95 corridor north of Baltimore, a team of observers found that about 17 percent of cars had black drivers and nearly 76 percent had white drivers and that the drivers observed traffic laws in similar proportions. Nevertheless, more than 80 percent of the cars stopped and searched by the Maryland State Police were driven by blacks and Hispanics, while cars driven by whites constituted fewer than 20 percent of the searches.[132] So much more likely were blacks to be pulled over than whites that the phrase "driving while black" came to signify African American drivers' feeling that they risked being treated as criminals on the roads. State and federal courts have specifically prohibited the use of race as a factor in "drug courier profiles."[133] Many suspect that the killing of Trayvon Martin in Florida resulted from racial profiling by a neighborhood watch captain.

Following the terrorist attacks of 9/11, profiling of Arabs and Muslims increased, particularly in matters of airline security. In efforts to identify potential terrorists, mistakes are often made.[134] In 2014, for example, New York City ended its practice of having undercover police officers spy on Muslims without probable cause.[135] In January 2016, the New York Police Department agreed to two settlements resulting from cases brought by citizens regarding the department's undercover operations. The settlement prohibits investigations in which race, religion, or ethnicity is a motivating factor in the surveillance. Adopting guidelines used by the FBI, a civilian will monitor police surveillance of religious groups.[136] Where issues of security are at stake, profiling is especially controversial.

Voting Rights for Felons

Since passage of the Civil Rights Act of 1964 and the Voting Rights Act of 1965, voting rights have been scrupulously protected, even as stricter requirements for voter identification have been enforced to prevent alleged fraud (see Chapter 11). But there remains a persistent inequality regarding whether felons have the right to vote, with each state making its own determinations (see Figure 5.7). At one end of the spectrum, Maine and Vermont

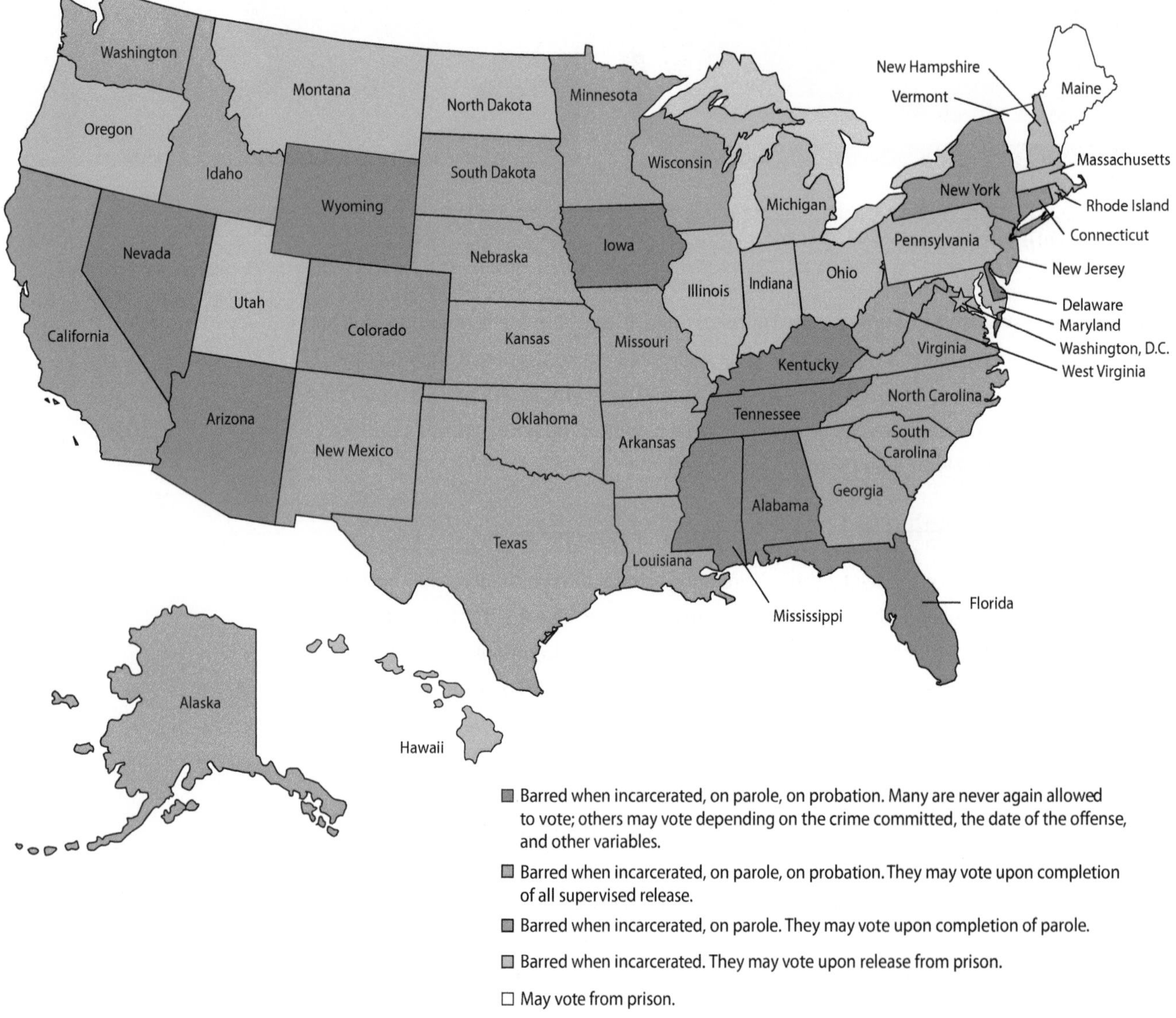

FIGURE 5.7 Voting Rights for Felons, 2016

Maine and Vermont allow incarcerated prisoners to vote. Many other states restore voting rights upon release from prison and after the parole period ends.

Source: Data from http://www.procon.org.

allow prison inmates to vote. Fourteen states and the District of Columbia allow felons to vote upon release from prison, and twenty-three more allow them to vote upon completion of probation or parole.[137] Thirteen states do not automatically restore voting rights, with the specifics of restoration varying among them. Recent estimates have placed the number of disenfranchised felons in the United States at approximately 5.8 million; this represents 2.5 percent of the voting-age population in the United States, or one in every forty adults.[138] Such laws markedly influence close elections because felons are more likely than the general population to be poor, and poor people are more likely to vote Democratic.[139] Thus, when Virginia Governor Terry McAuliffe, a long-time supporter of Bill and Hillary Clinton, restored voting rights to 206,000 felons in 2016, Republicans called it a move to support Hillary Clinton's 2016 presidential campaign.[140]

Undocumented Immigrants

The Fourteenth Amendment's equal protection clause prohibits states from denying to *any* person—in other words, not just citizens—equal protection under the law. Thus even undocumented immigrants receive some degree of legal protection in the United States, as in *Plyler v. Doe* (see Supreme Court Cases, Chapter 1). The level of that protection is deeply controversial, especially as the number of undocumented immigrants, estimated to be about 11.7 million, has leveled off after having peaked at about 12.2 million in 2007, with the recession the most likely cause for the drop-off.[141] With Congressional gridlock leaving it unable to pass any immigration measures, President Obama issued executive orders requiring Deferred Action for Parents of Americans (DAPA), to protect from deportation undocumented residents whose children are citizens, and Deferred Action for Childhood Arrivals (DACA), to cover the young children who came to the United States prior to June 15, 2012. Twenty-six states challenged the orders on the grounds that the president does not have legislative authority. The Obama administration replied that it is inherent in the president's authority as chief executive to set priorities for law enforcement, and that if he does not wish to use scarce resources to deport parents of U.S. citizens, or children who came here on their own, that is within his discretion. In 2016 the Supreme Court affirmed the lower court decision that the president does not have the authority to issue such executive orders (see Chapter 16, Economic, Domestic, and Foreign Policy, for further discussion of immigration policy).[142]

Congress has been considering a number of actions, including creating easier paths to citizenship for illegal immigrants or, alternatively, denying natural-born citizenship to U.S.–born children of undocumented immigrants. Sixty-two percent of Americans believe that children born in the United States under such circumstances should automatically be granted citizenship, with 31 percent opposed.[143] The constitutionality of a law that would deny them citizenship, given the Fourteenth Amendment's citizenship clause, remains unclear.[144]

While the Court reviews laws that discriminate against legal immigrants under its strictest level of scrutiny, it reviews laws that discriminate against undocumented immigrants under the easier rational-basis standard. Yet, the Court has held that states may not deny public education to undocumented immigrants,[145] and federal law requires hospitals to provide emergency care to undocumented immigrants through Medicaid, the federal program that supports health care to poor people. The growth of civil rights to cover undocumented immigrants is surely one of the most controversial of the frontiers we have examined.

Civil Rights and Democracy

The core demand of civil rights is equal opportunity under the law. When laws discriminate or allow discrimination, people are effectively excluded from civic life. The demands for equal opportunity are often made to government, which alone has the authority to prohibit discrimination.

While a democratic system of government works to be responsive to its citizens, responsiveness to minorities is harder to obtain when majorities seek to limit minority rights. As noted in Chapter 2, The Constitution, James Madison saw a large republic with varied interests as a cure for the mischiefs of faction. But when factions form on the basis of majority group versus minority group, such as white versus black, heterosexual versus gay and lesbian, or native-born versus immigrant, responsiveness to minority preferences has been achieved through the gateways of lawsuits, protests, and other forms of civic engagement by the minority group. In response, the government has struck down laws that discriminated and passed laws that prevented other people from discriminating.

Out of all the activities by groups seeking equal rights, voting might be key. With the vote, declared Martin Luther King Jr. in 1965, comes accountability. Blacks could "vote out of office public officials who bar the doorway to decent housing, public safety, jobs, and decent integrated education. It is now obvious that the basic elements so vital to Negro advancement can only be achieved by seeking redress from government. . . . To do this, the vote is essential."[146]

While voting rights provide accountability by allowing citizens to "throw the bums out," they also provide responsiveness. A minority group's elected opponents are not as forceful once a group has the right to vote. Former Texas Governor Rick Perry, who twice unsuccessfully sought the Republican nomination for president, was never known as a supporter of civil rights. Indeed, one of the controversies from his 2012 campaign was a piece of family property Perry inherited that included a landmark rock at the entrance that included the "n-word." The parcel of property where the rock is located was officially known by that name. While Perry decried the name on the rock when first running for president, he took no steps to change the name when he originally became its owner, when a private citizen, when elected a Texas state official, or even when elected governor. With less than 12 percent of the Texas population being African American, he was not offending a very large group. He did, however, support in-state tuition for children of undocumented Texas residents. Latinos made up nearly 40 percent of Texas's population when Perry was governor.[147] More generally, the voting patterns of southern House and Senate members on issues related to civil rights have moderated over the past forty years, proving that King was certainly correct about the value of the ballot.[148] While members of Congress representing southern states once voted in lockstep opposition to civil rights issues, their votes on such issues now differ only slightly from those of representatives of other states.[149]

These changes are part of a larger evolution in the idea of equality that has proceeded over the course of the nation's more than two centuries. Americans once believed that slaveholding was not inconsistent with demands for equality; today African Americans, women, and others once discriminated against have achieved full participation in the nation's civic life. But the frontiers of civil rights will continue to evolve. Some Americans believe that equal opportunity is not enough, that the government must take stronger measures to ensure greater equality of outcome. Because there is no constitutional right to equal results, the battle over this meaning of equality will be fought not in the courts, but in democratically elected legislatures.

Martin Luther King Jr. once declared that the "arc of the moral universe is long, but it bends toward justice." Two recent examples from the world of sports show how far we have come. When light middleweight boxing champion Manny Pacquiao declared in 2016 that gay people are "worse than animals," he lost his $1 million annual endorsement deal with Nike.[150] When Donald Sterling, the owner of the San Diego Clippers basketball team, scolded his girlfriend for bringing African American superstar Magic Johnson to Clippers games, he was roundly condemned by nearly everyone, north and south, Republican and Democrat, and was forced to give up his interest in the team. Considering that segregation in public facilities was legal in much of the United States until 1965, and that until the *Lawrence v. Texas* (2003) case states were free to make homosexual relations illegal, the arc of the moral universe appears to be opening more gateways for Americans than ever before.

Political Science Reasoning

Question 1

Practice 1, Practice 2

> *Plessy v. Ferguson* (1896)
>
> By the Fourteenth Amendment, all persons born or naturalized in the United States, and subject to the jurisdiction thereof, are made citizens of the United States and of the State wherein they reside; and the states are forbidden from making or enforcing any law which shall abridge the privileges or immunities of citizens of the United States, or shall deprive any person of life, liberty, or property without due process of law, or deny to any person within their jurisdiction the equal protection of the laws. . . .
>
> We consider the underlying fallacy of the plaintiff's argument to consist in the assumption that the enforced separation of the two races stamps the colored race with a badge of inferiority. If this be so, it is not by reason of anything found in the act, but solely because the colored race chooses to put that construction upon it. The argument necessarily assumes that if, as has been more than once the case, and is not unlikely to be so again, the colored race should become the dominant power in the state legislature, and should enact a law in precisely similar terms,

it would thereby relegate the white race to an inferior position. We imagine that the white race, at least, would not acquiesce in this assumption. The argument also assumes that social prejudices may be overcome by legislation, and that equal rights cannot be secured to the negro except by an enforced commingling of the two races. We cannot accept this proposition. If the two races are to meet upon terms of social equality, it must be the result of natural affinities, a mutual appreciation of each other's merits, and a voluntary consent of individuals. . . .

Brown v. Board of Education (1954) "Brown I"

Segregation of white and colored children in public schools has a detrimental effect upon the colored children. The impact is greater when it has the sanction of the law, for the policy of separating the races is usually interpreted as denoting the inferiority of the negro group. A sense of inferiority affects the motivation of a child to learn. Segregation with the sanction of law, therefore, has a tendency to [retard] the educational and mental development of negro children and to deprive them of some of the benefits they would receive in a racial[ly] integrated school system.

Whatever may have been the extent of psychological knowledge at the time of *Plessy v. Ferguson,* this finding is amply supported by modern authority. Any language in *Plessy v. Ferguson* contrary to this finding is rejected.

We conclude that, in the field of public education, the doctrine of "separate but equal" has no place. Separate educational facilities are inherently unequal. Therefore, we hold that the plaintiffs and others similarly situated for whom the actions have been brought are, by reason of the segregation complained of, deprived of the equal protection of the laws guaranteed by the Fourteenth Amendment. This disposition makes unnecessary any discussion whether such segregation also violates the Due Process Clause of the Fourteenth Amendment.

1. Explain the reasoning used in each of the above Supreme Court decisions.
2. How does the Court change its views on segregation between *Plessey* and *Brown*?
3. Why could the Court's decision in *Brown* not be used to desegregate public accommodations?

Question 2

Practice 1, Practice 2

Brown v. Board of Education (1955) "Brown II"

While giving weight to these public and private considerations, the courts will require that the defendants make a prompt and reasonable start toward full compliance with our May 17, 1954, ruling. Once such a start has been made, the courts may find that additional time is necessary to carry out the ruling in an effective manner. The burden rests upon the defendants to establish that such time is necessary in the public interest and is consistent with good faith compliance at the earliest practicable date. To that end, the courts may consider problems related to administration, arising from the physical condition of the school plant, the school transportation system, personnel, revision of school districts and attendance areas into compact units to achieve a system of determining admission to the public schools on a nonracial basis, and revision of local laws and regulations which may be necessary in solving the foregoing problems. They will also consider the adequacy of any plans the defendants may propose to meet these problems and to effectuate a transition to a racially nondiscriminatory school system. During this period of transition, the courts will retain jurisdiction of these cases.

The judgments below, except that, in the Delaware case, are accordingly reversed, and the cases are remanded to the district courts to take such proceedings and enter such orders and decrees consistent with this opinion as are necessary and proper to admit to public schools on a racially nondiscriminatory basis with all deliberate speed the parties to these cases.

1. Identify the question at stake in this case, then explain the Supreme Court's reasoning in the above decision.
2. What was the impact of the above decision on the Civil Rights Movement?

Focus on AP® Success

5 Civil Rights

Must Know: Key Concepts

- Civil Rights Act of 1964
- Voting Rights Act of 1965
- Title IX of the Civil Rights Act Amendments (1972)
- *Brown v. Board of Education I* (1954) "Brown I"
- Equal Protection Clause
- Letter from Birmingham Jail
- *Roe v. Wade* (1973)
- National Organization for Women
- Busing
- Affirmative Action

Thinking Politically

Concept Application

While serving as a law clerk for Justice Jackson, future Chief Justice William Rehnquist wrote a memo in which he stated, "To the argument . . . that a majority may not deprive a minority of its constitutional right, the answer must be made that while this is sound in theory, in the long run it is the majority who will determine what the constitutional rights of the minorities are." While some might argue that this is morally objectionable, there is some truth to the political reality of this statement. Guaranties of civil rights and civil liberties are not self-executing. They require implementation on the part of political actors and political institutions. What institutions in the U.S. political system are best situated to afford minority groups their rights?

Concept Application

The decision in *Brown v. Board of Education* (1954) was based on the Supreme Court's interpretation of the Fourteenth Amendment's equal protection clause. However, segregation was still legally practiced in public accommodations (hotels, restaurants, theaters, etc.) until the passage of the Civil Rights Act of 1964. Explain why the *Brown* decision required desegregation in those facilities as well as public school?

Understanding Learning Objectives with Key Concepts

PRD – 1.A Explain how constitutional provisions have supported and motivated social movements.

- The concept of civil rights deals with the protection that individuals have based on factors such as race, national origin, religion, and sex. Civil rights are protected by the Fifth Amendment's due process clause, the equal protection clause of the Fourteenth Amendment, and legislation passed by Congress.
- The struggle for equality continues beyond the Civil Rights Movement to also include women's and LGBT movements.
- Martin Luther King's "Letter from Birmingham Jail," explains his strategy of nonviolence in the face of discrimination and the obligation to resist unjust laws.
- The modern women's rights movement began in the 1970s and then led to the foundation of the National Organization for Women.
- The 1973 Supreme Court decision in *Roe v. Wade* that legalized abortion nationwide has worked to promote reproductive rights including access to abortion.

- The pro-life (anti-abortion) movement has also rallied around the equal protection clause, using it to justify limitations on abortion in order to protect the unborn.

PMI – 3.A Explain how the government has responded to social movements.

- The push for equality has resulted in significant legislation and litigation, such as:
  - In *Brown v. Board of Education* ("Brown I," 1954), the Supreme Court held that segregation in public schools violates the equal protection clause of the Fourteenth Amendment. The case partially overturned *Plessy v. Ferguson*. After the case, segregation was still allowed in businesses.
  - The Civil Rights Act of 1964 included among its provisions prohibition of businesses from discrimination based on race, color, religion, sex, or national origin and an authorization for the attorney general to sue segregated school districts.
  - Title IX of the Civil Rights Act Amendments (1972) prohibits sex-based discrimination in educational institutions.
  - The Voting Rights Act of 1965 prohibits racial discrimination in voting, bans literacy tests, and attempts to prohibit any voting regulation that might have the effect of denying the right to vote based on race.

CON – 6.A Explain how the Supreme Court has at times allowed the restriction of the civil rights of minority groups and at other times has protected those rights.

- At various times in U.S. history, the Court has allowed discriminatory practices to exist, only later to overturn those decisions.
  - In the period after the Civil War, many Southern states enacted discriminatory laws aimed at segregating African Americans. These laws were challenged based on the Fourteenth Amendment. The 1896 *Plessy v. Ferguson* decision allowed states to have segregation, provided that the facilities provided for each race were "separate but equal." In 1954, however, the Supreme Court overturned that precedent in *Brown v. Board of Education* (Brown I), ruling that segregation in public schools violated the equal protection clause.
  - In *Brown v. Board of Education* (1954), the Supreme Court held that segregation in public schools violates the equal protection clause of the Fourteenth Amendment. This case set the stage for passage of the Civil Rights Act of 1964.
  - The Supreme Court has prohibited the creation of majority-minority districts.
  - Further controversy over affirmative action's use of racial classifications to promote minority hiring and admission to educational institutions reveals a continued tension over the rights of the majority and those of minorities. As such, the court permits racial distinctions that benefit minorities but does not permit racial distinctions that harm minorities.

Making Connections

The study of the civil rights movement and the women's rights movement serve as case studies of how interest groups and social movements can achieve their goals. Take particular note of how these movements and the associated interest groups utilize lobbying, elections, and litigation to achieve their policy goals. This will deepen your understanding of Chapter 8, Interest Groups.

Going Deeper: Letter from Birmingham Jail

During the struggle for racial equality, the civil rights leader Martin Luther King was jailed for intentionally violating racially discriminatory laws in a nonviolent manner. This practice is known as civil disobedience. On one such occasion in 1963, he wrote an open letter to explain his actions. This letter has come to be known as "Letter from Birmingham Jail" or "The Negro is Your Brother." Some of its key points include:

Unjust laws or practices in a particular jurisdiction are, in and of themselves, detrimental to justice in all places. King eloquently writes:

> *Injustice anywhere is a threat to justice everywhere. We are caught in an inescapable network of mutuality, tied in a single garment of destiny. Whatever affects one directly affects all indirectly.*

Action is necessary to secure rights that are being abridged:

> *We know through painful experience that freedom is never voluntarily given by the oppressor; it must be demanded by the oppressed.*

Individuals have a right to defy unjust laws in a nonviolent manner:

> *I submit that an individual who breaks a law that conscience tells him is unjust, and who willingly accepts the penalty of imprisonment in order to arouse the conscience of the community over its injustice, is in reality expressing the highest respect for law.*

6 Public Opinion

AP® Learning Objectives

MPA – 1.A Explain the relationship between core beliefs of U.S. citizens and attitudes about the role of government.

MPA – 1.B Explain how cultural factors influence political attitudes and socialization.

MPA – 2.A Describe the elements of a scientific poll.

MPA – 2.B Explain the quality and credibility of claims based on public opinion data.

PMI – 4.A Explain how the ideologies of the two major parties shape policy debates.

PMI – 4.B Explain how U.S. political culture (e.g., values, attitudes, and beliefs) influences the formation, goal, and implementation of public policy over time.

PMI – 4.C Describe different political ideologies regarding the role of government in regulating the marketplace.

PMI – 4.D Explain how political ideologies vary on the government's role in regulating the marketplace.

PMI – 4.E Explain how political ideologies vary on the role of the government in addressing social issues.

PMI – 4.F Explain how different ideologies impact policy on social issues.

Performance Tasks

Upon the completion of this chapter, you must be able to do the following:

- Explain the socialization process.
- Explain how American culture has influenced political values in the United States and how those values are reflected in policy formulation and implementation.
- Explain the differences between liberalism, conservatism, and libertarianism with regard to the role of government in the economy and citizens' private lives.
- Explain the ideologies of the two major political parties.

B. O'Kane/Alamy Stock Photo

"We let the voters speak to us."

J. ANN SELZER
University of Kansas

J. Ann Selzer's gateway to American politics has been her ability to accurately measure public opinion in the state of Iowa—the home of the nation's first presidential caucus. Iowa, being the first contest, shapes the presidential race in important ways. Candidates spend huge amounts of time and money courting Iowans. Selzer understood the importance of this battle and realized that good estimates of what Iowans thought about the candidates prior to voting would be invaluable to the democratic process. She has been involved with the *Des Moines Register* Iowa caucus poll for over three decades, predicting in 2016 that Hillary Clinton would beat Bernie Sanders. Eight years earlier, she stunned the political world by anticipating Barack Obama's easy victory over Hillary Clinton.

Selzer's curiosity about people's attitudes and how best to capture those opinions began when she was five years old. Unhappy with a nickname her parents had given her, she asked neighborhood mothers about their opinions on it.[1] Her question was, "Do you think it is a good name for a witch?" Her results showed maternal support for making her parents abandon her nickname, cementing her interest in public opinion.

Selzer grew up in an upper-middle-class setting in Topeka, Kansas. She was a competitive and driven child who wanted to stand out among her four siblings.[2] After graduating from the University of Kansas, she earned her PhD in Communication Theory and Research from the University of Iowa. She started her career in Des Moines,[3] briefly working as director of research for Starr and Associates, a research institute and law office, before moving to Washington, D.C., to work for a public opinion research firm.[4]

In 1987, she moved back to Des Moines and took a job running the Iowa Poll for the *Des Moines Register*.[5] She understood that this position offered a chance to influence politics through the ability to assess accurately the thinking of Iowans. When she took over, the poll was a unit within the paper's operation and included surveys of people who had participated in previous polls, who were likely to be repeat caucus-goers. But Selzer wondered if the opinions of newly found caucus-goers matched those of people the Iowa Poll had surveyed before. She looked at the data and determined that they did not. She urged the editors to end the practice of re-interviewing previous poll participants. This approach helped to establish her credibility as a trusted pollster.[6] With this methodology, Selzer predicted that Bob Dole would win the 1988 Republican caucus over George H. W. Bush, the favorite in almost every other poll the newspaper had conducted. From this point on, her innovative methodologies and attention to detail helped her gain a reputation of pursuing the truth with new techniques.

She worked for the *Register* until 1992, when she left to develop her own polling firm, Selzer & Company.[7] In 1997 her company won the bid to conduct the *Des Moines Register* Iowa Poll when the newspaper decided to outsource the operation, and from there she has solidified her reputation as a preeminent pollster.[8] Some of the races that have helped cement her prowess are the 2004 last-minute victory of John Kerry in the Democratic caucus and Joni Ernst's 8.5-point victory over Bruce Braley in the 2014 Iowa senate race.[9] In the 2008 Democratic caucus polls, her firm's research indicated that caucus attendees would include a high proportion of first-time caucus-goers and independents—enabling them to reach a voice underrepresented in campaign projections and other polls. Her controversial projection that Obama would easily win led the Hillary Clinton and John Edwards campaigns to question her credibility.[10] But her accurate prediction proved that this methodology enabled her firm to out-predict other leading polls.

Selzer's gateway to participation in the American political system—measuring public opinion with accuracy—highlights its importance in a democracy. The expression of the public will is the bedrock of democracy. For politicians, knowing which way the public leans is a gateway to power. For citizens, expressing an opinion and knowing it is being heard is a gateway to influence. But reading public opinion correctly is not easy. Polls can be a great help, but they can easily be flawed. It is also worth noting that even if well measured, public opinion does not always point toward the best path for the country; the public can make the wrong call. To guard against such outcomes, it is critical the public be informed so they can make wise choices. In this chapter, we investigate the contours, sources, and impact of public opinion.

6.1 The Power of Public Opinion

Decide why public opinion is powerful

Essential Knowledge

In a democratic society, public opinion can impact elections and policy debates.

"Our government rests on public opinion," claimed Abraham Lincoln. "Public sentiment is everything. With public sentiment, nothing can fail. Without it, nothing can succeed."[11] The nation's sixteenth president (1861–65) was the great champion of "government of the people, by the people, and for the people," as he expressed it in his Gettysburg Address. He understood that democratic government must be responsive to the will of the people. The hope in a democracy is that each citizen has an equal voice and that those voices, collectively, will be heard by government officials and will guide their actions. Knowing what the public is thinking and having public support are a powerful combination. Writing more than one hundred years ago, James Bryce, a famous observer of U.S. politics, contended that public opinion is "the greatest source of power" in the United States, more important than the power of presidents, Congress, and political parties.[12]

The Power of Presidential Approval

approval rating: *Job performance evaluation for the president, Congress, or other public official or institution that is generated by public opinion polls and is typically reported as a percentage.*

Perhaps no one appreciates the power of public opinion more keenly than former President George W. Bush (2001–09). He came to office in 2001, following a contested election in which more than half the electorate had voted against him. However, following the terrorist attacks on September 11 of that year, the country rallied to his side.[13] President Bush then enjoyed the approval of 90 percent of the public. No president had ever scored higher—not Ronald Reagan (1981–89), not John F. Kennedy (1961–63), and not Franklin Delano Roosevelt (1933–45). With this unprecedented level of public support, Bush was able to get Congress to agree to nearly everything he wanted. It passed the PATRIOT Act, which expanded the powers of the federal government in the area of national security, and it approved his call for a new cabinet-level Department of Homeland Security. But such popularity is always short-lived. Bush, for example, tumbled in popularity during his remaining years in office. By the time he left office, Bush's approval stood in the mid-20s, and one CBS/*New York Times* poll indicated only 20 percent of Americans approved of his job—the lowest rating for any president since the start of scientific polling in the 1930s.

Handout/Getty Images News/Getty Images

IMAGE 6.1 Standing in the Control Room, President Obama watches the unfolding of events after ordering the assassination of Osama bin Laden in May 2011.

President Obama's **approval rating**, by contrast, was much more stable than President Bush's. As Figure 6.1 shows, Obama's popularity was pretty stable for the first 7 years of his presidency, usually hovering in the mid-40-percent range. He did enjoy a brief surge immediately following the assassination of Osama bin Laden on May 2, 2011, and his successful reelection in 2012. Over the last year of his presidency, his approval moved above 50 percent. That gain likely reflects improvement in the

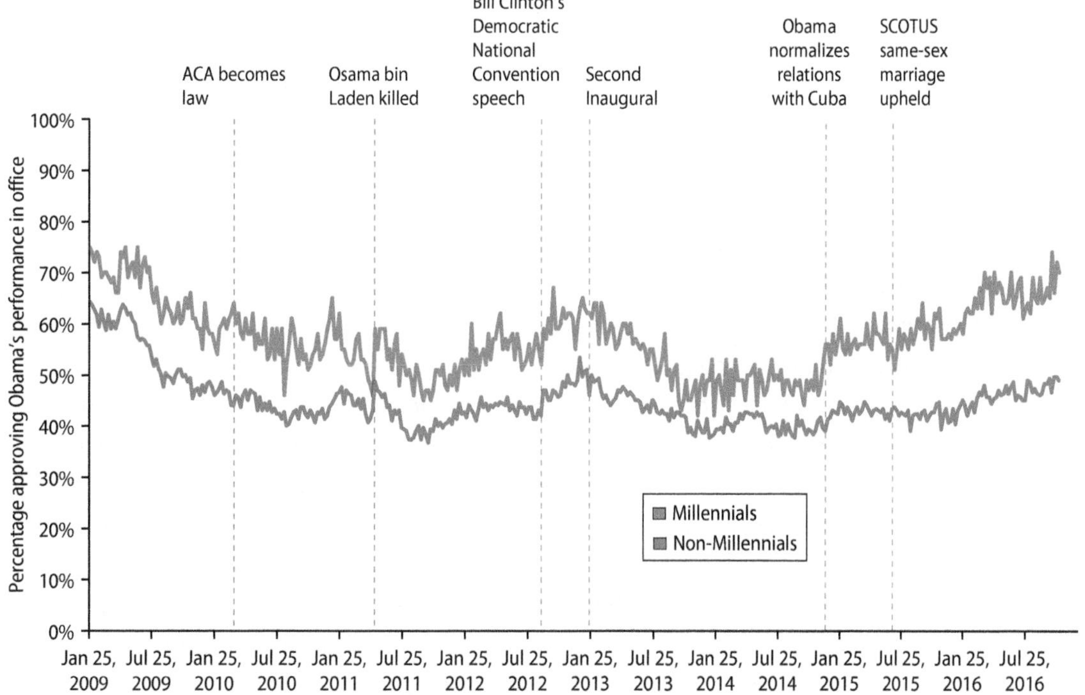

FIGURE 6.1 Approval Ratings of President Barack Obama, 2009–2016

Presidents' approval ratings generally decline during their time in office, but President Obama's popularity experienced a brief surge after the assassination of Osama bin Laden. Millennials have a higher approval of the president than older Americans.

Source: Gallup, http://www.gallup.com/poll/121199/Obama-Weekly-Job-Approval-Demographic-Groups.aspx

economy and inevitable comparisons to Hillary Clinton and Donald Trump, who were both very unpopular candidates. Obama does enjoy greater popularity among Millennials; the gap at times was as much as 20 percentage points. The trend over the course of Obama's presidency was much the same for Millennials and non-Millennials, which means both groups were reacting much the same to changing events. But it is clear that younger Americans were bigger fans, especially among African Americans.

Presidents, for the most part, start off with public support during the so-called honeymoon period. But as time unfolds and governing continues, the public becomes more dissatisfied. It seems as if staying in office is costly for presidents. We certainly saw that with Obama, and this pattern is a common one for presidents. President Trump faces this same basic fate during this term. It is an enduring feature of American politics.

What Is Public Opinion?

Public opinion is recognized for its power, but it is ever-changing, hard to measure, harder to predict, and nearly impossible to control. **Public opinion** is the aggregate of individual attitudes or beliefs about certain issues or officials, and it is the foundation of any democracy.

public opinion: *Aggregate of individual attitudes or beliefs about certain issues or officials.*

Of course, the electorate expresses its opinion primarily through voting, and elections are the most visible means by which citizens hold elected officials accountable. But a democratic system should not rely just on elections to ensure that politicians are doing the people's will. Elections are not held very often. Further, they give signals but not directions. For example, the electoral success of the Republicans in the 2014 midterm elections was hailed as a sign that the public was unhappy with the Obama administration's handling of the economy, health care, and conflicts in the Middle East. But what does "unhappiness" say about specific policies? Did the people want big spending cuts? Or did they want additional government efforts to stimulate the economy? Did they want Obamacare reformed or just want it to work better? Election results do not send clear signals on such specific questions. Voters can indicate only whether they like one candidate more than the other; they cannot convey the reasons for their vote. So legislators and elected executives who want to stay in power expend considerable energy trying to find out what the public wishes and to respond accordingly. Because public opinion plays such an important role in forging responsiveness, it is central to understanding U.S. politics.

Today, public opinion polls are the most reliable indicators of what Americans are thinking, and a whole industry and science have grown up around measuring people's opinions on everything from presidents to toothpaste. Polls are not the only sources of public opinion; others are the size of rallies and protests, the tone of letters sent to elected officials or newspapers, the amount of money given to particular causes or candidates, the content of newspaper editorials, and information gleaned from day-to-day conversations with average Americans. Shifts in public opinion can also be detected in Supreme Court decisions, as cases pertaining to birth control, abortion, and marriage equality indicate (see Chapter 4, Civil Liberties, for specific cases).

The Public's Support of Government

The health and stability of a democracy rest with the public. Just as government must respond to what the people want, so citizens must view the system as legitimate and want to be part of it. If the public withdraws its support, the government collapses. For these reasons, political scientists have sought to measure the public's faith in the political system. Two of the most common efforts involve assessing whether the people trust their government and whether they believe their participation in government matters. Political scientists call the latter **efficacy**—the extent to which people believe their actions affect the course of government. **Political trust** is the extent to which people believe the government acts in their best interests. It has generally declined over the past fifty years, with steeper declines following the beginning of the Iraq War in 2003 and the financial collapse that began in 2008. One current estimate is that only 19 percent of Americans say they can trust the government in Washington to do what is right "just about always" (3 percent) or "most of the time" (16 percent).[14]

efficacy: *Extent to which people believe their actions can affect public affairs and the actions of government.*

political trust: *Extent to which people believe the government acts in their best interests.*

Efficacy has also declined. It stood at more than 70 percent in 1960; by 1994, it had fallen by half. In other words, only one-third of Americans felt that their opinions mattered to government. The figure rebounded to 60 percent by 2002 but then declined again during the Iraq War and financial crisis. It has fallen well below 40 percent in the current environment.[15] There is little doubt, as President Obama said in his first inaugural address, that there has been a "sapping of confidence across our land."[16]

Public trust and efficacy react to changes in government and whether the nation is experiencing good or bad times. Yet, through it all, Americans' commitment to the country and its core institutions has remained strong. Patriotism, for example, shows little decline. In 2014, 5 percent of Americans viewed themselves as unpatriotic.[17] In 2015, 95 percent of Americans had pride in being American.[18] Almost no one in the country favors overthrowing the government.[19]

SUPREME COURT CASES

Bowers v. Hardwick (1986)

Obergefell v. Hodges (2015)

QUESTION: *Bowers:* May states prosecute consensual sexual activity by members of the same sex? *Obergefell:* May states prohibit same-sex marriage?

ORAL ARGUMENT: *Bowers*: March 31, 1986 (listen at http://www.oyez.org/cases /1980-1989/1985/1985_85_140) *Obergefell*: April 28, 2015 (listen at http://www.oyez.org/cases/2014/14-556)

DECISION: *Bowers*: June 30, 1986 (read at http://caselaw.findlaw.com/us-supreme-court/478/186.html). *Windsor*: March 27, 2013 (read at http://caselaw.findlaw.com/us-supreme-court/14-556.html).

OUTCOME: *Bowers*: There is no right to homosexual sodomy (5–4) (1986). *Obergefell*: States may not prohibit same-sex marriage (5–4) (2015).

When the police came to Michael Hardwick's home looking for him, his roommate let them in. When the police got to Hardwick's room, they observed him engaged in sexual behavior with another male. They arrested him under Georgia's anti-sodomy statute, which prohibits "any sexual contact involving the genitals of one person and the mouth or anus of another." Hardwick argued that the statute violated the right to privacy that the Court established in the *Griswold* birth control case (1965), which the Court later held to protect rights that were "deeply rooted in this Nation's history and tradition."* Noting that prohibitions on sodomy had "ancient roots," the Court voted 5–4 against the claim, calling the argument that homosexual sodomy is among those traditions "facetious." Chief Justice Warren Burger concurred, approvingly citing medieval English sources that declared sodomy as an offense of "deeper malignity" than rape. At the time, only about 32 percent of the American public agreed with the opinion that homosexual relations should be legal.

The Supreme Court reversed that decision nearly twenty years later in *Lawrence v. Texas* (2003). With seven new members on the Court, the justices voted 6–3 that the Texas law prohibiting sodomy was unconstitutional, with the majority opinion resting the decision on the liberty protected by the due process clause of the Fourteenth Amendment.

In the *Obergefell* case (2015), the Supreme Court struck down state laws that prohibited same-sex marriage. Citing the Supreme Court's 1967 *Loving v. Virginia* decision striking bans on interracial marriage, as well as the Supreme Court's 2003 *Lawrence v. Texas* decision overturning *Bowers v. Hardwick*, the Supreme Court ruled that the liberty protected by the Fourteenth Amendment includes the right to marry a partner of the same sex.

In fewer than thirty years, the Supreme Court had gone from holding that states could criminalize homosexual activity to determining that states may not prohibit same-sex marriage. These changes coincide with a more than quadrupling of support for marriage equality in the United States during that time. Whether this new result was directly due to the change in public opinion or due to new justices from a different generation who reflected that changed opinion, the Court's decision aligned with changes in public opinion.§

**Griswold v. Connecticut*, 381 U.S. 479 (1965); *Washington v. Glucksberg*, 521 U.S. 702, 721 (1997).

§ Marriages with members of the same sex should be legalized, September 1985, 11 percent agree. Do you favor or oppose allowing gay and lesbian couples to marry legally? December 2015, 52 percent. Both polls accessed on February 2, 2016, from Roper Opinion index, ropercenter.cornell.edu/ipoll-database.

Thinking Critically

1. Should the justices of the Supreme Court be influenced by public opinion?
2. How should the Court decide which rights, among those not specifically listed in the Constitution, should be protected as fundamental rights?

6.2 Public Opinion Polls

Decide how well polls measure public opinion

Polls make it possible to gauge the public's thinking on a variety of issues or officials, but they have been scientifically conducted only since the 1930s. Even today, a poorly designed or executed poll can produce misleading results. Moreover, so much information is available from surveys that it is important to know which findings warrant attention and which warrant caution. Poll results can be biased, contradictory, and confusing (see, for example, the polls unanimously showing a Clinton victory over Sanders in the 2016 Michigan Democratic primary), which is why Ann Selzer's accurate assessments of Iowans' political views were so valued during the presidential election season.

Gauging Public Opinion in the Past

In the eighteenth and nineteenth centuries, the contents of letters, the sizes of crowds at rallies, and people's willingness to sign petitions were used to gauge public opinion. They were crude indicators. Politicians had to go to great lengths to secure information about the public mood. George Washington (1789–97) was so frustrated with not being able to sense what voters thought about his policies as president that he literally mounted his horse and rode into the countryside to talk to the people. Abraham Lincoln held public meetings at the White House "to renew in me a clearer and more vivid image of that great popular assemblage out of which I sprung," he said, and he called these receptions his "public opinion baths."[20] President William McKinley (1897–1901) had his staff clip newspaper articles and put the clippings in a folder at night so he could read them to gauge the public's thinking.[21] Franklin Roosevelt also paid close attention to newspapers. And both Lincoln and Roosevelt, presidents in times of crisis, learned what the people thought through the many letters that citizens wrote to them. Even in the twenty-first century, citizens still write to the president. President Obama receives thousands of letters a day, and his staff selects ten a day for him to read.[22]

COMMON GROUND

Arizona Republic and Phoenix Gazette, September 27, 1941

IMAGE 6.2 Presidents—such as Franklin D. Roosevelt, depicted here—often got their information on public opinion by reading the newspaper.

Yet none of these sources of "public sentiment," as President Lincoln called it, gave very precise indicators. Lincoln once said that he wanted to "get done . . . what the people desire to have done," but the problem was that he did not know what they desired.[23] Given that public opinion was so difficult to determine, there were many disagreements about its shape and direction. Moreover, because it was based on the content of newspapers and letters, on petitions, and on conversations with political observers, it was really elite opinion.[24] In other words, the most activist and literate elements of society were defining public opinion. Those who could write letters, for example, and would take the time to do so were the ones whose voices were heard. Thus politicians had biased readings of public opinion because the views they heard tended not to represent the people equally.

Essential Knowledge

The quality of a poll (random sample, non-biased questions) can have a profound impact on the results. These results, when reported by the media, can then impact public opinion, public policy, and elections.

Scientific Polling and the Growth of Survey Research

In the 1800s, newspapers and other organizations polled the people to assess public opinion, but these polls were of limited help because it was unclear who was being surveyed. So-called straw polls, for example, sought to predict the outcome of elections. During the presidential campaign of 1824, the *Harrisburg Pennsylvanian* canvassed the opinion of newspaper readers and concluded that Andrew Jackson would get 63 percent of the vote and win easily.[25] As it turned out, Jackson received only about 40 percent of the popular vote.

Essential Knowledge

The media's use of polling results to convey popular levels of trust and confidence in government can impact elections by turning such events into "horse races," based more on popularity and factors other than qualifications and platforms of candidates.

Though straw polls were often inaccurate, newspapers and magazines continued to poll readers' opinions well into the twentieth century. During the 1936 presidential campaign, the *Literary Digest* conducted a poll that predicted Republican Alf Landon would win the election by 57 percent over President Franklin Roosevelt. The reverse happened: Roosevelt won with a landslide 61 percent of the vote. Why did the *Literary Digest* get it so wrong? It had sent out 10 million ballots. But it had sent them to names drawn from automobile registration lists and telephone books and asked recipients to mail the ballots back. The sample, as a result, was biased. First, in 1936 those who owned automobiles and had telephones were wealthier than average Americans and were more likely to be Republicans. Less wealthy Americans, responding favorably to Roosevelt's actions to end the Great Depression, were increasingly aligning themselves with the Democrats. Second, the poll asked respondents to mail in their ballots, introducing additional bias. Those who would take the time to do so would likely be better off, further increasing the Republican bias of the sample. Even though 2 million ballots were returned, the poll did not offer a very sound basis on which to make a prediction.

random sample: *Method of selection that gives everyone who might be selected to participate in a poll an equal chance to be included.*

George Gallup, who had founded the American Institute of Public Opinion in 1935, correctly predicted the outcome of the 1936 election by using a **random sample** to generate a way to select people to participate in surveys. He made his sample representative of the American public by giving, in effect, every American an equal chance to be part of it. The end product was a sample of 5,000, which was far smaller than the *Literary Digest's* sample but far more representative of average Americans. As a result of his innovative approach, Gallup is often considered the father of modern polling, and the best-known name in polling today remains the Gallup Poll. His scientific polling and survey research techniques have been refined over the years.

W. Eugene Smith/The LIFE Picture/Getty Images

IMAGE 6.3 In the 1930s, George Gallup developed a scientific approach to polling, greatly increasing its accuracy and authority.

The advent of scientific polling made it possible to assess the opinions of the public with some degree of ease and accuracy. V. O. Key, a leading scholar of public opinion in the 1950s and 1960s, described its impact this way:

> *In an earlier day public opinion seemed to be pictured as a mysterious vapor that emanated from the undifferentiated citizenry and in some ways or another enveloped the apparatus*

of government to bring it into conformity with the public will. These weird conceptions . . . passed out of style as the technique of the sample survey permitted the determination, with some accuracy, of the opinions within the population."[26]

Scientific polling also permitted greater equality in assessing public opinion because the polls had the ability to tap the opinions of all Americans. George Gallup understood this aspect of polling—that scientific polls democratized the measurement of public opinion.[27]

By the early 1940s, the federal government began to see the value of survey research, too, and in October 1941, the U.S. Army conducted a survey to understand the opinions of enlisted men and officers. Today, the federal government continues to undertake a wide variety of polls, ranging from surveys about health issues to tapping the public's thinking on the economy. Polls are undertaken by other organizations as well. After the end of World War II, the University of Michigan founded the Survey Research Center, now the academic center for all sorts of polling.[28] By the 1960s, John Kennedy was making use of pollsters, and both Lyndon B. Johnson (1963–69) and Richard M. Nixon (1969–74) followed his lead.[29] The news media also saw the value of information about the public's thinking. By the 1980s, all the major television networks had polling operations in conjunction with major newspapers or news services.

Today Americans are regularly surveyed on a wide range of things other than politics. Polls ask about sexual practices, television viewing preferences, car purchases, and how often people go bowling. Extensive polling has revealed what proportion of the nation believes in UFOs, what kind of soap people buy, and at what age children stop believing in Santa Claus. During 2015, a number of polling organizations asked questions about Caitlyn Jenner. There was much interest in her transition from being Bruce Jenner. For the most part, the public was split on reactions to Jenner and few changed their opinions about transgendered people.[30]

Types of Polls

In a nation of more than 200 million adults, gathering opinions from everyone is not practical. Even the U.S. census, a count of the population required by the Constitution every ten years, has trouble reaching every adult.[31] So polls draw a sample from a larger population. But first the population must be defined. It might be all adults over age 18, or only voters, or only citizens who contributed to Republican candidates in 2014.

The typical size of a sample survey is 1,000 people, though it can vary between 500 and about 1,500. Size does not matter as much as whether the sample is representative of the population being assessed. Having a representative sample means, in effect, that everyone in that population has an equal chance of being asked to participate in the poll. If a random 1,000 people are asked to be part of the survey, they should be representative of the population generally—in, say, wealth, ethnicity, or educational attainment. The key to a representative sample is the randomness. It should be much like drawing numbered balls for a lottery: Each ball has the same chance of being chosen.

There are various ways to collect the information being sought. For in-person interviews, survey researchers send interviewers into neighborhoods and communities to ask questions in person. This was long the favored method, but it became increasingly expensive. With the near-universal presence of telephones by the 1970s, calling people became a more viable and much less expensive option. Telephone polls have dominated survey research over the past thirty years and continue to be used much of the time. Automated telephone polls, the so-called robo-polls, are on the rise. They are cheaper but tend not to be very accurate.[32]

Essential Knowledge

Telephone polling using random digit dialing is the primary way people are selected for participation in a poll.

The latest platform for polling is the Internet. Internet polls have much potential, but the fact that older and poorer Americans may lack access to computers introduces bias. As with telephones in the past century, however, more and more people are using computers and the web, so in the future, Internet polling will likely become the dominant platform for survey research.

Call-in polls or write-in polls are other means of securing a sample. For the former, a telephone number is posted on the television screen, for example, and people are asked to call to register their views. In the latter, a newspaper publishes an appeal for subscribers to write letters offering their opinions. Such approaches can yield a large number of participants, but the size of the sample can be misleading, for those who are willing to call or write are different from those who are not. The samples yielded in these polls are not representative and, thus, are highly suspect.

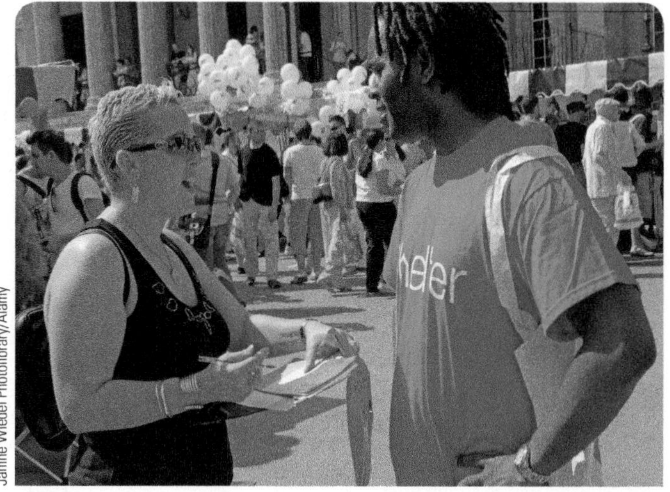
Janine Wiedel Photolibrary/Alamy

IMAGE 6.4 In-person interviews were long considered the best method for polling the people; despite the expense, they are still used occasionally.

Consider the following example of a call-in poll. The Miss America Beauty Pageant, which was owned by Donald Trump from 1996 to 2015, had long used a swimsuit competition to help decide who would win the much-coveted crown. However, critics demanded the elimination of the swimsuit segment because they believed it exploited women as sexual objects. Yet those who ran the contest knew that the swimsuit competition was very popular. The managers of the pageant decided to "let the public decide" by having a call-in poll asking whether the swimsuit competition should continue. The results were "clear": 87 percent voted to retain the swimsuit portion.[33] But did the public really speak here? Because the telephone number was posted only during the airing of the pageant, the respondents were people already watching the pageant and therefore were likely to be favorable to it. Those opposed to the swimsuit segment were more likely to be doing something else.

Essential Knowledge

The reliability of public opinion polls can be impacted by the type of poll and the representativeness of the sample set. Polls that underrepresent particular groups can yield results not reflective of the overall public opinion.

Presidential elections are awash in polls. In the heat of the fall campaign, nightly polls gauge changes in voters' preferences for the major contenders. These surveys are called **tracking polls**. Another type of survey involving elections is the **exit poll**, conducted as voters leave the polling booth. The goal here is to learn about the reasoning behind the votes citizens just cast but, more important, to predict the outcome of the election before all the ballots are formally counted.

tracking polls: *Polls that seek to gauge changes of opinion of the same sample size over a period of time; they are common during the closing months of presidential elections.*

exit polls: *Polls that survey a sample of voters immediately after exiting the voting booth to predict the outcome of the election before the ballots are officially counted.*

The most famous and consequential exit poll took place in Florida during the 2000 presidential elections, fueling one of the most controversial electoral struggles of all time. The major networks used an exit poll to predict that the Sunshine State would go to Vice President Albert Gore Jr. (1993–2001). Florida's electoral votes would put Gore over the 270 needed, making him the apparent winner of the presidency. These predictions started to roll in at 8 P.M. on election night. The campaign of Republican George W. Bush protested, saying it was too early to call the state and that the race was still too close to know who won. By 10 P.M., the earlier forecast was withdrawn, and the outcome of the presidential election was again unclear. By 2 A.M. the next morning, Fox News called the election for Bush, with the other major networks soon following. Just two hours later, however, the call was retracted. There followed a thirty-six-day legal battle over which candidate actually won in Florida. It was not settled until the U.S. Supreme Court halted the Florida recount in mid-December, giving Bush the presidency (see Supreme Court Cases: *Bush v. Gore*, in Chapter 10, Elections and Campaigns).

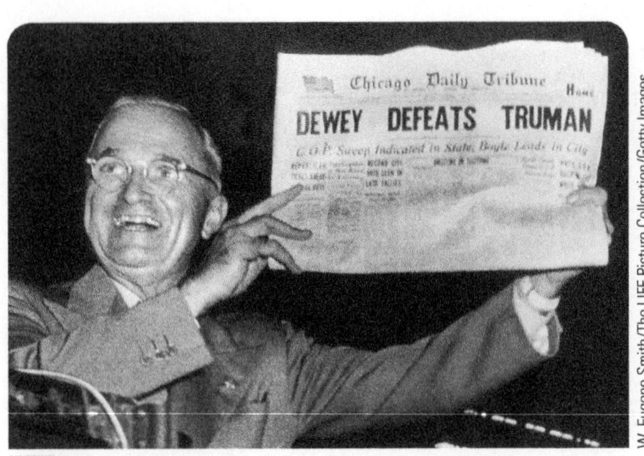

W. Eugene Smith/The LIFE Picture Collection/Getty Images

IMAGE 6.5 President Harry Truman holding up a newspaper proclaiming that he lost the 1948 presidential election to Thomas Dewey. The *Tribune's* polls were wrong, and Truman had actually won.

Many have wanted to blame exit polls for the confusion that election night, but the polls were not as big a problem as the news media's use of them. The networks feel real pressure to make early calls, and that pressure sometimes leads them to go beyond what the data support. So while CBS was making that first call around 8 P.M., its polling experts behind the scene were urging caution.[34] Twelve years later, the tables were turned. It was Karl Rove, the well-known Republican consultant from the 2000 campaign, who questioned Fox News when it called Ohio for President Obama. He did so on live TV and Megyn Kelly, the Fox News anchor on the air at the time, challenged Rove, going directly to the experts who made the prediction. The exit polls proved Rove wrong: Romney did, in fact, lose that crucial state.

push polls: *Polls that are designed to manipulate the opinions of those being polled.*

A final kind of election poll is actually a campaign strategy. **Push polls** are conducted by interest groups or candidates who try to affect the opinions of respondents by priming them with biased information. During the 2016 presidential primary in South Carolina, for example, Donald Trump claimed that Ted Cruz (R-TX) ran a push poll against him, trying to undermine his candidacy.[35] For these reasons and others, Trump started to call Cruz "lyin' Ted" on the campaign trail. Such polls seek to shift public opinion, not to measure it.

Error in Polls

confidence interval: *Statistical range with a given probability that takes random error into account.*

Pollsters, like Ann Selzer, do everything they can to ensure that their samples are representative. Even if the sample is drawn properly, however, there is still a chance of error. To capture this uncertainty, all poll numbers come with a **confidence interval** that captures the likely range 95 percent of the time. The poll produces a single estimate of the public's thinking, but the best way to think of that estimate is as a range of possible estimates. For a sample of 600 respondents, the sampling error is 4 percent. That 4 percent generates the confidence interval. Assume, for example, that 65 percent of those sampled support the efforts of Congress to reform the campaign finance laws. With a sampling error of 4 percent, the best way to think of the proportion is that, with 95 percent certainty, the actual amount of public support is somewhere between 61 percent and 69 percent. This range is the confidence interval. Note, however, that there is still a one in twenty chance (5 percent) that the true proportion is above or below that eight-point confidence interval. Hence, caution is always required when interpreting poll data.

Essential Knowledge

Sampling error is the error caused by examining the responses of the samples rather than the entire population.

In addition to sampling error, the wording of the question can introduce bias. The controversial issue of abortion offers a vivid example. What the public thinks about this issue depends a great deal on the way the question is asked. An NBC News/*Wall Street Journal* poll asked a representative sample of Americans the following question: "Which of the following best represents your views about abortion—the choice on abortion should be left up to the woman and her doctor, abortion should be legal only in cases in which pregnancy results from rape or incest or when the life of the woman is at risk, or abortion should be illegal in all circumstances?"

The answers show that 53 percent of the public felt that abortion was a decision best left to the woman and her doctor. Only 15 percent of Americans felt it should be illegal in all circumstances, with 29 percent wanting to have exceptions. In short, a majority of the public appeared to support abortion rights for women. That is an important finding.

But is it true? Consider the following question asked at about the same time by Fox News/Opinion Dynamics: "Once a woman is pregnant, do you believe the unborn baby or fetus should have all the same rights as a newborn baby?" The answers tell a different story. Nearly 60 percent of the public said yes, the unborn fetus should have the same rights as a newborn baby. Only 26 percent said no. According to this poll, a strong majority wants to protect the rights of the unborn and, therefore, to limit abortion rights for women.[36]

So what is American public opinion on abortion? Clearly, the answer depends on the wording of the question, specifically on whether respondents are asked to focus on the rights of women or the rights of the unborn. This same dynamic applies to other controversial issues, such as attitudes on race. Because of America's long and tortured history of race relations, people often try to give socially acceptable responses so as to suggest they are tolerant and not bigoted or racist. Although interviewers are trained to be neutral in their questioning, respondents sometimes try to give responses that they think the questioner wants to hear.

Another source of error in polls involves what political scientists call **nonattitudes**.[37] When asked, many people feel compelled to answer, even if they do not have opinions or know much about the question. They do not want to seem uninformed, but their responses create error in the survey.

Essential Knowledge

Polling questions cannot be asked in a manner that is biased. The question must present the respondent with choices in a non-biased or non-leading manner. Further, the results from closed ended questions are easier to calculate compared to the results from open ended questions.

nonattitudes: *Sources of error in public opinion polls in which individuals feel obliged to give opinions when they are unaware of the issue or have no opinions about it.*

The Future of Polls. The polls did not anticipate the upset win of Donald Trump in 2016, which casts a long shadow. The state polls, in particular, got it wrong. Wisconsin was supposed to be an easy win for Clinton; Trump instead won. This pattern held in a number of states, especially in the Rust Belt. It appears that many Trump voters were simply not counted in these polls. One explanation may be that these voters so distrusted the establishment that they would not agree to participate in polls. It is hard to know, but polls suffered a black eye in 2016.

Polling was in transition even before 2016. Representative sampling in telephone surveys is increasingly affected by the growing number of cell phones, especially for young people who usually do not have landlines. Telephone polls are increasingly moving toward cell phones and away from landlines. Even for those who continue to have landlines, the widespread use of caller ID and answering machines allows more and more Americans to screen their calls and refuse to participate in surveys. In fact, there is a general "polling fatigue" among the public.

People are asked to participate not only in political polls but also in surveys for insurance companies, health care providers, and an endless array of commercial products. Automobile service centers call customers to see if they are satisfied with their most recent visit; banks make similar calls. The result is that fewer people are willing to participate in telephone surveys. The declining response rate is lessening the ability of pollsters to capture public opinion accurately. In the 1990s, the rate of response was nearly 40 percent, and now it is about 15 percent.[38]

Traditional pollsters must find better ways to ensure accurate results. Internet-based polls represent the future. Through the Internet, polls can be done quickly and cheaply, but respondents may not be representative of the population. Statisticians have developed reliable ways to correct for bias, making the web a powerful tool to measure the public's thinking. As more people gain access to the web, the amount of bias will decline and this method will gain even wider favor. But the lessons of 2016 need to be kept in mind.

6.3 What Drives Public Opinion?

Identify who drives public opinion—citizens or elites

Where does public opinion come from? If it is the aggregate of citizen attitudes and beliefs, it starts with individuals. In this section, we examine the major forces that shape political thinking on a personal level, including the social and political environment in which one grows up and the generation and family into which one is born. Self-interest also affects political attitudes, as do the ideas of opinion leaders such as journalists, political observers, policy makers, and experts.

Social and Political Environment

Essential Knowledge
Some of the key agents of socialization are family, schools, peers, media, and social and religious organizations.

socialization: *Impact and influence of one's social environment on the views and attitudes one carries in life, a primary source of political attitudes.*

Independents: *Individuals who do not affiliate with either of the major political parties.*

Political attitudes are shaped by environment—the kind of place in which one grows up and lives. Someone who grew up in a small town in Alabama centered around the local Baptist church would be influenced by that setting and would be different from someone who grew up in, say, Seattle, Washington, in a family that was not religious. Attendance at a suburban private high school would yield differing influences than attendance at an urban public school. Each of us is a product of our family, friends, and community. We call the process by which our attitudes are shaped **socialization**.

The way we live our lives, the kinds of foods we eat, the types of vacations we enjoy, and the houses of worship we attend—they all shape how we are socialized. Our political attitudes are no different. The clearest embodiment of political socialization is partisanship, and evidence shows that parents pass their partisan views along to their children. If parents are Democrats, there is a two-thirds chance that their children will identify themselves as Democrats. They might identify as **Independents**, but there is just a 10 percent chance they will be Republicans. The impact of socialization depends, of course, on whether both parents identify with the same party. If the parents are split on partisanship, the chance of the children being Independents rises considerably.[39]

High divorce rates have changed family structure in recent years, but there is no evidence that they have interfered with the passing along of political values, even when children are exposed to many more potential influences. Recent research concludes that "despite [the] transformation in the political environment and the character of family life over the last thirty years, our findings about youth coming of age in the 1990s strongly parallel those based on youth socialization in the 1960s."[40]

It may be that political values are passed on in families by genes as well as by socialization. Recent research offers some tantalizing hints that genetics may shape political views.[41] Political scientists have been slow to embrace the possibility, but it should not be dismissed. That some people are more outgoing and more willing to build social networks appears to have a basis in one's genes.[42] If so, such a tendency could explain a willingness to become involved in politics, and it may even shape political views. Data show that identical twins, who share their entire genetic code, expressed more similar political attitudes than did fraternal twins, who are no more similar than any set of siblings. Such data are far from conclusive but still worth thinking about.[43] The bottom line is that this new area of research offers fascinating possibilities for understanding the sources of public opinion.[44]

Ryan Anson/afp/Getty Images

IMAGE 6.6 Parents generally pass political attitudes, including party identification, on to their children.

Whether through family socialization or genes, parents have the biggest impact during a child's early life, but, starting in the teenage years, friends also influence attitudes and behavior, as do schools and communities. Communities that are homogeneous, in which most people share many of the same views and opinions, are likely to reinforce the attitudes of parents. Colleges, too, influence attitudes, and college attendance often offers students a chance to break out of the homogeneous settings of their early years. Students meet people from different states or communities, as well as people with different backgrounds and attitudes. College classes and experiences can also shape political leanings (see Chapter 4, Political Analytics on page 134).

Socialization does not end at college graduation, however. It continues as young people pursue careers and choose where and how they will live. Consider people who live in San Francisco versus those who live in Dallas. Those different environments will surely have different effects on residents. Of course, those who choose to live in San Francisco may have different attitudes from those who move to Texas. But for the most part, it is between the ages of 18 and 24 when people's worldviews begin to crystallize and shape how they view work, family, and politics.

Generational Effects

Major events can change an entire generation's thinking about politics. The Great Depression, for example, which started in 1929 with the crash of the stock market, shaped the attitudes of millions of Americans. It was an economic calamity that even the severe economic downturn of 2008–09 did not match. Millions lost their savings and their homes. In 1932, one of every four Americans was out of work, and incomes had declined by 50 percent. One consequence was that the public blamed the party in power, the Republicans, and switched party allegiance. The Democrats, as a result, became the majority party for the first time in generations.

Essential Knowledge

Major political, social, and economic events can have a profound impact on a person's socialization.

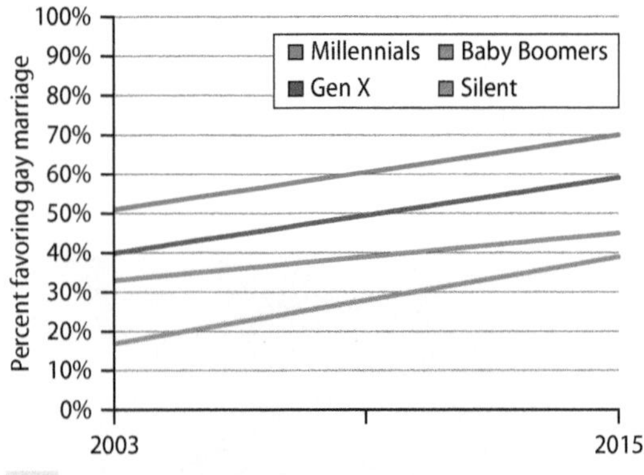

FIGURE 6.2 Shift in Public Opinion on Same-Sex Marriage, 2003–2015

Respondents were asked, "Do you strongly favor, favor, oppose, or strongly oppose allowing gays and lesbians to marry legally?"

Source: http://www.pewforum.org/2015/07/29/graphics-slideshow-changing-attitudes-on-gay-marriage/

The public's thinking on same-sex marriage has changed greatly over the past decade, as Figure 6.2 suggests. The public support for same-sex marriage has surged across the board, but opinions vary greatly by age. Millennials have long been supportive of same-sex marriage. Even in 2003, about 50 percent of the youth favored same-sex marriage. That proportion is now about 75 percent. Among the oldest Americans, support for same-sex marriage has been much more limited. In 2003, fewer than one in five of the "silent generation" favored it. But within a decade, this support more than doubled. The speed with which this issue has changed is impressive, and it shows no signs of slowing up, especially with the Supreme Court making same-sex marriage legal nationwide.

Generational effects are also tied to the era in which one is young and first active as a citizen. Those who were young during the presidency of Republican Ronald Reagan are likely to think of politics differently from those who came of age during the presidency of Democrat Barack Obama. The former will be more likely to hold favorable views about Republicans; the latter will likely be favorable to Democrats. Exit polls from 2008 indicated that 66 percent of all 18- to 29-year-old voters supported Obama.[45] By historical standards, this level of support was quite high. Four years later, Obama won 60 percent of the youth vote, which is still a substantial chunk.[46] In 2016, Hillary Clinton secured 55 percent of the youth favor, compared to 37 percent for Donald Trump.[47]

Essential Knowledge

Generational effects impact the development of a person's political beliefs and attitudes.

Although it remains to be seen whether being a member of what may be called the "Obama generation" will have an enduring effect on partisan identification and politics, America's **Millennial** generation does seem distinctive. Millennials seem to be more trusting of government than previous generations were. There is also evidence that suggests this group is less patient than previous generations and has "a thirst for instant gratification."[48] Perhaps having a world of information at one's fingertips has altered the expectations held by this new generation of Americans.

Millennials: *Generation born between 1982 and 2003.*

Self-Interest and Rationality

Forming political opinion is much more than just a psychological process tied to socialization, however. People also respond to the context in which they find themselves. That is, to a certain extent people are "rational" in that they act in a way that is consistent with their **self-interest**. For example, as income rises, the chance of someone being a Republican increases. Why? The Republicans have pursued tax policies that protect individual wealth, while the Democrats pursue tax policies that tax the wealthy at higher rates to pay for social programs that benefit the less wealthy. In fact, one could argue that although the transmission of partisanship reflects socialization, the reason it sticks is that it is in one's self-interest.

self-interest: *Concern for one's own advantage and well-being.*

Examples of **rationality** and self-interest abound. Couples with school-age children get interested in education policy. Homeowners become more focused on issues tied to property taxes than do individuals who rent. As citizens approach retirement age, they become protective of Social Security and Medicare benefits. Recently, young people, too, have been concerned about these benefits, but in ways that reflect their

rationality: *Acting in a way that is consistent with one's self-interest.*

self-interest. They wonder if the entitlement programs will be bankrupt before they are of age to receive the benefits. Gay Americans are more interested in debates over whether same-sex couples can get married than straight Americans are. Similarly, Latinos show greater concern for reforms in immigration laws than do Americans who are not recent immigrants.[49]

Self-interest clearly shapes political attitudes, but that does not mean that people are selfish. It means that they are trying to advance and protect their own interests, and that in itself is encouraging. Because a democracy rests on the sound judgments of the electorate, it is good to know that there is some evidence that citizens act rationally.

Elites

One of the big questions in the field of public opinion is what role elites—leaders of opinion—play in shaping citizens' thinking. A democracy is supposed to be a system in which the average person has a say in government, and the people's preferences drive public policy. Yet some people worry that experts, policy makers, political observers, journalists, and others in the news media have an undue influence in shaping public opinion. If elites shape public opinion, can the United States be a democratic nation? One way to approach the question of what political scientists call elite theory is to recognize, first, that it is not so simple a matter as elites offering an opinion and the public swallowing it. That assumption attributes far too much influence to elites and far too little credit to the people. Instead, it appears that elites can influence citizens if two conditions are met: first, citizens must be exposed to the message, and, second, they must be open to it.[50]

Let's assume that scientists find clear evidence that being gay is completely genetic. Such evidence does not exist, but if it did, that would mean that sexual orientation is fixed, just as eye color is fixed. If true, the public's attitudes toward homosexuality would surely change, as it is harder to justify discrimination against homosexuals if sexual orientation is an inborn characteristic. Yet some citizens, when learning this new information, would be resistant to the idea due to their moral beliefs. Social conservatives, for example, would on average be far less likely to accept this information than social liberals would. The prior beliefs of social conservatives would serve as a check on accepting it. By comparison, social liberals would have preexisting views that would fit better with the new information. They would be open to it.

This theory of who changes opinions and who does not has a number of implications. First, massive change in public opinion is not likely because the public is not made up of puppets. There is stability to opinion, although a major event such as 9/11 can and will shift the public's thinking on a number of important topics. Second, elites' ability to change public opinion is a product of the intensity and consistency of the message. Disagreement among elites on a new issue will decrease the potential for change. The public, for example, remained divided on global warming in the 1990s. Liberals were more willing to believe that climate change was caused by human activity. Conservatives had more doubts. As the scientific evidence mounted and more elites embraced the notion, the public collectively began to shift its thinking. In 1997, 60 percent of Americans felt that more research about global warming was needed to be sure of its effects, and only 28 percent felt that it was a serious problem. Ten years later,

POLITICAL ANALYTICS

Latinos' Views on Social Issues: Not So Conservative

AS WE HAVE SEEN, LATINOS ARE AN important and emerging part of the electorate that both major political parties would like to attract. Because Latinos are most likely to be Catholic, it has followed that their views on social issues such as abortion and same-sex marriage are conservative. Efforts to attract Latinos based on their presumed social conservatism began in earnest in the 1980s when the Reagan campaign produced political ads emphasizing Latinos' natural affinity for the conservative values of Republicans.[51]

The data from 2012 to 2014 shown in Figure 6.3, however, suggest a Latino electorate whose views on social issues have shifted from their conservative moorings. A majority of Latinos now support same-sex marriage, and the percentage is even higher for Catholic Latinos (54 percent). More than two-thirds of Latinos between the ages of 18 and 24 support same-sex marriage, which is significant because almost half of the eligible Latino electorate are Millennials.

On the issue of abortion, Latinos have long held the view that it should be illegal in all cases.[52] The data from 2014, however, show that among registered voters, Latinos are split, with 48 percent now believing abortion should be legal and 44 percent believing it should be illegal. On this issue, younger Latinos deviate slightly from all Latinos (approximately 4 percent) and about the same from other Millennials. It is also evident from the figure that among Catholic Millennials, the percentage saying abortion should be legal is reduced, suggesting that religion plays a role in their views. Taken together, we see a Latino electorate whose views on social issues may be evolving in a moderate direction.

Examine the graph and notice the views held by Latinos about same-sex marriage and abortion. Also notice the views held by different groups of Latinos about same-sex marriage.

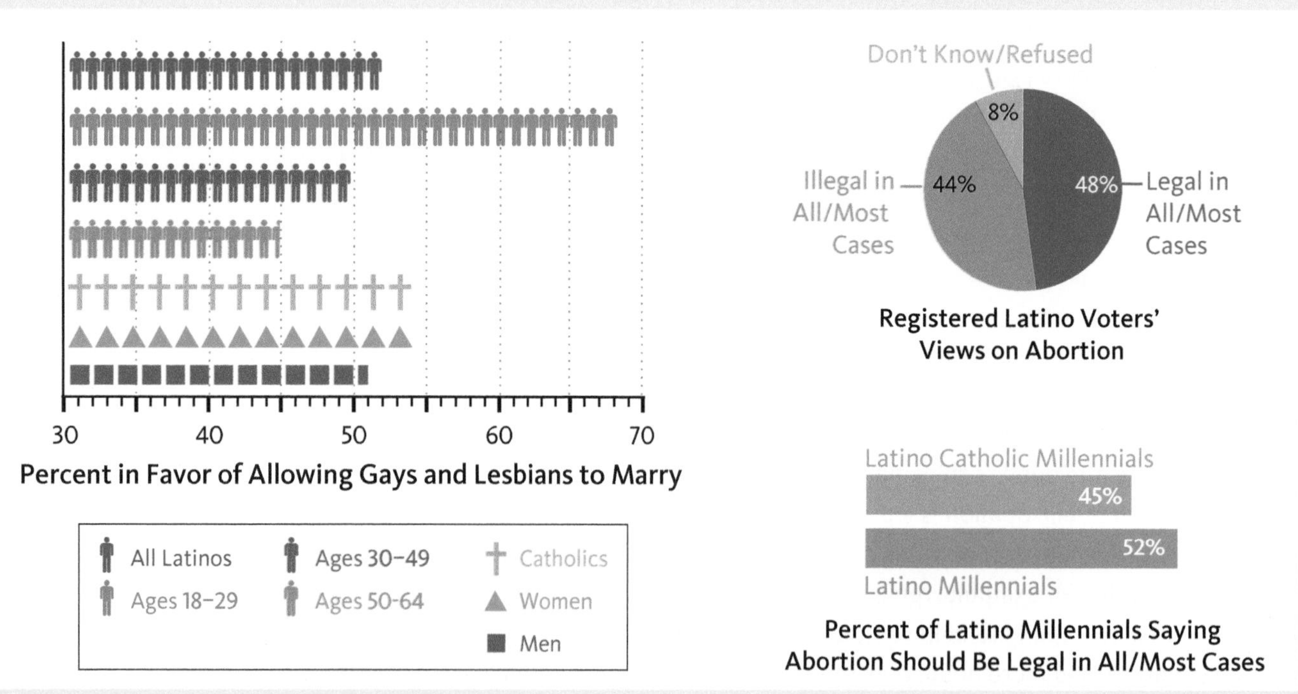

FIGURE 6.3 Latinos' Shifting Views on Social Issues

Thinking Critically

1. What positions on social issues should candidates and political parties take if they wish to attract Latino voters?
2. Are the shifting views on social issues seen among Latinos part of a broader trend among the American electorate?

Sources: Pew Research Center, "U.S. Hispanics: Religious, Social and Political Differences," May 7, 2014, http://www.pewforum.org/2014/05/07/hispanic-religious-social-political-differences; Mark Hugo Lopez and Danielle Cuddington, Pew Research Center, "Latinos' Changing Views of Same-Sex Marriage," June 19, 2013, http://www.pewresearch.org/fact-tank/2013/06/19/latinos-changing-views-of-same-sex-marriage; Mark Hugo Lopez, Jens Manuel Krogstad, Eileen Patten, and Ana Gonzalez-Barerra, Pew Research Center, "Latinos' Views on Selected 2014 Ballot Measure Issues," October 16, 2014, http://www.pewhispanic.org/2014/10/16/chapter-2-latinos-views-on-selected-2014-ballot-measure-issues; Jens Manuel Krogstad, Mark Hugo Lopez, Gustavo Lopez, Jeffrey Passel, and Eileen Patten, Pew Research Center, "Millennials Make Up Almost Half of Latino Eligible Voters in 2016," January 19, 2016, http://www.pewhispanic.org/2016/01/19/millennials-make-up-almost-half-of-latino-eligible-voters-in-2016; Robert P. Jones and Daniel Cox, Public Religion Research Institute, "How Race and Religion Shape Millennial Attitudes on Sexuality and Reproductive Health," March 27, 2015, http://publicreligion.org/site/wp-content/uploads/2015/03/PRRI-Millennials-Web-FINAL.pdf; Federico A. Subervi-Velez, Richard Herrera and Michael Begay. "Toward an Understanding of the Role of the Mass Media in Latino Political Life," March 1987, *Social Science Quarterly* 68: 185–96

only 25 percent felt that more research was needed, and 64 percent felt that action needed to be taken to address climate change.[53] With the spate of bad weather in 2014 and 2015, the public views climate change as an increasingly serious problem. In 2016, 56 percent of Americans were concerned or extremely concerned about climate change, a 5-point increase from 2015.[54]

Elites do influence public opinion, but they are not members of a monolithic group seeking to advance its own interests; in fact, elites often disagree among themselves and that disagreement can change as well. When there is consensus among elites, however, it probably means that the position has merit. Moreover, people respond only to ideas that they find appealing and that fit with their own values and opinions. As a model for how people change opinions in response to events, acting out of both self-interest and rationality, we can look at how different groups of Americans hold different opinions.

Essential Knowledge

Americans tend to share certain core values such as individualism, equality, free enterprise and limited government. However, not all citizens agree on the meaning of these concepts. These differences impact citizens' views on what constitutes an appropriate role for the government.

6.4 The Shape of Public Opinion

Discover how ideology and partisanship shape public opinion

To understand public opinion, it is essential to appreciate the ways it is shaped by partisanship and ideology. These two variables can, to a large extent, explain the opinions of citizens. Although not everyone is partisan or ideological, these forces provide useful frameworks for understanding the public's thinking on issues. With a firm understanding of partisanship and ideology in place, we can address two major questions about public opinion: How informed is the public? And is the public polarized?

Partisanship

party identification: *Psychological attachment to a political party; partisanship.*

Party identification, or partisanship, is central to understanding how people think politically. Party identification represents an individual's allegiance to a political party. This psychological attachment usually forms when an individual is young. The attachment, through what is called the perceptual lens, shapes the way partisans view the political world and process information. The perceptual lenses of partisans act like prisms that bend light. Democrats have prisms that bend light in one direction; Republicans' prisms bend it in another direction. The result, for example, is that Republicans are far less sympathetic to Obamacare than are Democrats.[55]

By knowing party identification, political scientists can predict—with considerable accuracy—attitudes on a range of issues. Republicans, for example, are less likely than Democrats to support government spending to help the poor and elderly. Republicans are not opposed to helping such people, but they want to do so through private charities and individual initiative. More generally, Republicans are less supportive of an activist federal government, while Democrats are more open to giving government an active role in the lives of citizens.

An easy indicator of the power of partisanship is the public's approval of President Obama. In the week before the 2016 election, about 53 percent of Americans approved of the job Obama was doing as president, but that proportion hides a much more powerful finding about partisanship. Among Democrats, 91 percent approved of his performance in the Oval Office. By contrast, just 11 percent of Republicans supported the president—a gap of 80 percentage points.[56] President George W. Bush experienced the same kind of gap in public opinion, with Republicans approving of his performance at far higher rates than Democrats did. But the partisan gap Obama generated in 2016 hit historic highs.

Because party identification is central to understanding public opinion, pollsters have been asking about partisanship since the 1940s. The American National Elections Studies, a premier academic survey organization, has been asking the same question since 1952: "Generally speaking, do you usually think of yourself as a Republican, a Democrat, an Independent, or what?"[57] This question asks respondents how they think about themselves in order to capture political identification and the general tendency, or the perceptual lens, of their thinking. The theoretical underpinnings are psychological. Partisanship can also be likened to loyalty, like the loyalty to sports teams or to friends that lasts through ups and downs. Partisanship can change over a person's life, but it tends to be stable, especially when compared to other political attitudes.

In the past few years, there has been much discussion in the press about Independents, with claims that they are the "largest group in the electorate."[58] With the rise of the Tea Party movement, their numbers are increasing. The view that Americans are mostly Independents has largely been viewed as a myth, however. Most citizens who claim to be Independents actually behave like partisans; that is, most of them lean toward one party or the other.[59]

Figure 6.4 suggests that Millennials are tilting toward the Democrats. At the start of the century, there was a relatively even split between the

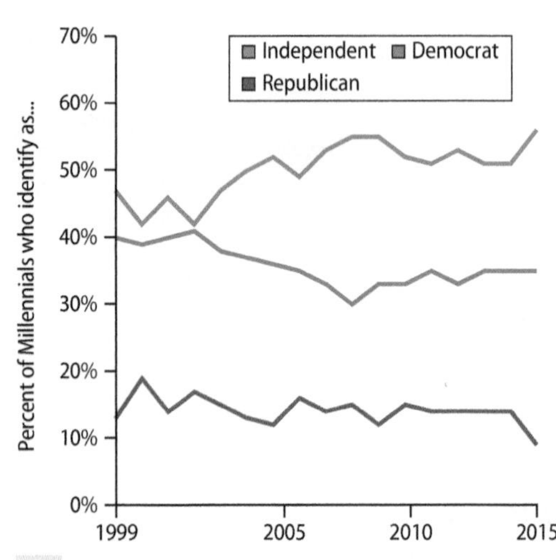

FIGURE 6.4 Trends in Partisanship Among Millennials

Among Millennials, Democrats have held a steady lead over Republicans during the past decade.

Source: 1999–2014 Pew Party Identification trends, http://www.people-press.org/2015/04/07/party-identification-trends-1992-2014/#generation; Pew Political Surveys, January–July 2015.

two parties. Now the Democrats enjoy about a 20 percentage point lead, and very few people identify as "pure" Independents—just 9 percent in 2015.

Ideology

political ideology: *Set of coherent political beliefs that offers a philosophy for thinking about the scope of government.*

liberals: *Individuals who have faith in government to improve people's lives, believing that private efforts are insufficient. In the social sphere, liberals usually support diverse lifestyles and tend to oppose any government action that seeks to shape personal choices.*

conservatives: *Individuals who distrust government, believing that free markets offer better ways than government involvement to improve people's livelihood. In the social sphere, conservatives have more faith in government's ability to enforce traditional values.*

moderates: *Individuals who are in the middle of the ideological spectrum and do not hold consistently strong views about whether government should be involved in people's lives.*

levels of conceptualization: *Measure of how ideologically coherent individuals are in their political evaluations.*

Political ideology has a complex relationship with partisanship. **Liberals** tend to be Democrats, and **conservatives** tend to be Republicans, but ideology speaks to both political and social values. Conservatives view a good society as one that allows individuals to pursue their economic interests in an unfettered fashion. Liberals worry that, without some governmental regulation to curb abuse and moderate economic cycles, the rich will get very rich and the poor will get very poor. This concern leads liberals to believe that government can improve people's lives and prevent inequalities that harm society and the economy as a whole. Conservatives are much more leery of government and view it as a problem in and of itself. They contend that less government interference will give the poor the opportunity to improve their lives by themselves. On social issues, the tables are turned. That is, liberals tend to believe that people should be able to make personal choices free from government interference. Conservatives, by contrast, value more traditional lifestyles and want government, at times, to enforce such choices.

Not all citizens think of themselves as liberals or conservatives. In 2016, about 35 percent of Americans viewed themselves as ideological **moderates**, 24 percent as liberals, and 37 percent as conservatives.[60]

There is an important debate among political scientists about whether citizens think ideologically at all. That is, do people have coherent views about politics? One famous effort to measure the ideological foundations, or **levels of conceptualization**, of the public's thinking found little evidence of such organized opinions. Data from the 1950s indicated that only about 12 percent of the public viewed the political parties in ideological terms, whereas more than 40 percent judged the parties by the groups (such as social classes or racial and ethnic groups) they were thought to represent rather than the policies they pursued.[61] This general pattern has remained much the same over the ensuing sixty years.

It is hard to argue that a majority of the public has a coherent, ideologically driven view of politics. Nevertheless, it is still worth looking at the public's overall policy mood. Is the public, collectively, becoming more liberal or more conservative? Such changes should aid understanding of the general direction of the country. Figure 6.5 maps changes in the public's ideological mood between 1952 and 2014.

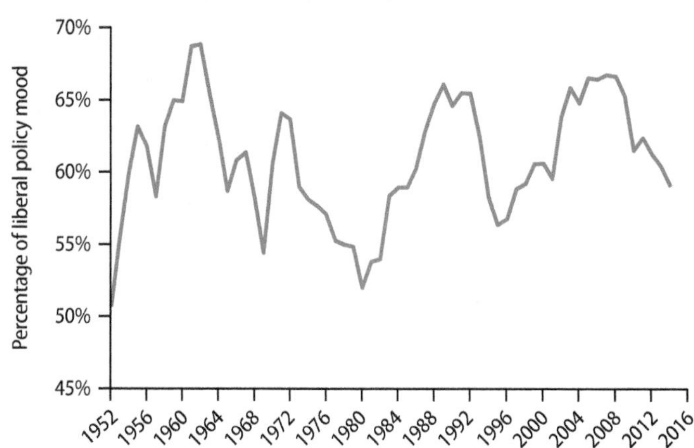

FIGURE 6.5 Liberal Policy Mood of Americans, 1952–2016

The policy mood of Americans is rarely fixed. It moved toward liberalism following George W. Bush's election in 2000 and then toward conservatism following Barack Obama's election in 2008.

Source: http://kelizabethcoggins.com/mood-policy-agendas/

This sixty-two-year time period reveals some interesting trends. The increasingly liberal nature of public opinion was apparent between 1952 and 1964—an era dominated by the Democrats. In the mid-1960s, with the unpopularity of the Vietnam War and growing concerns about civil rights, crime, and excessive government involvement in the economy, conservatism grew—and grew quickly. The pattern between 1980 and the early 1990s was a move back toward liberalism, culminating in the election of Bill Clinton in 1992. During the Clinton years, the public veered toward conservatism again. Following the election of George W. Bush in 2000, the public shifted more toward liberalism. And following Barack Obama's election in 2008, the pendulum swung back toward conservatism, which continues to the present. The rise of the Tea Party and Donald Trump certainly gives credibility to this recent shift. It is an interesting pattern, underscoring the different moods of the public. These different moods do not, however, last long, leading to frequent changes in the party that controls the White House.

Is the Public Informed?

A democracy depends on having an engaged and well-informed electorate. Otherwise, how can the public make good choices? If the power is to rest with the people, the people need to be knowledgeable about the issues of the day and the candidates who compete for public office.

The Framers were definitely concerned about the public's capacity to be informed and make good choices, especially because only 10 percent of Americans at the time were literate.[62] These concerns were one of the driving forces behind the gates and gateways in the Constitution, a document that sought to represent the public's views but also to establish institutions that would, according to James Madison, "refine and enlarge" them (see *Federalist* 10 in the Appendix). By that Madison meant that elected officials would react to public sentiment but not be a slave to it. Instead, they would debate it in a way that would improve it and allow for better government. Over time, the amount of input by citizens has increased; senators, for example, are now voted into office by direct election, not by state legislatures. Education levels have also greatly increased. Literacy in 2014 stood at about 99 percent,[63] suggesting that citizens are better able today than in the eighteenth century to meet the demands of being "informed."

But are they really "informed"? When survey research began in the 1940s, it became possible to gather systematic information on the public's knowledge about politics. The early evidence was not encouraging. In a detailed study of the 1940 presidential campaign, scholars from Columbia University assumed that voters would act like consumers and would look for the best deal and that the campaign would be an important source of information as they made their choices. But the data told a different tale. Instead, most voters made up their minds before the campaign, and their choices were driven by where they lived and whom they knew.[64] In a subsequent study, the Columbia researchers went so far as to argue that low turnout in elections might actually be a good thing because the uninformed would not be involved in choosing the nation's leaders.[65] This argument has strong elitist overtones and certainly strays far from the assumptions about government responsiveness and citizen equality on which American democracy rests. Together with previous findings about levels of conceptualization,[66] the argument suggested that the public may not be capable of meeting its democratic responsibilities. What ensued was a debate over the accuracy and interpretation of these core findings.

Political scientists went, in effect, in search of the "informed voter." It is clear that citizens do not know many details about politics. Only 10 percent of the public knows the name of the Speaker of the House. Only about a third can name one U.S. Supreme Court justice. Only about half of Americans know which party controls Congress, and fewer than half know the name of their own congressional representative.[67]

Should these data be taken as evidence that the public is not able to meet its democratic responsibilities? Let us consider some findings that give reason for optimism.

First, the public, *collectively*, seems to make reasonable choices. For example, when the economy is doing poorly, the party in power suffers. Voters hold presidents and legislators accountable; failures are punished, and successes are rewarded. Further, Americans do not favor costly wars, and they tend to reward candidates who pursue peace.[68]

Second, although individuals do not know all the details about candidates' views on all the issues, they do tend to know candidates' views on the issues that are salient to them. Hunters are much more likely to know candidates' views on gun control; college students are much more likely to know candidates' views on student loans. One study estimates that when an issue is salient to an individual, that individual knows candidates' views on that issue correctly more than 90 percent of the time.[69]

Third, the public can learn quickly about important issues, especially given the attention they receive from the news media. The public quickly learned about AIDS when it started to become a public health crisis in the 1980s. Following 9/11, the public understood the need to consider some curtailment of civil liberties to ensure security (see Public Policy and Public Opinion: Antiterrorism).

Fourth, public opinion is more stable than is suggested by the shifting answers individuals give to the same question asked just a few months apart. Such instability in an individual's answers does not mean that the public is fickle or poorly informed; instead, it appears that polls themselves may be at fault.[70] That is, survey questions and the normal error associated with asking questions make people's attitudes appear more unstable than they really are. Further, most issues are complex and leave many people genuinely conflicted. Being conflicted is not a sign of lack of information, but perhaps a realization that some problems are thorny and not easily answered. The following is one example:

> *Vincent Sartori cannot decide whether or not the government should guarantee incomes because he cannot decide how much weight to give the value of productivity. He believes that the rich are mostly undeserving and . . . yet he is angry at "welfare cheats" who refuse to work. . . . Caught between his desire for equality and his knowledge of existing injustice, on the one hand, and his fear that a guaranteed income will benefit even shirkers, on the other, he remains ambivalent about policies toward the poor.*[71]

So Sartori could easily give different answers to the same survey question, depending on what he is thinking about at the time. But different answers say more about the issue's complexity than about his lack of information.

Last, decisions we make on personal matters are rarely based on complete information, so why should political decision making be expected to conform to such high standards? Individuals often rely on cues and instincts to make decisions, rather than on analyses of detailed information. Scholars have termed such thinking "low information rationality."[72] There are two famous examples from presidential campaigns. In 1976, President Gerald R. Ford (1974–77), campaigning in Texas, bit into a tamale with the husk still on, a gaffe suggesting that he knew little about the foods and habits of the Latino community he was hoping to court. In 2016, Hillary Clinton claimed that about half of Donald Trump's supporters were a "basket of deplorables." Her comment suggested she was out of touch with ordinary Americans and was quick to label people unfairly. Simple things like

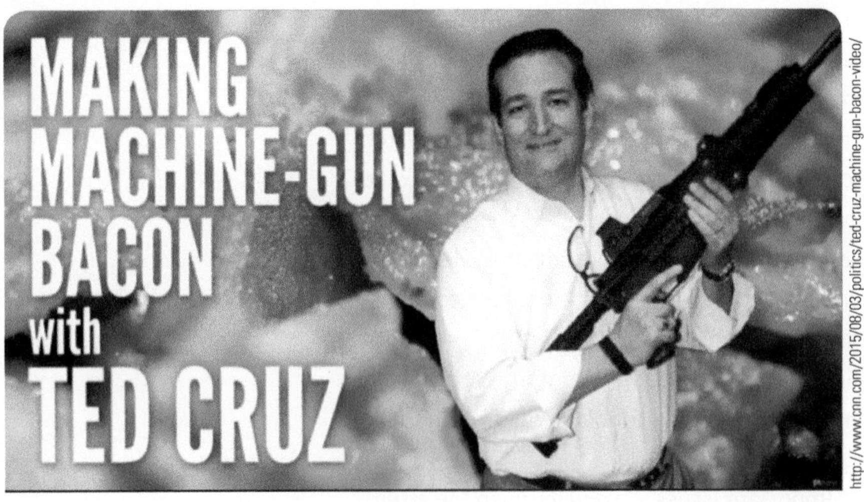

IMAGE 6.7 In an unorthodox effort to draw attention to his presidential candidacy, in 2015 Senator Ted Cruz produced a short video where he fired a machine to cook some bacon.

not knowing how to eat a tamale or off-handed comments can turn voters against political candidates. The public concludes that these contenders are not like them and, thus, are not likely to understand their problems. Small bits of information can be informative.

It is easy to make any member of the public—even a president—look uninformed, and of course it would be better if the public knew more about politics. But individuals do appear to learn about the issues that matter to them. Gaining information is a gateway to influence because, individually, people learn what they need to know to advance their interests, and collectively voters do hold government officials accountable.

Is the Public Polarized?

The engaged and informed citizens of a democracy cannot be expected to agree on everything. They will naturally have different views on issues. When the differences become stark, however, the danger is that **polarization** will fuel controversy and personal attacks to the point that compromise and consensus become impossible. Congress has clearly become more polarized over the past thirty years. Figure 6.6 tries to capture the idea of polarization on a simple left–right continuum. In the 1970s, the parties adopted positions that were closer to the middle; forty years later, their positions are more at the extremes. And these differences continue to grow. In fact, Democrats and Republicans disagree on more issues now than at any time since the end of the Civil War.[73]

polarization: *Condition in which differences between parties and/or the public are so stark that disagreement breaks out, fueling attacks and controversy.*

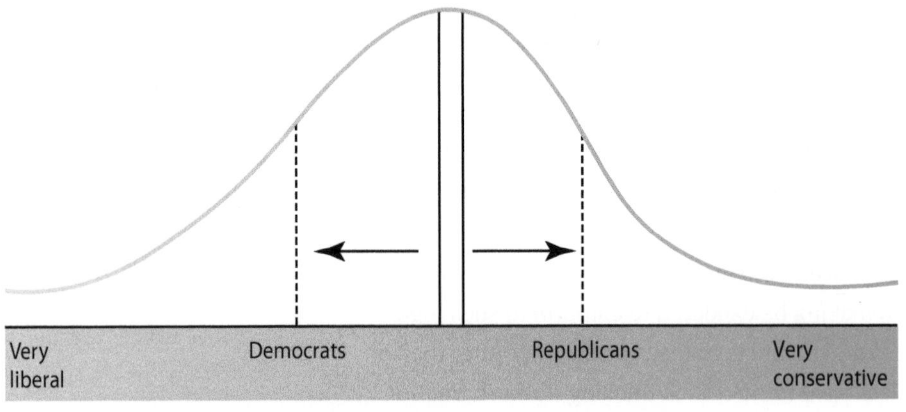

FIGURE 6.6 How Polarization Works

When the parties are polarized, they move toward the tail of these distributions. When parties are depolarized, they adopt positions near each other. Currently the parties are polarized, but that was not the case in the 1970s.

Source: John G. Geer, © Cengage Learning.

In the 1970s, there were numerous liberal Republicans and conservative Democrats. By 2008, these two groups were nearly extinct. In 2009, for example, Pennsylvania Senator Arlen Specter, one of the few moderate Republicans in Congress at the time, bolted from the Republican Party and became a Democrat. He switched parties because of what he saw as a swing to the right by the Republicans. The differences between the parties have continued to grow (see Figure 6.7),[74] evidenced by victories by candidates from the Tea Party

FIGURE 6.7 Party Polarization, 1879–2015

Since 1975, polarization in the U.S. Congress has been on the rise.

Source: http://voteview.com/Weekly_Constant_Space_DW-NOMINATE_Scores.htm

movement in the 2010 and 2014 congressional elections.[75] There is little doubt that the parties have polarized since the 1970s, along the lines described in Figure 6.7.

What is less clear is whether the public is also polarized. Some scholars have argued that the public has polarized along with parties, but the evidence is mixed. It depends very much on the issue. Consider the long-standing debate over the role of government. In November 2015, members of both parties very much believed the government should keep the "country safe from terrorism." When they were asked about maintaining "infrastructure," though, some differences started to emerge: 71 percent of Republicans and 81 percent of Democrats thought the government should maintain roads and bridges (that is, infrastructure). Polarization arose over the government's role in "ensuring access to health care": 83 percent of Democrats but just 34 percent of Republicans thought it should play a role.[76] Given how different issues have different patterns, it is no surprise that scholars disagree about the extent of differences among the electorate, with some suggesting that the political center has collapsed.[77]

Even some who think that the public is not as polarized as the parties are worried that polarization will yield more personal attacks and greater incivility. Others offer a more optimistic view, arguing that increasing polarization will activate

Mike Simons/Getty Images News/Getty Images

IMAGE 6.8 At town hall meetings held on police shootings in Cincinnati, community leaders protested the death of Nathaniel Jones. Such meetings occasionally become very contentious, highlighting the consequences of the continued polarization of the American political system.

PUBLIC POLICY AND PUBLIC OPINION

Antiterrorism

To see how public opinion affects the policies pursued by government, we examine foreign policy—in particular, antiterrorism. With continuing terrorist attacks around the world, it is important to consider the public's support for policies that advance our security and how public opinion impacts policy making in this area. This issue came even more into focus following the domestic terrorist attack in San Bernardino, California, in December 2015.

The September 11, 2001, terrorist attacks prompted a huge increase in government's efforts to secure U.S. citizens at home and abroad. In general, public opinion was highly supportive of the steps that President George W. Bush took to fight terrorism. These steps were taken with advice from Defense Department agencies, the Federal Bureau of Investigation, and the Department of Justice. The Bush administration authorized the detention of suspects, whether U.S. citizens or not, without charges or trials, and wiretapping (eavesdropping) without a warrant. With the onset of the 2003 war in Iraq, the measures employed in the name of antiterror security increased. Then, in 2004, CBS News and the *New Yorker* magazine broke the story about the Abu Ghraib facility in Iraq, where Iraqi prisoners were subject to activities that violated international norms of treatment and might be considered torture.[78] Subsequently, it was revealed that the U.S. interrogators used waterboarding, a near-drowning technique, as a means of getting information from prisoners about potential terrorist plots. The international community considers waterboarding to be torture, and many Americans were shocked by the news and demanded an end to the practice. The Bush administration also argued that suspected terrorists detained at the Guantánamo Bay facility located in Cuba, outside the United States, were not entitled to protections guaranteed to all prisoners of war by the Geneva Convention. In the 2006 *Hamdan v. Rumsfeld* case, the Supreme Court ruled that the detainees were protected by Article 3 of the Geneva Convention. Yet allegations of torture continued.

The issue of the treatment of detainees has become a major issue in recent presidential campaigns, such as when the Republican nominee, Donald Trump, said he would support reforming laws to allow more extreme use of torture against ISIS. After he took office, President Obama declared that the United States would no longer engage in any practice that violated international norms. The president also announced that the Guantánamo Bay facility would be closed. Despite an early consensus in the White House to close this controversial facility, deciding what to do with existing detainees and how best to handle others who may be engaged in terrorism has proven difficult.[79]

One of the reasons that these policies are hard to pursue is that Americans remain conflicted about the type of force necessary to preserve national security. In 2015, a Pew Research Poll reported that barely a majority of respondents supported the use of harsh interrogation techniques on suspected terrorists.[80] The core dilemma is that antiterrorism policies must remain secret to be effective, and the only opportunity the public has to register an opinion about government action is after that action has been taken. If harsh interrogation techniques save American lives by uncovering and then preventing a terrorist attack, the public will support the use of these techniques. But how can we be sure that such efforts are really effective? Does the government go too far sometimes? These are tough questions. How much liberty should we sacrifice to be safe?

Public uncertainty can also be seen in regards to the public's reaction to Edward Snowden's release of intelligence information. In January 2014, 46 percent of Americans thought what he had done was "bad for the country" and 40 percent thought it was good.[81] These are not easy issues, and the public's thinking reflects this kind of division. The public wants society to be open but realizes that security demands some secrecy. It is easy to see, therefore, why people can have different opinions about how to approach such a tough topic. The tragic events in San Bernardino are only the latest reminder about the importance of this long-standing debate and how the public changes in reaction to such events. Americans, for example, were more likely to feel we need to go farther to protect the country even at the expense of undermining people's liberties.[82]

The debate over secrecy is now taking place in a very different context than it was just a decade ago. The public is generally less inclined these days to get involved in international affairs. More than 50 percent of the public in 2013 wanted the United States to "mind its own business," which represented an all-time high over the past fifty years. Following the 9/11 terrorist attacks in 2001, for example, the proportion of citizens who held such views stood at just 30 percent.[83] This broader context has important implications for U.S foreign policy and how we approach antiterrorism measures.

Public Policy Connections

1. Should public officials disregard public opinion if they believe that following it would have a negative impact on the United States?
2. To what extent should public officials follow public opinion if they believe that doing so would violate the U.S. Constitution?

people's interest in elections, which in turn will spur more interest in politics. In fact, the share of the public that cares about which party wins the presidential election has increased since 1988. Interest in elections, generally, also seems to be on the rise. In 1988, 44 percent of the public paid "a lot" of attention to the presidential campaign. In 2000, the proportion stood at 53 percent, a notable gain.[84] In 2016, the proportion jumped, with two-thirds of Americans paying "a lot" of attention to the Clinton-Trump battle.[85]

Having a clear choice engages people and gives them a stake in an election outcome. If the system became depolarized, as in the 1950s, the public would no longer face a stark choice. It would matter far less whether Democrats or Republicans won because they would do similar things once in office. For these reasons, many scholars in the 1950s called for parties that would offer the public a real choice (see Chapter 9, Political Parties). Citizens, under such conditions, can more effectively hold officials accountable for misdeeds and reward successes.

6.5 Group Differences

Describe how demographic characteristics influence public opinion

Public opinion is shaped by more than partisanship and ideology. Demographics also matter—that is, the tendency for certain groups within the American population to hold similar views. In this section, we look at the ways socioeconomic status, religion, gender, race and ethnicity, and education tend to organize public opinion.

Socioeconomic Status

Socioeconomic status is a combined measure of occupation, education, income, wealth, and relative social standing or lifestyle. It influences where one lives, what kind of work one does, whom one knows, the kinds of schools one attends, and the kind of opportunities one can take advantage of. These matters inevitably mold political attitudes. Working-class people are more likely than wealthier people to favor more government programs to help the poor and provide child care, more funding for public education, and more protection for Social Security. Around 70 percent of Americans earning between $15,000 and $35,000 support increased spending by government on such social services. Among those earning between $75,000 and $105,000, the proportion drops to about 55 percent.[86]

Part of the reason for the strong differences in opinion among different income groups is that political parties have a class bias. Republicans draw far more support from those who come from higher socioeconomic strata than do Democrats. Starting in the 1980s, however, Republicans also began to draw support from working-class people who supported a conservative social agenda and a decreased role for government welfare-based programs. These so-called Reagan Democrats were central to Republican success in the ensuing decades. The candidacy and election of Donald Trump have in many ways reinvigorated the Reagan Democrats, as he draws support from lower-middle-class segments of the electorate who have been unhappy with stagnant wages and the way Washington works.

Age

Essential Knowledge

Life-cycle effects can impact a person's political beliefs. Political beliefs can sometimes change as a person ages.

Age also influences opinions on issues because the stage of one's life affects how one thinks about issues. For instance, 70 percent of people under 30 years of age favor increased spending on student loans. That drops to 42 percent among those over 55. This gap makes sense because younger people are more likely to need student loans. Younger people are much more likely to favor making marijuana legal than are older people. As of 2015, around 56 percent of those Americans 18 to 29 years old, according to a YouGov survey, favor making marijuana legal. For those 65 and older, the percentage drops to about 39 percent.[87] In general, older citizens are more socially conservative than are younger citizens,[88] and there is evidence that people tend to become more conservative as they age.

Religion

Religious affiliation is another indicator of opinion. Overall, for example, Protestants are more conservative than Catholics or Jews. Only 12 percent of Jews describe themselves as conservative, compared to 36 percent of Protestants. On some issues, Muslims have been found to be more liberal than the general population and significantly more liberal than Protestants and Catholics. For example, 70 percent of Muslims favor an activist government, whereas just 43 percent of the public as a whole subscribes to that view. On social issues, however, Muslims show a much more conservative tendency. When asked "Which comes closer to your view? Homosexuality is a way of life that should be accepted by society, or homosexuality is a way of life that should be discouraged by society," 61 percent of Muslims said that homosexual lifestyles should be discouraged, but only 38 percent of all Americans gave that response.[89]

Recent studies of religion and public opinion have focused on differences within denominations, particularly with the rise of evangelical Christianity among Protestants. Starting in the 1970s, and especially after the *Roe v. Wade* Supreme Court decision made abortion legal under some conditions in 1973, evangelicals became more active in politics. They strongly oppose abortion and gay rights, and they support school prayer. On the issue of same-sex marriage, in 2004 evangelical Protestants were six times more likely to oppose same-sex marriage than were non-evangelical—or "mainline"—Protestants.[90] Table 6.1 explores differences among Protestants, Catholics, and those not affiliated with a religious group on the issue of abortion. There are big differences, with evangelical Protestants very much more opposed to abortion than non-evangelicals.

Gender

Starting in 1980, a **gender gap** emerged in U.S. politics. Before 1980, the differences in political attitudes among men and women were not large and did not draw much attention. However, in elections since Ronald Reagan's 1980 victory over Jimmy Carter (1977–81), women have been generally more supportive of Democrats than of Republicans. In 1980,

gender gap: *Differences in the political attitudes and behavior of men and women.*

TABLE 6.1 Differences of Opinion on Abortion Among Religious Groups, 2014

Abortion Should Be ...	Legal in (most) All Cases	Illegal in (most) All Cases
Mainline Protestant	60%	35%
Evangelical Protestant	33%	63%
Historically Black Protestant	52%	42%
Catholic	48%	47%
Jewish	83%	15%
Muslim	55%	37%
Unaffiliated	73%	23%
Total	53%	43%

http://www.pewforum.org/religious-landscape-study/views-about-abortion/

the gap was 8 percentage points: 54 percent of men backed Reagan, and only 46 percent of women backed him. The gap has varied from 4 percent in 1992 to 11 percent in 1996. In 2008, Barack Obama secured 56 percent of the female vote and just 49 percent of the male vote. There was a 13-point gap in 2016, with 54 percent of women supporting Clinton and just 41 percent of men supporting her.[91] This gender gap has been enduring: If only women were allowed to vote, the Democrats would have won every presidential election since 1980 save for Reagan's landslide against Walter Mondale in 1984.[92]

In general, women are more liberal than men, and gender gaps are also evident on specific issues. Women tend to favor more spending on social programs than men. In 2013, more men favored cutting Medicare to reduce the deficit than did women.[93] Men are much more likely to support the death penalty than are women (62 percent versus 38 percent). This gap disappears when it comes to abortion: In 2013, around 20 percent of women and men thought abortion should be illegal in all circumstances.[94]

Race and Ethnicity

Another divide in public opinion involves race and ethnicity. The issue of slavery tore the nation apart, and more than one hundred years after the Civil War, Americans remained divided about issues involving race. In 1964, African Americans overwhelmingly endorsed desegregation, whereas white Americans were split on the issue. In 1974, only 23 percent of white Americans felt "government should help blacks," whereas 69 percent of African Americans believed that government should take that role.[95] Similar gaps exist today in regard to support for affirmative action policies that grant preferences to people (not only African Americans but also women) who have suffered discrimination in the past in job hiring, school admissions, and contracting. In 2015, 53 percent of whites, 77 percent of blacks, and, interestingly, 61 percent of Latinos favored "affirmative action."[96]

The term *Latino* is used to describe a broad array of groups that do not necessarily share common experiences, so opinion among Latinos tends to be divided. Some Latino families have lived in the Southwest for centuries, since before the area became part of the United States in 1848. Others have come to the United States within the past few years from homelands throughout Central and South America. Cuban immigrants, who left their homeland following the rise of Fidel Castro and the Communists in the late 1950s, tend to be much more conservative than Puerto Ricans and Mexican Americans. According to one study, about 47 percent of Cuban Americans are Republican identifiers, compared to only about 27 percent of Mexican Americans.[97] Latinos are divided in other ways as well. According to one group of prominent scholars:

CBS Photo Archive/Getty Images

IMAGE 6.9 Senator Elizabeth Warren is a favorite among liberals. In 2016, she used her notoriety to attack Donald Trump and others she disagreed with.

On many key domestic issues, significant majorities of each [Latino] group take the liberal position. On other issues, there is no consensus and, depending on the issue, Mexicans may be on the right, while Cubans and many Puerto Ricans are on the left of the nation's current political spectrum. Thus, labels such as liberal or conservative do not adequately describe the complexity of any one group's political views.[98]

Thus, both parties compete for the support of the Latino community. In 2004, Latino support for President George W. Bush helped him defeat John Kerry. In 2008, however, Barack Obama gained two-thirds of the Latino vote, a shift partly owing to actions by Republicans in Congress to block immigration reform. The importance of this group will only grow, as suggested by Figure 6.8. In the key battleground states of Pennsylvania and Florida, the share of the Latino vote jumped, as it did nationally and across all states. As Latinos make up more and more of the electorate, issues salient to them will also become increasingly important. For example, Latinos support bilingual education and policies that favor immigration more than do Anglos. In 2016, Donald Trump's controversial call for building a wall to stop Mexican immigration greatly complicated Republican efforts to secure the Latino vote for president as they did in 2004. Given Trump's rhetoric, it is no surprise that Clinton won the Latino vote by a record-breaking 79 percent to 18 percent margin.[99]

Asian American public opinion has not drawn the same level of attention as that of other groups. Asian Americans are, however, a growing segment of the population and constitute a sizable part of the population of some states, especially California. Like Latinos, the Asian American population is diverse, including people from Korea, Vietnam, Japan, and China. In general, however, Asian Americans are a bit more liberal than white Americans. In 2012, for example, about 73 percent of Asian Americans supported President Obama, whereas only 39 percent of white Americans did so. This support of Democrats by Asian Americans is on the rise as well. Hillary Clinton continued this pattern, attracting about two-thirds of the support of Asian Americans.[100]

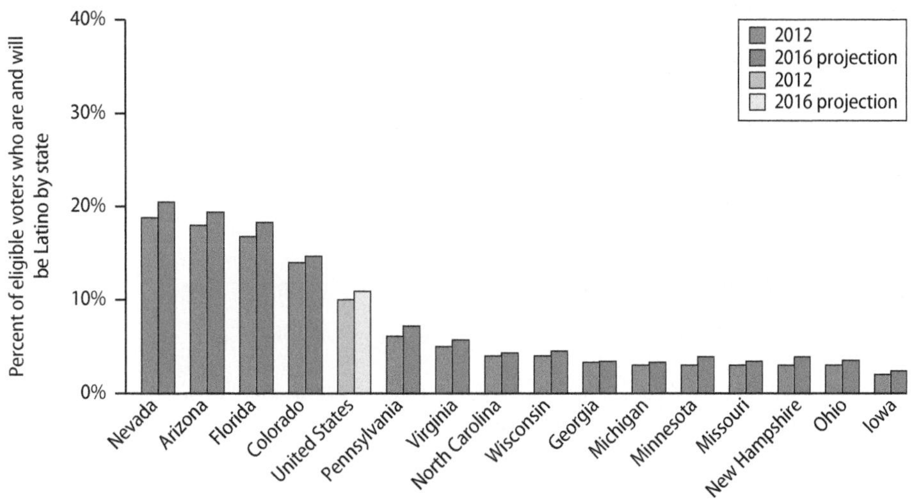

FIGURE 6.8 Latino Electorate Projected to Grow in Key States

Both parties need to find ways to reach out to Latino voters if they want to win elections in the coming years.

Source: http://cookpolitical.com/story/8608

ELECTION 2016

The "Latino" Identity

DEMOCRATS AND REPUBLICANS are in a long-standing battle to attract Latino voters, especially as this group continues to become a bigger part of the electorate. The 2016 presidential election saw a huge amount of attention paid to these voters, especially given the harsh anti-immigrant rhetoric of Donald Trump. Political observers use the terms *Hispanic* and *Latino* (which we treat interchangeably) to refer to this increasingly powerful set of voters. But does this label provide an accurate indication of the thinking of this "group"? This question becomes even more important to ask when we realize that some members of this group think of themselves as Mexican American or Cuban American. What political effects arise from these different identities?

The use of Hispanic and Latino labels began more than forty years ago when Congress added "Americans of Spanish origin" to the types of social statistics that would be collected by the federal government. When asked about their identity, however, most Latinos prefer to use their family's country of origin rather than terms like Latino or Hispanic. Moreover, large majorities of Latinos (69 percent) see differences within those catchall labels. That is, Mexican Americans do not believe they share a common identity with, say, Cuban Americans.

These differences do yield some political differences. Surveys in 2012 revealed overwhelming identification with the Democratic Party among Latinos, 70 percent among registered Hispanic voters[101] (see Table 6.2). However, unpacking these data to see how Latinos of different national origin view the parties reveals a slightly different story. While most groups of Latinos identify with the Democratic Party, Cuban Americans more closely identify with the Republican Party.

Of the generational groupings we identified in this chapter, members of the Latino baby boomer and silent generations are most likely to identify with the Democratic Party (70 percent) while the Millennial generation shows the lowest, though still strong, level of attachment (61 percent). Ten percent of this youngest generation of Latino voters chooses neither party, perhaps providing a glimmer of hope to Republican Party efforts to woo them into their camp.[102] Dampening that glimmer, possibly, is the trend that as non-citizen Latinos move toward citizenship, roughly half identify or lean toward the Democrats—a trend that will likely continue in light of the 2016 presidential election.

As we think about different groups in American politics, we need to be sensitive to key differences within the group as we offer general claims. The case of Latinos is an example: Key subgroup differences yield a more nuanced story, especially as we think about Cuban Americans. But 2016 may prove to be a watershed election for Latinos in light of the views on immigration of Donald Trump. There is recent evidence that this harsh rhetoric activates the Latino community.[103] If true, that may lead to significant realignment of this group in American politics that will have important effects in future elections.

TABLE 6.2 Political Party Affiliation Among Hispanics, 2014, in Percentages

	Identify with a Major Party			Don't Identify but Lean Toward One			Don't Identify with/ Lean Toward Either
	Total	Dem.	Rep.	**Total**	Dem.	Rep.	
All Hispanics	**46**	35	11	**33**	21	12	15
Hispanic registered voters	**61**	46	15	**12**	7	5	10

Source: http://www.pewhispanic.org/files/2014/10/2014-10-29_NSL-latino-politics_topline.pdf.

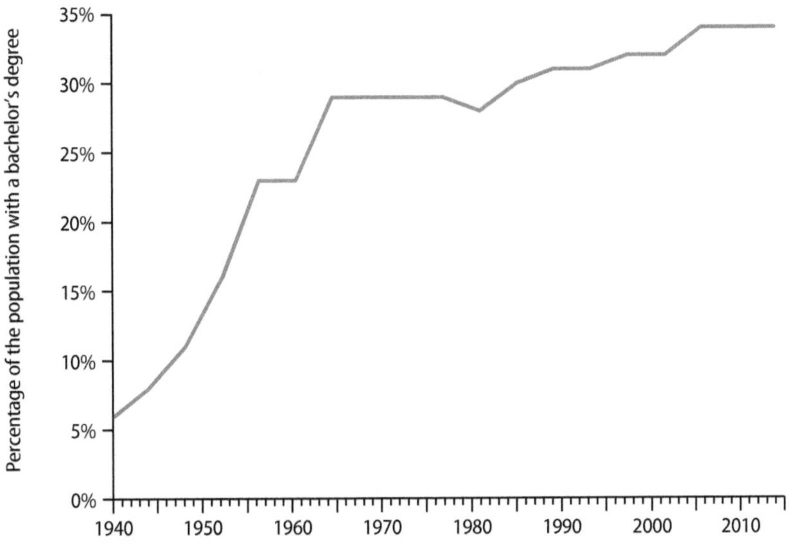

FIGURE 6.9 Percentage of Population with Bachelor's Degree, 1940–2015

Since the end of World War II, education levels have steadily increased. Level of education is a factor affecting public opinion on a range of specific issues.

Source: National Center for Education Statistics, http://nces.ed.gov/programs/digest/d14/tables/dt14_104.20.asp (Table 104.20: Percentage of persons 25 to 29 years old with selected levels of educational attainment, by race/ethnicity and sex: Selected years, 1920 through 2014).

Education

One important change in the American population is the increasing level of education. Figure 6.9 charts the share of Americans who had graduated college over the last seventy-five years. The pattern is striking. In 1940, about one in fifteen Americans had college degrees. By 2015, more than one in three Americans had graduated college. And more than seven of ten Americans had attended college—another vast increase from the 1940s. The upward trend has been continuous since the end of World War II in 1945 for two key reasons. The first is that more young people have access to a college education. The second is what is called "generational replacement"—that is, older, less-educated citizens have passed on, and the average level of education of the American public has thus increased.

It matters that people in the United States are more educated. In broad strokes, there is a long-standing belief that a democracy is best able to endure when its citizens are engaged and informed. With more education, the public should be more aware of politics and better able to find ways to ensure that government responds to them. In the language of this book, a better-educated public should be in better position to travel through the gateways of influence and find ways around the many gates in the American political system.

Education level is also connected to public opinion. Views on the controversial issue of immigration reform offer an instructive example. Among college graduates, three-quarters favored making it possible for those here illegally to become citizens (providing they pass background checks, pay relevant fines, and have jobs). Among those with a high school education or less, the proportion falls to just over half.[104] The 20-percentage-point gap is significant. Individuals with a higher level of education generally take a more liberal position on a variety of social and economic issues, ranging from government spending to defense policy to gay marriage.[105]

Public Opinion and Democracy

Essential Knowledge

In a democratic society, public policy should reflect the policy preferences of citizens. However, policy most likely will reflect the preferences of those who choose to participate in the political process.

For a country to be considered democratic, the views of the public must affect the course of government. For this reason, the public must be sufficiently well informed to be able to make good decisions and to ensure that politicians act in a way consistent with public preferences. Average Americans do not know a lot of details about politics, but the nation's many successes indicate that the public is equal to the task of self-government. As V. O. Key observed fifty years ago, "Voters are not fools."[106] In 2008, when most people thought the country was on the wrong track, they voted for change and put Barack Obama in office. By supporting Obama, the public signaled a desire for a clear break from the policies of the Bush administration. In 2016, most Americans still thought the country was on the wrong track, and that judgment fueled Donald Trump's rise to the presidency as he called for a real shakeup in Washington.

Elections are one means by which the public expresses its will, but on a year-to-year, even day-to-day, basis, public officials can stay in touch with what the public thinks through public opinion polls. Scientific polling permits researchers to measure people's thinking with considerable accuracy and gives average Americans a chance to speak out on policy and contribute to policy making. Scientific polling, introduced eighty years ago, not only created greater equality but also provided the gateways through which the public could affect the course of government. Polls are not perfect, but they do open up the democratic process.

Although it is clear that public officials are generally responsive to public opinion,[107] there are legitimate questions about the responsiveness of American government. Some observers suggest that the connection between opinion and policy is weak. Others point out that the public has mixed feelings on many issues and does not have concrete opinions about some of the toughest questions and can thus offer little guidance. Still others argue that politicians use policy to manipulate public opinion. That interaction is troubling and not the way a democratic system in which the government is accountable to the people should work. These concerns are why it is so instructive to look at the general patterns and the nation's general successes.

It is also important to recognize that, in a democracy, politicians know the kinds of issues the public will respond to and rebel against, and so they adopt views that will not arouse the electorate's anger. They are aware, in other words, of what political scientists call latent public opinion,[108] and this awareness makes them responsive and accountable. The ability to anticipate public opinion is an invaluable skill, helping officials avoid quagmires and stress issues that hit a responsive chord with the public. Thus the power of public opinion in a democracy is both direct and indirect. It is also imperfect in that there are both gates and gateways that shape how citizens direct the course of government.

Political Science Reasoning

Question 1

Practice 4

Speaker 1

So here's the question: Without a change in leadership, why would the next four years be any different from the last four years?

The first troubling sign came with the stimulus. It was President Obama's first and best shot at fixing the economy, at a time when he got everything he wanted under one-party rule. It cost $831 billion–the largest one-time expenditure ever by our federal government.

It went to companies like Solyndra, with their gold-plated connections, subsidized jobs, and make-believe markets. The stimulus was a case of political patronage, corporate welfare, and cronyism at their worst. You, the working men and women of this country, were cut out of the deal.

What did the taxpayers get out of the Obama stimulus? More debt. That money wasn't just spent and wasted–it was borrowed, spent, and wasted.

Maybe the greatest waste of all was time. Here we were, faced with a massive job crisis–so deep that if everyone out of work stood in single file, that unemployment line would stretch the length of the entire American continent. You would think that any president, whatever his party, would make job creation, and nothing else, his first order of economic business.

But this president didn't do that. Instead, we got a long, divisive, all-or-nothing attempt to put the federal government in charge of health care.

Obamacare comes to more than 2000 pages of rules, mandates, taxes, fees, and fines that have no place in a free country.

The president has declared that the debate over government-controlled health care is over. That will come as news to the millions of Americans who will elect Mitt Romney so we can repeal Obamacare.

And the biggest, coldest power play of all in Obamacare came at the expense of the elderly.

You see, even with all the hidden taxes to pay for the health care takeover, even with new taxes on nearly a million small businesses, the planners in Washington still didn't have enough money. They needed more. They needed hundreds of billions more. So, they just took it all away from Medicare. Seven hundred and sixteen billion dollars, funneled out of Medicare by President Obama. An obligation we have to our parents and grandparents is being sacrificed, all to pay for a new entitlement we didn't even ask for. The greatest threat to Medicare is Obamacare, and we're going to stop it.[1]

---

[1]Paul Ryan, speech to Republican National Convention, August 29, 2012.

Speaker 2

Today, after almost a century of trying, today, after over a year of debate, today, after all the votes have been tallied, health insurance reform becomes law in the United States of America—today . . .

This year, tens of thousands of uninsured Americans with preexisting conditions, the parents of children who have a preexisting condition, will finally be able to purchase the coverage they need. That happens this year.

This year, insurance companies will no longer be able to drop people's coverage when they get sick or place—[applause]. They won't be able to place lifetime limits or restrictive annual limits on the amount of care they can receive.

This year, all new insurance plans will be required to offer free preventive care. And this year, young adults will be able to stay on their parents' policies until they're 26 years old. That happens this year.

. . .

And we have now just enshrined, as soon as I sign this bill, the core principle that everybody should have some basic security when it comes to their health care. And it is an extraordinary achievement that has happened because of all of you and all the advocates across the country.[2]

1. What is the likely ideology of the first speaker? Cite specific textual evidence from the quote to support your assertion.
2. What is the likely ideology of the second speaker? Cite specific textual evidence from the quote to support your assertion.
3. Consider both speakers. Which speaker would be more likely to support changing the Social Security program to a private pension? Why?

---

[2]Barack Obama Remarks on Signing the Patient Protection and Affordable Care Act, March 23, 2010.

Focus on AP® Success

6 Public Opinion

Must Know: Key Concepts

- Socialization
- Liberalism
- Conservatism
- Libertarianism
- Tracking Poll
- Exit Poll
- Focus Groups
- Scientific Polling
- Sampling Error
- Keynesian Economic Theory
- Supply Side Economics

Thinking Politically

Data Analysis

Refer to Figure 6.5. To what extent does U.S. public policy reflect the trend(s) presented in the figure?

Concept Application

Refer to the information on public opinion presented in Chapter 6. What elements of U.S. public opinion have remained the same over time? What elements of U.S. public opinion have changed over time? What accounts for this change?

Understanding Learning Objectives with Key Concepts

MPA – 1.A Explain the relationship between core beliefs of U.S. citizens and attitudes about the role of government.

- Core values of U.S. citizens include individualism, equality of opportunity, capitalism, rule of law, and limited government. Not all citizens believe in all of these concepts equally. Various subgroups may hold values that conflict with some of these core beliefs. All of these values impact policies that citizens expect from their government.

MPA – 1.B Explain how cultural factors influence political attitudes and socialization.

- Individuals acquire political values and culture through a process known as socialization. The primary agents of socialization are family, school, civic groups, religious organizations, media, and social environments.
- The exposure to other cultures and beliefs systems that has come at the hands of globalization can impact political values as well. For example, as people become familiar with other cultures, they tend to become more socially tolerant.
- An individual's political values can, and often do, change over time. This is the result of major social events and simply the process of ageing itself. Generally speaking, people tend to become more socially conservative over time.
- Major political or social events can impact a person's political beliefs. For example the Great Depression changed people's views on the proper role of the national government.

MPA – 2.A Describe the elements of a scientific poll.

- For a poll to be scientific, it must utilize a randomly selected sample, a large enough sample size (typically 1,000–1,500), and a sample that is demographically reflective of the universe to be measured. Further, the questions must be unbiased. Sample error can occur even in properly conducted polls. Other ways to measure public opinion include focus groups, exit polls, and tracking polls.

MPA – 2.B Explain the quality and credibility of claims based on public opinion data.

- There is a relationship between polling and elections. However, polling does not always reflect electoral outcomes due to a variety of reasons: voter turnout, the reliability of the poll, and voter apathy with regard to certain political issues.

PMI – 4.A Explain how the ideologies of the two major parties shape policy debates.

- The Democratic Party is largely influenced by liberalism and the Republican Party is largely influenced by conservativism.

PMI – 4.B Explain how U.S. political culture (e.g., values, attitudes, and beliefs) influences the formation, goals, and implementation of public policy over time.

- The diversity of values in the United States is reflected in the public policy that is produced by the national government. However, the views of those who choose to participate are most reflected. Groups that participate at lower levels can have their policy preferences ignored.

PMI – 4.C Describe different political ideologies regarding the role of government in regulating the marketplace.

- There are different views on how the government should regulate the economy. Those individuals who subscribe to Keynesian economic theory hold that the Congress and president, through fiscal policy, should engage in deficit spending during economic downturns in an effort to stimulate the economy. Those individuals who subscribe to supply-side economic theory believe that economic activity can be stimulated through the reduction of taxes.

PMI – 4.D Explain how political ideologies vary on the government's role in regulating the marketplace.

- Liberals tend to hold that the government should play a greater role in the economy. They are more likely to support Keynesian economic practices and greater intervention of the Federal Reserve's ability to set monetary policy as way to stimulate the economy. They also tend to favor greater governmental regulation of businesses. Those individuals who are economically conservative believe that the government should play a less active role in the economy and generally oppose government spending as a way to stimulate the economy. Further, they believe that the Federal Reserve's ability to set monetary policy should be typically restricted to regulating inflation and acting as a "lender of last resort." Conservatives tend to be opposed to many governmental attempts to regulate businesses. Libertarians tend to be opposed to most all government intervention in the economy other than government protection of property rights.

PMI – 4.E Explain how political ideologies vary on the role of the government in addressing social issues.

- Individuals who believe in social liberalism tend to support less government intervention into issues of personal morality and more governmental action to increase social and economic equality. Conservatives, on the other hand, tend to be more supportive of governmental regulation of personal morality and less supportive of government attempts to increase social and economic equality. Libertarians are opposed to governmental regulation of personal morality as well as opposed to governmental attempts to increase social and economic equality.

PMI – 4.F Explain how different ideologies impact policy on social issues.

- The policies that Congress enacts generally reflect the ideology of the ruling party, but over time also reflect the changing balance of conservative and liberal views within the major parties.

Making Connections

There are connections between ideologies and U.S. political parties. Generally, Democrats tend to be more liberal and Republicans tend to be more conservative. However, even with increased party polarization, there still are many conservative Democrats and liberal Republicans. Further, there are many people who are ideologically libertarian in the Republican Party. Keep this in mind when studying Chapter 9, Political Parties.

Many opinion polls are conducted by media organizations. When studying Chapter 7, The News and Social Media, refer back the requirements of scientific polling. Their overemphasis on polling is referred to as horse race journalism.

Going Deeper: Measuring Public Opinion

Scientific polling as it is known today was developed by George Gallop in the 1930s. A key component of this is the random sample. The random sample is found by the use of randomly selected telephone numbers. However, cell phones have traditionally been excluded from the sample. This can result in underrepresentation of demographic groups that do not have traditional landline phones and rely exclusively on cell phones. Polling companies are now beginning to deal with this problem.

Another problem with polling is the limitation on the types of questions that can be asked. Most questions are "closed ended." That is to say, questions where the interviewer provides the respondent a range of answers from which to choose. For example "If the election were held today, would you vote for Mr. X or Ms Y?" It is often difficult for pollsters using traditional polling to obtain qualitative information on public opinion.

In an effort to obtain qualitative information, polling organizations will use focus groups. A focus group is a group of 10 to 15 people to which a trained moderator will ask open a series of open-ended questions. For example "What is the most pressing problem facing the United States today?" Over the span of one to two hours, group members will share and discuss their answers to these questions.

7 The News and Social Media

AP® Learning Objectives

PRD – 3.A Explain the media's role as a linkage institution.

PRD – 3.B Explain how increasingly diverse choices of media and communication outlets influence political institutions and behavior.

Performance Tasks

Upon the completion of this chapter, you must be able to do the following:

- Explain how the media connects citizens with the government.
- Citing specific examples, explain how the changing nature of the media has impacted the political process.

BRIAN KERSEY/UPI/Newscom

"... you have one thing that may save you, and that is your youth. This is your great strength. It is also why I hate and fear you."

STEPHEN COLBERT
Northwestern University

Richard Ellis/Alamy

Stephen Colbert has literally laughed his way to influence in politics. In 2015, he took over from David Letterman as the host of CBS's *The Late Show*, conducting poignant interviews and poking fun at Donald Trump as a presidential candidate in 2015 and 2016. Colbert's influence originally took off during *The Colbert Report*, a satirical news show that many young Americans found more compelling than traditional news shows that sought to inform the public.

Colbert's gateway to influence underscores the many changes in the media over the past twenty-five years. It used to be that "the media" were dominated by a handful of outlets (e.g., *New York Times*, CBS News) that sought to describe the day's events. The media have multiplied and decentralized, seeking often to interpret the news and entertain. The days of striving for serious, unbiased coverage are long gone.

Consider one example of Colbert's influence: In 2011, he drew attention to the rise of so-called super PACs by forming the Colbert Super PAC. His goal was to raise awareness about new election laws that allowed PACs to form and inject money into the political process. In an e-mail to supporters in October 2011, he wrote, "As you know, when we began Colbert Super PAC, we had a simple dream: to use the Supreme Court's *Citizens United* ruling to fashion a massive money cannon that would make all those who seek the White House quake with fear and beg our allegiance... in strict accordance with federal election law."[1] By poking fun at *Citizens United*, Colbert helped inform the public about PACs and their possible role in politics.

More recently, during a September 2015 interview on *The Late Show*, Colbert had a heartfelt conversation with Vice President Joe Biden. Biden, who was considering running for president, came across as caring and informed—so much so that Colbert urged him to become a candidate. The process would be better off if Biden ran, contended Colbert. Although Biden ultimately decided not to run, that interview shows how Colbert, by hosting important guests and asking probing questions, is able to shine a light on the workings of American politics.

Few would have thought that Colbert was on a path that would lead to such political influence. He grew up in South Carolina, the youngest of eleven children. His father was a physician and died when Colbert was just 10 years old.[2] Colbert first attended Hampden-Sydney College in Virginia, a small, private liberal arts college for men. This college has a deep history, striving to instill in its students a desire to "behave as gentleman at all times and in all places."[3] In retrospect, that may not have been a good fit for Colbert, and he transferred to Northwestern University. In 1986, he graduated with a degree in theater.[4]

His time at Northwestern was transformative. He began doing improv on campus and around Chicago. *Second City* gave him a big break, where he served as understudy to Steve Carell. In 1995, he began his career at Comedy Central, joining *The Daily Show* two years later as a correspondent, where he developed his now-famous Colbert persona.[5] *The Colbert Report* started as a spinoff from *The Daily Show* in 2005. Early on, he introduced "Truthiness"[6] to the political discourse. He used the concept to lob satirical bombs at the personalities and issues of the day. The term caught on so much that it became the "Word of the Year" in 2006.[7] Even if Colbert gave guests a hard time, people relished the chance to be on the show. Why? The Colbert Bump: There is evidence that guests got a boost in popularity.[8]

While Colbert is first and foremost an entertainer, he cares about issues and takes his gateway to influence seriously. For example, he testified before the House Judiciary Committee's Subcommittee on immigration, citizenship, and border security in 2010[9] because he likes "talking about people who don't have any power." He said, "migrant workers who come and do our work, but don't have any rights... yet we still invite them to come here and at the same time ask them to leave. And that's an interesting contradiction."[10]

Colbert's humor-infused partisanship is a symbol of the many changes in the media that we map out and assess in this chapter. We do so with a keen understanding of the critical role that the news media play in a democracy: They inform us. Colbert may do it differently from many in the past, but like other media sources, he acts as a watchdog, scrutinizing our political system. To discuss "the media," we analyze the functions and impact of the press, survey its history, and describe and evaluate new forms of communication. By so doing, we can better understand whether and how the news media promote democracy.

7.1 Political News

Determine why the media are important in a democracy

Essential Knowledge

Advances in communication technology have altered the way citizens acquire political information.

In a democracy such as the United States, citizens are supposed to be the ultimate source of power. The decisions made by the public shape the course of government. The public, therefore, needs information about politics to make good choices. Most people cannot directly observe political events, so they rely on the mass media for information about politics and government.

What Are the Mass Media?

mass media: *News sources, including newspapers, television, radio, and the Internet, whose purpose is to provide a large audience with information about the nation and the world.*

news media: *Subset of the mass media that provides the news of the day, gathered and reported by journalists.*

The **mass media** represent the vast array of sources of information that are available to the public, including newspapers, television, radio, blogs, online sources, cell phones, and social media such as Facebook or Twitter. The **news media** (also called the press) are a subset of the mass media that have traditionally provided the news of the day, gathered and reported by journalists. With all the new technologies of the twenty-first century, however, the news media are changing; now the average citizen is able to participate in politics through Instagram, Twitter, Tumblr, or Facebook. These types of social media have recast journalism by providing a proliferation of news outlets without a monolithic entity that shapes and defines political reporting. In this chapter, we use the term *mass media* to describe the many ways citizens learn about government and politics.

Essential Knowledge

The media functions as a linkage institution in American politics. A linkage institution connects citizens with policy-making institutions. The media does this by providing citizens with information about politics and government actions.

One aspect of the mass media today is speedy communication. What used to take days, weeks, and sometimes months, now takes seconds. For example, it took up to four days for some Americans to learn about the assassination of President Abraham Lincoln (1861–65) in April 1865. But no longer: Twitter feeds, for instance, bring information nearly as quickly as it happens. There is no need to wait for the evening news on TV. Most young people today (the Millennials born between 1982 and 2003) grew up with the 24-7 news cycle, an information world that is very different from that of their parents (and their professors). This chapter takes those changes into account.

watchdog: *Role of the press in monitoring government actions.*

Access to information is important because an enduring and effective democracy demands a knowledgeable public.[11] For the people to be informed, the press needs to be able to do its job free from government interference, and journalists must feel free to be critical of the government. This **watchdog** role of the press lies at the very heart of a democracy. In 1787, Thomas Jefferson observed, "Were it left to me to decide whether we should have a government without newspapers, or newspapers without a government, I should not hesitate a moment to prefer the latter."[12] What Jefferson meant is that only a well-informed public is capable of self-governing. Freedom of the press is intertwined with the very idea of democratic government, and the First Amendment to the Constitution protects it.

Functions of the News

The mass media help ensure government accountability and responsiveness by performing three important tasks: informing, investigating, and interpreting the news.

Informing. Journalists, simply put, inform. Coverage of ISIS from 2016, for example, might include stories about casualties or about military options for reducing the impact of this terrorist organization. Coverage of a political campaign, on the other hand, might include information about candidates' previous experience, their personal temperaments, or their views on important issues. If there is a crisis in the economy, journalists provide information about the problem, explain the solutions being proposed, and indicate what can be expected in the future. In August 2008—just a month before a financial crisis rocked the nation—about 5 percent of news stories dealt with the economy. In September 2008 that proportion soared to nearly 30 percent.[13] Domestic terrorism was also suddenly given much more coverage by journalists following a mass shooting in San Bernardino, California, in December 2015. A quick scan of any newspaper or news website can inform readers about a wide range of topics.

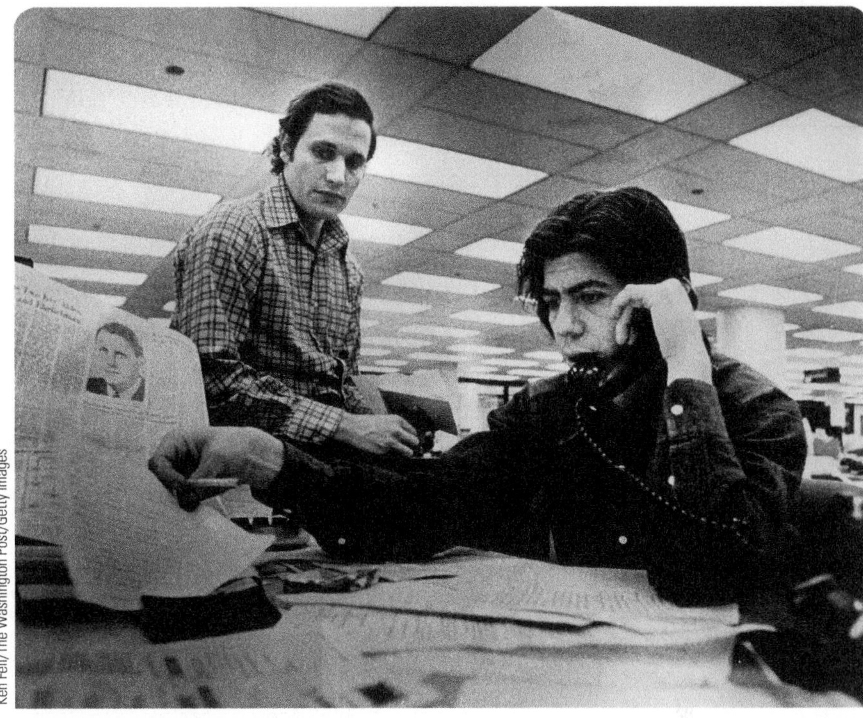

Ken Feil/The Washington Post/Getty Images

IMAGE 7.1 *Washington Post* reporters Bob Woodward and Carl Bernstein became legends for their work in following up on a news story about what seemed to be a routine break-in. But it was the Democratic campaign headquarters that was broken into on June 17, 1972, and the trail they picked up led to the White House. Certain to be impeached, President Richard M. Nixon resigned on August 9, 1974.

Investigating. The media can also *make* news by researching and revealing information about events. The Watergate scandal, uncovered by two reporters from the *Washington Post*, revealed questionable activities in the Richard M. Nixon administration (1969–74; see also Chapter 13, The Presidency). Bob Woodward and Carl Bernstein played the ultimate role of watchdog, creating a news story that gripped the country for more than a year. The episode ended with Nixon's resignation on August 9, 1974, the only time a U.S. president has resigned. This scandal would never have been uncovered without the tireless efforts of the *Post's* investigative reporters.[14] More recently, the *Boston Globe* in 2002 launched a series of investigations into the Catholic Church and possible sexual abuse by priests of children. Their efforts exposed a cover-up and a disturbing pattern of sexual abuse, leading to a major worldwide scandal for the church. The efforts of these journalists were captured in the Academy Award–winning movie *Spotlight* (2015).

Because of the importance of the press, politicians often court journalists, as they seek favorable coverage. They want reporters to share their accomplishments with voters. Yet journalists and politicians are usually in an adversarial relationship because journalists want to report new stories on topics of interest to the public. Those topics often include information unfriendly to candidates, which they want to downplay or ignore. In addition, reporters love to unearth scandals—something that politicians desperately want to avoid. Scandals are fresh and exciting, and uncovering them gives journalists real influence. The investigative function not only allows the press to fulfill its role as the watchdog of democracy, but it also makes reporters' jobs interesting and important. Also, scandals attract an audience, increasing profits. As you can see, the interests of politicians and the press often do not align.

Essential Knowledge

Many accuse the media of being a "score keeper" or engaging in "horse race journalism." In this role the media focuses on polling data and day-to-day activities of candidates to the exclusion of more substantive analysis of the candidates' policy positions.

Interpreting. When the media inform, they also interpret the news. Just giving one story front-page coverage and relegating another to an inside page involves interpreting what is more and less important. The role of interpretation has taken on even greater significance in the past few decades. In 1960, for example, journalists covered presidential campaigns in a very descriptive fashion: About 90 percent of campaign stories focused on describing what happened in the campaign that day. But in the following decades, journalists started to interpret events more frequently, assessing *why* something happened.[15] Cable news, for example, tends to deliver far more commentary than hard news. MSNBC, however, has sought to lessen its left-leaning coverage and provide more news,[16] which was clear during its coverage of the 2016 presidential campaign.

7.2 The Law and the Free Press

Analyze how the law protects the press

The First Amendment to the Constitution states that "Congress shall make no law . . . abridging the freedom . . . of the press." This protection is not unlimited, however. During times of war (or threat of war), national security concerns may require that the press not publish a story. The government, however, is often too eager to stop publication of controversial stories, whereas the press may be too willing to report on controversial stories that will boost sales. This conflict plays out in debates over prior restraint—government's ability to restrict the publication of sensitive material (see Chapter 4, Civil Liberties). When can government invoke prior restraint? At what point does prior restraint become censorship and thus undermine the ability of the press to be a watchdog?

libel: *Publishing false and damaging statements about another person.*

actual malice: *Supreme Court test for libel of a public figure, in which the plaintiff must prove that the publisher knew the material was false or acted with reckless disregard of whether it was true or false.*

Answers to these difficult questions have been shaped by Supreme Court decisions. In the early 1930s, for example, the state of Minnesota stopped a small newspaper from publishing controversial claims about the mayor of Minneapolis and convicted the publisher, Jay Near, under state libel laws. Near appealed the conviction all the way to the Supreme Court. In *Near v. Minnesota* (1931), the Court ruled that only in exceptionally rare cases could the government stop the printing of a story, overturning Near's conviction and invalidating the Minnesota law that led to his conviction.[17] The Court has reinforced the protections of press freedom in a **libel** case, *New York Times v. Sullivan* (1964), which also set a very high standard—proof of **actual malice**—to convict in a libel suit. Justice William J. Brennan wrote, "We consider this case against the background of a profound national commitment to the principle that debate on public issues should be uninhibited, robust, and wide open, and that it may well include vehement, caustic, and sometimes unpleasantly

SUPREME COURT CASES

New York Times v. Sullivan (1964)

QUESTION: What level of negligence must be found when public officials sue newspapers for libel?

ORAL ARGUMENT: January 6–7, 1964 (listen at http://www.oyez.org/cases/1960-1969/1963/1963_39)

DECISION: March 9, 1964 (read at http://caselaw.lp.findlaw.com/scripts/getcase.pl?navby=case&court=us&vol=376&page=254)

OUTCOME: Actual malice must be found to convict for libel, thus overturning the libel conviction of the *New York Times* (9–0).

Libel is the publication of false and damaging information about someone. Prior to libel laws, the defamed person often responded to libel by challenging the libeler to a duel, as when Vice President Aaron Burr challenged *Federalist* author and former Treasury Secretary Alexander Hamilton to a duel and killed him. To prevent such acts, various states made libel a criminal act. Today libel is almost exclusively a question for a civil suit, in which one person sues another for monetary damages.

The *Sullivan* case derived from an advertisement placed in the March 29, 1960, *New York Times* by an ad hoc group of civil rights supporters called the Committee to Defend Martin Luther King. The ad condemned the "wave of terror" against nonviolent civil rights activists by unnamed "southern violators." Because some of the actions against King included arresting him, the chief of the Montgomery, Alabama, police department claimed that all of the allegations were about him and that he had been libeled.

Under Alabama law, once damaging statements were found, the only defense was for the publication to prove that all the particulars were true. The ad in this case was not true in all the particulars. For example, it claimed that protesting students sang "My Country 'Tis of Thee" when they actually sang "The Star-Spangled Banner." The jury thus found against the *Times*, awarding the police chief $500,000 in damages.

The Supreme Court reversed the verdict, declaring that a law holding a newspaper liable for criticism of a public official only if the paper could prove that every statement in the article was true would lead to massive self-censorship by the press. Instead, the Court declared that libel against a public official required a finding of actual malice—that is, knowledge that the statement was false or reckless disregard of whether it was true or false. Under this standard, the Court found that the ad was substantially true, but even if it had not been substantially true, there was no evidence that the *Times* acted with malice.

This decision has made it much easier for newspapers to criticize public officials. The Court has expanded the ruling to cover public figures as well. When a supermarket tabloid trashes a popular actor or singer, the individual thus harmed has to prove actual malice to win a suit for libel.

Thinking Critically

1. What would happen if the media were held legally responsible for any false statement they made?
2. Should the burden of proof for proving libel of public officials be treated equally to the burden of proof for libel of private people?

sharp attacks on government and public officials" (see Supreme Court Cases: *New York Times v. Sullivan*).

The modern landmark case on the freedom of the press was the *Pentagon Papers* case (1971).[18] During the Vietnam War, the *New York Times* secured a copy of a top-secret Department of Defense analysis detailing U.S. involvement in Vietnam and began publishing it, believing that the information, some of which contradicted official statements, was essential to public understanding of government policy. Citing national security, the Nixon administration secured a court injunction forcing the *Times* to cease publication, but the newspaper appealed, and the case quickly went to the Supreme Court. While not denying the possibility that censorship can be warranted, the Court in this instance rejected the government's argument that national security took precedence over the right to publish documents embarrassing to the government. The government, said the Court, had not met the extraordinary burden of proof needed for prior restraint.

While journalists are protected by the *Pentagon Papers* decision, a new brand of "journalists" has arisen in the form of bloggers. A recent federal case held that bloggers are afforded the same protections as journalists working for established news outlets. This case expanded First Amendment protections beyond those in previous rulings to include persons other than "institutional media defendants."[19]

In general, the courts have tended to give the edge to the press in the belief that, in the long run, it is better to protect press freedoms so that the press can, in turn, help inform the public, which can then hold elected officials accountable. Consistent with this general predisposition, there are very few laws that constrain the print media, such as newspapers and magazines. The electronic media, however, are more heavily regulated by government. As early as the 1920s, Congress sought to regulate radio to ensure it would serve the public interest. It was a new medium, and Congress wanted to guard against it being used in a way that might undermine equality and fairness. In 1934, Congress created the Federal Communications Commission (FCC), now a powerful agency that regulates all forms of electronic media, including radio, broadcast television, cable television, cell phones, and even wireless networks. Anyone can start a newspaper, but starting a radio station requires a license from the FCC.

The FCC monitors media ownership as well. For a long time, the FCC worked to ensure that ownership of the news media was not concentrated in just a few hands; it was concerned that a monopoly would undermine the ability of the media to be fair and able to perform its watchdog function. The Telecommunications Act of 1996 eased the rules concerning multiple ownership, and the FCC has started to relax this standard. As a result, there has been a trend toward greater concentration of media ownership in the past decade. In 1995, major companies generally owned around ten television stations each; ten years later, each owned nearly forty. The ownership of radio has also changed. Clear Channel Communications owned 520 radio stations in 1999; a decade and a half later, the number stood at 840.[20]

This recent concentration of media ownership is not unique. Concerns about the consequences of control of the news by just a few people date to the late nineteenth century, when individuals such as William Randolph Hearst controlled major news organizations. Without genuine competition, the press, some fear, will become lapdogs, not watchdogs. But even the changes of the past few years have not eliminated competition. It is true that newspapers are now dominated by seven major chains; Gannett alone has a presence in over 100 media markets across the country.[21] But with so many outlets for news in the twenty-first century, one person or company is not able to control information. The public has access to a wide range of information.

Any effort to monopolize the press or curtail its freedom will be met by strong protests from citizens fearing a trend toward authoritarian rule (see Public Policy, the News, and

Social Media: Censorship). A government that limits press freedom seeks to insulate itself from criticism, thereby decreasing the chance for the public to hold leaders accountable. The absence of a robust press means that government will no longer be responsive, but that it will instead pursue policies that advance the interests of the few rather than the many. In this situation, greater inequality arises between those in power and those out of power. It is for all these reasons that an evaluation of how democratic a nation is rests on how much freedom its press enjoys.

7.3 The History of the Press in America

Define trends in the history of the press

The press in America has always been dynamic. Newspapers have developed from occasional pamphlets in the early 1700s, to comprehensive daily publications that aimed for objective reporting of political news, to today's online enterprises filled with a mix of news and entertainment. By the 1900s, journalism emerged as a profession with a commitment to objectivity. In the twentieth century, radio and then television changed how Americans received the news and how they reacted to it. Throughout, the press has at times supported government and elected officials and at times assumed an adversarial role as it has given citizens the information they need to make government accountable and responsive.

The Colonial Era, 1620 to 1750

In the early colonial period, newspapers were not widely available, and there were few printing presses. *Public Occurrences,* which began publication in Boston in 1690, had only a few pages and was more a pamphlet than a newspaper. Circulation was small, usually fewer than two thousand copies.[22] Newspaper publication was more of a hobby for publishers than anything else, and the notion that the press had the right to criticize government was not widely accepted. In fact, colonial governments feared that harsh criticism would incite the public and create instability, so publishers who attacked those in power could be thrown into jail and have their printing presses confiscated.

In 1734, John Peter Zenger was jailed for criticizing the colonial governor of New York in his *New York Weekly Journal*. When his case came to trial the next year, his lawyer, Andrew Hamilton of Philadelphia, decided on a bold strategy. Zenger would admit guilt—he had published the critical statements—and then argue that the jury should find him not guilty because the statements were true. In other words, the press had a fundamental right to criticize government, and a free press was more important than the law against **seditious libel** that had put Zenger behind bars. Much to the surprise of the governor and his supporters, the jury agreed and freed Zenger. The case is a landmark in advancing the idea of a free press.

seditious libel: *Conduct or language that incites rebellion against the authority of a state.*

In the same decade, in Philadelphia, Benjamin Franklin was laying the groundwork for the press as a viable institution in America with his *Philadelphia Gazette*. The paper would

PUBLIC POLICY, THE NEWS, AND SOCIAL MEDIA

Censorship

Any effort by government to control the media or to curtail the freedom of the press faces an immediate debate and often strong protest. The advent of radio and television and the recent proliferation of electronic media have brought new challenges to determining what kinds of content should be restrained and what kinds should be allowed to flow freely. No government agency regulates the print media, but the FCC has the authority to regulate the content and ownership of radio, television, the Internet, and all electronic media. One area of special concern has been what might be considered obscene, offensive, or harmful material.

The landmark Supreme Court decision in *FCC v. Pacifica Foundation* (1978) established the precedent that the FCC has the legal authority to fine any media outlet that knowingly allows the expression of obscene content, under certain circumstances. The background of the case was that in 1973 a New York radio station aired George Carlin's monologue "Filthy Words," which included seven words that could not be said on the public airwaves. The station had prefaced the monologue with a warning to listeners that it included "sensitive language which might be regarded as offensive to some." A listener who was in the car with his young son when he heard the broadcast filed a complaint with the FCC.

The underlying question in this case was whether the First Amendment inhibits the power of the government to restrict the public broadcast of indecent language under any circumstances. The Supreme Court ruled in a 5–4 decision that the government could invoke limited civil sanctions against the radio broadcast of patently offensive words dealing with sex and excretion without violating the First Amendment. The Court also said that the words did not have to be obscene to warrant sanction and that, in decisions on whether sanctions on media content are fair and justified, other factors such as audience type, the time that the broadcast was aired, and how it was transmitted are relevant.[23]

In today's television, music, and video climate, the boundaries for socially acceptable visual and verbal content are constantly evolving. In *FCC v. Fox Television Stations*, Fox Broadcasting Company appealed fines that the FCC imposed for its broadcasts of the Billboard Music Awards, during which participants uttered expletives. Fox claimed that participants on previous broadcasts had used similar language and that the FCC had ruled that the use was "fleeting" and was not seriously harmful. The Supreme Court ruled that the FCC needed to prove only that its new policy was justifiable and reasonable.[24] In response, network television and radio stations have taken to "bleeping" or "buzzing" over words that might be viewed as harmful by the FCC. In live broadcasts, networks typically use a five-second delay in sending their signals over the airways to make sure they have time to bleep out offensive language. Cable television outlets are not under this same type of restriction because they broadcast to paid subscribers who thus have more control over the content they choose to view.

Social networking and the Internet present new challenges, particularly in the area of child safety. The Internet is not exactly a broadcast medium, but given its wide availability to the general public, Congress has sought to restrict its content. In 1996, Congress passed the Communications Decency Act, which established broadcast-style content regulations for the Internet. The act banned the posting of "indecent" or "patently offensive" materials in a public forum on the Internet, including in newsgroups, chat rooms, web pages, and online discussion lists. The American Civil Liberties Union (ACLU) challenged the law, and in 1997, the Supreme Court ruled unanimously that it was unconstitutional because it imposed sweeping restrictions that violated the free speech protections of the First Amendment.[25]

In 1998, Congress tried for a second time to limit content on the Internet when it passed the Child Online Protection Act (COPA).[26] The act made it a crime for anyone using an Internet site or e-mail over the Internet to make any communication for commercial reasons considered "harmful to minors" unless the person had prohibited access by minors by requiring a credit card number to access the material. Again, the legislation was ultimately struck down, this time by the Court of Appeals for the Third Circuit. Further, in 2009, the U.S. Supreme Court refused to hear the government's appeal of this decision.

Congress subsequently responded by passing the Children's Online Privacy Protection Act (COPPA), which requires sites directed to children under the age of 13 to gain parental consent before collecting, maintaining, or using children's information. Parents can review their children's online activity under COPPA. The act also requires such a site to post a privacy policy on its home page and a link to the privacy policy on every page where personal information is collected.[27] In addition, Congress passed a law designed to prevent the exploitation of children by prohibiting pornographic websites from showing sexually explicit material involving children on their home pages.[28]

Given the vastness of the Internet and the speed at which technology evolves, it becomes fundamentally harder to keep the Internet "safe" for users of all ages as well as to preserve the security of information that is passed over it. Because the Internet is an engine of commerce as well as a media outlet, it is also regulated by the Federal Trade Commission (FTC).[29] The FTC offers detailed information to consumers about what information they should never release on the Internet, what websites are not secure, how to determine secure websites, and how to report wrongdoing. Citizens who fail to read privacy policies or are not careful about the information they release are vulnerable, and the FTC is the government agency responsible for helping to prevent Internet abuse and fraud.

Public Policy Connections

1. In a free society, what should the limits be on government censorship of the media?
2. Should all forms of media (newspapers, television, Internet, etc.) be subjected to the same level of regulation?

set the standard for American news with its ability to present news accounts in an interesting and enlightening manner. Franklin had a gift for writing and a flair for satire and parody. His accounts of government and stories of personal interest, including crime, sex, violence, and mysteries, became the foundation for modern American news coverage. He is considered by many to be one of America's first sensationalist journalists. But Franklin was trying to do much more than simply pique the interest of readers: He also believed that the news was critical to educating the public. His "An Apology for Printers" (1731) defended objectivity in journalism. Though it contradicted the prevailing view at the time, it helped set the standard for the future of American journalism.[30]

The Founding Era, 1750 to 1790

As tensions between the colonies and Britain increased, interest in politics grew as well, and the press responded. The circulation of newspapers grew twice as fast as the population

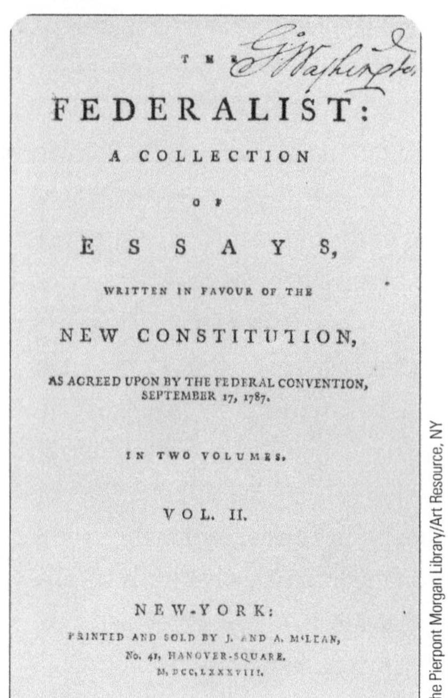
THE FEDERALIST: A COLLECTION OF ESSAYS, WRITTEN IN FAVOUR OF THE NEW CONSTITUTION, AS AGREED UPON BY THE FEDERAL CONVENTION, SEPTEMBER 17, 1787. IN TWO VOLUMES. VOL. II. NEW-YORK: PRINTED AND SOLD BY J. AND A. M'LEAN, No. 41, HANOVER-SQUARE, M,DCC,LXXXVIII.

The Pierpont Morgan Library/Art Resource, NY

IMAGE 7.2 *The Federalist Papers* are an early example of the power of the press in America. Writing as "Publius," James Madison, Alexander Hamilton, and John Jay published seventy-seven essays in New York newspapers arguing for the ratification of the Constitution. In 1788, these and eight other essays were republished in two volumes. They are still read today for insights into the interpretation of the Constitution and the Framers' vision for a republic.

between 1760 and 1776.[31] That year, when Thomas Paine published *Common Sense*, a pamphlet attacking King George, it sold 150,000 copies, far more than the 2,000 copies political documents normally sold.[32] Given that there were only 2.5 million people in the colonies, that is the equivalent of 18 million copies today.

The press helped spread the idea of independence because newspapers served as networks for sharing information. They reached not only subscribers but also many people who could not read, for the papers were read aloud in taverns and town squares. During the Revolution, some papers backed independence; others supported the British Crown.[33]

Partisanship in the press carried over to the battle for ratification of the Constitution, and newspapers provided a vital forum for debate. The Antifederalists waged a fierce campaign against the Constitution,[34] and those supporting the Constitution responded, most famously in a series of essays published in New York newspapers, which are today known as the **Federalist Papers**.

The Partisan Era, 1790 to 1900

Following the adoption of the Constitution, most newspapers allied themselves with the Federalists or with the newly emerging Jeffersonian party. In this era of the partisan press, writers made no effort to adjudicate between the claims and ideas of competing parties. Consequently, rhetoric was often harsh. During George Washington's time in office (1789–97), he was attacked constantly by the Jeffersonian press.

Even worse criticism was leveled at the second president, John Adams (1797–1801), who was not as universally admired as Washington. Adams was called a liar and feebleminded, among other things.[35] His administration's Sedition Act (1798) made it illegal to print or publish any "false, scandalous, and malicious writing" about the federal government, either house of Congress, or the president.[36] At the time, the United States was engaged in a limited and undeclared war with France over trade issues, and the Federalists believed that attacks on Adams and the government were ripping apart the new nation, which was barely a decade old. The Articles of Confederation had not even lasted ten years; might not the same fate await the Constitution? But the Jeffersonians were equally adamant that laws suppressing criticism of the government violated the Constitution. Jeffersonian publishers did not cease their attacks, and some went to jail and paid fines. After he and his party won the 1800 presidential election, Thomas Jefferson (1801–09) pardoned all publishers convicted under the act, and Congress refunded their fines.

Federalist Papers: *Series of essays written by James Madison, Alexander Hamilton, and John Jay arguing for the ratification of the Constitution; today a leading source for understanding the Constitution.*

Now it was Jefferson and his party's turn to be attacked. The Federalist opposition was very critical of Jefferson, calling him the "anti-Christ."[37] While Jefferson had long been a proponent of a free press and had severely criticized the Sedition Act, the attacks he endured were so vicious that he began to question the merits of this partisan press. In 1807 he conceded, "The man who never looks into a newspaper is better informed than he who reads them."[38] This was quite a change for a man who, twenty years earlier, had argued that newspapers were more important than the institutions of republican government itself. Jefferson's dilemma reveals a core issue about the press. The media do inform, playing a vital function. But informing almost always carries some bias, and when informing is deliberately intended to manipulate public opinion, the public responds with distrust.

Newspapers continued to have close alliances with political parties in the next decades of the nineteenth century. They not only served to attack the opposition but also provided a way for presidents and party leaders to express their opinions on the issues of the day. Some presidents, such as James K. Polk (1845–49), even started their own newspapers to get out their message.[39]

During the 1830s and 1840s, new steam presses reduced the cost of publishing newspapers. In 1833, Benjamin Day sold his *New York Sun* for a penny per issue, initiating the era of the **penny press**. At the same time, literacy throughout the nation was growing, and newspaper owners began to realize that they could make higher profits through circulation and advertising than as arms of political parties.[40] They also saw that partisanship drove away customers who did not share their political views. So to increase circulation, newspapers began to move toward sensationalism, printing news of crimes and scandals and stories about personalities, much as tabloids do today and as Ben Franklin did in the 1700s. In 1870, for example, only about 13 percent of all newspapers were independent of a political party. By 1900, that proportion had swelled to nearly 50 percent.[41]

penny press: *Newspapers sold for a penny, initiating an era in which the press began to rely on circulation and advertising for income and not on political parties.*

yellow journalism: *Style of journalism in the late-nineteenth century characterized by sensationalism intended to capture readers' attention and increase circulation.*

The circulation of newspapers rose from about 1.4 million in 1870 to more than 8 million within the next thirty years. The quest for market share led to competition over which newspaper could grab the most attention with sensational headlines and stories. Known as **yellow journalism**, this form of news reporting distorted the presentation of events and could mislead the public, all in the interest of boosting sales. Joseph Pulitzer and William Randolph Hearst, the most famous newspaper publishers at the time, used large type, provocative headlines, pictures, and color to attract readers. Hearst introduced comics as a way to sell more papers. The competition became particularly fierce over American relations with Spain, as stories of Spanish atrocities in Cuba inflamed the public. When the USS *Maine* sank in Havana Harbor on February 15, 1898, the newspapers quickly blamed Spain. The U.S. Navy launched a four-week investigation, finding that the *Maine* had been destroyed by an underwater mine but placing no blame. However, the American public, fed by the press, continued to blame Spain, and on April 25, the U.S. Congress declared war on Spain. Many observers credit these sensational newspaper stories with fueling the start of the Spanish-American War.[42]

863,956 The World. 863,956

MAINE EXPLOSION CAUSED BY BOMB OR TORPEDO?

Capt. Sigsbee and Consul-General Lee Are in Doubt---The World Has Sent a Special Tug, With Submarine Divers, to Havana to Find Out---Lee Asks for an Immediate Court of Inquiry---Capt. Sigsbee's Suspicions.

CA I. SIGSBEE, IN A SUPPRESSED DESPATCH TO THE STATE DEPARTMENT, SAYS THE ACCIDENT WAS MADE POSSIBLE BY AN ENEMY.

Dr. E. C. Pendleton, Just Arrived from Havana, Says He Overheard Talk There of a Plot to Blow Up the Ship---Capt Zalinski, the Dynamite Expert, and Other Experts Report to The World that the Wreck Was Not Accidental---Washington Officials Ready for Vigorous Action if Spanish Responsibility Can Be Shown---Divers to Be Sent Down to Make Careful Examinations.

The New York World a day after

who had been Populists and those who became Progressives — clamored for the United States to rescue the Cuban people from the Spanish malefactors.

President William McKinley and the conservative Republican leaders in Congress reluctantly gave way before this pressure. Senator Henry Cabot Lodge warned McKinley, "If the war in Cuba drags on through the summer with nothing done we [the Republican party] shall go down in the greatest defeat ever known."

Already, in November 1897, Spain, at the urging of President McKinley, had granted

Bettmann/Corbis

IMAGE 7.3 William Randolph Hearst's *New York Journal* and Joseph Pulitzer's *New York World* competed for circulation with sensational news and screaming headlines. The frenzy they stirred up over the sinking of the USS *Maine* in Havana Harbor in February 1898 helped lead to war with Spain. It is now generally believed that the explosion on the *Maine* was not caused by a Spanish bomb or torpedo but was accidental, a spontaneous combustion in inadequately vented coal bunkers.

The Professional Era, 1900 to 1950

The development of mass circulation newspapers also led journalism to develop into a serious profession with an ethic of objective reporting. Pulitzer, despite his role in advancing yellow journalism, was a key figure in this transition, believing that a vibrant independent press was essential for a democracy to endure. In 1904, he observed that "our Republic and its press will rise or fall together. An able, disinterested, public-spirited press... can preserve that public virtue without which popular government is a sham and a mockery."[43]

The idea of a public-spirited press was increasingly realized in efforts to investigate wrongdoing in government, business, and industry. Adolph Ochs purchased the *New York Times* in 1896 with the goal of pursuing objective reporting. Such commitments led journalists, with the backing of people such as Ochs and Pulitzer, to expose corruption and encourage genuine reform. Although President Theodore Roosevelt (1901–09) labeled such efforts as **muckraking**—after a character in *Pilgrim's Progress* who rakes "muck," looking for the worst rather than the best—he came to appreciate the service these investigative journalists provided. Perhaps the most famous example was Upton Sinclair's *The Jungle* (1906), a novel that exposed the horrors of the meatpacking industry. Roosevelt, who had read an advance copy of the book, called for government regulation of the food industry.[44] In response, Congress passed the Pure Food and Drug Act and the Meat Inspection Act to help ensure food safety.

muckraking: *Journalistic practice of investigative reporting that seeks to uncover corruption and wrongdoing.*

The rise of professional journalism is also tied to an ethic of objectivity. The goal of being impartial and unbiased in reporting became part of the journalist's creed, especially as taught in new schools of journalism. The American Society of Newspaper Editors adopted a set of principles declaring that "news reports should be free from opinion or bias of any kind."[45] Reporters were trained to present facts, not personal opinions, and to describe, not judge.

With the rise of investigative journalism, a key goal became to "get the scoop"—to write a story that presented the public with new and important information that was well researched and carefully documented. Journalists sought to cultivate politicians for access to news and stories, and this cultivation led to a different dynamic between politicians and the press. It remained adversarial, but both sides knew they needed each other. As the press and politicians formed closer relationships, the potential for conflicts of interest increased. To retain the relationship, politicians made certain statements "off the record," with the understanding that journalists would not use them in a story except as background, information that could help set the context and provide a broader understanding for the story. As a result, journalists have a strong ethic about not revealing confidential sources.

The press took some topics off the table, including the personal lives of politicians. For example, few Americans realized that President Franklin Delano Roosevelt (1933–45) was paralyzed from polio; the press chose not to cover his physical challenge and rarely photographed him being carried from his car. Journalists did not deem Roosevelt's condition relevant to governing, and his paralysis did not interfere with his performance as president, seemingly justifying the press's decision.

This practice did have costs, however. Using the same example, one could argue that the press relinquished its role of watchdog in not covering Roosevelt's health, especially as it declined. Roosevelt died in April 1945, three months after taking the oath of office for his fourth term. There were clear signs that he was ill, but the press chose not to report them.[46]

The Television Era, 1950 to 2000

The rise of television recast the news media and the information available to the public. At mid-century, the *New York Times* was the most influential newspaper and clearly the leader in American journalism. News magazines such as *Time* and *Life* had nationwide circulations, but they were not daily sources of information. Most people got their daily news from local newspapers and radio stations that broadcast news summaries—usually five minutes of news, weather, and sports on the hour. Then television began to nationalize the news. That is, the evening broadcasts from the three major networks—ABC, CBS, and NBC—gave Americans across the country access to the same news, and by the 1960s, they relied on television for political information.[47]

TV news was shaped by a handful of "anchormen." In fact, there were no women on the national networks, nor were there any anchors of color, in the first few decades of television. In 1976, Barbara Walters became the first woman to anchor the evening news (ABC). It was not until 2015 that an African American, Lester Holt, solo-anchored an evening news program.[48]

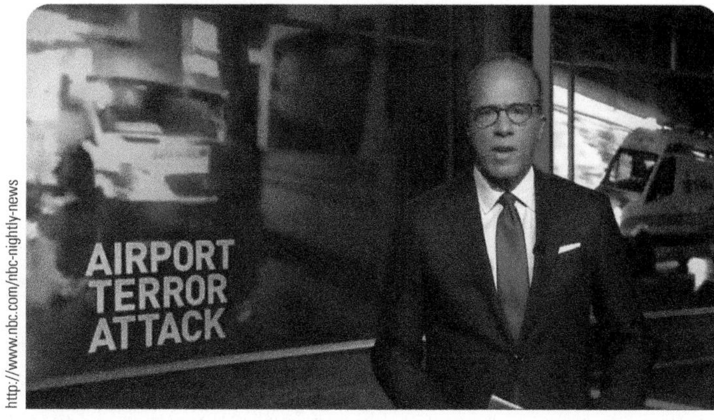

http://www.nbc.com/nbc-nightly-news

IMAGE 7.4 In 2015, Lester Holt became the first African American solo news anchor in the United States.

When TV news anchors are discussed, Walter Cronkite's name is soon to follow. Walter Cronkite, anchor of the *CBS Evening News,* was an icon. Not only was he famous, but he was also widely admired and trusted. In 1973, Americans rated him "the most trusted man in America."[49] Can you imagine that happening today? Cronkite represented both the height of what might be called "objective" journalism and the dominance of TV network news. Most Americans assumed that Cronkite provided the facts and did not let partisanship shape his reporting. He closed his evening news show by saying "and that's the way it is," and viewers agreed.

Television's visuals also redefined the news and even political events. Politicians now aimed to look good on television because viewers could detect nervousness and judge body language. The 1960 presidential campaign is a well-known example of the new emphasis on the visual side of politics. Most viewers of the televised presidential debates between Senator John Kennedy and Vice President Richard Nixon thought that Kennedy performed better.[50] He looked tanned and rested; in fact, he had spent a few days before the debate resting on a beach. Nixon, by contrast, had continued to campaign and had spent time in the hospital for a very sore leg. He was tired and in pain. He also refused to wear makeup. Nixon was not at his best, while Kennedy looked presidential. People who listened to the debate on the radio, however, thought that Nixon had won, further suggesting the power of visuals. Many commentators attribute Kennedy's razor-thin victory in the election to his performance in the debates.[51]

AP Images

IMAGE 7.5 Television proved its importance as a source for political information when the NBC board chair invited the 1960 presidential candidates to debate the issues on television. John F. Kennedy accepted first, saying, "I believe you are performing a notable public service in giving the American people a chance to see the candidates of the two major parties face to face." More than 70 million Americans watched the Kennedy–Nixon debates, and today presidential debates are fixtures of the fall campaign.

The general rule is that visuals in debates (and other campaign events) remain central to campaigns. It is important to look presidential. Some may now, however, question that rule in light of Donald Trump's approach in the 2016 presidential debates. He was widely criticized for his lack of policy knowledge and his often harsh rhetoric in those debates. Yet he won the presidency.

7.4 Mass Media in the Twenty-First Century

Explain how changes in the mass media have changed the information environment

The media have always been a dynamic institution, but the speed of changes in the past few decades is truly staggering. The impact of television, for example, changed further with the rise of cable television from the 1970s to the 1990s. It was now possible to bring news to the public any time of day, reshaping the American news environment. Recent advances in technology have opened up additional avenues of communication—nearly all at the same time. The pace and the depth of these changes make the information environment of the twenty-first century different from those that preceded it.

The Changing Media Environment

The options open to Americans for gathering information about politics have constantly expanded. Figure 7.1 displays the changing media environment and suggests two main lessons. First, Americans adopt new media quickly. In the early 1920s, there were only five radio stations, and few households owned radios. By 1927, there were seven hundred stations, and ownership was rapidly increasing.[52] By the end of the 1930s, almost everyone in the United States had access to a radio. Television caught on even more quickly. Only 10 percent of Americans had TV sets in their homes in the early 1950s; by 1960, the figure was 90 percent. Today, nearly all American households have not one TV but often two or three. Internet access also shows a steep upward trend, from few households in the mid-1990s to currently around 90 percent of Americans.[53]

The speed by which these new media have entered the marketplace itself increases. It took television thirteen years to reach 50 million users. In just three years on the market, more than 50 million iPods were sold, and when the iPad was released in 2010, about 3 million were sold in eighty days.[54] The number of Twitter users has jumped tenfold, from about 30 million in March 2010 to 320 million in February 2016.[55] Of course, among the younger generation, Twitter is a much more common feature of daily lives: Estimates are that about one-third of Millennials use Twitter and three in five have accounts.[56]

Second, there are more options for gathering news than ever before. In the 1930s, newspapers and radio were the main sources. In the 1950s, television was a new option, but there were only three networks, and they broadcast the news only in the evening. Now cable TV, satellite TV, and the Internet make news available night and day.

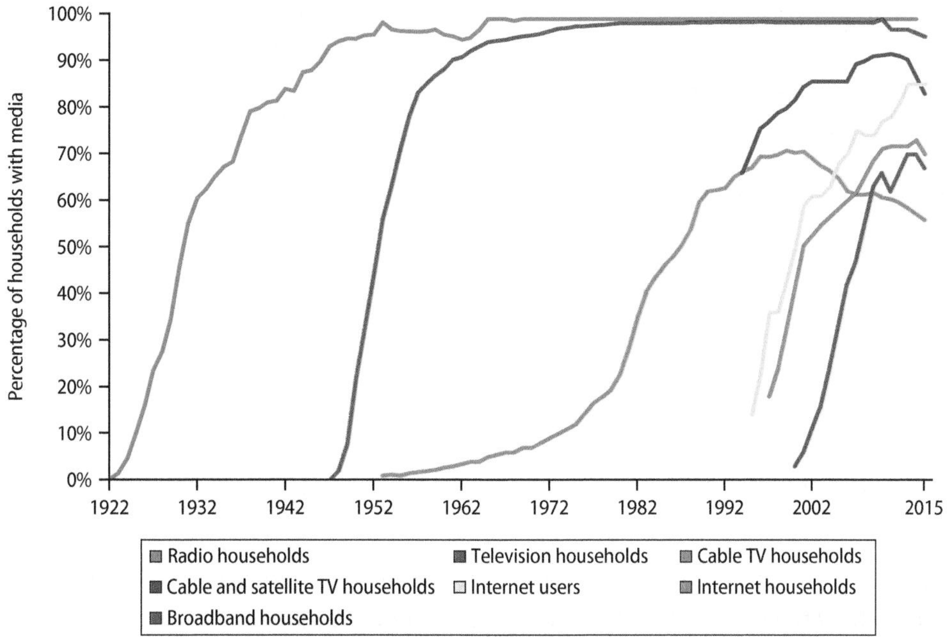

FIGURE 7.1 The Changing Media Environment, 1922–2015

When a new medium arises, the public quickly adopts it.

Source: http://www.nytimes.com/2011/05/03/business/media/03television.html?_r=0, http://www.nielsen.com/us/en/insights/news/2015/nielsen-estimates-116-4-million-tv-homes-in-the-us-for-the-2015-16-tv-season.html, http://tvbythenumbers.zap2it.com/2007/08/28/us-television-households-by-season/273, http://www.tvb.org/media_comparisons/4729/72512, http://www.nielsen.com/content/dam/corporate/us/en/newswire/uploads/2009/07/tva_2008_071709.pdf, http://www.tvhistory.tv/Cable_Households_77-99.JPG, http://www.ibtimes.com/forget-cable-cord-cutting-83-percent-american-households-still-pay-tv-2081570, http://www.pewinternet.org/2015/06/26/americans-internet-access-2000-2015, http://www.pewinternet.org/three-technology-revolutions, and http://www.pewinternet.org/2015/12/21/home-broadband-2015.

The Decline of Newspapers

Traditional printed newspapers are in decline. The number of daily papers has been dropping since 1990.[57] Newspaper readership is also declining. Figure 7.2 shows the drop in readership since the turn of the century. This decline has been going on for forty years. In the mid-1970s, about 70 percent of the public read newspapers. This decrease in the last decade and a half is true for all generations, but there are notable differences by age in regards to newspaper readership. Currently, about 25 percent of the Millennial generation are newspaper readers as compared to nearly about 55 percent of those over 65 years of age.[58] This gap suggests a grim future for the print version of the news as generational replacement unfolds. The decline of newspapers and newspaper readership raises concerns because newspapers tend to contain more **hard news**—fact-based stories, as opposed to interpretive narratives—than what is reported on TV. Alex Jones, one of the leading observers of the press, indicated that 85 percent of hard news comes from newspapers rather than from TV.[59] Will the decline of newspapers deprive Americans of hard news, of the facts they need to hold government accountable?

hard news: *Political news coverage, traditionally found in the printed press, that is more fact-based, opposed to more interpretive narratives and commentary.*

Some observers counter that readers are simply migrating from printed newspapers to online versions. In January 2004, online newspapers had about 41 million visitors; within the next decade the number had jumped to well over 100 million.[60] Although the move from the printed to online versions may offer some hope about the continued significance of the newspaper industry, it has not solved the industry's financial difficulties. With revenue plummeting, newspapers survive only by cutting staff. The *Boston Globe* no longer sends journalists overseas to report on international events. The *Los Angeles Times* has seen

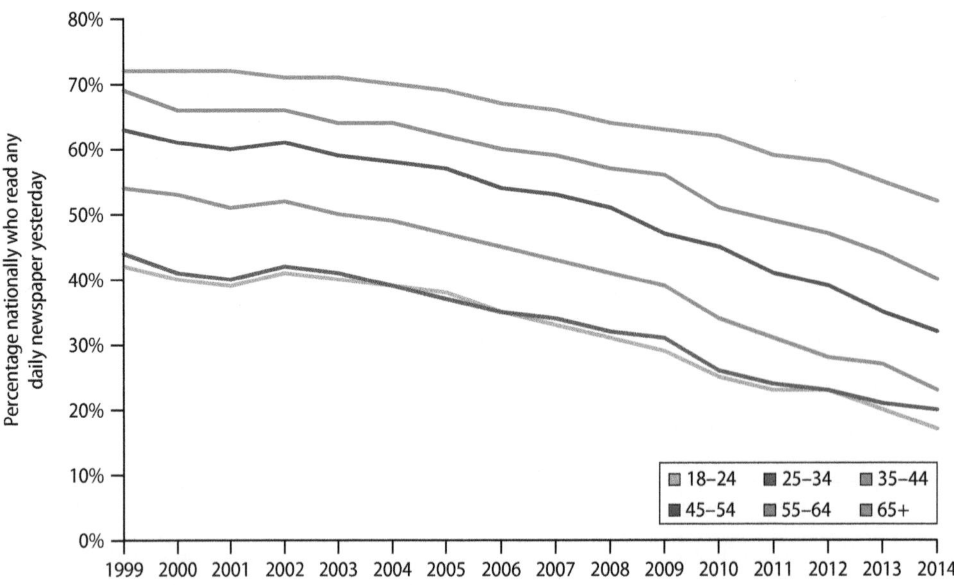

FIGURE 7.2 Newspaper Readership by Age, 1999–2014

Newspaper readership is declining across all ages.

Source: http://www.journalism.org/media-indicators/newspaper-readership-by-age.

its newsroom decline from 1,200 to 850 reporters.[61] Over the past decade, there has been a loss of 18,000 jobs in newsrooms, from 56,000 in 2003 to 36,000 in 2013.[62] Fewer reporters, editors, and other journalists mean that newspapers have less ability to inform and investigate. If the press cannot perform its watchdog role, the people stand to lose the means by which they hold government accountable.[63]

Despite these concerns, Americans want the news and continue to seek it out, so newspaper owners have an incentive to develop new ways to make a profit. In recent years, income has stabilized and better use of digital advertising has improved.[64] The bleeding, in other words, has stopped, and that may be a hopeful sign. But even for those who see a grim future for newspapers (as we currently think of them), it is important to remember that today's leading newspapers, such as the *New York Times,* have been powerful for only about seventy-five years, whereas American democracy has survived for 230 years. The press, in other words, will endure, regardless of form.

The Durability of Radio

In many ways, radio is underappreciated as a medium of communication; current debates center on newspapers, television, and the Internet. But radio remains important, especially considering how often Americans listen to the radio in their cars. The percentage of Americans who listen to the radio has remained unchanged in the past decade. In 1998, 95 percent of the American public tuned into an AM or FM station at least once a week; thirteen years later, 93 percent had listened to the radio in the previous seven days. Radio is expanding its reach by means of satellite radio and streaming audio on desktop and laptop computers. In fact, it is possible that "radio" is becoming "audio," reflecting advances in digital technology (see Figure 7.3).[65] These data underscore the growth in this area and this trend should continue.

Political talk radio, a medium dominated largely by conservatives, is increasingly popular.[66] In recent years, around 60 million Americans listened to talk radio,[67] most to

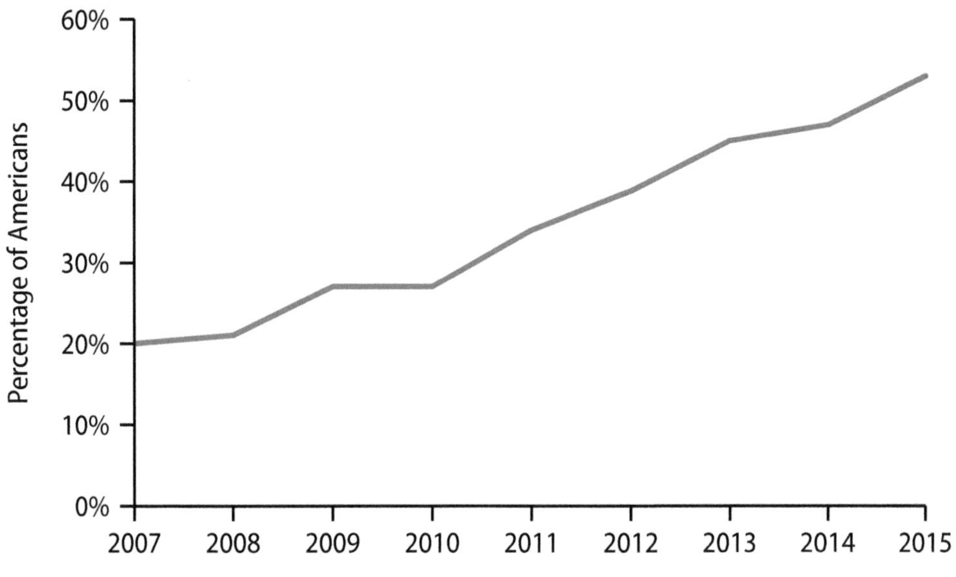

FIGURE 7.3 Monthly Online Radio Listeners, 2007–2015

The use of online radio is on the rise.

Source: http://www.journalism.org/2015/04/29/audio-fact-sheet.

conservative programs. In fact, as Table 7.1 shows, conservatives dominate the airwaves of talk radio. No "liberal" shows are even close to the popularity of the top-rated conservative commentators. Rush Limbaugh is by far the best known and the most controversial. Liberals at one time tried to make inroads into talk radio with the Air America radio network, but it did not last long. The reasons for this lack of success are unclear. Perhaps it is because there

TABLE 7.1 Top Talk Radio Hosts, 2009–2016 (in millions of listeners)

Host	Political Leaning/ General Topic	2009	2012	2016
Rush Limbaugh	Conservative	15.00	14.75	13.25
Sean Hannity	Conservative	14.00	14.00	12.50
Michael Savage	Conservative	9.00	8.75	5.25
Glenn Beck	Conservative	9.00	8.25	7.00
Mark Levin	Conservative	8.50	8.25	7.00
Dave Ramsey	Financial Advice	8.00	8.25	8.25
Neal Boortz	Libertarian	6.00	5.75	—
Laura Ingraham	Conservative	6.00	5.75	2.00
Jim Bohannon	Ind./Moderate	3.75	3.75	2.75
Jerry Doyle	Conservative	3.50	3.75	1.25

Source: Adapted from *Talker Magazine*, http://www.talkers.com/top-talk-radio-audiences, cited in Pew Research Center's Project for Excellence in Journalism's report, *The State of the News Media 2011*. And http://stateofthemedia.org/2013/audio-digital-drivers-listener-experience/19-limbaugh-audience-dips-slightly-but-still-tops-talk-radio/, Pew Research Center's Project for Excellence in Journalism, *State of the News Media 2013*.

are more conservatives than liberals in the United States. In addition, conservatives tend to live in the suburbs and rural areas and therefore spend more time in their cars than do city dwellers. Their greater opportunities for listening may be another reason for the dominance of conservative programming.[68]

The Transformation of TV News

Newspapers are not the only news outlets facing a decline in customers; the audience for the TV network evening news is also shrinking (see Figure 7.4). Nearly 25 percent of Americans watched the evening news in 1980; by 2013, that figure was around 10 percent.[69] The downward trend is likely to continue because older Americans make up the current audience for TV news. Young people, who represent the future audience, are not big consumers of network news. Their habits are not likely to change, painting a bleak picture for the industry in the coming years.

This decline, like that of newspapers, generates concern about how well informed the public is about politics. But these concerns are counterbalanced by the availability and uses of other sources of news (see Figure 7.4). TV news, which includes cable, has been on the decline, but look at the trend for "online/mobile" news and for radio as well.

The availability of news has been transformed. Cable news, for example, is not like the evening news shows of the 1970s, which were thirty-minute broadcasts around dinnertime. Cable news is available twenty-four hours a day. Events are covered live, transforming the news cycle. No longer do politicians time public appearances to appear on the evening news. News now comes at viewers at a rapid-fire rate, and cable news networks include interpretation in their constant programming. MSNBC's *Hardball with Chris Matthews* and

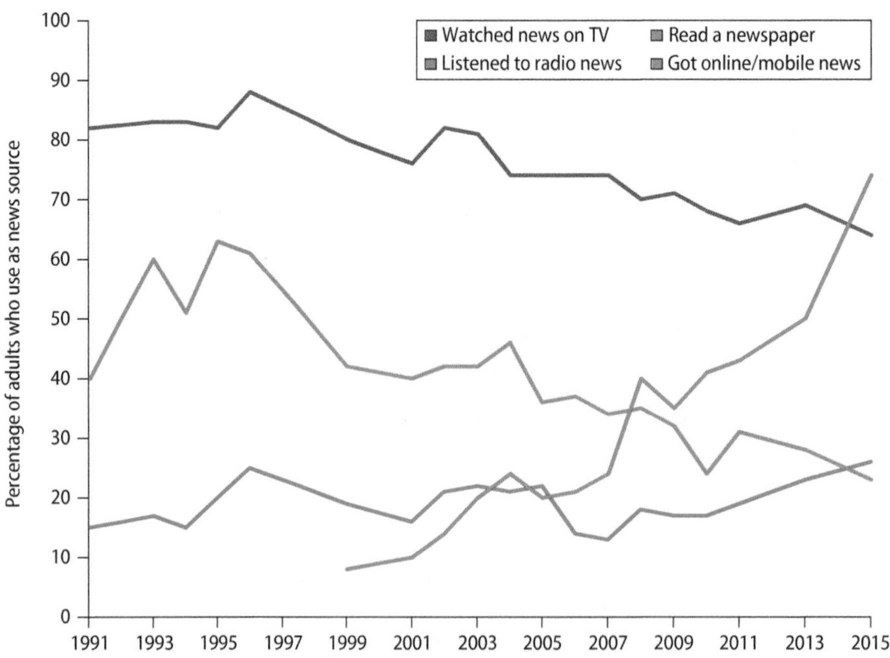

FIGURE 7.4 Different Sources of News, 1991–2015

Americans are getting their news increasingly from digital and online sources.

Sources: http://www.people-press.org/files/legacy-pdf/8-8-2013%20Media%20Attitudes%20Release.pdf; http://www.digitalnewsreport.org/survey/2015/sources-of-news-2015.

The Rachel Maddow Show are examples. Cable news has taken the interpretive function of the news media to a whole new level in response to the demands of 24-7 news programming. All these kinds of news, and others, can be gathered from handheld devices.

Infotainment

Television viewers also get political news through talk shows, such as *The Tonight Show starring Jimmy Fallon* and *Jimmy Kimmel Live*. We already know about Stephen Colbert's influence and popularity. These sources offer what is called "infotainment" or **soft news**, which is news with fewer hard facts of the kind newspapers generally report and more emphasis on personal stories that engage (or shock) the public and often appeal to the emotions rather than the intellect.

soft news: *News stories focused less on facts and policies than on sensationalizing secondary issues or on less serious subjects of the entertainment world.*

For example, about 3 million people, mostly younger Americans, watch the *Late Show with Stephen Colbert*, which delivers the news with humor and satire in the evening.[70] These kinds of shows often ask some tough questions, however, so it is an overstatement to claim that the news such shows provide is "soft." The guests who appear, for example, on *Real Time with Bill Maher* cover the full ideological spectrum, and Maher subjects those in power—regardless of party—to his rapier wit. In 2016, his popularity was challenged by *Last Week Tonight with John Oliver*, which has as many as 4 million viewers.[71]

http://www.americanbazaaronline.com/2015/04/10/reena-ninan-will-co-anchor-america-this-morning-and-world-news-now-on-abc/

IMAGE 7.6 Over the last few decades, TV news anchors have become increasingly diverse. In 2015, Reena Ninan became co-anchor of *World News Now* and *America This Morning*, ABC's early morning broadcast news shows.

Blogs

Blogs provide a forum for bottom-up commentary, descriptions of events, video postings, and general conversation. Through blogs, average citizens are able to express their opinions to a wider audience, and they offer a gateway for people to influence politics. In fact, blogs have given rise to a new category of journalists—citizen-journalists—who, although not professional journalists, circulate opinions and interpretations that clearly influence political debates. There are all kinds of blogs, with political blogs representing a subset. Of the fifteen most popular blogs in 2016, two are political: the *Huffington Post* (number 1) and the *Daily Beast* (number 8).[72]

In many ways, blogging symbolizes the modern transformation of the mass media. Blogs capture the interest of people of all ages, and some observers hope that they will provide a forum for more participation and deliberation. While there is some evidence that blogs do foster participation, they do not seem to foster deliberation. Liberals read liberal blogs, and conservatives read conservative blogs—in fact, 94 percent of people read blogs that share their ideological viewpoint. These data suggest that blogs reinforce existing preferences and do not provide opportunities to hear the other side.[73] In addition, blogs usually have clear ideological leanings. Conservative blogs include those of Matt Drudge and Rush Limbaugh.[74] *Daily Kos* and *Huffington Post* are liberal blogs.

Blogs have the potential to spread false information. Because no one checks the accuracy of a posting, individuals—some call them trolls—can say outrageous things merely to get attention without penalty.[75] In contrast, the traditional press has a well-established set of norms for vetting the accuracy of information; when false statements do get through, the journalists are likely to pay a heavy penalty. Trolls, on the other hand, often gain notoriety for lying.

Nevertheless, the importance of blogs continues to increase. Bloggers write about business news, iTechnology, political news, trends in Hollywood, and so on. News that is not picked up in the mainstream media often gets play in the blogosphere and can force the mainstream media to cover the story. Politicians understand the powerful effects blogs can have on the news. In modern presidential campaigns, candidates established blogs on their websites (e.g., tedcruz.org) with commentary on topics ranging from the cost of college tuition to how best to achieve peace in the Middle East.

Social Networking

The Internet has also enabled new social networks for sharing information. Just as personal conversations are important sources of information, social networking websites are increasingly important ways to spread political news. Facebook is, of course, the leading platform for social networking. Its website announces that its mission is "to give people the power to share and make the world more open and connected."[76] And for millennials, Facebook remains an important source of information for Americans.[77] As Figure 7.5 shows, Facebook increased in importance from 2013 to 2015. But as the figure also shows, Twitter has made real inroads, becoming a more common way to stay abreast of breaking news than Facebook.

Mark Zuckerberg started Facebook from his Harvard dorm room in February 2004 as a social networking service limited to the Harvard campus. By the end of the year, the network had more than 1 million users, and it reached 5.5 million by the end of 2005 when it was extended to all universities and high schools in the United States and Canada. In 2016 Facebook had more than 1.4 billion monthly users. Facebook is a worldwide phenomenon with launches in more than fifteen different languages.

In 2016, Zuckerberg predicted that Facebook would have 5 billion users by 2030. With worldwide population estimated to be 8.5 billion by then, the Harvard graduate is anticipating usage by 60 percent of all humans.[78] But all these platforms are dynamic and undergoing constant change. Consider the growing use of Snapchat, especially among those who are under 34 years of age. Just a few years ago, it did not exist, but by 2015 it had more than 200 million users, 71 percent of them under the age of 35.[79]

Politicians are making increased use of social media to communicate with the public. Donald Trump took this to a new level during his quest for the presidency in 2016. Nearly all presidential candidates use Twitter, but Trump made it an art form: His tweets often drove the coverage of the campaign and forced candidates to respond to his claims and ideas. In November 2016, Trump enjoyed nearly 13 million followers on Twitter.[80] Every attack or self-promotion claim he made through Twitter drew comment from journalists, activists, competing candidates, and the average voters. If you Googled "Donald Trump and Twitter" in October 2016, you would get nearly 175,000 hits.

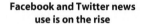

Facebook and Twitter news use is on the rise

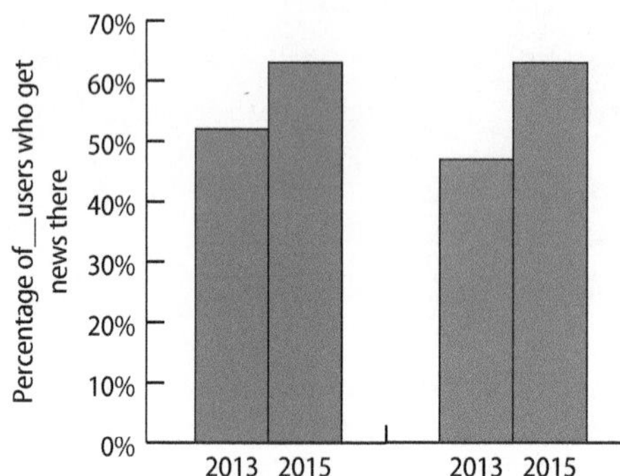

Of those who get news from__in 2015, percent who have kept up with a news event as it was happening

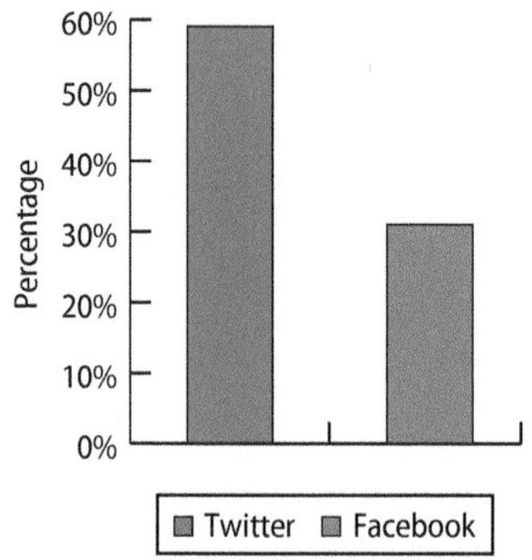

FIGURE 7.5 Rising Use of Facebook and Twitter as News Sources

Facebook and Twitter matter in today's political climate, with Twitter showing very steep user gains recently.

Source: http://www.journalism.org/2015/07/14/the-evolving-role-of-news-on-twitter-and-facebook.

POLITICAL ANALYTICS

Media Consumption Among Liberals and Conservatives

PEOPLE OBTAIN NEWS AND INFORMATION from a variety of sources, from radio talk shows to blogs to other Internet sources. But when it comes to news about government and politics, are there patterns to the sources people rely on and trust? Recent evidence suggest that liberals and conservatives differ in the number and sources of news they consume. It seems that the political polarization discussed in Chapter 6, Public Opinion, carries over to where people get their news.

Figure 7.6 shows stark differences between those who are consistently liberal and their conservative counterparts. Liberals tend to rely on multiple sources for news about politics, whereas conservatives go to Fox News as their primary source. People's ideological dispositions also affect the news sources they tend to trust. For example, when asked about the trustworthiness of thirty-six different news sources (from the BBC to the Rush Limbaugh show to BuzzFeed), consistent conservatives expressed distrust in two-thirds of them, while consistent liberals expressed trust in more than two-thirds of them.

Examine the reported main sources for news about government and politics for conservatives and liberals, as well as the difference in the number of main sources that liberals versus conservatives consume.

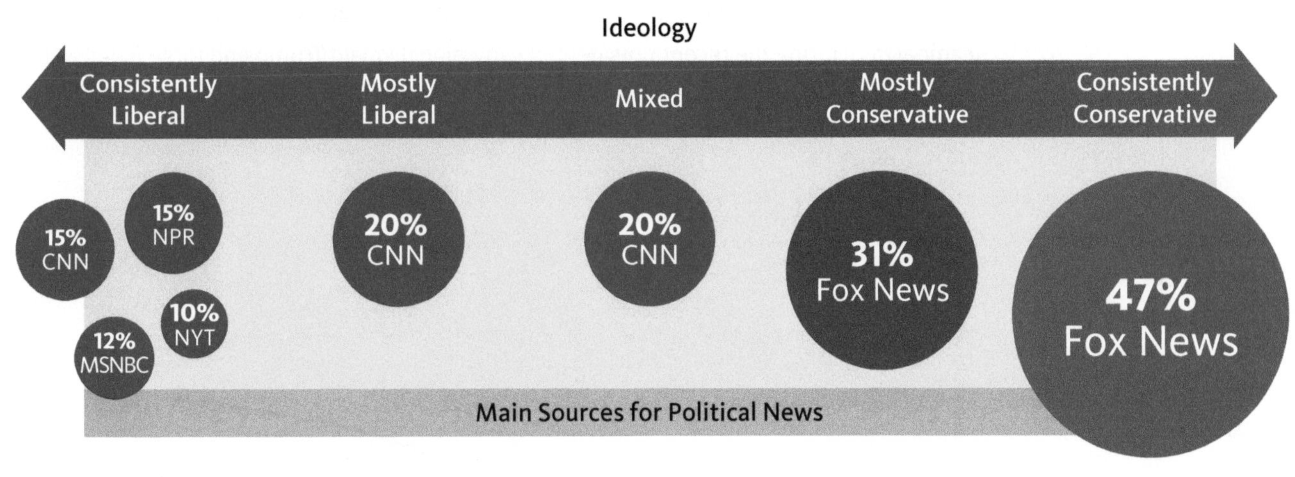

FIGURE 7.6 Media Habits of Liberals and Conservatives

Sources: Amy Mitchell, Jeffrey Gottfried, Jocelyn Kiley, and Katerina Eva Matsa, "Political Polarization and Media Habits," Pew Research Center. October 21, 2014, http://www.journalism.org/2014/10/21/political-polarization-media-habits.

Thinking Critically

1. Why do you think liberals tend to rely on more sources for news about government and politics than do conservatives?
2. What do you think are the consequences, if any, to trusting fewer or more media sources?

Donald Trump's use of Twitter transformed the campaign and the news media's coverage of it. In previous elections, political ads shaped the narrative of the campaign, but Trump drove the narrative during the 2016 presidential election by sending multiple tweets on any given day.

The News Media and Latinos

Latinos, as the fastest-growing ethnic group in the United States, are also prompting change in the media environment. One recent trend in the dissemination and consumption of news is the increase in viewership for the two major Spanish language networks, Univision and Telemundo.[81] The two networks reach over 5 million Spanish-speaking viewers in more than forty markets in the United States. To compete, other outlets are reaching out to Latino audiences. The growth in Spanish-language television now includes, for example, MundoFox, CNN Latino, and Fusion, a twenty-four-hour cable news channel that broadcasts content in English that is directed at English-speaking Latino Millennials.

Fusion, a joint venture between ABC News and Noticias Univision, reflects that many Latinos continue to rely on both English and Spanish sources of news (see Figure 7.7). Public broadcasting also has responded to the growing number of Latino viewers who consume news in English and Spanish. In Arizona, for example, PBS produces the public affairs program *Horizonte*, an English-language public affairs program about political issues of interest to Latinos.

Of course, the news media's attention to politics is heightened during presidential campaigns. During the recent presidential campaign, Donald Trump and Jorge Ramos, the most influential Latino anchorman (Univision), had a heated exchange during a 2015 news

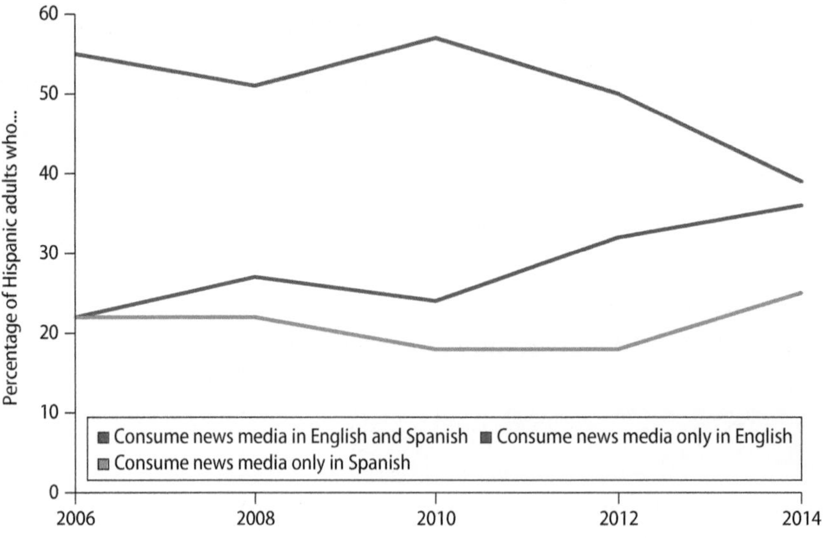

Note: Based on those who consume news on a typical weekday from at least one of four platforms tested–network, local, or cable television news; print newspapers; radio; and the Internet (n = 1,706 for 2012, n = 1,347 for 2010, n = 1,944 for 2008, n = 1,943 for 2006).

FIGURE 7.7 Bilingual News Viewership Among Latinos

Most Latinos continue to get their news in both English and Spanish, but the share is on the decline.

Source: http://www.journalism.org/2015/04/29/hispanic-media-fact-sheet.

conference. Trump had Ramos escorted out of the room, only to be let back in ten minutes later. This incident drew wide attention and underscored not only Trump's testy relationship with the press but also the reach of Univision. Presidential candidates cannot ignore that network or the audience it reaches.

In 2016, Univision announced an effort to register more Latino voters, which reflects its commitment to empowering this voting bloc. In the Romney–Obama battle in 2012, 11 million Latinos voted, and Univision was hoping to register many new voters for the 2016 election. Those efforts paid off in that over 13 million Latinos voted in 2016, with four of five voting for Hillary Clinton. These changing demographics will continue to shape American politics.[82]

The News Media and Millennials

The changes in the media environment do not affect all citizens equally, as suggested by Figure 7.8. The Millennial generation, for example, is more than three times more likely to get its news from BuzzFeed than are baby boomers. Google News is much more heavily used by Millennials than either Generation Xers or baby boomers. By contrast, PBS's audience draws far more heavily from baby boomers than Millennials.

When younger Americans read a newspaper or listen to a radio program, they do so for a much shorter period of time than do those who are older than 50. The youth seem to do more channel surfing, while older Americans are more likely to sit down and watch an entire news program. These habits may reflect differences in lifestyles between, for example, college students and adults with full-time jobs and families.[83] It could also reveal enduring differences between the generations.

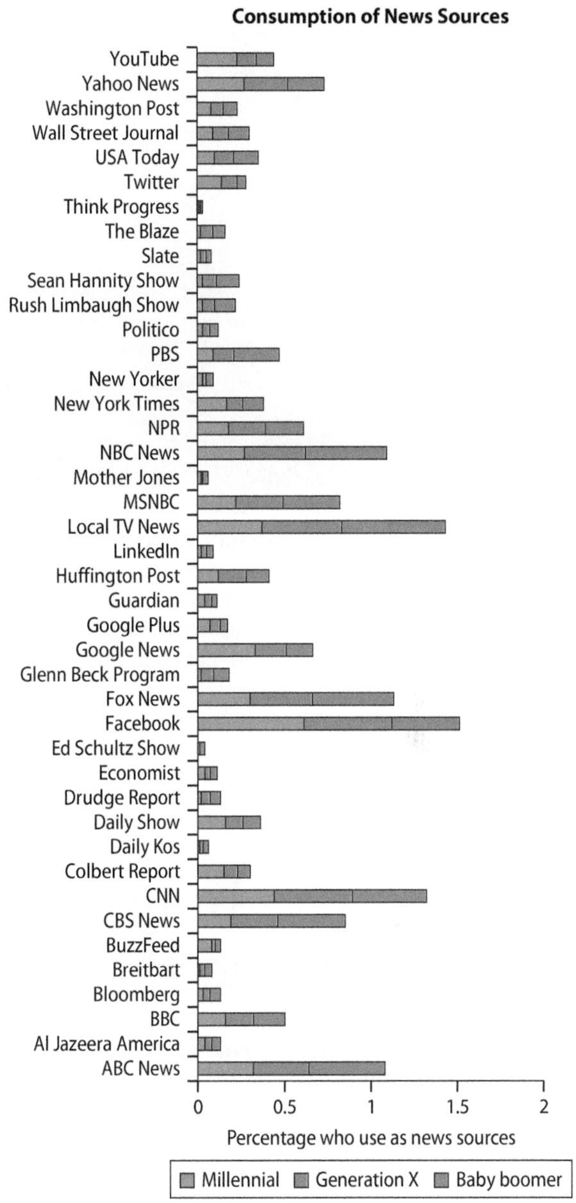

Conventional wisdom has always said that young people are less interested in politics than older Americans are, but Millennials appear to be more interested in politics at this point in their lives than were previous generations. This interest is not gauged by whether they watch the evening news or read newspapers, but by the ways they use new media to share information and learn about and express interest in politics.[84] Young adults tend to reject the top-down approach to learning about politics in which the news is filtered by professional journalists and trusted news anchors such as Cronkite. Instead, they seem much more interested in the bottom-up approach made possible by the wide-open availability of new media for citizen participation.

These changes are going to become more important over time as more Millennials become eligible to vote and older generations pass on. Technological change continues to spread, making the Internet and all of its information increasingly available to more Americans. The United States is in the midst of a major transformation in the media environment,

FIGURE 7.8 Main Sources of News by Age

Millennials tend to get their news from different sources than do older citizens.

Source: http://www.journalism.org/interactives/generational-media-habits/.

IMAGE 7.7 After her Democratic rival purportedly made a derogatory comment about Iowa farmers that was leaked and viewed on YouTube, 2014 Republican candidate for the U.S. Senate Joni Ernst aired a campaign ad that went viral. In the ad, she describes her experience growing up "castrating pigs" as a way to emphasize her proud Iowa farmer roots and her ability to "cut pork" (needless spending). She won the 2014 election by a large margin.

and observers are only beginning to understand the changes in how Americans transmit and consume the news.

One of the new ways that Millennials and other voters become aware of political information is through viral videos. In Iowa, for example, the Democrat running for U.S. Senate was "caught" on a video describing Iowa Senator Charles Grassley as a "farmer who never went to law school."[85] That video went viral, and Republican Senate hopeful Joni Ernst alluded to it in her ad in which she touted her credentials as a candidate who grew up "castrating hogs on an Iowa farm."

7.5 The Impact of the News Media on the Public

Assess how the news media affect public opinion

Essential Knowledge

How the news media cover events and provide analysis can impact political participation.

The press provides information, investigation, and interpretation of the news. The news media, both old and new, make decisions about what to cover, what not to cover, and how to cover it. How does the public respond to this information? This section looks at several models ranging between two extremes: that the mass media have no effect on the public and that the mass media dominate the public's thinking.

The Propaganda Model

Few people believe that the media have no influence on citizens. To hold such a view, one must either believe that the public ignores the media or that citizens learn about politics by observing the events themselves. Neither is true, so we can confidently label this the "naïve model" and dismiss it.

propaganda model: *Extreme view of the media's role in society, arguing that the press serves the interest of the government only, driving what the public thinks about important issues.*

The polar opposite has been called the **propaganda model**. This approach is exemplified by the Nazi dictatorship in Germany in the 1930s and 1940s. The Nazi Party controlled the content of newspapers and radio. It dictated the information available to citizens, affecting the direction and shape of public opinion. Through controlled programming, the German people often heard about the greatness of Adolf Hitler and the dangers of racial impurity. By holding a monopoly on information, the government could easily marshal public support. This is a dangerous model, and it is also inconsistent with how the press works in open societies. In the United States, media sources control programming, and they compete for audience share; the government does not control the flow of information.

The Minimal Effects Model

Toward the end of World War II, having seen the powerful effects of propaganda in Nazi Germany, scholars in the United States began to study public opinion and the influence of the media on it. Paul Lazarsfeld and others examined the media's influence on voting in the 1940 presidential election. The results were surprising: The researchers discovered that people had made up their minds before the campaign, and new information altered only a handful of people's choices.[86] Lazarsfeld's study gave rise to what has been called the **minimal effects model**. Lazarsfeld and his colleagues contended that the news media had only marginal influence on the public's thinking about politics. The public did not have much information about politics, and attitudes were shaped by long-standing forces such as partisanship or the neighborhood in which people lived.

minimal effects model: *View of the media's impact as marginal because most people seek news reports to reinforce beliefs already held rather than to develop new ones.*

According to this model, in a process described as **selective exposure**, people secured information from sources that agreed with them, leading to the reinforcement of beliefs, not to a change of beliefs. The minimal effects model was also based on a complementary process called **selective perception**—a concept developed in a study of the American voter published by Angus Campbell and three coauthors in 1960.[87] Selective perception describes partisans as interpreting the same information differently. In other words, partisanship involves a perceptual lens (see Chapter 6, Public Opinion) that shapes how outside events are viewed. So, for example, in May 2014, 79 percent of Democrats supported President Obama's health care reform legislation, passed in 2010, whereas only 8 percent of Republicans did.[88]

selective exposure: *Process whereby people secure information from sources that agree with them, thus reinforcing their beliefs.*

selective perception: *Process whereby partisans interpret the same information differently.*

The Not-So-Minimal Effects Model

In the 1970s, scholars started to gather better data that could more effectively test for the impact of the news media. This next generation of research produced the **not-so-minimal effects model**. While not overstating the power of the news media, the model acknowledges that the coverage of politics by the press matters in subtle and important ways. In particular, there are three kinds of media effects: agenda setting, priming, and framing.

not-so-minimal effects model: *View of the media's impact as substantial, occurring by agenda setting, framing, and priming.*

Agenda Setting. By stressing certain issues, the media influence what the American public views as the most pressing concerns. This effect is called **agenda setting**. Given that on any particular day there are literally hundreds of stories that could be reported, journalists' decisions about which stories to cover (and which story to lead with, and which to bury inside the paper or at the end of a newscast) matter considerably. Politicians and their advisers make a huge effort to convince the media to cover some stories and ignore others. Should the news lead with a story about casualties in the war in Afghanistan or about growing problems in the nation's public education system? As one scholar explains, the media "may not be successful most of the time telling people what to think, but it is stunningly successful in telling its readers what to think about."[89] The evidence is compelling. If the media talk about crime, the public starts to care about it. If the press starts paying additional attention to the federal budget deficit, the issue becomes more salient to citizens.

agenda setting: *Ability of the media to affect the way people view issues, people, or events by controlling which stories are shown and which are not.*

© Randy Glasbergen
www.glasbergen.com
GLASBERGEN
"Today in school we learned about the three main branches of government: lobbyists, fund-raisers and media."
Randy Glasbergen

IMAGE 7.8 Many think the media have more power than the president or Congress.

Since only about 1 percent of news coverage is dedicated to the topic of education, it is not surprising that education policy rarely rises to the top of politicians' agendas.[90]

Priming. An extension of agenda setting is **priming**. Emphasis by the media can alter the criteria that citizens use when evaluating political leaders. Following 9/11, for instance, the news media's coverage of terrorism was the most powerful force shaping President Bush's popularity.[91] The public gave Bush credit for dealing effectively with these tragic events. So when terrorism was the focus of the media, Bush's approval rating was high. But late in Bush's second term, when the primary topic covered by the media shifted to the economy, the public was less supportive of the president.

priming: *Process whereby the media influence the criteria the public uses to make decisions.*

Priming can also affect how people vote. In the 2016 campaign, Republicans wanted the public to focus on stagnant wages and terrorism, while the Democrats sought to focus on gains in the economy and Donald Trump's harsh rhetoric. The election was decided by a razor-thin margin, with Trump effectively tapping into the anger the public had with politics as usual.

framing: *Ability of the media to influence public perception of issues by constructing the issue or discussion of a subject in a certain way.*

Framing. **Framing** is the ability of the media to alter the public's view on an issue by presenting it in a particular way. If the battles waged in Afghanistan are framed as an issue of fighting terrorism, the public thinks about the war in a much more favorable light than if these conflicts are framed by the casualties incurred. Framing can have a very powerful effect, actually changing public opinion on an issue.

Perhaps the most famous example of framing comes from the work of Amos Tversky and Daniel Kahneman.[92] These scholars showed in a powerful way that one could produce very different policy solutions based solely on how the options were presented. In other words, "spin" or "framing" matters. Tversky and Kahneman told research subjects that the United States was preparing for the outbreak of an unusual disease, which was expected to kill six hundred people. The research subjects were asked how to combat it. Two comparable groups of research subjects were given different policy options to compare.

The first group was told that if program A were adopted, two hundred people would be saved; if program B were adopted, there was a one-third probability that six hundred people would be saved and a two-thirds probability that no one would be saved. Of those surveyed, 72 percent favored program A and 28 percent favored program B. It appears that citizens favor the sure thing of saving two hundred people and not taking the chances represented by program B. Such a strong result suggests that the government, if responsive to public opinion, should adopt program A.

The second group of research subjects were also given a choice between two policy options. If program C were adopted, four hundred people would die. If program D were adopted, there was a one-third probability that nobody would die and a two-thirds probability that six hundred people would die. Here, 22 percent of the subjects favored program C and 78 percent favored program D. These results suggest that the public does not respond favorably to the idea that four hundred people will die, leading them to favor option D.

Yet compare closely program C to A. While there is a 50-percentage-point difference in the number of people willing to support program A versus program C, the programs actually yield the exact same policy outcome: Two hundred people live, and four hundred people die. The *only* difference is that the description of program A stressed saving people, while the description of program C stressed the deaths of people. This experiment underscores the power of framing—that the public reacts to a news event or a policy depending on how it is presented. These data offer a powerful statement about the potential impact of the press and how they cover events can shape our thinking about them.

7.6 Evaluating the News Media

Evaluate the news media

"The American Press is in crisis," wrote Lance Bennett and his colleagues in their book *When the Press Fails.*[93] Concerns about the modern news media are widespread.[94]

Worries about the news media often center on two general concerns. One is that the media are biased and do not present objective information. The second, which is related, focuses on the general quality of information available to the public. The emphasis on soft news, for example, worries observers who do not think the public has enough exposure to more substantive hard news. Without enough hard news, these observers fear, the public will not be well enough informed to hold elected officials accountable.

Whether these concerns are valid or not (we examine them later), it is clear that the public's faith in the press has declined (see Figure 7.9). Just in the last twenty years, the share of Americans who had confidence in the press has dropped by 50 percent. As of 2015, only one in five Americans have faith in journalists.[95]

Is there reason to worry about the media? Are the mass media of the twenty-first century less able to fulfill their watchdog role? This section looks at media bias, the quality of information, and the implications of the Internet and media choice.

Are the Media Biased?

The press claims to be objective, and professional journalists subscribe to an ethic of neutrality. Yet, given that even the selection of stories covered influences public opinion, bias

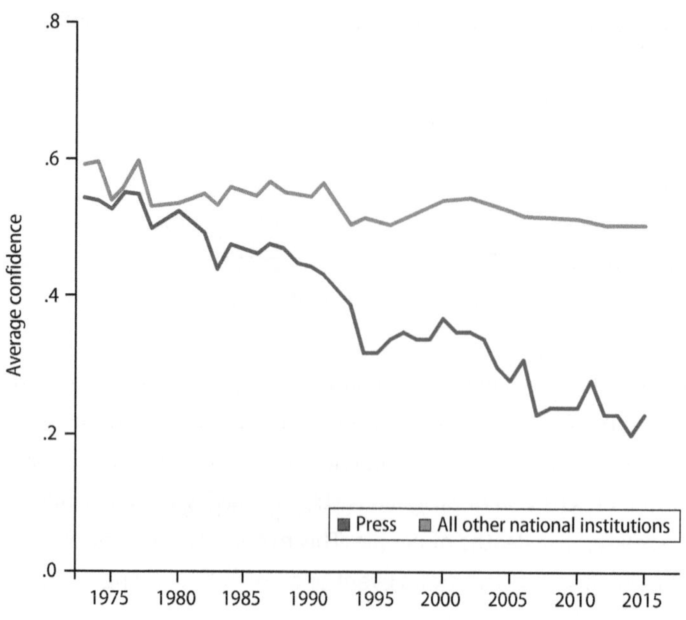

Note: The "other institutions" are the institutions of government, broadly defined.

FIGURE 7.9 Public Confidence in the Press, 1973–2015

The public's confidence in the press continues to decline.

Source: Jonathan M. Ladd, *Why Americans Hate the Media and Why It Matters* (Princeton, N.J.: Princeton University Press, 2012). Reprinted by permission of Princeton University Press; updated data provided by Johnathan M. Ladd.

Essential Knowledge

The demand for media and political communications from an ideologically diverse audience has led to debates over media bias and the impact of media ownership and partisan news sites.

may be inevitable. Nevertheless, it need not be evil or ideological. David Broder, one of the leading journalists of his time, attributed bias to the speed with which journalists have to act. "The process of selecting what the reader reads involves not just objective facts but subjective judgments, personal values, and, yes, prejudices," he confesses. Broder points out that:

> *the newspaper that drops on your doorstep is a partial, hasty, incomplete, inevitably somewhat flawed and inaccurate rendering of some of the things we have heard about in the past 24 hours—distorted, despite our best efforts to eliminate bias, by the very process of compression that makes it possible for you to lift it from the doorstep and read it in about an hour.*[96]

With the rise of the 24-7 news cycle, bias in selecting what to cover becomes even more evident. A common claim of "media bias" comes from politicians themselves. A good example comes from the feud between Fox News's Megyn Kelly and then Republican nominee Donald Trump. Trump claimed in 2015 that Kelly was biased and unfair in her treatment of him, asking him, for example, about his statements about women as "fat pigs." She pressed him on this matter, and Trump fought back. Yet she stood her ground, leading him to ramp up the rhetoric through Twitter and other platforms and to skip a Fox News–sponsored debate prior to the Iowa caucuses. Kelly tried to calm things down, telling ABC's George Stephanopoulos, "It was bizarre because I became the story. He was so very focused on me that I became the story and, you know, you never want to be the story when you're a news person."[97] This battle underscores the power of the media and how politicians often react negatively to criticism. Even so, the Trump–Kelly feud is unusual, but we may be entering a new era of relations between the press and politicians with President Trump now in office.

A broader point is that, for many years, conservative commentators have claimed that the news media are liberal. Accuracy in Media (www.aim.org), a conservative watchdog organization, contends that more than 80 percent of mainstream journalists support the Democratic Party. Such partisan loyalties, according to critics, drive the liberal bias.[98] Yet the people who own the most major media outlets—such as Rupert Murdoch, whose media properties include the *Wall Street Journal* and Fox News—are conservative. Should one assume that because most news outlets are owned by conservatives, the media are really conservative? It is far from clear whether the media are liberal or conservative.

Yet complaints about a liberal press seem to resonate with the public. Gallup Poll data measuring the public's belief about ideological bias in the news media indicate that about half the public believes the news media have a liberal bias and perceive a liberal tilt to the press's coverage of politics. The proportion has been quite stable. More than 40 percent of the public tends to think the press is too liberal, while only about 20 percent view journalists as too conservative.[99]

The debate over whether the news media are too liberal or too conservative misses the central point about the news today. With so many sources of information, it is easy to find news with a liberal spin and news with a conservative spin. In fact, in the second decade of the twenty-first century, much news reporting is partisan, more like the party-dominated press of the nineteenth century than the objective and neutral press of the twentieth century. Media choice and multiple outlets mean that a Democrat can find a Democratic-leaning source for news and a Republican can find a Republican-leaning source. It is fair to conclude that individual news outlets are biased, but collectively the media provide a full range of ideological viewpoints.

Quality of Information

The idea that people are getting news from Stephen Colbert rather than from Walter Cronkite is disconcerting to political observers. The general worry is that people are getting less hard news and instead are relying on what we earlier called soft news—feature stores that are more personal and less focused on policy, more sensationalized and less objective, than the political facts of hard news.[100] News about crime or natural disasters can fit the soft news category when the focus is about the drama surrounding the event (such as loss of life or homes) rather than a discussion of public policy that could reduce crime or perhaps provide a quicker government response to disasters.[101]

Part of this underlying concern is the emphasis on image as opposed to substance. The assumption here is that visuals (television and Internet news, in contrast to print news) appeal to the emotions more than to the intellect, so visual news formats are in themselves less "hard" and more superficial. It is true that visual images convey impressions that go beyond the facts, but that does not mean that such information is not valuable. In the 1950s, for example, televised congressional hearings gave the public a chance to see Senator Joseph McCarthy in action and undid his credibility (see Chapter 4, Civil Liberties). While newspapers had covered the excesses of his charges about Communist infiltration of the government, his actions on camera were much more harmful to his reputation.[102] There is a great deal to be learned from images.

All media of communication shape how information is shared and digested. Radio, for example, puts a premium on the quality of people's voices. Franklin D. Roosevelt probably

Bettmann/Corbis

IMAGE 7.9 During the Great Depression, President Franklin D. Roosevelt used radio to speak directly to the American people. His first fireside chat was broadcast on March 12, 1933, a week after he took office. Addressing the banking crisis, he explained government's response in clear terms: "We have provided the machinery to restore our financial system," he said, "and it is up to you to support and make it work. … Together we cannot fail."

made the most famous use of radio with his compelling and reassuring voice. He was the first president to use radio to communicate directly with the people, broadcasting what he called "fireside chats" from the White House in which he explained what he was doing to end the Great Depression.[103] Other politicians with less appealing voices would not have been able to put radio to such good use. Consider politics before the invention of the microphone. Who were the most effective politicians? Perhaps it was individuals with deep voices that could project to a large audience. A soft-spoken politician would have been at a real disadvantage.

It is also important to realize that images did not begin with the advent of television. Although it may be easier to engage in "image" politics in an era of video, politicians have always wanted to convey a favorable image and have done so using the media of their time. Abraham Lincoln sought to project himself as the self-made man that he was, so his 1860 campaign distributed pictures depicting him working with his hands as a rail-splitter.[104] Andrew Jackson (1829–37) built a successful run to the White House in part on his reputation as a tough military leader. Image has always been important to politicians.

The Granger Collection, NYC

IMAGE 7.10 During the presidential campaign of 1860, Republican candidate Abraham Lincoln sought to portray himself as a common man with a humble background who understood the needs of the people. To develop this image, Lincoln's campaign stressed that as a young man he split rails to build a fence around his home. The image became part of campaign lore.

In the same way, so-called sound bites—very brief snippets of information—did not begin with the advent of television. Many observers fear that by stressing short catchy statements rather than more detailed substantive statements, sound bites undermine the quality of information. Campaigns, however, have always made effective use of simple slogans. In 1900, for example, President William McKinley (1897–1901) sought reelection with the slogan "A full dinner pail," reminding voters about the economic prosperity they enjoyed during his first term.[105]

The purpose of this discussion is to urge caution in making hasty judgments about differences in the kinds of information available via the news media over the past two centuries. Soft news may be more informative than hard news because people find it easier to understand and more enjoyable. It is important, therefore, not to let the definition of what counts as news shape judgment of the press. Despite recent changes in the mass media, evidence suggests that Americans have as much information about politics as they did before the arrival of the Internet and the 24-7 news cycle. According the Pew Research Center for the People & the Press, "the coaxial and digital revolutions and attendant changes in the news audience behaviors have had *little* impact on how much Americans know about national and international affairs."[106] Americans do not appear less informed; they simply secure information in new ways.

Implications of the Internet

There is evidence that the Internet and social media have not changed the overall amount of information the public possesses, but it is important to acknowledge that new media are not equally available to all Americans. In 2016, 64 percent of low-income Americans had a smart phone versus 84 percent of high-income Americans. Age is an even bigger divide: Ninety-two percent of those younger than 35 had a smart phone versus 65 percent of those older than 35, and this divide only grows for the 65-and-up group.[107] A similar pattern exists in regards to Internet access. In 2015, 84 percent of Americans overall used the web versus 60 percent of senior citizens. Income differences exist as well.[108] But these patterns are changing as access to smart phones and the Internet spreads, which will help to bridge the digital divide.[109]

These data suggest a further inequality—that those with Internet access may be much better informed than the public generally just twenty years ago, whereas those without access may be even less informed. Variations among groups buried in discussions of the public as a whole are significant, but these variations will likely decrease as more people secure access to the Internet. Figure 7.1, which shows the many options people have for information, suggests that Americans will move toward universal access. There will always be a gap between the well informed and the poorly informed, but in time, the Internet will give older and less wealthy Americans a better chance to become more informed about politics than they currently are.

The Era of Media Choice

Perhaps the best word to describe today's media environment is *choice*.[110] The spread of cable television, the Internet, and satellite radio means that people have many possible sources for political information, as well as a huge array of entertainment programming that may lead them to opt out of political news altogether. In the mid-twentieth century, when the network evening news was the source of information, viewers had fewer choices and less opportunity to opt out. They might change channels at dinnertime, but they would get similar news from a different network. The evening news was the only show available during the dinner hour. The lack of choice may have given people more exposure to politics than they wanted.[111]

Essential Knowledge

Increased media choice and consumption have impacted political discussions. Citizens have access to media options that vary by many factors, including ideological preferences. As such, citizens can choose to only engage with media that aligns with their ideological preferences, which can reinforce their own values.

The TV network news standardized the information that many Americans had access to. With the wide array of choices now available, information is more polarized today. Viewers who choose a conservative TV network such as Fox and listen to Rush Limbaugh on the radio will have different information from those who watch MSNBC and tune in to National Public Radio. Those who lack interest in politics can avoid political news altogether. In other words, media choice cuts two ways: polarizing the type of information available, and making it possible to receive no political information at all.

The consequences of media choice are complex and are only beginning to be understood. New technologies in the future could further fragment what Americans as a people know. Efforts to make political news more interesting may mean a further "softening" of the news. The main point is that Americans have access to a vast amount of information, but the availability of more information does not necessarily mean that the public as a whole is better informed. Moreover, people follow news outlets that conform to their existing

ELECTION 2016

The Role of the Media

The 2016 presidential election was historic and path breaking. The upset that denied Hillary Clinton the presidency and gave Donald Trump the keys to the White House will be discussed for decades to come. The rise of President Trump is a story about the changing news media, the role of social media, and his unconventional approach to campaigning.

Trump challenged conventional wisdom about the role of the media. The typical presidential campaign since the 1950s had been focused on staying on message and avoiding gaffes. Television and then the Internet put a magnifying glass on mistakes, and candidates were advised to avoid them at any cost. But Donald Trump ignored that advice. He waged a war against the establishment using very harsh rhetoric. He comments about immigration at the launch of his campaign were seen by members of the news media as evidence that he was out of touch and that his campaign was destined to fail. Instead, he hit a chord with many Americans, especially those who were alienated and angry with the inability of the national government to improve the lives of those struggling with stagnant wages and the changing structure of the economy.

Trump continued to make controversial statements, including attacks against war heroes such as John McCain, gold-star families, former Miss Universes, prominent journalists, and his presidential adversaries (e.g., "Little Marco," "Lying Ted," and "Crooked Hillary"). He often made statements that were not consistent with evidence. But again, that did little to derail his candidacy. It was as if the news media were focused on the small stuff, while he kept his eye on the big picture—that the country wanted an end to politics as usual.

Trump's use of Twitter was controversial but also creative. By sending out incendiary tweets, he captured the attention of the news media. His speeches also drew substantial coverage from the press because he would raise doubts about the establishment in a caustic tone that had not been seen since the 1800s. If Trump called in to a morning news show, they would take his call, giving him another chance to talk about the need for change.

In the end, Trump was able to get unprecedented coverage from the news media. Rather than spending millions of dollars on political ads, he used cable news and the Internet to get his message out. He had, as a result, billions of dollars of *free* media coverage. Whether President Trump has introduced a new era in media politics is far from clear; we must wait and see what happens in the 2018 and 2020 elections. But no matter how one slices it, Trump was truly innovative in his campaign's approach to news media and social media.

---

ideological preferences. This self-selection can fuel further polarization, because many people are not getting information from the other side.

Essential Knowledge

The ability of citizens to hold their government accountable and participate in political discourse is directly impacted by things such as: media choices, new technologies, ideologically oriented telecasts, and questionable credibility of news sources.

The News, Social Media, and Democracy

The news media, as watchdogs, are a central player in democratic politics. In the twenty-first century, the mass media are far more open than they were just a few decades ago, providing additional chances to forge accountability, responsiveness, and equality. But these are only chances because the media are in the midst of a transformation whose repercussions are not yet known.

For example, nearly all public appearances and statements of political figures can now be caught on video or audiotape. As a result, politicians have a tougher time ducking responsibility; they are more easily held accountable for their actions and words. However, the threat of being caught on tape in an embarrassing moment may encourage politicians to stay in "the bubble," sheltered from public scrutiny and shielded from assertive journalists or potentially harmful situations. Politicians build staffs and organizations designed to keep them from making mistakes and from interacting with journalists and citizens. They want to appear at staged events where they can control the message. Of course, Donald Trump's approach to the 2016 presidential election has led some to think the "bubble" may have been popped. Trump ignored anyone who tried to handle him. His willingness to say what he thought resonated with many Americans.

The more open and more democratic new media thus have the potential to let citizens know more about the politicians who lead them; they also give people more opportunities to express opinions for politicians to consider as they develop and enact laws. Thus blogs and other new media may help forge responsiveness. But these gateways have potential costs: The opinions may come from people who are not representative of the American mainstream. Information offered as fact in these settings has not been checked and is potentially filled with errors.

The many changes in the news media have also led to a decline in the number of professional journalists who are covering politics. With fewer professional journalists, the press may be less able to investigate stories that might unearth corruption or provide a more complete account of some politicians' backgrounds.

The decline in investigative reporting could, in short, undermine accountability. But there is reason for optimism. While it is true that the days of Woodward and Bernstein are gone, the Internet offers new ways to forge accountability. For example, politifact.com tracks whether presidents keep their promises and also assesses the accuracy of claims by candidates during campaigns. When candidates are not telling the truth, the website labels the statement as "pants on fire." In 2016, politifact.com evaluated statements by Donald Trump. As of April that year, only 2 percent were deemed as truthful, with nearly 20 percent earning the label "pants on fire."

Such use of information and the Internet should ease some worries about democratic accountability. It is also worth noting that current doubts about the media's ability to advance democratic government comes mostly from people who favor a top-down approach for providing political information. For those who see the merit and appeal in a bottom-up approach that can be advanced by the Internet, the changes seem far less worrisome. On average, the Millennial generation will not be so worried; these young people have grown up with the transformed mass media. They see the potential that the Internet and other media have for promoting equality—and for providing more chances to be part of the process. But until access to the Internet becomes universal, these changes offer more hope than reality.

Political Science Reasoning

Question 1

Practice 1, Practice 4

> *The tumults in America I expected would have produced in Europe an unfavorable opinion of our political state. But it has not. On the contrary, the small effect of those tumults seems to have given more confidence in the firmness of our governments. The interposition of the people themselves on the side of government has had a great effect on the opinion here. I am persuaded myself that the good sense of the people will always be found to be the best army. They may be led astray for a moment, but will soon correct themselves. The people are the only censors of their governors: and even their errors will tend to keep these to the true principles of their institution. To punish these errors too severely would be to suppress the only safeguard of the public liberty. The way to prevent these irregular interpositions of the people is to give them full information of their affairs thro' the channel of the public papers, and to contrive that those papers should penetrate the whole mass of the people. The basis of our governments being the opinion of the people, the very first object should be to keep that right; and were it left to me to decide whether we should have a government without newspapers, or newspapers without a government, I should not hesitate a moment to prefer the latter. But I should mean that every man should receive those papers and be capable of reading them.*[1]

1. Citing textual evidence, what is Jefferson's opinion of the role of the media?
2. To what extent have Jefferson's views about the role of the media manifested in the Constitution and in subsequent Supreme Court interpretations?
3. There can be little doubt that the nature of the media has dramatically changed from the time of Jefferson to today. Based upon these changes, is it likely that Jefferson would hold the same opinion of today's media (cable news and social media) as he did of newspapers in the 1780s?

---

[1]Thomas Jefferson, 1787.

Focus on AP® Success

7 The News and Social Media

Must Know: Key Concepts

- Linkage Institution
- Social Media
- Broadcast Television
- Cable Television
- Agenda Setting
- Narrowcasting
- Echo Chambers
- Prior Restraint

Thinking Politically

Argumentation

The Supreme Court typically will allow the restriction of a fundamental right if a state or the national government can show a "compelling interest." On questions of national security or in promoting access to broadcast television for diverse viewpoints, the Court has allowed some limitations on the freedom of the press, but generally they are highly suspect. The political importance of social media such as Twitter is almost indisputable. With this increased importance, is there now a compelling interest for greater governmental regulation of social media? If so, in what regard?

Data Analysis

Figure 7.8 in the text presents a graph that shows how people obtain political information. What additional information could have been provided to make this figure more informative?

Source Analysis

Refer to Image 7.8. What is the perspective of the cartoonist? Assuming the cartoonist's perspective is correct, does this represent a change in the U.S. political system?

Understanding Learning Objectives with Key Concepts

PRD – 3.A Explain the media's role as a linkage institution.

- A linkage institution is an institution that connects citizens with the government. The media is one such organization. Traditionally, the term media has referred to newspapers, radio, and broadcast television. However, over the last 40 years the media has changed and grown. New technology such as cable and satellite television, as well as the Internet and social media, have influenced how citizens obtain information about their government and interact with government officials.

- Polling used by the media can cause over emphasis on the polling data rather than on the qualifications and policy position of the candidate themselves. In this regard the media is criticized as creating "horse races" out of elections.

PRD – 3.B Explain how increasingly diverse choices of media and communication outlets influence political institutions and behavior.

- The level of political participation is impacted by the type and amount and media coverage. There is a positive correlation between consumption of political information from media and the likelihood of voting.

- Due to the demand for greater choice in news outlets, there is now a range of options from which citizens can choose to receive information. The business model of traditional broadcast television was to appeal to as many viewers as possible. With the advent of cable television, a new business model has emerged called "narrowcasting." With this model, the news organization attempts to capture a small segment of the population and focus on that group's desires. This has led some to accuse these media outlets of ideological bias. Also, during this time there has been greater concentration in the ownership of media outlets. This has led some to question if the range of opinions represented and the diversity of issues that receive coverage has been reduced.

- The changing nature of the media has also changed the democratic debate in the United States. People have more access to newsmedia than ever, but their choices are increasingly ideologically oriented (which has implications on the general level of knowledge of society). Furthermore, consumer-driven media outlets cater to the desires, interests, and biases of their audiences, and social media has a tendency to reinforce existing beliefs in a kind of echo chamber. This further polarizes the very information that citizens are absorbing and contributes to ideological polarization. Finally, growing questions about the credibility of the news that contradicts existing beliefs threatens public confidence in the media as a whole.

Making Connections

The media is but one of four linking institutions in American politics. The others are elections, political parties, and interest groups.

Much of the president's power stems from his power as an opinion leader. Theodore Roosevelt used the term "bully pulpit" to describe the president's unique position to influence the formation of public opinion. When studying the Chapter 13, The Presidency, think about how the rise of broadcast radio and television have increased the power of the presidency.

The constitutional protections of the First Amendment are absolutely necessary for the functioning of the media in the U.S. political system. From Chapter 4, Civil Liberties, review the few acceptable limitations on free expression, such as national security, and content restrictions on broadcast radio and television.

Political campaigns rely on advertising to disseminate information about their candidates. When studying Chapter 10, Elections and Campaigns notice that as the media changed from newspapers to broadcast radio and television to the Internet, so has political advertising and campaign strategy.

Recall from Chapter 6, Public Opinion, that one of the criticisms of the media is that it tends to focus on the "horse race" of a political campaign rather than the candidates and their policy positions.

Going Deeper: *New York Times v. United States*

The case of *New York Times v. United States*, also known as the "Pentagon Papers Case," is a landmark case involving the First Amendment's protection of a free press.

In 1967, the government commissioned a report to study the U.S. involvement in Vietnam. By 1971, the 7,000-page top-secret report was complete. The report was critical of many of the decisions made by the Johnson administration.

In March of 1971, the report was read to a reporter for the *New York Times*. The paper began publishing information contained in the report in June of 1971. The government of the United States immediately sought a restraining order to stop further publication of the information contained in the reports stating that further publication would cause "irreparable injury" to the interests of the United States. A federal district court judge granted the order.

Eventually the dispute arrived at the Supreme Court. The question that the Court had to decide was, did the government show a compelling interest in its censorship of the *New York Times*. The Court had recognized in the past that there exists a compelling interest to protect national security. As such, previous decisions had allowed an exception to its virtually universal prohibition of prior restraint.

However, the Court held that while the so-called *Pentagon Papers* were embarrassing to the U.S. government, they did not jeopardize U.S. security interests.

There was not an opinion given for the Court. Rather, in this case the opinions were delivered *per curiam* (each justice wrote his own opinion).

Justice Black (with Justice Douglas) wrote: "In the First Amendment the Founding Fathers gave the free press the protection it must have to fulfill its essential role in our democracy. The press was to serve the governed, not the governors. The Government's power to censor the press was abolished so that the press would remain forever free to censure the government."

Justice Brennan wrote: "The entire thrust of the Government's claim throughout these cases has been that publication of the material sought to be enjoined 'could,' or 'might,' or 'may' prejudice the national interest in various ways. But the First Amendment tolerates absolutely no prior judicial restraints of the press predicated upon surmise or conjecture that untoward consequences may result."

Chief Justice Burger in his dissent writes: "In these cases, the imperative of a free and unfettered press comes into collision with another imperative, the effective functioning of a complex modern government, and, specifically, the effective exercise of certain constitutional powers of the Executive. Only those who view the First Amendment as an absolute in all circumstances — a view I respect, but reject — can find such cases as these to be simple or easy."

8 Interest Groups

AP® Learning Objectives

PMI – 5.E Explain the benefits and potential problems of interest-group influence on elections and policy making.

PMI – 5.F Explain how variation in types and resources of interest groups affects their ability to influence elections and policy making.

PMI – 5.G Explain how various political actors influence public policy outcomes.

Performance Tasks

Upon the completion of this chapter, you must be able to do the following:

- Explain how interest groups impact the policy making process in Congress and other governmental institutions.
- Explain how interest groups impact the electoral process.

Meg Lessard/www.meglessardphotography.com

"Regardless of whether we swing an election or not, we are working with the next generation of leaders on the Democratic and Republican side to learn how to work together and to problem solve jointly."

SAM GILMAN
Brown University

Photograph by Francis Tatem

On forty campuses across the United States, college chapters of Common Sense Action (CSA) formed to take back politics for the Millennial generation. What began as an idea tossed around by Brown University undergrads Sam Gilman, Andrew Kaplan, and Heath Mayo turned into one of the most innovative student-run interest groups trying to change politics. Their mission was to expand "opportunities for Millennials by bringing our generation to the policy-making table and building a movement of Millennial voters committed to advancing generational fairness, investing in Millennial mobility, and repairing politics."

After working as an intern at the Bipartisan Policy Center in Washington, D.C., Gilman realized the importance of workforce development. The Millennial generation had twice the unemployment rate of the national average, and yet members of Congress were not discussing this issue, mostly because it would not lead to more votes. No community present in Washington, D.C. was pushing for the interests of young people, so Gilman convinced Kaplan and Mayo to form their own bipartisan organization.

A key moment for Gilman occurred on September 11, 2012, at 1:30 P.M., when his closest friend went to vote in the primary election on campus thirty steps from the campus center and told him that he was only the seventeenth voter that day. "And that really hit me. And when I voted in the general election two days before we officially launched CSA, I was the 130th voter at 10:15 A.M. The critical moment was realizing what happens if we can mobilize Millennials in and around primary elections for issues that impact our generation, in a world in which so few people vote in primary elections, and they are increasingly becoming the most important elections in our country, particularly as districts are becoming more polarized."

Through dorm meetings, Gilman, Kaplan, and Mayo were able to get a sense of the issues their generation cared about. At the subsequent CSA National Summit, the group established a core principle—respecting where people come from—so that liberals and conservatives alike can come together and find common ground on issues that affect their generation the most. Their bipartisan Agenda for Generational Equality seeks to advance generational fairness via a national entitlement solution, encourage Millennial mobility by making college more affordable, invest in the employment of Millennials, and repair politics through increased Millennial political participation.

Their bipartisan approach paid off. With their chapter model and grassroots organizing, CSA built legitimacy as the first bipartisan advocacy group of Millennials in Washington, D.C., expanded to twenty states, and engaged over ten thousand people in policy discussions at a time when it has become increasingly difficult to convene Democrats and Republicans to talk substantively about key issues.

All three graduated from college, and Gilman has retained his leadership role in CSA. He recognized that CSA needed an electoral counterpart in order to make a direct effort to break the gridlock in Washington, D.C. In January 2016, the organization merged with another grassroots group called Run for America, which Gilman describes as a "citizen-powered movement to reimagine politics and expand the electorate through political campaigns." The newly merged organization, named Action for America (AFA), combined its policy advocacy and a nationwide call to recruit candidates from both parties who are willing to cross the aisle to work together to run for the House of Representatives. In its first electoral cycle, AFA had two candidates running on the platform of Millennial engagement and bipartisan cooperation. For AFA, finding strong leaders in the Millennial generation is key to not only running the group but also making real bipartisan changes in politics. The grassroots origins and activities of AFA are examples of students engaging in collective action to generate change and using university and political resources to raise awareness and support for issues relevant to the Millennial generation, as well as actively recruiting individuals to run for political office who share their commitment to positive policy change and reducing political polarization.[1]

Small or large, student-run or long-established national organizations, interest groups are a mechanism of representation in a democracy because they help translate individual opinions and interests into outcomes in the political system. Interest groups form for many reasons: to advance economic status, express an ideological viewpoint, influence public policy, or promote activism in international affairs. In a democracy, the most crucial role of interest groups is their attempt to influence public policy, which is one of the express interests of the student-run AFA. In this chapter, we examine the history of interest groups, why they form, what they do, and their impact on democratic processes. We also identify how and why some groups are more influential than others. We focus on interest groups as gateways to citizen participation and, at the same time, point out how they can erect gates when they pursue narrow policy interests.

8.1 Interest Groups and Politics

Outline how interest groups have developed over time

In 1831, the French political theorist Alexis de Tocqueville came to the United States to observe American social and political behavior. He stayed for more than nine months and later published his study as *Democracy in America,* a classic of political literature. He wrote, "The most natural right of man, after that of acting on his own, is that of combining his efforts with those of his fellows and acting together. Therefore the right of association seems to me by nature almost as inalienable as individual liberty."[2] Tocqueville noticed that Americans in particular liked to form groups and join associations as a way of participating in community and political life. To Tocqueville, the formation of group life was an important element of the success of the American democracy.

What Are Interest Groups?

interest groups: *Groups of citizens who share a common interest—a political opinion, religious or ideological belief, a social goal, or an economic characteristic—and try to influence public policy to benefit themselves.*

Essential Knowledge

Interest groups represent a range of interests, both broad and narrow, and seek to impact policy making. This can be accomplished through citizen education, drafting proposed legislation, lobbying both Congress and the bureaucracy, as well as litigation.

Tocqueville used the term *association* to describe the groups he observed throughout his travels in America; today we call them interest groups. An **interest group** is a group of citizens who share a common interest—whether a political opinion, religious affiliation, ideological belief, social goal, or economic objective—and try to influence public policy to benefit its members. Other types of groups form for purely social or community reasons, but this chapter focuses on the groups that form to exert political influence.

Most interest groups arise from conditions in public life. A proactive group arises when an enterprising individual sees an opening or opportunity to create the group for social, political, or economic purposes. A reactive group forms to protect the interests of members in response to a perceived threat from another group, to fight a government policy that the members believe will adversely affect them, or to respond to an unexpected external event. Groups whose members share a number of common characteristics are described as homogeneous, whereas groups whose members come from varied backgrounds are described as heterogeneous. All interest groups are based on the idea that members joining together in a group can secure a shared benefit that would not be available to them if they acted alone.

Citizens most often join groups to advance their personal economic well-being, to get their voices heard as part of a larger group's efforts on an issue, or to meet like-minded citizens who share their views. There is no legal restriction on the number of groups that people can join, and citizens are frequently members of a number of organizations. On the large scale, citizens join groups as a gateway toward participating in democratic society.

The Right to Assemble and to Petition

right of association: *Right to freely associate with others and form groups, as protected by the First Amendment.*

The First Amendment states that Congress cannot prohibit "the right of the people peaceably to assemble, and to petition the Government for a redress of grievances." This right to assemble is the **right of association**. The Framers believed that the opportunity to form groups was a fundamental right that government may not legitimately take away. At the same time, however, they were fearful that such groups, which Madison called **factions**, might divide the young nation. Although Madison recognized that such groups could not be suppressed without abolishing liberty, he also argued in *Federalist* 51 that, in a large and diverse republic, narrow interests would balance out each other and be checked by majority rule. (See *Federalist* 10 and *Federalist* 51 in the Appendix.) Madison feared that factions could have the same divisive or polarizing effect in a democracy. Nevertheless, the Bill of Rights contains protections for the rights of association and petition because these rights are essential for citizens to be able to hold their government accountable, ensure the responsiveness of elected officials, and participate equally in self-government.

faction: *Defined by Madison as any group that places its own interests above the aggregate interests of society.*

The **right of petition** gives individuals with a claim against the government the right to ask for compensation, and it also includes the right to petition to ask for a policy change or to express opposition to a policy. It was the earliest and most basic gateway for citizens seeking to make government respond to them, and it has been used from the beginning of government under the Constitution. For example, in the First Congress, cotton growers asked the government for direct payment of subsidies to allow them to keep their farms in years with low crop yields. Owners of shipping companies petitioned Congress to limit the amount of goods that foreign ships could deliver to the United States so they could maximize their share of the carrying trade. Even the makers of molasses got together to ask the government to impose higher taxes on imported molasses so they would face less competition.[3] In the nineteenth century, petitions were used for broader and more sweeping issues, such as appeals to end slavery, to ban alcoholic beverages, and to secure the right to vote for women. In the twenty-first century, groups such as change.org use the Internet to make it possible for individuals to directly "ask" Congress for a benefit via e-mail or to sign a "virtual" petition that can be presented to Congress. Interest groups also use their high membership numbers as a proxy for the direct expression of support that once came from petitioners' personal visits to lawmakers.

right of petition: *Right to ask the government for assistance with a problem or to express opposition to a government policy, as protected by the First Amendment.*

lobbying: *Act of trying to persuade elected officials to adopt a specific policy change or maintain the status quo.*

Today the rights of association and petition most often take the form of **lobbying**, or trying to persuade elected officials to adopt or reject a specific policy change. Lobbying is a legitimate form of petitioning, and interest groups of all sizes and purposes engage in it, from Action for America, to big companies such as Uber and Google, to large-scale grassroots groups such as the Sierra Club. The term *lobbying* was coined more than three hundred years ago when individuals seeking favors from the British government would pace the halls, or lobbies, of the Parliament building, waiting for a chance to speak with members. The practice was immediately adopted in the new United States.

Interest groups lobby the legislative, executive, and even judicial branches of government at the state and

The Granger Collection, NYC

IMAGE 8.1 Citizens have been using their right to petition to influence government since the earliest days of the democracy. Here female lobbyists in the late nineteenth century are trying to persuade members of Congress in the Marble Room of the U.S. Capitol. Although women did not yet have the right to vote, they still went to Washington, D.C. to make their voices heard on issues that were important to them.

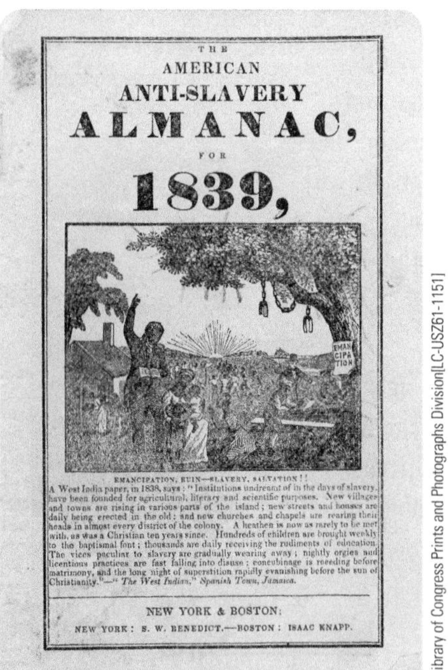

THE
AMERICAN
ANTI-SLAVERY
ALMANAC,
FOR
1839,

EMANCIPATION, RUIN—SLAVERY, SALVATION!!

A West India paper, in 1838, says: "Institutions undreamt of in the days of slavery, have been founded for agricultural, literary and scientific purposes. New villages and towns are rising in various parts of the island; new streets and houses are daily being erected in the old; and new churches and chapels are rearing their heads in almost every district of the colony. A heathen is now as rarely to be met with, as was a Christian ten years since. Hundreds of children are brought weekly to the baptismal font; thousands are daily receiving the rudiments of education. The vices peculiar to slavery are gradually wearing away; nightly orgies and licentious practices are fast falling into disuse; concubinage is receding before matrimony, and the long night of superstition rapidly evanishing before the sun of Christianity."—"*The West Indian*," *Spanish Town, Jamaica.*

NEW YORK & BOSTON:
NEW YORK: S. W. BENEDICT.—BOSTON: ISAAC KNAPP.

IMAGE 8.2 Abolitionists used stark imagery and words to rally citizens against slavery. In 1843, Lydia Maria Child compiled *The American Anti-Slavery Almanac*. Its cover alone makes the case for abolition. Child was a writer and editor who was also active in the women's suffrage movement.

federal levels. For example, when groups lobby Congress or state legislatures, they typically meet with members' staff aides to make the case for their policy goals. Lobbyists may also try to influence the executive branch by meeting personally with key bureaucrats and policy makers. Lobbying of the judicial branch takes the form of lawsuits against government policies that interest groups see as fundamentally unconstitutional or that go against the original intent of the law. Such lawsuits can be high profile and are initiated by groups of all political ideologies. For example, cases orchestrated by the National Association for the Advancement of Colored People (NAACP), the Mexican-American Legal Defense and Education Fund, and other progressive interest groups ended school segregation (see Chapter 5, Civil Rights). For other cases, interest groups can also submit *amicus curiae* briefs ("friend of the court") that record their opinions even if they are not the primary legal participants in a case. Interest groups also lobby for and against judicial nominees, especially Supreme Court appointments. Lobbying strategies and tactics differ according to the branch of government at the state and federal levels, but no government entity is outside the scope of lobbyists' efforts.[4]

The History of Interest Groups

As the nation expanded its geographic borders, its population, and its economic base, government took on more responsibilities that affected individual lives. Issues that were once considered local became nationally important, and improvements in travel and communications enabled citizens with a national concern to band together. Slavery was the most divisive of these national issues, and citizens who opposed slavery formed the American Anti-Slavery Society in 1833. Soon many other groups were urging the abolition of slavery, creating the abolitionist movement. Abolitionists held rallies, distributed pamphlets, and collected signatures on petitions to persuade Americans, specifically members of Congress, to abolish slavery.

Advocates for women's suffrage (the right to vote) paid close attention to antislavery efforts, seeing in them an example of the power of organization. In 1848, the women's suffrage movement was officially launched at Seneca Falls, New York.[5] To the members of this group, the refusal to allow women to vote was a gate that stood in the way of true political equality among all citizens. The abolitionist and the women's movements paralleled each other in relying on the principle of equality as a rationale for supporting their policy goals.

Later in the nineteenth century, as America industrialized, the business community began to strengthen its efforts to influence policy. Large trade associations formed, both regional and national, with members that included sugar manufacturers, mining companies, and railroad owners. These businesses combined to form interest groups based on their common economic interests, and these groups gave wealthy owners of corporations a disproportionate influence over public policy.

unions: *Interest groups of individuals who share a common type of employment and seek better wages and working conditions through collective bargaining with employers.*

To counteract the power of wealthy business corporations, workers organized **unions** to protect their interests, which were different from the interests of the people who owned industries but at the same time were interconnected with them. The International Ladies' Garment Workers' Union (ILGWU) is an instructive example. It was formed in 1900 by workers (mostly women) who assembled women's clothing. By 1910, workers in this industry had staged several strikes against employers to secure better working conditions. The turning point for the union came in 1911, when 141 workers died in a fire at the Triangle Shirtwaist Factory in New York City because they were trapped on the factory's upper floors. The fire escapes were inadequate, and the elevator was broken. Most of the victims were young, immigrant women who needed this kind of work because it did not require English reading or writing skills.[6] Leaders of the union saw a chance to turn tragedy into accomplishment by expanding its membership and lobbying the government to force manufacturers to improve worker safety. In part due to the efforts of the ILGWU, the Department of Labor was created as a separate cabinet-level department in 1913. It enforces mandatory standards for worker safety and oversees bargaining agreements between management and labor unions.[7] In 1935, unions were successful at getting more protections for workers through the National Labor Relations Act, which allowed unions to engage in collective bargaining. The act also provides that only one union can be selected to represent workers in a specific location, so that after a union successfully organizes a work location, those workers have to abide by that union's decisions.[8]

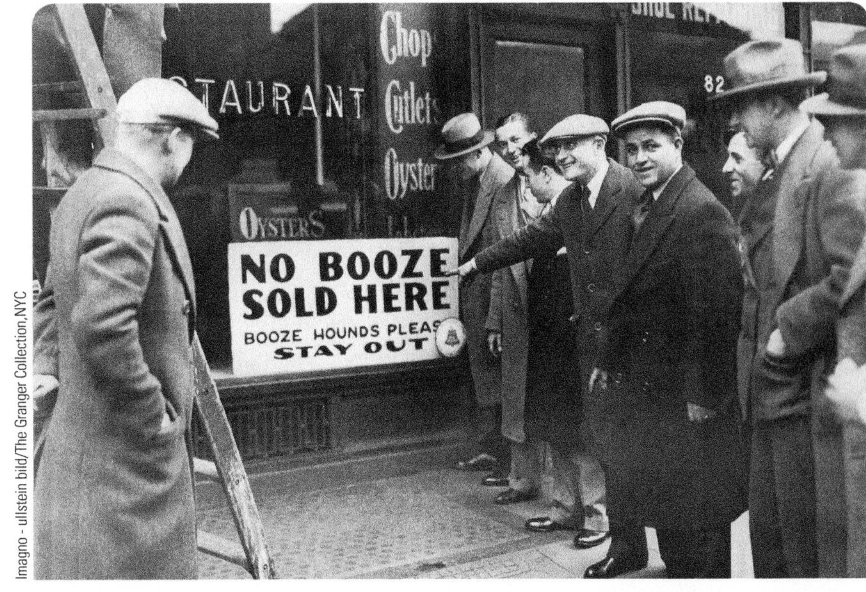

Imagno - ullstein bild/The Granger Collection, NYC

IMAGE 8.3 Prohibition was enacted by the Eighteenth Amendment to the Constitution in 1919. Here a restaurant owner in New York City makes it clear that no alcohol is sold on the premises. Prohibition was hard to enforce and was ultimately repealed by the Twenty-First Amendment to the Constitution in 1933.

Today business and trade associations, unions, citizens' organizations, and **grassroots movements** are a familiar part of the landscape of interest group politics. With the growth in the economy and in the size and scope of government in the American democracy, citizens have responded by forming more groups. The Chamber of Commerce, the National Rifle Association (NRA), AARP (formerly known as the American Association of Retired Persons), the League of United Latin American Citizens (LULAC), and the Sierra Club have existed for more than fifty years. Each claims to have millions of members, and each has different policy goals. However, not all modern interest groups are national in scope, and some are newly formed, so it is difficult to know how many groups are in existence at any one time. One study by political scientists estimated that there are approximately seven thousand groups operating in the American political system.[9] Their methods of communication and persuasion may differ from those of the very first petitioners of Congress, but they share the common role of serving as a gateway through which the opinions of ordinary citizens are expressed to their elected officials.

grassroots movement: *Group that forms in response to an economic or political event but does not focus on only one issue.*

8.2 Types of Interest Groups

Identify the types of interest groups that have evolved

Because the universe of interest groups is so large and diverse, it can be helpful to categorize groups by their core organizing purposes and the arenas in which they seek to influence public policy. In this section, we survey three types of interest groups—economic, ideological, and foreign policy–focused—to illustrate and explain differences in interest group policy goals and strategies.

Economic Interest Groups

economic interest group: *Group formed to advance the economic status of its members.*

Economic interest groups form to advance the economic status of their members and are defined by a specific set of financial or business concerns. Their membership bases tend to be exclusive because their purpose is to secure tangible economic benefits for themselves; if they grow too large or too inclusive, members' benefits are necessarily diluted. However, if the underlying industries represented by these groups disappear or merge with others, the groups have to adapt in order to attract new members.

Trade and Professional Associations. Trade associations focus on particular businesses or industries and make up a subcategory of economic interest groups. Examples include the National Association of Manufacturers, the Chamber of Commerce, the National Retail Federation, and the Semiconductor Industry Association. Trade associations form because business owners believe that they will have more influence on the policy process collectively than they would individually.

Professional associations are formed by individuals who share similar jobs. Examples include the American Bar Association (lawyers), the American Medical Association (doctors), and the American International Automobile Dealers Association (car dealers). These associations are frequently responsible for setting guidelines for professional conduct—from business practices to personal ethics—and for collectively representing the members in the policy process.

Corporations. Large corporations are a type of economic interest group in that they try to influence policy on their own as well as by joining trade associations comprising businesses with similar goals. Corporations such as Walmart, Comcast, and Boeing have thousands of employees, and that fact alone encourages politicians to listen to their concerns. Recently, corporations have aggressively contributed to political campaigns to influence policy, as will be discussed in detail later in this chapter. (For more on campaigns, see Chapter 10, Elections and Campaigns.)

Unions. Unions are a type of economic interest group that aims to protect workers through safer working conditions and better wages. They are traditionally organized as local chapters that are part of a national organization representing workers in specific fields and industries. For example, autoworkers might join the United Auto Workers (UAW), truck drivers might join the International Brotherhood of Teamsters, health care workers might join the Service Employees International Union, and high school teachers might join the National Educational Association. Unions typically require dues from all the people employed in a workplace that they represent in collective bargaining whether or not they voted in support of unionization. Typically collective bargaining can yield better wages and benefits for workers than when they are not represented as a collective. In March 2016 the Supreme Court, in *Friedrichs v. California Teachers Association*, left in place a lower court ruling that upheld the right of unions to charge fees to non-members who work in a unionized workplace in return for securing benefits for them through collective bargaining.

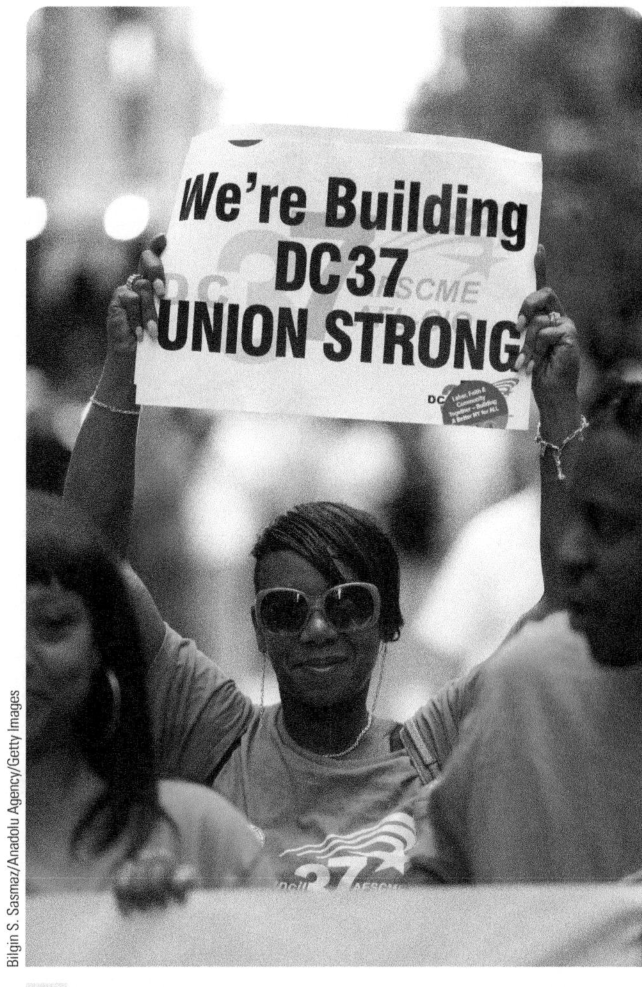

Bilgin S. Sasmaz/Anadolu Agency/Getty Images

IMAGE 8.4 Unions organize to provide collective benefits to workers in specific industries and professions. Here a union member expresses support for her union by marching in a Labor Day parade.

Unions' strength comes from their ability to call or threaten strikes and to bargain collectively with employers over wages and working conditions. For example, in 2015, the UAW successfully unionized workers at the Volkswagen plant in Chattanooga, Tennessee. This unionization was the first of its kind at a foreign automaker in the South, which typically has a less favorable climate for unions. The victory by the UAW means that workers who voted to form the union can now be represented in collective bargaining negotiations with the automaker.[10] Over the past decade, however, collective bargaining by public sector unions has come under attack by advocates for smaller government. In Indiana, Wisconsin, and Ohio, Republican governors and state legislators have severely curtailed the collective bargaining rights of state workers. Unions have fought back, however. In November 2011, Ohio voters repealed a law they viewed as too restrictive on the rights of union workers.[11] And in Wisconsin, Governor Scott Walker faced a recall election in June 2012 that was instigated primarily by supporters of collective bargaining rights, but he defeated the Democratic challenger 53 to 46 percent.[12] Walker later ran for the Republican nomination for president for the 2016 presidential election in part on the strength of his record against unions, but his campaign failed to catch on with the GOP base and he dropped out early in the process.

The biggest threat to unions, however, is the loss of jobs in the industries they represent. For example, the UAW was formed to represent the growing auto industry in the United States in 1935.[13] Over time, automation, foreign competition, and periodic economic downturns have resulted in the loss of thousands of jobs in this industry, which has in turn reduced the membership in the UAW. Just in the past decade, the union has lost nearly 250,000 members; that is one reason their victory at the Volkswagen plant in Tennessee was so important to the union. To combat their general membership loss, the UAW has branched out to other industries ranging from dining service employees at colleges to workers in gambling venues.[14]

Overall, private sector union membership has been declining (see Figure 8.1). Part of the reason for this decline is that government regulations now require the protections

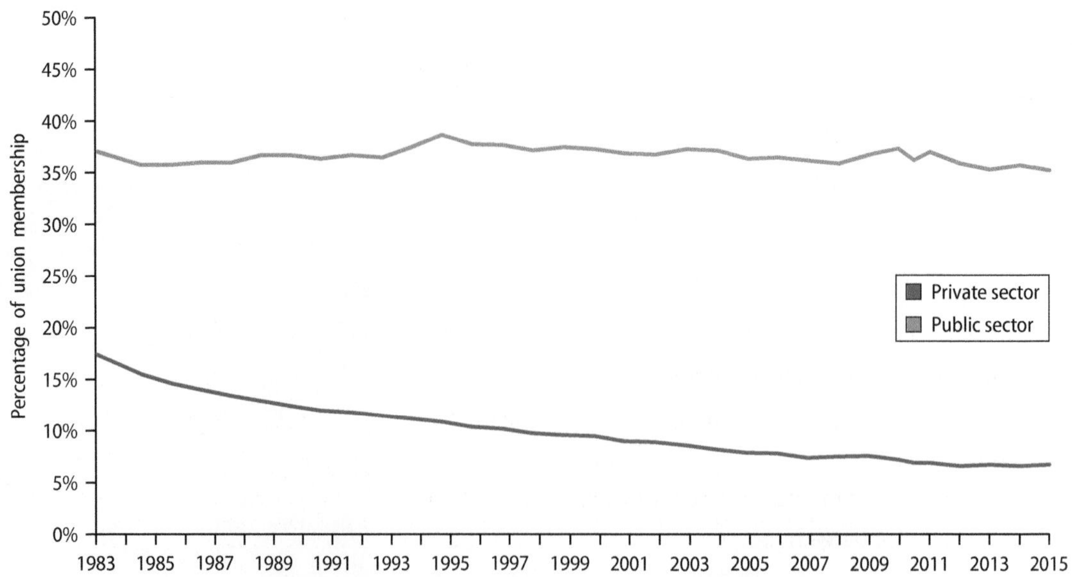

Notes: Data refer to the sole or principal job of full- and part-time workers. All self-employed workers are excluded, regardless of whether or not their businesses are incorporated. Data for 1990–93 have been revised to reflect population controls from the 1990 census. Beginning in 2000 data reflect population controls from census 2000 and new industry and occupational classification systems. Beginning in 2000 private sector data refer to private sector wage and salary workers; private sector data for earlier years refer to private nonagricultural wage and salary workers.

Percentages are based on the percentage employed.

FIGURE 8.1 Percentage of Wage and Salary Workers with Union Membership, 1983–2015

Private-sector union membership has been declining over time, while public-sector union membership has increased.

that unions long sought in terms of safe working conditions, overtime compensation, and nondiscrimination. In a sense, unions have been victims of their success in pushing for government regulations, and workers do not have to join a union to receive these protections. Consequently, over time the incentive for union membership has decreased.

Additionally, as of 2016, twenty-five states have right-to-work laws that allow individuals to choose not to join a union even if their workplace has a designated union in place.[15] As in the case of the UAW, unions have responded to this downturn in membership by seeking to represent workers in a wider range of industries. Despite the downturn in membership in large industrial and manufacturing unions, unions in other sectors of the economy, both public and private, representing teachers, health service workers, communications workers, and government employees have all made large gains over the past two decades. Table 8.1 lists the top six unions in the country, which together have nearly 11 million members. Today unions represent 11.1 percent of the overall workforce in the United States.[16]

American unions are both economically and politically powerful because they can mobilize their members to vote for candidates they see as favorable on issues such as higher minimum wages, standards for overtime pay, better access to health care insurance, worker safety, and international trade agreements. In recent years, public employee unions have come under increasing challenge over issues related to wages and pensions with efforts to reduce their bargaining power with state and local governments. Unions have countered these challenges with a combination of legal challenges and grassroots mobilization.

TABLE 8.1 Unions with the Largest Membership, 2015

Union	Number of Members (in millions)
National Education Association (NEA)	3.0
Service Employees International Union (SEIU)	2.0
American Federation of State, County and Municipal Employees (AFSCME)	1.6
American Federation of Teachers (AFT)	1.6
International Brotherhood of Teamsters (IBT)	1.4
United Food and Commercial Works International Union (UFCW)	1.3

Source: National Education Association, http://www.nea.org/home/2580.htm; Service Employees International Union, http://www.seiu.org/about; American Federation of State, County and Municipal Employees, http://www.afscme.org/union; American Federation of Teachers, http://www.aft.org/about/; International Brotherhood of Teamsters, http://www.opensecrets.org/orgs/summary.php?id=D000000066; United Food and Commercial Workers International Union, http://www.ufcw.org/about_ufcw/.

Essential Knowledge

Single issue groups seek to not only influence policy making but public opinion as well.

Ideological and Issue-Oriented Groups

Ideological interest groups form among citizens with the same beliefs about specific issues. We describe these groups as ideological rather than economic because economic benefits are not the primary basis for their existence. This category can include **citizens' groups** (Common Cause, Public Citizen), **single-issue groups** (NRA, Right to Life), and grassroots movement groups (MoveOn.org, National Organization for Women). Citizens' groups, sometimes called public interest groups, are typically formed to draw attention to public issues that affect all citizens equally, such as environmental protection, transparency in government, consumer product safety, ethics reform, and campaign finance reform. Single-issue groups form to present one view about a highly salient issue that is intensely important to its members, such as the national debt and the federal deficit to members of the American Family Association (AFA). In contrast, broader organizations typically emerge in response to an economic or political event but do not focus solely on one issue. For example, MoveOn.org was founded by two wealthy men who were angry that President William Jefferson (Bill) Clinton (1993–2001) was impeached even though most people opposed the proceedings. MoveOn.org called for an end to the Iraq War during the George W. Bush administration (2001–09). During the Obama administration (2009–17), the group worked hard to promote the health care exchanges and Medicaid expansion set forth under the Affordable Care Act.[17]

ideological interest groups: *Groups that form among citizens with the same beliefs about a specific issue.*

citizens' groups: *Groups that form to draw attention to purely public issues that affect all citizens equally.*

single-issue groups: *Groups that form to present one view on a highly salient issue that is intensely important to members, such as gun control or abortion.*

Ideological groups provide a way for individual members to express their opinions on issues more forcefully than would be possible for any one person alone. Members of ideological groups benefit from knowing that others share their views and from feeling empowered. In this way, ideological groups can encourage political participation in a democratic society. At the same time, these groups contribute to the polarization of the American public. Because a group of this type gets its power from agreement within its ranks on a highly salient issue, it discourages debate and disagreement within the group and any type of compromise on that issue.

For example, NARAL (formerly known as the National Abortion Rights Action League) takes the position that a woman has the right to terminate a pregnancy without limitations, whereas the Right to Life organization holds that all abortions should be forbidden except when the life of the mother is endangered by the continuation of the pregnancy. Individual members in each group may hold more moderate views, but the leadership believes that any public compromise will alienate core members and diminish the group's status on the issue within the media and government. In this case, ideological groups not only balance out each other but also block the way forward. The intensity with which each side holds its position discourages cross-group dialogue and makes it harder for elected officials to achieve a reasonable and widely acceptable resolution of the issue. Because an interest group seeks a favorable government response on a narrowly defined issue important to that group, the group can also create imbalances that verge on inequalities.

Foreign Policy and International Groups

Some interest groups address cross-border concerns. Foreign policy groups form to generate support for favorable U.S. policies toward one or several foreign countries. International aid groups encourage citizens to provide voluntary assistance to people in need all over the world. International groups concerned with human rights work to call attention to violations in the hopes of ending oppression.

Groups That Influence Foreign Policy. One of the best-known organizations that seek to influence foreign policy is the American Israel Public Affairs Committee (AIPAC). This group aims to ensure a strongly pro-Israel American foreign policy and uses public advocacy, member mobilization, and campaign contributions to influence members of Congress to support its goals. AIPAC first formed in the early 1950s, and it claims credit for getting the first aid package to Israel—$65 million to help relocate Holocaust refugees—passed by Congress in 1951.[18] Today, AIPAC has more than one hundred thousand active members and is widely considered to be one of the most influential groups of its kind in Washington.

Groups That Advocate International Aid and Support for Human Rights. Religious organizations often encourage members to provide international assistance. For example, Catholic Relief Services sponsors the Global Solidarity Network, which allows college students to communicate with people living in small villages or towns in developing countries. The National Council of the Churches of Christ in the USA provides funding and coordinates religious and humanitarian missions to foreign countries.[19]

STR/Newscom/European Pressphoto Agency/HOMS/SYR/Syrian Arab Republic

IMAGE 8.5 Humanitarian groups are often essential to providing services to civilians in war-torn areas. Here members of the International Organization for Migration (IOM) work with the United Nations to help refugees caught in the Syrian conflict.

Other interest groups, such as Amnesty International and Human Rights Watch, focus attention on human rights violations or starvation in certain areas of the world. Many are

nongovernmental organizations (NGOs), which are not affiliated with any government and work hard to preserve their neutrality so that they can operate in as many parts of the world as possible. These groups monitor human rights abuses and wartime violence around the world, most recently paying close attention to the conflicts in Syria and Iraq.[20] Other groups focus their efforts more specifically. The International Rescue Committee has worked to help relocate refugees who are fleeing violence in their countries; most recently their efforts have focused also on the violence in Syria.[21] They illustrate the power of interest groups to draw attention to a situation occurring in a foreign land and to solicit a powerful response from both average citizens and elected officials.

nongovernmental organizations (NGOs): *Organizations independent of governments that monitor and improve political, economic, and social conditions throughout the world.*

8.3 What Interest Groups Do

Describe activities interest groups engage in

Interest groups perform a number of functions in the political process. They collect information about the implications of policy changes and convey that information to lawmakers and other policy makers. Their lobbying efforts aim to construct policies in ways that will most benefit their members. This section examines the tactics of lobbying, from providing information, to contributing to campaigns, to orchestrating grassroots movements that increase political participation on an issue. Lobbying is one of the fundamental gateways for expressing views and securing a favorable response from government officials.

Inform

All interest groups provide information about the issues they care about to their members, the media, government officials, and the general public. The type of interest group dictates the kind of information it disseminates. Before the Internet, groups provided members with information about government policies and new developments in their issue areas through newsletters and sessions at annual conventions. Today they disseminate such information on their websites and try to limit access by requiring members to register and sign in to the websites. Social media, such as Facebook, Snapchat, Vine, Twitter, and Instagram, also enable groups to keep members informed and to rally them to take action on the group's behalf.

Interest groups do more than merely report on current policy developments; they also provide members with interpretations of how the developments will affect their mission and goals. For example, in the area of environmental and energy policy, interest groups are very active in keeping their members up to date on policy developments. For example, in November 2015, when then President Obama denied the application to build the Keystone Pipeline XL, which was considered a strong stance against climate change, the Sierra Club issued a press release claiming credit for its efforts to help defeat the pipeline and informing its members that their support of the Sierra Club made a difference.[22] (For more on climate change, see Chapter 16, Economic, Domestic, and Foreign Policy.)

Interest groups also work hard to inform government officials about the impact of specific public policies. Most of the time, lobbyists have pro or con positions on a policy proposal, and their goal is to persuade government officials to agree with their perspective. Legislators and government officials are generally knowledgeable in their areas of expertise, but the vast size of the federal and state governments makes it hard to know the impact of policies on every citizen. Economic and ideological groups constantly monitor policies that might affect their members in a positive or negative way and strive to make legislators and government officials aware of the impact of policy proposals (see Public Policy and Interest Groups: Fracking).

Groups convey information via e-mail; telephone; personal meetings with staff, elected officials, and bureaucrats; and testifying before Congress and state legislatures. Groups also use the bureaucratic regulatory process to respond to regulations with comments to influence how laws are carried out by the executive branch (see Chapter 14, The Bureaucracy). For example, the National Education Association (NEA), a teachers' union, sent a letter to the Obama administration commenting on its proposed rules for implementing the Race to the Top program, which is designed to provide funds to local communities to improve education. In this letter, the NEA supported some of the provisions but was critical of others, in this way conveying the views of its members to bureaucrats.[23] The NEA then posted the letter on its website to inform teachers across the country about the specific ways that the program might impact their schools and school systems.

Groups also can engage in several of these types of activities at once. For example, LULAC (mentioned above) has a long history of engaging and informing its members in several political arenas. They were active in bringing the court case *Hernandez v. State of Texas* (featured in Chapter 5) to the Supreme Court to secure the right of Mexican Americans to participate on juries. More recently, LULAC has worked to mobilize Latino voters by informing them of registration and voting procedures in their communities. And LULAC was very supportive of President Obama's successful nomination of Sonia Sotomayor to the Supreme Court.[24]

Lobby

Almost every kind of group with every kind of economic interest or political opinion—including business firms, trade and professional organizations, citizens' groups, labor unions, and universities and colleges—engages in one form of lobbying or another.[25] State, county, and city government officials maintain lobbying offices in Washington, D.C., both separately and as part of larger national groups such as the National Governors Association or the United States Conference of Mayors. Lobbyists for these government entities frequently visit with the state's congressional delegation to keep the representatives informed about how federal programs are operating back home and to ask for legislation that will benefit their states. Mayors and county executives do the same thing, trying to influence their state legislators and governor by keeping them informed about how policies affect their constituents.

The Lobbyists. Groups can use their own employees as lobbyists or contract with firms that specialize in lobbying. According to the Center for Responsive Politics, in 2015, there were 11,169 individuals registered as active lobbyists in Washington, D.C. That amounts to nearly twenty-one lobbyists for each member of the House and Senate.[26] The offices of many of these lobbyists are concentrated in an area of northwest Washington known as the K Street corridor; when people say they work on K Street, it is safe to assume that they are lobbyists.

Although lobbyists are frequently stereotyped as representing only the narrow interests of their clients, they are typically individuals who have held public service jobs at some point in their careers. There are three common pathways to becoming a Washington lobbyist: working on Capitol Hill, working in the executive branch, or working on a political campaign. Lobbyists may start out on a political campaign for a congressional candidate or work in a congressional office, and then leave to join a corporation, lobbying firm, or a law firm with a branch that lobbies on specific legal matters. Or lobbyists may start out as practicing attorneys, then go to work in Congress or the executive branch, and subsequently join a company or lobbying firm.

AP Images/Rich Pedroncelli

IMAGE 8.6 At the end of a legislative session, lobbyists gather in a hallway outside the state capitol in California to see how their proposals fared.

In 2015, interest groups and lobbying firms spent nearly $2.4 billion on a wide range of expenses associated with lobbying, including salaries for in-house lobbyists, consulting fees charged by lobbying firms, overhead for office space, and travel costs of staff (see Table 8.2).[27] In the past, the costs of lobbying also included paid trips for members of Congress and their staffs (known as junkets), as well as expensive meals. Lobbyists justified these expenses as a way of getting to know members of Congress in a smaller and more relaxed setting, which they claimed would enable them to enhance their or their client's influence in the policy process. A

TABLE 8.2 Top Spenders on Lobbying, 2016

Lobbying Client	Issues	Dollars Spent
U.S. Chamber of Commerce	Product liability, finance, copyright, patent and trademark	$79,205,000
National Association of Realtors	Taxes, finance, housing	$45,255,769
Blue Cross/Blue Shield	Health issues, taxes, Medicare and Medicaid	$19,058,109
American Hospital Association	Health issues, Medicare and Medicaid, federal budget and appropriations	$15,454,734
American Medical Association	Health issues, taxes, Medicare and Medicaid	$15,290,000
Pharmaceutical Research and Manufacturers of America	Health issues, Medicare and Medicaid, pharmacy	$14,717,500
Boeing Corporation	Defense and aerospace	$12,870,000
AT&T	Telecommunications	$12,666,000
National Association of Broadcasters	Radio and TV, Copyright	$12,118,000

Source: Adapted from Center for Responsive Politics, "Top Spenders, 2016," https://www.opensecrets.org/lobby/top.php?indexType=s&showYear=2016, accessed November 7, 2016.

PUBLIC POLICY AND INTEREST GROUPS

Fracking

The struggle for power over policy decisions is ongoing, and interest groups are always moving forward to accomplish their agendas within the larger policy-making arena. The issues within the energy and environmental arena are vast, and in this section, we focus on the interest group activity surrounding the use of hydraulic fracturing, otherwise known as fracking, which is a technique that extracts oil and natural gas. Since 1997, the use of fracking has expanded greatly, bringing with it increases in jobs and overall production of oil and gas nationwide, which has contributed to economic growth in some areas.[28] At the same time, there have been serious allegations that fracking poses a threat to the environment, particularly safe drinking water. In response to concerns expressed by residents in areas with fracking, in 2010 Congress requested that the Environmental Protection Agency (EPA) conduct a study of the effects of fracking on drinking water. The EPA then launched a study and focused on locations in four states (North Dakota, Pennsylvania, Texas, and Colorado) where fracking had already been occurring for some time.[29] In June 2015, the EPA released its draft report of the study's findings and concluded that although hydraulic fracking does interact and rely on water systems that also provide drinking water, they did not identify any serious negative effects from the process to date.[30] In this way, the issue of fracking presents a clear case study of the trade-offs between jobs, energy production, and environmental protection and how interest groups try to influence public policy in these areas.

Both America's Natural Gas Alliance (ANGA), a group that promotes the use of natural gas, and the Natural Resources Defense Council (NRDC), an environmental advocacy group that opposes fracking, responded to this investigation in ways that advance their own perspective. ANGA is an example of a corporate interest group designed to advance the policies preferred by its industry members. NRDC is typical of a public interest nonprofit group that addresses issues of public policy that affect a wide group of citizens.

Each group is committed to representing the views of its members. For ANGA that consists of oil and gas companies, and for NRDC, that consists of individual and group donors, as well as foundations that support NRDC's environmental protection stances.[31]

In response to the EPA study, ANGA issued an extensive report on the question of water pollution and its ties to fracking. The report focused on one community, Washington County, Pennsylvania, an area that engaged in coal mining before turning to fracking. In this report, which was shared with other major oil and gas interest groups, ANGA argued that any existing water contamination could be a result of a number of industrial activities,

Mark Ovaska/Redux

IMAGE 8.7 Fracking is becoming more widespread across previously undeveloped lands. Here a fracking site known as the Marcellus Shale Well sits among farmland in Pennsylvania.

not solely tied to fracking, and that if this were true for Washington County, it could be true for other such affected areas.[32]

In contrast, NRDC created the Community Fracking Defense Campaign (CFDC), which raises money and awareness of the issue and focuses on the impacts on residents of Pennsylvania as well as other states, including New York, Ohio, California, Illinois, and Texas.[33] CFDC posts videos on its website featuring residents of areas with fracking talking about the degraded quality of the water and air in their communities. These videos are human interest stories designed to gain sympathy for these residents and persuade viewers to support NRDC's efforts to oppose fracking.[34] In addition to trying to generate grassroots opposition to fracking, the group also responds to government action on this issue. CFDC severely criticized the EPA study and pointed to dissenting voices in the scientific community to support their ongoing efforts to limit fracking.[35]

Each group's strategy reflects its core organization. As an industry-based organization, ANGA issued a comprehensive study that relies heavily on technical evidence designed to be used to oppose EPA restrictions on fracking. As a public issue group, NRDC works to build grassroots support for its position and inform its members, which the group hopes in turn will influence regulators and lawmakers. Overall, the struggle to sway public opinion on the issue of fracking is just one illustration of how interest groups try to influence public policy on key issues.

Public Policy Connections

1. How should the government decide when the interests of different groups conflict?
2. What should be done when a small group gains an inordinate amount of political influence?

decade has passed since congressional ethics reforms prohibited paid trips and meals for members and staff.[36] Still, lobbyists can use money to maintain their influence in other ways. For example, their salaries typically include allocations to make strategic campaign contributions to members of Congress who preside over issues that are important to their companies or clients.

During a typical day, lobbyists phone, e-mail, or meet with congressional staffers, their clients, and possibly members of the media to gather information about relevant issues for their clients or to promote their clients' policy positions. Lobbyists also attend congressional hearings, executive branch briefings, and even committee markups in which members of Congress write legislation. Interest groups, businesses, and industries do not survive by lobbying only, but lobbying is a natural outgrowth of their purpose because members expect their leaders to advocate for them when necessary.

Lobbying Strategies. Lobbying frequently involves a multipronged strategy. Groups usually try an inside lobbying strategy first, in which they deal directly with legislators and their staff to ask for a specific policy benefit or to try to stop a policy that they oppose. These insider meetings require access to policy makers, which typically comes about as a result of longtime interactions that build mutual trust. The key aspect of the **inside strategy** is to keep the policy request narrowly tailored to the group's needs because the broader the policy request, the more likely other groups will become involved in the negotiations, and complications can ensue. Either the policy request has to expand, so that

inside strategy: *A strategy employed by interest groups to pursue a narrow policy change and influence legislators directly rather than using a wider grassroots approach.*

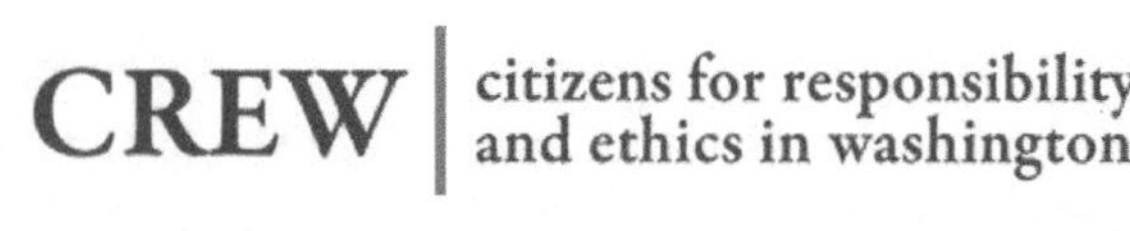

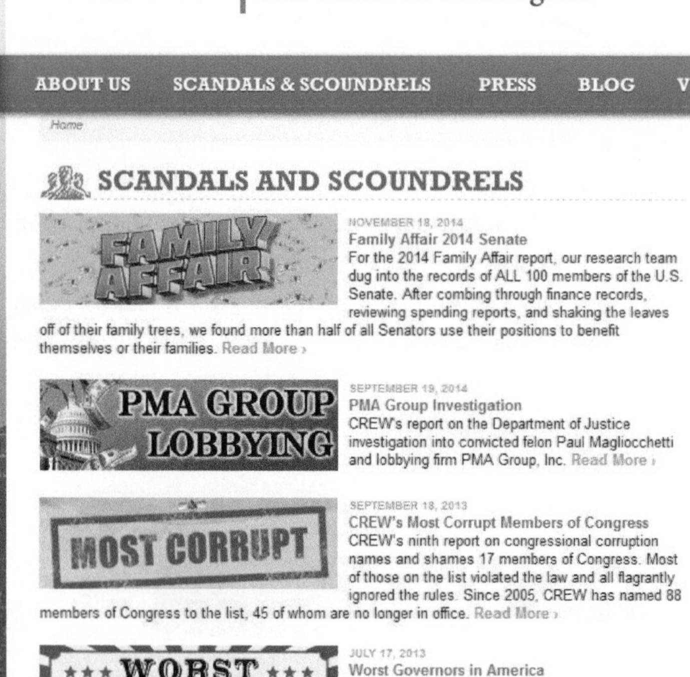

ABOUT US
SCANDALS & SCOUNDRELS
PRESS
BLOG
Home
SCANDALS AND SCOUNDRELS
FAMILY AFFAIR
NOVEMBER 18, 2014
Family Affair 2014 Senate
For the 2014 Family Affair report, our research team dug into the records of ALL 100 members of the U.S. Senate. After combing through finance records, reviewing spending reports, and shaking the leaves off of their family trees, we found more than half of all Senators use their positions to benefit themselves or their families. Read More ›
PMA GROUP LOBBYING
SEPTEMBER 19, 2014
PMA Group Investigation
CREW's report on the Department of Justice investigation into convicted felon Paul Magliocchetti and lobbying firm PMA Group, Inc. Read More ›
MOST CORRUPT
SEPTEMBER 18, 2013
CREW's Most Corrupt Members of Congress
CREW's ninth report on congressional corruption names and shames 17 members of Congress. Most of those on the list violated the law and all flagrantly ignored the rules. Since 2005, CREW has named 88 members of Congress to the list, 45 of whom are no longer in office. Read More ›
WORST GOVERNORS
JULY 17, 2013
Worst Governors in America
After examining all 50 executives, CREW names the 18 governors who have turned their states into a political circus. Read More ›

IMAGE 8.8 Watchdog groups hold public officials accountable for their behavior. Citizens for Responsibility and Ethics in Washington (CREW) publishes a website listing major scandals committed by public officials.

each group gets a high level of benefits, or each group has to be satisfied with less, and few groups are ever satisfied with less. Nevertheless, if several groups share the same policy goals, they may form a temporary coalition, working together to improve their chances of success.

When an inside strategy does not work, groups adopt a more public or outside lobbying strategy by getting the press and their members more directly involved. A group may go straight to the press to provide details about the adverse effects of the proposal, hoping that the journalists will inform the general public. In this way, interest groups try to make use of the press's watchdog role over the government. For example, a non-profit group called Citizens for Responsibility and Ethics in Washington (CREW) consistently tries to get the press to focus on whether government officials are obeying ethics and campaign finance laws.[37] They monitor the use of campaign funds by members of Congress and frequently call for investigations into what they see as misuse of funds in a section on their website entitled "Scandals & Scoundrels," where they post an updated list of members of Congress who are under ethics investigations either by Congress itself, the Federal Election Commission, or the Department of Justice as well as under scrutiny for other ethical violations.[38]

Through publicity and coordinated activities, groups also try to promote grassroots lobbying by encouraging action by their own members and the larger public. Energizing constituents in congressional districts used to be the work of regional offices. Today interest groups can generate citizen involvement through the Internet, asking that a message be sent by e-mail, text messaging, or cell phone, or show their members how to start their own Internet petitions. MoveOn.org, for example, gets grassroots support by asking members to e-mail, call, or send letters to their local legislator as well as to others who might be sympathetic to their cause. In addition, marches and rallies show strength in numbers to elected officials and also generate publicity that can attract new people to join advocacy efforts. In these ways, groups directly give their membership a stronger voice in the policy-making process.

The core organizational purpose also helps shape a group's lobbying strategy. For example, economic groups typically adopt an insider lobbying strategy and limit their activity to key actors in Congress and the executive branch. In contrast, citizens' groups typically adopt the outsider strategy to take advantage of the strength that comes from their large memberships. If they can mobilize their members to communicate with elected officials and simultaneously use the media to spread their message, they believe they will be successful.

Campaign Activities

Interest groups also promote their views by engaging in campaign activities, although federal law regulates their participation through the Federal Election Commission (FEC). Candidates and their campaign organizations must comply with reporting and disclosure requirements, which are monitored by the FEC. Groups with tax-exempt status are prohibited from engaging in any activity on behalf of a candidate or party in an election campaign. These groups, commonly referred to as **501(c)(3) organizations** after the section of the Internal Revenue Code that governs their activities, are likely to be charities, religious organizations, public service organizations, employee benefit groups, and fraternal societies, which are exempt from paying federal tax. Although they cannot engage in lobbying in any significant way, they can produce voter education guides or other nonpartisan educational materials that explain issues brought up during a political campaign and keep the public informed.[39]

Lisa Werner/Alamy

IMAGE 8.9 Peaceful protests are frequently an effective way of voicing opinion on an issue. This gathering was organized to show opposition to fracking.

501(c)(3) organizations: *Tax-exempt groups that are prohibited from lobbying or campaigning for a party or candidate.*

There are also groups that fall under the **501(c)(4) organization** category, which are nonprofit and are supposed to be focused on public policy issues, not politics. These groups are not required to reveal their contributors. Such groups include the Sierra Club, the NRA, and, more recently, chapters of the Tea Party movement. Their status as "apolitical" nonprofit groups came under close scrutiny by the Internal Revenue Service in 2012 and 2013, leading some to allege that the Democratic Obama administration was targeting conservative groups. However, the Obama administration claimed that all groups who were seeking this status were subject to intense investigation and responded by proposing new regulations that more closely restricted what kinds of activities these groups could engage in so that it would be clear they could not be overtly political.[40]

501(c)(4) organizations: *Tax-exempt groups that exist to promote social welfare and can advocate for specific policy issues.*

Essential Knowledge

Interest groups attempt to influence elections through the use of PACs. With PACs' contributions, interest groups attempt to gain access to winning politicians.

Groups that fall outside the tax-exempt category are free to engage in lobbying and campaign activities. But to set boundaries between the group's core mission and politics, they generally create parallel organizations that make campaign contributions to legislators. These **political action committees (PACs)** and their larger versions, Super PACs, raise funds to support electoral candidates and are subject to campaign finance laws (see Chapter 10). In one sense, PACs serve as gateways for expanding interest groups' political influence through financial involvement in campaigns.

political action committees (PACs): *Groups formed to raise and contribute funds to support electoral candidates and that are subject to campaign finance laws.*

PACs began growing in number and force after the Supreme Court's landmark decision *Buckley v. Valeo* (1976) upheld limits on donations to congressional campaigns.[41] As the costs of campaign spending rose over time, groups realized that creating or expanding an affiliated PAC to make campaign contributions could increase their influence over elected officials. Unaffiliated PACs, groups that make campaign contributions but are not associated with specific interest groups, also grew in size as a means of coordinating campaign contributions from individual citizens who wanted to express their campaign support as part of a larger group. All PACs make campaign contributions to the candidates they believe will be supportive of their policy goals (see Table 8.3). Thus PACs expand the

TABLE 8.3A Top 5 PAC Contributors to Republican Candidates, 2015–16

PAC Name	Total Amount Given to Republicans
National Association of Realtors	$2,702,170
National Beer Wholesalers Association	$2,205,200
Majority Committee PAC	$2,203,687
National Auto Dealers Association	$1,982,250
AT&T Inc.	$1,982,000

TABLE 8.3B Top 5 PAC Contributors to Democratic Candidates, 2015–2016

PAC Name	Total Amount Given to Democrats
International Brotherhood of Electrical Workers	$2,587,250
Machinists/Aerospace Workers Union	$2,182,000
National Association of Realtors	$1,837,980
American Association for Justice	$1,718,500
Plumbers/Pipefitters Union	$1,656,080

Source: Center for Responsive Politics, www.opensecrets.org, adapted from data released by the Federal Election Commission, accessed November 7, 2016, http://www.opensecrets.org/pacs/index.php?party=D&cycle=2016

reach of interest groups well beyond lobbying to include active engagement in the electoral arena.

Given the amount of money that PACs spend on campaign support, many observers have expressed concern that PACs exert a disproportionate influence over legislators, which creates an imbalance in government responsiveness toward some groups. In the age of so-called Super PACs and 501(c)(4) groups that can spend nearly unlimited money on issue ads directed at persuading the public to support their policy position, interest group interaction can get captured by big money battles among these groups. Supporters of open and equal democratic participation fear that such money battles could simply favor the richest and loudest groups and slant policy making to benefit specific groups rather than the majority of the people.

For example, in 2013, much was made of the influence of Club for Growth, a PAC devoted to lowering taxes, because of its influence on Republican members who were advocating for lower government spending. The Club for Growth, founded by Stephen Moore in 1999, is a PAC that collects funds and makes campaign contributions to members who support its platform. In October 2013, the federal government shut down for 16 days at an estimated cost of $2 billion because a group of these congressmen refused to vote to fund it and refused to raise the borrowing limit for the federal government (the debt ceiling). The Club for Growth was widely credited with supporting these congressmen at that time.

Essential Knowledge

Debates have increased over free speech and competitive and fair elections, specifically related to money and campaign funding (including contributions from individuals, PACs, and political parties).

More generally, however, scholars have had difficulty establishing exactly what PACs are getting for their money. Although campaign contributions can make it easier for groups

SUPREME COURT CASES

Citizens United v. Federal Election Commission (2010)

QUESTION: Can the government limit campaign spending by corporations and unions without violating First Amendment rights?

ORAL ARGUMENT: March 24, 2009, reargued September 9, 2009 (listen at http://www.oyez.org/cases/2000-2009/2008/2008_08_205)

DECISION: January 21, 2010 (read at http://caselaw.lp.findlaw.com/scripts/getcase.pl?court=US&vol=000&invol=08-205)

OUTCOME: No, governmental restrictions on corporate speech violate First Amendment rights (5–4).

In an attempt to equalize finances in political campaigns, Congress passed the Bipartisan Campaign Reform Act of 2002, also called the McCain-Feingold Act after its two leading sponsors. In 1976, the Supreme Court upheld limits on contributions to congressional campaigns but struck down limits on what independent groups unaffiliated with the campaign could spend. In response, McCain-Feingold restricted corporations and unions from using television or radio ads for "electioneering communications"—commercials that refer to a candidate by name—within thirty days of a primary or sixty days of a general election.

While corporations are often for-profit operations, such as General Motors or Microsoft, nonprofit and political entities such as the NAACP also organize as corporations under the tax code. One such political organization is Citizens United, a conservative interest group "dedicated to restoring our government to citizen control." During the 2008 Democratic primary campaign, it released a documentary called *Hillary: The Movie,* which was severely critical of Senator Clinton (D-NY). Citizens United planned to show the documentary on pay-per-view television and to market it in advertisements on broadcast television. Concerned about violating McCain-Feingold, Citizens United sued the FEC, seeking an injunction prohibiting enforcement of the act as a violation of the First Amendment rights of corporations.

In a break with past decisions, the Supreme Court declared that corporations and unions had the same First Amendment rights as U.S. citizens. Using the compelling interest test (see Chapter 4, Civil Liberties), the Court ruled that Congress cannot disfavor certain subjects or different speakers. While recognizing that corporations may have more money to spend than individual citizens do, the Court ruled that First Amendment protections do not depend on the speaker's "financial ability to engage in public discussion." Such limitations violate the marketplace of ideas that the First Amendment is designed to protect. The ruling left open the question of whether Congress could limit the speech rights of foreign corporations operating within the United States.

The dissenters claimed that money is not equivalent to speech and that the law was a reasonable attempt to level the playing field in campaigns.

Thinking Critically

1. Why is campaign spending a form of speech?
2. Should corporations receive the same free speech protections as ordinary citizens?

to get access to legislators, they generally do not buy results in terms of policy outcomes—at least not directly. For example, an auto maker and a union might team up to lobby for a policy that benefits their industry and their affiliated PACs may also contribute money to elected officials. The combination of lobbying and campaign money may get lawmakers' attentions, but it is also the case that those lawmakers want to secure benefits for any

ELECTION 2016

The Libre Initiative

ONE NEWER EXAMPLE OF A 501(c)(4) organization that was founded to mobilize voters is the Libre Initiative (www.thelibreinitiative.com). According to its website, this group was founded with the purpose of "informing the U.S. Hispanic community about the benefits of . . . limited government . . . and free enterprise"; their slogan is #BeLibre.[42] Typically Latinos have been viewed as more progressive, and approximately 71 percent of Latino voters voted for President Obama in the 2012 election.[43] This organization exists to encourage community networks of economic and political support among Latinos and to build support for conservative policy positions such as school choice and less regulation of small business. At the same time, it supports a moderate immigration reform policy that opposes mass deportations while calling for stronger enforcement of the legal immigration laws. Located in nine states, it also provides information about a range of issues, including where to finish high school and how to get a driver's license.[44]

The Libre Initiative was founded by Daniel Garza, who serves as its executive director. He previously served in the George W. Bush administration and worked in Spanish-language television before taking on the job of heading an organization that was geared up to play a significant role in the 2016 election cycle. With two Latino presidential candidates, Ted Cruz (R-TX) and Marco Rubio (R-FL), contesting for the GOP nomination, 2016 presented a major opportunity for a Latino conservative organization to gain attention and potential supporters in the Latino community. As with any interest group, that requires informing and persuading individuals that the group best represents their opinions and policy goals. Some of their efforts include rallying their members around immigration reform and the more fiscally conservative policies that they support, and they include a direct appeal to women with their #MsLibre campaign designed to attract Latina women supporters. The Libre Initiative also works with other conservative groups and has received funding from the Koch brothers, who have been very public about wanting to expand the reach of their conservative fiscal message to the Latino community.

In terms of outcomes, the Libre Initiative was poised to exert influence in the 2016 election with its location in several key swing states, such as Florida, Colorado, Nevada, and Virginia. It ultimately proved to be successful in a broad sense in that Latino turnout increased in the general election, and 29 percent of Latinos voted for the GOP presidential candidate.[45] The Libre Initiative is one example of how interest group participation has expanded significantly among Latino groups along the range of ideological viewpoints in American politics.

Essential Knowledge

While portions of the McCain-Feingold Bipartisan Campaign Reform Act were struck down, the Court allowed other provisions to stand. One of those provisions requires candidates to state on their advertisements, "I approve this message."

employees in their districts who work in the auto industry. Interest groups tend to lobby and contribute to members of Congress who are leaning in their direction, and who have constituents who may be employed in the areas represented by the interest groups, so it is difficult to prove the impact of a campaign contribution.[46]

Campaign finance laws impose limits on what interest groups can do in terms of issue advocacy, the practice of running advertisements or distributing literature on a policy issue rather than for a specific candidate. In general, the Supreme Court ruled that campaign spending is a form of speech and that, as with other forms of speech, Congress must show a compelling interest before it can pass laws to regulate it. The McCain-Feingold Bipartisan Campaign Reform Act (2002) restricted corporations and unions from using television and radio ads for "electioneering communications"—commercials that refer to a candidate by name—within thirty days of a primary and sixty days of a general election. Since 2002, many groups have run ads that could be interpreted as issue advocacy or as outright campaigning. In 2007, in *Federal Election Commission v. Wisconsin Right to Life, Inc.*, the Supreme Court ruled that if a campaign advertisement could be reasonably viewed as issue-based, it was protected under the guarantee of free speech and could not be prohibited under the McCain-Feingold Act.[47]

Running issue ads has become a regular feature of interest group activity, even in nonelection years. Before 2010, interest groups could run issue ads on specific issues within a certain time frame prior to an election according to federal election laws; many interest groups used these ads to generate support or opposition to then President Obama's health care plan before it became law. Although they served the purposes of interest groups, they also encouraged elected officials to be more responsive to constituents' needs because they focused attention on issues of importance to constituents. In 2010, the Supreme Court removed virtually all limits on issue ads, and individuals, corporations, and unions can spend as much money as they want on issue ads. (See this chapter's Supreme Court Cases: *Citizens United v. Federal Election Commission*, as well as the discussion of issue ads in Chapter 10.) In 2014, the Supreme Court went even further, in their ruling in *McCutcheon et al. v. Federal Election Commission*, by removing the overall limits on the amount of money one individual can contribute to all federal elections; there are still limits on how much money can be given to one candidate, but an individual can now contribute to every single candidate running for federal office, as well as political parties.[48]

8.4 The Impact of Interest Groups on Democratic Processes

Analyze what balances out power among interest groups

"I have often admired the extreme skill," wrote Tocqueville, "with which the inhabitants of the United States succeed in proposing a common object to the exertions of a great many men, and in inducing them voluntarily to pursue it."[49] Both Tocqueville and James Madison assumed that voluntary association or the forming of factions was a natural process of citizens interacting in a free society. Scholars have been interested in the same process, examining why interest groups form and what effects they have in a democratic society. In this section, we survey various perspectives on interest groups that relate to government responsiveness and citizen equality.

Essential Knowledge

The policy-making process is influenced by a variety of forces, including: single issue groups, social movements, and protest movements.

Natural Balance or Disproportionate Power

Over the past seven decades, scholarly debate has centered on the process of interest group formation and its consequences. In the 1950s, David Truman agreed with Tocqueville and Madison, describing interest group formation as natural. He observed that when individuals have interests in common, they naturally gravitate toward each other and form a group. As long as those individuals share a characteristic, opinion, or interest, the group continues to exist, but if the commonality disappears, the group disappears.[50]

Writing in the mid-1960s, however, Mancur Olson argued that merely having something in common with other people was not enough to give a group life and keep it going

Essential Knowledge

Not all groups impact the policy-making process equally. The influence of interest groups professional organizations, social movements, government agencies (including the military) varies from group to group and issue to issue.

pluralist: *View of democratic society in which interest groups compete over policy goals, and elected officials are mediators of group conflict.*

special interests: *Set of groups seeking a particular benefit for themselves in the policy process.*

as an effective organization.[51] Olson focused on the costs of organizing and maintaining a group, noting that costs increase as a group grows in size and reach. The people who pay membership dues expect benefits in return. Since the governmental decisions that interest groups obtain are "public goods" that apply whether one has joined the group or not, Olson argues that the cost–benefit structure that underlies group formation contradicts Truman's claim that all groups naturally form and sustain themselves.

The debate between Truman and Olson raises the fundamental issue of whether interest groups are natural and can compete on an equal basis or artificial because they distort public policy in favor of some citizens over others. Other scholars have addressed this question in different ways. Robert Dahl argued that in a **pluralist** society, the battles over public policy by the varied interest groups that emerge to represent their members will produce a consensus that serves the public's common interest.[52] Scholars such as C. Wright Mills worried that a power elite controlled power in the American democracy.[53] His concerns were echoed by Theodore Lowi, who argued that in a democracy, some voices are louder than others and that government is more responsive to louder voices and will consistently serve such groups at the expense of those who cannot make their voices heard.

According to Lowi, this kind of policy making is elitist and fundamentally antidemocratic.[54] More recently, political scientists Larry Bartels and Martin Gilens have each written extensively about the disproportionate impact of the wealthy on public policy making and demonstrated that ideas put forth by groups that represent the interests of the wealthy, especially in the issue areas of tax policy and social welfare, receive more attention from lawmakers than other groups.[55]

Traditionally, the narrow focus of interest groups has engendered a sense of illegitimacy. Interest groups form and survive by appealing to a particular segment of society (economic, ideological, or social), so they are inherently exclusive. Exclusive groups act only in the best interests of their members, even if nonmembers thereby lose out. E. E. Schattschneider described this aspect of interest groups as an actual threat to democracy. He argued that if interest groups are given legitimacy because they claim to represent citizens' interests, but in fact they seek narrow benefits for their members at the expense of nonmembers, there is an inherent unfairness to them. Moreover, citizens will be lulled into a false sense of security about living in an "interest group society" because they believe that every interest group has an equal opportunity to be influential.[56]

There is a middle ground between these contrasting views. Given the approximately seven thousand registered groups in America today, it is clear that group formation is a natural outgrowth of the freedom to associate and of community life in which human beings share social, economic, and political goals. But if Olson is right, and successful cost–benefit strategies determine whether a group can survive or grow, groups led by individuals with sufficient time and money stand a greater chance of winning a policy fight than do groups without such resources. In this view, interests become **special interests**, a term with negative connotations that is more frequently used during campaign season to suggest that some groups exert a disproportionate amount of power in the American democracy. To the extent that a well-funded interest group can more easily pressure the government to produce policies that are beneficial to its members, government responds unequally across all citizens. In this view, financial advantage creates an artificial imbalance of influence that acts as a gate against equality.

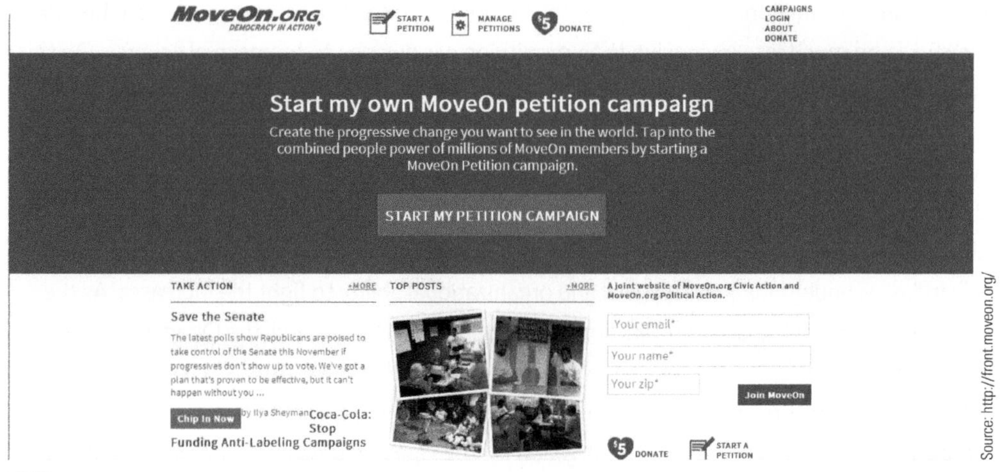

Source: http://front.moveon.org/

IMAGE 8.10 As their website indicates, MoveOn.org is a nonprofit grassroots organization that is geared toward increasing political participation on a wide range of issues.

When a group is founded explicitly to represent one group of people or set of interests, does that mean that its activities will not benefit the society as a whole? Take, for example, Black Lives Matter, a group that formed out of a mass social movement protesting the deaths of Michael Brown in Ferguson, Missouri, and Eric Garner in New York City. Although the group's core focus was the deaths of unarmed African Americans during interactions with law enforcement, its message spread further and wider into discussions of racism more generally, from schools to the workplace to the judicial arena. In moving from a broad social movement to an interest group that changes policy, Black Lives Matter may experience the challenges of all interest groups in voicing the concerns of those it represents while maintaining its effectiveness in gaining the support of a broad enough coalition to secure policy change in these arenas.

Self-Service or Public Service

In assessing the relative power of interest groups in a democratic political system, it is essential to remember that interest groups do not pass or implement laws; they try to influence state and federal governments to enact their policy goals. To do so, they constantly interact with political parties, members of Congress, executive branch bureaucratic agencies, and even the judicial system. The question of legitimacy of an interest group's activities comes when a victory for one group means a loss for another, or more broadly a loss for the general public.

For example, during most of the 1990s and 2000s, car manufacturers—acting alone and as part of their larger trade association, the American Association of Automobile Manufacturers—successfully lobbied to block efforts by environmental groups to secure an increase in government-mandated fuel efficiency standards. These standards, known by the general term *corporate average fuel economy* (CAFE), are designed to ensure that automobiles use as little fuel as possible to run efficiently. The government has an interest in requiring such efficiency in order to promote energy conservation more generally. However, automobile manufacturers argued that increased fuel efficiency is more expensive to produce and that CAFE standards would cut into their profits and might even decrease sales. In other words, the auto manufacturers would pay the price for accomplishing the public goal of promoting energy conservation. When auto companies violate these standards they have to pay monetary fines to the federal government; between 1991 and 2012, those fines added up to more than $873 million.[57] But to automobile manufacturers, the total sum of these fines was viewed to be much less expensive than modifying car designs to increase efficiency. On this issue, the self-interest of the auto manufacturers conflicted with that of the general public.

In 2007, with high increases in fuel prices and a general increased awareness of global warming, then President George W. Bush agreed to a modest increase in fuel efficiency standards to 33.6 miles per gallon by 2012. When President Obama took office in 2009, he reiterated support for those standards. At the same time, an economic crisis hit the American automobile industry, undermining its financial and organizational ability to fight the increases. As the economic health of the domestic automobile industry slowly improved, the Obama administration felt freer to speed up the timetable for implementing those standards. As a result, the EPA issued regulations, first in 2010 and again in 2012, that require automobile manufacturers to produce vehicles that get 54.5 miles per gallon by 2025 (see Figure 8.2).[58] To help understand and evaluate CAFE standards for automobiles, the EPA developed a separate website to inform consumers called CAFE PIC; this website not only helps aid consumers but also keeps a public record of which automobile manufacturers are complying with the standards.

The regulatory process is one gateway for interest groups to offer comments directly to the federal government on public policy proposals. The case of CAFE standards is one example of how time and circumstances almost always shift the playing field and the balance of power in the interest group arena.

The frustrating aspect of the role that interest groups play in a democracy is that groups contesting a single issue frequently talk over each other, not with each other. It is often left to members of Congress and the executive branch to balance their own responses to interest group requests and still maintain responsiveness to constituents and the nation at large. Over

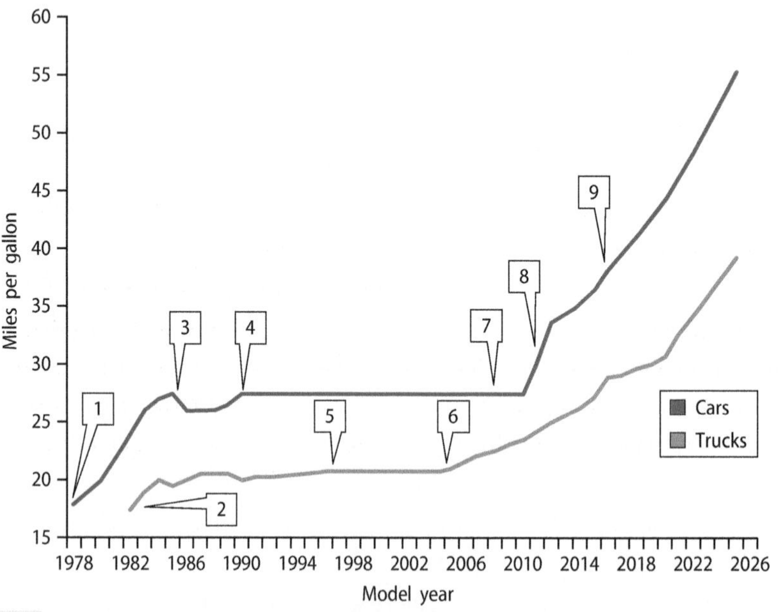

FIGURE 8.2 Fuel Economy Standards

Over time, the government has steadily increased the standards for fuel economy for cars and trucks. The numbered boxes indicate times when the federal government has taken action to regulate fuel economy.

Source: Center for Climate and Energy Solutions, "Federal Vehicle Standards," accessed March 16, 2014, http://www.c2es.org/federal/executive/vehicle-standards#timeline.

time, most interest groups experience wins and losses in the policy system; the necessary condition for a democracy is that every group has a chance to make its case.

Open or Closed Routes of Influence

Although interests may ultimately balance each other, and changing conditions may ultimately level the playing field, the fact that a tightly knit group of specialists often controls policy areas raises concern about fairness both inside and outside interest group organizations. For example, lobbyists work to build good relationships with legislators and officials in the bureaucracy. Given their knowledge of particular policy areas, many of them move in and out of government. Are lobbyists always thinking of their groups' members when they engage in their activities, or are they thinking about their next jobs? Do they constitute an insider group that is ultimately self-serving rather than serving the public?

Essential Knowledge

Interest groups accomplish much of their work by interacting with specific congressional committees and bureaucratic agencies. These alignments are known as iron triangles.

Scholars have long used the phrase **iron triangle** to describe the relationship among interest groups, members of Congress, and federal agencies. In essence, an iron triangle is a network forged by members in three categories that works to seal off access to public policy making. Lobbyists and interest groups want to maximize their benefits from federal programs; members of Congress want to maximize their power to shape the programs; and federal bureaucrats want to maximize their longevity as administrators of these programs.

iron triangle: *Insular and closed relationship among interest groups, members of Congress, and federal agencies.*

Critics of the influence of interest groups in a democracy often describe iron triangles as unbreakable and argue that they contribute to the inefficiency of the federal government because they sustain programs that should be eliminated or enlarge programs beyond what is necessary to meet their intended purposes. The criticism is not limited to scholars. In his farewell address in 1961, President Dwight D. Eisenhower (1953–61) warned of what he called the military–industrial complex, a self-serving interconnection among branches of the U.S. military, the defense manufacturing industry, and federal agencies overseeing scientific research. Eisenhower was greatly concerned that the defense industry had undue influence that would be used to unnecessarily increase spending on defense programs. "This conjunction of an immense military establishment and a large arms industry is new in the American experience," he said. "The total influence—economic, political, even spiritual—is felt in every city, every State house, every office of the Federal government. We recognize the imperative need for this development. Yet we must not fail to comprehend its grave implications. Our toil, resources, and livelihood are all involved; so is the very structure of our society."[59] President Eisenhower's stature as a decorated general who commanded U.S. and Allied forces in World War II gave him credibility on the issue of defense spending, and his depiction of the military–industrial complex as a type of iron triangle drew a great deal of notice. Even today, efforts by the Secretary of Defense to reduce the size of the armed forces and eliminate military equipment are met with stiff resistance by the members of the iron triangle that Eisenhower identified more than fifty years ago.[60] Moreover, today the term *iron triangle* is applied to a wide range of issue areas, including health care and prescription drugs (see Figure 8.3).

Essential Knowledge

Another metaphor to describe the relationship between interest groups and the government is the term "issue network." It can include a wider variety of actors (such as think tanks, media personalities, etc.) and is more open.

Yet the well-known interest group scholar Hugh Heclo claims that the interconnection of interest groups and the government is more benign, suggesting that the term **issue networks** is better than *iron triangle* to describe the relationship.[61] Heclo argues that interest groups, members of Congress, and bureaucrats all share information constantly, and that their interactions are open and transparent, not closed. Heclo wrote thirty years ago, before the advent of the 24-7 news cycle, Twitter messaging, and other telecommunications

issue network: *View of the relationship among interest groups, members of Congress, and federal agencies as more fluid, open, and transparent than that described by the term* iron triangle.

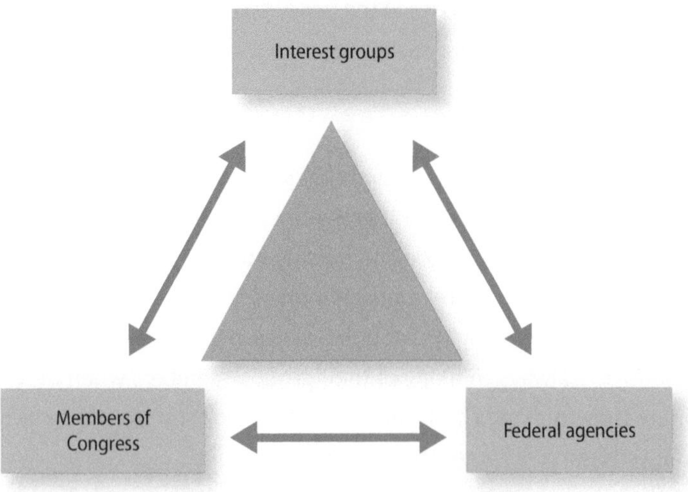

FIGURE 8.3 Iron Triangle

The *iron triangle* is a policymaking structure that includes congressional committees, federal agencies, and interest groups.

innovations, so it stands to reason that it is harder than ever for self-serving interconnections to go unnoticed. In addition, citizens' watchdog groups, such as Common Cause, and policy institutes, such as the Center for Responsive Politics, monitor interest group influence on government activities and policies. When these groups find evidence of wrongdoing in government, they loudly blow a whistle by issuing reports and holding press conferences to inform the media and the general public.

What remains true is that lobbyists, members of Congress and their staffs, and members of the executive branch do pass through what scholars describe as a revolving door of paid positions in one another's organizations, with knowledge and experience on a specific issue as the valued commodity. The term **revolving door** has a negative connotation, suggesting that an iron triangle of influence consists of the same set of people moving from one branch of government to another and then to the private sector. The image of a revolving door also suggests that the system does not stop to include outsiders with new perspectives; in other words, it can act as a gate against wider political participation.

revolving door: *Movement of members of Congress, lobbyists, and executive branch employees into paid positions in each other's organizations.*

Take, for example, Jim DeMint, a Republican from South Carolina who resigned in January 2013, early in his second term as a U.S. Senator, to become head of the Heritage Foundation, a conservative think tank. DeMint had been a leader among the conservative Republicans in the Senate, especially those affiliated with the Tea Party, and political observers were surprised to see him leave that position of power in the Senate. However, in his new position DeMint's salary is close to $1 million per year, compared to his previous salary of $174,000. DeMint used his position at the Heritage Foundation to more actively promote conservative policies on two fronts. First, he focused the efforts of the Heritage Foundation on opposing the Affordable Care Act. Second, he increased the role of the political arm, known as Heritage Action, by raising money for it and using it to support political candidates who oppose the Affordable Care Act.[62] DeMint represents a new version of the revolving door where elected officials who are closely tied to ideological agendas leave their

POLITICAL ANALYTICS

Top National Associations in the United States

THOUSANDS OF INTEREST GROUPS in the United States try to influence public policy at all levels of government. Interest groups amplify the voice of like-minded citizens to policy makers in Congress, in state legislatures, and at local levels. There is a wide variety of interest groups, each representing the views of citizens and groups in the electoral, legislative, judicial, and executive arenas of government.

Figure 8.4 shows two ways of looking at important resources interest groups have in their attempts to affect public policy to benefit their members: their membership size and their budget. Interest groups provide information to their members about the activities of their elected officials. They may also call on their membership to contact their representatives to express their views. The larger the membership, the more influence the group may enjoy. Likewise, associations with large budgets may be able to direct large-scale efforts to keep up with government activity and support candidates more effectively than those with fewer resources. Notice the variety of associations and the interests they represent, as well as the overlap between the two categories of associations shown.

Thinking Critically

1. Which of the associations do you think are most effective at lobbying members of Congress?
2. The associations in the graphic are the largest by membership and by budget. What other characteristics might be important for associations?

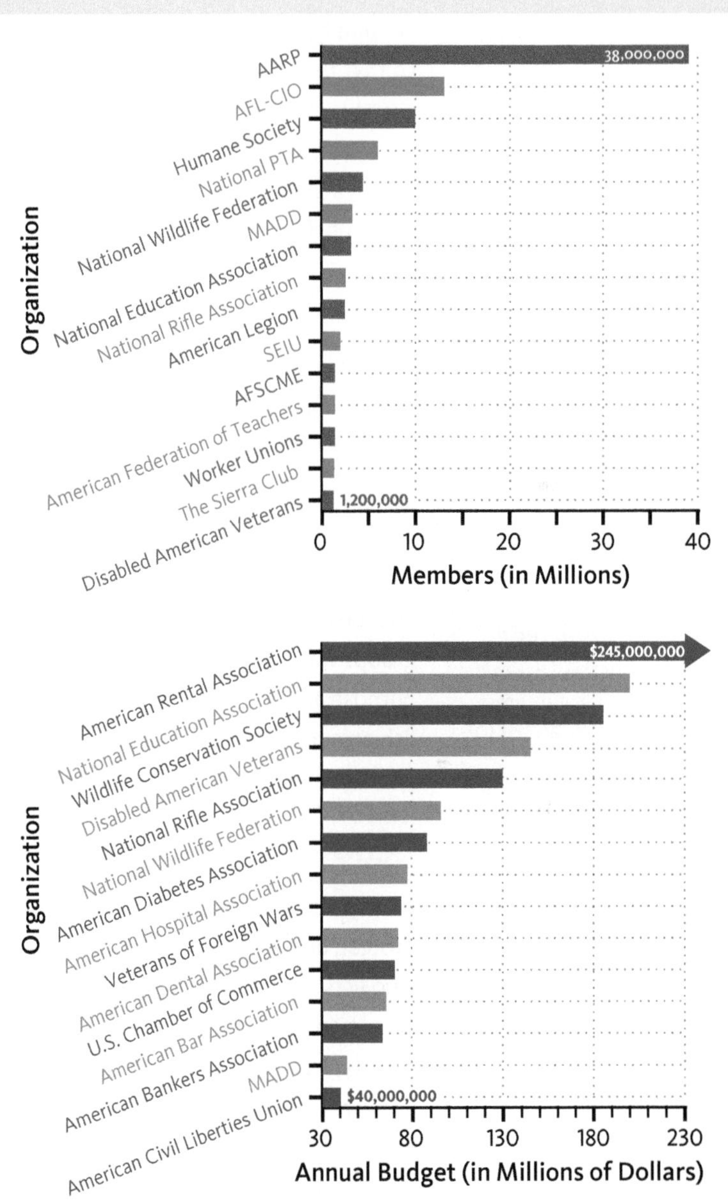

FIGURE 8.4 Selected Top Interest Groups by Membership and Budget, 2015

Sources: Encyclopedia of Associations, National Organizations of the U.S. 54th edition, 2015, Gale Publishing; Open Secrets: Influence and Lobbying. The Center for Responsive Politics, http://www.opensecrets.org/influence/, accessed March 10, 2016.

office to head organizations that seek to influence public policy at the grassroots level as well as inside the Beltway—and earn a much higher salary in the process.

Sometimes that can be very successful for the organization that hires former members of Congress; however, in the case of DeMint, it has also produced conflict at times. In 2015, Republican members of Congress complained about Heritage Action's "scorecard," which assigns ratings to members based on a series of roll call votes that they take to advance the group's ideas, saying that it was not realistic and could damage their electoral prospects. DeMint had to ensure that the members viewed the two parts of his organization separately so that the Heritage Foundation could maintain its influence over policy making.[63]

It is also essential to remember that not all relationships among lobbyists, members of Congress, and federal officials are tainted or suspicious. Congress and the federal bureaucracy each have elaborate rules governing their behavior with respect to interest groups and lobbyists, and most members and bureaucrats follow them closely.

8.5 Characteristics of Successful Interest Groups

Assess what makes an interest group successful

Essential Knowledge

A variety of factors impact the effectiveness of interest groups: resources, access to politics, and free riders.

The measure of a successful interest group is how well it accomplishes its goals. Some groups want to stay in existence forever, but other groups form temporarily for a specific purpose and disband after they accomplish their goal. For the groups that want to establish an enduring voice in a democracy, success can be measured in four ways: leadership accountability, membership outreach, financial stability, and public influence.

Leadership Accountability

As anyone who has tried to get a group of students together to perform a task, lodge a protest, or plan an event knows, coordination can be difficult. It typically takes an individual who acts as an interest group entrepreneur to organize citizens into a formal group that agrees on a united purpose. In return for organizing the group, the interest group entrepreneur typically takes a leadership role in directing the group's activities. For example, in 1985 Grover Norquist founded the group Americans for Tax Reform, which is dedicated to lowering taxes, and he has remained its leader and public voice ever since.[64]

Benefits that come from being a group leader range from salary as a paid staff member to prestige and influence over the group's goals and strategies. The interest group scholar Robert Salisbury calls the trade-off between the work and the benefits of being a leader the "exchange theory of interest groups," and he argues that no one would rationally expend the energy and time to start a group if he or she could not take a prominent role in directing it.[65] Members are willing to pay their group leaders and give them power in the group in return for accomplishing the group's collective goals.

Transparency about the group's political and financial activities in pursuit of its goals is an important democratic element of an interest group; without it, there is a risk that the leaders could act in ways that do not properly serve the members. However, leaders do sometimes act in their own self-interest (by misusing group finances, for example), or they may take the group in an ideological direction that does not mirror the majority opinion in the group. More than a hundred years ago, Robert Michels coined the phrase **iron law of oligarchy** to describe this behavior. When leaders take such actions at the expense of rank-and-file members, the internal governance of the interest group breaks down. Flaws in interest group management can be a major problem for a democracy if citizens join a group with the expectation that the group will accurately represent their opinions and interests, and it does not.

iron law of oligarchy: *Theory that leaders in any organization eventually behave in their own self-interest, even at the expense of rank-and-file members; the larger the organization, the greater the likelihood that the leader will behave this way.*

Members must be able to register satisfaction or dissatisfaction with the group's leadership. The simplest way to do that is to leave the group, but in doing so, the individual may lose the benefits that the group provides. Using the group's website, members can convey their opinions to the leadership, but members cannot really control the group's actions, especially if the group is large. Citizens have a right to expect accountability from interest group leaders, and interest groups that want to sustain themselves understand that their membership needs to remain satisfied over time.

Membership Stability

Whether a group is small or large, attracting members and keeping them over time are essential to its survival. People join groups because they share similar interests or political viewpoints or because they want to protect their economic livelihoods. For the leaders of groups, the challenge is to find the right balance between membership size and the organization's purpose. Having too many members may create internal disagreements about policy goals, but having too few may weaken the group's ability to exert influence in the policy system.

Selective Benefits. One way to attract and keep members is to provide **selective benefits** exclusive for members.[66] These can include *material benefits*, such as direct monetary benefits from policies that the group advocates, discounts on travel or prescriptions, and even monthly magazines. *Solidary benefits* are less tangible. They range from the simple pleasure of being surrounded by people with similar interests and perspectives to the networking benefits of interacting with people who share professional or personal concerns. *Expressive benefits* are the least tangible in that they consist of having a specific opinion expressed in the larger social or political sphere. When individuals join a group, they know that their viewpoint is being actively represented in the policy system, and that knowledge can be gratifying all by itself.

selective benefits: *Benefits offered exclusively to members of an interest group.*

The Free Rider Problem. Many of the benefits that large interest groups seek on behalf of their members—clean air by the Sierra Club or gun rights by the NRA—are **public goods**. In other words, they are available to all people, whether they have contributed toward the provision of that good or not. Public goods are typically the spillover effects of public policies that affect all citizens. If a group lobbies for public goods or collective benefits that are so widespread that members and nonmembers alike receive them, incentives to join the group disappear. Olson addressed this collective action dilemma, calling it the **free rider problem**.[67] Why pay to join a group if one can get the benefits for free? Why join if the group is so large that it does not actually need an additional member?

public goods: *Goods or benefits provided by government from which everyone benefits and from which no one can be excluded.*

free rider problem: *Problem faced by interest groups when a collective benefit they provide is so widespread and diffuse that members and nonmembers alike receive it, reducing the incentive for joining the group.*

The Economic and Political Change Problem. Changes in the economy and the political environment can also have a negative impact on a group's membership stability.

The decline of membership size of the UAW discussed earlier is an example of what can happen to union membership when an industry experiences job losses. From a political standpoint, groups can "succeed" their way out of existence but then reemerge when policies turn against their cause. For example, after the passage of McCain-Feingold campaign finance reform (noted earlier), Common Cause lost some influence because it had succeeded in lobbying Congress to address its core issue of the role of money in campaigns.

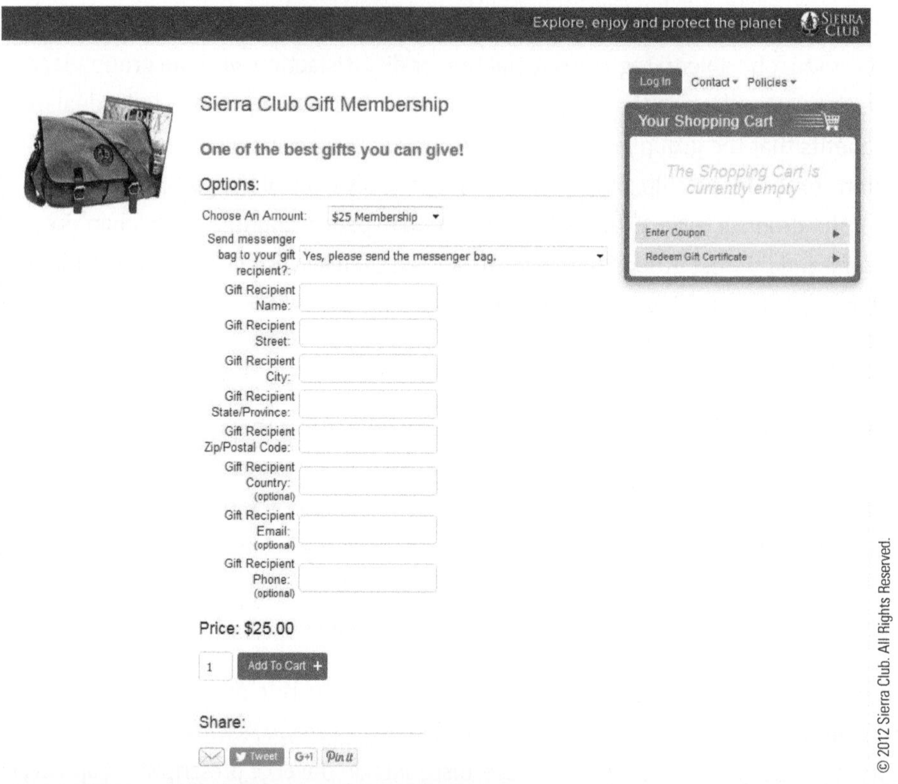

IMAGES 8.11 AND 8.12 Interest groups offer tangible benefits to individuals to encourage them to join. Messenger bags and totes with the organization's name also provide free advertising.

However, within a decade, the Supreme Court drastically weakened the regulation of money in campaigns with its rulings against core provisions of the legislation. In response, Common Cause increased its visibility in leading the fights to reverse the Supreme Court decisions and to reinstate limitations on the donation and use of money in campaigns.

Concern for survival in an increasingly crowded interest group society can sometimes bring an interest group into conflict with its core principles. Groups can try to counteract declining membership by creating new issues to rally members around or by portraying serious threats to the issues most important to members, although such actions can be criticized as "disinformation campaigns."

Financial Stability

Together with keeping a membership base, a group must also maintain financial stability. Groups of all types require money to sustain their staffing, lobbying, and information distribution. The Internet has made fundraising easier because it allows groups to solicit money without incurring costs for printed advertising, mailers, and postage. Most organizations also rely on dues. Grassroots groups that seek to attract as many members as possible keep their dues relatively modest. For example, in 2016 the NRA raised its annual dues from $35 to $40.

Interest groups also achieve financial stability by creating not-for-profit businesses within the organization. AARP is a classic example of a large interest group that wears two hats: a politically powerful lobby on policies that affect senior citizens and a multimillion-dollar business that provides health insurance, life insurance, and discounts on movies, travel, and prescriptions to members, who must be at least 50 years old to join. A basic AARP membership costs only $16 a year, and it provides the opportunity to purchase the other services at discounted rates. In turn, AARP receives payments from businesses that it contracts with to provide services to its members. AARP is among the most successful large-scale interest groups in American history; in 2015, it claimed a membership of nearly 38 million.[68]

The financial challenge for many groups is to keep their operating costs in line with their expected income. For the very largest interest groups, such as AARP, a single year's operating budget can be more than one billion dollars; in 2015 the group took in $1.54 billion and spent $1.49 billion.[69] For most other groups, the operating budget ranges from thousands to millions of dollars per year. Groups can experience financial difficulty as a result of financial mismanagement by group leaders, or, in some cases, they may simply outlive their usefulness and members cease paying dues. In such cases, they may be forced to scale back their activities and close local chapter offices.

Influence in the Public Sphere

The extent to which an interest group appears to influence public debate is a sign of its success. One indicator of influence is being quoted in the press. Earlier we discussed Club for Growth, a group devoted to lowering taxes. In late 2014 they decided to change their leadership, replacing Chris Chocola with a former Congressman from Indiana, Dave McIntosh, who was known for being an outspoken champion of fiscal conservatism. The group also sought to increase their direct influence over supporting incumbents in Congress who agreed with their positions rather than trying to punish, or threatening to withdraw support from, members who did not support their policy positions. The Club for Growth is responding to competition from other conservatives, namely the billionaire Koch brothers, who have become very strong financial backers of fiscal conservatism as well.[70] For the Club for Growth to maintain its own supporters, it has to demonstrate that it has not lost influence to the Koch brothers and others who advocate for similar policy positions. Groups face constant pressure to signal to members, as well as to the public at large, that they have a significant role in policy formation on the issues about which members are most concerned.

Interest Groups and Democracy

Interest groups are a powerful instrument of democracy because they crystallize the opinions and interests of average citizens and present those views to elected officials during the policy-making process. It was precisely this power to influence policy that Madison feared so much and why he hoped that in a large republic, competition among interest groups would prevent any one of them from gaining too much influence. Interest groups contribute to a democracy by holding the government accountable for its actions, pressuring elected officials to be responsive to their constituents, and serving as a vehicle to equalize the influence of different groups of citizens in the policy process.

A group can channel the power of separate individuals into a single collective voice that is more likely to be heard throughout the policy system. In addition, the very existence of an interest group can keep citizens informed about the direct impact of policy on their lives; with that information, constituents can better hold their elected officials accountable for those policies.

Interest groups engage in several methods to influence economic, social, and foreign policy, including direct lobbying, media campaigns, legal challenges, and grassroots organizing. When interests clash, as in the case of education reform or energy policy, elected officials, bureaucrats, and even the judiciary often act as intermediaries. In Congress, political parties adopt positions that are favored or opposed by specific interest groups and thus create alliances between parties and interest groups. Although there are more interest groups today than ever before, political parties serve as a counterweight to the influence of interest groups. As partisanship has grown stronger in the House, the Senate, and even the White House, members who are asked to choose between an interest group and a political party choose the party. However, given that political parties tend to align very closely with supportive interest groups, members do not have to make that choice very often. To the extent that interest groups can influence politicians to address narrow or exclusive interests to the detriment of what is best for all citizens, they can be viewed as a negative aspect of the U.S. democracy.

Yet interest groups also represent a positive aspect of democracy when they serve to express wide-ranging viewpoints, and they continue to be an effective way of giving voice to citizens' needs and concerns. Interest groups continuously win and lose within the American policy-making system, and they reinvent their lobbying strategies in response to changing political and economic conditions. However, sole reliance on interest groups as a means of citizen participation is dangerous because some groups have more resources—time, money, and membership—than others and consequently win more often. In this way, interest groups can be both gateways and gates to citizen equality and the securing of policy benefits. Ultimately, citizens must hold both their interest group leaders and their elected officials accountable for public policy outcomes.

Political Science Reasoning

Question 1

Practice 1, Practice 4

> The latent causes of faction are thus sown in the nature of man; and we see them everywhere brought into different degrees of activity, according to the different circumstances of civil society. A zeal for different opinions concerning religion, concerning government, and many other points, as well of speculation as of practice; an attachment to different leaders ambitiously contending for pre-eminence and power; or to persons of other descriptions whose fortunes have been interesting to the human passions, have, in turn, divided mankind into parties, inflamed them with mutual animosity, and rendered them much more disposed to vex and oppress each other than to cooperate for their common good.
>
> So strong is this propensity of mankind to fall into mutual animosities, that where no substantial occasion presents itself, the most frivolous and fanciful distinctions have been sufficient to kindle their unfriendly passions and excite their most violent conflicts. But the most common and durable source of factions has been the various and unequal distribution of property. Those who hold and those who are without property have ever formed distinct interests in society. Those who are creditors, and those who are debtors, fall under a like discrimination. A landed interest, a manufacturing interest, a mercantile interest, a moneyed interest, with many lesser interests, grow up of necessity in civilized nations, and divide them into different classes, actuated by different sentiments and views. The regulation of these various and interfering interests forms the principal task of modern legislation, and involves the spirit of party and faction in the necessary and ordinary operations of the government.[1]

1. Citing textual evidence, what is Madison's reasoning for why factions should be regulated?
2. According to Madison, how can interest groups be regulated?
3. What provisions of the Bill of Rights protect interest groups?

Question 2

Practice 1, Practice 4

> It is of great importance in a republic not only to guard the society against the oppression of its rulers, but also to guard one part of the society against the injustice of the other part. Different interests necessarily exist in different classes of citizens. If a majority be united by a common interest, the rights of the minority will be insecure. There are but two methods of providing against this evil: the

[1]James Madison, *Federalist* 10.

one by creating a will in the community independent of the majority—that is, of the society itself; the other, by comprehending in the society so many separate descriptions of citizens as will render an unjust combination of a majority of the whole very improbable, if not impracticable. The first method prevails in all governments possessing an hereditary or self-appointed authority. This, at best, is but a precarious security because a power independent of the society may as well espouse the unjust views of the major, as the rightful interests of the minor party, and may possibly be turned against both parties. The second method will be exemplified in the federal republic of the United States. Whilst all authority in it will be derived from and dependent on the society, the society itself will be broken into so many parts, interests, and classes of citizens, that the rights of individuals, or of the minority, will be in little danger from interested combinations of the majority. In a free government the security for civil rights must be the same as that for religious rights. It consists in the one case in the multiplicity of interests, and in the other in the multiplicity of sects. The degree of security in both cases will depend on the number of interests and sects; and this may be presumed to depend on the extent of country and number of people comprehended under the same government. This view of the subject must particularly recommend a proper federal system to all the sincere and considerate friends of republican government, since it shows that in exact proportion as the territory of the union may be formed into more circumscribed confederacies, or States oppressive combinations of a majority will be facilitated: the best security, under the republican forms, for the rights of every class of citizens, will be diminished: and consequently the stability and independence of some member of the government, the only other security, must be proportionately increased.[2]

1. How does federalism address the issues brought on by factions?
2. What are the implications of the increased concentrations of power described in Chapter 3, Federalism?

---

[2]James Madison, *Federalist* 51.

Focus on AP® Success

8 Interest Groups

Must Know: Key Concepts

- Interest Group
- Linkage Institution
- Iron Triangle
- Issue Network
- Free Rider
- Political Action Committees
- Single-issue Group
- Social Movement

Thinking Politically

Concept Application

Both iron triangles and issue networks are involved in the policy-making process. They are both composed of interest groups and other political actors. Explain the differences between iron triangles and issue networks.

Concept Application

Interest groups attempt to exert influence over policy makers in both Congress and the bureaucracy. Explain why members of Congress and bureaucrats are receptive to the influence of lobbyists.

Concept Application

There are various models of American democracy: participatory democracy, pluralist democracy, and elitist democracy. Explain how the activities of interest groups exemplify one of these models.

Concept Application

Interest groups that attempt to secure public policies that could be defined as public goods are frequently plagued by the free rider problem. Explain how interest groups attempt to overcome this problem.

Concept Application

One of the frequent criticisms of interest groups is that they tend to only represent the views of their members rather than the public interest. This can be particularly problematic when a small group gains an inordinate amount of influence. What constitutional methods exist to limit interest group influence?

But politicians who talk about failed policies are just blowing smoke. Government policies succeed in doing exactly what they are supposed to do: channeling resources bilked from the general public to politically organized and influential interest groups.

— Robert Higgs

Concept Application

What is the perspective of the above author? To what extent would the author agree with the Supreme Court's decision in *Citizens United v. Federal Election Commission*?

Understanding Learning Objectives with Key Concepts

PMI – 5.E Explain the benefits and potential problems of interest-group influence on elections and policy making.

- Interest groups, regardless of whether they represent either narrow or broad interests, engage in a range of activities. Interest groups provide information to both citizens and government officials. They draft legislation that can be introduced in Congress by supportive members of Congress. They also apply political pressure to policy makers by organizing the members of the interest group.

- Frequently, interest also work in political parties as part of the coalition of groups that make up each party. Additionally, they form relationships with congressional committees and bureaucratic agencies known as iron triangles. They also partner with other interest groups and political actors (like think tanks, congressional staffers, media elites, bureaucrats and other officials, etc.) in what are called issue networks. Issue networks tend to be more free flowing than iron triangles and are typically formed around a specific issue for a short time, whereas iron triangles tend to be permanent.

PMI – 5.F Explain how variation in types and resources of interest groups affects their ability to influence elections and policy making.

- The political impact of an interest group can be caused by a range of factors including the amount of resources the group has access to, the ability of the group to secure access to policy makers, and the free rider problem. For example, smaller groups that have access to a large sum of money may focus on lobbying Congress and the bureaucracy. Groups that have been marginalized in society may seek to achieve their goals through litigation in the less political judiciary rather than trying to influence elected members of Congress.

PMI – 5.G Explain how various political actors influence public policy outcomes.

- Policymaking can be influenced by single-issue groups (such as the NRA), ideological movements and social movements (such as the conservative movements of the 1980s and the civil rights movement), and protest movements (such as the antiwar movement of the 1960s).

- Political actors compete with each other to influence policy. These actors include interest groups, administrative agencies including the defense department, as well as social movements. The impact of the actors varies.

- Periodically in the United States there is a "critical election." This election marks realignment in the voting behavior of various interests. These realignments are often accompanied by a change in the composition of the major parties.

Making Connections

Interest groups engage in a practice called "electioneering," which means they are engaged in activities that are designed to influence elections. They do not nominate candidates but do engage in activities such as voter mobilization and give campaign contributions. Be sure to connect the information in this chapter with Chapter 10, Elections and Campaigns and Chapter 11, Voting and Participation.

Special interest groups are involved in the policy making process in both Congress and bureaucratic agencies. When studying Chapter 12, Congress and Chapter 14, The Bureaucracy, pay attention to the role of special interest groups.

The civil rights movement and women's rights movement (along with their accompanying interest groups), as illustrated in Chapter 5, Civil Rights, serve as case studies of how social movements and interest groups obtain their goals. Review the methods these groups used to achieve their policy goals.

Students frequently confuse the roles of political parties and interest groups. When studying Chapter 9, Political Parties, be sure to contrast the function of political parties with interest groups.

While not specifically mentioned in the Constitution, interest groups and their activities are constitutionally protected. Review Chapter 4, Civil Liberties and be sure you are able to explain how these groups are protected.

Going Deeper: *Citizens United v. Federal Election Commission*

In 2002, Congress passed the Bipartisan Campaign Reform Act, commonly referred to as the McCain-Feingold Act. This piece of legislation sought to diminish the impact of money in politics. Corporations and labor unions are not allowed to take money from their general funds and make direct disbursements to political candidates.

To get around the limitation, some corporations were making what were known as issue advocacy ads or officially "electioneering communications." These advertisements mentioned the candidates by name and, under the guise of providing information to voters, acted as essentially campaign ads. Under McCain-Feingold these advertisements, if paid for by a corporation (including most interest groups), would be prohibited 30 days before a primary election and 60 days before a general election. Prohibited from being run right before an election, these advertisements would be essentially meaningless.

The legislation also prohibited the use of so called soft money by political parties. Soft money was money that was spent by party committees for the benefit of a candidate. To be legal, soft money expenditures could not be coordinated with the candidate.

Finally, the legislation required that candidates make a statement on their advertisements stating their name and that they approved of the advertisement. This is commonly referred to as the "stand by your ad" rule.

The prohibition on issue advocacy advertisements was challenged in the case of *Citizens United v. Federal Election Commission*. In its decision, the Court overturned the restriction on advocacy advertisements by corporations. Previously, the Court declared that how a person spends his or her money for political purposes is a form of political speech protected by the First Amendment. Further, as corporations have been legally considered "people," they are now also entitled to have their political expression protected.

The so called soft money that once flowed through parties has now been changed to other independent expenditure committees such as Super PACs and 527s. This has decreased the strength and importance of political parties and strengthened the role and power of interest groups. The only lasting impact of McCain-Feingold has been the "stand by your ad" provision.

9 Political Parties

AP® Learning Objectives

MPA – 3.C Explain the roles that individual choice and state laws play in voter turnout in elections.

PMI – 5.A Describe linkage institutions.

PMI – 5.B Explain the function and impact of political parties on the electorate and government.

PMI – 5.C Explain why and how political parties change and adapt.

PMI – 5.D Explain how structural barriers impact third-party and independent-candidate success.

PRD – 2.A Explain how the different processes work in a U.S. presidential election.

Performance Tasks

Upon the completion of this chapter, you must be able to do the following:

- Explain how political parties connect citizens with the government.
- Explain how and why the composition of each of the two major parties has changed.
- Explain how parties have adapted to changes in campaign laws, candidate-centered campaigns, and changes in communication technology.
- Explain why third parties and independent candidates seldom enjoy electoral success.
- Explain why various demographic groups align with each party and tend to support that party's candidates.
- Explain how the following operate in the U.S. electoral system: caucuses, conventions, (open and closed), primary elections, and general elections (presidential and midterm).

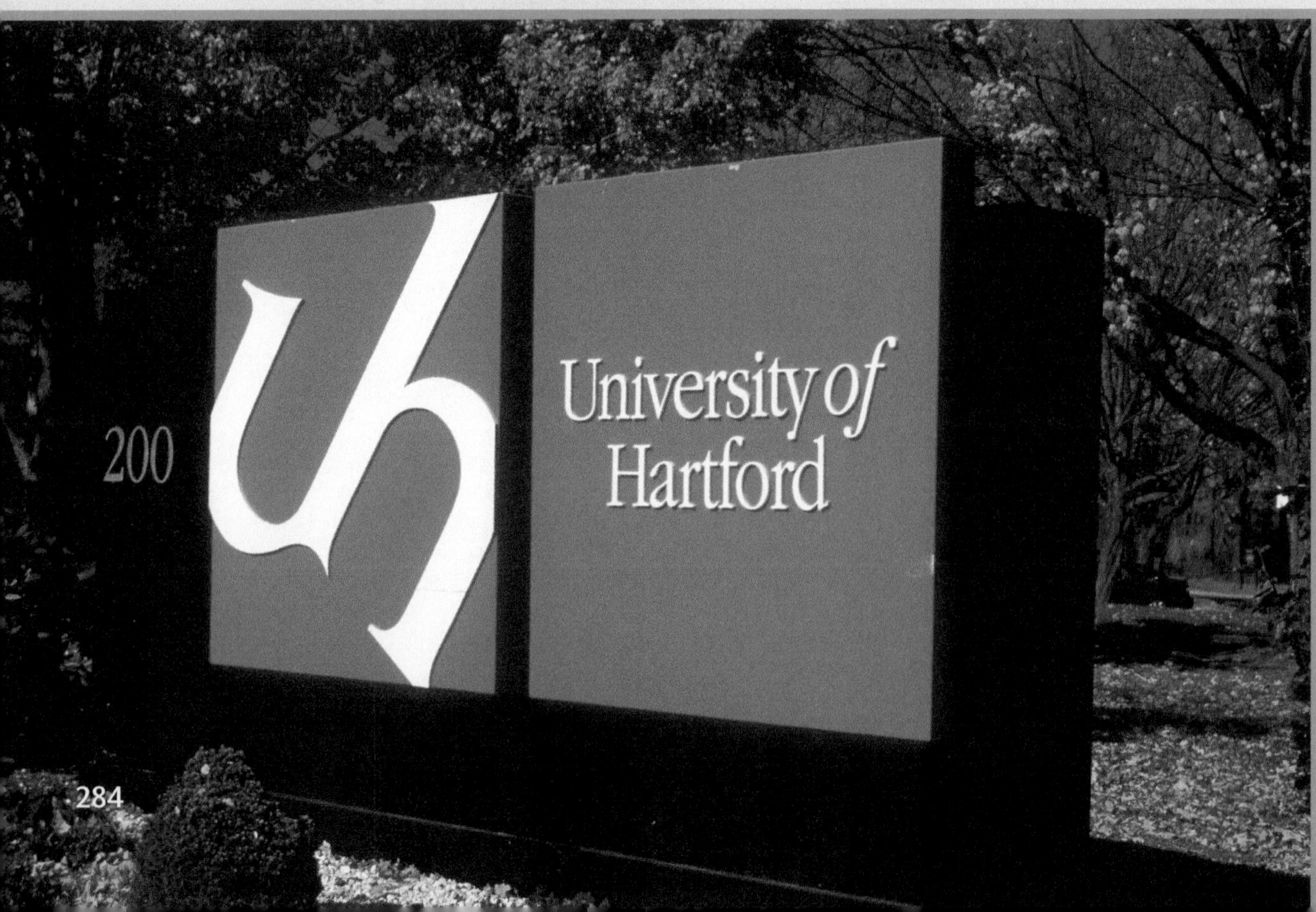

FOTOSEARCH RM/AGE Fotostock

“The America I know is great—not because government made it great but because ordinary citizens like me, like my father and like you are given the opportunity every day to do extraordinary things.”

MIA LOVE
University of Hartford

AP Photo/Rick Bowmer

Ludmya “Mia” Love is the newest member of the House of Representatives from the state of Utah. Congresswoman Love won the Fourth District of Utah in 2014, defeating Democrat Doug Owens in an open seat election. With that victory, Love became the first African American Republican to serve in the House of Representatives and the first African American to be elected to Congress from Utah. This was Love’s second attempt at winning the Fourth District seat, which was created after the 2010 census when Utah was allocated an additional congressional district. In her first run against incumbent and Democrat Jim Matheson, she fell short by less than 800 votes. In the open seat contest in 2012 she won with 50 percent of the vote.

Mia Love is the daughter of Haitian immigrants born in Brooklyn, New York. Her parents fled Haiti and the repressive regime of François “Papa Doc” Duvalier. Love (then Bourdeau) grew up in Connecticut, where her father worked multiple jobs so she could attend and graduate from the University of Hartford with a degree in fine arts. When she began college, her father admonished her, “Mia, your mother and I never took a handout. You will not be a burden on society. You will give back.” It would not take long for Mia Love to discover how to give back.

Love grew up Roman Catholic but converted to the Church of Jesus Christ of Latter-day Saints soon after graduation in 1997. Mia Love’s journey to Congress did not begin with a passion for politics. After graduation, she worked as a flight attendant with Continental Airlines and moved to Utah. There she met her future husband, Jason Love. It was in Saratoga Springs, Utah, and with the encouragement of her family, that Mia Love took up the challenge of her father to “give back.”

As a parent and homeowner, Mia Love became active in neighborhood issues. Specifically, she led the “War of the Midges,” demanding that developers take greater efforts to control bug infestations in her neighborhood. This gateway into activism led Love to become involved in the Republican Party through the work of her husband’s family. She found that the values of the party resonated with the values imparted to her by her parents: “All of the things my parents were teaching me, it kind of fit [the Republican philosophy]. It started clicking, so even though I knew very early on I was Republican, I started actively getting engaged after I met my husband.” Her foray into local politics continued when she sought a seat on the city council. As she put it, “I guess really the only way to make things happen is to be part of the decision making.” Her first campaign was in 2003 and she served on the city council for two terms before seeking and winning the mayoral seat in 2010. As mayor of Saratoga Springs, Mia Love’s political profile rose significantly. Republicans in Utah and elsewhere took notice of the rising star in Utah politics. She was introduced to the nation at the 2012 Republican National Convention, where fellow Utahan Mitt Romney was formally nominated for the presidency.

Upon beginning her term in the House of Representatives, Mia Love was assigned to the Financial Services Committee. Love hit the ground running and in her first year, she introduced five bills and cosponsored over a hundred, ranging from reducing the cost of higher education to a cosponsored Jobs in America bill with Democrat Kyrsten Sinema (D-AZ; profiled in Chapter 10, Elections and Campaigns). Mia Love’s political views are conservative. She is a so-called Tea Party conservative (discussed later in this chapter). Love advocates the repeal of the Affordable Care Act, is a proponent of a balanced federal budget, is pro-life, and supports limited government.[1]

Mia Love found a way to “give back” through political participation and becoming, as she said, a decision maker. The Republican Party provides her with an avenue to channel her political convictions but, as her cosponsorship of legislation demonstrates, Love is not tied to giving back to just some in her community but to all of her constituents. Political parties, as you will read, attempt to aggregate the views of voters and try to be inclusive in those efforts. The move to inclusiveness is strategic in regards to winning elections, a primary focus of political parties, but also serves as a gateway for those, like Mia Love, seeking ways to give back.

9.1 The Role of Political Parties in American Democracy

Outline how political parties evolved in American politics

Essential Knowledge

Political parties function as a linkage institution. That is to say they connect citizens with the policy-making institutions (Congress, president, bureaucracy, judiciary). Parties do this by providing information to citizens and facilitating citizen involvement in the political process. Parties also represent citizen preferences to policy makers.

A democratic government must be responsive to its citizens, and for government to be equally responsive, every citizen must have an equal opportunity to influence it. But mobilizing the more than 319 million people in the United States to take an active role in monitoring their government is a truly momentous challenge. In the United States, political parties fill an essential need by shaping the choices that voters face in elections, which serve as the key mechanism by which voters hold their government accountable. With so many public offices to fill, voters need some sort of road map to compare candidates and make the choices that will serve their best interests. The potential danger of relying on parties to shape these choices is that parties become interested only in winning office, not in serving the interests of the people. It takes action and vigilance on the part of voters to ensure that parties do not go in this direction.

In this section, we look at the role that parties play in the American democratic system. Specifically at the way they organize the electorate, shape the elections that determine whether their candidates win office, and guide the actions of elected officials.

What Are Political Parties?

political parties: *Broad coalitions of interests organized to win elections in order to enact a commonly supported set of public policies.*

party platform: *Document that lays out a party's core beliefs and policy proposals for each presidential election.*

A **political party** is a group of individuals who join together to choose candidates for elected office—whether by informal group voting or a formal nominating process. These candidates agree to abide by the **party platform**, a document that lays out the party's core beliefs and policy proposals. Parties operate through national, state, and county committees; members include party activists, citizen volunteers, and elected officials. A party's main purpose is to win elections in order to control governmental power and implement its policies; this fundamental goal distinguishes parties from interest groups, who also seek to influence electoral outcomes but do not formally run candidates for office.

At the national level, the party issues its platform during presidential election years. In their 2016 platforms, for example, the Republican Party (www.gop.org) and the Democratic Party (www.dnc.org) stated their positions on national security, health care, energy policy, the environment, and taxes. These platforms not only define the positions of the presidential and vice presidential candidates but also serve as a general guide to the policy positions of all the candidates running under the party label. From time to time, individual candidates may disagree with elements of the party's platform, but, in general, candidates who choose to run under a party label are defined by it. Using party labels as a shortcut for the party platform, voters can hold the elected officials accountable for their policy successes and blame them for policy failures.

Citizens tend to vote for one party over the other in somewhat predictable patterns. Classic political scientists, such as V. O. Key Jr., use the term *party in the electorate* to describe the general patterns of voters' party identification and their behavior on Election

Day. A main goal of any political party is to maximize party affiliation among voters so that it translates into a solid majority of the party in the electorate, which can in turn translate to a solid majority of the *party in government*. To accomplish this goal, the *party as an organization* is created, with internal structures that guide how the party functions.[2] The modern American political party is multilevel, with committees at the federal, state, and local levels.

What Political Parties Do

In this section, we move from theoretical ideas about political parties to what they actually do in the American political system.

Essential Knowledge

Political parties perform a range of functions in the United States, including recruiting and training candidates, providing campaign support services, fund-raising, proving information to voters, and issuing party platforms.

Parties in the Electorate. Parties offer several layers of opportunity for political participation. Most simply, a person can claim to be a member of a party by stating that he or she identifies with it, for example, by saying "I am a Republican." That statement is an acknowledgment of party identification—an attachment or allegiance to a political party. Voters identify with parties for several reasons. The simplest is the belief that the policies put forth by one party will serve their interests better than the policies proposed by other parties in the political arena. Another reason to join a party stems from family or social environment, in which being a member of a party is similar to other personal characteristics. As Chapter 6, Public Opinion, explains, many young people adopt the party identification of their parents. Although parties always ask for contributions, there are no membership fees. For this reason, parties provide the broadest and most open gateway to participation in American politics.

A more formal step of party identification is stating party affiliation when registering to vote. Voter registration rules vary by state, but they typically require a citizen to show proof of identity and address to an official government office. In some places, voters can register by mail or when they get their driver's licenses, but in others, they must fill out the forms in person at a local board of elections.

At the next level of participation, voters can become active in the party at the town, county, state, and federal level. Parties encourage people to volunteer on campaigns at every level—making phone calls to prospective voters, passing out bumper stickers, or maintaining e-mail contact through the campaign website. Of course, political parties expect their members to vote on Election Day and to bring their friends, coworkers, and family members to the polls with them. Parties also rely on supporters to build up the organization and candidates by making financial contributions.

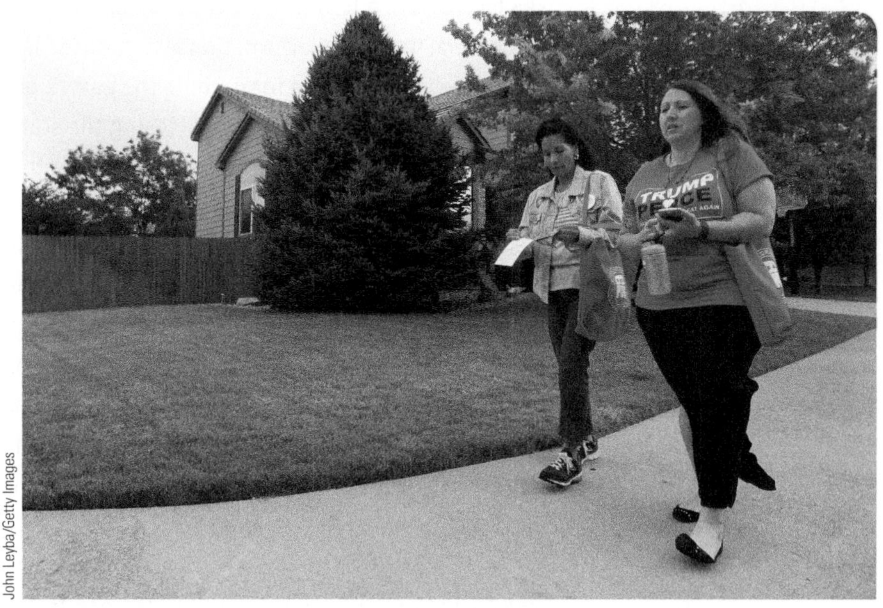

John Leyba/Getty Images

IMAGE 9.1 Get-out-the-vote efforts are a crucial part of local party organization work. Campaigns with organized "ground games" are essential in ensuring their candidates' voters vote in early balloting and on election day. These supporters of the Trump-Pence campaign are canvassing a neighborhood in Thornton, Colorado, a battleground state.

Political parties also serve as a gateway to elected office. Mia Love, for example, got her start in politics through volunteer work with a local party on a campaign, and then she ran for the House of Representatives. Many candidates who seek public office start out by affiliating with a party in college and rise through the ranks of party organizations. Parties also actively recruit individuals in their county, district, or state to run for elected office. Candidate recruitment involves party leaders at all levels trying to identify people who would make good candidates for elected office because they are well known in the community, have personal wealth, or have a professional record that speaks to current issues and would appeal to voters.

party caucus: *Group of party members in a legislature.*

Parties in Government. Parties also serve to organize members of Congress and state legislatures into cohesive groups, known as **party caucuses**, which consistently vote, year after year, for the policies that the parties promise in their platforms. The party in government is made up of the elected officials who share the same party affiliation and work together to accomplish the party's electoral and policy goals. Elected officials often hold positions in party organizations as well. For example, Terry McAuliffe, who served as the chair of the national Democratic Party from 2001 to 2005, was elected governor of Virginia in 2013. Even the president, whose primary responsibility is to govern, is expected to serve as leader of his political party by setting the agenda according to party policy goals. The president is also increasingly expected to engage in political support for party candidates, from campaign appearances to party fundraisers.

Essential Knowledge

The effectiveness of party leadership in the legislature and the national committee is the primary factor in determining the success of parties in translating citizen preferences into public policy.

national committee: *Top level of national political parties; coordinates national presidential campaigns.*

Party Organization. The modern political party is structured as a multilevel organization with units at the federal, state, and local levels. **National committees** are at the top of the party organization, and their members are chosen by each state party organization (see Figure 9.1). A new president can select the national committee chair; in the case of the presidential "out" party, the national committee itself elects the party chair. The national committee is responsible for running the party's presidential nominating convention every four years. Key to that effort is overseeing the states' primary delegate selection process and officially recognizing a state's delegation at the convention.

The main job of the national committee is to do everything possible to elect the party's presidential nominee every four years, which requires strengthening all party organizations from the national down to the local levels. The national committee runs training workshops on party-centered activities, such as candidate recruitment and fundraising. It has to raise money; for example, in the 2016 presidential campaign, the Democratic National Committee raised $986 million, and the Republican National Committee raised $756 million.[3] The national party can spend its money on coordinated expenditures (that is, in cooperation with the presidential campaign), and it can make independent expenditures, which are funds spent separately on general efforts to increase voter turnout for the party's nominee.

Each major political party has a committee dedicated to raising money for incumbent House and Senate members. For the Democrats, it is the Democratic Congressional Campaign Committee and the Democratic Senatorial Campaign Committee; for the Republicans, it is the National Republican Congressional Committee and the National Republican Senatorial Committee. These congressional party committees are also responsible for recruiting qualified challengers to run for seats held by the opposing party and helping to fund their

Essential Knowledge

The organization of American political parties has been affected by a host of factors, including but not limited to campaign finance law, regional realignments, and changes in communication and data-management technology.

Essential Knowledge

Although the role of the party organization is less today than what it has been in the past, parties still engage in a range of voter mobilization activities. The evolution of the candidate-centered campaign has forced the parties to adapt and change. They also provide candidates with services such as data management.

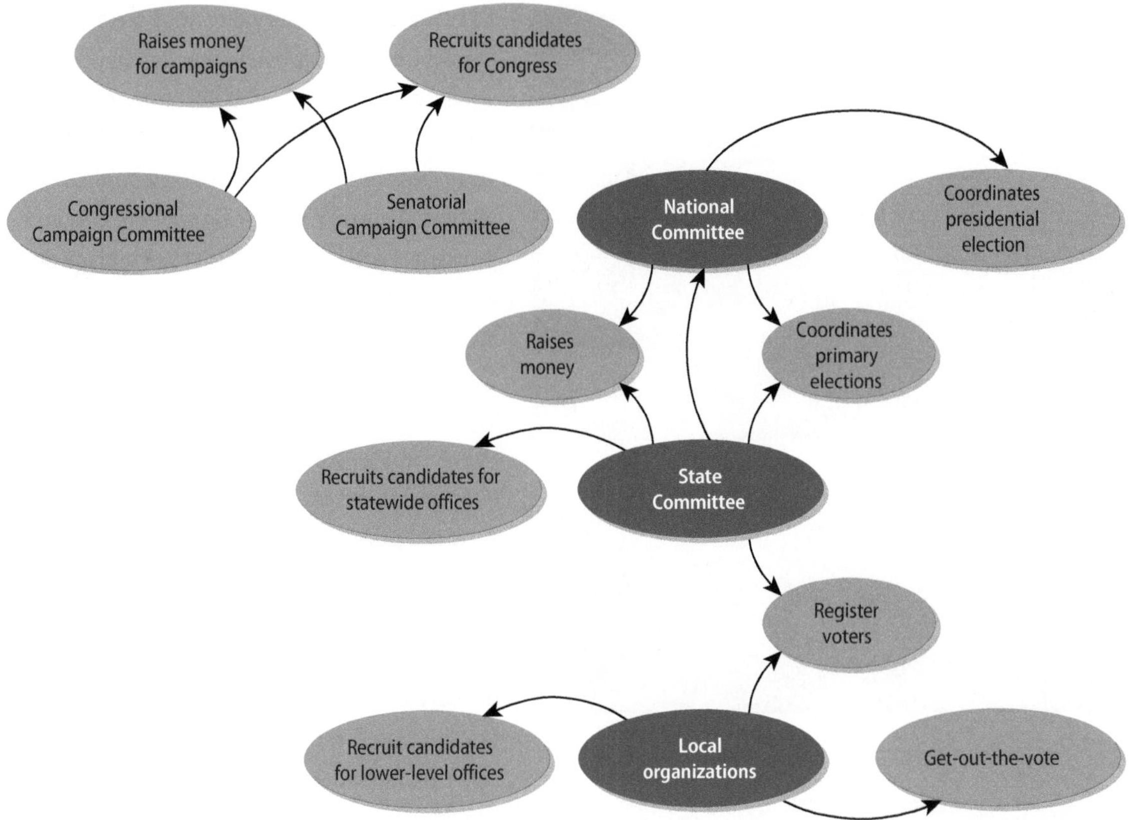

FIGURE 9.1 Party Organization at the National, State, and Local Levels

This figure shows the three levels of political party organizations and their primary functions. American political parties are interconnected and work to elect their candidates to office.

campaigns. Through November 9, 2016, the four congressional party organizations raised approximately $592 million in the 2015–16 cycle.[4]

State political parties are the next level of party organization, and they are regulated by state law, so their responsibilities can vary by state. Typically a political party has a state central committee that tries to elect candidates to statewide office and also works with local organizations to recruit new voters and raise money. As you can see from the websites of the Texas Republican and Democratic parties in Images 9.2 and 9.3, each state party organization displays the structure of the state party organization, provides information about how to become involved with the party, and provides information about the key issues. Each state party organization has its own website, which displays the structure of the state party organization and provides information about how to become involved with the party.

Local party organizations exist at the county, town, and precinct or ward levels. The essential functions of local party organizations are to recruit candidates for lower-level elected offices, register voters, and, most important, ensure that voters get to the polls on Election Day.[5]

> ***Essential Knowledge***
>
> Who parties nominate can have a direct impact of voter turnout. Candidate characteristics such as charisma and experience can increase voter turnout.

The Party Nomination Process

One of the most important functions of parties is to nominate candidates for office and then elect them, a process accomplished in two stages. In elections with more than one candidate seeking the party's nomination, states hold **primary elections**, in which voters determine the party's choice to run in the next stage—the **general election**.

primary election: *Election in which voters select the candidates who will run on the party label in the general election; also called direct primary.*

general election: *Election in which voters choose their elected officials.*

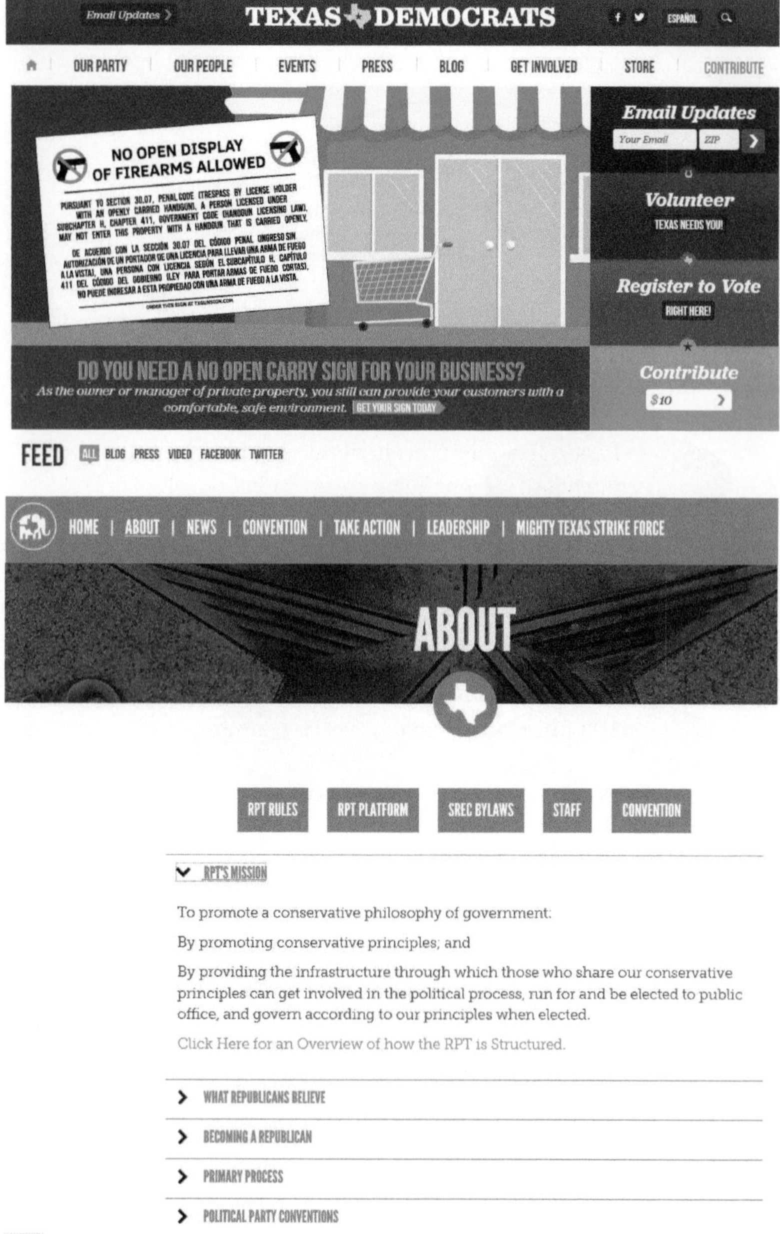

IMAGES 9.2 AND 9.3 State political parties can be powerful in shaping state politics. They help recruit candidates for the state legislatures; after the primaries, they work hard to elect their party's nominees to statewide office. Here the websites of the Texas Democratic Party and the Texas Republican Party announce news, activities, and opinions on issues.

Primaries. Primary elections are a very important way that each voter can have an equal voice in nominating his or her party's candidates for elected office. Although most states rely heavily on the primary, some states authorize nominating conventions and primaries, with the primaries taking place only if the challenger to the party nominee receives a certain percentage of votes at the convention or a certain number of citizen petition signatures.[6]

As noted, state laws regarding elections vary, and there are several types of primaries. A closed primary is one in which voters must affiliate with a party before casting a vote (either by registering before the election or on the day of the primary). A semiclosed primary is one in which party-affiliated voters cast votes in their party's primary, and nonaffiliated voters can choose which party's primary to vote in. In an open primary, voters do not have to affiliate with a party before voting. Instead, they are given **ballots** with each party's list of candidates, and they can choose which ballot to use but are restricted to voting for only one party's nominees. In a blanket primary, voters are given the ballots from all parties and allowed to cast votes for any party's candidates as long as they cast only one vote per elective office. But, in 2000, the Supreme Court ruled that blanket primaries were unconstitutional if the parties themselves wished to keep their nominations to actual party members (see Supreme Court Cases: *California Democratic Party v. Jones*). Currently some states use a modified version of a blanket primary, known as the nonpartisan blanket primary, in which all the candidates, from all parties, who are running for office are listed without identifying their party affiliation, and if no majority winner emerges, the top two vote-getters face each other in a runoff election.

ballot: *List of candidates who are running for elected office; used by voters to make their choice.*

Primary elections are a fact of political life, but insofar as they create competition within a political party and encourage candidates to reveal negative aspects of each other's professional or personal lives, they can weaken the party's eventual nominee when he or she faces opponents in the general election. Because party organizations want the candidate who is most likely to win the election nominated under the party

SUPREME COURT CASES

California Democratic Party v. Jones (2000)

QUESTION: Do blanket primaries, in which voters can vote for any party's candidate regardless of their own party affiliation, violate the right of association of political parties that want to limit their primaries to those who belong to the party?

ORAL ARGUMENT: April 24, 2000 (listen at http://www.oyez.org/cases/1990-1999/1999/1999_99_401)

DECISION: June 26, 2000 (read at http://caselaw.lp.findlaw.com/cgi-bin/getcase.pl?court=US&navby=case&vol=000&invol=99-401)

OUTCOME: Yes, the right of association means that states cannot force parties to open their primaries to voters who are not party members (7–2).

In 1996, voters in California approved Proposition 198 (see Chapter 3, Federalism, on citizen initiatives), which established a blanket primary in which each voter can vote in any primary election, regardless of party affiliation. In 2000, to prevent Republicans from voting in its primary, the California Democratic Party went to court, claiming that California's blanket primary law violated the state Democratic Party's right to freedom of association as guaranteed by the First Amendment.

Ultimately, the case reached the Supreme Court, where Justice Antonin Scalia wrote the majority opinion in favor of the California Democratic Party. The Court ruled blanket primaries to be unconstitutional because they violated the First Amendment. The majority argued that a blanket primary violated a political party's right to associate exclusively with its members, which can be extended to mean that political parties have the right to allow only registered party members to choose their party's nominees in a primary. Scalia wrote that "Proposition 198 forces political parties to associate with—to have their nominees, and hence their positions, determined by—those who, at best, have refused to affiliate with the party, and, at worst, have expressly affiliated with a rival."

Thinking Critically

1. Should a political party be forced to give voters who are not members the same privileges that party members have?
2. Why might a political party want to be responsive to voters who are not members?

banner, they try to exert control over the primary election process in several ways. First, state laws govern party ballot access—literally, who can actually get on the primary election ballot. The relationship between elite state party members and state legislators is very close, so the party controls the gate by determining how open or restrictive ballot access is for candidates seeking to run for office on the party label. Second, although party organizations remain technically neutral during the primary election season, they can steer donors toward their preferred candidates and away from candidates who do not agree with their goals. As a consequence, individuals who are perceived as weak or as not loyal to the party may run into major roadblocks set up by the party organization. Later in this chapter, we discuss an example of intraparty conflict as it applies to the Republican Party and the Tea Party movement, which acts as a type of conservative faction within it.

The Presidential Nomination. The process by which each party nominates its presidential candidate has evolved from one that was concentrated in the hands of a small group of elites to the modern process that allows millions of voters to participate directly in choosing the party's presidential nominee (see Figure 9.2).

In a presidential primary, voters cast a vote for a particular candidate, but what they are really doing is choosing delegates who will support that nominee at the party's national nominating convention. In a presidential **caucus**, which serves the same nominating purpose, the process is less formal and more personal in that party members meet together in town halls, schools, and even private homes to choose a nominee. Each state is awarded a number of delegates to the convention by the national party organization based largely on the number of Electoral College votes the state has but also on the size of party support in that state. The candidate who wins a majority of the delegates from the primary and caucus elections is selected at the national convention as the party's nominee for president.

caucus: *Meeting of party members in town halls, schools, and private homes to select a presidential nominee.*

The Democratic Party and Republican Party allocate their delegates within the primaries and caucuses differently. The Democratic Party has had a more tumultuous nominating process due in large part to some key rule changes in the 1970s and 1980s. In the 1960s, members of underrepresented groups, such as women and African Americans, began calling for a change in the presidential nominating procedures for the Democratic Party. Specifically, they objected to the use of the unit rule, or **winner-take-all system**, which meant that whoever won the majority of primary or state nominating convention votes would win the entire state's delegates. Activists believed that the unit rule allowed conservative white men to dominate the nominating process. In response to this grassroots movement, the Democrats formed the McGovern-Fraser Commission, which recommended changes in the way that delegates were chosen and awarded to candidates during the primary season. In 1972, the Democratic Party instituted requirements that states' delegations accurately reflect the distribution of preferences for presidential candidates in the state. For the 1976 election,

winner-take-all system: *Electoral system in which whoever wins the most votes in an election wins the election.*

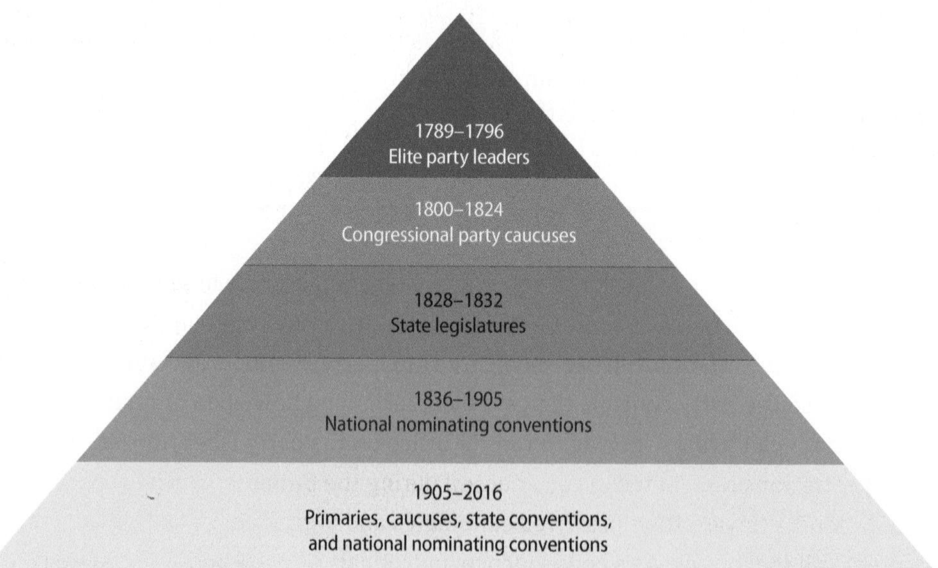

FIGURE 9.2 The Evolution of the Presidential Nominating Process, 1789–2016

This figure depicts the changing nature of the way American political parties nominate candidates for president. The decision-making process in American parties has evolved from small groups of elites, called cadres, to large, mass-based decision making in caucuses and primaries.

the Democrats formally instituted **proportional representation**; that is, the number of delegates that a candidate receives is based on the percentage of the vote received in the primary or caucus, either at the state level or in each congressional district. In most states, delegates are committed to a candidate before the primary election takes place.

proportional representation: *An electoral system that assigns party delegates according to vote share in a presidential primary election or that assigns seats in the legislature according to vote share in a general election.*

To further address the activists' concern that the nominating process was dominated by white men, the 1972 reforms required a certain percentage of each state's delegates to be women, African Americans, young people (defined as eligible voters under 30), and other underrepresented groups based on their proportion in each state's population.[7] If states did not comply with this requirement, the national party reserved the right not to "seat" or count their delegates in the final nominating vote held at the party's national convention. Although the party stated the goal of increasing delegates from underrepresented groups, it did not really increase African American convention participation until 1984, when Jesse Jackson, an African American, ran for the Democratic presidential nomination. Although the nomination went to former Vice President Walter Mondale, Jackson was successful enough to insist that more people of color be delegates to the convention. The cumulative effect of these reforms created a gateway for members of underrepresented groups to exert influence in determining the Democratic Party presidential nominee.

In 1981, the Democratic Party made several other changes, including requiring that each state's delegation comprise an equal number of men and women, and creating a category of delegates known as superdelegates. The superdelegates are not chosen through the primary voting process but rather are active members of the party who will be instrumental in turning out party voters in the general election. Most superdelegates are elected officials in the party, such as governors and members of Congress from each state, as well as state party committee chairs and key activists in interest groups that are loyal to the Democrats. They are uncommitted and free to choose whomever they wish to support at the convention.[8]

In contrast to the Democratic Party, the Republican Party had rarely faced an internal demand for more diverse representation, so it had not significantly changed its nominating system. But in 2010, the Republican Party adopted proportional representation in its nominating system in the hopes of generating more competition and a lengthier campaign season, both of which would increase turnout and enthusiasm among Republican voters.[9] States that did not abide by this system, including Florida and Arizona, were penalized by losing some of their delegates to the national convention. Republicans have no requirements as to the racial or gender composition of a state's delegates, and they have no

ROBYN BECK/Getty Images

IMAGE 9.4 In 2016, the field of potential GOP presidential nominees was so large, with sixteen candidates, that the Republican Party held two separate debates. The ten highest-polling candidates participated in a debate in Boulder, Colorado, in October 2015. The other candidates for the nomination, who were not demonstrating sufficient support in the polls at that point, held a separate debate earlier in the evening.

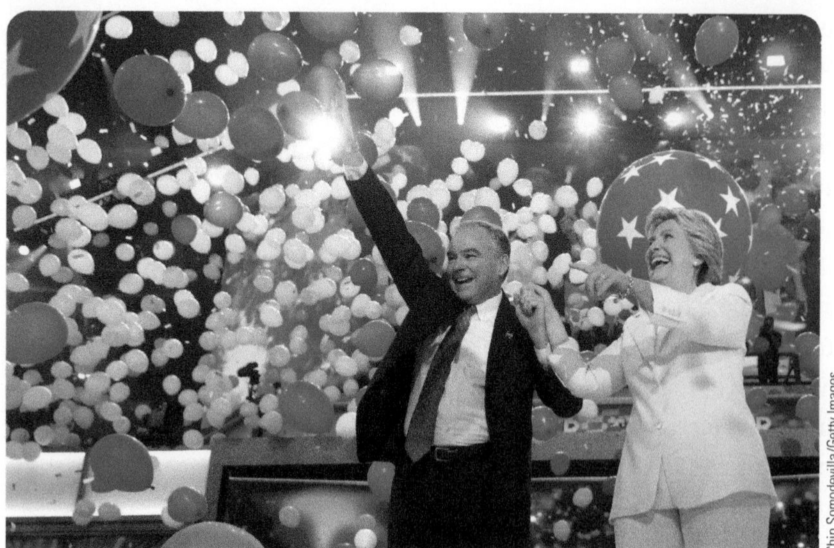

Chip Somodevilla/Getty Images

IMAGE 9.5 In 2016 Hillary Clinton broke the political "glass ceiling" when she became the first woman to be nominated for President of the United States by a major political party. Clinton chose Senator Tim Kaine (D-VA) as her vice-presidential running mate. The Clinton and Kaine Democratic Party ticket was celebrated at their national party convention in Philadelphia.

superdelegates. However, they did add a category of bonus delegates to the 2012 nominating process, awarding these to states based on the percentage of votes cast for the Republican presidential candidate in past elections; in general, bonus delegates are often elected officials and loyal party activists.

However, the 2012 GOP nomination process proved to be too drawn out and conflictual, and turnout among Republicans did not increase appreciably in the general election. Throughout fall 2011 and early 2012, momentum shifted across a number of contenders, including Newt Gingrich and Rick Santorum, before Mitt Romney, former governor of Massachusetts, secured the necessary number of delegates (1,144) in June 2012. There is no question that proportional representation, combined with the role of Super PACs, allowed candidates who did not have a strong majority to stay in the nomination contest and collect delegates longer than under a winner-take-all system (see Chapter 10 for a discussion of Super PACs).

For the 2016 nomination process, the Republicans made more changes to their rules, including scheduling the New Hampshire and South Carolina primaries and Iowa and Nevada caucuses all in February and barring all other states from holding their nominating contests earlier than those four states. States holding their contests between March 1 and March 14 awarded all their delegates proportionate to the vote received by the candidates; states holding contests from March 15 on could choose either a proportional or a winner-take-all system. Those states chose the two systems in almost equal numbers, with Pennsylvania and Wisconsin using a mixed process of allocating delegates. Due to concerns that the many debates (twenty-seven) in the 2012 Republican nomination process damaged the eventual nominee, Mitt Romney, the the Republican Party chose to hold fewer debates among the candidates vying for the party's nomination, reducing the number to twelve, less than half the number in 2012.[10]

Tasos Katopodis/Getty Images

IMAGE 9.6 Donald J. Trump was the 2016 Republican Party presidential nominee, a billionaire businessman who had never held elected office. Here he is seen with his running mate, Indiana Gov. Mike Pence, as they are formally recognized at the Republican National Party convention in Cleveland, Ohio.

9.2 The Dynamics of Early Party Development

Identify which issues divided the first political parties

Political parties in 2016 seem well established, as if they have existed as long as the nation itself. But parties were not intended to be part of the original fabric of the political system. They emerged from disagreements among the Framers. Today, two large parties include a broad swath of the electorate and must make internal compromises to stay unified. In this section, we trace the background to these developments.

Political Factions: Federalist Versus Antifederalist

James Madison, writing in *Federalist Papers* 10 and 51 (see the Appendix), predicted the rise of factions, groups of individuals who share a common political goal and ally with each other on a temporary basis to accomplish that goal. Although factions were not considered the same thing as political parties of the kind that had emerged in Britain, the Framers feared that both factions and parties might encourage divisions in the young democracy that could threaten its existence.

Yet factions emerged even before the Constitution was adopted. In the debate over ratification (see Chapter 2, The Constitution), those who argued for the Constitution called themselves Federalists. They believed that a stable federal government that could collect tax revenue, raise and maintain an army and navy, regulate foreign and domestic trade, and stabilize currency would make the American democratic experiment a success. Opponents of a strong national government, however, viewed the future of the United States in terms of loosely affiliated but sovereign states that governed themselves, managing their own tax policies and internal security. These were the Antifederalists. In their view, the United States had just fought a war to overturn a strong monarch, and they did not want to put themselves under the rule of an oppressive new centralized government that would govern from the top down (see Table 9.1).

Ultimately, the Federalist viewpoint triumphed, and the Constitution was ratified. But the debate did not end there. The nation's first president, George Washington (1789–97), formed a government that included proponents of a strong national government (led by

TABLE 9.1 Federalist and Antifederalist Policies

Federalist	Antifederalist
Ratify the Constitution	Oppose ratification of the Constitution
Establish central bank	Oppose central bank
Protect commercial interests	Support agricultural interests
Assert federal supremacy	Preserve state power
See no need for Bill of Rights	Pass Bill of Rights

Source: Adapted from John H. Aldrich and Ruth Grant, "The Antifederalists, the First Congress, and the First Parties," *Journal of Politics* 55 (1993): 295–326.

Alexander Hamilton and John Adams) and strong state governments (led by Thomas Jefferson). Washington worried that opposing views could lead to organized political parties that would cause conflict in the new nation.[11]

IMAGE 9.7 Andrew Jackson originated the modern political party by encouraging grassroots participation by voters and party organizations in his election campaigns and by building the Democratic Party while he served as president from 1829 to 1837.

Thomas Jefferson, Andrew Jackson, and the Emergence of the Democratic Party

After winning the election of 1800, Thomas Jefferson used his victory to transform his fledgling political party into a viable long-term organization known as the Democratic-Republicans (most candidates shortened the name to Republican), while the supporters of Adams and Hamilton united around the Federalist Party.[12] The Democratic-Republicans occupied the White House for the next twenty-eight years with the terms of Jefferson (1801–09), James Madison (1809–17), James Monroe (1817–25), and John Quincy Adams (1825–29). The Federalist Party slowly faded away as a force in politics.

The Democratic-Republicans soon split over the nomination process for president. Specifically Andrew Jackson, an ambitious politician, wanted to take the party to a new level of inclusiveness and use that wider reach to become president. Jackson, from Tennessee, had served in both the House and the Senate, but he made his national reputation during the War of 1812, especially as the hero of the Battle of New Orleans. After his military service ended, Jackson returned to Congress and attempted to win the presidential nomination of the Democratic-Republicans in 1824.[13] At that time, presidential nominations were decided by party caucuses in Congress. Only about a fourth of the members of the party showed up to cast their votes, and no one won a majority. As a result there were four Democratic-Republican "nominees": Andrew Jackson, John Quincy Adams, William Crawford, and Henry Clay.[14] None of the candidates received a majority of electoral votes, and the House of Representatives chose John Quincy Adams as president. (See Chapter 11, Voting and Participation, for a discussion of that election.)

By 1828, the nomination process had begun to change, with nominations by parties located at the state level, in legislatures and state conventions, rather than the national Congress. By locating the nomination process in the states instead of in Congress, parties enlarged the number of people involved in making the decision about who could run for president. In 1828, using a grassroots state-level strategy to attract both the support of state legislators and the voters themselves, Jackson worked closely with Martin Van Buren, a powerful New York politician, to challenge Adams for the nomination of the Democratic-Republicans; this time, Jackson won the nomination and the presidential election. Then, as now, it is rare for a challenger to defeat the incumbent president in American politics.

As president, Jackson worked closely with Van Buren to knock down the gates that stood in the way of public access to party decisions, to make their political party more accessible to the general public, and to attract the votes of an ever-expanding nation. They recognized that parties could be more than mere coalitions of politicians who agreed on policy; they could be full-fledged grassroots organizations.[15] To accomplish that goal, they had to offer incentives to individuals to join the party organization, including the patronage system discussed later in this chapter. They even shortened the name of the party to the Democratic Party to signal that they were building a new kind of political party organization.

By 1832, the end of Jackson's first term in office, politics had changed in fundamental ways because of the nation's rapid geographic and population growth.[16] The Jackson-led Democrats emerged as a large grassroots majority political party, and Jackson used all the powers of the presidency to strengthen his political party around the country. In the meantime, the anti-Jackson wing of the old Democratic-Republicans had taken the name National Republicans. In the presidential election of 1832, the National Republicans nominated Henry Clay, a U.S. senator from Kentucky, to run against Jackson.

Although Henry Clay lost that election to Jackson, he returned to the Senate and started laying the groundwork for a new political party that would oppose Jackson's policies. He encouraged members of the National Republicans to join forces with others who opposed Jackson and to form the Whig Party, which objected to what they viewed as Jackson's abuse of presidential power for partisan gains. From 1832 to 1856, the Democrats and the Whigs dominated American politics and presidential elections. However, the issue of slavery soon emerged to shake up the party balance.

The Antislavery Movement and the Formation of the Republican Party

The Democratic Party's general strategy for opening a larger gateway for citizen participation in politics inadvertently encouraged alternate groups and political parties to emerge on the political scene. In 1833, William Lloyd Garrison, a white journalist, formed the American Anti-Slavery Society to press for the abolition of slavery. Former slave Frederick Douglass and other African Americans in the North also led efforts to end slavery, and the abolitionist movement grew large and vocal enough to pressure the Democrats and Whigs to take a formal position on slavery, especially the extension of slavery into western territories.

Northern and southern Democrats were united against the abolitionist movement, but for different reasons. Northern Democrats recognized that if the slavery question came to the forefront of politics, the nationally dominant Democratic Party would be split between the North and the South. Southern Democrats opposed abolishing slavery outright or limiting its expansion because the plantation economy of the South was heavily dependent on slave labor. The Whig Party was also divided along northern and southern lines for the same reasons.

Further complicating party politics were smaller **third parties** that arose in the North, some explicitly antislavery. Third parties are minor political parties that present an alternative to the two dominant political parties in the American political system. They have been a part of the political system since the early nineteenth century. Typically, third parties focus on a

third parties: *Minor political parties that present a third alternative to the two dominant political parties in the American political system.*

single issue; the Liberty Party, for example, was explicitly antislavery, while the Green Party, active today, focuses on environmental protection (we discuss third parties in greater depth later in this chapter). As frequently happens in American politics, however, third parties are absorbed into larger parties; the Liberty Party was absorbed into a larger coalition of groups, led by the Free Soilers, which opposed the expansion of slavery in the territories. Meeting in Ripon, Wisconsin, in 1854, these groups were also joined by some antislavery northern Democrats, and the modern Republican Party was born. In the words of one activist, Alvan E. Bovay, "We went into the little meeting held in a schoolhouse Whigs, Free Soilers, and Democrats. We came out of it Republicans."[17] Six years later, the Republican Party had consolidated its support and elected Abraham Lincoln (1861–65) to the presidency.

Shortly after Lincoln's election, seven southern states seceded from the union, and the Civil War erupted. The Confederacy dissolved after the war ended in 1865, but southerners resented northerners and the Republican Party because of both the South's physical and economic losses and the continued occupation of the South by northern troops. Since that time, the Democrats and the Republicans have been the nation's two major political parties.

Party Loyalty and Patronage

patronage system: *Political system in which government programs and benefits are awarded based on political loyalty to a party or politician.*

Andrew Jackson set an example of how to build a political party organization using government resources. Just as Jackson worked to expand the electorate, he sought to expand the size of the federal government in order to increase the number of federally funded jobs his party could control. The Jacksonian era provided many opportunities to bring the federal government into the state and local arena by establishing programs to build forts, post roads (for mail delivery), customhouses, and lighthouses. Whoever controlled the jobs associated with these federal programs could also demand political allegiance from those who filled them. By the late nineteenth century, a system emerged whereby the politician became the "patron" of the businessmen and workers who were on the payrolls of the federal or the state governments. Jobs built party loyalty, and those hired often had to declare their political allegiance to the politician who arranged for the job and promise to vote for him. Such a system is commonly referred to as a **patronage system**.

THE BALLOT
IN COUNTING THERE IS STRENGTH
"THAT'S WHAT'S THE MATTER."
Boss Tweed. "As long as I count the Votes, what are you going to do about it? say?"
Provided courtesy HarpWeek

IMAGE 9.8 William Marcy "Boss" Tweed was the head of the Democratic Party machine in New York City in the 1850s and 1860s. He was notorious for using political office to hand out favors and benefits to loyal party members and to accumulate personal wealth. The editorial cartoons of Thomas Nast helped expose the graft and corruption of the "Tweed Ring."

As the government expanded, so did the party organization. At each level—federal, state, and local—there were parallel party committees. Parties became the organizations they are today, with a national committee, state committees, and local chapters at the county, ward, town, or precinct level. At each level, leaders who had power within the party acted as party bosses, controlling the distribution of public funds and making sure to reward supporters and withhold funds from opponents. The key element in this system was the loyalty of supporters who voted for the boss's preferred set of candidates on Election Day. Voter support in this kind of system was so reliable and predictable that it became known as machine politics; it ran like a well-oiled machine.

The expansion of party machines was fueled by a huge influx of new immigrants in the late nineteenth century who mostly settled in large cities of the North and Midwest. Democratic bosses in these cities recognized that immigrants, once naturalized, would be a major source of new voters and courted their loyalty through patronage. In turn, parties served as a type of gateway for immigrants to become integrated into American political life. As city populations increased at a much faster rate than rural populations, Democrats gained political power in cities, while Republican power in the North and Midwest tended to be concentrated in rural areas.

Reform and the Erosion of Party Control

A critical factor in the success of machine politics was party control of voting. In contrast to today's system—in which states manage most aspects of elections, including ballot design and ballot counting—local parties in the late nineteenth century printed their own ballots, called party strip ballots, which listed only their candidates, and gave them to voters on their way into the polling places. In many places, party officials counted the votes as well, further manipulating the voting process to their advantage.

Essential Knowledge
Progressive era reforms have tended to weaken American political parties. These reforms have produced the candidate-centered campaign.

However, three developments eroded party organizations' control over government jobs and elections: the creation of a merit-based system of government employment, the introduction of ballot reforms, and a change in the way nominees for elected office were selected. All three reforms were led by Progressives, coalitions of Democrats and Republicans who believed that government had been captured by corrupt elites who were using government resources to enrich themselves rather than to serve citizens.

Since Andrew Jackson's day, bosses in the old patronage system had taken for granted the right to distribute government jobs to their supporters. But in 1883, the Pendleton Act reformed the civil service by requiring that government jobs be filled based on merit, not on political connections (see Chapter 14, The Bureaucracy, for more on the civil service). This was the first of several laws that slowly transformed the federal bureaucracy from a corrupt insider organization to a neutral, policy-based organization.[18]

Voting procedures were also reformed between 1888 and 1911 as states adopted the so-called **Australian ballot** system, which originated in Australia in 1858, to replace the party strip ballots[19] (see Figure 9.3). When parties had printed the ballots and had given them to voters, who then put them in the ballot box, there was no privacy, and party officials monitored citizens' votes. The Australian ballot system introduced the secret ballot; each ballot listed all of the candidates from all of the parties who were running for office, and voters marked their choices in private. In addition, poll watchers and ballot counters were expected to perform their tasks without favoring a specific party and without intimidating voters. This reform greatly reduced party boss control over election outcomes.[20]

Australian ballot: *Voting system in which state governments run elections and provide voters the option of choosing candidates from multiple parties; also called the secret ballot.*

Last, Progressives launched grassroots campaigns for direct primaries run by the state for nominating party candidates. These primaries aimed to replace the nomination of candidates in local and state party conventions, which were typically dominated by party bosses. Although states were relatively slow to adopt direct primaries, eventually this system became the dominant means of choosing party candidates. The effect of direct primaries was to greatly reduce the control that party bosses and machines had over the choices offered in elections.

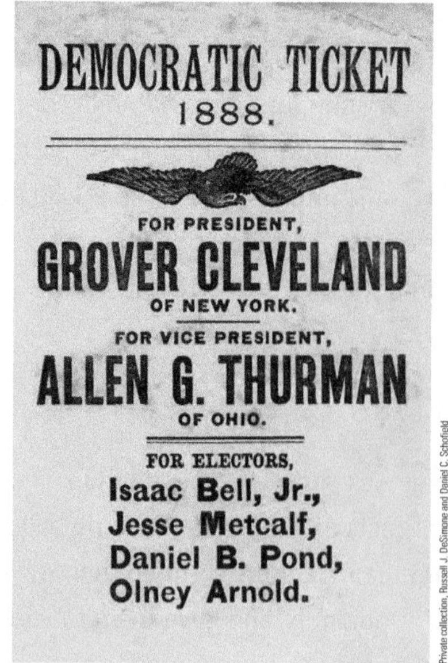

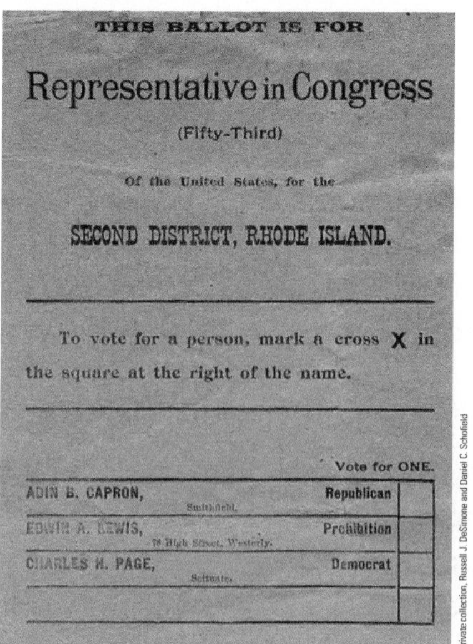

FIGURE 9.3 Ballot Reform

On the left are examples of party strip ballots used in Rhode Island in 1888. These types of ballots were printed by political parties and handed to voters on Election Day. They gave voters no opportunity to split their vote among different parties. On the right is an example of the so-called Australian ballot. Like this ballot used in Rhode Island in 1892, Australian ballots were printed by state governments rather than by political parties. They listed all candidates for elected office, not just candidates from a single party, and therefore allowed voters to split their vote among different parties.

Source: Russell J. DeSimone and Daniel C. Schofield, "Rhode Island Election Tickets: A Survey," Technical Services Department Faculty Publications (Kingston: University of Rhode Island, 2007), Private collection, Russell J. DeSimone and Daniel C. Schofield.

9.3 The Effects of a Two-Party System

Explain why two parties dominate the U.S. political system

Following the Civil War, party divisions ran largely along geographic lines, with Republicans dominant in the Northeast and West and Democrats dominant in the South and increasingly in the nation's largest cities. Today, the Democratic and Republican Parties have reversed their geographic strongholds, but the two-party system remains intact. In this section, we examine the effects of a two-party system not only on citizens' choices but also on the ways that government can respond. We also examine the reasons why the United States, even before the Civil War, never had more than two major parties, and we explore the role of the third parties that have occasionally arisen to challenge two-party dominance.

Limited Political Choice

Surely, there are more than two views on how to solve important policy problems. If a group of students has a conversation about a political issue, whether it is war, civil liberties, education, crime, or same-sex marriage, there will likely be more than two opinions expressed. It might seem logical, therefore, that a large democracy such as the United States should have many parties that vie with each other to capture political offices. But the United States has only two major parties.

In 1957, the scholar Anthony Downs argued that voters whose views fall between the two parties were actually represented in a two-party system. His **median voter theorem** proposed that, in a two-party race, if voters select candidates on the basis of ideology and everyone participates equally, the party closer to the middle will win. As candidates from each party seek to attract a majority of votes, and because most voters fall in the middle of the ideological spectrum, both parties move toward a compromise, or middle position. In this way, moderates have a great deal of potential political influence in a two-party system.[21]

median voter theorem: *Theory that, in a two-party race, if voters select candidates on the basis of ideology and everyone participates equally, the party closer to the middle will win.*

Nevertheless, the impact of ideologically extreme campaign activists and interest groups that align with a party can pressure parties and candidates to move away from the center.[22] In today's highly partisan atmosphere, it seems as though the political center has almost entirely disappeared. Each party appears to be so dominated by its more extreme wing that there is little opportunity within each to make moderate views known or to compromise. The current polarization in the two-party system increasingly appears to contradict Downs's expectations about convergence to the middle. In regions where one party is very dominant, elected officials may not be responsive to voters from the other party.

The Structural Limits

The two-party system is built into the American electoral system. As the political scientist Maurice Duverger explains, the American electoral system is a **single-member plurality system**, in which one legislative seat (on a city council, in a state assembly, in the House of Representatives) represents citizens who live in a geographically defined district.[23] To win that seat, a candidate usually needs only a **plurality of votes**, not a pure **majority**—that is, more votes than any other candidate, but not necessarily 50 percent plus 1. Because there is only one seat to be won in a district, only the party or parties with the strongest support have a chance to win a seat. In the United States, many districts are noncompetitive—that is, one of the two major parties dominates. Other districts are competitive; the two major parties vie for electoral support. As a result, voters have become accustomed to choosing between candidates from the two major parties.

single-member plurality system: *Electoral system that assigns one seat in a legislative body to represent citizens who live in a defined area (a district) based on which candidate wins the most votes.*

plurality vote: *Vote in which the winner needs to win more votes than any other candidate.*

majority vote: *Vote in which the winner needs to win 50 percent plus 1 of the votes cast.*

Other electoral systems work differently. Many democracies assign the number of seats a party wins according to proportional representation, based on the percentage of votes it receives in a particular election. This type of electoral system encourages smaller parties to form around specific issues and to field candidates for office. Voters are likewise encouraged to support smaller parties. With so many parties fielding candidates, no single party is likely to receive a majority, and parties govern by forming coalitions.

Essential Knowledge

Single-member plurality electoral systems ("winner-take-all") tend to produce two major parties. The role of minor parties is thus effectively diminished.

In the United States, however, the single-member plurality system encourages a two-party system, and the two-party system in turn encourages political debates that ask Americans to take a "for" or an "against" position on an issue. During an election, there is little effort to arrive at the middle ground, although there is often debate within a party as to what its position will be. In fact, the two-party system works to transfer the battleground from between parties to within parties. Each party—rather than government itself—is a coalition.

The Role of Third Parties

> ***Essential Knowledge***
> While third parties have little chance of winning electorally, occasionally popular ideas championed in their platforms have been adopted by the major parties. Though this is a victory for third parties, it also serves as a barrier to third party and independent candidate success.

Scholars have debated whether this two-party system adequately reflects the range of views among citizens. In one sense, a two-party system stands as a gate that blocks the emergence of alternative viewpoints and reduces the choices available to voters in terms of perspectives on how to govern. On the other hand, when the two parties together do not offer policy proposals that a significant number of voters want to see enacted, third parties form. These third parties can mount challenges so significant that the major parties are compelled to act, often by incorporating the third party's policy proposal into their platforms.

We have already seen how the antislavery ideas of the Liberty Party and the Free Soil Party were absorbed into the Republican Party when it was founded in 1854. A second example occurred in the late nineteenth century, when farmers were in an uproar about declining crop prices, the lack of available credit, and the constricting use of gold rather than silver as the collateral for U.S. currency. Splinter parties rose up around these issues. Of these, the Populist Party was the largest and most viable; its presidential candidate in the 1892 presidential election, James Weaver, won four states outright and split the vote in two other states.[24] In the 1896 election, the Democrats thought they saw an opportunity to win votes by incorporating into their party platform the Populist demand for free and unlimited coinage of silver, which would drive up prices, thus helping those who were in debt. They even nominated the Populist candidate, William Jennings Bryan, as their own. Bryan lost the election, and with that defeat, the "free silver" movement, which had been strong in the West, rapidly declined.

A little over a decade later, Theodore "Teddy" Roosevelt ran for president as the Progressive Party candidate. Roosevelt, a Republican, had served as president from 1901 to 1909. He decided to run for president again in 1912 to mobilize voters around a host of

Dennis MacDonald/age fotostock/Alamy

IMAGE 9.9 Protesters assemble at the Capitol building in Washington, D.C., to rally against what they deem an intrusive federal government.

progressive reforms that would weaken party machines, most notably the idea of popular elections for U.S. senators. At that time, U.S. senators were elected in state legislatures rather than directly by the voters. Although Roosevelt lost, the Progressives were successful in getting Congress to pass and the states to ratify the Seventeenth Amendment on April 8, 1913, which allowed for the direct election of U.S. senators.

Since Teddy Roosevelt's run, five contenders representing significant third parties have entered presidential elections, but none has been able to build a sustained organization over time. Two of these candidates, Strom Thurmond (Dixiecrats) and George Wallace (American Independent Party), ran on segregationist platforms of parties that were splinter groups of the Democratic Party. John Anderson (National Unity Party) and Ross Perot (United We Stand) each ran on a platform that favored moderate social policy and strict fiscal discipline. Ross Perot was given credit for using his United We Stand Party to force the two major party candidates in 1992, President George H. W. Bush (1989–93) and William Jefferson (Bill) Clinton (1993–2001), to address the federal deficit, the amount by which annual government spending exceeds incoming revenue. Ralph Nader ran for president on the Green Party ticket in 2000, 2004, and 2008, promoting a platform that called for stronger environmental and consumer protections. Although Nader did not win, his messages of change and open government were clearly echoed by the mainstream Democratic candidate, Barack Obama, in his successful first campaign for president. For a compact list of significant parties in American politics, see Figure 9.4.

Though third parties have not fared well in national electoral contests, they sometimes find success in lower-level elections. The Libertarian Party, for example, claimed more than 143 elected officials as of early 2016.[25] Most are members of school boards and

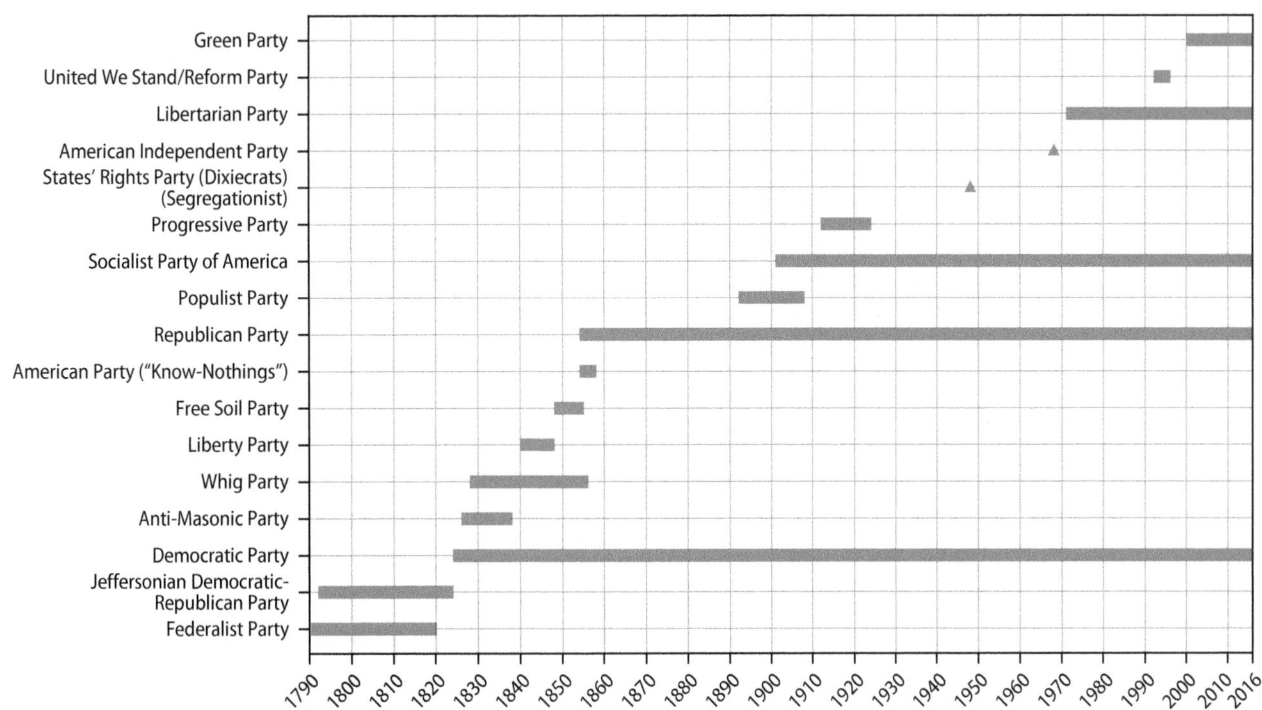

FIGURE 9.4 American Political Parties, 1789–2016

Note that the Democratic Party is the nation's oldest political party. The graph shows it beginning under President Andrew Jackson, but some argue that it actually began with President Thomas Jefferson's Democratic-Republicans.

town councils, with mayors holding the highest offices. Another example of a third party that found success in local elections was the La Raza Unida Party (LRUP) in the 1970s.[26] The LRUP organized in 1970 in the south Texas counties of Zavala, Dimmitt, and La Salle, all near the U.S.–Mexico border. Its founders' goals were to advance the economic, social, and political interests of Mexican Americans. Their mobilizing efforts led to electoral victories in the Crystal City, Cotulla, and Carrizo Springs school boards and town councils, all areas heavily populated by Latinos yet whose local offices Anglos had historically held. The LRUP spread throughout the Southwest into rural and urban areas from Texas to California, electing members to various local offices. Part of its legacy is the activation of Latinos into the political process and providing a gateway for Latinas; one notable veteran of the party is Rosie Castro, former Bexar County LRUP chairwoman and mother of Secretary of Housing and Urban Development Julián Castro and his twin brother, Congressman Joaquín Castro (D-TX, who is featured in Chapter 12, Congress).

The Tea Party

Third parties do not have to stand by themselves to have an impact on party politics; they can also be an influential force within one or more parties. For example, in 2010 and 2012, the Tea Party movement was very effective at supporting challengers to incumbents in primary elections in the Republican Party or supporting a third candidate in the general election. By one count, 129 candidates running for the House of Representatives and 9 candidates running for the U.S. Senate in the 2010 Congressional elections affiliated themselves with the Tea Party.[27] Its message was fiscal responsibility, lower taxes, and paying down the national debt, and the Tea Party was successful in electing members of Congress, such as Senator Rand Paul (R-KY), who share its concern that the federal budget ought to be at the top of the American political agenda.[28] The results from the 2014 midterm elections, however, may have revealed some cracks in the Tea Party movement as many Republican incumbent U.S. Senators successfully fought back against Tea Party–backed challengers.[29]

At the presidential level, members of the Tea Party movement were also active in the Republican nominating process and were vocal in demanding that the Republicans commit to their concerns. In the 2016 Republican nomination process, multiple candidates courted and claimed to be supported by the Tea Party, including Ted Cruz (R-TX), Rand Paul (R-KY), Marco Rubio (R-FL), and Donald Trump. Donald Trump's nomination by the Republican Party and subsequent election as president may be seen as evidence of the Tea Party movement's continued influence.

As mentioned, the established wing of the Republican Party started to fight back against efforts to undermine incumbent Republicans or candidates who did not subscribe entirely to the Tea Party's agenda. In March 2014, Senator Mitch McConnell (R-KY), who was facing a Tea Party challenger in his primary, was quoted as saying, "I think we will crush them everywhere." The first test of that came in Texas, where a Tea Party challenger, Representative Steve Stockman, was in fact overwhelmingly defeated by the incumbent Republican candidate, John Cornyn, in the Senate primary. In the face of the enormous resources of the mainstream Republican Party, the Tea Party had more difficulty in 2014 recruiting and funding strong challengers to Republican incumbents in the House and Senate.[30]

The Tea Party movement, although not officially a political party, illustrates how third parties can force the two major political parties to be more responsive; in this case, the Tea

Party has given voice to more conservative voters. When they are large enough, these groups have the potential to move the party platforms in new directions and, in turn, to change federal laws.[31] The Tea Party movement's success in defeating incumbent Republicans in primaries and in electing Republicans who espoused more conservative views has created a more polarized and less effective governing environment in Congress (see Chapter 6, Figure 6.7, and Chapter 12).

Ilya B. Mirman/Shutterstock.com

IMAGE 9.10 As an outsider candidate for president in 2016, Donald Trump campaigned untraditionally, relying heavily on social media and his status as a nonpolitician. Trump drew on the frustration some voters felt in 2016, which is described in Chapter 1. Here he is pictured speaking to a crowd in New Hampshire in 2015 while campaigning for the GOP nomination.

Party Control of Presidential Nominations

Donald Trump's candidacy in 2016 proved problematic for the Republican Party's ability to steer the nomination process. Though not the preferred candidate of the so-called Republican Party establishment, Trump was nevertheless able to earn primary and caucus victories. Though the parties set the rules of the nomination process, such as the number of debates held and how states allocate delegates (proportional vs. winner-take-all), no apparatus has ultimate control over Republican voters' choice of nominee.

Donald Trump's election to the presidency raises questions about the future of the Republican Party. His nomination prompted a backlash among a significant number of "establishment" Republicans who either passively refused to endorse him or actively opposed him throughout his campaign. His victory, however, placed him as the leader of the Republican Party. Will divisions within the GOP be reconciled by President Trump and members of Congress? Speaker of the House Paul Ryan, an "establishment" Republican, will have to work with President Trump. Their relationship will shed light on the nature and future of the Republican Party coalition.

Obstacles to Third Parties and Independents

Because third-party candidates can act as spoilers, the two major parties do everything they can to discourage them, from challenging signatures for ballot access in court to preventing them from participating in presidential debates. The Democrats and Republicans have controlled state legislatures and Congress for so long that they have successfully established gates within state electoral laws that favor a two-party system over a multiple-party system. In addition, without the backing of a major party to get out the vote, collect campaign contributions, and arrange for media coverage, most third-party and Independent candidates do not stand much chance of being elected. Consequently, voters who consider themselves

PUBLIC POLICY AND POLITICAL PARTIES

Assault Weapons Ban

In Chapter 4, Civil Liberties, we explained how the Supreme Court has interpreted the provisions of the Second Amendment to allow individuals to own firearms. As we noted, gun control is a highly contested public policy area, especially between the Democrats and the Republicans. However, tragic events such as the shooting of former Congresswoman Gabby Giffords and six other people in Arizona; the Aurora, Colorado, movie theater shootings; and the Newtown school shootings have precipitated a national discussion over whether assault weapons should be banned.

Although not all party members agree, a majority of self-described Democrats favor most stricter gun laws. Among Republicans, attitudes vary depending on the type of policy proposal. In a 2016 Pew Research Center Poll, majorities of both party identifiers agreed on requiring background checks at gun shows; 86 percent of Democrats and 78 percent of Republicans.[32] On the question of an assault weapon ban, though, the margin was much wider, with 67 percent of Democrats favoring such a ban, compared with 35 percent of Republicans in favor.[33]

During the 2016 presidential election, the Democratic Party made gun control part of its party platform, stating that "To build on the success of the lifesaving Brady Handgun Violence Prevention Act, we will expand and strengthen background checks and close dangerous loopholes in our current laws; repeal the Protection of Lawful Commerce in Arms Act (PLCAA) to revoke the dangerous legal immunity protections gun makers and sellers now enjoy; and keep weapons of war—such as assault weapons and large capacity ammunition magazines (LCAM's)—off our streets."[34] The Republican Party had a contrasting statement in their platform about the assault weapons ban, stating that "We oppose ill-conceived laws that would restrict magazine capacity or ban the sale of the most popular and common modern rifle. We also oppose any effort to deprive individuals of their right to keep and bear arms without due process of law."[35] By including these statements in their party's platforms during a presidential candidate, each party was staking out a distinct policy position designed to attract support from its base.

In Congress, these party differences are also strongly visible. For example, in the 113th Congress, Senator Dianne Feinstein (D-CA) introduced a bill to reinstate the assault weapons ban that would outlaw a number of types of firearms capable of holding large amounts of ammunition. Her bill, the Assault Weapons Ban of 2013, had twenty-four Senate cosponsors, all of them Democrats. In the House of Representatives, Representative Carolyn McCarthy (D-NY) introduced a bill with the same language, and there were eighty-one House cosponsors, all of them Democrats. However, because the House of Representatives was controlled by the Republicans, and Republicans in the Senate could filibuster the legislation, there was little to no chance that it would have passed. Despite the odds against passage, the assault weapons ban was an important focal point for Democrats to mobilize supporters of gun control. Since the attempt in 2013, only one similar piece of legislation was introduced to curb assault weapons. Congressman David N. Cicilline (D-RI) introduced the Assault Weapons Ban of 2015. One hundred twenty-five Democrats signed as cosponsors, while no Republicans did so. There was no companion legislation introduced in the Senate.

Interest groups influence gun policy as well. The National Rifle Association (NRA), which is a large grassroots group and one of the most effective in the nation, figures prominently in the national discussion on a ban on assault weapons. Like many interest groups, the NRA has formed a PAC to contribute to campaigns. Most PACs contribute to incumbents, current members of Congress who are much more likely to win than challengers. Most PACs support incumbents from both parties. Unlike many groups, however, the NRA's PAC contributes overwhelmingly to candidates from one party: the Republican Party. In the 2014 congressional election cycle, the NRA's affiliated PAC contributed a total of $800,050 to congressional campaigns, with 95 percent going to Republicans and 5 percent going to Democrats. Safari Club International, a group that promotes wildlife conservation and protects the rights of hunters, also throws its support primarily behind Republican candidates. Its Arizona-based PAC contributed $449,811 with 94 percent going to Republicans and 6 percent going to Democrats. There was only one group, the Brady Campaign to prevent gun violence, that overwhelmingly supported Democrats, contributing a total of $46,746 to pro–gun-control Democrats in 2014 and no funds to Republicans.[36] Campaign contributions are important and so is the potential to bring voters out the door to vote for candidates who support their policy positions. Political parties depend on interest groups who agree with their policy stances to help mobilize voters; without them, that job becomes much more difficult. The issue of thwarting gun violence through gun control, with specific measures such as the assault weapons ban, will likely remain a strong source of division in parties at the top levels of the organizations, among party identifiers, and among members of Congress.

Public Policy Connections

1. Is it wise for a political party to take such a definitive stand on a controversial issue?
2. Does PAC money undermine the influence of political parties to the detriment of democracy in the United States?

Independents do not have the opportunity to vote for candidates who might be closest to them in terms of policy preferences.

Candidates who are elected from third parties have little influence in legislatures because parties shape the internal power structure there. The party that wins the majority of seats in the legislature becomes the majority party and consequently controls the legislative process. After the legislative session begins, members are asked to express their opinions in subcommittees, in committees, and on the floor by voting with or against their party's proposed legislation, and it is rare that an alternative to the major party proposal is considered (see Chapter 12). Those who are elected as Independents, such as Senator Bernie Sanders (I-VT), have no party organization to join in the legislature. Independents must pledge to support one of the two major parties in order to sit on committees and perform their other responsibilities as legislators. When he was elected to the Senate in 2006 and reelected in 2012, Sanders chose to caucus with the Democrats. When Angus King was elected to the Senate from Maine in 2012 as an Independent, he chose to caucus with the Democrats as well.

In 2016, Sanders even sought the nomination of the Democratic Party, though not officially a Democrat. Sanders appealed to Democrats claiming to be the "authentic" Progressive in the race. His campaign resonated with the progressive wing of the party. That segment of the Democratic Party, many of whom are younger voters, supported his candidacy. Though he was unsuccessful in winning the party's nomination, Sanders campaigned vigorously for Hillary Clinton, urging his supporters to elect the Democratic nominee and prevent Donald Trump from winning the presidency.

Challenges to Party Power from Interest Groups

In addition to challenges from third parties, the two major parties face challenges from established interest groups and from broader social groups formed at the grassroots of

American politics (see Chapter 8, Interest Groups). These groups and movements draw attention to each party's failings in specific issue areas and engage in activities from staging protest rallies to nominating alternative candidates to run in primaries in order to get parties to move closer to the policy positions the group or movement advocates.

Essential Knowledge
Social movements can sometimes force parties to change their platforms.

Over the past two decades, interest and social movement groups have become more tightly aligned with specific political parties, and that alignment has undermined their capacity to serve as independent checks on—or competitors with—political parties. For example, unions such as the Service Employees International Union (SEIU) and environmental groups such as the Sierra Club are generally supportive of the Democratic Party, whereas business groups such as the Chamber of Commerce and the National Rifle Association (NRA) are supportive of the Republican Party.

For interest groups, the risk in continuously supporting one party is that the party will take their support for granted. In fact, parties are most responsive to interest groups when they threaten to withdraw their support or start their own party organizations. Consequently, interest groups maintain their influence with political parties by constantly expressing their preferences on policies to party leaders and providing support only when the party is responsive to their concerns. For example, on the issue of gun control, interest groups on both sides of the issue have been very active in lobbying elected officials and trying to persuade the public to support their preferred policy position.

9.4 Party Alignment and Ideology

Define partisan affiliation and ideology

Throughout U.S. history, there have been long stretches of time during which the party affiliations of voters remained stable, but there have also been key elections in which parties lost or gained significant blocs of voters. Scholars have tried to identify the factors that explain why voters make large, permanent shifts from one party to another. Shifts in party allegiance can occur when there is an external shock to the nation, such as an economic depression or a foreign military attack. Shifts can also occur when public attitudes change considerably and one party appears to respond more quickly to those changes than another.

Essential Knowledge
Party identification and voting behavior are influenced by a range of variables, including demographic variables (sex, age, race, etc.) and ideology.

The Parties After the Civil War

party alignment: *Voter identification with a political party in repeated elections.*

Following the Civil War, as we have seen, the Republicans were dominant in the Northeast and West and the Democrats were dominant in the South and increasingly in large cities with big immigrant populations. This **party alignment**—voters identifying with a party in repeated elections—was relatively stable until 1896, when a number of smaller parties challenged the Republican and Democratic Parties. The Republican Party emerged from that election with a victory, and the smaller parties faded from the national political scene.

From 1896 to 1932, the basic geographic pattern of party alignment stayed the same, but the combination of the stock market crash of October 24, 1929, the global depression that followed, and a drop in worldwide agricultural prices brought political trouble to the Republican Party. By 1932, voters in every part of the country were ready for a change, not only in political leadership but also in the entire approach to government.

The New Deal and the Role of Ideology in Party Politics

During the election of 1932, voters were exposed to a new political ideology, or set of consistent political views, about the way that the federal government could work. Today's voters might describe themselves as liberal or conservative, but voters before 1932 typically identified themselves with a political party. In that election year, Franklin Delano Roosevelt (1933–45), governor of New York, ran for president on a platform designed to reverse the effects of the Great Depression. The idea that the federal government would help individuals to help themselves was transformative in American politics. The Democratic Party platform resonated with voters, and Roosevelt won the election.

After he took office, Roosevelt championed a vast array of new government programs that are commonly referred to as the New Deal. These programs were designed to help individuals who were jobless, homeless, or otherwise in financial need. Essentially the New Deal was a promise by the federal government to provide a safety net for workers and their families who fell on hard times. Following his electoral victory in 1932, Roosevelt built a coalition of white southerners, working-class ethnic northerners, advocates for liberal social policies, and northern African Americans who had previously been Republicans. This was a radical shift for African Americans, who since the Civil War had followed the party of Abraham Lincoln and shunned the Democrats, whom they associated with racism and slavery. This electoral coalition was large but fragile, and Roosevelt engaged in a great deal of political balancing and a wide distribution of government benefits to maintain it.

AP Images

IMAGE 9.11 In his campaign for president in 1932, Franklin Delano Roosevelt introduced an innovative campaign platform. "I pledge you," he said, "I pledge myself, to a new deal for the American people." The term "New Deal" came to describe federal programs that took an active role in helping individual citizens find jobs, save for retirement, and benefit from fair working conditions.

In supporting the New Deal, voters came to accept the ideological viewpoint that government involvement in the economic aspects of individuals' lives was legitimate and, on balance, a good thing. As we noted in Chapter 1, Gateways to American Democracy, this perspective on government serves as a foundation for the modern definition of a liberal. Today the liberal viewpoint builds on the New Deal perspective by favoring government redistribution of income through higher taxes on the wealthy to provide social benefits, such as health care, unemployment insurance, and welfare payments to the poor. Those who opposed the New Deal are the forefathers of the modern conservatives, who believe in lower taxes and less government involvement in economic life.

Essential Knowledge

The key constituencies of each party occasionally shift. This is known as a realignment. Realignments can occur as a result of major economical, social, and policy-related changes.

In response to Roosevelt's big government approach, the Republicans seized what they saw as the main weakness of the New Deal, which was the high cost of all these newly created programs. To pay for them, the federal and state governments would have to raise taxes on businesses and workers alike. The Republicans recognized that they had an opportunity to reshape their party platform to exploit the Democrats' weakness.

In the aftermath of 1932, the two parties transformed; it was almost as if they had switched places. The Democrats changed from a party that believed in states' rights, low taxes, and little government intervention in individuals' lives to the party that created a large social safety net that relied on the federal government to ensure personal economic stability. The Republicans changed from a party that believed in a strong central federal government and in intervention in the economy when necessary to the party of a strictly limited federal government and fiscal responsibility.

realignment: *Long-term shift in voter allegiance from one party to another.*

Voters responded to these partisan and ideological changes by changing their own party allegiances over time, essentially producing a **realignment** of the electorate. In the broadest sense, today's Democrats generally support expanding the size of government to accomplish specific policy goals, even if it means raising taxes, and support liberal social values. In contrast, Republicans generally support limiting the size of government by keeping taxation and regulation of the economy to a minimum and support preserving conservative social values.

Civil Rights, the Great Society, and Nixon's Southern Strategy

The Democratic and Republican Parties remained divided mainly along this economic dimension until the early 1960s, when the Democratic Party established itself as the party of civil rights for African Americans. During the presidency of Lyndon Baines Johnson (1963–69), the Civil Rights Act of 1964, the Voting Rights Act of 1965, the Department of Housing and Urban Development Act of 1965, and the Fair Housing Act of 1966 were all signed into law. These acts gave the federal government strong enforcement powers to guarantee African Americans the fullest extent of the civil rights afforded to every American and served as a key gateway for full political participation by African Americans. Johnson's policies brought a second dimension to liberal ideology: now the federal government was granted the power not only to help individuals in need economically but also to take affirmative steps to overrule state and local governments to prevent discrimination on all levels. As noted in Chapter 5, Civil Rights, the government's role evolved from preventing unequal treatment under the law to ensuring equality in all walks of life, from education to employment to housing.

By putting the stamp of the Democratic Party on the pledge to preserve civil rights, Johnson appealed to those who opposed segregation. Today African Americans remain the most loyal of any demographic constituency in the Democratic Party. In 2004, 88 percent of African American voters chose the Democratic candidate, John Kerry, over President George W. Bush.[37] In 2008, 95 percent of African American voters chose the Democratic candidate,

POLITICAL ANALYTICS

Latinos and the Political Parties: Votes and Issues

LATINOS ARE AN IMPORTANT AND GROWING group of voters in the United States. Both major U.S. political parties have a large stake in attracting their affinity and votes. Democrats have enjoyed strong support from Latinos in presidential elections, and Latinos most often identify with them. Latinos also see Democrats as the party best able to handle important political issues.

Figure 9.5 shows three ways in which to gauge Latinos' preference for the two major political parties. Though Democrats have an edge in Latino support, the data on party identification among Latinos suggest that a growing number of Latinos may be choosing the Republican Party. In the 2016 election, Democrat Hillary Clinton garnered 65 percent of the Latino vote according to some exit polls, less than did President Obama in 2012. This underscores the extent to which Latino voters may be a group for which both parties will actively compete. However, other scholars claimed that Latinos supported Clinton by as much as 80 percent.* If the actual figures are somewhere in that range, it is likely that Latinos continued their support for Democrats.

Consider the data on voting patterns as well as the trend and magnitude of difference in Latino party identification and beliefs.

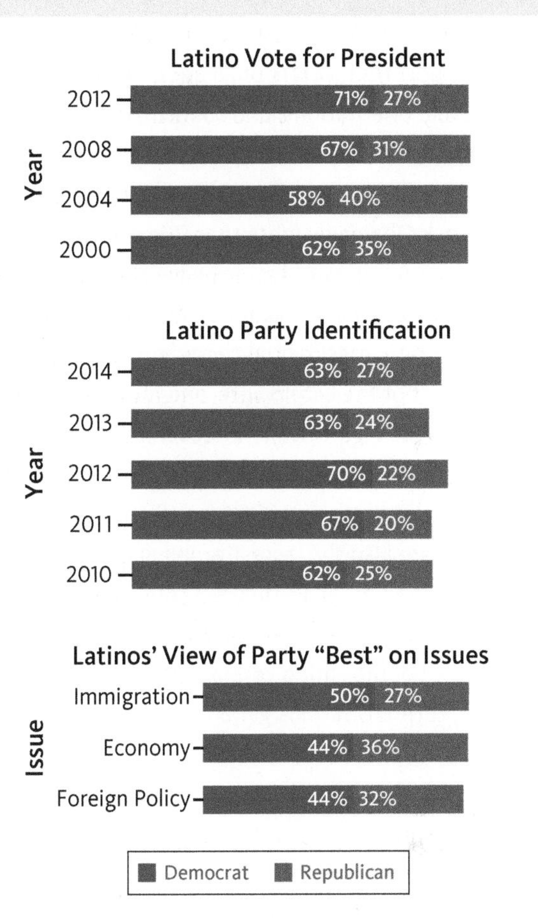

FIGURE 9.5 Democrats, Republicans, and Latinos

Sources: Pew Hispanic Center analysis of national exit poll data, 1980–2012; Pew Research Center, 2002–2014 National Survey of Latinos; Pew Research Center, 2002–2014, National Survey of Latinos, September 11–October 9, 2014.

*Alec Tyson and Shiva Maniam, "Behind Trump's victory: Divisions by race, gender, education," Pew Research Center, November 9, 2016. http://www.pewresearch.org/fact-tank/2016/11/09/behind-trumps-victory-divisions-by-race-gender-education/; Jon Huang, Samuel Jacoby, K. K., Rebecca Lai, and Michael Strickland, "Election 2016: Exit Polls," *New York Times*, November 8, 2016. http://www.nytimes.com/interactive/2016/11/08/us/politics/election-exit-polls.html; "The Rundown on Latino Voter Election Eve Polling and Latino Exit Polls," Latino Decisions, November 9, 2016. http://www.latinodecisions.com/blog/2016/11/09/the-rundown-on-latino-voter-election-eve-polling-and-latino-exit-polls.

Thinking Critically

1. How do you think the 2016 presidential election campaign affected Latinos' views about the way in which the Democratic and Republican Parties handle key issues?
2. In the long term, do you think Republican efforts to attract Latino voters will succeed?

Barack Obama, who was elected as the nation's first African American president.[38] In 2012, 93 percent of African American voters cast their ballot for the Democratic incumbent, President Obama.[39] In 2014, a nonpresidential election year, 90 percent of African American voters cast their ballots for Democratic candidates for Congress.[40] And in the 2016 presidential election, 88 percent of African Americans supported Hillary Clinton.[41]

ELECTION 2016

The Partisan Inclinations of Latinos

DEMOCRATS AND REPUBLICANS WOULD, of course, like to have support from voters of all ages, races, ethnicities, sexual orientations, and so forth. At least since the 1960s, most African Americans have supported Democrats. The same is true of Latinos, who, for example, supported Barack Obama by more than 70 percent in 2012. Like African Americans, Latinos have become a vital part of the Democratic Party's coalition of voters. Since 2000, the Democratic presidential candidate has received at least 58 percent of the Latino vote, and much more in recent elections (see Figure 9.5). Moreover, Latinos tend to self-identify as Democrats and have for some time and by large margins: 63 percent in 2014 (see Figure 9.5). Because Latinos are also the fastest-growing group of eligible voters (see Chapter 1), they are considered an important part of both major parties' electoral fortunes.

The influence of the Latino vote is a function of party preference and turnout. Latinos generally see Democrats as "better" for them in some key areas, such as immigration policy (see Figure 9.5). Heading into the 2016 election, Republicans needed to make significant inroads into the Latino vote. Mitt Romney received only 27 percent of the Latino vote in 2012. Some estimates of the Latino vote share that Republicans need to be competitive in 2016 were as high as 47 percent, a figure higher than any Republican presidential candidate has ever received.[42]

Did Latinos' affinity for Democrats translate into support for Hillary Clinton? Probably. While exit polls showed that 65 percent of Latinos voted for the Democratic candidate, a drop from President Obama's support, other evidence suggests the figure was much higher. Most likely, Democrats continue to have substantial allegiance among Latinos.[43] But past support does not guarantee continued votes. Some signs, although slight, suggest that there is room for Republican inroads. Figure 9.5 indicates that Latinos are self-identifying less as Democrats since a high point in 2012. The trend toward identifying with the Republican Party shows an upward trajectory since around 2011. As new generations of Latinos become eligible to vote—the estimate is around 800,000 per year become eligible[44]—they become potential Republican identifiers. Complicating this scenario, however, was Donald Trump's presidential campaign, which many Latinos viewed as hostile. His comments that Mexicans entering the United States illegally were rapists and murderers did not encourage Latinos to support him or the Republican Party, and some polls indicated that upwards of 80 percent of Latinos viewed Trump unfavorably.[45]

The partisan inclinations of Latinos may not be as clear-cut as it seemed at first glance. Add to that the other factor that affects the extent of the Latino influence: voter turnout. Even with a large influx of Latinos eligible to vote, if they do not go to the polls, their influence is muted. The data show an apparent ceiling to voter turnout among Latinos in the high 40 percent range.[46] In the long term, the numbers of potential new Latino voters who become eligible to vote will only increase, and Latinos will continue to be sought after by both parties.

In addition to advancing civil rights and earning the enduring loyalty of African American voters, the Johnson administration also expanded federal programs that granted aid to individuals and to state and local governments in the areas of health care, education, housing, job training, and welfare to families with children (see Chapter 13, The Presidency, for an extensive discussion of Johnson's programs). This set of policies was called the Great Society and was founded on the idea that federal expansion would strengthen American society by helping all citizens reach their potential. By expanding the reach of the federal government this way, Johnson reinforced the liberal ideological underpinnings of the Democratic Party.

As this shift in Democratic policies occurred, Republicans saw a new opportunity to attract support from voters who opposed the expansion of the federal government into race relations or the regulation of the economy. Beginning with the campaign of Barry Goldwater in 1964 and continuing with the campaigns of Richard M. Nixon (1969–74) in 1968 and, to a more limited extent, of Ronald Reagan (1981–89) in 1980, the Republicans employed a so-called southern strategy, presenting themselves to southern white voters as holding views on civil rights and race that were opposite those of the Democrats.

Although Republicans did not sanction racism and discrimination, they made it clear that they would not take the same strong steps as the Democrats to impose federal law on states to remedy these problems. Republicans extended their philosophy of limited government intervention by asserting that each state was responsible for enforcing civil rights and that the federal government was overstepping its bounds by interfering at the state and local levels. At the same time, Republicans opposed the Great Society policies as too expensive, and they were philosophically opposed to the federal government giving so much aid directly to individuals without asking for something in return. In this way, the Republican Party continued to move toward a more conservative ideology that sought to limit the powers and programs of the federal government.

The Reagan Revolution and Conservative Party Politics

In 1980, Ronald Reagan, former Republican governor of California, defeated the incumbent President Jimmy Carter (1977–81), a Democrat, partly by appealing to those who opposed the Supreme Court's legalization of abortion in *Roe v. Wade* (1973). Following the ruling, the national stance of the parties diverged, with the Democratic Party publicly supporting the decision and the Republican Party split on the issue. When Reagan won the Republican Party's presidential nomination, he moved the Republicans more firmly into the anti-abortion camp. In the general election, Reagan's campaign offered a consistent conservative ideology that focused on limiting the size of the federal government, opposing abortion, and allowing prayer in public schools, which had been prohibited by the Supreme Court ruling in *Engel v. Vitale* in 1962 (see Chapter 4 for further discussion of prayer in school).[47] Reagan's campaign strategy was designed to attract conservative Democrats who were alienated by their party's official position on abortion and to attract the growing numbers of active evangelical Christian voters, especially in the South.

Reagan also took advantage of the instability in foreign relations that marked Jimmy Carter's four years in office. Although Carter had increased defense spending for the military while in office, he focused on protecting human rights. For Reagan, protecting individual political freedom was a moral obligation for the United States. Reagan campaigned on a strong defense and tough foreign policy that actively promoted freedom, and he made it clear that, under his administration, the United States would work to undermine the Communist political and economic system that was dominant in the then-Soviet Union, eastern Europe, and Cuba.

The combination of these issues brought Reagan the support of many working-class, ethnic, northern voters and southern white voters. These voters were subsequently referred to as Reagan Democrats, and it was in large part due to them that he won the presidential election of 1980.

Digital focus/Alamy

IMAGE 9.12 During his two terms as president from 2009 to 2017, Barack Obama pursued a policy agenda that included the Affordable Care Act, the promotion of marriage equality, and the negotiation of a nuclear treaty with Iran. The extent to which these policy initiatives will remain, however, was in doubt with the election of Donald Trump who, as a presidential candidate, vowed to overturn many of the Obama administration's defining achievements.

Although the Republicans held the presidency for the next twelve years, many of the voters who supported Republicans at the national level stayed loyal to the Democrats in congressional, state, and local elections, especially in the South. This split-ticket voting made it hard for parties to sustain complete voter allegiance at all levels of elected office.

The Modern Partisan Landscape

Bill Clinton was governor of Arkansas when he successfully ran for president in 1992. As had Reagan, Clinton changed his party's direction with a campaign platform that advocated dropping opposition to the death penalty, facilitating free trade, and promising a middle-class tax cut. These policies moved the Democrats away from liberal policies, but Clinton still ran under the established Democratic Party label. Clinton thus appealed to a wider range of voters, and he was able to recapture some electoral territory the Democrats had lost in the southern states.

Essential Knowledge

Political parties will sometimes change their platform and messaging techniques to appeal to different demographic groups.

In office, however, Clinton lost popularity by veering away from core issues such as the middle-class tax cut and economic growth to address socially liberal policies on abortion and gays in the military, to which he had given far less emphasis on the campaign trail. This political misstep set the stage for a Republican Party resurgence.

In the 1994 midterm congressional elections, Republicans took control of both the House and the Senate for the first time since 1954. Led by Newt Gingrich, a Republican House member from Georgia, the Republicans put forth a party platform called the Contract with America, which promised ten major policy initiatives, such as a balanced federal budget and less federal regulation. Every Republican candidate for the House signed it, and by coordinating candidates this way, the Republican Party presented a single national message to voters about what it would do if it won control of Congress. In addition, Gingrich strategically targeted seats in the South that were held by conservative Democrats, trying to appeal to the same set of southern voters who elected Ronald Reagan. Republican efforts were successful, finally overcoming the split-ticket voting of southern voters who had previously voted Democratic in congressional elections.[48] At the presidential level, George W. Bush, the son of former President George H. W. Bush and a conservative Republican governor of Texas, built on the momentum of the Republicans to launch a successful bid for the presidency in 1999.

In 2006, the Democrats began to regain electoral momentum with voters who self-identified as Democrats but had not been voting that way in recent elections, as well as with Independent voters. That year, powerful short-term forces, such as corruption scandals and the Iraq War, put voters in a particularly sour mood toward incumbent Republicans.

The results of the 2008 elections, however, were a sign that the party landscape was shifting again[49] (see Figure 9.6). Clearly the election of an African American president was a significant turning point in race relations; Barack Obama received 43 percent of the white vote in 2008, 2 percentage points higher than John Kerry, a white Democrat, received in 2004. Obama won five states that had been considered solidly Republican in previous presidential elections: Florida, Indiana, North Carolina, Ohio, and Virginia.

However, when voters give one party majority party control of the White House and Congress, they have high expectations for a strong governing track record. In one way, that is what political scientists mean by **responsible parties**; if the parties offer voters clear choices, voters can hold the party in charge responsible for policy outcomes. When President Obama and the Democrats took charge of government in 2009, they faced some of the greatest economic challenges since the Great Depression, as well as ongoing wars in Iraq and Afghanistan. Additionally, Obama and the Democrats in Congress set out to build on the Great Society legacy of government social policy by passing the Affordable Care Act to make health insurance available to all Americans. The 2010 congressional midterm elections were the first opportunity that voters had to register their satisfaction

responsible parties: *Parties that take responsibility for offering the electorate a distinct range of policies and programs, thus providing a clear choice.*

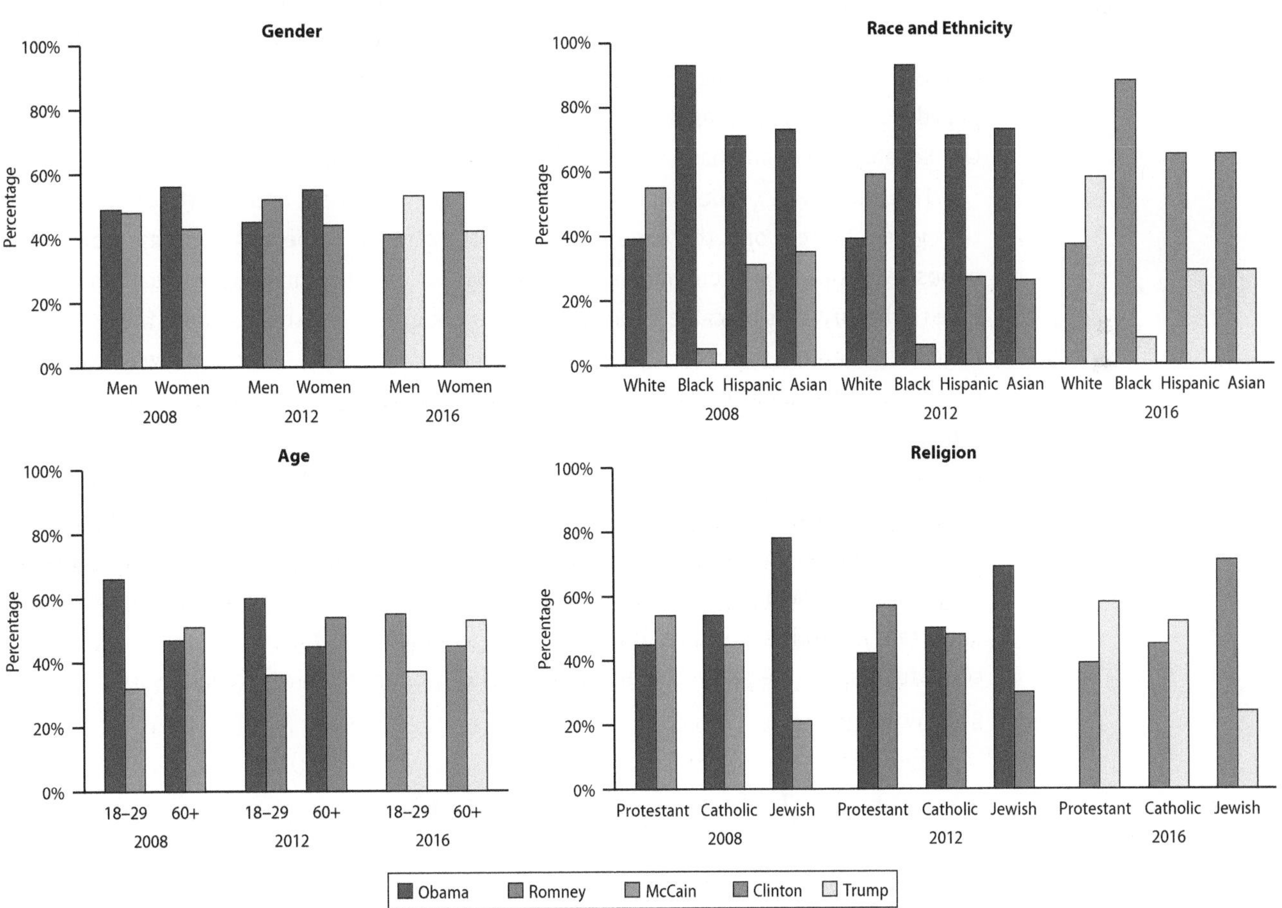

FIGURE 9.6 Votes for President by Demographic Group

Patterns of support among voters can change over time but have remained relatively consistent for the last three election cycles.

Source: New York Times, http://elections.nytimes.com.

or dissatisfaction with the president and his party, and they did so by giving Republicans control of the House of Representatives and electing more Republicans to the Senate. The Democratic losses and Republican gains showed the responsible party system in action, because voters held the incumbent majority party accountable for its performance on the economy, health care, and the ongoing wars.

However, in 2012, Barack Obama won reelection by a margin of 51 to 47 percent and a margin of 5 million votes, although his share of the white vote declined to 39 percent.[50] From the president's perspective, winning reelection as an incumbent was a reaffirmation of his—and by extension the Democratic Party's—policy agenda. At the same time, Republicans held on to their majority control of the House of Representatives and the Democrats held on to the U.S. Senate, which made responsible party government difficult to achieve.

The 2014 midterm elections saw the continuance of divided government, with Republicans in the majority in both houses of Congress and Obama holding the executive branch. The continued divided government led to little bipartisanship and culminated in the decision of the Republican-held U.S. Senate not to act on President Obama's nomination of Merrick Garland to replace Justice Antonin Scalia, who died on February 13, 2016. In the fall of 2016, voters were faced with an open seat in the White House because Barack Obama could not run for president a third time. America again faced a choice between the two parties' candidates with differing visions of the role of government in American society. The 2016 election results significantly changed party control of government. With Donald Trump winning the presidency and Republicans retaining control of both the House of Representatives and the U.S. Senate, the country has a united party government for the first time since 2009.

There is a trade-off between responsible party government and bipartisan cooperation; where there is one, there is almost never the other. Members of Congress from opposite parties rarely communicate directly with each other anymore; instead, they take to the airwaves on cable TV and Twitter to criticize each other. Despite the wide divide between the two major parties, within each party, members do not always agree on issues, and party leaders are not always able to forge internal cooperation. Elected officials are constantly exposed to a wide range of opinions, and they face pressures to respond both to the voters and to party elites. Politicians and party activists can communicate directly with voters, and citizens have many ways to register their opinions on most issues. In addition, party activists are able to track elected officials and monitor how well they adhere to the party's policies. Although increased participation in the deliberation of important issues is a welcome development in a democracy, it makes it hard to represent constituents, toe the party line, and still be able to compromise when necessary to enact good public policy.

Political Parties and Democracy

Political parties, which emerged in the nation's first decade, now play a major role in American democracy. The Democrats and the Republicans together claim the allegiance of almost 90 percent of voters when one includes strong identifiers and voters who consistently lean toward one party.[51] Political parties determine the choices voters have at the polls by crafting the laws that allow candidates to be on the ballot and overseeing the primaries that allow voters to choose candidates. Parties also recruit candidates for elected office, raise funds for campaigns, register voters, and organize get-out-the-vote drives. In sum, parties shape the selection of candidates who seek, run for, and win elected office.

Do political parties make it easier for voters to hold elected officials accountable? Party platforms tell voters what candidates intend to do if elected, and voters can compare their actions against their campaign pledges. If pledges and policies match up, voters typically reelect the officials; if they do not, voters can vote for the opponents in the next election. One advantage of clear dividing lines between the parties is that it makes the job of monitoring the government easier for the average voter. However, such clear divisions also bring the disadvantages of conflict and stalemate that make bipartisan policy making difficult.

Parties do a mixed job of promoting equal political participation among all citizens. On the one hand, they are a gateway to participation because membership in a political party is free, and citizens can work a little or a lot on behalf of the party. Primaries and caucuses give every party member a say in determining who will represent the party in elected office, and they force candidates who seek the party's endorsement to shape their campaign platforms according to party voters' preferences. Because voters are free to join and leave political parties as frequently as they wish, parties are always seeking to represent their members' viewpoints.

On the other hand, parties can discourage political participation by acting as gatekeepers in the way of third-party formation. The U.S. party system is structured around two major parties, and even though third parties have arisen at various times, they are quickly subsumed or defeated by one of the two major parties. The two-party system reduces major policy issues to two-sided questions, when, in fact, the complexity of these issues warrants multiple perspectives. The problem for democracy is that there is no formal venue for presenting multiple perspectives in elections or in the governing institutions.

The larger question is whether the twenty-first-century U.S. party system fulfills the role of enabling widespread participation in the governing process. In terms of responding to changes in public opinion, political parties fall short of meeting their responsibilities as agents of democratic government. They are large, entrenched organizations with multiple layers—federal, state, and local—that can differ in their viewpoints on specific issues. The breadth of the national parties makes it difficult to reach internal consensus on issues at every level of government.

The combination of intraparty divisions with interparty polarization and conflict has produced a party-dominated democracy that is not consistently responsive to voters' interests and opinions. However, in a democracy, power rests on winning elections, and for that, parties will always depend on voters like you, who hold the power to change them by staying loyal or switching your allegiance.

Political Science Reasoning

Question 1

Practice 1, Practice 3

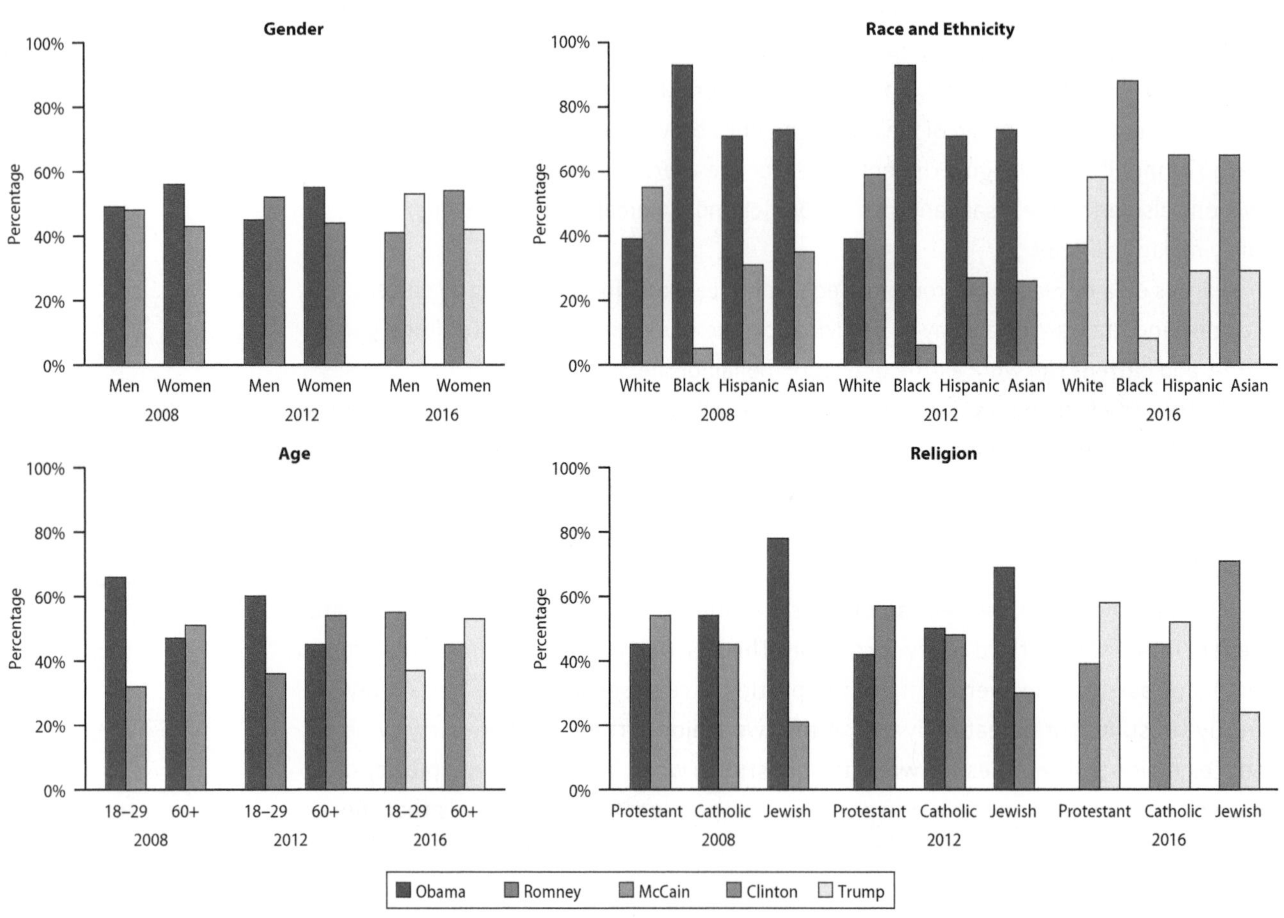

FIGURE 9.6 Votes for President by Demographic Group (*taken from HED text*)

1. Based on votes for president, which groups appear to be the key constituencies of the Democratic Party and the Republican Party?
2. Which groups appear to be changing their preferences?
3. How might the impacted political parties change their platforms based on these changes?

Question 2

Practice 1, Practice 4

THE BALLOT
IN COUNTING THERE IS STRENGTH
"THAT'S WHAT'S THE MATTER."
Boss TWEED. "As long as I count the Votes, what are you going to do about it? say?"

IMAGE 9.8 William Marcy "Boss" Tweed (*taken from HED text*)

The above political cartoon of William "Boss" Tweed was drawn by Thomas Nast and published in *Harper's Weekly* in October of 1871.

1. Citing specific evidence from the cartoon, what Nast's opinion of electoral procedures of that time?
2. What specific reforms were instituted to address the issues identified in the cartoon?
3. What has been the impact of these reforms on the strength of American political parties?

Focus on AP® Success

9 Political Parties

Must Know: Key Concepts

- Linkage Institution
- Party Platform
- Party Organization
- Party in Government
- Party in the Electorate
- Micro Targeting
- Winner Take All Elections
- Proportional Representation Elections
- Duverger's Law
- Open Primary
- Closed Primary
- Party System/Party Era
- Party Realignment
- Candidate-Centered Campaign
- Third Party

Thinking Politically

Argumentation

The "candidate-centered campaign" has been a hallmark of modern American politics. It is largely caused by the direct primary, which has tended to weaken political parties. Among the many problems associated with weakened parties is the increased difficulty in policy making in Congress. This is not to say that the direct primary is not without benefits. Some would argue that the increased level of democratic participation in choosing candidates is a good thing. Do the benefits of the direct primary outweigh the disadvantages?

Data Analysis

Examine the data displayed in Figure 9.5. Based upon this information and the information displayed in Figure 6.8 from Chapter 6, what are the implications for both the Democratic and Republican parties?

Data Analysis

Examine the data displayed in Figure 9.6. Who are the typical voters for each party? Which demographic group is the most Democratic? Which demographic group is the most Republican?

Understanding Learning Objectives with Key Concepts

MPA – 3.C Explain the roles that individual choice and state laws play in voter turnout in elections.

- Voter choices can be influenced by party identification as well as things such as characteristics of the candidate, political issues, and various demographic factors such as race, sex, age, income level, and education.

PMI – 5.A Describe linkage institutions.

- Linkage institutions are institutions that connect citizens to policy-making institutions. These linkage institutions facilitate communication and involvement of citizens in the political process. In the United States, politics linkage institutions include media, political parties, elections, and interest groups.

PMI – 5.B Explain the function and impact of political parties on the electorate and government.

- American political parties interact with the electorate and the government in several ways:
    - Parties educate voters by providing information to them about candidates, issues, and governmental

policies. Parties also mobilize and organize citizens for political action.

- Parties write platforms that explain their positions on political issues.
- Parties recruit, train, and support candidates for public office.
- Parties also provide support services to candidates in the form of training campaign managers, assisting with fundraising, and developing a media strategy.

PMI – 5.C Explain why and how political parties change and adapt.

- Historically parties, specifically the party organization, nominated candidates for public office, usually through a caucus or convention. This changed with advent of the direct primary. Now members of the party in the electorate, regular citizens who affiliate with a party, select candidates for public office. This has contributed to the "candidate-centered campaign." As such, the role of the party organization has been weakened. Parties have adapted to this change to the candidate-centered campaign by supporting the candidates rather than taking a dominant role in running the campaign.
- Parties have recognized the increasing demographic diversity of the United States by appeals to people based on things such as race, sex, class, etc.
- Parties have adapted their structure to recognize new campaign legislation (such as bans of soft money), changes in regional alignments (such the Republican Party in the southeast), and the development of information technology.
- Due to advances in information technology, political parties keep voter databases that contain detailed demographic information. Utilizing data analytics, parties are able to refine and customize their message to individual voters in a process known as micro targeting.

PMI – 5.D Explain how structural barriers impact third-party and independent-candidate success.

- The electoral system of the United States is a single-member plurality system (also known as winner take all or first past the post). In this system, a candidate either wins or loses an election. This is different from a proportional representation system where candidates from political parties are elected to legislative office based on the relative strength of the performance of their party. According to Duverger's law, single-member district systems will tend to favor the creation of two large parties. This fact serves as barrier to the success of third-party candidates.
- The two dominant parties in American politics have also been adept at incorporating issues that were raised by third parties into their own platforms. Deprived of a unique set of issues, third party candidates have difficulty securing votes, and the third party dies away.

PRD – 2.A Explain how the different processes work in a U.S presidential election.

- Parties have a direct influence on U.S. elections. They organize nominating elections, called primaries, in each state. Some states have open primaries and some have closed primaries.
- Open primary – Citizens declare on primary election day the primary in which they wish to participate
- Closed primary – Citizens declare their party preference at the time of voter registration

Making Connections

American political parties are election centered. As such, there is tremendous overlap between content of this chapter and Chapter 10, Elections and Campaigns and Chapter 11, Voting and Participation. Upon the conclusion of those chapters, you should review this chapter to make deeper connections regarding the role that parties play in elections, political campaigns, and voting.

Interest groups and political parties are similar yet have distinct functions. Learn to distinguish between the functions and characteristics of the two.

The election of the president has two distinct phases: nomination (the contest for national convention delegates) and the general election (the contest for presidential electors). This chapter will discuss the nomination process briefly. It will be more fully discussed in the next chapter, as will be the general election process. Learn to distinguish between the different strategies needed to win each phase.

Going Deeper: Party Systems

It is important to remember that American parties are coalitions of interests. They are not monolithic. There are distinct periods when these interests are aligned with a political party. These periods are known as party systems or party eras.

Periodically in American politics, the electorate goes through what is known as realignment. This occurs when the groups that form the coalitions that makes up each party shift. This usually happens when there has been some sort of economic and or social upheaval. For example, there was realignment in 1932 that produced a period of Democratic Party dominance until 1968.

The election that marks the change is called a realigning election or critical election. During this election, one or more groups begin to change their party allegiance. Using the above example of 1932, African Americans, who had historically voted Republican since the Civil War, began to a show a preference for the Democratic Party.

10 Elections and Campaigns

AP® Learning Objectives

PRD – 2.A Explain how the different processes work in a U.S. presidential election.

PRD – 2.B Explain how the Electoral College impacts democratic participation.

PRD – 2.C Explain how the different processes work in U.S. congressional elections.

PRD – 2.D Explain how campaign organizations and strategies affect the elections process.

PRD – 2.E Explain how the organization, finance, and strategies of national political campaigns affect the election process.

Performance Tasks

Upon the completion of this chapter, you must be able to do the following:

- Explain how the following models describe voter behavior: rational choice, retrospective voting, prospective voting, and party line voting.
- Explain how fund-raising and increasing campaign costs impact elections and policy making.
- Explain how campaigns have evolved to the point that they now require professional staffs and modern communications strategies.

George Frey/Getty Images

> *"It's my hope I'll be reelected to serve this community. . . . There's a lot of work we still have to do to fight for the middle class and make sure every Arizonan has a shot at the American dream."*
>
> **KYRSTEN SINEMA**
> Brigham Young University

AP Images/Matt York

Congresswoman Kyrsten Sinema (D-AZ) is unconventional. Just consider her educational background. She graduated high school at the age of 16 in Arizona as valedictorian and graduated Brigham Young University (BYU) in 1995 at the age of 18. She earned a master's degree in social work in 1999, a JD in 2004, and her PhD in Justice Studies in 2012—all from Arizona State University. Sinema also has a strong bipartisan streak—again something unusual these days. She first ran for state legislature in 2002 as an independent, but after losing the race, ran as a Democrat in 2004 and won. In the Arizona state legislature, she worked closely with Republicans on legislation tied to human trafficking. In her first race for Congress, the *Arizona Republic*, the local Phoenix newspaper, endorsed her for her nonpartisan style, arguing that for "Sinema, it's always about the issue, not the personalities."[1] Finally, Sinema's personal choices make her unique: Although raised in a conservative Mormon family, she is the first openly bisexual person elected to Congress. In an era when the country has become quite used to openly gay politicians, her sexuality drew quite a bit of attention. She was not fond of the attention either, explaining that "I'm not a pioneer. I'm just a regular person who works hard."[2]

Yet Sinema is a pioneer. She uses the political process as a gateway to make a difference. During her childhood, she faced some hard times, living for a while in an abandoned gas station without electricity or running water.[3] Those early experiences shaped her life and convinced her to get involved and make the lives of people better. She supported the DREAM Act as a member of the Arizona state legislature. She also fought to rein in Maricopa County Sheriff Joe Arpaio's hardline immigration stances, which often drew attention across the entire country.[4] She hired undocumented DREAM activist Erika Andiola (featured in Chapter 5, Civil Rights) on her staff—a strong signal about her position on that issue. Since being in the U.S. Congress, she has focused a good deal of attention on issues tied to veterans. She argues that "our country has a moral responsibility to do right by the men and women who serve in our military."[5]

Her congressional career started in 2012 when she won in a new district that arose from the redistricting following the 2010 census. In this fairly competitive district, she won the election with about 49 percent of the vote. Her Republican opponent, Vernon Parker, garnered 45 percent, and a Libertarian candidate secured about 6 percent of the vote. As a first-term member of Congress from a competitive district, she knew she would face a tough battle for reelection. Having tackled the difficult issues in Congress and being openly bisexual, she faced harsh attacks. But knowing that her reelection would not be easy, she raised a good deal of money not only to respond to any attacks but also to scare off potential challengers.

Sinema won 54 percent of the vote in 2014, beating her opponent by 13 points. She won by only 4 points two years earlier. In 2016 she did even better, winning by over 20 percentage points and securing 61 percent of the vote against her opponent, David Giles.

Elections and campaigns, as Kyrsten Sinema knows, offer a gateway into the American political system. They provide many opportunities for participation, not only running for office but also volunteering and working at the polls. During campaigns, candidates offer competing visions of the role of government and promise to enact specific policies. The people decide to support a candidate and a campaign program when they go to the polls. Elections provide the most common (and easiest) gateway for the people to express their opinions and to hold elected officials accountable, shaping the course of government. In this chapter, we examine how elections and campaigns work, asking whether, and how, these institutions both promote government responsiveness and foster accountability.

10.1 The Constitutional Requirements for Elections

Describe the ideas that molded the Framers' thinking about elections

Given the importance of elections to the democratic process, it is surprising that the Constitution says so little about them. The requirements that the Constitution lays out for elections indicate that the Framers wanted to set up barriers against direct democracy. Only the House of Representatives was to be elected directly by the people. In elections for the president and for the Senate, the public's role was indirect and complex. Today, senators are elected directly by the people. Presidential elections also give citizens more say in the process, but these contests continue to be shaped by constitutional requirements that serve as a gate between the people and the presidency. In this section, we explain the constitutional requirements for American elections as background for understanding the ways in which presidential and congressional campaigns are run.

Presidential Elections

The constitutional rules governing the selection of the president reflect three fundamental themes that guided the Framers' thinking. First, the states were given broad discretion on key matters regarding presidential elections to ensure their importance and to counterbalance the power of the national government. Second, the Framers designed the presidency with George Washington in mind and did not spell out all aspects in great detail, including elections. Over time, the details were filled in. Third, the presidency was intended to stand above party politics, doing what was right for the nation rather than supporting one faction over another. That assumption went awry early on, and parties formed almost from the start.

Essential Knowledge

To win the Electoral College, the nominees of each party focus on the "swing states." These states are very often different from the states they focused on to win the nomination.

The Electoral College. The means by which the president of the United States is selected was born of compromise between the interests of the states and the interests of the people, yielding a system that even today is indirect and confusing. Like the Connecticut Compromise that produced a legislature with an upper chamber to represent the states and a lower chamber to represent the people, the system for electing the president was intended to be similarly balanced. The formal selection of the president is in the hands of electors, who collectively constitute the **Electoral College**.

Electoral College: *The presidential electors, selected every four years to represent the votes of their respective states, who meet to cast the electoral votes for president and vice president.*

The Constitution gave state legislatures the responsibility of deciding how best to choose electors, either by choosing the electors themselves or granting the people the right to choose the electors. Because state legislators were, for the most part, elected by the people, this arrangement gave the public an indirect say in the choice. The idea was that the Electoral College would serve as a gatekeeper against rash or ignorant voters. There was little support among the Framers for letting the people choose the president directly. In fact, during the debates at the Constitutional Convention, George Mason said that allowing the people to select the president would be like referring "a trial of colors to a blind man."[6] Today the people of each state, not the members of state legislatures, choose the electors in an arrangement that has given citizens a new gateway for influence (see Figure 10.1).

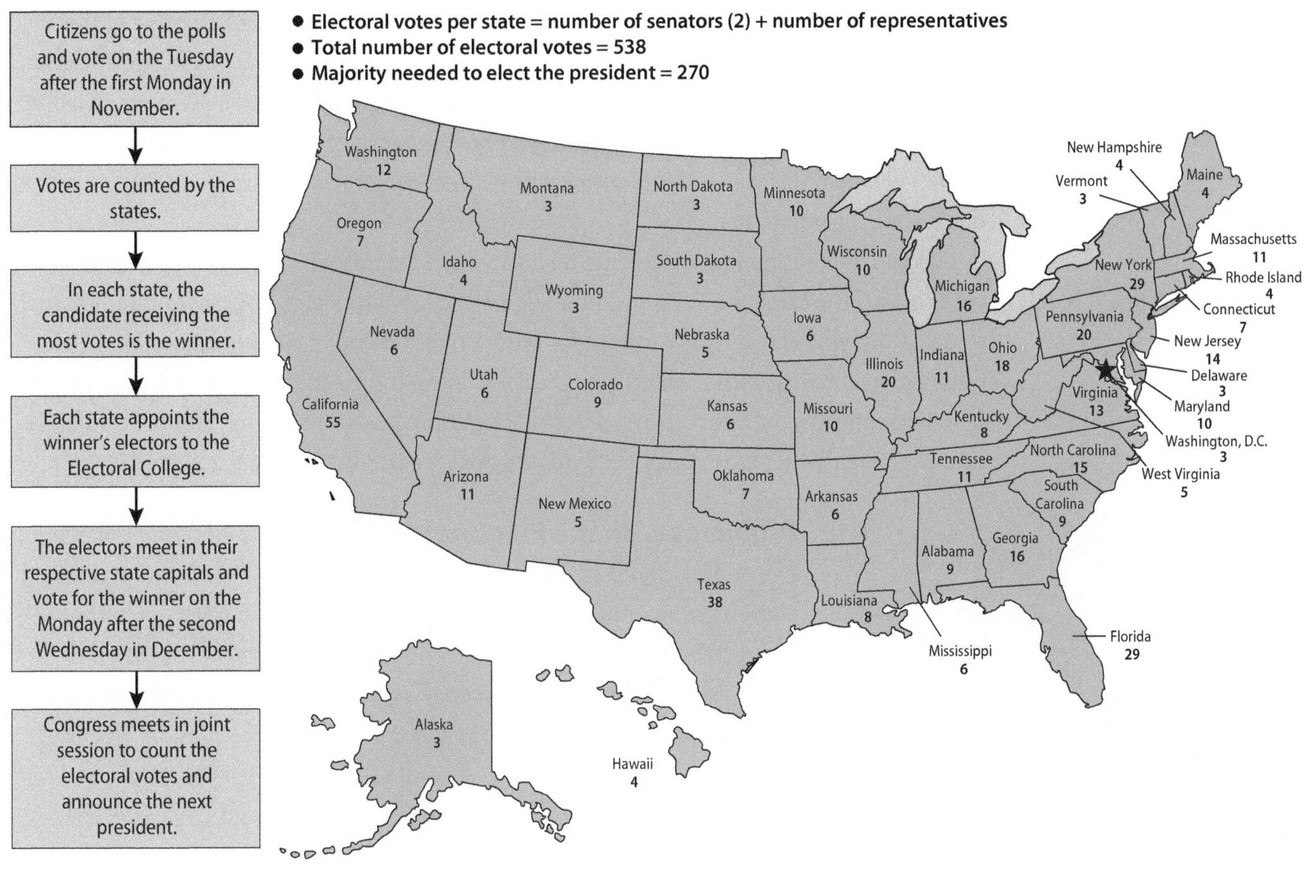
Citizens go to the polls and vote on the Tuesday after the first Monday in November.
Votes are counted by the states.
In each state, the candidate receiving the most votes is the winner.
Each state appoints the winner's electors to the Electoral College.
The electors meet in their respective state capitals and vote for the winner on the Monday after the second Wednesday in December.
Congress meets in joint session to count the electoral votes and announce the next president.
• Electoral votes per state = number of senators (2) + number of representatives
• Total number of electoral votes = 538
• Majority needed to elect the president = 270
Washington 12
Oregon 7
California 55
Idaho 4
Nevada 6
Montana 3
Wyoming 3
Utah 6
Arizona 11
Colorado 9
New Mexico 5
North Dakota 3
South Dakota 3
Nebraska 5
Kansas 6
Oklahoma 7
Texas 38
Minnesota 10
Iowa 6
Missouri 10
Arkansas 6
Louisiana 8
Wisconsin 10
Illinois 20
Michigan 16
Indiana 11
Ohio 18
Kentucky 8
Tennessee 11
Mississippi 6
Alabama 9
Georgia 16
Florida 29
South Carolina 9
North Carolina 15
Virginia 13
West Virginia 5
Pennsylvania 20
New York 29
Vermont 3
New Hampshire 4
Maine 4
Massachusetts 11
Rhode Island 4
Connecticut 7
New Jersey 14
Delaware 3
Maryland 10
Washington, D.C. 3
Alaska 3
Hawaii 4

FIGURE 10.1 How the Electoral College Works

This map shows each state's number of electors for the 2016 election, allocated on the basis of the 2010 census. In every state but two, the winner of the popular vote takes all of the electoral votes. Maine and Nebraska allocate votes by congressional district and so can split their electoral votes. The flowchart on the left shows the process by which popular votes are transferred to Electoral College votes.

The electors, however, remain the formal decision makers for choosing the president. In fact, they meet in December to vote formally for the president—five or so weeks after election day in November. These electors are selected in a variety of ways in the fifty states. It is very much a state-centered process. Before the election, each party lines up electors for its nominee. In the 2016 presidential elections, when Hillary Clinton won the most votes in the state of California, her electors were then eligible to vote in December's meeting of the Electoral College. Republican candidate Donald Trump had different electors ready to serve if he had won. Presidential nominees seek to identify people who will be loyal to them. This is important because many states allow electors to vote their conscience, meaning they are not legally bound by the results of the election in their state. Electors rarely deviate from supporting the candidate to whom they are pledged, but the possibility for defection remains.

> ***Essential Knowledge***
>
> The fact that all but two states (Maine and Nebraska) award all of their electoral votes to the top candidate raises questions about whether the Electoral College facilitates or impedes democracy.

Each state receives a number of electoral votes equal to its number of senators and members of the House of Representatives. The minimum is three, because every state has at least one House member and two senators. In 2016, seven states (Alaska, Delaware, Montana, North Dakota, South Dakota, Vermont, and Wyoming) and the District of Columbia had only three votes each in the Electoral College. With fifty-five electoral votes, California had the most. In all but two states, all the state's electoral votes are allocated to the candidate who finishes first in the voting. This winner-take-all system means that if a candidate wins California by just a single vote, that candidate gets all fifty-five of the state's electoral votes. The two exceptions are Nebraska and Maine, which allocate votes by congressional district and so can split their electoral votes. In 2008, Barack Obama won one congressional district in Nebraska, securing one of Nebraska's five electoral votes. In 2016, Maine split electors for the first time, awarding three electoral votes to Hillary Clinton and one to Donald Trump.

To win the presidency, a candidate needs to win a majority (270) of the 538 electoral votes (538 is the total of 435 representatives and 100 senators plus 3 votes from the District of Columbia, whose residents can vote for president but do not have representation in Congress). If no nominee wins a majority of electoral votes, the election is thrown into the House of Representatives. At this point, each state delegation gets a single vote, and the candidate who wins a majority of the states becomes the next president. That last happened in 1824.

IMAGE 10.1 Following passage of the Twelfth Amendment, presidential and vice presidential candidates campaigned on the same ticket. This campaign poster from the 1872 election shows President Ulysses S. Grant and his vice presidential candidate using their humble beginnings to appeal to workingmen.

Problems with the Electoral College. The Electoral College has never worked as the Framers envisioned, as an institution that would allow a group of independent decision makers to get together in the many states and deliberate over who would make the best president. The Framers viewed the presidency as a contest between individuals, not between political parties, and in the first four presidential elections (1789, 1792, 1796, and 1800), electors cast ballots for their top two choices; the winner became president, and the second-place finisher became vice president. The process ignored the parties of the candidates; the goal was to select the most qualified person. In 1796, the process yielded John Adams (1797–1801) as president and his chief rival, Thomas Jefferson, as vice president. Just imagine Hillary Clinton serving as Donald Trump's vice president!

Serious problems arose in 1800, when political parties had fully emerged. Thomas Jefferson and Aaron Burr, both running as Democratic-Republicans, received the same number of Electoral College votes, even though everyone knew that Jefferson was seeking the presidency and Burr the vice presidency. To achieve that outcome, one of the Democratic-Republican electors needed to withhold a vote from Burr, giving Jefferson the most votes and Burr the second most. That did not happen. Adams, who was also running again as a Federalist, finished third. Because no candidate had an outright majority in the Electoral College, Burr decided to try to become president. The election, as a result, was sent to the House of Representatives, since there was no majority winner. A lengthy battle in the House ensued, lasting thirty-seven ballots before Thomas Jefferson (1801–1809) finally won the presidency. The Twelfth Amendment, adopted in 1804, fixed this problem by combining the vote for president and vice president into one ballot, with the person running for each office named.

Another source of problems in the system was that states were free to set their own rules for selecting electors. In the first presidential election in 1789, four states (Delaware, Maryland, Pennsylvania, and Virginia) held direct popular elections to choose electors.[7] Other states used their legislatures to select electors. Further, there was no agreed-upon time for holding these elections. In 1800, voting took place any time between April and November. New York selected its electors in April, and Pennsylvania and South Carolina did not even have rules for selecting theirs until November. States also frequently changed their methods of selecting electors. Only Maryland used a **popular vote** for selecting electors in the first four presidential contests.

popular vote: *Tally of total votes from individual citizens, as opposed to the electoral vote.*

Because of this odd hodgepodge of frequently changing rules, the presidential contest in the early nineteenth century was very different from the campaigns of today. Now states hold elections all on the same day—the first Tuesday after the first Monday in November—and electors meet in December to choose the next president. The Electoral College is an historical artifact of the Framers' constitutional design. But the hodgepodge of state rules, as noted earlier, always makes it possible for some new twist to unfold that would fuel controversy surrounding the formal selection of the president.

Electoral College Reform. The biggest problem with the Electoral College occurs when winning the nation's popular vote does not automatically translate into a win in the Electoral College, meaning that the individual who received fewer votes could become the president. This happened in the 1824, 1876, 1888, 2000, and 2016 presidential elections. Such outcomes raise questions about equality. If a democracy rests on the idea of majority rule—that is, the candidate with the most support in the public wins the election—then about 10 percent of our presidential elections have been "undemocratic."

Some may wonder why the country does not just change the rules to select the president through the popular vote. This method would appear more democratic because all votes would be treated equally. But the current system has some advantages. For example, the Electoral College system encourages candidates to secure support in all corners of the country, not just in areas with dense populations. A system of popular votes would privilege Los Angeles over Oklahoma. In America's federal system, the states do matter. Eliminating the Electoral College would decrease the role of the states, dampening the significance of state interests. There are also practical problems. Doing away with the Electoral College through a constitutional

Library of Congress Prints and Photographs Division [LC-DIG-ggbain-03138]

IMAGE 10.2 The 1876 election was contested, and its outcome was determined by an electoral commission. Some feared public disturbances at the inauguration, so Rutherford B. Hayes, who had won the Electoral College but not the popular vote, took the oath of office privately in the White House. The formal ceremony at the Capitol, two days later, was peaceful.

SUPREME COURT CASES

Bush v. Gore (2000)

QUESTION: Does Florida's subjective recount mechanism violate equal protection of the law? If so, should there be a recount using more objective standards?

ORAL ARGUMENT: December 11, 2000 (listen at http://www.oyez.org/cases/2000-2009/2000/2000_00_949/)

DECISION: December 12, 2000 (read at http://caselaw.lp.findlaw.com/scripts/getcase.pl?court=us&vol=000&invol=00-949)

OUTCOME: Yes, Florida's recount procedures violate the equal protection clause (7–2), and no, there is insufficient time to conduct a recount (5–4).

The presidential election of 2000 came down to Florida's electoral votes. The candidate who won the state—Republican Governor George W. Bush of Texas or Democratic Vice President Al Gore—would win the election. The early counts were excruciatingly close, with the news networks first calling the election for Gore, then declaring it undecided, then declaring Bush the winner, and then putting it back in the undecided column.

Due to the closeness of the race, an automatic machine recount took place. Bush led Gore by 537 votes out of nearly 6 million cast. Because elections, even for federal office, are administered under state law, Gore went to state court in Florida, asking for a hand recount in four counties that would require election officials in those counties to determine, from each ballot, the intent of the voter. In punch card ballots, the machine will not read a ballot unless the chad—the area that is to be punched out by the voter—is completely removed. But a hand count might be able to determine the voter's intent from a "hanging" or "dimpled" or "pregnant" chad—indented but not sufficiently punched out so as to break off or even break the corners.

The Florida Supreme Court ruled for Gore by a 4–3 vote on December 8. Bush then filed suit in federal court, claiming that the standard of the intent of the voter that Florida used, which could mean different standards by different officials, was so arbitrary as to violate the equal protection clause. The Bush legal team asked for an injunction, an order blocking further recount. Both the U.S. District Court and the U.S. Court of Appeals rejected Bush's request. Bush then appealed to the Supreme Court.

The Supreme Court agreed to hear the case, and on December 9, it decided, by a 5–4 vote, to halt the recount before the Court's decision. The Court heard oral arguments on December 11 and announced its decision at 10 p.m. on December 12.

The Supreme Court ruled by a 7–2 vote that the absence of specific standards for gauging the intent of the voter was so arbitrary as to violate the equal protection clause. The Court also declared by a 5–4 vote that Florida's legislature intended all recounts to be completed by December 12, thus making a recount impossible.

The dissenters declared that the machinery of running elections is a state question that should not involve the federal courts; that the Court's prior interpretation of the equal protection clause has allowed differential treatment as long as there is no intent to discriminate against certain groups; and that the Court's December 12 deadline was never stated in Florida law.

Vice President Gore conceded the election the next day.

Thinking Critically

1. Why was the Supreme Court so rushed in its decision?
2. In what way did Florida's recount plan violate equality?

amendment would be difficult because it is unlikely that three-quarters of the states, needed to ratify an amendment, would support such a reform. Small states see merit in the system, since it forces presidential candidates to consider their needs and gives them a chance for more influence.

AP Images/Marta Lavandier

IMAGE 10.3 Election workers in Miami manually recount votes while representatives of both parties observe. The 2000 Florida recount was fraught with difficulty, and a series of court cases regarding the election culminated in a Supreme Court decision on December 12 that halted the recount and essentially made George W. Bush the winner of the election.

The 2000 Presidential Election. Because elections are a centerpiece of democracy, it is important for them to be viewed as fair. The events surrounding the 2000 presidential election tested the credibility of the American electoral process. The margin between Vice President Albert Gore Jr. and George W. Bush (2001–09) was razor thin. In the popular vote, Gore received nearly 600,000 more votes than Bush—just a 0.5 percentage point difference (48.4 percent to 47.9 percent). The number of electoral votes did not identify a winner on election night because the state of Florida was too close to call, and without that state's electoral votes, neither candidate had the necessary 270 votes. Bush led in Florida by 537 votes out of 5.8 million votes cast—a 0.0001 percent difference. Demands for a recount ensued, and the Florida recount revealed how difficult it is to produce an accurate vote count. A series of court cases resulted in a Supreme Court decision that determined the outcome of the election (see Supreme Court Cases: *Bush v. Gore*).

Many votes had not been counted in Florida, and some had been counted for the wrong candidate. Citizens across the country lost faith in American elections. Since that time, the public's confidence had been restored. But the 2016 presidential election raised the issue again. Hillary Clinton won more votes than Trump but did not win the Electoral College. Many see this outcome as unfair, but both sides understood the rules of the game. The faith in elections following 2000 was restored, and that will likely happen after this last presidential election as well.

Essential Knowledge

Most states use the direct primary to nominate candidates for public office. These primaries can be "closed" or "open." In a closed primary citizens can only vote in the primary of the party that they declared when they registered to vote. In an open primary citizens decide on primary election day in which primary they wish to participate. A majority is usually needed to win a primary.

The ultimate winner of the contest is decided in a general election. A plurality is usually required to win a general election.

Congressional Elections

The constitutional guidelines for congressional elections also reflect the compromise between the interests of the states and the interests of the people. The Framers intended that the Senate would bring state interests to bear on the legislative process, while they intended that the House would represent "the people." Each state, regardless of size, has two senators, while representatives are elected from congressional districts within states whose boundaries are adjusted to accommodate changes in population. Senators serve staggered six-year terms, while House members serve two-year terms.

Senate Elections. The Constitution originally gave the choice of senators to state legislatures. Again the Framers inserted a gate between the people and those who were to serve their interests in the Senate. In the late nineteenth century, however, Progressive reformers called for elimination of this gate, arguing that the people ought to have a direct say in the election of senators. This reform became a reality with the adoption of the Seventeenth Amendment in 1913. Even with this change, however, there are barriers against overwhelming change in the composition of the Senate because Senate elections are staggered; only one-third of senators are up for election at a time. This arrangement ensures that the Senate is insulated from large shifts in public sentiment.

Essential Knowledge

Gerrymandering, redistricting, and unequal representation of constituencies have increased partisanship and decreased accountability, partially addressed by such Court decisions as the one-person, one-vote ruling in *Baker v. Carr* (1961) and the no-racial-gerrymandering decision in *Shaw v. Reno* (1993).

House Elections and Redistricting. In contrast to the Senate, the entire House of Representatives is up for election every two years. Also in contrast to the Senate, House members have always been elected directly by the people.[8]

The Constitution requires that states apportion representatives by population, which is counted every ten years in a census. Originally, each member was to represent no more than thirty thousand people. As the population grew, the House of Representatives grew as well, from 65 members in 1789 to 237 members in 1857. The House continued to grow until 1911, and in 1929, the number was capped at 435. A member now represents, on average, more than seven hundred thousand people, as set by the 2010 census. Every ten years, states draw new district lines following a census. Depending on patterns of population growth or decline, states win or lose congressional seats with each new census. Currently seven states have populations so small that they qualify for only one member of the House of Representatives (Alaska, Delaware, Montana, North Dakota, South Dakota, Vermont, and Wyoming). These states do not need to worry about drawing new congressional districts.

redistricting: *Process whereby state legislatures redraw the boundaries of congressional districts in the state to make them equal in population size.*

State legislatures are responsible for drawing the district lines in a process known as **redistricting**. While the official aim of redistricting is to try to keep districts equal in population, the majority party in the state legislature tries to construct each district in such a way as to make it easier for its candidates to win congressional seats. Although citizens are not required to disclose party affiliation in the census, past voting patterns give parties a strong indication of where they have the advantage. In addition to equal population in districts, another important constraint facing the redistricting is that the boundaries must be contiguous (uninterrupted).

Redistricting has also been used as a tool to achieve greater minority representation in the House of Representatives. Following passage of the Voting Rights Act (VRA) in 1965, some states sought to dilute the effect of minority voters by drawing district lines so as to split their voting strength. In 1982, amendments to the VRA forbade this practice, and in response, state legislatures created majority-minority districts, in which African Americans or Hispanics would constitute a majority of the voters in the district, thereby increasing the possibility of their electing African American or Hispanic candidates. In 2012, for example, Joaquín Castro won election to the House from the 20th Congressional District in Texas, which is a Latino majority-minority district (see Chapter 12, Congress). In the past decade, however, the federal courts have ruled that state legislatures overemphasized the racial composition of these districts to the point that the districts made no geographic sense. As a result, current guidelines on redistricting call for the consideration of race in drawing district lines, but not to the extreme that it had been employed in the past.[9]

gerrymandering: *Redistricting that blatantly benefits one political party over the other or concentrates (or dilutes) the voting impact of racial and ethnic groups.*

Any change to the size and shape of a district can have political implications because shifts in its partisan makeup alter which party might be able to capture the seat. For these reasons, there are major battles over the composition of districts. The politicization of drawing districts is called **gerrymandering**. Chapter 12 provides more details about this process

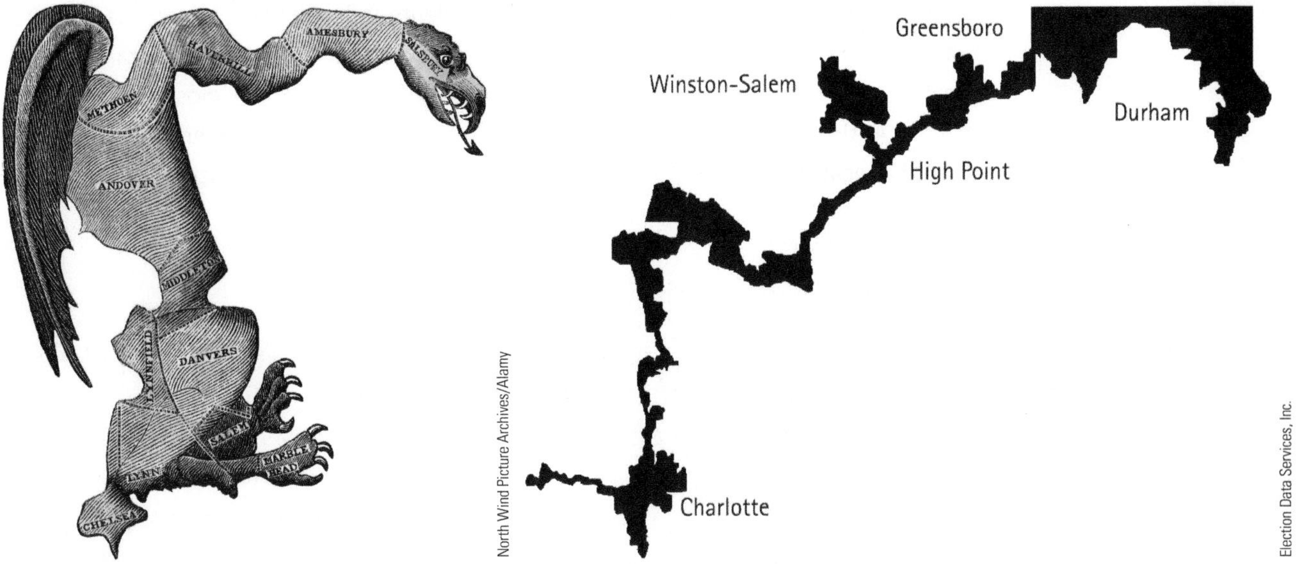

IMAGES 10.4 AND 10.5 The term *gerrymander* comes from the salamander-shaped district in Massachusetts (above left), which Governor Elbridge Gerry approved following the census of 1810. Political rivals denounced the blatant seeking of political advantage that had produced such an oddly shaped congressional district, and the taunt stuck, passing into common usage in politics. Nevertheless, gerrymandered districts remain. In 1991, a North Carolina redistricting was designed to create a district with African Americans in the majority (above right). Federal courts later ruled that North Carolina had to revise these district lines so that the congressional district was more compact.

and explains how different compositions of districts can alter the kind of gateway congressional elections offer.

For example, the Supreme Court in *Thornburg v. Gingles* unanimously struck down a North Carolina redistricting plan. It had a discriminatory effect (a discriminatory intent is not necessary for a violation of the VRA, just a discriminatory effect) of diluting the ability of African Americans to choose state representatives of their choice by splitting "politically cohesive groups of black voters" into districts where blocs of white voters would consistently defeat the black candidates.[10] Twenty years later, the Supreme Court, in *LULAC v. Perry,* upheld a partisan gerrymandering by the Texas legislature but struck down one of the districts where a Latino majority had been diluted by moving a bloc of Latinos into a different district.[11]

Other Elections

The only type of election mentioned in the Constitution in which the people could directly participate is the election of members of the U.S. House of Representatives. Today, however, U.S. citizens elect the president (through electors), members of Congress, governors, state legislators, and a range of local officials, including at the city, town, or village level. In some states, voters can cast ballots on specific policies through initiatives and referenda[12] (see Chapter 3, Federalism). In addition, we have primary elections where parties ask citizens to vote for the nominee for the general election (see Chapter 9, Political Parties). Further, in thirty-eight of the fifty states, some sort of election is involved in the selection or the retention of judges for the state's highest court.[13] No other developed country has as many elections as the United States.[14]

There are three reasons for this heavy reliance on the ballot. First, the public views elections as legitimate devices for making political choices.[15] Second, the Constitution was vague about rules surrounding the choice of presidents and members of Congress, allowing states to make greater use of elections, and many have done so. Third, the federal system created layers of government and multiple political offices to fill them, most of which are elected. At the local level, the people generally elect school board members and commissions that deal with various public tasks, such as water and road construction.

10.2 Presidential Campaigns

Outline the steps in presidential campaigns

Presidential campaigns capture the interest of the vast majority of Americans. In September 2016, two months before the presidential election, 85 percent of the electorate paid at least some attention to the contest between Donald Trump and Hillary Clinton.[16] Every move a presidential candidate makes is watched and assessed. This focus on the presidency would have surprised the Framers, who expected the legislative branch to be the center of attention. But as the executive branch has gained power, so has the importance of the contest to fill the office of president.

The course of the modern presidential campaign is long and difficult. From the decision to run to the final victory and concession speeches, the road to the White House is shaped by constitutional requirements, interparty struggles, and strategies for attracting votes that highlight the many gates and gateways along the way.

Evolution of the Modern Campaign

As in so many matters of custom and protocol, George Washington shaped the way future presidential aspirants would campaign for president. Like others at the Constitutional Convention, he worried that a chief executive could morph into a monarch, so he deliberately avoided doing anything to advance his candidacy. He took these steps even though he and all the Framers knew that they created the office of president with him in mind. Washington stayed at Mount Vernon, his estate on the Potomac River, and let others work on his behalf. The electors met on February 4, 1789, and the vote for Washington was unanimous. Only then did Washington proceed to New York City, then the new nation's capital, where he took the oath of office on April 30.

Washington's conduct continued to influence presidential campaigns until the start of the twentieth century. Candidates allowed their political parties to campaign on their behalf but avoided looking too ambitious. In 1896, William McKinley (1897–1901) stayed home in Canton, Ohio, speaking to well-wishers from his front porch. This so-called front porch campaign proved successful, but only because his campaign manager, Mark Hanna, and the Republican Party were raising funds and securing votes behind the scenes.

Although candidates in the early nineteenth century sought to appear aloof and above the fray, their supporters took every opportunity to advance their candidacies. Buttons and slogans promoted favorites, and parades and barbeques sought to convince the undecided.

Participation had much more of a social component than it does now. Many observers argue that the high rate of voting in the late nineteenth century reflected the fact that campaigns were often fun.[17]

By the early twentieth century, presidential contenders began to campaign actively, too, and campaigning started earlier and earlier. The 2016 presidential campaign officially began in March 2015, when Senator Ted Cruz (R-TX) formally announced his intention to seek the presidency. He was hoping an early start would help him win.[18] Throughout 2015, seventeen candidates announced their decision to seek the White House, including Jeb Bush, Ben Carson, Rand Paul, Mike Huckabee, Donald Trump, John Kasich, Carly Fiorina, and Marco Rubio. Starting the day after the 2016 election, speculation began about who might run in 2020. Will Senator Elizabeth Warren, Senator Cory Booker, or First Lady Michelle Obama try for the Democratic nomination? It is no wonder that many observers have expressed concern over what has been called the **permanent campaign**,[19] a worry that politicians, especially presidents, spend too much time working toward reelection and not enough time governing. Some argue that if politicians spent more time governing and less time running for elections, the nation would be better off. Nevertheless, politicians must win elections to be able to govern, and constant campaigning may be an indication of responsiveness.

The Granger Collection, NYC

IMAGE 10.6 In 1896, William McKinley, former House member and governor of Ohio, ran for president from his front porch in Canton, Ohio. Visitors arrived by train, and he spoke to groups of them, sometimes several times a day. In contrast, his opponent, William Jennings Bryan, traveled all over the country by train, speaking to crowds from the back of train cars. McKinley won.

The Decision to Run and the Invisible Primary

The decision to seek the presidency is a serious one. The presidency is the highest elective office in the land and a position that offers a chance both to influence the course of the nation and to leave a legacy as the leader of the free world. It is perhaps for these reasons that so many of the nation's political leaders consider running for this great office. The decision is not, however, an easy one to make, and potential candidates must ask themselves many difficult questions:

permanent campaign: *Charge that presidents and members of Congress focus more on winning the next election than on governing.*

- How will a presidential campaign affect my family?
- Will my indiscretions in college come back to haunt me?
- Can I build a team of advisers that will allow me to win the presidency?
- Can I raise enough money to be competitive?
- Who else might run for the office?
- What do I want to accomplish if elected?
- Am I prepared to campaign eighteen hours a day for nearly two years straight?
- Am I capable of handling the pressure that comes with being in the Oval Office?
- Can I win?
- What happens if I lose?

These are some of the questions that swirl in a potential candidate's mind when he or she thinks about throwing "my hat in the ring," a phrase from the sport of boxing that Theodore Roosevelt used to announce his candidacy in 1912. The campaign for president is unlike that for any other office. The demands are intense. Every move a major candidate makes is discussed and analyzed by journalists and political pundits. Presidential campaigns are pressure cookers—perhaps appropriately, because the office is so demanding. The American public wants to know whether a candidate has the toughness to serve as commander in chief and the wisdom to identify the best policies. Candidates often describe the process as being put through a meat grinder. For an overview of the two- to three-year-long ordeal, see Table 10.1.

invisible primary: *Period just before the primaries begin during which candidates attempt to capture party support and media coverage.*

After a candidate decides to run for president, he or she enters what is called the **invisible primary**. No votes are cast, but candidates are jockeying for position so they can be ready to do well in the initial primaries and caucuses. Usually, candidates must line up party support, financial backing, and credibility with journalists in the news media. Candidates who can get attention from the news media can raise more money and secure more endorsements from party leaders. Over the last fifty years, the invisible primary has been very much an insider's game, but that was not the case for Donald Trump. He stormed the Republican Party from the outside, with few endorsements (at first), limited fundraising, and doubts from journalists about the viability of his campaign. Yet he took his case to the broader public and hit a chord with many voters that sparked his campaign during the invisible primary. Hillary Clinton, by contrast, was very traditional in her approach to the nomination. She raised money, collected numerous endorsements, and built an organization designed to turn out the vote. What is not clear is whether Trump's unique approach can be duplicated in future campaigns or whether it was tied to his own personal flair and the unusual context of 2016.

Essential Knowledge

During the invisible primary, the media focus on polling results and fund-raising numbers. This focus by the media on the horse race rather than the issues is a source of criticism.

Incumbent presidents usually win their party's nomination for a second term. If that part of the contest is a struggle, as it was in 1980 for President Jimmy Carter (1977–81), it is a sign that the incumbent is in trouble, and he usually goes on to lose the general election. But when the seat is open—when an incumbent is in his second term or decides not to run again, as Lyndon Baines Johnson (1963–69) did in 1968—a

TABLE 10.1 The Road to the White House

Time Frame	Event
Beginning two to three years prior to the election year	Decision to run, in which candidates weigh their options and make formal announcements Invisible primary, in which candidates jockey for position and try to build momentum
Beginning in the election year	Caucuses and primaries, in which the people vote, and one candidate in each party emerges as the front-runner
Summer of election year	National party conventions, in which the front-runner in each party is formally nominated and gives an acceptance speech that kicks off the fall campaign
Fall of election year	National campaign, during which televised presidential debates are a highlight
November of election year	Election Day, in which the people vote
December of election year	Electoral College, in which electors meet in their state capitals and formally choose the president
January after election year	Inauguration Day

battle unfolds. These struggles tend to be multicandidate affairs, often with numerous serious contenders seeking the nomination. In 2016, both parties' nominations were open, meaning that neither the sitting president nor the sitting vice president was seeking the nomination—a situation that has occurred only two times since 1928 (1952 and 2008). As noted above, seventeen Republicans sought the 2016 nomination. On the Democratic side, Hillary Clinton's stature in the party kept many candidates from seeking the presidency, including Vice President Joe Biden. Senator Bernie Sanders (I-VT), who most thought was a long shot for the Democratic nomination, ended up being a major challenger to the former Secretary of State.

Michael Ciaglo-Pool/Getty Images

IMAGE 10.7 Republican held many debates, with Trump usually coming out on top.

Caucuses and Primaries

To win a party's nomination, a candidate must secure a majority of delegates to the national party convention. The national party allocates delegates to each of the fifty states (plus the District of Columbia, Guam, and Puerto Rico) and sets guidelines on how the states may choose their delegates. (See Chapter 9 for more details about the delegate distribution process.)

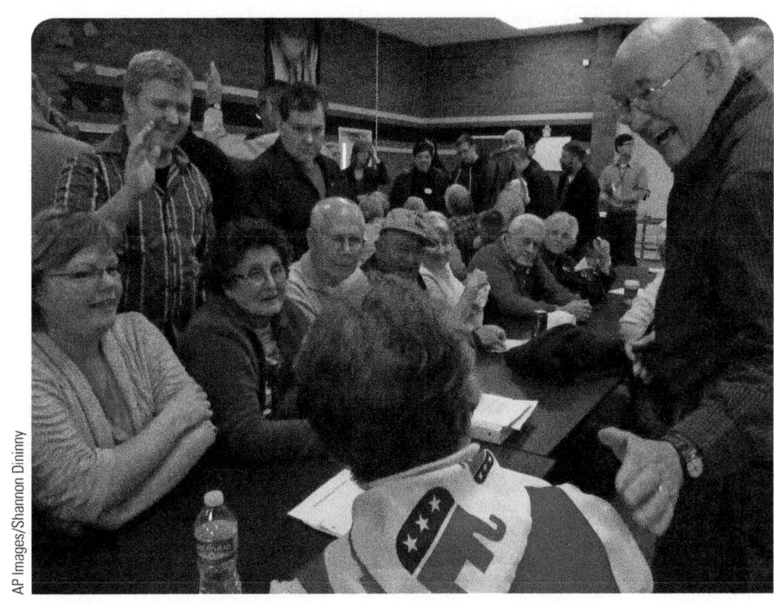

AP Images/Shannon Dininny

IMAGE 10.8 Republicans meet to discuss who should be their party's nominee for president. A caucus allows people to talk about their views, which is one of its advantages.

About 70 percent of the states use some form of primary election in which citizens go to the polling booths and vote for their favorite party candidates. The other 30 percent use caucuses, which are something like town meetings. During the Iowa caucus, the nation's first and most famous caucus, each party requires people to attend a lengthy meeting in which they indicate their preferences. Because caucuses demand more time from voters, the rate of participation is lower than in primaries.

Caucuses and primaries take place over six months, from January through June of the election year. The first states to hold these events wield a good deal of influence, since the early contests provide momentum for those who do well and force those who do poorly to drop out. After the 2016 New Hampshire primary, for example, Governor Chris Christie (R-NJ) ended his bid for the presidency. Governor Martin O'Malley (D-MD) quit following a disappointing showing in Iowa. Iowa and New Hampshire are critical states in the process, since the former is the first state to hold a caucus and the latter holds the first primary (for more on this process, see Chapter 9).

ELECTION 2016

Insiders Versus Outsiders as Presidential Candidates

PRESIDENTIAL NOMINATIONS are often a battle between "insiders" and "outsiders." The insiders are candidates with ties to the party establishment. The outsiders are seeking to force change in the party by challenging the existing leadership. Over the last half-century, party "insiders" have been more successful than the "outsiders," having won over 80 percent of presidential nominations (see Table 10.2). Some outsiders have, however, had notable successes. Both Ronald Reagan (1980) and Barack Obama (2008) challenged the party establishment, went on to win the nomination and the general election, and forged change in the party. The 2016 election saw both an insider (Hillary Clinton) and an outsider (Donald Trump). Trump captured the party with his successful bid to be president, and he will now be able to transform the party.

It should come as no surprise that party insiders, in general, do better than party outsiders. To win the nomination, it is important to have the support of existing party organization. The "party organization" includes current officeholders, party officials, and interest groups attached to the parties like unions or business organizations. These stakeholders can provide access to important resources. Candidates need volunteers to organize rallies, knock on doors, and call prospective voters. These activists may also have fundraising networks that candidates can tap into to finance their campaigns.[20]

One way to evaluate the influence of the party establishment is to catalog the number of endorsements a candidate receives. Endorsements not only indicate public support for a candidate and a willingness to help this person win, they also signal to other party insiders that this is the endorser's preferred candidate, helping to generate additional support for the candidate within the party. The general rule is simple: the more endorsements, the better.

Hillary Clinton had more than five hundred elected officials endorse her in 2016. Bernie Sanders had fewer than twenty.[21] Donald Trump—a true outsider—had only a handful of endorsements from GOP insiders when the campaign began. When New Jersey Governor Chris Christie endorsed Trump in late February 2016, it was big news because he was the first prominent Republican insider to support the real-estate mogul.

TABLE 10.2 Outsider Candidates (shown in boldface) in Presidential Elections, 1968–2016

Year	Republican	Democrat
1968	Richard Nixon	Hubert Humphrey
1972	Richard Nixon	**George McGovern**
1976	Gerald Ford	**Jimmy Carter**
1980	**Ronald Reagan**	Jimmy Carter
1984	Ronald Reagan	Walter Mondale
1988	George H. W. Bush	Michael Dukakis
1992	George H. W. Bush	Bill Clinton
1996	Robert Dole	Bill Clinton
2000	George W. Bush	Albert Gore
2004	George W. Bush	John Kerry
2008	John McCain	**Barack Obama**
2012	Mitt Romney	Barack Obama
2016	**Donald Trump**	Hillary Clinton

Party insiders, on average, have real advantages over candidates who challenge the establishment. Outsiders can, however, succeed if the public wants change and they tap into that desire to shake things up. Trump's success in 2016 was tied in large part to his ability to connect directly to the public. In fact, the party establishment spent much of the first four months in 2016 looking for ways to stop Trump. But those efforts failed: The Republican primary voters were angry and wanted change. Trump understood that and parlayed that sentiment into a successful campaign that led to his nomination in July 2016 in Cleveland.

The National Convention

Following the primary season, each party meets in a national convention. Before the 1960s, conventions were often exciting because it was uncertain who the nominee would be. Conventions often started with numerous contenders, which meant no candidate had enough delegates to win the nomination on the first round of voting at the convention. In 1924, for example, it took the Democrats 124 ballots to select their nominee (John W. Davis from West Virginia). Over the last six decades, however, the likely nominee was known except for a handful of cases. In 1976, there was a big battle between then Governor Ronald Reagan and President Gerald Ford. Ford ended up prevailing in a very close contest. During the early part of 2016, there was much speculation about a so-called open convention for Republicans. Trump did manage to secure enough delegates to win the nomination, but that was not clear until early May.

National conventions do more than select the presidential nominee. They provide a chance for activists and party leaders to get together to discuss strategy and policy behind the scenes. They approve the party platform and also approve the vice presidential nominee. A highlight of these four days is the acceptance speech, in which the party's nominee speaks directly to the nation, laying out a vision for the country. There is much excitement surrounding these events. Because the party dominates the news for these four days, the convention is both an advertisement for the party and its candidate and an important springboard for the fall campaign.

Starting in the 1960s, conventions began to be televised. Party leaders, therefore, wanted to ensure that they were orderly. To avoid projecting an unruly image that might cost votes in the upcoming general election, parties work to forge consensus and avoid public disagreements. Convention planners do not want to impress television viewers but instead want to use this gathering of party electors to jumpstart the general election campaign.

Both the Democratic and Republican conventions in 2016 posed challenges to having orderly gatherings of delegates. Donald Trump had detractors from the more mainstream Republicans, while Hillary Clinton faced real unhappiness from her left from Bernie Sanders' supporters. But for the most part, these differences were papered over during the conventions.

Essential Knowledge

Parties nominate a candidate for president at national conventions. Delegates at a party's national convention are "pledged" to a candidate based on the results of a primary or caucus. To win the nomination of their party, candidates focus on delegate rich states and states whose primary or caucus occurs early.

Presidential Debates

With both party nominees chosen, campaigning for the general election formally starts and the election battle ensues on many fronts. One significant event in the fall is the series of televised presidential debates. In 2016, more than 220 million people watched Hillary Clinton and Donald Trump address the issues in a debate format.[22] Today these events, as well as a vice presidential debate, are managed by the nonpartisan, nonprofit Commission on Presidential Debates, which was established in 1987. The commission chooses the locations and sets the rules.

The first presidential debate was between John Kennedy and Richard Nixon in 1960, and many felt that Kennedy's performance was critical to his narrow win.[23] Thereafter, incumbent candidates were reluctant to participate in televised debates, fearing that they might have more to lose than to win. But in 1976, President Gerald R. Ford (1974–77),

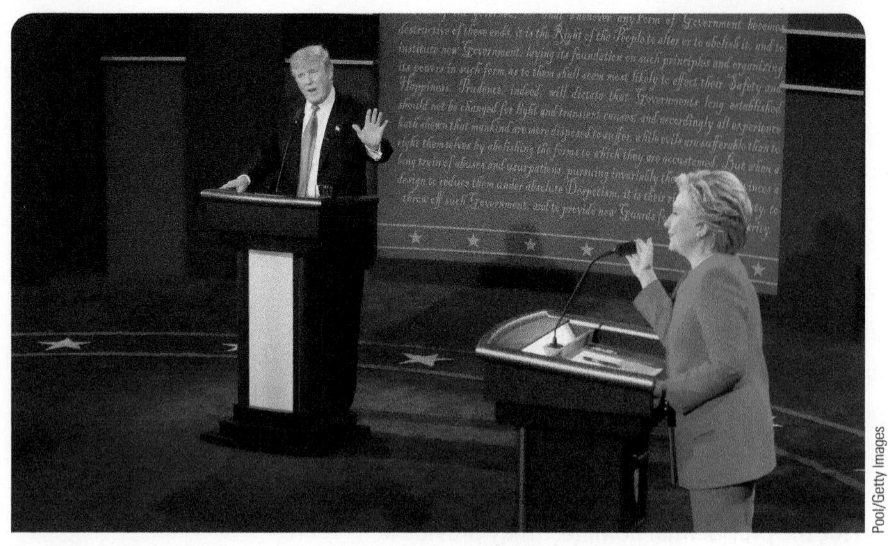

Pool/Getty Images

IMAGE 10.9 Debates are a staple of presidential campaigns.

behind in the polls, viewed the debates as a chance to narrow Jimmy Carter's lead. Since that time, the presidential debates have been a regular feature of the fall campaign.

The debates draw tremendous amounts of attention from the news media. Any mistake by a candidate generates scrutiny. In 1992, President George H. W. Bush (1989–93) was caught looking at his watch during one of the debates, giving the impression that he was bored. That perception fueled the belief that Bush was out of touch, causing him problems in his reelection bid against Arkansas Governor Bill Clinton. In 2012, Mitt Romney turned in a very good performance against President Obama in their first debate in Denver. Obama seemed disengaged. The debate made Romney look presidential and gave his campaign a short-term boost. Hillary Clinton scored well in her debates with Donald Trump, but there were no long-term effects. Debates usually have much more risk than reward, and campaign insiders usually hope for no more than an error-free performance by their candidate.

10.3 Issues in Presidential Campaigns

Identify the issues that shape presidential campaigns

Citizen participation in American politics peaks during presidential campaigns. Supporters and people who are undecided have the chance to attend rallies, hear speeches, read commentary, and watch the never-ending advertisements on television. There seems to be almost no way for the public not to be involved. Because the campaigns are important gateways for public participation, we look in particular at fundraising and campaign strategies that make public engagement possible but may also introduce inequalities.

Fundraising and Money

Of course, no one could run for president without funding. How candidates raise money, how much money they raise, and the influence of money in presidential elections have been concerns of Congress and voters for decades, especially as the amount of spending on campaigns has risen sharply. Some believe these huge sums inject inequalities into presidential campaigns, as it seems candidates who lack personal fortunes and established fundraising operations are less likely to be able to compete.

In 1971, Congress tried to put candidates on an equal financial footing and make them less beholden to special interests by passing the Federal Election Campaign Act (FECA). This law transformed campaigns, since it requires candidates and political parties to disclose their campaign financial records. In 1974, Congress amended the law to set strict limits on how much money could be contributed by individuals and parties to campaigns, and created the Federal Election Commission (FEC) as an independent agency to monitor campaign finance.[24] Under the rules, candidates seeking their party's nomination are given public funds for the campaign in the form of matching funds: a dollar amount equal to the amount the candidates raise from private contributors, with a limit per individual contributor and an overall cap. In 2016, the limit per contributor was $2,700 in the primary and $2,700 in the general campaign.[25] After the Supreme Court's ruling in *McCutcheon, et al. v. FEC*, individuals have no limit on the number of campaigns to which they may contribute.[26]

There are complicated rules for the public financing of presidential nomination campaigns, but they have not really mattered over the last few presidential elections. Candidates now tend to raise huge amounts of money outside of the public system, spending as they see fit in the primaries and caucuses. This change has introduced a lot more money into the political system. As of March 2016, Bernie Sanders, for example, had raised $182 million in his quest to win the Democratic nomination.[27] On the Republican side, Ted Cruz raised nearly $80 million by the end of March.[28] There are reasons to worry about the amount of money now in the election process, but raising these amounts of money does open some gates to influence. Consider Bernie Sanders. By March 2016, 4 million individuals had contributed to his campaign, with the average donation being just $27.[29] This level of engagement is impressive. The Internet makes it efficient to raise small amounts of money, and presidential candidates welcome that kind of broad-based support.

John McCain in 2008 was the last major party nominee to use public funds, receiving about $80 million from the government. Barack Obama that year opted out of general election funding for the first time since the system began in 1976. By so doing, he spent far more money than did McCain. In the 2012 presidential election, both nominees raised their own money for the general election. That pattern continued in 2016 and appears very likely to continue for the foreseeable future, unless some new law arises to check the spending.

Figure 10.2 documents the huge surge in spending that began about a decade ago and shows little sign of abating. Just consider that in 1996 about $200 million was spent by presidential candidates. In 2016, it was about $2 billion—ten times the amount spent in 1996.[30]

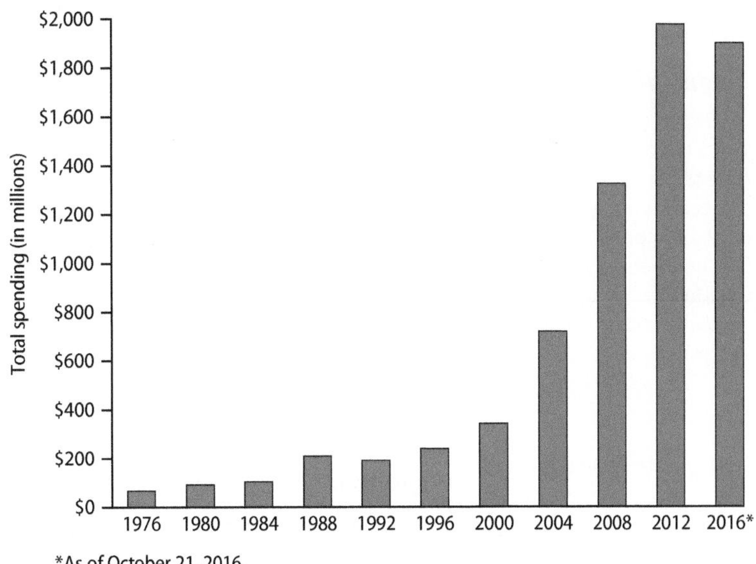

*As of October 21, 2016.

FIGURE 10.2 Total Spending by Presidential Candidates, 1976–2016

Spending in presidential campaigns has been increasing greatly in the past four decades, with particularly large increases in the past decade. A few weeks before Election Day in 2016, spending by presidential candidates had reached almost $1.9 billion.

Source: From "Presidential Fundraising and Spending 1976-2008," Center for Responsive Politics, 2008; https://www.opensecrets.org/pres12; https://www.opensecrets.org/pres16.

Essential Knowledge

In the *Citizens United* decision, the Supreme Court held that corporations, associations, and labor unions had a right to free speech. This led to the rise of Super PACs.

Super PACs: *Independent groups that can raise unlimited amounts of money from individuals, labor unions, and corporations and can spend it to support or oppose political candidates but cannot coordinate directly with candidates or political parties.*

Essential Knowledge

There is increasing debate over the corrosive impact of money on elections and free speech. Allowing corporate spending as free speech has the potential to drown out the free speech of individuals.

Essential Knowledge

In 1976, the Supreme Court ruled that the First Amendment's speech protections apply to campaign spending, meaning that how people spend their money is a form of constitutionally protected expression.

swing voters: *Voters who are neither reliably Republican nor reliably Democratic and who are pursued by each party during an election, as they can determine which candidate wins.*

swing states: *States that are not clearly pro-Republican or pro-Democrat and therefore are of vital interest to presidential candidates, as they can determine election outcomes.*

Most of this surge in money can be tied to the Supreme Court ruling in *Citizens United v. Federal Election Commission* (2010; see Supreme Court Cases in Chapter 8, Interest Groups). This landmark case allowed for increased campaign fundraising (and spending) as it undid many of the restrictions formerly placed on corporations and unions. One critical consequence was the rise of **Super PACs**, which—unlike PACs—can raise funds from corporations, unions, interest groups, and individuals without legal limits.[31] These organizations are not allowed to coordinate directly with the candidates they support, but often those who run a Super PAC are friends and former aides to the candidates, making the distinction questionable. This has given the wealthy a chance to influence the electoral process in dramatic ways, since a single individual can fund a Super PAC. In April 2016 more than 40 percent of all campaign contributions had been made by just fifty donors.[32] This concentration of funding in a handful of mega-donors poses a problem for the election process and stands in sharp contrast to the breadth of participation that Sanders' campaign represented.

In the 2016 Republican presidential primary alone, Trump's Super PACs spent $42.5 million, and in the Democratic primary, Clinton's Super PACs spent $12 million.[33] Trump did run a leaner campaign in 2016, relying on less spending than his opponents.[34] But this may be an aberration.

Many observers worry about the influence of money on the election process and believe that these huge amounts raise questions about fairness and equality, as people who have money will have more gateways than those who do not. But it is far from clear that candidates are being "bought" with this influx of money. Big donors often give money to the candidate they agree with on the largest number of issues. In addition, it is worth remembering that most of this money is being spent on getting candidates' messages out to the public and building organizations to get out the vote—so one could argue that additional money in the electoral system informs people and activates them to participate.[35] Campaign spending, as a result, can stimulate interest in the election, which is also a benefit. Like most of American politics, these changes in the landscape of campaign fundraising and spending are a mix of gates and gateways.

The real problem with Super PACs and the issue ads they sponsor is that voters do not always know where the money is coming from. Under the new campaign rules, there is less transparency. Thus, as noted above, it is possible for one or two wealthy donors to fund a Super PAC, and to the extent that the Super PAC's issue ads impact an election outcome, some observers contend that these results distort the electoral process. It should be noted that despite all the Super PAC spending against Donald Trump during the 2016 primaries and caucuses ($381,776,844[36]), he continued to do well. The same was true for Barack Obama in 2012. The Republicans used Super PACs to attack the president relentlessly in 2012, and it did not keep him from winning reelection.

Swing Voters and States

Although partisanship remains high, **swing voters** still exist—people who do not fall into either the Republican or Democratic camp—and so do **swing states** that might vote either Democratic or Republican in an election. Parties avidly pursue swing voters during a presidential election, as they can swing the results one way or the other. In the past, swing voters have constituted about 20 percent of the electorate, but that share has been falling. Two weeks before the November 2016 election, less than 15 percent of the electorate was undecided between Donald Trump and Hillary Clinton.[37] Partisanship remains an anchor driving the preferences of most Americans, leaving only a handful of "persuadable" or swing voters.

Regardless of the percentage of swing voters, perhaps the more critical strategic feature of presidential campaigns are swing states. These states can mean the difference between victory and defeat. Because of the Electoral College's winner-take-all system, presidential candidates invest time and effort only in states that they can win. In 2016, for example, it made no sense for Hillary Clinton to campaign in Tennessee, a reliably Republican state that she could not win. At the same time, she did not spend much time in Massachusetts—a state that she was able to win easily. But both Clinton and Trump campaigned hard in Pennsylvania—a **battleground state** that each thought they had a chance to win; winning Pennsylvania was critical to securing 270 votes in the Electoral College.[38]

battleground state: *State in which the outcome of the presidential election is uncertain and in which both candidates invest much time and money, especially if its votes are vital for a victory in the Electoral College.*

Citizens in these close states got lots of attention. Nearly 90 percent of campaign visits by presidential candidates are to battleground close states.[39] TV viewers were deluged with campaign ads, and party-based get-out-the-vote organizations were active in even the smallest towns. This flurry of activity filtered down to the public. Citizens in these close states were well informed and increasingly interested in the campaign. But the strategy of pursuing votes in swing close states yields an important inequality, for citizens in close states other than swing close states do not get such attention, and interest in the campaign lags, especially among the poor. In 2016, eleven close states were considered to be battleground close states: Colorado, Florida, Iowa, Michigan, Nevada, New Hampshire, North Carolina, Ohio, Pennsylvania, Virginia, and Wisconsin. Only 28 percent of the nation's population resides in these close states.[40] It is a problem that voters in different close states are treated differently by the campaigns. Theoretically, all voters should receive equal treatment, yet about one in five Americans is the focus of attention of presidential candidates.

Essential Knowledge

Parties use communication technology and voter data management to disseminate, control, and clarify political messages and to enhance outreach and mobilization efforts.

Microtargeting

Since the 1960s, when consumer behavior became a popular field of study, direct marketers have refined the practice of gathering detailed information about different cross sections of consumers to sell their products.[41] Today, the technique of **microtargeting** has become a boon to political parties and electoral campaigns. By identifying and tracking potential supporters, campaign strategists can design specific political messages tailored for each of the voting profiles developed from the data. In 1996, for example, President Bill Clinton's reelection campaign sought to reach so-called soccer moms—"busy suburban women devoted to their jobs and kids, who had real concerns about real presidential politics."[42] Polls and other information suggested that these voters could be moved into the Clinton camp, although men, for the most part, seemed to have already made up their minds. In 2004, the focus was on "NASCAR dads"—working-class white males who lived mostly in the South. Many thought the Democrats had to win this group to capture the presidency. In the 2012 campaign, both Mitt Romney and Barack Obama microtargeted Latino voters, believing that this growing bloc of voters was critical to the election outcome.[43] In the 2016 campaign, Latino voters were important "targets," as were women and Millennials.[44] The Clinton campaign pursued more microtargeting than did Trump's team, which relied more on free media to get their message out.

microtargeting: *Gathering detailed information on cross sections of the electorate to track potential supporters and tailor political messages for them; also called narrowcasting.*

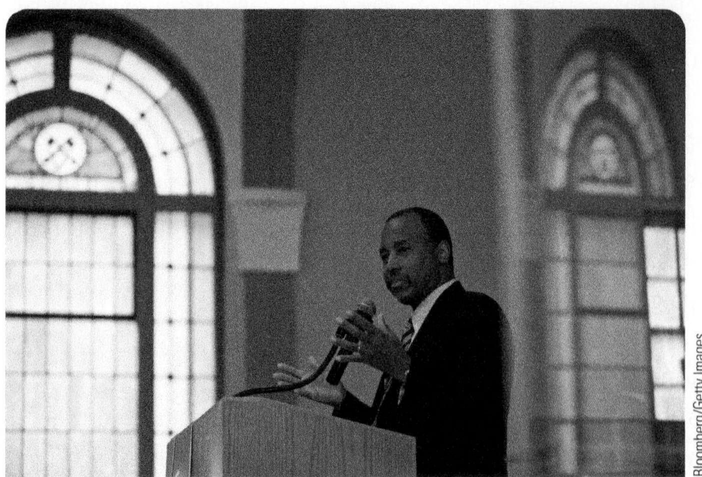
Bloomberg/Getty Images

IMAGE 10.10 In Ben Carson's bid to become president in 2016, he focused on health care as one of his main campaign issues.

As a campaign strategy, microtargeting has begun to replace traditional polling techniques and precinct-by-precinct get-out-the-vote drives (see Chapter 6, Public Opinion). By combining information from polling surveys with political participation and consumer information obtained from data-gathering companies such as Acxiom and InfoUSA, political parties and campaigns can establish profiles of the many different types of voters and the issues they support. The resulting database can then be "mapped" to get a geographic depiction of the trends in voting habits and political interests of different voters. Each party builds its own database that it can share with candidates: The Democratic National Committee's database is called VoteBuilder, and the Republican National Committee's database is called GOP Data Center.[45]

Rather than a general political message sent through a specific medium, campaigns are now able to send dozens of versions of the message using various methods—mail, phone calls, e-mail, text messages, home visits—to reach targeted audiences. This strategy takes a person-by-person view of the electorate rather than a view of the electorate en masse. So, instead of targeting a broad category such as women, campaigns can now focus on narrow subgroups such as undecided iPhone owners in their 30s who follow the news and hence are open to a message from a campaign.

The strategy is not entirely new. John Kennedy used an early form of this strategy in the 1960 election when his campaign targeted messages to African American voters.[46] But with more and more information becoming available about voters, microtargeting has become easier and more cost-effective. Detailed information about the partisan composition of the audience for various media can be used to target key groups of voters.

Campaign Issues

Issues shape campaigns. Many observers think that the personalities of the candidates frame elections, but that view is not consistent with the evidence. In general, about half of the content of advertising in presidential campaigns involved policy, with a quarter concerning the personal traits of the candidates, and the remaining quarter focusing on general values such as freedom, hard work, and patriotism.[47] In 2008, the economy dominated the discussion between John McCain and Barack Obama. According to one estimate, more than 50 percent of the appeals made by these contenders dealt with the economy alone.[48] That should be no surprise with the crash of the stock market in September 2008. The ensuing "Great Recession" made the economy the main issue in 2012. In 2016, the economy remained front and center, but the two nominees gave substantial attention to other issues such as terrorism, immigration, and trade.[49]

valence issues: *Noncontroversial or widely supported campaign issues that are unlikely to differ among candidates.*

position issues: *Political issues that offer specific policy choices and often differentiate candidates' views and plans of action.*

To understand how issues influence campaigns, political scientists have drawn a distinction between **valence issues** and **position issues.**[50] A valence issue is a vague claim to a goal, such as "a strong economy," "improved education," or "greater national security." These are goals all candidates talk about and voters seek: No candidate has ever opposed a strong economy or called for less national security. Valence issues provide limited insight into the policies a candidate might pursue once in office. A position issue is different. Here candidates adopt views that allow voters to understand specific plans for government. Two examples from the 2016 campaign are Hillary Clinton's support for making college debt free for students and Donald Trump's opposition to the Affordable Care Act. Because taking clear positions on issues may drive some votes away, presidential candidates rely more heavily on valence issues. According to one study, about three-quarters of their TV ads highlight valence issues.[51]

Candidates can use issues strategically to win votes. But candidates rarely agree on the issues that should define the campaign. Imagine if an incumbent is running for reelection and the economy is growing at a brisk pace. That nominee will want to talk about the economy at every stop and use his or her political ads to remind voters about this economic growth. The challenger will not share that view: He or she will duck that issue in favor of other issues that the campaign thinks will work for him or her. Therefore, campaigns are often about not just the positions candidates adopt on issues but also which issues define the campaign. Trump sought to tar Clinton with terrorism, while Clinton pushed questions about temperament against the then Republican nominee.

Because campaigns are competitive struggles for votes, candidates look for ways to secure extra votes while maintaining existing support. This dynamic is especially true for candidates who trail because they need to find some way to break up the support for the candidate in the lead. One strategy is to use a **wedge issue** that has the potential to break up the opposition's coalition.[52] Wedges usually involve controversial policy concerns, such as affirmative action, that divide people rather than build consensus. In 2012 and 2014, the Democrats also sought to use various gender issues as wedges against the Republicans, including debates over contraception and equal pay, and race was the wedge issue of 2016.[53]

wedge issue: *Divisive issue focused on a particular group of the electorate that candidates use to gain more support by taking votes away from their opponents.*

negativity: *Campaign strategy of telling voters why they should not vote for the opponent and of highlighting information that raises doubts about the opponent.*

Negativity

Candidates are very good at telling voters why they should vote for them. They are also pretty good at telling the public why they should not vote for their opponents. Candidates' use of claims against the opposition is labeled **negativity**.

One of the most famous examples of negativity is the so-called Daisy spot. This was a television commercial aired only once by President Lyndon B. Johnson in his 1964 campaign against the Republican nominee, Arizona Senator Barry Goldwater. The implication in the ad was that if Goldwater were elected president, he would start a nuclear war. It was a very hard-hitting claim that many thought unfair.[54] But was it? Goldwater had called for the tactical use of nuclear weapons and made some loose statements about attacking the Soviet Union with nuclear weapons. This issue was among the most important facing the nation—much like terrorism

The Granger Collection, NYC

IMAGE 10.11 Negative campaigning is not new. This poster from the 1864 election shows Abraham Lincoln defining his opponent, General George McClellan, as the ally of Confederate President Jefferson Davis and perpetuator of the slave system. Lincoln, on the other hand, is for the workingman and freedom. Notice the integrated school with happy children.

AP Images/Democratic National Committee

IMAGE 10.12 The "Daisy spot" is perhaps the most famous negative ad in American history. It was aired only once by President Lyndon Johnson in the 1964 campaign, and it never explicitly mentioned his opponent, Senator Barry Goldwater. But Goldwater had made statements about the possible use of nuclear weapons, and those statements made the meaning of this ad clear and emotionally resonant.

is now. The public needed to know Goldwater's views, and this negative ad helped generate a debate.

In recent years, the amount of negativity in presidential campaigns has been on the rise (see Figure 10.3). In the 2008 election, less than 30 percent of campaign ads were positive, and another 20 percent were a mix of negative and positive appeals (so-called contrast ads). That means half the ads were negative. Over 60 percent of the ads in the 2012 presidential campaign were negative, with just 14 percent of spots being purely positive.[55] In 2016, only 60 percent of ads were negative, which is largely a result of Trump running primarily positive ads. Of the Trump campaign's ads, only 37 percent were negative, versus more than half of the Clinton campaign's ads.[56] Many observers worry about negativity, viewing attacks on the opposition as weakening the fabric of democracy, especially since about 80 percent of the public say they dislike negative ads.[57]

Negative ads, however, serve a purpose. To ensure accountability, candidates need to be able to criticize the other side. In 2016, Donald Trump reminded the public of the job losses in some areas of the economy that were associated with the trade deals cut under Democratic administrations working with Republican Congresses and argued that Hillary Clinton would just bring more of the same (see Chapter 16, Economic, Domestic, and Foreign Policy for more on trade policy). This was potentially important information that forced Clinton to respond. At the same time, Clinton questioned whether Trump could be trusted with the presidency given his inflammatory statements about women, Muslims, and Mexicans. Such attacks demand a response and can thus increase accountability.

In other words, negative appeals contain information about the candidates that voters need to know. After hearing each side attack the other during a campaign, voters are better able to make informed decisions. It is also important to know that although negativity is on the rise, it is not new. In 1948, President Harry S. Truman (1945–53) equated the Republicans with the Nazi leadership in Germany during World War II.[58] In 1800, the Federalist Party claimed that Thomas Jefferson was the Antichrist.[59] These attacks make Trump's claims about Clinton's flip-flops look tame.

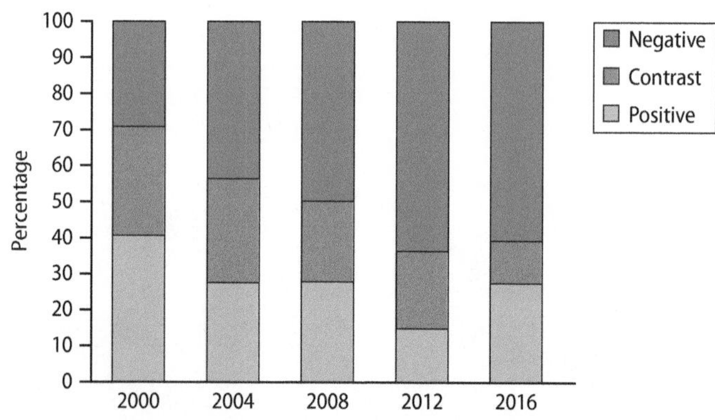

Note: Data from 2000, 2004 and 2008 come from the Wisconsin Advertising Project. Data from 2012 and 2016 come from the Wesleyan Media Project.

FIGURE 10.3 Share of Positive, Contrast, and Negative Ads in Presidential Campaigns, 2000–2016

Negativity in presidential campaigns is generally on the rise. In 2016, only 60 percent of ads were negative ads, but this was largely a result of Donald Trump running primarily positive ads. Of the Trump campaign's ads, 37 percent were negative, whereas 51.5 percent of the Hillary Clinton campaign's ads were negative.

Polls and Prediction Models

Given Donald Trump's victory in 2016, it is easy to overestimate his skill and Hillary Clinton's lack of skill. The winners always look brilliant and the losers misguided. Such simplistic judgments are not, however, very useful, since we are letting the outcome shape the evaluation of the process. To take a more systematic look at how campaigns work, political scientists have developed prediction models that yield specific estimates of the vote share in presidential elections. The goal is to provide a general understanding of who wins and why. In 2008, nearly all models predicted an Obama win. The economy was bad and the public was ready for a change. In 2016, the fundamentals of these prediction models sent more mixed signals. The economy was growing, which helped the Democrats. But Obama had been in office for eight years and that helped the Republicans—the country was ready for a change in the party that controlled the presidency. Five of the seven models predicted a Clinton win, but it was narrow.[60] It is important to remember that these models predict the national popular vote.[61] So in that regard, these models actually did pretty well.

The best prediction models use some combination of the following key structural factors:

1. **The economy.** What is the condition of the economy? A strong economy leads voters to support the incumbent party. A struggling economy gives an edge to the challenger.
2. **Presidential popularity.** How popular is the sitting president? An unpopular president will hurt the chances for his party's candidate.
3. **The incumbent party's time in office.** How long has the incumbent party controlled the presidency? The American public has shown a consistent preference for change. A party that has been in power for a long time usually has made enough mistakes to lead citizens to vote for the other side.

Considering these three factors, it is easy to see why 2012 would be a close race. Although incumbent presidents tend to win reelection, their chance for success decreases if the economy is weak, as the examples of Jimmy Carter and George H. W. Bush demonstrate. In a process called **retrospective voting**, voters tend to judge incumbents on their performance and vote accordingly.[62] At the same time, Barack Obama was reasonably popular and respected, and these qualities, coupled with voters' reluctance to oust incumbent presidents, contributed to his victory in 2012.

retrospective voting: *Theory that voting is driven by a citizen's assessment of an officeholder's performance since the last election.*

10.4 Congressional Campaigns

Outline the steps in congressional campaigns

Nearly all congressional campaigns start with a primary election in which the party's official candidate is selected. The general election follows. These campaigns occur every two years. In the Senate, one-third of all seats are contested every two years. For the House of Representatives, every member faces reelection every two years.

Essential Knowledge

Both modern congressional and presidential campaigns are characterized by the "constant campaign": rising campaign costs, intensive fund-raising, professional consultants, and the growing importance of social media.

The Decision to Run and the Primaries

People who choose to run for Congress are usually visible residents of their district or state. Often they already hold local or state-level elected offices (see the Political Analytics

POLITICAL ANALYTICS

Latina Elected Officials in the United States

AS DISCUSSED IN CHAPTER 1, Gateways to American Democracy, a primary reason for identifying gateways to participation is to provide the citizenry a voice in the governing process. This chapter and the following one discuss voting as a means for citizens to register their preferences about whom they wish to make policy decisions on their behalf. As the saying goes, "Elections have consequences," and one of them is how well the policy preferences of voters are translated into actual policies. For some (as discussed in Chapter 12, Congress), demographic representation of the citizenry is crucial to the link between those who govern and those who are governed. Many people believe that representatives should look like a cross section of the American public.

Figure 10.4 showcases the status of one particular American demographic group, Latinas, and how successful

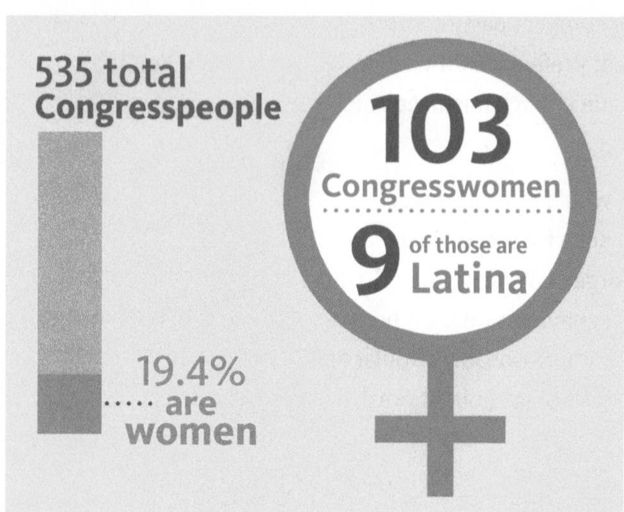

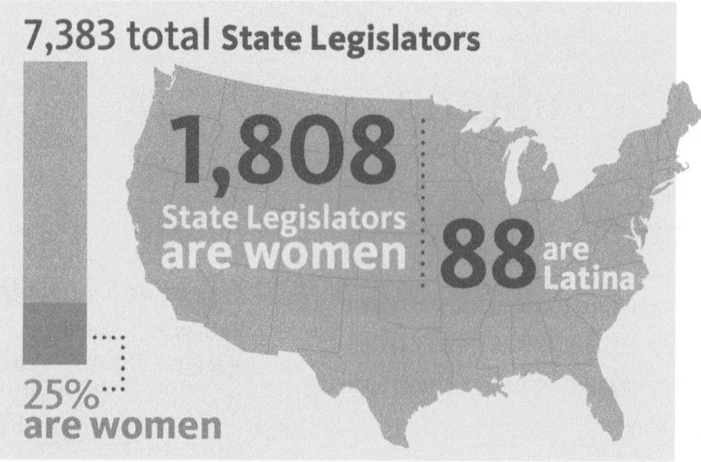

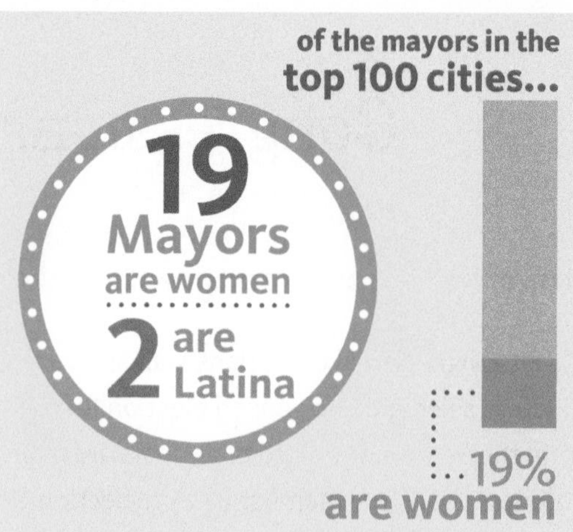

FIGURE 10.4 Latinas in Politics

they have been in gaining elected office at different levels of government. As the graphic demonstrates, Latinas hold very few elected offices. Only one is a governor—Susana Martinez from New Mexico. Only nine Latinas serve in Congress and none in the U.S. Senate. Given that Latinos make up about 17 percent of the U.S. population (and Latinas about half of that), Latinas are underrepresented demographically. To the extent that descriptive representation is a good indicator of policy representation, Latinas appear to be lacking a political voice commensurate with their numbers in the population.

One encouraging sign is that close to two thousand Latinas serve on city councils and in other local political offices and they might run for higher office in the near future. Further, no less than four national organizations—LatinasRepresent, Political Parity, the National Hispanic Leadership Agenda, and Emily's List—have launched efforts to increase the number of Latinas elected to office in 2016.

Examine Figure 10.4 to see the proportion of female and Latina elected officials compared with the total number of available elected seats at each level of office.

Thinking Critically

1. What do the data about Latinas suggest regarding the status of their political careers?
2. What are the consequences, if any, of the relatively low numbers of Latinas who hold elected positions at the various levels of government?

Sources: Nia-Malika Henderson, "Report: Latinas Vastly Underrepresented in Elected Offices," *Washington Post*, February 6, 2014, https://www.washingtonpost.com/blogs/she-the-people/wp/2014/02/06/report-latinas-vastly-underrepresented-in-elected-offices; "Emily's List Announces New Initiative to Get More Latinas Elected to Office," Fox News Latino. March 2, 2016, http://latino.foxnews.com/latino/politics/2016/03/02/emily-list-announces-new-initiative-to-get-more-latinas-elected-to-office; "Latina Representation in National Elected Office," LatinasRepresent, https://latinasrepresent.org; Brianna Dimas, "Latina Leadership Institute Launches in San Antonio," LatinasRepresent, July 6, 2015, https://latinasrepresent.org/latina-leadership-institute-launches-san-antonio; "Women in Elective Office 2016," Center for American Women and Politics, http://www.cawp.rutgers.edu/women-elective-office-2016; "Women of Color in Elective Office 2016," Center for American Women and Politics, http://www.cawp.rutgers.edu/women-color-elective-office-2016.

sections in Chapter 3, Federalism, and in this chapter). They might—like Kyrsten Sinema—be schoolboard members, city council members, or state legislators. Many grew up in the district or state and can claim long-standing ties to it; this was certainly true of Sinema. Contenders with strong local roots can organize core supporters who volunteer time, and often money, to advance their candidacies.

Although candidates do not have to declare their intention to run for Congress until about a year before the election, both incumbents—those already holding the office—and challengers generally begin campaigning nearly two years before Election Day. For House members, that means the campaign never stops—yet another manifestation of the permanent campaign. The contests that occur in between the four-year presidential election cycles are called **midterm elections**.

midterm elections: *Congressional elections held between the presidential elections.*

Party primaries nearly always determine which candidate will gain the party endorsement for a House or Senate seat, although a handful of states, such as Colorado, Connecticut, New Mexico, New York, and Utah, hold preprimary conventions to determine who can compete in the primary. To win the primary election, a candidate generally shapes his or her campaign messages to please core party members in the district or state. For Democrats, that typically means slanting toward a more liberal set of policies and, for Republicans, toward a more conservative set of policies. But the message also depends on the number and type of candidates in the primary contest. If there are more than two candidates, each has to identify a message that considers all competitors in the race.

The Fall Campaign

Following the primaries, the two winning candidates often revise their campaign messages to attract more moderate voters. Anthony Downs explained this shift in message with the median voter theorem, which argues that candidates in their quest for votes should adopt moderate positions on issues. If one candidate fails to do so, the other candidate can move to the center, winning a majority of votes and the election.[63] To win the general election, candidates usually need votes from party members as well as from Independents and members of the opposing party. It is for these reasons that elections are often battles over the so-called middle.

Running for Congress requires attending local gatherings such as town meetings, parades, festivals, and high school sporting events. Candidates meet with as many key businesspeople, members of the press, and local interest groups as possible. They give speeches, and their campaigns develop slogans and TV ads. Elections to the House of Representatives typically focus more on local issues intrinsic to the district and less on national programs and issues. Senate elections pay more attention to national issues because the Senate is viewed as more nationally focused. In elections where an incumbent is running, the contest becomes an evaluation of his or her performance in office compared to what the challenger promises to do if elected.

The geographic size of a congressional district or state can affect campaign strategy. Some urban districts are small, such as in New York City, but often very expensive to campaign in due to costs of television. Other districts involve much more territory to cover: Crisscrossing Wyoming to meet voters is a much larger task than driving across Rhode Island. Because it is so difficult to establish a personal relationship with constituents in large districts and states, congressional campaigns in these areas are typically less about the personal characteristics of the candidates and more about issues and party policies.[64]

10.5 Issues in Congressional Campaigns

Determine which issues shape congressional campaigns

Congressional elections do not draw as much attention as presidential elections, but they involve many of the same issues. Money and fundraising are concerns, and again the FEC sets limits. Political parties attempt to work within—or get around—these limits to help their candidates. Voters usually reelect House and Senate members, so whether congressional elections actually serve to hold Congress accountable is a question for American democracy. Voters know less about these candidates than about the candidates in presidential elections, suggesting perhaps that there is not much accountability. Nevertheless, the composition of Congress changes in response to conditions in the country. If times are good, voters reward the party that controls the presidency. In general, the pattern of Republican and Democratic gains and losses indicates that voters hold members of Congress accountable and that Congress is, therefore, a responsive institution.

Fundraising and Money

A key element in launching and running a congressional campaign is fundraising. Every campaign needs an office, staff members, computers, posters and pamphlets, a website, and money for television and radio ads. Senate campaigns generally cost more than House campaigns because they seek to reach voters across an entire state rather than just a district.

Federal campaign finance laws set the same limits on congressional elections as on presidential elections: An individual could contribute up to $2,700 to a candidate for the primary election in 2016, and the same amount for the general election for as many campaigns as he or she wishes. Candidates also raise money from PACs, which are limited to donating $5,000 for a primary election, and $5,000 for a general election, to a single candidate.[65] In the 2016 Senate elections, the cost of running for office continued to climb. Consider that Mitch McConnell (R-KY) and Alison Lundergan Grimes (D) spent $45 million in the Kentucky Senate race. Major candidates in the 8th District of Ohio spent about $17 million. In the 2002 midterm elections, total spending in congressional races was about $2 billion. Just twelve years later the amount spent by candidates had more than doubled.[66]

The amount of money required to wage a competitive contest for a seat in Congress is formidable, and it gives an advantage to people who are personally wealthy and able to make good use of personal or business connections. Name recognition also helps in fundraising. For example, a local sports hero or decorated war veteran who chooses to run for office gets enough free publicity to attract interest. Clay Aiken, a runner-up on *American Idol*, ran for Congress in North Carolina in 2014; although his campaign was ultimately unsuccessful, his preexisting fame helped him launch his bid. Translating fame into credibility for office holding is not always easy, but name recognition is clearly an advantage.

vanishing marginals: *Trend marking the decline of competitive congressional elections.*

safe seat: *Seat in Congress considered to be reliably held by one party or the other.*

term limits: *Rule restricting the number of terms an elected official can serve in a given office.*

The Role of Political Parties

Of the other sources of financial support available to candidates, the most important is the political party. Parties are forbidden by campaign finance laws from actively coordinating a specific individual's congressional or senatorial campaign, but local parties can engage in general activities, such as voter registration drives, partisan rallies, and get-out-the-vote efforts on election day that help party-endorsed candidates at every level.

Incumbency Advantage

Incumbents almost always win,[67] and in the past two decades, more than 70 percent of House incumbents won by 60 percent or more of the vote [68] (see Figure 10.5). Since the 1960s, the number of competitive races has been in decline, a trend called **vanishing marginals**. Fewer and fewer congressional elections are competitive. Noncompetitive districts are often referred to as **safe seats**. The high rates of incumbent reelection may indicate that incumbents are doing a good job, especially with constituent services that build support with voters (see also Chapter 12).

Concerns about incumbency advantage have led some observers to fear a lack of accountability and to call for **term limits**, which would force members to retire after serving a maximum number of terms. Presidents, for example, can serve only two terms, and most governors

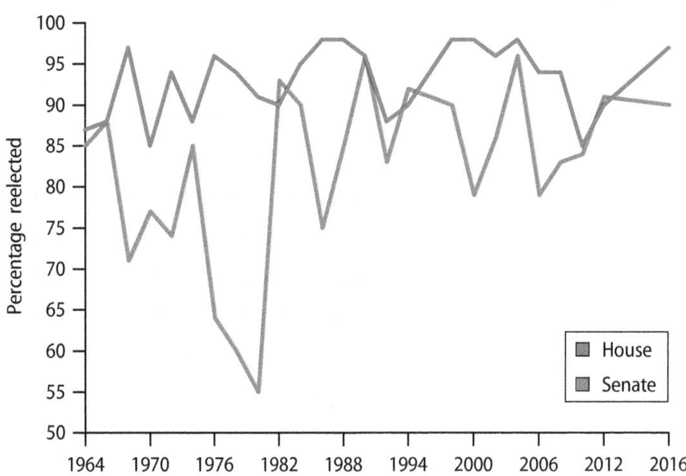

FIGURE 10.5 Reelection Rates of Incumbents in Congress, 1996–2016

Once elected, U.S. Senators and Representatives often are reelected to office as many times as they choose to run again.

Source: https://www.opensecrets.org/bigpicture/reelect.php.

are similarly constrained. But chief executives have more concentrated power than do legislators, so ensuring turnover in the executive branch does keep gateways to responsive government open.

Further, more turnover actually occurs in the House than the 90 percent reelection rate suggests. Members often engage in strategic retirement, deciding not to run for reelection when the outcome is likely to be unfavorable. It is also unclear what reelection rates exactly mean. For example, the lower reelection rates of senators do not imply that the Senate is more responsive than the House. Instead, the gap may be a function of differences between the two chambers. A seat in the Senate, the upper house, is a more coveted position than a seat in the House, and Senate races generally attract higher-quality challengers than do House races. Better challengers yield more competitive elections and more defeats for incumbents. The ability of challengers to do better in Senate races than in House races is also related to the additional media attention these races receive; quite simply, voters learn more about the challengers. Finally, the difference in terms—six years as opposed to two—may indicate that House members stay in closer touch with constituents than do senators, and their constituents reelect them.[69]

Incumbents also win reelection at high rates because their constituents know them. Name recognition for House and Senate incumbents is often higher than 80 percent. Senate challengers do better than House challengers, but still about a quarter of the electorate does not recognize their names.[70] Compare these percentages to those of the 2016 presidential election, in which basically every American knew the names of the two nominees.[71]

Additional explanations have been advanced to explain incumbency advantage. For example, with the bureaucracy growing in size and reach, people expect more from their government. As a result, citizens need a mediator to handle issues that arise with the bureaucracy. Members of Congress serve as a conduit to help connect people with government services. Thus a citizen who fails to receive a Social Security check or has trouble with a passport calls his or her member of Congress for help. The result is constituent loyalty and an increased willingness to support that official's reelection. Other scholars have offered a more sinister interpretation: In this view, members of Congress deliberately design bureaucratic agencies and programs in ways that ensure they will be unable to carry out the tasks that constituents demand. In a sense, the bureaucracy is built to fail, so constituents have to contact their representative or senator to make it work; when help arrives, loyalty to the incumbent is built.[72] There is also a simple explanation for why reelection rates of incumbents are so high: Candidates who win once obviously have the skills to be elected, and these serve them well in reelection campaigns.[73]

In addition, recent evidence suggests that members of Congress may be the beneficiaries of the migration of Americans. That is, incumbency advantage appears to be increasing because districts are becoming "deep red" (Republican) and "deep blue" (Democratic) due to people's decisions about where to live. The assumption is that a Republican who has a choice to live, for example, in San Francisco or Dallas will tend to choose Dallas because it offers a political culture more in line with his or her preferences. In this sense, because of the redrawing of district lines and the desire of individuals to live near people with similar values and political leanings, congressional districts are becoming heavily Democratic or heavily Republican. The result is that fewer races are competitive and incumbents are more successful.[74]

Relative Lack of Interest

Voting rates in congressional elections, particularly in midterm elections, are always lower than in presidential elections. Presidential elections are high-stimulus elections, whereas congressional elections are low-stimulus ones. The attention and excitement of a presidential election means that voters are bombarded with information about the contest. Congressional elections generate far less attention. A major consequence of these differences is that voters in congressional elections often do not know much about the candidates.

As a result, voting is driven largely by two major forces: partisanship and incumbency. Voters follow party identification and vote for their party's candidates. And, as we have seen, voters also tend to vote for incumbents. There is also the effect of **presidential coattails**—that is, a popular president running for reelection brings additional party candidates into office. Voters going to the polls in high-stimulus elections to vote for president cast ballots for other members of the party for lower-level offices. While scholars debate this effect, it is clear that the partisan makeup of Congress reflects the popularity of the president or presidential candidate.[75] In 2016, Donald Trump was able to keep the Republicans in control of both houses of Congress despite a good deal of speculation that the Democrats would capture the Senate.

presidential coattails: *Effect of a popular president or presidential candidate on congressional elections, boosting votes for members of his or her party.*

Is voting in congressional elections a means by which citizens in a democracy hold government responsible? Does voting in congressional elections yield the will of the majority? Figure 10.6 shows the frequent shifts in the share of seats the president's party has in the

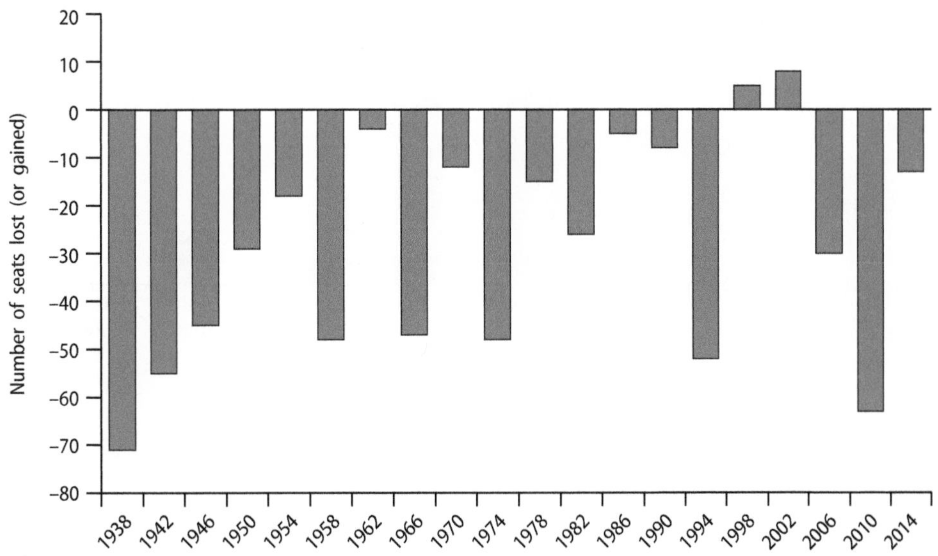

FIGURE 10.6 Loss of Seats in the House of Representatives by the President's Party in Midterm Elections, 1938–2014

The president's party usually loses seats in midterm elections, sometimes with the consequence that the majority in the House of Representatives or the Senate changes hands.

Source: Gerhard Peters, "Seats in Congress Gained/Lost by the President's Party in Mid-Term Elections," The American Presidency Project, ed. John T. Woolley and Gerhard Peters, Santa Barbara: University of California, 1999–2012, http://www.presidency.ucsb.edu/data/mid-term_elections.php. © 1999–2012, Gerhard Peters, The American Presidency Project. Reproduced by permission. Data for 2014, http://www.realclearpolitics.com/elections/live_results/2014/house/.

PUBLIC POLICY, ELECTIONS, AND CAMPAIGNS

Party Platforms

Elections and campaigns are the key instruments of American democracy because they allow voters to judge their elected officials and replace them if enough voters disapprove of their job performance. One key part of this electoral process is the **party platform**. The platform lays out the party's thinking on key issues and can be usefully thought of as a set of promises the party makes about their plans for governing (see Chapter 9, Political Parties). Those issues, as a result, can be used to attract the support of voters and activists and also serve as a basis to judge performance once in office. Further, the creation of the platform provides an opportunity for participation, especially among the more politically active segments of the public. In this section, we will analyze how the platforms are formed and whether candidates, once elected, do follow through on their own and their party's promises.

The party platform is officially adopted at the party's national convention every four years (which nominates a presidential and vice presidential candidate). The platform is a document that tends to be driven by party activists. These actors care about policy and work hard to ensure their views are reflected in the platform. The writing of the platform takes place months prior to the convention in an array of meetings among activists.

Since party platforms are one indicator of promises made by parties and their candidates, do candidates fulfill these promises once elected to office? According to one study, about 66 percent of campaign promises in congressional campaigns have been enacted, only about 10 percent were ignored, and the remaining 20 percent or so were blocked in Congress.[76]

Another study comparing campaign appeals in House elections to subsequent introduction and cosponsorship of legislation finds that House members also keep their promises.[77] It appears that even images in television advertisements aired in congressional elections, which are usually thought of as vague and empty, serve to guide the policies House members support.[78] In short, platforms matter.

Is this also true for presidents? This question is a bit more challenging to answer, since presidential candidates make so many visible public speeches and statements. The data in Figure 10.7 suggest that President Obama did

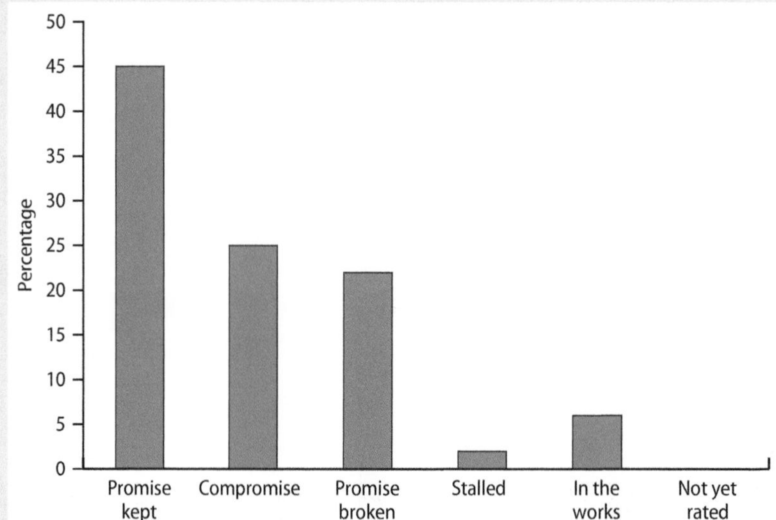

FIGURE 10.7 President Obama's Campaign Promises Kept and Broken

Despite the common perception that politicians do not keep their campaign promises, these data suggest that President Barack Obama did keep most of the promises he made during his presidential campaigns. This pattern applies for politicians in general, including recent presidents George W. Bush and Bill Clinton.

Note: PolitiFact compiled more than five hundred promises that Barack Obama made during the campaign and has tracked their progress, rating those that are completed as "promise kept," "compromise," or "promise broken," and the others as "not yet rated," "in the works," or "stalled."

Source: PolitiFact, "The Obameter: Tracking Obama's Campaign Promises," PolitiFact.com. Copyright © 2012 by *Tampa Bay Times*. All rights reserved. Reproduced by permission. http://www.politifact.com/truth-o-meter/promises/obameter/.

a reasonable job of doing what he said he would do. Of more than five hundred promises he has made, he broke about 20 percent of them, while keeping or compromising on about 70 percent of them.

The larger takeaway from the preceding data on party platforms is that politicians do try to keep their promises. They are not perfect, but these data offer a bit of optimism about the connection between campaigns and public policy.

When the president or other elected officials do stray too far from their party platform or campaign promises, the public can vote them out of office in the next election. Perhaps the most famous example of breaking a promise occurred in 1991, when President George H. W. Bush agreed to a tax increase as part of a budget deal with congressional Democrats. In his acceptance speech at the 1988 Republican National Convention, Bush had pledged he would not raise taxes, saying, "Read my lips, no new taxes." This emphatic statement was his best-known line, and it came back to haunt him. In his bid for reelection, Democratic ads played video recordings of his promise over and over to discredit him. Although he regretted breaking his promise, it is not clear that his actions were wrong: Political, economic, and social situations change, and elected officials need to change with them. In response to external events, such as a foreign policy crisis or a downturn in the economy, responsive and responsible politicians act accordingly.

Every democratic government rests on fair and open elections. Elections serve an important public policy purpose because they allow voters to change the course of government. Politicians recognize that they have to offer voters some blueprints for their future actions in office, and they do so during the campaign. Voters then choose the candidate they think will do the best job. This linkage is one of the fundamental gateways of democracy. It is important that each citizen make the most of this gateway to ensure that elected officials are responsive to the needs of the public. It is also important that the rules governing elections make it possible for this gateway to function well.

Public Policy Connections

1. Should candidates be tied to their party's platforms or be allowed to define their own stances on issues?
2. How can voters effectively hold candidates accountable for their performance in office?

House of Representatives. These shifts are often attributed to the state of the economy and the popularity of the incumbent president. According to estimates from political scientists, a party can lose up to forty-six seats when its president is highly unpopular. At the same time, a gain of 2 percent in people's income can produce eleven more seats in Congress for the incumbent party.[79]

party platform: *Document that lays out a party's core beliefs and policy proposals for each presidential election.*

Because of these aggregate shifts in midterm congressional elections, many scholars have viewed midterm elections as referenda on the sitting president. But given the fact that the president's party has just come off a victory in the previous election, winning seats that might often go to the other party, the normal occurrence is that the president's party loses seats in the midterm election. The president's party has gained seats only three times in the past twenty midterm elections (1938–2014). The average seat loss for the president's party in midterm elections is about twenty-five (see Figure 10.6). The extent of these losses, or whether they can even be turned into gains, depends on the approval rating of the president. So in 1994, the sweep by Republicans was interpreted as a repudiation of President Bill Clinton's policies, and the Republican success in the midterm elections in 2002 was viewed as a vindication of President George W. Bush. In 2010, voters were unhappy with President Obama, whose approval ratings had slipped throughout the year. To signal their discontent, voters handed the Republicans control of the House of Representatives. In 2014, the public again showed unhappiness with Obama by handing Senate control to the GOP.

Economic conditions and presidential popularity indirectly influence voters in another way. Because politicians are ambitious and want to run for office when the prospects for success are high, they survey conditions when deciding whether to run. In December 2001, with President George W. Bush's sky-high popularity, conditions looked good for Republicans in the 2002 midterm elections, and many high-quality Republican candidates decided to run. In contrast, in December 2013, President Obama's popularity was sagging and the economy continued to struggle, so many high-quality Democratic contenders decided not to run in 2014, waiting for a more favorable time. The aggregate effect of these decisions produces an outcome for congressional elections that correlates with economic conditions and presidential popularity. Political scientists call this influence the **strategic politician hypothesis**.[80]

strategic politician hypothesis: *Effect that the strength of the economy and the popularity of the sitting president have on the decision to run for Congress.*

Much has been written on the exact mechanisms that drive voters and congressional elections. While there is disagreement over the specifics, it is clear that the composition of Congress changes in response to economic conditions. When there are good times, the president's party benefits. When times are bad, the president's party suffers. It is also true that big issues can matter. In 2014, the controversy over the Affordable Care Act certainly shaped a lot of congressional campaigns and outcomes in those elections as well.

Elections, Campaigns, and Democracy

American elections and the campaigns that precede them are the means by which citizens participate in selecting those who will govern them. It is inevitable that they are at the center of concerns about American democracy. Many observers worry that campaigns are too long, that candidates spend too much money, and that the voters are not very well informed. These concerns often focus on the fairness of the process and of the outcome. In the long term, the process has worked reasonably well. In the short term, those who lose see the process as unfair.

In any assessment of the American political system, your own partisanship needs to be set aside. In 1980, for example, many Americans were unhappy with the state of the economy and foreign affairs. More than 70 percent of the electorate felt that the nation was on the wrong track.[81] The 1980 campaign offered the public a chance to correct course by changing presidents, and the public did so by electing Ronald Reagan. Reagan promised to end the era of big government by slashing taxes and domestic spending. Four years later, only 26 percent of the electorate felt that America was on the wrong track,[82] and President Reagan won the 1984 election in a landslide, losing only one state. In 2008, the public again was very dissatisfied with the direction of the country—only 14 percent felt the nation was on the right track.[83] The Republicans lost control of the White House, giving Barack Obama a chance to correct course. In 2016, the discontent in the country gave rise to Trump's presidency. More than 60 percent of Americans thought the country was on the wrong track, and around 30 percent felt we were on the right track.[84]

The general lesson is that elections and campaigns, although imperfect, provide a real chance to ensure government responsiveness and have done so over many years and decades. Candidates seek the support of the public through speeches, ads, press releases, and other methods of campaigning. The public digests that information and chooses a candidate. People's votes are a blunt instrument, but they help to forge accountability. If elected officials want to stay in office, they need to act in a way that will increase the chances of continued support. Of course, the party out of office would like to get back in, and it, too, seeks the support of the public. It is through this competitive struggle that American democracy works. Critics worry that the public does not know many of the details of candidates and their platforms, and that is clearly true. But the American public should not be underestimated. That the country has not only survived for more than two centuries but thrived suggests just the opposite. The fact that the public collectively seems to act in reasonably coherent ways is testimony to political scientist V. O. Key's classic observation that "voters are not fools."[85]

Political Science Reasoning

Question 1

Practice 1, Practice 4

> It was desirable that the sense of the people should operate in the choice of the person to whom so important a trust was to be confided. This end will be answered by committing the right of making it, not to any preestablished body, but to men chosen by the people for the special purpose, and at the particular conjuncture.
>
> It was equally desirable, that the immediate election should be made by men most capable of analyzing the qualities adapted to the station, and acting under circumstances favorable to deliberation, and to a judicious combination of all the reasons and inducements which were proper to govern their choice. A small number of persons, selected by their fellow-citizens from the general mass, will be most likely to possess the information and discernment requisite to such complicated investigations.
>
> It was also peculiarly desirable to afford as little opportunity as possible to tumult and disorder. This evil was not least to be dreaded in the election of a magistrate, who was to have so important an agency in the administration of the

government as the President of the United States. But the precautions which have been so happily concerted in the system under consideration, promise an effectual security against this mischief. The choice of several, to form an intermediate body of electors, will be much less apt to convulse the community with any extraordinary or violent movements, than the choice of one who was himself to be the final object of the public wishes. And as the electors, chosen in each State, are to assemble and vote in the State in which they are chosen, this detached and divided situation will expose them much less to heats and ferments, which might be communicated from them to the people, than if they were all to be convened at one time, in one place.

Nothing was more to be desired than that every practicable obstacle should be opposed to cabal, intrigue, and corruption. These most deadly adversaries of republican government might naturally have been expected to make their approaches from more than one quarter, but chiefly from the desire in foreign powers to gain an improper ascendant in our councils. How could they better gratify this, than by raising a creature of their own to the chief magistracy of the union? But the convention have guarded against all danger of this sort, with the most provident and judicious attention. They have not made the appointment of the President to depend on any preexisting bodies of men, who might be tampered with beforehand to prostitute their votes; but they have referred it in the first instance to an immediate act of the people of America, to be exerted in the choice of persons for the temporary and sole purpose of making the appointment. And they have excluded from eligibility to this trust, all those who from situation might be suspected of too great devotion to the president in office. No senator, representative, or other person holding a place of trust or profit under the United States, can be of the numbers of the electors. Thus, without corrupting the body of the people, the immediate agents in the election will at least enter upon the task free from any sinister bias. Their transient existence, and their detached situation, already taken notice of, afford a satisfactory prospect of their continuing so, to the conclusion of it. The business of corruption, when it is to embrace so considerable a number of men, requires time as well as means. Nor would it be found easy suddenly to embark them, dispersed as they would be over thirteen States, in any combinations founded upon motives, which though they could not properly be denominated corrupt, might yet be of a nature to mislead them from their duty.[1]

1. What was Hamilton's view of the ability of average citizens to select the president?
2. Does the Electoral College function today as it was described in *Federalist* 68? Explain why or why not.

[1]Alexander Hamilton, *Federalist* 68.

Focus on AP® Success

10 Elections and Campaigns

Must Know: Key Concepts

- Caucus
- National Convention
- General Election – Presidential
- General Election – Midterm
- Electoral College
- Presidential Coattails
- Bipartisan Campaign Reform Act
- *Citizens United v. Federal Election Commission*
- Incumbency Advantage
- PAC (Political Action Committee)
- Super PAC

Thinking Politically

Argumentation

In the last 20 years, two candidates (George W. Bush in 2000 and Donald Trump in 2016) won the Electoral College without winning the popular vote. These events have added to the call for the elimination of the Electoral College. Should the process of selecting the president be changed? If so, how? If not, why not?

Understanding Learning Objectives with Key Concepts

PRD – 2.A Explain how the different processes work in a U.S. presidential election.

- U.S. elections are impacted by various factors such as:
  - Primary Election – Used by a political party to select candidates to represent the party on the general election ballot. In a closed primary, only registered party members can vote. In an open primary, voters may participate without previously registering as a member of a party.
  - Caucuses – Meetings at which party members discuss issues and declare their preference for the nomination of their party's presidential candidate. The results of these caucuses are used to pledge or "assign" delegates to candidates. These delegates will be sent to the national convention, where the nomination will take place.
  - Party Conventions – At the national convention, delegates from state parties select a nominee for president and vice president as well as approve a platform. The winner of the national convention is usually known well in advance of the actual start of the convention. This is because there is almost always a candidate who has a majority of pledged delegates prior to the beginning of the convention.
  - General Election – The general election is the election that determines the actual winner of the office. During the general election in presidential election years, voters will select presidential electors, as well as other officials such as members of congress.
  - Electoral College – Presidential electors are the only individuals who actually vote for the office of president. Each state receives a number of electors based on the size of its congressional delegation (senators plus representatives). Electors are selected by voters. The presidential candidate with a plurality of the popular vote in a state will receive all of that state's electoral vote (except in Maine and Nebraska). This is referred to as "winner take all" and tends to force the focus of the election into swing states.

PRD – 2.B Explain how the Electoral College impacts democratic participation.

- All states except for two (Main and Nebraska) award all of their electoral votes to the candidate who captures a plurality of the popular vote in that state. Further, it is possible for a candidate to win the Electoral College without winning the popular vote. This process has called into question the degree to which the Electoral College reflects democratic values.

PRD – 2.C Explain how the different processes work in U.S. congressional elections. Sever factors impact congressional elections. These include:

- Incumbency Advantage – The incumbent is the person who currently holds an elected office. It is far more likely that the incumbent will be reelected than that the challenger will win. This is because the incumbent enjoys greater name recognition and easier access to PAC money and perks of the office (i.e. constituency service, franking privilege, etc.).

- Most states use primary elections as the means to nominate candidates. Primaries can be either open or closed. Primary elections usually have much lower turnout than general elections. Individuals who vote in a primary election are more likely to be politically active than those who vote only in the general election.

- Some states still use caucuses as a means to nominate candidates. To participate in a caucus, party members must attend the caucus and remain present through the entirety of the meeting. As such, the time requirement for participation is much greater than for a primary. Individuals who participate in a caucus tend to be far more partisan and better educated than the average citizen.

- The general election is the election that determines who will win the office. It is typically a contest between the nominees of the Democratic Party and the Republican Party. Occasionally, minor party candidates and independents may be on the ballot as well. General elections for national offices occur every two years. During this election, one third of the U.S. Senate and all of the members of the U.S. House of Representatives will be chosen. Depending on the state, voters may also elect various state and local officials. Turnout during general elections where the president is also chosen is typically in the range of 55 to 60 percent. During presidential elections, the winning president's party usually also makes gains in Congress, a phenomenon known as the "presidential coattail effect."

- Midterm general elections occur two years after a presidential election. During this election, voters will choose one third of the Senate and all of the members of the House of Representatives. Depending on the state, voters may also elect various state and local officials. Turnout during these elections is typically between 35 and 40 percent, made up of voters who are less diverse, more educated, and more partisan than the body of voters who participate in presidential elections. During midterm elections there is generally a decrease in Congress of members who are the same party as the president.

PRD – 2.D Explain how campaign organizations and strategies affect the election process. Modern campaigns are characterized by:

- Professional Consultants – Modern campaigns require a staff of professionals that have been trained in activities such as media, fundraising, communication, logistics, etc. These professionals are paid by the campaign. This presents an impediment to candidates who have limited access to funds.

- Increased Campaign Costs – Campaign costs have increased faster than the rate of inflation. This is due to the factors such as increased use of paid consultants and increased costs of media.

- Election Cycles – Members of the House of Representatives are said to be engaged in the "constant campaign." This because by the time they take the oath of office during the first week of January, they will typically have a primary election less than two years away. Individuals who want to be president typically start the process two to three years in advance of the next general election.

- Social Media – Over the last ten years, social media has changed the campaign landscape. Professional consultants now manage a candidate's social media presence in an effort to maximize this platform for communication, organizing, and fundraising.

PRD – 2.E Explain how the organization, finance, and strategies of national political campaigns affect the election process.

- The role of money in federal elections is a controversial topic. Both Congress and the Supreme Court have made policy that regulates the rules of money for political purposes.

- Bipartisan Campaign Reform Act of 2002 – Also known as McCain-Feingold, this law requires that candidates state on their advertisements that they have approved the content of the advertisement.
- *Citizens United v. Federal Elections Commission* – This ruling held that corporations, labor unions, and associations can spend money for political purposes as long as it is independent of a candidate for public office. This spending is a form of free speech protected by the First Amendment.

- There is ever-increasing debate about the role of money in politics. Many critics believe that the current system of campaign finance and independent expenditures calls into question the fairness of elections.

- Interest groups attempt to influence elections by distributing campaign contributions through organizations known as political action committees (PACs). Political action committees are organizations that raise money to contribute to electoral campaigns of candidates for public office. These contributions are limited by federal election laws. Interest groups that make these contributions are usually seeking to obtain access to public officials.
- Groups can also raise and spend money independent of campaign organizations. This is done through Independent Expenditure-Only Committees (IEOCs), more commonly known as Super PACs. There is no limit on how much money a Super PAC can raise and spend in support of a candidate as long as there is no coordination between the Super PAC and the candidate and the candidate's campaign.

Making Connections

There is tremendous amount of overlap between the content contained in this chapter and Chapter 8, Interest Groups, Chapter 9, Political Parties, and Chapter 11, Voting and Participation. Consider, for example, how interest groups and political parties work to influence elections.

Going Deeper: "Money Is Speech"

A phrase heard frequently in U.S. politics is that "money is speech." At first blush, this might sound ridiculous. However, the Supreme Court through a series of decisions has interpreted the First Amendment in such a manner.

In 1974, Congress passed amendments to the Federal Election Act of 1971. These amendments attempted to limit the influence of money in politics. Some of the key provisions of these amendments were contribution limits, disclosure requirements for political contributions, limits on the overall amount of money that a candidate can spend, limits on the amount of money that a candidate can contribute to his or her own campaign, and a limit on independent expenditures. Independent expenditures are expenditures made by a third party and not coordinated with the candidate.

These provisions were challenged in the case of *Buckley v. Valeo*. In its decision, the Court struck down limits on total spending by candidates, limits on the amount of money a candidate can contribute to his or her own campaign, and limits on independent expenditures.

In interpreting the First Amendment, the Court reasoned that how a person spends his or her money could be viewed as a form of political expression. This expression is therefore entitled to constitutional protections. This is the reasoning that has given rise to the oft used phrase "money is speech."

The *per curium* decision in *Buckley v. Valeo* resulted in several dissents, including Justice White. In his dissent he states:

> *The act of giving money to political candidates, however, may have illegal or other undesirable consequences: it may be used to secure the express or tacit understanding that the giver will enjoy political favor if the candidate is elected. Both Congress and this Court's cases have recognized this as a mortal danger against which effective preventive and curative steps must be taken.*

This line of reasoning is echoed in other Supreme Court decisions including *Citizens United v. Federal Election Commission*. The consequence of these cases is that it is incredibly difficult for Congress, or state governments, to limit the use of money in politics.

11 Voting and Participation

AP® Learning Objectives

MPA – 3.A Describe the voting rights protections in the Constitution and in legislation.

MPA – 3.B Describe different models of voting behavior.

MPA – 3.C Explain the roles that individual choice and state laws play in voter turnout in elections.

Performance Tasks

Upon the completion of this chapter, you must be able to do the following:

- Citing specific amendments, legislation, and cases, explain how the right to vote has been expanded.
- Explain what demographic variables are correlated with voter turnout.
- Explain how the following impacts voter turnout: political efficacy, voter registration, and midterm versus presidential elections.
- Compare voter turnout in the United States with that of other democracies.
- Explain how the following models describe voter behavior: rational choice, retrospective voting, prospective voting, and party line-voting.

B Christopher/Alamy

"... *we should seek not a world where the black race and the white race live in harmony, but a world in which the terms* black *and* white *have no real political meaning.*"[1]

TA-NEHISI COATES
Howard University

Ta-Nehisi Coates was born in 1975 and grew up in segregated northwest Baltimore. While he did not grow up poor, he was surrounded by urban violence. His sense of racial consciousness developed at an early age, and he used to listen to Malcolm X's "The Ballot or the Bullet" speech on a portable audiocassette player that was called a Walkman. Though not a campaign organizer or political operative, Coates has emerged as a prominent social and political voice of a generation of African Americans.[2] His primary and most visible means of participating in politics is through writing.

Coates arrived at Howard University in 1993, pursuing his interest in poetry and writing. He reached out to several older black writers connected with the university who helped to mentor and shape his writing. His in-depth research and his willingness to immerse himself in the material grew out of this period of mentorship at Howard. Inspired by the faculty he met at Howard, Coates went to the library each morning and immersed himself in books about nationalism, integration, and the American experience. He often recalls this time as painful, but an extremely necessary pain that was integral to writing and the development of his writing process: "The process of getting conscious for me was a very, very uncomfortable, disturbing and something physically painful process. And so that's the standard to which I write, because it was what I've experienced over my time."[3] Coates left Howard to begin a career in journalism. Though he did not graduate from Howard, the school afforded him to the ability to read, to learn, and to develop a clear ideological position on critical issues of importance to him. He credits his time spent at Howard as the key juncture in his development as a writer.

After working as a freelance writer for about seven years, Coates began working at *The Atlantic* in 2008 and is now a national correspondent. His influential piece "The Case for Reparations" sparked a new national conversation about the lasting effects of slavery on the African American community. Coates was described as being adept at "digest[ing] the central paradox of the time: how, within an increasingly progressive era, a country led by a black president could still act with such racial brutality."[4] For Coates, writing became his gateway to political participation.

Coates's 2015 book *Between the World and Me* propelled him further into the spotlight, offering a powerful perspective on race relations in the United States. In this extended message to his 14-year-old son, Coates writes about his fears of what his son will have to experience as an African American. He notes that the history of the African American experience is one of a tradition of destroying the black body. He reminds his son, "you must always remember . . . that the sociology, the history, the economics, the graphs, the charts, the regressions all land, with great violence, upon the body." This powerful imagery led observers to note that Coates "speaks unpopular, unconventional and sometimes even radical truths in his own voice, unfiltered."[5]

Coates continued to voice opinions on issues such as mass incarceration, reparations, and the 2016 presidential election. He credits his influence to his growing audience and the community that is forming around him. "There is some group of Americans who are really, really curious to understand how we ended up at this point," he said, explaining that these are the people who have contributed to his recent popularity. While he does not believe they will immediately "go forth and create some sort of long-lasting policy,"[6] there does seem to be some hope in the way that he addresses his readers, hope that maybe his ability to reach this broader audience is helping to educate and bring conscious awareness to at least some of the nation. His goal, in short, is to encourage Americans to participate in this important conversation.

This chapter describes the many gateways to political participation, ranging from voting to campaigning to protest. Coates's story highlights an additional means of participating in the political process: His writing has opened new conversations about race in the United States. His voice is an important one, and he found his gateway through his investment at Howard University to understand his place in the American experience and in communicating his thoughts as a writer.

11.1 The Practice and Theory of Voting

Explain why there are battles over ballot access

Americans enjoy near-universal opportunities to vote. Even so, no one should assume that such opportunities have always existed or that they are permanent. Despite the widespread belief in the importance of elections for democratic institutions, some Americans have argued that voting rights should not be universal. Who votes shapes the outcome of elections and the conduct of government. Voting, in short, is a central gateway to power, so there are always battles over who gets access to the ballot.

The Constitution and Voting

Essential Knowledge

While the question of who gets to vote is fundamentally a state issue, the U.S. Constitution has been amended several times to increase suffrage and other opportunities for participation.

The Constitution is nearly silent on the rules about voting in elections, leaving such choices to the states. As Article I, Section 4, of the Constitution states, "The Times, Places and Manner of holding Elections for Senators and Representatives, shall be prescribed in each State by the Legislature thereof." The Constitution does spell out in some detail the workings of the Electoral College, which chooses the president (see Chapter 10, Elections and Campaigns). But state legislatures were given nearly complete latitude about how to select their members for the Electoral College. Similarly, the Constitution makes the states the prime players in setting voting requirements.

The consequence of this delegation of authority is a system of voting that is very complicated because state rules vary considerably. The differing rules also lead to inequalities among the states. It is, for example, easier to vote in some states than in others. We explore some of these issues in this chapter and in Chapter 10.

Competing Views of Participation

suffrage: *Right to vote; also called* franchise.

Debates about voting and the removal of obstacles to voting have often centered on whether potential voters would be qualified to cast ballots. For example, in the nineteenth century, many lawmakers did not think women would make wise political choices and were therefore reluctant to consider granting them **suffrage**.[7] Others worried that too much participation yields too many demands on government, making government less able to respond. It seems that those opposed to removing obstacles to voting feared that too much democracy could be bad for democracy.[8]

We label these ideas the Hamiltonian model of participation. Alexander Hamilton represents a perspective that sees risks in greater participation and, thus, favors a larger role for elites. In this model, not only would the quality of the decision be diluted by more participation, but government would be less able to advance the national interest because it would be responding to uninformed voters. The Hamiltonian model stands in stark contrast to the Jeffersonian model, which holds that more participation yields a more involved and engaged public and that, in turn, produces better outcomes.[9] In other words, democracy thrives with more democracy. Thomas Jefferson had more faith than Hamilton did in the people's ability and worried that excessive reliance on elites would make government less responsive to its citizens.

Figure 11.1 offers a summary of these competing views. Proponents of the Hamiltonian model do seek accountability, but they place much more faith in the ability of elites than in the ability of the general public to make the right decisions. The people, they contend, are often uninformed and cannot make the best choices. In contrast, proponents of the Jeffersonian model want to see more participation, believing that the people can be trusted and that getting more people involved will push government to be more responsive to the people's interests. They contend that if certain groups of people are disenfranchised, government will be less responsive. People may not be well informed about politics, but if they have a chance to be involved, they will become better informed. An informed citizenry that actively participates in politics will ensure that government is both accountable and responsive.

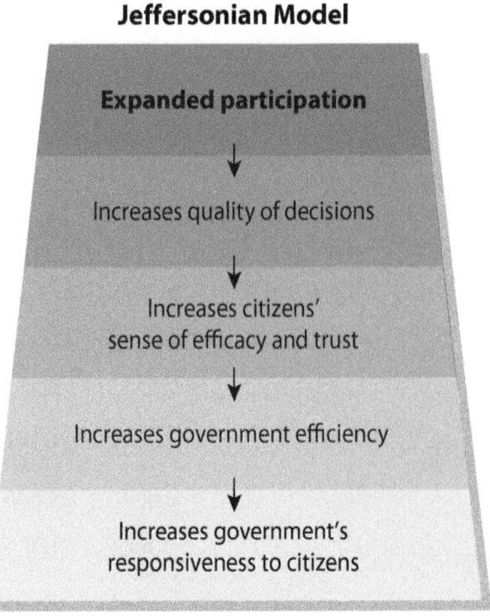

FIGURE 11.1 Hamiltonian and Jeffersonian Models of Participation

This figure shows two ways of thinking about how citizens' participation in government affects various aspects of politics and governance. The two models offer contrasting viewpoints about the value and consequences of political participation.

Obviously the Jeffersonian model holds equality as an important political value, whereas the Hamiltonian model places more emphasis on efficient and effective outcomes. These competing visions of citizen involvement have played out in nearly all debates about expanding the opportunity for more citizens to cast ballots. In the course of the nation's history, proponents and opponents of expanding the right to vote have each achieved victories. Although the overall trend has been constant expansion, the contest has been fraught with conflict—not only debate in Congress and the courts but also violence in the streets, as the following section will attest.

11.2 The History of Voting in America

Outline how the right to vote has expanded

The history of voting in America falls into three general eras.[10] First, from the 1790s to 1870, voting rights expanded, and by 1860 universal white male suffrage had been achieved. After the Civil War, voting rights were extended to African American males by means of the Fifteenth Amendment. But states, localities, and political parties sought by various means to block African Americans, Asian immigrants, and others from voting. From the 1870s until 1920, the barriers to voting often increased. Reforms were under way as well, and beginning with the Nineteenth Amendment in 1920, which granted women the right to vote, voting rights began to expand again. The civil rights movement of the 1950s and 1960s culminated in the passage of laws protecting voting rights for African Americans, Latinos, and others, and a Constitutional amendment in 1971 extended the right to vote to 18-year-olds. In 1961, citizens of the District of Columbia were given the opportunity to vote in presidential elections (see Figure 11.2). Thus, in the twentieth century, there was a second wave of expansion of voting rights.

These three eras suggest that voting and the electorate have expanded in the long run, though not consistently and with contractions that have violated civil rights (see Chapter 5, Civil Rights). In this section, we survey these developments by looking at the first era of expanding voting rights, women's suffrage, the denial and then protection of voting rights for African Americans and Latinos, and voting restrictions and opportunities for other groups.

Expansion of Voting, 1790s to 1870

George Washington (1789–97) was elected to the presidency twice, unanimously both times.[11] By all accounts, he was a popular president and the overwhelming choice of the public. Yet a close look at the first presidential elections shows that very few citizens actually voted for Washington. In fact, for the first nine presidential elections (1789–1820), popular votes were not even recorded across all the states. Most states did not allow the public to cast ballots for president; state legislators chose the electors who voted in the Electoral College. State legislators also chose U.S. senators. The people could vote for representatives to the House of Representatives, but eligibility to vote was largely limited to white males who owned a certain amount of property or paid a certain amount of taxes. Slaves could not vote, and free black males often did not have the right to vote. South Carolina, Georgia, and Virginia blocked free blacks from voting when the Constitution was first adopted. In New Jersey, women who owned property could vote from 1776 until 1807, when the right was rescinded.[12]

franchise: *Right to vote; also called* suffrage.

Not until the rise of Jacksonian democracy in the 1820s did the **franchise** (the right to vote) begin to expand significantly. In the 1824 presidential election, only about 366,000 votes were cast, representing just over 25 percent of eligible voters.[13] None of the four candidates won a majority in the Electoral College, though Andrew Jackson won the most

Color Code: Participation Equality

Fifteenth	1870	Prohibits states from denying the right to vote on account of race
Seventeenth	1913	Gives the people (instead of state legislatures) the right to choose U.S. senators
Nineteenth	1920	Guarantees women the right to vote
Twenty-Third	1961	Grants residents of the District of Columbia votes in the Electoral College
Twenty-Fourth	1964	Prohibits poll taxes
Twenty-Sixth	1971	Guarantees 18-year-olds the right to vote

FIGURE 11.2 Constitutional Amendments That Pertain to the Right to Vote

These six amendments to the Constitution were designed to increase the role of citizens in governance. They removed obstacles from voting and expanded suffrage, and the Seventeenth Amendment provided for direct election of U.S. Senators.

popular votes (41 percent), so the election was decided by the House of Representatives. In one of the most controversial deals in American politics, Henry Clay, who had come in third, threw his support to John Quincy Adams, who had come in second, thereby enabling Adams to win the presidency. Once in office, President Adams (1825–29) named Clay secretary of state.

Jackson's supporters charged that Adams and Clay had made a "corrupt bargain," generating widespread outrage over the "deal."[14] Determined to get Jackson elected to office the next time, they pursued a number of strategies (see also Chapter 9, Political Parties). One was to press states to remove property requirements for voting and to allow citizens, instead of state legislatures, to vote for president. This effort paid off. In the presidential election of 1828, turnout tripled to more than 1.1 million votes cast and produced a landslide for Jackson (1829–37), who won 56 percent of the popular vote and two-thirds of the Electoral College vote. By the time of the Civil War, property and tax qualifications had been largely eliminated, but the franchise was still limited largely to white males. Women could not vote, nor could many free blacks. Those who voted for president in 1860, consequently, were almost exclusively white males.

IMAGE 11.1 When the 1824 presidential election produced no majority in the Electoral College, the House of Representatives selected John Quincy Adams, who had received fewer votes than Andrew Jackson. Jackson's supporters, angered at this outcome, worked to expand the right to vote before the next election. In 1828, Jackson beat Adams in the popular vote and in the Electoral College. Following Jackson's inauguration on March 4, 1829, crowds of supporters celebrated at the White House.

Following the Civil War, the Fifteenth Amendment, ratified in 1870, gave African American males the right to vote. Efforts by southern states to deny that right (covered later in this chapter) have shaped American politics into the present.

The Road to Women's Suffrage, 1848 to 1920

In 1848 in Seneca Falls, New York, the first women's rights meeting initiated a movement for women's suffrage. The movement gained energy after the Civil War, as women individually and through suffrage organizations pressured state legislatures to change state laws to allow women to vote. Susan B. Anthony, a leader in the National Woman Suffrage Association, worked tirelessly for most of her life to secure women the right to vote. In 1872, for example, she went to the polls in her hometown of Rochester, New York, and cast a ballot, claiming that the Fourteenth Amendment's statement that "all persons [not just men] born or naturalized in the United States . . . are citizens" gave women the right to vote. Later, she was arrested (as she hoped she would be), and her trial gave the issue of suffrage for women much attention. She was found guilty of breaking the law, but not before she had used the trial as a platform for her cause.[15]

The efforts of the suffrage movement were gradually successful. In 1869, the territory of Wyoming granted the right to vote to women, and that right was retained when Wyoming became a state in 1890. By 1916, eleven states, all in the West, allowed women to vote (see Figure 5.2, Women's Suffrage Before 1920, in Chapter 5). The piecemeal approach of statewide campaigns came to an end on August 26, 1920, when the Tennessee legislature ratified the Nineteenth Amendment by a single vote. With Tennessee, three-quarters of the states had ratified the amendment, giving constitutional protection to women's suffrage. The amendment states, "The right of citizens of the United States to vote shall not be denied or abridged by the United States or by any State on account of sex." Some southern states used the late date of the Tennessee ratification, only ten weeks before the presidential election, to deny women's access to the ballot until the next election cycle.[16]

The effect of women's vote was debated and even feared at the time. There was speculation that women were not well-suited to be active participants in the political process and that allowing them to vote would provide "an unpredictable or volatile addition to the electorate."[17] Others were concerned about nearly doubling the voting electorate and the additional demands that would place on government. Such views are closely associated with the Hamiltonian model of voting. But evidence gathered by political scientists suggests that these worries were unfounded. Women in the 1920s voted in ways that reflected their interests just as much as men's did.[18] The adoption of the Nineteenth Amendment did not, in other words, undermine the basic stability of electoral politics—a finding supportive of those who favor the Jeffersonian approach to participation.

turnout: *Share of all eligible voters who actually cast ballots.*

With women able to vote, overall **turnout** did drop in the short term. From 1904 to 1916, the average rate of turnout in presidential elections was about 63 percent.[19] With the inclusion of women as eligible voters, turnout fell to 49 percent in both 1920 and 1924. But then it started to climb as women increasingly exercised their right to vote, reaching 57 percent in both 1928 and 1932. By 1940, the turnout rate was 62 percent—essentially at the pre-1920 level. These data strongly suggest that women quickly became involved in the political process. By 1984, women voted at a slightly higher rate than men—a trend that continues today.[20]

The Granger Collection, NYC

IMAGE 11.2 In the early 1870s, suffragists such as Susan B. Anthony tried to exercise the right to vote. When Virginia Minor was blocked from registering to vote in Missouri, she sued. Her case, decided by the Supreme Court in 1875, determined that women were citizens but that the Constitution does not confer a right to vote. In this drawing, Victoria Claflin Woodhull points to the Constitution as she tries to vote in a local New York City election; her sister, Tennessee Claflin, stands behind her.

Denial of African American Suffrage, 1870 to 1965

The story of gates against African American participation is long and agonizing. Five years after the Civil War ended, Congress and the states ratified the Fifteenth Amendment, which reads, "The right of citizens of the United States to vote shall not be denied or abridged by the United States or by any State on account of race, color, or previous condition of servitude." With such constitutional protection, African Americans should have been able to exercise their right to vote. During Reconstruction (1865–77), the period when the federal government effectively controlled the state governments in the South, southern blacks were able to vote. Their votes made it possible for South Carolina—the first state to secede and the first to fire on federal troops—to elect the first African American member of the House of Representatives, Joseph Rainey, in 1870.

IMAGE 11.3 Segregation was a harsh reality throughout the United States, but in the South, states passed laws formally separating the races. These examples are reminders of those laws, and that era is referred to as "Jim Crow."

The presidential election of 1876 ended any hope of integrating blacks into American political life. Neither the Democrat Samuel Tilden nor the Republican Rutherford B. Hayes won a majority in the Electoral College. Contested votes in three southern states and Oregon, with charges of fraud, led Congress to appoint an Electoral Commission to resolve the matter of who should count the votes of the electors (the Constitution does not say who should resolve disputed votes). In an unofficial bargain, all the disputed votes went to Hayes (1877–81) in return for his promise that federal troops would be removed from the South and the region would return to self-governance. With this agreement, Reconstruction was effectively over, and so was African American participation in the political process.

In an era known as **Jim Crow**, southern state legislatures, no longer under federal authority, started to pass laws that denied African Americans basic political rights. State and local laws systematically undermined the political, economic, and social standing of African Americans by requiring segregation of the races in public schools, parks, accommodations, and transportation. Those who disobeyed segregation laws were subject not only to fines and jailing but also to lynching and other acts of brutal violence. Between 1889 and 1930, more than 3,700 lynchings were reported, most of them of southern blacks, and many other lynchings and mob actions were not reported in the press.[21]

Jim Crow laws: *Southern laws that established strict segregation of the races and gave their name to the segregation era.*

The law-based means of denying African Americans the right to vote included the following strategies.

Literacy Tests. **Literacy tests**, which required potential voters to prove they could read, were applied differently to whites and blacks. African Americans were often given

literacy tests: *Tests requiring reading and interpretation skills in order to vote.*

harder tests to ensure they would not pass. In some cases, the tests were set up to guarantee failure, as there were no correct answers. Figure 11.3 reproduces some questions from the Louisiana literacy test, a test that is impossible to pass.

poll taxes: *Tax on voting; prohibited by the Twenty-Fourth Amendment (1964).*

Poll Taxes. **Poll taxes** were another means of discouraging blacks from voting. In the 1890s, an individual had to pay $1 in Mississippi and $2 in South Carolina to vote, an amount that may seem small today but was huge in the poverty-stricken postwar South, where the average annual income was equivalent to $86 in today's dollars; the South Carolina poll tax would be equivalent to about $1,000 today.[22] For most blacks, almost all poor farmers, this tax made voting impossible.[23]

The State of Louisiana

Literacy Test (This test is to be given to anyone who cannot prove a fifth grade education.)

Do what you are told to do in each statement, nothing more, nothing less. Be careful as one wrong answer denotes failure of the test. You have 10 minutes to complete the test.

1. Draw a line around the number or letter of this sentence.
2. Draw a line under the last word in this line.
3. Cross out the longest word in this line.
4. Draw a line around the shortest word in this line.
5. Circle the first, first letter of the alphabet in this line.
6. In the space below draw three circles, one inside (engulfed by) the other.

7. Above the letter X make a small cross.

8. Draw a line through the letter below that comes earliest in the alphabet.

Z V S B D M K I T P H C

9. Draw a line through the two letters below that come last in the alphabet.

Z V B D M K T P H S Y C

10. In the first circle below write the last letter of the first word beginning with "L".

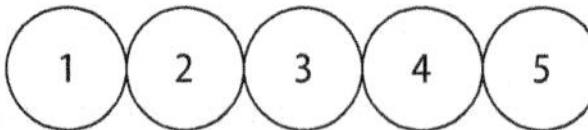

11. Cross out the number necessary, when making the number below one million.

10000000000

12. Draw a line from circle 2 to circle 5 that will pass below circle 2 and above circle 4.

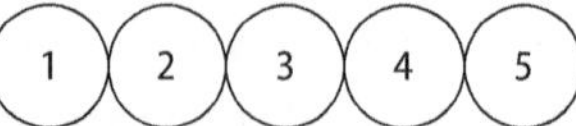

13. In the line below cross out each number that is more than 20 but less than 30.

31 16 48 29 53 47 22 37 98 26 20 25

FIGURE 11.3 Louisiana Literacy Test

These questions, excerpted from a three-page test, make it clear that the test was not intended to test literacy but to deny African Americans the right to vote.

Source: Rethinking Schools, http://www.rethinkingschools.org.

Grandfather Clauses. To help keep literacy tests and poll taxes from discouraging white voters, exemptions were allowed for those whose grandfathers had voted. Because the grandfathers of most African Americans had been slaves with no voting rights, these **grandfather clauses** never benefited them.

grandfather clauses: *Election rules that exempted people from difficult literacy and interpretation tests for voting if their grandfathers had been eligible to vote.*

The White Primary. Following the Civil War, the Democratic Party dominated in the South. By restricting its primary to white voters, it kept black voters—even if they could exercise the right to vote—from having any influence because whoever won the Democratic primary always won the general election. In 1944, the U.S. Supreme Court, in *Smith v. Allwright*, ruled the **white primary** unconstitutional.[24]

white primary: *Election rules that prohibited blacks from voting in Democratic primaries.*

The Civil Rights Movement and African American Voting, 1950s and 1960s

The era of Jim Crow lasted for decades because, despite the guarantee of the Fifteenth Amendment, states retained authority over voting laws, and these laws were not challenged. In addition, Democratic Party dominance ensured the continuation of the so-called Solid South, a voting bloc critical to all Democratic presidential candidates from Woodrow Wilson (1913–21) to Franklin Delano Roosevelt (1933–45) to John F. Kennedy (1961–63), who therefore did not push for civil rights. Southern senators had the power to block efforts to end Jim Crow laws, given their seniority and the option (or threat) of using the filibuster (see Chapter 12, Congress).[25]

Beginning in the 1950s the civil rights movement challenged the denial of basic political rights. Boycotts, sit-ins, and marches called attention to the lack of equal treatment for African Americans in the South (see Chapter 5), and public support for ending the legal barriers grew. For instance, in October 1963, 86 percent of the American public approved of "a federal law that requires negroes be given equal rights in voting."[26] In 1964, support by the public helped give Congress the impetus to pass the Civil Rights Act, which protected voting rights and put severe restrictions on the administration of literacy tests. To strengthen protections of voting rights, Congress passed the Voting Rights Act in 1965, which effectively ended literacy tests and other strategies that had discriminated against African Americans at the polls and gave the Justice Department the authority to supervise **voter registration** in locales that had discriminated (see also Chapter 5). The Twenty-Fourth Amendment, ratified in 1964, banned poll taxes.

voter registration: *Enrollment required prior to voting to establish eligibility.*

One consequence of these measures was a huge upswing of voter participation in the South. From 1920 to 1960, the turnout rate in southern states averaged 23 percent in presidential elections, whereas in the rest of the country it was 65 percent. The low turnout in the South was due not only to the exclusion of blacks; the South was also poorer than much of the rest of the country, and poverty generally depresses turnout. In addition, Democratic Party dominance meant that elections were not competitive and generated little public interest. But **voter apathy** in the South has declined as wealth has risen, and Democratic Party dominance has ended as well. The participation of southerners in elections is much the same as for the rest of the nation now.[27]

voter apathy: *Lack of interest in voting and in politics generally.*

Those with the Hamiltonian model mind-set worried that African Americans would not have the necessary education and skills to recognize how their interests could be best served at the polls. But, as in the case of women, the worries were unfounded. The political revival of African Americans gave them reason to become more attentive, more informed, and

SUPREME COURT CASES

Katzenbach v. Morgan (1966)

QUESTION: May Congress prohibit states from enforcing English-language literacy tests?

ORAL ARGUMENT: April 18, 1966 (listen at http://www.oyez.org/cases/1960-1969/1965/1965_847)

DECISION: June 13, 1966 (read at http://laws.findlaw.com/us/384/641.html)

OUTCOME: Yes, Congress has the authority (7–2).

Section 4(e) of the Voting Rights Act of 1965 prevented states from establishing English-language literacy tests for voting if the resident had finished the sixth grade in an accredited school in the U.S. Commonwealth of Puerto Rico in which the language of instruction was "other than English" (this almost always meant Spanish). Although voting qualifications were traditionally left to states, the Fourteenth Amendment, which, among other things, prohibited states from denying to any person the equal protection of the laws, also gave Congress the authority to enforce its provisions through "appropriate legislation." As many people of Puerto Rican heritage had been denied the right to vote in New York due to an inability to read and write English, Congress added the above-noted protection.

Morgan and other registered voters in New York City brought the lawsuit to challenge Congress's authority to prohibit English-language voting requirements. A special three-judge district court struck down the congressional requirement. U.S. Attorney General Nicholas Katzenbach appealed that decision directly to the Supreme Court, as the Voting Rights Act allows.

The Supreme Court ruled that the enforcement provision of the Fourteenth Amendment gave Congress the same broad powers to enact legislation to protect voting rights that the necessary and proper clause did for the enumerated powers in the Constitution (see Supreme Court Cases: *McCulloch v. Maryland* in Chapter 3, Federalism). The Court declared that legislation prohibiting discrimination in voting on account of language fell within the constitutional authority of Congress.

Thinking Critically

1. What reasons, valid and invalid, might New York have had for restricting the right to vote to those who can read or write in English?
2. Why might the Voting Rights Act have protected Americans educated in Spanish in Puerto Rico but not Americans educated in Spanish in Mexico?

better citizens overall. As one study reports, "African-Americans developed the attitudes and skills necessary to 'learn the trade' of politics in a remarkably short period of time."[28] In 2012, black turnout was higher than white turnout for the first time in a presidential election, 66 percent to 64 percent. In the 2016 election, turnout among blacks dropped slightly yet remained relatively high.[29] The fact that blacks overcame the informational and educational disadvantages imposed on them in the Jim Crow era casts doubts on the Hamiltonian theory of participation, giving advocates of the Jeffersonian school reason for optimism.

The Latino Vote

The Jim Crow laws designed to limit the franchise of blacks had the same effects on Latinos. Poll taxes placed an additional, and relatively high, cost on Latinos wanting to vote. One of the major gates to Latino voter participation involved language. After Reconstruction and well into the twenty-first century, many Latinos speak Spanish as their first language.[30] Literacy tests, as applied to Latinos, were English-language tests. These tests constructed a real gate to participation. As we saw in Chapter 5, in the 1960s, New York's English requirements prevented Puerto Rican Americans from registering to vote prior to 1955 (see Supreme Court Cases: *Katzenbach v. Morgan*).[31] That decision, while important, did not break down all the gates because it did not require that voter registration, ballots, and other voting materials be made available to non-English-speaking voters in their native language.

In 1975, Congress extended the Voting Rights Act to include "Language Assistance Amendments." Those laws ensured that in areas in which more than 5 percent of the citizens of voting age are members of a single language minority and have limited English proficiency, governments must provide election materials and assistance in their native language (as well as in English).[32] This change opened a significant gateway for Latinos and other non-English speakers to participate in elections. In comments before the Senate Judiciary Committee, Senator Orrin Hatch (R-UT) explained his support for the provisions this way:

> *The right to vote is one of the fundamental human rights. Unless government assures access to the ballot box, citizenship is just an empty promise. Section 203 of the Voting Rights Act, containing bilingual election requirements, is an integral part of our government's assurance that Americans do have such access.*[33]

Considering the many gates facing Latino voters, their socialization into the electoral arena has been stilted. Gates such as Jim Crow laws, Mexican Repatriation, and language requirements, for example, discouraged Latinos from voting and inevitably passed this uneven and constrained sense of citizenship to succeeding generations. Even so, the Voting Rights Act proved a boon to the participation of Latinos. Together with voter mobilization, Latinos are overcoming these early gates and now voting in much larger numbers. Although it seems that there are now more gateways to participation, new efforts in the form of voter identification laws have been enacted by some states, constructing new gates that will hinder many Latinos (and others) from exercising the right to vote. (See Public Policy and Voting: Voter ID Laws.)

Figure 11.5 provides some clear data on Latino voting by comparing the rates of participation to other relevant groups. As the figure shows, Latino voting in presidential elections continues to lag behind the rates of both white and African American voters. Over the past four election cycles, whites have voted at rates between 60 and 70 percent, while African American turnout has increased from 52 percent to an historic 66 percent in the 2012 election. In the same time period, voting rates for Latinos have hovered in the range of 45 to 51 percent. The gap between black and Latino turnout has increased in recent years, surely reflecting the mobilization of the African American community with the Obama candidacy.

However, this lower turnout masks the fact that Latinos represent an ever-growing segment of the total voting population. While turnout rates have been pretty flat, the number of eligible Latino voters has grown from 13.2 million to 23.7 million since the year 2000. While the 2000 Latino turnout rate of 45 percent brought around 6 million people to the polls, the 2012 turnout rate of 48 percent resulted in around 11 million Latino voters. Latinos now constitute about 12 percent of the electorate,[34] and the percentage will only grow in the coming years.[35]

PUBLIC POLICY AND VOTING

Voter ID Laws

To avoid voter fraud, many states have instituted voter identification requirements. As of 2016 thirty-three states have voter identification laws in force.[36] Of these, seventeen states require voters to show a photo ID, and sixteen states require a nonphoto ID, such as a bank statement with the voter's address. Other states ask voters to show ID with or without a photo but do not prevent individuals from voting if they do not present a ballot ID at the polling stations. (See the Political Analytics section in Chapter 5.) Voter ID laws, however, are controversial as some argue that it creates a gate to participation. The poor and less educated, for example, may find it harder to meet these new standards and, if so, may be disenfranchised. Even for those who are better educated and have ID, 2016 showed that these requirements greatly lengthened the time it takes to vote, creating very long lines at polling places across America.

Opponents of Indiana's 2005 photo identification law sought to block its implementation through a lawsuit. The fundamental issue in this case was whether state laws that were intending to prevent voter fraud had the result of preventing citizens who were legally entitled to vote from doing so. Indiana argued that the requirement of a photo ID was not unduly burdensome because the state provided voter identification cards to citizens who had no other photo IDs. But opponents argued that the process of getting such a card was too complicated and that the overall effect of the law would be to disenfranchise thousands of citizens. In 2008, the Supreme Court upheld the Indiana law by a 6–3 vote. Justice John Paul Stevens wrote on behalf of the majority, "The state interests identified as justifications for [the law] are both neutral and sufficiently strong to require us to reject" the lawsuit. However, Justice David Souter wrote in dissent that the law "threatens to impose nontrivial burdens on the voting right of tens of thousands of the state's citizens."[37]

The issue is still not settled. Starting in 2012, the American Civil Liberties Union filed suit against Pennsylvania's strict new voter ID law, and the State Supreme Court struck down the law.[38] In addition to not "[assuring] fair and free elections," as the Pennsylvania judge wrote, these laws may have a disproportionate effect on some groups of voters.

For example, elderly, poorer citizens, and even women whose surnames may change as they marry, divorce, or simply maintain their maiden names[39] may not have acceptable forms of photo identification. Latinos may also be less likely than other voters to have valid photo identification. In Texas, for example, scholars showed that not only were Latinos less likely to have such IDs, but they were also less likely to have the documents necessary to obtain them (see Figure 11.4).[40] In a federal court case brought by the Texas State Conference of the NAACP and the Mexican American Legislative Caucus of the Texas House of Representatives, the courts used such evidence to strike down a Texas law requiring citizens to present photo identification to vote. At issue was whether the Texas law violated Section 2 of the Voting Rights Act that prohibits voting practices or procedures that discriminate on the basis of race, color, or membership in one of the

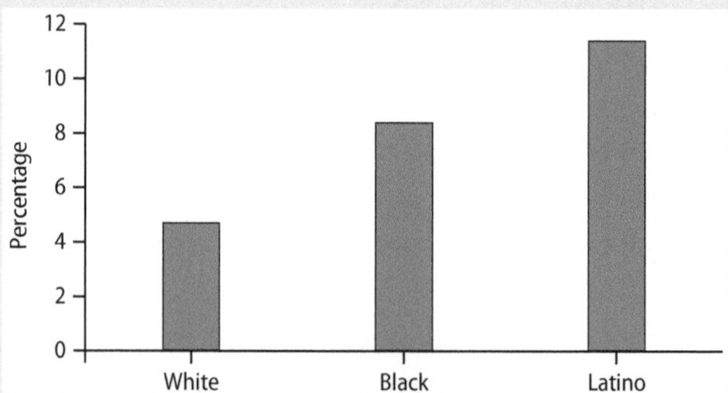

FIGURE 11.4 Percent of Eligible Voters in Texas Who Lack an Accepted Photo ID

This figure shows recent data from Texas about who is affected by voter identification laws. It is clear from the data that Blacks and Latinos are least likely to hold an acceptable form of photo identification that would allow them to vote.

Source: Matt A. Barreto and Gabriel R. Sanchez, "Accepted Photo Identification and Different Subgroups in the Eligible Voter Population, State of Texas," Expert Report Submitted on Behalf of Plaintiffs in *Veasey v. Perry*, Case 2:13-cv-00193, June 27, 2014, http://www.latinodecisions.com/blog/wp-content/uploads/2014/10/Texas-Voter-ID-Expert-Report_Barreto_Sanchez.pdf.

language groups identified in the VRA.[41] The Texas law was temporarily stayed for the November 2014 election and was since reinstated following the *Shelby County v. Holder* (2013) decision. (See the discussion of the *Shelby* case and the Political Analytics feature in Chapter 5.)

These are all complicated issues and as such must be thoughtfully assessed, especially as they affect differentially the ability of certain groups to influence the political process. Political considerations also come into play. The two political parties may see their electoral fortunes tied to either increased or decreased voter participation and thus have different incentives to cooperate with each other on voting requirements. Latinos, for instance, are substantially more likely to vote Democratic than Republican.

With the Hamiltonian and Jeffersonian views of voting in mind, it is important to decide what standards should be imposed for citizens to vote. Clearly, the federal government has taken steps to make the voting process easier and more convenient. But ultimately states and localities administer and oversee elections, and states have responded inconsistently to the federal efforts. Some appear to have made it easier to vote, but others, such as Indiana, have made it harder by requiring photo identification at the polling place. It would seem that, in a democracy, all citizens should have an equal opportunity to cast their votes because voting is the fundamental mechanism by which we hold government accountable. As states introduce more laws regarding identification, disparities in the opportunity to vote may be growing.

Public Policy Connections

1. Do voter ID laws disenfranchise portions of the electorate?
2. Should the national government establish a standard for voter identification?

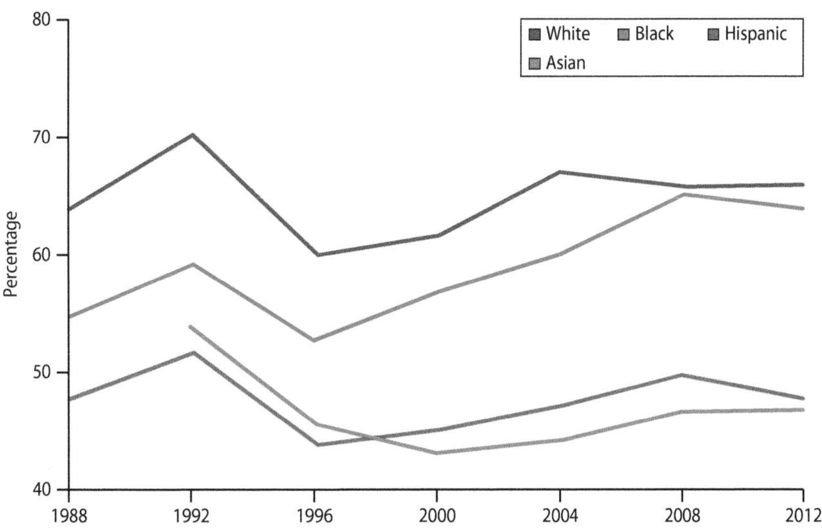

Note: Hispanics are of any race. For the years 1988 through 2008, whites, blacks, and Asians include only non-Hispanics. For 2012, blacks and Asians include Hispanics. Data for non-Hispanic Asians were not available in 1988.

FIGURE 11.5 Voter Turnout Rates in Presidential Elections, by Race and Ethnicity

This figure demonstrates the disparities in turnout rates among four racial and ethnic groups. Latinos and Asian Americans have continued to exert less of an effect on elections than their growing populations might suggest.

Source: Pew Resource Center, http://www.pewresearch.org/fact-tank/2013/05/08/six-take-aways-from-the-census-bureaus-voting-report/

The Vote for 18-Year-Olds, 1971

Until 1971, nearly all states set the minimum age for voting at 21,[42] but with the adoption of the Twenty-Sixth Amendment that year, the Constitution mandated that states could not deny the right to vote to anyone age 18 or over. The impetus for this extension of the franchise was the Vietnam War, which heightened awareness of the fact that young men were being sent off to fight at age 18 but could not participate in elections. The call for the 18-year-old vote also took place in the context of campus antiwar protests and student demands for greater rights and in the wake of African American achievements in civil and voting rights—protests that had achieved protection of the right to vote. At that moment in the country's history, people were receptive to arguments in favor of greater participation. Unlike the extension of the franchise to women and African Americans, the amendment was not controversial. President Richard M. Nixon (1969–74) supported it even though he knew from polling data that the young voters were not likely to support him in the upcoming 1972 presidential election.

11.3 Who Votes?

Identify who tends to turn out in American elections

Voting is an important gateway to influence, but not everyone has the inclination or the desire to participate. Failure to vote has real implications for the political process; it affects which representatives govern and make laws, and who governs has policy consequences that affect everyone in the United States. Low turnout raises questions about government's responsiveness, and unequal turnout by various demographic groups suggests that government's response is unequal, too. Low turnout among young people, for example, in contrast to older Americans, means that elected officials may give more attention to issues affecting senior voters, such as Social Security, than to issues affecting younger voters, such as the costs of education. Figure 11.6 documents that the youngest voters have the lowest turnout and that voters turn out more often as they age. In this section, we examine turnout rates generally and then look at turnout rates by various demographic groups.

Turnout

Even with widespread opportunity to cast ballots and shape the course of government, Americans often choose not to vote. In 1996, fewer than half of eligible voters (about 48 percent) took the time to vote in the presidential contest between William Jefferson (Bill) Clinton (1993–2001) and Senator Robert Dole (R-KS). In 2012, the rate of participation improved to about 58 percent.[43] While that proportion was higher than in 1996, it was less than in 2008. Presidential elections are high-stimulus events (see Chapter 10) that generate more interest and voting than any other American election. In midterm congressional elections, which are low-stimulus elections, turnout is usually less than 40 percent. For

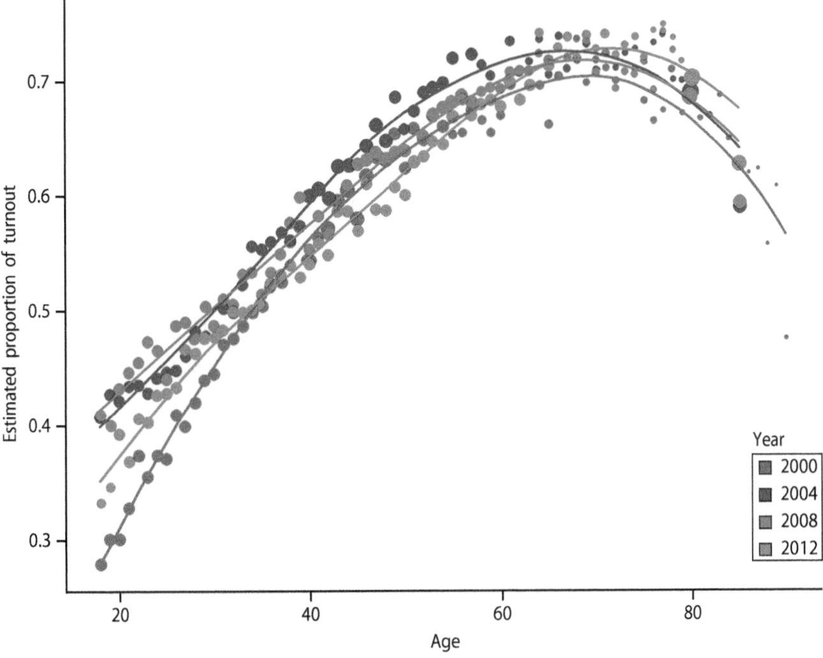

FIGURE 11.6 Turnout by Age in Presidential Elections

Young voters have turned out in greater numbers in the past three presidential elections, but their rate of turnout is still considerably lower than that of people over 30, decreasing the likelihood that government will be responsive to their interests.

Source: Census Current Population Surveys.

primary elections during presidential nominations, turnout is even lower. In 2016 in the all-important New Hampshire presidential primary, turnout was 52 percent, an all-time high perhaps due to the high stimulus created by the candidacy of Donald J. Trump. Still, in other states, turnout remained low, never reaching 40 percent. Texas had a turnout of less than 25 percent, and Florida had only 28 percent.[44] For local school board elections, the electorate is even smaller: Often fewer than 10 percent of eligible citizens vote in such contests. A general assessment of turnout in the United States is offered later in the chapter. Here, we turn to the demographics of turnout.

The Demographics of Turnout

Given the important power that voting brings in a democracy, the following becomes a central question: Who votes? Do various demographic groups vote in equal proportions? If not, what are the consequences for government responsiveness?

Essential Knowledge

Not all demographic groups vote at the same rate. Political efficacy and engagement can impact the likelihood that a person will vote.

The data suggest that people who are most likely to vote tend to be better educated, better paid, and older than those who are unlikely to vote. There are some modest race, ethnicity, and gender differences, but when scholars control for differences in education and income, differences in race pretty much disappear.[45] The key lesson is that the driving force of participation is the development in young people of the kinds of skills and habits that prepare an individual for active citizenship.

Sex. Women turn out at a higher rate than men, by perhaps 3 to 5 percentage points. According to one estimate, 59 percent of women reported voting in 2012 compared to

54 percent of men.[46] The gender gap is important in American politics, but it relates to the tendency of women to support Democrats over Republicans, not to the difference in turnout between women and men.

Age. Age affects rates of participation. Turnout peaks once voters are about 60 years old (see Figure 11.6). Even when differences in education and income are controlled for, participation remains higher for older Americans. In 2012, around 70 percent of citizens older than 65 claimed to have voted. The proportion is just 41 percent for those 24 and younger, and it is even lower for those 21 and younger.[47] Such findings are tied to the fact that younger citizens are often more mobile and less integrated into the community than are older citizens.[48]

It is worth noting that participation by the very youngest voting-age citizens (18–24) climbed to more than 49 percent in 2008, from 36 percent in 2000. Much of this gain was among young blacks, whose rate of participation jumped in response to Obama's candidacy. But the excitement of the youth faded four years later, with 38 percent turnout in 2012.[49] One has to be cautious in making too much of these changes, but it does suggest that younger people can, under some conditions, become more active in politics. The general shift from the mid-1990s, where turnout was about 35 percent, to now being around 40 percent is in line with some of the early patterns of greater participation that have been found among the Millennials, the youngest cohort of voting-age citizens.

Race and Ethnicity. Patterns of turnout vary by the race and ethnicity of voters. Figure 11.5 shows the turnout rates for four racial/ethnic groups. There is a clear increase in the turnout of African American voters, most notably since 1996. Latino and Asian Americans continue to lag behind whites and African Americans in their propensity to vote. It is also important to remember that once we take into account the education levels of all of these groups, the variation in turnout diminishes. For example, Latino and white voters who both hold college degrees have about the same likelihood of voting.

A closer look at a pattern regarding white voters is shown in Figure 11.7. Because of changing demographics in the U.S. population, the percentage of the total vote composed of white voters has declined dramatically from 1980 to 2012. This trend is significant because the two political parties' coalitions are, to some extent, composed of the different racial and ethnic groups. The Republican Party, for example, has found more support among white voters. In contrast, the Latino vote in 2012 and in 2016 reached 10 and 11 percent of the total vote, respectively, and Latinos supported Barack Obama and Hillary Clinton by substantial margins.[50] As the share of the white vote declines and the share of nonwhite voters rises, the electoral consequences may shape the future electoral fortunes of both political parties.

Income. The higher one's income, the more likely one is to vote. More income generally means that people believe they have more at stake and thus more reason to vote. Individuals with higher incomes are also likely to be in environments in which politics is frequently discussed and that provide greater opportunities for learning about the political process. Political knowledge is strongly correlated with the propensity to vote. Further, individuals with higher incomes are more likely to be able to arrange to vote than are those with low-paying jobs, who may be less able to take time off from work to go to the polls.

Data from the U.S. Census Bureau in Table 11.1 strongly confirm this relationship. In 2012, about 75 percent of people with total family incomes between $100,000 and $150,000 reported that they went to the polls. For people whose incomes fell in the range that represents the annual median family income in America—$40,000 to $50,000—turnout was 62 percent. For the least well off (those earning less than $15,000), 48 percent said they voted.

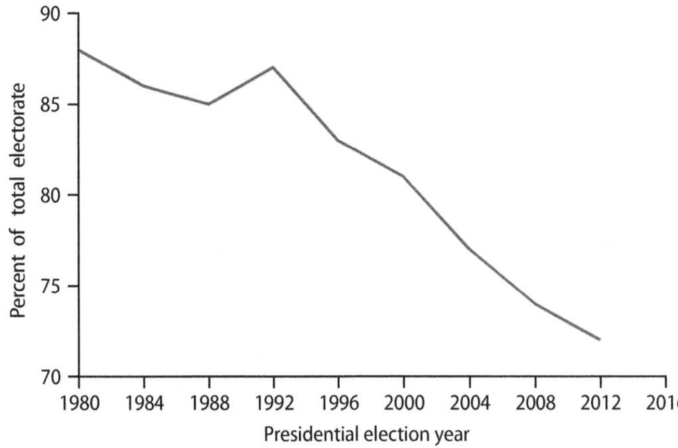

FIGURE 11.7 White Share of the Vote in Presidential Elections

Between 1980 and 2012, the percentage of voters in U.S. presidential elections who were white dropped from 88 percent to 72 percent. The way proposed policies affect African American, Latino, and Asian American voters will be an important factor in determining which candidates win future elections.

Source: Roper Center for Public Opinion Research, "How Groups Voted," Cornell University, http://ropercenter.cornell.edu/polls/us-elections/how-groups-voted/.

Education. Although race and ethnicity, sex, age, and income have some effects on the propensity of people to vote, the number of years of formal education seems to be the most important influence. Social science research has documented the connection between education and voting.[51] The youngest voting-eligible citizens (18- to 24-year-olds) who have college degrees have turnout rates 20 percentage points higher than the rates of older citizens (65–74) who do not have a high school education.[52] Table 11.2 shows the propensity to vote by educational level. The gap between people with the least education and those with the most is about 50 percentage points—a huge difference. Nearly three-fourths of college-educated people vote, whereas less than a quarter of those with just a grade-school education do so.

The relationship between education and voting may not be as simple as these data suggest, however. New evidence indicates that going to college does not matter as

TABLE 11.1 Turnout by Income in the 2012 Presidential Election

	Turnout
Less than $15,000	48%
$15,000–$19,999	52%
$20,000–$29,999	56%
$30,000–$39,999	58%
$40,000–$49,999	62%
$50,000–$74,999	66%
$75,000–$99,999	70%
$100,000–$150,000	74%
More than $150,000	76%

Source: U.S. Census. *Voting and Registration in the Election of 2012*, https://www.census.gov/hhes/www/socdemo/voting/publications/p20/2012/tables.html.

TABLE 11.2 Turnout by Education in Recent Presidential Elections

Years of Education	1988	1992	1996	2000	2004	2008	2012
8 years or fewer	37%	35%	30%	27%	24%	23%	22%
Less than high school	41%	41%	34%	34%	34%	27%	32%
High school	55%	58%	49%	49%	50%	50%	49%
Less than college	65%	69%	61%	60%	66%	65%	61%
College or more	78%	81%	73%	72%	74%	73%	72%

Source: Harold Stanley and Richard Niemi, *Vital Statistics on American Politics* (Washington, D.C.: CQ Press, 2013).

much as childhood socialization, which imbues the values of citizenship and similarly affects the decision to attend college. It is not, therefore, spending four years in college that makes college graduates more likely to vote; rather, it is having been raised in an environment that stresses the importance of education that shapes willingness to vote.[53]

The gap in turnout between people who are more educated and those with little education has increased over the past forty or so years. The increase can be explained by expanded access to education. Individuals who lack a high-school education are at a much larger disadvantage than in the past. These patterns suggest that inequalities may result as government responds more effectively to those who vote than to those who do not.

11.4 Why Citizens Vote

Articulate the main theoretical approaches that explain voting

With the right to vote guaranteed and widely available, why do some people choose not to vote? Perhaps we can start to answer that question by reversing it—that is, by looking at why people *do* vote. Political scientists have developed three approaches to explain why eligible voters choose to cast ballots. One model draws from the field of economics, the second draws from psychology, and the third focuses on the rules and context of the election. In this section, we present these explanations as well as some new ideas about the relationship of genetics and voting. Last, we briefly discuss the impact of weather on voting.

Economic Model of Voting

self-interest: *Concern for one's own advantage and well-being.*

The economic model of voting starts with the assumption that all choices involve calculations about **self-interest** that balance costs and benefits. In choosing a college, students consider the price of tuition, the location of the school and its reputation, the quality of the education, and the potential social life. The decision to vote is no different. According to the economic model, citizens consider the costs and benefits of voting; when the benefits exceed the costs, they turn out to vote. So, according to this model, if voting becomes less costly to all citizens, there should be an increase in participation. If it becomes more costly, fewer people will turn out. Under this model, voters act in a rational, self-interested fashion.

However, economic voting is not straightforward. In *An Economic Theory of Democracy* (1957), Anthony Downs describes **rational voting** as a puzzle. He points out that there are some costs tied to voting, such as the time it takes to become informed, to register to vote, and to go to the polls.[54] Costs could also involve lost work time and the cost of gas to drive to the local polling place. These costs are not huge, but they are real.

rational voting: *Economic model of voting wherein citizens weigh the benefits of voting against the costs in order to take the most personally beneficial course of action.*

The benefits of voting are less clear. If benefits are defined in a narrow, self-interested fashion, there are no tangible benefits to be had from voting. A voter may favor a candidate (or party) because of a specific policy, such as the promise of a tax cut that would provide a big financial benefit. But a tax cut is a public good that is shared by all in society, including those who do not vote. In addition, and perhaps most important, the chance that one vote will alter the outcome of the election is very small—so small, in fact, that there is a greater chance of being killed in an accident on the way to the polls than of changing the outcome of the election. Even in the razor-thin contest in Florida in the 2000 presidential election, the margin was 537 votes.[55] One vote did not make the difference. Thus, given that there are some financial costs to voting, why should a self-interested person participate?

Essential Knowledge

Voters who vote based upon a candidate or party's past performance are said to engage in retrospective voting.

In short, the conclusion of the economic model is that voting is not in one's self-interest and in fact is irrational. If the decision to vote is driven by a self-interested assessment of costs and benefits, people should not take the time to vote. That is a troubling conclusion for the workings of democratic government. Obviously, if citizens do not bother to vote, government cannot be responsive, and public officials will not be held accountable.

Essential Knowledge

Voters who vote for a candidate or party based upon promises of future performance are engaging in prospective voting.

Downs understood the troubling implications of his model and claimed that people voted because they knew that the system would collapse if no one voted. To save the system from collapse, it was rational to vote. This observation has appeal at first glance, but the logic is flawed: One vote will not save the system from collapsing. So even if the system is about to crumble, it remains rational to abstain from voting.

The prediction from Downs's model has drawn much attention from scholars. William Riker and Peter Ordeshook sought to save the model by introducing the idea of **civic duty** as a benefit of voting. The notion of civic duty is important, but the argument describes a psychological attitude voters might have.[56] Thus Riker and Ordeshook's argument does not solve the problem in Downs's model.[57] Narrow self-interest does not explain why people vote. As a consequence, political scientists tend to view voting as more of a psychological process than as a narrow economic or self-interested process.

civic duty: *Social force that binds a person to actively participate in public and political life.*

Psychological Model of Voting

The psychological model views participation in elections as a product of citizens' attitudes about the political system. These attitudes are often a product of socialization

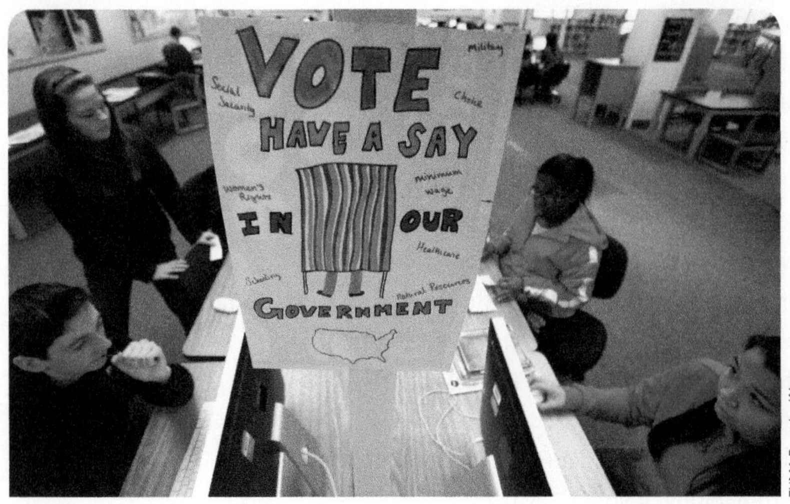

ZUMA Press Inc/Alamy

IMAGE 11.4 Kids Voting USA is a national organization that promotes civic learning in schools and communities. In 2012, more than 1.2 million children participated by "voting" in the presidential election and chose Barack Obama over Mitt Romney by more than 2 to 1. Votes were also cast for libertarians and socialists running for various small parties, as well as for Independents and the Green Party. Here an 8-year-old "votes" in Tallahassee, Florida.

and early political experiences. People who are raised in households in which voting is important are likely to think that participation matters. Those who have a strong sense of trust in government or believe that their votes matter are more likely to participate. The focus here is on what we called **civic interest** in Chapter 1, Gateways to American Democracy.

Riker and Ordeshook's concept of civic duty fits well in this psychological model of voting. Many people who vote recognize that being a citizen in a democracy carries the obligation to vote. In 2012, for example, 90 percent of the public believed that "it's my duty to always vote."[58] The act of voting makes citizens feel good and feel that they are part of the political system. Surveys have found a strong correlation between civic-mindedness and the propensity to vote. In fact, there is often guilt associated with not voting, so much so that people tend to over-report the frequency with which they go to the polls.[59]

civic interest: *Concern for the well-being of society and the nation as a whole.*

Another psychological component tied to the act of voting is partisanship. Citizens who align themselves with the Democratic Party or the Republican Party are more likely to vote. Being a partisan implies an engagement in politics, and partisans see importance in the outcomes of elections. Partisanship increases the prospects that an individual will vote.

Both civic duty and partisanship are attitudes formed in childhood. One survey found that a person's attitude about citizenship expressed in 1965 was a powerful predictor of his or her voting in the 1980 presidential election.[60] The relationship between socialization and voting holds even after education and other important variables that drive participation are taken into account. In addition, parents' electoral activism in 1965 also explains their children's willingness to vote in 1980. Much has changed since 1980, but socialization continues to have a long and powerful reach. For these reasons, some states have Kids Voting, a program designed to instill the habit of voting in grade-school children.[61]

It is also clear that citizens who express greater trust in government are more willing to participate. In addition, people who think they have a voice in government are more likely to vote. Political scientists call this attitude **efficacy**—the belief that one's involvement influences the course of government.

efficacy: *Extent to which people believe their actions can affect public affairs and the actions of government.*

institutional model: *Model of voting that focuses on the context of the election, including whether it is close and whether the rules encourage or discourage participation.*

Institutional Model of Voting

A third explanation of voting looks at political context. In the **institutional model**, voting is understood to be shaped by the rules of the system, by political party behavior, by the ways candidates run their campaigns, and by the context of the election.[62] This model does not ignore individuals' personal resources or psychological attitudes; it simply points out that the political environment is a factor that shapes participation.

It is clear, for example, that the popularity and appeal of the candidates affect turnout.[63] Contenders who are viewed as unexciting, even boring, offer voters few reasons to participate. But both very popular and very unpopular candidates might spur turnout. A highly controversial candidate might lead people who are strongly opposed to show up in great numbers on Election Day. A highly popular candidate likewise brings out supporters.

The competitiveness of an election also influences motivation. Elections that look to be close draw voters' interest and attention, especially if they think their votes might influence the outcome. A close race is exciting, and people like to be part of it. But elections often are not competitive, lessening citizens' incentive to make time to cast their ballots.

Because voting takes time, the efforts by parties, interest groups, and civic organizations to bring people to the polls can make a difference. Get-out-the-vote drives seem to pay big dividends, especially at the local level. For example, direct personal contact, such as going door to door, may increase the rate of voting by 7 to 10 percentage points in local elections.[64] Even text messaging seems to increase turnout by about 3 percentage points, according to a recent study.[65] The size of these effects is not likely to apply to presidential elections because many people are already inclined to vote in these high-stimulus elections. Parties, too, can increase turnout by mobilizing their base to participate.[66] Canvassing by telephone or in person not only may lower information costs but also may activate citizens' sense of civic duty. In some cases, parties or other organizations pick up people and bring them to the polls, lowering the costs of voting.

Essential Knowledge

Some individuals make the choice as to who to vote for based overwhelmingly on party identification. Most likely, they will vote for candidates of the same party for all offices. This is known as party-line voting.

Is Voting in Your Genes?

It makes sense that voting is a product of psychological forces or perhaps of the costs and benefit of participating. But might the choice to be active in politics have a deeper cause? Might it be in your genes? More than two thousand years ago, Aristotle contended that "man is by nature a political animal." Political scientists have tended to believe that citizens are "blank slates," nurtured by socialization, education, and environment. Recent evidence, however, has suggested a genetic component to participation. James Fowler and his colleagues found a strong relationship between genes and turnout.[67]

Daniel Acker/Bloomberg/Getty Images

IMAGE 11.5 Campaigns try many methods to encourage younger citizens to participate. Here popular singer and songwriter Katy Perry rallies Hillary Clinton supporters before the annual Jefferson-Jackson Dinner in Iowa on October 24, 2015.

Another study reported "that two extensively studied genes are significant predictors of voter turnout."[68] These new data are important because they suggest that scholars may need to move beyond looking at the nurture side of the equation and start to consider the role nature plays in shaping individuals politically. Even so, much more evidence is needed before a genetic model of participation is accepted. In fact, a recent study called into question this relationship between genes and voting.[69] Nevertheless, the idea is intriguing and worth considering as an alternative way of thinking about voting.

Weather

There has been a long-standing view that weather affects why some people vote and others do not. With bad weather, potential voters may ask: Why bother voting? Is it worth dealing with the unpleasant weather? People who would have to travel through an ice storm in Oklahoma may have less incentive to turn out than those in Arizona on a day with sunny skies and pleasant temperatures.

The impact of weather has produced much speculation. People deal with varying weather conditions all the time, and perhaps bad weather has little effect on them. Recently, three political scientists have undertaken a comprehensive examination of this question using data "from over 22,000 weather stations to provide election day estimates of rain and snow for each U.S. County." The results are clear: Rain significantly reduces voter participation by a rate of just less than 1 percent per inch, and an inch of snowfall decreases turnout by almost 0.5 percent. These scholars go on to show that bad weather benefits Republicans slightly by discouraging less-well-off voters from participating, giving weather a potential partisan bias.[70]

11.5 Assessing Turnout

Evaluate how low turnout is in American elections

As this chapter has established, most Americans do not vote in most elections. Even in presidential elections, for which turnout is highest, only slightly more than half of eligible voters go to the polls. In this section, we assess turnout in the United States. Is it too low for responsive and responsible government? Even more important, does turnout increase the prospects of governmental action that ensures equality?

Is Turnout Low?

There is a widespread belief among political scientists, political observers, and journalists that turnout in American elections is low. Consider the titles of the following books on the topic of voting in the United States: *Why Americans Still Don't Vote, Where Have All the Voters Gone?*, and *The Vanishing Voter*.[71] When just 37 percent of the American public took the time to vote in the 2014 congressional elections, the concern about low turnout expressed in these books seems justified. Even with all the attention and interest surrounding the 2016 presidential elections, turnout of the voting-age population was about 58 percent.[72] Such data strike many as disappointing. But further investigation of turnout can offer a different way to interpret the situation.

The United States Compared to Other Democracies. Compared to other democracies, turnout in the United States is low. Between 1948 and 2016, the average rate of turnout in U.S. presidential elections was about 58 percent,[73] while in other democracies it was 90 percent or more. These numbers compel an assessment of why U.S. turnout is so low.

One reason has to do with the rules for voting. Australia has **compulsory voting**—citizens are required by law to vote. Those who do not vote must pay a $20 fine, and the fine increases to $50 if the nonvoter does not answer the Australian Election Commission's inquiry about why he or she did not vote. New Zealand requires all citizens to register to vote. In most of the countries of Western Europe, the government is responsible for registering citizens to vote. In the United States, by contrast, both voting and registering are voluntary, and only about 70 percent of the public is registered. That means that nearly one-third of potentially eligible voters cannot cast votes on Election Day even if they want to do so.

Another reason has to do with the convenience of voting. Most European countries lessen the costs of voting by allowing it to take place on Sunday. In the United States, voting takes place on Tuesday, a workday for most people. Federal law stipulates that the first Tuesday after the first Monday in November is the day on which voting for president and members of Congress will take place, and most states have also selected Tuesdays as the day for voting in primaries and in state and local elections. The costs of voting are increased because people may be at work and may have difficulty finding the time to vote. With more costs to voting, turnout is lower in the United States than in many European democracies. This discussion highlights the importance of considering the context of each election, which is the theoretical focus of the institutional model of voting.

According to one estimate, turnout in the United States would be 27 percentage points higher (or more than 80 percent) if the nation had laws and rules that foster voting.[74] At the least, this figure suggests that comparisons of turnout in various democracies require a careful accounting of the rules and institutions that shape the willingness of citizens to go to the polls.

Essential Knowledge

Voter turnout in the United States, relative to other democracies, is relatively low. This is caused by a variety of factors, including registration requirements, lack of incentives or penalties, and different types of elections (presidential versus midterm). Higher voter turnout in other democracies varies with the degree of registration requirements, as well as presidential/parliamentary types and electoral systems.

compulsory voting: *Practice that requires citizens to vote in elections or face punitive measures such as community service, fines, or imprisonment.*

Trends in Turnout. A second way turnout in American elections looks problematic is the trend over the past fifty years. One of the lines in Figure 11.8 represents the percentage of turnout in presidential elections measured against the **voting-age population (VAP)**, an estimate of those old enough to vote. In the United States, all citizens 18 or older constitute the VAP. The graph shows a lot of change—a decline in the 1970s, a surge in 2004 and 2008, a drop-off in 2012. This pattern is much the same for midterm elections. In 1962, turnout for congressional elections was 48 percent. It fell to a low of 38 percent in 1986, with a slight rebound to about 41 percent in 2010. But regardless of how you want to interpret these shifts, one thing is clear: Turnout today is less than it was fifty years ago.

voting-age population (VAP): *Used to calculate the rate of participation by dividing the number of voters by the number of people in the country who are 18 and over.*

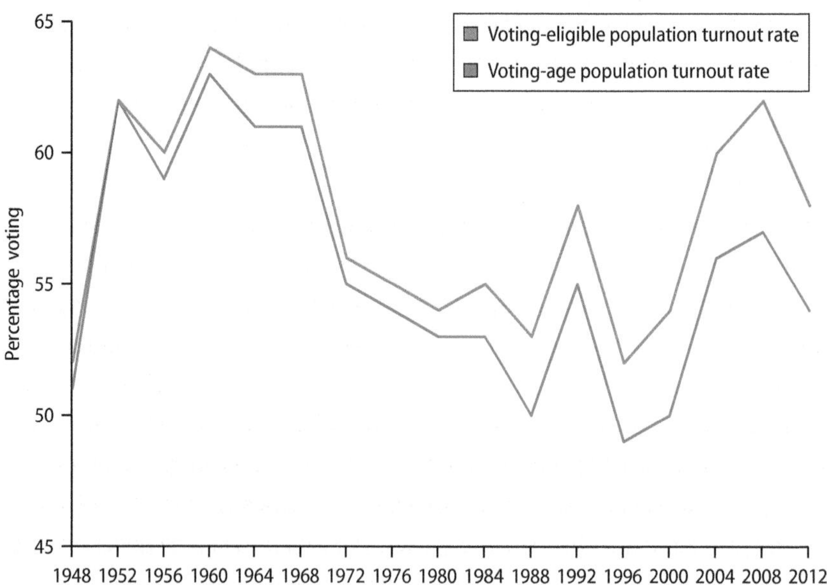

FIGURE 11.8 Presidential Turnout Rates

The VAP measure is the traditional approach to assessing turnout, dividing the number of voters by the voting-age population. The VEP seeks to correct for overcounting in the voting-age population by removing noncitizens and people in jail who are not eligible to vote. Until 1972, this correction made only a modest difference. But given the surge of immigration and the growth in the number of convicted felons since then, the VEP measure is more accurate. Turnout in the 2004 and 2008 elections was actually comparable to turnout in the 1950s and 1960s, but turnout dropped in 2012.

Source: "Presidential Turnout Rates, 1948–2012," United States Elections Project, accessed January 28, 2014, http://elections.gmu.edu /voter_turnout.htm.

This pattern becomes more worrisome in light of rising levels of education since 1960, as education is one of the strongest predictors of turnout. Even though education levels have increased over the past fifty years (see Table 11.2), the rate of participation in elections has not increased.

These kinds of data have led political scientists to study why fewer Americans seem to be voting.[75] Explanations have varied. One explanation looks at the difference between those who enter the electorate and those who leave. The concept of **generational replacement** describes a trend in which older voters who pass away are replaced in the electorate by less reliable young voters.[76] It is difficult, however, to sort out generational differences from changes in self-interest. That is, do older voters turn out to vote because of the generation they were part of, because they are older and have more experience in dealing with politics, or because they want to protect their interests or expand the benefits that directly affect them, such as Medicare and low payments for prescription drugs?

generational replacement: *Cycle whereby younger generations replace older generations in the electorate.*

A second explanation has been the decline of party organizations.[77] Local parties have been less able to turn out the vote on Election Day than they were in the late nineteenth and early twentieth centuries, and therefore the voting rate has declined. Some scholars have estimated that half of the decline in turnout can be attributed to the drop in mobilization efforts.[78] This explanation has appeal, but parties in many ways are stronger today than they were in the past, although the days of big-city bosses and urban political machines are gone (see Chapter 9). Obama and the Democratic Party were successful in turning out the vote in 2012, especially in key states such as Ohio, and citizens are voting along party lines more than any time since scientific surveys began in the 1950s. So a decline in party strength (perceived or real) is not an adequate explanation for low turnout.

A third explanation for declining turnout is the increasingly harsh tone of political campaigns. Some argue that negative campaigns have fueled voter apathy. It is clear that negative advertising on TV often fosters voters' disgust with politics. About 80 percent of people say they do not like these campaign tactics.[79] Initial studies suggested that negative campaigns could decrease turnout by about 5 percentage points.[80] In addition, there is clear evidence that negativity in campaigns has been on the rise since the 1960s (see Chapter 10), so there has been an apparent correlation between the two trends.[81] Scholars and pundits rushed to endorse this hypothesis, but subsequent studies have called it into question.[82] A harsh campaign is likely to be competitive, and competitive campaigns draw interest and therefore increase turnout. Further, negative attacks can activate partisanship, which also increases turnout. People often choose to affiliate with a party in part because they do not like members of the opposite party. An attack ad by the Republicans can remind their supporters why they oppose the Democrats, giving them more reason to participate. A recent comprehensive study of all research on this topic shows clearly that negativity is not responsible for lowering turnout.[83]

A New Way to Measure Voting. There is another explanation that actually contends that turnout has *not* declined over the last forty years: The VAP measure has been in error because it does not take into account increases in the number of immigrants and convicted felons who are ineligible to vote. Over the last few decades, there has been a steep increase in the number of undocumented immigrants. With the sagging economy of the last few years, the numbers have declined, but even so, in 2014 the number of undocumented immigrants was estimated to be just over 11 million (or about 3.5 percent of the population).[84] Though there have been some recent declines, over the last thirty years there has also been nearly a threefold increase in the number of people in prison (from 585,000 to 1.5 million), reflecting tougher sentencing in American courts of law.[85]

A new measure called the **voting-eligible population (VEP)** corrects for these trends. The top line in Figure 11.8 presents the VEP estimates for turnout. It indicates that aggregate turnout in the 2008 presidential election was actually about 62 percent. By this measure, turnout has not declined over the last thirty years. In fact, turnout is now a full 10 percentage points higher than in the presidential election of 1948, when it was 52 percent. These revised estimates put a new spin on what has been perceived as a problem with U.S. elections, suggesting that Americans are not less willing to vote than in the past or than citizens in other democracies.[86]

voting-eligible population (VEP): *Used to calculate the rate of participation by dividing the number of voters by the number of people in the country who are eligible to vote rather than just of voting age.*

In 2016, the Supreme Court rejected a challenge to Texas's voting law that would have required states to apportion districts based on VEPs. The Supreme Court unanimously declared that state legislatures may include all residents in determining legislative districts (including children, felons, whether incarcerated or free, and noncitizens) and not just residents who are eligible to vote.[87]

Do Turnout Rates Create Inequality?

Voting is a hallmark of democratic politics and is certainly a cherished American value. The idea is simple. Each person has one vote, and each vote should be equal. The fact that those who are better educated or better off participate at a greater rate is a potential source of concern (see Table 11.1 and Table 11.2). That the wealthy are more likely to vote than the poor is an especially troubling trend because the income gap between the rich and the poor is increasing.[88] As the rich become richer, they become better able to contribute more money to parties and candidates.[89] Such donations only further advance their potential influence.

That individuals with more resources participate more is not a new idea. Its implications have fueled much speculation but were supported by little evidence until Larry Bartels provided a systematic account of the impact of these differences. Focusing on the behavior of U.S. senators, Bartels shows that they respond more to the rich, less to people of middle income, and not at all to the poor.[90] Others have gone even further, showing that rich Americans have much more influence on public policy than those less well off.[91] It makes sense that politicians respond to people who participate and do not respond to those who do not. That is why it is so important for people to get involved in politics and also why the increasing rate of participation in the past decade or so is such good news.

11.6 Voting Laws and Regulations

Analyze how changes in voting laws have affected rates of participation

The rules surrounding voting alter participation rates. Voting policies are made at both the federal and state levels. State governments continue to manage most voting laws and procedures, although the federal government steps in to prevent discrimination at the polls. The federal government is committed to increasing participation by making voting as easy as possible. At the same time, both state and federal governments work to prevent voter fraud, as we saw when we examined voter ID laws. Thus, voting policies have the effect of both expanding and potentially contracting turnout. This section reviews policies that have altered the way voting works in the United States.

Reforms to Voting Laws in the 1890s

Rules matter, as the institutional model of voting suggests. Any change in the laws governing voting (or any process related to voting) will alter how that process works. A classic example of the power of rules can be found in the late nineteenth century, when the Progressives called for a series of reforms to the voting process to end corrupt practices. The reforms affected who was eligible to vote and the way people actually voted. In other words, they altered who participated in elections.

Corrupt voting practices needed to end. Big-city political machines routinely "stuffed" the ballot box,[92] and party members manipulated the results to ensure victory. Turnout in some cities exceeded 100 percent, meaning that not only were some people voting who should not have been but also that some were voting multiple times. Party members often rounded up people and brought them, in sequence, to various polling precincts around the city, making sure they voted in each one. Someone who had died would remain on the rolls, and the party machine would "allow" that person to vote. This corrupt practice has been referred to as **graveyard voting**.[93]

graveyard voting: *Corrupt practice of using a dead person's name to cast a ballot in an election.*

In response to these excesses, Progressives called for voter registration.[94] The idea was that voters would have to preregister with a government official to be placed on an official list of voters. The list would be updated when someone died, and it would be used at the polls on Election Day to ensure that a potential voter had the right to vote and had not already voted. This reform spread rapidly. Today, all states except North Dakota require voter registration. The specific rules of registration vary a great deal among the states. For example, in only eleven states can a person register and vote on Election Day.[95] All other states require earlier registration.

Voter registration laws prevented outright fraud at the polls. An additional consequence was that they prevented immigrants from voting. Party machines had benefited greatly from the support of immigrants in city elections, and many of the newcomers to America who came in great numbers in the late nineteenth and early twentieth centuries were among those whom parties encouraged to vote multiple times. Some states, such as Wisconsin, allowed white immigrants to vote, providing they declared their intention to become citizens.[96] But the new registration laws made voting a two-step process, requiring potential voters to document, before the election, that they met the conditions for voting. Voter registration added a new gate to the system. While it reduced fraud, decreased the strength of the party machines, and pleased Americans who were worried about the impact of immigrants, it caused an overall decline in turnout. In 1888, turnout in presidential elections stood at 81 percent. By 1912, it had fallen to 59 percent. It is surely true that the 81 percent turnout was inflated due to corrupt voting practices, but the introduction of voter registration had negative effects on participation as well.[97]

An important change in voting rules was the adoption in 1888 of the Australian ballot, also known as the secret ballot (see Figure 9.3, Ballot Reform, in Chapter 9). Like voter registration, it was adopted as a reform intended to prevent the corrupt practices of political machines. In the early nineteenth century, voting was public and was often done by "party strips." That is, voters would enter a polling precinct and ask for a ballot from one party or the other, thereby indicating their preferences. It was easy to cast and count such ballots, but voters were also subjected to pressure from party bosses. Those who operated the polling precincts would know how voters planned to vote by observing which party strip they requested. The introduction of the secret ballot meant that voters faced less intimidation, but voting also became more complicated. Voters now could choose candidates for each office separately; they no longer had automatic access to party-line voting as they did with the strip ballot. With a more complicated process, once again turnout declined. Despite decreasing turnout, the secret ballot has become a cornerstone of American democracy.

The National Voter Registration Act

In 1993, Congress sought to streamline voter registration procedures so that more Americans would exercise their right to vote, at least in federal elections. The National Voter Registration Act, commonly known as the "Motor Voter" law, requires states to allow citizens to register to vote at the same time they apply for or renew their driver's licenses.

This law also requires states to inform citizens who are removed from the approved voter rolls and limits removal to a change of address, conviction for a felony, and, of course, death. These requirements were in response to charges that local governments, controlled by political parties, improperly removed voters from the voter rolls without their knowledge; under the guise of updating voter registration lists, officials of one party were disqualifying voters who would tend to vote for the other party's candidates. The 1993 law imposes criminal penalties on anyone who tries to coerce or intimidate voters on their way to the polling place or tries to prevent registered voters from casting their ballots.[98] This law has been in place for more than two decades with little change.

New Forms of Voting

As indicated earlier, some states are experimenting with laws that make voting easier. Some have instituted early voting, allowing voters to cast ballots before the Tuesday on which a general election is held. This flexibility helps working people, who might find it hard to find time to vote on a Tuesday. It also provides more than a single day for voting, so that schedule conflicts (such as a dental appointment or a sick child) do not interfere. In Texas, for example, citizens can vote any time between seventeen and four days before election day, "to make the voting process more convenient and accessible"[99] Other states, such as Oregon, have started to make use of a **vote-by-mail (VBM) system**. Voters get ballots in the mail two weeks before the election, giving them a chance to research the candidates and cast their ballots. They can make their choices at home and avoid the often long lines at the polling booth. This innovation, proponents argue, lowers the cost of voting, and there is some evidence it has increased participation. Oregon has had a very high rate of voting, although it did drop from about 70 percent in 2008 to about 64 percent in 2012.[100] California has had less success with voting by mail. Some now worry that, under the rules of VBM systems, less-educated people are less likely to vote.[101]

vote-by-mail (VBM) system: *Method of voting in an election whereby ballots are distributed to voters by mail, and voters complete and return the ballots by mail.*

Over the past three decades, nearly two-thirds of states passed "early voting" provisions that allow citizens to cast ballots prior to election day (see Figure 11.9).[102] The idea was that limiting participation to a single day kept many people from participating. The idea seemed sensible, and a lot of states followed suit. Although there is little evidence that early voting increases turnout, the provisions clearly lower the costs of voting.[103] Recently, however, some states have begun to reverse those laws and reduce the availability of early voting, eliminated same-day voter registration, and enacted new strict photo identification requirements.[104] Opponents say these new laws increase the cost of voting, making it more difficult for some citizens to vote. Others say the laws are necessary to protect the integrity of the ballot box.

Nevertheless, new technologies, including the Internet, Twitter, and cell phones, may be used in the future, and they could make it easier for some people to vote (elderly and disabled people, for example), thus increasing turnout. However, opponents of using these technologies argue that they would be too susceptible to voter fraud for two reasons. First, there would be no way to identify the person who is casting the vote, unless citizens are given individual PIN codes or use their Social Security numbers. Given the number of Internet security breaches, opponents argue that such a system would not guard personal privacy. Second, votes at polling places are counted by election officials, but Internet and

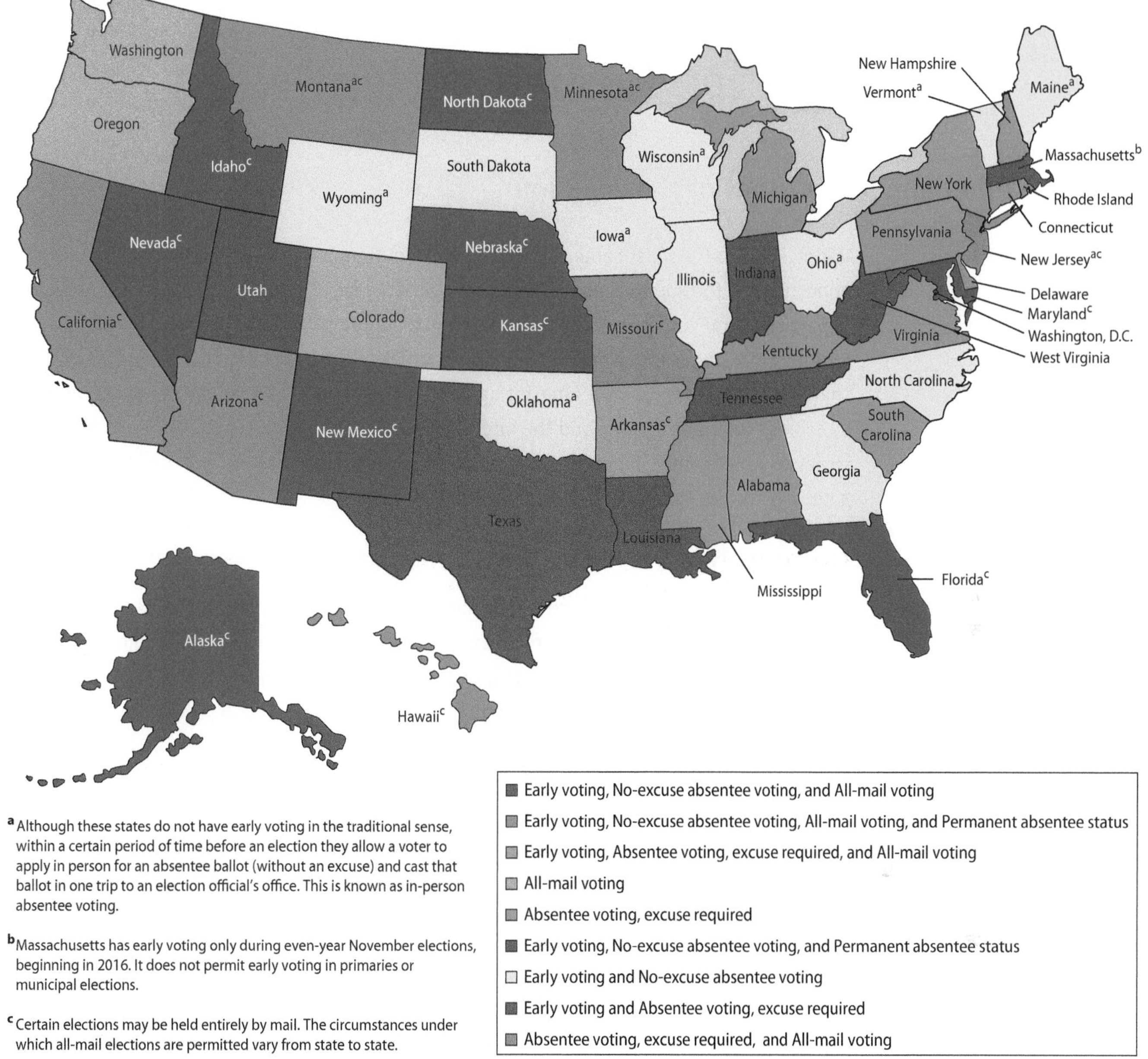

FIGURE 11.9 Absentee and Early Voting by State

States determine most of the rules about forms of voting. This map shows which states have embraced new forms of voting such as early voting, no-excuse absentee voting, and vote by mail—all of which are designed to ease the voting process.

Source: http://www.ncsl.org/research/elections-and-campaigns/absentee-and-early-voting.aspx

cell phone voting data would likely be collected and counted by computer servers, which are vulnerable to hacking and other security breaches.

In considering the effects of voting by new technologies, the beneficial effects on community and civic life of having everyone vote on a single day should also be considered. The act of standing in line and talking with fellow voters, or discussing the act of voting with friends and family at the end of the day, can reinforce the sense of political efficacy and provide a foundation for the democratic process. Voting by mail, cell phone, or Twitter may detract from this shared experience, and that cost must be weighed against the added benefits of increased voter participation.

11.7 Participation Beyond Voting

Describe other important forms of participation

Voting is by far the most common form of participation, but in a democracy, citizens have opportunities to express their views in other ways. In fact, voting is a very constrained form of participation: Voters select one person from a limited set of candidates. There is no way to tell from a single vote whether the citizen agrees or disagrees with the candidate on the key issues of the day. But the American political system gives individuals the opportunity to express their preferences and the intensity of those preferences in other ways. Although far fewer Americans join political campaigns or protest movements, both are important gateways for the expression of political views.

Involvement in Political Campaigns

Campaigns give citizens a chance to talk about politics, volunteer, promote issues they care about, and make financial donations to candidates and causes. The weeks leading up to an election allow candidates and interest groups to connect with the public. The campaign is an important gateway that allows the public to influence politics and politicians to influence the public.

As a result, political scientists try to understand the motivations for people's involvement in campaigns and the nature of their involvement. Do Americans try to influence other citizens? According to a survey done in 2014, about 70 percent of Americans indicate that they discuss politics at least a few times a month.[105] Table 11.3 reports that 28 percent of Americans claimed in 1996 that they tried to influence others to vote a certain way. This

TABLE 11.3 Nonvoting Measures of Political Participation

Year	Tried to Influence Others' Votes	Attended a Political Meeting	Worked for a Party or a Candidate	Wore a Button or Displayed a Bumper Sticker	Gave Money to a Campaign
1980	36%	8%	4%	7%	8%
1984	32%	8%	4%	9%	8%
1988	29%	7%	3%	9%	9%
1992	37%	8%	3%	11%	7%
1996	28%	5%	2%	10%	8%
2000	34%	5%	3%	10%	9%
2004	48%	7%	3%	21%	13%
2008	45%	9%	4%	18%	14%
2012	37%	5%	3%	14%	10%

Source: American National Election Study, 1948–2012.

was the lowest rate over the last seven presidential elections and probably reflects the fact that few doubted that President Bill Clinton would beat the Republican nominee, Bob Dole. In 2008, 45 percent of Americans said they tried to influence others' votes, a greater than 50 percent jump from 1996. The 2008 contest between Democrat Barack Obama and Republican John McCain captured the public's interest. Four years later, the numbers declined to 37 percent, which is much more typical for presidential elections.

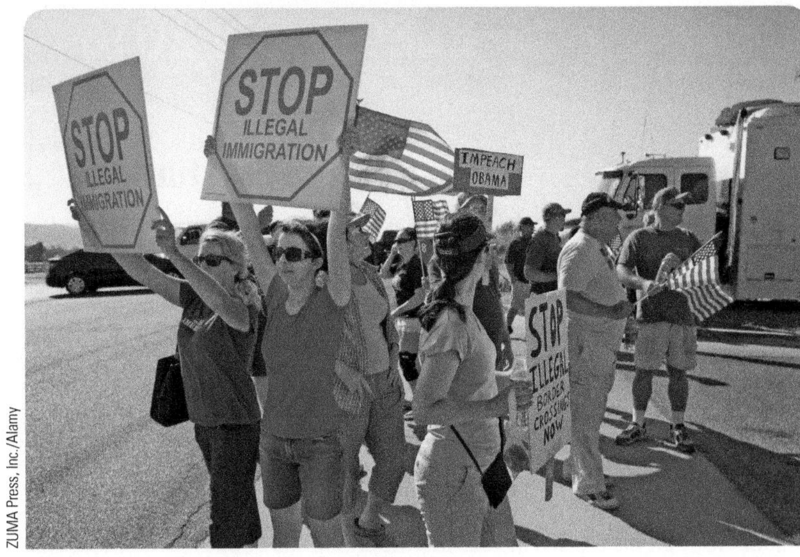

IMAGE 11.6 Residents of Murrieta, California, protest the immigration policy and call for the impeachment of President Obama at a U.S. Border Patrol station in July 2014.

By contrast, as shown in Table 11.3, the proportion of people who work in a campaign has been small and very stable over the past three decades, hovering around 3 percent. About one in twenty Americans attended a political meeting during the course of the 2012 campaign. Willingness to give money to a campaign was higher, hitting 10 percent in 2012.

This evidence about political participation suggests that Americans do get involved in elections in a number of different ways. If active citizens are defined as individuals who vote and engage in at least one of the activities reported in Table 11.3, about 40 percent have met the standard over this twenty-eight-year period. More than 15 percent of the public voted and engaged in two of the activities. One may want to debate whether these numbers are high or low, but regardless of interpretation, Americans do more than just vote come election time.

Protest Politics

Political protests are an important means of expressing opinions and bringing about change. The Boston Tea Party, in which protesters dumped tea into Boston Harbor rather than support the British government-backed monopoly, is perhaps the first and most famous American protest. This protest was not about taxes, but rather about the fact that the British were undermining local merchants. Throughout American history, abolitionists seeking an end to slavery, women seeking the vote, working people seeking the right to strike and organize unions, civil rights activists calling for an end to segregation and discrimination, antiwar activists seeking to end the wars in Vietnam and Iraq, and many others have called attention to their causes though marches, street demonstrations, petitions, and advertising campaigns.

Most recently, the Tea Party movement has recast American politics. It began with protests against the nearly $800 billion stimulus package, which Congress passed in 2009 in the hopes of ending the steep economic downturn that began in 2008. The protests quickly coalesced into a movement that became active in politics. During the 2010 midterm elections, a number of Tea Party–backed candidates were elected to office, including Senator Rand Paul (R-KY). The movement played a key role in the 2012 Republican nomination and

ELECTION 2016

Do College Freshmen Represent a New Protest Generation?

THOUGH VOTING IS THE most common form of political participation, there are other forms beyond voting in which some Americans also choose to engage. Ta-Nehisi Coates, for example, participates by communicating his views and raising awareness about issues through his stories in *The Atlantic* and in his books. Table 11.3 shows the rate of participation in a variety of forms of participation beyond voting. Protest politics is, as the text indicates, also an important, and nontraditional, means of political expression with a long history in the United States, dating back at least to the original Tea Party protest of 1773.

At various times in history, the American people chose to use this form of participation to raise awareness and demand change from policy makers. Martin Luther King Jr. encouraged the "March on Washington" in 1963, rallying more than 200,000 Americans to the nation's capital in the name of jobs, freedom, and civil rights. (See Chapter 5 for a description of King's famous "I Have a Dream" speech at that event.) Young Americans protested American involvement in the Vietnam War in the 1960s led, in part, by Students for a Democratic Society.[106] That generation of Americans was dubbed by some as a "protest generation."[107] What about your generation? How do you and your peers feel about protest behavior?

For the past fifty years, incoming college freshmen have been surveyed about a variety of topics ranging from financial concerns to political engagement. In fall 2015, more than 140,000 students were surveyed by the Higher Education Research Institute at UCLA. The 2015 Freshman Survey revealed a notable increase in the percentage of college freshmen who expect to engage in student protest and demonstrations.[108] Figure 11.10 shows the percentage of freshmen who believe there is a "very good chance" they will participate in student protests and

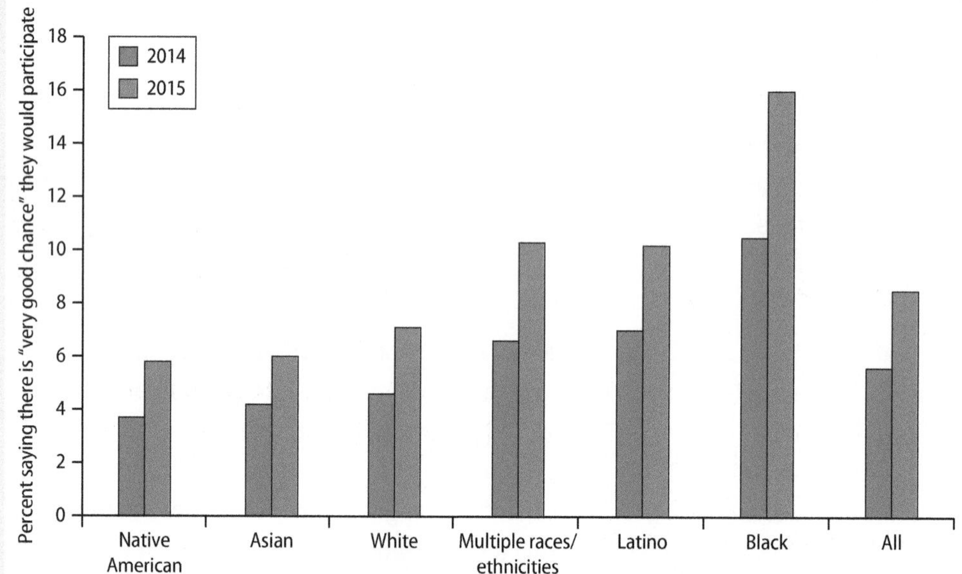

FIGURE 11.10 Expectation of Participating in Student Protests and Demonstrations, by Race and Ethnicity

Freshmen who entered college in fall 2015 were notably more likely than previous classes to believe they would be involved in protests or demonstrations, particularly blacks, Latinos, and multiple-race students. The last group of young Americans similarly inclined toward this form of political participation protested the Vietnam War and marched in favor of civil rights.

Source: Kevin Eagan, Ellen Bara Stolzenberg, Abigail K. Bates, Melissa C. Aragon, Maria Ramirez Suchard, and Cecilia Rios-Aguilar, *The American Freshman: National Norms Fall 2015*, Cooperative Institutional Research Program, Higher Education Research Institute. University of California, Los Angeles.

demonstrations, compared to their fall 2014 freshman counterparts. Regardless of ethnic or racial group, the 2015 cohort showed significant increases in their expectations of protesting. Combining those figures with those who believe there is a "good chance" of protesting raises the percentage to over 30 percent. These responses represent the highest level recorded since the questions were first asked of freshmen in 1967.

Are today's college students poised to be the new protest generation? There are already signs that college students are willing to raise their voices in campus demonstrations. As the student protest at the University of Missouri in September 2015 showed, students are responding positively to calls from fellow students to take action to protest what they see as disturbing incidents of racial intolerance.[109] Students at the Columbia, Missouri, campus claimed that university officials were not doing enough to stop incidents of racism on campus. Other students joined the protests, including the football team, supported by their coach. Their protests led to the resignation of the president of the university. Some protesters indicated that they have been inspired by other demonstrations, including the Black Lives Matter movement.[110]

There are signs of increased political engagement by younger voters. Senator Bernie Sanders' presidential nomination campaign, for example, engaged many younger voters. As the text notes, younger voters have tended to be less engaged politically than older Americans. Perhaps the newest generation of college students will be distinguished by their increased propensity to engage in politics.

---

congressional elections, including providing support for Senator Ted Cruz (R-TX) in his victorious Senate campaign. It continues to shape American politics, especially within the Republican Party.[111] Tea Party supporters were not happy with the nomination of Mitt Romney in 2012,[112] but his choice of Paul Ryan to be his vice presidential running mate mitigated Tea Party activists' doubts about Romney's commitment to their issues. By 2014, the influence of the Tea Party had started to wane, as more establishment Republicans won nearly all the important senatorial primaries. But even so, the Tea Party remains capable of upsetting the apple cart, as suggested by the stunning upset of Republican Majority Leader Eric Cantor in the 2014 primary by newcomer Dave Brat, who went on to win in the general election. Still, the themes set forth by the Tea Party remain resonant in American politics and have been echoed frequently by members of Congress and Senator Ted Cruz as a presidential candidate in 2016.

Andrew Burton /Getty Images News/Getty Images

IMAGE 11.7 Sometimes incidents prompt concerned Americans to attend rallies and demonstrations. Here protesters hold a rally in Baltimore after charges were announced against the officers involved in the April 2015 arrest of Freddie Gray, a 25-year-old African American man who died due to injuries he sustained while being taken to the police station.

Protests sometimes backfire. In 1932, in the midst of the Great Depression, Army veterans seeking early payment of their World War I bonuses descended on Washington, D.C. Thousands camped out in tents and shacks. The House of Representatives agreed to early payment, but the Senate refused, and the protesters were ordered to go home. When some

POLITICAL ANALYTICS

Discussing Politics

AS SHOWN IN TABLE 11.3, a little more than one-third of Americans report trying to influence others' votes. People often attempt to exert that influence through conversations with others. Moreover, 70 to 80 percent of those with stronger ideological beliefs tend to engage and enjoy political discussions. One way Americans share their views about politics and government is through social media.

Figure 11.11 shows that those who are consistently liberal or conservative tend to want to read about the views of only those who share their views. Forty-four percent of consistent liberals, for example, report blocking or otherwise ending engagement with those with whom they disagree politically. Further, when it comes to conversations about politics, two-thirds of consistent conservatives report that most of their close friends share their views. Those whose political views are mixed tend to have friends with a wider variety of political views. When it comes to political dialogue, those with strongly held ideological beliefs choose to hear views that are mostly in line with their own.

Examine how conservatives and liberals differ in the likelihood of blocking posts in their Facebook feeds from those with whom they disagree, as well as the degree to which members of each group share the political views of their friends.

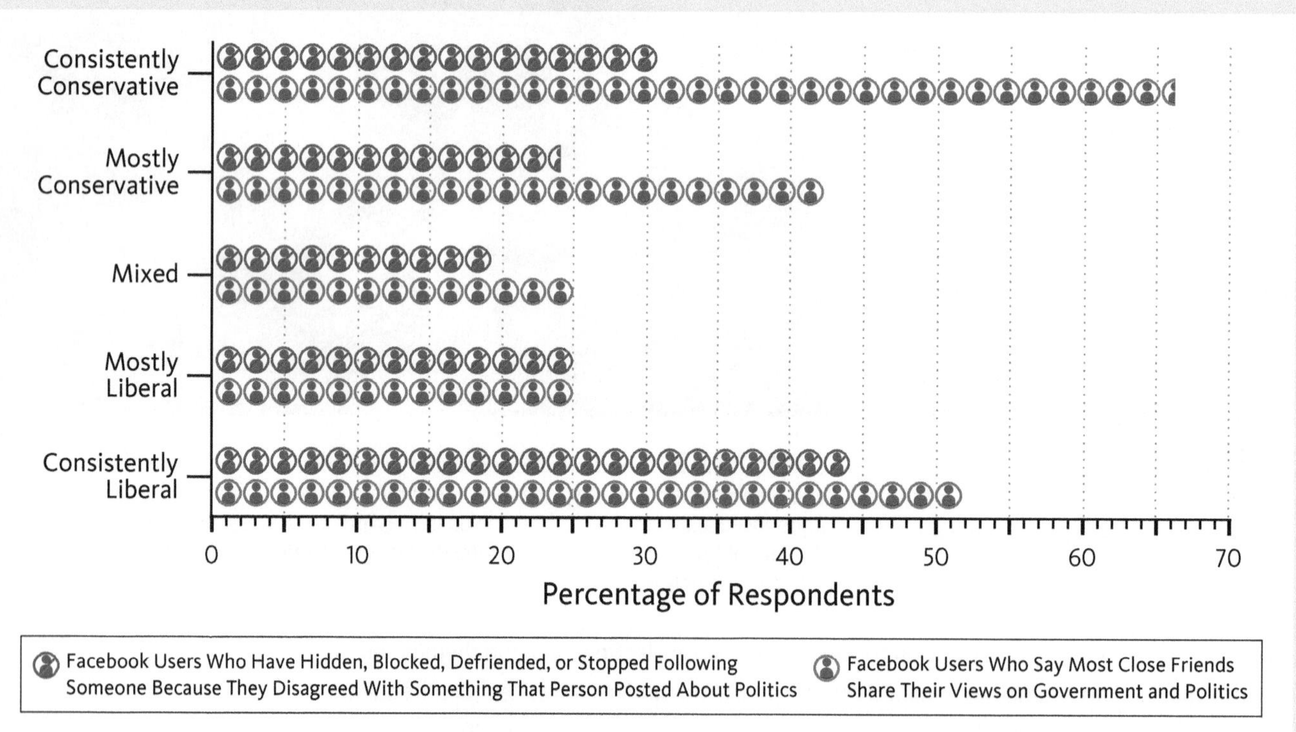

FIGURE 11.11 Liberals and Conservatives, Social Media, and Politics

Thinking Critically

1. What can you conclude from the social media and politics patterns among different groups of Americans? Do most people communicate only with those they agree with?
2. What are the consequences (if any) of limiting your circle of friends, through social media or otherwise, to those who share your political views?

Sources: Amy Mitchell, Jeffrey Gottfried, Jocelyn Kiley, and Katerina Eva Matsa, "Political Polarization & Media Habits," Pew Research Center, October 21, 2014, http://www.journalism.org/2014/10/21/political-polarization-media-habits; Amy Mitchell, Jeffrey Gottfried, Jocelyn Kiley, and Katerina Eva Matsa, "Talking Politics: Leaders vs. Listeners and the Views People Hear," Pew Research Center, October 21, 2014, http://www.journalism.org/2014/10/21section-3-talking-politics-leaders-vs-listeners-and-the-views-people-hear.

did not, President Herbert Hoover (1929–33) called out federal troops. Using tanks, cavalry, and tear gas, General Douglas MacArthur sought to disperse the veterans in an action that led to the death of one veteran.[113]

Protests can become so controversial and stir up such strong emotions that the government takes steps to limit them. Such action, one could argue, constrains First Amendment rights of speech and assembly (see Chapter 4, Civil Liberties). But do protesters have the right to undermine the freedoms of others? This is not an easy question to answer. The courts have weighed in on such debates, seeking to balance competing rights. One of the most controversial cases concerns the right of anti-abortion protesters to protest outside abortion clinics and in particular to try to convince women coming to the clinics for services to change their minds. For instance, in *Hill v. Colorado* (2000), the Supreme Court upheld the right of states to limit protests near sites that conduct abortions.[114] But in 2014, the Supreme Court's *McCullen v. Coakley* decision cut back on *Hill* by unanimously striking a Massachusetts law that had kept anti-abortion protestors at least 35 feet from health facilities that perform abortions.[115]

In general, very few Americans participate in protests. Overall, only about 10 percent of Americans claim to have ever participated in a protest.[116] However, the propensity of Americans to engage in nontraditional forms of political participation may be changing. The Occupy Movement that took place in 2011, the protests in Ferguson, Missouri, and the subsequent Black Lives Matter movement suggest a willingness to protest policies and practices Americans deem unfair. Recent student protests on the campuses of the University of Missouri, Harvard University, Princeton University, and other campuses suggest that younger Americans, in particular, may be poised to become more engaged in traditional and nontraditional forms of participation.[117]

E-Participation

In the past decade, many Americans have engaged in politics through e-mail and the Internet. It is easier and cheaper to send an e-mail message to a member of Congress than to write a letter, and Americans do so with increasing frequency. In 1998, members of Congress received more than 23 million e-mails; two years later that number had doubled to 48 million.[118] Recent estimates put the figures at well over 100 million, demonstrating that the use of e-mail to contact members of Congress has exploded over the past decade, underscoring the ease and convenience of e-mail and transforming the way voters communicate with politicians.[119] Members of Congress facilitate this gateway by encouraging citizens through their websites to contact them via e-mail.[120]

Beyond e-mail, people express their opinions through blogs. As Chapter 7, The News and Social Media, demonstrates, blogs have become an important way to share information and to influence the political process. Candidates now hire their own bloggers in an effort to influence the direction of these exchanges. Most recently, politicians now use Twitter to share information with the public. In 2014, Monica Wehby, a Republican Senate candidate in Oregon, posted a photo on Twitter of her marked ballot. She was encouraging people to vote for it. But this tweet posed some problems, since Oregon law does not allow you to show your marked ballot to another person. Wehby went on to win the primary election but lost to incumbent Democratic Senator Jeff Merkley after a series of missteps in her campaign.[121] Participating in politics by writing a blog, tweeting, or using other electronic communications will continue to rise. In 2014, about 40 percent of Americans claimed to have a Twitter account.[122] Those involved in social media do participate in politics more than those who do not, but whether that difference is due to social media or just a preexisting desire to participate is far from clear.

The Internet has also transformed fundraising and campaign involvement. Former Vermont Governor Howard Dean's 2004 campaign for the Democratic presidential nomination was the first to tap successfully into the power of this new technology. Since then, other candidates have made use of the Internet and social media to raise money. Obama in 2008 broke all records for fundraising with about $500 million. Just four years later, he raised nearly $700 million through e-mail, the Internet, and social media.[123]

Fundraising for presidential campaigns in 2012 was different due to a change in regulations following the Supreme Court's 2010 decision in *Citizens United v. Federal Election Commission* (see Chapter 8, Interest Groups). While 2008 can be thought of as the year of the small Internet donor, 2012 can be thought of as the year of the mega-donor. New regulations permit the rich, including corporate entities, to form Super PACs and contribute unlimited amounts to support or oppose political candidates as long as they do not coordinate directly with candidates or parties. It is not yet clear what will be the impact of all this money. Certainly the millions of dollars spent to defeat President Obama in 2012 did not work. In 2014, over $600 million was spent by Super PACs and other independent groups. It is unclear whether those funds made a difference in the congressional elections since the groups spent money on behalf of Republicans and Democrats.[124]

In 2016, large expenditures by Super PACs across all elections continued, reaching nearly $1 billion. Hillary Clinton was the beneficiary of close to $200 million in Super PAC money, three times as much as was spent to support Donald Trump. Overall, more than $2 billion were spent in the 2016 presidential election by the political parties, Super PACs, and the candidates' campaigns. Though the Clinton campaign saw almost twice as much money spent on her behalf, Donald Trump nonetheless won the election.[125]

Voting, Participation, and Democracy

The U.S. government has lasted more than two centuries. This longevity is not an accident. It is attributable in large part to the fact that Americans have, collectively, taken the time to participate. There have been many barriers, from limited suffrage to rules that discourage voting. But the long-term trend has been increased participation, and that speaks to the health of American democracy. Now suffrage—the right to vote—is available to all citizens except those convicted of a felony (see Chapter 5).[126] The rate of voting in the United States is not as low as many observers tend to assert. Further, looking at participation more broadly, Americans do more than just vote in elections: They are engaged in political campaigns and in making their communities better at the local level. The Internet offers a world of possibilities for increased participation in different forms.

There is a danger to a democracy from a distortion in turnout; the rich participate more than the poor, and this gap seems to be growing. With nonvoters being poorer and less educated, their failure to participate may help explain why government is not as responsive to their needs. Put another way, the government may be overly responsive to the needs of the well-off. This disparity in responsiveness threatens the underpinnings of a democratic and egalitarian society. If the political system responds to one segment of the population and systematically ignores other segments, general support for democracy, based on principles of fairness, could drop significantly.

With the Internet's growing influence, there may be other dangers to democracy. Wealthier citizens have more access to the information and resources on the Internet and therefore become even more informed and better able to make government responsive to their needs. The rich have always had advantages, but their advantages may be growing. At the same time, the Internet might be used to extend participation. As recent presidential campaigns have demonstrated, this technology can be used to expand the number of contributors to include people who have only a few dollars to contribute or who might want to show up at a local meeting to learn about an issue of relevance to them.

Let us return to Figure 11.1, which offered two models of participation. The Hamiltonian model argued that more participation is not always a good thing and that government works best with limited involvement from the public. The Jeffersonian model contended that greater participation improves both the quality of the input and the lives of citizens. Within our book's gateway approach, the participatory model of voting has more appeal than the elite model. Democracy becomes more responsive, more accountable, and more equal if more people participate. The cycle is reinforcing. Citizens themselves need to do all they can to encourage participation; doing so is in their self-interest and their civic interest. Democracy rests on the active and healthy participation of the citizenry. In other words, as the number of gateways increases, so does the quality of American civic life.

Political Science Reasoning

Question 1

Practice1, Practice 2

Oregon v. Mitchell (1970)

For the reasons set out in Part I of this opinion, I believe Congress can fix the age of voters in national elections, such as congressional, senatorial, vice-presidential and presidential elections, but cannot set the voting age in State and local elections...

[T]he Constitution was also intended to preserve to the States the power that even the Colonies had to establish and maintain their own separate and independent governments, except insofar as the Constitution itself commands otherwise. My Brother HARLAN has persuasively demonstrated that the Framers of the Constitution intended the States to keep for themselves, as provided in the Tenth Amendment, the power to regulate elections. My major disagreement with my Brother HARLAN is that, while I agree as to the States' power to regulate the elections of their own officials, I believe, contrary to his view, that Congress has the final authority over federal elections. No function is more essential to the separate and independent existence of the States and their governments than the power to determine within the limits of the Constitution the qualifications of their own voters for state, county, and municipal offices and the nature of their own machinery for filling local public offices. Moreover, Articles I, 2, is a clear indication that the Framers intended the States to determine the qualifications of their own voters for state offices because those qualifications were adopted for federal offices unless Congress directs otherwise under Articles I, 4. It is a plain fact of history that the Framers never imagined that the national Congress would set the qualifications for voters in every election from President to local constable or village alderman. It is obvious that the whole Constitution reserves to the States the power to set voter qualifications in state and local elections, except to the limited extent that the people through constitutional amendments have specifically narrowed the powers of the States.... The Equal Protection Clause of the Fourteenth Amendment was never intended to destroy the States' power to govern themselves, making the Nineteenth and Twenty-fourth Amendments superfluous. My Brother BRENNAN's opinion, if carried to its logical conclusion, would, under the guise of insuring equal protection, blot out all state power, leaving the 50 States as little more than impotent figureheads. In interpreting what the Fourteenth Amendment means, the Equal Protection Clause should not be stretched to nullify the States' powers over elections which they had before the Constitution was adopted and which they have retained throughout our history...

In enacting the 18-year-old vote provisions of the Act now before the Court, Congress made no legislative findings that the 21-year-old vote requirement was used by the States to disenfranchise voters on account of race. I seriously doubt that such a finding, if made, could be supported by substantial evidence. Since Congress has attempted to invade an area preserved to the States by the Constitution without a foundation for enforcing the Civil War Amendments' ban on racial discrimination, I would hold that Congress has exceeded its powers in attempting to lower the voting age in state and local elections. On the other hand, where Congress legislates in a domain not exclusively reserved by the Constitution to the States, its enforcement power need not be tied so closely to the goal of eliminating discrimination on account of race...

1. What did the Supreme Court decide in *Oregon v. Mitchell*?
2. According to the original text of the U.S. Constitution, who has the primary responsibility for setting voter requirements?
3. To what extent, and why, has this responsibility changed (if at all)? If you believe that there has been little to no change in responsibility, explain why this policy preference has remained constant.

Exercise 2

Practice 1, Practice 4

Amendment XV

Section 1. The right of citizens of the United States to vote shall not be denied or abridged by the United States or by any State on account of race, color, or previous condition of servitude.

Section 2. The Congress shall have the power to enforce this article by appropriate legislation.

Amendment XVII

The Senate of the United States shall be composed of two Senators from each State, elected by the people thereof, for six years; and each Senator shall have one vote. The electors in each State shall have the qualifications requisite for electors of the most numerous branch of the State legislatures.

When vacancies happen in the representation of any State in the Senate, the executive authority of such State shall issue writs of election to fill such vacancies: Provided, That the legislature of any State may empower the executive thereof to make temporary appointments until the people fill the vacancies by election as the legislature may direct.

This amendment shall not be so construed as to affect the election or term of any Senator chosen before it becomes valid as part of the Constitution.

Amendment XIX

The right of citizens of the United States to vote shall not be denied or abridged by the United States or by any State on account of sex. Congress shall have power to enforce this article by appropriate legislation.

Amendment XXIV

Section. 1. The right of citizens of the United States to vote in any primary or other election for President or Vice President, for electors for President or Vice President, or for Senator or Representative in Congress, shall not be denied or abridged by the United States or any State by reason of failure to pay any poll tax or other tax.

Section. 2. The Congress shall have power to enforce this article by appropriate legislation.

Amendment XXVI

Section. 1. The right of citizens of the United States, who are eighteen years of age or older, to vote shall not be denied or abridged by the United States or by any State on account of age.

Section. 2. The Congress shall have power to enforce this article by appropriate legislation.

1. Explain how the above amendments *collectively* represent changing American political values.
2. The above amendments were received with varying degrees of resistance. Explain the difference between the results and effects of the implementation of Fifteenth Amendment and those resultant of the implementation of the Nineteenth Amendment.

Focus on AP® Success

11 Voting and Participation

Must Know: Key Concepts

- Rational Choice Voting
- Retrospective Voting
- Prospective Voting
- Party-line Voting
- Voting Rights Act of 1965
- Fifteenth Amendment
- Seventeenth Amendment
- Nineteenth Amendment
- Twenty-Fourth Amendment
- Twenty-Sixth Amendment
- Political Efficacy
- Voter Registration

Thinking Politically

Data Analysis

Examine Figure 11.5. What are the overall voter turnout trends for the four groups presented in the chart? What are the implications for both the Democratic and Republican Parties?

Data Analysis

Examine Figure 11.6. What is the trend that is being presented in the chart? What other information would be helpful to have in order to better understand the trend displayed in the chart?

Concept Application

Review the material from both this chapter and Chapter 6. Explain how the process of political socialization can impact voter turnout and behavior.

Understanding Learning Objectives with Key Concepts

MPA – 3.A Describe the voting rights protections in the Constitution and in legislation.

Over the course of U.S. history, the right to vote has been expanded. This has taken the form of both legislation and constitutional amendments.

- Fifteenth Amendment – This amendment was passed in the aftermath of the Civil War. It prohibited discrimination in voting based on "race, color, or previous condition of servitude." It was largely circumvented in the American South by means of literacy tests and other discriminatory practices. Congress used section 2 of the amendment as the basis for the passage of the Voting Rights Act of 1965.

- Seventeenth Amendment – The Seventeenth Amendment provided for direct election of U.S. senators. Prior to the ratification of this amendment, U.S. senators were selected by state legislatures.

- Nineteenth Amendment – Prohibited sex discrimination in voting. It was ratified in 1920 during the Progressive period in American history. Many women were legally voting prior to ratification of this amendment, particularly in western states.

- Twenty-Fourth Amendment – The Twenty-Fourth Amendment, ratified in 1964, prohibited the use of poll taxes. A poll tax is a tax that is paid to vote. In the American South these taxes were primarily intended to suppress minority voting because minorities are disproportionately poor and less able to pay the tax.

- Twenty-Sixth Amendment – Prohibited discrimination in voting based on age if a person was 18 years or older.

- Congress has passed significant legislation to facilitate voting and protect voting rights. These laws include:
  - Voting Rights Act of 1965 – Legislation passed by Congress that banned discriminatory practices in voting.
  - National Voter Registration Act ("Motor Voter") – Required that states offer voter registration to qualified individuals when applying for their driver's licenses or applying for various other governmental services.

MPA – 3.B Describe different models of voting behavior.

- Political scientists have developed models that attempt to explain voting behavior. These models include:
  - Rational Choice Voting – In this model, a person votes based upon what he or she perceives as his or her self-interest.
  - Retrospective Voting – In this model of voting, a person seeks to reward or punish parties and candidates based upon how he or she perceives their performance over the last few years.
  - Prospective Voting – This model of voting is based on how a person believes the candidate or party will behave in the future.
  - Party-Line Voting – In party-line voting, a person casts his or her ballot for all members of the same party. This form of voting has been in decline as there has been weakened party identification since the mid-twentieth century.

MPA – 3.C Explain the roles that individual choice and state laws play in voter turnout in elections.

- There are ranges of factors that can impact the likelihood that a person will vote. Among these are structural barriers such as time and place of elections, political efficacy (the belief that one's participation makes an impact on the outcome), and demographics. Generally speaking, the following characteristics are more correlated with voting: older, better-educated, wealthier, white as opposed to nonwhite. Other factors impact voter turnout, in the United States and worldwide, including:
  - Election laws are diverse. In the United States, the states have great control over election procedures and some states' policies make it easier to register and vote while others work to place more demands on a hopeful voter.
  - Most states require voter registration. Before a person can vote, he or she must register, and this must typically be done in advance of an election. This is generally seen as a barrier to voting. The United States is one of the only democracies in the world that requires voter registration.
  - Other democracies provide incentives to voters or fine individuals who do not vote, though the United States does not. This has a tendency to increase voter turnout.
  - There is a presidential election every four years. During this election voters select presidential electors, one third of the U.S. Senate, and all 435 members of the U.S. House of Representatives. There may also be various state offices on the ballot. Voter turnout in presidential elections runs 50 to 60 percent of the voting age population. In the United States, voter turnout is higher for presidential elections and lower for midterm elections. This is likely a result of the higher level of media attention garnered by presidential candidates.
  - Midterm elections occur two years after a presidential election. During this election, voters will choose one third of the Senate and all of the members of the House of Representatives. Depending on the state, voters may also elect various state and local officials. Turnout during these elections is typically between 35 and 40 percent, made up of voters who are less diverse, more educated, and more partisan than the body of voters who participate in the presidential elections. During midterm elections there is generally a decrease in Congress of members who are the same party as the president.

Making Connections

Refer back to Chapter 5, Civil Rights, to review how the Fifteenth Amendment, Voting Rights Act of 1965, and the Nineteenth Amendment expanded the right to vote.

Much of the content presented in this chapter overlaps with the content presented in Chapter 8, Interest Groups, Chapter 9, Political Parties, and Chapter 10, Elections and Campaigns. Consider how the expansion of suffrage has impacted the two major parties.

Going Deeper: Voter Participation

During the Progressive period of American history, many states began to adopt registration laws in an attempt to counteract voter fraud. Most registration procedures require voters to complete the process in advance of an election, sometimes several weeks in advance.

This system has led to concerns that participation has been decreased. To combat this, some states have instituted same day registration. This allows a person to register and vote on the same day. Congress attempted to increase access to voting in 1993 with passage of the National Voter Registration Act, more commonly referred to as "Motor Voter." The law required that states offer the opportunity to register to vote when a person gets his or her driver's license or applies for other governmental services.

Some data has indicated that Motor Voter has had little impact on voter turnout. Indeed, the percentage of eligible voters who turn out for a presidential election continues to fluctuate without any sustained increase. For midterm elections, the overall decline from the highs of the 1960s continues. It may well be that there are other factors that influence voter turnout other than the perceived barrier of voter registration.

As the text points out, there are a number of demographic factors that impact turnout such as race, sex, age, etc. When examining other democratic systems, it appears that there are other variables associated with rates of voter turnout. Proportional representation systems tend to have higher voter turnout when compared with single-member district "winner take all" systems." The number of elections can also be a factor. Countries that have fewer elections tend to have higher turnout. When considering primary, state, and local elections, the United States has more elections than do countries that have higher voter turnout.

12 Congress

AP® Learning Objectives

CON – 3.A Describe the different structures, powers, and functions of each house of Congress.

CON – 3.B Explain how the structure, powers, and functions of both houses of Congress affect the policy-making process.

CON – 3.C Explain how congressional behavior is influenced by election processes, partisanship, and divided government.

PMI – 2.C Explain how Congress uses its oversight power in its relationship with the executive branch.

Performance Tasks

Upon the completion of this chapter, you must be able to do the following:

- Describe the powers of Congress with regard to economic policy making.
- Describe the powers of Congress in the areas of military and foreign policy.
- Describe how the necessary and proper clause expands the power granted by the Constitution to Congress.
- Compare and contrast the House of Representatives and the Senate with regard to representation, debate procedures, and the special roles of each chamber.
- Explain how the committee system operates.
- Explain the differences between the following views of representation: delegate, trustee, and political.
- Explain how elections, redistricting, and ideology impact congressional decision making.
- Explain how Congress exercises legislative oversight.

"Just as there are streets and highways that help us get to where we want to go on the road, there is an infrastructure of opportunity in America that allows us to get to where we want to go in life."

JOAQUÍN CASTRO
Stanford University

ZUMA Press, Inc./Alamy

Very few people can claim that their sibling is the Secretary of Housing and Urban Development, but even fewer can say this while they are already a sitting member of the U.S. House of Representatives. Joaquín Castro (D-TX) from Texas's 20th District was born in 1974 to a community activist mother and a schoolteacher father. As a second-generation Mexican American, Representative Castro and his identical twin brother Julián were well aware of the sacrifices their grandparents had to make to give their children a better life in America. His family history has deeply affected how he serves his congressional district.

Public service did not come naturally for one of the Castro brothers: Joaquín Castro was uninterested in politics despite growing up in a political household. Only after they left Texas and went to school at Stanford did both the Castro brothers recognize the importance of public service. After earning law degrees from Harvard Law School, they returned home and joined a private law firm. Representative Castro ran for the state legislature in District 125, while Julián Castro entered city politics, running for the city council seat his mother lost three decades before. Julián went on to be elected the mayor of San Antonio and then served in President Obama's cabinet as Secretary of Housing and Urban Development. During his five terms in the state legislature, Joaquín Castro took a deep interest in education and health care, and he served as the vice chairman of the Higher Education Committee.

During his 2012 campaign for the U.S. House, Representative Castro promised to pursue his "Infrastructure of Opportunity," a program that he believes "allows each of us to pursue our American dreams." Castro wants to see the United States build an infrastructure of exemplary public schools and universities, a strong health care system, and an economy that pays people well so they can support their families.

As Representative Castro passionately declared from the House floor after he won election to Congress with nearly 64 percent of the vote, the infrastructure of opportunity is just as important for the future of America as is a sound transportation infrastructure. Representative Castro put his support behind bills that will help improve the infrastructure of opportunity, such as his sponsorship of the Student Aid Expansion Act of 2013 and the Paycheck Fairness Act. He even spends a large portion of his free time improving education opportunities in his home district, which includes parts of San Antonio. He has raised money for underprivileged youths to go to college through the Trailblazers College Tour, and he created SA READS, which has provided more than 200,000 books to more than 150 schools and shelters in San Antonio.

Beyond education and health care, Representative Castro also cares deeply about the nation's defense and military needs. Through his assignments on the House Armed Services Committee and the House Foreign Affairs Committee, Representative Castro was able to visit Afghanistan as it was holding elections in March 2014. Castro's service on the House Armed Services Committee is particularly important for his constituents, as the city of San Antonio has three military bases, and the state of Texas has more than 120,000 active military personnel and 1.7 million veterans.

Representative Castro was reelected in 2014 with 76 percent of the vote and again in 2016 with 80 percent of the vote. In 2015, he introduced a bipartisan bill with two Republican Congressmen, the Reduce Homelessness for Female Veterans Act. The bill authorizes the Department of Housing and Urban Development and the Department of Veterans Affairs to conduct research into the numbers and causes of homelessness among female veterans. Castro's committee service as well as his prior service in the state legislature have distinctly positioned him as a trusted leader willing to give voice to the needs of his constituents and act as an advocate for the many servicemen and women whom he represents.[1]

In this chapter, we explain how members of Congress navigate the gates and gateways embedded in the legislative branch to best serve the interests of their constituents. The fact that members of Congress must repeatedly return home to ask the voters to reelect them helps keep them responsive to their constituents, who hold them accountable for the policies they enact into law. But the process of congressional representation—that is, of putting good ideas into practice as law—is difficult and complex. Structural gates are embedded in a separation of powers system of government and in a democratic legislative process that encourages competition among groups with conflicting interests. Navigating this terrain is not easy, but Joaquín Castro's efforts to represent his district show how an individual member of Congress seeks to be an advocate as well as a legislator.

12.1 Congress as the Legislative Branch

Describe how Congress has developed

In Chapter 2, The Constitution, we discussed the ideas of representation that shaped the Framers' thinking. They believed that a democratic government had to be responsive and accountable to the people. In such a government, leaders would not inherit power; rather, they would be chosen by the people at regular intervals, and these elections would be the key way that voters would hold government officials accountable for their actions. The Framers of the Constitution designed Congress to be the legislative branch of the federal government, and they gave it broad powers to enact laws. At the same time, they wanted the process of lawmaking to be complex and deliberative so that members of Congress would not succumb to impulsive actions that might harm constituents or violate fundamental constitutional rights. Over time, Congress has increased the scope and range of its powers, but the new responsibilities have added a layer of complexity that makes it harder than ever to pass laws.

Representation and Bicameralism

Essential to understanding how Congress facilitates representation in the American democracy is to recognize that it is bicameral; that is, it is divided into two separate chambers: the House of Representatives and the Senate. This structure reflects the Framers' fear that the power of the legislative branch might grow to the point where it could not be controlled by the other two branches. Because the legislative branch is closest to the people—its members represent specific population groups, by region, and can be removed by election—the Framers believed that Congress would have a democratic legitimacy that neither the executive nor the judicial branches would possess.

Essential Knowledge

The Senate represents the states equally, with each state receiving two members. The House of Representatives represents the states based on their populations. Larger states receive more members, with each state receiving at least one member.

The solution, according to James Madison, was to divide the legislature into two parts that would check each other. In *Federalist* 51 he explained that this would "render them . . . as little connected with each other, as the nature of their common functions, and their common dependence on the society, will admit." The House of Representatives would be a large body that reflected population size within states and was directly elected at frequent intervals (every two years). The Senate would be an elite chamber, with two senators for every state regardless of population size elected by state legislatures for six-year terms. In that way, both the popular opinions of average voters and the elite opinions of the well-educated and the wealthy would be represented in Congress. This arrangement also guaranteed that large states could not overwhelm smaller states in determining the content of laws. The specific differences between the two parts of Congress are discussed in the next section.

Constitutional Differences Between the House and Senate

To accomplish Madison's goal, the Constitution establishes four key differences between the two chambers of Congress: qualifications for office, mode of election, terms of office, and constituencies (see Table 12.1).

Qualifications for Office. To serve as a member of the House of Representatives, an individual must be at least twenty-five years old, reside in the state that he or she represents, and have been a U.S. citizen for seven years before running for office. The qualifications for the Senate are that an individual must be at least thirty years old, reside in the state he or she represents, and have been a U.S. citizen for nine years before taking office. Senators are expected to be older and to have lived in the United States for a longer period of time than House members because the Framers believed those characteristics would make the Senate the more stable partner in the legislative process.

Although the members of the First Congress (1789–91) were all white men, no provision in the Constitution delineates a specific race, gender, income level, or religion as a prerequisite for serving in Congress. Twenty-first-century Congresses have been much more diverse, with female, African American, Hispanic, Pacific Islander, and Native American members in the House (see Figure 12.1). Nevertheless, note that women held only 20 percent of the seats in the 114th Congress (House and Senate combined), although they constituted 51 percent of the nation's population. African Americans hold forty-six House seats and two Senate seats, while Latinos hold thirty-two House seats and four Senate seats. Despite the advancements made by underrepresented groups in electing members to Congress, it is still predominantly white and male.[2] The average age of a House and Senate member is nearly sixty. House members tend to serve an average of four terms (ten years) and Senators an average of close to two terms (ten years).[3] The twenty-first-century House has included members from the Protestant, Catholic, Hindu, Jewish, Greek Orthodox, Mormon, Buddhist, Quaker, and Muslim faiths. The religious background of senators has been slightly less varied but has also included members from the Protestant, Roman Catholic, Mormon, Buddhist, and Jewish faiths.[4]

House members have more varied prior experience than their Senate colleagues. A majority of House members served in their state legislatures before coming to Congress;

TABLE 12.1 Comparison of House and Senate Service

Characteristic	House	Senate
Minimum age	25 years old	30 years old
Citizenship	7 years	9 years
Term of office	2 years	6 years
Geographic constituency	District	State
Redistricting	Every 10 years	—
Mode of election until 1914	Direct	Indirect through state legislatures
Mode of election after 1914	Direct	Direct

POLITICAL ANALYTICS

Who Are Your Representatives?

WHEN THE U.S. CONSTITUTION WAS BEING DEBATED, Antifederalists complained that the Congress would comprise people who were unrepresentative of the American population. They worried that only a select and unrepresentative few would be chosen to represent the views of the electorate.[5] One way to judge whether the legislative branch is equipped to reflect the American people's views on public policy is to examine who represents us.

Figure 12.1 shows the demographic composition of the 114th Congress and of the U.S. population. Some disparities exist when we compare the demographic profile of the American population with those who represent us in Congress. For example, while women are a majority of population, they make up only 20 percent of the representatives in Congress. Of course, demographic representation is only one form of representation, albeit an important one. How House members and Senators represent the public policy views of Americans is the key to our representative democracy.

Examine the demographic composition of the U.S. House of Representatives and the U.S. Senate. Notice how the profile of Congress compares with the population characteristics of the United States.

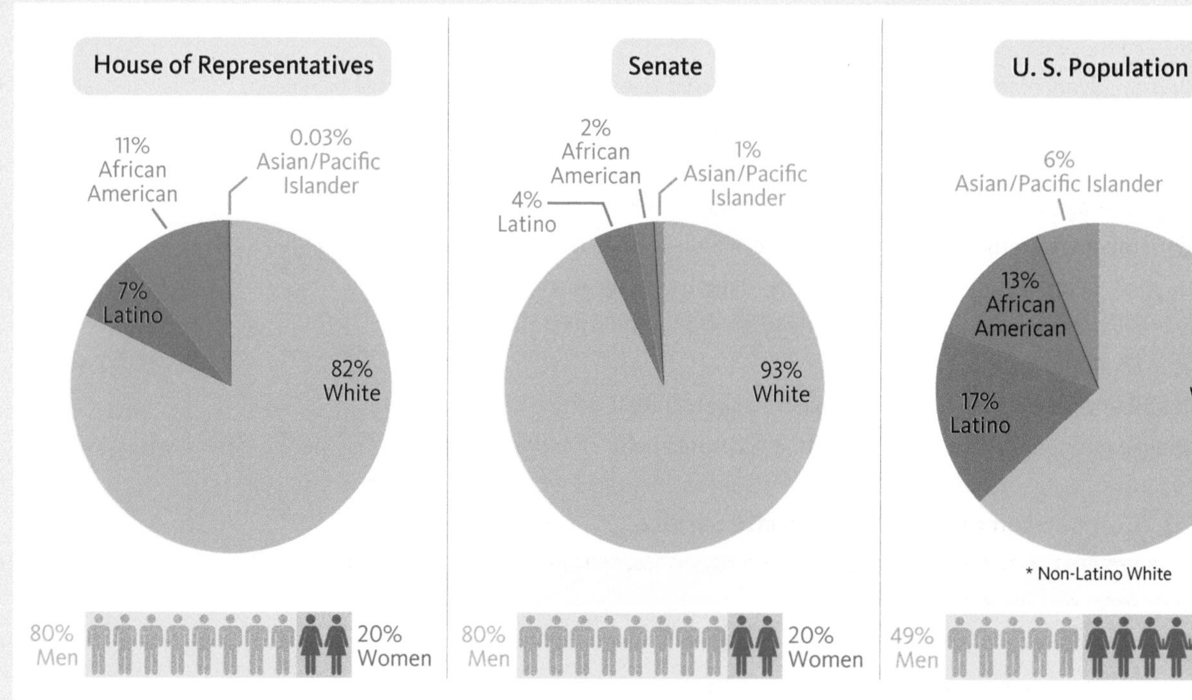

FIGURE 12.1 Profile of Members of the 114th House and Senate

Thinking Critically

1. Would public policy be "better" if Congress looked more like the demographic profile of the U.S. population?
2. Are men able to represent the views of women as well as women are? Who would you prefer to represent your views on public policy?

Sources: Jennifer E. Manning, *Membership of the 114th Congress: A Profile*, Congressional Research Service, October 31, 2015, https://www.fas.org/sgp/crs/misc/R43869.pdf; U.S. Census, http://www.census.gov/quickfacts/table/PST045215/00.

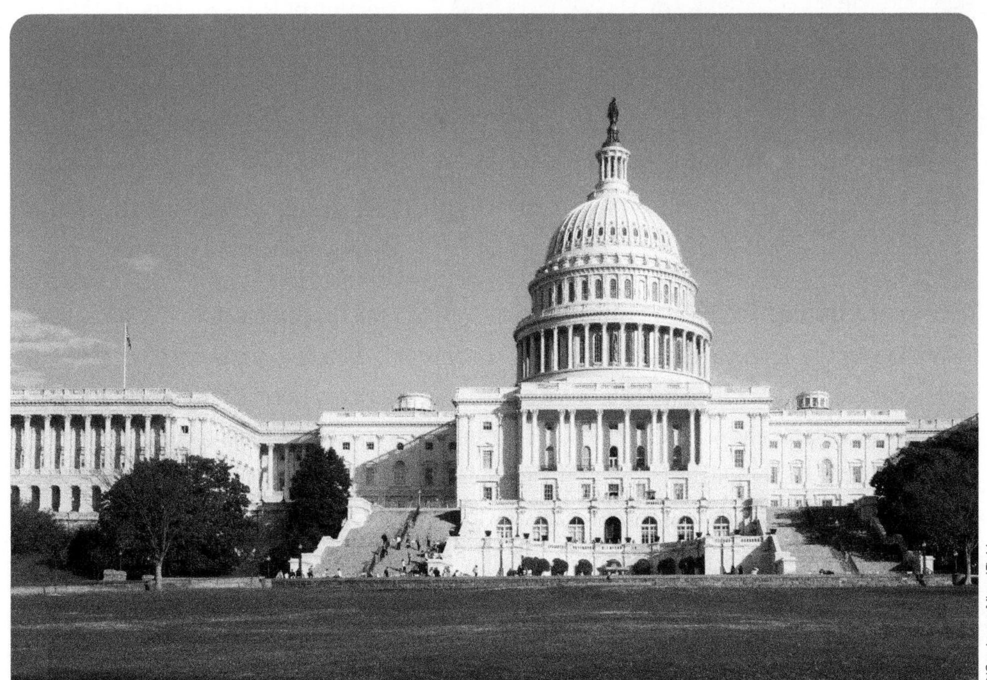

©iStock.com/VisualField

IMAGE 12.1 The Framers created the House of Representatives and the Senate as separate chambers of Congress, but both are located in the U.S. Capitol. In this view from the National Mall, the Senate chamber is on the left and the House chamber is on the right. There are six office buildings for members of Congress and their staff members, three on each side of the Capitol.

others were mayors, law enforcement officers, teachers, doctors, ministers, radio talk show hosts, accountants, Peace Corps volunteers, software business executives, and ranchers. Just as House members use state legislatures as stepping-stones, senators use the House of Representatives to launch their bids for the Senate. In the 114th Congress, fifty-three senators had previously served in the House of Representatives, and others had been mayors, governors, and attorneys general and even cabinet secretary.

Mode of Election. House members are elected directly by citizens. Senators are elected directly as well, but that is a more recent development. From 1789 to 1914, the mode of election for the Senate was indirect: Citizens voted for members of their state legislatures, who then selected the U.S. senators. The mode of election for the House and Senate was different on purpose. The House was supposed to be more immediately responsive to the opinions of the people, but the Framers designed the Senate to insulate senators from the

Chip Somodevilla/Getty Images

IMAGE 12.2 Barbara Mikulski (D-MD) was the longest-serving woman in Congress. She served in the House of Representatives from 1977 to 1986, when she was elected to the Senate. Throughout her career, she championed women's health and labor issues. She was also a strong advocate for her home state of Maryland. Her Senate seat was won by Chris Van Hollen (D) in 2016.

direct voice of the people—in other words, to make them less directly responsive to the people.

The mode of election for the Senate changed from indirect to direct with the ratification of the Seventeenth Amendment in 1913. At the end of the nineteenth century, in response to charges of deadlock and corruption during the election of U.S. senators in state legislatures, Progressives led a movement to allow voters to directly elect their senators.[6] The amendment opened up a much more direct gateway of influence for constituents over their U.S. senators.

Essential Knowledge

The fact that senators serve longer terms leads to coalitions of members that are more long-lasting than in the House of Representatives.

Terms of Office. A term of office is the length of time that an elected official serves before facing the voters again in an election. The term of office for House members is two years, and the term of office for U.S. senators is six years. The difference in term of office leads to key differences in how each chamber operates. House members have a shorter amount of time to demonstrate their effectiveness before they face reelection, so the House of Representatives as a whole is usually in a greater hurry to pass legislation than is the Senate. Senators know they have six years before they have to face their voters, so they have a bit more flexibility in working out disagreements among their constituents and balancing constituents' interests against the interests of the nation as a whole. Because senators know they have a longer time in which to establish a good reputation among their home state voters, the Senate takes more time to deliberate over legislation.

In any given election year, the entire membership of the House of Representatives must face the voters, but only one-third of senators stand for reelection. To guarantee that the whole Senate would never stand for reelection all at once, the Constitution divided the first Senate, which met in 1789, into three classes of senators who would be elected at different six-year intervals.[7] To this day, the maximum number of senators who stand for regularly scheduled reelection in the same year is 34 (out of a possible 100), thereby ensuring that a majority of the Senate is never up for reelection at the same time as the entire House of Representatives.[8] This electoral condition reinforces the stability of the Senate's membership; it also limits the electoral incentives for House and Senate members to cooperate with one another to pass legislation.

Constituencies. A constituency is the set of people that officially elects the House or Senate member; in the United States, constituency is defined geographically. Each member of the House of Representatives represents a congressional district with established geographic boundaries within the state (except for seven states with populations so small that they have just one congressional district; see Figure 12.2). Each U.S. senator represents an entire state, and two U.S. senators are elected from each state.

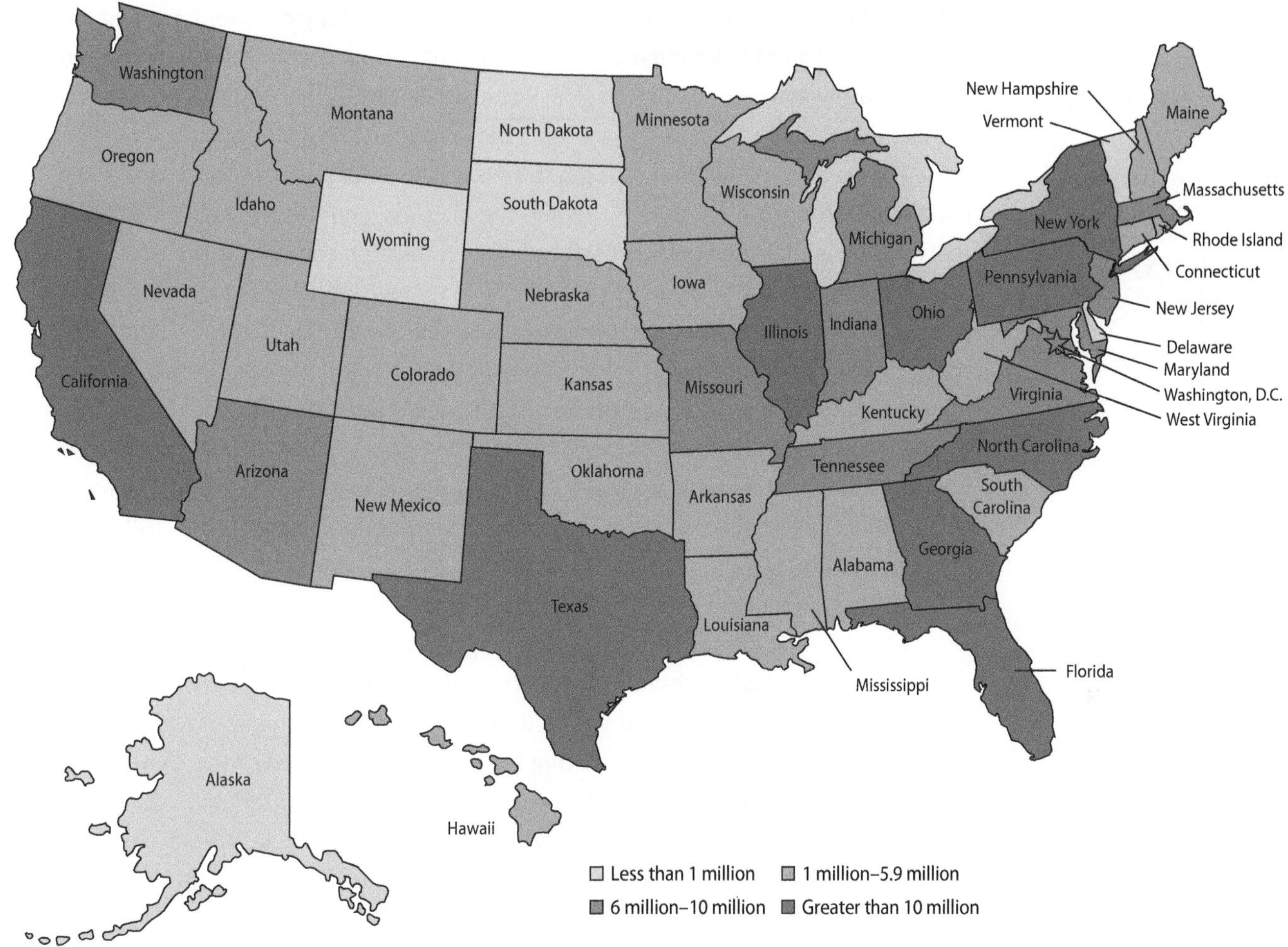

FIGURE 12.2 States by Population, 2015

The U.S. Senate has two senators for every state, regardless of population. This arrangement makes states equal in Senate votes: Wyoming has the same number of votes as California. But it also means that the less than 1 million citizens of Wyoming have the same voice in the Senate as the more than 39 million citizens of California. Equal representation in the Senate did not seem as imbalanced when states had more similar population sizes, but today, with such huge differences, some observers think representation in the Senate is inherently unfair.

Source: © Cengage Learning; data from U.S. Census Bureau, "Population Estimates," accessed February 17, 2016, http://factfinder.census.gov/ces/tableservices/jsf/pages/productview.xhtml?pid=PEP_2015_PEPANNRES&src=pt.

In 1789, the average size of a congressional district was about 30,000 people and the average size of a state was about 300,000 people; in 2016, a congressional district had about 711,000 people and the nation's largest state, California, had approximately 39 million residents.[9] Because the Framers knew that the country's population would change, they required a count, or census, of the population every ten years. Following the census, the number of congressional districts in each state would be adjusted to reflect population changes. The House started with 65 members and, when capped by Congress at 435 in 1929, had increased by 670 percent.[10] Congress was concerned that if the House grew any larger it would not be possible to conduct legislative business.[11] Today, because there is an absolute limit on the total number of House members, population growth or decline has a direct bearing on a state's representation, increasing or decreasing the state's number of representatives and thus its relative influence in the House.

Essential Knowledge

The case of *Baker v. Carr* and subsequent cases also demand that congressional districts be equal in population. This tends to prevent overrepresentation of rural areas. This can impact the policy decisions made by Congress.

Redistricting. Only the House of Representatives is subject to redistricting, which is the redrawing of the boundaries of congressional districts in a state to make them approximately equal in population size. Because the size of the House is limited to 435, the overall number of congressional seats per state must be adjusted following a census if there have been population changes. Based on the state's allocation of congressional districts, the state legislature redraws the districts, and the only real limitation on redistricting is that the boundaries of the district must be contiguous (uninterrupted). During redistricting, the majority party in the state legislature tries to influence the process to construct each district in such a way that a majority of voters favors its party, thereby making it easier for its candidates to win, in a process known as gerrymandering. Sometimes the majority party will combine two existing districts that have House members from the other party, forcing them to run against each other. In a limited number of states there are bipartisan redistricting commissions that seek to draw district lines in a nonpartisan way, but the vast majority of redistricting is still done by state legislatures.

Essential Knowledge

In the case of *Shaw v. Reno*, the Supreme Court prohibited the creation of districts that were overwhelmingly based on race.

Redistricting has also been used as a tool to achieve greater minority representation in the House of Representatives following the theory of descriptive representation, whereby an individual represents a constituency not just in terms of geography but also in terms of race or ethnicity. The Voting Rights Act of 1965 prohibits states and political subdivisions from denying or limiting "the right of any citizen of the United States to vote on account of race or color"; it was later amended to protect the voting rights of non-English-speaking minorities—referring to Latinos—as well. This act is discussed in detail in Chapters 5, Civil Rights; 10, Elections and Campaigns; and 11, Voting and Participation; here we focus on the fact that many states initially responded to the law by redrawing congressional districts to group minority voters in a way that would deny them the voting strength to elect a minority member of Congress. In 1982, Congress amended the Voting Rights Act to prevent this kind of manipulation. In response, some state legislatures created so-called majority-minority districts in which African Americans or Latinos would constitute a majority of the voters and would have enough votes to elect an African American or Latino candidate.[12] The Texas district that Congressman Castro represents is considered a majority-minority district, with 69 percent of the population there identifying as Latino.[13] Since then, the federal courts have ruled that state legislatures overemphasized the racial composition of these districts to the point that the districts made no geographic sense. Current guidelines on redistricting call for the consideration of race in drawing district lines but not to the extent that it was employed in the past.[14]

Because representation in the Senate is related to state boundaries, not to population size, some scholars have argued that the Senate is less responsive than the House. It is true that there are vast differences in population size among the states[15] (see Figure 12.2). As we explore later in this chapter, the rules of the Senate amplify this imbalance of influence by granting each senator equal power to delay, or block, legislation. As a result, a senator who represents a state such as Wyoming, with fewer than six hundred thousand people, can delay, or in the final day of a session actually prevent, the passage of a policy that might benefit a state such as California, with 39 million people.

12.2 The Powers of Congress

Define the powers of Congress

As Chapter 2 describes, the Framers granted Congress powers that were necessary to construct a coherent and forceful federal government. Some of these, such as the power to tax and to regulate commerce among the states, had been denied to Congress under the Articles of Confederation, and their absence had weakened the new republic. At the same time, the Framers worried that the legislative branch would grow too powerful, so they limited the powers of Congress to a list in Article I, Section 8, of the Constitution, together with a few stated responsibilities in other sections. The following discussion highlights the most important powers of Congress. It also examines the ways that Congress has used its constitutional powers to expand its role in the policy-making system and ways that Congress is balanced and checked by the executive and judicial branches.

Essential Knowledge

Congress only has the power to legislate on those topics assigned to the national government by the Constitution (enumerated powers) and those topics that are related to the enumerated powers (implied powers by way of the the necessary and proper clause).

Taxation and Appropriation

Congress has the power "To lay and Collect Taxes." In a division of this important power, the Constitution states that all bills for raising revenue should originate in the House of Representatives, but the Senate "may propose or concur with Amendments, as on other Bills." Initially, the Framers thought that tax revenue would come primarily from levies placed on imported goods. As the industrial economy grew, so did the need for government services and programs that cost money. With the Sixteenth Amendment, ratified in 1913, Congress gained the power "to lay and collect taxes on incomes," whatever the source. This amendment overturned prohibitions on certain types of income taxes.

Essential Knowledge

While most powers are shared between the House of Representatives and the Senate there are a few unique powers assigned to each house.

Paralleling the power to tax, Congress also has the power to spend—"to pay the Debts and to provide for the common Defence and general Welfare." The general welfare clause has proven to be a major means by which Congress's power has expanded. Congress **appropriates** (or allocates) federal monies on programs it **authorizes** (or creates) through its lawmaking power. This "power of the purse" has been instrumental in the expansion of Congress's relative strength among the branches of government.[16] The Constitution also gives Congress the authority to borrow money, to coin money, and to regulate its value, and it requires a regular accounting of revenue and expenditures of public money.

appropriate: *Congress's power to allocate a set amount of federal dollars for a specific program or agency.*

authorize: *Congress's power to create a federal program or agency and set levels of federal funds to support that program or agency.*

War Powers

The Constitution gives Congress authority to "provide for the common Defence." In reality, the war powers are shared with the president. For example, Congress has the sole power to declare war, but this power is typically used only after the president has requested a declaration of war. In many cases, the president may ask Congress for specific authorization to take military action; under its power of taxation and appropriation, Congress has the authority to fund or refuse to fund military operations. Generally, Congress also has the power "to raise and support Armies," "to provide and maintain a Navy," "to provide for

Essential Knowledge

Congress has the power to declare war.

calling forth the Militia," and to make rules and regulations regarding the armed forces and their organizations. Relations between Congress and the president over war powers have sometimes been harmonious, but in recent decades, they have become contentious. The struggle between the president and Congress over the war powers is examined in detail in Chapter 13, The Presidency.

Regulation of Commerce

The Constitution gave Congress an important power that it did not have under the Articles of Confederation: the power "to regulate Commerce with foreign Nations, and among the several States, and with the Indian Tribes." Using the power in this commerce clause, Congress established a national set of laws regulating commerce that are applicable to all states equally.[17] In time, the authority to regulate interstate commerce has allowed Congress to expand its power to the point that almost no economic activity is beyond its reach. For example, in 1942 the Supreme Court upheld Congress's power to regulate wheat production even when that wheat is not sold or transported in interstate commerce but is consumed on the farm where it was planted and harvested.[18] In the name of regulating interstate commerce, Congress has passed laws that permit the federal government to break up monopolies, protect labor unions, set a minimum wage, and outlaw racial discrimination by businesses and commercial enterprises. In 2012, the Court ruled that Congress's requirement, set forth in the Patient Protection and Affordable Care Act, that individuals purchase health insurance went beyond Congress's commerce clause authority but upheld most of the act as within Congress's taxing authority (see Supreme Court Cases: *National Federation of Independent Business et al. v. Sebelius*).

Appointments and Treaties

Essential Knowledge

Most major appointments by the president to the executive branch and judicial branch must be approved by the Senate.

Treaties must also be ratified by a two-thirds majority vote of the Senate.

In recognition of the Senate's perceived wisdom and stability, the Framers gave the Senate, and not the House, the power of advice and consent. In the appointment of high-level executive branch appointees, such as cabinet secretaries and ambassadors, this power allows the Senate to evaluate the qualifications of a presidential nominee and, by majority vote, to approve or reject the nominee. Similarly, the appointment of all federal judges, from district courts to the Supreme Court, is subject to the approval of the Senate (see Chapter 15, The Judiciary, for more details on this process). Additionally, the Senate acts as a check on the president's power to make treaties with foreign nations: Treaties must be approved by a two-thirds vote, or they fail to take effect (see Chapter 13 for more on treaty negotiation and ratification). The advice and consent role of the Senate acts as a gateway for citizen influence over presidential appointments and treaties because senators are more likely to block appointments and treaties that they believe are unpopular with their constituents.

Impeachment and Removal from Office

Congress's ultimate check on the executive and judicial branches is its power to remove officials and judges from office by impeachment. The president, vice president, and high-level officials are subject to impeachment for "Treason, Bribery, or other high Crimes and Misdemeanors." This power is rarely used. In Chapter 13, we examine the two cases in which presidents have been impeached but not removed from office. In the case of

SUPREME COURT CASES

National Federation of Independent Business et al. v. Sebelius (2012)

QUESTION: May Congress impose a mandate to purchase health insurance on those who do not wish to carry it? Did Congress exceed its spending authority with the Medicaid expansions?

ORAL ARGUMENT: March 26–28, 2012 (listen at http://www.oyez.org/cases/2010-2019/2011/2011_11_400)

DECISION: June 28, 2012 (read at http://www.oyez.org/cases/2010-2019/2011/2011_11_400)

OUTCOME: Yes, the authority is within Congress's taxing power (5–4). Yes, Congress exceeded its spending authority (7–2). Overall, however, the law is constitutional.

The Obama administration argued that because the decisions of individuals not to purchase health insurance have a substantial effect on hospitals and insurance companies involved in interstate commerce, Congress has the right to mandate the purchase of such insurance. Those opposed to the act argued that if Congress could make people purchase health insurance because of the substantial effect it has on interstate commerce, why couldn't it, under the same reasoning, make people buy broccoli? As a fallback, the administration argued that even if the act was not itself a regulation of commerce, it was necessary and proper to the regulation of commerce (see Supreme Court Cases: *McCulloch v. Maryland* in Chapter 3, Federalism). As a second fallback, the administration argued that the mandate was a valid exercise of Congress's authority to tax to provide for the general welfare. Opponents pointed out that when Congress was debating the bill, the Obama administration insisted that the payments for not purchasing health insurance were a penalty and not a tax, so that members of Congress could not be accused of passing unpopular tax increases. Additionally, opponents claimed that the threat states faced of losing all Medicaid funding if they did not voluntarily expand their Medicaid coverage was coercive, in violation of the Tenth Amendment (see Chapter 3).

In a complicated decision, Chief Justice John Roberts, joined by the Court's four more conservative justices (Samuel Alito, Anthony Kennedy, Antonin Scalia, and Clarence Thomas), declared that Congress did not have the authority under the commerce clause or the necessary and proper clause to mandate that individuals enter the insurance market. This part of the opinion weakens Congress's commerce clause powers. Crucially, however, Chief Justice Roberts, joined by the Court's four more liberal justices (Stephen Breyer, Ruth Bader Ginsburg, Elena Kagan, and Sonia Sotomayor), ruled that the penalty for not purchasing insurance could be considered a tax, and that as a tax, it was well within Congress's authority.

Finally, by a 7–2 vote, all justices except Ginsburg and Sotomayor argued that Congress cannot rescind previously committed funds to states that refuse to accept the new Medicaid requirements, imposing the first limits on Congress's spending power in seventy-five years. But by a 5–4 vote, with Roberts joining the liberal bloc, the Court upheld the withholding of new funds from states that did not accept the new Medicaid expansion, as well as the rest of the law.

In 2015, in *King v. Burwell*, the Supreme Court ruled that citizens in the thirty-four states that did not establish statewide exchanges for the purchase of insurance could receive insurance subsidies even though the law stated that the subsidies would be granted through "state-run exchanges."

Thinking Critically

1. Why does it matter whether the payment for not having health insurance is a "penalty" or a "tax"?
2. What was unusual about the Court's decision involving Congress's spending authority?

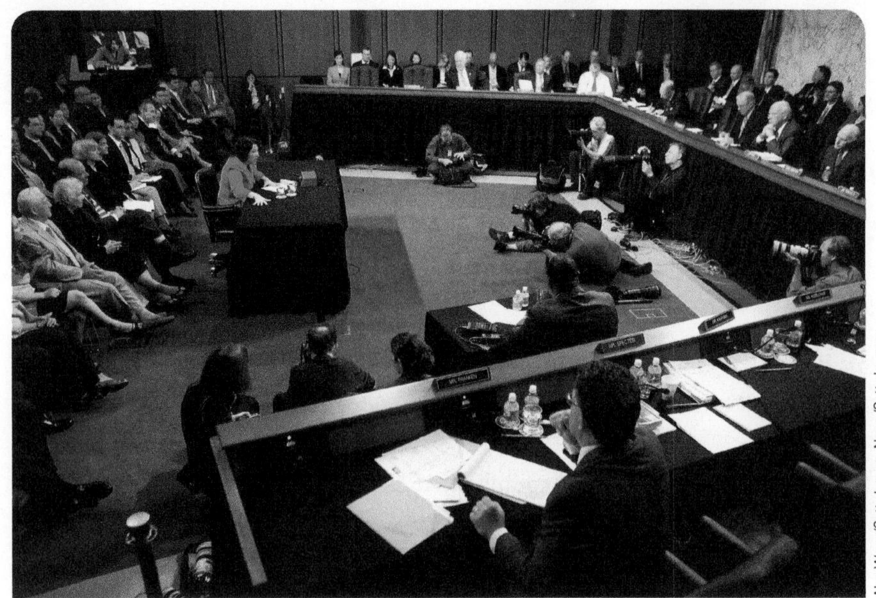

IMAGE 12.3 The Senate exercises its advice and consent powers when it holds hearings on presidential nominees and then votes to approve or reject them. In the summer of 2009, senators questioned President Barack Obama's first Supreme Court nominee, Sonia Sotomayor, an appeals court judge from New York. She was confirmed on August 6, 2009, by a vote of 68 to 31, and she is the first Latina Supreme Court justice.

President Richard Nixon (1969–74), the threat of impeachment was credible enough that he resigned from office.

The process of impeachment and removal from office takes place in two steps. First, a majority of the House of Representatives votes to bring formal charges against the president or other federal official, an action called impeachment. Then the Senate conducts the trial, with the chief justice of the United States presiding in the case of the president's impeachment, and votes to convict or acquit. If two-thirds of the senators present vote to convict, the president or the federal official will be removed from office.

Lawmaking

Congress, as the legislative branch, is responsible for lawmaking. Unlike the enumerated powers listed at the beginning of Article I, Section 8, and explained previously, the final paragraph of Section 8 gives Congress broad authority "to make all Laws which shall be necessary and proper for carrying into Execution the foregoing Powers." In combination with the general welfare clause and the commerce clause, this necessary and proper clause allows Congress a great deal of leeway to carry out its responsibilities under the assumption that additional powers are implied in these clauses, although not explicitly stated in the Constitution. Over time, Congress has made full use of this flexibility to expand its authority in a wide range of areas, such as regulating interstate railroads, establishing civil rights protections, funding school lunch programs, limiting greenhouse gases, and providing student loans. Essentially, if an argument can be made that a service or program is reasonably tied to an enumerated power, Congress has used its powers to create that service or program.

Authorization of Courts

In Article I, the Constitution also gives Congress the power to "constitute Tribunals inferior to the Supreme Court." Article III, the section on the judiciary, reiterates congressional control by saying that Congress may "ordain and establish" courts at levels lower than the Supreme Court. In 1789, Congress used this power to pass the Judiciary Act, which established federal district courts and circuit courts of appeal. Today, there are ninety-four district courts and thirteen appellate circuits.[19]

The federal judicial branch asserted more authority over the other two branches in the Supreme Court case of *Marbury v. Madison* (see Chapter 2). This case established judicial review, which is the federal judiciary's power to declare laws passed by Congress as unconstitutional. The *Marbury* decision gave the courts the power to interpret the Constitution and determine how congressional laws (and even executive branch actions) conform to its explicit language and its intent (see Chapter 15 for further explanation of this decision).

In recent years the Senate has tried to reassert its influence over the federal courts through the nomination process.[20] As we discuss later in the chapter, individual senators can try to defeat presidential nominees for federal judgeships with whom they disagree on key constitutional questions. More broadly, senators in the opposite party from the president can refuse to hold hearings or vote on a presidential nominee, even to the Supreme Court.

Oversight

After a bill becomes a law, the executive branch, headed by the president, is supposed to carry out the law according to Congress's wishes. But the executive branch is a bureaucracy with many departments and agencies that have authority to implement laws. The sheer size and complexity of the federal bureaucracy make it difficult for Congress to determine whether laws are being administered according to the intent behind them (see Chapter 14, The Bureaucracy, for more details). Over time, Congress has asserted its oversight authority to monitor the ways in which the executive branch implements law. This authority stems from Congress's responsibility to appropriate money to provide for the general welfare of the nation. Congress constantly exercises this authority, but less so under unified government, when the same party controls Congress and the White House, than under **divided government**, when the party that controls Congress is not the party of the president. Under unified government, members of Congress assume that because they share the same partisan affiliation as the president, his administration is more likely to implement laws according to congressional intent.

In contrast, legislatures in countries that have parliamentary systems typically choose their executives from among the members of the majority party, so that the executive and legislative branches always share the same policy goals. Consequently, legislative oversight is not a fundamental element of those political systems.

Members of Congress engage in oversight activities in several ways. They hold hearings with cabinet officials and bureaucrats to analyze how well programs are working, and they frequently invite members of the public to describe how federal programs operate in their communities. Members of Congress regularly write letters to executive branch agency heads to inquire about specific programs, and they keep careful track of the responses they receive. In cases of oversight hearings, special investigations, or suspected wrongdoing by members of the executive branch, Congress can legally require members of the administration to testify. For example, in May 2014, the House of Representatives created a Select Committee on Benghazi, chaired by Representative Trey Gowdy (R-SC), to investigate the death of U.S. Ambassador Christopher Stevens and three other U.S. workers near diplomatic facilities in Benghazi, Libya, in 2012 in an attack by alleged terrorists. In doing so the Republican leadership argued that the Obama administration had not been forthcoming about the nature, causes, and response to the attacks that killed these individuals and the House had a right to exercise its oversight authority in this area. Nearly three decades earlier, the Democrats in the House and Senate created a special committee, known as the Iran-Contra Committee (see Chapter 13 for more details), to investigate actions involving members of

Essential Knowledge

During times of divided government, it is difficult for either party to achieve its legislative goals, especially during the lame duck period of an outgoing president. Presidential appointments are also frequently blocked in the Senate. This is often referred to as gridlock.

divided government: *Situation in which one party controls the executive branch and the other party controls one or both parts of the legislative branch.*

Essential Knowledge

Through the use of committee hearings and through Congress's power of the purse (control over spending), legislators exercise oversight over the executive branch, as well as the president.

President Reagan and his staff in the sale of military weapons to support an insurgency in Nicaragua. These congressional oversight investigatory committees have the power to subpoena key government personnel whom they believe might provide information about the conduct of the executive branch. In these ways, Congress provides a gateway for the people to constantly monitor and hold the federal government accountable for how it implements policy or reacts to foreign affairs.

12.3 The Organization of Congress

Outline how Congress is structured

The House and the Senate have evolved into very different institutions by virtue of their differences in size, rules, structure, and responsibilities. The Constitution establishes few guidelines for how the House and Senate should operate, so it was left to the members to determine how to choose their leaders and how much power to give them. Some aspects of leadership are shared by the House and Senate, but there are important differences in the amount of power each grants to its leaders. Notably, the power of political parties to shape policy is vastly different in each chamber.

The Role of Political Parties

In today's political world, political parties seem natural and intrinsic to the organization of Congress. Indeed, members of Congress align more closely with their political parties in the House and Senate than in any time in the past 100 years (see Chapter 6, Figure 6.7). But this degree of difference between the political parties did not always exist in Congress. The House did not organize itself along strict partisan lines until well into the nineteenth century. As Congress scholars Sarah Binder and Eric Schickler each show, not until after the Civil War did the House change its internal rules to give the majority party the ability to get its preferred policies passed over the objections of the minority party.[21] Since then, party affiliation and party loyalty have become the defining features of how policy is made in the House of Representatives.

The reason parties could become so powerful inside the House chamber was that they were important outside Washington, back home in local districts. Being identified with a political party became an essential stepping-stone to political office. Political parties controlled the nomination process for Congress, and anyone who wanted to run on a party ticket had to pledge support for the party's policies. Consequently, each individual member had a strong incentive to align with a political party both at home in the district and in Washington (see Chapter 9, Political Parties, for more on party affiliations).

With the rise in party strength at the district level, House members were increasingly judged on the performance of their party in office, and elections became centered on gaining majority control of the chamber. If the majority party could pass policies that it favored and prevent those who disagreed with them (the minority party) from gaining any power, majority party members could return to their districts and claim credit for being effective legislators.

Although the Senate also became more party-oriented at the end of the nineteenth century, its members never changed the rules of the chamber to give the majority party complete dominance. Because the number of senators has remained small, it is still possible to conduct legislative business in a personal manner, and each senator exerts individual influence over policy outcomes. Senators also have the chance to make individual impressions on voters over a longer time (six years) and from a more visible vantage point, as they represent entire states rather than just one district. In this age of increased polarization, voters weigh a senator's ideology and party affiliation more heavily than they used to, but it is still not as important as in House elections. Consequently, senators have had fewer incentives to hand over their individual powers to a single party leader to accomplish party goals.

As a result, members of the minority party in the Senate have far more power in the policy-making process than do their counterparts in the House.[22] In essence, getting any legislation passed in the Senate usually requires compromise and cooperation among all senators—majority and minority party members—in one way or another.

Essential Knowledge

Increasing polarization can result in gridlock, which increases the need for compromise.

Essential Knowledge

The Speaker of the House is the most powerful member of the House and perhaps the most powerful member of Congress. Among the Speaker's powers are presiding over the House and assigning bills to committee.

The House of Representatives

As is the case with any large organization, success requires leadership. To maximize party cohesion, members of the House meet in a party caucus ("to caucus" literally means "to gather") of the members of their political party. Each party's caucus chooses its party leaders: For the majority party, the top party leader is the Speaker of the House, and for the minority party, it is the minority leader.

Speaker of the House: *Constitutional and political leader of the House.*

The Speaker of the House.

Speaker of the House is the only formal leadership position written into the Constitution. Article I, Section 2, states that "the House of Representatives shall chuse their Speaker and other Officers," but there the official description ends. The Speaker is elected by a majority of House members every two years, on the first day of the first session of each new Congress. The position first became organizationally powerful under the tenure of Thomas Brackett Reed (R-ME), who served as Speaker from 1889 to 1891 and again from 1895 to 1899.[23] Reed was elected to the House in 1876, and by the early 1880s he was already displaying political ambition.

As Speaker, Reed implemented a set of procedural changes known as Reed's Rules that strengthened the power of the majority party over the minority party. Because the House ran on majority rule, the party that had the most votes could pass a bill outright. Reed's party granted him the power to appoint all committee chairmen, approve all members' committee assignments, refer bills to committee, bring bills that reflect the majority party's ideas to the House floor, and refuse to allow the minority party to delay legislation.[24] Both former Speaker of the House Nancy Pelosi (D-CA) and current Speaker Paul Ryan (R-WI) used many of the same powers to run the House, although they each presided over a more complex decision-making environment than did Reed.

Library of Congress Prints and Photographs Division[LC-USZ62-132187]

IMAGE 12.4 Thomas Brackett Reed (R-ME) served as Speaker of the House from 1889 to 1891 and again from 1895 to 1899. He changed the rules of the House to give the majority party the advantage in setting the policy agenda and passing bills that accomplished its goals.

In the century following Reed, the leadership styles of Speakers varied according to how much power the rank-and-file party members wanted to give to their leaders. The scholar David Rohde and others argue that the variation in leadership style can be explained by the underlying coherence of the majority party during these years. When the rank-and-file membership of the majority party is unified in its policy goals, it hands power to party leaders, especially the Speaker, to accomplish those goals under what Rohde called conditional party government.[25] The leadership of Speaker Newt Gingrich (1995–98) represents this model of party leadership because he came to power with a large class of newly elected Republicans on a party platform called the Contract with America. They captured control of the House from Democrats after forty years in the minority and produced a cohesive ideological party that was willing to give Gingrich strong powers to accomplish policy goals. However, just three years later, Gingrich resigned the Speakership after the 1998 midterm elections; the Republicans lost seats as a result of an unpopular attempt to impeach President Clinton (see Chapter 13).

After Gingrich, the Republicans chose a less powerful Speaker, Dennis Hastert (R-IL), and moved from a conditional party government system to what scholars call a party cartel system. According to Gary Cox and Mathew McCubbins, in this system, the power of party leaders rests on their ability to set the legislative agenda and provide services, such as campaign finance funds, and organizational positions, such as committee positions, to party members in exchange for their loyalty.[26] This type of cartel system worked better for the Republicans after 2001, when a Republican was elected to the White House and set the policy agenda for members of the party. Typically under unified government, members of the majority party in the House use the president's agenda as a starting point. As a result, the Speaker can lose independence in setting the policy direction for the House. A case in point is the Hastert Rule, named after former Speaker Dennis Hastert. The Hastert Rule states that when the Republicans are in majority control of the House, they will not bring a bill to the House floor without a majority of Republicans (i.e., a majority of the majority) agreeing to do so. In adopting that rule, the House Republican Party as a whole was ensuring that the Speaker would only bring bills to the House floor that followed their preferences.

KEVIN DIETSCH/Newscom/United Press International (UPI)/WASHINGTON DC UNITED STATES

IMAGE 12.5 Nancy Pelosi (D-CA) was elected the first female Speaker of the House of Representatives in 2007 and served as Speaker until 2011; since then she has served as Minority Leader. She was generally considered a strong Speaker because she exerted control over committee chairs and the conditions under which bills were considered on the House floor.

After the Democrats won control of the House in the 2006 elections, Nancy Pelosi was elected the first female Speaker of the House. She lost that post after the Republicans gained a House majority in 2010 and elected John Boehner as Speaker. The ability of the Speaker to make the most of party power depends a great deal on how unified the party is on any given issue, or a whole range of issues, and on whether he or she represents the same party as the president. In the 112th and 113th Congresses, Speaker Boehner, with an opposite-party president, had the most difficulty holding his majority party together on votes related to federal spending and deficit reduction. On these issues, he faced both an internal party division and a small wing of the Republican majority, led by Tea Party–affiliated members, that did not want to cooperate with President Barack Obama under any circumstances.

In fact, cooperation broke down so severely over the federal budget and national debt in late 2013 that the government shut down for sixteen days (see Chapter 16, Economic, Domestic, and Foreign Policy, for a full discussion). To resolve this impasse, Speaker Boehner had to violate the Hastert Rule in order to make sure the government was funded and the debt ceiling was increased. These problems persisted throughout the 114th Congress until finally the pressure on Speaker Boehner grew so great that he resigned his office (and his seat in Congress) in October 2015. He was replaced as Speaker by Paul Ryan (R-WI), who had run for vice president with Mitt Romney on the Republican ticket in 2012 and subsequently served as chair of the House Ways and Means Committee before being elected Speaker.[27]

Bloomberg/Getty Images

IMAGE 12.6 Paul Ryan (R-WI) was elected Speaker of the House in October 2015 after John Boehner (R-OH) stepped down due to internal party divisions over his leadership. Ryan, who ran for vice president with Mitt Romney in 2012, is viewed as being better able to bridge the differences within the Republican majority in the House.

Whether he or she works with a same- or an opposite-party president, the Speaker's most important responsibility is to maintain power in the House for the majority party, and that means getting the members of the majority party reelected. To do so, the Speaker supports a set of policies that he or she believes are popular with voters, and he or she tries to get those policies enacted into law. For example, during the consideration of health care reform in the House, the Democrats shared the goal of passing a health care reform bill, so they allowed the Speaker to use all the tools at her disposal to get the bill passed. The Democrats suffered big losses in the 2010 elections in part due to voter backlash on this issue. For Speaker Boehner, the 2012 elections represented his first test of holding on to power in the House, and he focused his efforts on bringing bills to the House floor on issues such as federal aviation, transportation, and insider trading in Congress, all of which he knew had support within Congress and were popular with voters. By the time the 2014 elections came around, Boehner and the Republicans were more secure in holding the majority. Still, Pelosi and Boehner shared the dubious distinction of presiding over Congresses with some of the lowest approval ratings ever recorded; in early 2014, only 12 percent of Americans approved of the job that Congress was doing.[28] The numbers in 2016 were not much improved; only 27 percent of voters believed that incumbent members of Congress deserved to be reelected. For their own Congressional representatives, voters were a bit more generous, with a bare majority (51 percent) saying that their own member deserved reelection.[29]

House majority leader: *Leader of the majority party in the House and second in command to the Speaker.*

House Party Leaders. The **House majority leader**, as second in command, works with the Speaker to decide which issues the party will consider. He or she also coordinates with committee leaders on holding hearings and reporting bills to the House floor for a vote. The House majority leader must strike a compromise among many competing forces, including committee chairs and external interest groups. He or she is also expected to raise a significant amount of campaign contributions for party members, and that role produces more pressure to appease as many interest groups as possible. The majority leader also has nine majority whips to help "whip up" support for the party's preferred policies and keep lines of communication open between the party leadership and the rank-and-file membership. The majority leader and whips work hard to track members' intended votes—in a process called the whip count—because they want to bring to the floor only those bills that will pass; any defeat on the floor could weaken voter confidence in the majority party.[30]

House minority leader: *Leader of the minority party in the House.*

The minority party in the House is the party that has the largest number of House members who are not in the majority party. The highest-ranking member of the minority party is the **House minority leader**, and his or her main responsibility is crafting the minority party's position on an issue and serving as the public spokesperson for the party. If the minority party is the same as the president's party, the House minority leader is also expected to garner support for the president's policies among minority-party members. The House minority leader works with minority whips, who are responsible for keeping all the minority members in line with the party's public positions.

The challenge for the minority party in the House of Representatives is that it has very little institutional power; the majority party uses its numerical advantage to control committee and floor actions. Because of its institutional disadvantages, the minority party in the modern House of Representatives rarely has the power to stop majority party proposals from passing. Minority party members can vote no, but their real power lies in making speeches, issuing press releases, and stirring up grassroots opposition to majority party proposals.

The Senate

The Senate has always been a smaller chamber than the House because it is based on the number of states in the union and does not adjust according to population growth. Since 1959, when Hawaii and Alaska joined the union, the Senate has had 100 members, and the magic number to secure majority control in the Senate has been 51 senators. Not until the 1910s did senators formally appoint individual senators to speak for them as majority and minority party leaders. However, the Senate majority leader has fewer formal powers to advance the party's agenda compared to the Speaker of the House. Because the Senate never grew to be as large and unwieldy as the House, the individual members have rarely seen the benefit of giving up power to party leaders to make the Senate run efficiently or enact the party's agenda.

President Pro Tempore. Article I, Section 3, of the Constitution states that the vice president shall be the president of the Senate, but that in his absence the Senate may appoint a president pro tempore (temporary president) to preside over the Senate. For most of the Senate's history, the vice president presided over the Senate, and his main functions were to recognize individual senators who wished to speak and to rule on which procedural motions were in order on the Senate floor. The vice president can also break a tie vote in the Senate, a power that can give the president's party control of the outcome on the floor. But in the 1950s, the vice president became more active in executive branch business and less active in the Senate. Subsequently, the Senate began appointing the oldest serving member from the majority party as the president pro tempore. The president pro tempore is closely advised by the Senate parliamentarian, who is responsible for administering the rules of the Senate.

Senate Party Leaders. The majority party elects the **Senate majority leader**, but unlike the Speaker of the House, this position is not written into the Constitution. The job of the Senate majority leader is to make sure the Senate functions well enough to pass legislation. To accomplish that goal, the Senate majority leader tries to craft legislation as close to the preferred policies of his or her party as possible, necessitating a great deal of compromise and the "power of persuasion."[31]

Senate majority leader: *Leader of the majority party in the Senate.*

Essential Knowledge

The majority leader is the most powerful powerful person in the Senate. Although not as influential as the Speaker of the House, the majority leader has several key functions such as scheduling bills for consideration.

Still, the Senate majority leader does have several formal powers. For instance, he or she is the official scheduler of Senate business and is always recognized first to speak on the Senate floor. Every senator has the right to speak on the Senate floor, but senators must speak one at a time. Being recognized first, before any other senator, gives the majority leader the power to control the floor and prevent any other senator from speaking. But because the Senate majority leader relies on the senators' voluntary cooperation to conduct the business of the Senate, there are limits on how tough he or she can be on Senate colleagues. If a Senate majority leader tries to bully senators, they might retaliate by constantly using their individual floor powers to try to delay or block key legislation.

The **Senate minority leader** is the leader of the minority party in the Senate and is expected to represent minority-party senators in negotiations with the majority leader on which bills are brought to the Senate floor and under what circumstances. Similar to the House counterpart, the Senate minority leader's job is to organize minority-party senators into a coherent group that can present viable alternatives to the majority party's proposals.

Senate minority leader: *Leader of the minority party in the Senate.*

The extended leadership structure of the Senate looks similar to that of the House (see Figure 12.3). It consists of an assistant majority leader, majority and minority whips, and conference chairs, all of whom are responsible for uniting the senators in their respective parties and crafting legislative proposals that can garner enough support to pass the Senate.

Essential Knowledge

Each committee is run by a chair selected by the majority party, usually according to seniority. Furthermore, each committee has a majority of its members selected from the majority party.

The Committee System

Almost all legislation that passes the House or Senate goes through a committee. The House and Senate are organized into separate committees to deal with the different issues, such as agriculture, energy, and education. The party that has the majority in the entire House or Senate also has the majority of seats on each committee, and the committee chair is chosen from the majority party, with the approval of the party caucus. Typically, each House member or senator gives the party leadership a list of desired committee assignments, and the leadership assigns committee seats according to seniority and the availability of seats on specific committees.

The House and Senate each have several types of committees. A standing committee is a permanent committee with the power to write legislation and report it to the full chamber. Select committees, joint committees, and special committees are usually focused on a more narrow set of issues, such as aging or tax policy, but none has the same legislative clout and authority as a standing committee. In the House, there are twenty standing committees, and the average House committee has forty-three members. In the Senate, there

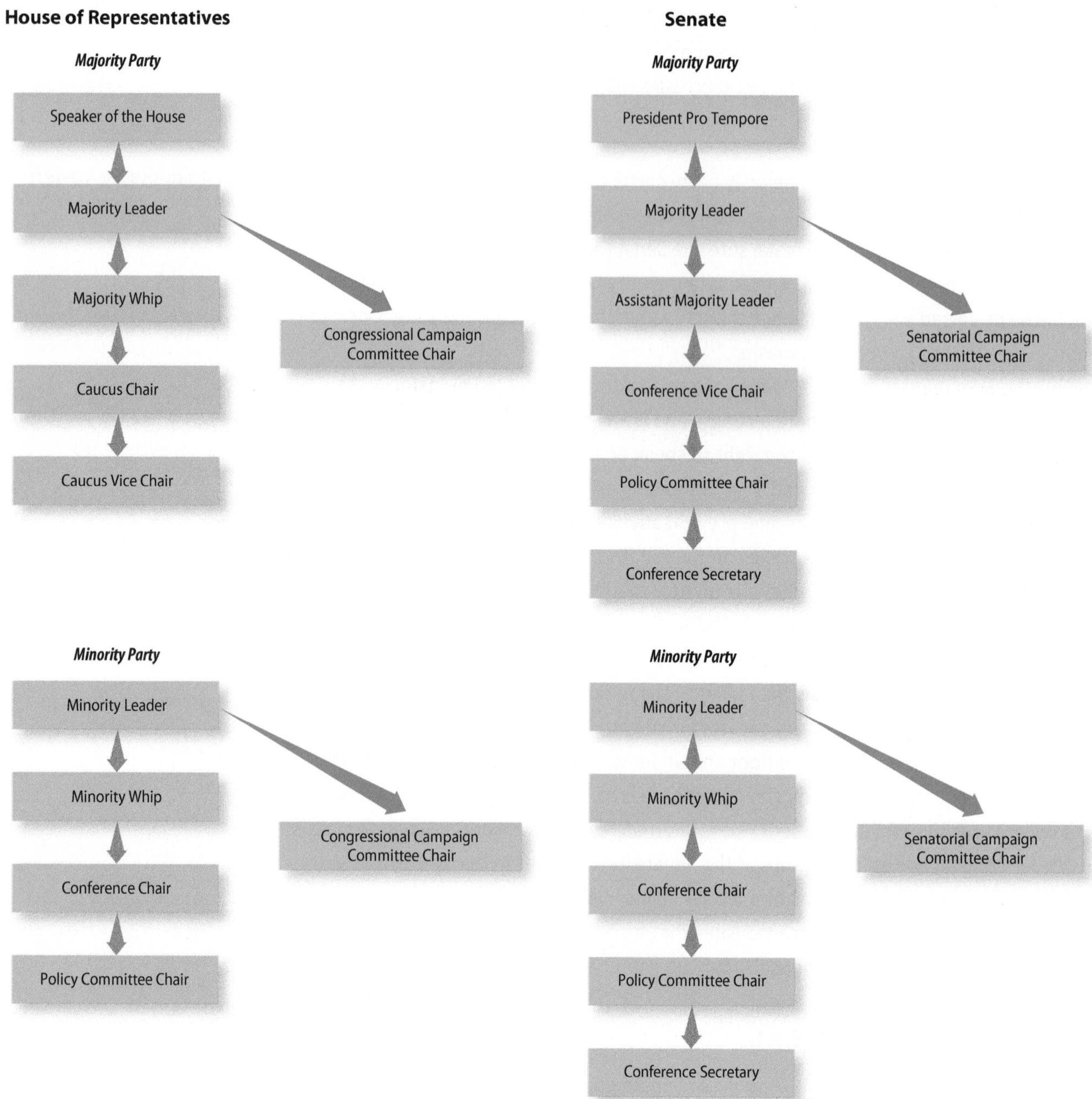

FIGURE 12.3 The Structure of Party Leadership in Congress

Each chamber of Congress has its own separate party leadership structure designed to help party leaders keep rank-and-file members united and accomplish the party's policy goals.

are sixteen standing committees, and the average Senate committee has twenty members. The committee system is the central hub of legislative activity in Congress.[32] Committees hold hearings to consider members' bills, to conduct oversight of the executive branch, or to draw attention to a pressing issue. Committees also write the legislation that is eventually considered on the House and Senate floors. Table 12.2 lists the standing committees in each chamber.

During committee hearings, committee members hear testimony on the content and impact of a bill from other members of Congress, executive branch officials, interest groups,

TABLE 12.2 Standing Committees in Congress

House of Representatives (20 committees)	Senate (16 committees)
Agriculture	Agriculture, Nutrition, and Forestry
Appropriations	Appropriations
Armed Services	Armed Services
Financial Services	Banking, Housing, and Urban Affairs
Budget	Budget
Education and the Workforce	Health, Education, Labor, and Pensions
Energy and Commerce	Commerce, Science, and Transportation Energy and Natural Resources Environment and Public Works
Foreign Affairs	Foreign Relations
Homeland Security	Homeland Security and Governmental Affairs
Oversight and Government Reform	
House Administration	Rules and Administration
Judiciary	Judiciary
Natural Resources	
Transportation and Infrastructure	
Rules	
Science, Space, and Technology	
Small Business	Small Business and Entrepreneurship
Ethics	
Veterans' Affairs	Veterans' Affairs
Ways and Means	Finance

Source: U.S. House of Representatives, http://www.house.gov/committees/; U.S. Senate, http://www.senate.gov/pagelayout/committees/d_three_sections_with_teasers/committees_home.htm. See the committee membership lists.

businesses, state and local government officials, and citizens' groups. For the public, hearings are a direct gateway for influence on members of Congress because important information is conveyed in a public setting. Committee hearings serve five basic functions for members of Congress: They draw attention to a current problem or issue that needs public attention, inform committee members about the consequences of passing a specific bill, convey constituents' questions and concerns about an issue, exert oversight of the executive branch to determine whether congressional intent is being honored, and provide an arena in which individual members make speeches to attract media attention that is often used later in a campaign as evidence that the member is doing his or her job. Committee chairs decide which bills receive hearings and which go on to **markup**, a meeting in which committee members write the version of the bill that they may send to the entire chamber for a vote. In both the hearing and markup process, the committee chair gives preference to the views of the majority-party members of the committee.

markup: *Process by which bills are literally marked up, or written, by the members of the committee.*

Committee chairs have powerful roles. The chair is typically the majority-party member who has the most seniority (longest time) on the committee. However, the Speaker or the Senate majority leader reserves the right to suggest a less senior member as chair if he or she believes that person will better serve the party's interests. One of the most dramatic uses of this power came in 2010, when the Republicans selected Fred Upton (R-MI) as chair of the Energy and Commerce Committee, passing over Joe Barton (R-TX), who had served as **ranking member**—the member of the committee from the minority party with the greatest seniority—since 2006. The party leadership believed that Congressman Barton's views were out of sync with the party majority, especially after his public apology to the BP oil company for the federal government's demand for a monetary settlement to pay for the cleanup of the Gulf oil spill. This case illustrates the steps that party leaders will take to maintain control over committee agendas through the selection of committee chairs. Additionally, the Republicans have a three-term limit on committee chairmanships; the Democrats do not. Term limits on chairmanships sustain the party's power to make a change in leadership of committees on a regular basis; in fact, Fred Upton ended his term as chair of the Energy and Commerce Committee in 2017 because his three terms were up.

ranking member: *Leader of the minority-party members of a committee.*

In general, when a bill is referred to a committee, it is assigned to a subcommittee, a smaller group of committee members who focus on a specific subset of the committee's issues. Subcommittees can consider legislation, but only the full committee can report a bill to the chamber floor for consideration. In 1973, the House expanded the number of subcommittees and subcommittee chairs, largely as a result of the efforts of young representatives who wanted to enact policies that older committee chairs opposed. By creating more subcommittees, the House created smaller centers of power in which individual members could exert influence over the content of legislation.[33] The Senate did not make similar changes; each senator already had individual power and did not see the need to make changes in the committee structure.

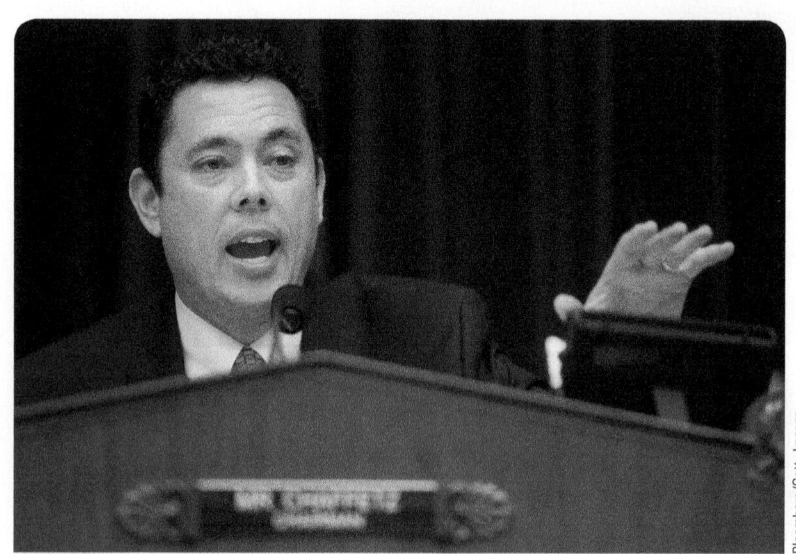

Bloomberg/Getty Images

IMAGE 12.7 Representative Jason Chaffetz (R-UT), chair of the House Committee on Oversight and Government Reform, presides over an investigative hearing.

Advocacy Caucuses

In addition to committees in the House and Senate, there are also advocacy caucuses, groups whose members have a common interest and work together to promote it. Members might have similar industries located in their districts and states, such as coal mining; share a background, such as the Hispanic Caucus, of which Representative Castro is a member; or hold similar opinions on issues, such as abortion or land conservation. Members join an advocacy caucus because it gives them an opportunity to work closely with colleagues to represent specific interests and to draw attention to issues of concern to them and to their constituents. Many advocacy caucuses are bipartisan—that is, both Democrats and Republicans join as members. Advocacy caucuses are important to the interactions of Congress because they bring together members from different parties and regions that might not otherwise work closely with each other.[34]

Nearly three hundred advocacy caucuses are registered with the Committee on House Administration. In contrast, the Senate has only one official caucus, on international narcotics control. However, the Senate has a number of informal caucuses, such as the Senate Air Force Caucus and the Senate Steel Caucus, with members from both parties.

Advocacy caucuses have no formal legislative power, but they can be influential on a bill, especially in the House, because they represent a bloc of members who could vote together in support or opposition. As an alternative to joining a caucus, senators can join together in a temporary coalition and call a press conference to draw attention to the group, industry, or issue that unites them. Senators can also join a congressional caucus even though it is lodged in the House. When he was a senator from Illinois (2005–08), former President Barack Obama joined the Congressional Black Caucus.

12.4 The Lawmaking Process

Explain how a law is made in Congress

In this section, we examine the lawmaking process. The process by which a policy proposal becomes a bill and then a law is long and winding, and the Framers designed it deliberately to ensure that laws were reasonable and well thought out. The gates against passage are almost too successful. In the 113th Congress (2013–14), members introduced 5,899 public bills in the House of Representatives and 3,020 public bills in the Senate. Of the total 8,919 bills, Congress enacted only 297—or 3.3 percent—into law.[35] Passing a law requires compromise and cooperation; for an overview of the process, see Figure 12.4.

Essential Knowledge

The constructional rules and the legislative procedures of each house make it very difficult to pass legislation. The number of chamber and debate rules set the bar high for building majority support.

The Procedural Rules of the House and Senate

Just as the roles of political parties and leaders differ in the House and Senate, so do the internal rules of these chambers. Over time, House and Senate members have adopted different procedures for considering legislation, and these procedures can make compromise between the two chambers more difficult.

Essential Knowledge

The House Rules Committee writes a rule for each bill, which regulates debate time and amendments.

The House Committee on Rules. To proceed from committee to the House floor, all bills must pass through the House Rules Committee. Because the House is so large, bills cannot proceed to the floor from committee unprotected; otherwise, the number of legislative amendments that could be offered by the 435 members of the House would overwhelm lawmaking.

The Rules Committee maintains control before the bill goes to the floor by issuing a **rule** dictating how many amendments may be considered. A closed rule means that no amendments may be offered; a modified closed rule allows a few amendments; and an open rule, as its name suggests, allows any number of amendments. The most typical rule is a

rule: *Guidelines issued by the House Rules Committee that determine how many amendments may be considered for each bill.*

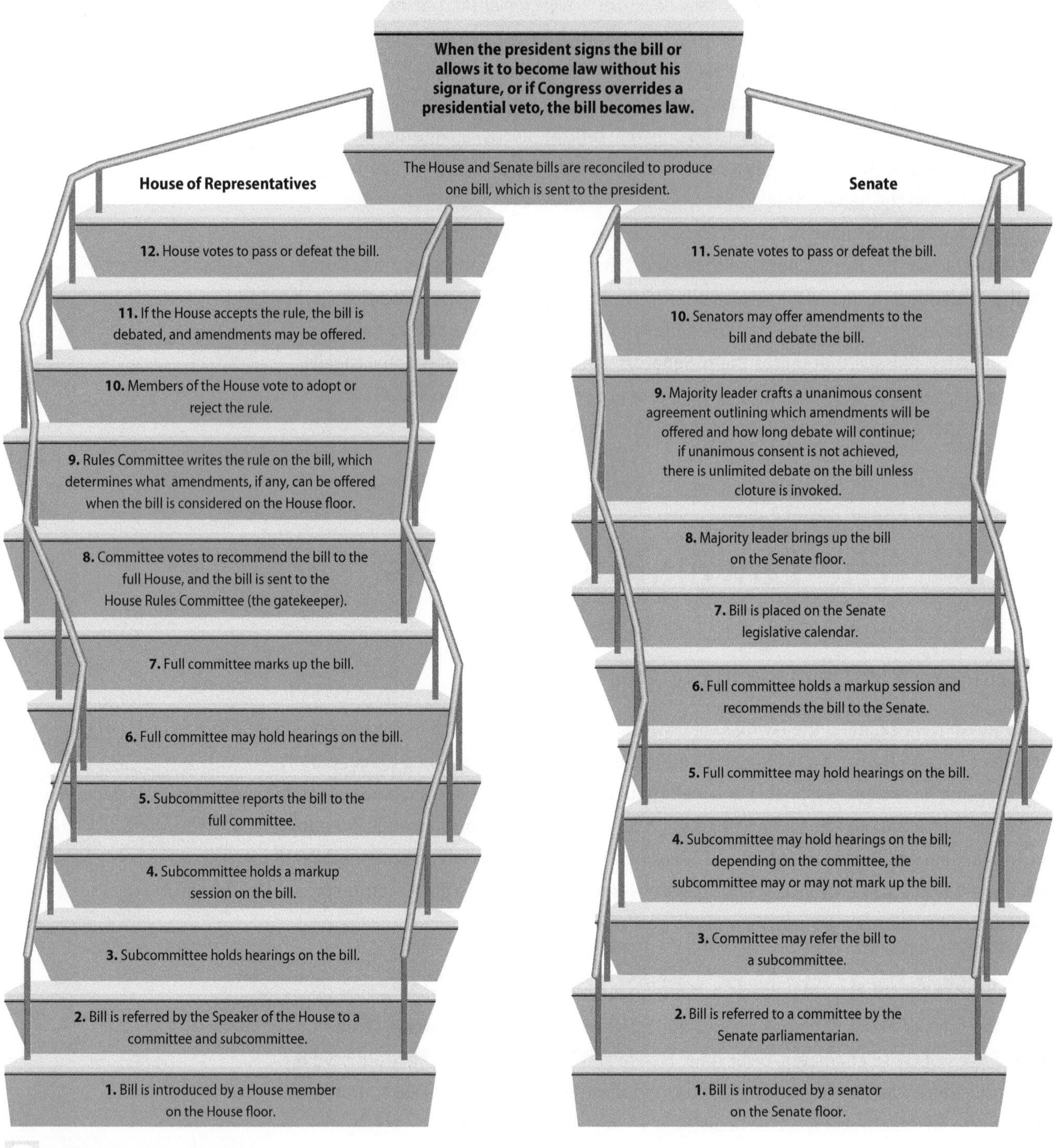

FIGURE 12.4 How a Bill Becomes a Law

The path by which a bill becomes a law is a long and winding one with lots of obstacles in the way to final enactment. Members of the House and Senate introduce thousands of bills in each Congress, but a very small percentage of them are ever signed into law.

modified closed rule, which allows the minority party to offer at least one alternative to the bill supported by the majority party. The rule is voted on by all members of the House; if it is approved, debate on the bill begins. If the rule is defeated, the bill is returned to the House Rules Committee or the originating committee for further consideration.

The majority party has learned over time how to use the Rules Committee to maintain policy advantages over the minority party. The majority party uses its numerical advantage on the Rules Committee (9–4 in the 113th Congress) to structure floor debate to limit the minority party's opportunity to amend or change a bill. The Speaker appoints all the majority-party members to the Rules Committee, and they are expected to use their powers to advance the party's preferred version of a bill.

Agenda-Setting Tools in the Senate. The Senate does not have a gatekeeper committee like the Committee on Rules in the House, and all senators have the power to try to amend legislation on the floor. The tool that they use is Rule XIX of the Standing Rules of the Senate, which grants senators the right to speak on the Senate floor. Over time, senators have used this right to make speeches, offer amendments to bills, object to consideration of a bill on the floor, or engage in a **filibuster**, an extended debate that members start with the purpose of delaying or even preventing the passage of a bill.[36] All senators in the majority and the minority parties can use the filibuster. Throughout Senate history, a wide range of bills, from civil rights legislation to product liability legislation, have been delayed or defeated by filibusters.[37]

filibuster: *Tactic of extended speech designed to delay or block passage of a bill in the Senate.*

The only way to stop a filibuster is by invoking **cloture**, a motion to end debate that requires a supermajority of sixty votes to pass. In November 2013, the Democratic majority, led by Senator Harry Reid (D-NV), changed the threshold for cloture on presidential nominations and judicial nominations for district and appeals court judges to fifty-one rather than sixty. This made it easier for President Obama to get his nominees confirmed because the Democrats had a working majority of fifty-five members, which meant that approval for these nominees was virtually guaranteed and could not be blocked by the Republicans. This was an historic change; the Senate had not changed the cloture threshold since 1975, when it lowered it from two-thirds of the Senate (sixty-seven) to three-fifths (sixty).

cloture: *Vote that can stop a filibuster and bring debate on a bill to end.*

However, this cloture change was not without significant controversy. Typically major rules changes in the Senate require two-thirds of Senators to agree, but in this case, the majority party used procedural tools to get around this requirement. When the Republicans blocked an Obama judicial nominee for the Court of Appeals, Senator Reid made a motion to reduce the threshold for cloture for judicial nominations other than for the Supreme Court to fifty-one votes rather than sixty votes. The presiding officer of the Senate, who chairs the proceedings, ruled that Reid's motion was out of order. Reid in turn asked for a roll call vote; it takes only a majority of the Senate to accept or reject the ruling of the chair. The Democrats had fifty-five votes, and fifty-two of them voted to reject the ruling of the chair, which allowed Reid's motion to replace existing rules and effectively eliminate the filibuster on presidential executive branch nominees and federal judges (except for the Supreme Court).[38]

However, it is important to note that the Democrats did not seek to eliminate the sixty-vote threshold for filibustering legislation. Given that the majority control of the Senate and the White House can change hands, it was deemed too risky to shut off the option in case the Democrats became the minority party in the Senate and lost the White House in 2016. It is clear from the action by the Democrats that a simple majority of the Senate has the authority to eliminate the filibuster at any point that it desires. After cloture has been invoked on a bill, no more than thirty additional hours of debate are permitted. All amendments must be germane to the bill's issues, and a time for a final vote is set. Figure 12.5 illustrates the variation in the number of cloture motions in the Senate over time.

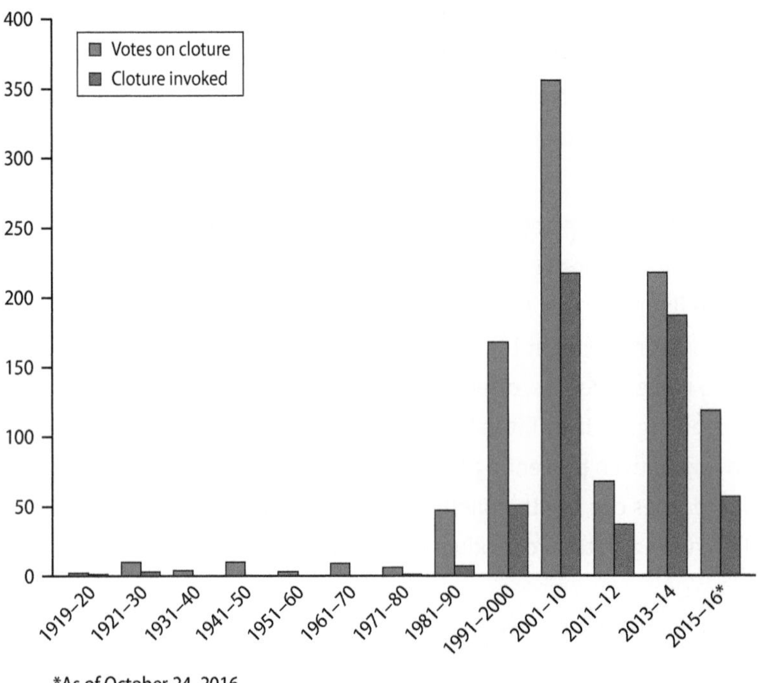

FIGURE 12.5 Senate Action on Cloture Motions, 1919–2016

In November 2013, the number of votes required to invoke cloture on executive nominations and federal judicial nominations lower than the Supreme Court was lowered from sixty votes to fifty-one votes.

Source: U.S. Senate, http://www.senate.gov/pagelayout/reference/cloture_motions/clotureCounts.htm.

In addition, Senate rules no longer require those seeking to block a bill to speak continuously on the floor. Senators who oppose a bill can merely state their intention to filibuster, and that will be sufficient to block the bill from consideration on the floor. Senators also use the threat of a filibuster to block the president's Supreme Court nominations, a practice that has come under increasing scrutiny. Filibusters of this type are an expression of partisanship or ideology, and they can disrupt the operation of the federal courts.[39] To counteract the filibuster in recent years, the Senate has resorted to a two-track system in which a bill that is being filibustered can be set aside to allow the Senate to proceed to other bills. But even with this two-track system, the filibuster has imposed substantial costs on the Senate, both in terms of the legislation that has failed to pass and the legislation that could not be brought to the floor.

Some scholars have argued that the filibuster has been used too frequently as a way of blocking action on important public policies and is not a legitimate democratic instrument of power. Others argue that filibustering is a responsive and effective means of representation in Congress; if there is intense opposition to a bill in a senator's state, or from a minority of voters nationwide, the senator may consider it a responsibility to block the bill's passage.[40]

Without a gatekeeper like the House Committee on Rules and with the constant threat of a filibuster, there are few restrictions on a bill when it comes to the Senate floor. When the Senate majority leader wishes to bring a bill up for consideration, he or she must ask for unanimous consent. Consequently, the Senate typically operates under **unanimous consent agreements** to establish guidelines for debating a bill. Senators strike a deal about how a bill will be debated on the Senate floor, how and when amendments will be offered, how much time will be allocated to debate and vote on amendments, and at what time on what date the final vote on the complete bill will take place. Senators have accepted this form of limitation on their rights to amend or block a bill because it requires their consent and enables the Senate to move forward and pass key legislation.

unanimous consent agreement: *Agreement among all 100 senators on how a bill or presidential nomination will be debated, changed, and voted on in the Senate.*

Nevertheless, a senator can object to a unanimous consent request to bring a bill to the Senate floor in a practice known as a **hold**. A hold is a less drastic measure than a filibuster, but it can be used by any senator to delay a bill for a minimum of twenty-four hours. The majority leader can circumvent a hold by requesting a vote on cloture; if sixty senators agree, the Senate proceeds to consider the bill. Typically, senators hold up bills to extract concessions from Senate leaders or from the president's administration on the legislation being considered. They also use the hold to draw increased attention to a bill in the hope that public opposition will develop. Twenty-four hours may not seem like a long time, but in an age of 24-7 media and the Internet, public impressions can form quickly. For example, in March 2010, Senator Jim Bunning (R-KY) used his power to object to unanimous consent to delay a bill that would have extended benefits to unemployed workers. Although he explained that he was doing so to avoid increased deficit spending, the bill was perceived by members of both parties to be vital. Senate leaders managed to bring sufficient public pressure to bear on Bunning, and he dropped his objection; in fact, he subsequently decided to retire from the Senate. As we noted previously, ironically, his replacement, Senator Rand Paul (R-KY), has made full use of his individual powers to delay legislation by exercising the hold and filibustering.

hold: *Power available to a senator to prevent the unanimous consent that allows a bill or presidential nomination to come to the Senate floor, which can be broken by invoking cloture (currently sixty votes on most items).*

Legislative Proposals

The lawmaking process starts with an idea. Ideas for legislation can come from a number of sources, including constituents, interest groups, local or national newspaper stories, state or local governments, staff members, and the members' own personal interests.[41] When an idea is agreed on, the House or Senate member's staff consults with the Office of Legislative Counsel, which turns the general outlines of a bill into the technical language that will alter the U.S. Code, the set of federal laws that governs the United States. After approving the final legal language of a bill, the member introduces the bill into the respective chamber (House or Senate), an action known as bill sponsorship. After a bill is introduced, other members can sign on to be cosponsors (sponsorship of legislation is discussed in more detail later in this chapter). In reality, many freestanding bills that are introduced separately are later incorporated into larger omnibus bills that are passed by Congress. Combining bills into omnibus legislation can be useful, especially in periods of divided government. These big bills allow Congress to pass numerous provisions that might not pass if each were presented separately.[42]

Essential Knowledge

Congress is often described as "government by committee." Committees in Congress are where the real work of legislating takes place. This is also where hearings are conducted and where most debate takes place.

Committee Action

After a member introduces a bill, it is referred to one or more committees or subcommittees that have jurisdiction over its subject matter. The first step in getting the bill enacted into law is to secure a hearing on a bill in subcommittee or full committee. In general, a

Essential Knowledge

Occasionally, the entire House of Representatives will act as a committee. This process is called Committee of the Whole. During this time there are fewer rules on debate and amendments.

committee tends to act first on bills that are sponsored by the chair of the committee, then on those sponsored by the subcommittee chairs, and last on bills sponsored by regular members of the committee. If the sponsor is not on the committee to which the bill is assigned, it is much harder to get action on the bill. This arrangement also makes sense because committee members are more likely to have expertise on the issues covered by the committee than are other legislators, so their bills are taken more seriously by their fellow committee members.[43] In rare cases, however, as a result of intense interest group lobbying or media pressure, a committee might hold a hearing on a bill sponsored by someone who is not a committee member, but the committee typically drafts its own bill to address the same issue.

Essential Knowledge

If a bill is stalled in committee in the House of Representatives, the bill can be removed from the committee and advanced to the floor through the use of a discharge petition.

After the hearings, the committee may move to the markup. At this point, the stakes intensify in terms of what the bill will ultimately look like, so the stakeholders in the policy process try to exert influence. In this era of increased partisanship and party leadership control, committees have less freedom to craft legislation that differs from the leadership's goals. After the full committee approves a bill, it and an accompanying committee report are sent to the full House or Senate for consideration by all members.

Floor Action and the Vote

When a bill is sent to the full House or Senate—commonly known as "going to the floor"—all the members of the chamber gather to debate and vote on it. Debate takes different forms in each chamber. In the House, it is heavily structured, and most members are allowed no more than five minutes to speak on a measure, leaving almost no time for actual deliberation among members. In contrast, the Senate has few limits on the time allowed for members to speak on an issue on the floor. If the Senate is operating under a unanimous consent agreement or cloture, time is limited; otherwise, senators can make speeches and even engage in active debate on an issue for much longer than their House counterparts. Unfortunately for the current political system, real debate rarely occurs on the floor; instead, representatives and senators use their opportunity to speak to make partisan speeches or to direct their remarks to their constituents back home, knowing that the proceedings are televised by C-SPAN and C-SPAN2.

Essential Knowledge

Because the House is larger, debate there is highly structured (or formal). There are strict time limits. In the Senate, which is smaller, there are fewer rules for debate.

During a roll call vote, the clerks of the House or Senate call the name of each member, who registers his or her vote electronically. Members cast up or down votes to pass or reject legislation, to table (set aside) legislation, or to approve a motion to recommit (send it back to committee with instructions to rewrite it). In addition to individually recorded votes, general voice votes can be taken when a consensus exists and there is no perceived need to record each member's vote.

Essential Knowledge

Members of Congress may perceive themselves as delegates, focused on carrying out the wishes of their constituents, trustees whose task is instead to exercise independent judgment of what would be best for constituents, or as politicos who balance the two methodologies as is expedient.

A roll call vote is the most fundamental way that a member of Congress represents his or her constituents. When members of Congress cast their votes, they can act as trustees who exercise independent judgment about what they believe is best for the people or as delegates who do exactly as the people wish. Over time, congressional representation has evolved into a hybrid of both types of representation; thus, members of Congress act as both trustees and delegates. Roll call voting is therefore a key gateway for citizen influence in the legislative process.

Scholars have long characterized roll call voting by partisan dimension and by ideological or spatial dimension because in the past both the Democratic and Republican Parties contained both liberals and conservatives.[44] Currently, the vast majority of Democratic members are liberal and the vast majority of Republican members are conservative. Consequently, scholars now can examine roll call voting through both the partisan and ideological lens simultaneously. They confirm that most members of the House and Senate vote along party lines; in the 113th Congress, in the House, 92 percent of Republicans and 89 percent of Democrats voted with their party; in the Senate, 84 percent of Republicans and 90 percent of Democrats voted with their party. Overall, 70 percent of all votes taken in the House and 68 percent of all votes in the Senate divided along party lines.[45] Party leaders in Congress frame the content of bills and the choices for roll call votes along the lines of party platforms and ideology. Essentially, they are engaging in what is called message politics, designing legislation to push members into casting votes that may later be used in campaigns against them.[46] This framework reflects a responsible parties system (see Chapter 9) in which voters can clearly distinguish Democratic and Republican legislative policy goals. Although the increased emphasis on partisanship makes it easier for citizens to more clearly hold Congress accountable, it decreases the likelihood of bipartisan cooperation and makes passing legislation more difficult.

Conference Committee

For a bill to become law, the House and Senate have to pass an identically worded version of it to send to the president for his or her signature. The last stage in the congressional legislative process takes place when the House and Senate meet in conference committee to resolve any differences in the versions that passed each chamber. The Speaker of the House and the Senate majority leader typically appoint the chairs and ranking members from the committees that originated the bills, plus other members who have been active on the bill. If the bill is very important to the party leaders, they also have the power to appoint themselves to the committee. If the conferees can reach agreement, the conference committee issues a conference report that must be voted on by the entire House and Senate. Because the conference report represents the end of the negotiation process between the two chambers, members cannot offer amendments to change it. However, if a majority of members of the House or Senate are displeased with the final results of the conference, they can defeat the report outright or vote to instruct the conference committee to revise the agreement.

In the past twenty years, Congress has decreased its use of conference committees. Instead, party leaders take on the responsibility of producing a final bill themselves. In choosing this path, they concentrate power in the hands of fewer members of Congress than in the traditional conference committee system.[47] Although this alternative provides a more streamlined way of legislating, it also acts as a gate against input from committee members who wish to represent their constituents' views on the final version of the bill.

The Budget Process and Reconciliation

federal budget deficit: *Difference between the amount of money the federal government spends in outlays and the amount of money it receives from revenues.*

Although the federal government tries to spend about as much money as it takes in from revenues, it does not typically succeed. Instead, it usually runs a **federal budget deficit**, which requires it to borrow money to meet all its obligations (see Chapter 16 for more detail on current deficits and national debt). Although the process is complex, essentially

PUBLIC POLICY AND CONGRESS

Unemployment Insurance

In times of economic difficulty, Congress is often asked to act quickly to help individuals in need of income support. During the Great Depression, President Franklin Delano Roosevelt (1933–45) proposed a number of programs that would try to help workers get back on their feet and provide a safety net for their retirement years. The Social Security Act of 1935 set out to accomplish a number of these goals, and we discuss it in depth in Chapter 16. As part of the Social Security Act, Congress enacted a program designed to provide temporary cash payments to unemployed workers who have lost their jobs, due to downsizing or layoffs, known as Unemployment Insurance. Workers who quit their jobs or are fired from their jobs are not eligible for Unemployment Insurance. In nearly all states, Unemployment Insurance is funded by a tax on employers, which is collected by the federal government and placed in the Unemployment Trust Fund, but the program is administered by state governments. Although the federal government gives states the power to run the program, it sets basic rules for its administration.

Since its creation, the Unemployment Insurance program has grown from covering businesses that employ eight or more workers to any business that employs one or more workers, essentially covering the entire workforce. Typically, unemployment benefits are available for twenty-six weeks before an individual exhausts his or her benefits. However, during economic crisis periods, Congress has agreed to extend unemployment insurance for longer periods of time and provide federal funding to states to pay for the extra weeks of benefits for unemployed workers.

Such was the case in 2008 when the housing and stock market declines left a lot of people without work. President George W. Bush worked with a Democratic-controlled House and Senate to pass a federally funded extension program, called Emergency Unemployment Compensation (EUC), that allowed workers to collect Unemployment Insurance for up to seventy-three weeks on top of the twenty-six weeks normally allowed, for a total of ninety-nine weeks of eligible benefits. In February 2009, shortly after President Obama took office, the unemployment rate stood at 8.3 percent, and he requested that Congress extend EUC as part of the American Recovery and Reinvestment Act of 2009, otherwise known as the stimulus package.[48] The Democratic-controlled Congress passed that bill, and the extended time frame for benefits lasted until June 1, 2010. However, the unemployment rate had increased in the intervening year, and after several short-term renewals, in December 2010, President Obama worked with Congress to renew EUC through June 2012.

After the House Republicans took control of the House of Representatives in 2011, it was unclear whether future renewals of extended unemployment would be possible because of their general opposition to longer-term government relief programs. Proponents of extended unemployment benefits argue that by giving cash benefits to individuals who are out of work, the government is helping to keep the economy afloat. By some estimates every dollar paid out in unemployment benefits generates $1.60 in return.[49] However, opponents argue that extending unemployment benefits beyond twenty-six weeks discourages individuals from taking jobs that might pay less than the value of their unemployment benefits. In turn, individuals who stay out of the workforce for longer periods of time have a more difficult time finding jobs, thereby creating an entrenched cycle of long-term unemployment.

Despite these objections, the Republicans in the House did agree to renew EUC through January 2, 2013, because unemployment continued to be very high, but they insisted on reducing the total number of weeks a recipient could receive benefits.[50] As it was set to expire at the end of 2012, Congress and President Obama agreed to renew the program for one more year as part of a larger bill that also extended tax cuts that were enacted in the Bush administration.

However, in December 2013, as EUC was again set to expire, the unemployment rate stood at 6.7 percent, and Republicans in the House and Senate argued that it was no longer necessary to extend unemployment benefits past the traditional twenty-six weeks. Because the Republicans controlled the House of Representatives, it was not possible to renew the program without their support. In the months that followed in 2014, President Obama negotiated with the U.S. Senate, which was controlled by the Democrats, and asked for bipartisan support from Republican Senators to put pressure on the House Republicans to support a limited extension of EUC. The Senate did pass a temporary extension in April 2014, but the House did not take up the measure; with unemployment rates falling steadily through September 2014, the Congress adjourned without passing the extension. The extension of unemployment insurance was an effective tool in helping individuals who lost their jobs during the Great Recession, but in times of job growth, the political incentive to extend these benefits is reduced. In fall 2016, the national unemployment rate stood at 5 percent.

Public Policy Connections

1. To what extent does the national government have an obligation to intervene in the economy by created welfare programs?
2. How can Congress control the growth of entitlements considering that once established, entitlement programs are difficult to eliminate?

this means that the federal government pays interest on outstanding loans, and the loans and interest that accumulate over time constitute the **national debt**.

The modern Congress operates under a budget process created in the Congressional Budget and Impoundment Control Act of 1974, which was enacted to give Congress more power over the federal budget.[51] It was passed at a time of relatively low deficits, but many new government programs were being implemented and government financial obligations were steadily rising. The act created the House and Senate Budget Committees and the Congressional Budget Office so that Congress could construct its own budget blueprint as an alternative to the president's annual budget.

The federal government's fiscal year begins on October 1 and ends on September 30, and the key aspect of the budget process is that the congressional budget, known as the **concurrent budget resolution**, is supposed to be approved by both chambers by April 15. Because the budget resolution does not have the force of law, it is not sent to the president for his or her signature; rather, it serves as general instructions to congressional committees about how much money can be allocated for federal programs in the fiscal year. The authorizing committees take this blueprint into account when they reauthorize existing programs or create new ones, and the appropriations committees in the House and Senate use it to allocate funds in twelve separate bills. They typically begin their work in May in the hope of enacting all appropriations bills by September 30. If Congress and the president fail to agree on any one of the twelve appropriations bills, Congress enacts a **continuing resolution** that funds the government temporarily while disagreements about spending are worked out.

national debt: *Sum of loans and interest that the federal government has accrued over time to pay for the federal deficit.*

Essential Knowledge

The budget created by Congress covers both discretionary and mandatory spending. As mandatory spending (particularly entitlements) increases, the availability of funds for discretionary items will decrease.

concurrent budget resolution: *Congressional blueprint outlining general amounts of funds that can be spent on federal programs.*

continuing resolution: *Measure passed to fund federal programs when the appropriations process has not been completed by September 30, the end of the fiscal year.*

From 2009 to 2012, the House of Representatives passed a budget resolution, but the Senate did not. This failure to produce a concurrent budget resolution left the appropriations process less structured. As a result, Congress relies more heavily on continuing resolutions than on passing separate appropriations bills. Congress's failure to produce a budget resolution makes it more difficult for voters to hold it accountable for federal budget policy. In December 2013, Congress broke the trend and passed a two-year budget bill that essentially lasted until October 1, 2015. In November 2015, after the new Speaker of the House had taken office, Congress passed a new budget bill that President Obama signed, which funded the government until October 1, 2016. In September 2016, Congress and the president agreed to a short-term continuing resolution to fund the government through December 9, 2016. For more details on the conflicts surrounding budget bills, see Chapter 16.

The new Speaker also secured several big legislative victories by passing a multiyear infrastructure bill that had been stuck in Congress for several years and passing a revised multiyear reauthorization of the Elementary and Secondary Education Act. For a Congress that had been virtually at a standstill in working with a Democratic president, these were significant legislative accomplishments.

reconciliation: *A measure used to bring all bills that contain changes in the tax code or entitlement programs in line with the congressional budget.*

The 1974 Budget Act created a parallel budget bill, known as **reconciliation**, which does require the president's signature. Reconciliation was specifically designed as umbrella legislation to bring all bills that contain changes in the tax code or entitlement programs in line with the congressional budget. Entitlement programs, such as Social Security, Medicare, and Medicaid, are considered mandatory because they pay out benefits to individuals based on a specified set of eligibility criteria. When Congress wants to make a change to one of these programs, it must pass a reconciliation bill. The reconciliation bill has special procedural protections in the Senate: It cannot be filibustered, and it can be debated for no more than twenty hours. A bill that cannot be filibustered was a tempting target for those who wanted to add nonbudget-related provisions. Consequently, in 1985, the budget process was modified to include the Byrd Rule, which required that reconciliation be used only to reduce the federal deficit, which at the time was $212.3 billion.[52] In subsequent years, the Byrd Rule has been interpreted to mean that all provisions of reconciliation must be directly related to the budget.[53]

Despite the Byrd Rule, Congress has found ways to use the reconciliation process to pass controversial legislation. In 2010, the Democratic majority in Congress used it to pass part of its comprehensive health care reform, commonly known as Obamacare. Both Democrats and Republicans have used the reconciliation process to go beyond changes in the tax code, or to balance the budget, on issues ranging from welfare reform to children's health insurance.[54]

Presidential Signature or Veto, and the Veto Override

In the last step in the legislative process, the bill is sent to the president for his approval or rejection. A president can actively reject, or veto, a bill. If Congress will be going out of session within ten days, the president can wait for the session to end and simply not sign the bill, a practice known as a pocket veto. If Congress remains in session and the president neither vetoes the bill nor signs it, the bill becomes law.

override: *Congress's power to overturn a presidential veto with a two-thirds vote in each chamber.*

The veto is a powerful balancing tool for the president against the overreach of Congress; however, the Framers also gave Congress the **override**, which is the power to overturn a presidential veto with a two-thirds vote in each chamber. When the president vetoes a bill, it is returned to the chamber from which it originated; if two-thirds of the members of that chamber vote to override the veto, it is sent to the other chamber for a vote. A two-thirds vote by each chamber, rather than just a majority vote, is required for an override because the Framers wanted to enable the president to block a bill passed by Congress if he does not believe that it is in the best interest of the nation as a whole. The president can use the veto either to prevent a bill from becoming law or to pressure Congress into making changes that are closer to his policies.[55]

12.5 The Member of Congress at Work

Assess what a member of Congress does

The cardinal rule of succeeding in the House or Senate is simple: Never forget where you came from. Representative Joaquín Castro has shown how a member tries to balance the competing demands of legislating with the core responsibility of serving constituents. The following sections describe exactly what the job of a House or Senate member entails.

Offices and Staff

For all newly elected members in the House and Senate, the first steps are to set up an office and hire staff members. In the House, each representative receives about the same amount of money for office operations. In the Senate, the office budget is determined by the population of the senator's state, based on the reasoning that senators from larger states have more constituents and more issues to deal with than their smaller-state colleagues. Most members bring some of their campaign workers to Washington to work on their staffs and try to hire people from their districts or states. New members of Congress also seek out individuals with prior Capitol Hill experience to help orient them to their new surroundings and provide specific issue expertise.

Generally, a member of Congress's Washington office has a chief of staff who oversees the entire office, a scheduler who makes the member's appointments, a press secretary who handles all interactions with the media, and a legislative director who supervises the member's legislative work. In addition, legislative assistants handle specific issues, and legislative correspondents are responsible for answering constituent letters, phone calls, and e-mails.

House and Senate members aim to be responsive to constituents, and that means providing prompt and extensive constituent services. To do so, they establish district offices in the congressional district for representatives and around the state for senators. These offices help constituents navigate federal agencies if they have difficulty—for example, getting a Social Security check or a passport—and advise constituents on how to win federal contracts. Specific requests for help are assigned to caseworkers. These local offices serve as direct and important links between voters and members of Congress and affect both accountability and responsiveness.[56]

Legislative Responsibilities

A successful legislator typically fulfills four responsibilities: securing desired committee assignments and performing committee work, sponsoring and cosponsoring bills, casting votes, and obtaining federal funds for the district or state.

Committee Work. Just before the start of each new Congress, members are asked which committees they would like to join, and party leaders try to accommodate their wishes, although freshman members rarely get their most favored committees immediately. Freshman members choose committee assignments based on the needs of their district or state, their professional background, their personal experience, and their desire to increase chances for reelection. A House member from Oregon might seek a seat on the House Natural Resources Committee because that committee oversees logging and other land use issues that are important to constituents. A senator from Iowa might seek membership on the Senate Agriculture, Nutrition, and Forestry Committee because farming is a key economic interest in that state. However, a new senator has to accommodate his or her committee assignment wish list to the reality of the existing committee assignments of the senior senator from the state. All members of the House and Senate try to put themselves in the best possible institutional position to address issues that matter to their constituents.

Committee work consists of attending hearings and participating in markups as well as initiating ideas for legislation for consideration by the committee. Committee members also meet with interest groups, businesses, and citizens' groups that are specifically concerned about bills to be considered in the committee. The extent to which members participate actively in committee business varies according to the local concerns of their constituents, their personal interests, and whether the committee might provide an opportunity for political advancement.[57]

Committees themselves provide different gateways for members to serve their constituents and advance their careers. For example, the Appropriations Committee and the Environment and Public Works Committee distribute federal funds for a wide range of programs and projects and thereby provide an opportunity for members to influence how these funds are spent. Serving on other committees, such as the Armed Services Committee, can provide members with credentials in the area of defense policy, which can be useful if they represent areas with high military employment or envision themselves running for president one day.

Bill Sponsorship. Members can sponsor a bill by themselves, or they can ask colleagues to cosponsor bills with them; the more cosponsors, the greater the show of support for the bill. Members sponsor and cosponsor bills for three important reasons. First, bill sponsorship is an effective tool for giving voters in a district or state a voice in the federal policy-making system. Second, it is a means of staking out specific territory that members can claim as their area of expertise and can be a means of fulfilling campaign promises.[58] Third, it attracts the attention of the media, relevant interest groups, and the press and thereby can help House and Senate members build their reputations as legislators.

Roll Call Votes. Each representative and senator is expected to cast a roll call vote on the bills and amendments that reach the floor of the House and Senate. In the House alone, members cast 547 roll call votes during the 113th Congress, and senators cast 657 roll call votes.[59] Given the large number of roll call votes, voters have difficulty identifying how their members of Congress voted on bills that affect them directly. Because most members of Congress vote the party line, party identification can be helpful in holding members accountable for their roll call votes. If members do not vote the party line, they risk losing the support of party voters in their district or state. However, most members will not vote for a measure that goes against their constituents' opinions or interests. For this reason, majority party leaders try to construct bills that will benefit the constituents of the members of their party.

Federal Funds. Most members of Congress try to secure federal funds for their districts and states. The effort to carve out some piece of the federal financial pie is typically referred to as "bringing home the bacon" or pork barrel spending, and it can work through funding formulas for federal programs or **earmarks**, which are narrowly defined federally funded projects.[60] Federal funds can be used to rebuild a highway, build a fairground, fund a local orchestra, construct a research center on the effects of pig odor, and even support a water taxi service in Connecticut. One of the most controversial earmarks ever was the so-called bridge to nowhere in Alaska championed by the late Senator Theodore (Ted) Stevens (R-AK). A bipartisan group of members of Congress, as well as public watchdog groups, raised media awareness about the enormous cost of this bridge. In response, the House and Senate directed the state of Alaska to spend the money allocated for the bridge on more important transportation projects.[61] Over the past decade, spending on earmarks has increased; in fiscal year 2010, $16.5 billion was authorized to fund 9,129 earmarks.[62] When the Republicans won control of the House of Representatives, they proposed a total ban on earmarks beginning in 2011, which the Senate also adopted. It is not clear that this ban actually eliminates the kind of localized spending that earmarks directed toward constituents because now legislators find ways to hide their efforts to direct federal dollars back home. For this reason, it may be that the ban on earmarks actually makes it harder for voters to hold Congress accountable for federal spending.

earmark: *Federal dollars devoted specifically to a local project in a congressional district or state.*

Essential Knowledge

Pork barrel legislation and logrolling affect lawmaking in both chambers. Earmarks and other forms of "pork" are ways in which coalitions are assembled to pass legislation.

Despite the conflict over the earmark and federal funding process generally, one could argue that obtaining federal dollars for the district is a form of responsiveness to the local needs of voters. Voters are taxpayers, and members of Congress are simply seeking to bring some of that tax money back home in a directed fashion. On the other hand, many of the projects are not necessary to most voters, and they create waste and inefficiency that can make the federal government less effective.

Tom Williams/Getty Images

IMAGE 12.8 All members of Congress try to build a good reputation among their constituents. Part of that effort includes going back to the district and meeting with voters to hear their concerns. Here Joaquín Castro is shown meeting with residents of his district.

Communication with Constituents

Congressional representation depends on good communication between constituents and their representatives and senators. It is important to remember that members of Congress have two distinct places of work: Washington, D.C., and their home district or state.

In Washington, members take advantage of technological innovations, such as e-mail and the Internet, to stay in touch with their constituents. Before e-mail and the rise of social media, members used the franking privilege, which is free mail service, to respond to constituent letters and to send quarterly newsletters as updates on their activities. Today the vast majority of members of Congress use social media such as Twitter, Instagram, and Facebook to transmit information about their activities to constituents, in addition to hard-copy mailings. To help members stay in touch with their constituents, the federal government pays for House and Senate members to return home to their districts or states approximately thirty-three times a year. These trips home are crucial for building bonds with voters, and members make sure to meet with individuals, speak to local interest groups, attend local parades and business openings, and attract local media coverage.

home style: *The way in which incumbents portray themselves to constituents.*

Cultivating direct links with constituents and making a good impression on them is what the political scientist Richard Fenno calls **home style**, or the way members portray themselves to constituents.[63] Members can choose to emphasize their local work for constituents, or they can emphasize their influence on national policy; some try to do both. Members can be very good at giving charismatic speeches, or they can be quiet, unassuming workers; successful members adapt their home style to the expectations and customs of constituents.

The Next Election

As political scientist David Mayhew explains, members of Congress are always looking ahead to the next election.[64] Elections are the means by which constituents express approval or disapproval of the job members of Congress are doing, and they are the fundamental tool that voters use to hold their members accountable for individual legislative work and the collective performance of their party in office. House members have only two years to show that they can manage to gain influence in the House and be responsive to local concerns at the same time. Senators have six years, but a senator has to share the job with another senator from the same state and compete for voter support, media attention, committee assignments, and the chance to be the "go-to" senator on key issues affecting the state. Because Senate elections are staggered, voters in a state elect each senator separately, at different times. A newly elected senator almost always finds that the senior colleague is established on key committees and well positioned on issues that are important to the state. Junior senators, therefore, are left to scramble for the leftovers and to establish good reputations among constituents in the shadows of their senior colleagues.[65]

Despite the fact that congressional job approval has fallen, constituents typically like their own senator or House member. 2014 was a bit different from prior years in that Republican incumbents held on to their seats at a consistently high rate, while a number of Democratic incumbents lost their seats and had a lower reelection rate; 95 percent of House incumbents and 82 percent of Senate incumbents won reelection, and control of the Senate went to the Republicans, which gave them unified control of both chambers of Congress.[66]

Congressional campaigns are typically divided into two categories: those with an incumbent seeking reelection and those with open seats, where no incumbent is seeking reelection. In elections in which an incumbent is running, the contest becomes an evaluation of the job he or she has done in office compared to what the challenger promises

ELECTION 2016

Increased Party Competition in the Senate

ELECTION YEAR 2016 WAS a very competitive year at both the congressional and presidential levels. The presidency was open because Barack Obama could not seek reelection. The House was firmly in Republican hands and not expected to change party control, but the U.S. Senate was a different story. Recall that Senate elections are staggered so that typically no more than one-third of the Senate is up for reelection in any federal election year. In some years, such as 2014, there are more Democratic incumbents up for reelection. Republicans took full advantage of it by defeating five Democratic incumbent senators and winning a total of nine Democratic-controlled seats to take majority control of the Senate.

Just two years later, in 2016, the situation was reversed. The Republicans had many more incumbent senators seeking reelection. In total, there were ten Democratic-held seats (with seven Democratic incumbents running) and twenty-four Republican-held seats (with twenty-two Republican incumbents running) contested.

The complicating aspect to the 2016 elections for Congress, especially the Senate, is to estimate the impact of the presidential election on these contests. With strong competitive presidential candidates at the top of the party ticket on the ballot, both parties can expect high voter turnout among their bases, which produces greater competition at both the presidential and congressional levels. But if one party nominates a candidate who is popular with the party base but not with independents or swing voters, then that party can risk negative effects in congressional elections as well.

As we interpret the outcome of congressional elections, it is also important to examine the role of key groups of voters, especially in light of the changing demographics of the American electorate. In the 2016 elections, about 58 percent of eligible voters turned out to cast their ballots. Among them, Latinos represented only 11 percent of the total voter turnout when they are 11.9 percent of the eligible voting population, and African Americans represented 12 percent of the voter turnout, while they are 13 percent of the eligible voting population. Turnout among these groups can affect both the presidential electoral outcome and the election outcome in congressional races. For example, in 2016, Latinos in Nevada were thought to play a large role in electing Catherine Cortez Masto to the U.S. Senate; she is the first Latina U.S. Senator ever elected.[67]

Consequently, reelection is a product of many forces—some of which are outside of candidates' control. Part of the incumbent advantage rests on incumbents' efforts to use all their resources to serve their constituents responsively. Members' concern for their local districts or states can be one of the biggest gates standing in the way of a productive Congress. Parties provide a collective set of policy goals that will benefit or appeal to party members at the local level. For a member of Congress, however, tying his or her electoral fortunes to the political party can be risky if the majority party falls out of favor with voters who hold it accountable for policy outcomes. Holding a high-ranking party position will require a lot of time away from the district and cause the member to lose touch with his or her reelection base. Former House Majority Leader Eric Cantor (R-VA) served in that role from 2011 to July 2014 but was defeated in a primary by a little-known college professor who ran a campaign saying that Cantor was out of step with the views of the district; he subsequently resigned his seat in Congress before his term ended. Although these types of primary election upsets are infrequent, they are powerful reminders that incumbents must constantly balance the needs of their constituents with their party and stay responsive, or risk losing the next election.

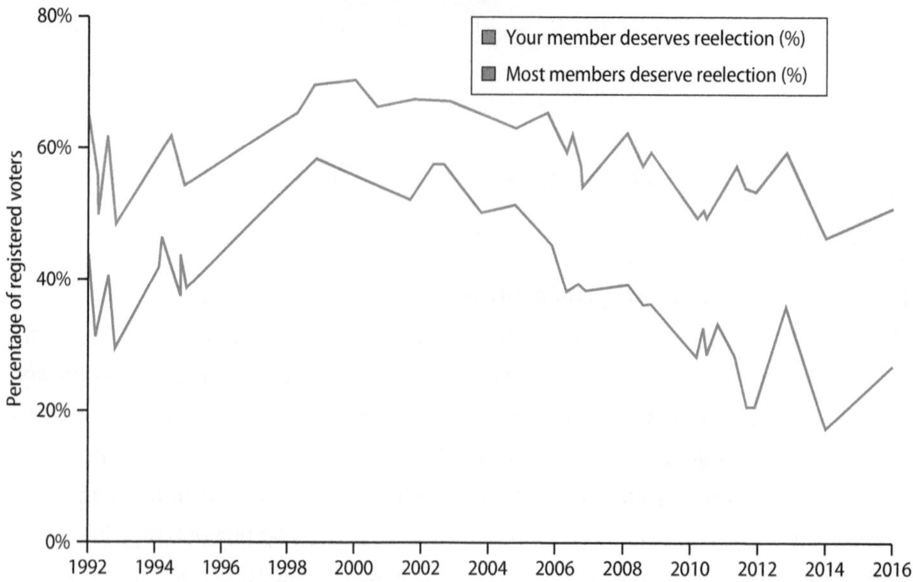

FIGURE 12.6 Voter Opinion of Congressional Incumbents, 1992–2016

Although congressional incumbents typically enjoy high reelection rates, negative impressions of Congress as an institution can reduce voter support.

Source: Gallup poll, http://www.gallup.com/poll/167024/record-low-say-own-representative-deserves-election.aspx; http://www.gallup.com/poll/189215/anti-incumbent-mood-toward-congress-going-strong.aspx?g_source=POLITICS&g_medium=topic&g_campaign=tiles.

to do if elected. Incumbents have major advantages because they have already won at least one election in the district, they are likely to have moderate name recognition, and they have the power to use their congressional offices to provide services to constituents. However, incumbents can also suffer if the reputation of Congress suffers (see Figure 12.6), and so they work to stake out individual reputations that contrast to the institution as a whole.

Congress and Democracy

The composition of Congress has changed considerably over the nation's history. The lawmaking body is five times larger and now includes men and women from a wide range of ethnic, racial, and religious backgrounds. From the standpoint of equality of opportunity in a democracy, the increased diversity in Congress is a positive step.

Is Congress a responsive decision-making body? Individual members clearly work hard to address the concerns of their constituents, both at home in the district or state and in their Washington offices. But Congress as a whole is not always capable of addressing the immediate needs of the nation in a timely fashion. The bicameral nature of the institution, with each chamber's separate rules of operation, makes the legislative process time-consuming and complex. In the House, the majority party almost always succeeds in passing legislation that reflects the party's policy goals. In the Senate, the minority has much greater power to block the majority through the threat of a filibuster, so minority-party views are typically incorporated into legislation. These differences offer advantages and disadvantages; if Congress acts too hastily, it can pass harmful legislation, but if it acts too slowly, it can fail to meet its fundamental responsibilities to address issues that citizens care about.

Are individual members of Congress accountable for the collective output of Congress as a whole? Not always. The fundamental difficulty with the representative structure of Congress is that each member is elected separately, so that voters may reelect their own representative or senator but still be unhappy with Congress as a whole. It is too easy for one member of Congress to say to constituents, "I am working hard to help you; it is all those other men and women who are not doing their jobs." Only in the rarest of election years do voters actually hold all the members of the Congress accountable for their collective performance. This lack of collective accountability can be a significant obstacle or gate to Congress's productivity and responsiveness to important policy needs.

Is Congress equal in its treatment of each citizen relative to all others? Because each state has the same number of senators regardless of population size, are the citizens of small states more powerful in the Senate than citizens who live in large states? Are the laws that Congress passes fair and balanced, or do they benefit one group more consistently than another? There are no simple answers to these questions. Some voices in society are louder and more prominent than others, and members of Congress tend to respond to citizens whom they perceive to be supportive, who donate more money, and who vote regularly. In some issue areas, the more prominent members of society win out over citizens who are less active and less visible. It is not clear that Congress sets out to give some people greater advantages than others, but the process of balancing the different individual and regional interests in national policy making produces winners and losers. The fundamental challenge to Congress is to make sure that there are no permanent winners or losers, and the challenge to all citizens is to monitor their members of Congress to be sure they are performing their legislative responsibilities.

Political Science Reasoning

Question 1

Practice 1, Practice 4

> What GAO Found U.S. Department of Education (Education) grant staff did not consistently document in the official grant files key required monitoring activities, according to GAO's review of a nongeneralizable sample of 75 discretionary grants. As a result, about $21 million in discretionary grant funds lacked correct documentation of grantee performance in the official grant files GAO reviewed. Specifically, compared to Education's requirements for these files, almost all—69 of 75—were incomplete in terms of certain key documents (that is, grant award notifications, post-award conference records, and annual performance reports) that should have been contained in them. Further, the three principal offices GAO

reviewed—the Offices of Postsecondary Education, Elementary and Secondary Education, and Innovation and Improvement—have not established detailed written procedures for the supervisory review of official grant files, contrary to federal internal control standards, which call for entities to provide reasonable assurance that internal control objectives, such as grant monitoring, are achieved and clearly documented. By developing and implementing detailed supervisory review procedures for official grant files, Education would be better positioned to ensure the proper stewardship of its discretionary grants.

Education spent about $700,000 to develop features within the Post-Award Monitoring (PAM) Module of its grants management system that allow staff to, for example, identify and share performance information to a central location, but it has not developed guidance on its effective use by grant staff working across programs and offices. Education described several ways staff share performance information, but according to a review of official grant files and interviews with Education officials, GAO found that staff rarely used PAM to disseminate information about grantee performance, such as notable results achieved in specific grant projects. Additionally, while Education officials said they offer staff training on PAM, they have not developed guidance to clarify use of features related to grantee performance. Federal internal control standards call for pertinent information, such as grantee performance information, to be identified, captured, and distributed in a form and time frame that permits people to perform their duties efficiently. Absent guidance on how to effectively use PAM Module features to share information about grantee performance, Education will likely not be able to achieve the full potential benefits of its grants management system.[1]

1. What is the claim of the authors of the above document?
2. What reasoning is used to support their claim?
3. What methods does Congress have at its disposal to exercise of legislative oversight?
4. How might the Department of Education attempt to counteract the oversight of Congress?

Question 2

Practice 1, Practice 4

H. Res. 22

In the House of Representatives, U. S.,

January 5, 2017.

Resolved, That at any time after adoption of this resolution the Speaker may, pursuant to clause 2(b) of rule XVIII, declare the House resolved into the Committee of the Whole House on the state of the Union for consideration of the bill (H.R. 26) to amend chapter 8 of title 5, United States Code, to provide

[1]Government Accountability Office. (2017). *Discretionary Grants: Education Needs to Improve its Oversight of Grants Monitoring* (GAO-17-266). Retrieved from https://www.gao.gov/assets/690/684173.pdf.

that major rules of the executive branch shall have no force or effect unless a joint resolution of approval is enacted into law. The first reading of the bill shall be dispensed with. All points of order against consideration of the bill are waived. General debate shall be confined to the bill and shall not exceed one hour equally divided and controlled by the Majority Leader and the Minority Leader or their respective designees. After general debate the bill shall be considered for amendment under the five-minute rule. The bill shall be considered as read. All points of order against provisions in the bill are waived. No amendment to the bill shall be in order except those printed in the report of the Committee on Rules accompanying this resolution. Each such amendment may be offered only in the order printed in the report, may be offered only by a Member designated in the report, shall be considered as read, shall be debatable for the time specified in the report equally divided and controlled by the proponent and an opponent, shall not be subject to amendment, and shall not be subject to a demand for division of the question in the House or in the Committee of the Whole. All points of order against such amendments are waived. At the conclusion of consideration of the bill for amendment the Committee shall rise and report the bill to the House with such amendments as may have been adopted. The previous question shall be considered as ordered on the bill and amendments thereto to final passage without intervening motion except one motion to recommit with or without instructions.

Section 2. Upon adoption of this resolution it shall be in order without intervention of any point of order to consider in the House the resolution (H. Res. 11) objecting to United Nations Security Council Resolution 2334 as an obstacle to Israeli-Palestinian peace, and for other purposes. The resolution shall be considered as read. The previous question shall be considered as ordered on the resolution and preamble to adoption without intervening motion or demand for division of the question except one hour of debate equally divided and controlled by the chair and ranking minority member of the Committee on Foreign Affairs.

1. What committee is responsible for this resolution?
2. What is the function of this resolution?
3. How does the Senate enforce similar rules for debate and amendments? Explain.
4. Which method (House or Senate) provides members of the minority party more input into deciding the way in which legislation will be considered? Why?

Focus on AP® Success

12 Congress

Must Know: Key Concepts

- Fiscal Policy
- Monetary Policy
- Declaration of War
- *McCulloch v. Maryland* (1819)
- Majority Leader
- Minority Leader
- Whips
- Filibuster
- Cloture
- Holds
- Unanimous Consent
- Rules Committee
- Committee of the Whole
- Discharge Petition
- Delegate
- Trustee
- Politico
- Pork Barrel
- Log Rolling
- *Baker v. Carr* (1961)
- *Shaw v. Reno* (1993)
- Enumerated Powers
- Implied Powers
- Necessary and Proper Clause
- Gerrymandering
- Divided Government
- Oversight
- Power of the Purse

Thinking Politically

Concept Application

Each house of Congress has unique characteristics that can be attributed to its size, constituencies, and term of office. These characteristics impact how each house functions. Compare the leadership of each house. Explain why the leadership of the House of Representative tends to be more powerful than the leadership of the Senate.

Understanding Learning Objectives with Key Concepts

CON – 3.A Describe the different structures, powers, and functions of each house of Congress.

- States are represented equally in the Senate and are represented based on population in the House of Representatives. A census occurs every ten years to determine the population of each state.

- The size of each chamber impacts the way that it functions. The smaller Senate is said to be less formal, meaning it regularly sets aside its rules. It also typically allows unlimited debate and non-germane amendments (riders). The larger House of Representative is said to be more formal, strictly following its rules. It places time limits on debate and insists that amendments to bills relate to the main topic of the legislation.

- Coalitions of members in the Senate tend to be longer lasting than in the House of Representatives due to the longer terms that Senators serve.

- Congress makes public policy in the areas that are assigned to the national government by the Constitution. These areas are either specifically mentioned in the Constitution (enumerated) or related to the powers that are specifically mentioned (implied).

  - Congress possess the power to set fiscal policy (budget, tax, spend, borrow) and the power to set monetary policy (coin money and regulate its value).

- Congress has the power to declare war and fund the military.
- Congress has powers that go beyond the powers listed in the Constitution due to the necessary and proper clause as interpreted in the case of *McCulloch v. Maryland.*

CON – 3.B Explain how the structure, powers, and functions of both houses of Congress affect the policy-making process.

- The two houses of Congress are distinctly different from one another. There are differences in procedures and Constitutional prerogatives. These differences impact the policy-making process.
- Most of the legislative work of both houses occurs in committee. Different responsibilities of each house specified by the Constitution impacts the policy-making process. The unique confirmation and foreign policy responsibilities of the Senate tend to make Senate committees slightly more powerful than similar committees in the House. The constitutional requirement that revenue bills start in the House of Representatives means that the House Committee on Ways and Means is more influential than the Senate Committee on Finance.
- Rules specific to each house impact how Congress functions.
    - The rules of each chamber make it difficult to build the coalitions necessary to pass legislation.
    - The Speaker of the House is the leader of the majority party as well as the presiding officer of the House. The parties in each house elect leaders and whips whose job it is to help organize party members to vote for bills that advance their party's agenda. The Senate Majority Leader is the most powerful member of that house. Committee membership is assigned by each party. The majority party selects the chair of each committee.
    - The rules of the Senate allow for unlimited debate, which can give rise to a filibuster. A filibuster is an attempt to "talk a bill to death." Filibusters are ended by cloture.
    - Members of the Senate can prevent a bill from coming to the floor though the use of a hold. Most Senate business is dispensed with using unanimous consent.
    - The House Rules Committee determines the schedule and conditions under which bills will be considered in the House. The House Committee of the Whole allows the House to operate with more flexibility. A discharge petition removes a bill from a House committee and advances it to the full House of Representatives.
    - The Senate has specialized functions relating to treaty ratification and confirmation of executive nominations.
- Congressional attempts to balance the budget are complicated by the growth of entitlement programs. The ability to fund discretionary items will decrease unless taxes are increased.
- Coalition building can occur through pork barrel legislation and logrolling.

CON – 3.C Explain how congressional behavior is influenced by election processes, partisanship, and divided government.

- The functioning of government and congressional behavior is impacted by:
    - Ideological division inside of and between parties causes gridlock in Congress. This is reflective of the increased polarization in the electorate.
    - Gerrymandering, redistricting, and malapportionment have tended to increase partisanship and to decrease the accountability of Congress.
    - Divided government has become common since 1968 and has led to increased partisanship and difficulty in confirmation of executive appointments. This is a result of the dealignment of the electorate and split ticket voting.
    - The terms delegate, politico, and trustee describe the varying degrees to which members feel compelled to "vote their constituencies."

PMI – 2.C Explain how Congress uses its oversight power in its relationship with the executive branch.

- Congress supervises the bureaucracy to see if its legislation is being implemented in a manner that Congress approves. The process is called oversight and can take the form of committee hearings and the use of the power of the purse (the ability to control an agency's budget).
- Congress can check the power of the president though oversight similar to how it checks the bureaucracy as well as the confirmation process.

Making Connections

A key to understanding both the Congress and the presidency is to see their interaction. Do not expect to fully understand Congress until you have studied the presidency. The reverse is true as well.

Going Deeper: Malapportionment and Gerrymandering

The U.S. Supreme Court dealt with the issue of malapportionment in the case of *Baker v. Carr* (1961). In this case, the Court required that districts be devised so that each district be as nearly equal in population as possible. This then will ensure that a citizen's vote in one district will be weighed the same as vote in another district.

In the case of *Shaw v. Reno*, the Court struck down a congressional districting plan in South Carolina where the state legislature had diluted minority voting strength by concentrating a large segment of the African American population into one district.

13 The Presidency

AP® Learning Objectives

CON – 4.A Explain how the president can implement a policy agenda.

CON – 4.B Explain how the president's agenda can create tension and frequent confrontations with Congress.

CON – 4.C Explain how presidents have interpreted and justified their use of formal and informal powers.

CON – 4.D Explain how communication technology has changed the president's relationship with the national constituency and the other branches.

PMI – 2.D Explain how the president ensures that executive branch agencies and departments carry out their responsibilities in concert with the goals of the administration.

Performance Tasks

Upon the completion of this chapter, you must be able to do the following:

- Explain how the president can use formal and informal power to achieve the administration's policy agenda.
- Explain the sources of conflict and tension between the president and Congress.
- Explain how various factors have increased presidential power beyond those powers listed in the Constitution, including appointment power, single rather than plural executive, various interpretations of presidential power, presidential use of the media (including social media), ideology, and control of the bureaucracy.
- Explain the powers that enable the president to direct the bureaucracy and how those powers only provide for limited control.

Barry Winiker/Photolibrary/Getty Images

"As a second-generation Greek immigrant, I was raised to be thankful for the gifts that this great nation gave to me and to my parents before me. Throughout my childhood in Hinton, West Virginia, my father, an optometrist and small business owner, and my mother, a teacher, were both engaged in service through our community and church. . . . I look forward to working alongside the remarkable men and women of the Department [of Health and Human Services] to continue to ensure that children, families, and seniors have the building blocks of healthy and productive lives."[1]

SYLVIA MATHEWS BURWELL
Harvard University

AP Images/J. Scott Applewhite

From a very young age, Sylvia Mathews Burwell showed a keen interest in politics. In elementary school, she helped campaign for a friend's father, and at age 11, she volunteered for Jay Rockefeller's bid for governor. Later her mother ran for mayor of her hometown, Hinton, West Virginia, at age 65, and won, without ever having run for public office before. Sylvia graduated from Harvard with a degree in government and became a Rhodes Scholar at Oxford University, which introduced her to the world of professional politics. In 1992, she worked on Bill Clinton's presidential campaign. She led Clinton's economic transition team, and after he won the election, became a staff director on the National Economic Council (NEC).

Burwell was promoted to the chief of staff for the Treasury Secretary and then served as Clinton's deputy chief of staff. In 1998, she assumed the position of deputy director in the Office of Management and Budget (OMB). When Republican candidate George W. Bush won the 2000 presidential election, she turned her focus to the world of nonprofit foundations, initially working for the Bill and Melinda Gates Foundation. As president of the Walmart Foundation, she tackled global health issues. Her past experience with the OMB put her on the top of a short list of candidates to head the agency after Democratic President Barack Obama was reelected in 2012. In 2013, Obama nominated her for the position. Burwell's appointment as OMB director was impressively smooth, and she was confirmed by the Senate in a 96–0 vote on April 24, 2013. On April 11, 2014, President Obama nominated Burwell as the next Secretary of Health and Human Services (HHS). The president put one of his most important policy legacies—the Affordable Care Act—in her hands. The Senate Finance Committee approved her nomination by a vote of 21–3 on May 21, 2014, and the full Senate confirmed her on June 5, 2014, by a vote of 78–17.

Burwell's career exemplifies the gateways that open when you get involved in politics: the political networks that talented and hardworking volunteers establish on campaigns. Her experience demonstrates how campaign work can be the beginning of a lifetime of public service. As Secretary of HHS, Burwell carried out the remainder of the health care law that had yet to be implemented, and Republicans used her nomination to reiterate their criticisms of the law. Burwell's appointment is also the perfect example of how the gates of Congress can get in the way of executive branch policy implementation, even for laws that have already passed through their chambers.[2]

In this chapter, we examine how the president governs and how responsive he can be to the people. We look at his constitutional powers and the way he uses the executive power to achieve his policy goals, from nominating appointees such as Burwell to issuing executive orders to accomplish policy goals. We also look at the limits on presidential power. As presidential scholar Charles Jones has argued, successful presidents work within a separation-of-powers system and alongside the legislative and judicial branches, compromising, persuading, and overcoming opposition. The most successful presidents are strong leaders with clear policy visions and excellent communication and negotiation skills. In the twenty-first century, the American president has to implement existing law and, equally important, leads the effort to turn his policy goals into law and achieve his visions for the nation.

13.1 Presidential Qualifications

Outline the requirements to serve as president

The American presidency was invented at the Constitutional Convention in 1787. The Framers had no definitive models to help them determine what sort of person should serve as a democratically elected head of state because nations were still run by monarchs whose power to rule was hereditary. But the Framers had George Washington, the hero of the Revolutionary War, in mind for the office, and he helped shape the idea of what a president should be. Still, they left the qualifications as open as possible, and men with diverse experiences have served as president.

Constitutional Eligibility and Presidential Succession

Article II, Section 1, of the Constitution states that the president must be a natural-born citizen (or a citizen at the time the Constitution was adopted), at least 35 years old, and a resident of the United States for at least 14 years. The original Constitution did not specify eligibility for the vice presidency, as the person who came in second in the vote for president would be vice president. But in 1800, Thomas Jefferson (1801–09) and Aaron Burr ended up in a tie in the Electoral College when in fact supporters wanted to elect them as a team, with Jefferson as president and Burr as vice president. The Twelfth Amendment, ratified in 1804, changed the process so that candidates are elected for president and vice president separately. The amendment also directs that the vice president must meet the same eligibility requirements as the president and that electors cannot vote for both a president and a vice president from the elector's home state. This requirement makes it difficult for parties to nominate presidents and vice presidents from the same state.

The Constitution also states that when the president is removed from office by death, resignation, or inability to perform the duties of the office, the vice president becomes president. It stipulates that if neither the president nor the vice president is able to complete the elected term, Congress should designate a successor by law. In 1792, Congress passed the Presidential Succession Act, which designated the president pro tempore of the Senate as next in line, and then the Speaker of the House. In 1841, John Tyler (1841–45) became the first elected vice president to succeed a president when President William Henry Harrison insisted on giving a two-hour inaugural speech in the freezing rain while wearing no hat or coat, and consequently came down with a cold. Besieged by candidates hoping that he would appoint them to public office, he had little time to rest. Only one month after assuming office, the new president died after his cold developed into pneumonia. The order of succession today is illustrated in Table 13.1.

There was no constitutional provision for replacement of the vice president, and in the course of the nation's history, the office has occasionally been vacant. Eventually, the Twenty-Fifth Amendment, ratified in 1967, required the president to nominate a replacement vice president, who must be approved by a majority vote of the House and the Senate.

The first vice president to assume office in this manner was Gerald R. Ford, nominated by President Richard M. Nixon (1969–74) in 1973, following the indictment and subsequent resignation of Vice President Spiro T. Agnew on charges of tax fraud.

The amendment also allows for a temporary transfer of power from the president to the vice president in cases of incapacity when invoked by either the president or vice president and a majority of the cabinet. To date, only the president has invoked this clause and then only when he has had to have surgery that would require sedation. For example, in 1985, when President Ronald Reagan (1981–89) had a colonoscopy, Vice President George H. W. Bush was acting president for eight hours.[3] In contrast, no one invoked the clause when President Reagan was shot in a failed assassination attempt in 1981; Vice President Bush stood in for him at official functions and meetings for approximately two weeks but did not serve as the official acting president during this time.

Today another constitutional amendment, the Twenty-Second (1951), limits the president to two elected terms. For a century and a half, presidents followed the precedent established by George Washington (1789–97) when he stepped down after two terms. But in 1940, President Franklin Delano Roosevelt (1933–45) chose to run for a third term and won, and also won election to a fourth term in 1944. Though the dangers of World War II were a factor in his staying in office, many Americans, especially Republicans, worried that a long-standing president could expand executive branch power too much, so they sought a way to limit presidential terms of service. In 1946, Republicans captured a majority in the House and Senate, and on the very first day the new Congress met, they proposed a constitutional amendment limiting the president to two full terms in office.[4] For a list of constitutional amendments that pertain to the presidency, see Figure 13.1.

TABLE 13.1 Presidential Order of Succession

1. Vice president
2. Speaker of the House
3. President pro tempore of the Senate
Cabinet Secretaries
4. State
5. Treasury
6. Defense
7. Attorney General
8. Interior
9. Agriculture
10. Commerce
11. Labor
12. Health and Human Services
13. Housing and Urban Development
14. Transportation
15. Energy
16. Education
17. Veterans' Affairs
18. Homeland Security

Essential Knowledge

The Twenty-second Amendment limits a president to two terms in office. Long an informal practice, with the growth in power of the office, many thought it important to formalize this limitation.

Presidential term limits enforce turnover and open opportunity for new leadership, but they also act as a gate that prevents voters from reelecting a popular president whom they want to keep in office. Because a president in his second term cannot seek reelection, he is commonly referred to as a **lame duck**. Lawmakers know that the president's time in office is limited, so they are less likely to cooperate or compromise with him. On the other hand, a president who wants to chart a policy course that is unpopular may be more likely to do so when he does not have to face the voters. Lame-duck status therefore has the advantage of giving the president more political freedom, but the disadvantage of making him less directly responsive to public opinion. Barack Obama (2009–17) provides an example. During his second term, public opinion was unfavorable toward continuing troop involvement in Afghanistan, but President Obama maintained U.S. commitments in that area even after declaring the end of U.S. combat there. Some critics believe he should have heeded the public and withdrawn troops, but others argue that he was taking the unpopular but correct course of action for the nation. Absent the pressure of seeking reelection to a third term,

lame duck: *Term-limited official in his or her last term of office.*

The Granger Collection, NYC

IMAGE 13.1 George Washington was a successful military general who led American troops in the Revolutionary War. He was widely admired and was chosen to be the first president of the United States because it was believed that his experience and personal characteristics would be a model for the future. He took the oath of office on April 30, 1789, on the balcony of Federal Hall in New York City, then the nation's capital.

Obama had the flexibility to pursue a policy on what he perceived to be its merits. Indeed, in his nomination of Merrick Garland to serve on the Supreme Court, Obama justified his choice as being in the best interest of the judicial system, despite intense Republican opposition to it in the Senate.

Background and Experience

In keeping with the democratic spirit of the founding of the United States, the Framers did not specify qualifications for the presidency beyond age and citizenship, and in the ensuing two centuries, men of varying backgrounds have served in the office. Presidents have come from all walks of life and from almost all regions of the country. Harry S. Truman (1945–53), born in Missouri, was a farmer and owner of a men's clothing store. Ronald Reagan, born in Illinois, was a radio sports announcer and actor. Barack Obama, born in Hawaii, was a community organizer and constitutional law professor. Until John F. Kennedy (1961–63), a Catholic, was elected in 1960, all presidents were from Protestant backgrounds. Until Barack Obama, an African American, was elected in 2008, all presidents were white and male. In 1984 Walter Mondale made history by selecting Geraldine Ferraro as the first woman to run for vice president. In 2008, Hillary Clinton ran for the Democratic Party presidential nomination but lost to Obama. In 2016 she ran again for the Democratic Party nomination and was successful; in November 2016, she lost the presidential election to Donald Trump. Overall, it has taken more than two centuries, but women and minorities have joined white men as viable candidates for the presidency.

The clearest path to the White House is through the office of the vice president, but most presidents have some combination of service in the military, in a state legislature, or

Twelfth	1804	Requires that electors cast separate votes for president and vice president and specifies requirements for vice presidential candidates
Twentieth	1933	Declares that presidential term begins on January 20 (instead of March 4)
Twenty-Second	1951	Limits presidents to two terms
Twenty-Fifth	1967	Specifies replacement of the vice president and establishes the position of acting president during a president's disability

Of the twenty-seven Amendments to the Constitution, four pertain directly to the presidency: the twelfth, twentieth, twenty-second, and twenty-fifth.

FIGURE 13.1 Constitutional Amendments Pertaining to the Presidency

as governor; in the U.S. House of Representatives and Senate; or in a prior presidential administration. For example, James Monroe (1817–25) was a soldier in the Revolutionary War, a U.S. senator, minister to France, secretary of state, and secretary of war. Herbert Hoover (1929–33) was an international food relief worker and Secretary of Commerce.[5]

There are advantages and disadvantages for presidents, depending on their prior experience. Lyndon Baines Johnson (1963–69) was very successful in passing his domestic policy agenda, in large part due to his experience as a House member, U.S. senator, and Senate majority leader. His prior experience taught him crucial negotiating skills with members of Congress, and he used his skills to their fullest extent. In contrast, Jimmy Carter (1977–81) was generally considered to have failed in getting his domestic policy agenda enacted because of his lack of experience in Washington. He came to the White House from the governor's mansion in Georgia, where he exercised executive power with little challenge from the legislature. When he faced a Congress that did not embrace his agenda, he lacked the negotiating skills to be successful. Of course, no single set of qualifications or experiences can guarantee success as a president. When voters cast their ballots for president, they take a leap of faith that the person who wins will be trustworthy, accountable, and responsive to their needs and will implement the laws equally for every citizen. For a list of the presidents of the United States, see Table 13.2.

The Granger Collection, NYC

IMAGE 13.2 Being born in a log cabin was an asset for presidential hopefuls in the nineteenth century, and candidates liked to portray their humble origins and demonstrate that they were men of the people. In 1840, William Henry Harrison cultivated the connection with campaign images such as this one, although he was born in an elegant plantation manor house. But the claims of other presidents, such as Abraham Lincoln, were legitimate. The log cabin birthplace of James Buchanan still stands.

Essential Knowledge

The power of the presidency has generally expanded over time. The desirability of this expansion continues to be a source of controversy.

Essential Knowledge

Plural executives (multiple elected executives) were common in many of the states. The Framers, however, opted for a single executive for the United States, for reasons set forth in Federalist 70. There, Hamilton argues that a single executive is necessary for accountability and to prevent Congress from encroaching on the power of the president.

Expansion of the Presidency

President George Washington had the enormous responsibility of setting the standard for how a president should govern in a democracy, and he was very careful not to infuse the office with airs of royalty or privilege. The Framers anticipated that the executive branch would be led by one person whose primary responsibility would be the defense of the United States. As commander of the Continental Army during the Revolutionary War, Washington had military experience, but he was also a cautious and thoughtful statesman who wanted to establish a precedent for how the chief executive should operate.

In the course of the nineteenth century, from the presidencies of Thomas Jefferson, to Andrew Jackson (1829–37), to Abraham Lincoln, and finally to William McKinley (1897–1901), the nation grew in size, population, and economic power. The job of the chief executive grew accordingly, but, though increasingly demanding and complex, it remained

TABLE 13.2 Presidents of the United States, 1789–2017

President	Term Dates	Party	Prior Experience
1 George Washington	1789–97		General, delegate to First Continental Congress
2 John Adams	1797–1801	Federalist	Vice president
3 Thomas Jefferson	1801–09	Democratic-Republican	Vice president, Secretary of State
4 James Madison	1809–17	Democratic-Republican	Secretary of State, U.S. House, state legislator
5 James Monroe	1817–25	Democratic-Republican	Secretary of War, Secretary of State, U.S. Senate
6 John Quincy Adams	1825–29	Democratic-Republican	Secretary of State, U.S. Senate
7 Andrew Jackson	1829–37	Democrat	U.S. Senate, general, U.S. House
8 Martin Van Buren	1837–41	Democrat	Vice president, U.S. Senate
9 William Henry Harrison	1841 (died in office)	Whig	U.S. Senate, general, territorial governor
10 John Tyler	1841–45	Whig	Vice president, U.S. Senate, governor, U.S. House
11 James K. Polk	1845–49	Democrat	Governor, U.S. House
12 Zachary Taylor	1849–50 (died in office)	Whig	General
13 Millard Fillmore	1850–53	Whig	Vice president, U.S. House
14 Franklin Pierce	1853–57	Democrat	U.S. Senate, U.S. House, state legislator
15 James Buchanan	1857–61	Democrat	Secretary of State, U.S. Senate, U.S. House
16 Abraham Lincoln	1861–65 (died in office)	Republican; National Union	U.S. House
17 Andrew Johnson	1865–69	Democrat; National Union	Vice president, U.S. Senate, U.S. House
18 Ulysses S. Grant	1869–77	Republican	General
19 Rutherford B. Hayes	1877–81	Republican	Governor, U.S. House, general
20 James A. Garfield	1881 (died in office)	Republican	U.S. Senate, general, U.S. House, state legislator
21 Chester A. Arthur	1881–85	Republican	Vice president, collector of the port of New York
22 Grover Cleveland	1885–89	Democrat	Governor, mayor
23 Benjamin Harrison	1889–93	Republican	U.S. Senate
24 Grover Cleveland	1893–97	Democrat	U.S. President, governor, mayor
25 William McKinley	1897–1901 (died in office)	Republican	Governor, U.S. House
26 Theodore Roosevelt	1901–1909	Republican	Vice president, governor
27 William Howard Taft	1909–13	Republican	Secretary of War, governor general of the Philippines, federal judge
28 Woodrow Wilson	1913–21	Democrat	Governor, university president
29 Warren G. Harding	1921–23 (died in office)	Republican	U.S. Senate, lieutenant governor, state legislator
30 Calvin Coolidge	1923–29	Republican	Vice president, governor
31 Herbert Hoover	1929–33	Republican	Secretary of Commerce

TABLE 13.2 Continued

President	Term Dates	Party	Prior Experience
32 Franklin Delano Roosevelt	1933–45 (died in office)	Democrat	Governor, Assistant Secretary of the Navy, state legislator
33 Harry S. Truman	1945–53	Democrat	Vice president, U.S. Senate
34 Dwight D. Eisenhower	1953–61	Republican	University president, general
35 John F. Kennedy	1961–63 (died in office)	Democrat	U.S. Senate, U.S. House
36 Lyndon Baines Johnson	1963–69	Democrat	Vice president, U.S. Senate, U.S. House
37 Richard M. Nixon	1969–74 (resigned)	Republican	Vice president, U.S. Senate, U.S. House
38 Gerald R. Ford	1974–77	Republican	Vice president, U.S. House
39 Jimmy Carter	1977–81	Democrat	Governor, state legislator
40 Ronald Reagan	1981–89	Republican	Governor, actor, union president
41 George H. W. Bush	1989–93	Republican	Vice president, CIA director, U.S. House
42 William J. Clinton	1993–2001	Democrat	Governor, state attorney general
43 George W. Bush	2001–2009	Republican	Governor
44 Barack Obama	2009–2017	Democrat	U.S. Senate, state legislator
45 Donald Trump	2017–	Republican	Businessman

essentially focused on national defense and economic growth. In the twentieth century, however, the United States became a leading international military and economic power. Its role in World War II and the subsequent Cold War against the Soviet Union expanded the authority of the presidency. Historian and presidential adviser Arthur Schlesinger Jr. used the term **imperial presidency** to describe the power of the president to speak for the nation on the world stage and to set the policy agenda at home.[6] Schlesinger's view suggests that as long as the United States is engaged in military conflicts all over the world to promote and protect its interests, the president will be considered the most important figure in American politics. However, after two very long wars, public opinion has shifted against intervening in foreign conflicts (see Chapter 6, Public Opinion), which leaves less support for presidential military action on foreign soil. As the public looks more inward and focuses on domestic policy, Congress and the president stand on more balanced scales.

imperial presidency: *Power of the president to speak for the nation on the world stage and to set the policy agenda at home.*

13.2 Presidential Power: Constitutional Grants and Limits

Identify the powers of the president and explain how they are limited

As we saw in Chapter 12, Congress, the Framers enumerated Congress's powers, both to assert powers that were missing under the Articles of Confederation, such as the powers to collect taxes and to regulate commerce, and to constrain the branch they anticipated

Essential Knowledge

Although the formal powers of the executive are fairly limited, modern presidents have used informal powers to significantly expand their power in pursuit of policy goals.

would be the most powerful. The Framers expected the executive branch to be smaller and less powerful and did not believe it necessary to enumerate the executive powers as they did the legislative powers (see Table 13.3). Instead, in the very first sentence of Article II, they "vested" the president with a general grant of "executive Power" and then, later in the article, stated certain additional powers and responsibilities. The general grant of executive power has allowed the presidency to become the powerful office it is today. In this section, we look at the constitutional sources of the president's powers, the ways in which presidents have sought to expand their constitutional powers, and the ways in which the other branches, especially Congress, act to check and balance the president.

Commander in Chief

commander in chief: *Leader of the armed forces of the United States.*

The president is the **commander in chief** of the armed forces of the United States, which includes the Army, Navy, Air Force, Marine Corps, and Coast Guard, plus their Reserve and National Guard units. An elected commander in chief, rather than an appointed military officer, is a distinctly important element of American democracy. The president directs all war efforts and military conflict. Congress, however, has the power to officially declare war

TABLE 13.3 A Comparison of Legislative and Executive Authority Under the Constitution

While the Constitution grants specific legislative authority to Congress, it provides a general grant of authority to the president that does not require specific enumerated grants of power, nor is there an executive equivalent of Article I, Section 9, which specifically limits congressional authority.

	Legislative	Executive
Authority	"All legislative Powers herein granted shall be vested in a Congress of the United States"	"The executive Power shall be vested in a President of the United States"
Specific Powers	Article I, Section 8, including: • lay and collect taxes • provide for the common defense • regulate interstate and foreign commerce • authorize courts • set uniform rules for naturalization and bankruptcy • establish post offices • make all laws that are "necessary and proper" for carrying out the listed powers	Article II, Section 2, including: • act as commander in chief of armed forces • grant pardons • make treaties • receive foreign ministers • appoint ambassadors, judges, cabinet-level officials Article II, Section 3: • ensure that the laws are faithfully executed Article I, Section 7: • veto legislation
Limits on Power	Explicit limits on powers: Article I, Section 9, including: • no bills of attainder • no ex post facto laws • no titles of nobility Bill of Rights: • substantive limits of the First through Eighth Amendments Ninth Amendment: • enumeration of rights does not grant general authority Tenth Amendment: • people and states retain reserved powers not granted to Congress	Mostly through checks and balances: • veto override • Senate confirmation on appointments • Senate treaty ratification • removal by impeachment

and to authorize funding for the war effort. Because the war powers that are divided between the president and Congress are so contentious, we examine them later in the chapter.

Power to Pardon

The president has the power to grant clemency, or mercy, for crimes against the United States, except in the case of impeachment from federal office. Clemency is a broad designation that includes a **pardon**, which is forgiving an offense altogether, and a commutation, which is shortening a federal prison sentence; in general, pardoning someone is considered a more sweeping act of clemency than commuting a sentence. Election considerations can also come into play because presidents who are in their first term may want to appear tougher on crime than in their second term, when they will not be seeking reelection. For example, in his first term in office, President George W. Bush issued 19 pardons and commuted 2 sentences, but in his second term, Bush granted 170 pardons and commuted 7 sentences. In comparison, President Obama issued 22 pardons and commuted 1 sentence in his first term, but through August 2016, he had issued 70 pardons and commuted 673 sentences.[7]

pardon: *Full forgiveness for a crime.*

The crimes for which people are pardoned also differ across presidencies. Under George H. W. Bush, many of the pardon recipients had been part of the Iran-Contra scandal under President Reagan. In contrast, his son, President George W. Bush, refused to pardon a former White House staff member, I. Lewis Libby, who had been convicted of lying and obstruction of justice in a federal investigation about a leak of confidential information (although he did commute his prison sentence).[8] President Bill Clinton's most famous pardon was to a wealthy campaign contributor, Marc Rich, who had been indicted for tax evasion and fraud. President Obama focused most of his pardons on less prominent individuals who were convicted of crimes and served their sentences but who petitioned to have their full citizenship rights reinstated.

Treaties and Recognition of Foreign Nations

The president or his designated representative has the power to negotiate and sign treaties with foreign nations, but he must do so with the "Advice and Consent of the Senate," as specified by the Constitution. For a treaty to be valid, two-thirds "of the Senators present" must approve. Historically, the Senate has refused to approve some notable treaties, ranging from the Treaty of Versailles ending World War I signed by President Woodrow Wilson (1913–21), to the Kyoto Protocol on climate change signed by Vice President Albert Gore Jr., who was representing President William Jefferson (Bill) Clinton (1993–2001).

Essential Knowledge

A treaty is a formal agreement between two or more countries. Treaties are negotiated by the president (or someone on his behalf) and must be approved by the Senate.

These examples illustrate how the requirement that the Senate approve treaties serves as a gateway for public input into presidential actions, and how it can be a gate that blocks a president's attempt to reach agreements with foreign nations. Today, with the expansion of globalization, the president's representatives negotiate treaties over a wide range of areas, such as military alliances, human rights accords, environmental regulations, and trade policies. For example, President Obama spent considerable time and energy negotiating the Trans-Pacific Partnership trade agreement with twelve nations, foremost Japan, while in office, but as of November 2016, the agreement had not been ratified by Congress. The president also enters into executive agreements, which do not require Senate approval and tend to be less expansive in scope than treaties.

Essential Knowledge

An executive agreement is an agreement between the leaders of countries. Presidents often prefer to use executive agreements to conduct foreign policy rather than treaties because executive agreements do not require Senate approval.

POLITICAL ANALYTICS

A Day in the Life of the President

MOST AMERICANS KNOW THAT THE PRESIDENT of the United States resides and works in the White House in Washington, D.C. Many people probably assume that the president spends his day immersed in international and domestic policy discussions and decisions. But what does a president's daily schedule actually look like? Do all presidents follow the same schedule? Is every minute of the day filled with an activity?

Figure 13.2 shows a day in the life of former Presidents George W. Bush and Barack Obama. President Bush's schedule from his presidency is available through his presidential library archives and includes his "daily diary." As you can see, it is very detailed, with every meeting timed and scheduled from early in the morning until evening. President Obama's schedule, because he was the sitting president at the time of this publication, is much less detailed. The whereabouts of the current president are much more guarded. Still, we can see similarities in the two schedules. For example, both start their day with what is termed the "President's Daily Brief," a report the president receives from the CIA and the State Department regarding national security.

Notice the length of the president's daily routine and the variety of events and duties of the president. Find the similarities and differences between the schedules of Presidents Bush and Obama.

President George W. Bush, March 7, 2008

Time	Activity
6:57–6:59	Talked with his Assistant and Chief of Staff Joshua B. Bolten and Secretary of State Condoleezza Rice
6:59–7:09	Met with Mr. Bolten; Stephen J. Hadley, Asst. for Nat'l Security Affairs; Lt. Gen. Douglas E. Lute, Asst. & Deputy National Security Advisor for Iraq & Afghanistan
7:09–7:26	Met with Mr. Bolten, Mr. Hadley, Lt. Gen. Lute (out at 7:14), and Edward W. "Ed" Gillespie, Counselor
7:26–7:31	Participated in National Security Council (NSC) pre-brief
7:31–7:50	Talked on a secure conference call with Vladimir V. Putin, President of the Russian Federation
7:53–7:59	Participated in a taping session for a radio address to the nation on FISA
8:08–8:33	Met for daily intelligence briefing
8:37–9:11	Participated in a National Security Council meeting on Afghanistan
9:37–10:14	Participated in a secure conference call with Hamid Karzai, Pres. of Afghanistan; Mr. Hadley; Lt. Gen. Lute; John P. Hannah, Asst. to the Vice Pres. for National Security Affairs; & John K. Wood, Sr. Dir. for Iraq & Afghanistan
10:17–10:53	Met for daily communication briefing
10:53–11:12	Participated in a taping session for 2008 American Red Cross National Convention
11:17–11:43	Participated in an interview with Jeff Spaulding, Sr. Producer, Major League Baseball Productions
11:45–11:53	Participated in an NSC briefing
1:01–1:10	Met with the chair of the Council of Economic Advisers
1:10–1:15	Participated in a pre-brief with Carlos Gutierrez, Secretary of Commerce
1:15–1:35	Met with a family of Cuban political prisoners
1:35–1:46	Made a statement on Cuba
1:55–1:57	Made a statement on the economy
2:14–4:06	Participated in U.S. Department of Defense briefings
4:29–4:58	Met with Dr. Rex W. Chowdry, Maryland Health Care Commission
7:00–9:00	With the first lady, hosted a social dinner with Ambassador Mel Sembley and family

FIGURE 13.2 What Is the President Doing Today?

President Barack Obama, March 31, 2016

Early am	With the vice president, began the day with the Presidential Daily Briefing, White House, Oval Office
10:35	Held a trilateral meeting with President Park Geun-Hye of the Republic of Korea and Prime Minister Shinzo Abe of Japan; the vice president also attended Walter E. Washington Convention Center, Washington, DC
2:10	Held a bilateral meeting with President Xi Jinping of the People's Republic of China; the vice president also attended Walter E. Washington Convention Center, Washington, DC
4:15	Held a brief bilateral meeting with President Francois Hollande of France, Walter E. Washington Convention Center, Washington, DC
7:15	Held a working dinner with heads of delegations at the Nuclear Security Summit; the vice president also attended White House, East Room

FIGURE 13.2 What Is the President Doing Today? (Continued)

Sources: Schedules were adapted from https://www.whitehouse.gov/blog and https://www.georgewbushlibrary.smu.edu/~/media/GWBL/Files/Digitized%20Content/2014-0098-F/2008/t003-026-080307-2014-0098-f.ashx.

Thinking Critically

1. What do you think are the most important parts of the president's day?
2. What do you expect the details of President Obama's schedule to look like when they are released after his term in office?

The president's authority in foreign affairs includes the power to "receive Ambassadors and other public Ministers," which allows the president to recognize the legitimacy of foreign regimes. Such decisions are frequently based on the internal political system of the foreign nation. For example, revolutionaries overthrew Russia's czarist regime in 1917, but the new Soviet Union, a Communist nation, was not recognized by the United States until 1933, through the action of President Franklin Roosevelt. In contrast, in 2008, when the young democracy of Kosovo declared its independence from Serbia, President George W. Bush immediately recognized it as an independent nation.[9] However, the president also reserves the power not to recognize self-declared independent nations, as in the case of Russian separatists who took over control of the Crimean peninsula and eastern parts of Ukraine.

Essential Knowledge

Most high-level presidential cabinet appointments require Senatorial confirmation. This can set the stage for conflict between the president and Senate with the Senate refusing to confirm nominees on policy grounds. Some presidential appointments are more controversial. However, the vast majority of White House staff appointees do not require confirmation.

Executive and Judicial Nominations

The president has the power to appoint all federal officers, including cabinet secretaries, heads of independent agencies, and ambassadors. The presidential appointment process has two steps: (1) nomination and (2) subsequent approval by a majority of the Senate. The appointed officers are typically referred to as political appointees, and they are expected to carry out the president's political and policy agenda (in contrast to civil servants, who are hired through a merit-based system and are politically neutral; see Chapter 14, The Bureaucracy). During Senate recesses, the president can make appointments that will expire when the Senate officially adjourns at the close of a Congress (adjourns *sine die*), unless the appointee is subsequently confirmed. Presidents have sometimes used recess appointments to bypass the Senate, as President Obama did in appointing Richard Cordray director of the Consumer Financial Protection Bureau in 2012. Obama used the recess appointment power to get around strong Republican opposition to Cordray's appointment and the creation of the bureau he was nominated to lead (for more on this bureau, see Chapter 14). In order to prevent the president from making recess appointments when the Senate is on short breaks, the Senate has taken to officially staying in session but not conducting any business. In response, President Obama has acted as if the Senate were in recess and made a set of appointments to several agencies, including the National Labor Relations Board. In the 2014 case *National Labor Relations Board v. Noel Canning*, the Supreme Court ruled that only the Senate can decide when it is in recess, thus striking down three of Obama's appointments.

Essential Knowledge

Perhaps the most lasting impact of presidents is who they appoint to the bench; these appointments are lifelong. This power is checked by the Senates ability to advise and consent.

The president also nominates judges in the federal judicial system, from the district court level to the Supreme Court, and they too must receive majority approval in the Senate (see Chapter 15, The Judiciary, for more details on the judicial nomination process). In recent years, this process has become more ideological and contentious; rather than considering only qualifications for the job, presidents and members of the Senate also consider a nominee's ideological views on key issues. As we discussed in Chapter 12, the Senate changed its rules in 2013 to make it easier to confirm district and Appeals Court nominees but did not change the process for Supreme Court nominations; the 2016 nomination of Merrick Garland to the Supreme Court is an example of how this process can result in stalemate or the rejection of the president's nominee. As with the treaty process, the Senate's advice and consent role in appointments and nominations is a gateway for citizen influence.

The president has the power to fire federal officers but not to remove judges, who can be removed only by impeachment. Even though they have the formal power to do so, presidents rarely remove cabinet members because that would entail an admission of error in making the appointment in the first place. Some cabinet secretaries who disagreed with presidents about policies or, worse, committed acts of corruption were subsequently fired or were asked to resign. President Andrew Johnson fired his secretary of war, who disagreed with him about the policy of Reconstruction in the South after the Civil War.

Veto and the Veto Override

veto: *Authority of the president to block legislation passed by Congress. Congress can override a veto by a two-thirds majority in each chamber.*

pocket veto: *Automatic veto that occurs when Congress goes out of session within ten days of submitting a bill to the president and the president has not signed it.*

The president has an important role in the enactment of legislation. He has the power to **veto** bills passed by Congress before they become law by refusing to sign them and sending them back to the chamber in which they originated with his objections. If Congress will be going out of session within ten days, he can simply not sign the bill, a practice known as a **pocket veto**. If the president refuses to sign the bill and Congress remains in session, the bill is enacted into law.

To counter the power of the veto, the Framers gave Congress the veto override, the power to overturn a presidential veto with a two-thirds vote in each chamber. Because the two-thirds threshold is higher than the majority vote needed to pass a bill in the first place, it is difficult for Congress to overcome presidential opposition to a bill. The high threshold reinforces the power of the president in blocking congressional action and so serves as a gateway for presidential influence in the legislative process. One could also see the veto as a gate that legislation must pass through to become law, which can be unlocked only with a congressional supermajority.

The veto is the most direct way that the president checks the power of Congress. Presidents use the veto power either to prevent a bill from becoming law or to pressure Congress into making changes to bring the bill closer to his policies and his view of the national interest[10] (see Table 13.4). For most of the twentieth century, Congress sent the president a large number of single-issue or narrowly drawn bills each year. In recent decades, however, Congress has learned to get around the threat of a presidential veto by passing **omnibus bills** that include provisions affecting a number of issue areas. These bills are costly to veto because they affect a wide range of voters and generate a lot of public support, so they give Congress an advantage in negotiating with the president.[11]

omnibus bill: *One very large bill that encompasses many separate bills.*

Presidents naturally tend to veto more bills when Congress is controlled by the opposite party, a condition known as divided government. One of the most dramatic veto battles occurred in the fall of 1995 and early winter of 1996 between Democratic President Bill Clinton and the Republican-controlled Congress led by then-Speaker Newt Gingrich (see Chapter 3, Federalism). President Clinton and Congress differed over the size of cuts in **entitlement programs** such as Medicare, the health care program for the elderly (see Chapter 16, Economic, Domestic, and Foreign Policy, for a longer discussion of entitlement programs). Clinton vetoed two omnibus funding bills that Congress sent him, resulting in the shutdown of the entire government both times. The second shutdown lasted several weeks

entitlement programs: *Federal programs, such as Social Security, Medicare, or Medicaid, that pay out benefits to individuals based on a specified set of eligibility criteria.*

TABLE 13.4 Presidential Vetoes, 1945–2016

President	Congresses	Regular Vetoes	Pocket Vetoes	Total Vetoes	Vetoes Overridden
Harry S. Truman	79th–82nd	180	70	250	12
Dwight D. Eisenhower	83rd–86th	73	108	181	2
John F. Kennedy	87th–88th	12	9	21	0
Lyndon Baines Johnson	88th–90th	16	14	30	0
Richard M. Nixon	91st–93rd	26	17	43	7
Gerald R. Ford	93rd–94th	48	18	66	12
Jimmy Carter	95th–96th	13	18	31	2
Ronald Reagan	97th–100th	39	39	78	9
George H. W. Bush	101st–102nd	29	15*	44	1
William Jefferson Clinton	103rd–106th	36	1	37	2
George W. Bush	107th–110th	11	1	12	4
Barack Obama**	111th–114th	12	0	12	1
Total		488	310	798	52

*President George H. W. Bush attempted to pocket veto two bills during intrasession recesses. Congress considered the two bills enacted into law because the president had not returned the legislation. These two disputed vetoes are not included in Table 13.4.

**As of October 24, 2016.

Source: Kevin R. Kosar, *Regular Vetoes and Pocket Vetoes: An Overview*, CRS Report for Congress, RS22188 (Washington, D.C.: Congressional Research Service, November 18, 2010), 2–4, https://www.hsdl.org/?view&did=740060; source for veto information is John T. Woolley and Gerhard Peters, "Presidential Vetoes: Washington–Obama," The American Presidency Project, accessed March 2, 2016, http://www.presidency.ucsb.edu/data /vetoes.php.

and affected veterans' hospitals, all national parks and monuments, and other government-run services. The public blamed the Republican Congress, not the president, for the impasse, and many of the voters who generally supported the Republicans lived in areas that were hard hit by the shutdown. In January 1996, Congress compromised by agreeing to a funding bill that was closer to President Clinton's position. For the rest of 1996, President Clinton and the Republican majority in Congress worked to produce key legislation on welfare reform, health insurance portability, and the minimum wage. In this case, the president used the threat of more vetoes to get members of Congress to produce legislation closer to his policy positions.[12]

Essential Knowledge

The State of the Union address is a primary example of the president's utilization of the bully pulpit to set the political agenda.

Other Powers

State of the Union address: *Speech on the condition of the country given by the president to Congress every January.*

The president works within this framework of formal powers and constraints to lead the nation, and in doing so becomes the chief agenda setter for domestic and foreign policy. In a later section of this chapter, we discuss agenda setting in more detail; here it is important to note that, over time, smaller tasks assigned to the president in the Constitution have evolved into powerful tools for influencing legislation. One tool is the **State of the Union address**, which is authorized in Article II, Section 3: The president "shall from time to time give to the Congress Information of the State of the Union, and recommend to their Consideration such Measures as he shall judge necessary and expedient." Nothing in this passage requires the president to inform Congress on a yearly basis or to do so in person. Presidents George Washington and John Adams (1797–1801) delivered the State of the Union address in person, but subsequent presidents began sending a written message instead, a tradition that lasted until 1913, when President Wilson went to Congress once again to give the report as an address.[13] Over the past century, presidents have turned this obligation into an opportunity to outline a broad policy agenda for the nation. That same passage also says that the president "may, on extraordinary Occasions convene both Houses, or either of them." Thus the president can call Congress into a special session to consider legislation or to hear him deliver an important speech.[14]

Congress's Ultimate Check on the Executive: Impeachment

Congress has general oversight of the executive branch (a power discussed in Chapters 12 and 14), but its ultimate check on the president is its power to remove him from office. As discussed in Chapter 2, The Constitution, Article II, Section 4, of the Constitution stipulates that the president, vice president, and all civil officers (including cabinet secretaries and federal judges) are subject to removal for "Treason, Bribery, or other high Crimes and Misdemeanors." Should these officers be removed from office, they may be subject to normal criminal charges and proceedings, where applicable.

impeachment: *Process whereby the House brings charges against the president or another federal official that will, upon conviction by the Senate, remove him or her from office.*

The process of removal begins with **impeachment** in the House of Representatives. Typically, the House Judiciary Committee investigates charges and recommends to the full House whether to impeach or not. If the House votes to impeach a federal officer, the Senate holds a trial, and if the president is impeached, the chief justice of the Supreme Court presides. If two-thirds of the senators vote to convict, the official is removed from office.

At the highest level of federal office, two presidents—Andrew Johnson and Bill Clinton—have been impeached, but neither was convicted by the Senate, and both remained in office. Impeachment resolutions have been introduced by individual members of the House of Representatives against other presidents, but they were not acted on. The greatest impact stemming from the power to impeach came in the case of Richard M. Nixon, which shows how the threat of impeachment can be enough to remove a president from office. Knowing he was about to be impeached, Nixon resigned instead. In addition to charges of wrongdoing, partisan disagreements can influence some members of Congress in their votes to move forward with impeachment proceedings.

As the following discussion of Richard Nixon will show, impeachment is a rarely used but powerful instrument that makes it possible for Congress to hold the president accountable for his actions. In a democratic nation guided by the rule of law, all citizens are equally obligated to obey the laws of the land, including the president.

Richard M. Nixon. President Richard Nixon was embroiled in a serious scandal known as Watergate, after the name of a complex in Washington where the Democratic National Committee had its headquarters. It was there that the scandal began with a break-in on June 17, 1972. In August, the *Washington Post* reported that the bank account of one of the five men caught in the act and arrested had $25,000 in funds originally given to the Nixon 1972 reelection campaign.[15]

Nixon denied any connection and was reelected in the fall, but all the while he and his aides were working to cover up the fact that his reelection committee had ordered the break-in to install listening devices on Democratic Party phones. Two *Washington Post* reporters, Bob Woodward and Carl Bernstein, continued to investigate the story (see Chapter 7, The News and Social Media). As connections between Nixon and the break-in were revealed, several of his aides were convicted of conspiracy, burglary, and wiretapping, and others resigned. In May 1973, the Senate's newly formed Watergate Committee began televised hearings on the Watergate break-in and cover-up, and the Justice Department appointed Archibald Cox as the special prosecutor in charge of the Watergate investigation.

In the months that followed, a Nixon staffer revealed that the president had tape-recorded all of his White House conversations, and both the Senate Watergate Committee and the House Judiciary Committee formally issued subpoenas demanding that Nixon turn over the recordings. The turning point in what became known as the Watergate scandal came on Saturday, October 20, 1973, when President Nixon asked his attorney general, Elliot Richardson, to fire Archibald Cox and abolish the office of special prosecutor entirely. Richardson refused, as did the deputy attorney general. Both resigned. Solicitor General Robert Bork, next in command, then carried out the president's wishes. What had been a struggle for information became a question of obstruction of justice by the president.

President Nixon turned over a limited number of tapes, but there was an eighteen-and-a-half-minute gap on one tape, and Congress wanted to know what was discussed during that time and why it was erased. The administration claimed that the tape was erased by mistake. During the next months, Nixon released only partial transcripts and said that others were protected by **executive privilege**—the president's right to engage in communications with his advisers that he does not have to reveal. The justification for this privilege is that the president must make difficult choices and, without the guarantee of privilege,

executive privilege: *President's right to engage in confidential communications with his advisers.*

IMAGE 13.3 When Richard Nixon resigned the presidency in August 1974, it was the first time in U.S. history that a president had relinquished his office. President Nixon left office under charges of abuse of power arising from a cover-up of the Watergate scandal, which forever changed the nation's faith in the presidency as a trustworthy institution.

may not receive or deliver the fullest information in the course of his deliberations.

The Supreme Court created an exception to this privilege in *United States v. Nixon* when on July 24, 1974, it unanimously ruled that executive privilege is not absolute and must give way when the government needs the information for a trial. The tapes showed that Nixon and his aides had conspired to cover up the Watergate break-in. Three days later, the House Judiciary Committee approved three articles of impeachment against Nixon.[16] With the full House of Representatives ready to vote on the articles, President Nixon resigned on August 9, 1974.

In 1975, Nixon's successor, former Vice President Gerald R. Ford (1974–77), pardoned Nixon of all federal offenses he might have committed. The Watergate scandal had a negative impact on the American presidency, raising public mistrust of the office and of the federal government more generally. However, the process leading up to Nixon's resignation also revealed the ways in which members of both parties can work together in Congress to exercise congressional oversight of the executive.

Impeachment is not a power to be used lightly. However, it does serve as a gateway for the public, through its elected officials in Congress, to hold the president, cabinet officials, and federal judges accountable for abuses of power.

13.3 The Growth of Executive Influence

Describe the growth of executive influence

With all the formal constitutional restrictions on the president, one has to wonder how the modern presidency became so powerful. The answer lies in the general grant of executive power and the constitutional provision that the president "take Care that the Laws be faithfully executed," which he promises to do when he takes the oath of office. Presidents have found ways to unlock the enormous powers inherent in these constitutional provisions to expand their informal powers over policy making and implementation. The president's veto power and Congress's power to override and to impeach the president counteract each other and help ensure that each branch remains responsive to its governing responsibilities.

However, Congress has no formal means to balance and check the president's growing executive power, though at times the judicial branch has been able to do so.

Essential Knowledge

Presidential actions (such as executive orders and signing statements) can set the stage for conflict with Congress.

Presidential Directives and Signing Statements

Presidents use the executive power to issue **presidential directives** that give specific instructions on a federal policy and do not require congressional approval. Recent presidents have used this unilateral power much more frequently than previous presidents, especially under conditions of divided government or interbranch policy conflict.[17] Presidential directives might take the form of executive orders, proclamations, or military orders. They are the primary way that presidents shape policy implementation, and they are the instruments presidents use to act quickly in national emergencies.[18]

presidential directive: *Official instructions from the president regarding federal policy.*

The best-known type of directive is the **executive order**, which can be used for a wide range of purposes. Typically, executive orders instruct federal employees to take a specific action or implement a policy in a particular way. Some scholars argue that executive orders are an important source of "independent authority" that is used solely at the discretion of the president.[19] Even though presidents since Washington have issued executive orders, the orders were not officially numbered until 1862 and not published in the *Federal Register* until 1935.[20] In 1948, President Truman integrated the armed forces with Executive Order 9981, stating "there shall be equality of treatment and opportunity for all persons in the armed forces, without regard to race, color, religion, or national origin."[21] Truman used the power of executive order to bypass congressional and some military opposition to integration of the armed forces because he believed it was the right thing for the country.

executive order: *Presidential directive that usually involves implementing a specific law.*

Essential Knowledge

The president's power to issue executive orders is, depending on the case, derived from the Constitution or delegated by Congress. Although not statutory law, these orders can have the same effect as statutory law.

Similarly, in 1957, President Dwight D. Eisenhower (1953–61) used a combination of executive orders, proclamations, and military orders to enforce school integration in Little Rock, Arkansas. Following the 1954 and 1955 *Brown v. Board of Education* Supreme Court rulings that struck down the practice of segregation in public schools, the governor of Arkansas, Orval Faubus, called up the Arkansas National Guard to block nine African Americans from attending Central High School in Little Rock. President Eisenhower responded by issuing a proclamation calling on the governor to cease and desist, and when the governor ignored the proclamation, Eisenhower issued Executive Order 10730 to send the 101st Airborne Division to Little Rock to ensure that the students would be allowed into the school (see also the Supreme Court Case *Cooper v. Aaron* in Chapter 15). He also used his authority as commander in chief to take command of the Arkansas National Guard and order it to assist in the school's integration. Eisenhower intervened because he believed it was his obligation as president to enforce the laws of the land as set forth by the rulings of the Supreme Court.[22]

Still, a presidential directive is not completely immune from scrutiny or accountability. In 1952, during the Korean War, the United Steelworkers union threatened to stop work at steel mills. In response, President Truman used his executive powers to order the seizure of steel mills and put them under the control of the U.S. government. Although the steel workers were willing to put off the strike and work in the newly government-controlled mills, the steel mill owners sued to challenge the legality of the seizure. In *Youngstown Sheet and Tube Co. v. Sawyer,* better known as the Steel Seizure case, the Supreme Court ruled against the president, claiming he had no statutory authority from Congress to seize the mills and that his commander in chief status did not allow him to seize domestic property

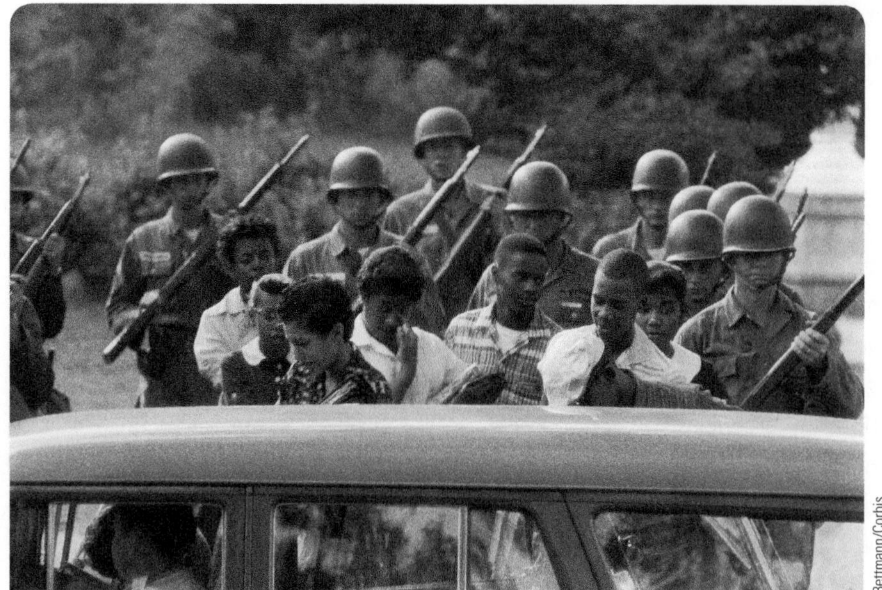

Bettmann/Corbis

IMAGE 13.4 In September 1957, in a move that demonstrated federal power over state power as well as the authority of the commander in chief, President Dwight D. Eisenhower sent the 101st Airborne Division to Little Rock, Arkansas, to protect nine African American students attempting to attend previously all-white Central High School. He also nationalized the Arkansas National Guard for the same purpose.

when the United States was at war in a foreign land (see Supreme Court Cases: *Youngstown Sheet and Tube Co. v. Sawyer*).

In foreign and military affairs, presidents can issue presidential directives on national security; these have a similar purpose to executive orders but are not published in the *Federal Register,* which is the official record of government regulations (see Chapter 14). These directives can announce specific sanctions against individuals who are considered enemies of the United States or make larger statements about U.S. policy toward a foreign country. President George W. Bush used this power frequently in what he described as a war on terror and in the conduct of the wars in Afghanistan and Iraq. For example, he issued an order in 2001 to create military tribunals that would try suspected enemy combatants and terrorists, rather than allowing them to be tried in a regular military court. He also created a special subcategory called homeland security presidential directives, which are not as widely publicized as other directives and deal only with homeland security policy.

signing statements: *Written remarks issued by the president when signing a bill into law that often reflect his interpretation of how the law should be implemented.*

When a president signs a bill into law, he can issue **signing statements**, written remarks that reflect his interpretation of the law that are not required or authorized by the Constitution. Signing statements can be classified as nonconstitutional and constitutional. Nonconstitutional statements are typically symbolic, celebrating the passage of the law or providing technical instructions for implementing a new law. Constitutional statements are more serious in that the president uses them to indicate a disagreement with Congress on specific provisions in the law. In constitutional signing statements, the president may go so far as to refuse to implement specific provisions of laws. This kind of statement is a challenge to Congress's constitutional authority to legislate.[23] Even when the presidency and the Congress are controlled by the same party, signing statements can be used to shift the implementation of policy toward presidential preferences. President Obama recognized the controversy over signing statements, and he issued a memorandum early in his first term stating that he would use signing statements "to address constitutional concerns only when it is appropriate to do so as a means of discharging my constitutional responsibilities."[24] In issuing this memorandum, President Obama was trying to alleviate concerns about abusing executive power but at the same time preserving the presidential power to interpret legislation that is inherent in signing statements. As of November 2016, President Obama had issued 35 signing statements and 249 executive orders.[25]

Presidential directives and signing statements create tension between the president and Congress and between the president and the judiciary because they are an expansion of presidential power. At times they have been deemed illegal.[26] Many presidents, from Lincoln to Franklin D. Roosevelt to George W. Bush, have taken temporary actions that have violated constitutional rights in the name of national security, from suspending *habeas corpus* to interning Japanese Americans and repatriating Latinos to eavesdropping on U.S. citizens (see Chapter 4, Civil Liberties, and Chapter 5, Civil Rights, for expanded discussions of these actions). Judging the merit of such actions is difficult because citizens have to decide whether the president is acting in good faith on behalf of the country or seeking to expand his own power and agenda.

Essential Knowledge

The president is uniquely situated in American politics to impact public opinion. The president can use his power to influence Congress; presidents frequently rely on the informal powers of bargaining and persuasion to work with Congress.

Power to Persuade

Presidents understand that communicating well with the public is essential to building support for their policies. They also face the challenge of using their personal reputations and negotiating skills to generate support among members of Congress. President Theodore Roosevelt (1901–09) described the office of the president as a **bully pulpit**, where presidents could use the attention associated with the office to make a public argument in favor of or against a policy.[27] The key to using the bully pulpit effectively is to explain a policy in simple and accessible terms, to get the public's attention, and to frame an issue in a way that is favorable to the president's policy position. Using the bully pulpit can accomplish the president's goals only if he already has a receptive audience. In today's highly partisan and divided political climate, there is no guarantee that the president's detractors will listen to his message.[28]

bully pulpit: *Nickname for the power of the president to use the attention associated with the office to persuade the media, Congress, and the public to support his policy positions.*

A president's relationship with the members of the news media is a crucial factor in successful communication, and it has evolved dramatically over time. Samuel Kernell, a presidential media scholar, argues that over the past seventy years, presidents have increased the extent to which they control their interactions with the press. Press conferences are one important way of sustaining a relationship with the news media, and presidents have tried to use them to their advantage. Some presidents are more comfortable with the press than others. Franklin D. Roosevelt held an average of eighteen solo press conferences per year, Lyndon Johnson held twenty-five, Ronald Reagan held six, Bill Clinton held six, and George W. Bush held five. President Obama averaged five press conferences per year in his first term and averaged four press conferences per year through November 2016.[29] Press conferences are somewhat risky because, unlike speeches, presidents do not control the content of the questions that are asked, and they can sometimes make unrehearsed statements that have political consequences. In addition to press conferences and televised speeches, President Obama also used new technologies to bypass the media and speak directly to the people. Recognizing that many voters get their news and political information from sources such as Facebook and Twitter instead of from traditional network television, he created a blog on the

Bettmann/Corbis

IMAGE 13.5 President Theodore Roosevelt was a larger-than-life figure who challenged corporate monopolies, sought to strengthen U.S. international power, and increased federal efforts at land conservation. He was known for using the office of the president as a bully pulpit to persuade the public to support his policies.

SUPREME COURT CASES

Youngstown Sheet and Tube Co. v. Sawyer (1952)

QUESTION: Can the president seize steel mills to prevent a strike during wartime?

ORAL ARGUMENT: May 12, 1952

DECISION: June 2, 1952 (read at http://caselaw.lp.findlaw.com/scripts/getcase.pl?court=US&vol=343&invol=579)

OUTCOME: No, the seizure was overturned (6–3).

After North Korea's invasion of South Korea in June 1950, President Harry Truman sought and received a United Nations resolution permitting intervention on behalf of South Korea. In 1952, with the Korean War still raging, the United Steelworkers announced plans for an April strike. President Truman feared that the strike would severely harm America's war effort. One alternative for putting off the strike was to seek a temporary court order prohibiting a strike when national security is at stake, a provision allowed under the Taft-Hartley Labor Act.

Uncomfortable with what was perceived to be an anti-labor policy, Truman instead ordered Secretary of Commerce Charles Sawyer to seize the steel mills and run them under the flag of the United States. Because the steelworkers preferred working at the steel mills under the government to the Taft-Hartley alternatives, they agreed to come back to work after the seizure.

The steel mill owners then brought suit challenging the seizure. Truman claimed the authority to do this under his power to make sure that the laws were faithfully executed and under his power as commander in chief of the armed forces. The Court's decision rejected the president's authority to seize the steel mills, noting that Congress had not passed a law allowing the seizure, so there were no laws involving the seizure to be faithfully executed. The Court also ruled that the president's authority to rule as commander in chief did not extend to domestic seizures during foreign wars. Without congressional authorization, the president could not seize the steel mills. A separate concurring opinion, since treated as the heart of the case, noted that the president's authority is at its peak when he acts under the express authority of Congress, is in a middle category when Congress has not acted, and is at its lowest when the president acts contrary to congressional will. As Congress had rejected granting the president the authority to seize property in labor disputes, Truman was acting under the lowest level of authority. Without congressional authorization, the president could not seize the steel mills.

The Steel Seizure case still stands as the leading decision on presidential authority. The Supreme Court relied heavily on it in deciding that President George W. Bush did not have the authority to hold enemy combatants from the war in Afghanistan at the U.S. naval base at Guantánamo Bay, Cuba, without a hearing, since Congress had not authorized the action.*

Thinking Critically

1. Why did the Court block President Truman's seizure of the steel mills?
2. Did the decision place the president above Congress, below Congress, or equal to Congress in terms of making policy?

**Hamdan v. Rumsfeld*, 548 U.S. 557 (2006).

White House website, posted videos of his speeches, and sent mass e-mails to citizens who inquired about specific proposals.[30]

In conjunction with public outreach, the president also tries to personally persuade members of Congress and other policy makers to support his policies. Political scientist Richard Neustadt has argued that this personal persuasion is the root of presidential power.

Several factors affect a president's power to persuade, notably his professional reputation and his approval ratings.[31] A presidential approval rating is usually expressed as the percentage of the American people who say the president is doing a good job. A president's professional reputation is a combination of his prior experience and the steps he takes throughout his term. When a president comes to the Oval Office with executive experience or a strong reputation as a productive legislator, he is likely to have a reservoir of respect from members of Congress, the public, and the media. That reservoir can become depleted if the president makes missteps and is not successful with his legislative agenda.

Lawmakers are more likely to pass a president's policy proposals when his approval rating is high, and they are less cooperative when the president is unpopular. Members of Congress pay attention to presidential approval ratings because national polls are a barometer of public opinion. Members of Congress from districts or states in which a majority of voters chose the incumbent president generally want to support him. It follows, then, that a large presidential electoral victory will yield a greater number of supportive members of Congress. Even members of Congress from districts that did not support the incumbent president want to be careful in the way that they oppose a popular president for fear of looking unpatriotic or unresponsive to majority public opinion. Public approval can be essential to presidential policy success, which is why the president tries to maintain public support throughout his years in the White House[32] (see Chapter 6 for more on presidential approval ratings and presidential effectiveness).

To be persuasive, a president has to balance his own policy preferences with those of members of Congress and convince the American public that he is leading the country in the right direction.[33] The stakes can be very high for presidents as they navigate the legislative process (see Chapter 12). The president's need to be responsive to public opinion serves as a gateway for influence by the public on his decision making.

head of state: *Title given to the president as national leader.*

Agenda Setting

As the chief executive officer of the entire federal government, the president has an obligation and an opportunity to work with Congress to set the foreign and domestic policy agenda for the nation, from determining how to configure military strength, to overseeing economic growth, to ensuring the health and safety of individual citizens. The president is the sole occupant of his elected office, as compared with 535 members of the House and Senate. Consequently, the president has the power to focus the nation's attention on his or her ideas and policy proposals.

In dealing with foreign powers, the president is **head of state** and commander in chief of the military. As head of state, the president oversees a vast organization of employees in the State Department and the office of the U.S. Trade Representative who lay the groundwork for negotiations with foreign leaders on issues ranging from nuclear weapons control to trade policy. Upon their recommendation, the president proposes new treaties or revisions to existing agreements as needed. Ultimately, the president is the public face of and the authority behind U.S. foreign policy decisions. He must establish working

Bettmann/Getty Images

IMAGE 13.6 President John F. Kennedy was completely at ease with the press and held sixty-four press conferences during his time in office. They were televised, and not only White House reporters but also the American public looked forward to the lively exchanges between the press and the president, who was known for his sense of humor and ready wit.

NICHOLAS KAMM/Getty Images

IMAGE 13.7 The president, as head of state, engages in direct diplomacy with foreign leaders in a number of different settings. Such formal functions expose world leaders to elite members of the American political and economic arenas. These events can serve to enhance diplomatic relations between the United States and its allies. At this state dinner in March 2016, President and Mrs. Obama welcomed Justin Trudeau, the prime minister of Canada, and his wife, Sophie.

relationships with foreign leaders and demonstrate an understanding of how other nations' political systems operate, especially the extent to which the executive power is placed in one person or shared, as it is in parliamentary systems (see Chapter 12).

Because the president is presumed to serve the best interest of the entire nation, the American public frequently supports most of his foreign policies—at least initially. The main congressional counterweights to the president's powers in these areas are the power of the Senate to ratify treaties and the power of Congress to appropriate money for federal programs, including foreign aid and diplomatic programs. These congressional powers come in the form of responses to the president's proposals. Congress can have some influence on the president's foreign policy agenda through hearings and press statements, but if the president is able to persuade the public to support his or her positions, he is typically able to forge his or her own path on foreign policy.

In the area of domestic policy, the president uses the State of the Union address, the federal budget, the power to make executive appointments, the bully pulpit, the executive power to implement laws, and the veto power as his agenda-setting tools. He issues his federal budget in early February, shortly after he delivers the State of the Union address. The budget is a blueprint that indicates his spending priorities for all areas of the federal government. Congress does not have to abide by this budget, and Congress frequently ignores it and constructs its own federal budget (see Chapter 12 for a discussion of the budget). All measures that raise taxes and spend federal money can be vetoed by the president, and, as we have seen, the veto or the threat of a veto gives the president a means of exerting pressure on Congress to follow his budget priorities.

The president engages in domestic policy agenda setting in other ways as well. For example, as in the case of President Obama and health care, presidents can propose legislation that changes existing programs or creates new ones and ask Congress to consider his suggestions. He can also be even more proactive by issuing presidential directives that direct the bureaucracy to implement laws as he sees fit. The president's major speeches, press conferences, interviews, social media communication, and travels always command media attention, so he has a constantly open forum to try to persuade voters to support his proposals.[34]

13.4 The President in Wartime

Analyze why the president is so powerful during wartime

As executive branch powers have grown, presidents have increasingly come into conflict with the judicial branch and Congress, especially in times of national crisis and war (see also Chapter 4). In this section, we examine the power struggle between the president and Congress over war powers, which the Constitution divides between the two branches, and the power struggle between the president and the judiciary on the scope of presidential powers and civil liberties. It is crucial to understand that the balance of power among the three branches of the federal government is constantly evolving in response to changing internal and external conditions.

Power Struggles Between the President and Congress

The Constitution gives Congress the power to declare war, but it has been the practice for presidents to first formally ask Congress for a declaration of war. After Congress declares war, the president as commander in chief has the authority to direct the conflict. Through its constitutional powers in Article I, Section 8, "to raise and support Armies" and "to provide and maintain a Navy," Congress retains the power to cut off the flow of money for the war effort. Generally, the president and Congress have worked together in times of military conflict, but in the late 1960s, opposition to the Vietnam War brought about significant divisions between the executive and legislative branches over war powers.

Essential Knowledge

Term-of-office and constitutional-power restrictions, including the passage of the Twenty-second Amendment, demonstrate changing presidential roles.

Vietnam and the War Powers Act. Vietnam had been a divided nation since 1954, with Communist forces controlling North Vietnam and anti-Communists controlling South Vietnam, and a civil war had erupted between them. President Eisenhower and then Presidents Kennedy and Johnson believed that containing Communism and keeping the North Vietnamese Communists from taking over South Vietnam were important, but the U.S. troop buildup was slow at first. In 1964, however, President Johnson presented evidence to Congress that the North Vietnamese were attacking U.S. ships on patrol duty in international waters in the Gulf of Tonkin off the shore of North Vietnam. Johnson asked Congress for the authority to fight back, and Congress responded with the Tonkin Gulf Resolution, stating that "The Congress approves and supports the determination of the President, as Commander in Chief, to take all necessary measures to repel any armed attack against the forces of the United States and to prevent further aggression."[35] Congress passed the resolution with only two dissenting votes, few restrictions, and no time limit on how long the United States would stay involved in the conflict.[36]

By 1968, the United States had more than five hundred thousand troops in Vietnam, and the conflict was commonly referred to as the Vietnam War, although there was never a formal declaration of war by Congress. The conflict had become highly unpopular, and President Johnson was forced to give up his bid for reelection. That year, Richard Nixon was elected president and promised to end the Vietnam War; however, he actually broadened the conflict to the neighboring countries of Cambodia and Laos in his efforts to win the war.

By 1971, Congress had repealed the Tonkin Gulf Resolution, and, following the Paris Peace Accords signed in January 1973, U.S. troops were withdrawn from Vietnam. In October 1973, Congress passed a more formal proposal to limit presidential authority to engage in military conflict. This **War Powers Act** states that the president cannot send troops into military conflict for more than a total of ninety days without seeking a formal declaration of war, or authorization for continued military action, from Congress. President Nixon vetoed the act, but Congress overrode the veto.

War Powers Act: *The 1973 act that provides that the president cannot send troops into military conflict for more than a total of ninety days without seeking a formal declaration of war, or authorization for continued military action, from Congress.*

The War Powers Act was ostensibly a gate that would stand in the way of a president's decision to launch a war without first gauging congressional support. Although the act tried to clarify presidential authority and limits, the scholar Louis Fisher argues that it is flawed because the ninety-day limit does not begin until the president has officially reported the troop engagement to Congress. A president could send troops into a conflict and not report it to Congress, thereby avoiding a trigger of the War Powers Act.[37] In addition, the act did not really give Congress the power to end a military conflict except by denying all funding for it, as it ultimately did with Vietnam. However, if there is considerable public support for an ongoing military engagement, the president can make the case that it is too dangerous to cut off all funding, and Congress would be reluctant to cut off funding when troops were still in the field and could be harmed. The irony of the War Powers Act is that it gives presidents an incentive to seek a declaration of war or authorization to use military force, after which time Congress loses much of its control of the operation of the conflict.[38] In other words, once Congress gives the president permission to go to war, it is next to impossible for Congress to stop the war.[39]

The Iraq War. The United States was involved in major military conflicts in Iraq and Afghanistan for the first decade (and beyond) of the twenty-first century. The two wars ran parallel to each other, but their origins are quite different. The Iraq War began in 2003, but its origins date back to August 1990, when Iraq, led by Saddam Hussein, invaded Kuwait. This act of aggression prompted multilateral military action known as the Gulf War, which aimed to push Iraq out of Kuwait. The Gulf War was short-lived; as part of the peace settlement, Iraq was prohibited from developing weapons of mass destruction and was required to submit to constant United Nations (UN) monitoring.

By 2002, it had become increasingly difficult for UN inspectors to accurately assess Iraq's capabilities for producing weapons of mass destruction. Although there had been no concrete evidence of such weapons, President George W. Bush argued that a preemptive strike against Iraq was necessary to preserve the security of the United States. In accordance with the War Powers Act, President Bush asked Congress for a resolution authorizing military action. On October 10, 2002, the House of Representatives approved a joint resolution that gave the president the authority to use all military force to "defend the national security of the United States."[40] The Senate approved the resolution the next day by a vote of 77–23.

The Iraq War was launched on March 19, 2003; Saddam Hussein was captured in December 2003 and was tried and hanged for war crimes. Nevertheless, instability in Iraq continued. By 2006, with violence in Iraq at a high level, the Democrats in Congress—many of whom had initially supported the war—withdrew their support and called for the return of all U.S. troops and an end to the war. During the midterm congressional elections that year, Democrats made ending the war a campaign issue, and they won majority control of the House and the Senate. However, in January 2007, President Bush increased the number of troops in Iraq in an effort known as the "surge," which was intended to reduce violence there.

As of January 2009, the three dominant groups in Iraq—the Sunnis, the Shiites, and the Kurds—were operating under a parliamentary system of government, and the U.S. government worked with the Iraqis to end the war and transfer full governmental control to them. On August 31, 2010, President Obama announced the end of the nation's formal combat involvement, and by the end of December 2011, the last official combat personnel departed from Iraq, although some U.S. soldiers are there in an advisory role. Since then, the Iraqi government has struggled to maintain security among the different factions vying for power, in addition to the incursions by the extremist group ISIS, which has led to violence and casualties. Iraq today represents a nation forever changed by U.S. involvement; what remains uncertain is whether that change will enable or prevent democratic government there.

The Afghanistan War. The war in Afghanistan began after the September 11, 2001, terrorist attacks were traced back to al-Qaeda operatives harbored by the Afghan Taliban regime. President George W. Bush addressed Congress on September 20, 2001, indicating that the Taliban would be held responsible for the attacks, and, in October, the United States and its allies launched a military action on Afghanistan designed to find those responsible for the 9/11 attacks and bring down the Taliban regime. However, Bush did not ask for a declaration of war against the nation of Afghanistan. Although the Taliban regime was subsequently toppled and a new leader, Hamid Karzai, was elected and later reelected, the Taliban mounted a resurgence in Afghanistan. In 2009, President Obama, as commander in chief, responded to resurgent Taliban-sponsored attacks on U.S. troops and civilian Afghans by ordering a surge of thirty thousand additional troops to Afghanistan, bringing the total there to nearly a hundred thousand.[41] In the next two years, as the number of American and Afghan casualties increased, public support for the war decreased, and it was hard for President Obama to maintain U.S. involvement there. The Republicans' takeover of the House of Representatives in the 2010 election complicated his decision making because they publicly resisted efforts to reduce the U.S. presence in Afghanistan until the government could demonstrate it had defeated the Taliban and al-Qaeda.

On May 1, 2011, President Obama announced that Osama bin Laden, who had claimed to be the head of al-Qaeda and the coordinator of the 9/11 attacks, had been killed in a military operation in Pakistan. With the death of bin Laden, public support for the war diminished further. In 2012, President Obama and Secretary of Defense Leon Panetta announced their intention to work with the Afghanistan government to reduce the number of U.S. troops in Afghanistan at a faster rate. As of August 2016, the number of U.S. troops stationed in Afghanistan was approximately 8,400.[42]

Uprisings in Foreign Lands. Ongoing military conflicts such as those in Iraq and Afghanistan have spillover effects that can limit the president's flexibility in responding to conflicts in other foreign nations. Protests in 2011 known as the Arab Spring that threatened to topple authoritarian regimes offer an example. Seeking UN approval and international cooperation, the U.S. military became involved only in Libya. When in March 2011 President Obama authorized the use of air strikes and drones in Libya, he was acting in conjunction with NATO forces to enforce a UN Security Council resolution that authorized international military action to enforce a no-fly zone to stop the Libyan leader, Muammar al-Qaddafi, from committing violence against his own people. The decision to intervene in Libya was controversial given ongoing involvement in Afghanistan, so Obama gave a national address to explain his decision and inform the American people that U.S. ground troops would not be deployed. Nevertheless, some members of Congress argued that the air strikes violated the War Powers Act because the president had not formally notified Congress of military involvement there. The president moved forward anyway, and by October 2011, the rebel forces had prevailed, and Qaddafi was killed as he resisted capture.[43] Without a strong leader, the country fell into chaos. The power vacuum enabled ISIS to control substantial amounts of Libyan territory.

Unlike Libya, President Obama did not propose intervening in the Syrian conflict, although the United States did support a UN resolution condemning the violence committed by President Bashar al-Assad's regime against opposition forces. That resolution was vetoed by Russia and China, and without multilateral or congressional support for intervention, Obama lacked the same justification for entering that conflict that he did in the case of Libya.[44] However, Obama worked with the United Nations and Russia to broker a deal whereby Syria agreed not to use chemical weapons and to turn over all chemical weapons to the United Nations for safe destruction. Although that turnover has been completed, the civil war rages on in Syria. Meanwhile, the Obama administration has supplied Syrian rebels with light arms and humanitarian aid, while Russia has sold advanced aircraft and missile systems to the Syrian government. With the rise of ISIS, the United States has played a much larger role in the Syrian conflict. The United States led a coalition of nations in air strikes against ISIS and provided weapons to groups fighting against ISIS.

Beha el Halebi/Anadolu Agency/Getty Images

IMAGE 13.8 The conflict in Syria was a major issue in President Obama's second term in office. While the United States focused its efforts on ISIS in Syria, Russian forces aided the Assad regime by engaging in air strikes across Syria. Here we see the aftermath of a Russian strike in the town of Aleppo, which had been the site of strong resistance to Assad.

Tensions with Russia intensified when Ukrainian rebels ousted their pro-Russian president. Ukraine, Russia's neighbor to the West, is home to many individuals of Russian heritage. Subsequently, Russian separatists staged takeovers of Ukrainian government buildings in southern and eastern Ukraine, essentially declaring them part of Russia. The Ukrainian government was not well prepared to stop these takeovers, which Russia actively supported. In response, President Obama and leaders of European nations imposed economic sanctions on Russia in an effort to pressure them to withdraw their support of these separatists. President Obama and Congress understood that the United States is expected to take the lead in responding to international crises of the type that occurred in Ukraine as well as Syria. However, the American public are weary of war and international conflict. At the same time, Americans view global instability as a threat to their safety. In recent years, it became increasingly clear to both Obama and Congress that public opinion among the American people leaned more strongly against intervention in foreign conflicts; 57 percent of Americans opposed sending ground troops to combat ISIS.[45] This broader context has important implications for U.S. foreign policy because presidents, and members of Congress, recognize the difficulty of waging a military intervention without public support.

These examples demonstrate that tension between the presidency and Congress over war powers compels the president to make the case to Congress that military action is necessary. Moreover, as in the case with Ukraine and Syria, presidents face challenges in persuading a war-weary nation to intervene with military force. In such cases, the Obama administration sought to actively intervene only with strong international support and with as little involvement as possible of U.S. ground troops.

Power Struggles Between the President and the Judiciary

Power struggles between the president and the judiciary in wartime generally focus on civil liberties. In Chapter 4, we examined the Court's rejection of Abraham Lincoln's argument about the suspension of *habeas corpus*, and in Chapter 5, we discussed the Court's acquiescence in President Roosevelt's executive order on the internment of Japanese Americans. In this chapter, we have already noted the limits on presidential actions imposed by the Steel Seizure case.

The most significant recent clash between the president and the judiciary over wartime powers arose during President George W. Bush's declared war on terror. Following 9/11, President Bush greatly expanded the powers of the executive branch. As we have seen in previous chapters, he created separate military tribunals to try captured terrorists, claimed exemption from the Geneva Convention rules on the treatment and detainment of prisoners, and authorized the National Security Agency to monitor conversations of suspected terrorists with residents of the United States without obtaining warrants. President Bush's justification was that, as commander in chief, he had the foremost responsibility to protect American citizens and actions taken for that purpose should not be subject to the approval of Congress or the courts.

A combination of congressional action and Supreme Court decisions following the guidelines of the Steel Seizure case constrained most of these presidential actions. In 2004, the Supreme Court's *Hamdi v. Rumsfeld* decision rejected Bush administration attempts to deny *habeas corpus* protections to an enemy combatant who was a U.S. citizen because federal law prohibits such denial to U.S. citizens.[46] That same day, the Court also rejected the administration's authority to deny *habeas corpus* to an enemy combatant who was not a U.S. citizen.[47] The Bush administration then established special military tribunals to review the detention of enemy combatants at Guantánamo Bay, but the Court rejected the authority of the tribunals because Congress had not authorized them.[48] The Court rejected congressional and presidential efforts to limit the Court's jurisdiction to hear

PUBLIC POLICY AND THE PRESIDENCY

Use of Drones

Since the terrorist attacks of 9/11 and subsequent terror attacks in the United States, such as the Boston Marathon bombings, and others around the world, the United States has sent ground forces into Iraq and Afghanistan, and also used alternative means of warfare such as drones—unmanned aircraft that are guided remotely and can be used to target individuals who are viewed to be engaged in terrorist activities directly against the United States and its allies. However, these aircraft are not 100 percent accurate and have resulted in the deaths of innocent civilians.

As commander in chief, the president has the authority to order a drone strike. President Obama has starkly increased the number of these attacks in Pakistan, Yemen, and Somalia, where known terrorist groups, such as al-Qaeda, have set up bases of operations. In 2014, President Obama began targeting drone strikes against ISIS, which was then a new and ultraviolent terrorist group operating in Syria and Iraq. A British organization, the Bureau of Investigative Journalism, has reported that more than three thousand people have been killed by drone attacks, including civilian men, women, and children.

Drone strikes became controversial as the media began to report on civilian casualties. In 2011, a drone strike in Yemen killed two American citizens, Anwar Al-Awlaki, a known leader of al-Qaeda, and his associate, Samir Kahn.[49] That same year, a U.S. drone strike also killed Al-Awlaki's 16-year-old son, also a U.S. citizen, in Yemen.[50] Some people claim that as American citizens, these individuals should have been captured and tried in an American court of law, and these drone attacks deprived them of their rights under the U.S. Constitution. Others argue that by engaging in activities designed to harm U.S. security, they relinquished those rights.

President Obama defended the use of drones as a more effective way of combating individuals and groups that are intent on killing Americans and that as commander in chief, his first obligation was to take any and all steps that he believed would protect Americans. After signing a type of presidential directive known as a Presidential Policy Guidance statement on the use of drones in May 2013, President Obama said this:

> Nevertheless, it is a hard fact that U.S. strikes have resulted in civilian casualties, a risk that exists in every war. . . . But as commander in chief, I must weigh these heartbreaking tragedies against the alternatives. To do nothing in the face of terrorist networks would invite far more civilian

TABLE 13.5 U.S. Drone Strikes and Related Casualties in Selected Countries, 2004–15

	Pakistan (June 2004 to date)	Yemen (Nov. 2002 to date)*	Somalia (Jan. 2007 to date)*	Afghanistan (Jan. 2015 to date)
U.S. drone strikes	419	99–119	9–13	13–38
Total reported killed	2,467–3,976	460–681	23–105	99–342
Civilians reported killed	423–965	65–97	0–5	14–42
Children reported killed	172–207	8 or 9	0	0–20
Reported injured	1,152–1,731	92–221	2–7	18–27

Source: Bureau of Investigative Journalism, Monthly Updates on the Covert War, July 1, 2015, https://www.thebureauinvestigates.com/2015/07/01/drone-war-report-january-june-2015-controversial-signature-strikes-hit-yemen-and-pakistan/

casualties—not just in our cities at home and our facilities abroad, but also in the very places like Sana'a and Kabul and Mogadishu where terrorists seek a foothold. Remember that the terrorists we are after target civilians, and the death toll from their acts of terrorism against Muslims dwarfs any estimate of civilian casualties from drone strikes. So doing nothing is not an option.[51]

Presidents weigh the costs of ensuring the safety of American citizens, both in terms of dollars and the lives of American soldiers, against the costs of using tactics that may result in civilian deaths.

The American Civil Liberties Union (ACLU) and the Center for Constitutional Rights filed lawsuits on behalf of Al-Awlaki both before and after his death in an attempt to block the president and the executive branch from targeting American citizens. However, federal courts have dismissed these suits. Moreover, American public opinion indicates strong bipartisan support for drone strikes, with 74 percent of Republicans and 52 percent of Democrats approving Obama's decision.[52] In such an atmosphere, future presidents are likely to continue to use this advanced technology; however, if public opinion shifts dramatically, support for such policies may be harder to find.

Public Policy Connections

1. Does the president have an unlimited right to use force against those suspected of engaging in terrorist acts, even on American citizens? If yes, how does that align with the Constitutional right to due process? If no, how can the president protect citizens against major terrorist attacks?
2. To what extent should Congress regulate the president's war-making power granted by the Constitution?

such appeals, claiming that those limits did not apply to cases that had been filed before Congress passed the law. Even when Congress and the president authorized tribunals, the Supreme Court declared that neither Congress nor the president has the authority to suspend the writ of *habeas corpus*, which the Constitution allows only during "Cases of Rebellion or Invasion."[53] Thus, in cases involving terrorism, the Court has put gates in the way of Congress and the president in their efforts to restrict civil liberties in the name of national security. (For a broader discussion of the balance between laws against terrorism and civil liberties, see Chapter 4.)

13.5 Organization of the Modern White House

Summarize how the White House is organized

The way that a president organizes the Executive Office and the cabinet reveals a great deal about his management style as well as his policy preferences. The president relies on his White House advisers for policy recommendations. The modern president has the challenge of encouraging cooperation between political appointees and members of the civil service and making sure that employees in each category are held accountable for their decisions.

The Executive Office of the President

The president runs a large organization known as the Executive Office of the President (EOP), a loosely knit unit of several key organizations that report directly to him. These include the White House Office; the Office of Management and Budget (OMB), which Sylvia Mathews Burwell led until she became Secretary of HHS; the National Security Council (NSC); and the Council of Economic Advisers. Each office has influence over budgetary, military, and economic policies.

Essential Knowledge

The president's ideology, the Constitution, legislation, and the appointments made by the president all impact the ways in which federal agencies will implement the president's goals.

The growth of the president's staff in the past seventy-five years is stunning. President Franklin Roosevelt established the EOP, and his decision in 1939 to move the Bureau of the Budget from the Treasury Department to the EOP gave him more direct control over the federal budget. At that time, there were about sixty people working in the EOP; under President Obama, there were nearly eighteen hundred.[54] A key change in the structure of the EOP occurred when President Eisenhower, a highly decorated army general who was accustomed to a formal chain of command, appointed the first **chief of staff**, Sherman Adams. Eisenhower also raised the status of the NSC and the Bureau of the Budget to full advisory roles reporting directly to his office.

chief of staff: *Person who coordinates and oversees interactions among the president, his personal staff, and his cabinet secretaries.*

Staff organizations can have a real impact on the success of a presidential administration. For many presidents, the choice of how to organize their staffs rests with their own personalities and operating styles. These personal characteristics can make a president more or less likely to take advice from one adviser, or balance the advice from several advisers and come to a final decision on his own; how much presidents rely on their advisers often depends on how much they trust their own judgment.[55]

In general, a tightly organized White House staff organization yields a productive presidency, and the chief of staff is central to that effort in several ways. He serves as a gatekeeper by controlling the flow of staff and paperwork, and focuses the president's attention on key issues. The chief of staff also monitors the coherence of presidential policies across cabinet departments and can serve as a referee for disagreements among members of the president's senior staff. Last, he can be important in forming bridges between the president and Congress.

Another important element in presidential productivity is staff continuity, and new presidents often bring former executive branch personnel into their administrations. These staff members bring personal experience to a new president's organization. They also bring policy expertise that will help bolster the president in dealing with members of Congress who specialize in specific policy areas. One of the effects of a lame-duck presidency is that many members of the president's inner circle start to leave the administration as it enters its final two years. However, presidents can counteract that loss by replacing the departed advisors with staff who have also worked for the administration, just in different positions. President Obama did so when he appointed Jacob Lew Secretary of the Treasury after he served as OMB director and chief of staff, and with Sylvia Mathews Burwell when he appointed her Secretary of HHS after she replaced Jacob Lew as OMB director.

The Office of the Vice President

Traditionally, the office of the vice president has not had many important responsibilities. It was not until the twentieth century that vice presidents were chosen by presidential candidates to enhance their electoral prospects, and even then, once they were in office, they were given little more than ceremonial tasks. However, with the increasing complexity and international significance of the presidential role following World War II, President Eisenhower assigned his vice president, Richard Nixon, the task of traveling around the world to meet with foreign leaders. Twenty years later, Walter Mondale, President Jimmy Carter's vice president, expanded the role of the office by serving as a close adviser to the president on issues ranging from national security to domestic policy.[56]

Twenty years after the Carter presidency, George W. Bush allowed his vice president, Richard (Dick) Cheney, to play a prominent role in the nation's military and foreign policy. Cheney had been secretary of defense under Bush's father, George H. W. Bush (1989–93), and oversaw the Gulf War; he was widely perceived to be highly influential on such issues as the Iraq War, antiterrorism policies, and energy development. The fact that George W. Bush relied so heavily on Cheney to make key decisions elevated the power, visibility, and even controversy of the role of the vice president.[57] Joseph Biden, who served as vice president under President Obama, was also given considerable responsibility for foreign affairs. Vice presidents can push policies forward even when the president is reluctant to do so. For example, in 2012, Vice President Biden's public support for same-sex marriage pressured President Obama to speed up his announcement of support. Ultimately, however, even if a vice president exerts influence, it is the president who ultimately bears the responsibility for the outcomes.

The Office of the First Lady

The role of the first lady has evolved over the history of the presidency, paralleling in some ways the increasing public roles available to women over the past century. Although the wife of the president has always been seen as an important partner in the president's social and diplomatic activities and as caregiver in the event of a health crisis, her role as a public advocate on policy issues emerged in the twentieth century. Eleanor Roosevelt, the wife of Franklin Roosevelt, was widely believed to hold considerable sway over her husband's views, but her most public moment as first lady came in 1939 when she came to the defense of Marian Anderson, a famous African American opera singer. When the Daughters of the American Revolution canceled a performance by Anderson at Constitution Hall on account of her race, Eleanor Roosevelt arranged for Anderson to perform on the steps of the Lincoln Memorial in front of thousands of cheering listeners.[58] Eleanor Roosevelt's action was interpreted as a strong stand for civil rights, despite the fact that her husband's administration was not actively pursuing civil rights as part of the domestic agenda.

Alex Wong/Getty Images News/Getty Images

IMAGE 13.9 Michelle Obama, the first African American first lady, came to the White House from a career as a practicing attorney. She is also the mother of two daughters. The first lady has a wide range of duties as the wife of the president, including hosting dignitaries, overseeing White House events, and advancing social causes. As first lady, Michelle Obama has emphasized healthy eating habits. Here she is shown working with young people in the vegetable gardens she planted on the White House grounds.

The modern office of the first lady has no formally stated responsibilities, but the first lady has a staff that includes a press secretary, a scheduler, and speechwriters. Since Eleanor Roosevelt, first ladies have often taken on single issues to champion, such as Lady Bird Johnson on nature conservation; Betty Ford on alcoholism; Rosalynn Carter on mental health; Nancy Reagan on drug addiction; Barbara Bush on literacy; Hillary Clinton on health care, women's rights, and child welfare; and Laura Bush on reading and education. Michelle Obama took a broad approach to her role by emphasizing the contribution each individual can make in his or her community on a range of issues from homelessness, to education, to childhood nutrition.

13.6 Presidential Greatness

Assess presidential greatness

President Donald Trump is the forty-fifth president of the United States. The preceding presidents served with varying degrees of success as leaders in foreign and domestic policy. Presidential leadership is judged by whether a president is able to get his or her preferred policies passed by Congress and enacted into law and by how well he or she oversees the bureaucracy to make the government run effectively and efficiently (for more on the bureaucracy, see Chapter 14).

Scholars typically judge presidential greatness by looking at the clarity of a president's vision for policy, his communication and negotiation skills, and the effectiveness of his use of presidential powers, especially the general grant of executive power. Good presidents do not have to excel in every one of these categories, but they have to compensate for a weakness in one area with greater strength in another. Stephen Skowronek argues that presidents have opportunities to continue the policies of their predecessors or forge new paths, but that a president's success is often determined by external events, such as a terrorist attack or a global economic downturn.[59] The scholar Aaron Wildavsky suggested that there are actually "two presidencies": a foreign policy presidency and a domestic policy presidency.[60] On foreign policy, the president often must work quickly and in private, as negotiations must be conducted discreetly. Domestic politics rarely require immediate action and usually entail open debate, with many citizens and interest groups vested in the outcome.[61]

The following discussion focuses on three presidents who are frequently singled out for their impact on domestic and foreign policy: Franklin D. Roosevelt, a Democrat from a wealthy, elite New York family; Lyndon Johnson, a Democrat from a very poor Texas family; and Ronald Reagan, a Republican from a middle-class family in Illinois.[62] Each had strengths and weaknesses, and each knew how to maximize his greatest asset—intellect, negotiating skills, public communications—to try to accomplish his goals.

New Deal: *Franklin Delano Roosevelt's program for ending the Great Depression through government intervention in the economy and development of a set of safety-net programs for individuals.*

Roosevelt: The New Deal and World War II

When Franklin D. Roosevelt took office in 1933, the nation was experiencing the Great Depression. Unemployment had reached 25 percent, and Americans, many of them homeless and hungry, were suffering. To combat the effects of the depression, FDR had a clear policy vision, which he called the **New Deal**. In the first three years of his presidency, he succeeded in getting Congress to pass legislation that radically altered the size and shape of the federal government. His immediate need was to find a way to get cash into the hands of individual citizens, but he opposed handouts. Instead, he created job programs, including the Conservation Corps, the Works Progress Administration, and the Tennessee Valley Authority, all of which both employed and trained workers.

FDR also expanded the government's role in regulating the economy. The creation of the Securities and Exchange Commission and other laws relating to banking and finance helped restore confidence in banks and the stock market. The National Labor Relations Act established federal oversight of working conditions, labor standards, and labor disputes. This legislation brought the government and the business and labor sectors closer together. The Social Security program, a pension program to which workers contributed through a payroll tax that was also paid by employers, further entwined business and government.

FDR used the bully pulpit and advanced the use of communication technology in the office of the president. He invented the fireside chat, a radio address to voters explaining the reasoning behind his governing decisions. Because fewer than half of all Americans owned radios at this time, FDR also turned the chats into newsreels that were shown in movie theaters. Ever since, presidents have found direct communications with voters to be an effective governing device.[63] President Roosevelt was also open and available to the Washington press corps, and his very first press conference in 1933 was a success. As a media-savvy president, FDR created the formal position of White House press secretary.[64]

Roosevelt took a personal role in negotiating legislative deals with members of the House and Senate, which were controlled by the Democrats. He allowed his staff to lay out the conditions for a compromise, but Roosevelt would finish the negotiations himself.[65] During his first five years in office, Roosevelt had great success in getting legislation through Congress, but in 1937, he overstepped by proposing to expand the size of the Supreme Court. The Court had struck down several of Roosevelt's favored policies, often by closely divided votes, and his so-called Court-packing plan would have allowed him to appoint additional justices and secure a majority favorable to him. Congress rejected Roosevelt's attempt to circumvent the checks and balances, and after that, his relationship with Congress began to falter.

On December 7, 1941, Japan attacked the United States at Pearl Harbor in Hawaii, drawing the United States into World War II. From that point on, foreign affairs dominated Roosevelt's presidency, but the New

PhotoQuest/Getty Images

IMAGE 13.10 Franklin Delano Roosevelt faced the worst economic crisis in the nation's history during the Great Depression. He proposed a series of policies known as the New Deal to provide economic opportunity and financial security in old age for America's workers. Here people lined up for food provided for the unemployed by private organizations.

Deal legislation of the previous decade laid the groundwork for the modern structure of domestic programs in the United States. On April 12, 1945, President Roosevelt died in office and was succeeded by Vice President Harry Truman.

Hulton Archive/Stringer/Getty Images

IMAGE 13.11 Lyndon Baines Johnson proposed sweeping changes to the nation's civil rights laws, as well as domestic health and welfare programs. Here he is signing the Civil Rights Act on July 2, 1964; Dr. Martin Luther King is standing behind him.

Johnson: The Great Society and Vietnam

Great Society: *Lyndon Johnson's program for expanding the federal social welfare programs in health care, education, and housing and for ending poverty.*

As president, Lyndon B. Johnson focused his mission on improving race relations and ending poverty because he believed they stood in the way of social, political, and economic progress. Most of his programs, which he called the **Great Society**, built on the infrastructure of FDR's New Deal, but they went much further in connecting the individual to the federal government. Johnson believed that as president he had an obligation to try to guarantee civil rights to all Americans.[66] In the area of race relations, he persuaded Congress to pass the Civil Rights Act of 1964, the Voting Rights Act of 1965, and the Fair Housing Act of 1968, which together formed a powerful set of laws protecting the rights of African Americans and subsequently the rights of other minority groups as well (see Chapter 5).

As 2014 marked the fiftieth anniversary of the passage of the Civil Rights Act (see Chapter 5), it also brought renewed attention to President Johnson's legacy, especially on current issues such as income inequality and fair pay. LBJ believed that it was possible for people to work very hard but still remain poor and that poor people were severely disadvantaged in terms of education, access to jobs, and affordable housing. He transformed the relationship between the individual and the federal government into one that included pure need, rather than merit based on work. He created two major federal health insurance programs: Medicaid, a health insurance program for the poor, and Medicare, a health insurance program for the elderly. He was also responsible for creating the Food Stamp Program, the School Lunch Program, Head Start, the Job Corps, and the Elementary and Secondary Education Act.

Johnson was not a skilled communicator or comfortable giving speeches, and he did not come across well on television, which by this time had succeeded radio as the dominant form of political communication. He compensated for his lack of communication skills by relying more heavily on his very strong negotiation skills. From his prior experience as a member of Congress and Senate majority leader, Johnson understood how to convince members of Congress that it was in their best interests to pass legislation. Johnson made sure that his programs would benefit all poor people, white and black, rural and urban. By creating wide eligibility criteria, Johnson almost guaranteed that every congressional district in the country would receive some benefit from the programs. For example, both Medicaid and Medicare legislation included subsidies to rural hospitals and to big inner-city hospitals for services and capital expenditures such as improving facilities and building new ones. School lunch programs benefited school children as well as farmers, who sold the federal government their meat, milk, cheese, and grains at a guaranteed price, so they always had a market.

Johnson also used his presidential powers to distribute and award federal contracts and federal funds to key members of Congress and key state officials in return for their support of his programs. He understood that if a member of Congress needed to explain his vote in support of a liberal bill, he could do so more easily if he could point to some other federal benefit he had secured, such as a bridge, a Navy or Army base, or a new hospital wing.

Although Johnson's personal relationship with the press and the public started out reasonably well, as U.S. involvement in the Vietnam War escalated, the press began to distrust him, and many journalists believed he was not being candid about the war with them and the American people. By the end of his presidency, Johnson's relationship with the press was downright hostile. In fact, negative reporting on the progress of the Vietnam War, combined with significant health concerns, was among the reasons that Johnson ultimately chose not to seek reelection, a decision he announced on March 31, 1968. He died five years later, on January 22, 1973.

Reagan: The Reagan Revolution and the End of the Cold War

Ronald Reagan's vision of the relationship between the individual and the federal government was different from the views of Roosevelt and Johnson, and it is still invoked to this day by conservative Republicans seeking to limit the size and scope of the federal government. President Reagan believed that the New Deal and the Great Society had combined to weaken individual initiative and responsibility. When he took office, he mounted an aggressive campaign to scale back federal programs that provided benefits to individuals without asking for anything in return. He believed that big government and high taxes were crushing personal initiative, creativity, and innovation. "Government is not the solution to the problem. It is the problem," Reagan announced in his first inaugural address.

Dennis Brack/Newscom

IMAGE 13.12 Ronald Reagan was known for his tough foreign policy and pressuring the Soviet Union to withdraw from nations that it had controlled since World War II. Here he is at the Brandenburg Gate at the Berlin Wall, which separated free West Germany from Communist East Germany. It is at this spot that he uttered the famous words, "Mr. Gorbachev, open this gate; Mr. Gorbachev, tear down this wall."

Tax cuts were the first thing on Reagan's agenda for two reasons. First, he believed that if taxes went down, the economy would flourish. Second, he knew that if tax revenue went down and spending increased, federal deficits would be created. These deficits would serve as justification for proposing cuts in entitlement programs, such as Social Security, Medicaid, and Aid to Families with Dependent Children (replaced in 1996 by the Temporary Aid to Needy Families program). Entitlement programs put a strain on the federal budget, especially as the number of people living in poverty grew and the elderly lived

ELECTION 2016

The Legacy of Barack Obama

THE ELECTION THAT OCCURS after an incumbent president has served two full terms is always in some part a referendum on that president's job performance over the previous eight years. The presidential election of 2016 was no different, with the Democratic candidate, Hillary Clinton, who served as Secretary of State in Obama's first term, praising his record and promising to preserve and continue his policies. Her opponent, Donald Trump, a businessman with no prior elected experience, criticized the Obama administration and ran on a platform of changing or repealing Obama's policies.

Action Sports Photography/Shutterstock.com

IMAGE 13.13 Donald Trump was elected president of the United States in November 2016. Here we see him making one of many speeches on the campaign trail during the presidential election in 2016.

Every presidency is subject to differences of opinion, and as we have noted in this chapter, presidents have some policy authority when they issue regulations and executive orders to implement laws. But in general all presidents must work with Congress to enact laws to meet the basic responsibilities of the federal government such as taxes and spending, and maintaining a national defense.

Obama inherited policies from his predecessor George W. Bush: the Iraq and Afghanistan wars, the auto industry and banking industry bailouts, and a major recession. President Obama ended active military combat in both Iraq and Afghanistan, and by the end of his time in office, the auto and bank industries were back on steadier footing. Since 2009, the unemployment rate dropped from a peak of more than 10 percent to 5 percent. President Obama's most significant legislative accomplishment is the Affordable Care Act (Obamacare) enacted in 2010, which by 2016 covered nearly 20 million additional people who had previously been unable to get health insurance. Obama nominated three Supreme Court justices, two of whom were confirmed, and worked with Congress to reduce the deficit and, at the same time, invest in infrastructure. Separate from the president's direct efforts, same-sex marriage also become legal across all fifty states.

In terms of foreign policy, President Obama had mixed success. While the U.S. role in the Iraq and Afghanistan wars officially ended, the United States was still actively engaged in fighting terrorism in several countries at the end of his second term. In addition, a number of terrorist attacks, from the Boston Marathon bombings to the 2015 San Bernardino shootings to the Orlando nightclub massacre, shook American voters' confidence in their own security.

Hillary Clinton shaped her presidential campaign in part by running on Obama's successes in domestic areas such as the economy and health care, and arguing that the world had become less safe due to forces outside U.S. control. She argued that her experience as Secretary of State uniquely qualified her to take on foreign policy and national security, but she also walked the fine line of discussing how she might take different approaches from Obama. Trump argued that Clinton must be held responsible for the failure of the Obama administration to reduce terrorism and make Americans feel safer. He argued that an entirely new foreign policy needed to be put in place, even going so far as to advocate for torture of suspected terrorists. While the Trump policies may sound extreme, they resonated with a portion of the electorate who perceived the United States to be far less safe under the Obama administration.

Ultimately voters chose to elect Donald Trump, which was in part a rejection of the policies of the eight years of the Obama administration. However, as we discuss in Chapter 10, Elections and Campaigns, every presidential candidate also runs on his or her own platform, and Trump will be held accountable for his own decisions, successes, and failures in dealing with Congress as the President of the United States.

longer. Reagan managed to make cuts in the programs for the poor and elderly by restricting eligibility for benefits, but he did not succeed in dismantling them.

At the same time Reagan was implementing his domestic policy vision, he was also implementing his foreign policy vision. He took a firm stand against the Soviet Union, which he perceived as a direct threat to the United States and as a major promoter of Communism throughout the world. The defense buildup he ordered set off a military spending race that strained the Soviets' state-controlled economy to the breaking point. By the end of Reagan's second term, it was clear that the Soviet Union was moving toward collapse and could no longer control its satellite nations in Eastern Europe. Reagan's foreign policy was arguably an important factor in the end of Communism and the Cold War.

Reagan was referred to as the "Great Communicator" because he came across very well on television; as a former actor, he was able to give engaging, persuasive, and even comforting speeches. He won American hearts in 1981 during a failed assassination tempt, when he turned to his wife, Nancy, and quipped, "Honey, I forgot to duck."[67] In January 1986, when the space shuttle *Challenger* blew up shortly after takeoff as millions of Americans watched their TVs in horror, Reagan's words eased the national pain: "The crew of the space shuttle *Challenger* honored us by the manner in which they lived their lives. We will never forget them, nor the last time we saw them, this morning, as they prepared for their journey and waved goodbye and slipped the surly bonds of earth to touch the face of God."[68] The power of speech cannot be overestimated in an analysis of presidential success because it is the most basic way that the president tries to connect with the people.

Reagan did not hesitate to use his formal presidential powers to their fullest. Early in his presidency, when the air traffic controllers' union went on strike in 1981, he ordered the controllers back to work. When they refused, he fired all of them and replaced them with Air Force and civilian (private) air traffic controllers. Eventually, the union relented, and most of the air traffic controllers were hired back, but with fewer benefits and at lower salaries. This action sent a clear signal to members of Congress and to interest groups that Reagan was not afraid to take a potentially unpopular stand to accomplish his goals.

President Reagan delegated much of the actual negotiating over policy to staff members. He also enhanced the power of the OMB director to negotiate with Congress on budgetary matters. Reagan and his staff were frequently successful in these negotiations, but on issues on which they were at a public disadvantage, Reagan knew when to compromise. During his last two years in office, he worked with a Democratic-controlled Congress to pass trade legislation, welfare reform, and the first comprehensive AIDS funding and treatment bill.

Reagan's presidency was not without controversy, however. In late 1986, the Iran-contra scandal erupted when it was revealed that NSC members were selling U.S. weapons to Iran for cash, which was then given to the contra resistance movement in Nicaragua that was fighting the Communist-leaning Sandinista regime. Congress had passed a law expressly prohibiting aid to the contras and held hearings to investigate the administration's actions. President Reagan himself was never directly implicated, but the scandal raised questions about the accountability of the president for his staff's actions, and it tarnished the last two years of his presidency. Although Reagan enjoyed relatively consistent popularity and was perceived as highly responsive to his base of supporters, his record came under greater scrutiny after he left office because his policies produced higher federal budget deficits and reduced funding for programs for the disadvantaged.

The example of Reagan, in the context of Roosevelt and Johnson, shows how the office of the presidency can shape domestic and foreign policy for future generations. Thirty-five years after Roosevelt died and eleven years after Johnson left office, Reagan ran for president on a campaign platform of scaling back the New Deal and the Great Society. In turn, Reagan left a conservative political legacy about the limited role of the federal government that remains a powerful rallying cry for Republicans today. Ronald Reagan died on June 5, 2004.

The Presidency and Democracy

From George Washington to Barack Obama, the presidency has evolved from an institution with strictly limited responsibilities to the large and powerful institution it is today. Donald Trump's presidency will have to address an ever-changing and increasingly complicated policy landscape. Certainly the Framers would be surprised by the growth of the presidency, and they might wonder whether the executive branch is too focused on serving the president individually and not focused enough on the needs of citizens more generally.

Nevertheless, the president operates in a separation-of-powers system, and laws must be passed with the cooperation of Congress, so the president cannot be rewarded or blamed entirely for the federal government's policies.[69] Moreover, individuals have gateways of influence on the presidency. Voters can render their direct verdict on the president's job performance when they choose whether to reelect him, provided he runs for a second term. Voters also indirectly register their opinions in congressional midterm elections, which focus on members of the House and Senate but are also interpreted as judgments on the president's record. Because high presidential approval ratings help presidents sway Congress, presidents are frequently responsive to public opinion. Because there is no possibility of a third term in office, presidents in their second term are typically freer from public accountability. In cases of very serious wrongdoing, Congress has the power to impeach and convict the president, but the threshold for impeachment is extremely high, and it happens very rarely.

In the course of the nation's history, presidents have grown less accessible to the average voter. However, technological innovations as simple as fast airplane travel and, more recently, e-mail, texting, and social networking websites, provide many more modes of communication between voters and the president or the president's staff. Although the president will not meet most of the people he represents, each town meeting he holds and public speech he gives is an opportunity for an exchange of views. And the job of the presidential staff is to keep him or her as well-informed on public opinion as possible.

Essential Knowledge

Presidents use modern technology as a way to connect with voters and help shape public opinion.

In the modern age, presidents are considered their political party's leaders, and they want their records to reflect well on other elected officials from their party. All presidents see it as their responsibility to do what they believe to be best for the country, even in the face of opposition from the media, the public, and Congress. At times, this opposition can result in a less effective president than some might want, but the operation of checks and balances on presidential power accords with the Framers' vision of presidential leadership.

Overall, the modern presidency acts as both a gate and a gateway to democracy at the same time. It is a gate in that the president oversees a very large federal government that can be complex and difficult to change in response to public needs. It is a gateway in that any natural-born citizen can run for the most powerful office in the land, and although wealth, education, and connections are extremely helpful in winning, they are not prerequisites for victory. To date, the men who have been elected president have come from a wide range of economic, educational, and professional backgrounds. With the election of an African American president, and most recently, a man with no prior political experience, major entry barriers to the presidency have been broken; one might argue that the path to the White House is more open than ever before.

Political Science Reasoning

Question 1

Practice 1, Practice 4

EXECUTIVE ORDER

ENFORCING STATUTORY PROHIBITIONS ON FEDERAL CONTROL OF EDUCATION

By the authority vested in me as President by the Constitution and the laws of the United States of America, and in order to restore the proper division of power under the Constitution between the federal government and the States and to further the goals of, and to ensure strict compliance with, statutes that prohibit federal interference with State and local control over education, . . . it is hereby ordered as follows:

Section 1. Policy. It shall be the policy of the executive branch to protect and preserve State and local control over the curriculum, program of instruction, administration, and personnel of educational institutions, schools, and school systems, consistent with applicable law . . .

Section 2. Review of Regulations and Guidance Documents. (a) The Secretary of Education (Secretary) shall review all Department of Education (Department) regulations and guidance documents . . .

(b) The Secretary shall examine whether these regulations and guidance documents comply with federal laws that prohibit the department from exercising any direction, supervision, or control over areas subject to State and local control, including:

(i) the curriculum or program of instruction of any elementary and secondary school and school system;
(ii) school administration and personnel; and
(iii) selection and content of library resources, textbooks, and instructional materials.

(c) The Secretary shall, as appropriate and consistent with applicable law, rescind or revise any regulations that are identified pursuant to subsection (b) of this section as inconsistent with statutory prohibitions. The Secretary shall also rescind or revise any guidance documents that are identified pursuant to subsection (b) of this section as inconsistent with statutory prohibitions . . .

DONALD J. TRUMP
THE WHITE HOUSE
April 26, 2017

1. What is the legal basis of the above executive order?
2. Based upon the above executive order, to what extent would President Trump support further involvement by the federal government in education? Cite specific textual evidence to support your answer.
3. What is the legal basis by which the federal government can make education policy?

Question 2

Practice 1, Practice 4

> My opinion originally was that the President of the United States should have been elected for seven years, and forever ineligible afterward. I have since become sensible that seven years is too long to be irremovable, and that there should be a peaceable way of withdrawing a man in midway who is doing wrong. The service for eight years, with a power to remove at the end of the first four, comes nearly to my principle as corrected by experience; and it is in adherence to that, that I determine to withdraw at the end of my second term. The danger is that the indulgence and attachments of the people will keep a man in the chair after he becomes a dotard, that reelection through life shall become habitual, and election for life follow that. General Washington set the example of voluntary retirement after eight years. I shall follow it. And a few more precedents will oppose the obstacle of habit to any one after a while who shall endeavor to extend his term. Perhaps it may beget a disposition to establish it by an amendment of the Constitution. I believe I am doing right therefore in pursuing my principle. I had determined to declare my intention, but I have consented to be silent on the opinion of friends, who think it best not to put a continuance out of my power in defiance of all circumstances. There is, however, but one circumstance which could engage my acquiescence in another election; to wit, such a division about a successor, as might bring in a monarchist. But that circumstance is impossible.[1]

1. Consider the author's belief about presidential terms. What would the author think of the Twenty-second amendment?
2. What would be the implications of a seven-year presidential term? List several potential differences and explain.

---

[1]Thomas Jefferson to John Taylor, January 6, 1805.

Focus on AP® Success

13 The Presidency

Must Know: Key Concepts

- Veto
- Agenda Setting
- Executive Order
- Bully Pulpit
- Office of Management of Budget
- Pocket Veto
- Executive Agreement
- Treaty
- Formal Power
- Informal Power
- Signing Statement
- *Federalist* No. 70
- Twenty-Second Amendment

Thinking Politically

Concept Application

Compare the following theories on the power of the president: constitutional, stewardship, prerogative. Which theory allows for a greater range of presidential action?

Argumentation

Does the Twenty-Second Amendment's term limitations on the president unnecessarily interfere with a democratic society's ability to select its leaders? Or is the amendment necessary to protect a democratic society from the development of a dictator?

Understanding Learning Objectives with Key Concepts

CON – 4.A Explain how the president can implement a policy agenda.

- Presidents have a variety of powers they use to accomplish their policy goals.
- These powers are both formal (specified in the Constitution or through legislation) or informal (derived from custom and practice).
    - The president has the power to veto legislation passed by Congress. It is extremely difficult for Congress to override a veto. A pocket veto occurs when the president does not act by the time Congress has adjourned. In such a case, the bill dies.
    - The president has the ability to negotiate treaties with other countries. The president may also enter into executive agreements with the *leaders* of other countries, although these agreements have less force than a ratified treaty and last only so long as both leaders are in office.
- The president frequently relies on the informal power of persuasion and his role as an opinion leader to facilitate negotiation with Congress. This can be a significant power, especially if the president is popular. The president has an advantage over Congress here because he speaks with one voice, whereas Congress cannot.
- The president has power to issue executive orders. This implied executive power of the president is derived from the Constitution's take care clause and legislation passed by Congress that gives him or her the ability to unilaterally act in certain circumstances. These orders allow the president to set policy and manage the operation of the national government.

- President can also issue signing statements. This informal power allows the president to comment on his or her interpretation of the law.

CON – 4.B Explain how the president's agenda can create tension and frequent confrontations with Congress.

- Senators, responding to their constituencies, may disagree with a president's nominations based on experience, policy opinions, or partisanship. Cabinet appointments garner the most public attention and are often the most hotly contested.
- The Senate's ability to confirm executive and judicial nominations is a check on presidential power. Perhaps the most lasting impact that a president makes is his or her appointments to the judiciary.
- Even when the president and Congress are of the same party, their differing goals or differing constituencies may result in a struggle over the final character of legislation or of legislative priorities.

CON – 4.C Explain how presidents have interpreted and justified their use of formal and informal powers.

- The need for a single executive is set forth in *Federalist* 70. In this essay, Hamilton states that a single executive is needed to, among other things, preserve governmental accountability.
- The Founders feared the concentration of power into the hands of one person. As such, they limited the power of the presidency through the system of checks and balances. As the power of the presidency has increased, other restrictions, such as term limits from the Twenty-Second Amendment, have been put in place.
- There are several different theories as to the nature of presidential power. Constitutional theory holds that the only real powers that the president has are stated in the Constitution. The stewardship theory holds that presidents are stewards of the American people and should take whatever action is necessary to meet their needs unless that action is forbidden by the Constitution. The prerogative theory states that certain things should be left to the discretion of the chief executive. The executive should then exercise these prerogatives to protect the interests of the people even if that means exceeding the authority granted under law or, in extraordinary situations, violates the law if necessary to save the country.

CON – 4.D Explain how communication technology has changed the president's relationship with the national constituency and the other branches.

- The ability of the president to communicate has a direct impact on his or her ability to achieve policy goals.
- Modern presidents have enjoyed greater access to the public than have prior presidents due to expansion of the mass media such as radio, television, and the Internet (including social media).
- Most presidents use the State of the Union address to outline their major policy initiatives. Presidents also us the "bully pulpit" as a means to advance their policy goals. The term "bully pulpit" refers to the unique position in American politics that the president has that enables him or her to act as an opinion leader.

PMI – 2.D. Explain how the president ensures that executive branch agencies and departments carry out their responsibilities in concert with the goals of the administration.

- The president's appointees will usually reflect his or her policy implementation priorities, but not every president is equally successful in controlling the bureaucracy, which is generally independent.
- The Office of Management of Budget exists to help the president supervise the executive branch. Even with the assistance of this agency, the task is difficult due to the expansive nature of the federal bureaucracy and its range of activities.

Making Connections

While the president is the head of the executive branch, he or she is structurally separated from the rest of it due to limits on the power of appointment and removal of federal workers. When studying Chapter 14, The Bureaucracy, make a note of how the bureaucracy can maintain its independence.

Both Congress and the president have a role in setting foreign and military policy. These two institutions can conflict in these policy areas. Review the foreign and military power of Congress in Chapter 12. Chapter 16, Economic, Domestic, and Foreign Policy, will also illustrate the interplay between these two institutions in these policy areas.

Much of the president's power is based on the ability to persuade. As such, the ability to access the media is critical. Review the role media plays in American politics in Chapter 7, The News and Social Media.

Going Deeper: Office of Management and Budget

The Office of Management and Budget (OMB) assists the president in the supervision of the federal bureaucracy and in the development of a budget that will be submitted to Congress.

Federal agencies submit their budget request to the OMB, which will then analyze them to ensure that they are in alignment with the president's policy priorities. OMB also does economic forecasting as a means to estimate future revenue and estimates the impact of new fiscal policy proposed by the president.

OMB provides the president information on the performance of executive agencies. This is a necessary check on performance as information obtained from the agencies themselves may be biased because they have a vested interest in painting themselves in the best light possible.

14 The Bureaucracy

AP® Learning Objectives

PMI – 2.A Explain how the bureaucracy carries out the responsibilities of the federal government.

PMI – 2.B Explain how the federal bureaucracy uses delegated discretionary authority for rule making and implementation.

PMI – 2.C Explain how Congress uses its oversight power in its relationship with the executive branch.

PMI – 2.D Explain how the president ensures that executive branch agencies and departments carry out their responsibilities in concert with the goals of the administration.

PMI – 2.E Explain the extent to which governmental branches can hold the bureaucracy accountable given the competing interests of Congress, the president, and the federal courts.

Performance Tasks

Upon the completion of this chapter, you must be able to do the following:

- Explain how the bureaucracy makes and enforces public policy.
- Explain why Congress has delegated policy making to the bureaucracy and how the bureaucracy exercises that power.
- Explain how the Congress, president, and judiciary hold the bureaucracy accountable.

Danny Moloshok/Reuters

> *"If front-line, non-intelligence government employees cannot disclose wrongdoing to the public that was never classified and then that information can be stamped years later with a classified TSA marking, the First Amendment is now meaningless."*[1]
>
> **ROBERT MACLEAN**
> Air Force

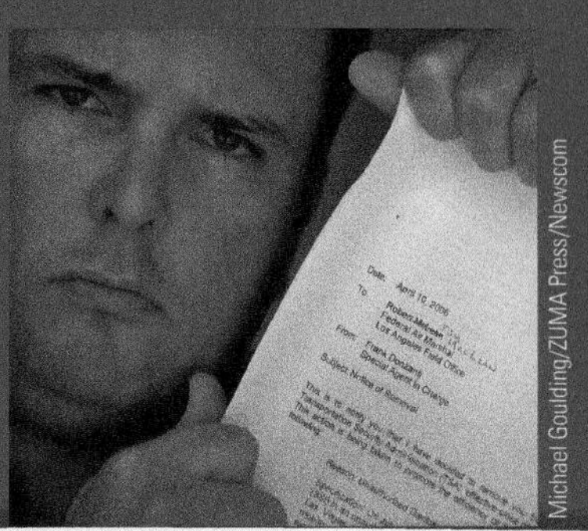

Michael Goulding/ZUMA Press/Newscom

Every day, Americans board domestic and international flights with men and women whose sole job is to protect the passengers, crews, and airlines in the air. Federal air marshals carry out their jobs silently, unbeknownst to their fellow airline passengers. After being honorably discharged from the military, Robert MacLean became a federal air marshal (FAM), a position that has become increasingly important since the September 11, 2001, terrorist attacks.

MacLean's career as a FAM changed forever when he became a whistleblower following serious security concerns in 2003. In July 2003, various U.S. security agencies received elevated terrorist threats. The Transportation Security Administration (TSA) was notified of the threats and conducted meetings with air marshals during which they were briefed on the nature of the threats. Despite the elevated danger, the TSA cancelled months of air marshal missions, citing budget concerns. They notified the air marshals via unencrypted text messages to their cell phones. This greatly concerned MacLean, and he took his concerns to his direct supervisor and finally to the Inspector General of the Department of Homeland Security, to no avail. Feeling it was his duty to protect the American public in light of these security breaches, MacLean anonymously leaked the text message he received that canceled the air marshal missions to MSNBC. After the leak, many congressional members raised concerns about the canceled missions, and in response to that criticism, the TSA quickly moved to reinstate them.

MacLean did not stop there, though. One year later, he anonymously went on television to discuss his concerns on the air marshal dress code, which he felt made the marshals conspicuous to potential terrorists. His concerns over the air marshal dress code, in tandem with a report by the Government Accountability Office, resulted in changes to the air marshal dress code to better conceal marshals' identities. After his television appearance, the TSA recognized MacLean, and they were also able to link him to the earlier text message leak in 2003. In 2006, MacLean was fired from his position as a marshal. When MacLean contested his dismissal, he discovered that the text message he had leaked was retroactively classified, which was a large part of the reason he was fired.

Ever since his dismissal, MacLean has fought the TSA to be reinstated, arguing he is a protected whistleblower under the Whistleblower Protection Act of 1989. As a federal employee, MacLean argued it was not only legal but expected to disclose any wrongdoing taking place in the agency he was employed by, especially if his disclosure could save American lives. His removal as a marshal is a violation of this law, which is supposed to protect him from any retaliation.

Two Merit Systems Protection Board chairmen upheld MacLean's termination, as did an administrative judge in May 2010. MacLean appealed to the Federal Circuit Court of Appeals, which ruled in his favor. The circuit court argued that the main reason for MacLean's termination was a regulation and not a statute, which the whistleblower act protects MacLean from. The Department of Justice appealed the decision to the Supreme Court. The case, *Department of Homeland Security v. MacLean,* was heard on November 4, 2014, and on January 21, 2015, by a 7–2 vote, the Supreme Court ruled that MacLean should not have been dismissed because his "disclosure was not specifically prohibited by law."[2] MacLean was subsequently reinstated by the TSA.

MacLean's case is unique because it directly questions the difference between a statute created by the legislature and a regulation, which is issued by the bureaucracy. According to the Federal Circuit Court and the Supreme Court, laws created by Congress trump regulations created by agencies and departments, even if they make those regulations to fill the holes in a statute. The events surrounding MacLean's disclosure of TSA information demonstrate the gates that Congress can put in the way of bureaucratic regulation and the amount of power those regulations can wield when left unchecked by the legislature.[3]

In this chapter, we examine the cabinet-level departments, agencies, and other organizations that constitute the executive branch. We look at their structure, characteristics, rationale, procedures, accountability, and responsiveness to citizens' concerns. A fundamental question for students of American government is whether the sprawling nature of the bureaucracy makes it a gate or a gateway to serving the people effectively.

14.1 The American Bureaucracy

Explain what the bureaucracy does

Essential Knowledge

Even with the assistance of the Office of Management and Budget and the rest of the Executive Office of the President, it can be difficult to ensure the bureaucracy is responsive to presidential directives.

Just mention the word *bureaucracy* and most people roll their eyes and utter phrases like "red tape" or "slow as molasses." Of all the components of American government, the bureaucracy is most likely to be perceived as annoying and daunting, as a gate against getting things done. Yet the bureaucracy is also the most likely to have a direct impact on citizens' lives. Most Americans have never met a president or a member of Congress or a federal judge, but every American has likely interacted with an employee of the government. Whether the interaction involves showing identification to a TSA agent in the airport or waiting in line at the post office, the rules and regulations of the federal bureaucracy present numerous opportunities for frustration.

Essential Knowledge

Congress gives bureaucratic agencies the authority to issue administrate regulations. They also have the authority to assess fines when those regulations are violated.

Bureaucracies generally are not afforded much respect because they seem so complicated and impenetrable, and bureaucrats are often portrayed as faceless robots who merely enforce the rules. Yet enforcing the rules is the bureaucracy's job; as an extension of the presidency, bureaucratic implementation is how the president executes the law. Rules must be enforced equally across all citizens. In the most obvious example, a first-class stamp costs the same in every state and will take a letter to any place in the nation, just across town or from Houston to Honolulu.

bureaucracy: *Executive branch departments, agencies, boards, and commissions that carry out the responsibilities of the federal government.*

Despite the well-known problems associated with bureaucracies, organization is essential to modern government. In the late nineteenth century, the German sociologist Max Weber described bureaucracies as highly rational organizations that enabled large numbers of people to get difficult jobs done efficiently.[4] If the federal bureaucracy does not seem efficient today, that may be because of the enormous responsibilities it bears, not only to implement complex policy and law established by the president and Congress, but also to do so in a way that is orderly, predictable, fair, equal for all citizens, and transparent. The formal aspects of bureaucratic structure promote accountability, while the informal operations—the bureaucratic culture—determine how well the organization carries out its own mission and how well it interacts with other organizations. We discuss these elements in detail to draw a practical road map not only to understand the federal government but also to actually make it work better for ordinary citizens.

Chip East/Reuters/Corbis

IMAGE 14.1 The federal bureaucracy has a direct impact on your life. Most Americans are familiar with waiting in line at the post office, but not many people think about the fact that the quality of the grains in their breakfast cereal, the safety of the highways they drive on, and the purity of the water they drink are also regulated by government agencies.

What Is the Bureaucracy?

The **bureaucracy** is the large collection of executive branch departments, agencies, boards, commissions, and other government organizations that carry out the responsibilities of the federal government. At first, the nation did not require many employees to fulfill the government's duties, which were limited to large national issues such as defense, tariffs on imported goods, and settling western lands. As the nation's lands and economy grew, so did the need for a more complex structure at the federal level to oversee government activities. These responsibilities are established by laws passed by Congress and signed by the president; however, for execution, they often entail expertise, so the legislature relies on specialists—the bureaucrats—to write the **regulations** that implement the law.

regulations: *Guidelines issued by federal agencies for administering federal programs and implementing federal law.*

In 2016, the number of federal employees, including the armed services, totaled almost 4.1 million people.[5] Federal employees do a wide variety of jobs. A national park ranger is a federal employee, as is a TSA officer, a border patrol officer, a bridge designer with the Army Corps of Engineers, an accountant with the Securities and Exchange Commission, and a lawyer with the Department of Justice. For every federal job classified as "professional," there are also staff jobs, including clerks, office managers, janitors, mechanics, and delivery personnel, who keep the bureaucracy running. Skills and specialties in almost any type of work can be a gateway to employment in the federal government, which we discuss in more detail later in the chapter.

One simple way to understand the basic structure of the bureaucracy is to imagine a piece of furniture called a cabinet that stores different types of items in different drawers. It is no accident that the term *bureaucracy* has *bureau* at its base, an old-fashioned term for a cabinet. President Thomas Jefferson (1801–09) had a separate room in the White House that he called his cabinet, and the centerpiece of the room was a long table with drawers on each side that served as his desk, in which he stored all important federal papers according to issue area.[6] A modern president could not fit all the paperwork of the federal bureaucracy in a single desk, but the idea of compartmentalizing federal responsibilities has endured over time.

Today, a president builds a **cabinet**—his set of key advisers who are responsible for the areas under their jurisdiction. As noted in Chapter 13, The Presidency, the cabinet is distinct from the president's White House staff, which works directly for the president, because cabinet members oversee entire departments constructed to implement federal policy. Most cabinet members are **cabinet secretaries** and head executive departments, but presidents may select additional advisers for cabinet-rank status. In the Obama administration, these included the vice president, the chief of staff, the heads of the Environmental Protection Agency and of the Office of Management and Budget, the U.S. trade representative, the U.S. ambassador to the United Nations, and the chair of the Council of Economic Advisers.[7] When a new president is elected, he or she typically selects new membership for the cabinet, although there have been cases where a president has asked a cabinet member to stay on. Notably, President Obama asked Robert Gates, who was Secretary of Defense under George W. Bush, to stay on in that position to ensure that the leadership of U.S. military involvement in Iraq and Afghanistan remained consistent despite the transition to a new commander in chief.

cabinet: *Set of executive departments responsible for carrying out federal policy in specific issue areas.*

cabinet secretaries: *Heads of cabinet departments and chief advisers to the president on the issues under their jurisdiction.*

Constitutional Foundations

The word *bureaucracy* does not appear in the U.S. Constitution, but the foundations of the federal bureaucracy can be traced to a few key sentences in Article II that relate to the powers of the president.

Appointments. Article II, Section 2, gives the president the power to "nominate, and by and with the Advice and Consent of the Senate, . . . appoint . . . all other Officers of the United States, whose Appointments are not herein otherwise provided for, and which shall be established by Law." This section goes on to state that Congress can "by Law vest the Appointment of such inferior Officers, as they think proper, in the President alone, in the Courts of Law, or in the Heads of Departments." Thus the discussion of the president's appointment power implies the existence of executive departments.

Opinions on Federal Policies. Article II, Section 2, references the executive branch more directly when it authorizes the president to "require the Opinion, in writing, of the principal Officer in each of the executive Departments, upon any subject relating to the Duties of their respective Offices." The Framers envisioned that the president would manage a staff of federal officers who would oversee executive departments managing the operations of government, although it is doubtful that they expected the president's staff to be as large as it is today.

Execution of the Laws. Article II, Section 3, gives the president broad powers to "take Care that the Laws be faithfully executed." At the same time that the Framers wanted to make sure that the president would follow the intent of Congress, they also gave him wide discretion in how he carried out the laws. This broad executive power is the foundation for the growth of the federal bureaucracy as well as for the growth of the presidency, as discussed in Chapter 13.

Structure of the Bureaucracy

For more than two centuries, the federal bureaucracy has been changing, growing, and developing into today's interlinked set of organizations that implement federal policy. Some organizations are vast, such as the executive departments, and some are small advisory boards and commissions. Coordinating the authority and operations of these different types of organizations is a significant challenge for the executive branch as it carries out its constitutional duties. The structure of the U.S. bureaucracy and the challenges it faces are not unique. Bureaucratic organization is essential for the operation of modern governments and organizations.

Executive Departments. Today there are fifteen executive, or cabinet-level, departments in the federal bureaucracy. A cabinet department is an executive branch organization led by a cabinet secretary appointed by the president. Cabinet departments are responsible for implementing laws and policies in specific areas through the regulatory and enforcement process. Regulations are the guidelines that detail how a law will be carried out, and what has to be done to comply with the law (see Chapter 16, Economic, Domestic, and Foreign Policy, for a full description). Regulations go through several versions, and after a lengthy review process, the final regulations are printed in the **Federal Register**, which is the federal government's official publication for implementation of laws.

Federal Register: *Official published record of all executive branch rules, regulations, and orders.*

The job of the secretary is to oversee implementation, provide advice to the president about the issues under the department's control, and develop an annual budget for the department. Congress has the authority to create a cabinet department, but once it is created, it is under the control and supervision of the president as head of the executive branch. Table 14.1 lists each department, the year it was created, its website, and its number of employees.

Each cabinet department consists of subdivisions arranged in a hierarchical form to divide up its tasks and theoretically maximize efficiency and responsiveness. Figure 14.1 shows how the Department of Health and Human Services (HHS) is organized. This organizational chart makes it clear that each department has many subdivisions, or layers, with each assigned a specific federal policy to implement. HHS oversees 300 programs, with more than 72,000 employees and a budget of $1.2 trillion.[8] This massive and complex organization is necessary to respond to the needs of all the individuals affected by the programs that HHS manages.

The responsibilities of HHS grew even broader when President Obama signed the Patient Protection and Affordable Care Act into law on March 23, 2010. Because HHS oversees Medicaid, Medicare, and other federal health-related programs, it bears the bulk of the responsibility to implement the new programs associated with this legislation. For example, HHS tries to remedy deficiencies in the Medicare prescription drug program for senior citizens and inform citizens about expanded eligibility for health insurance through Medicaid. It also coordinates health insurance exchanges, works with states to enhance existing state-based insurance programs, and joins with other federal agencies to encourage wellness and disease-prevention programs.[9] Health care reform is just one example of federal policy that is implemented by a cabinet department, in conjunction with state governments. For an in-depth discussion of the Affordable Care Act, see Chapter 16.

TABLE 14.1 Cabinet Departments, 2016

Department	Year Established	Website	Employees (in thousands)
State	1789	http://www.state.gov	34.2
Treasury	1789	http://www.treasury.gov	99.0
Defense (originally War)	1789	http://www.dod.gov	738.1
Interior	1849	http://www.interior.gov	65.6
Agriculture	1862	http://www.usda.gov	90.1
Justice	1870	http://www.justice.gov	118.3
Commerce	1903	http://www.commerce.gov	44.1
Labor	1913	http://www.dol.gov	16.9
Housing and Urban Development	1965	http://www.hud.gov	8.3
Transportation	1966	http://www.transportation.gov	55.7
Energy	1977	http://www.energy.gov	16.0
Education	1979	http://www.education.gov	4.3
Health and Human Services	1980	http://www.hhs.gov	72.6
Veterans Affairs	1989	http://www.va.gov	349.8
Homeland Security	2003	http://www.dhs.gov	184.0

Source: The White House, http://www.whitehouse.gov; The White House, Office of Management and Budget, *Fiscal Year 2017 Analytical Perspectives, Budget of the U.S. Government* (Washington, D.C.: U.S. Government Printing Office, 2016), Table 8-2, Federal Civilian Employment in the Executive Branch, p. 82, http://www.whitehouse.gov/sites/default/files/omb/budget/fy2017/assets/spec.pdf. For the history of each department, see the websites listed.

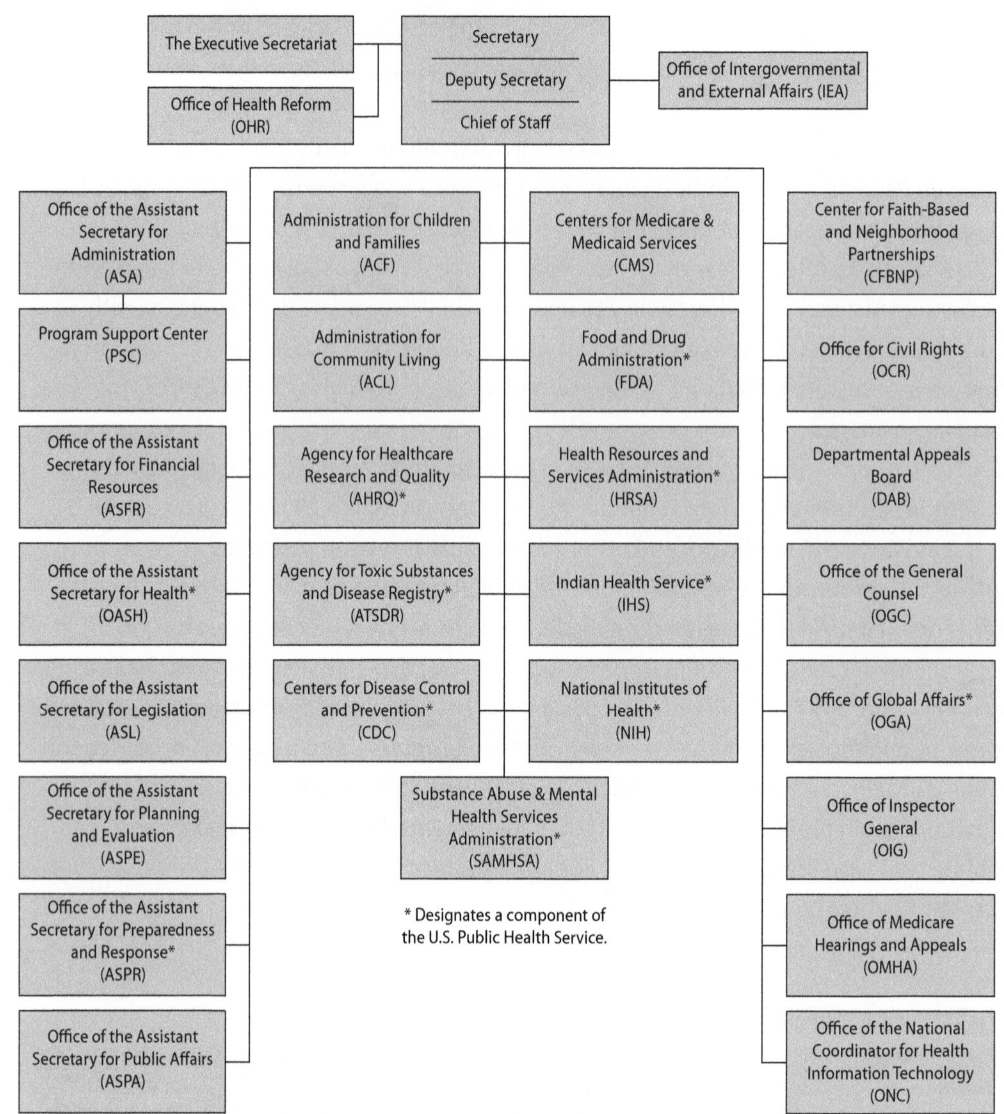

FIGURE 14.1 Organizational Chart of the Department of Health and Human Services

Cabinet departments are complex hierarchical organizations with layers of authority and sublevel agencies that have jurisdiction over specific federal programs and policies. This organizational chart of the Department of Health and Human Services shows sublevel agencies with lines of responsibility.

Source: U.S. Department of Health and Human Services, Organizational Chart, accessed April 1, 2016, http://www.hhs.gov/about/orgchart/index.html.

Office of Management and Budget (OMB): *Federal agency that oversees the federal budget and all federal regulations.*

Other Types of Federal Organizations. In addition to cabinet-level departments, there are numerous independent organizations that constitute the federal government, including agencies, commissions, administrations, boards, corporations, and endowments (see Table 14.2). These organizations vary by structure, mission, and degree of independence from the president. For example, the **Office of Management and Budget (OMB)** has final authority over the entire federal budget, and each agency and department must submit its proposed budget to OMB for approval before it is included in the president's official proposed budget. The OMB's director is part of the president's cabinet, although OMB is not a cabinet department. Additionally, all regulations must go through OMB before they take effect.

TABLE 14.2 Selected Independent Agencies and Commissions, 2016

Department	Year Established	Website	Employees (in thousands)
Environmental Protection Agency (EPA)	1970	http://www.epa.gov	15.5
Equal Employment Opportunity Commission (EEOC)	1965	http://www.eeoc.gov	2.3
General Services Administration (GSA)	1949	http://www.gsa.gov	11.7
National Aeronautics and Space Administration (NASA)	1958	http://www.nasa.gov	17.4
National Labor Relations Board (NLRB)	1935	http://www.nlrb.gov	1.6
National Science Foundation (NSF)	1950	http://www.nsf.gov	1.4
Office of Personnel Management (OPM)	1978	http://www.opm.gov	5.6
Securities and Exchange Commission (SEC)	1935	http://www.sec.gov	4.6
Small Business Administration (SBA)	1953	http://www.sba.gov	3.3
Social Security Administration (SSA)	1935	http://www.socialsecurity.gov	65.5

Source: The White House, http://www.whitehouse.gov; The White House, Office of Management and Budget, *Fiscal Year 2017 Analytical Perspectives, Budget of the U.S. Government* (Washington, D.C.: U.S. Government Printing Office, 2016), Table 8-2, Federal Civilian Employment in the Executive Branch, p. 82, accessed March 29, 2016, http://www.whitehouse.gov/sites/default/files/omb/budget/fy2017/assets/spec.pdf.

The Environmental Protection Agency (EPA) is an **independent agency**, a type of federal organization established by Congress with authority to regulate an aspect of the economy or a sector of the federal government. Independent agencies do not operate within a cabinet department. Congress designs such agencies to operate with their own authority. The EPA bears the responsibility for preserving the quality of the air, water, and land. It can issue regulations and create policy in a wide range of areas, including limiting emissions from coal-fired plants and auto fuel emissions. Its regulations are subject to OMB approval, just like regulations from any cabinet department.

independent agency: *Federal organization that has independent authority and does not operate within a cabinet department.*

A **federal regulatory commission** is an agency typically run by a small number of officials, known as commissioners, who are appointed by the president for fixed terms and are responsible for overseeing a sector of the economic or political arena. One example is the Securities and Exchange Commission (SEC), which is responsible for monitoring all business practices involving the stock market. The SEC has five commissioners who serve staggered five-year terms and together manage 4,600 employees.[10] The SEC oversees the work of accountants, stockbrokers, hedge fund managers, financial advisers, and small business owners. It has legal authority to demand information from these professionals, impose fines for bypassing investment rules, and even bring formal charges for serious violations of the law.

federal regulatory commission: *Federal agency typically run by a small number of officials, known as commissioners, who are appointed by the president for fixed terms and oversee economic or political issues.*

A federal administration is responsible for running a federal program or overseeing specific areas of federal responsibility. The Transportation Security Administration (TSA), which Robert MacLean worked for, is a type of federal administration that was created after the attacks of 9/11 and later placed under the Department of Homeland Security (discussed later in this chapter).

A federal board typically has a more narrow scope of authority but can possess the power to require changes in operating procedures and to suggest fines. It usually consists of individuals who are appointed for a specific term and who, ideally, have expertise in the area of the board's jurisdiction. For example, the National Transportation Safety Board (NTSB) is

IMAGE 14.2 The National Transportation Safety Board investigates the causes of accidents, such as the bird strike that forced US Airways Flight 1549 to land in the Hudson River on January 15, 2009. Not all accidents have such fortunate outcomes, and the NTSB makes recommendations for preventing similar accidents in the future.

responsible for investigating transportation-related accidents such as the emergency landing of US Airways Flight 1549 (dubbed the "Miracle on the Hudson," the jet's engines lost power after encountering a flock of geese) or train accidents such as the Amtrak derailment outside Philadelphia in 2015, and another Amtrak crash nearby in 2016. Whenever an accident involves any form of transportation, one of the NTSB's five board members is appointed to oversee an investigation of the event. When the investigation is completed, the agency issues a report that includes findings about the accident's cause and recommendations for avoiding a similar event. Despite its authority in these investigations and its members' knowledge of safe transportation practices, the NTSB does not have the power to issue federal regulations.

A federal corporation is a type of federal organization similar to a private business in that it provides a service or commodity for a price to the public, but it also receives federal funding. For example, the National Railroad Passenger Corporation, better known as Amtrak, is essentially a for-profit railroad, but it receives federal funding and is subject to federal restrictions and controls.

A national endowment is also a type of federal organization that uses funds specifically allocated to promote a public good or service. The National Endowment for the Arts, for example, was created to support scholarship and art that would be available to the general public, but it does not have any formal responsibility to monitor private- and public-sector activities in a specific set of issue areas. Because endowments are funded by the federal government, they are expected to serve as gateways for the expression of a wide range of viewpoints and perspectives in the work that they support.

14.2 Core Components of the Bureaucracy

Outline the essential elements of a bureaucracy

All these bureaucratic organizations share four core components that determine how government implements policy and, more immediately, how government responds to the individual needs of citizens. These components are mission, hierarchical decision-making process, expertise, and bureaucratic culture.

Mission

Each federal agency has a stated mission that defines its role and responsibilities within the federal bureaucracy. For example, the mission of the Department of Health and Human Services is stated on its website:

> *THE DEPARTMENT OF HEALTH AND HUMAN SERVICES (HHS) is the United States government's principal agency for protecting the health of all Americans and providing essential human services, especially for those who are least able to help themselves.*[11]

A mission statement is important as the public face of the department, and it is the measure by which members of Congress and the general public can hold the department accountable for the success or failure of its efforts.

Hierarchical Decision-Making Process

To carry out its mission, every federal organization has a hierarchical decision-making process that structures the way policy is implemented. The hierarchy of authority in a bureaucracy means that an employee's decision on the implementation of policy is reviewed at each higher level in the organization. For example, HHS contains the following levels of authority, in ascending order: bureau chief, assistant secretary, deputy secretary, secretary. Each of these officials puts his or her expert input into policy implementation and then sends the decision up to the next level for approval. Not every department uses these levels of authority in the same way, but each leads up to the secretary, who is responsible for all of the policy decisions that come out of a department, and, ultimately, to the president.

The hierarchical decision-making process has advantages and disadvantages. It ensures that the unit responds consistently and predictably. The process also requires careful consideration of a policy before it is implemented. These two structural characteristics, taken together, are designed to ensure that policies are administered equally across citizens. However, this same hierarchical structure can present an obstacle to speedy decision making. Despite efforts to streamline the process, the step-by-step review of decision making inevitably slows down the implementation of federal laws.

Expertise

Fundamental to the core of the federal bureaucracy is the presumption that the people who hold bureaucratic positions have expertise in the issue areas they oversee and implement. This expertise can come from a number of sources. Individuals can enter the bureaucracy at the lowest possible levels and stay in their jobs long enough to acquire knowledge about federal programs. An employee might have worked in a particular industry, such as nuclear energy, and then have brought his or her preexisting knowledge to the bureaucracy—in this case, the Nuclear Regulatory Commission—as a mid-level employee. Other bureaucrats may have studied a federal policy area in academia or at policy think tanks and then may have been offered government positions. Congress, with members who chaired or served on relevant congressional committees, is a major source of cabinet secretary appointments.

Bureaucratic Culture

The fourth core component of a bureaucracy is the bureaucratic culture. As one political scientist explained, "Every organization has a culture, that is, a persistent, patterned way of thinking about the central tasks of and human relationships within an organization. Culture is to an organization what personality is to an individual. Like human culture, it is passed on from one generation to the next."[12]

Fundamental to bureaucratic culture is the constant drive to self-perpetuate; employees in a bureaucratic organization want to preserve their jobs and their influence in the policy-making system. For this reason, bureaucratic culture can act as a gate that prevents efficiency and responsiveness in government because it can create situations in which employees in different organizations duplicate tasks, counterbalance one another's efforts, and ultimately fail to accomplish their agency's or department's mission.

At its worst, bureaucratic failure can result in a terrible loss of life, as in the case of the 9/11 terrorist attacks. Many politicians, members of the media, and citizens blamed the federal agencies that oversee intelligence gathering—the Federal Bureau of Investigation (FBI), the Central Intelligence Agency (CIA), and the National Security Agency (NSA)—for failing to uncover and prevent the attacks. Each agency detected warning signs of such an attack, but the agencies did not work together. The bureaucratic culture of each agency was insular and distrustful, and lack of coordination among them resulted in an intelligence failure.[13]

To remedy the lack of coordination among the nation's national security and disaster relief agencies, Congress created the cabinet-level Department of Homeland Security in 2003. The hope was that a single large federal organization, presumably with one culture and one overarching mission, would be more effective. The new department consolidated several key units that had been operating independently, including the Coast Guard, U.S. Citizenship and Immigration Services, Customs Service, Secret Service, and Federal Emergency Management Agency, and also created new intelligence offices that would try to serve as bridges between the FBI and the CIA.

Other types of disasters do not involve as large a loss of life but still reflect mismanagement of risk by the government. In 2010, the Deepwater Horizon oil rig exploded in the Gulf of Mexico near Louisiana, killing eleven workers and unleashing approximately 4.9 million barrels of oil into Gulf waters.[14] The oil rig was leased by the British-owned company BP. At first it appeared that the oil spill would be contained, but the rig sank, creating complications in the cleanup effort, and the oil spill grew larger and approached U.S. shores from Florida to Texas. This bureaucratic failure began in the office of the Minerals Management Service, the agency in the Department of the Interior that gave BP permission to drill without first requiring assessments from other federal agencies, specifically the National Oceanic and Atmospheric Administration, about the risks to endangered species in the area, as well as the overall probability of an accident similar to the one that occurred.[15]

This lack of coordination, a clear example of bureaucratic culture getting in the way of good policy implementation, has proved costly to the environment and to the people who live along the shores of the Gulf of Mexico. As a result of the disaster, the chief federal bureaucrat responsible for overseeing offshore drilling resigned, as did the head of the Minerals Management Service. President Obama responded by issuing an executive order to form a commission to investigate the failure, instituted a temporary ban on all offshore drilling projects, and addressed the nation to explain how the federal government was addressing the crisis. On October 12, 2010, he lifted the ban on offshore drilling but put greater safeguards into permit approval and safety guidelines.[16] In 2012, BP initially agreed to a total $7.8 billion settlement with individuals who claimed economic and medical hardship as a result of the spill; as of September 2015, $5.6 billion has been paid out.[17]

In addition to addressing natural and man-made disasters, the federal government also oversees a wide range of safety compliance for everyday activities such as driving. The National Highway Transportation Safety Administration (NHTSA) is responsible for regulating car and truck safety, including mechanical issues, airbags, seat belts, and child restraints, as well as promoting road safety by trying to limit drunk driving. In recent years, the NHTSA has come under fire from consumer advocates and members of Congress because of its failure to forcefully address a major ignition flaw that cut off power to automobiles spontaneously. The flaw potentially affected well over 1 million vehicles manufactured by General Motors between 2003 and 2007. There were 260 incidents of faulty ignition switches reported to NHTSA, and 13 deaths have been attributed to them. Even in the face of congressional inquiries on behalf of constituents, NHTSA did not launch any systematic investigation because they claimed that they did not receive accurate information from General Motors as to the extent and potential life-threatening nature of the problem. In May 2014, NHTSA issued a $35 million fine to General Motors for not issuing a recall for these cars; although this is the largest fine ever imposed on an auto manufacturer, consumer advocates said it was too little too late.[18] The investigations into this bureaucratic failure of oversight did not end with the fine; in September 2015, the Department of Justice announced that GM would pay an additional $900 million in fines to settle a criminal investigation into the faulty ignition switches.[19] Subsequently, both NHTSA and GM stated that they would refine their safety compliance and regulatory processes.

The safety arena is not the only way in which the federal government regulates automobiles. In 2015, the Environmental Protection Agency (EPA) found that Volkswagen rigged the engines on their diesel cars to perform differently when being tested on emission standards. The scandal forced a recall of at least 500,000 cars in the United States and millions more around the world. The EPA had the legal power to impose fines on Volkswagen of $37,500 per car, which would have amounted to $18 billion. Rather than imposing the fines outright, the EPA joined with the Department of Justice to sue Volkswagen over their violations of emissions standards; in addition, the Federal Trade Commission sued Volkswagen for false advertising of their diesel cars as "clean diesel." All parties were trying to work out a

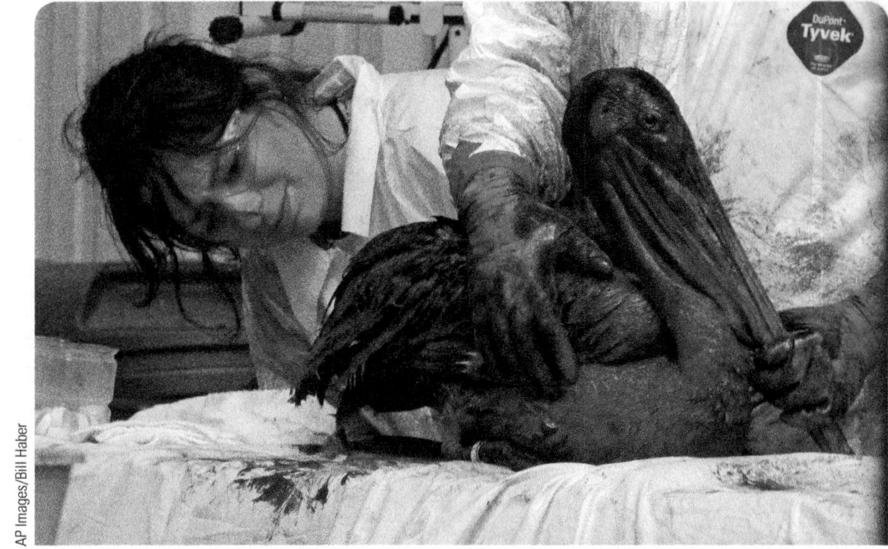

AP Images/Bill Haber

IMAGE 14.3 On April 20, 2010, the Deepwater Horizon oil rig, leased by the BP oil company, exploded in the Gulf of Mexico, killing eleven workers and unleashing millions of gallons of oil into Gulf waters. Controversy still surrounds this massive environmental disaster, with the states asking how such an event could have been allowed to occur. Here emergency responders clean pelicans at a Louisiana facility.

settlement and in June 2016, Volkswagen agreed to pay approximately $14.7 billion in fines and payments to consumers.[20]

Although each of the disasters just discussed was brought about by entirely different circumstances, a common lack of communication and expert direction exposed the inherent dangers of a flawed bureaucratic culture. If such failings are serious enough, the president may ultimately be held accountable for them. Federal agencies may continue to resist change, not wanting to give up any authority. Change in any long-standing organization is difficult to achieve and generally happens only when the people at the top of the chain of command tear down the barriers to cooperation.

Bureaucratic culture can be shaped by the type of person drawn to work in a government bureaucracy. Bureaucrats are often depicted as narrow-minded and resistant to innovation, but many different types of people seek jobs in the bureaucracy.[21] A person who works in a long-standing government division may seek job security and stability, but someone who joins a newly formed department or agency might seek opportunities for creativity. In addition, policies evolve over time in response to changing external conditions. For example, twenty years ago, the Department of Energy might have focused on more efficient ways of drilling for oil and subsequently hired geologists; today, with the emphasis on reducing national dependence on fossil fuels, the Department of Energy seeks to hire individuals with expertise in new energy technologies. There is no single personality type in the bureaucracy. The bureaucracy is so complex and diverse that individuals with a wide range of skills and interests choose to work within it.

One counteracting force to the drawbacks of bureaucratic culture and its tendency to block cooperation among agencies is bureaucratic reputation. Federal agencies want to develop good reputations for their effective implementation of federal policy. Most people take pride in the jobs they do, and bureaucrats are no different.[22]

14.3 Historical Evolution of the Bureaucracy

Describe the growth of the bureaucracy over time

The federal bureaucracy is as old as the nation itself, but it has evolved in ways that some of the Framers would barely recognize. Although they understood that the population would increase and the country's borders would expand, they could never have imagined that the federal government would have so many responsibilities and be so integral to citizens' daily lives. Over time, in tandem with economic, social, and technological developments, Congress passed laws creating new executive departments and other bureaucratic organizations. Here we trace the growth of the federal bureaucracy and the development of professional staff positions to implement federal policy.

Expansion of Executive Branch Departments

The first departments created by Congress in 1789 were State, Treasury, and War. The attorney general also sat on the president's cabinet, though he did not yet head a department.

In addition, the Post Office, first created in 1775 by the Continental Congress to serve the vital function of establishing communication routes among the colonies, became a permanent government organization in 1794.[23] Through these organizations, Congress intended to fulfill the constitutional responsibilities set forth in Article I, Section 8—to regulate commerce among the states and with foreign nations, to provide for defense, to collect taxes and borrow money, and to establish post offices and post roads.

In 1849, Congress created the Department of the Interior to deal with the demands of western expansion, such as sale of federal lands and the management of Indian affairs. The Department of Agriculture was created in 1862 to mitigate the hardships caused by crop and price fluctuations through crop subsidies that remain in place today. In 1870, the Office of the Attorney General, first set up in 1793, was transformed into the Department of Justice to handle the legal business of the nation.

The next two departments, Commerce and Labor, represented economic concerns. Congress addressed them by creating a single department in 1903, but within a decade, the issues of child safety and workers' standards became so important that Congress divided the department, giving Labor its own cabinet status. This sequence was paralleled later in the twentieth century by the creation of the Department of Health, Education, and Welfare in 1953 and its subsequent division into two departments—the Department of Education, created in 1979, and the Department of Health and Human Services in 1980 to oversee health care and welfare programs. In 1949, the War Department was transformed into the Department of Defense, coordinating the Army, Navy, and Air Force. In 1965, Congress created the Department of Housing and Urban Development to oversee federal programs designed to build more affordable housing for people with low incomes and to help restore inner cities that were losing residents. The Department of Transportation was created in 1966, following a decade of interstate highway building authorized by the Highway Act of 1956. Increases in trucking also put pressure on the federal government to maintain highways and regulate business and labor practices in trucking and the air travel industry. As a direct response to the energy crisis of the early 1970s, the Department of Energy was created in 1977 to promote fuel conservation as well as the development of alternatives to fossil fuels, including nuclear, ethanol, and solar power.

Essential Knowledge

Agencies are given discretion as to how to enforce laws passed by Congress. Further, Congress gives them the authority to issue administrative regulations. For example, the U.S. Department of Education makes rules (administrate regulations) for the administration of student loans.

In 1989, the Department of Veterans Affairs was created with the support of President George H. W. Bush (1989–93). Finally, as noted earlier, Congress created the Department of Homeland Security in 2003 in a direct response to the widely perceived intelligence failures associated with the terrorist attacks of 9/11.

Growth of Regulatory Agencies and Other Organizations

In addition to the formal cabinet departments, the executive branch contains numerous regulatory agencies and other organizations that are responsible for administering the details of laws in specific areas, as well as for overseeing the practices of businesses and individuals involved in all facets of economic and political life. These agencies serve as gateways for the federal government to respond to citizens in targeted ways on a localized level, and they are especially important in ensuring safety and economic fairness for citizens in daily life. Among the concerns these agencies address are highway and air travel, food inspection and product labeling, and bank and stock market practices.

PUBLIC POLICY AND THE BUREAUCRACY

Consumer Financial Protection

The federal bureaucracy has grown, in part, because Congress has continually responded to changes in the economy and society that have required government action. However, at times, industries that are regulated by the government create new technologies or businesses practices that become widely adopted so quickly that the government cannot keep up with them in terms of regulation. One example of this kind of innovation is the packaging of risky mortgages (known as sub-prime) into bundles that could be purchased by investors who counted on the high interest from these mortgages to make large profits. The problem with these risky mortgages was that when the economy slowed down, many homeowners could no longer pay the interest or even the basic principal payment. Homeowners lost their homes, and investors lost all their investments. The collapses of both the housing industry and the investments in mortgages are considered to be major causes of the recent recession, and many voters blamed large banks and mortgage companies.

In response, Congress and President Obama passed comprehensive financial reform legislation known as the Dodd-Frank Wall Street Reform and Consumer Protection Act. This legislation made a number of important changes designed to place the banking industry under greater federal supervision and protect against future financial crises. It prohibits banks and other companies from engaging in unethical lending practices, such as offering high-interest mortgages and credit cards to individuals who do not have the incomes or assets to afford them. It requires banks to set aside large sums of money to guard against losses from risky or highly unprofitable investments. Additionally, the law requires large banks to organize their investment practices as separate entities apart from their more traditional banking functions, so if investments, such as derivatives and credit-default swaps, go bad, the entire bank will not be put at risk. All these provisions illustrate the way the president and Congress as institutions try to adapt to the invention of new products, services, and economic practices. Opponents of regulation, however, including major banks and financial institutions affected by the legislation, argued that the new law interferes with the free market and, during a recession, could slow recovery.

The law also created a new Consumer Financial Protection Bureau, an independent bureau within the Federal Reserve, to ensure that banking and credit-related businesses operate in a way that is transparent and fair to consumers and businesses alike through enforcement and consumer education. However, it took a year for the Consumer Financial Protection Bureau to begin operations. The delay was due to a provision in the law requiring that a director be confirmed before any regulations could be issued. Opponents of the law in the Senate blocked President Obama's first nominee and were delaying action on the second nominee when, in January 2012, the president appointed Richard Cordray as the bureau's first director as a recess appointment. Some of the most important parts of the law, such as the regulations to ensure that lenders do not give mortgages to people who cannot repay them, have been finalized and were put into effect in January 2014.

The regulatory process is never easy, and delays are common, but the implementation of the Dodd-Frank Act has been especially complex because it involves the overhaul and installment of financial regulations and the establishment of a new agency. The act has a wide impact, ranging from protecting homeowners to safeguarding consumers against unfair credit and debit card fees. The regulatory process has been prolonged by another factor as well—the degree of coordination required among the other agencies involved, including the Federal Reserve and the SEC, each of which has time and workload constraints. Finally, the public comment periods and the backlash from financial institutions have made the process even more complicated, with many vigorously opposing the regulations that will force them to adopt new practices to achieve fairness and transparency. To date, only 274 of the 390 regulations had been finalized, demonstrating that laws that are a gateway for consumer protection may have to work past the gates that the regulatory process, interest group lobbying, and partisan politics might put in their way.[24]

Public Policy Connections

1. Which form of policy making is more reflective of democratic values: legislation passed by Congress or regulations created by the bureaucracy?
2. Which policy-making process is based more on expertise?

One of the most familiar types of regulatory agency is the Food and Drug Administration (FDA), which monitors food safety and handling practices as well as pharmaceutical development and approval procedures. The motto of the FDA summarizes its mission, "Protecting and Promoting *Your* Health." The agency fulfills its mission by issuing guidelines and standards for companies to follow. Well-publicized cases of *E. coli* contamination in ground beef and salmonella in raw tuna, which resulted in illness and even death, illustrate just how difficult it is for the FDA to monitor food safety. Americans consume billions of pounds of ground beef each year, most of it processed by private companies that are subject to FDA inspection but are expected to do most of the food quality and safety monitoring themselves.[25]

As the nation's economy has grown, so has the number of industries, products, and services that may warrant government regulation. This growth has expanded the workload of existing agencies and may require the creation of new ones. For example, Congress established the Federal Trade Commission to protect consumers from unfair financial and marketplace practices and the Consumer Product Safety Commission to ensure that basic goods purchased by consumers are safe.[26] In 2010, President Barack Obama and Congress worked together to create a new regulatory agency—the Consumer Financial Protection Bureau—that would help consumers navigate mortgage and other housing loans as well as real estate investments.[27] This new government agency was included in the Dodd-Frank Wall Street Reform and Consumer Protection Act, which overhauled the banking and investment industries.

There are limits to the effectiveness of regulatory agencies. They have government authority to monitor practices, issue fines, and even shut down businesses, but the government must rely on voluntary cooperation by the vast majority of private businesses in following agency guidelines. The distinct separation between the government and private businesses that is the hallmark of the American economy can also stand as a gate against effective government regulation and **oversight**. Nevertheless, regulatory agencies are gateways through which citizens can ask government to protect them from fraudulent and unsafe products sold in the marketplace.

oversight: *Powers of Congress to monitor how the executive branch implements the laws.*

From Patronage to the Civil Service

For the nation's first forty years, jobs in the executive branch were filled by wealthy elites who had personal political and social connections to members of Congress and the

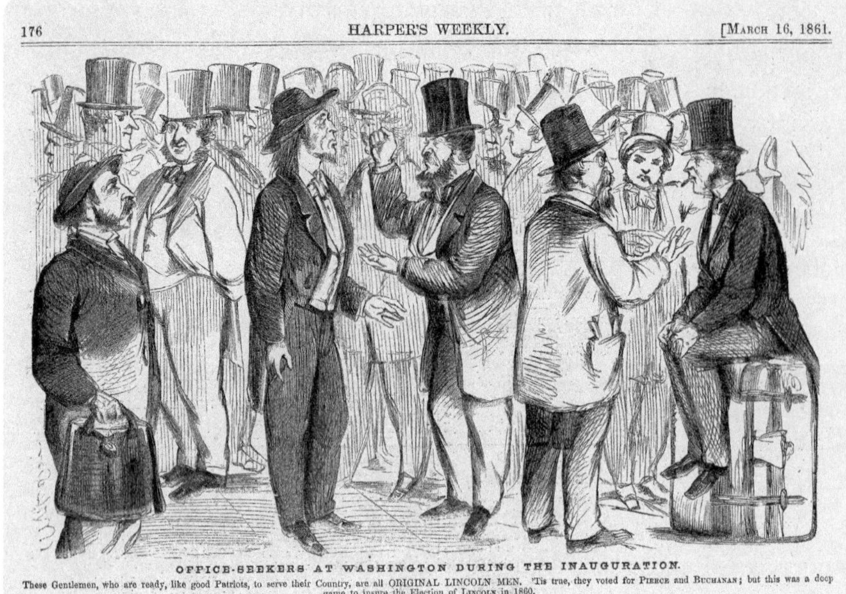

176
HARPER'S WEEKLY.
[MARCH 16, 1861.
OFFICE-SEEKERS AT WASHINGTON DURING THE INAUGURATION.
These Gentlemen, who are ready, like good Patriots, to serve their Country, are all ORIGINAL LINCOLN MEN. 'Tis true, they voted for PIERCE and BUCHANAN; but this was a deep game to insure the Election of LINCOLN in 1860.

Provided courtesy HarpWeek

IMAGE 14.4 Nineteenth-century presidents complained of being besieged by office seekers, men who hoped their connections with members of Congress or the president could help them land lucrative or powerful positions in the executive departments. In this engraving, office seekers wait to see Abraham Lincoln.

president.[28] But President Andrew Jackson (1829–37) used the executive powers of the president to appoint people from wider social and economic backgrounds to federal positions. He also demanded political loyalty from federal employees; to get a job in the Jackson administration, one had to be an active political supporter of Jackson and the Democratic Party. This arrangement, in which the politician appoints employees who pledge loyalty to him, is generally referred to as the patronage system. Jackson's political enemies called it the spoils system, charging Jackson with awarding jobs to political friends in the manner of the saying, "To the victor belong the spoils."

Essential Knowledge

The replacement of patronage with the merit system has increased the effectiveness and professionalism of the bureaucracy. However, some critics believe that is has also led to a decline in responsiveness.

For most of the nineteenth century, Congress and the president shared the patronage power; the president allowed members of Congress to recommend individuals for government posts. With each election in which a different party assumed office, there was a large turnover in staff. The federal patronage system allowed politicians to manipulate federal programs and positions for political and private gain.[29] For example, the Republican-controlled Congress created programs to provide pensions for Civil War veterans who had fought for the North, which was heavily Republican.

As the nation grew larger and the economy more complex, the federal bureaucracy needed more expertise and stability. The assassination of President James A. Garfield in 1881 by an individual who had sought, but had not received, a federal job caused a public outcry against patronage in government employment. Although the assassin had had no direct contact with Garfield, he evidently held the president responsible for his failure to secure a federal job. In response, Congress passed the **Pendleton Act**, which was signed into law by President Chester A. Arthur (1881–85) on January 16, 1883. It was the first of the reforms that slowly changed the federal bureaucracy from a corrupt and partisan insider organization to a neutral, policy-based organization.[30]

Pendleton Act: *1883 act that established a merit- and performance-based system for federal employment.*

However, there are examples of federal agencies being accused of overstepping their authority for political purposes. The Internal Revenue Service (IRS) has been under scrutiny for targeting groups that claim to be nonprofit but might also be engaged in political activity; in the past decade, the IRS has been accused of giving extra scrutiny to groups ranging from the NAACP to Tea Party–affiliated nonprofit organizations. It could be argued that these actions stem from a deeply ingrained culture at the IRS of auditing individuals, businesses, and groups to make sure they comply with tax laws, but to the public, it looked as if the bureaucracy failed to maintain its mission of neutrality in implementing the law.

The Pendleton Act created the **Civil Service Commission** to administer entrance exams for the federal civil service and set job requirements and promotion standards based on a **merit system** and performance, not political affiliation. At first the civil service covered only a small fraction of federal jobs; the rest were controlled primarily by powerful members of Congress who used their influence to direct federal jobs to loyal supporters. But over time, successive presidents wrested more control over the federal bureaucracy from Congress by issuing executive orders to classify a greater percentage of jobs as merit-based and as part of the **civil service**. By 1897, 50 percent of federal jobs were covered by the civil service, and by 1951, 88 percent of federal jobs were civil service jobs.[31] The remaining federal employees are **political appointees** appointed by the president to carry out his political and partisan agenda within the federal policy-making system.

Civil Service Commission: *Created by the Pendleton Act to administer entrance exams for the federal civil service and set standards for promotion based on merit.*

merit system: *System of employment under which employees are chosen and promoted based on merit.*

civil service: *The nonpartisan federal workforce employed to carry out government programs and policies.*

political appointees: *Federal employees appointed by the president with the explicit task of carrying out his political and partisan agenda.*

career civil servants: *Federal employees who are hired through a merit-based system to implement federal programs and who are expected to be neutral in their political affiliations.*

Career Civil Service

Career civil servants are nonpolitical personnel who must pass an exam to secure their jobs and compete on an equal playing field with anyone else who has the same credentials. For the number of executive branch employees, and other members of the federal workforce, see Figure 14.2. The largest percentage of executive branch employees are located in the metropolitan Washington, D.C., area.[32] In general, federal civil service employees fall into three categories: blue-collar, white-collar, and senior executive positions. Blue-collar jobs consist of "craft, repair, operator, and laborer jobs," and employees in this category are under the Federal Wage System, which sets pay levels associated with specific jobs. Executive-level management employees are governed by the Senior Executive Service guidelines, which generally follow the General Schedule (GS) pay scale. All federal employees are subject to performance evaluations and may receive gradual raises, promotions up the career ladder, and incentive and merit bonuses for outstanding job performance.[33]

Some departments and agencies are staffed by career employees who are not in the civil service but nonetheless operate under similar structures. For example, the State Department oversees a corps of diplomats known as Foreign Service officers who are sent all over the world to manage U.S. embassies and consulates. To join the Foreign Service, one must meet certain qualifications and pass an entrance exam, similar to the procedure for entering the civil service generally. However, the Foreign Service has its own pay scale and promotion criteria.

Although politics may permeate any workplace, the civil service is designed to protect employees from partisanship, and employees are expected to be objective as they carry out their job responsibilities. Civil servants remain in their positions from one administration to the next, and they cannot be asked to resign for partisan reasons.

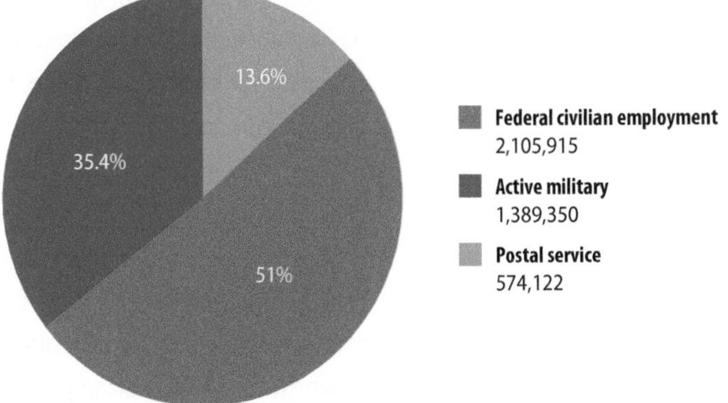

FIGURE 14.2 Distribution of Federal Government Workforce, 2016

Federal employment is divided into several categories: executive branch, active military forces, and the U.S. Postal Service.

Source: The White House, Office of Management and Budget, *Fiscal Year 2017 Analytical Perspectives Budget of the U.S. Government*, Table 8-3, "Total Federal Employment," p. 83, http://www.whitehouse.gov/sites/default/files/omb/budget/fy2016/assets/spec.pdf.

Political Appointees

Political appointees, unlike civil servants, get their jobs because they are members of the same party that controls the executive branch, they have connections to politically powerful people, or they have served in a prior presidential administration. Political appointees can occupy a wide range of positions, from cabinet secretary to commissioner to administrator. Although it is uncommon, political appointees can also come from the opposition party, especially when they have particular expertise in a policy area or a president wants continuity in department leadership early in his administration. Regardless of their personal views, political appointees are expected to carry out the president's policy agenda.[34]

Political appointees can come from a variety of backgrounds. Typically they are members of the president's inner circle or campaign team, served as congressional committee chairs, or served in former presidential administrations. In some cases, they come from the private sector. There are advantages and disadvantages to the president in choosing people from any of these backgrounds. Sometimes a president's trusted campaign advisers are not talented administrators; sometimes members of the private sector find government work too frustrating. Presidents try to make the best choices possible, but occasionally a cabinet secretary is replaced during a presidential term, especially if he or she has become a lightning rod for a broader controversy or an unpopular position.

When a president is reelected for a second term, he customarily requests the resignations of his entire cabinet and then chooses which resignations to accept and which to reject. This custom gives presidents the opportunity to change policy direction and bring fresh perspectives into the executive branch at the start of a second term. For example, in President Obama's second term, many cabinet secretaries left the administration, including the secretaries of State, Defense, Treasury, Commerce, HHS, and Homeland Security. In some cases, members of the cabinet will leave one position to assume another; in 2014, Secretary of Housing and Urban Development Shaun Donovan left that job to head OMB. Donovan was replaced by Julián Castro, the former mayor of San Antonio (see Chapter 12, Congress, for more on Castro and his brother Joaquín, who is a congressman from Texas).

Top-level political appointees require Senate confirmation, a process made slightly easier when the Senate is controlled by the president's party and by the Senate rules change that reduced the cloture threshold to fifty-one votes for presidential nominees and judicial appointments lower than the Supreme Court (see Chapter 12 for more details). Under Franklin Delano Roosevelt (1933–45), the number of such employees was 73, but it has risen to 499 under President Obama. But there are hundreds of other jobs that are considered political appointments. For example, President Dwight D. Eisenhower (1953–61) appointed a layer of federal employees, known as **Schedule C appointees**, to oversee civil service employees. By some accounts, in creating this category Eisenhower was able to add approximately one thousand politically appointed positions to the bureaucracy over the course of his administration.[35] Subsequently, Presidents John F. Kennedy (1961–63), Lyndon Baines Johnson (1963–69), and Richard M. Nixon (1969–74) added more political appointees.

Schedule C appointees: *Federal employees appointed by the president to oversee civil service employees.*

Senior Executive Service (SES): *Senior management personnel in the federal government appointed by the president.*

In 1978, President Jimmy Carter (1977–81) created the **Senior Executive Service (SES)**, experienced personnel who can be assigned by the president to senior management positions throughout the federal bureaucracy. For SES positions, the president generally chooses career civil service employees who have shown expertise in their jobs, but the president also has the authority to bring in individuals from the private sector. The SES provides a layer of administration over federal programs that is directed by the president, infusing the federal bureaucracy with political perspectives that can clash with the goal of objective implementation of federal policy. Since 1980, the total number of political appointees has averaged about three thousand.[36] Although that may not seem like a high number compared to the total federal workforce, the category of political appointee has been used successfully by many presidents to expand their direct influence within the bureaucracy.

Diversity in the Federal Bureaucracy

Presidents Clinton, George W. Bush, and Obama explicitly aimed to diversify the federal workforce. Figure 14.3 shows the percentage of ethnic, racial, gender, and LGBT groups that make up the federal bureaucracy.[37] Within these statistics, one can argue that women, at 51 percent of the population, and Latinos, at 17 percent of the population, are the groups that are least well represented proportionally. In addition to high-ranking appointments, the Obama administration also tried to recruit members of underrepresented groups to lower-level federal jobs, both political and in the civil service, to ensure that future administrations will have as diverse a talent pool to hire from as possible.

Building a diverse federal workforce serves as a gateway to the advancement of women and minorities within the public and private sectors, as these employees can later obtain political appointments to the president's cabinet. At this highest level of cabinet appointees, President Obama can lay claim to having had the greatest number of women to date. However, he was criticized by advocates for failing to attract other underrepresented groups such as Latinos and African Americans. The head of the National Council of La Raza, Janet Murguia, pointed out that these groups heavily supported Obama in 2008 and 2012 and should have been rewarded with a greater number of prominent appointments in the administration.[38] In Obama's first term, cabinet-rank officials consisted of seven women and fifteen men, including four African Americans, one Latino, one Asian American, and one Pacific Islander. In 2016, at the end of his second term, his cabinet consisted of seven women and fifteen men, including four African Americans and four Latinos. When Julián Castro was appointed to be Secretary of HUD, many believed that the administration did so to address the concerns of the Latino community about high-level representation within President Obama's cabinet.

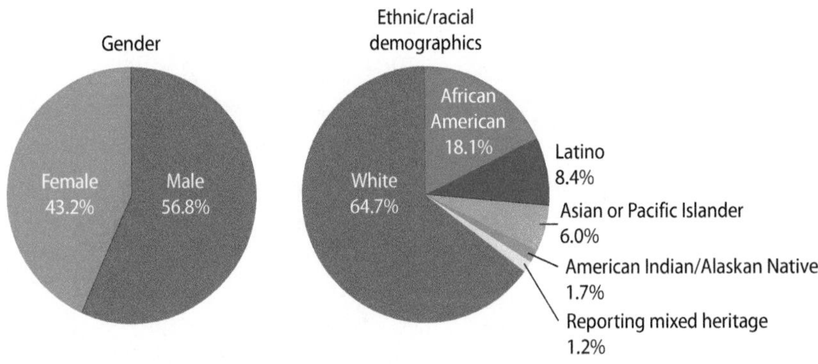

FIGURE 14.3 Composition of the Federal Workforce

These charts show the demographics of the federal workforce. For the first time, statistics on lesbian, gay, bisexual, and transgender (LGBT) workers are available, with 2.8 percent of the federal workforce identifying in this category. Additionally, 9.0 percent of all federal workers have a designated disability.

Source: https://www.opm.gov/policy-data-oversight/diversity-and-inclusion/federal-workforce-at-a-glance.

POLITICAL ANALYTICS

Younger Americans in the Federal Workforce

JUST AS THE FEDERAL WORKFORCE CAN BE A gateway for the advancement of women and minorities, it can also serve that purpose for Millennials and others preparing to enter the workforce. Diversity in the federal bureaucracy furthers goals of representing the population in public service and may present opportunities for those employed. A broad workforce may also be important as a mechanism for the input of new ideas and personnel into the bureaucracy.

Figure 14.4 features data about Millennials and Generation Xers in the federal workforce (defined here as people born from 1976 to 1990, or those under 40 years old). Taken from an annual survey of federal workers, the data show that these two groups make up almost

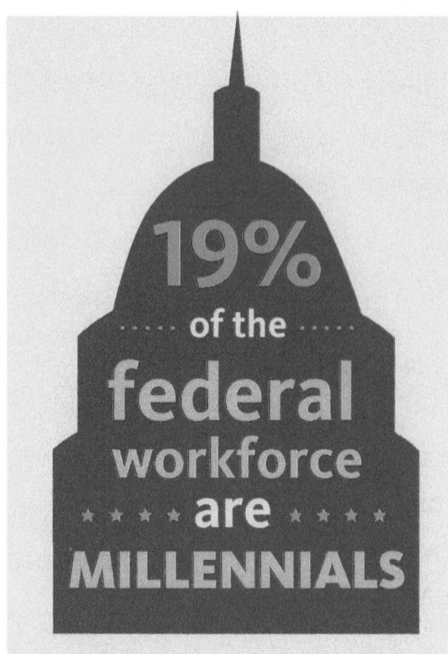

64%
report positive job satisfaction
87%
feel the work they do is important
81%
see how their work relates to their agency's goals & priorities

MILLENNIAL minorities =

25% of the total workforce

35% of the federal workforce

35% earned bachelor's degrees or higher

FIGURE 14.4 Millennials and Generation Xers in the Federal Bureaucracy

Sources: https://www.fedview.opm.gov; U.S. Department of Labor, Bureau of Labor Statistics, http://www.bls.gov/cps/demographics.htm#age.

20 percent of the federal bureaucracy. Those who found employment with the federal government report high levels of satisfaction with their jobs and believe that the work they do is important. Millennials and Generation Xers who are also racial or ethnic minorities are also well represented in the federal bureaucracy as compared to the overall U.S. workforce. Examine the data about how much of the federal workforce is made up of those under 40 years of age, how younger Americans feel about working in the federal bureaucracy, and the percentages of younger federal workers who are minorities.

Thinking Critically

1. How do you think the job satisfaction levels for these groups of federal workers are related to how they view the promise of government?
2. What do you think Millennials bring to the federal bureaucracy?

Sources: Office of Personnel Management, *2015 Federal Employee Viewpoint Survey*, https://www.fedview.opm.gov; U.S. Department of Labor, Bureau of Labor Statistics, http://www.bls.gov/cps/demographics.htm#age.

Private-Sector Contract Workers

In addition to civil service employees and political appointees, the federal government hires thousands of individuals and companies from the private sector to administer programs and carry out tasks associated with specific policies. These companies can range from nonprofit community organizations, to midsize security firms, to large health care conglomerates. They are not under the direct control of the federal bureaucracy, but they carry out crucial tasks for it. President Bill Clinton was the first Democrat since the 1930s to suggest that some of the services provided by the federal government could be more efficiently done by the private sector. In addition, incentive programs were put in place to reward federal civil servants for efficiency, in the same way that employees in the private sector receive bonuses.

President George W. Bush continued this trend of contracting out the performance of government tasks to private companies. For example, during the Iraq War, the federal government contracted with major construction companies to work with the Army Corps of

Umit Bektas/Reuters

IMAGE 14.5 The federal bureaucracy often employs private-sector workers and organizations to administer federal programs or help support military operations. Here private security personnel help government officials in Afghanistan. Although there is a need for more personnel to supplement U.S. efforts, controversies can arise in terms of oversight of private workers, as well as the dangers they encounter on the job.

Engineers to rebuild war-torn areas of Iraq. It also contracted with private security firms to provide additional security for U.S. diplomatic and civilian personnel in both Iraq and Afghanistan. At home, much of the actual administration and provision of benefits under the Medicare and Medicaid programs is carried out by large private health maintenance organizations (HMOs) and other private service providers. When such large programs are run by private-sector organizations, it is sometimes more difficult to conduct proper oversight to prevent cost overruns or unnecessary billing charges.[39]

There are costs and benefits to the privatization of federal services. One concern is that the federal government does not have close oversight over the quality, experience, or job performance of the employees who work in the private companies. Although company employees have an incentive to do their jobs well, fraud, waste, and abuse can go undetected for years because of the lack of direct federal oversight. Sometimes the federal government ends up paying more for the provision of services through private contractors than it would if federal employees administered the program directly. The benefit of using private firms is that they do not technically count as additional federal employees, so when they are used, the overall size of the federal workforce appears smaller, and costs associated with job-related benefits are reduced. In some cases, it is more efficient to use a private firm that has expertise in an area to provide a service at a lower cost than to use permanent employees and achieve the same outcome. That allows the government to increase or decrease employment for specific projects; it is much more difficult to eliminate federal positions.

Bureaucrats and Politics

The civil service was created to protect federal employees from partisan politics, but by 1939 it had become clear that political influence was still rampant throughout the bureaucracy, not only at the federal level but at state and local levels as well. In response, Congress passed the Hatch Act, which prohibited government employees from working on political campaigns, using their positions to solicit campaign donations, or promoting candidates for elected office. This mandated separation of politics from the bureaucracy was designed to eliminate the last vestiges of patronage. It took pressure off bureaucrats, who could tell campaigning politicians that they were prohibited from engaging in certain political activities. In 1993, the Hatch Act Reform Amendments significantly loosened restrictions on political activities by government employees as long as the activities occurred while they were off duty. Now political appointees are explicitly allowed to engage in political activities on behalf of the president so long as the costs for these activities are not paid with tax dollars. However, bans on political activities remain in force for employees in law enforcement and intelligence agencies as well as for employees of the Federal Election Commission, which monitors federal campaign activities.[40]

Conflict between civil servants, who take a programmatic approach and aim to make programs work efficiently over the long term, and political appointees, who want to carry out the president's partisan agenda while the president is in office, was addressed by the Civil Service Reform Act of 1978. President Jimmy Carter proposed the act to encourage cooperation between political appointees and civil servants and to make sure that each was held accountable for decision making. The act created the Office of Personnel Management to oversee both categories of federal employees. The Office of Personnel Management, under the direct control of the Executive Office of the President, can expand the number of political appointees and reduce the number of career civil servants. With more politically appointed personnel in the bureaucracy, presidents assert greater control over how federal policy is formulated and implemented. To preserve the essential political neutrality of the career civil service, the act also created the Merit Systems Protection Board, which ensures that the protections afforded to career civil servants through the merit system remain in place.

Nevertheless, bureaucrats do face conflicting pressures when Congress is controlled by one political party and the executive branch is controlled by the other political party, a condition known as divided government. Under divided government, federal bureaucrats are frequently caught in the middle because they are pressured by Congress to implement policy one way and by political appointees in their agencies to implement policy in a different way. Objectively, policy is supposed to be implemented in a manner that will produce the most efficient and responsive results, but trying to please two powerful bosses can result in inefficient and ineffective policy. Fortunately, the career nature of the civil service, with its built-in protections against political pressure, helps mitigate the negative consequences of divided government. In addition, because career civil servants frequently outlast presidents and some members of Congress, they have a longer-term perspective on the impact of their decisions.

At the same time, bureaucrats tend to form long-term working relationships with members of Congress and even with interest group lobbyists in the policy areas in which they specialize. In Chapter 8, Interest Groups, we explored the concepts of iron triangles (see Figure 8.3) and issue networks, both of which are used to describe these relationships. Bureaucrats want to maximize their longevity as administrators of federal programs, so they try to be as responsive as possible to the other members of the network, and each member constantly shares information with the others.[41] Critics of iron triangles and issue networks argue that they contribute to the inefficiency of the federal government because they sustain programs that may be duplicative or outdated, and they may encourage corruption within the government. However, given the 24-7 news cycle and the amount of government information available on the Internet, the public, the media, and watchdog groups are able to monitor such relationships, and they are now more transparent than ever before. Nevertheless, iron triangles are another indication that, despite the protections of a merit-based civil service, politics will always influence, to some degree, the bureaucrats who implement federal policy.

Essential Knowledge

Iron triangles and issue networks are two models that represent the interaction of the bureaucracy with political actors.

14.4 Accountability and Responsiveness in the Bureaucracy

Assess how the bureaucracy is both accountable and responsive, and how it can fail

Typically, the power of the vote in regularly scheduled elections is used to monitor elected officials, but there are no ways for the average voter to register an opinion about the collective job performance of employees of the federal bureaucracy. Because the bureaucracy varies by type of agency, size of agency, and type of employee, it is difficult for citizens to evaluate job performance and hold bureaucrats collectively accountable for their actions. At the individual level, the job performance of civil servants is reviewed by supervisors at regular intervals, and political appointees can be removed by the president if the president is unhappy with their work. But democracy requires that citizens be able to hold their entire government accountable for the policies it implements, and there is no readily available mechanism for the public to hold civil servants accountable for their job performance. There are, however, certain standards and procedures that Congress has put in place to hold the bureaucracy accountable and encourage responsiveness. Legal challenges to regulations are another means by which the bureaucracy can be held accountable.

Roles of the Legislative and Judicial Branches

Essential Knowledge
The Congress, the president, and the judiciary each have mechanisms to ensure the accountability of the bureaucracy.

Essential Knowledge
Cabinet members and other executive branch officials frequently testify before Congress, providing them with information necessary for the development of legislation.

Congress contributes to the accountability and responsiveness of the bureaucracy through its oversight of implementation and its so-called power of the purse. Congressional committees with jurisdiction in a set of issue areas can request that agency and cabinet officials testify before them to explain the way they implement programs under their jurisdiction.[42] The congressional investigations into the terror attack in Benghazi, Libya, in 2012, which resulted in the death of the U.S. Ambassador Christopher Stevens and three private security personnel, serve as an illustration of this process. Both the Democratic-controlled Senate and the Republican-controlled House held hearings to investigate the attack. At one of the Senate hearings, then Secretary of State Hillary Clinton testified about how those deaths occurred, whether the State Department had provided sufficient security, and whether the administration had been fully truthful in its explanation of the event. Benghazi became a lightning rod for Republicans who sought to criticize what they viewed as the administration's unwillingness to provide sufficient answers about the attack.

The issue persisted through 2014 when the House of Representatives, controlled by the Republicans, formed a Select Committee on Benghazi comprising both Republicans and Democrats. Their rationale for continuing to investigate the administration was that Congress had not been provided a full explanation, and no persons had been brought to justice for the deaths of U.S. personnel. However, U.S. forces captured a key suspect in those attacks on June 15, 2014, in Libya, and he was brought to the United States to be charged and stand trial for planning the attack. Although congressional criticism continued, it could no longer be argued that the Obama administration had done nothing to find the perpetrators of the attack.[43] When Hillary Clinton ran for president in 2016, the issue was once again brought up during the campaign and was viewed to be effective against her by her opponent, Donald Trump. Not all oversight

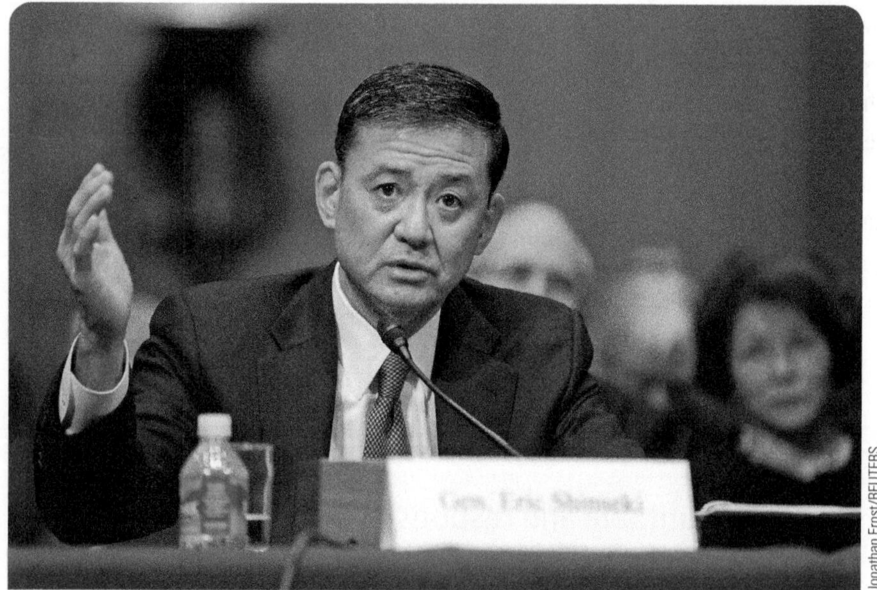

Jonathan Ernst/REUTERS

IMAGE 14.6 In 2014, the Department of Veterans Affairs came under heavy criticism when it was discovered that thousands of veterans were forced to wait months for health care services and that VA personnel had falsified records to hide these delays. Here General Eric Shinseki is testifying before the Senate Veterans Affairs Committee about the scandal; he resigned two weeks later.

issues are so politically charged, but Benghazi does represent an example of how Congress can try to use its powers to exercise oversight of the executive branch.

A serious issue of bureaucratic failure came to light closer to home in 2014 when the Department of Veterans Affairs was accused of systematically denying or delaying care to veterans at a dozen or more VA hospitals across the country.[44] In Phoenix, Arizona, for example, VA employees allegedly tried to cover up the fact that between 1,400 and 1,600 veterans were on long waiting lists to see doctors, and that at least 40 veterans died waiting to be seen for care.[45] Typically veterans are expected to receive care between fourteen and thirty days after they request an appointment.[46] After the delays in care in Phoenix and other centers around the country were brought to light by the news media, the House and Senate Veterans Affairs Committees each held hearings where Secretary Eric Shinseki, a decorated veteran in his own right, testified before Congress. Veterans' groups called for bureaucratic accountability at the VA and asked President Obama to seek Secretary Shinseki's resignation. President Obama maintained his support for his cabinet secretary, but as more information came out in public, the pressure grew to the point that he accepted Shinseki's resignation; two more high-ranking officials resigned shortly thereafter. When Congress exercises its oversight power and an agency becomes viewed as incompetent, it risks budget and personnel cuts, being rolled into a larger agency, or being dissolved altogether. Or, as in the case of the VA, members of the executive branch can be asked to resign or be impeached if there is sufficient evidence of incompetence or illegal activity.

Another way Congress can hold the bureaucracy accountable is through its powers to authorize and appropriate. Authorization and appropriation hearings give Congress a chance to evaluate federal agencies and to withhold or reduce funds if there are dissatisfactions. Agency heads are fully aware of this congressional power, and it is a key reason that they take congressional opinion into account when they implement federal programs. Congressional influence of this type thus serves as a gateway for the public—which elects members of Congress—to hold the bureaucracy accountable for its actions.

The judicial branch, too, helps hold the bureaucracy accountable. The courts can serve as effective monitors of implementation because they are a gateway for groups adversely affected by a federal regulation to argue their case against it. Typically, the courts intervene when there is a dispute between Congress and the executive branch on the interpretation of a law, and not when the two branches agree (see Supreme Court Cases: *Chevron U.S.A. v. Natural Resources Defense Council*).

Efficiency and Transparency

One of the biggest challenges a bureaucratic organization faces is carrying out its mission efficiently while maintaining transparency to the American public. A chronic complaint about the bureaucracy is that it is slow. Yet issuing rules and regulations takes so long because the process solicits input from all sectors, including members of Congress, businesses and industries that are being regulated, and average citizens with a stake in the issue. For example, it took President Obama six years into his administration to issue sweeping regulations to reduce emissions from coal-fired power plants by 20 percent as part of his policies on climate change. As stated earlier, though, even after regulations are issued, they are subject to the kind of input described previously

SUPREME COURT CASES

Chevron U.S.A. v. Natural Resources Defense Council (1984)

QUESTION: Can the Environmental Protection Agency (EPA) allow pollution-producing plants to update equipment at some sources of pollution at a plant without requiring that it update all equipment at the plant?

ORAL ARGUMENT: February 29, 1984 (listen at http://www.oyez.org/cases/1980-1989/1983/1983_82_1005)

DECISION: June 25, 1984 (read at http://www.law.cornell.edu/supremecourt/text/467/837)

OUTCOME: Yes, the EPA can adjust regulations because courts recognize a responsibility to defer to agency decisions in the absence of specific congressional instructions to administer the law differently (6–0; three justices did not participate).

Congress establishes agencies to handle both routine administrative chores and highly technical decisions. Because Congress cannot foresee all questions that may arise, it delegates rule-making authority to agencies. These rules are subject to review by the federal judiciary to ensure that they are consistent with the intent of Congress.

Under the Carter administration, the EPA made rules governing the emission of air pollution from sources such as plants and factories. Under those rules, replacing any equipment at a source would mean that all equipment at the source would have to meet the stringent standards of the 1977 amendments to the Clean Air Act. During the Reagan administration, the EPA loosened the rules so that plants with multiple sources of pollution could update some of the sources as long as total pollution from the plant did not increase.

The National Resources Defense Council sued Chevron U.S.A., claiming that the EPA's decision to loosen the rules violated congressional intent. The Court of Appeals for the District of Columbia agreed, striking the new EPA rule and restoring the older rule. Chevron appealed the court of appeals decision to the Supreme Court.

The Supreme Court reversed the decision of the court of appeals. Although the decision allowed looser regulations of pollution control, it also stated that federal courts should grant a great deal of deference to the decisions and rules made by federal agencies. Specifically, the Court declared that if Congress has explicitly expressed a preference on an issue, the agency must follow that intent. If, however, as is often the case, Congress has not explicitly expressed a preference on the issue, courts must accept the agency's rule as long as the rule is reasonable. In the *Chevron* suit, the Supreme Court declared that it was reasonable for the EPA to allow plants to replace equipment at some sources without having to replace equipment at all sources. Otherwise, plants might simply put off any improvements in equipment. Reasonableness is a very broad standard, so this decision grants federal agencies a great deal of flexibility in how to implement federal law.

Thinking Critically

1. Why would the Supreme Court generally want to defer to the judgment of bureaucracies on a rule?
2. How might responsiveness suffer when Congress and the Court delegate authority to the bureaucracy?

and may not even be finalized until the end of his second term. The government can justify the slowness of the decision-making process on the grounds that it considers many points of view in implementing policy. Unfortunately, inclusiveness comes at the expense of efficiency.

In addition, the issues related to food and drug safety, transportation safety, working conditions, and antiterrorism measures can be matters of life and death. Citizens expect the federal government to act in their best interests, but such issues require caution, and caution can lead to delay. On the other hand, if the government fails to make its practices transparent and does not consider all the implications of its decisions, citizens may lose trust in government.

These concerns were part of the rationale behind a series of bills designed to open up the workings of the federal bureaucracy to the general public. In 1966, the Freedom of Information Act established a procedure by which ordinary citizens can directly request documents and reports from the federal government by paying a nominal fee, as long as the documents are not classified. Access to a classified document or report is automatically restricted to federal employees who hold security clearances and have a legitimate need to see the document. In times of military conflict, such as during the Vietnam and Iraq wars, presidents typically restrict access to public documents relating to war efforts. In response to the mistrust of the federal government that grew out of the Vietnam War and the Watergate scandal, in 1976 Congress enacted the Government in the Sunshine Act, which tried to increase transparency by requiring government agencies to hold open forums to allow the public to comment on their decisions, regulations, and performance.

To highlight the tension between efficiency and transparency, let us return to the Food and Drug Administration, discussed earlier in the chapter. One of the agency's most important responsibilities is monitoring pharmaceutical development from the initial testing of drugs to final approval for widespread use. Even before a drug is submitted to the FDA for approval, pharmaceutical companies have conducted three phases of clinical trials, which are experiments and applications on human subjects that measure the efficacy and safety of the drug. If the drug shows promise, the company submits a New Drug Application to the FDA. If agency employees agree that the clinical trial results are reliable, the FDA forms a review panel whose members have different types of expertise about the potential effects of the drug. The panel serves as a gateway for nonemployees of the agency to participate in the drug approval process. Members of the panel consider all the results of the trials and offer opinions as to whether the drug can be approved for sale. Ultimately, the FDA makes the final decision.

This process illustrates the trade-off between efficiency and transparency.[47] When a new drug is effective against disease, the public wants access to that drug as soon as possible. However, every new drug has unforeseen side effects, some of which may not be visible in the short term, so the more information the FDA has, the more likely the drugs it approves for the market will be safe. Forming review committees with members from outside the agency is one way of collecting a wide range of information about the possible impacts of the drug. Yet this process is time-consuming; the more participants, the more slowly it moves. Like many federal agencies, then, the FDA must weigh the cost of efficient decision making against the cost of approving a drug before it has been thoroughly tested. The FDA is constantly updating consumer advisories about a wide range of food and medical products. For example, the FDA issued a warning to diabetics using a specific type of glucose test strip because it was found to be inaccurate.[48] In most, if not all, instances when the FDA issues such an advisory to the public, the manufacturer withdraws the product from the market.

Whistleblowing

Most federal employees are careful, dedicated, and hardworking. However, as in all organizations run by human beings, there can be inefficiency, error, abuse of power, and corruption. Each federal agency has an Office of Inspector General that monitors the activities of the agency's employees. But unless a wrongdoing is identified and brought to the inspector general's attention, it frequently goes unpunished.

whistleblowers: *Employees who report mismanagement, corruption, or illegal activity within their agencies.*

To encourage more candid disclosure of wrongdoing in federal agencies, Congress passed the Whistleblower Protection Act in 1989 to protect **whistleblowers**, government employees who report mismanagement, corruption, or illegal activity within their agencies.[49] Before the passage of this act, whistleblowers had no real protection against reprisals from their colleagues, especially from those at higher levels of authority. The act established grievance and appeal procedures for employees who believe they have been retaliated against for reporting wrongdoing in their agencies. In 2010, Congress extended protections to employees in the financial services industry who act as whistleblowers, but they did not extend such protection to TSA workers or federal marshals; Robert MacLean (see beginning of chapter) sued the federal government to get such protection, and won.

Bureaucratic Failure

Whether whistleblowers come from inside or outside the federal government, it is up to the federal government to respond to them in an effective fashion. Unfortunately, there are serious cases in which a government agency has failed to respond. What happens when an entire agency fails to accomplish its mission?

One of the realities of federal management and oversight is that a federal agency or a congressional committee needs to be aware of a problem in order to address it. The dual responsibilities of accountability and responsiveness in the federal bureaucracy require the bureaucracy to do its job well enough to protect citizens from physical and financial harm. Unfortunately, the American people are so familiar with the failures of the federal bureaucracy that its successes are overlooked. The fact that 325 million people live in relative peace and security; experience safe and reasonable working conditions; trust that the medications they take are well tested; travel on trains, buses, and planes without incident; drink clean water; and receive their mail every day is a testament to the ways in which the federal bureaucracy meets its obligations. It is up to the voters to hold their elected officials—in Congress as well as the president—accountable for the performance of the federal bureaucracy.

Science Source

IMAGE 14.7 The Food and Drug Administration conducts onsite inspections of food products both domestically produced and imported. Here two FDA field employees are inspecting fish shipments at Los Angeles International Airport.

ELECTION 2016

Holding the Federal Government Accountable

IN 2016, INCUMBENT PRESIDENT Barack Obama had completed his two terms in office and could not run for another term. Even though Obama did not run for president again, voters still considered the success of his administration, and his running of the federal bureaucracy, as part of their decision to elect a new president from his political party. The Democratic nominee for president, Hillary Clinton, was even more tied to Obama than simply sharing the same party affiliation because she had served as Secretary of State during his first four years in office. So in that way, voters had a chance to offer their assessment of how well she did as part of the federal bureaucracy in deciding whether or not to vote for her.

But the vast size and reach of the federal bureaucracy and its impact in the daily lives of voters make elections about more than just choosing a new president; they are a verdict on how well the federal government does its job. In 2015, a Gallup survey was taken asking Americans to rate specific business sectors positively or negatively, and the federal government was included. Twenty-five percent of Americans viewed the federal government in a positive light, 18 percent were neutral, and 54 percent viewed it negatively.[50] Those kind of numbers always worry incumbent federal elected officials because they expect to be held accountable, even indirectly, for the job performance of the federal government.

But voters also have different priorities and concerns, so they may be more attentive in some areas of the bureaucracy. For example, senior citizens will be more concerned with how well Medicare works, veterans will pay attention to the VA, college students will worry about the federal student loan program, people seeking health insurance through the Affordable Care Act will be concerned about accessing health insurance exchanges, and medical researchers will want the FDA to be careful and efficient in the drug approval process. On the financial side, most Americans will want the financial and banking system to be secure, stable, and fair, which is why consumer advocates were so supportive of the Dodd-Frank law. And although the federal government does not have direct control of the economy and job growth, certain policies can be credited with making improvements or slowing it down.

During the election in 2016, many of these types of programs were discussed by the candidates from both major parties, as well as candidates running for Congress, both incumbents and challengers. Bernie Sanders was a candidate for the Democratic nomination for president, and he focused his campaign largely on criticizing the Obama administration for failing to punish Wall Street banks for the recession, and promising to find a way to reduce student loan costs to attend college. Donald Trump was the Republican Party nominee for president, and while he did not get into many specifics, he generally criticized the Obama administration for failing to be effective in the key areas of federal responsibility, including national defense, trade and economic growth, and the fight against terrorism. Members of Congress tried to separate themselves from the presidential contest by focusing on their individual efforts to help constituents navigate the federal bureaucracy in areas where they may need assistance, such as filing a Social Security or Medicare claim or securing a federal grant for a bridge or highway. However, given that Congress and President Obama were unable to agree on so many key issues for most of his second term in office, Congress in 2016 had a much sparser record of legislative accomplishments to run on than in past years.

Ultimately it is up to voters to decide what they actually expect from the federal government, in specific issue areas of concern to them. For politicians seeking their support, it is crucial to make sure that as many areas as possible of the federal government function well, because they never know which part of the government a voter will come into contact with on any given day. The results of the 2016 election showed that when voters are frustrated with government across all levels, presidential candidates who emphasize their effectiveness, as Donald Trump did, can resonate enough to help win control of the White House.

The Bureaucracy and Democracy

The federal government that started with three cabinet departments has grown to include fifteen cabinet departments and many powerful independent agencies. The federal bureaucracy, including the armed services, employs nearly 4.1 million people. Their jobs affect the lives of all citizens, from the quality of the food they eat, to the safety of the highways they drive, to the purity of the water they drink.

In some important ways, the federal bureaucracy has become far more responsive to the needs of average individuals in the course of the nation's history, especially in the areas of social benefits, health care, environmental protection, and civil rights enforcement. The federal bureaucracy has tried to be more transparent in its operations by placing comprehensive information on the Internet for the public to access at any time. However, the responses to the Gulf of Mexico oil spill and the GM ignition switch case show that there have been notable and serious failures in the government's action to secure the safety of citizens.

The structure of the bureaucracy includes many gates against speedy implementation of federal policy. That there are so many layers of authority even within one agency, much less an entire cabinet department, adds considerable delay to the process of policy implementation. Multiple agencies can have jurisdiction over the same federal program or share responsibility for responding to natural disasters such as hurricanes. Such overlap can lead to miscommunication and to competition over authority and power. The hierarchy and procedural barriers that come with a large federal bureaucracy can stand in the way of efficient government.

At the same time, the rules and guidelines governing decision making in the bureaucracy are designed to ensure equal implementation of the law, which is a crucial element of a democracy. Americans expect federal laws to be applied in a consistent manner, with openness, and vigilant congressional and public oversight. Understanding how laws are implemented, especially the gateways through which federal regulations are issued and enforced, gives citizens the power to hold the government accountable.

Citizens such as Robert MacLean have the opportunity, in a democracy, to pressure the government to be responsible and implement the laws with vigor in all areas. But one might also argue that advocates should not be needed to ensure that the bureaucracy works with efficiency and transparency, and that the average citizen should not experience frustration in trying to navigate the gateways of the bureaucracy. Fortunately, it is possible to overcome these gateways—with enough persistence.

Political Science Reasoning

Question 1

Practice 1, Practice 4

> A vital element in keeping the peace is our military establishment. Our arms must be mighty, ready for instant action, so that no potential aggressor may be tempted to risk his own destruction. Until the latest of our world conflicts, the United States had no armaments industry. American makers of plowshares could, with time and as required, make swords as well. But now we can no longer risk emergency improvisation of national defense; we have been compelled to create a permanent armaments industry of vast proportions. Added to this, three and a half million men and women are directly engaged in the defense establishment. We annually spend on military security more than the net income of all United States corporations.
>
> This conjunction of an immense military establishment and a large arms industry is new in the American experience. The total influence—economic, political, even spiritual—is felt in every city, every statehouse, every office of the federal government. We recognize the imperative need for this development. Yet we must not fail to comprehend its grave implications. Our toil, resources and livelihood are all involved; so is the very structure of our society. In the councils of government, we must guard against the acquisition of unwarranted influence, whether sought or unsought, by the military–industrial complex. The potential for the disastrous rise of misplaced power exists, and will persist. We must never let the weight of this combination endanger our liberties or democratic processes. We should take nothing for granted. Only an alert and knowledgeable citizenry can compel the proper meshing of the huge industrial and military machinery of defense with our peaceful methods and goals so that security and liberty may prosper together.[1]

1. What is the author's primary claim in the address above? Cite specific textual evidence to support your answer.
2. In his address, Eisenhower makes reference to an iron triangle. How do bureaucratic agencies and special interest groups mutually support each other?
3. To what extent can Congress and the president effectively check the mutually supportive relationships between bureaucratic agencies and special interest groups?

---

[1]Dwight Eisenhower, Farewell Address to the Nation, January 17, 1961.

Question 2

Practice 1, Practice 4

Public Law 115–13
115th Congress

Joint Resolution

Providing for congressional disapproval under chapter 8 of title 5, United States Code, of the rule submitted by the Department of Education relating to accountability and State plans under the Elementary and Secondary Education Act of 1965.

Resolved by the Senate and House of Representatives of the United States of America in Congress assembled,

That Congress disapproves the rule submitted by the Department of Education relating to accountability and State plans under the Elementary and Secondary Education Act of 1965 (published at 81 Fed. Reg. 86076 (November 29, 2016)), and such rule shall have no force or effect. Approved March 27, 2017.

1. What is the purpose of the above piece of legislation?
2. Under what authority do administrative agencies issue regulations?
3. What are the implications of Congress rather than the bureaucracy making more public policy?

Focus on AP® Success

14 The Bureaucracy

Must Know: Key Concepts

- Secretary
- Department
- Independent Regulatory Commission
- Government Corporation
- Administrative Regulations
- Issue Network
- Iron Triangle
- Legislative Oversight
- Patronage System
- Civil Service
- Merit System
- Pendleton Act
- Congressional Budget Office
- General Accounting Office
- Office of Management and Budget

Thinking Politically

Concept Application

Explain how the civil service shifted from patronage to merit based appointment. What are the implications of this switch?

Concept Application

Explain how the judiciary can oversee the bureaucracy.

Concept Application

Why has Congress delegated so much policy-making authority to the bureaucracy?

Understanding Learning Objectives with Key Concepts

PMI – 2.A Explain how the bureaucracy carries out the responsibilities of the federal government.

- After a law has been enacted, the next step is to implement policies set forth in the legislation. This task falls on the bureaucracy. The bureaucracy is composed of the various agencies in the federal government.
  - A department is a cabinet level collection of agencies that is supervised by a secretary. For example, the Treasury Department is composed of many agencies including the Internal Revenue Service and Bureau of Engraving and Printing.
  - Some agencies are not part of cabinet departments, for example the Central Intelligence Agency. Some agencies, independent regulatory commissions, are structurally removed from direct presidential oversight, for example the Federal Reserve. Some agencies provide services to the general public in exchange for fees paid for by individuals that use those services. Examples of these government corporations are Amtrak and the Postal Service.
- These agencies perform a wide range of activities:
  - In addition to enforcing statutory law, agencies are authorized by Congress to issue and enforce their own administrative regulations. These regulations must be within the scope of authority that Congress has granted to the agency.
  - Agencies also issue fines for violations of the regulations that they issue.

- Agencies provide information to Congress by testifying before congressional committees. This is done to facilitate the drafting of new legislation and legislative oversight.

- Bureaucratic agencies form relationships with congressional committees and interest groups known as iron triangles. They also partner with other political actors in what are called issue networks. These political actors include think tanks, congressional staffers, media elites, state and local government officials, etc. Issue networks tend to be more free flowing than iron triangles and are typically temporary whereas iron triangles tend to be permanent.

- Most employees of the national government are career civil servants. These individuals obtain their positions through merit, often through an examination process.

- This process, known as the merit system, began with the passage of the Pendleton Act. Before that time, governmental positions were awarded based on political patronage. Elected officials rewarded supporters by giving them government jobs.

- The shift to the merit system has allowed the development of professionalism and specialized knowledge on the part of the bureaucrats, which can improve policy implementation.

- The merit system also promotes bureaucratic neutrality because few members of the bureaucracy are dependent upon the president for their jobs, and in fact, civil servants are protected from being fired for political reasons.

PMI – 2.B Explain how the federal bureaucracy uses delegated discretionary authority for rule making and implementation.

- Congress vests agencies with the ability to issue rules (formally known as administrative regulations) to carry out legislative mandates of Congress. Examples of types of administrative regulations issued include:

  - Department of Homeland Security – Under authority granted to it by Congress issues regulations that set specific requirements for the type and storage of information collected by states to be in compliance with the Real ID Act.

  - Department of Transportation – Under authority granted to it by Congress, the Federal Aviation Administration in the Department of Transportation issues regulations that provide general operating and flight rules for private and commercial aircraft.

  - Department of Veterans Affairs – Under authority granted to it by Congress issues regulations that relate to veterans' benefits.

  - Department of Education – Under authority granted to it by Congress issues regulations for the various federal student loan programs.

  - Environmental Protection Agency (EPA) – The EPA is an independent executive agency that, with authority granted by Congress, enforces environmental regulation.

  - Federal Elections commission (FEC) – Congress created the FEC and authorized it to enforce laws related to federal elections as well as make and enforce administrative regulations relating to federal elections. The FEC is an independent regulatory commission.

  - Securities and Exchange Commission (SEC) – The SEC is an independent regulatory commission created by Congress to regulate the securities industry (stock market, investment banks, etc.) through the issuance of administrative regulations. It also enforces federal statutory law.

PMI – 2.C Explain how Congress uses its oversight power in its relationship with the executive branch.

- The Senate confirms executive appointments to the leadership of bureaucratic agencies. Congress controls an agency's budget and has the ability investigate an agency's performance through a process called oversight. This typically occurs in congressional committee hearings. Congress has also created agencies that assist it in overseeing the bureaucracy, such as the Congressional Budget Office, which helps Congress evaluate budget requests from agencies. Congress has also created the Government Accountability Office, which assists Congress in evaluating agency performance.

PMI – 2.D Explain how the president ensures that executive branch agencies and departments carry out their responsibilities in concert with the goals of the administration.

- The president appoints the leadership of bureaucratic agencies and can remove these individuals as well. The president can issue executive orders that direct how an agency operates. The president is assisted in reviewing agency performance and budget requests by the Office of Management and Budget in the Executive Office of the President.

PMI – 2.E Explain the extent to which governmental branches can hold the bureaucracy accountable given the competing interests of Congress, the president, and the federal courts.

- The three constitutional branches have the formal and informal powers to oversee the bureaucracy. Both the Congress and the president can draw public attention to bureaucratic inefficiency and abuses. Agencies often respond to this negative attention by internal reforms in an attempt to avoid formal action by the Congress and the president. The court system can also exercise the power of judicial review over administrative regulations. Further, the judiciary can review regulations to determine if they fall outside of the grant of authority given to the agency by Congress.

Making Connections

Young students are often told that "Congress makes law, the president enforces the law, and the court system interprets the law." While this is factually correct, it is overly simplistic. A more accurate view is to see the bureaucracy as being functionally separate from the president. Further, you should recognize that and be able to explain how Congress, the president, bureaucracy, and judiciary all make public policy. Indeed, there are far more administrative regulations than there are laws passed by Congress.

Review iron triangles and issue networks again. They are covered in Chapter 8, Interest Groups. Review from Chapter 12, Congress, the ways in which Congress exercises legislative oversight.

Review from Chapter 13, The Presidency, the ways in which the president can direct the bureaucracy.

Interest groups have unique relationships with administrative agencies. Because agencies make public policy in the form of administrative regulations, they are lobbied just like Congress. Interests seek to develop long-standing relationships with agencies by providing information and political cover to the agency. In exchange for this, the interest group can gain an inordinate amount of influence over the agency. This is referred to as agency capture or regulatory capture.

Going Deeper: Legislative Oversight

The Constitution gives Congress the power to oversee the federal bureaucracy, such as by controlling an agency's budget. However, to effectively use these powers Congress needs information on the performance of the agency. This can be obtained from the agency itself.

Congress routinely requires that bureaucratic officials testify in front of congressional committees providing information on how the agency is implementing congressional directives and on any challenges that the agency faces.

However, this information is not without bias. It is in the best interest of these officials to paint their agencies in the best light possible and to always advocate for more money. As presidential appointees spend more time in their agencies, they can be accused of "going native." This is when an official begins to identify more with the perspective of the agency and its client's special interests than with larger public interest.

In 1921, Congress created the Government Accountability Office (GAO). Originally named the General Accounting Office, and nicknamed the watchdog agency, the GAO provides Congress an independent source of information on agency performance. The Office of Management and Budget performs a similar function for the president.

15 The Judiciary

AP® Learning Objectives

CON – 5.A Explain the principle of judicial review and how it checks the power of other institutions and state governments.

CON – 5.B Explain how the exercise of judicial review in conjunction with life tenure can lead to debate about the legitimacy of the Supreme Court's power.

CON – 5.C Explain how other branches in the government can limit the Supreme Court's power.

Performance Tasks

Upon the completion of this chapter, you must be able to do the following:

- Explain how the Supreme Court uses the Constitution to establish the power of judicial review and how the Supreme Court uses it to check Congress, the president, and the bureaucracy.
- Explain why the exercise of judicial review is controversial.
- Explain how and why the Supreme Court seeks to protect its legitimacy.
- Explain how *stare decisis*, judicial activism, and judicial restraint impact judicial decision making.
- Explain how Congress and the president can check the power of the judiciary.

Martin Shields/Alamy

"Theresa, I think this fish has found her pond."

SONIA SOTOMAYOR, TO A PROFESSIONAL FRIEND AFTER OVERCOMING HER FEARS ABOUT BEING A JUDGE
Princeton University

Many gates blocked Sonia Sotomayor's path to the Supreme Court. She was female (no female had served on the Court until Sandra O'Connor in 1981), she was Puerto Rican (no Latino had ever served on the Court until Sotomayor), she had juvenile diabetes (which, at the time, substantially lowered life expectancy), and she had an alcoholic father who died when she was 9. Sotomayor used her intelligence and diligence to overcome what for others would have been disadvantages. As she noted in her memoir, despite these setbacks, "I did have sources of deep happiness, and these bred in me an optimism that proved stronger than any adversity." That inner strength led her to become high school valedictorian; attend Princeton University, where she won the prestigious Pyne Prize, the highest general distinction Princeton confers on an undergraduate; and then attend Yale Law School. She has readily admitted that she probably got admitted to Princeton due to its affirmative action program.

In 2014, affirmative action faced one of its most recent challenges at the Supreme Court. In 2006, the voters of Michigan passed an amendment to their state constitution banning race- and gender-based affirmative action in public education, public employment, and public contracting. The Coalition to Defend Affirmative Action filed suit against the amendment, and, in 2012, a federal district court ruled that the ban was unconstitutional. Michigan's attorney general, Bill Schuette, appealed the ruling, and the U.S. Court of Appeals declared the amendment unconstitutional. Schuette then appealed the Court of Appeals decision to the Supreme Court, which agreed to hear the case. On April 22, 2012, the day that the case came before the U.S. Supreme Court. Sonia Sotomayor found herself sitting in judgment over the constitutionality of efforts to block racial- and gender-based affirmative action.

The 2014 case, *Schuette v. Coalition to Defend Affirmative Action*, culminated from two prior cases involving the University of Michigan. In 2003, the Supreme Court struck down the affirmative action plan at Michigan's undergraduate college (*Gratz v. Bollinger*) but upheld the constitutionality of the affirmative action plan at the University of Michigan Law School (*Grutter v. Bolinger*). One of the litigants, or parties to the suit, Jennifer Gratz helped organize the initiative for the 2006 statewide constitutional amendment that banned the state of Michigan or any of its public universities from taking race or gender into account in hiring or admissions.

On April 22, Sonia Sotomayor was in the minority as she argued that the Michigan amendment banning affirmative action was unconstitutional. The Supreme Court upheld that amendment in a 6–2 vote in 2014. Justice Clarence Thomas joined the concurring opinion of Justice Scalia, which cited an earlier opinion of Justice Thomas that disputed whether affirmative action plans *ever* helped minority students (emphasis in original). Justice Sotomayor, on the other hand, read her dissent from the bench, a rare occurrence for any justice and the first time Justice Sotomayor had ever done so. She took issue with Chief Justice Roberts' statement that "the way to stop discriminating on the basis of race is to stop discrimination on the basis of race," declaring it to be "out of touch with reality." Sotomayor insisted that it is the role of the judicial system to protect minorities from the tyranny of the majority. She wrote, "The Court abdicates that role, permitting the majority to use its numerical advantage to change the rules mid-contest and forever stack the deck against racial minorities in Michigan."

For a Puerto Rican girl raised in the poverty-stricken South Bronx, affirmative action was a gateway to an Ivy League education. That gateway eventually led to Sonia Sotomayor being the first Latino to sit on the U.S. Supreme Court.[1]

As the Court's **affirmative action** cases show, the judicial system of the United States, because of its authority to rule on the constitutionality of federal and state laws and policies, has an extraordinary amount of power in the American political system. As the highest court in the land, the Supreme Court not only decides whether affirmative action may be allowed but also decides other issues, such as whether health insurance can be mandated (yes), same-sex marriage can be prohibited (no), or the death penalty inflicted (yes, with restrictions). The justices on the Court make important decisions that affect the lives of individuals and the policies of the nation at large despite the fact that they are not elected by the people and cannot be removed from office if the people disagree with the decisions they make. In this chapter, we investigate the structure and procedures of the judicial system; the factors that influence judicial decisions; how judges are selected; how representative of American society the Court is; the role that race, ethnicity and gender might have in judicial decision making; and the role the Supreme Court has played in determining public policy and federal authority. Thus we examine, too, the controversial role and power of the judiciary in a democracy.

15.1 The Role and Powers of the Judiciary

Describe what the judicial branch does

The job of courts is to resolve legal disputes. The American legal system is based largely on the English system, which is the system that the colonists were familiar with. The legal system under the Constitution kept many of the same practices but added some innovations.

affirmative action: *Policies that support greater equality, often by granting racial or gender preferences in hiring, education, or contracting.*

English Legal Traditions

adversary process: *Confrontational legal process under which each party presents its version of events.*

Resolution of legal disputes follows an **adversary process**. In an adversarial system, each party, usually represented by an attorney, presents its version of events, with virtually all attempts to slant information short of lying under oath deemed acceptable.

Essential Knowledge

The legal system operates under the rule of *stare decisis*. This means the cases will be decided upon precedents created in prior cases. This is typical in common law legal systems.

Although in some cases a judge decides which side is correct, a group of ordinary citizens usually determines the outcome. The right to trial by jury dates back in England to the Magna Carta (1215), where it replaced trial by ordeal, the practice of subjecting people to drowning or burning to see if they were innocent. Trial by jury is crucial to liberty because it inserts a gate of citizen judgment between the accused person and the government that protects the accused from arbitrary detention and unjust punishment. It also provides a gateway of citizen involvement through juror participation.

appeal: *Legal proceeding whereby the decision of a lower court on a question of law can be challenged and reviewed by a higher court.*

courts of appeals: *Intermediate federal courts that are above the district courts and below the Supreme Court.*

Trials involve questions of fact (for example, did the University of Michigan set different standards for white and minority students?) and questions of law (for example, do such differing standards violate the Fourteenth Amendment?). Trial court decisions about questions of fact are presumed to be valid because the trial judge or the jury directly hears the evidence in the case. But because trial courts sometimes make mistakes about questions of law, the American legal system has followed the British practice by allowing **appeals** from trial court rulings. In the U.S. federal system, the **courts of appeals** and the Supreme Court hear appeals, which involve issues of law. These courts do not retry the facts as established by the trial court.

criminal case: *Government prosecution of an individual for breaking the law.*

civil suit: *Lawsuit by a person, organization, or government against another person, organization, or government.*

Trials resolve two distinct types of disputes. In a **criminal case**, the government prosecutes an individual for breaking the law. Criminal cases are based almost exclusively on prohibitions on behavior written into statutes (laws) passed by federal, state, or local legislatures. In a **civil suit**, a plaintiff, such as Jennifer Gratz, sues a defendant, such as the University of Michigan, to enforce a right or to win monetary damages.

common law: *Judge-made law in England and the United States that results from gaps in statutory law.*

precedent: *Practice of reaching decisions based on the previous decisions of other judges.*

Criminal law is based on statutory authority, but statutory authority cannot cover all possible civil disputes between individuals. Many disputes involve actions that no legislative authority could have ever imagined. When there are gaps in statutory law, courts rely on judge-made law known as **common law**. Common law requires judges to accept and rely on previous decisions (if each judge makes his or her own decisions on each case, there can be no common law). Thus, British royal judges developed the practice of reaching decisions based on **precedents**, the previous decisions of other royal judges. Deciding cases based on precedents means that similar cases are decided similarly. Precedent is perhaps the most fundamental feature of English and American law. Because similar cases get decided similarly, following precedent promotes greater equality, predictability, and stability in law.

Constitutional Grants of Power

Article III of the Constitution establishes the judicial branch of government. It briefly refers to a Supreme Court of the United States and grants Congress the authority to create lower courts at its discretion. The Constitution grants the federal courts the authority to hear "cases" or "controversies." The Supreme Court has interpreted this provision to require that people who initiate lawsuits have standing. That is, they must establish that they have suffered a harm that the law protects them against. Standing is a gate that limits access to the judicial system.

Because the Constitution says so little about the judicial branch, one of the early acts of the First Congress, the Judiciary Act of 1789, established thirteen **district (trial) courts** and three circuit courts with both trial and appellate authority that serve at an intermediate level between the district courts and the Supreme Court. Today, there are 678 district court judges serving in 94 separate district courts and 179 court of appeals judges serving in thirteen intermediate appellate circuits.[2] The thirteen intermediate appellate courts include eleven numbered courts, a court of appeals for the District of Columbia, which handles most litigation involving federal agencies, and the Court of Appeals for the Federal Circuit, which handles customs and patent claims. In addition, Congress established the Foreign Intelligence Surveillance Court in 1978 (see Chapter 4, Civil Liberties) and the Court of International Trade in 1980. Separately, Congress has established six so-called Article I or legislative courts whose purpose is to help Congress perform its Article I duties. Unlike Article III judges, Article I judges do not serve for life. These courts are listed in Table 15.1.

district courts: *Federal trial courts at the bottom of the federal judicial hierarchy.*

The lawful authority of a court to hear a case is its **jurisdiction**. In general, jurisdiction for any federal court requires either that the case involves federal law (including the Constitution and treaties); or that the parties include the United States, ambassadors, or other public ministers; or that the parties are residents of different states. The Constitution further divides the Supreme Court's jurisdiction into original jurisdiction, the authority to hear a case directly from a petitioning party (as in a trial), and appellate jurisdiction, authority

jurisdiction: *Lawful authority of a court to hear a case.*

TABLE 15.1 Article I Courts

Name	Jurisdiction	Location
Bankruptcy Court	All bankruptcy cases	Each federal district
Military Appeals	Appeals of court-martial trials	Washington, D.C.
Veteran Appeals	Appeals of veterans and survivors' benefits	Washington, D.C.*
Federal Claims	Suits against the United States for more than $10,000	Washington, D.C.
Tax Court	Taxpayer lawsuits	Washington, D.C.*
Territorial Courts	U.S. trial courts for Guam, U.S. Virgin Islands, and Northern Mariana Islands	In their respective territories

*Can hear cases outside Washington, D.C.

Source: http://www.lectlaw.com/def/a148.htm; http://www.uscourts.gov/FederalCourts/Bankruptcy.aspx.

Essential Knowledge

Judicial review is not specifically mentioned in the Constitution, but Hamilton wrote in *Federalist* 78 that the judiciary must have the power to rule on the constitutionality of law. In the 1803 case *Marbury v. Madison*, the Supreme Court asserted this power for the first time.

judicial review: *Authority of courts to declare laws passed by Congress and acts of the executive branch to be unconstitutional.*

Marbury v. Madison: *An 1803 Supreme Court decision that established the Supreme Court's power of judicial review.*

to hear cases on appeals from lower courts. The Supreme Court has original jurisdiction in "all Cases affecting Ambassadors, other public Ministers and Consuls, and those in which a State shall be Party" (Article III, Section 2). The Constitution then declares that "in all the other Cases" properly before the Court, it would have appellate jurisdiction subject to such exceptions and regulations that Congress shall make.

The Constitution grants the federal courts the authority to hear cases of law and equity. Cases of law and equity can involve (1) the common law when there are gaps in legislative authority; (2) statutory interpretation, where the courts have to determine what Congress meant by a statute (for example, is discrimination on the grounds of pregnancy included in the prohibition on sex discrimination in the Civil Rights Act of 1964?); and (3) constitutional interpretation, where the courts must decide whether a law or practice violates a provision of the Constitution.

Constitutional interpretation brings forth the greatest power of the federal judiciary, **judicial review**. Judicial review, established by ***Marbury v. Madison*** (1803), is the power of courts to declare actions of Congress, the president, or state officials unconstitutional and therefore void (see Chapter 2, The Constitution). The Supreme Court, for example, has exercised the power of judicial review on laws pertaining to affirmative action (see Public Policy and the Judiciary: Affirmative Action).

15.2 State and Lower Federal Courts

Explain how state and lower federal courts operate

en banc: *Decision by an entire Court of Appeals circuit, typically following an original judgment by a three-judge panel of the circuit.*

While the Supreme Court is the highest court in the United States, it hears only a small percentage of the cases filed in federal court. The overwhelming majority of federal cases are resolved in the district courts, which conduct civil and criminal trials. Cases appealed from the district courts go to one of the U.S. Courts of Appeals, in which three-judge panels usually decide cases. From those panels, losing parties can appeal cases to the entire circuit for an ***en banc*** ("by the full court") hearing, or they can appeal directly to the U.S. Supreme Court (see Figure 15.1).

State Courts in the Federal Judicial System

petition for a writ of *certiorari*: *Request to the Supreme Court that it review a lower court case.*

Each state has its own judicial system, and unless a case involves federal law or the type of parties that create federal jurisdiction, cases get resolved in state courts, each of which has its own hierarchy of trial and appellate courts. Cases that involve federal issues that begin in one of the fifty separate state court systems can be appealed to the federal court system in one of two ways. First, criminal defendants who have exhausted their state appeals (that is, have gone through their last appeal at the state level) can file a writ of *habeas corpus* with a U.S. District Court, which then allows the court to determine whether one or more of the defendant's federal legal rights have been violated. Second, any parties who have exhausted their state appeals can file a request for review, known as a **petition for a writ of *certiorari***, directly with the Supreme Court.

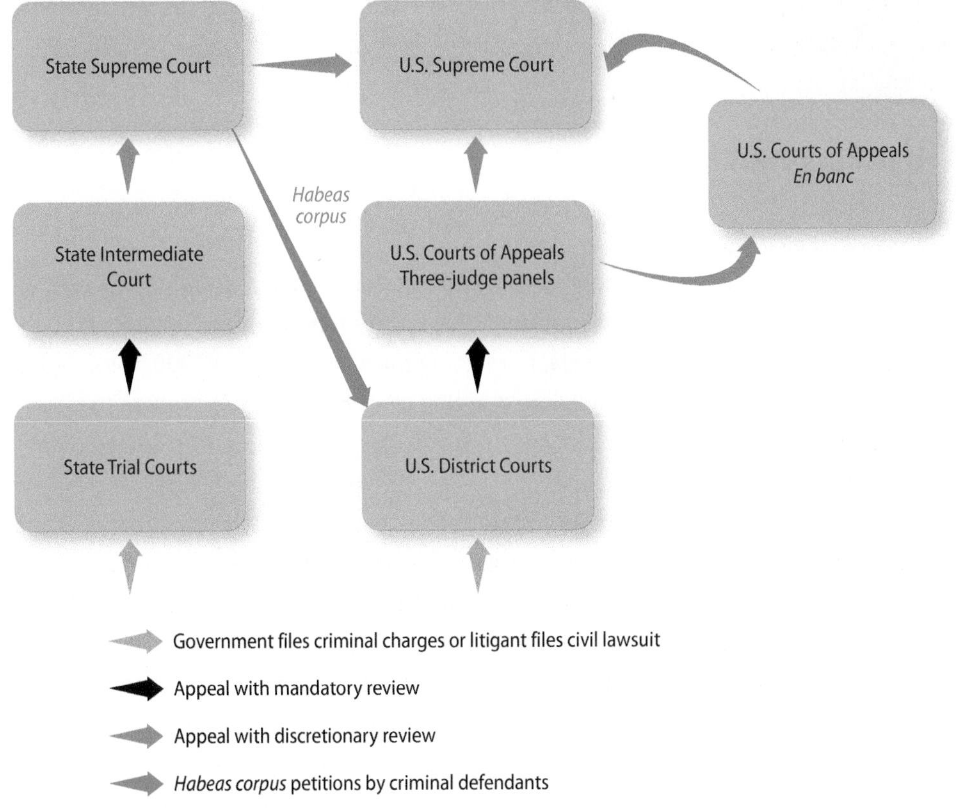

FIGURE 15.1 Judicial Organization in the United States

Cases can reach the U.S. Supreme Court from both the federal and state judicial systems.

Source: Adapted from Lee Epstein, Jeffrey A. Segal, Harold J. Spaeth, and Thomas G. Walker, *The Supreme Court Compendium*, 5th ed. (Washington, D.C.: CQ Press, 2010), Figure 7-3.

District Courts

The Judiciary Act of 1789 established thirteen district courts for the thirteen states. Today, there are ninety-four districts. Many states have more than one district, but no district covers more than one state. Districts that cover only part of a state receive geographic names, such as the Northern District of Illinois. Altogether there are 667 district judgeships. Many districts have only one judge, but the Southern District of New York has twenty-eight, and the Central District of California has twenty-seven. Nevertheless, with rare exceptions, district judges oversee trials alone, not in panels.

Trials in the district courts are either criminal or civil. In civil suits, plaintiffs (the parties bringing the suit) often request monetary damages to compensate for harm done to them, such as by a broken contract or a defective product. When rights are alleged to have been violated, they may ask that the practice be stopped. Litigants filed more than 281,000 civil suits in the district courts in 2015, and the federal government initiated approximately 80,000 criminal prosecutions.[3]

When Gratz and Grutter sued the University of Michigan over its admissions policies, the first stop for each was the U.S. District Court. Both had standing to sue, as their rejections by the university were real injuries, and because they claimed that their rights to equal protection under the Fourteenth Amendment had been violated, their cases raised a constitutional issue and entered the federal court system. Gratz and Grutter sought not

PUBLIC POLICY AND THE JUDICIARY

Affirmative Action

An overly simple view of American politics holds that the legislative branch makes the law, the judicial branch interprets the law, and the executive branch enforces the law. However, in interpreting the law, judges often go beyond mere interpretation and get actively involved in policy making. While Presidents John F. Kennedy and Lyndon Johnson first proposed affirmative action plans, the Supreme Court has interpreted what that means for private business, government contracting, and public education.

With regard to private businesses, the Supreme Court has ruled that businesses and unions can agree to establish voluntary affirmative action programs where there has been a substantial racial imbalance in the workforce. In the famous case of *Steelworkers v. Weber* (1979), white steelworker Brian Weber was turned down for a promotion to craft worker. In a workforce that was 39 percent black, fewer than 2 percent of the skilled craft workers were black. Kaiser Aluminum and the United Steelworkers had agreed that 50 percent of future promotions would go to blacks, even if that bypassed whites with higher seniority. Weber sued, but the Supreme Court upheld the affirmative action plan.[4] On the other hand, the Court ruled that seniority cannot be overridden when it comes to layoffs: Whites with higher seniority cannot be laid off ahead of minorities with lower seniority, even if seniority-based layoffs will harm racial balance and even if minorities had less seniority because original hiring practices discriminated against them.[5]

National and state governments have established preferences for minority-owned businesses when they grant contracts and licenses, although the Court has wobbled. In 1987, the Court upheld a plan, similar to the one in the *Steelworkers* case, that granted preferences to women.[6] A 1980 decision allowed the federal government to require 10 percent of its grants to state and local governments for public works projects to go to minority-owned businesses.[7] Nine years later, however, a more conservative Court prohibited the city of Richmond, Virginia, from doing the same thing.[8] In 1990, the Court upheld the granting of radio license preferences to minority broadcasters; six years later, the Court reversed that decision.[9]

As colleges and universities actively sought racial and gender balances in their student bodies, several controversial cases arose. The Supreme Court first confronted college affirmative action plans in 1978. The medical school at the University of California, Davis, had eighty-four seats in each entering class for which anyone could apply and sixteen seats set aside for minority candidates only. Allan Bakke, a white male, was denied admission although he had a 3.5 grade point average (GPA) and a Medical College Admission Test (MCAT) score in the 90th percentile, whereas the average scores for the sixteen minority seats were a 2.6 GPA and an MCAT score in the 20th percentile. Bakke sued, and a split Court decreed in *Regents v. Bakke* that this sort of quota system violated the Civil Rights Act. Nevertheless, the Court held that affirmative action plans in which race is a "plus" in an applicant's overall file did meet the state's compelling interest in establishing a diverse student body.[10]

In 1996, a Court of Appeals panel in Texas declared affirmative action unconstitutional within the Fourth Circuit.[11] The University of Texas responded by implementing a program that guarantees admission to the University of Texas to anyone who graduates in the top 10 percent of his or her high school class. Because public schools are highly segregated in Texas, the university believed this would be an effective means of obtaining a diverse student body.

In the meantime, the Supreme Court revisited the *Bakke* decision in a pair of 2003 cases (*Gratz* and *Grutter*), discussed in this chapter. Despite surpassing the average qualifications required by the University of Michigan to gain entrance, Jennifer Gratz and Barbara Grutter were both rejected—Gratz from the undergraduate program and Grutter from the law school. With the legal assistance from the Center for Individual Rights, a conservative legal group that actively sought students looking to fight affirmative action, both women sued the university. As we saw earlier, the Supreme Court struck down the undergraduate and upheld the law school admissions policy.

In the case of the law school, then sitting Justice Sandra Day O'Connor, the first woman appointed to the Supreme Court (1981), expressed the belief that the Constitution required affirmative action programs to be temporary solutions only and the hope that by 2028 they would no longer be necessary. Opponents of affirmative action, such as Ward Connerly, chair of the American Civil Rights Institute, hope that such plans will not last that long. Connerly has launched state-level initiatives in Arizona, California, Colorado, Michigan, Nebraska, and Washington to let voters decide whether such programs should be allowed. Voters rejected affirmative action in all those states except Colorado.

California voters passed their amendment in 1996. Since that time, and despite fears that the initiative would reduce the number of underrepresented minorities in colleges and universities, Latino students have become the largest ethnic group at the University of California.[12]

In 2014, the Michigan case reached the Supreme Court, which declared in *Schuette v. Coalition to Defend Affirmative Action* that the people of Michigan had the right to pass a constitutional amendment via initiative that prohibits the state's public universities from using race as a factor in admissions or public employment.[13]

While the University of Texas largely replaced its affirmative action program with guaranteed admission to anyone who finished in the top 10 percent of his or her high school class, it was unable to fill all entering spots with this plan. To fill the remaining spots, the University used an admissions plan that gave preferences based on race and ethnicity. Abigail Fisher, a white female whom the University rejected for admission despite scores that were higher than many of the nontraditional admittees, filed suit claiming that the continuing use of race violated her rights under the equal protection clause of the Fourteenth Amendment. Both the district court and the Court of Appeals upheld the University's admission plan under the precedent established in *Grutter v. Bollinger*. Because the lower courts did not use the strict-scrutiny standard that the Supreme Court had required in cases involving racial or ethnic classifications, the Supreme Court sent the case back (remanded) to the lower courts for reconsideration using the appropriate standard.[14]

The Fifth Circuit reheard the case and again ruled in favor of the University of Texas. Fisher appealed to the Supreme Court and once again the Court granted review. Only seven justices participated. Justice Antonin Scalia passed away after the oral arguments, so even if the Senate had quickly confirmed Merrick Garland, President Obama's nominee to replace Scalia, Garland would not have been able to vote on the case. Justice Kagan also did not participate due to her prior involvement in the case while serving in President Obama's Justice Department. The Supreme Court's 2016 decision upheld the University's program.[15]

Public Policy Connections

1. How active should an unelected judiciary be in the area of civil rights?
2. How democratic is the power of judicial review? Reflect on specific examples of tension between democratically elected legislature's passage of laws and the subsequent overturning of those laws.

---

only their own admission to the University of Michigan but also an end to the university's use of race in admissions decisions. The district courts allowed both suits to move forward as **class action lawsuits**, meaning that Gratz and Grutter were suing not only on behalf of themselves but also on behalf of all people denied admission at Michigan on account of

class action lawsuit: *Lawsuit filed by one person on behalf of that person plus all similarly situated people.*

their race. Class action lawsuits can open the gateways of access to groups of citizens in the same circumstances, thus broadening the impact over the possible result of an individual lawsuit.

Civil Procedure. The overwhelming majority of lawsuits filed in federal court settle out of court with a negotiated agreement between the plaintiff and the defendant. In 2014, the district courts terminated over 250,000 civil cases.[16] Litigants settled nearly 99 percent of these cases before going to trial. Of the few cases that went to trial, nearly two-thirds were decided by juries. The other third were bench (nonjury) trials, as the *Gratz and Grutter* cases were.

After a case is assigned to a judge, the next step in a civil suit is discovery. Discovery grants each side access to information relevant to its suit held by the other side. Crucial to the *Gratz* and *Grutter* suits were University of Michigan documents showing differential admission rates for whites and minorities who had similar grades and standardized test scores. During discovery, the attorneys for each side can also question witnesses for the other side in a process known as deposition. Following discovery, litigants file briefs with the court, laying out their arguments.

amicus curiae: *Latin term meaning "friend of the court" that is used to describe individuals or interest groups who have an interest in a lawsuit but are not themselves direct parties to the suit.*

solicitor general: *Official in the Justice Department who represents the president in federal court.*

Outside interests can file ***amicus curiae*** ("friend of the court") briefs, stating their concerns in a case.[17] The most influential *amicus* briefs are those filed in the name of the United States, as represented by the Office of the **Solicitor General** in the Justice Department.[18] In the *Gratz* and *Grutter* cases, the Clinton administration filed briefs in favor of the University of Michigan, which argued that affirmative action was necessary to obtain a diverse student body. General Motors also filed a brief in favor of the university's affirmative action program, stating that it needed a diverse pool of highly qualified attorneys, managers, and the like. Eventually, Microsoft and nineteen other Fortune 500 companies signed briefs supporting the university.[19]

Civil trials begin with opening statements by the plaintiff and respondent. The plaintiff then calls its witnesses, who can be cross-examined by the respondent's attorney. Once the plaintiff rests the case, the respondent calls its witnesses, who can be cross-examined by the plaintiff's attorney.

Kevin Lamarque/Reuters

IMAGE 15.1 Abigail Fisher sued the University of Texas over its affirmative action policy, which she claimed denied her equal protection under the law.

Trial courts make determinations as to fact and as to law, whereas appellate courts generally make determinations only as to law, applying the facts as determined by the trial court. That would normally mean that it would be up to the district court to determine factually whether race played a role in admissions at Michigan and how much of a role it played. Then it would decide as a matter of law whether that role was allowable or not. The parties in the *Gratz* and *Grutter* cases made the decision a bit easier for the judges, for the University of Michigan readily admitted—indeed, strongly defended—its use of race in admissions. Therefore, the question for the trial judge was not a question of fact, but a question of law: Does the equal protection clause of the Fourteenth Amendment prohibit the use of race as a factor in university admissions?

While trial judges or juries have nearly complete discretion in deciding questions of fact, they are constrained by the courts above them on questions of law. In affirmative action, the key precedent was the 1978 Supreme Court decision in *Regents of the University of California v. Bakke*.[20] A divided Court ruled in *Bakke* that the University of California's quota system of reserving a certain number of seats for minorities was unconstitutional, but that a system in which race was a "plus" in admissions could be justified due to the benefits that a diverse student body provides all the students.

In December 2000, Judge Duggan ruled in the *Gratz* case that the point system used by the university—in which each applicant could receive up to 150 points, including 20 for being from an underrepresented minority group—was a valid and necessary means of obtaining a diverse student body. On the other hand, Judge Friedman ruled in March 2001 that the law school's use of race in admissions violated the Constitution, finding that it was an "enormously important factor" in admissions and not the mere plus approved by the Supreme Court in *Bakke*. The University of Michigan appealed Friedman's decision to the Sixth Circuit Court of Appeals, while the Center for Individual Rights backed Gratz's appeal to the same circuit.

Criminal Procedure. Beyond civil cases such as the Michigan affirmative action suits, trial courts also conduct criminal trials. A federal criminal prosecution begins with an alleged violation of federal criminal law. In the U.S. federal system, states have primary authority over law enforcement, but the federal government frequently prosecutes drug, weapons, terrorism, and immigration cases, plus other crimes that involve interstate commerce or the instrumentalities of the federal government, such as the post office and government buildings.

The clearance rate for state and federal crimes—that is, the percentage of reported crimes in which someone is arrested, charged, and turned over for prosecution—is highest for violent crimes (47.4 percent in 2014) but much lower for property crimes such as burglary (13.6 percent).[21] Under the Constitution, an accused criminal in a federal court has a right to indictment by a grand jury, a specially empanelled jury consisting of between sixteen and twenty-three citizens who determine whether the government has sufficient evidence to charge the suspect with a crime. In the rare occasions in which a grand jury chooses not to indict, the suspect is freed.

Following indictment, the accused is arraigned, or informed of the charges against him or her, and asked to enter an initial plea of guilty or not guilty. About 90 percent of federal criminal cases are resolved through **plea bargains**, in which the accused person pleads guilty, usually in exchange for reduced charges or lesser sentences.[22] This arrangement greatly enhances the ability of trial courts to deal with large criminal caseloads.

plea bargain: *Agreement by a criminal defendant to plead guilty in return for a reduced sentence.*

In the small number of cases that proceed to trial, the accused person has the right to a trial by jury but is free to request a bench trial, in which the judge decides guilt or innocence. A jury in a federal felony case consists of twelve individuals who must reach a verdict unanimously. (Neither twelve people nor unanimity is required in a state court.) The defendant can appeal a guilty verdict, but the double jeopardy clause of the Constitution prohibits the government from appealing a verdict of not guilty. If the defendant is found guilty, the judge determines the sentence based on guidelines that depend on the nature of the offense, the number of prior convictions, and other factors as recommended by the U.S. Sentencing Commission. In death penalty cases, the decision on the punishment is left to the jury. That is, following a guilty verdict, the jury hears new testimony by the prosecutor and defense attorney about whether death is the appropriate punishment.

Courts of Appeals

Sitting hierarchically above the ninety-four district courts are the U.S. Courts of Appeals. Congress has divided the Courts of Appeals into eleven numbered circuits plus a circuit for the District of Columbia and a "federal circuit" that hears appeals from specialized lower courts that deal with patents and customs (see Figure 15.2). Each of the numbered courts of

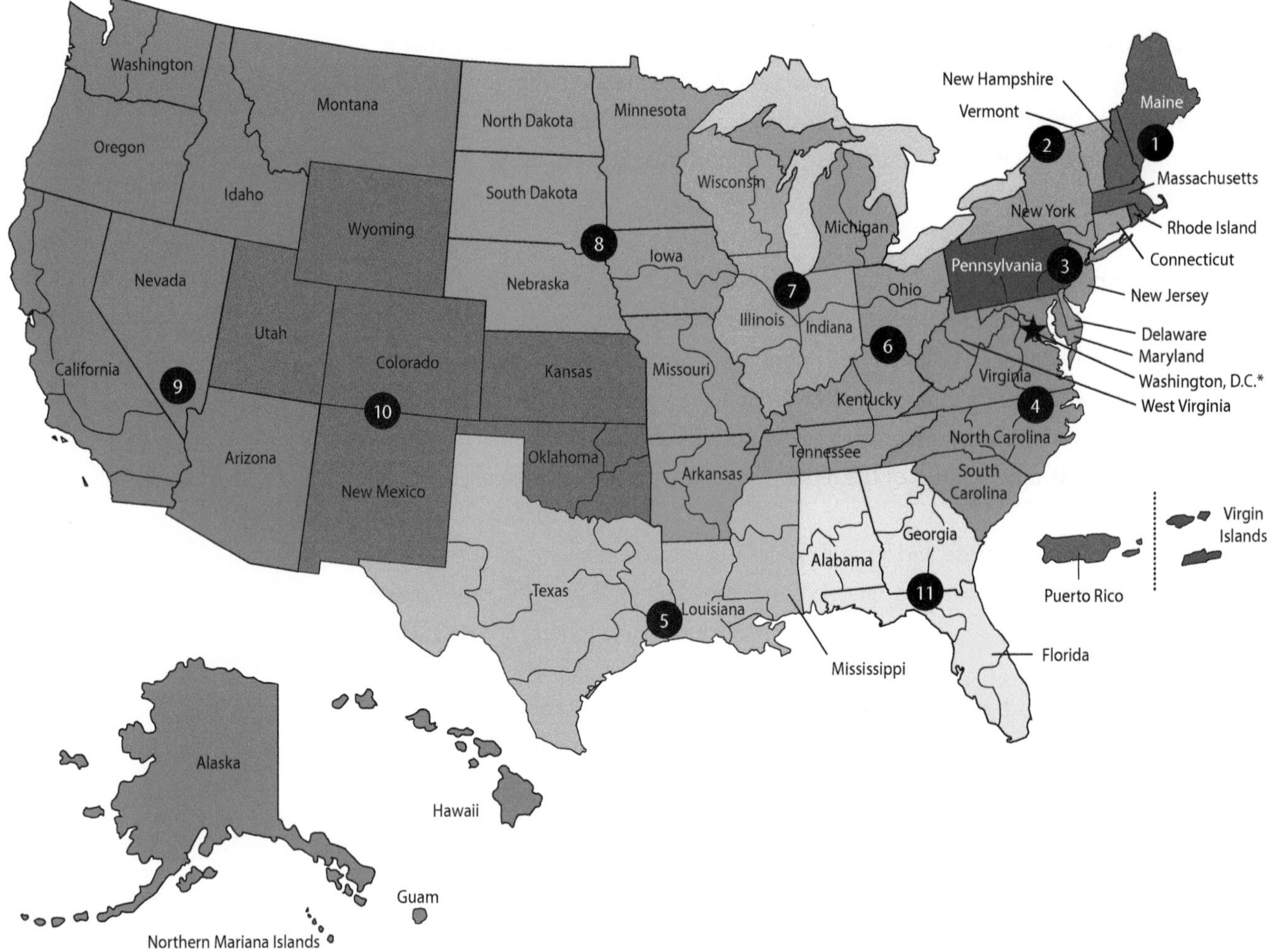

*U.S. Court of Appeals for the District of Columbia
The Federal Circuit Court, in Washington, D.C., hears appeals in trade and patent cases.

FIGURE 15.2 U.S. Courts of Appeals and U.S. District Courts

Every state has one (Colorado, Wyoming, Kansas) or more (Texas, California, Florida, New York) district courts. Every Court of Appeals Circuit covers several states.

Source: Data from U.S. Courts, Court Locator, http://www.uscourts.gov/court_locator.aspx.

appeals has jurisdiction over several states. For example, the Sixth Circuit Court of Appeals, which sits in Cincinnati, hears appeals from district courts in Kentucky, Michigan, Ohio, and Tennessee.

The number of judgeships in each circuit ranges from six in the First Circuit, which covers some of the New England states, to twenty-nine in the Ninth Circuit, which covers California and six other western states, plus Alaska and Hawaii. Regardless of the number of judgeships, randomly assigned three-judge panels usually hear appeals from the district courts.

The courts have mandatory jurisdiction over cases appealed to them. That is, if a losing party from the district court appeals to the appropriate court of appeals, the court must hear the case. Because the circuit courts are in the middle of the federal judicial hierarchy, cases can be both appealed to the court of appeals and appealed from the court of appeals (refer to Figure 15.1). Appeals from a court of appeals can happen in two ways. First, losing litigants at the court of appeals who believe that the three-judge panel that heard their case did not represent the judgment of the circuit as a whole can request an *en banc* review. Alternatively, losing litigants can request review by the Supreme Court. In both cases, further review is at the discretion of the court that is being petitioned.

Given the importance of the *Grutter* and *Gratz* cases, the cases made it through the U.S. Court of Appeals in anything but a normal manner. Rather than a hearing with a three-judge panel, possibly followed by *en banc* and/or Supreme Court review, the Center for Individual Rights, which represented Gratz and Grutter, requested and was granted an immediate *en banc* review. On May 14, 2002, the Sixth Circuit ruled in favor of the university in the law school case by a 5–4 vote. The **majority opinion** argued that the law school's approach resembled the plus system approved by the Supreme Court in the *Bakke* case. All three Republicans on the circuit sided with Grutter; five of the six Democrats sided with the university, consistent both with generally greater support among Democrats than Republicans for equality of outcome over equality of opportunity and with evidence that such attitudes often influence judicial decisions. Not surprisingly, Barbara Grutter appealed the decision to the Supreme Court.

majority opinion: *Opinion of a court laying out the official position of the court in the case.*

On October 1, 2002, ten months after oral arguments, the court of appeals still had not issued its ruling in the undergraduate case. In an unusual step, Gratz's attorneys asked the Supreme Court to bypass the court of appeals and rule directly on their appeal. On December 1, the Supreme Court accepted review in both cases.

15.3 The Supreme Court

Review the procedures the Supreme Court uses

The Supreme Court's procedure in handling cases consists of deciding whether to grant review and, if review is granted, of receiving briefs, hearing oral arguments, deciding who wins, and writing the majority opinion. If desired, justices who do not agree with the decision of the Court majority (that is, the decision about who wins the case) can write dissenting opinions. Those who agree with the majority opinion on who should win but differ as to the reasoning can write concurring opinions. The majority opinion, however, stands as the precedent for lower-court judges to apply in similar cases dealing with the same issue.

Granting Review

Each year, about eight thousand losing litigants ask the Supreme Court to review their cases. Most have lost in one of the U.S. Courts of Appeals or one of the fifty state supreme courts. The vast majority of appeals to the Supreme Court come in the form of petitions for writs of *certiorari*, often shortened to petitions for "cert." The Supreme Court's decision to grant cert is purely discretionary, but its rules suggest that a grant of cert is more likely when a lower court resolves issues of law differently from the way other lower courts have or issues a decision that conflicts with decisions of the Supreme Court. The Supreme Court is also more likely to grant review when the U.S. government, represented by the solicitor general's office, requests it, either as a petitioning party or as *amicus curiae*. The filing of *amicus* briefs by other parties can also be important to the Court, as it signals that the case involves important questions of public policy.[23]

The large number of petitions for cert prevents the justices from fully reviewing each one. Instead, they rely on their clerks, who are usually recent law school graduates, to write summaries. Most of the justices' chambers have joined the "cert pool," which splits the cert petitions among the clerks of the justices in the pool.

The large number of petitions also prevents the justices from fully discussing each one. Rather, the chief justice passes around a "discuss list," a set of cases he thinks worthy of discussion. Any justice can add any other case to the list if he or she wishes. Cases not

Mug Shot/Alamy

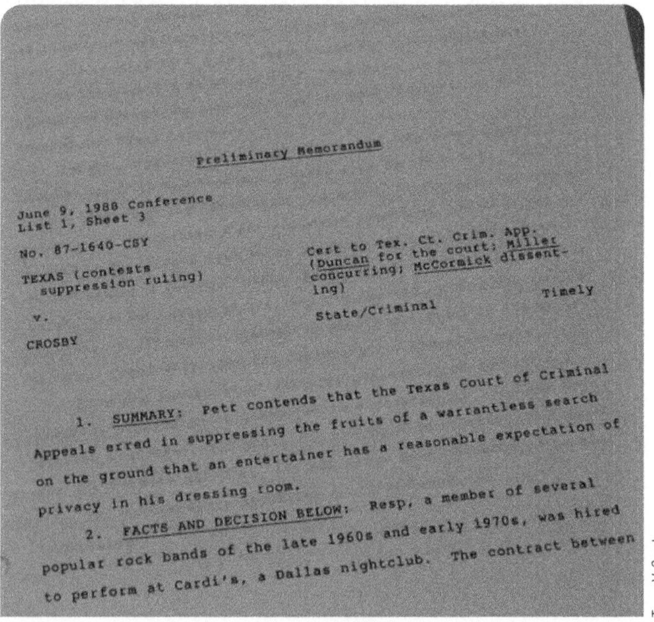

Preliminary Memorandum

June 9, 1988 Conference
List 1, Sheet 3

No. 87-1640-CSY

TEXAS (contests suppression ruling)

v.

CROSBY

Cert to Tex. Ct. Crim. App. (Duncan for the court; Miller concurring; McCormick dissenting)

State/Criminal

Timely

1. SUMMARY: Petr contends that the Texas Court of Criminal Appeals erred in suppressing the fruits of a warrantless search on the ground that an entertainer has a reasonable expectation of privacy in his dressing room.

2. FACTS AND DECISION BELOW: Resp, a member of several popular rock bands of the late 1960s and early 1970s, was hired to perform at Cardi's, a Dallas nightclub. The contract between

Texas V. Crosby

IMAGES 15.2 AND 15.3 At left is a mug shot of 1960s rock star David Crosby; at right is a Pool Memo regarding the cert petition by the State of Texas appealing the Texas Supreme Court decision excluding evidence of crack cocaine smoking and possession by Crosby, who was smoking the crack in his dressing room before a show. The Texas Supreme Court ruled that a dressing room was akin to a hotel room and as such Crosby had a legitimate expectation of privacy there. As no justice thought the appeal even worthy of consideration, the case did not make the Court's "discuss list," leaving the Texas Supreme Court decision in favor of Crosby standing. The full pool memo is available at http://epstein.wustl.edu/research/blackmunMemos/1987/Denied-pdf/87-1640.pdf.

on the discuss list are automatically denied cert, leaving the lower court's decision as final. The justices then meet in conference to consider each of the cases on the discuss list. The Court grants cert through a **rule of four**. That is, although five votes constitute a majority, the Court will agree to hear a case if any four justices vote to grant cert. Overall, the Court grants only about 1 percent of cert petitions, leaving the lower court decision as final in the remaining 99 percent of the cases.

rule of four: *Supreme Court rule that grants review to a case if as few as four of the justices support review.*

The justices' votes on petitions for *certiorari* remain secret unless a justice leaves his or her papers to the public, as justices sometimes do after they retire. To date, the justices' votes in the *Gratz* and *Grutter* cases are unavailable, but the importance of the issue plus a split between the Sixth Circuit Court upholding affirmative action and an earlier Fifth Circuit decision striking it down at the University of Texas made a grant highly likely.[24] On December 2, 2002, the Court granted review to both cases.

Oral Arguments

Following a grant of cert, the justices receive written briefs from the litigants explaining why their position should win. Other parties may file *amicus curiae* briefs urging the Court to affirm or reverse the lower-court decision. Again, the most influential of these briefs come from the solicitor general's office, which represents the current presidential administration at the Supreme Court. Thus, while the Clinton administration sided with the university at the district-court level in the *Gratz* and *Grutter* cases, the George W. Bush administration switched sides and asked the Supreme Court to strike down the law school and undergraduate admissions programs. On the other hand, seventy-four organizations filed *amicus* briefs supporting the university, which, until the 2015 same-sex marriage case, *Obergefell v. Hodges*,[25] was the most ever in a Supreme Court case.[26] One of the briefs in the affirmative action case came from a group of high-ranking military officers, who wrote about the need for a diversified officer corps and thus the need for diversified service academies. Critically, they argued that without affirmative action, the service academies would be overwhelmingly white.

Parties normally receive thirty minutes each for oral argument, although the justices frequently interrupt with questions. The quality of oral argument varies enormously, and not surprisingly, can influence which party wins.[27]

The Supreme Court heard oral arguments in the *Gratz* and *Grutter* cases on April 1, 2003, hearing the *Grutter* case first. Grutter's attorney, Kirk Kolbo from the Center for Individual Rights, spoke first, arguing that the Constitution prohibits distinctions based on race. Justice O'Connor immediately interrupted, asking the attorney about Court precedents holding that race could be used if the government had a compelling interest in doing so. Kolbo responded that the school could legally achieve a diverse student body without using racial preferences by using factors that are not explicitly racial, such as economic status. U.S. Solicitor General Theodore Olson spoke next, opposing the University of Michigan's (hereafter just "Michigan") use of affirmative action but, under President Bush's directive, not calling for a complete ban on the use of race. Olson chose not to answer questions about the military's use of affirmative action, stating that he had not examined military policies. Michigan's attorney, Maureen Mahoney, a former law clerk for Chief Justice Rehnquist, tried to distinguish between the university's attempt to obtain a diverse student body and the type of quota system declared unconstitutional in the *Bakke* case. "She's very good," Justice Ginsburg whispered to Justice David Souter after the arguments ended. "She's fabulous," replied Souter.[28] Her ability, of course, would help Michigan's chances; political science studies have demonstrated that the attorneys' abilities at oral argument significantly influence the justices' decisions.[29]

Kolbo represented Gratz as well as Grutter, arguing in Gratz's case that the use of race as a factor must be extraordinary and rare, and that diversity does not meet that extraordinary standard. Michigan's attorney in the undergraduate case defended the need for a "critical mass" of minority students so that those students would not feel like tokens.

The Decision

Within a few days of oral argument, the justices meet in conference to vote on the merits of the case (that is, to decide which side wins) and to assign a justice to write the Opinion of the Court in the case. If the chief justice is in the majority, he determines who will write the opinion. If the chief justice is not in the majority, the assignment is made by the most senior justice who is in the majority.

The opinion is the heart of the Court's legal and policy-making power. It explains the Court's justification for its decision and sets guidelines for other courts to follow in subsequent cases. To have this authority, it must become a majority opinion by gaining the assent of a majority of the justices.

Assigning the writing of the Opinion of the Court to a justice does not mean that a majority opinion will result. If a justice writes an opinion siding with one side, and other justices agree with the result (that is, agree on who wins) but not with the reasoning, they can concur in the judgment. That means that they are not joining the Opinion of the Court. Such justices will typically write a **concurring opinion** that explains their reasoning or join the concurring opinion of another justice. Justices who disagree with the result reached by the majority can write a **dissenting opinion** explaining why they believe the Court's decision was in error. If, due to a combination of concurring and dissenting justices, fewer than five justices join the Opinion of the Court, that opinion becomes a plurality judgment rather than a majority opinion. Plurality judgments have less value as precedents than majority opinions.

concurring opinion: *Opinion that agrees with the results of the majority opinion (that is, which party wins) but sets out a separate rationale.*

dissenting opinion: *Opinion that disagrees with the majority opinion as to which party wins.*

The vote in the affirmative action cases revealed a split in the justices' preferences: 5–4 in favor of the law school program, but 6–3 against the undergraduate program. As Figure 15.3 shows, four conservative justices thought that both the undergraduate and the law school affirmative programs violated the Fourteenth Amendment and were unconstitutional, whereas the three most liberal justices thought that both programs were acceptable because of the university's compelling interest in creating a diverse student body and the narrow tailoring of the affirmative action programs to meet that interest. Justices Sandra Day O'Connor and Stephen Breyer were the swing justices. They agreed that diversity constituted a compelling interest but did not believe that the undergraduate program, which automatically gave a set number of points to minority applicants, was narrowly tailored to meet that interest. They thus voted with the more conservative justices to strike the undergraduate program. But O'Connor and Breyer voted with the liberals to uphold the law school program, which overall gave strong preferences to underrepresented minorities but was more careful in considering the importance of race in each individual's application.

Because the conservative former Chief Justice William Rehnquist dissented in the law school case, Justice Stevens, then the senior justice in the majority, assigned the opinion. Given former Justice O'Connor's role as the swing justice in the case, he assigned the opinion to her. O'Connor declared that while racial categorizations could be used only if the state had

FIGURE 15.3 Ideology and Votes of Supreme Court Justices in the *Gratz* and *Grutter* Cases

The justices are aligned from most liberal to most conservative. The six justices to the right of the blue vertical line voted with Gratz to strike the undergraduate affirmative action program at the University of Michigan. The five justices to the left of the orange vertical line voted with the University of Michigan in upholding the law school's affirmative action program.

Source for justices' ideology: Martin-Quinn scores, http://mqscores.berkeley.edu. Jeffrey A. Segal. *Photos*: Ginsburg, Breyer, Kennedy, Scalia, Stevens, and Thomas by Steve Petteway, Collection of the Supreme Court of the United States; Souter by Joseph Bailey, National Geographic Society, Collection of the Supreme Court of the United States; O'Connor and Rehnquist by Dane Pennland, Smithsonian Institution, Collection of the Supreme Court of the United States.

a compelling interest in doing so, the need for diversity was such an interest. She quoted from *amicus* briefs by businesses, which cited the need for a diverse workforce in the global economy, and she cited extensively from the military brief's stated need for a diverse officer corps.

Chief Justice Rehnquist was in the majority in the undergraduate case, and he assigned the majority opinion to himself. His opinion accepted the notion that diversity was a compelling interest—he did not have the votes to declare otherwise—but wrote that the automatic granting of twenty points toward admission to every minority student did not meet the precedent required in *Bakke* of considering each particular applicant as an individual.

Though Gratz won her case, she had by this point graduated from a different Michigan campus, the University of Michigan–Dearborn. The University of Michigan changed its admissions procedures to be more like the law school's procedures: Race would still be used as an admissions factor, but there would be no automatic point total added just because of an applicant's race.

15.4 Judicial Decision Making

Identify factors that influence judicial rulings and the impact those decisions have

We have now discussed the structure of the court system and the procedures it follows in both civil and criminal cases. In this section, we will examine how judges make decisions about a case and the impact those decisions have on public policy. Because judges are unelected and serve for life, they are not accountable to the people in the same way that presidents and members of Congress are. Nevertheless, they have an extraordinary power—the power of judicial review. Judicial review allows an unelected branch of government to strike the laws and actions of the elected branches of government—Congress and the president. This authority by the judicial branch is questionable in a democracy, where the people are supposed to have the final say. Therefore, along with judicial review comes what law professor Alexander Bickel has labeled the **countermajoritarian difficulty**.[30] We expect the judiciary to enforce limits on governmental power, but when it does so, it acts in a countermajoritarian manner because unelected judges are using this power to strike the actions of democratically elected executives and legislatures.

countermajoritarian difficulty: *Alexander Bickel's phrase for the tension that exists for representative government when unelected judges have the power to strike laws passed by elected representatives.*

The Supreme Court first held an act of Congress unconstitutional in 1803, and then did not hold another one unconstitutional until 1857. Since that time, however, the Court has struck down 191 congressional laws, slightly more than one per year, with 7 laws struck down in 1935 during the height of the Court's battle with the New Deal (see Figure 15.4). Since the 1986 term, the Court has struck down more than twice as many state and municipal laws (144) as federal laws (57).[31]

Essential Knowledge

The degree of activism on the part of the members of the Court is a source of controversy.

Given the undemocratic nature of judicial review, politicians frequently decry **judicial activism**, judges who go beyond what the law requires and seek to impose their own policy preferences on society through their decisions. These critics insist that judges should act with **judicial restraint**—that is, judges should respect the decisions of other branches or, through the concept of precedent, the decisions of earlier judges.

judicial activism: *Decisions that go beyond what the law requires, made by judges who seek to impose their own policy preferences on society through their judicial decisions.*

judicial restraint: *Decisions by judges respecting the decisions of other branches or, through the concept of precedent, the decisions of earlier judges.*

We will explore two broad approaches to understanding judicial policy making: a legal approach, which suggests that courts rely on legally relevant factors, and an extralegal

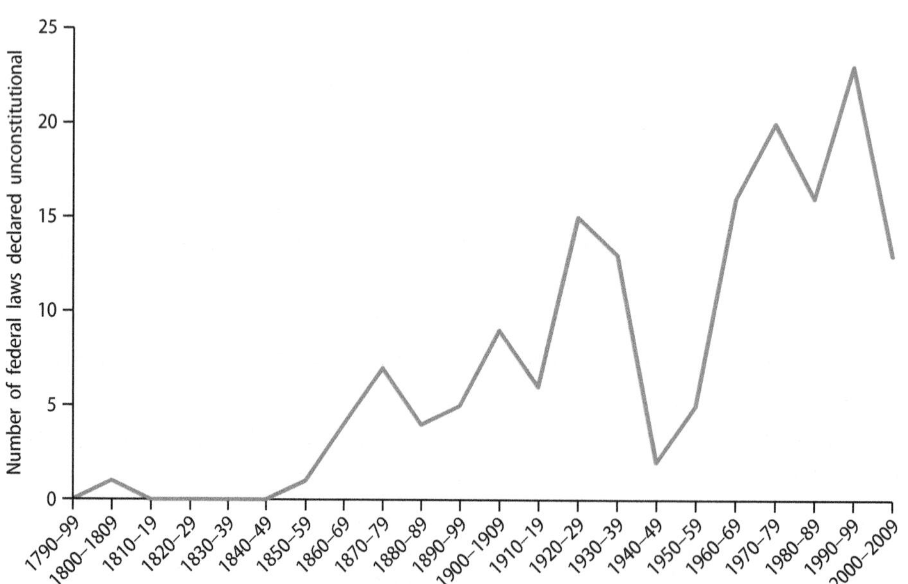

FIGURE 15.4 Number of Federal Laws Declared Unconstitutional, 1790–2014

The Supreme Court declared two federal laws unconstitutional in the 2010 term, three in the 2011 term, three in the 2012 term, one in the 2013 term, two in the 2014 and none in the 2015 term.

Sources: Harold W. Stanley and Richard G. Niemi, Eds., *Vital Statistics on American Politics*, 3rd ed. (Washington, D.C.: CQ Press, 1992); Lawrence Baum, *The Supreme Court*, 8th ed. (Washington, D.C.: CQ Press, 2004), 170, 173; Harold J. Spaeth, Lee Epstein, Andrew D. Martin, Jeffrey A. Segal, and Thomas W. Walker, U.S. Supreme Court Database, scdb.wustl.edu. Jeffrey A. Segal, © Cengage Learning.

approach, which suggests that courts rely on legally irrelevant factors. We then examine the consequences for a democracy of the reliance on extralegal factors by an unelected judiciary.

Judicial Restraint: The Legal Approach

According to the legal approach, justices base their decisions on legally relevant materials, such as prior court precedents, the plain meaning of the text of the law under consideration, and the intent of the framers of the law, rather than on their own preferences. This viewpoint is known as judicial restraint.

As we explained earlier in the chapter, precedent means a reliance on the prior decisions of the Court. In the *Grutter* case, the Court accepted the arguments from the *Bakke* case that the government had a compelling interest in achieving a diverse student body but concluded that systems that establish racial quotas go too far. Reliance on precedent creates stability in law: Decisions change gradually rather than abruptly. Reliance on precedent also generates a degree of equality and fairness. If you slip on your neighbor's walkway, it is not necessarily clear whether your neighbor is at fault for a slippery surface or you are at fault for not being careful. It is hard to say in advance that ruling one way is just and ruling the other way is unjust. But if the judge rules that the owner is not liable and the next week under similar conditions the neighbor slips on your walkway, fairness demands that the judge should again rule that the owner is not liable. That is what ruling based on precedent accomplishes. Lower courts are bound by Supreme Court precedents, but the Supreme Court does not necessarily consider itself strictly bound to its own precedents. Otherwise, there would be no growth in the law, and, for example, the United States might still have the separate-but-equal school systems that were declared unconstitutional in *Brown v. Board of Education*.

Beyond precedent, legal-based approaches consider the plain meaning of the law being interpreted. In recent history, the late Justice Antonin Scalia was the Court's foremost proponent of this approach. If there is no right to privacy written in the Constitution, he claimed, then the Supreme Court should not be creating privacy rights. As Scalia argued, if such rights are to be protected, they should be granted by democratically elected legislatures, not by life-appointed judges. However, while a textual approach makes some issues perfectly clear—for example, that a 34-year-old cannot be president—it does not necessarily answer whether affirmative action plans designed to increase diversity or fair representation in an unequal society violate equal protection of the law.

Similarly, Justice Clarence Thomas often argues for decision making based on the intent of the Framers. This approach places the meaning of the Framers ahead of the literal meaning of the words that they wrote. Thus, while dissenting in a case that upheld federal prohibitions on medicinal marijuana under Congress's authority to regulate interstate commerce, Thomas ignored more than seventy years of precedent that had expanded the scope of the commerce clause. He argued that local activities such as the medical use of homegrown marijuana were not what the Framers meant by commerce.[32] This may well be true, but in many circumstances, it is difficult to know what the Framers meant or what they would have thought if they could have envisioned modern American society. For example, does the Fourth Amendment's protection of one's person, houses, papers, and effects against unreasonable searches and seizures include telephone wires, cell phones, and wireless e-mail?

Judicial Activism: The Extralegal Approach

Legal approaches often fail to provide a good indicator of what the Supreme Court will do. While some precedents, notably the 1978 *Bakke* decision, supported affirmative action, more recent cases prior to *Grutter* had pushed in the opposite direction. The text of the Fourteenth Amendment guarantees equality, but there is no evidence that the Framers of the amendment intended it to prohibit policies that tried to help disadvantaged groups.

Alternatively, we can consider extralegal approaches to Supreme Court decision making. Extralegal factors go beyond the legal factors that courts are supposed to consider. The most important sets of extralegal considerations include the justices' own preferences and strategic considerations based on the preferences of others. Many, if not most, justices may be labeled activists, justices who decide cases based on their own policy preferences.[33]

The Justices' Preferences. In the affirmative action cases, the four most conservative justices voted to strike both the undergraduate and the law school plans, the three most liberal justices voted to uphold both, and the two justices in the middle voted to uphold the law school program but to strike the undergraduate program. (For the ideology of the justices currently on the Court, see Figure 15.5.)

This sort of relationship between the justices' ideology and their votes is fairly common. But because Supreme Court scholars cannot obtain information from the justices themselves about their ideology, they use indirect measures. As Figure 15.6 shows, there exists a very strong relationship between the justices' ideology and their votes once on the Court.[34] Note, however, that this strong relationship does not necessarily apply to state courts or lower federal courts, both of which must follow precedents established by the Supreme Court, at least on matters of federal law.

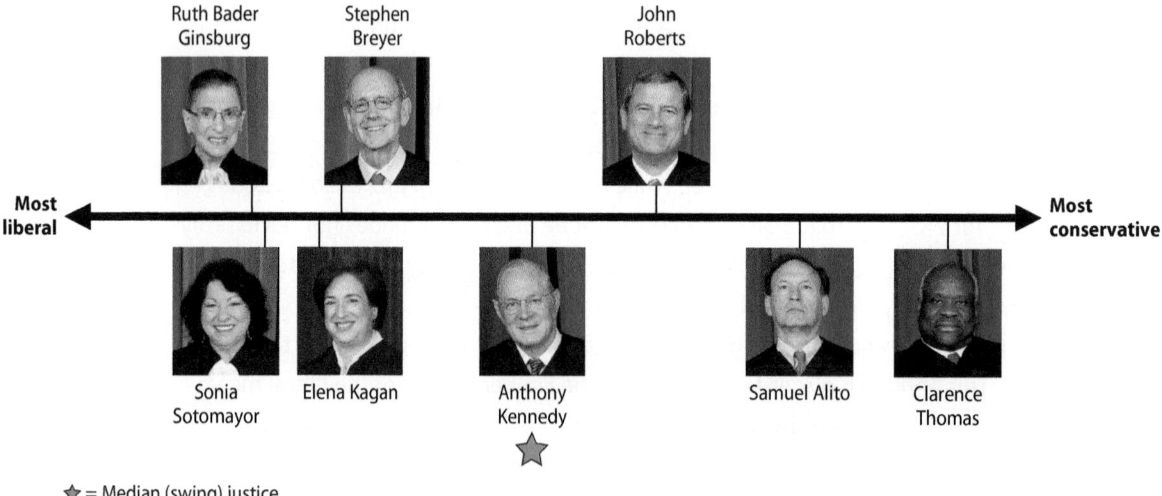

FIGURE 15.5 Estimated Ideology of the Supreme Court Justices, 2015–2016 Term

Statistical analysis of Supreme Court justices by Andrew Martin and Kevin Quinn places Justices Ginsburg and Sotomayor at the left (liberal) end of the scale while Justice Thomas anchors the right (conservative) end of the scale. With Justice Scalia's passing, there were only eight justices on the Court as of November 2016.

Source: Justices' ideology: Martin-Quinn scores, http://mqscores.berkeley.edu. Jeffrey A. Segal, © Cengage Learning. Photos: Steve Petteway, Collection of the Supreme Court of the United States.

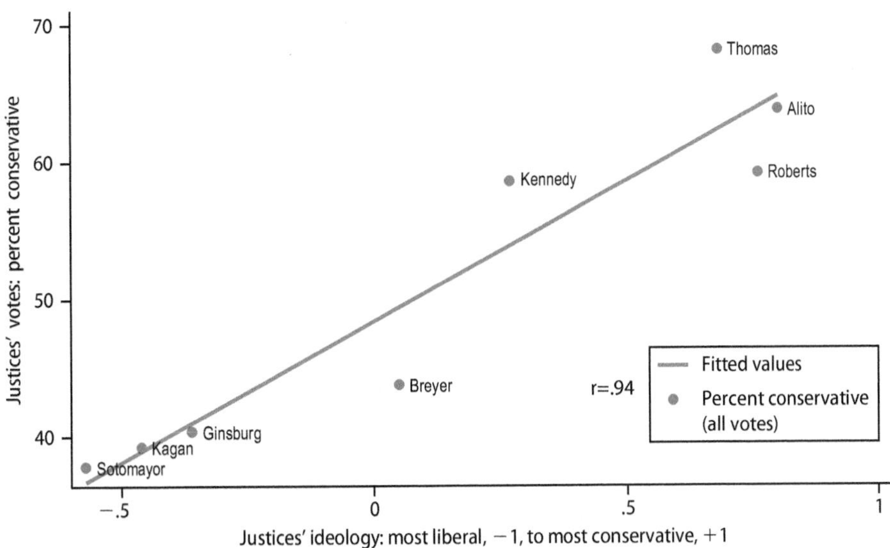

FIGURE 15.6 Justices' Votes by Their Ideology, 1987–2015

The graph shows that, as the justices' ideologies line up from the left (most liberal) to the right (most conservative), the percentage of the time they vote conservatively increases substantially. Generally speaking, the most liberal justices, those farthest to the left on the graph (Sotomayor, Kagan, and Ginsburg), vote in the liberal direction (toward the bottom of the graph), whereas the most conservative justices (Alito, Roberts, and Thomas) vote conservatively most of the time (toward the top of the graph).

Source: Justices' ideology: Data updated by Jeffrey Segal from Jeffrey Segal and Albert Cover, "Ideological Values and the Votes of Supreme Court Justices," *American Political Science Review* 83 (1989): 557–65. Justices' votes: Harold J. Spaeth, Lee Epstein, Andrew D. Martin, Jeffrey A. Segal, Theodore J. Ruger, and Sara C. Benesh, 2014 Supreme Court Database, Version 2014, Release 01, http://Supremecourtdatabase.org. Jeffrey A. Segal, © Cengage Learning.

Strategic Considerations. Justices cannot behave solely on the basis of their ideological preferences. Justice Rehnquist (1972–2005), while writing the *Gratz* opinion, may have preferred to declare that virtually all affirmative action plans are unconstitutional, but if he had done so, he might have lost the support of Justices O'Connor (1981–2006) and Breyer (1994–). So he compromised and accepted diversity as a rationale, but nevertheless was able to strike down the undergraduate program. Negotiations over the content of the majority opinion are a routine part of Supreme Court decision making.[35]

A justice may need to consider not only the preferences of other justices but also the preferences of other actors in the political environment. The efforts of President Franklin Delano Roosevelt (1933–45) to pack the Court in the face of the Court's rejection of his New Deal programs assuredly played a role in the Court's about-face and subsequent approval of such programs, as we will see later in the chapter. Similarly, the Court backed down from efforts to limit congressional investigations into Communism in the 1950s when Congress threatened to remove the Court's jurisdiction from such cases. Considerations about the legitimacy of its decisions may have led to Chief Justice John Roberts's purported switch from striking the Affordable Care Act to upholding it.[36]

Essential Knowledge

Any challenge to the Court's legitimacy or the legitimacy of its decisions can lead to changes in the types of people appointed to the Court, altering the Court's jurisdiction, or refusal to implement the decision.

As the *Gratz* and *Grutter* cases show, the courts have a major role in the American policy-making process, balancing equality of opportunity against affirmative action policies aimed at providing greater equality of outcome. Given the play of extralegal factors in such decisions, are judges, in fact, policy makers?[37] When the Supreme Court decides for the nation that affirmative action programs are allowed as long as they provide individualized assessments of students' records, they are making policy. The fact that this is not merely interpretation of the law is supported by the fact that the justices' ideological preferences overwhelmingly explain their votes on the Court.

But we might reach a different conclusion regarding the lower courts. Consider a district court judge faced with a suit by a white student to gain admission to a university that has an affirmative action program similar to the Michigan law school program. The judge applies the precedent from *Grutter* and rejects the student's challenge. Although that judge has made a decision that is crucial to the student, both the scope of the decision (which applies only to that student) and the low level of discretion involved in reaching it (the judge felt bound by the Supreme Court precedent in *Grutter*) make this sort of behavior distinct from policy making.

Restraint and Activism in Judicial Decision Making

Contemporary research suggests that justices respect the decisions of legislatures and earlier judges when those decisions are consistent with the justices' ideology. Thus, for example, liberal justices such as Ginsburg and Breyer overwhelmingly vote to uphold liberal precedents[38] or federal laws favored by liberals.[39] But when conservative precedents or laws favored by conservatives are under consideration, liberal justices are more than willing to strike them. Similarly, conservative justices such as Alito and Thomas overwhelmingly vote to uphold conservative precedents or the constitutionality of federal laws favored by conservatives. But when precedents are liberal in direction or when liberals favor the laws under review, conservative justices are more than willing to strike them.

The vast majority of justices are restrained toward laws and precedents that they agree with ideologically but are quite willing to overturn laws and precedents that they are distant from ideologically. Does this bode poorly for a democratic society that expects its judicial system to exhibit impartiality? Perhaps, though as we shall see later, our elected representatives appoint judges and so indirectly the people help choose which judges will make judicial policy in the United States.

The Impact of Court Rulings

Now that we understand how judges make decisions, we will examine what impact those decisions have for our democratic system. The fact that the federal court issues a decision does not necessarily mean that government officials charged with implementing it will comply. The courts have no power of enforcement. The Supreme Court's school desegregation decision in *Brown*, for example, met with massive resistance from supporters of segregation: Elected officials urged disobedience, local boards of education ignored the decision, and lower courts complied with the decision halfheartedly at best. All the while, citizens rallied in the streets in opposition (see Supreme Court Cases: *Cooper v. Aaron*; see also Chapter 13, The Presidency). In part because of these reactions, very few schools desegregated in the ten years following *Brown*.[40] And the fact that a decision might be complied with does not necessarily mean that it will have the impact that the Court intended. The advances in school desegregation over time have not meant that educational equality has been achieved in the United States.

Additionally, many types of court decisions can be overturned by Congress, state legislatures, or other legislative mechanisms such as state-level referenda. When a court's decision is based on the meaning of a statute (for example, is carbon dioxide considered a pollutant under the Clean Air Act?), Congress can simply overturn the court's decision if it disagrees with the court's conclusion.

In the constitutional realm, if the Court declares that a practice is not unconstitutional, as in the law school affirmative action case, that practice can still be prohibited through the legislature or, if the state allows, through a referendum. So when the Supreme Court rules that affirmative action is not prohibited by the Constitution, that does not mean that the university is required to implement an affirmative action program or that the state is required to allow such a program. As we saw earlier, following the Supreme Court decision in her case, Jennifer Gratz used the gateway provided by Michigan's initiative procedure, organizing a statewide proposal in Michigan that banned the use of race, gender, or ethnicity for admissions or hiring in higher education.

On the other hand, when the Supreme Court declares that the Constitution prohibits an activity, legislatures find that prohibition difficult to overturn. For example, when the Court declared that Congress did not have the authority to set the voting age at 18 for state elections, the only recourse was for Congress and the states to pass a constitutional amendment overturning that decision. Only five of the Supreme Court's constitutional decisions have ever been overturned via amendment (see Table 15.2). While relatively more of the Court's statutory decisions get overturned by Congress, such instances are still fairly rare.

In addition, most Supreme Court decisions are complied with, even when the consequences for the losing litigants are serious. Following the Supreme Court's Watergate

Essential Knowledge

The Congress and the president have several checks on the Court: the power to appoint and confirm (or refuse to confirm) justices, the power to propose constitutional amendments to overturn judicial interpretations, and the power to change or limit the Court's jurisdiction by law.

Furthermore, since the Court relies upon the executive branch to enforce its decisions, inaction on the part of the president or state governments can limit the effectiveness of its decisions.

TABLE 15.2 Constitutional Amendments Overturning Supreme Court Decisions

Supreme Court Decision	Amendment
Chisolm v. Georgia (1793) allowed citizens to sue other states in federal court.	Eleventh Amendment (1795) establishes sovereign immunity for states.
Dred Scott v. Sandford (1857) denied citizenship to African Americans.	Fourteenth Amendment (1868) makes all people born in the United States citizens of the United States.
Minor v. Happersett (1874) denied voting rights to women.	Nineteenth Amendment (1920) guarantees women the right to vote.
Pollock v. Farmers' Loan and Trust (1895) limited Congress's authority to tax income.	Sixteenth Amendment (1913) grants Congress the authority to tax income from whatever source derived.
Oregon v. Mitchell (1970) prompted Congress to set the voting age at 18 for all elections. The case struck the law as applied to state elections.	Twenty-Sixth Amendment (1971) sets the voting age at 18 for all elections.

SUPREME COURT CASES

Cooper v. Aaron (1958)

QUESTION: Does the threat of violence negate a school district's obligation to desegregate?

ORAL ARGUMENT: September 11, 1958 (listen at http://www.oyez.org/cases/1950-1959/1958/1958_1)

DECISION: September 12, 1958 (read at http://laws.findlaw.com/us/358/1.html)

OUTCOME: No, desegregation is required, even when mobs threaten violence (9–0).

Despite substantial opposition in the South to the 1954 *Brown* desegregation decision, the Little Rock school board approved a plan in May 1955 that would begin to integrate its schools as of September 1957. In response, the state legislature declared that no student could be required to attend an integrated school. Nevertheless, the National Association for the Advancement of Colored People (NAACP), a civil rights interest group, selected John Aaron, his sister Thelma, and seven other exceptional African American students to attempt to integrate Central High School.

As September 1957 approached, Governor Orval Faubus called out the Arkansas National Guard to physically prevent the students from entering the school. For three weeks, the Guard kept the school off limits to the nine students. This action encouraged segregationists, who took to the streets around the school to protest integration.

On September 20, 1957, a federal district court issued an order prohibiting the Arkansas Guard from interfering with desegregation efforts. In response, Faubus withdrew the Guard, leaving the streets under the control of a dangerous and angry mob.

On September 23, the African American students entered school under police protection, but the police were unable to control the mob and quickly removed the students. Two days later, President Dwight D. Eisenhower sent the 101st Airborne Division to Little Rock to disperse the mobs and protect the students. Eight of the nine black students remained at the school for the remainder of the school year. Given the unrest, William Cooper and other members of the Arkansas Board of Education filed suit to thwart the board's own desegregation plan. In June 1958, the district court upheld its request. In August, the court of appeals reversed the district court. The Supreme Court granted the board's petition for a writ of *certiorari*.

In an unusual opinion signed the day after oral argument by all nine justices, the Supreme Court refused to allow the board to back out of its desegregation plan due to the threat of violence. The Court declared that the U.S. Constitution and the Supreme Court's interpretation of the Constitution are the supreme law of the land. In response, Governor Faubus closed the school for the year, but it reopened as an integrated school in 1959. The Court's expansion of its authority—adding its interpretation of the Constitution to those items that are the "supreme law of the land"—has drawn criticism of judicial overreaching from people on the right and the left.

Thinking Critically

1. Why is the judiciary the branch of government best able to make decisions that a majority of citizens strongly oppose?
2. Can the Supreme Court be effective in guaranteeing equality when the majority of citizens actively oppose equality?

decision, President Richard M. Nixon (1969–74) turned over the Watergate tapes, even though doing so meant the end of his presidency.[41] Following the Supreme Court's decision in reapportionment cases, state legislatures reapportioned their states, even though it meant that many of the legislators would be reapportioned out of their seats.[42] Similarly, states stopped prosecuting doctors for providing abortions following *Roe v. Wade*.[43]

Thus, the federal court system and the Supreme Court in particular play an important role in determining public policy. Yet, as we have seen, the people play an indirect role in choosing federal judges. We will now take a closer look at how the selection process occurs.

Bob Daemmrich/Newscom/Polaris Images/Austin/Texas/United States

IMAGE 15.4 Chief Judge Roy Moore of the Alabama Supreme Court begins court sessions with prayer and has mounted a plaque of the Ten Commandments in his courtroom. After the Supreme Court's 2015 decision legalizing same-sex marriage, Moore ordered Alabama probate judges not to issue same-sex marriage licenses. Moore's order has since been overturned.

15.5 The Appointment Process for Federal Judges and Justices

Discuss how federal judges get selected

The Constitution grants the president the authority to nominate judges, but these nominations are subject to the advice and consent of the Senate. Judges confirmed by the Senate serve during "good behavior," which, short of impeachment, essentially means a life term. The House has impeached only one Supreme Court justice, Samuel Chase (1805), in an attempt by the Democratic-Republicans to remove an ardent Federalist from the bench. The Senate rejected every charge against Chase (just three votes short of the required two-thirds majority on one of the counts),[44] establishing a custom crucial to **judicial independence** that judges would not be removed due to partisan disagreements with their decisions.

judicial independence: *Ability of judges to reach decisions without fear of political retribution.*

As procedures have evolved, the president and the Senate accommodate each other on district court appointments, but they sometimes clash at the appeals court level. At the Supreme Court level, presidential nominees face intense scrutiny by the Senate, which often reflects concerns by citizens and interest groups.

District Courts

When a vacancy occurs in a district court, the president consults the senators from the state in which the court is located. If one of them is opposed to the nomination, he or she can invoke the norm of senatorial courtesy and receive the support of other members of the Senate in blocking that nominee. When the two senators are from different parties, the

UNITED STATES SENATE

COMMITTEE ON THE JUDICIARY

12-Mar-99

Dear Senator Moynihan

You will kindly give me, for the use of the Committee, your opinion and information concerning the nomination of:

Robert A. Katzmann to be United States Circuit Judge for the Second Circuit

Please return this form as soon as possible to the nominations office in Dirksen G-66. No further proceedings on this nominee will be scheduled until both blue slips have been returned by the nominee's home state senators.

Respectfully

Orrin G. Hatch
Chairman

Via courier to: SR-464

REPLY

TO: Senator Hatch, Chairman

X I approve

____ I oppose

Comments: Superb choice! (Ours, that is!)

U.S. Senator

Courtesy of Robert A. Katzmann

IMAGE 15.5 Senator Daniel Patrick Moynihan (D-NY) signed a blue slip approving the appointment of Robert Katzmann to the Second Circuit Court of Appeals. The photocopy that Judge Katzmann gave us was white.

senator from the president's party sometimes offers the other senator a percentage of the appointments, hoping the favor will be returned if the other party wins the presidency.

This norm is enhanced by the chair of the Judiciary Committee sending "blue slips," so called because of the color of the paper, to the senators of the president's party of a nominee's home state, asking whether they approve of the choice. Without a positive response, the Judiciary Committee generally will not hold a hearing on the nominee; with no hearing, there is no vote. Even with a positive response to the blue slip, the Judiciary chair may choose not to hold a hearing, particularly if he or she is of the opposite party of the president.

Sonia Sotomayor, who would go on to become President Barack Obama's first Supreme Court nominee, received her district court nomination during the presidency of Republican George H. W. Bush (1989–93) due to an appointment-sharing deal between New York's two senators at the time, Republican Alfonse D'Amato and Democrat Daniel Patrick Moynihan. Like the president, senators use a variety of criteria in naming district court judges, including ideology, qualifications, and the rewarding of party loyalty.[45]

Confirmation of district court judges is generally routine, with nearly 90 percent of nominees between the administration of Jimmy Carter (1977–81) and Barack Obama approved.[46] With an increasingly partisan confirmation environment following the 2010 elections, and a Republican majority in the Senate following the 2014 election, the confirmation rate during the Obama administration was closer to 80 percent.[47] Following the nomination, the Senate Judiciary Committee conducts hearings on nominees. At the hearings, the American Bar Association (ABA), an organized interest group representing the nation's attorneys, evaluates the merits of nominees. District court nominees may also be requested to testify. If the Judiciary Committee approves the nomination, it moves to the Senate floor for a vote. Under recent rules changes that prohibit filibusters on lower-court nominees, a majority is all that is needed for approval.

Courts of Appeals

The formal process of appointment for court of appeals judges is the same as that of district court judges, but the greater authority of court of appeals judges means that the Senate and outside interest groups pay much closer attention to the president's nominees. While court of appeals judges formally represent multiple states, seats are informally considered to belong to particular states. Thus, senatorial courtesy still applies.

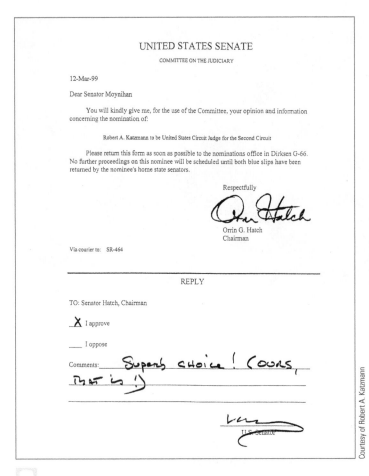

Senate Democrats twice blocked the nomination of current Chief Justice John Roberts, a conservative Republican, to the U.S. Court of Appeals. Only after a third nomination in 2003, at which point Republicans controlled the Senate (and thus the Judiciary Committee), did Roberts receive a hearing and a vote. Overall, the Senate has failed to confirm more than 20 percent of court of appeals nominees since Clinton's administration (1993–2001), with the overwhelming majority being blocked in the Judiciary Committee.[49] In 2010, Senate Republicans began extensive use of holds, a process by which a single senator can block the unanimous consent agreements by which the Senate operates, to delay votes on many of President Obama's nominees. The Democrats responded in November 2013 by changing Senate rules to prohibit filibusters on all executive or judicial nominations except those for the Supreme Court.

Scott J. Ferrell/Getty Images

IMAGE 15.6 Born in Honduras, Miguel Estrada immigrated to the United States at age 17. Despite a limited command of English, he graduated with honors from Columbia University in 1983 and Harvard Law School in 1986. After Estrada clerked for Justice Kennedy and worked in the Justice Department, President George W. Bush nominated him to the U.S. Court of Appeals in 2001. Democrats in the Senate blocked a vote on his nomination. Among the reasons, according to a leaked memo from the office of then Senate majority whip Richard Durbin (D-IL), was that "he has a minimal paper trail, he is Latino, and the White House seems to be grooming him for a Supreme Court appointment."[48]

The federal courts were for many years the exclusive province of white men. Not until President Franklin Roosevelt nominated Florence Allen to the U.S. Court of Appeals in 1934 did a female serve as either a district or circuit court judge.[50] No African American served on the federal courts until President Harry Truman nominated William Hastie to the U.S. Court of Appeals in 1949.[51] President John F. Kennedy made Reynoldo Garza the first Latino federal judge to serve on the U.S. District Court. In 1978, President Jimmy Carter made Garza the first Latino to serve on the U.S. Court of Appeals.[52]

Today, the federal courts increasingly reflect the diversity of the United States. Women make up 32 percent of district and court of appeals judges, and African Americans make up 13 percent of district and circuit court judges. Latinos make up 8 percent of court of appeals judges and 10 percent of district court judges.[53] Table 15.3 presents the female and minority appointment records of Presidents George W. Bush (2001–09) and Obama.

Does such diversity matter? While it is not the case that judges' votes are generally caused by their gender, race, or ethnicity, on certain issues there are substantial effects. Women are substantially more likely than men to support sex-discrimination claimants[54]—in fact, judges who have daughters are more likely to support pro-female positions than judges who only have sons.[55] African American judges are more likely to rule "liberally on cases having a substantive racial dimension."[56] Latino and white judges do not decide similarly to each other, with

TABLE 15.3 Federal Court Appointments of Presidents G. W. Bush and Obama

Demographic	Bush (Total: 324)	Obama (Total: 324)
Gender		
Male	253 (78%)	188 (58.1%)
Female	71 (22%)	136 (41.9%)
Race or Ethnicity		
African American	24 (7.4%)	61 (18.4%)
Native American	0 (0%)	1 (0.3%)
Asian American	4 (1.2%)	20 (6.0%)
Latino	30 (9.3%)	36 (10.9%)
Pacific Islander	0 (0%)	1 (0.3%)
White	266 (82.1%)	212 (64.0%)

Source: http://www.fjc.gov/history/home.nsf/page/research_categories.html. Accessed August 22, 2016.

POLITICAL ANALYTICS

Increasing Diversity on the Federal Courts

FOR THE FIRST 178 YEARS OF THE REPUBLIC, the U.S. Supreme Court was composed of all white men. Thurgood Marshall became the first African American when he was named to the court in 1967. The Supreme Court was all male until 1981, when Justice Sandra Day O'Connor was appointed. You read about political career ladders for women in Chapter 3, Federalism (see Election 2016: Beyond the Presidential Race). There is also a pool of persons who are prepared to serve on the Supreme Court. Though no particular judicial experience is required, nominees are vetted by the American Bar Association, and their judicial experience is usually relevant to the confirmation process. Like members of Congress who gain political experience in local offices and state legislatures, Supreme Court nominees have usually served on lower federal courts. To the extent that those courts contain a diverse pool of judges, presidents have a greater pool from which to draw when choosing nominees for the Supreme Court.

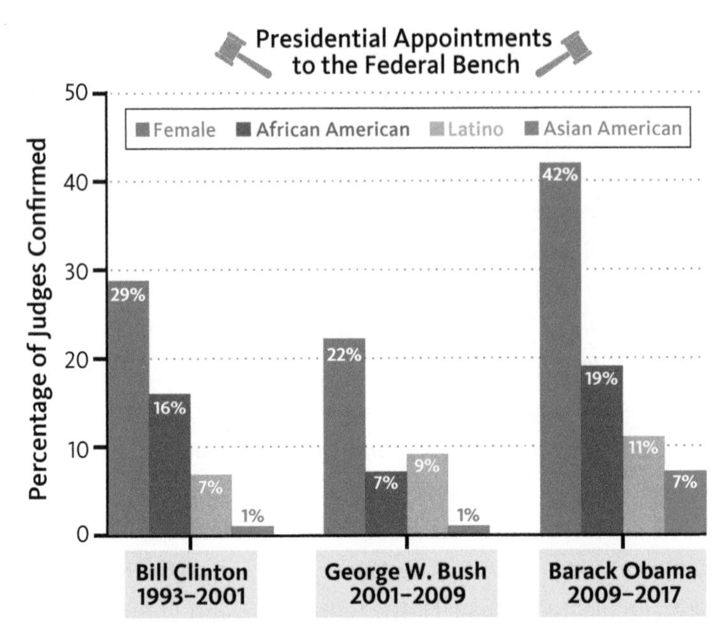

FIGURE 15.7 The Changing Face of the Judiciary

Figure 15.7 shows how the past three presidents' appointments have affected the diversity of the pool of lower-court judges. The demographic profiles of Presidents Clinton, G. W. Bush, and Obama show how the pool of judges in the federal courts is changing. In addition to these changes, the Senate has confirmed eleven judges nominated by President Obama who are openly gay or lesbian, compared to one prior to his presidency. The face of the U.S. federal courts is changing and beginning to more closely resemble the total U.S. population.

Examine the demographic profiles of judges nominated by Presidents Clinton, G. W. Bush, and Obama.

Thinking Critically

1. How important is it for the federal courts to include judges who resemble the general population of the United States?
2. Do you think the demographic characteristics of federal court judges will continue to change and lead to changes in the composition of the Supreme Court?

Sources: "Infographic: President Obama's Judicial Nominees," The White House, September 24, 2013, https://www.whitehouse.gov/share/judicial-nominees; "This is the First Time Our Judicial Pool Has Been this Diverse," The White House, December 17, 2015, https://www.whitehouse .gov/share/judicial-nominations; "Women in the Federal Judiciary: Still a Long Way to Go," National Women's Law Center, http://nwlc.org/resources/women-federal-judiciary-still-long-way -go; "Broadening the Bench: Professional Diversity and Judicial Nominations," Alliance for Justice, March 18, 2016, http://www.afj.org/wp-content/uploads/2014/11/Professional-Diversity-Report. pdf; Barry J. McMillion, "U.S. Circuit and District Court Judges: Profile of Select Characteristics," Congressional Research Service, March 19, 2014, https://www.fas.org/sgp/crs/misc/R43426.pdf.

Latino judges often granting more conservative decisions in criminal justice and civil liberties cases.[57] Latino judges also decide differently than African American judges, voting more conservatively in criminal cases, race discrimination cases, and cases involving economically disadvantaged litigants.[58] The fact that both African Americans and Latinos are members of discriminated-against minorities in the United States is not enough to result in similar decision making.

The Supreme Court

Given the Supreme Court's authority, the appointment of a Supreme Court justice is a high-stakes affair with extensive media coverage, interest group mobilization, public opinion polls, and the occasional scandal. As President Nixon correctly noted, "The most important appointments a President makes are those to the Supreme Court of the United States."[59] While Nixon was no doubt referring to the ideological and policy implications of such appointments, presidents also use Supreme Court appointments for electoral advantage.

Essential Knowledge

Who the president appoints to the Court can change the ideological makeup of the Court. This then can impact the decisions the Court makes.

This was undoubtedly the case in October 1956, a month before the general election, when Republican President Dwight D. Eisenhower (1953–61), burnishing his above-politics credentials, nominated Democrat William Brennan to the Court. Brennan was a Catholic, and Cardinal Spellman of New York had been lobbying hard for a Catholic nominee.[60] Presidential candidate Ronald Reagan promised to nominate the first woman to the Court and did so with his 1981 appointment of Sandra Day O'Connor. Fear that George W. Bush would get credit for nominating the first Latino to the Supreme Court was one of the factors that led Democrats to oppose Miguel Estrada's court of appeals nomination,[61] and he was thus denied the judicial experience that would be important for a Supreme Court nomination. President Obama received credit for nominating the first Latino to the Supreme Court with Sonia Sotomayor's appointment in 2009.

Although electoral advantage certainly influences presidential decisions, presidents also try to choose nominees who are close to them ideologically, hoping to shape the direction of the Court for years to come. Ronald Reagan had this in mind when he nominated the conservatives Robert Bork (whom a Democratic-controlled Senate rejected) and Antonin Scalia (whom a Republican-controlled Senate approved). Considerations of ideology are not new. George Washington named eleven consecutive Federalists to the first Supreme Court, and Franklin Roosevelt appointed only supporters of his New Deal programs, most of whom were Democrats.

In recent times, nominees for the Supreme Court always receive hearings before the Senate Judiciary Committee, though Merrick Garland has not received one as of November 2016. These hearings include testimony by the ABA on the qualifications of the nominee, comments by organized interests for and against the nominee, and testimony by the nominee. Every nominee since 1986 has received a unanimous vote of "well qualified" from the ABA except Robert Bork (of the fifteen members of the ABA Standing Committee on Federal Judiciary, ten voted that he was well qualified, one voted not opposed, and four voted that he was not qualified), Clarence Thomas (twelve voted qualified, two not qualified, and there was one recusal), and Harriet Miers, who withdrew her nomination in the face of substantial opposition to her ties to the president and her lack of qualifications.

Other interest groups mobilize for and against nominees, too. When President Obama nominated Sonia Sotomayor to the Court in 2009, various interest groups spoke against her, including Americans United for Life, the libertarian Independence Institute, the conservative Cato Institute, and the New Haven Fire Department due to a vote she cast against a white plaintiff in an affirmative action case. On the other hand, she received support from representatives of the ABA, the Leadership Conference on Civil Rights, the Federal Bureau of Investigation, the Fraternal Order of Police, and the National Association of Women Lawyers. Overall, representatives from 210 groups supported her confirmation whereas representatives from only 8 groups opposed it. Having 210 groups in favor is substantially more than any other nominee has ever received.[62]

Once the nomination is on the floor, senators debate the pros and cons of the nominee until the vote is set. Floor votes can be postponed indefinitely through a filibuster, a tactic used with increasing frequency for court of appeals nominees, but Abe Fortas's chief justice nomination (1968) is the only Supreme Court nomination to be defeated by a filibuster.

The confirmation process has also become a much more partisan process over the years. While Chief Justice John Roberts received unanimous support from Republicans, then-Senator Barack Obama (D-IL) and seventeen other Democrats opposed him. Similarly, while Sonia Sotomayor, nominated by Democratic President Obama, received unanimous support from Democrats (57 of 57), only 9 out of 40 Republicans supported her.

This partisanship as to Supreme Court nominations continued into 2016. Just hours after Justice Antonin Scalia passed away, Republican Senate majority leader Mitch McConnell (R-KY) declared that the Senate would not consider any nomination made by President Obama.

Among opposition-party senators, ideology can sometimes be decisive. In the Roberts vote, only 25 percent of liberal Democrats supported him whereas more than 80 percent of more moderate Democrats did so. With Sotomayor, however, support was below 40 percent for both moderate Republicans (33 percent) and more conservative Republicans (10 percent; see Figure 15.8). Constituent preferences matter too[63];

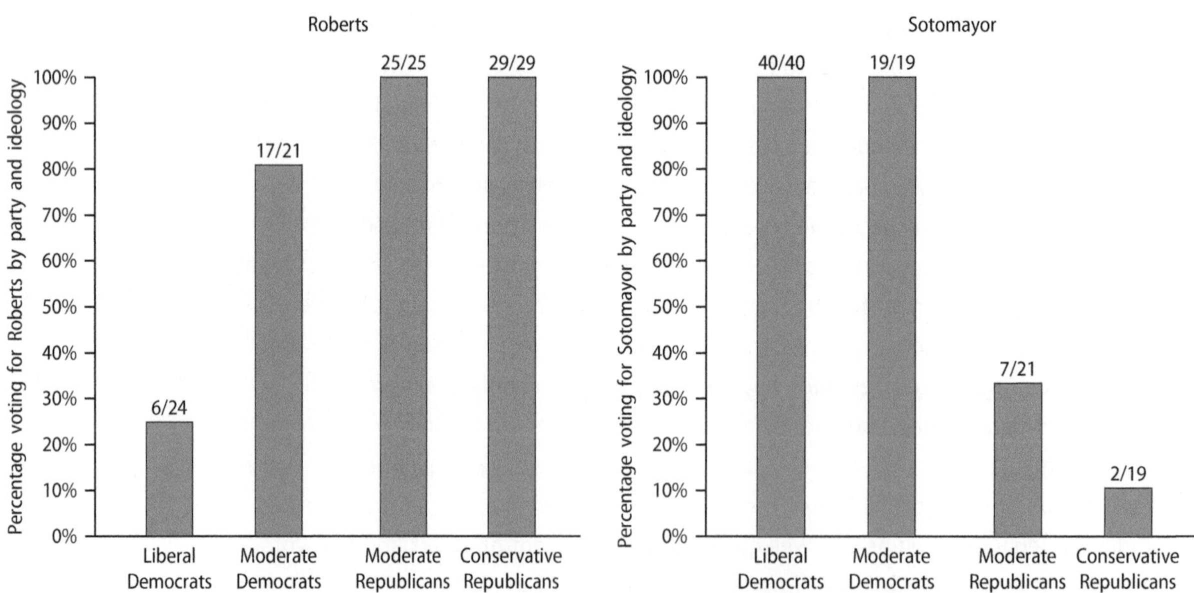

FIGURE 15.8 Ideology and Partisanship in the Roberts and Sotomayor Confirmation Votes

Every Republican voted to confirm John Roberts for chief justice, while moderate Democrats were more likely to support him than liberal Democrats. Similarly, all Democrats voted to confirm Sonia Sotomayor for associate justice, while moderate Republicans were more likely to support her than conservative Republicans.

Source: Data collected by Lee Epstein, Jeffrey A. Segal, and Chad Westerland, http://epstein.wustl.edu/research/Apptldeology.html.

ELECTION 2016

The Supreme Court and the 2016 Election

DESPITE THE ENORMOUS ROLE THE Supreme Court plays in American life, barely a word was mentioned about it in early presidential debates. Following the passing of Justice Antonin Scalia on February 13, 2016, the Court quickly rose to be one of the leading issues in this year's campaign. Within twenty-four hours of Justice Scalia's passing, Republican senators declared that no replacement should be named until after the 2016 election. Nevertheless, on March 16, President Obama nominated Merrick Garland, chief judge on the U.S. Court of Appeals for the District of Columbia, to fill Scalia's seat.

Garland—like Justices Roberts, Kennedy, Breyer, Kagan, and Ginsburg—attended Harvard Law School. Ginsburg transferred to Columbia, but the others have Harvard Law degrees (the remaining justices—Sotomayor, Thomas, and Alito—went to Yale). Following law school, Judge Garland served as a Supreme Court clerk (for William Brennan), as did Justices Roberts (William Rehnquist), Kagan (Thurgood Marshall), and Breyer (Arthur Goldberg), Like Justices Roberts, Ginsburg, and Thomas, Garland was sitting on the U.S. Court of Appeals for the District of Columbia (commonly labeled the second most important court in the nation) when nominated. Like every single member of the current Supreme Court, Garland has not served in the military, nor has he ever held elective office. He did, however, graduate from Harvard College as its undergraduate valedictorian. Nevertheless, the Republicans showed no signs of even being willing to consider his nomination. They have not requested the traditional FBI investigation that is conducted on all judicial nominees and, with minor exceptions, they have not granted him the courtesy meetings in their offices that all nominees get in the days following their nomination.

We could note the hypocrisy on both sides as to whether Garland should receive an up or down vote. When George W. Bush was president and Democrats controlled the Senate, Republicans insisted that the Senate was obligated to vote, while Obama's Vice President Joseph Biden, then chair of the Senate Judiciary Committee, argued in 1992 that President George H. W. Bush should not try to fill a Supreme Court nomination should one arise, but if he did, it would be "essential" that the Senate not act. More instructive than this game of "gotcha" (which both sides delight in playing) is to look at the consequences of a left-of-center Supreme Court nominee to replace Justice Scalia. Some of the 5–4 decisions in which Justice Scalia was in the majority include:

- *District of Columbia v. Heller* (2008),[64] in which the Supreme Court ruled that the Second Amendment protects an individual right to own guns, as well as *McDonald v. Chicago* (2010),[65] in which the Court held that right to be binding on state governments
- *Citizens United v. FEC* (2010),[66] in which the Supreme Court ruled that corporations have the same First Amendment rights as individuals to make unlimited campaign contributions to causes and candidates they support
- *Printz v. United States* (1997),[67] which required state law enforcement officers to assist federal law enforcement by conducting background checks on prospective handgun purchasers
- *Friedrichs v. California Teachers Association* (2016).[68] This case came down after Scalia's passing, but evidence from the oral arguments indicates that Scalia was ready to join four other justices in declaring that public employee unions violate the First Amendment rights of their members by requiring them to pay union dues. Voluntary union dues for state and local employees such as teachers inevitably would have led to a substantial decrease in power and influence for public employee unions. The Court split 4–4 in this case. When that happens the lower court's decision stands—in this instance, upholding mandatory union dues—but no precedent is set outside the circuit of the lower court.

Elections have consequences, and one of the biggest consequences of the 2016 election will be that Donald Trump will get to nominate the successor to Justice Scalia.

only three of the Republicans who voted for Sotomayor came from a state that Obama lost in 2008. Given the highly partisan nature of Supreme Court nominations over hot-button issues such as affirmative action, many Republicans reacted negatively to an earlier statement expressing her hope that "a wise Latina with the richness of her experiences would more often than not reach a better conclusion than a white male who hasn't lived that life."[69]

The nominees' perceived qualifications are no less important than ideology. While the high-quality nominees of recent years—Kagan, Sotomayor, Alito, and Roberts—all received substantial opposition, the Senate confirmed all of them. Alternatively, Merrick Garland had not received a Judiciary Committee hearing as of November 2016, much less a vote. Lower-qualified nominees have long faced decisive trouble; a case in point was G. Harrold Carswell, a little-known federal judge whom Richard Nixon nominated to the Supreme Court in 1970.

The question of qualifications includes not just ability, but also ethics. The Reagan administration withdrew the nomination of Douglas Ginsburg in 1987 following media reports that he had smoked marijuana while a professor at Harvard Law School. Much larger ethical questions surrounded the nomination of Clarence Thomas in 1991. During the televised hearings for Thomas, Anita Hill, who had worked for him at the Department of Education and later at the Equal Employment Opportunity Commission (EEOC), charged Thomas with sexual harassment. Thomas vociferously denied the charges and accused Democrats in the Senate of engaging in a "high-tech" lynching. Many people watching the hearings were disturbed by the harshness of the attacks on Anita Hill by the all-male Judiciary Committee. The senators acted the way elected officials of both parties normally do in such circumstances: Those who were ideologically close to the nominee—in this case, conservatives—believed him, whereas those who were ideologically distant did not.[70] The end result was that the Senate approved Thomas by a 52–48 vote.

Bettmann/Corbis

IMAGE 15.7 In 1991, President George H. W. Bush nominated Clarence Thomas to the Supreme Court to replace the retiring Thurgood Marshall. Thomas was not a supporter of affirmative action, and civil rights and feminist groups objected to his nomination. Then Anita Hill, who had worked for Thomas at the Department of Education and the Equal Employment Opportunity Commission, accused him of sexual harassment. Despite her testimony, the Senate confirmed Thomas by a narrow margin.

Demographic Diversity on the Court

In a Court long dominated by white males, Clarence Thomas was only the second African American to serve; the first was Thurgood Marshall (1967), a distinguished lawyer for the National Association for the Advancement of Colored People (NAACP) who argued *Brown v. Board of Education* (1954) before the Court. The Senate has confirmed 112 justices to seats on the Supreme Court. Of those 112, only 4—Sandra Day O'Connor (1981), Ruth Bader Ginsburg (1993), Sonia Sotomayor (2009), and Elena Kagan (2010)—have been female. Sotomayor is the first and only Latino. By some measures, the current Supreme Court, with three women, one African American, and one Hispanic, is the most diverse ever.

The first thirty-two Supreme Court nominations went to Protestants, long the dominant religious group in American politics. The first Roman Catholic was Roger Taney in 1836; the first Jew was Louis Brandeis in 1916. Today, in a sign that the gateways to prominent positions have opened dramatically, the Court has five Roman Catholic justices, three Jewish justices, and no Protestants. Merrick Garland, if confirmed, would be the fourth Jewish justice on the current Court.

This diversity matters in a number of ways, both on lower courts and at the Supreme Court.[71] As Justice Sotomayor's "wise Latina" comment suggests, judges' backgrounds and experiences can influence their views on the proper outcome of a case. Given that the Court has tremendous discretion about which cases to hear, greater diversity means that the Court may be more responsive to the issues that matter most to an increasingly diverse national population. Historic appointments such as O'Connor's or Sotomayor's can also have an influence on how their colleagues vote.[72] As more women serve on the U.S. Supreme Court, the bias found against female attorneys might lessen.[73]

On the other hand, for the first time in history, not one member of the Supreme Court held elective office prior to service on the Court. This lack of experience in electoral politics might play into their decisions striking down campaign finance laws (see *Citizens United v. Federal Election Commission*, in Chapter 8, Interest Groups). The educational background of the current justices also is fairly narrow. Every one of them, including nominee Garland, attended either Harvard or Yale Law School, though Justice Ginsburg transferred to and graduated from Columbia Law School. Professionally, only Sotomayor served as a trial judge, and all the justices except Kagan came to the Supreme Court from federal appeals courts, as did nominee Garland. This narrowness of background has not always been the case. In the past, many Supreme Court nominees graduated from modestly ranked law schools, and the justices often came to the Court from governorships, cabinet positions, the Senate, and private practice. To people who believe that the justices simply make decisions that are commanded by the Constitution, this narrowness does not matter. But to those who believe that experience does matter, the lack of this form of diversity hurts both the Court and the nation.

15.6 Historical Trends in Supreme Court Rulings

Outline how the Supreme Court has expanded and contracted national powers

In *Federalist* 78, Alexander Hamilton described the judiciary as "the least dangerous branch" because it has no power over the sword or the purse. But, as we have seen, due to the power of judicial review, the Supreme Court has actually played a major role in policy making: dividing authority between the nation and state, between Congress and the president, and between local and state governments and the people. Through the Court's history, its interpretations have expanded, then contracted, and once again expanded national powers. After a long and slow start, it has also moved, fairly consistently, toward greater protections of equality. In this section, we will take a look at the policies issued by this least dangerous but also least democratic branch of American government.

Expansion of National Power Under the Marshall Court

During George Washington's administration (1789–97), the Supreme Court had so little power or status that its first chief justice, John Jay, resigned to become governor of New York. Not until the fourth chief justice, John Marshall, did the Court begin to establish itself as a major player in national politics. The Marshall Court (1801–35; Courts are often named after the sitting chief justice) did so not only by affirming its power of judicial review in the *Marbury* case but also by setting forth a broad interpretation to the scope of national power in the cases of *McCulloch v. Maryland* (1819) and *Gibbons v. Ogden* (1824) and by limiting the authority of state judiciaries in a series of decisions culminating in *Cohens v. Virginia* (1821; see Supreme Court Cases: *McCulloch v. Maryland* in Chapter 3).[74]

The decision in *McCulloch v. Maryland* expanded national power in two ways: by granting the national government the right to create a bank through the necessary and proper clause, and by limiting state power by denying the states the authority to tax activities of the national government. Similarly, in *Gibbons v. Ogden*, the Court took an expansive view of national power, declaring that the commerce clause, which granted the national government the authority to regulate commerce "among the several States," would be broadly defined to include not just the shipping of goods across state lines but also the economic activities within a state that concern other states. As in *McCulloch*, what the Constitution grants as a legitimate object of national authority (here, interstate commerce) could not be regulated by a state. By establishing judicial review, expanding national power, and ensuring the uniformity of federal law, the Marshall Court set the United States on the path to a strong and unified nation.

Limits on National Power, 1830s to 1930s

Starting in the 1830s, the Supreme Court began limiting national power over slavery and, later, civil rights, as well as governmental efforts to regulate the economy. Although the Constitution permitted slavery, the justices did not address the issue directly until the case of *Dred Scott v. Sandford* (1857).[75] As noted in Chapter 5, Civil Rights, the Supreme Court declared that no black person could be an American citizen and that Congress did not have the authority to regulate slavery in the territories.

Following the Civil War, Congress proposed and the states ratified the Fourteenth Amendment, which prevented states from denying any person due process of law or the equal protection of the laws and from abridging the privileges or immunities of citizens of the United States. The Supreme Court interpreted the Fourteenth Amendment narrowly, thus limiting national power. For example, the *Slaughterhouse Cases* restricted the privileges or immunities clause that states could not abridge to the right of access to the seat of government, the right to pass freely from state to state, and the right to demand the protection of the federal government on the high seas or abroad, but little more.[76] Through precedent, the limited reading of the clause largely remains in effect today.

In *United States v. Cruikshank*, the Supreme Court reversed federal charges against the perpetrators of the Colfax massacre (see Chapter 5), arguing that the right to enforce the Fourteenth Amendment's due process clause gave Congress the authority to act only against states, not against individuals.[77] Similarly, in the *Civil Rights Cases,* the Court refused to grant Congress the authority to prohibit discrimination by private individuals under the equal protection clause, declaring that state-sponsored inequality was all that the amendment prohibited.[78]

The Supreme Court limited national authority in the economy, too. Following the Civil War, as the American economy shifted from agriculture to industry, powerful business and industrial interests sought to limit attempts by Congress and the states to regulate economic activity and labor. The Supreme Court generally backed business and industrial interests by setting up barriers to regulation. It promoted *laissez-faire*, the belief that the government should not intervene in the economy.

Strengthened National Power, 1930s to the Present

Following the onset of the Great Depression in 1929, citizens called on the states and the national government to try to regulate the economy and to assist workers, but the Supreme Court held firm in creating a constitutional gate that declared much of the economic legislation passed in the early years (1933–36) of Franklin Roosevelt's administration unconstitutional. Under pressure from Congress and Roosevelt, the Court eventually reversed itself, opening a gateway by allowing government greater leeway in regulating the economy. During this same period, the Court began restricting state government limits on civil rights and liberties, while strengthening national power to protect civil rights.

Economic Regulation. Elected president in 1932 on a platform of economic recovery and reform, Franklin Roosevelt saw several pieces of his New Deal legislation—which aimed to alleviate the nation's economic hardships—struck down by the Court, often by closely divided votes. After his 1936 reelection, Roosevelt struck back at the Court, proposing a so-called Court-packing plan that would have allowed him to appoint a new justice for every justice older than 70 who failed to resign. This scheme would have increased the Court's size to fifteen and guaranteed judicial support for his economic plans.

In the historic "switch in time that saved nine," two of the moderate backers of the Court's *laissez-faire* policies, Owen Roberts and Chief Justice Charles Evans Hughes, proved themselves responsive to the hostile political environment facing the Court. They began to change their votes, providing majorities for both national and state plans to regulate the economy, thereby removing the need for the Court-packing plan. In a series of cases decided in 1937, the Court upheld state-level minimum wage laws. Nationally, the Court recognized the right of unions to organize and bargain collectively as within the powers of Congress to regulate under the commerce clause.

Increased Protections for Civil Liberties and Civil Rights. With the government's authority over the economy established, cases before the Court dealt increasingly with questions of civil rights and civil liberties, topics discussed more fully in Chapters 4 and 5. The Court incorporated various provisions of the Bill of Rights, making them binding on the states. This selective incorporation doctrine began slowly, with First Amendment rights among the few incorporated before the 1950s. The doctrine expanded during the liberal Warren Court (1953–69), which made most of the criminal procedure guarantees of the Bill of Rights binding on the states.

Outside of incorporation, the Warren Court greatly expanded the interpretation of liberties involving the First Amendment, equal protection, the right to privacy, and criminal procedure. In First Amendment cases, the Court protected the speech rights of those advocating violence against religious and racial minorities, the press rights of newspapers against libel suits by public figures, and the right to publish allegedly obscene materials as long as they had even the slightest amount of redeeming social value. It also limited prayer and Bible readings in the schools.[79] Regarding equal protection, beyond the momentous *Hernandez v. Texas* and *Brown v. Board of Education* decisions, the Court launched a reapportionment revolution, setting forth a "one person, one vote" requirement.[80] The Warren Court also created a right to privacy that is not explicitly in the Constitution.[81] Finally, regarding criminal justice, the Warren Court demanded that evidence obtained by police in violation of the Fourth Amendment's protection against unreasonable searches or seizures should be excluded at trial (the exclusionary rule) and that subjects in custody not be interrogated without being informed of their rights to remain silent and to have an attorney (the so-called *Miranda* warnings, after the plaintiff in the case).[82]

Neither the more conservative Burger (1969–86) nor Rehnquist (1986–2005) Courts undid what the liberal Warren Court had done. For a summary of the Supreme Court's leading decisions, see Table 15.4. The Burger Court allowed children to be bused away from their neighborhood schools to increase integration. The Burger Court also established abortion rights, limited the death penalty, protected women's rights under the equal protection clause of the Fourteenth Amendment, and, in a precursor to the *Gratz* and *Grutter* lawsuits, first allowed affirmative action at colleges and universities.[83] On the other hand, the Burger Court chose not to extend equal protection rights to the unequal funding of school districts and, in the criminal justice area, limited the reach of the exclusionary rule and the *Miranda* warnings.[84]

Although conservative, the Rehnquist Court, over Chief Justice William Rehnquist's dissent, first extended privacy rights to homosexual conduct.[85] On the other hand, the Rehnquist Court limited, however slightly, the scope of abortion rights and cut back, again only slightly, the scope of congressional authority under the commerce clause and sovereign immunity.[86] And perhaps most important, as noted in Chapter 10, Elections and Campaigns, it ended the dispute over the 2000 presidential election with its decision in *Bush v. Gore*.[87]

The Roberts Court has been decidedly pro-business, hearing more such cases than previous courts and ruling on them in a decidedly pro-business direction.[88] It protected Walmart against a large discrimination lawsuit.[89] Even more important, it ruled that corporations have the same speech rights as citizens, enabling corporations to spend unlimited amounts of money on political campaigns[90] (see Chapters 8 and 10). On the other hand, the Court upheld Obama's health care plan in 2012, in what was not the conservative position in the case.[91] It also ruled that state denial of marriage licenses to same-sex couples was a violation of the equal protection clause of the Fourteenth Amendment.[92] In 2014, it upheld the Michigan initiative that banned affirmative action in that state.[93]

TABLE 15.4 Leading Decisions of the Marshall, Taney, Warren, Burger, Rehnquist, and Roberts Courts

Court	Case (Year)	Description
Marshall (1801–35)	*Marbury v. Madison* (1803)	Established judicial review
	McCulloch v. Maryland (1819)	Used implied powers to allow Congress to establish a national bank
	Cohens v. Virginia (1821)	Declared that federal courts have final say on meaning of federal law
	Gibbons v. Ogden (1824)	Established expansive interpretation of commerce clause
Taney (1836–64)	*Dred Scott v. Sandford* (1857)	Stated that "negroes of the African race" cannot be citizens and that Congress cannot prohibit slavery in the territories
Warren (1953–69)	*Hernandez v. Texas* (1954)	Recognized Latinos as a separate class for equal protection purposes
	Brown v. Board of Education (1954)	Prohibited segregation of public schools
	Wesberry v. Sanders (1964)	Required equality in the size of legislative districts
	New York Times v. Sullivan (1964)	Made it very difficult for public officials to sue newspapers for libel
	Miranda v. Arizona (1966)	Required that criminal defendants be told of their rights
	Griswold v. Connecticut (1965)	Established the right to privacy
Burger (1969–86)	*Reed v. Reed* (1971)	Granted women rights under the equal protection clause
	New York Times v. United States (1971)	Set extremely high bar for government censorship of newspapers
	Roe v. Wade (1973)	Extended privacy rights to cover abortion rights
	United States v. Nixon (1974)	Required President Richard M. Nixon to hand over incriminating evidence in Watergate case
	Regents v. Bakke (1978)	Allowed universities to use race-based affirmative action admissions
	Plyler v. Doe (1982)	Guaranteed right of undocumented children to attend public schools
Rehnquist (1986–2005)	*Planned Parenthood v. Casey* (1992)	Cut back but did not eliminate abortion rights established in *Roe v. Wade*
	Bush v. Gore (2000)	Ended the Florida presidential recount with George W. Bush holding a small lead, leading to Al Gore's concession
	Lawrence v. Texas (2003)	Extended privacy rights to homosexual conduct
	Gratz/Grutter v. Bollinger (2003)	Upheld race-based affirmative action as long as racial considerations are made on a case-by-case basis
Roberts (2005–present)	*District of Columbia v. Heller* (2008)	Upheld the right to bear arms as an individual right
	Citizens United v. FEC (2010)	Declared that corporations and unions have the same First Amendment rights to contribute to political campaigns as individuals
	National Federation of Independent Business v. Sebelius (2012)	Upheld the constitutionality of the Affordable Care Act
	Obergefell v. Hodges (2015)	Struck down state bans on same-sex marriage, legalizing same-sex marriage throughout the United States

Source: Adapted from John H. Aldrich and Ruth Grant, "The Antifederalists, the First Congress, and the First Parties," Journal of Politics 55 (1993): 295–326.

The Judiciary and Democracy

The judicial system of the United States promotes the equal right of participation by allowing a single individual who has been harmed by a law to challenge its constitutionality. People who have financial resources or who can find support from organized interests may fare better than those who have to act on their own. The action may not be successful. Nevertheless, the judiciary provides a separate gateway to the political system, one that is different in kind from the gateway to the legislative or executive branch. By filing a suit through the judiciary, a single individual—such as Oliver Brown (in the *Brown v. Board* school desegregation case) or the anonymous "Jane Roe" (in the *Roe v. Wade* abortion decision)—can have an enormous influence on the American political system.

Representative democracy requires government to be accountable and responsive to the public. Yet the judicial branch is not accountable in any meaningful way: Even if the public is dissatisfied with justices' decisions, Congress has not successfully used the impeachment process to remove justices for those decisions. Yet this does not mean that the Court is not responsive to the public or to the public's representatives. Responsiveness can happen through four different gateways.

The first gateway is through the electoral process.[94] During the 1960s, the Warren Court made a series of decisions on contentious issues such as criminal procedure and religious freedom that were significantly more liberal than many Americans might have preferred. Richard Nixon campaigned for president in 1968 with promises to appoint justices who were significantly more pro-police and significantly less pro-defendant. Nixon won the election and, in his first term, appointed four justices, all of whom were considerably more conservative on criminal procedure than the rest of the Court. The result was a conservative shift in Supreme Court decisions in criminal cases that mirrored public preferences as expressed in the 1968 election.

Second, in cases in which the Court is unresponsive to congressional preferences, Congress can threaten the Court's institutional authority. During the Civil War, Congress took away the Court's appellate jurisdiction over *habeas corpus* appeals. In the 1930s, Franklin Roosevelt threatened to dilute the Court by adding six new members. In both cases, the Court backed down and responded favorably to congressional (and thus, presumably, public) preferences.

The third gateway is through current events, which can move public opinion and judges' behavior in the same direction. During the Vietnam War, as events in Southeast Asia led American citizens to oppose the war in greater numbers, those events also led federal judges to impose shorter sentences on draft dodgers.[95] As society became more progressive on women's rights and same-sex marriage, judges, who themselves are members of society, presumably became more progressive on those issues, too. Immediately after the attacks of September 11, 2001, Americans were increasingly willing to allow the government to examine personal mail and Internet activity (see Chapter 6, Public Opinion), and judges moved in the same direction.

Fourth, judges might believe that they have an obligation to rule consistently with public opinion, even if they are not subject to electoral sanctions. It is probably no accident that the Supreme Court's split decision in the Michigan affirmative action cases reflected America's ambivalence about whether equality meant treating everybody exactly the same or whether, to promote equality of outcomes, underrepresented groups should be given advantages in admissions. Justice O'Connor, who split the difference over what can be done in the name of equal protection in the *Gratz* and *Grutter* cases, has spoken often about the need of the Supreme Court not to vary too far from public preferences.

That argument cuts both ways. As Justice Robert Jackson declared in a 1943 case striking down mandatory flag salutes, "The very purpose of a Bill of Rights was to withdraw certain subjects from . . . political controversy, to place them beyond the reach of majorities and officials and to establish them as legal principles to be applied by the courts. One's right to life, liberty, and property, to free speech, a free press, freedom of worship and assembly, and other fundamental rights may not be submitted to vote; they depend on the outcome of no elections."[96] If justices are responsive, it is not because the Constitution's framework requires it; it is because they choose to be.

Political Science Reasoning

Question 1

Practice 1, Practice 3

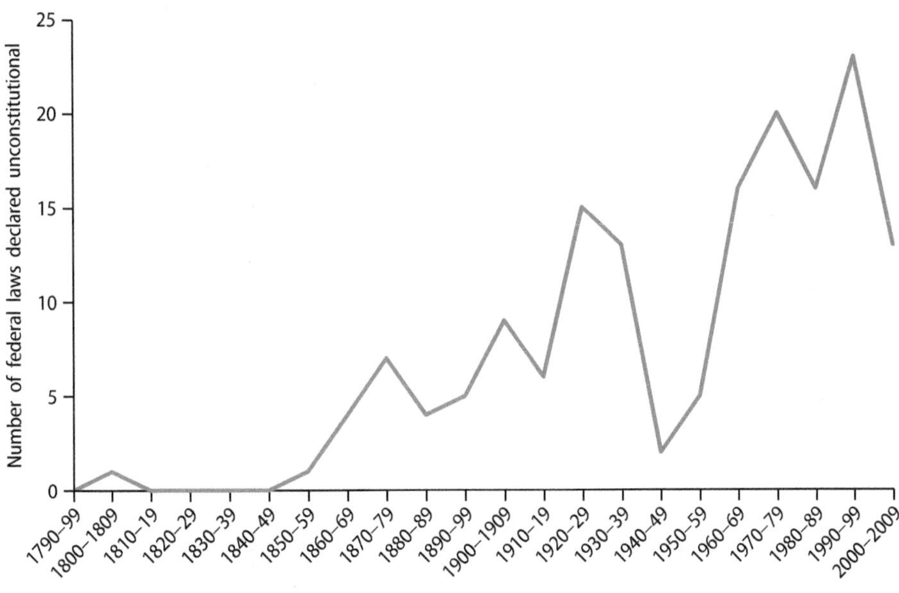

FIGURE 15.4

1. What is the general trend of the data displayed in the above figure?
2. What does the data reveal about the propensity of the Court to overturn federal laws?
3. What other date or information might be useful in understanding the above figure?

Question 2

Practice 1, Practice 4

> [T]he courts were designed to be an intermediate body between the people and the legislature, in order, among other things, to keep the latter within the limits assigned to their authority. The interpretation of the laws is the proper and peculiar province of the courts. A constitution is, in fact, and must be regarded by the judges, as a fundamental law. It therefore belongs to them to ascertain its meaning, as well as the meaning of any particular act proceeding from the legislative body. If there should happen to be an irreconcilable variance between the two, that which has the superior obligation and validity ought, of course, to be preferred; or, in other words, the Constitution ought to be preferred to the statute, the intention of the people to the intention of their agents.
>
> Nor does this conclusion by any means suppose a superiority of the judicial to the legislative power. It only supposes that the power of the people is superior to both; and that where the will of the legislature, declared in its statutes, stands in opposition to that of the people, declared in the Constitution, the judges

ought to be governed by the latter rather than the former. They ought to regulate their decisions by the fundamental laws, rather than by those which are not fundamental . . .[1]

The Constitution, on this hypothesis, is a mere thing of wax in the hands of the Judiciary, which they may twist and shape into any form they please. It should be remembered, as an axiom of eternal truth in politics, that whatever power in any Government is independent, is absolute also; in theory only at first, while the spirit of the people is up, but in practice as fast as that relaxes. Independence can be trusted nowhere but with the people in mass. They are inherently independent of all but moral law. My construction of the Constitution is very different from that you quote. It is, that each department is truly independent of the others, and has an equal right to decide for itself what is the meaning of the Constitution, in the cases submitted to its action, and especially where it is to act ultimately and without appeal. I will explain myself by examples, which, having occurred while I was in office, are better known to me, and the principles which governed them.[2]

1. Which of the above two excerpts supports the concept of judicial review? Cite specific textual evidence to support your position.
2. What would be the implications of allowing each branch to judge the constitutionality of its own actions, both generally and specifically in the area of civil rights?
3. How might Jefferson react to the assertion that the Supreme Court has become too "activist"?

[1]Alexander Hamilton, *Federalist* 78.
[2]Thomas Jefferson letter to Judge Roane, September 6, 1819.

Focus on AP® Success

15 The Judiciary

Must Know: Key Concepts

- Judicial Review
- *Marbury v. Madison* (1803)
- Supremacy Clause
- *Stare Decisis*
- Precedent
- Lifetime Tenure
- Judicial Activism
- Judicial Restraint
- *Federalist* 78

Thinking Politically

Argumentation

Compare judicial activism with judicial restraint. Which judicial philosophy best represents democratic values?

Concept Application

Explain how judicial review acts as a check on policy making by the legislative and executive branches.

Argumentation

Congress has several tools that it can use to check judicial decision making. However, not all of these tools are equally effective. Some tools might be relatively easy to use yet not be very strong. On the other hand, a tool might be incredibly strong but virtually impossible to use. Two of the tools that Congress possesses to check judicial decision making are constitutional amendment and statutory amendment. Which tool is more effective?

Concept Application

Explain how the American value of "rule of law" impacts the status of the judiciary's legitimacy relative to the other constitutional branches: Congress and the president.

Understanding Learning Objectives with Key Concepts

CON – 5.A Explain the principle of judicial review and how it checks the power of other institutions and state governments.

- The judicial branch of the national government is tasked with interpreting and applying laws passed by Congress, treaties, and the U.S. Constitution. Judicial review is the ability of the judiciary to review actions of the other two constitutional branches (Congress and executive branch) to determine if those actions are in accordance with the Constitution. Judicial review also allows the national court system to review actions of state governments to determine if those actions are in agreement with the U.S. Constitution.
    - Article III of the Constitution establishes the Supreme Court and allows Congress to create other courts that are inferior to it. It also provides that once appointed by the president and confirmed by the Senate, judges shall hold their offices for life during good behavior. This provision insulates the judiciary from politics and is the basis of their independence.
- In *Federalist* 78, Hamilton spelled out the need for judicial review as a means to preserve the will of the people as expressed through the Constitution. Further, Hamilton argued that judges should be bound by precedent and have lifetime terms.
- *Marbury v. Madison* is the first time that the Supreme Court asserted the power of judicial review. While not explicitly stated in the Constitution, it flows logically from it. Judicial review can be inferred from the Constitution's grant of judicial power to the court

system in Article III and the supremacy clause, which states that the Constitution and laws made pursuant to it, shall be the supreme law of the land.

CON – 5.B Explain how the exercise of judicial review in conjunction with life tenure can lead to controversy about the legitimacy of the Supreme Court's power.

- Judicial decision making in the United States is highly bound by precedents. That is to say that once the Court determines the meaning of a law or constitutional provision in one case, that interpretation can and should be used in other cases. This gives the law continuity and the judiciary legitimacy. When deciding cases in this manner, courts are said to be following the rule of *stare decisis*, which translates loosely as "let the decision stand." This tends to add predictability to the legal process.

- Changes in the composition of the Court can lead to different policy outcomes. The ideology of the members of the Court impact the decisions that are made and the opinions that explain those decisions. By changing the composition of the Court in appointing new members to fill vacancies, presidents have a profound influence on judicial policy making. The judicial term of office of life during good behavior insulates judges from political pressure. As such, they are to make decisions without the need to be concerned with reelection. However, many citizens question the right of the judiciary to act in a manner not in agreement with popular views. Congress and the president have several options in such situations.

  - The president can attempt to impact future decision making by the Court through the use of his or her appointment power. Congress can amend previous legislation if the Court has interpreted it in a manner inconsistent with the intent of Congress.

  - Congress can change the Court's jurisdiction, denying them the ability to hear similar cases in the future. This is known as jurisdiction stripping.

  - Once the Court has issued a decision, it is the job the of the executive to enforce it. However, if a president were to refuse to enforce it, there is nothing the Court can do.

- How judges make decisions can be a source of controversy, especially since they are insulated from accountability and public opinion. Judicial activism is a philosophy whereby a judge allows his or her views on public policy to impact the interpretation of existing law or precedence. Judicial restraint can be viewed as somewhat the opposite of this. Judges who believe in judicial restraint are less likely to inject their public policy views in to the judicial decision-making process. Further, they are more respectful of the importance of precedents and less likely to overturn legislation.

CON – 5.C Explain how other branches in the government can limit the Supreme Court's power.

- Congress can amend legislation that has been interpreted by the Court and, in effect, negate any precedent created by the Court in that case.

- Congress can propose by a two-thirds vote of both houses a constitutional amendment to counteract a Supreme Court decision. This proposed amendment would then need to be ratified by three-quarters of the states. The Eleventh, Fourteenth, Sixteenth, and Twenty-Sixth Amendments are examples of this.

- Perhaps the best way to regulate judicial decision making is with the appointment process. While not entirely effective, examining past decisions and political actions by a prospective judge is a fairly reliable way to predict future behavior. Presidents tend to nominate to the bench individuals who share their political beliefs. In recent years there have been increasing partisan struggles in the Senate for confirmation of judicial and other nominees.

- States and presidents can occasionally ignore judicial decisions that they find objectionable.

- The Constitution vests Congress with the power to restrict the jurisdiction of the court system.

Making Connections

A deeper understanding of the role of the judiciary in American society can be developed when it is viewed through the lens of the struggle for equality by various marginalized groups. You should be able to explain why these interest groups and social movements utilize the judiciary more so than they do the other policy-making institutions. This is covered in Chapter 5, Civil Rights.

Going Deeper: Noncompliance

One of the more interesting checks on the judiciary is noncompliance. What can the Court do to a president who ignores its decisions? The simple answer is nothing. The judiciary has no power to enforce its decisions. It must rely on the executive branch.

Could a president directly defy a Supreme Court decision today? The best answer is it would depend on the political situation. While the Court lacks the power of enforcement, Congress has the power of impeachment. If a president with a low approval rating directly defies a popular Supreme Court decision with the Congress controlled by the opposition party, the House of Representatives might begin the impeachment process.

However, if the circumstances were a little different, such as a popular president ignoring an unpopular decision with Congress being the same party of the president, it is doubtful that House would begin impeachment.

A more likely scenario is what is known as "foot dragging." In such a situation, a president would slowing and loosely enforce only some the provisions of the decision.

At the state and local level, governments can sometimes ignore judicial decisions until someone complains. For example, prayers at public high school athletic events and graduation ceremonies have been generally ruled to be an unconstitutional establishment of religion. However, in smaller communities they still occur. In this situation, elected local offices are reluctant to defy what might be widely supported by the community. In such a situation, litigation on the part of an aggrieved party would be necessary. Until such time as this occurs, the practice will continue.

16 Economic, Domestic, and Foreign Policy

AP® Learning Objectives

To perform well on the exam, students must understand how public policy engages and is informed by the concepts contained in the Curriculum Framework. This chapter on public policy provides students that opportunity.

Some of the learning objectives previously covered that apply here include:

CON – 2.A Explain how societal needs affect the constitutional allocation of power between the national and state governments.

CON – 3.A Describe the different structures, powers, and functions of each house of Congress.

CON – 4.A Explain how the president can implement a policy agenda.

CON – 4.B Explain how the president's agenda can create tension and frequent confrontations with Congress.

Performance task

- Citing specific examples, explain how the constitutionally created tension between the president and Congress works to create public policy in the U.S. political system.

Whittier College

"Our government is not designed for people who have fallen through the cracks."

"We will never solve homelessness. That's just a fact . . . But that doesn't mean we don't try."

MIGUEL SANTANA
Whittier College

Miguel Santana, currently the chief administrative officer for Los Angeles, California, is one of eight children whose parents emigrated from Mexico. His parents came to the United States without documentation but applied and received amnesty under a program established by the 1986 Immigration Reform and Control Act; he and all his siblings were born in the United States. Life experiences gave him perspective on how the government could help or hinder individuals who are trying to carve out lives in America.

Santana attended Whittier College, where he double-majored in sociology and Latin American studies and worked as a volunteer with the homeless. He subsequently got a job working with the Mexican American Legal Defense and Education Fund and then worked for L.A. County Supervisor Gloria Molina. He was able to take time off from that job to attend Harvard University to get a master's degree in public administration. He returned to Molina's office and then moved on to be deputy chief executive officer for Los Angeles County, which involved working with programs that served vulnerable populations such as children, individuals on public assistance, and veterans with special needs. All told, his portfolio included a budget close to $9 billion. Not only did Santana help manage large government budgets, he also had the opportunity to learn which programs were effective in carrying out the intent of specific policies and which programs needed an overhaul.

In 2009, Mayor Antonio Villaraigosa asked Santana to take the job of city administrator, which reports to both the mayor and the Los Angeles City Council. It would prove to be a challenging time to take the reins of the budget of Los Angeles, which is the main job of the city administrator. Los Angeles, like other cities at the time, was facing a budget deficit of nearly $500 million. Together with other city officials, Santana proposed unpopular budget cuts in services and public employee benefits, and eventually the city ended up on a sounder fiscal footing. He became a well-known figure in city politics, and when Villaraigosa left office, the new mayor, Eric Garcetti, asked Santana to stay on as city administrator.

Santana's volunteer work during his college years left him with a strong imprint and a desire to try to address the issue of homelessness. In his job with L.A. County, he implemented a program that sought out the least healthy among the homeless who were most vulnerable to chronic illness and gave them apartments and made sure they had consistent access to social services, which would keep them from returning to the streets without shelter or health care. Not only did it improve their lives, but it improved public policy by delivering services to those who needed them.

The issue also hit home for him, as he is a resident of downtown Los Angeles, which has experienced a recent rise in homelessness. Santana passed homeless people on his way to and from work every day, which made him realize that he had to take action that exceeded his job description. He sought more than $3 million in funds to help the homeless who were living in an area known as "skid row." A short time later, he issued a public report on the $100 million that Los Angeles spends on programs that serve the homeless and pointed out flaws in the way the city coordinated services as well as its dominant focus on law enforcement in its overall efforts to address the problem. While Santana recognizes that homelessness cannot be eradicated quickly, if ever, he refuses to give up on his commitment to making public policies more effective in this area.[1]

Throughout this text, we have learned about individuals from a wide range of backgrounds and have shown how they have transformed the policies that affect our daily lives. We have examined the minimum wage, fracking, gun control, the use of drones, the death penalty, and voter ID laws. In this chapter, we bring it all together and provide an in-depth description of the policy-making process in the domestic, economic, and foreign arenas. We look at how government interacts with the private sector in implementing domestic and economic policy as well as the effectiveness of foreign policy in promoting U.S. interests and security around the globe. A fundamental question for students of American government is whether public policy making serves as a gate or a gateway to effectively serving the people's interests.

16.1 Public Policy Under a Constitutional System

Outline the steps in the policy-making process

public policy: *Intentional actions of government designed to achieve a goal.*

Public policy can be described as the set of laws and regulations that govern American political and social life to meet a specific need and accomplish a goal. It is in the arena of public policy—in determining who gets what, when, and how, and with what result—that we can see whether the constitutional system created by Madison and the Framers really works. Can the people pursue policies that advance their own interests? Can the people's representatives, while pursuing policies that advance their constituents' interests, produce a nation that looks out for the welfare of all the people?

With a government deliberately designed to represent competing interests, public policy has tended to cycle. One argument gains favor, driving policy in one direction. But new problems arise, calling for a redirection of policy. In the early years of the American republic, for example, Congress raised tariffs (taxes on imports) to help support new manufacturing enterprises, which could then undersell foreign competitors. But when agricultural interests complained about having to pay high prices for foreign goods, Congress lowered tariffs. Banking policies were similarly adjusted, sometimes to favor debtors and other times to favor creditors.

The Process of Policy Making

The development of good public policy is always difficult and complex. A policy, for example, of providing tax benefits to homeowners to spur home ownership sounds like a good thing, as would policies that make it easier for people to obtain mortgages. It would help homeowners, support the home construction industry, and create jobs, building more stable communities. But what sounds simple rarely is that simple because there are usually unintended consequences. A policy of tax benefits for homeowners can also encourage sprawl that turns agricultural land into suburbs, thus decreasing crop yields and altering food production, while leaving cities with vacant housing and declining tax bases. Making it easier for people to obtain mortgages means more people default on their loans when the economy goes into a downturn, as happened during the most recent recession (2007–09). Subsequently, government responds to these new problems by developing additional policies to revitalize agriculture, urban infrastructure, and the banking system.

With so many competing interests and the potential for unintended negative consequences, government seeks to pursue policies that maximize benefits and minimize costs. This is not easy and often does not happen. Political scientists—scholars who study politics and the processes of government—have categorized the steps in policy making to make the process more understandable.

problem identification: *The first step in the policy-making process, in which a problem in politics, the economy, or society is recognized as warranting government action.*

The main stakeholders in the policy-making process include members of Congress, the president, the executive branch agency that deals with the issue, the courts, political parties, interest groups, and interested citizens. These stakeholders attempt to formulate a policy that will address the problem (see Figure 16.1).

Although presidents and members of Congress formally appear to be in command of the federal policy-making process, they face a complex set of gates standing in the way of implementing policy. In Chapter 3, Federalism, we explained how governmental powers are shared among the federal, state, and local governments. Frequently, policy changes at the federal level require cooperation from these other governmental units, and that can be a complicated task across all fifty states. Encouraging all the states to adopt the same policy is not always possible; the federal government may need to step in and implement the policy itself. In this chapter, we discuss economic, domestic, and foreign policy and show how public policy is an outcome of all the actions taken by a wide array of stakeholders at the federal, state, and local levels.

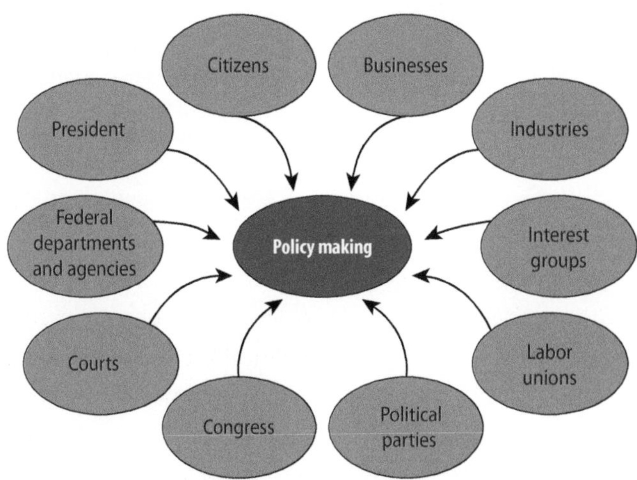

FIGURE 16.1 Stakeholders in the Policy-Making Process

The U.S. policy-making process includes people and groups with a wide range of different interests, ranging from the president to average citizens.

The first step is **problem identification**. For example, constituents might complain to members of Congress that the cost of college is too high. The second step is for the issue of the cost of higher education to make it to the **policy agenda** of policy makers.[2] Of all the problems that government might be able to solve, only a small fraction can receive attention at any one time. Those that make it onto the policy agenda get the attention of Congress, the president, the executive branch agency that deals with the issue, the courts, political parties, interest groups, and interested citizens. These stakeholders attempt **policy formulation** that will solve the problem. In the example of the high cost of college, the stakeholder network considered three proposals: direct federal loans to college students; promoting private loans by paying banks the interest on student loans while the student is in college; and guaranteeing the loans if students are unable to repay them.

In a fourth step, **policy enactment**, the legislative branch passes a law that enacts one or more of those proposals, as Congress did with student loans in 2010. Following passage, the legislature grants the executive branch **policy implementation** authority over the program. In this case, the Department of Education was given the authority to direct the student loan program. After a few years, Congress may engage in **policy evaluation** of the program. Following this policy evaluation, the cycle of policy making might begin again with new legislation to adjust the program to make it work better (see Figure 16.2).

In this chapter, we will focus on domestic, economic, and foreign policies. In each of these domains, the stakeholders mentioned earlier wield influence in different ways, depending on the characteristics of the issue being considered. In most cases, the origins of an implemented policy start with Congress when it passes a law and the president approves it (discussed in more depth in Chapter 12, Congress). But in other cases, the president can use his executive regulatory power to effect change without a new congressional law, or Congress can decide to change funding allocations for specific programs in order to slow down or prevent their implementation. In the next section, we will examine more closely this second method of policy implementation.

Essential Knowledge

There are several agenda setters in American politics, such as the president and the media.

policy agenda: *The second step in the policy-making process, in which a problem that has been identified gets the attention of policy makers.*

policy formulation: *The third step in the policy-making process, in which those with a stake in the policy area propose and develop solutions to the problem.*

policy enactment: *The fourth step in the policy-making process, in which Congress passes a law that authorizes a specific governmental response to the problem.*

policy implementation: *The fifth step in the policy-making process, in which the executive branch develops the rules that will put the policy into action.*

policy evaluation: *The final step in the policy-making process, in which the policy is evaluated for its effectiveness and efficiency; if changes are needed, the issue is placed back on the policy agenda, and the cycle starts again.*

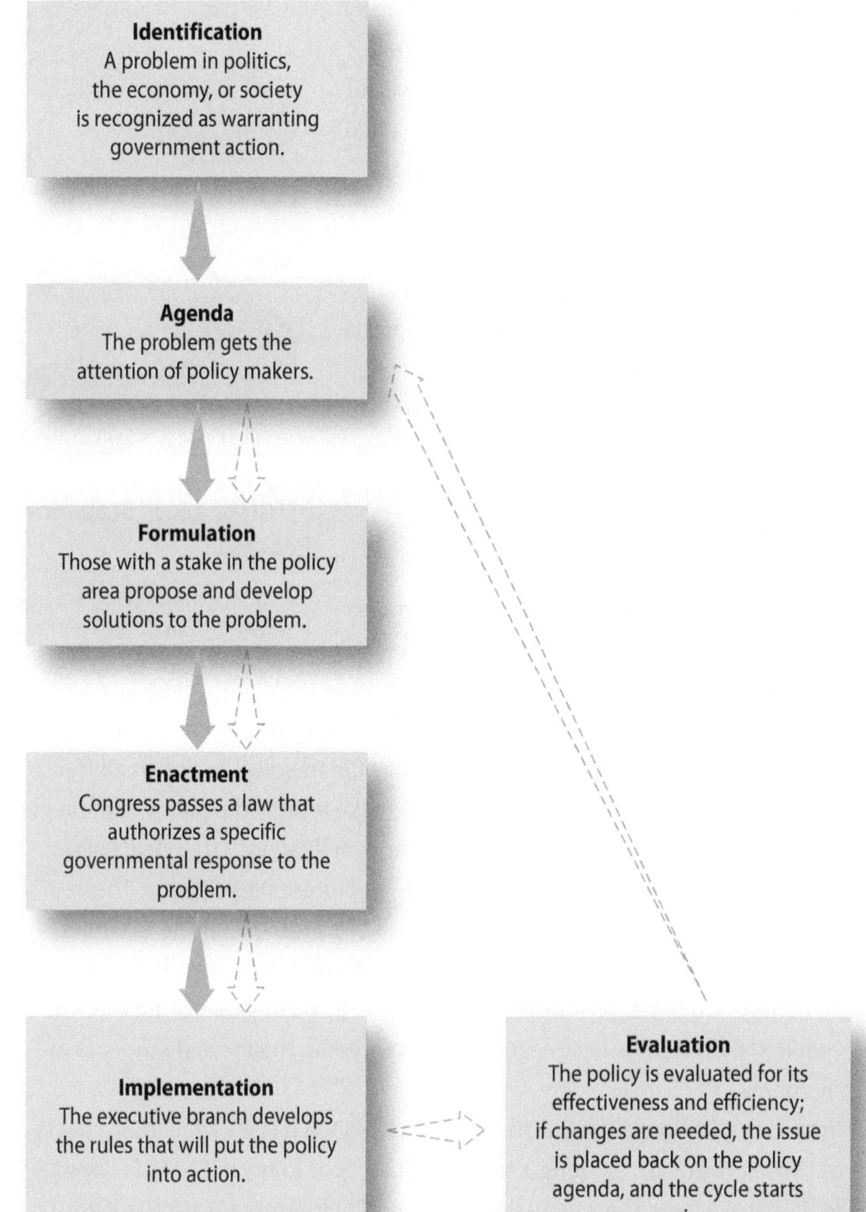
Identification
A problem in politics, the economy, or society is recognized as warranting government action.
Agenda
The problem gets the attention of policy makers.
Formulation
Those with a stake in the policy area propose and develop solutions to the problem.
Enactment
Congress passes a law that authorizes a specific governmental response to the problem.
Implementation
The executive branch develops the rules that will put the policy into action.
Evaluation
The policy is evaluated for its effectiveness and efficiency; if changes are needed, the issue is placed back on the policy agenda, and the cycle starts again.

Essential Knowledge

Congress has delegated policy-making power to the bureaucracy. It makes policy through the issuance of regulations.

Essential Knowledge

The OMB assists the president in the supervision of the bureaucracy. Even with assistance this agency, monitoring the bureaucracy is a challenge.

FIGURE 16.2 The Public Policy-Making Process

The process by which policy is made has six major steps: identification, agenda, formulation, enactment, implementation, and evaluation.

regulatory process: *System of rules that guide how a law is implemented; also called the rule-making process.*

The Regulatory Process

regulations: *Guidelines issued by federal agencies for administering federal programs and implementing federal law.*

For laws to be implemented, there must be rules to instruct policy makers, government officials, organizations, and businesses. The formal responsibility for policy implementation falls to the bureaucracy in what is commonly called the **regulatory process** (see Figure 16.3). The current framework for the regulatory process has its foundation in the Administrative Procedures Act that Congress passed in 1946 to provide a consistent blueprint for all federal agencies in the issuing of regulations.

The federal government typically issues regulations when a law is first enacted and when a new circumstance or policy need arises that requires updates to the way the law is implemented. One such circumstance might be a change in the political control of the White House. Frequently, an incoming president of a different party issues new regulations to reverse the previous administration's policies. More commonly, a new president instructs federal agencies and the Office of Management and Budget (OMB), which oversees budgetary and regulatory issues, to revise existing regulations to better reflect his policy preferences. For example, in September 2015, President Obama issued an executive order requiring private contractors doing business with the federal government to offer paid sick leave to the men and women whom they employ.

The bureaucracy produces these regulations by working within a process that begins with identifying the agency that has jurisdiction. The agency in charge will then offer preliminary **regulations**, and the political appointees of the agency will determine whether they are in line with the president's policy views. Although the bureaucracy is theoretically supposed to be insulated from direct political pressure, the reality is that the president's policy preferences are considered during this process.

When there is some agreement on the content of the preliminary regulations, they are submitted to the Office of Information and Regulatory Affairs within the OMB for approval to be printed in the ***Federal Register***, the official published record of all executive branch rules, regulations, and orders. As noted previously, the OMB must review all regulations before they take effect. When preliminary regulations appear in the *Federal Register*, a period for public comment is defined (typically outlined in the originating legislation) ranging from thirty to ninety days. During this period, ordinary citizens, interest groups, and relevant industries and businesses can submit their opinions to the agency about the regulations. In addition, the agency or its local affiliate can hold public hearings in locations across the country to solicit opinions on the regulations.

Based on all the responses it receives, the responsible agency revises the preliminary draft regulations and issues final regulations. These are once again sent to the OMB and then are published in the *Federal Register* thirty days in advance of taking formal effect. Once the final regulations are issued, the program is officially ready to be implemented. A current example of this process concerns the disposal of coal ash from coal-burning power plants. After a major coal ash spill into local rivers and streams in Tennessee, environmental groups pushed the Environmental Protection Agency (EPA) to issue new regulations outlining the requirements for safe coal ash disposal. The preliminary regulations were issued in October 2009, but after the public comment period was up, the EPA still had not issued final regulations. In response, environmental groups, led by Earthjustice, sued the EPA, and a judge forced the agency to agree to issue the final regulations by December 19, 2014, which it did. Only a few days later, a second major coal ash spill occurred in North Carolina, adding more pressure for the EPA to act in a timely manner.[3] It was not until October 19, 2015, however, that the EPA regulations on safe coal ash disposal took effect. Such extreme delays in issuing and implementing final regulations are not typical, but this example shows how the regulatory process itself can act as a gate to effective oversight of industry and environmental protection.

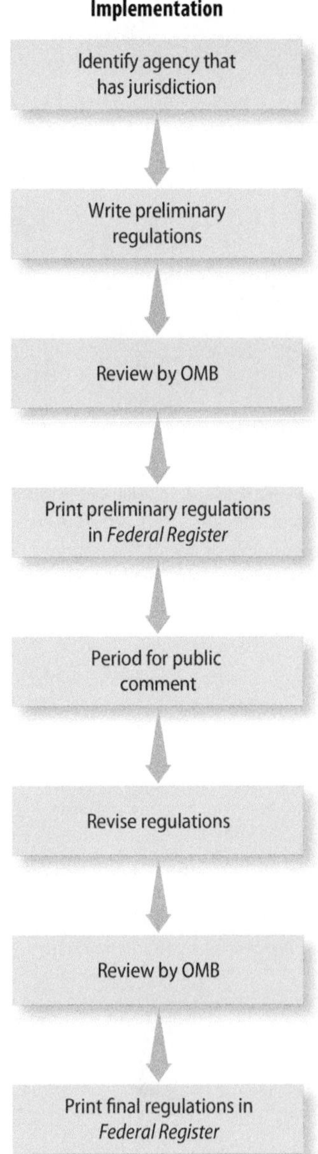

FIGURE 16.3 The Regulatory Process

After policies are enacted, they need to be implemented and regulated under a structure that is overseen by the Office of Management and Budget (OMB). This figure outlines the regulatory process from start to finish.

Federal Register: *Official published record of all executive branch rules, regulations, and orders.*

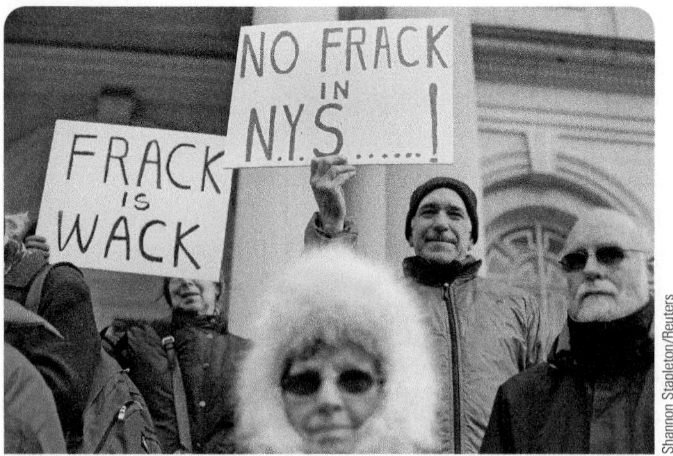

IMAGE 16.1 Public comments are a vital part of the regulatory process because they are a gateway by which citizens can communicate their opinions about the impact of policy to regulators. Here residents of communities affected by fracking offer their comments on proposed regulations to the Environmental Protection Agency.

Blocking Implementation

Even after final regulations are issued, groups can challenge the legality of them in the federal court system. For example, in 2016, the Supreme Court considered a challenge to regulations issued requiring the inclusion of contraception in employer-sponsored health insurance plans under the Affordable Care Act (ACA). The case, *Zubik v. Burwell*, involved the Little Sisters of the Poor; this religious group refused the ACA's accommodation, which only required it to notify the government that the ACA violated its religious views. In April 2016, in the wake of a likely 4–4 split, the Court asked for more briefs so that a compromise could be reached. In addition to court action, the House or Senate can pass appropriations bills with language that prevents an agency or department from using federal money to implement the regulations. However, the president typically threatens to veto the bill if this type of language is included because it undermines his policy priorities and, more broadly, his executive power to implement laws. As a result, legislative leaders usually remove such language in the final version of appropriations bill sent to the president (see Chapter 12 for more on the appropriations process).

State Governments and Public Policy

As we noted in Chapter 3, it is important to understand how the federal government interacts with state governments in implementing policy and, at the same time, how states interact with each other. In this section, we will take a closer look at how states can influence each other through processes referred to as policy diffusion and the race to the bottom.

Policy Diffusion. In a 1932 opinion, Supreme Court Justice Louis Brandeis wrote, "It is one of the happy incidents of the federal system that a single courageous State may, if its citizens choose, serve as a laboratory; and try novel social and economic experiments without risk to the rest of the country."[4] As far back as the Revolutionary era, New Jersey experimented with women's suffrage, as did several western states at the end of the nineteenth century. Nebraska has a unicameral legislature, and Wisconsin experimented with an unemployment insurance program in the 1920s. A little more than a decade later, the federal government created a national unemployment insurance program. More recently, four states have legalized the use of recreational marijuana, and at least another dozen states have legal medical marijuana. When one state adopts a policy and then other states follow, such policy adoption at the state level often encourages the federal government to see the benefits of such policies as well.

The main benefit of states serving as laboratories of change is that other states can learn about successful programs and copy them or learn what not to do if an experimental program fails. This takes place through a process known as **policy diffusion**, and it typically starts with states that border one another. Examples are numerous, including the Children's Health Insurance Program,[5] regulation of air pollution,[6] school choice plans (allowing students to choose which school in a district to attend),[7] health care reform,[8] and Native American

policy diffusion: *Process by which policy ideas and programs initiated by one state spread to other states.*

casinos.[9] States learn not only from neighboring states but also from their local governments. Such was the case with antismoking ordinances, which cities and towns successfully adopted before states did, and currently, localities are adopting higher minimum wage laws before entire states are doing so.[10]

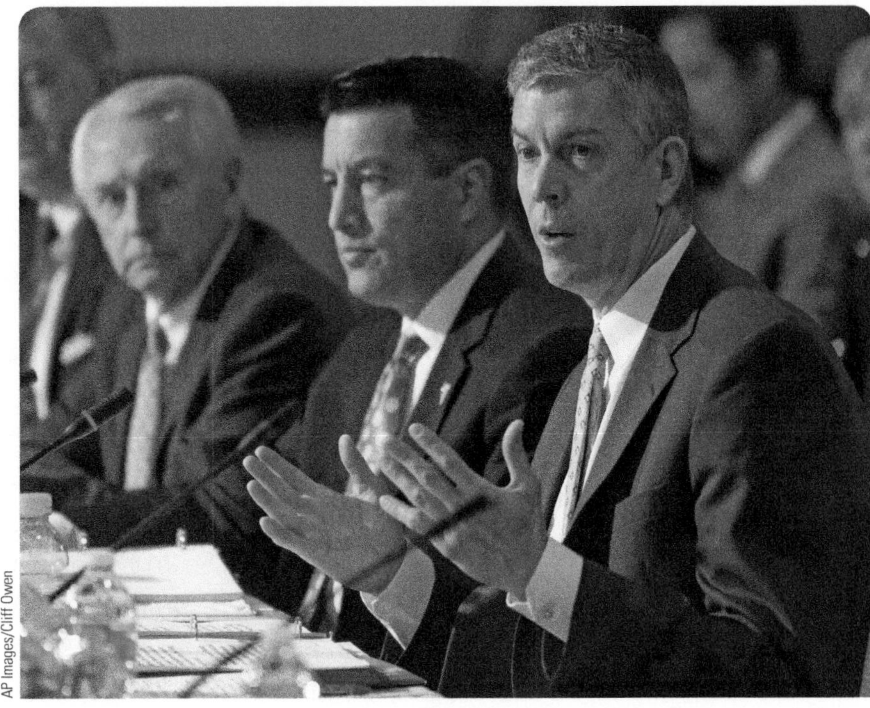

AP Images/Cliff Owen

IMAGE 16.2 The federal system of government requires cooperation between the national and state governments, and federal policy is frequently implemented by state governments. Here governors meet with then-Secretary of Education Arne Duncan, right, to discuss proposed changes to federal educational guidelines during a meeting of the National Governors Association.

The Race to the Bottom. If diffusion is the good side of policy making in a federal system, the race to the bottom can, depending on one's point of view, potentially involve negative consequences. A race to the bottom exists when states compete against each other to reduce taxes, environmental protections, or welfare benefits in order to create incentives for businesses to come to the state or disincentives for poor people to come. For example, lower tax rates draw people to a state, yet to keep people there, the state cannot raise taxes even when the public might desire more spending.[11] When states compete economically with one another, if one state decreases environmental enforcement, a neighboring state may be forced to do so as well.[12] In terms of welfare benefits, individuals seeking benefits move to the most generous states. This situation led states to establish residency requirements for welfare until the Supreme Court prohibited them.[13] Consequently, states that want to increase welfare benefits for their own citizens hesitate to do so unless neighboring states also do so, lest they attract an overload of recipients from those other states.[14] Alternatively, the Obama administration established a "Race to the Top" in education, whereby states that implement education reforms, such as increasing the number of charter schools, receive more federal aid. This action coincides with increasing federal involvement in education over the past fifty years.

16.2 Domestic Policy

Identify the key federal programs that make up domestic policy

The term "domestic policy" covers a wide range of policy areas in which the government plays a role, at the federal, state, and local levels, in the lives of average citizens. Table 16.1 lists the major federal programs generally considered under the category of domestic policy, when they were enacted into law at the federal level, and a brief description of what they do.

TABLE 16.1 Major Federal Programs

Names	Year	Description
Social Security	1935	Old-age retirement insurance program that pays a monthly amount to retired workers
Unemployment Insurance	1935	Temporary replacement income for job loss
Social Security Disability Insurance	1935	Payments to individuals who can no longer work due to disability
Supplemental Security Income	1972	Subsidy for low-income individuals who are over 65, blind, or disabled
Medicare	1965	Health care insurance for the elderly and disabled
Medicaid	1965	Health care insurance for low-income individuals
Temporary Aid to Needy Families	1935	Subsidy for low-income individuals with children; originally known as Aid to Families with Dependent Children but replaced in 1996 by TANF
Food Stamps	1964	Subsidy for low-income individuals for food purchase
Public Housing Assistance	1937	Subsidy for low-income individuals for housing
Immigration and Nationality Act	1952	Laws governing documented entry and citizenship into the United States
Clean Air Act	1963/ 1970	Laws requiring minimum standards for air quality; amended in 1970 to create the Environmental Protection Agency
Clean Water Act	1972	Regulations for the discharge of potential contaminants into water sources
Medicare Prescription Drug Act	2003	Expanded Medicare to provide insurance coverage for prescription drugs for the elderly and disabled
Affordable Care Act	2010	Mandate that requires every individual to have health insurance coverage and provides access and subsidies through exchanges and expanded Medicaid

Throughout the book, we have covered major issues in domestic policy, including public education (see Chapter 3), affirmative action (Chapter 15, The Judiciary), and workplace equality (Chapter 5, Civil Rights). In this chapter, we explore three major areas of domestic policy that are sparking intense debate today: entitlement programs, income security, and health care; immigration; and energy and environmental policy. In each of these issue areas, we will provide an overview of public policy and analyze an example of how a specific policy has been crafted and implemented (see the Public Policy features).

Entitlement Programs, Income Security, and Health Care

Social Security: *Federal pension program that makes a monthly payment to retired elderly workers and disabled persons.*

During the twentieth century, the federal government enacted laws to create a social safety net to provide income stability for the elderly and disabled, and assistance with food, health care, and housing for the poor. **Social Security** is one of the largest and likely best-known federal domestic policy programs; it is essentially a federally guaranteed pension program funded by taxes imposed by employers and workers. Social Security was created in 1935 as part of the set of policy programs known as the New Deal proposed by President Franklin Delano Roosevelt (1933–45; see Chapter 13, The Presidency). The New Deal represented a major change in the relationship between the federal government and individuals by establishing a set of programs that would guarantee payment to an individual if he or she met certain criteria (for example, age, children, low income, or disability). This type of program is commonly known as an **entitlement program**, which means that individuals are "entitled" to receive the benefit as long as they qualify under these criteria. The passage of the Social Security Act marked the beginning of the transformation of the role of the federal and state governments in providing a social safety net for individuals in need of financial assistance as well as aid to secure food, housing, and health care.

entitlement programs: *Federal programs, such as Social Security, Medicare, or Medicaid, that pay out benefits for individuals based on a specified set of eligibility criteria.*

Social Security itself is a mandatory retirement account for all workers that is funded by taxes paid by both employers and workers. The amount of Social Security retired workers receive is calculated based on the amount of time they worked while paying into the program; when they retire, they receive a monthly payment directly from the federal government. The drive to provide this kind of income security for individuals was in large part a response to the dire effects of the Great Depression, which left millions of people without jobs and income. At the same time, the federal government created Unemployment Insurance, which is run by state governments according to federal guidelines; it provides short-term payments to workers who lose their jobs and is funded by taxes imposed on employers.

In addition to these programs, which are targeted at the working population, the Social Security Act of 1935 and its subsequent legislative expansions have created several other programs that are designed to help individuals who need assistance supporting themselves or their families. Two of these, Social Security Disability Insurance and Supplemental Security Insurance, are designed to help those who are no longer able to work or who have a disability that prevents them from working full time. Another major program is Temporary Aid to Needy Families (TANF), which is a program to provide payments to women in poverty with children (it was originally called Aid to Families with Dependent Children). The majority of this program's costs are funded by the federal government through a single amount of funding per year, known as a block grant, although states are expected to contribute a minimum amount of money to help administer the program.

Essential Knowledge

The national government can influence state policy making through block grants, categorical grants, and mandates.

In addition to income security, as part of the New Deal, the federal government also put in place sets of programs to help individuals get mortgages to buy houses through the Fannie Mae Corporation and to build affordable housing by offering subsidies to developers. These programs were aimed at helping people buy houses because that was believed to help ensure financial stability and help the economy through new housing construction.[15]

In the 1960s, under President Johnson's Great Society initiative (see Chapter 13), these types of income security programs were expanded to include health care, food security, and expanded housing assistance. In terms of health care, **Medicare** was created as a federal program, funded through a payroll tax that provided health insurance to people over the age of 65. **Medicaid** was created as a shared program between the federal and state governments, funded through general taxation, to provide health care coverage for low-income people.[16] The Food Stamp Program, today known as the Supplemental Nutritional Assistance Program, was designed to provide money to low-income families to purchase food and household items and is fully funded through general taxation.

Medicare: *Federal health insurance program for the elderly and disabled.*

Medicaid: *Shared federal and state health insurance program for low-income persons.*

Lastly, federal housing assistance was expanded under the Section 8 program to provide payments to housing developers to cover the rental costs of housing for low-income individuals, who typically must pay a minimum of $25 or 30 percent of their income toward rent under the program.[17]

It has been nearly eighty years since the passage of the Social Security Act, and the federal government has expanded many of the programs the act first established, but not without controversy and opposition. When the act was passed, opponents claimed it was an overreach of federal power to take money from individuals only to give it back to them in their later years. Moreover, establishing other anti-poverty subsidies that would be paid directly to lower-income individuals might create a dependency on that payment that would discourage them from securing independent financial security. Lastly, opponents of expanding the role of the federally guaranteed safety net have argued that as the population expands and lives longer, the cost of these programs is unsustainable; for example, Social Security alone accounted for 24 percent ($888 billion) of the FY 2015 federal budget.[18] The federal bureaucracy, specifically the Department of Health and Human Services (HHS), is largely responsible for administering these programs in conjunction with state and local government. We provide a brief overview of HHS in Chapter 14, The Bureaucracy, but here we embed it in the larger context of the expansion of the federal role in health care over the past decade. The most recent such expansion came with the ACA, which was enacted in 2010 and requires all individuals to purchase health insurance, either on their own or, if they are low income, with subsidies from the federal government. When the ACA was enacted, there were approximately 44 million Americans without access to health insurance coverage.[19] In 2016, 20 million of those formerly uninsured people had access to health insurance through the ACA. Moreover, some of the largest gains in health insurance coverage from the ACA are among Latinos and African Americans.[20]

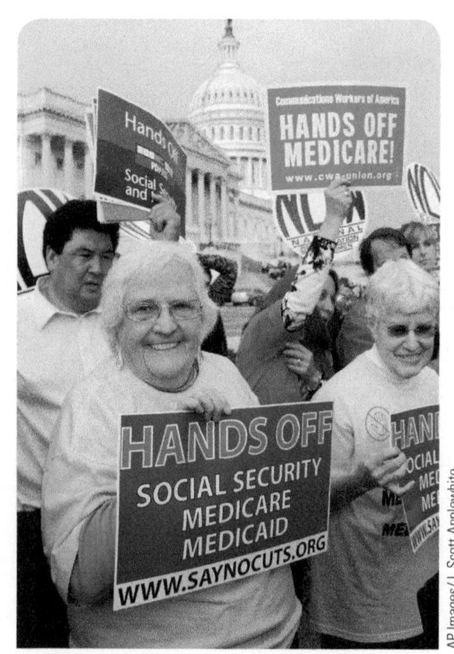

AP Images/J. Scott Applewhite

IMAGE 16.3 Senior citizens who are recipients of Social Security and Medicare are very vocal in seeking to protect their benefits. This group of elderly activists traveled to Capitol Hill in Washington, D.C., to oppose proposed cuts to those programs.

The American health care system includes private and public health care insurance components. Most Americans receive health insurance through their employment or purchase it independently from private insurance companies; as noted previously, federal programs are available to help cover the costs of health insurance. At the federal level, HHS is responsible for overseeing these programs, as well as implementing new ones. Each state also has a department of health, as do many cities and counties; importantly, states also have the power to regulate insurance providers who provide coverage there.

The process by which the ACA (otherwise known as Obamacare) moved from proposal to bill to law was long and winding, as lawmaking always is, and it was especially complicated because of the fragmented nature of America's health care system, party politics and partisanship, and the heightened political rhetoric that surrounded the effort (see Chapter 12). Ultimately, the Democrats used their majority party power in the House and Senate to pass the law, with no Republican support.

The primary impetus of the law was to provide access to health insurance to the nearly 10 percent of Americans who did not have it. They did not have health insurance for a range of reasons: their employer did not offer it; they were self-employed and could not afford to purchase it; they were unemployed but not poor or old enough to qualify for a government program; or they were deemed ineligible by private insurance companies because they had health conditions that made them high risk and expensive to cover.[21]

The Affordable Care Act (ACA)

The ACA established a number of new programs, the most notable of which extended access to health insurance coverage to uninsured citizens and legal immigrants through an expansion of Medicaid eligibility and the provision of federal subsidies to workers to purchase private health insurance through health insurance exchanges that would be set up by states or, if the states refused, by the federal government directly.[22] The act provided for increased regulation of the medical services covered by private health insurance companies, mandated that individuals carry health insurance, required that young adults under the age of 26 be able to stay on a parent's insurance policy, and banned the denial of health insurance or an increase in premiums based on a preexisting condition. The act also increased payment levels to doctors who participate in the Medicaid program and helped senior citizens by closing a loophole in Medicare coverage for prescription drugs. The ACA is an important example of how the domestic policy process works, from the passage of the law to its implementation.

The implementation of the act came in stages, with some of the regulations issued very soon after the bill passed and others taking much longer to finalize. Part of the delay was attributable to a key lawsuit filed against the bill claiming that some of its provisions were unconstitutional. Twenty-six state attorneys general signed on to a lawsuit challenging the constitutionality of the federal health insurance mandate included in the law. The lawsuit made its way to the Supreme Court, which upheld the mandate in 2012 (see Chapter 12).

The Court case cleared the way for implementation of the insurance provision through health care exchanges under ACA. However, only fourteen states set up their own health insurance exchanges; the federal government established exchanges in the remaining thirty-six states. The ACA also encouraged states to expand Medicaid to cover individuals at or below 138 percent of the poverty level because the federal government paid the extra costs of the expansion for up to three years. As of September 2016, thirty-one states agreed to the Medicaid expansion and nineteen states refused it.[23] Additionally, individuals at 100 to 400 percent of the poverty level are eligible for subsidies (the federal government will pay part of their premiums).[24] Traditionally underserved communities, such as Latinos, are estimated to comprise nearly 25 percent of those eligible for coverage under ACA, and the Obama administration made it a point to engage in targeted outreach to encourage them to enroll.[25] As we noted above, the ACA has enabled significant expansion of health care coverage in these communities.

The dynamics surrounding the ACA reflect the complexity of implementing health care policy for millions of Americans across states. The ACA brings up the larger question of whether major policy overhauls can be accomplished without bipartisan support in the American federalism structure because states are so vital in the implementation process. Without their full cooperation, it becomes much more difficult for a federal program to succeed.

Immigration Policy

Another very important and often contentious issue in the public policy sphere is immigration policy—for both legal and unauthorized immigration. The Department of Homeland Security, the Department of Justice, and the Department of State share jurisdiction over immigration policy. Immigration has fueled U.S. population growth since the nation's founding, and the United States now comprises citizens with ancestries from many different foreign lands. The most recent data available indicate that there are 13.1 million legal permanent residents in the United States—people born outside of the United States who have been granted legal status and reside in the United States.[26] The largest percentage of foreign-born people come from Latin America (mostly Mexico), followed by Asia and then Europe. Immigration laws serve simultaneously as gates regulating entry into the United States and as gateways to eventual citizenship. For those individuals who entered the United States without authorization and have put down roots, there is no current pathway to legal citizenship available. However, children who are born to unauthorized immigrants living in the United States are legal citizens because of the Fourteenth Amendment to the Constitution.

The Legal Immigration Process. The legal immigration process is jointly administered by the Department of State and the U.S. Citizenship and Immigration Services (USCIS), an agency of the Department of Homeland Security. Immigrants seeking to come to the United States apply for visas, which are granted by the Department of State; once they arrive, their journey toward citizenship is overseen by USCIS.[27]

To come to the United States with the intention of staying on a permanent basis, individuals can apply for a general immigration visa, a family relations visa, or an employment visa. The Immigration and Nationality Act of 1990 sets an annual limit of between 416,000 and 675,000 on these types of visas; in addition, 50,000 visas are set aside for people born in countries that have recently had the lowest numbers of immigrants to the United States.[28] In 2014, 481,392 individuals entered the United States as legal permanent residents.[29]

To become a naturalized citizen, an immigrant must first apply to be a legal permanent resident of the United States, a step known as getting a green card, which is the permanent resident card issued to those who are eligible. (The green card is no longer green, but the name has remained.) To get a green card, an individual must secure a sponsor who will attest that the individual has some means of financial support. The individual must also take a medical exam and secure proof of employment if he or she intends to hold a job in the United States. This criterion can present a significant barrier to permanent residency: The federal government requires an individual seeking permanent residence to have talents or skills for a particular job that a current U.S. citizen could not provide. Marriage to an American citizen can also serve as a gateway to a green card, although the federal government has imposed stricter oversight on such marriages to counteract fraud. In 2013, the federal government also extended this gateway to apply to same-sex marriages, in response to a Supreme Court ruling that struck down discrimination against same-sex partners under federal law.[30] To become a fully naturalized U.S. citizen, a green card holder must reside in the United States continuously for at least five years; be able to read, write, and speak English; pass a citizenship test on the history and government of the United States (see Chapter 5); and pledge support for the United States.[31]

The Debate over Unauthorized Immigration. In recent years, pressure to reform immigration laws to address the issue of unauthorized immigration has mounted because of the millions of individuals who have entered the United States outside the legal immigration process.[32] Proponents of reform argue that individuals who arrived illegally but have since established productive lives should be legally incorporated into society and have the opportunity to be full and active citizens, a position that opponents refer to as "amnesty." Opponents tend to counter-argue that individuals who broke the law to enter the United States must be forced to return to their country of origin and apply for legal immigration status, and that without stronger border security, the hope of amnesty will just drive greater unauthorized immigration. The Republican and Democratic Parties are split along these lines as well; Democrats are stronger supporters of immigration reform that includes a gateway to amnesty and citizenship, while Republicans typically support a stronger border enforcement program with no amnesty and no gateway to citizenship.

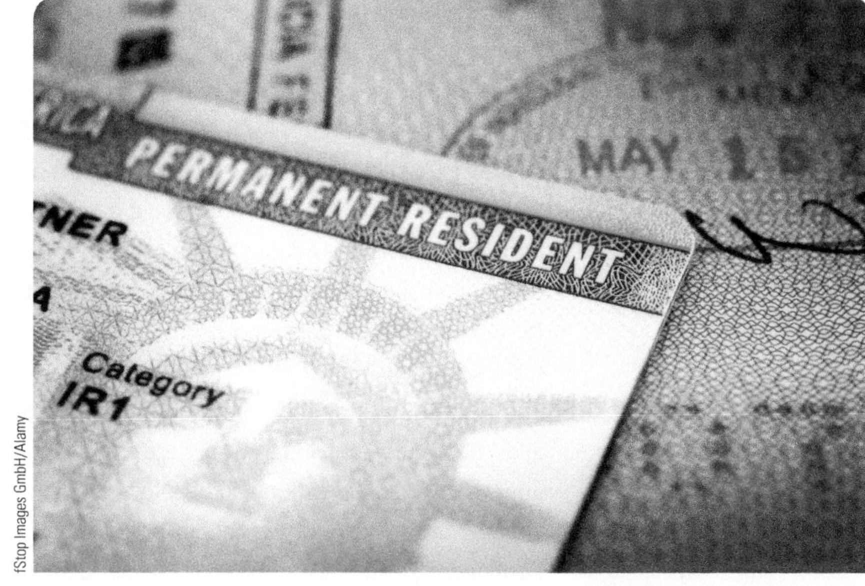

fStop Images GmbH/Alamy

IMAGE 16.4 "Green card" is a commonly used term for the legal document that authorizes an immigrant to live in the United States as a permanent resident and makes him or her eligible to become a naturalized citizen.

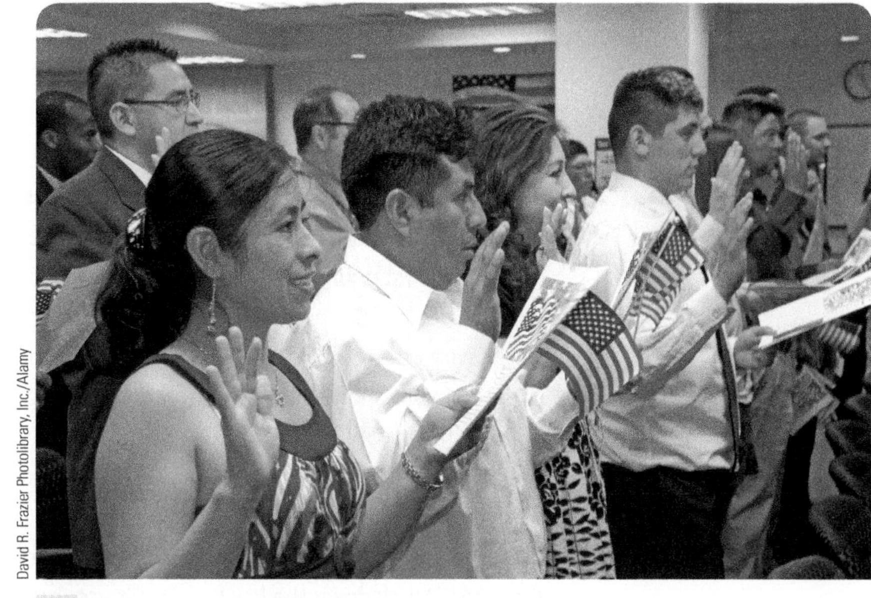

David R. Frazier Photolibrary, Inc./Alamy

IMAGE 16.5 An immigrant goes through a long and complex process to become a naturalized U.S. citizen. In this photo, immigrants who have come from many different nations are sworn in as U.S. citizens.

The last law that was enacted to specifically address unauthorized immigration was the 1986 Immigration Reform and Control Act, which passed with bipartisan support and was signed into law by President Ronald Reagan (1981–89). The act granted amnesty, or forgiveness, to almost 2.8 million individuals who had entered the country without authorization and wished to stay as legal residents.[33] The 1986 reform bill did not stem the flow of unauthorized immigrants to the United States. In 2007, President George W. Bush (2001–09), a Republican, and the Democratic-controlled Congress tried to produce a new immigration reform bill that would give unauthorized immigrants who were already in the United States an opportunity to become citizens but would, at the same time, discourage future unauthorized immigration. They failed to reach agreement.

One reform bill that gained traction was the Development, Relief, and Education for Alien Minors proposal, known as the DREAM Act, which would allow children who entered the country illegally with their parents to get on a path to legal citizenship at age 16 if they have been in the country for five years, have graduated from high school, and have no criminal record.[34] In his first term, President Obama announced his support for the DREAM Act. By June 2012, Congress had not passed it, so, using his authority over border control and national security, President Obama ordered the Department of Homeland Security to stop deporting young people who met the criteria of the DREAM Act and to allow them to apply for temporary work permits. Although it did not create a full path to citizenship, President Obama's action did partially implement the policy goals of the DREAM Act.[35]

In 2014, President Obama went further when he announced a program that would allow parents of individuals who were citizens by birth or legal permanent residents to apply to avoid deportation and be allowed to submit applications for work permits in the United States. The plan was called Deferred Action for Parents of Americans and Lawful Permanent Residents. Before the plan could be fully implemented, Texas sued in federal court to stop the program, arguing that President Obama had exerted authority that was constitutionally held by Congress; twenty-five other states joined in the lawsuit.[36] The case, *United States v. Texas*, made it all the way to the Supreme Court, which in June 2016 upheld the lower court decision stating that President Obama's orders went beyond his executive authority.

Local and Federal Action on Unauthorized Immigration. States and localities, especially those along the border with Mexico, have tried to address unauthorized immigration in their own ways and in opposite policy directions. States with Republican-dominated legislatures have taken more punitive action than those controlled by Democrats. The most publicized effort took place in Arizona, where in April 2010 then-Governor Jan Brewer signed a law, S.B. 1070, that allowed police officers to ask about immigration status when they stopped individuals for any other police inquiry. Under the law, it was a crime to fail to show documentation establishing legal residence in the United States, and police officers could hold someone until their immigration status was verified.[37] Later that year, the U.S. Justice Department sued to get the law struck down in federal court on the basis that the state was infringing on the proper role of the federal government on immigration. The case made its way to the Supreme Court in 2012, and in *Arizona v. United States*, the court struck down the law because it assumed state powers over immigration that are granted to the federal government.

The state of Alabama also enacted a law that not only allowed police officers to inquire about immigration status but also required local schools to report on the number of students enrolled who were unauthorized immigrants and prohibited any business in Alabama from doing business with unauthorized immigrants. Reaction to this law was mixed, inside and outside of Alabama. Community groups, immigrant advocates, and businesses all complained that it was too strict and was hurting the Alabama economy because unauthorized immigrants were too frightened to leave their homes.[38] The federal government and activist groups sued to overturn the law; as in the case of Arizona, the federal courts struck down most of the provisions of the law, and their decision was upheld by the Supreme Court, which refused to hear Alabama's appeal.

SUPREME COURT CASES

Arizona v. United States (2012)

QUESTION: Does the supremacy clause prevent the state of Arizona from supplementing federal immigration law?

ORAL ARGUMENT: April 25, 2012 (listen at http://www.oyez.org/cases/2010-2019/2011/2011_11_182)

DECISION: Decided June 25, 2012 (read at http://caselaw.lp.findlaw.com/scripts/getcase.pl?court=US&vol=000&invol=11-182)

OUTCOME: 5–3. The Supreme Court struck down three restrictions in the law.

As noted in Chapter 3, the national government has only those powers granted to it in the Constitution. While the remaining powers remain with the states, the supremacy clause declares that where federal and state laws conflict, federal law is supreme.

In response to a large influx of undocumented persons across the border with Mexico into Arizona, the Arizona state legislature passed S.B. 1070. The United States believed that the law encroached on federal power to regulate immigration and sought to prohibit enforcement of its provisions. A federal district court found four provisions to be beyond the constitutional authority of Arizona to regulate: (1) creating a state-law crime for being unlawfully present in the United States, (2) creating a state-law crime for working or seeking work while not authorized to do so, (3) requiring state and local officers to verify the citizenship or alien status of anyone who was lawfully arrested or detained, and (4) authorizing warrantless arrests of aliens believed to be removable from the United States.

All eight of the justices hearing the case (Justice Kagan did not participate due to her prior work on issues related to the case while in the Justice Department) agreed that the provision requiring local police officers to check the immigration status of anyone lawfully arrested was constitutional. With Justices Scalia, Thomas, and Alito dissenting in part, a majority of the justices held that the rest of the provisions violated the supremacy clause given Congress's regulation of the subject.

The Court, in an opinion by Justice Kennedy, held that the Constitution's grant to Congress to "establish an uniform Rule of Naturalization," combined with Congress's extensive regulation of immigration, deprives states of the authority to: (1) make it illegal under state law for people to enter the United States without legal documentation, (2) make it illegal under state law for people without proper documentation to find employment, or (3) allow warrantless arrests of people believed to be in the United States without proper documentation. In all three provisions, the Court ruled that Congress's regulation of those facets of immigration was so extensive that states were "preempted" from adding to those regulations.

Thinking Critically

1. Why do you think the Arizona legislature might have passed the law in question?
2. Do you think any of the Arizona provisions were in fact unconstitutional (that is, they would be invalid even if Congress had not extensively regulated the areas in question)?

Not all state responses to unauthorized immigration have been punitive. For example, California, Texas, and New Mexico each adopted policies that allow unauthorized immigrants to receive private and public aid to attend state colleges and universities. Their justification is that it is better to educate residents who are in the United States so that they can contribute to society than it is to put up gates against their educational and economic advancements.

Ultimately it will be a major challenge for policy makers in both major political parties to construct a holistic immigration policy that is both fair and practical. Although there is general agreement within the core membership of each party, there are enough dissenting voices on how best to cope with illegal immigration that a clear policy position may not emerge. One factor that might affect the future of immigration reform is the growing number of Latinos in the United States, who typically express strong opposition to punitive measures on unauthorized immigration. As the number of Latino voters grows, the United States may see more convergence on a single policy position by the parties in an effort to win this increasingly important voting bloc.

Energy, Environmental Policy, and Climate Change

The public policy sphere of energy and environmental issues is ever expanding, from the domestic production of energy in the coal, oil, and natural gas sectors, to the protection of clean air and water, to the cleanups of toxic waste, to the global concern over climate change. Over the course of the twentieth century, these issues became ever more important with the expansion of manufacturing, population growth, geographic mobility, technology, and consumer consumption of natural resources. As Figure 16.4 shows, Americans chiefly relied on wood as a source of energy to heat their homes and businesses until coal helped power the second industrial revolution during the late nineteenth century. During the twentieth century, the discovery of oil and natural gas as well as the construction of hydroelectric dams through New Deal projects, such as the Tennessee Valley Authority, helped satisfy the growing demands for energy. Following the Manhattan Project and the first explosions of the atomic bomb, the United States spearheaded research into nuclear power and built nuclear power plants to supplement fossil fuel (coal, oil, and natural gas) production.

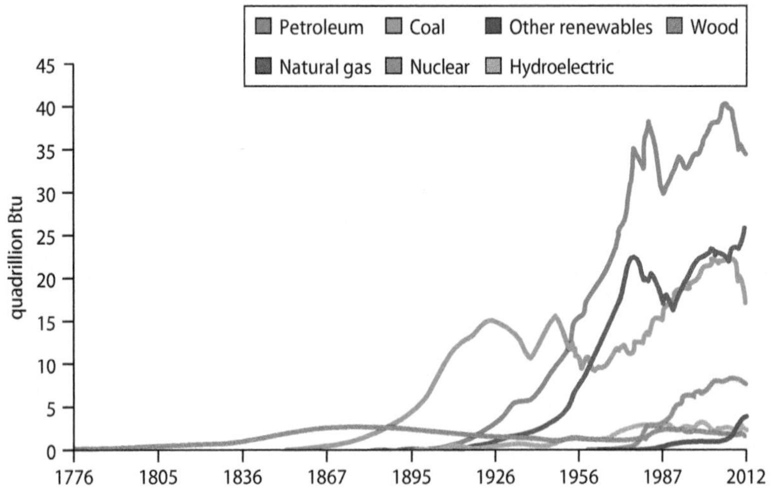

FIGURE 16.4 History of Energy Consumption in the United States

Energy sources have evolved over the course of American history, starting with wood and coal and moving toward oil, natural gas, and nuclear energy.

Source: U.S. Energy Information Administration, "Energy Sources Have Changed Throughout the History of the United States," http://www.eia.gov/todayinenergy/detail.cfm?id=11951#.

In the 1960s, however, Americans became increasingly concerned about the impact of new energy and other technologies on the environment. Rachel Carson's epic study of the effects of pesticides on the bird population, called *Silent Spring*, provoked an intense debate between large chemical companies and the scientific community and created national concern that gave rise to the environmental movement. The United States took sweeping steps to regulate the effects of energy use on the environment in 1963, when Congress passed the **Clean Air Act** to reduce pollution in response to growing public concerns and calls for stricter government controls.[39] However, in order to effectively oversee the government's role in regulating the environment, it became necessary to create an agency with jurisdiction specifically designed to protect the environment. Consequently, Congress revisited the Clean Air Act in 1970 and created the Environmental Protection Agency (EPA) to implement the Act. In 1972, the **Clean Water Act** was passed; it was based on a 1948 act that gave the government the authority to regulate the quality of both drinking water and navigational waters. Together, the Clean Air and Water acts provide a significant amount of power to the federal government to regulate pollution in our air and water.

Clean Air Act: *Broad federal legislation that expanded the federal government's ability to monitor and protect the environment against pollution.*

Clean Water Act: *Broad federal legislation that expanded the federal government's ability to monitor and protect the safety and quality of water.*

Since that time, the federal government has grappled with balancing the need to protect the environment and the nation's need for energy sources to fuel the economy and everyday living. Over the past forty years, the nation has experienced several energy crises where the demand for and cost of energy (for example, gasoline prices) rose so high that businesses and consumers suffered. In response, the government has encouraged alternative sources of energy as well as the expanded development of fossil fuels in the United States. Today, the nation is almost to the point where it is entirely energy self-sufficient, which somewhat reduces the reliance on foreign nations for energy and at the same time decreases the chances of getting involved in international conflicts waged over energy.[40]

Just as the United States depends on energy to drive its economy, developing nations around the world also require energy as their economies grow. As nations around the world expand their economies and increase the standard of living for their residents, pressure builds on both the supply of energy that is required to fuel that economic growth and the environmental impact of that growth. Fears regarding global climate change are fueled not only by the continued reliance of developed countries on fossil fuels but also by the increased consumption of fossil fuels by nations such as India and China in their efforts to develop industrialized economies.[41] There is an inherent tension between industrialized nations that have used the world's energy resources freely for more than a hundred years and more recently developed nations that are seeking to industrialize their economies. Now that more advanced nations are concerned about the environment—and climate change in particular—they want to encourage, even require, all nations to use energy-efficient technology. However, this type of technology can be expensive and add to the costs of production, which developing nations fear would slow their economic growth. Although the international community has tried to forge agreements with developing nations to limit pollution and other damage to the environment, those efforts have not been widely successful.

The United States has had more success pursuing domestic energy policies. Within the federal government, the EPA shares jurisdiction with the Department of Energy and the Department of Interior over federal energy and environmental policy, from regulating carbon emissions and auto fuel efficiency to granting leases to drill for oil and

POLITICAL ANALYTICS

Lead Exposure in the United States

ACCORDING THE CENTERS FOR DISEASE CONTROL and Prevention (CDC), even low levels of lead in children's blood can affect their IQs and academic achievement. Because the negative effects of lead in people's blood are irreversible, the CDC recommends preventing exposure to lead if at all possible. As the 2016 case of Flint, Michigan, illustrates, lead exposure and possible poisoning is a serious problem in some areas of the United States.

Figure 16.5 shows the states with a low, moderate, and high risk of lead exposure. Using a method designed by the State of Washington's Department of Health, researchers are able to use data from the U.S. Census to estimate the risk for lead exposure on a scale of 1 to 10, where 10 represents the highest risk. The states on this map are ranked (by color) on the proportion of census tracts in the states that are in categories 8 to 10 on the scale.

The risk of exposure to lead is lowest in the western states and highest in the nation's older urban areas. In states such as New York and Illinois (that is, with New York City and Chicago), therefore, more than 40 percent of the census tracts are at high risk of lead exposure. In states such as Arizona, in contrast, only 15 percent of the tracts are at high risk. Though

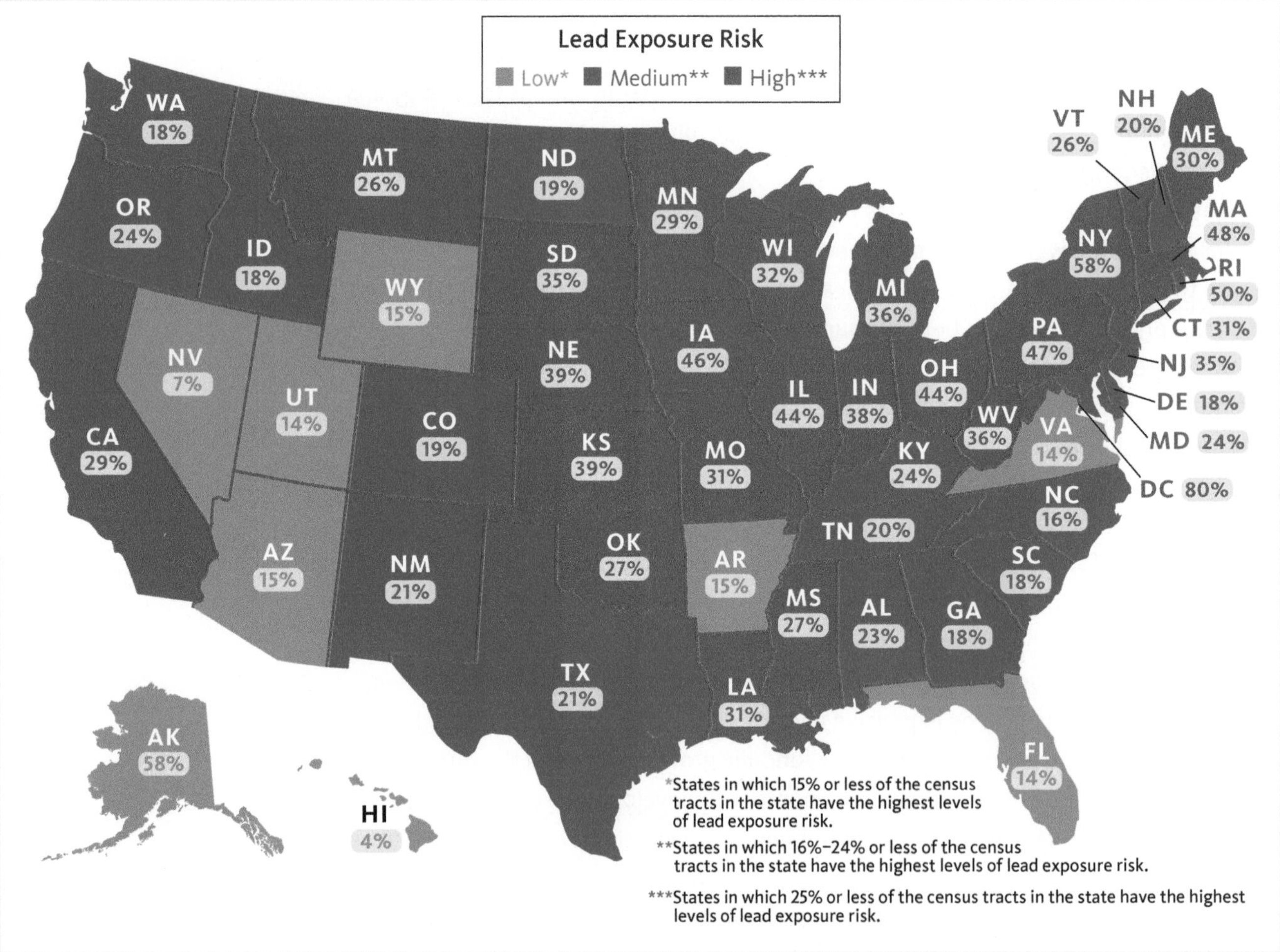

Lead Exposure Risk

Low* Medium** High***

*States in which 15% or less of the census tracts in the state have the highest levels of lead exposure risk.

**States in which 16%–24% or less of the census tracts in the state have the highest levels of lead exposure risk.

***States in which 25% or less of the census tracts in the state have the highest levels of lead exposure risk.

FIGURE 16.5 Risks of Lead Exposure

the states are categorized to correspond to high, medium, and low levels of risk, the CDC and other health professionals contend that no level of exposure to lead is safe for children.

Examine the risks of lead exposure throughout the United States, noticing the pattern of high- to low-risk states moving from east to west across the country.

Thinking Critically

1. As a matter of health policy, is the risk of exposure to lead a national issue?
2. How should policy makers address issues such as exposure to lead that affect some areas of the nation more than others?

Sources: Sarah Frostensen and Sarah Kliff, "The Risk of Lead Poisoning Isn't Just in Flint. So We Mapped the Risk in Every Neighborhood in America," *Vox*, April 6, 2016, http://www.vox.com/a/lead-exposure-risk-map; "What Do Parents Need to Know to Protect Their Children?" Centers for Disease Control, http://www.cdc.gov/nceh/lead/acclpp/blood_lead_levels.htm; Washington Tracking Network, "A Source for Environmental Public Health Data," Washington State Department of Health, https://fortress.wa.gov/doh/wtn/WTNIBL; data in map derived from https://github.com/voxmedia/data-projects/tree/master/vox-lead-exposure-risk.

natural gas both on- and offshore of the continental United States. In rare instances, the Department of State might also be involved in environmental policy if it will have an international impact. We discuss one such case in this chapter (see Public Policy and the Environment: Keystone XL Pipeline). Once an agency has been created, it is responsible for policy implementation within its jurisdiction. When the federal government proposes a policy change in an issue area, whether independently or as a response to a new law passed by Congress, the agency with jurisdiction in that issue area issues regulations to guide implementation.

Domestic policy, such as health care, immigration, and environmental protection, has several important layers. Congress and the president enact laws, which are then implemented by the executive branch through the regulatory process. At the same time, state and local governments are also helping to implement federal policies, as well as put in place policies that fall under their own set of powers (see Chapter 3). There are advantages and disadvantages to this layering; on the one hand, layering acts as a gateway for a wide range of voices to be heard in the policy process, but on the other hand, layering can serve as a gate that stands in the way of quickly and efficiently addressing important policy issues.

A glaring example of this type of gate occurred in Flint, Michigan, where bureaucratic decision making and cost-cutting measures posed a real danger to the residents in terms of the quality of their drinking and bathing water. Flint is a city of approximately 99,000 residents, 42 percent of whom live in poverty.[42] In April 2014 city officials in Flint decided to use the Flint River as the main water source for the city, even though the water from the river would flow through potentially corrosive pipes.[43] City officials decided not to put corrosion control technology in place unless evidence emerged of contaminants in the water. Over the next two years, that is exactly what happened: Tests first showed bacteria, then corrosive elements, then toxic chemicals, and finally lead. In fact, samples of water taken from Flint showed nearly three times the limit recommended by the EPA, and the percentage of children found to have higher amounts of lead in their blood doubled.

The reaction among local and public officials to the revelations about the drinking and bathing water in Flint were mixed: Some officials denied they knew about the problem, others said the problem was not widespread or severe, and still others claimed that they had warned city officials but did not get a response. By October 2015 the city of Flint switched its water supply and officials stated that the proper corrosion controls were in place, but many of the old pipes in Flint were not replaced. In January 2016, both Governor Snyder (R-MI) and President Obama declared a state of emergency at the state and federal levels. In April 2016, three individuals involved with the water scandal were indicted, and in July 2016, 6 more individuals were indicted for providing false information about water safety levels and trying to block the subsequent investigation.

For the residents of Flint who were harmed by pollutants in their water, the policy-making system, with all its oversight and safeguards, clearly failed them. And the case of Flint shows the limits of the government's power to regulate the environment at the local level. Whether the Flint crisis will serve as a wakeup call to communities and the elected officials who govern them remains to be seen.

16.3 Economic Policy

Explain how the federal government intervenes in the economy

Ever since the founding, Americans have debated whether and how the federal government should intervene in the economy. For the first hundred years of the nation's existence, the major source of government intervention in the economy was to impose taxes (known as tariffs) on goods imported from outside the country. Tariffs served as a way both to protect domestic industries and to raise revenues. But as the economy grew in the late 1800s, pressure mounted to regulate the growth of big business and to improve working conditions, which resulted in a series of laws dealing with antitrust (against big monopolies) to safety in the workplace. In the twentieth century, the federal income tax replaced tariffs as the key financing mechanism for federal government spending. The reality in today's world is that the government is heavily involved in the economy and that U.S. fiscal and monetary policy has a major impact in the national and international arena. The federal government intervenes in the economy to support economic development, regulate business practices, oversee banking and finance, and maintain a safety net of retirement, unemployment, and disability benefits.

Intervention in the Economy

Beginning with Theodore Roosevelt (1901–09), presidents have overseen the federal role in the nation's economy; some have wanted more intervention and some have wanted less. Republican presidents typically want to lower all taxes, a policy that provides less revenue to the federal government and subsequently decreases federal spending. Democratic presidents have typically wanted to cut taxes for individuals with lower incomes and to raise taxes on wealthier citizens to support federal programs. The key advisors to the president on economic policy are the Secretary of the Treasury, the National Economic Council, and the Council of Economic Advisers. The president also appoints the chairman of the Federal Reserve (discussed later in this section), which has a major role in monetary policy. The set of stakeholders in federal economic policy includes the president, Congress, business interests, and consumers (see Figure 16.7).

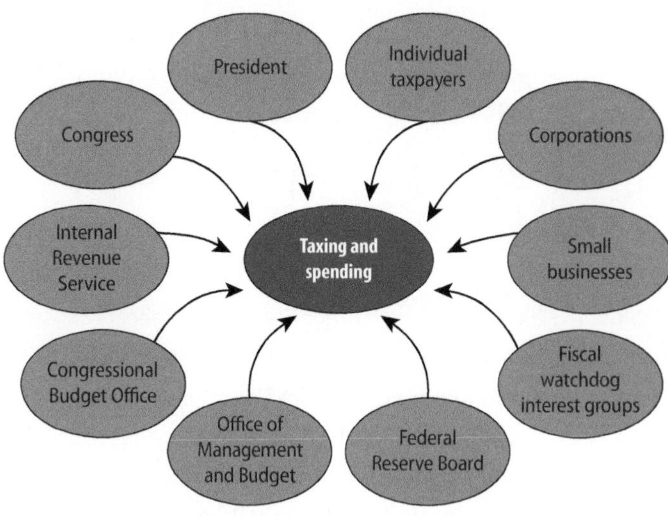

FIGURE 16.7 Stakeholders in Federal Economic Policy

A diverse set of public and private organizations and individuals impact economic policy.

When the economy is weak, there is pressure on the president to take extraordinary steps to strengthen it. This is what President Franklin Roosevelt did during the Great Depression and what President Obama did nearly a decade ago in response to the 2007–2009 recession. A **recession** is typically defined as a downturn in economic activity, with declines in employment levels, income, retail spending, and industrial production. The 2007–2009 recession was attributed largely to inflated housing prices, irresponsible lending by banks, and excessive borrowing by consumers, all of which led to widespread foreclosures and the collapse of major sectors of the financial and construction industries. When people lose jobs, consumer spending declines, forcing business and industry to cut back production and lay off workers, potentially leading to a vicious circle in which consumer spending declines even further, forcing businesses and industry to cut back production even more and lay off even more workers.

recession: *A period of time marked by successive quarters of lower economic output.*

President Obama responded to the economic crisis by adopting a mixed strategy on taxes and spending. He continued President George W. Bush's program, which effectively bailed out banks, and he instituted a bailout program for the auto industry; the majority of those funds have been paid back to the government with interest. Additionally, he worked with Congress to enact a nearly $800 billion stimulus bill that was a combination of spending increases favored by Democrats and tax credits (which amount to tax cuts) favored by Republicans to boost the economy. Because raising taxes during a recession is widely believed to have a negative impact on consumer spending and job growth, Obama and Congress extended tax cuts in 2010 and 2012.

Just as there are specific stakeholders that often participate in the formation and implementation of economic policy, there are also specific tools that have been developed over time to achieve specific economic goals.

Fiscal Policy

Government can use fiscal policy to intervene in the economy through taxing and spending. Fiscal policy can also be used to manipulate the money supply to avoid recession. More spending or lower taxes increase the money supply, while lower spending or more taxes decrease the money supply. In times of severe economic crises, the president may support a policy of increasing the money supply to ward off a recession. Alternatively, an increase in prices can cause workers to demand raises. Higher wages will lead to even larger increases in prices, setting off inflation. In this case, the president may support a decrease in the money supply to ward off or reduce the extent of inflation. It also remains true in the American economic system that there is a business cycle, based on innovation, production, and consumer demand, that operates independently but simultaneous to the

PUBLIC POLICY AND THE ENVIRONMENT

Keystone XL Pipeline

Against the backdrop of higher energy costs, projects such as the Keystone XL oil pipeline, a Canadian-funded oil pipeline that would have run from Canada to the Texas coast, underscore the way in which federal policy has to balance the nation's demand for energy and employment against competing demands to live in a clean and safe environment. Energy projects such as the Keystone XL can act as a gateway for Americans today in terms of jobs, but it can be a gate against a future that ensures a clean environment in which to live and work. It served as an important example of the dynamics of domestic policy making because it involves the executive branch, Congress, interest groups, private industry, and even a foreign nation.

In 2008, the energy company TransCanada submitted an application to the State Department to build a 1,700-mile oil pipeline from Alberta, Canada, to Nederland, Texas[44] (see Figure 16.6). Because the project crossed over the border from a foreign nation, it fell under the jurisdiction of the U.S. State Department, which does not normally have a role in this policy area; the State Department required TransCanada to submit an application for a presidential permit.[45] The State Department also conducted a study for an environmental impact statement (EIS) to see if the pipeline would have any adverse environmental effects on the regions through which it would run. Although the State Department was designated as the lead agency for the review of the project, the EPA was also involved and reviewed the environmental impact of the project.[46]

Almost two years later, the State Department released a draft of its EIS, which stated that the construction and operation of the pipeline would have minimal environmental impacts. The State Department then solicited public comment on the draft. By the time the opportunity for public comment closed, it had received thousands of public comments from interest groups and industry members on the proposal. In 2011, the State Department released its final EIS, which concluded that the project was in line with President Obama's environmental policies.[47]

Although the State Department gave the go-ahead for the project, the EPA and numerous environmental interest groups were not persuaded by the State

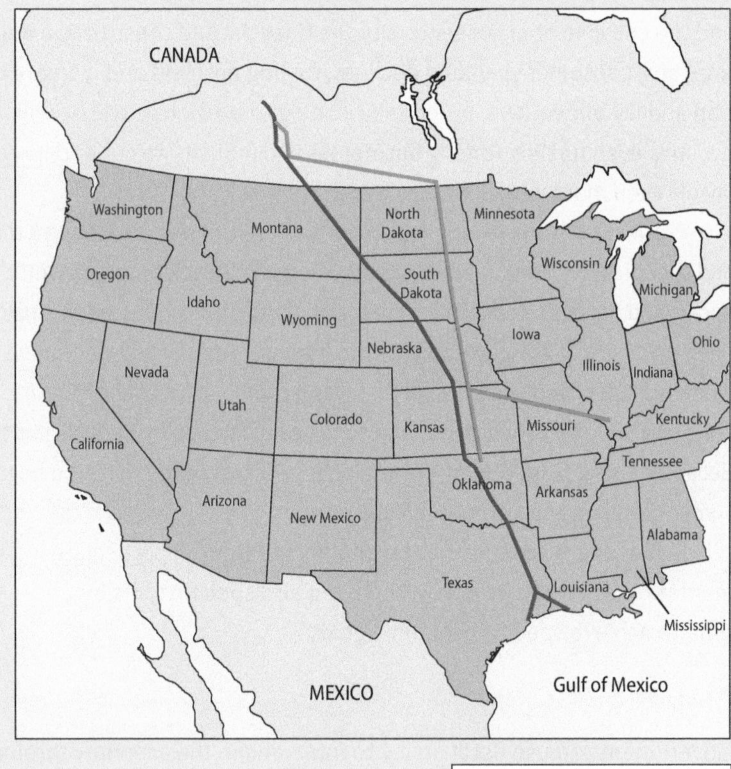

FIGURE 16.6 Keystone Pipeline Map

This map illustrates the proposed route of the Keystone XL Pipeline, which would have run from Canada to Texas. President Obama rejected the proposal.

Source: Laris Karklis/*The Washington Post*. http://www.washingtonpost.com/national/health-science/canadian-firm-to-push-ahead-with-part-of-keystone-pipeline/2012/02/27/glQavJftdr_story.html/; for the state of Nebraska, http://www.montrealgazette.com/technology/route+Keystone+pipeline+proposed+through+Nebraska/6486974/story.html.

Department's findings. Congress also reflected the division over the pipeline, where representatives from both sides of the aisle struggled over the project and its merits. Proponents of the project saw it as key to economic growth in the United States, while opponents had serious concerns about the potential for environmental damage from a pipeline leak. The Republican majority in the House of Representatives wanted to push President Obama into making a final decision on the project, so, as part of a bill to extend the payroll tax cut (see Chapter 13), they attached a provision requiring that the president issue a decision within sixty days. Obama responded by denying TransCanada the permit to build the pipeline, citing inadequate information to gauge its full environmental impact. One major concern was the pipeline's proximity to the Sand Hills region that covers the Ogallala Aquifer, which provides most of the drinking and irrigation water for the Midwest. In response, TransCanada reapplied for the permit, proposing a route that avoided the Sand Hills region in Nebraska.[48]

Throughout the presidential permit process, numerous interest groups, including labor unions, environmental activists, and energy producers, stated their positions on the pipeline. In an interesting twist, labor and energy interest groups were allies, as both supported the construction of the pipeline. Environmental groups vigorously voiced their objections. In contrast, both the House and Senate passed resolutions calling for the approval of the pipeline. In fact, the amount of public response was so great that Obama announced in 2014 that he had to delay his final decision on the pipeline because the public comments on the project numbered in the millions, and the administration needed more time to consider all the views expressed.

Ultimately, on November 6, 2015, President Obama accepted the recommendation by the State Department to reject the application to build the Keystone XL pipeline. In explaining his decision, Obama said that he believed that the pipeline would not have helped the economy or lowered gasoline prices. Instead, he believed that it would have extended the nation's promotion of fossil fuel energy and undercut its efforts to fight global warming. He stated, "America is now a global leader when it comes to taking serious action to fight climate change. And frankly, approving this project would have undercut that global leadership. And that's the biggest risk we face—not acting."[49] The Keystone XL pipeline case illustrates many of the major components of policy making, from the private sector to the federal bureaucracy, Congress, interest groups, and finally the office of the president.

Public Policy Connections

1. How does public opinion impact elected officials? Should it?
2. How should the political system respond to immediate demands from citizens who desire more jobs and economic development when those demands might conflict with the need to provide future generations with a clean environment?

implementation of government economic policy. In other words, both the private and public sectors shape the direction of the economy.

Monetary Policy

The president is limited in his or her power to directly influence the nation's economic conditions because monetary policy is under the control of the **Federal Reserve Board**, an independent agency that serves as the nation's central bank, increasing or decreasing the money supply by changing the reserve requirements—the amount of cash reserves that banks must keep on hand. To control the flow of money in the economy, Congress created the Federal Reserve in 1913 as a system of twelve regional banks in one national banking

Federal Reserve Board: *Independent regulatory commission that affects the money supply by setting the reserve requirements of member banks, establishing a discount rate for loans to member banks, and buying or selling government securities.*

TABLE 16.2 Comparison of Fiscal and Monetary Policy

Type of Policy	Policy Maker	Action	Direct Effect	Effect on Money Supply
Fiscal	Congress, president	Increase spending or cut taxes	Consumers have more money to spend.	Increases
	Congress, president	Decrease spending or increase taxes	Consumers have less money to spend.	Decreases
Monetary	Federal Reserve Board	Increase reserve requirement	Banks have less money to loan.	Decreases
	Federal Reserve Board	Decrease reserve requirement	Banks have more money to loan.	Increases
	Federal Reserve Board	Increase the discount rate	Loans are more expensive.	Decreases
	Federal Reserve Board	Decrease the discount rate	Loans are less expensive.	Increases

system. The Federal Reserve System is led by a seven-member board of governors, each nominated by the president and confirmed by the Senate. Members serve fourteen-year terms, and the president selects the board chair, who serves a four-year term, with the option of reappointment. Janet Yellen, the current chair of the Federal Reserve, is the first female to serve in that position.

When the Federal Reserve increases reserve requirements, banks have less money to lend, and the money supply decreases. This action tends to raise interest rates. When the Federal Reserve decreases reserve requirements, banks have more money to lend, and thus the money supply increases (see Table 16.2). This move tends to lower interest rates. The Federal Reserve Board also controls the money supply through the discount rate, which is the interest rate that the Federal Reserve charges other banks on loans. When the discount rate is lower, banks are not able to charge high interest rates on the money they lend to consumers and businesses.

Although the president can name people to the Federal Reserve, he or she cannot fire them if they promote monetary policy that differs from his policy preferences. His or her only power over them comes from the nomination process.

The power of the federal government to steer the economy has been debated since our nation's founding. In times of crisis, the president and Congress can enact programs that target specific problems, as in the case of the auto industry bailout and stimulus package. But more generally, it is the Federal Reserve that has a strong role in setting monetary policy by setting interest rates, which in turn controls the flow of money to businesses and individuals seeking to take out loans.

Trade Policy

International trade—the exchange of commerce with other nations—is also an integral component of our nation's economic policy. President Washington's Farewell Address in 1796 acknowledged the importance of international commerce to the new nation, and the Framers knew that trade with foreign nations was integral to its economic success and stability. Over time, the United States grew economically strong through innovation, exploitation of its vast natural resources, and an increasing population that expanded both its workforce and its consumer base. In the twentieth century, the United States built on its economic strength by becoming an innovator in intellectual and technical services. In the twenty-first century, trade remains an important gateway to economic, political, and cultural relationships with other nations, though in recent years the nation has begun to import more goods than it exports.

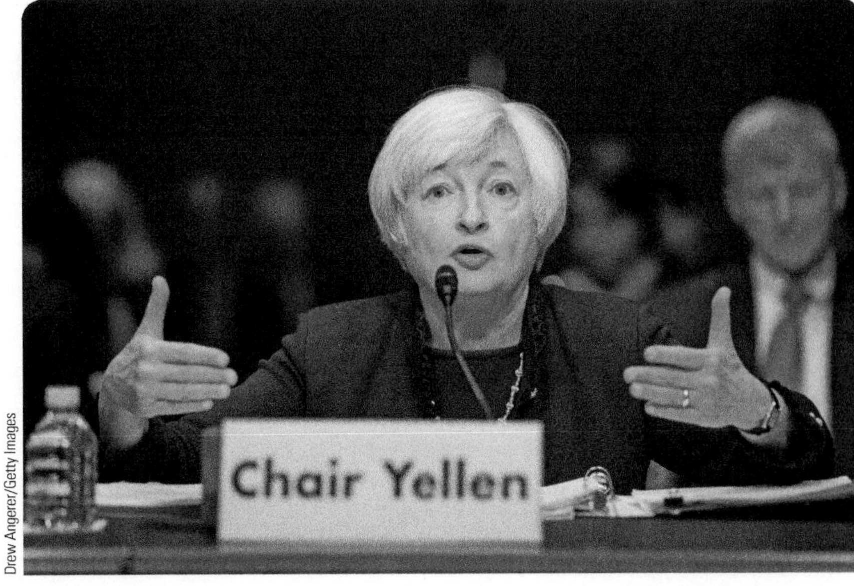

IMAGE 16.6 A number of Federal Reserve chairs have served multiple terms and under different presidents. The current chair of the Federal Reserve is Janet Yellen, who was nominated by President Obama in October 2013, was confirmed by the Senate, and took office in January 2014.

Protectionism Versus Free Trade. Trade policy has long been aligned with foreign policy and has been used by the United States to export both capitalism and democracy. International trade policy is complex because each nation wants to negotiate deals that give its industries the greatest advantages either to sell their goods abroad or to be protected from cheaper imports from foreign nations. A policy that protects against foreign imported goods more than it promotes exports is known as **protectionist**, and a policy that strikes down barriers on imported foreign goods is known as **free trade**. A third and relatively recent policy, **fair trade**, encourages foreign trade as long as there are comparable working conditions and wages within the industries in the trading nations. Environmental regulation has also become increasingly important in trade negotiations. If one nation exploits its workers with long hours, unsafe conditions, environmental pollution, and low pay to produce and sell goods more cheaply than another, it violates fair trade practices. When a nation violates fair trade practices, individuals may boycott its products, or, more significantly, other nations may refuse to trade with it.

protectionist: *Policy designed to raise import barriers for goods that are domestically produced.*

free trade: *Policy designed to lower import barriers to encourage trade across nations.*

fair trade: *Policy designed to make sure that the working conditions are relatively equal in nations that trade with each other.*

The president takes the lead in negotiating international trade agreements, either bilaterally (with one other country) or multilaterally through the office of the U.S. Trade Representative (USTR), an office created within the Executive Office of the President by President John F. Kennedy (1961–63) in 1963. The USTR is responsible for negotiating the terms of international trade agreements. To present a balanced position on behalf of the U.S. government, the USTR solicits information and feedback about the potential impact of the trade agreement from import- and export-related industries, cabinet departments, and members of Congress. Gathering such information is helpful not only in crafting an agreement that benefits U.S. industries but also in building the necessary support to get the trade agreement ratified by Congress.

During the late nineteenth and twentieth century, protectionist trade policies enabled U.S. industries to corner the consumer market and make huge profits. Businesses reinvested those profits in developing technology and in expanding so that the United States became the major supplier of manufactured goods throughout the world. It did not face strong competition in the world marketplace until the late 1980s, when Japan, China, and India developed their industrial capacity sufficiently to become competitive in a number of economic sectors. They replicated the U.S. policy of exporting their goods while maintaining trade barriers against the import of U.S. goods.

PUBLIC POLICY AND THE ECONOMY

Federal Deficit and the Debt Ceiling

Although many experts credit President Obama's policies with warding off an even deeper recession, or depression, these policies temporarily increased the federal deficit, which in turn increased the federal debt. As we noted in Chapter 12, the federal deficit is the difference between the amount of money that the government takes in and the amount of money that it spends. When the federal government runs a deficit, it must borrow money to make up the shortfall. Consequently, the federal government pays interest on this borrowed money, and the combined amount of the borrowed money and the interest that accumulates over time constitutes the national debt.

As the federal debt has risen in recent years, Americans have become increasingly concerned about burdening future generations with the task of paying it back. There are two components to the federal debt: (1) public debt, which is the money that comes from issuing debt instruments, such as U.S. Treasury bonds, that investors buy with a promise of getting a set amount of interest on the bonds at a later date; and (2) intragovernment held debt, which is the amount of money that the federal government borrows from itself when it transfers money from one program to another or uses built-up reserves in one program as collateral for borrowing. The **debt ceiling** is a cap on the amount of money that Congress authorizes the president to borrow to pay the federal government's bills. Before 1917, there was no legal limit on the government's ability to issue such debt. However, to fund operations for World War I, Congress passed the Second Liberty Bond Act, which allows the federal government to issue longer-term debt as long as Congress issues its approval for doing so.[50] Today the president must ask to raise the debt ceiling and cannot do so without congressional approval.

The issue of the debt ceiling has become a major source of contention between the president and Congress. When President Obama first took office, he inherited a federal deficit of $1.4 trillion and a total national debt of $11.9 trillion dollars (see Figure 16.8); both were the cumulative effect of past presidential policy making, including the Bush tax cuts and the Iraq and Afghanistan wars. But during the first two years of the Obama administration, the national debt climbed to $13.5 trillion.[51] In the 2010 midterm congressional elections, the Tea Party movement became active within the Republican Party in order to strengthen the GOP's existing commitment to reduce taxes and federal spending. When the Republicans won control of the House of Representatives, those members who were elected with Tea Party support stayed adamant in their position against raising the debt ceiling. As noted in Chapter 12, the majority of those members were reelected in 2012, and again in 2014, and President Obama was reelected as well, which maintained divided party control between Congress and the presidency. Since then, these conservative members have joined forces with other GOP members in the House and the Senate to continue their opposition to increased federal spending.

For fiscal year 2015, the federal deficit stood at $439 billion, which was less than half the size of what President Obama inherited in 2009, but the national debt had risen to $19.2 trillion. During Obama's two terms in office, the issue of the federal debt ceiling caused standoffs with Congress on two separate occasions.

In 2011 President Obama proposed a "grand bargain" that would have cut the debt by $4 trillion over ten years with a combination of spending reductions and increased taxes. Republicans in the House rejected any plan that included tax increases. Eventually, the president, Senate leaders, and then-Speaker John Boehner agreed to raise the debt ceiling in exchange for cutting $900 billion over ten years from the federal budget.

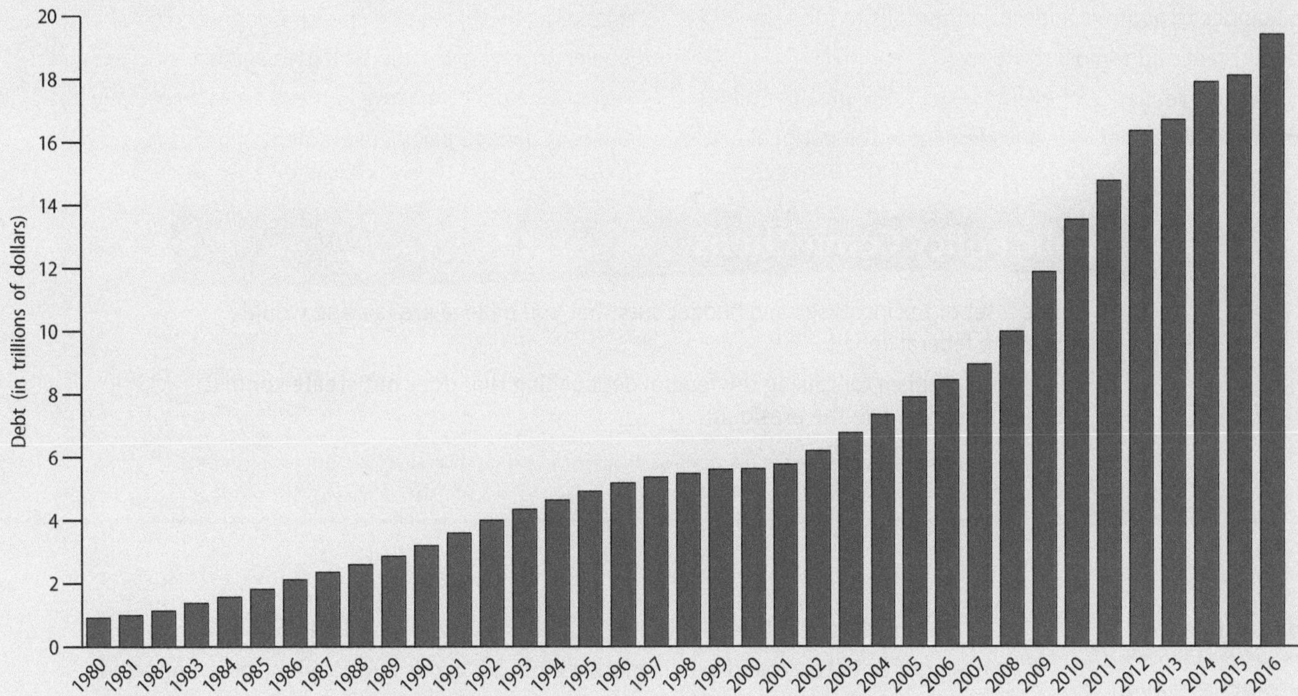

FIGURE 16.8 U.S. National Debt, 1980–2016

Over the past four decades, the national debt has grown much larger. In 1980 it was less than $2 trillion, but by 2016 it had risen to more than $18 trillion.

Source: The White House, Office of Management and Budget, Table 7.1, Federal Debt at the End of Year: 1940–2021, U.S. budget for FY 2017, http://www.whitehouse.gov/omb/budget/historicals.

In October 2013, a similar scenario occurred, but this time, the Republicans in the House tied all government spending to the debt ceiling and refused to act unless implementation of the ACA was delayed or repealed. The Senate was then controlled by the Democrats and supported the president's position to raise the debt ceiling with no strings attached. Still, the House GOP action resulted in a government shutdown that lasted sixteen days, and the United States came close to the brink of defaulting on its debt obligations. The public outcry over the government shutdown was so strong that Congress and the president came to a longer-term agreement about the federal budget to try to avoid future shutdowns.

In October 2015, a standoff between President Obama and the Republican-controlled House of Representatives and Senate was narrowly avoided through political deal making. As we discussed in Chapter 12, then-Speaker John Boehner, who was increasingly unpopular with the conservative wing of the House GOP, agreed to step down from his leadership post and Congress. Though there was a brief discussion about who would succeed him, Paul Ryan (R-WI) emerged as the consensus choice of the party to be the next Speaker. However, Ryan was hesitant to take the post if the House GOP continued to refuse to raise the debt ceiling and risk another government shutdown. Recall from Chapter 12 that the majority party must first vote to agree to consider a bill on the House floor (e.g., the Rule), and then a vote is taken to pass or defeat the bill. In this case, the House GOP agreed to the Rule, which brought a bill to the House floor to suspend the requirement that the president seek an official increase in the debt ceiling through March 2017. In effect, that meant that the federal government could continue borrowing money by issuing debt without seeking congressional permission to do so. The bill passed 266–167, with 79 Republicans voting for it and the rest of the votes to pass it coming from Democrats.[52] The next day, Paul Ryan was elected Speaker of the House. Later that year, Speaker Ryan once again had to persuade his Republican colleagues to approve appropriations bills to fund the government and avoid a shutdown.

As this sequence of events reveals, the president does not have sole power over any element of the national economy; he shares power with Congress. This shared power arrangement can be a gate against efficient and responsive policy making in these areas, especially in times of divided party government.

Public Policy Connections

1. Devise a set of tax increases and budget cuts that you believe are fair and would reduce the federal deficit.
2. Create a mechanism for raising the federal debt ceiling that does not create conflict between Congress and the president.

debt ceiling: *The congressionally authorized limit on federal borrowing.*

NAFTA: *Comprehensive multination trade agreement ratified in 1994 that knocked down trade barriers among Canada, the United States, and Mexico.*

In the decades since, the United States has forged multilateral trade agreements designed both to expand export markets for U.S. goods and to allow more imported goods. The Canada Free Trade agreement, followed by the **North American Free Trade Agreement (NAFTA)**, created a free trade zone of goods and services across the northern and southern borders of the United States, creating jobs nationwide. However, some industries, such as the domestic textile and steel industries, were adversely affected and lost jobs. Many businesses moved their production facilities to Mexico, where it was less expensive to produce goods. These goods could then be sold cheaply in the United States because, under the free trade agreement, no import duties could be charged. The impact of NAFTA is an example of the consequences of policies that are designed to integrate the U.S. economy into the global world of trade.

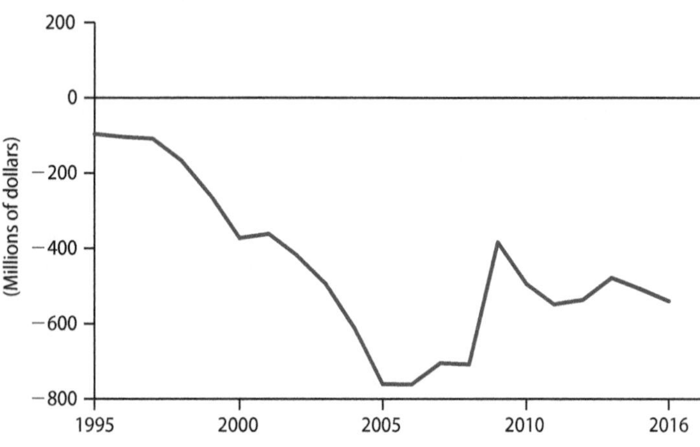

FIGURE 16.9 U.S. Balance of Trade, 1995–2016

The balance of trade is the difference between how much the United States imports from other countries and how much it exports to other countries. This graph shows the dollar value of all goods and services that the United States trades; negative numbers indicate that the country imports more than it exports.

Source: https://www.census.gov/foreign-trade/statistics/historical/gands.pdf

Six years after the passage of NAFTA, the United States normalized trade status with China, which reduced trade barriers and opened up Chinese markets to U.S. goods. In doing so, it also encouraged American producers of goods such as textiles, apparel, steel, and electronics to relocate their production facilities to China. More than a decade later, the United States has a large trade imbalance with China: At the end of 2015, U.S. imports exceeded exports to China by $367 billion.[53] A large trade imbalance means that the American consumers are buying far more goods made in China than Chinese consumers are buying goods made in the United States. Such an imbalance in trade can harm U.S. manufacturers who are trying to compete with Chinese imported goods (see Figure 16.9). In early 2016, President Obama and U.S. trade negotiators completed the terms of the Trans-Pacific Partnership with eleven Asian and Pacific nations to open up their economic borders to allow the imports of goods into their nations in exchange for more favorable trade terms for their products to enter other markets, including the United States. As of fall 2016, Congress had not ratified the trade deal, but there is a two-year window to complete the ratification process in all participating countries.

The increase in the number of economically developed nations as producers and consumers of goods, combined with the presence of U.S.-owned industries in these nations, has created a strong incentive for the United States to be a supportive partner in the international economy in order to encourage other countries to allow U.S. goods to be sold there.

Trade and International Economic Organizations. In addition to the unilateral trade agreements that it has struck with other nations, the United States also participated in the General Agreement on Tariffs and Trade (GATT), which governed multinational trade agreements between 1948 and 1994. In 1994, during the eighth round of GATT, the **World Trade Organization (WTO)** was created to deal with the explosive expansion of the global trade community and to establish a single international organization with the authority to resolve trade disputes.[54] If one country claims that another country is engaged in unfair trading practices, it can bring its case to the WTO; each party to the dispute must abide by the WTO's ruling or face monetary fines and trade limitations. For example, in 2009, China imposed a ban on broiler products, which covers chicken, from the United States, and the United States lodged a formal complaint with the WTO citing unfair trade practices. The WTO formed a panel to resolve the issue.

World Trade Organization (WTO): *International organization that considers and resolves trade disputes among member nations.*

It took nearly four years for the WTO to return a decision, and it ruled that China had violated fair trade practices and had to remove the barriers to imported chicken from the United States.[55] The slow pace of the WTO deliberation illustrates how an international organization can serve as a gate or obstacle to efficient resolution of economic disputes. Entering the WTO was a major change in U.S. trade policy because it required the United States to relinquish its right to act unilaterally in trade disputes. At the same time, by agreeing to abide by WTO rulings, the United States gave assurance to foreign nations that it would respect international rules and would be a fair and reliable trading partner while expecting other nations to do the same.

Another significant development in international trade relations was the creation of the **European Union (EU)**, a major expansion of a preexisting European economic organization known as the European Community.[56] In June 2016, Great Britain held a referendum, known as Brexit, on whether to exit the EU, a decision that would have global trade and economic implications. It was narrowly approved by a vote of 52 percent to 48 percent. Because the sitting Prime Minister had opposed Brexit, he stepped down and was replaced by another member of his party. There is a two year time frame to negotiate Great Britain's exit from the EU, and it remains to be seen how it will proceed.

European Union (EU): *Association of European nations formed to facilitate economic and political interactions across their borders.*

Economic policy is an enormously complicated arena in which the U.S. government tries to implement policies that will encourage stability and growth. In the past two decades especially, continuous deficit spending and severe swings in the economy have created a large national debt and pressure to reduce the government's spending and its overall role in the economy. Moreover, the expansion of U.S. businesses around the world has created a highly interdependent global economy, where another nation's trade and monetary policies may have direct effects on the U.S. economy. Navigating this ever-changing economic arena continues to be one of the great challenges facing U.S. policy makers.

16.4 Foreign Policy

Evaluate the effectiveness of U.S. foreign policy

The international arena in which the United States is positioned today is nothing like the world in which the Framers wrote the Constitution. Travel to Europe is now a matter of hours instead of months; communication with all parts of the world is instantaneous. Conflict, terrorism, disease, and poverty are not just localized problems but are international in scope. In this section, we examine how the United States came to its position as global leader and discuss the constitutional gates and international conditions that constrain its actions. As we noted in Chapter 13, the conduct of foreign policy is the purview of the executive branch led by the president as commander in chief but with significant input from Congress; the Department of Defense, the Department of State, the Department of Homeland Security, and the National Security Agency all play vital roles in our foreign and military policy.

International Relations and U.S. Foreign Policy Goals

globalization: *The interconnectedness of nations around the world on economic, political, cultural, social, and military dimensions.*

When the Framers wrote the Constitution, the United States, as a democracy, stood virtually alone in a world ruled by monarchs. Though independent and isolated by geography, the new nation was still vulnerable, and in its first years, it was caught up in European rivalries. In 1796, when he was leaving the presidency, George Washington (1789–97) warned against foreign entanglements: "The great rule of conduct for us in regard to foreign nations," he wrote in his Farewell Address, "is in extending our commercial relations, to have with them as little political connection as possible."[57] More than two hundred years later, Washington's isolationist tendencies have been swamped by the evolution of **globalization**, which intertwines the fate of the United States with hostilities, health crises and epidemics such as the Ebola and Zika viruses, and natural disasters and environmental degradation wherever they occur.

With globalization, regional economies, societies, and cultures have become increasingly integrated through trade, capital investment, labor flows, migration, travel, and, most strikingly, the Internet and instantaneous communication (for example, Twitter). In one sense, these changes opened the economic and political gates that long kept nations apart. People are today interconnected on multiple levels. Citizens of China drink Coke and eat McDonald's hamburgers, and Americans wear clothing with "made in China" on the label. Over the course of the late twentieth century and through today, developed nations have found it cheaper to manufacture goods in developing countries, and free trade is seen as a gateway to more open and democratic societies in nations previously closed to outside influences.

The interdependence of the new globalized world might sound like a formula for peace, but in fact the connections are complex. Being connected does not mean sharing political systems and religions, or even cultures below the level of popular culture. The differences that do exist have intensified in the new global age and have produced political, social, and military conflict. America has objective strategic interests that it must protect, such as maintaining its energy supplies from abroad. But it also has a strong commitment to human rights and democratic principles of government, and sometimes these guiding principles clash. As a leading military, diplomatic, and economic power, the United States has to balance the need to preserve its own interests against the benefits that arise from working with other nations under an international framework of laws and policies. To recognize the challenges the United States faces in achieving its goals today, we must first understand the nature of the international system and how it evolved.

IMAGE 16.7 Frequently residents of foreign nations complain about the "Americanization" of their food and culture, but at the same time, American businesses are very successful internationally. Here we see customers at a McDonald's in Beijing, China.

The Origins of U.S. Foreign Policy. The dawn of the twentieth century witnessed the first large-scale U.S. involvement in international conflicts on foreign soil with World War I (WWI). Prior to that, the United States had fought conflicts mostly within its contiguous geographic borders; in the late nineteenth century, the United States ventured into the Southern Hemisphere with the Spanish-American War, and annexed the Philippines. But full international involvement by the United States did not commence until WWI. In 1914, when WWI began in Europe, President Woodrow Wilson (1913–21) proclaimed neutrality, but German attacks on U.S. commercial shipping in international waters convinced him to change course. In asking for a declaration of war from Congress on April 2, 1917, Wilson argued, "The world must be made safe for democracy. Its peace must be planted upon the tested foundations of political liberty."[58]

Wilson had a vision for peace that inspired Americans and Europeans alike, and he took a leading role in writing the treaty that ended the war. One provision of the treaty created an international organization—called the League of Nations—that would help preserve the political independence of its members against aggressor nations. But in 1920, the Senate rejected the treaty and, with it, Wilson's vision of a role for America in the world. Politicians and voters alike feared that membership in the League of Nations would compromise the nation's sovereignty. WWI overturned old empires and established new nations. Despite President Wilson's efforts to engage the United States in international democracy building, the United States turned inward and adopted a policy of isolationism.

In Russia, a **Communist** revolution installed a political and economic system that used government management of the economy to prevent large concentrations of private wealth. A long-term goal of this system was economic security and equality for all citizens. The Communist Party was the only political party in the new Soviet Union, stifling virtually all dissent. In Germany, a new democracy struggled such that voters elected Adolf Hitler and the Nazi Party, who promised to restore Germany's economic and military power. Under Hitler's dictatorship, Germany became an aggressor once again, and in 1939, its invasion of Poland triggered the Second World War (WWII). In Asia, Japan had launched a similar course of aggression, and its air assault on Pearl Harbor on December 7, 1941, led President Franklin Delano Roosevelt (1933–45) to ask Congress for a declaration of war against Japan the next day (and against Germany and Italy on December 11, 1941, after those nations, in alliance with Japan, had declared war on the United States).

Communist: *Government management and ownership of key elements of a nation's economy.*

When World War II ended in 1945, Europe was on the brink of collapse. The United States emerged as a leading world power and could no longer sustain its isolationist policies. New weapons technologies, especially airpower, expanded the reach and level of destruction that one nation could impose on another. Like Wilson, Roosevelt envisioned a peace in which an international organization, stronger than the League of Nations, could prevent aggression and meet humanitarian needs. The **United Nations (UN)** was founded in April 1945, and Congress ratified U.S. membership in December. Its headquarters was built along the East River in New York City, and it became a gateway for nations to interact with each other and try to resolve disputes in a neutral environment.

United Nations (UN): *Organization formed after World War II to mediate disputes among nations around the world.*

Hopes for a peaceful world were shortly shattered, however, as rivalry between the United States with its Western democratic allies and the Soviet Union and Eastern European states provoked a **Cold War**. As new nations emerged from the aftermath of the war, they were forced to align themselves with the forces of democracy or Communism. On March 12, 1947, President Harry Truman (1945–53) spoke to a joint session of Congress convened to consider a growing economic crisis in Greece. He clearly stated his belief that the economic stability of Greece was essential to keeping it from falling to the Communists. During this speech, Truman set forth the policy that the United States would take active steps to preserve democracy and contain Communism throughout the world, a policy that became known as the Truman Doctrine or the policy of containment.

Cold War: *An era in history marked by conflict and distrust between the United States and Communist nations.*

For the next decades, U.S. efforts to contain Communism involved the nation in military interventions, most notably in Korea and Vietnam but also in the Middle East and Latin America. As we saw in Chapter 13, these military interventions were undertaken by the president in his role as commander in chief. Presidential power grew in accord with America's commitment to world leadership. In an age when atomic bomb capabilities called for split-second decisions, the president's authority to command military response went mostly unchallenged.

Beginning in 1989, facing enormous economic difficulties and organized political dissent, the Communist regimes of Eastern Europe began to fall, which was symbolically represented by the collapse of the Berlin Wall that separated East (Communist) and West (democratic) Germany. In 1991, the Soviet Union itself disintegrated into separate states, with the most powerful being Russia. Thus the United States could declare victory in the Cold War but now faced the challenge of winning and keeping the peace.

The context for international relations at the end of the Cold War was vastly different from earlier eras. After that struggle ended, the old bipolar world of the two superpowers quickly became **multipolar**, with numerous centers of power competing for regional dominance and with numerous regional conflicts. Since the end of WWII, many nations in addition to Vietnam and Iran had gained independence from such former colonial powers as France and the United Kingdom. Some of these nations—India and Indonesia, for example—had risen to prominence by attempting to remain neutral in the superpower struggle, forming the nonaligned movement. Modernization in China gave that huge nation new international stature. In the Middle East, tensions between Israel and the Arab states went unresolved. In Africa, decolonization had created a patchwork of new states across tribal lines struggling against corruption, poverty, and disease. And in the old Soviet bloc, especially in central Asia, new states struggled to suppress regional, religious, and ethnic hostilities and to resist Russian dominance. Cold War tensions still resonate when issues of sovereignty emerge, as they did with the Russian takeover of the Crimean peninsula, which was part of the country of Ukraine. In that case, the majority of residents in Crimea were of Russian descent and welcomed the aggressive takeover by the Putin-led government. Western nations responded by

multipolar: *A world system where there are distinct centers of political and military power.*

imposing economic sanctions on Russia, but tensions only escalated when Russian sympathizers in eastern Ukraine waged war against the government. Russia kept control of Crimea, but as of 2016, simmering tensions still existed in eastern Ukraine.

Foreign Policy Tools

Nations have a wide array of policy tools available to them. Some involve cooperation through bilateral or multilateral treaties, diplomatic relations, and aid; others entail conflict through the use of force or the threat of military action. In this section, we will examine how the United States uses these tools.

Military Action. The president, as commander in chief, has always made the decision to engage in military action. Although Congress has formally declared war only five times, U.S. troops have been sent into conflicts and potential conflicts about 250 times since the beginning of the nation.[59] Today, in making the decision to engage in military action, the president is heavily influenced by the recommendations of the secretary of defense, the national security adviser, and the director of the Central Intelligence Agency.

For military missions that are publicized, not secret, a president usually enjoys widespread support if the mission can be clearly tied to preserving national security. In cases in which the United States is attacked on its own soil, support for a military response is even higher. This so-called **rally-around-the-flag effect** is a surge in patriotic sentiment that translates into presidential popularity.[60] For example, when President George H. W. Bush commenced the first Gulf War, his approval ratings shot up to 89 percent.[61] His son, President George W. Bush, experienced a similar spike in popularity after 9/11; his job approval ratings went from 52 percent to 90 percent, and they remained above 70 percent for almost an entire year.[62]

rally-around-the-flag effect: *Surge of public support for the president in times of international crisis.*

The public's influence on the president's decision to engage in military action is always limited because the amount of information available to the public is purposely restricted, both to ensure the safety of the troops involved and to preserve military advantages in conflict. Simply put, the president and his or her military advisers have access to far greater amounts of information than does the average citizen, and in turn, the average citizen expects the president to act on this information in a way that preserves national security. Even when Congress debates sending troops or funding military action, most classified information is held in secret and not revealed to the public (but see Chapter 4, Civil Liberties, on the Snowden National Security Agency revelations). The fundamental imbalance of information held by the government and what the general public understands poses a major problem for the assumptions of a democracy because the people cannot hold the government fully accountable if they are not fully informed. Nevertheless, when a president decides to send troops, he or she has to anticipate public reaction and hope that the public maintains its trust and confidence in his or her decision to take such action.

The twenty-first century has ushered in new weaponry and new levels of violence committed by nations and **nonstate actors**, such as terrorist groups who take up violence against civilians as a means of attacking the United States and other Western nations.

nonstate actors: *Individuals or groups that do not represent any specific national government and may take action across borders.*

The Bush administration used this new reality to justify military action against the Taliban regime in Afghanistan. President George W. Bush went one step further to launch a preemptive attack—that is, an attack prior to an act of aggression by another—against Iraq in 2003 to remove Saddam Hussein from power and dismantle alleged weapons of mass destruction that might be used against the United States and its allies (see Chapter 13 for more on the Iraq and Afghanistan wars). In invading Afghanistan and Iraq, Bush was trying to leverage the full strength of the U.S. military to combat terrorism.

However, many critics argue that in conflicts between a state and nonstate actors, traditional military weapons and strategies are ineffective, and new tools, such as surveillance, intelligence gathering and analysis, and the use of unmanned drones, are the only way to prevent future attacks. This is perceived to be particularly true of efforts to combat terrorist groups such as ISIS and Boko Haram. As such, the policy infrastructure dedicated to addressing terrorism has grown dramatically over the past decade, with a greater reliance on cooperation among the Department of Homeland Security (see Chapter 14), Department of Defense, Department of Justice, and the president's National Security Council. Coordinating across such a vast portion of the federal government can produce both gates and gateways to effective antiterrorism policies, both at home and abroad (see Chapter 4 and Chapter 6, Public Opinion, for more on U.S. antiterrorism policy).

Anti-Nuclear Proliferation Measures. Compounding the challenges of fighting terrorism is the fear of nuclear proliferation among established nations and nonstate terrorist groups. In addition to the United States and Russia, the United Kingdom, France, China, India, North Korea, Pakistan, and Israel have nuclear capabilities. Because India and Pakistan have experienced border clashes and are generally unfriendly toward each other, their possession of nuclear weapons poses a threat to the stability of Southeast Asia. Most recently, the United States has focused intense concern on nuclear weapons development in Iran and North Korea (see Figure 16.10).

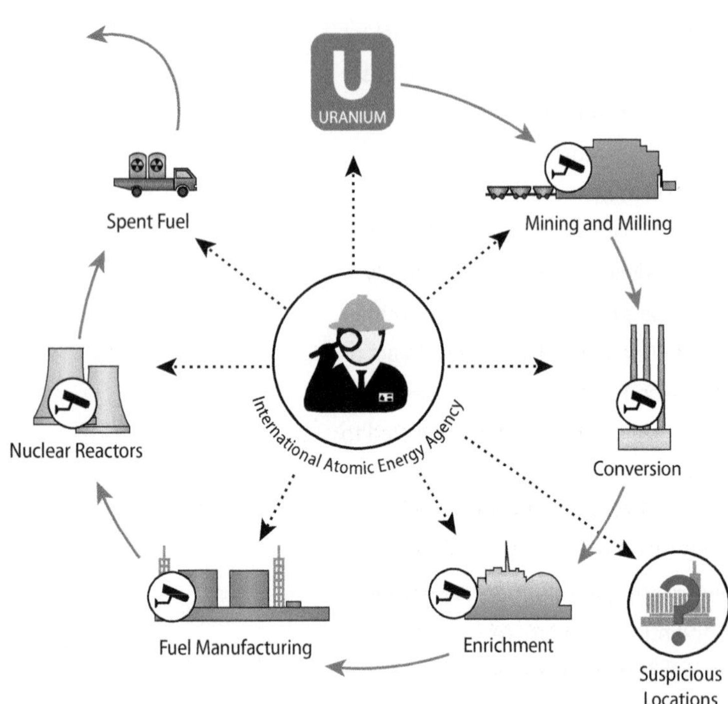

FIGURE 16.10 Monitoring Nuclear Facilities in Iran

Iran has been developing the capability to produce nuclear weapons but has not yet finished the process. The Iran deal is designed to prevent Iran from obtaining nuclear weapons for at least ten years. This figure shows how the international community will monitor Iran's compliance with the deal at every stage of nuclear development.

Source: https://www.whitehouse.gov/issues/foreign-policy/iran-deal

As the preeminent international peacekeeping organization, the United Nations has long led efforts to curb nuclear proliferation through treaties that would ban the testing of nuclear weapons and set up an official verification system whereby countries would be regularly inspected to make sure they were not developing nuclear capabilities. The Nuclear Non-Proliferation Treaty that went into effect in 1970 was designed to discourage nations from developing nuclear weapons technology; currently, 190 nations are signatories.[63] The key element of this treaty is the use of the International Atomic Energy Agency (IAEA) to monitor and inspect nations' weapons capability. The United States and the rest of the international community rely on this organization and its powers to monitor nuclear facility development in countries that do not currently have nuclear weapons, such as Iran.

To that end, President Obama instructed his Secretary of State, John Kerry, to participate in multilateral negotiations (which included China,

France, Germany, the Russian Federation, and Great Britain) with Iran to limit that country's progress toward acquiring a nuclear weapon. In July 2015, the United States and these other nations agreed to a Joint Comprehensive Plan of Action that required Iran to stop its progress toward developing a nuclear bomb for at least ten years and agree to regular inspections by the IAEA. Contingent on Iran's compliance and cooperation, the United Nations agreed to lift existing sanctions on Iran, which enabled it to participate in the world economic arena and gain access to funds that had been frozen by other nations.[64] As of January 2016, the IAEA had certified that Iran had taken the necessary first steps to limit its progress toward a nuclear bomb, and as a result, some sanctions were lifted. However, in his comments on the Iran deal at that time, President Obama reiterated that any violation of the agreement on Iran's part would result on an immediate reimposition of the sanctions.[65] Supporters of the Iran deal argued that keeping nuclear weapons out of Iran would make the Middle East more stable, but opponents warned that allowing Iran access to its previously frozen money, and allowing it to sell oil, would only make it more powerful in the region.

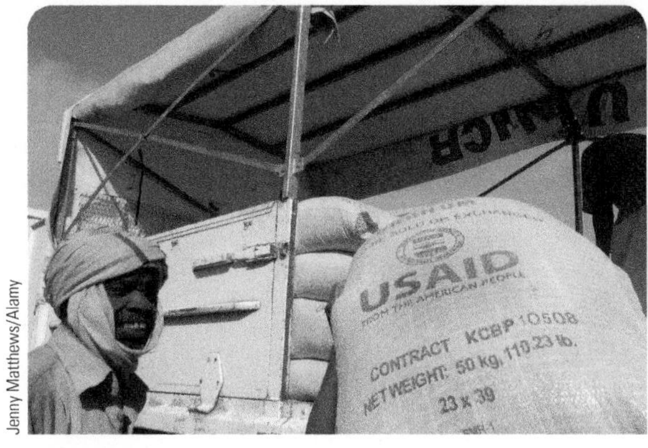

Jenny Matthews/Alamy

IMAGE 16.8 A number of U.S.-based organizations provide aid to individuals in need all around the world. Here workers with the U.S. Agency for International Development (USAID) help administer assistance to Sudanese refugees.

Diplomacy and Humanitarian Assistance. In addition to military actions, another cornerstone of U.S. foreign policy is diplomacy. The Department of State is responsible for formulating foreign policy using nonmilitary methods; these efforts are conducted by diplomatic personnel in U.S. missions, consulates, and embassies around the world. There are also agencies within the Department of State that oversee a key component of our foreign policy—the provision of humanitarian assistance. The interdependence of nations today provides an opportunity for Americans, from the average citizen to the president, to participate on a wider level and improve living conditions everywhere. A world with more stable nations that treat their citizens equally and with dignity benefits the United States because it means that fewer internal conflicts will emerge that warrant military intervention. Governmental and nongovernmental organizations that provide funds for economic, health, and educational development provide an avenue for the U.S. government, groups, and individual citizens to take an active role in international life.

For example, within the U.S. federal government, the U.S. Agency for International Development (USAID) is an independent agency with the mission of providing training, education, and materials to developing nations and of promoting democracy.[66] It is led by an administrator appointed by the president who works closely with other federal departments, including the Department of State, on international aid issues. USAID was created by President John F. Kennedy in 1961 as part of the Foreign Assistance Act. Today its activities include disaster relief, child health and nutrition, and disease treatment and prevention. For example, USAID disaster assistance response teams were very involved in fighting the Ebola virus in West Africa. In fiscal year 2015, USAID had an operating budget of $1.40 billion.[67]

In addition to unilaterally promoting economic development, the United States is also a member of the World Bank and the International Monetary Fund, two global economic organizations. The **World Bank** was founded in 1944 as an international aid and reconstruction organization to help rebuild nations that had been badly damaged during WWII.[68]

World Bank: *International organization that distributes grants and low-income loans in developing countries.*

PUBLIC POLICY AND INTERNATIONAL RELATIONS

Promotion of Democracy

President Woodrow Wilson's idea was that the United States should make the world "safe for democracy," and President Truman's view was that the United States should intervene militarily to promote and defend against Communist takeovers. Truman's approach drew strength from the theory of "democratic peace," which holds that the world is a safer place if nations are democratic. The core contention is that democracies, reflecting the will of the people, have almost never gone to war against other each other.[69] The public's desire for peace simply makes that outcome rare.

The federal government attempts to export democratic values through diplomatic and cultural programs. The Voice of America broadcasts news and programming in more than forty different languages across the world and cooperates with private organizations, such as Radio Free Asia, that provide a forum for democratic activists in Myanmar, China, and other nondemocratic states. American interest groups and nonprofit organizations also promote democracy abroad. Freedom House supports nonviolent civil initiatives in societies where freedom is denied or threatened. Since 1972, the organization has issued reports on every country around the world, classifying countries as free, partially free, or not free based on a freedom index that takes into account the electoral process, civil liberties, and human rights (see Figure 16.11).

Today, the question of what is justified in the name of preserving and promoting the American form of democracy

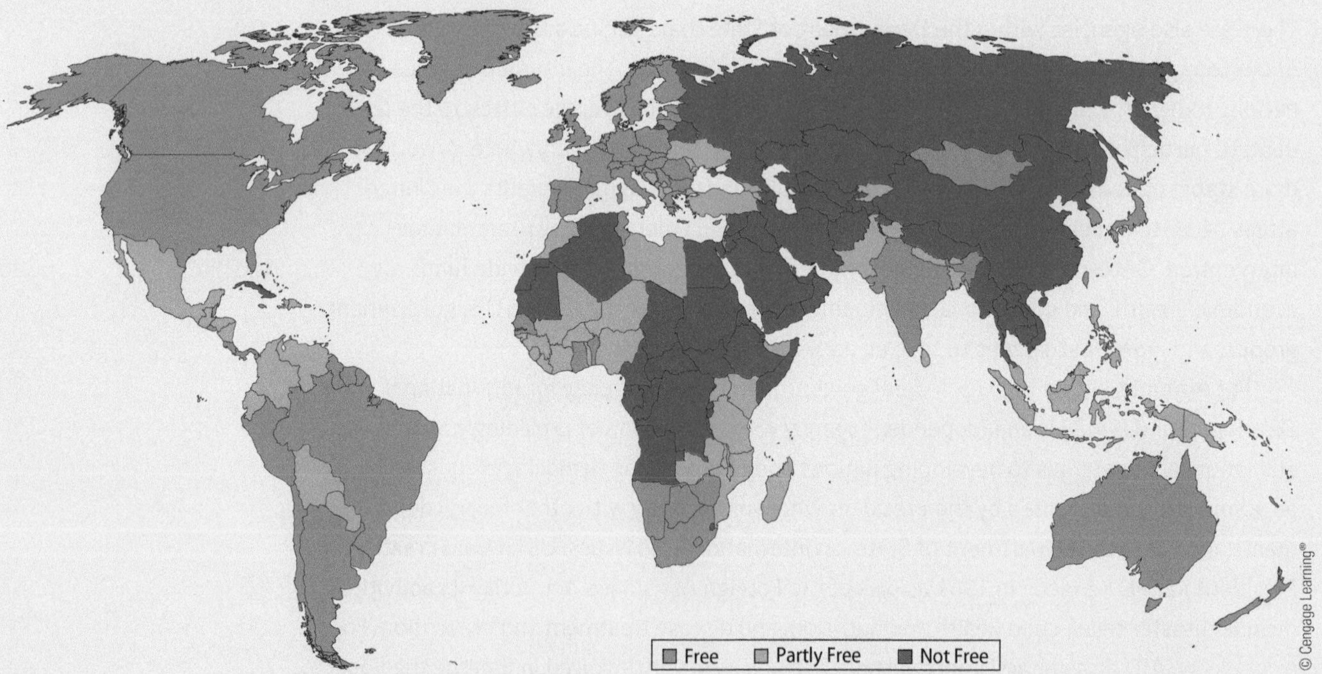

FIGURE 16.11 Freedom House Map

Freedom House is an organization that monitors freedom around the world. It produced this map to illustrate which countries were free, partly free, and not free as of 2016.

Source: https://freedomhouse.org/report/freedom-world/freedom-world-2016

remains unresolved, especially in the face of old and new conflicts in nations such as Iraq, Egypt, and Syria where internal forces are battling for control of their governments. Making the case to the American people that direct U.S. intervention is necessary in distant regions with long histories of conflict, such as the Middle East, is difficult to do, as we saw with the debate over punishing Syria for its use of chemical weapons. America's international reputation was tarnished by its unilateralism in the Iraq War, making it more difficult for the United States to gain cooperation from the international community for intervention.

For these and other reasons, President Obama tried to reshape U.S. foreign policy by becoming more reliant on international organizations such as the United Nations, and using the international economic system to impose financial penalties and block trade with nations that violate international law or harbor terrorist groups. In an address to West Point, Obama made it clear that the United States would intervene when its interests were directly threatened, but that it could not be expected to send forces to engage in every military action occurring around the world. However, as the upheaval in Iraq shows, the United States remains involved in military conflicts even after the formal cessation of its role in war. The promotion of democracy is a long and unstable process, and when countries in which the United States has had a military presence devolve into civil war, there is enormous pressure to reengage to prevent further bloodshed.

Public Policy Connections

1. To what extent should American foreign policy be concerned with promoting American political values? Should American foreign policy instead focus on promoting American economic interests?
2. Should Congress be more active in shaping American foreign policy?

Today it has 189 members, known as shareholders, and five divisions that work together to provide low-interest loans, grants, and investment capital to build and improve infrastructure and alleviate poverty. The United States is the largest shareholder in the World Bank and consequently has leadership responsibilities; the president nominates the head of the bank, who serves a five-year renewable term.[70] The World Bank funds specific projects to improve transportation, provide clean water, build energy utilities, modernize medical care, initiate crop development programs, and provide start-up money for new businesses in poor and developing countries. In fiscal year 2015, the World Bank provided $42.49 billion in grants, loans, and investment capital to nations around the world.[71]

International Monetary Fund (IMF): *International organization that works to stabilize currency values and government debt for nations in economic difficulty.*

The **International Monetary Fund (IMF)** was created alongside the World Bank in 1944 with a different mission. The IMF focuses on preserving economic stability, including currency values, among nations and makes short-term loans to nations that cannot balance their budgets or need immediate funds.[72] The IMF also works with nations to try to reduce their government debt by renegotiating loans or by providing loans on better terms. The IMF has the same set of members as the World Bank, and each member makes a financial contribution to the fund based on its share of the global economy. The IMF has a board of governors, which includes a governor from each member nation, but the daily operations of the fund are overseen by a managing director and a twenty-four-member executive board. In contrast to its role in the World Bank, the United States does not play a prominent role in directing IMF operations and does not nominate the managing director. However, the United States pays the largest single share (17.6 percent) of the IMF's fund, so it wields significant influence over lending decisions. In 2015, the IMF had $120 billion in outstanding loans to countries around the world.[73]

ELECTION 2016

Holding Steady or Changing Course?

PRESIDENTIAL ELECTIONS CAN BE THOUGHT OF AS referendums on the incumbent president's party policies. In 2016, Democratic nominee Hillary Clinton promised to continue the policies of Barack Obama's presidency in both the economic and foreign spheres as well as to preserve Obamacare. Republican nominee Donald Trump promised to change many of Obama's policies, including reforming or repealing Obamacare, changing U.S. positions on military interventions, reworking the NATO alliance, and altering trade policies to protect U.S. manufacturing industries. Voters had a stark contrast between the two candidates in terms of how they would each have upheld or reversed the White House policies of the previous eight years.

In the area of foreign policy, Clinton's challenge was in claiming credit for Obama's successes but explaining how she would fix his failures. For Trump, the challenge was keeping a promise to keep America out of war and still explain how he would fight terrorism and keep Americans safer at home. Voters were generally tired of war in foreign lands but fearful of terrorist attacks, such as those in San Bernardino and Orlando, at home. Although voters were supportive of President Obama's actions to end active U.S. combat in Iraq and Afghanistan and to open dialogue with nations such as Cuba, they remained nervous about the threat of terrorism and border security. Voters were also skeptical of containing Iran in terms of developing nuclear weapons despite Obama's diplomatic efforts with that nation.

In terms of domestic policy, Clinton argued that Obama's policies, and those of the Democratic Party generally, had repaired the American economy, so they should be continued. When Obama took office in January 2009, the economy was on the verge of a depression, with unemployment nearing 10 percent. In 2016, unemployment was around 5 percent, with monthly job growth averaging around two hundred thousand jobs. Still, many Americans remained skeptical of the condition of the economy and Obama's policies, including bailouts for large corporations and banks and using federal money to stimulate job growth. And there were still sections of the American workforce that remained unemployed or underemployed, such as people between the ages of 18 and 24, as well as declines in some sectors of the economy, such as manufacturing.[74]

Trump crafted his campaign around the idea that he was a businessman who knew how to bring back jobs across many sectors of the economy. Despite the fact that Trump did not provide specific proposals or policy suggestions to show how he would strengthen the U.S. economy, voters responded to his personal style as a leader who would produce better policies for them. It was not surprising that his message resonated with a significant portion of the electorate who believe that the policy-making process has gotten too big and inefficient to serve the average American. Revelations such as lead poisoning in Flint, Michigan, also provided examples of government failure of the type that Trump promised to fix if elected.

Ultimately, President Donald Trump faces the largest national debt in history and has the responsibility to produce domestic policy in an ever more complex nation. From health care to immigration to the environment, the landscape is always changing, and voters have to decide whether the current system of policy making is equipped to meet new challenges. The same is true of navigating foreign policy when governments all over the world are experiencing internal transition as well as increased threats to their security.

In this way, interpreting the outcomes of Election 2016 is more complicated than merely declaring victory for the out-party candidate Donald Trump. President Trump will govern in his own style and undoubtedly adopt new policy approaches. Voters will have their chance to register approval or disapproval with President Trump's policies when Congressional midterm elections take place in 2018.

The United States supports organizations that send individuals to foreign nations for peacekeeping, educational, and cultural purposes. The **Peace Corps** is perhaps the best known of these organizations. The Peace Corps was established in 1961; since then, more than 195,000 U.S. citizen volunteers have lived and worked in seventy-six countries all over the world.[75] The mission of the Peace Corps is to help train citizens of other nations in essential skills, establish communication about Americans with other nations, and bring more knowledge about foreign peoples back to America through the volunteers. Today the Peace Corps operates on a budget of $379.5 million, and it still attracts recent college graduates and others who work in wide-ranging fields, including teaching, agriculture, HIV/AIDS prevention, medicine, engineering, communications, environmental conservation, and construction.[76] The model of the Peace Corps has spurred the creation of domestic volunteer organizations such as AmeriCorps and Teach for America, which operate within the United States but pursue similar goals of education and economic development in underserved areas.

Peace Corps: *U.S. government-funded organization that sends individuals on educational and cultural missions around the world.*

However, the fact that nations are more connected to each other in our global world does not mean that they share political systems, religions, or cultures. The differences that do exist have come into the forefront through regime change in recent years, which has resulted in political, social, and military conflict. The scope of U.S. involvement in international relations is decided by each presidential administration, in consultation with Congress; in that way, every presidential election is a gateway through which the American voters have the opportunity to render their opinions on whether to reset the boundaries of engagement.

Public Policy and Democracy

Public policy covers a lot of territory in the language of American politics. It is essentially the set of outputs by federal, state, and local governments that address the interests and opinions of citizens. In this chapter, we have presented an overview of the federal regulatory system that serves as the main vehicle to implement the laws that Congress and the president enact. Once a law is passed, the executive branch produces a set of guidelines for how the law will work, and the public has a chance to comment on those regulations before they are finally put into place.

The three broad policy areas discussed in this chapter—domestic, economic, and foreign—all differ in the ways that policy outcomes can be directly controlled by policy makers. In domestic policy, our federal system of government has expanded over the past century to provide direct and indirect assistance to individuals in the area of income security, food security, housing, and health care. Our system of federalism allows states some leeway in how they implement federal law, especially when the policy overlaps with areas that are solely controlled by the states. The different ways that the ACA has been implemented or blocked at the state level illustrate the variation in the potential impact of federal policy.

In the economic sphere, the president, Congress, and the Federal Reserve all have a role to play in how much money the government spends and how cheaply consumers can borrow money. But the independent business cycle also has a strong impact on whether those policies succeed in contributing to economic growth and stability.

In the area of foreign policy, the United States has always had to balance its own principles regarding human rights and freedoms with its military and economic self-interest around the world. Also, military and humanitarian crises emerge frequently and fall out of direct U.S. control; however, the United States is still faced with the choice of whether to intervene and to what extent. As events in Ukraine, Syria, and Africa have shown, choosing the right policy is no easy task.

At times, it seems that there are more gates to influencing public policy in our system of government than there are gateways. Policy makers can be well-intentioned and sincerely interested in reflecting the interests and concerns of the majority of the people, but the process itself can be slower and less efficient than most of us would like. The policy-making process is complicated because it involves elected officials in multiple branches of government at all levels (federal, state, and local), the business community, interest groups, and private citizens who choose to make their opinions heard. Our system has about as much participation as James Madison would have expected; the question remains as to whether it is enough to address the pressing needs of the twenty-first century.

Political Science Reasoning

Question 1

Practice 1, Practice 4

President George W. Bush went to New York City on September 14, 2001, just after the 9/11 terrorist attacks. Addressing a crowd of rescue workers at "ground zero," he made the following remarks:

> Bush: Thank you all. I want you all to know—it [the bullhorn used by the president] can't go any louder—I want you all to know that America today, America today is on bended knee, in prayer for the people whose lives were lost here, for the workers who work here, for the families who mourn. The nation stands with the good people of New York City and New Jersey and Connecticut as we mourn the loss of thousands of our citizens.
>
> Rescue Worker: I can't hear you!
>
> Bush: I can hear you! I can hear you! The rest of the world hears you! And the people—and the people who knocked these buildings down will hear all of us soon!
>
> Rescue Workers: [Chanting] USA! USA! USA! . . .
>
> Bush: The nation—The nation sends its love and compassion—
>
> Rescue Worker: God bless America!
>
> Bush:—to everybody who is here. Thank you for your hard work. Thank you for makin' the nation proud, and may God bless America.
>
> Rescue Workers: [Chanting] USA! USA! USA! . . .

1. What was the purpose of the above speech?
2. What is the impact of major events, such as 9/11, on presidential power?
3. How do major events, such as 9/11, change the relationship between Congress and the president?

Question 2

Practice 1, Practice 4

> 107th Congress
> 2d Session
> S.J. Res 46
>
> Whereas in 1990 in response to Iraq's war of aggression against and illegal occupation of Kuwait, the United States forged a coalition of nations to liberate Kuwait and its people in order to defend the national security of the United States and enforce United Nations Security Council resolutions relating to Iraq . . .
>
> **SECTION 1. SHORT TITLE.**
>
> This joint resolution may be cited as the 'Authorization for Use of Military Force Against Iraq Resolution of 2002'.

SEC. 2. SUPPORT FOR UNITED STATES DIPLOMATIC EFFORTS.

The Congress of the United States supports the efforts by the President to—

(1) strictly enforce through the United Nations Security Council all relevant Security Council resolutions regarding Iraq and encourages him in those efforts . . .

SEC. 3. AUTHORIZATION FOR USE OF UNITED STATES ARMED FORCES.

(a) Authorization—The President is authorized to use the Armed Forces of the United States as he determines to be necessary and appropriate in order to—

> (1) defend the national security of the United States against the continuing threat posed by Iraq; and
>
> (2) enforce all relevant United Nations Security Council resolutions regarding Iraq...

(c) War Powers Resolution Requirements.—

> (1) Specific statutory authorization.—Consistent with section 8(a)(1) of the War Powers Resolution [50 U.S.C. 1547(a)(1)], the Congress declares that this section is intended to constitute specific statutory authorization within the meaning of section 5(b) of the War Powers Resolution [50 U.S.C. 1544(b)].
>
> (2) Applicability of other requirements.—Nothing in this joint resolution supersedes any requirement of the War Powers Resolution [50 U.S.C. 1541 et seq.].

SEC. 4. REPORTS TO CONGRESS.

(a) Reports—The President shall, at least once every 60 days, submit to the Congress a report on matters relevant to this joint resolution . . .

1. What is the purpose of the above document?
2. What constitutional power(s) is Congress exercising?
3. What power(s) does the president have that corresponds to the above congressional power(s)?
4. To what extent are the powers of the president and the Congress in conflict? How?

Focus on AP® Success

16 Economic, Domestic, and Foreign Policy

Thinking Politically

Argumentation

The Constitution vests Congress with the sole power to declare war. However, the president as commander in chief has ordered the military into conflict without congressional approval since the early days of the republic. With an exception for direct imminent attack upon the United States, should the Constitution be amended to require presidents to seek congressional approval before entering into any military conflict?

Argumentation

The U.S. Supreme Court has interpreted the Constitution to allow the judiciary to determine the constitutionality of actions of the executive and legislative branches. This power was established in *Marbury v. Madison* and is known as judicial review. However, the judiciary is unelected with lifetime terms while members of both the Senate and House of Representatives are held accountable by the people in regular elections. As the people's representatives, should the Congress have the ability to overturn, perhaps by a two-thirds majority vote, a judicial decision that declares a law unconditional?

Argumentation

The Constitution vests Congress with the power to set fiscal policy. How the national government taxes and spends money can have a profound impact on the economy. Should national government use fiscal policy to attempt to manage the economy? If so, should it engage in Keynesian or supply-side policies? If not, why?

Argumentation

The Constitution vests Congress with many powers to oversee the federal bureaucracy such as the power of the purse and authorization legislation. However, if attacked by Congress, the bureaucracy is not without resources. Agencies often have alliances with special interest groups that they can use to try and blunt actions by Congress. Does Congress possess adequate Constitutional power to oversee the federal bureaucracy?

Concept Application

Explain how military conflict tends to impact the approval rating of the president.

Concept Application

Explain how the Congress sets fiscal policy.

Concept Application

Compare liberal, conservative, and libertarian views on the role of the government in the economy.

Concept Application

The Constitution of the United States divides governmental power between the national government and the states in a framework known as federalism. Explain how federalism complicates the policy-making process.

Concept Application

Explain how the policy-making process in the United States provides for multiple points of access to policy makers.

Concept Application

Explain how who participates in politics impacts the policies that are made.

Making Connections

The previous chapters have illustrated how different institutions and features of the U.S. government operate. This chapter provides examples of how the institutions and features interact as *a system* to produce public policy.

Many students can become confused when thinking about public policy. These students tend to view public policy as only statutory law issued by some legislative body such as the U.S. Congress. However, a more accurate view defines public policy as official pronouncements by public institutes with citizen compliance being mandatory. Using this definition of public policy, it becomes evident that there are four national policy making institutions: Congress, the president, the bureaucracy, and the court system.

Think back on how the president can make public policy by issuing executive orders, how bureaucracy makes public policy by issuing administrative regulations, and how the judiciary makes public policy by deciding cases that create precedents.

Agenda setting is the process by which issues are selected to be addressed by the political system. In Chapter 7, The News and Social Media and Chapter 13, The Presidency, review how the media and the president impact the national agenda.

The constitutional division of power between the national government and the states can and does impact policy making. Review in Chapter 3, Federalism, how policy areas are divided between the national government and the states. Also review how the role of the national government has grown over time, in particular which constitutional provisions and which Supreme Court decisions have contributed to this increase in power.

Foreign and military policy is the product of the interaction of the Congress and the president. Typically, presidents take the lead; however, Congress has a role to play as well. After reviewing Chapter 12, Congress, and Chapter, 13, The Presidency, be able to explain the constitutional powers of each institution with regard to both foreign and military power.

Interest groups are intimately involved in policy development. In Chapter 8, Interest Groups, review the role the iron triangles and issue networks play in policy creation.

Americans approach public policy from different ideological perspectives. In Chapter 6, Public Opinion, review the liberal, conservative, and libertarian views on policy.

Going Deeper: Fiscal Policy

Fiscal policy is defined as the taxing and spending policy of the United States. The Constitution vests the Congress and the president with the power to set fiscal policy. Each year the president submits a proposed budget to Congress that sets forth his recommendation for fiscal policy. The Office of Management and Budget in the Executive Office of the President exists to help the president in this endeavor.

After receiving the president's proposed budget, the House and Senate Committees on the Budget begin the process of drafting their own budget resolutions. The Congressional Budget Office assists them in this process.

There several different parts to the budget. First is mandatory spending. Mandatory spending occurs automatically. If Congress never passed another piece of legislation, money will still be spent from the U.S. Treasury in accordance with existing mandatory-spending provisions in previously passed legislation. Mandatory spending is mainly comprised of entitlement programs of which Social Security, Medicare, and Medicaid are the largest. In fiscal year 2015, mandatory spending accounted for 64 percent of spending by the national government.

In fiscal year 2016, interest on the national debt comprised 6 percent of spending by the national government. While not categorized as mandatory spending, interest on the national debt occurs automatically as well. The Treasury Department is authorized to refinance the principal of the national debt with the issuance of new securities.

All other spending is categorized as discretionary. The largest area of discretionary spending is national defense, accounting for 15 percent of overall spending (half of the discretionary spending) in fiscal year 2016.

Legal authorization for the expenditure of government funds comes in the form of appropriations bills. These bills are written by the House and Senate appropriations committees. The House and Senate versions of these bills are reconciled in a conference committee. It is during the appropriations process that "pork barrel" spending is usually authorized. Frequently targeted by pundits for citizens' outrage, much of this spending may very well be wasteful. However, the impact on the overall budget is miniscule.

Budget resolutions previously adopted will be used as a blueprint for the drafting of appropriations bills. It is possible for appropriations bills to be drafted that exceed the amount set forth in the budget. As such, these budget resolutions are little more than guidelines.

Total income for the national government in fiscal year 2016 was $2.99 trillion, of which $2.49 trillion was already allocated to mandatory spending and interest on the national debt. This occurs *before* one dollar is spent for discretionary items. Total spending that fiscal year was $3.54 trillion. The difference between the amount spent and the amount received is called a deficit. The deficit for fiscal year 2016 was over half a trillion dollars. The national debt is comprised of the total of all of the previous deficits.

Obviously with the growth of entitlement programs due to an ageing population and increased interest payments due to increases in the national debt, attempts to balance the budget will be difficult.

APPENDIX A

The Declaration of Independence

In Congress, July 4, 1776

The Unanimous Declaration of the Thirteen United States of America

When, in the course of human events, it becomes necessary for one people to dissolve the political bands which have connected them with another, and to assume, among the powers of the earth, the separate and equal station to which the laws of nature and of nature's God entitle them, a decent respect to the opinions of mankind requires that they should declare the causes which impel them to the separation.

We hold these truths to be self-evident: That all men are created equal; that they are endowed by their Creator with certain unalienable rights; that among these are life, liberty, and the pursuit of happiness; that, to secure these rights, governments are instituted among men, deriving their just powers from the consent of the governed; that whenever any form of government becomes destructive of these ends, it is the right of the people to alter or to abolish it, and to institute new government, laying its foundation on such principles, and organizing its powers in such form, as to them shall seem most likely to effect their safety and happiness. Prudence, indeed, will dictate that governments long established should not be changed for light and transient causes; and accordingly all experience hath shown that mankind are more disposed to suffer, while evils are sufferable, than to right themselves by abolishing the forms to which they are accustomed. But when a long train of abuses and usurpations, pursuing invariably the same object, evinces a design to reduce them under absolute despotism, it is their right, it is their duty, to throw off such government, and to provide new guards for their future security. Such has been the patient sufferance of these colonies; and such is now the necessity which constrains them to alter their former systems of government. The history of the present King of Great Britain is a history of repeated injuries and usurpations, all having in direct object the establishment of an absolute tyranny over these states. To prove this, let facts be submitted to a candid world.

He has refused to assent to laws, the most wholesome and necessary for the public good.

He has forbidden his governors to pass laws of immediate and pressing importance, unless suspended in their operation till his assent should be obtained; and, when so suspended, he has utterly neglected to attend to them.

He has refused to pass other laws for the accommodation of large districts of people, unless those people would relinquish the right of representation in the legislature, a right inestimable to them, and formidable to tyrants only.

He has called together legislative bodies at places unusual, uncomfortable, and distant from the depository of their public records, for the sole purpose of fatiguing them into compliance with his measures.

He has dissolved representative houses repeatedly, for opposing, with manly firmness, his invasions on the rights of the people.

He has refused for a long time, after such dissolutions, to cause others to be elected; whereby the legislative powers, incapable of annihilation, have returned to the people at large for their exercise; the state remaining, in the mean time, exposed to all dangers of invasions from without and convulsions within.

He has endeavored to prevent the population of these states; for that purpose obstructing the laws for naturalization of foreigners; refusing to pass others to encourage their migration hither, and raising the conditions of new appropriations of lands.

He has obstructed the administration of justice, by refusing his assent to laws for establishing judiciary powers.

He has made judges dependent on his will alone, for the tenure of their offices, and the amount and payment of their salaries.

He has erected a multitude of new offices, and sent hither swarms of officers to harass our people and eat out their substance.

He has kept among us, in times of peace, standing armies, without the consent of our legislatures.

He has affected to render the military independent of, and superior to, the civil power.

He has combined with others to subject us to a jurisdiction foreign to our constitution, and unacknowledged by our laws, giving his assent to their acts of pretended legislation;

For quartering large bodies of armed troops among us;

For protecting them, by a mock trial, from punishment for any murders which they should commit on the inhabitants of these states;

For cutting off our trade with all parts of the world;

For imposing taxes on us without our consent;

For depriving us, in many cases, of the benefits of trial by jury;

For transporting us beyond seas, to be tried for pretended offenses;

For abolishing the free system of English laws in a neighboring province, establishing therein an arbitrary government, and enlarging its boundaries, so as to render it at once an example and fit instrument for introducing the same absolute rule into these colonies;

For taking away our charters, abolishing our more valuable laws, and altering fundamentally the forms of our governments;

For suspending our own legislatures, and declaring themselves invested with power to legislate for us in all cases whatsoever.

He has abdicated government here, by declaring us out of his protection and waging war against us.

He has plundered our seas, ravaged our coasts, burned our towns, and destroyed the lives of our people.

He is at this time transporting large armies of foreign mercenaries to complete the works of death, desolation, and tyranny already begun with circumstances of cruelty and perfidy scarcely paralleled in the most barbarous ages, and totally unworthy the head of a civilized nation.

He has constrained our fellow-citizens, taken captive on the high seas, to bear arms against their country, to become the executioners of their friends and brethren, or to fall themselves by their hands.

He has excited domestic insurrections among us, and has endeavored to bring on the inhabitants of our frontiers the merciless Indian savages, whose known rule of warfare is an undistinguished destruction of all ages, sexes, and conditions.

In every stage of these oppressions we have petitioned for redress in the most humble terms; our repeated petitions have been answered only by repeated injury. A prince, whose character is thus marked by every act which may define a tyrant, is unfit to be the ruler of a free people.

Nor have we been wanting in our attentions to our British brethren. We have warned them, from time to time, of attempts by their legislature to extend an unwarrantable jurisdiction over us. We have reminded them of the circumstances of our emigration and settlement here. We have appealed to their native justice and magnanimity; and we have conjured them, by the ties of our common kindred, to disavow these usurpations, which would inevitably interrupt our connections and correspondence. They, too, have been deaf to the voice of justice and of consanguinity. We must, therefore, acquiesce in the necessity which denounces our separation, and hold them, as we hold the rest of mankind, enemies in war, in peace friends.

We, therefore, the representatives of the United States of America, in General Congress assembled, appealing to the Supreme Judge of the world for the rectitude of our intentions, do, in the name and by the authority of the good people of these colonies, solemnly publish and declare, that these United Colonies are, and of right ought to be, FREE AND INDEPENDENT STATES; that they are absolved from all allegiance to the British crown, and that all political connection between them and the state of Great Britain is, and ought to be, totally dissolved; and that, as free and independent states, they have full power to levy war, conclude peace, contract alliances, establish commerce, and do all other acts and things which independent states may of right do. And for the support of this declaration, with a firm reliance on the protection of Divine Providence, we mutually pledge to each other our lives, our fortunes, and our sacred honor.

John Hancock, *President and delegate from Massachusetts*

Georgia

Button Gwinnett
Lyman Hall
George Walton

North Carolina

William Hooper
Joseph Hewes
John Penn

South Carolina

Edward Rutledge
Thomas Heyward Jr.
Thomas Lynch Jr.
Arthur Middleton

Maryland

Samuel Chase
William Paca
Thomas Stone
Charles Carroll of Carrollton

Virginia

George Wythe
Richard Henry Lee
Thomas Jefferson
Benjamin Harrison
Thomas Nelson Jr.
Francis Lightfoot Lee
Carter Braxton

Pennsylvania

Robert Morris
Benjamin Rush
Benjamin Franklin
John Morton
George Clymer
James Smith
George Taylor
James Wilson
George Ross

Delaware

Caesar Rodney
George Read
Thomas McKean

New York

William Floyd
Philip Livingston
Francis Lewis
Lewis Morris

New Jersey

Richard Stockton
John Witherspoon
Francis Hopkinson
John Hart
Abraham Clark

New Hampshire

Josiah Bartlett
William Whipple
Matthew Thornton

Massachusetts

Samuel Adams
John Adams
Robert Treat Paine
Elbridge Gerry

Rhode Island

Stephen Hopkins
William Ellery

Connecticut

Roger Sherman
Samuel Huntington
William Williams
Oliver Wolcott

APPENDIX B

The Constitution of the United States

We the People of the United States, in Order to form a more perfect Union, establish Justice, insure domestic Tranquility, provide for the common defence, promote the general Welfare, and secure the Blessings of Liberty to ourselves and our Posterity, do ordain and establish this Constitution for the United States of America.

Article I.

Section 1. All legislative Powers herein granted shall be vested in a Congress of the United States, which shall consist of a Senate and House of Representatives.

Section 2. The House of Representatives shall be composed of Members chosen every second Year by the People of the several States, and the Electors in each State shall have the Qualifications requisite for Electors of the most numerous Branch of the State Legislature.

No Person shall be a Representative who shall not have attained to the age of twenty five Years, and been seven Years a Citizen of the United States, and who shall not, when elected, be an Inhabitant of that State in which he shall be chosen.

Changed by the Fourteenth Amendment, Section 2.

Representatives and direct Taxes shall be apportioned among the several States which may be included within this Union, according to their respective Numbers, which shall be determined by adding to the whole Number of free Persons, including those bound to Service for a Term of Years, and excluding Indians not taxed, three fifths of all other Persons. The actual Enumeration shall be made within three Years after the first Meeting of the Congress of the United States, and within every subsequent Term of ten Years, in such Manner as they shall by Law direct. The Number of Representatives shall not exceed one for every thirty Thousand, but each State shall have at Least one Representative; and until such enumeration shall be made, the State of New Hampshire shall be entitled to chuse three, Massachusetts eight, Rhode-Island and Providence Plantations one, Connecticut five, New-York six, New Jersey four, Pennsylvania eight, Delaware one, Maryland six, Virginia ten, North Carolina five, South Carolina five, and Georgia three.

When vacancies happen in the Representation from any State, the Executive Authority thereof shall issue Writs of Election to fill such Vacancies.

The House of Representatives shall chuse their Speaker and other Officers; and shall have the sole Power of Impeachment.

Section 3. The Senate of the United States shall be composed of two Senators from each State, chosen by the Legislature thereof, for six Years; and each Senator shall have one Vote.

Changed by the Seventeenth Amendment.

Immediately after they shall be assembled in Consequence of the first Election, they shall be divided as equally as may be into three Classes. The Seats of the Senators of the first class shall be vacated at the Expiration of the second Year, of the second Class at the Expiration of the fourth Year, and of the third Class at the Expiration of the sixth Year, so that one third may be chosen every second Year; and if Vacancies happen by Resignation, or otherwise, during the Recess of the Legislature of any State, the Executive thereof may make temporary Appointments until the next Meeting of the Legislature, which shall then fill such Vacancies.

Changed by the Seventeenth Amendment.

No Person shall be a Senator who shall not have attained to the Age of thirty Years, and been nine Years a Citizen of the United States, and who shall not, when elected, be an Inhabitant of that State for which he shall be chosen.

The Vice President of the United States shall be President of the Senate, but shall have no Vote, unless they be equally divided.

The Senate shall chuse their other Officers, and also a President pro tempore, in the Absence of the Vice President, or when he shall exercise the Office of President of the United States.

The Senate shall have the sole Power to try all Impeachments. When sitting for that Purpose, they shall be on Oath or Affirmation. When the President of the United States is tried the Chief Justice shall preside: And no Person shall be convicted without the Concurrence of two thirds of the Members present.

Judgment in Cases of Impeachment shall not exceed further than to removal from Office, and disqualification to hold and enjoy any Office of honor, Trust or Profit under the United States: but the Party convicted shall nevertheless be liable and subject to Indictment, Trial, Judgment and Punishment, according to Law.

Section 4. The Times, Places and Manner of holding Elections for Senators and Representatives, shall be prescribed in each State by the Legislature thereof; but the Congress may at any time by Law make or alter such Regulations, except as to the Places of chusing Senators.

The Congress shall assemble at least once in every Year, and such Meeting shall be on the first Monday in December, unless they shall by Law appoint a different Day.

Changed by the Twentieth Amendment, Section 2.

Section 5. Each House shall be the Judge of the Elections, Returns and Qualifications of its own Members, and a Majority of each shall constitute a Quorum to do Business; but a smaller number may adjourn from day to day, and may be authorized to compel the Attendance of absent Members, in such Manner, and under such Penalties as each House may provide.

Each House may determine the Rules of its Proceedings, punish its Members for disorderly Behaviour, and, with the Concurrence of two thirds, expel a Member.

Each House shall keep a Journal of its Proceedings, and from time to time publish the same, excepting such Parts as may in their Judgment require Secrecy; and the Yeas and Nays of the Members of either House on any question shall, at the Desire of one fifth of those Present, be entered on the Journal.

Neither House, during the Session of Congress, shall, without the Consent of the other, adjourn for more than three days, nor to any other Place than that in which the two Houses shall be sitting.

Section 6. The Senators and Representatives shall receive a Compensation for their Services, to be ascertained by Law, and paid out of the Treasury of the United States. They shall in all Cases, except Treason, Felony and Breach of the Peace, be privileged from Arrest during their Attendance at the Session of their respective Houses, and in going to and returning from the same; and for any Speech or Debate in either House, they shall not be questioned in any other Place.

Amplified by the Twenty-Seventh Amendment.

No Senator or Representative shall, during the Time for which he was elected, be appointed to any civil Office under the Authority of the United States, which shall have been created, or the Emoluments whereof shall have been encreased during such time; and no Person holding any Office under the United States, shall be a Member of either House during his Continuance in Office.

Section 7. All Bills for raising Revenue shall originate in the House of Representatives; but the Senate may propose or concur with Amendments as on other Bills.

Every Bill which shall have passed the House of Representatives and the Senate, shall, before it become a Law, be presented to the President of the United States; If he approve he shall assign it, but if not he shall return it, with his Objections to that House in which it shall have originated, who shall enter the Objections at large on their Journal, and proceed to reconsider it. If after such Reconsideration two thirds of that House shall agree to pass the Bill, it shall be sent, together with the Objections, to the other House, by which it shall likewise be reconsidered, and if approved by two thirds of that House, it shall become a Law. But in all such Cases the Votes of both Houses shall be determined by yeas and Nays, and the Names of the Persons voting for and against the Bill shall be entered on the Journal of each House respectively. If any Bill shall not be returned by the President within ten Days (Sundays excepted) after it shall have been presented to him, the Same shall be a Law, in like Manner, as if he had signed it, unless the Congress by their Adjournment prevent its Return, in which Case it shall not be a Law.

Every Order, Resolution, or Vote to which the Concurrence of the Senate and House of Representatives may be necessary (except on a question of Adjournment) shall be presented to the President of the United States; and before the Same shall take Effect, shall be approved by him, or being disapproved by him, shall be repassed by two thirds of the Senate and House of Representatives, according to the Rules and Limitations prescribed in the Case of a Bill.

Section 8. The Congress shall have Power To lay and Collect Taxes, Duties, Imposts and Excises, to pay the Debts and provide for the common Defence and general Welfare of the United States; but all Duties, Imposts and Excises shall be uniform throughout the United States.

General welfare clause gives Congress the power to tax to provide for the general welfare.

To borrow Money on the credit of the United States;

To regulate Commerce with foreign Nations, and among the several States, and with the Indian Tribes;

Commerce clause gives Congress the power to regulate commerce with foreign nations, with Indian tribes, and among the various states.

To establish an uniform Rule of Naturalization, and uniform Laws on the subject of Bankruptcies throughout the United States;

To coin Money, regulate the Value thereof, and of foreign Coin, and fix the Standard of Weights and Measures;

To provide for the Punishment of counterfeiting the Securities and current Coin of the United States;

To establish Post Offices and post Roads;

To promote the Progress of Science and useful Arts, by securing for limited Times to Authors and Inventors the exclusive Right to their respective Writings and Discoveries;

To constitute Tribunals inferior to the Supreme Court;

To define and punish Piracies and Felonies committed on the high Seas, and Offences against the Law of Nations;

To declare War, grant Letters of Marque and Reprisal, and make Rules concerning Captures on Land and Water;

To raise and support Armies, but no Appropriation of Money to that Use shall be for a longer Term than two Years;

To provide and maintain a Navy;

To make Rules for the Government and Regulation of the land and naval Forces;

To provide for calling forth the Militia to execute the Laws of the Union, suppress Insurrections and repel Invasions;

To provide for organizing, arming, and disciplining, the Militia, and for governing such Part of them as may be employed in the Service of the United States, reserving to the States respectively, the Appointment of the Officers, and the Authority of training the Militia according to the discipline prescribed by Congress;

To exercise exclusive Legislation in all Cases whatsoever, over such District (not exceeding ten Miles square) as may, by Cession of Particular States, and the Acceptance of Congress, become the Seat of the Government of the United States, and to exercise like Authority over all Places purchased by the Consent of the Legislature of the State in which the Same shall be, for the Erection of Forts, Magazines, Arsenals, dock-Yards and other needful Buildings;—And

To make all Laws which shall be necessary and proper for carrying into Execution the foregoing Powers, and all other Powers vested by this Constitution in the Government of the United States, or in any Department or Officer thereof.

Necessary and proper clause gives Congress the power to pass all laws necessary and proper to the powers enumerated in Section 8.

Section 9. The Migration or Importation of such Persons as any of the States now existing shall think proper to admit, shall not be prohibited by the Congress prior to the Year one thousand eight hundred and eight, but a Tax or duty may be imposed on such Importation, not exceeding ten dollars for each Person.

The Privilege of the Writ of Habeas Corpus shall not be suspended, unless when in Cases of Rebellion or Invasion the public Safety may require it.

No bill of Attainder or ex post facto Law shall be passed.

No Capitation, or other direct, Tax shall be laid, unless in Proportion to the Census or Enumeration herein before directed to be taken.

Changed by the Sixteenth Amendment.

No Tax or Duty shall be laid on Articles exported from any State.

No Preference shall be given by any Regulation of Commerce or Revenue to the Ports of one State over those of another; nor shall Vessels bound to, or from, one State, be obliged to enter, clear or pay Duties in another.

No Money shall be drawn from the Treasury, but in Consequence of Appropriations made by Law; and a regular Statement and Account of the Receipts and Expenditures of all public Money shall be published from time to time.

No Title of Nobility shall be granted by the United States: And no Person holding any Office of Profit or Trust under them, shall, without the Consent of the Congress, accept of any present, Emolument, Office, or Title, of any kind whatever, from any King, Prince, or foreign State.

Section 10. No State shall enter into any Treaty, Alliance, or Confederation; grant Letters of Marque and Reprisal; coin Money; emit Bills of Credit; make any Thing but gold and silver Coin a Tender in Payment of Debts; pass any Bill of Attainder, ex post facto Law, or Law impairing the Obligation of Contracts, or grant any Title of Nobility.

No State shall, without the Consent of the Congress, lay any Imposts or Duties on Imports or Exports, except what may be absolutely necessary for executing its inspection Laws; and the net Produce of all Duties and Imposts, laid by any State on Imports or Exports, shall be for the Use of the Treasury of the United States; and all such Laws shall be subject to the Revision and Control of the Congress.

No State shall, without the Consent of Congress, lay any Duty of Tonnage, keep Troops, or Ships of War in time of Peace, enter into any Agreement or Compact with another State, or with a foreign Power, or engage in War, unless actually invaded, or in such imminent Danger as will not admit of delay.

Article II.

Vesting clause gives the president the executive power.

Section 1. The executive Power shall be vested in a President of the United States of America. He shall hold his Office during the term of four Years, and, together with the Vice President, chosen for the same Term, be elected, as follows

Each State shall appoint, in such Manner as the Legislature thereof may direct, a Number of Electors, equal to the whole Number of Senators and Representatives to which the State may be entitled in the Congress: but no Senator or Representative, or Person holding an Office of Trust or Profit under the United States, shall be appointed an Elector.

Changed by the Twelfth Amendment.

The Electors shall meet in their respective States, and vote by Ballot for two Persons, of whom one at least shall not be an Inhabitant of the same State with them-selves. And they shall make a List of all the Persons voted for, and of the Number of Votes for each; which List they shall sign and certify, and transmit sealed to the Seat of the Government of the United States, directed to the President of the Senate. The President of the Senate shall, in the Presence of the Senate and House of Representatives, open all the Certificates, and the Votes shall then be counted. The Person having the greatest Number of Votes shall be the President, if such Number be a Majority of the whole Number of Electors appointed; and if there be more than one who have such Majority, and have an equal Number of Votes, then the House of Representatives shall immediately chuse by Ballot one of them for President; and if no Person have a Majority, then from the five highest on the List the said House shall in like Manner chuse the President. But in chusing the President, the Votes shall be taken by States, the Representation from each State having one Vote; a quorum for this Purpose shall consist of a Member or Members from two thirds of the States, and a Majority of all the States shall be necessary to a Choice. In every Case, after the Choice of the President, the Person having the greatest Number of Votes of the Electors shall be the Vice President. But if there should remain two or more who have equal Votes, the Senate shall chuse from them by Ballot the Vice President.

The Congress may determine the Time of chusing the Electors, and the Day on which they shall give their Votes, which Day shall be the same throughout the United States.

No Person except a natural born Citizen, or a Citizen of the United States, at the time of the Adoption of this Constitution, shall be eligible to the Office of President; neither shall any person be eligible to that Office who shall not have attained to the Age of thirty five Years, and been fourteen Years a Resident within the United States.

Changed by the Twenty-Fifth Amendment.

In Case of the Removal of the President from Office, or of his Death, Resignation, or Inability to discharge the Powers and Duties of the said Office, the Same shall devolve on the Vice President, and the Congress may by Law provide for the Case of Removal, Death, Resignation or Inability, both of the President and Vice President, declaring what Officer shall then act as President, and such Officer shall act accordingly, until the Disability be removed, or a President shall be elected.

The President shall, at stated Times, receive for his Services, a Compensation, which shall neither be encreased nor diminished during the Period for which he shall have been elected, and he shall not receive within that Period any other Emolument from the United States, or any of them.

Before he enter on the Execution of his Office, he shall take the following Oath or Affirmation:—"I do solemnly swear (or affirm) that I will faithfully execute the Office of President of the United States, and will to the best of my Ability, preserve, protect and defend the Constitution of the United States."

Section 2. The President shall be Commander in Chief of the Army and Navy of the United States, and of the Militia of the several States, when called into the actual Service of the United States; he may require the Opinion, in writing, of the principal Officer in each of the executive Departments, upon any Subject relating to the Duties of their respective Offices, and he shall have Power to grant Reprieves and Pardons for Offences against the United States, except in Cases of Impeachment.

He shall have Power, by and with the Advice and Consent of the Senate, to make Treaties, provided two thirds of the Senators present concur; and he shall nominate, and by and with the Advice and Consent of the Senate, shall appoint Ambassadors, other public Ministers and Consuls, Judges of the supreme Court, and all other Officers of the United States, whose Appointments are not herein otherwise provided for, and which shall be established by Law: but the Congress may by Law vest the Appointment of such inferior Officers, as they think proper, in the President alone, in the Courts of Law, or in the Heads of Departments.

The President shall have Power to fill up all Vacancies that may happen during the Recess of the Senate, by granting Commissions which shall expire at the End of their next Session.

Section 3. He shall from time to time give to the Congress Information of the State of the Union, and recommend to their Consideration such Measures as he shall judge necessary and expedient; he may, on extraordinary Occasions, convene both Houses, or either of them, and in Case of Disagreement between them, with Respect to the Time of Adjournment, he may adjourn them to such Time as he shall think proper; he shall receive Ambassadors and other public Ministers; he shall take Care that the Laws be faithfully executed, and shall Commission all the Officers of the United States.

Take care clause requires the president to make sure that the laws are "faithfully executed."

Section 4. The President, Vice President and all civil Officers of the United States, shall be removed from Office on Impeachment for, and Conviction of, Treason, Bribery, or other high Crimes and Misdemeanors.

Article III.

Section 1. The judicial Power of the United States, shall be vested in one supreme Court, and in such inferior Courts as the Congress may from time to time ordain and establish. The Judges, both of the supreme and inferior Courts, shall hold their Offices during good

Behaviour, and shall, at stated Times, receive for their Services, a Compensation, which shall not be diminished during their Continuance in Office.

Section 2. The judicial Power shall extend to all Cases, in Law and Equity, arising under this Constitution, the Laws of the United States, and Treaties made, or which shall be made, under their Authority;—to all Cases affecting Ambassadors, other public Ministers and Consuls;—to all Cases of admiralty and maritime Jurisdiction;—to Controversies to which the United States shall be a Party;—to Controversies between two or more States;—between a State and Citizens of another State;—between Citizens of different States;—between Citizens of the same State claiming Lands under Grants of different States, and between a State, or the Citizens thereof, and foreign States, Citizens or Subjects.

Changed by the Eleventh Amendment.

In all Cases affecting Ambassadors, other public Ministers and Consuls, and those in which a State shall be Party, the supreme Court shall have original Jurisdiction. In all the other Cases before mentioned, the supreme Court shall have appellate Jurisdiction, both as to Law and Fact, with such Exceptions, and under such Regulations as the Congress shall make.

The Trial of all Crimes, except in Cases of Impeachment, shall be by Jury; and such Trial shall be held in the State where the said Crimes shall have been committed; but when not committed within any State, the Trial shall be at such Place or Places as the Congress may by Law have directed.

Section 3. Treason against the United States, shall consist only in levying War against them, or in adhering to their Enemies, giving them Aid and Comfort. No Person shall be convicted of Treason unless on the Testimony of two Witnesses to the same overt Act, or on Confession in open Court.

The Congress shall have Power to declare the Punishment of Treason, but no Attainder of Treason shall work Corruption of Blood, or Forfeiture except during the Life of the Person attainted.

Article IV.

Full faith and credit clause requires states to accept civil proceedings from other states.

Section 1. Full Faith and Credit shall be given in each State to the public Acts, Records, and judicial Proceedings of every other State. And the Congress may by general Laws prescribe the Manner in which such Acts, Records and Proceedings shall be proved, and the Effect thereof.

Privileges and immunities clause requires states to treat nonresidents equally to residents.

Section 2. The Citizens of each State shall be entitled to all Privileges and Immunities of Citizens in the several States.

A person charged in any State with Treason, Felony, or other Crime, who shall flee from Justice, and be found in another State, shall on Demand of the executive Authority of the State from which he fled, be delivered up, to be removed to the State having Jurisdiction of the Crime.

Fugitive slave clause required states to return runaway slaves; negated by the Thirteenth Amendment.

No Person held to Service or Labour in one State, under the Laws thereof, escaping into another, shall, in Consequence of any Law or Regulation therein, be discharged from such Service or Labour, but shall be delivered up on Claim of the Party to whom such Service or Labour may be due.

Section 3. New States may be admitted by the Congress into this Union; but no new State shall be formed or erected within the Jurisdiction of any other State; nor any State be formed by the Junction of two or more States, or Parts of States, without the Consent of the Legislatures of the States concerned as well as of the Congress.

The Congress shall have Power to dispose of and make all needful Rules and Regulations respecting the Territory or other Property belonging to the United States; and nothing in this Constitution shall be so construed as to Prejudice any Claims of the United States, or of any particular State.

Section 4. The United States shall guarantee to every State in this Union a Republican Form of Government, and shall protect each of them against Invasion; and on Application of the Legislature, or of the Executive (when the Legislature cannot be convened) against domestic Violence.

Guarantee clause provides a federal government guarantee that the states will have a republican form of government.

Article V.

The Congress, whenever two thirds of both Houses shall deem it necessary, shall propose Amendments to this Constitution, or, on the Application of the Legislatures of two thirds of the several States, shall call a Convention for proposing Amendments, which, in either Case, shall be valid to all Intents and Purposes, as Part of this Constitution, when ratified by the Legislatures of three fourths of the several States, or by Conventions in three fourths thereof, as the one or the other Mode of Ratification may be proposed by the Congress; Provided that no Amendment which may be made prior to the Year One thousand eight hundred and eight shall in any Manner after the first and fourth Clauses in the Ninth Section of the first Article; and that no State, without its Consent, shall be deprived of its equal Suffrage in the Senate.

Article VI.

All Debts contracted and Engagements entered into, before the Adoption of this Constitution, shall be as valid against the United States under this Constitution, as under the Confederation.

This Constitution, and the Laws of the United States which shall be made in Pursuance thereof; and all Treaties made, or which shall be made, under the Authority of the United States, shall be the Supreme Law of the Land; and the Judges in every State shall be bound thereby, any Thing in the Constitution or Laws of any State to the Contrary notwithstanding.

Supremacy clause makes federal law supreme over state laws.

The Senators and Representatives before mentioned, and the Members of the several State Legislatures, and all executive and judicial Officers, both of the United States and of the several States, shall be bound by Oath or Affirmation, to support this Constitution; but no religious Test shall ever be required as a Qualification to any Office or public Trust under the United States.

Article VII.

The Ratification of the Conventions of nine States, shall be sufficient for the Establishment of this Constitution between the States so ratifying the Same.

Done in Convention by the Unanimous Consent of the States present the Seventeenth Day of September in the Year of our Lord one thousand seven hundred and Eighty seven and of the Independence of the United States of America the Twelfth In witness whereof We have hereunto subscribed our Names,

George Washington, *President and deputy from Virginia*

Delaware

George Read
Gunning Bedford Jr.
John Dickinson
Richard Bassett
Jacob Broom

Maryland

James McHenry
Daniel of St. Thomas Jennifer
Daniel Carroll

Virginia

John Blair
James Madison Jr.

North Carolina

William Blount
Richard Dobbs Spaight
Hugh Williamson

South Carolina

John Rutledge
Charles Cotesworth Pinckney
Charles Pinckney
Pierce Butler

Georgia

William Few
Abraham Baldwin

New Hampshire

John Langdon
Nicholas Gilman

Massachusetts

Nathaniel Gorham
Rufus King

Connecticut

William Samuel Johnson
Roger Sherman

New York

Alexander Hamilton

New Jersey

William Livingston
David Brearley
William Paterson
Jonathan Dayton

Pennsylvania

Benjamin Franklin
Thomas Mifflin
Robert Morris
George Clymer
Thomas FitzSimons
Jared Ingersoll
James Wilson
Gouverneur Morris

[The first ten amendments, known as the Bill of Rights, were ratified in 1791.]

First Amendment

Establishment clause prohibits governmental establishment of religion.

Free exercise clause protects the free exercise of religion.

Congress shall make no law respecting an establishment of religion, or prohibiting the free exercise thereof; or abridging the freedom of speech, or of the press; or the right of the people peaceably to assemble, and to petition the Government for a redress of grievances.

Second Amendment

A well regulated Militia, being necessary to the security of a free State, the right of the people to keep and bear Arms, shall not be infringed.

Third Amendment

No Soldier shall, in time of peace be quartered in any house, without the consent of the Owner, nor in time of war, but in a manner prescribed by law.

Fourth Amendment

The right of the people to be secure in their persons, houses, papers, and effects, against unreasonable searches and seizures, shall not be violated, and no Warrants shall issue, but upon probable cause, supported by Oath or affirmation, and particularly describing the place to be searched, and the persons or things to be seized.

Fifth Amendment

No person shall be held to answer for a capital, or otherwise infamous crime, unless on a presentment or indictment of a Grand Jury, except in cases arising in the land or naval forces, or in the Militia, when in actual service in time of War or public danger; nor shall any person be subject for the same offence to be twice put in jeopardy of life or limb; nor shall be compelled in any criminal case to be a witness against himself, nor be deprived of life, liberty, or property, without due process of law, nor shall private property be taken for public use, without just compensation.

Double jeopardy clause prevents the government from retrying someone for a crime after an initial acquittal.

Self-incrimination clause protects people from having to testify against themselves at trial.

Due process clause prevents the federal government from denying any person due process of law.

Takings clause requires just compensation when the government seizes private property for a public purpose.

Sixth Amendment

In all criminal prosecutions, the accused shall enjoy the right to a speedy and public trial, by an impartial jury of the State and district wherein the crime shall have been committed, which district shall have been previously ascertained by law, and to be informed of the nature and cause of the accusation; to be confronted with the witnesses against him; to have compulsory process for obtaining witnesses in his favor, and to have Assistance of Counsel for his defence.

Seventh Amendment

In Suits at common law, where the value in controversy shall exceed twenty dollars, the right of trial by jury shall be preserved, and no fact tried by a jury, shall be otherwise reexamined in any Court of the United States, than according to the rules of the common law.

Eighth Amendment

Excessive bail shall not be required, nor excessive fines imposed, nor cruel and unusual punishments inflicted.

Cruel and unusual punishment clause prohibits cruel and unusual punishments.

Ninth Amendment

The enumeration in the Constitution, of certain rights, shall not be construed to deny or disparage others retained by the people.

Tenth Amendment

The powers not delegated to the United States by the Constitution, nor prohibited by it to the States, are reserved to the States respectively, or to the people.

Reserve powers clause reserves to the states or to the people those powers not delegated to the United States.

Eleventh Amendment (1798)

The Judicial power of the United States shall not be construed to extend to any suit in law or equity, commenced or prosecuted against one of the United States by Citizens of another State, or by Citizens or Subjects of any Foreign State.

Twelfth Amendment (1804)

The Electors shall meet in their respective states and vote by ballot for President and Vice President, one of whom, at least, shall not be an inhabitant of the same state with themselves; they shall name in their ballots the person voted for as President, and in distinct ballots the person voted for as Vice President, and they shall make distinct lists of all persons voted for as President, and of all persons voted for as Vice President, and of the number of votes for each, which lists they shall sign and certify, and transmit sealed to the seat of the government of the United States, directed to the President of the Senate;—The President of the Senate shall, in the presence of the Senate and House of Representatives, open all the certificates and the votes shall then be counted;—The person having the greatest number of votes for President, shall be the President, if such number be a majority of the whole number of Electors appointed; and if no person have such majority, then from the persons having the highest numbers not exceeding three on the list of those voted for as President, the House of Representatives shall choose immediately, by ballot, the President. But in choosing the President, the votes shall be taken by states, the representation from each state having one vote; a quorum for this purpose shall consist of a member or members from two-thirds of the states, and a majority of all the states shall be necessary to a choice. And if the House of Representatives shall not choose a President whenever the right of choice shall devolve upon them, before the fourth day of March next following, then the Vice President shall act as President, as in the case of the death or other constitutional disability of the President.—The person having the greatest number of votes as Vice President, shall be the Vice President, if such number be a majority of the whole number of Electors appointed, and if no person have a majority, then from the two highest numbers on the list, the Senate shall choose the Vice President; a quorum for the purpose shall consist of two-thirds of the whole number of Senators, and a majority of the whole number shall be necessary to a choice. But no person constitutionally ineligible to the office of President shall be eligible to that of Vice President of the United States.

Changed by the Twentieth Amendment, Section 3.

Thirteenth Amendment (1865)

Section 1. Neither slavery nor involuntary servitude, except as a punishment for crime whereof the party shall have been duly convicted, shall exist within the United States, or any place subject to their jurisdiction.

Section 2. Congress shall have power to enforce this article by appropriate legislation.

Fourteenth Amendment (1868)

Citizenship clause makes all persons born in the United States citizens of the United States and of the state in which they reside.

Privileges or immunities clause prohibits states from abridging certain fundamental rights.

Due process clause prevents state governments from denying any person due process of law.

Equal protection clause prevents states from denying any person the equal protection of the laws.

Section 1. All persons born or naturalized in the United States and subject to the jurisdiction thereof, are citizens of the United States and of the State wherein they reside. No State shall make or enforce any law which shall abridge the privileges or immunities of citizens of the United States; nor shall any State deprive any person of life, liberty, or property, without due process of law; nor deny to any person within its jurisdiction the equal protection of the laws.

Section 2. Representatives shall be apportioned among the several States according to their respective numbers, counting the whole number of persons in each State, excluding Indians not taxed. But when the right to vote at any election for the choice of electors for President and Vice President of the United States, Representatives in Congress, the Executive and Judicial officers of a State, or the members of the Legislature thereof, is denied to any of the male inhabitants of such State, being twenty-one years of age, and citizens of the United States, or in any way abridged, except for participation in rebellion, or other crime, the basis of representation therein shall be reduced in the proportion which the number of such male citizens shall bear to the whole number of male citizens twenty-one years of age in such State.

Changed by the Nineteenth and Twenty-Sixth Amendments.

Section 3. No person shall be a Senator or Representative in Congress, or elector of President and Vice President, or hold any office, civil or military, under the United States, or under any State, who, having previously taken an oath, as a member of Congress, or as an officer of the United States, or as a member of any State legislature, or as an executive or judicial officer of any State, to support the Constitution of the United States, shall have engaged in insurrection or rebellion against the same, or given aid or comfort to the enemies thereof. But Congress may by a vote of two-thirds of each House, remove such disability.

Section 4. The validity of the public debt of the United States, authorized by law, including debts incurred for payment of pensions and bounties for services in suppressing insurrection or rebellion, shall not be questioned. But neither the United States nor any State shall assume or pay any debt or obligation incurred in aid of insurrection or rebellion against the United States, or any claim for the loss or emancipation of any slave; but all such debts, obligations and claims shall be held illegal and void.

Section 5. The Congress shall have power to enforce, by appropriate legislation, the provisions of this article.

Fifteenth Amendment (1870)

Section 1. The right of citizens of the United States to vote shall not be denied or abridged by the United States or by any State on account of race, color, or previous condition of servitude.

Section 2. The Congress shall have power to enforce this article by appropriate legislation.

Sixteenth Amendment (1913)

The Congress shall have power to lay and collect taxes on incomes, from whatever source derived, without apportionment among the several States, and without regard to any census or enumeration.

Seventeenth Amendment (1913)

The Senate of the United States shall be composed of two Senators from each State, elected by the people thereof, for six years; and each Senator shall have one vote. The electors in each State shall have the qualifications requisite for electors of the most numerous branch of the State legislatures.

When vacancies happen in the representation of any State in the Senate, the executive authority of such State shall issue writs of election to fill such vacancies: *Provided*, That the legislature of any State may empower the executive thereof to make temporary appointments until the people fill the vacancies by election as the legislature may direct.

This amendment shall not be so construed as to affect the election or term of any Senator chosen before it becomes valid as part of the Constitution.

Eighteenth Amendment (1919)

Repealed by the Twenty-First Amendment.

Section 1. After one year from the ratification of this article the manufacture, sale, or transportation of intoxicating liquors within, the importation thereof into, or the exportation thereof from the United States and all territory subject to the jurisdiction thereof for beverage purposes is hereby prohibited.

Section 2. The Congress and the several States shall have concurrent power to enforce this article by appropriate legislation.

Section 3. This article shall be inoperative unless it shall have been ratified as an amendment to the Constitution by the legislatures of the several States, as provided in the Constitution, within seven years from the date of the submission hereof to the States by the Congress.

Nineteenth Amendment (1920)

The right of citizens of the United States to vote shall not be denied or abridged by the United States or by any State on account of sex.

Congress shall have power to enforce this article by appropriate legislation.

Twentieth Amendment (1933)

Section 1. The terms of the President and Vice President shall end at noon on the 20th day of January, and the terms of Senators and Representatives at noon on the 3rd day of January, of the years in which such terms would have ended if this article had not been ratified; and the terms of their successors shall then begin.

Section 2. The Congress shall assemble at least once in every year, and such meeting shall begin at noon on the 3d day of January, unless they shall by law appoint a different day.

Section 3. If, at the time fixed for the beginning of the term of the President, the President elect shall have died, the Vice President elect shall become President. If a President shall not have been chosen before the time fixed for the beginning of his term, or if the President elect shall have failed to qualify, then the Vice President elect shall act as President until a President shall have qualified; and the Congress may by law provide for the case wherein neither a President elect nor a Vice President elect shall have qualified, declaring who shall then act as President, or the manner in which one who is to act shall be selected, and such person shall act accordingly until a President or Vice President shall have qualified.

Section 4. The Congress may by law provide for the case of the death of any of the persons from whom the House of Representatives may choose a President whenever the right of choice shall have devolved upon them, and for the case of the death of any of the persons from whom the Senate may choose a Vice President whenever the right of choice shall have devolved upon them.

Section 5. Sections 1 and 2 shall take effect on the 15th day of October following the ratification of this article.

Section 6. This article shall be inoperative unless it shall have been ratified as an amendment to the Constitution by the legislatures of three-fourths of the several States within seven years from the date of its submission.

Twenty-First Amendment (1933)

Section 1. The eighteenth article of amendment to the Constitution of the United States is hereby repealed.

Section 2. The transportation or importation into any State, Territory, or possession of the United States for delivery or use therein of intoxicating liquors, in violation of the laws thereof, is hereby prohibited.

Section 3. This article shall be inoperative unless it shall have been ratified as an amendment to the Constitution by conventions in the several States, as provided in the Constitution, within seven years from the date of the submission hereof to the States by the Congress.

Twenty-Second Amendment (1951)

Section 1. No person shall be elected to the office of the President more than twice, and no person who has held the office of President, or acted as President, for more than two years of a term to which some other person was elected President shall be elected to the office of the President more than once. But this Article shall not apply to any person holding the office of President when this Article was proposed by the Congress, and shall not prevent any person who may be holding the office of President, or acting as President, during the term within which this Article becomes operative from holding the office of President or acting as President during the remainder of such term.

Section 2. This Article shall be inoperative unless it shall have been ratified as an amendment to the Constitution by the legislatures of three-fourths of the several States within seven years from the date of its submission to the States by the Congress.

Twenty-Third Amendment (1961)

Section 1. The District constituting the seat of Government of the United States shall appoint in such manner as the Congress may direct:

A number of electors of President and Vice President equal to the whole number of Senators and Representatives in Congress to which the District would be entitled if it were a State, but in no event more than the least populous State; they shall be in addition to those appointed by the States, but they shall be considered, for the purposes of the election of President and Vice President, to be electors appointed by a State; and they shall meet in the District and perform such duties as provided by the twelfth article of amendment.

Section 2. The Congress shall have power to enforce this article by appropriate legislation.

Twenty-Fourth Amendment (1964)

Section 1. The right of citizens of the United States to vote in any primary or other election for President or Vice President, for electors for President or Vice President, or for Senator or Representative in Congress, shall not be denied or abridged by the United States or any State by reason of failure to pay any poll tax or other tax.

Section 2. Congress shall have power to enforce this article by appropriate legislation.

Twenty-Fifth Amendment (1967)

Section 1. In case of the removal of the President from office or of his death or resignation, the Vice President shall become President.

Section 2. Whenever there is a vacancy in the office of the Vice President, the President shall nominate a Vice President who shall take office upon confirmation by a majority vote of both Houses of Congress.

Section 3. Whenever the President transmits to the President pro tempore of the Senate and the Speaker of the House of Representatives his written declaration that he is unable to discharge the powers and duties of his office, and until he transmits to them a written declaration to the contrary, such powers and duties shall be discharged by the Vice President as Acting President.

Section 4. Whenever the Vice President and a majority of either the principal officers of the executive departments or of such other body as Congress may by law provide, transmit to the President pro tempore of the Senate and the Speaker of the House of Representatives their written declaration that the President is unable to discharge the powers and duties of his office, the Vice President shall immediately assume the powers and duties of the office as Acting President.

Thereafter, when the President transmits to the President pro tempore of the Senate and the Speaker of the House of Representatives his written declaration that no inability exists, he shall resume the powers and duties of his office unless the Vice President and a majority of either the principal officers of the executive department[s] or of such other body as Congress may by law provide, transmit within four days to the President pro tempore of the Senate and the Speaker of the House of Representatives their written declaration that the President is unable to discharge the powers and duties of his office. Thereupon Congress shall decide the issue, assembling within forty-eight hours for that purpose if not in session. If the Congress, within twenty-one days after receipt of the latter written declaration, or, if Congress is not in session, within twenty-one days after Congress is required to assemble, determines by two-thirds vote of both Houses that the President is unable to discharge the powers and duties of his office, the Vice President shall continue to discharge the same as Acting President; otherwise, the President shall resume the powers and duties of his office.

Twenty-Sixth Amendment (1971)

Section 1. The right of citizens of the United States, who are eighteen years of age or older, to vote shall not be denied or abridged by the United States or by any State on account of age.

Section 2. The Congress shall have power to enforce this article by appropriate legislation.

Twenty-Seventh Amendment (1992)

No law varying the compensation for the services of the Senators and Representatives shall take effect, until an election of Representatives shall have intervened.

APPENDIX C

Federalist Papers 10 and 51

10

James Madison

November 22, 1787

To the People of the State of New York

Among the numerous advantages promised by a well constructed Union, none deserves to be more accurately developed than its tendency to break and control the violence of faction. The friend of popular governments, never finds himself so much alarmed for their character and fate, as when he contemplates their propensity to this dangerous vice. He will not fail therefore to set a due value on any plan which, without violating the principles to which he is attached, provides a proper cure for it. The instability, injustice and confusion introduced into the public councils, have in truth been the mortal diseases under which popular governments have every where perished; as they continue to be the favorite and fruitful topics from which the adversaries to liberty derive their most specious declamations. The valuable improvements made by the American Constitutions on the popular models, both ancient and modern, cannot certainly be too much admired; but it would be an unwarrantable partiality, to contend that they have as effectually obviated the danger on this side as was wished and expected. Complaints are everywhere heard from our most considerate and virtuous citizens, equally the friends of public and private faith, and of public and personal liberty; that our governments are too unstable; that the public good is disregarded in the conflicts of rival parties; and that measures are too often decided, not according to the rules of justice, and the rights of the minor party; but by the superior force of an interested and over-bearing majority. However anxiously we may wish that these complaints had no foundation, the evidence of known facts will not permit us to deny that they are in some degree true. It will be found indeed, on a candid review of our situation, that some of the distresses under which we labor, have been erroneously charged on the operation of our governments; but it will be found, at the same time, that other causes will not alone account for many of our heaviest misfortunes; and particularly, for that prevailing and increasing distrust of public engagements, and alarm for private rights, which are echoed from one end of the continent to the other. These must be chiefly, if not wholly, effects of the unsteadiness and injustice, with which a factious spirit has tainted our public administrations.

By a faction I understand a number of citizens, whether amounting to a majority or minority of the whole, who are united and actuated by some common impulse of passion, or of interest, adverse to the rights of other citizens, or to the permanent and aggregate interests of the community.

There are two methods of curing the mischiefs of faction: the one, by removing its causes; the other, by controlling its effects.

There are again two methods of removing the causes of faction: the one by destroying the liberty which is essential to its existence; the other, by giving to every citizen the same opinions, the same passions, and the same interests.

It could never be more truly said than of the first remedy, that it is worse than the disease. Liberty is to faction, what air is to fire, an aliment without which it instantly expires. But it could not be a less folly to abolish liberty, which is essential to political life, because it nourishes faction, than it would be to wish the annihilation of air, which is essential to animal life, because it imparts to fire its destructive agency.

The second expedient is as impracticable, as the first would be unwise. As long as the reason of man continues fallible, and he is at liberty to exercise it, different opinions will be formed. As long as the connection subsists between his reason and his self-love, his opinions and his passions will have a reciprocal influence on each other; and the former will be objects to which the latter will attach themselves. The diversity in the faculties of men from which the rights of property originate, is not less an insuperable obstacle to a uniformity of interests. The protection of these faculties is the first object of Government. From the protection of different and unequal faculties of acquiring property, the possession of different degrees and kinds of property immediately results: and from the influence of these on the sentiments and views of the respective proprietors, ensues a division of the society into different interests and parties.

The latent causes of faction are thus sown in the nature of man; and we see them every where brought into different degrees of activity, according to the different circumstances of civil society. A zeal for different opinions concerning religion, concerning Government and many other points, as well of speculation as of practice; an attachment to different leaders ambitiously contending for pre-eminence and power; or to persons of other descriptions whose fortunes have been interesting to the human passions, have in turn divided mankind into parties, inflamed them with mutual animosity, and rendered them much more disposed to vex and oppress each other, than to co-operate for their common good. So strong is this propensity of mankind to fall into mutual animosities, that where no substantial occasion presents itself, the most frivolous and fanciful distinctions have been sufficient to kindle their unfriendly passions, and excite their most violent conflicts. But the most common and durable source of factions, has been the various and unequal distribution of property. Those who hold, and those who are without property, have ever formed distinct interests in society. Those who are creditors, and those who are debtors, fall under a like discrimination. A landed interest, a manufacturing interest, a mercantile interest, a monied interest, with many lesser interests, grow up of necessity in civilized nations, and divide them into different classes, actuated by different sentiments and views. The regulation of these various and interfering interests forms the principal task of modern Legislation, and involves the spirit of party and faction in the necessary and ordinary operations of Government.

No man is allowed to be a judge in his own cause; because his interest would certainly bias his judgment, and, not improbably, corrupt his integrity. With equal, nay with greater reason, a body of men, are unfit to be both judges and parties, at the same time; yet, what are many of the most important acts of legislation, but so many judicial determinations, not indeed concerning the rights of single persons, but concerning the rights of large bodies of citizens; and what are the different classes of legislators, but advocates and parties to the causes which they determine? Is a law proposed concerning private debts? It is a question to which the creditors are parties on one side, and the debtors on the other. Justice ought to hold the balance between them. Yet the parties are and must be themselves the judges; and the most numerous party, or, in other words, the most powerful faction must be expected to prevail. Shall domestic manufactures be encouraged, and in what degree, by restrictions on foreign manufactures? are questions which would be differently decided by the landed and the manufacturing classes; and probably by neither, with a sole regard to justice and the public good. The apportionment of taxes on the various descriptions of property, is an act which seems to require the most exact impartiality; yet, there is perhaps no legislative act in which greater opportunity and temptation are given to a predominant party, to trample on the rules of justice. Every shilling with which they over-burden the inferior number, is a shilling saved to their own pockets.

It is in vain to say, that enlightened statesmen will be able to adjust these clashing interests, and render them all subservient to the public good. Enlightened statesmen will not always be at the helm: Nor, in many cases, can such an adjustment be made at all, without taking into view indirect and remote considerations, which will rarely prevail over the immediate interest which one party may find in disregarding the rights of another, or the good of the whole.

The inference to which we are brought, is, that the *causes* of faction cannot be removed; and that relief is only to be sought in the means of controlling its *effects*.

If a faction consists of less than a majority, relief is supplied by the republican principle, which enables the majority to defeat its sinister views by regular vote: It may clog the administration, it may convulse the society; but it will be unable to execute and mask its violence under the forms of the Constitution. When a majority is included in a faction, the form of popular government on the other hand enables it to sacrifice to its ruling passion or interest, both the public good and the rights of other citizens. To secure the public good, and private rights, against the danger of such a faction, and at the same time to preserve the spirit and the form of popular government, is then the great object to which our enquiries are directed: Let me add that it is the great desideratum, by which alone this form of government can be rescued from the opprobrium under which it has so long labored, and be recommended to the esteem and adoption of mankind.

By what means is this object attainable? Evidently by one of two only. Either the existence of the same passion or interest in a majority at the same time, must be prevented; or the majority, having such co-existent passion or interest, must be rendered, by their number and local situation, unable to concert and carry into effect schemes of oppression. If the impulse and the opportunity be suffered to coincide, we well know that neither moral nor religious motives can be relied on as an adequate control. They are not found to be such on the injustice and violence of individuals, and lose their efficacy in proportion to the number combined together; that is, in proportion as their efficacy becomes needful.

From this view of the subject, it may be concluded, that a pure Democracy, by which I mean, a Society, consisting of a small number of citizens, who assemble and administer the Government in person, can admit of no cure for the mischiefs of faction. A common passion or interest will, in almost every case, be felt by a majority of the whole; a communication and concert results from the form of Government itself; and there is nothing to check the inducements to sacrifice the weaker party, or an obnoxious individual. Hence it is, that such Democracies have ever been spectacles of turbulence and contention; have ever been found incompatible with personal security, or the rights of property; and have in general been as short in their lives, as they have been violent in their deaths. Theoretic politicians, who have patronized this species of Government, have erroneously supposed, that by reducing mankind to a perfect equality in their political rights, they would, at the same time, be perfectly equalized and assimilated in their possessions, their opinions, and their passions.

A republic, by which I mean a government in which the scheme of representation takes place, opens a different prospect, and promises the cure for which we are seeking. Let us examine the points in which it varies from pure democracy, and we shall comprehend both the nature of the cure and the efficacy which it must derive from the union.

The two great points of difference, between a democracy and a republic, are, first, the delegation of the government, in the latter, to a small number of citizens, elected by the rest; secondly, the greater number of citizens, and greater sphere of country, over which the latter may be extended.

The effect of the first difference is, on the one hand, to refine and enlarge the public views, by passing them through the medium of a chosen body of citizens, whose wisdom may best discern the true interest of their country, and whose patriotism and love of justice, will be least likely to sacrifice it to temporary or partial considerations. Under such a regulation, it may well happen, that the public voice, pronounced by the representatives of the people, will be more consonant to the public good, than if pronounced by the people themselves, convened for the purpose. On the other hand the effect may be inverted. Men of factious tempers, of local prejudices, or of sinister designs, may by intrigue, by corruption, or by other means, first obtain the suffrages, and then betray the interest of the people. The question resulting is, whether small or extensive republics are most favorable to the election of proper guardians of the public weal, and it is clearly decided in favor of the latter by two obvious considerations.

In the first place, it is to be remarked that, however small the republic may be, the representatives must be raised to a certain number, in order to guard against the cabals of a few; and that however large it may be, they must be limited to a certain number, in order to guard against the confusion of a multitude. Hence, the number of representatives in the two cases not being in proportion to that of the constituents, and being proportionally greatest in the small republic, it follows, that if the proportion of fit characters be not less in the large than in the small republic, the former will present a greater option, and consequently a greater probability of a fit choice.

In the next place, as each Representative will be chosen by a greater number of citizens in the large than in the small Republic, it will be more difficult for unworthy candidates to practise with success the vicious arts, by which elections are too often carried; and the suffrages of the people being more free, will be more likely to center on men who possess the most attractive merit, and the most diffusive and established characters.

It must be confessed, that in this, as in most other cases, there is a mean, on both sides of which inconveniences will be found to lie. By enlarging too much the number of electors, you render the representatives too little acquainted with all their local circumstances and lesser interests; as by reducing it too much, you render him unduly attached to these, and too little fit to comprehend and pursue great and national objects. The Federal Constitution forms a happy combination in this respect; the great and aggregate interests being referred to the national, the local and particular, to the state legislatures.

The other point of difference is, the greater number of citizens and extent of territory which may be brought within the compass of Republican, than of Democratic Government; and it is this circumstance principally which renders factious combinations less to be dreaded in the former, than in the latter. The smaller the society, the fewer probably will be the distinct parties and interests composing it; the fewer the distinct parties and interests, the more frequently will a majority be found of the same party; and the smaller the number of individuals composing a majority, and the smaller the compass within which they are placed, the more easily will they concert and execute their plans of oppression. Extend the sphere, and you take in a greater variety of parties and interests; you make it less probable that a majority of the whole will have a common motive to invade the rights of other citizens; or if such a common motive exists, it will be more difficult for all who feel it to discover their own strength, and to act in unison with each other. Besides other impediments, it may be remarked, that where there is a consciousness of unjust or dishonorable purposes, communication is always checked by distrust, in proportion to the number whose concurrence is necessary.

Hence it clearly appears, that the same advantage, which a Republic has over a Democracy, in controlling the effects of factions, is enjoyed by a large over a small Republic—is enjoyed by the Union over the States composing it. Does this advantage consist in the substitution of Representatives, whose enlightened views and virtuous sentiments render them superior to local prejudices, and to schemes of injustice? It will not be denied, that the Representation of the Union will be most likely to possess these requisite endowments. Does it consist in the greater security afforded by a greater variety of parties, against the event of any one party being able to outnumber and oppress the rest? In an equal degree does the increased variety of parties, comprised within the Union, increase this security? Does it, in fine, consist in the greater obstacles opposed to the concert and accomplishment of the secret wishes of an unjust and interested majority? Here, again, the extent of the Union gives it the most palpable advantage.

The influence of factious leaders may kindle a flame within their particular States, but will be unable to spread a general conflagration through the other States: a religious sect, may degenerate into a political faction in a part of the Confederacy but the variety of sects dispersed over the entire face of it, must secure the national Councils against any danger from that source: a rage for paper money, for an abolition of debts, for an equal division of property, or for any other improper or wicked project, will be less apt to pervade the whole body of the Union, than a particular member of it; in the same proportion as such a malady is more likely to taint a particular county or district, than an entire State.

In the extent and proper structure of the Union, therefore, we behold a Republican remedy for the diseases most incident to Republican Government. And according to the degree of pleasure and pride, we feel in being Republicans, ought to be our zeal in cherishing the spirit, and supporting the character of Federalists.

Publius

51

James Madison

February 6, 1788

To the People of the State of New York

To what expedient then shall we finally resort for maintaining in practice the necessary partition of power among the several departments, as laid down in the constitution? The only answer that can be given is, that as all these exterior provisions are found to be inadequate, the defect must be supplied, by so contriving the interior structure of the government, as that its several constituent parts may, by their mutual relations, be the means of keeping each other in their proper places. Without presuming to undertake a full development of this important idea, I will hazard a few general observations, which may perhaps place it in a clearer light, and enable us to form a more correct judgment of the principles and structure of the government planned by the convention.

In order to lay a due foundation for that separate and distinct exercise of the different powers of government, which to a certain extent, is admitted on all hands to be essential to the preservation of liberty, it is evident that each department should have a will of its own; and consequently should be so constituted, that the members of each should have as little agency as possible in the appointment of the members of the others. Were this principle rigorously adhered to, it would require that all the appointments for the supreme executive, legislative, and judiciary magistracies, should be drawn from the same fountain of authority, the people, through channels, having no communication whatever with one another. Perhaps such a plan of constructing the several departments would be less difficult in practice than it may in contemplation appear. Some difficulties however, and some additional expense, would attend the execution of it. Some deviations therefore from the principle must be admitted. In the constitution of the judiciary department in particular, it might be inexpedient to insist rigorously on the principle; first, because peculiar qualifications being essential in the members, the primary consideration ought to be to select that mode of choice, which best secures these qualifications; secondly, because the permanent tenure by which the appointments are held in that department, must soon destroy all sense of dependence on the authority conferring them.

It is equally evident that the members of each department should be as little dependent as possible on those of the others, for the emoluments annexed to their offices. Were the executive magistrate, or the judges, not independent of the legislature in this particular, their independence in every other would be merely nominal.

But the great security against a gradual concentration of the several powers in the same department, consists in giving to those who administer each department, the necessary constitutional means, and personal motives, to resist encroachments of the others. The provision for defense must in this, as in all other cases, be made commensurate to the danger of attack. Ambition must be made to counteract ambition. The interest of the man must be connected with the constitutional rights of the place. It may be a reflection on human nature, that such devices should be necessary to control the abuses of government. But what is government itself but the greatest of all reflections on human nature? If men were angels, no government would be necessary. If angels were to govern men, neither external nor internal controls on government would be necessary. In framing a government which is to be administered by men over men, the great difficulty lies in this: You must first enable the government to control the governed; and in the next place, oblige it to control itself. A dependence on the people is no doubt the primary control on the government; but experience has taught mankind the necessity of auxiliary precautions.

This policy of supplying by opposite and rival interests, the defect of better motives, might be traced through the whole system of human affairs, private as well as public. We see it particularly displayed in all the subordinate distributions of power; where the constant aim is to divide and arrange the several offices in such a manner as that each may be a check on the other; that the private interest of every individual, may be a sentinel over the public rights. These inventions of prudence cannot be less requisite in the distribution of the supreme powers of the state.

But it is not possible to give each department an equal power of self defense. In republican government the legislative authority, necessarily, predominates. The remedy for this inconveniency is, to divide the legislature into different branches; and to render them by different modes of election, and different principles of action, as little connected with each other, as the nature of their common functions, and their common dependence on the society, will admit. It may even be necessary to guard against dangerous encroachments by still further precautions. As the weight of the legislative authority requires that it should be thus divided, the weakness of the executive may require, on the other hand, that it should be fortified. An absolute negative, on the legislature, appears at first view to be the natural defense with which the executive magistrate should be armed. But perhaps it would be neither altogether safe, nor alone sufficient. On ordinary occasions, it might not be exerted with the requisite firmness; and on extraordinary occasions, it might be prefidiously abused. May not this defect of an absolute negative be supplied, by some qualified connection between this weaker department, and the weaker branch of the stronger department, by which the latter may be led to support the constitutional rights of the former, without being too much detached from the rights of its own department?

If the principles on which these observations are founded be just, as I persuade myself they are, and they be applied as a criterion, to the several state constitutions, and to the federal constitution, it will be found, that if the latter does not perfectly correspond with them, the former are infinitely less able to bear such a test.

There are moreover two considerations particularly applicable to the federal system of America, which place that system in a very interesting point of view.

First. In a single republic, all the power surrendered by the people, is submitted to the administration of a single government; and usurpations are guarded against by a division of the government into distinct and separate departments. In the compound republic of America, the power surrendered by the people, is first divided between two distinct governments, and then the portion allotted to each, subdivided among distinct and separate departments. Hence a double security arises to the rights of the people. The different governments will control each other; at the same time that each will be controlled by itself.

Second. It is of great importance in a republic, not only to guard the society against the oppression of its rulers; but to guard one part of the society against the injustice of the other part. Different interests necessarily exist in different classes of citizens. If a majority be united by a common interest, the rights of the minority will be insecure. There are but two methods of providing against this evil: The one by creating a will in the community independent of the majority, that is, of the society itself, the other by comprehending in the society so many separate descriptions of citizens, as will render an unjust combination of a majority of the whole, very improbable, if not impracticable. The first method prevails in all governments possessing an hereditary or self appointed authority. This at best is but a precarious security; because a power independent of the society may as well espouse the unjust views of the major, as the rightful interests, of the minor party, and may possibly be turned against both parties. The second method will be exemplified in the federal republic of the United States. While all authority in it will be derived from and dependent on the society, the society itself will be broken into so many parts, interests and classes of citizens, that the rights of individuals or of the minority, will be in little danger from interested combinations of the majority. In a free government, the security for civil rights must be the same as for religious rights. It consists in the one case in the multiplicity of interests, and in the other, in the multiplicity of sects. The degree of security in both cases will depend on the number of interests and sects; and this may be presumed to depend on the extent of country and number of people comprehended under the same government. This view of the subject must particularly recommend a proper federal system to all the sincere and considerate friends of republican government: Since it shows that in exact proportion as the territory of the union may be formed into more circumscribed confederacies or states, oppressive combinations of a majority will be facilitated, the best security under the republican form, for the rights of every class of citizens, will be diminished; and consequently, the stability and independence of some member of the government, the only other security, must be proportionally increased. Justice is the end of government. It is the end of civil society. It ever has been, and ever will be pursued, until it be obtained, or until liberty be lost in the pursuit. In a society under the forms of which the stronger faction can readily unite and oppress the weaker, anarchy may as truly be said to reign, as in a state of nature where the weaker individual is not secured against the violence of the stronger: And as in the latter state even the stronger individuals are prompted by the uncertainty of their condition, to submit to a government which may protect the weak as well as themselves: So in the former state, will the more powerful factions or parties be gradually induced by a like motive, to wish for a government which will protect all parties, the weaker as well as the more powerful. It can be little doubted, that if the state of Rhode Island was separated from the confederacy, and left to itself, the insecurity of rights under the popular form of government within such narrow limits, would be displayed by such reiterated oppressions of factious majorities, that some power altogether independent of the people would soon be called for by the voice of the very factions whose misrule had proved the necessity of it. In the extended republic of the United States, and among the great variety of interests, parties and sects which it embraces, a coalition of a majority of the whole society could seldom take place on any other principles than those of justice and the general good; and there being thus less danger to a minor from the will of the major party, there must be less pretext also, to provide for the security of the former, by introducing into the government a will not dependent on the latter; or in other words, a will independent of the society itself. It is no less certain than it is important, notwithstanding the contrary opinions which have been entertained, that the larger the society, provided it lie within a practicable sphere, the more duly capable will be of self government. And happily for the *republican cause,* the practicable sphere may be carried to a very great extent, by a judicious modification and mixture of the *federal principle.*

PUBLIUS

APPENDIX

D Electoral Maps: 2000–2016

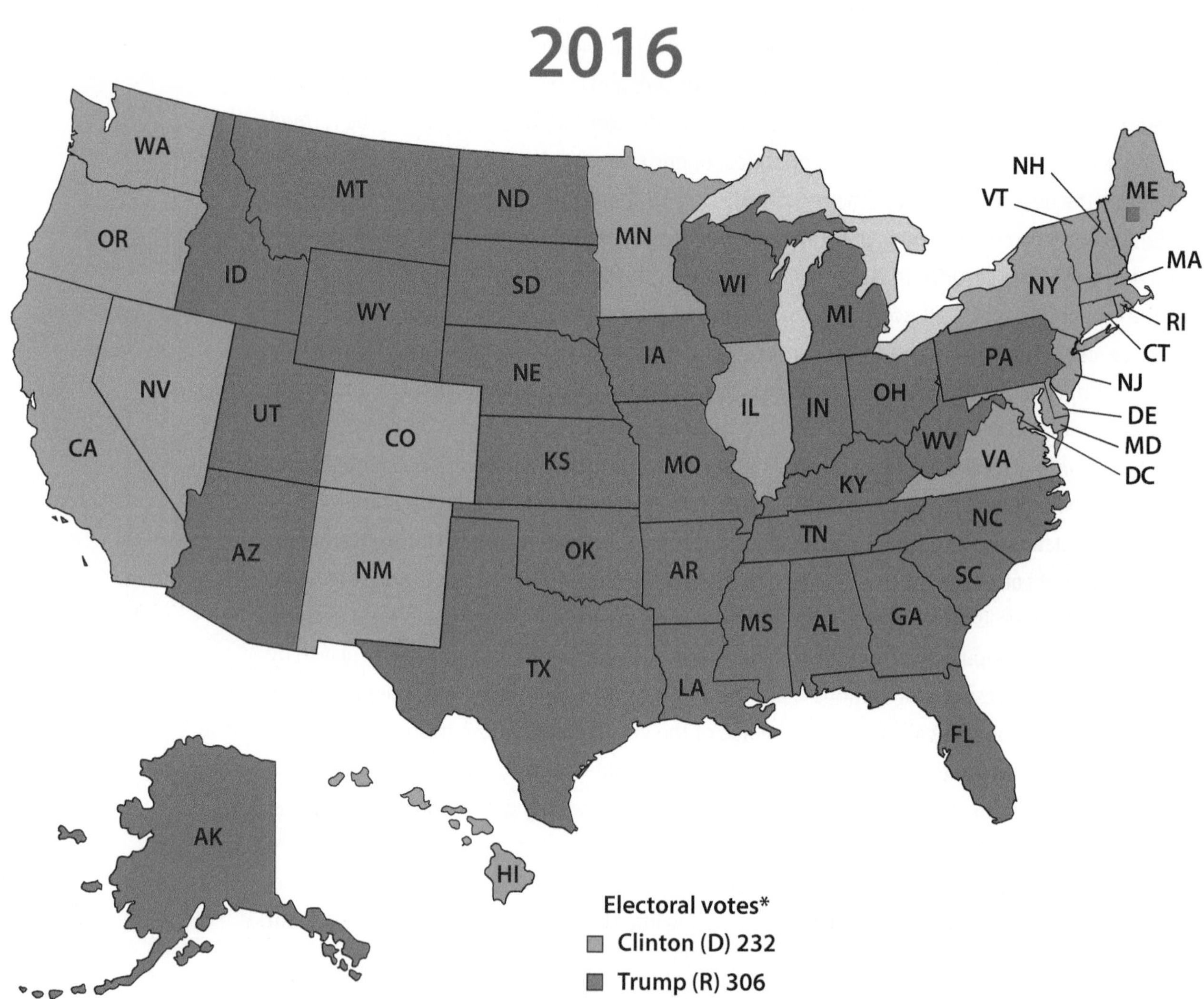

*Maine split its electoral votes, awarding three to Clinton and one to Trump. Information is current as of November 14, 2016.

2012

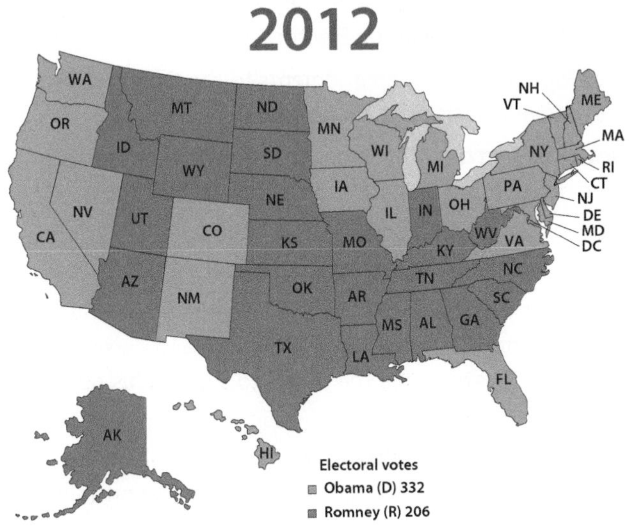

2008

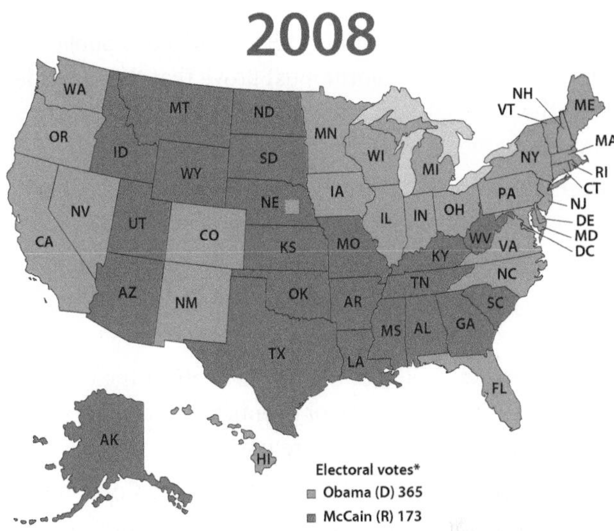

* Nebraska split its electoral votes, awarding one to Obama for carrying the second congressional district and four to McCain for carrying the state as a whole plus its other two congressional districts.

2004

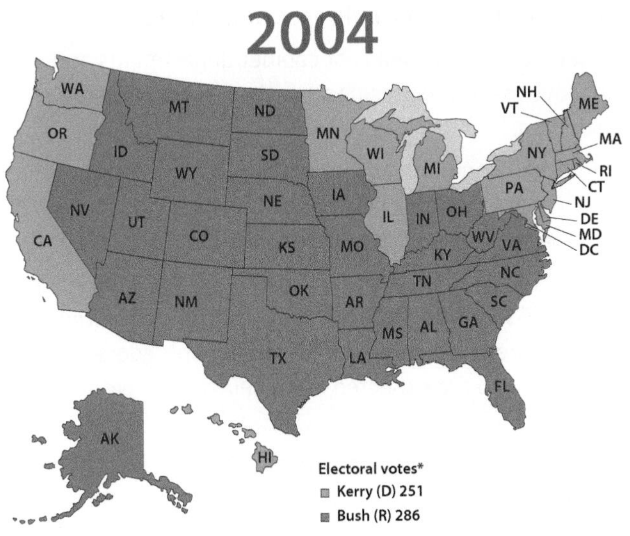

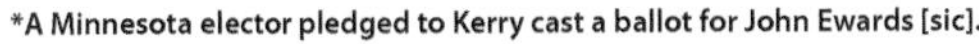
*A Minnesota elector pledged to Kerry cast a ballot for John Ewards [sic].

2000

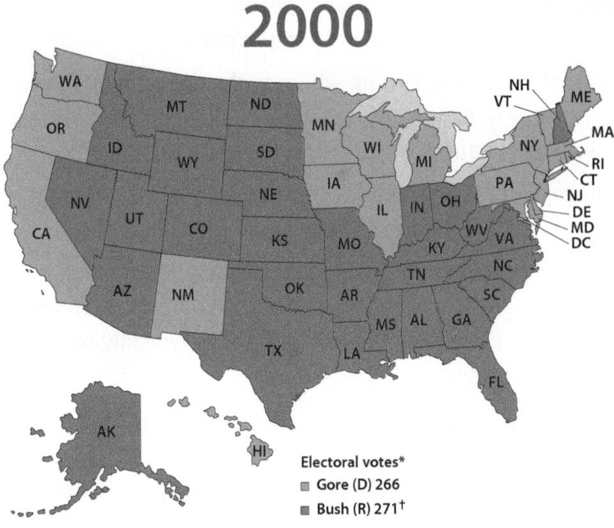

* A District of Columbia elector pledged to Gore cast no ballot as a protest against the District of Columbia's lack of representation in the U.S. Congress

† The state of Florida certified Bush the winner on November 26, a result that Gore contested in court.

Glossary

A

actual malice Supreme Court test for libel of a public figure, in which the plaintiff must prove that the publisher knew the material was false or acted with reckless disregard of whether it was true or false.

adversary process Confrontational legal process under which each party presents its version of events.

affirmative action Policies that support greater equality, often by granting racial or gender preferences in hiring, education, or contracting.

agenda setting Ability of the media to affect the way people view issues, people, or events by controlling which stories are shown and which are not.

amendment Formal process of changing the Constitution.

amicus curiae Latin term meaning "friend of the court" that is used to describe individuals or interest groups who have an interest in a lawsuit but are not themselves direct parties to the suit.

Antifederalists Those who opposed the new proposed Constitution during the ratification period.

appeal Legal proceeding whereby the decision of a lower court on a question of law can be challenged and reviewed by a higher court.

appropriate Congress's power to allocate a set amount of federal dollars for a specific program or agency.

approval rating Job performance evaluation for the president, Congress, or other public official or institution that is generated by public opinion polls and is typically reported as a percentage.

Articles of Confederation Initial governing authority of the United States, 1781–88.

Australian ballot Voting system in which state governments run elections and provide voters the option of choosing candidates from multiple parties; also called the secret ballot.

authorize Congress's power to create a federal program or agency and set levels of federal funds to support that program or agency.

autocracy System of government in which the power to govern is concentrated in the hands of an individual ruler.

B

ballot List of candidates who are running for elected office; used by voters to make their choice.

battleground state State in which the outcome of the presidential election is uncertain and in which both candidates invest much time and money, especially if its votes are vital for a victory in the Electoral College.

Bill of Rights First ten amendments to the Constitution, which provide basic political rights.

Black Lives Matter Movement that grew out of the perceived discounting of black lives by police and juries.

Brown v. Board of Education The 1954 Supreme Court decision striking down segregated schools.

bully pulpit Nickname for the power of the president to use the attention associated with the office to persuade the media, Congress, and the public to support his policy positions.

bureaucracy Executive branch departments, agencies, boards, and commissions that carry out the responsibilities of the federal government.

C

cabinet Set of executive departments responsible for carrying out federal policy in specific issue areas.

cabinet secretaries Heads of cabinet departments and chief advisers to the president on the issues under their jurisdiction.

capitalism Economic system in which businesses and key industries are privately owned and in which individuals, acting on their own or with others, are free to create businesses.

career civil servants Federal employees who are hired through a merit-based system to implement federal programs and who are expected to be neutral in their political affiliations.

caucus Meeting of party members in town halls, schools, and private homes to select a presidential nominee.

checks and balances Government structure that authorizes each branch of government (executive, legislative, and judicial) to share powers with the other branches, thereby holding some scrutiny of and control over the other branches.

chief of staff Person who coordinates and oversees interactions among the president, his personal staff, and his cabinet secretaries.

citizens' groups Groups that form to draw attention to purely public issues that affect all citizens equally.

citizenship Full-fledged membership in a nation.

civic duty Social force that binds a person to actively participate in public and political life.

civic interest Concern for the well-being of society and the nation as a whole.

civil liberties Those rights, such as freedom of speech and religion, that are so fundamental that they are outside the authority of government to regulate.

civil rights Set of rights centered around the concept of equal treatment that government is obliged to protect.

Civil Rights Act Prohibits discrimination in employment, education, and places of public accommodation (1964).

civil service The nonpartisan federal workforce employed to carry out government programs and policies.

Civil Service Commission Created by the Pendleton Act to administer entrance exams for the federal civil service and set standards for promotion based on merit.

civil society Voluntary organizations that allow communities to flourish.

civil suit Lawsuit by a person, organization, or government against another person, organization, or government.

class action lawsuit Lawsuit filed by one person on behalf of that person plus all similarly situated people.

Clean Air Act Broad federal legislation that expanded the federal government's ability to monitor and protect the environment against pollution.

Clean Water Act Broad federal legislation that expanded the federal government's ability to monitor and protect the safety and quality of water.

clear and present danger test First Amendment test that requires the state to prove that there is a high likelihood that the speech in question would lead to a danger that Congress has a right to prevent.

cloture Vote that can stop a filibuster and bring debate on a bill to end.

Cold War An era in history marked by conflict and distrust between the United States and Communist nations.

commander in chief Leader of the armed forces of the United States.

commerce clause Gives Congress the power to regulate commerce "with foreign Nations, and among the several States, and with the Indian Tribes" (Article I, Section 8).

common law Judge-made law in England and the United States that results from gaps in statutory law.

Communist Government management and ownership of key elements of a nation's economy.

compelling interest test Standard frequently used by the Supreme Court in civil liberties cases to determine whether a state has a compelling interest for infringing on a right and whether the law is narrowly drawn to meet that interest.

compulsory voting Practice that requires citizens to vote in elections or face punitive measures such as community service, fines, or imprisonment.

concurrent budget resolution Congressional blueprint outlining general amounts of funds that can be spent on federal programs.

concurrent powers Powers held by both the national and state governments in a federal system.

concurring opinion Opinion that agrees with the results of the majority opinion (that is, which party wins) but sets out a separate rationale.

confederal system System of government in which ultimate authority rests with the regional (for example, state) governments.

confidence interval Statistical range with a given probability that takes random error into account.

Connecticut Compromise Compromise on legislative representation whereby the lower chamber is based on population, and the upper chamber provides equal representation to the states.

conservatives Individuals who distrust government, believing that private efforts are more likely to improve people's lives. In the social sphere, conservatives usually support traditional lifestyles and tend to believe that government can play a valuable role in shaping personal choices.

constitution Document or set of documents that establish the basic rules and procedures for how a society shall be governed.

Constitutional Convention Meeting in 1787 at which twelve states intended to revise the Articles of Confederation but ended up proposing an entirely new Constitution.

constitutional system System of government in which people set up and agree on the basic rules and procedures that will govern them.

content-neutral Free speech doctrine that allows certain types of regulation of speech, as long as the restriction does not favor one side or another of a controversy.

continuing resolution Measure passed to fund federal programs when the appropriations process has not been completed by September 30, the end of the fiscal year.

countermajoritarian difficulty Alexander Bickel's phrase for the tension that exists for representative government when unelected judges have the power to strike laws passed by elected representatives.

Court-packing plan President Franklin Roosevelt's proposal to add new justices to the Supreme Court so that the Court would uphold his policies.

courts of appeals Intermediate federal courts that are above the district courts and below the Supreme Court.

criminal case Government prosecution of an individual for breaking the law.

D

debt ceiling The congressionally authorized limit on federal borrowing.

Declaration of Independence 1776 document declaring American independence from Great Britain and calling for equality, human rights, and citizen participation.

democracy System of government in which the supreme power is vested in the people and exercised by them either directly or indirectly through elected representatives.

direct democracy Form of democracy in which political power is exercised directly by citizens.

dissenting opinion Opinion that disagrees with the majority opinion as to which party wins.

district courts Federal trial courts at the bottom of the federal judicial hierarchy.

divided government Situation in which one party controls the executive branch, and the other party controls the legislative branch.

Dred Scott v. Sandford The 1857 Supreme Court decision declaring that blacks could not be citizens and Congress could not ban slavery in the territories.

dual federalism Doctrine holding that state governments and the federal government have almost completely separate functions.

E

earmark Federal dollars devoted specifically to a local project in a congressional district or state.

economic interest group Group formed to advance the economic status of its members.

efficacy Extent to which people believe their actions can affect public affairs and the actions of government.

egalitarianism Belief in human equality that disdains inherited titles of nobility and inherited wealth.

Electoral College The presidential electors, selected to represent the votes of their respective states, who meet every four years to cast the electoral votes for president and vice president.

en banc Decision by an entire Court of Appeals circuit, typically following an original judgment by a three-judge panel of the circuit.

entitlement programs Federal programs, such as Social Security, Medicare, or Medicaid, that pay out benefits to individuals based on a specified set of eligibility criteria.

enumerated powers Powers expressly granted to Congress by the Constitution.

equality Idea that all individuals are equal in their moral worth and so must be equal in treatment under the law and have equal access to the decision-making process.

equality of opportunity Expectation that citizens may not be discriminated against on account of race, gender, or national background and that every citizen should have an equal chance to succeed in life.

equality of outcome Expectation that equality is achieved if results are comparable for all citizens regardless of race, gender, or national background or that such groups are proportionally represented in measures of success in life.

Equal Pay Act Prohibits different pay for males and females for the same work (1963).

equal protection clause Prevents states from denying any person the equal protection of the laws (Fourteenth Amendment).

establishment clause First Amendment clause prohibiting governmental establishment of religion.

European Union (EU) Association of European nations formed in order to facilitate economic and political interactions across their borders.

exclusionary rule Supreme Court rule declaring that evidence found in violation of the Fourth Amendment cannot be used at trial.

executive branch The branch of the federal government that executes the laws.

executive order Presidential directive that usually involves implementing a specific law.

executive privilege President's right to engage in confidential communications with his advisers.

exit polls Polls that survey a sample of voters immediately after exiting the voting booth to predict the outcome of the election before the ballots are officially counted.

expectation of privacy test Supreme Court test for whether Fourth Amendment protections apply.

F

faction Defined by Madison as any group that places its own interests above the aggregate interests of society.

fair trade Policy designed to make sure that the working conditions are relatively equal in nations that trade with each other.

federal budget deficit Difference between the amount of money the federal government spends in outlays and the amount of money it receives from revenues.

federalism System of government in which sovereignty is constitutionally divided between national and state governments.

Federalist Papers Series of essays written by James Madison, Alexander Hamilton, and John Jay arguing for the ratification of the Constitution; today a leading source for understanding the Constitution.

Federalists Initially, those who supported the Constitution during the ratification period; later, the name of the political party established by supporters of Alexander Hamilton.

Federal Register Official published record of all executive branch rules, regulations, and orders.

federal regulatory commission Federal agency typically run by a small number of officials, known as commissioners, who are appointed by the president for fixed terms and oversee economic or political issues.

Federal Reserve Board Independent regulatory commission that affects the money supply by setting the reserve requirements of member banks, establishing a discount rate for loans to member banks, and buying or selling government securities.

filibuster Tactic of extended speech designed to delay or block passage of a bill in the Senate.

501(c)(3) organizations Tax-exempt groups that are prohibited from lobbying or campaigning for a party or candidate.

501(c)(4) organizations Tax-exempt groups that exist to promote social welfare and can advocate for specific policy issues.

Founders The people who were involved in establishing the United States, whether at the time of the Declaration of Independence or the writing of the Constitution.

Framers The people who were involved in writing the Constitution.

framing Ability of the media to influence public perception of issues by constructing the issue or discussion of a subject in a certain way.

franchise Right to vote; also called suffrage.

free exercise clause First Amendment clause protecting the free exercise of religion.

free rider problem Problem faced by interest groups when a collective benefit they provide is so widespread and diffuse that members and nonmembers alike receive it, reducing the incentive for joining the group.

free trade Policy designed to lower import barriers to encourage trade across nations.

fugitive slave clause Required states to return runaway slaves; negated by the Thirteenth Amendment (Article IV, Section 2).

G

gender gap Differences in the political attitudes and behavior of men and women.

general election Election in which voters choose their elected officials.

general welfare clause Gives Congress the power to tax to provide for the general welfare (Article I, Section 8).

generational replacement Cycle whereby younger generations replace older generations in the electorate.

gerrymandering Redistricting that blatantly benefits one political party over the other or concentrates (or dilutes) the voting impact of racial and ethnic groups.

globalization The interconnectedness of nations around the world on economic, political, cultural, social, and military dimensions.

grandfather clauses Election rules that exempted people from difficult literacy and interpretation tests for voting if their grandfathers had been eligible to vote.

grassroots movement Group that forms in response to an economic or political event but does not focus on only one issue.

graveyard voting Corrupt practice of using a dead person's name to cast a ballot in an election.

Great Society Lyndon Johnson's program for expanding the federal social welfare programs in health care, education, and housing and for ending poverty.

H

hard news Political news coverage, traditionally found in the printed press, that is more fact-based, opposed to more interpretive narratives and commentary.

head of state Title given to the president as national leader.

hold Power available to a senator to prevent the unanimous consent that allows a bill or presidential nomination to come to the Senate floor, which can be broken by invoking cloture (currently sixty votes on most items).

home style The way in which incumbents portray themselves to constituents.

House majority leader Leader of the majority party in the House and second in command to the Speaker.

House minority leader Leader of the minority party in the House.

I

ideological interest groups Groups that form among citizens with the same beliefs about a specific issue.

impeachment Process whereby the House brings charges against the president or another federal official that will, upon conviction by the Senate, remove him or her from office.

imperial presidency Power of the president to speak for the nation on the world stage and to set the policy agenda at home.

implied powers Powers not expressly granted to Congress but added through the necessary and proper clause.

incorporate Process of applying provisions of the Bill of Rights to the states.

independent agency Federal organization that has independent authority and does not operate within a cabinet department.

Independents Individuals who do not affiliate with either of the major political parties.

individualism Set of beliefs holding that people, and not government, are responsible for their own well-being.

inside strategy A strategy employed by interest groups to pursue a narrow policy change and influence legislators directly rather than using a wider grassroots approach.

institutional model Model of voting that focuses on the context of the election, including whether it is close and whether the rules encourage or discourage participation.

interest groups Groups of citizens who share a common interest—a political opinion, a religious or ideological belief, a social goal, or an economic characteristic—and try to influence public policy to benefit themselves.

International Monetary Fund (IMF) International organization that works to stabilize currency values and government debt for nations in economic difficulty.

invisible primary Period just before the primaries begin during which candidates attempt to capture party support and media coverage.

iron law of oligarchy Theory that leaders in any organization eventually behave in their own self-interest, even at the expense of rank-and-file members; the larger the organization, the greater the likelihood that the leader will behave this way.

iron triangle Insular and closed relationship among interest groups, members of Congress, and federal agencies.

issue network View of the relationship among interest groups, members of Congress, and federal agencies as more fluid, open, and transparent than that described by the term iron triangle.

J

Jim Crow laws Southern laws that established strict segregation of the races and gave their name to the segregation era.

judicial activism Decisions that go beyond what the law requires made by judges who seek to impose their own policy preferences on society through their judicial decisions.

judicial branch The branch of the federal government that interprets the laws.

judicial independence Ability of judges to reach decisions without fear of political retribution.

judicial restraint Decisions by judges respecting the decisions of other branches or, through the concept of precedent, the decisions of earlier judges.

judicial review Authority of courts to declare laws passed by Congress and acts of the executive branch to be unconstitutional.

jurisdiction Lawful authority of a court to hear a case.

L

lame duck Term-limited official in his or her last term of office.

Lawrence v. Texas 2003 Supreme Court case extending the right to privacy to homosexual behavior.

legislative branch The branch of the federal government that makes the laws.

Lemon test Test for determining whether aid to religion violates the establishment clause.

levels of conceptualization Measure of how ideologically coherent individuals are in their political evaluations.

libel Publishing false and damaging statements about another person.

liberals Individuals who have faith in government to improve people's lives, believing that private efforts are insufficient. In the social sphere, liberals usually support diverse lifestyles and tend to oppose any government action that seeks to shape personal choices.

libertarians Those who generally believe that government should refrain from acting to regulate either the economy or moral values.

liberty Political value that cherishes freedom from an arbitrary exercise of power that constricts individual choice.

literacy tests Tests requiring reading and interpretation skills in order to vote.

lobbying Act of trying to persuade elected officials to adopt a specific policy change or maintain the status quo.

M

majoritarian System of policy making in which those with a numerical majority hold authority.

majority opinion Opinion of a court laying out the official position of the court in the case.

majority rule Idea that a numerical majority of a group should hold the power to make decisions binding on the whole group; a simple majority.

majority vote Vote in which the winner needs to win 50 percent plus 1 of the votes cast.

Marbury v. Madison An 1803 Supreme Court decision that established the Supreme Court's power of judicial review.

marketplace of ideas Idea that the government should not restrict the expression of ideas because the people are capable of accepting good ideas and rejecting bad ones.

markup Process by which bills are literally marked up, or written, by the members of the committee.

mass media News sources, including newspapers, television, radio, and the Internet, whose purpose is to provide a large audience with information about the nation and the world.

McCulloch v. Maryland 1819 Supreme Court decision upholding the right of Congress to create a bank.

median voter theorem Theory that, in a two-party race, if voters select candidates on the basis of ideology and everyone participates equally, the party closer to the middle will win.

Medicaid Shared federal and state health insurance program for low-income persons.

Medicare Federal health insurance program for the elderly and disabled.

merit system System of employment under which employees are chosen and promoted based on merit.

microtargeting Gathering detailed information on cross sections of the electorate to track potential supporters and tailor political messages for them; also called narrowcasting.

midterm elections Congressional elections held between the presidential elections.

Millennials Generation born between 1982 and 2003.

Miller test Supreme Court test for determining whether material is obscene.

minimal effects model View of the media's impact as marginal because most people seek news reports to reinforce beliefs already held rather than to develop new ones.

minority rights Idea that majority should not be able to take certain fundamental rights away from those in the minority.

Missouri Plan Process for selecting state judges whereby the original nomination is by appointment, and subsequent retention is by a retention election.

moderates Individuals who are in the middle of the ideological spectrum and do not hold consistently strong views about whether government should be involved in people's lives.

monarchy System of government that assigns power to a single person who inherits that position and rules until death.

muckraking Journalistic practice of investigative reporting that seeks to uncover corruption and wrongdoing.

multipolar A world system where there are distinct centers of political and military power.

N

NAFTA Comprehensive multination trade agreement ratified in 1994 that knocked down trade barriers among Canada, the United States, and Mexico.

national committee Top level of national political parties; coordinates national presidential campaigns.

national debt Sum of loans and interest that the federal government has accrued over time to pay for the federal deficit.

natural (unalienable) rights Rights that every individual has and that government cannot legitimately take away.

necessary and proper clause Gives Congress the power to pass all laws necessary and proper to the powers enumerated in Article I, Section 8.

negativity Campaign strategy of telling voters why they should not vote for the opponent and of highlighting information that raises doubts about the opponent.

New Deal Franklin Delano Roosevelt's program for ending the Great Depression through government intervention in the economy and development of a set of safety-net programs for individuals.

news media Subset of the mass media that provides the news of the day, gathered and reported by journalists.

nonattitudes Sources of error in public opinion polls in which individuals feel obliged to give opinions when they are unaware of the issue or have no opinions about it.

nongovernmental organizations (NGOs) Organizations independent of governments that monitor and improve political, economic, and social conditions throughout the world.

nonstate actors Individuals or groups that do not represent any specific national government and may take action across borders.

not-so-minimal effects model View of the media's impact as substantial, occurring by agenda setting, framing, and priming.

nullification Right of states to invalidate acts of Congress they believe to be illegal.

O

Office of Management and Budget (OMB) Federal agency that oversees the federal budget and all federal regulations.

oligarchy System of government in which the power to govern is concentrated in the hands of a powerful few, usually wealthy individuals.

omnibus bill One very large bill that encompasses many separate bills.

order Political value in which the rule of law is followed and does not permit actions that infringe on the well-being of others.

override Congress's power to overturn a presidential veto with a two-thirds vote in each chamber.

oversight Powers of Congress to monitor how the executive branch implements the laws.

P

pardon Full forgiveness for a crime.

party alignment Voter identification with a political party in repeated elections.

party caucus Group of party members in a legislature.

party identification Psychological attachment to a political party; partisanship.

party platform Document that lays out a party's core beliefs and policy proposals for each presidential election.

patronage system Political system in which government programs and benefits are awarded based on political loyalty to a party or politician.

Peace Corps U.S. government-funded organization that sends individuals on educational and cultural missions around the world.

Pendleton Act 1883 act that established a merit- and performance-based system for federal employment.

penny press Newspapers sold for a penny, initiating an era in which the press began to rely on circulation and advertising for income and not on political parties.

permanent campaign Charge that presidents and members of Congress focus more on winning the next election than on governing.

***petition for a writ of* certiorari** Request to the Supreme Court that it review a lower court case.

plea bargain Agreement by a criminal defendant to plead guilty in return for a reduced sentence.

pluralist View of democratic society in which interest groups compete over policy goals, and elected officials are mediators of group conflict.

plurality vote Vote in which the winner needs to win more votes than any other candidate.

pocket veto Automatic veto that occurs when Congress goes out of session within ten days of submitting a bill to the president and the president has not signed it.

polarization Condition in which differences between parties and/or the public are so stark that disagreement breaks out, fueling attacks and controversy.

policy agenda The second step in the policy-making process, in which a problem that has been identified gets the attention of policy makers.

policy diffusion Process by which policy ideas and programs initiated by one state spread to other states.

policy enactment The fourth step in the policy-making process, in which Congress passes a law that authorizes a specific governmental response to the problem.

policy evaluation The final step in the policy-making process, in which the policy is evaluated for its effectiveness and efficiency; if changes are needed, the issue is placed back on the policy agenda, and the cycle starts again.

policy formulation The third step in the policy-making process, in which those with a stake in the policy area propose and develop solutions to the problem.

policy implementation The fifth step in the policy-making process, in which the executive branch develops the rules that will put the policy into action.

political action committees (PACs) Groups formed to raise and contribute funds to support electoral candidates and that are subject to campaign finance laws.

political appointees Federal employees appointed by the president with the explicit task of carrying out his political and partisan agenda.

political culture A shared way of thinking about community and government and the relationship between them.

political equality The idea that people should have equal amounts of influence in the political system.

political ideology Set of coherent political beliefs that offers a philosophy for thinking about the scope of government.

political parties Broad coalitions of interests organized to win elections in order to enact a commonly supported set of public policies.

political tolerance Willingness of people to put up with ideas with which they disagree.

political trust Extent to which people believe the government acts in their best interests.

politics Process by which people make decisions about who gets what, when, and how.

poll taxes Tax on voting; prohibited by the Twenty-Fourth Amendment (1964).

popular vote Tally of total votes from individual citizens, as opposed to the electoral vote.

populists Those who oppose concentrated wealth and adhere to traditional moral values.

position issues Political issues that offer specific policy choices and often differentiate candidates' views and plans of action.

power elite Small handful of decision makers who hold authority over a large set of issues.

precedent Practice of reaching decisions based on the previous decisions of other judges.

presidential coattails Effect of a popular president or presidential candidate on congressional elections, boosting votes for members of his party.

presidential directive Official instructions from the president regarding federal policy.

primary election Election in which voters select the candidates who will run on the party label in the general election; also called direct primary.

priming Process whereby the media influence the criteria the public uses to make decisions.

prior restraint Government restrictions on freedom of the press that prevent material from being published.

private discrimination Discrimination by private individuals or businesses.

private goods Goods or benefits provided by government in which most of the benefit falls to the individuals, families, or companies receiving them.

problem identification The first step in the policy-making process, in which a problem in politics, the economy, or society is recognized as warranting government action.

propaganda model Extreme view of the media's role in society, arguing that the press serves the interest of the government only, driving what the public thinks about important issues.

proportional representation An electoral system that assigns party delegates according to vote share in a presidential primary election or that assigns seats in the legislature according to vote share in a general election.

protectionist Policy designed to raise import barriers for goods that are domestically produced.

public discrimination Discrimination by national, state, or local governments.

public goods Goods or benefits provided by government from which everyone benefits and from which no one can be excluded.

public opinion Aggregate of individual attitudes or beliefs about certain issues or officials.

public policy Intentional actions of government designed to achieve a goal.

push polls Polls that are designed to manipulate the opinions of those being polled.

R

rally-around-the-flag effect Surge of public support for the president in times of international crisis.

random sample Method of selection that gives everyone who might be selected to participate in a poll an equal chance to be included.

ranking member Leader of the minority-party members of a committee.

rationality Acting in a way that is consistent with one's self-interest.

rational voting Economic model of voting wherein citizens weigh the benefits of voting against the costs in order to take the most personally beneficial course of action.

realignment Long-term shift in voter allegiance from one party to another.

recession A period of time marked by successive quarters of lower economic output.

reconciliation A measure used to bring all bills that contain changes in the tax code or entitlement programs in line with the congressional budget.

Reconstruction The period from 1865 to 1877 in which the former Confederate states gained readmission to the

Union and the federal government passed laws to help the emancipated slaves.

redistricting Process whereby state legislatures redraw the boundaries of congressional districts in the state to make them equal in population size.

regulations Guidelines issued by federal agencies for administering federal programs and implementing federal law.

regulatory process System of rules that guide how a law is implemented; also called the rule-making process.

representative democracy Form of democracy in which citizens elect public officials to make political decisions and formulate laws on their behalf.

republic Form of government in which power derives from citizens, but public officials make policy and govern according to existing law.

reserve powers Powers retained by the states under the Constitution.

responsible parties Parties that take responsibility for offering the electorate a distinct range of policies and programs, thus providing a clear choice.

responsiveness Idea that government should implement laws and policies that reflect the wishes of the public and any changes in those wishes.

retrospective voting Theory that voting is driven by a citizen's assessment of an officeholder's performance since the last election.

revolving door Movement of members of Congress, lobbyists, and executive branch employees into paid positions in each other's organizations.

right of association Right to freely associate with others and form groups, as protected by the First Amendment.

right of petition Right to ask the government for assistance with a problem or to express opposition to a government policy, as protected by the First Amendment.

right to privacy Constitutional right inferred by the Court that has been used to protect unlisted rights such as sexual privacy and reproductive rights, plus the right to end life-sustaining medical treatment.

Roe v. Wade 1973 Supreme Court case extending the right to privacy to abortion.

rule Guidelines issued by the House Rules Committee that determine how many amendments may be considered for each bill.

rule of four Supreme Court rule that grants review to a case if as few as four of the justices support review.

rule of law Legal system with known rules that are enforced equally against all people.

S

safe seat Seat in Congress considered to be reliably held by one party or the other.

Schedule C appointees Federal employees appointed by the president to oversee civil service employees.

secede To formally withdraw from a nation-state.

seditious libel Conduct or language that incites rebellion against the authority of a state.

selective benefits Benefits offered exclusively to members of an interest group.

selective exposure Process whereby people secure information from sources that agree with them, thus reinforcing their beliefs.

selective incorporation Doctrine used by the Supreme Court to make those provisions of the Bill of Rights that are fundamental rights binding on the states.

selective perception Process whereby partisans interpret the same information differently.

self-government Rule by the people.

self-interest Concern for one's own advantage and well-being.

Senate majority leader Leader of the majority party in the Senate.

Senate minority leader Leader of the minority party in the Senate.

Senior Executive Service (SES) Senior management personnel in the federal government appointed by the president.

separate-but-equal doctrine Supreme Court doctrine that upheld segregation as long as there were equivalent facilities for blacks.

separation of powers Government structure in which authority is divided among branches (executive, legislative, and judicial), with each holding separate and independent powers and areas of responsibility.

signing statements Written remarks issued by the president when signing a bill into law that often reflect his interpretation of how the law should be implemented.

single-issue groups Groups that form to present one view on a highly salient issue that is intensely important to members, such as gun control or abortion.

single-member plurality system Electoral system that assigns one seat in a legislative body to represent citizens who live in a defined area (a district) based on which candidate wins the most votes.

social contract Theory that government has only the authority accorded it by the consent of the governed.

Social Security Federal pension program that makes a monthly payment to retired elderly workers and disabled persons.

socialism Economic system in which the government owns major industries.

socialization Impact and influence of one's social environment on the views and attitudes one carries in life, a primary source of political attitudes.

soft news News stories focused less on facts and policies than on sensationalizing secondary issues or on less serious subjects of the entertainment world.

solicitor general Official in the Justice Department who represents the president in federal court.

Speaker of the House Constitutional and political leader of the House.

special interests Set of groups seeking a particular benefit for themselves in the policy process.

state action Action by a state, as opposed to a private person, that constitutes discrimination and therefore is an equal protection violation.

State of the Union address Speech on the condition of the country given by the president to Congress every January.

states' rights View that states have strong independent authority to resist federal rules under the Constitution.

Stonewall riots Street protest in 1969 by gay patrons against a police raid of a gay bar in New York; the protest is credited with launching the gay rights movement.

strategic politician hypothesis Effect that the strength of the economy and the popularity of the sitting president have on the decision to run for Congress.

suffrage Right to vote; also called franchise.

Super PACs Independent groups that can raise unlimited amounts of money from individuals, labor unions, and corporations and can spend it to support or oppose political candidates but cannot coordinate directly with candidates or political parties.

supremacy clause Makes federal law supreme over state laws (Article VI).

swing states States that are not clearly pro-Republican or pro-Democrat and therefore are of vital interest to presidential candidates, as they can determine election outcomes.

swing voters Voters who are neither reliably Republican nor reliably Democratic and who are pursued by each party during an election, as they can determine which candidate wins.

symbolic speech Actions, such as burning the flag, that convey a political message without spoken words.

T

term limits Rule restricting the number of terms an elected official can serve in a given office.

third parties Minor political parties that present a third alternative to the two dominant political parties in the American political system.

three-fifths compromise Compromise over slavery at the Constitutional Convention that granted states extra representation in the House of Representatives based on their number of slaves at the ratio of three-fifths.

tracking polls Polls that seek to gauge changes of opinion of the same sample size over a period of time, common during the closing months of presidential elections.

turnout Share of all eligible voters who actually cast ballots.

U

unanimous consent agreement Agreement among all 100 senators on how a bill or presidential nomination will be debated, changed, and voted on in the Senate.

unions Interest groups of individuals who share a common type of employment and seek better wages and working conditions through collective bargaining with employers.

unitary system System of government in which ultimate authority rests with the national government.

United Nations (UN) Organization formed after World War II to mediate disputes among nations around the world.

V

valence issues Noncontroversial or widely supported campaign issues that are unlikely to differ among candidates.

valid secular purpose Supreme Court test that allows states to ban activities that infringe on religious practices as long as the state has a nonreligious rationale for prohibiting the behavior.

vanishing marginals Trend marking the decline of competitive congressional elections.

veto Authority of the president to block legislation passed by Congress. Congress can override a veto by a two-thirds majority in each chamber.

vote-by-mail (VBM) system Method of voting in an election whereby ballots are distributed to voters by mail, and voters complete and return the ballots by mail.

voter apathy Lack of interest in voting and in politics generally.

voter registration Enrollment required prior to voting to establish eligibility.

voting-age population (VAP) Used to calculate the rate of participation by dividing the number of voters by the number of people in the country who are 18 and over.

voting-eligible population (VEP) Used to calculate the rate of participation by dividing the number of voters by the number of people in the country who are eligible to vote rather than just of voting age.

Voting Rights Act Gives the federal government the power to prevent discrimination in voting rights (1965).

W

War Powers Act The 1973 act that provides that the president cannot send troops into military conflict for more than a total of ninety days without seeking a formal declaration of war, or authorization for continued military action, from Congress.

watchdog Role of the press in monitoring government actions.

wedge issue Divisive issue focused on a particular group of the electorate that candidates use to gain more support by taking votes away from their opponents.

whistleblowers Employees who report mismanagement, corruption, or illegal activity within their agencies.

white primary Election rules that prohibited blacks from voting in Democratic primaries.

winner-take-all system Electoral system in which whoever wins the most votes in an election wins the election.

women's suffrage movement Movement to grant women the right to vote.

World Bank International organization that distributes grants and low-income loans in developing countries.

World Trade Organization (WTO) International organization that considers and resolves trade disputes among member nations.

***writ of* habeas corpus** Right of individuals who have been arrested and jailed to go before a judge, who determines whether their detention is legal.

Y

yellow journalism Style of journalism in the late nineteenth century characterized by sensationalism intended to capture readers' attention and increase circulation.

Endnotes

Chapter 1

1. Feb. 5 2008 Speech. http://www.nytimes.com/2008/02/05/us/politics/05text-obama.html?_r=0.
2. International Social Survey Program, as cited in Russell Dalton, *The Good Citizen* (Washington, D.C.: CQ Press, 2007), 144; Morley Winograd and Michael D. Hais, *Millennial Makeover: MySpace, YouTube and the Future of American Politics* (New Brunswick, N.J.: Rutgers University Press, 2008), 260–63. The caption for the photo on page 5 is drawn from this source.
3. Dalton, *The Good Citizen*, 153.
4. Larry Bartels, *Unequal Democracy* (Princeton, N.J.: Princeton University Press, 2008); David Cay Johnston, "The Gap Between Rich and Poor Grows in the United States," *New York Times,* March 29, 2007. The caption for the photo on page 5 is drawn from these sources: U.S. census data; Merrill Goozner, "Top 1 Percent Got Lion's Share of Income," *Fiscal Times,* March 5, 2012, http://www.thefiscaltimes.com/Blogs/Gooz-News/2012/03/05/Top-1-Percent-Got-Lions-Share-of-Income-Gains-in-2010.aspx; and Emmanuel Saez, "Striking It Richer: The Evolution of Top Incomes in the United States (Updated with 2009 and 2010 Estimates)," *Pathways Magazine* (Winter 2008): 6–7, http://www.stanford.edu/group/scspi/_media/pdf/pathways/winter_2008/Saez.pdf.
5. "Americans' Approval of Congress Drops to Single Digits," *New York Times,* October 25, 2011, http://www.nytimes.com/interactive/2011/10/25/us/politics/approval-of-congress-drops-to-single-digits.html.
6. Kerem Ozan Kalkan, Geoffrey C. Layman, and Eric M. Uslaner, "Attitudes Toward Muslims in Contemporary American Society," *Journal of Politics* 69 (2009): 847–62; Brett Benson, Jennifer Merolla, and John Geer, "Two Steps Forward, One Step Back?" *Electoral Studies* 30 (2011): 607–20.
7. "Obama Ratings Historically Polarized," Gallup Politics, January 27, 2012, accessed April 10, 2012, http://www.gallup.com/poll/152222/Obama-Ratings-Historically-Polarized.aspx.
8. See http://www.usdebtclock.org, accessed October 27, 2016.
9. Charles Beard, *American Government and Politics* (New York: Macmillan Company, 1915), 18.
10. Edmund Burke, "*Reflections on the Revolution in France,*" in *The Portable Edmund Burke,* ed. Isaac Kramnick (New York: Viking, 1999), 32.
11. John Adams to John Taylor, April 15, 1814, in *The Political Writings of John Adams: Representative Selections,* ed. George Peek Jr. (New York: Hackett Publishing, 2003), 67.
12. Quoted in David McCullough, *John Adams* (New York: Simon and Schuster, 2001), 68.
13. Jonathan Grossman, "Fair Labor Standards Act of 1938: Maximum Struggle for a Minimum Wage," U.S. Department of Labor, accessed April 1, 2014, http://www.dol.gov/dol/aboutdol/history/flsa1938.htm.
14. Amy K. Glasmeier, Amy K. "Living Wage Calculator." MIT. Accessed February 25, 2016, http://livingwage.mit.edu/
15. Josiah Ober, *Mass and Elite in Democratic Athens: Rhetoric, Ideology and the Power of the People* (Princeton, N.J.: Princeton University Press, 1991).
16. Harold Lasswell, *Politics: Who Gets What, When, How* (New York: McGraw-Hill, 1936).
17. See http://www.usnews.com/news/articles/2015/07/06/its-official-the-us-is-becoming-a-minority-majority-nation
18. Danielle Allen, quoted in "Here's Why Voters Are So Anxious This Election," NPR News, January 25, 2016, accessed January 25, 2016, http://www.npr.org/2016/01/25/464217330/heres-why-voters-are-so-anxious-this-election.
19. *Obergefell v. Hodges*, 2015 Supreme Court decision.
20. David Remnick, "The President's Hero," *New Yorker,* February 2, 2009, http://www.newyorker.com/talk/comment/2009/02/02/090202taco_talk_remnick.
21. *Garner v. Louisiana*, 368 U.S. 157 (1961), reversing convictions over attempts to desegregate a lunch counter in Baton Rouge, Louisiana; *Browder v. Gayle*, 142 F. Supp. 707 (1956), ending segregated buses in Montgomery, Alabama; and *Cooper v. Aaron* 358 U.S. 1 (1958), ordering the desegregation of Central High School in Little Rock, Arkansas.
22. Winograd and Hais, *Millennial Makeover;* Morley Winograd and Michael D. Hais, "The Boomers Had Their Day. Make Way for the Millennials," *Washington Post,* February 3, 2008, http://www.washingtonpost.com/wp-dyn/content/article/2008/02/01/AR2008020102826.html.
23. See https://www2.ed.gov/about/overview/budget/history/edhistory.pdf.
24. Darrell M. West, Grover J. Whitehurst, and E. J. Dionne Jr., "Invisible: 1.4 Percent Coverage for Education Is Not Enough," Brookings.edu, December 2, 2009, accessed April 10, 2012, http://www.brookings.edu/research/reports/2009/12/02-education-news-west.
25. John Leland, "Bernie Sanders and Donald Trump Voters Share Anger, but Direct It Differently," *New York Times*, January 31, 2016, accessed January 31, 2016, http://www.nytimes.com/2016/01/31/us/bernie-sanders-and-donald-trump-voters-share-anger-but-direct-it-differently.html.
26. James Madison to W. T. Barry, "Epilogue: Securing the Republic," August 4, 1822, in *The Founders' Constitution,* ed. Philip B. Kurland and Ralph Lerner (Chicago: University of Chicago Press, 1986), accessed April 25, 2012, http://press-pubs.uchicago.edu/founders/documents/v1ch18s35.html.

Chapter 2

1. Cited in Lupe S. Salinas, "Gus Garcia and Thurgood Marshall: Two Legal Giants Fighting for Justice," *Thurgood Marshall Law Review* 28 (2003): 145–73.
2. *Delgado et al. v. Bastrop Independent School District,* Civil No. 388, W.D. Texas (1948).
3. Michael A. Olivas (ed.), *Colored Men and Hombres Aqui:* Hernandez v. Texas *and the Emergence of Mexican-American Lawyering* (Houston, Tex.: Arte Público Press, 2006).
4. *Hernandez v. Texas*, 347 U.S. 475 (1954).
5. *Hernandez v. Texas*, at 475.
6. *Hernandez v. Texas,* at 479.
7. Gordon S. Wood, *The American Revolution* (New York: Modern Library Chronicles, 2002), 39.
8. Edmund Burke, "Speech to the Electors of Bristol," November 3, 1774, in *The Founders' Constitution*, ed. Philip B. Kurland and Ralph Lerner (Chicago: University of Chicago Press, 1986), accessed April 25, 2012, http://press-pubs.uchicago.edu/founders/documents/v1ch13s7.html.
9. Robert Middlekauff, *The Glorious Cause: The American Revolution, 1763–1789* (New York: Oxford University Press, 1982), 231.

10. Thomas Paine, *Common Sense* (Philadelphia, 1776), USHistory.org, accessed April 10, 2012, http://www.ushistory.org/paine/commonsense/sense4.htm.

11. Articles of Confederation, Article IX, Paragraph 5, U.S. Constitution Online, accessed April 10, 2012, http://www.usconstitution.net/articles.html#Article9.

12. Thomas Jefferson, "Notes on the State of Virginia," 1784, in *The Founders' Constitution*, ed. Philip B. Kurland and Ralph Lerner (Chicago: University of Chicago Press, 1986), accessed April 25, 2012, http://press-pubs.uchicago.edu/founders/documents/v1ch10s9.html.

13. Historical Census Browser, University of Virginia, Geospatial and Statistical Data Center, accessed April 10, 2012, http://mapserver.lib.virginia.edu/.

14. Middlekauff, *The Glorious Cause*, 624.

15. William Riker, "The Heresthetics of Constitution Making," *American Political Science Review* 78 (1984): 1–16.

16. "Variant Texts of the Plan Presented by William Patterson," in *Debates in the Federal Convention of 1787 Reported by James Madison*, ed. Gaillard Hunt and James B. Scott (New York: 1920), 102–4, quoted by the Avalon Project, Yale University, Lillian Goldman Law Library, accessed April 10, 2012, http://avalon.law.yale.edu/18th_century/patexta.asp.

17. "1790 Census of Slave and Free Population," U.S. Census of Population and Housing, Historical Census Browser, University of Virginia, Geospatial and Statistical Data Center, accessed April 10, 2012, http://mapserver.lib.virginia.edu/.

18. Quoted in Max Farrand, *The Framing of the Constitution of the United States* (New Haven, Conn.: Yale University Press, 1913), 1:486–7.

19. Garry Wills, *Negro President: Jefferson and the Slave Power* (Boston: Houghton Mifflin, 2003), 5–6.

20. James Madison, *Letters and Other Writings of James Madison: 1769–1793* (New York: Worthington, 1884), 1:186.

21. Quoted in Max Farrand, ed., *The Records of the Federal Convention of 1787* (New Haven, Conn.: Yale University Press, 1911), 3:359.

22. Wendy J. Schiller and Charles Stewart III, *Electing the Senate: Indirect Democracy before the 17th Amendment* (Princeton, N.J.: Princeton University Press, 2014).

23. Paul Finkelman, "Ted Cruz: Our First Foreign-Born President?," *Huffington Post*, January 12, 2016, accessed January 30, 2016, http://www.huffingtonpost.com/paul-finkelman/ted-cruz-our-first-foreig-b-8958476.html.

24. "An Act to establish an uniform Rule of Naturalization," 1790, ch. 3, 1 *Stat.* 103, accessed January 30, 2016, http://library.uwb.edu/static/USimmigration/1%20stat%20103.pdf.

25. Jack Maskell, "Qualifications for President and the 'Natural Born' Citizenship Eligibility Requirement," *Congressional Research Service*, November 14, 2011, accessed January 26, 2016, http://www.fas.org/sgp/crs/misc/R42097.pdf.

26. See Allison M. Martens, "Reconsidering Judicial Supremacy: From the Counter-Majoritarian Difficulty to Constitutional Transformations," *Perspectives on Politics* 5 (2007): 447–59.

27. Marco Rubio, "Convention Can Restore Limited Government," *USA Today*, January 6, 2016, retrieved February 8, 2016, http://www.usa-today.com/story/opinion/2016/01/06/marco-rubio-constitutional-convention-editorials-debates/78368672/.

28. James Madison, "*Federalist* 47," in *The Federalist Papers*, U.S. Constitution Online, accessed April 10, 2012, http://www.constitution.org/fed/federa47.htm.

29. James Madison, "*Federalist* 39," in *The Federalist Papers*, U.S. Constitution Online, accessed May 3, 2012, http://www.constitution.org/fed/federa39.htm.

30. Brutus, "Antifederalist 1," U.S. Constitution Online, accessed May 10, 2012, http://www.constitution.org/afp/brutus01.htm.

31. Ibid.

32. See http://www.constitution.org/rc/rat_va_08.txt.

33. James Madison, "*Federalist* 41," in *The Federalist Papers*, U.S. Constitution Online, accessed April 10, 2012, http://www.constitution.org/fed/federa41.htm.

34. "June 16, 1788: Patrick Henry Demands and Gets a Bill of Rights," Free Republic, accessed May 10, 2012, http://www.freerepublic.com/focus/f-news/1003306/posts.

35. *Wickard v. Filburn*, 317 U.S. 111 (1942).

36. *National Federation of Independent Business v. Sebelius*, 11–393 (2012).

37. See http://tinyurl.com/113th-congress-proposed-amend.

38. *Furman v. Georgia*, 408 U.S. 238 (1972).

39. *Gregg v. Georgia*, 428 U.S. 153 (1976).

40. "States With and Without the Death Penalty," Death Penalty Information Center, accessed January 16, 2016, http://www.deathpenaltyinfo.org/states-and-without-death-penalty.

41. *Hurst v. Florida*, 193 L. Ed. 2d 504 (2016).

42. See http://www.gallup.com/poll/1606/death-penalty.aspx.

43. "Federal Death Penalty," Death Penalty Information Center, accessed April 10, 2012, http://www.deathpenaltyinfo.org/federal-death-penalty?scid=29&did=147.

44. Alan Yuhas, "Dzhokhar Tsarnaev Sentenced to Death for Boston Marathon Bombing—As It Happened," *The Guardian*, May 15, 2015, accessed January 16, 2016, http://www.theguardian.com/us-news/live/2015/may/15/dzhokhar-tsarnaev-boston-marathon-bombing.

45. David Baldus, Charles A. Pulaski Jr., and George Woodworth, *Equal Justice and the Death Penalty* (Boston: Northeastern University Press, 1990).

46. *McCleskey v. Kemp*, 481 U.S. 279 (1987).

47. *Roper v. Simmons*, 543 U.S. 551 (2005); *Kennedy v. Louisiana*, 554 U.S. 407 (2008).

48. See http://www.innocenceproject.org/know/, accessed January 16, 2016.

49. *District Attorney's Office v. Osborne*, 174 L. Ed. 2d 38 (2009).

50. Daryl J. Levinson and Richard H. Pildes, "Separation of Parties, Not Powers," *Harvard Law Review* 119 (2006): 2311.

51. Alexander Keyssar, *The Right to Vote* (New York: Basic Books, 2000), 17.

Chapter 3

1. Marissa Evans, "The 25 Most Influential Women in State Politics, Kate Brown: 'A Voice for Those That Don't Have One'," *Roll Call*, February 8, 2016, accessed February 8, 2016, http://blogs.rollcall.com/news/influential-women-kate-brown/.

2. "Gays in Politics: Uncommon Clout," Summary: Oregon's gay and lesbian activists have forged one of the country's strongest political alliances, *The Oregonian*, April 11, 1994.

3. "Essay by Kate Brown" for *Out and Elected in the USA*, accessed January 24, 2016, http://outhistory.org/exhibits/show/out-and-elected/1992/kate-brown.

4. Jeremy W. Peters, "Openly Gay, and Openly Welcomed in Congress," *New York Times*, January 25, 2016, accessed February 6, 2016, http://www.nytimes.com/2013/01/26/us/politics/gay-lawmakers-growing-presence-suggests-shift-in-attitudes.html?pagewanted=all&_r=0.

5. "Women Who Lead: Governor Kate Brown," Equity Foundation, March 2015, accessed January 26, 2016, http://www.equityfoundation.org/blog/women-who-lead-governor-kate-brown/.

6. Kate Brown, "2016 Policy Agenda," prepared remarks, January 20, 2016, accessed January 30, 2016, http://www.oregon.gov/gov/media/Pages/speeches/2016-Policy-Agenda.aspx.
7. Colin Bonwick, *The American Revolution* (Charlottesville: University of Virginia Press, 1991), 194.
8. "The First Political Cartoons," Archiving Early America, accessed July 7, 2016, http://www.earlyamerica.com/earlyamerica/firsts/cartoon/.
9. William Riker, *Federalism: Origin, Operation, Significance* (Boston: Little Brown, 1964), 5.
10. Article 6, the Virginia Plan, accessed August 7, 2014, http://avalon.law.yale.edu/18th_century/vatexta.asp.
11. James Madison, "*Federalist* 39," in *The Federalist Papers,* U.S. Constitution Online, accessed April 13, 2012, http://www.constitution.org/fed/federa39.htm.
12. *Revenues and Expenditures for Public Elementary and Secondary Education: School Year 2011–12 (Fiscal Year 2012)* (Washington, D.C.: National Center for Education Statistics, January 2015), accessed January 25, 2016, http://nces.ed.gov/pubs2014/2014303.pdf.
13. Michael B. Berkman and Eric Plutzer, *Ten Thousand Democracies* (Washington D.C.: Georgetown University Press, 2005).
14. *Brown v. The Board of Education*, 247 U.S. 483 (1954).
15. *Cisneros v. Corpus Christi*, 404 U.S. 1211 (1971).
16. Joy Resmovits, "No Child Left Behind Waivers Granted to 33 U.S. States, Some with Strings Attached," *Huffington Post*, July 19, 2012, accessed July 20, 2012, http://www.huffingtonpost.com/2012/07/19/no-child-left-behind-waiver_n_1684504.html.
17. Fundamental Change, Innovation in America's Schools Under Race to the Top, November 2015, accessed January 25, 2016, http://www2.ed.gov/programs/racetothetop/rttfinalrpt1115.pdf.
18. Fundamental Change, Innovation in America's Schools Under Race to the Top, November 2015, accessed January 25, 2016, http://www2.ed.gov/programs/racetothetop/rttfinalrpt1115.pdf; American Recovery and Reinvestment Act of 2009. Pub. L. 111–5. 123 Stat. 115 17 February 2009, sections 14005–14007.
19. *Cohens v. Virginia*, 19 U.S. 264 (1821).
20. *Chisolm v. Georgia*, 2 U.S. 419 (1793).
21. Elinor Ostrom, *Governing the Commons: The Evolution of Institutions for Collective Action* (New York: Cambridge University Press, 1990), 106–10.
22. *United States v. Windsor*, 133 S. Ct. 2675 (2013).
23. Patrick Henry, Speech at the Virginia Ratifying Convention, June 4, 1788, http://press-pubs.uchicago.edu/founders/documents/v1ch8s38.html.
24. Christopher M. Parker, "Ideological Voting in Supreme Court Federalism Cases, 1953–2007," *Justice System Journal* 32, 2 (2011): 206–34.
25. See http://www.azleg.gov/DocumentsForBill.asp?Bill_Number=HB2201&Session_ID=115, accessed February 22, 2016.
26. *McCulloch v. Maryland*, 17 U.S. 316 (1819).
27. *Gibbons v. Ogden*, 22 U.S. 1 (1824).
28. Daniel Webster's statement is from his Senate debate with Robert Y. Hayne of South Carolina, January 27, 1830. The Jefferson Day dinner took place on April 13, 1830. See Richard B. Morris and Jeffrey B. Morris, eds., *Encyclopedia of American History*, 7th ed. (New York: HarperCollins, 1996), 189–90.
29. *Dred Scott v. Sandford,* 60 U.S. 393 (1857).
30. "Confederate States of America—Declaration of the Immediate Causes Which Induce and Justify Secession of South Carolina from the Federal Union," December 24, 1860, Avalon Project, Yale University, Lillian Goldman Law Library, accessed April 30, 2012, http://avalon.law.yale.edu/19th_century/csa_scarsec.asp.
31. See http://www.civil-war.net/pages/ordinances_secession.asp.
32. Andrew Johnson, "Veto of the Civil Rights Bill," March 27, 1866, Teaching American History, accessed April 13, 2012, http://teachingamericanhistory.org/library/document/veto-of-the-civil-rights-bill/.
33. Morton Grodzins, *The American System: A New View of the Government of the United States* (New York: Rand McNally, 1966), 8.
34. Wendy J. Schiller, "Building Careers and Courting Constituents: U.S. Senate Representation, 1889–1924," *Studies in American Political Development* 20 (2006): 1.
35. *National Labor Relations Board v. Jones & Laughlin Steel Corporation*, 301 U.S. 1 (1937).
36. *United States v. Darby Lumber Company*, 312 U.S. 100 (1941).
37. *Wickard v. Filburn*, 317 U.S. 111 (1942).
38. Grodzins, *in American System*, 8–9.
39. "American Independent Party Platform of 1968," October 13, 1968, Gerhard Peters and John Woolley, The American Presidency Project, accessed April 13, 2012, http://www.presidency.ucsb.edu/ws//index.php?pid=29570#axzz1rwnAcK5P.
40. Sean Nicholson-Crotty, "Rational Election Cycles and the Intermittent Political Safeguards of Federalism," *Publius: The Journal of Federalism* 38 (2008): 295–314.
41. Timothy Conlon, *New Federalism: Intergovernmental Reform from Nixon to Reagan* (Washington D.C.: Brookings Institution, 1988).
42. "Ronald Reagan, First Inaugural Address," January 20, 1981, American Rhetoric, accessed April 13, 2012, http://www.americanrhetoric.com/speeches/ronaldreagandfirstinaugural.html.
43. Bill Clinton, "The Era of Big Government Is Over," January 27, 1996, radio address, CNN, accessed April 13, 2012, http://www.cnn.com/US/9601/budget/01-27/clinton_radio/.
44. Tim Conlan and John Dinan, "Federalism, the Bush Administration, and the Transformation of American Conservatism," *Publius: The Journal of Federalism* 37 (2007): 279–303.
45. Scott F. Abernathy, *No Child Left Behind and the Public Schools* (Ann Arbor: University of Michigan Press, 2007), 23.
46. John Schwartz, "Obama Seems to Be Open to a Broader Role for States," *New York Times*, January 29, 2009, http://www. nytimes.com/2009/01/30/us/politics/30federal.html/; "DEA Pot Raids Go On; Obama Opposes," *Washington Times*, February 5, 2009, http://www.washingtontimes.com/news/2009/feb/05/dea-led-by-bush-continues-pot-raids/?page=1.
47. *Younger v. Harris*, 401 U.S. 37 (1971).
48. *United States v. Lopez*, 514 U.S. 549 (1995).
49. *South Dakota v. Dole*, 483 U.S. 203 (1987) at 211.
50. *National Federation of Independent Business v. Sebelius*, 132 S. Ct. 2566 (2012).
51. *National Federation of Independent Business v. Sebelius*, 183 L. Ed 2d 450 (2012).
52. Frances E. Lee, "Bicameralism and Geographic Politics: Allocating Funds in the House and Senate," *Legislative Studies Quarterly* 29 (2004): 185–213.
53. Per capita figures derived by authors from "2013 Annual Survey of State Governments State Government Finances," The Census Bureau, accessed January 25, 2016, http://www.census.gov/govs/state/ and http://www.census.gov/popest/data/state/totals/2013/index.html (state populations).
54. Per capita figures derived by authors from http://www.census.gov/prod/2011pubs/fas-10.pdf, p. 10 (antiterrorism aid) and http://

www.census.gov/popest/data/state/totals/2013/index.html (state populations), accessed January 25, 2016.

55. John Hudak, *Presidential Pork: White House Influence over the Distribution of Federal Grants* (Washington D.C.: Brookings, 2014).

56. *The Partial Veto in Wisconsin,* Information Bulletin 04-1 (Madison: State of Wisconsin Legislative Reference Bureau, 2004), http://legis.wisconsin.gov/lrb/pubs/ib/04ib1.pdf.

57. Michael Cooper, "Budget Is Job of Governor, Judges Rule," *New York Times,* December 17, 2004.

58. Congressional Budget Office, "The Underfunding of State and Local Pensions," May 2011, accessed March 21, 2014, https://www.cbo.gov/sites/default/files/cbofiles/ftpdocs/120xx/doc12084/05-04-pensions.pdf.

59. Michael Lewis, "California *and* Bust," *Vanity Fair,* November 2011, http://www.vanityfair.com/business/features/2011/11/michael-lewis-201111; Scott Malone, "Rhode Island's Central Falls Files for Bankruptcy," Reuters, August 1, 2011, accessed May 11, 2012, http://www.reuters.com/article/2011/08/01/us-rhodeisland-centralfalls-idUSTRE7703ID20110801; Michael Cooper and Mary Williams Walsh, "Alabama Town's Failed Pension Is a Warning," *New York Times,* December 23, 2010, http://www.nytimes.com/2010/12/23/business/23prichard.html?pagewanted=print.

60. Center for American Women and Politics, Rutgers University, Eagleton Institute of Politics, "History of Women Governors," accessed January 26, 2016, http://www.cawp.rutgers.edu/history-women-governors.

61. Julie Dolan, Melissa Deckman, and Michele Swers, *Women and Politics: Paths to Power and Political Influence* (Upper Saddle River, N.J.: Pearson Prentice Hall, 2007) and Richard Herrera and Karen Shafer, "Women in the Governor's Mansion," in *Women & Executive Office*, ed. Melody Rose (Boulder, Col.: Lynn Reiner, 2013).

62. Gary C. Jacobson, "Strategic Politicians and the Dynamics of U.S. House Elections, 1946–86," *American Political Science Review* 83 (1989): 773–93.

63. T. S. Last, "Voters Choose not to Retain Judge," *Albuquerque Journal North*, November 5, 2015, accessed January 25, 2016, http://www.abqjournal.com/491897/abqnewsseeker/voters-choose-not-to-retain-judge-raphaelson.html.

64. *Republican Party of Minnesota v. White*, 536 U.S. 765 (2002).

65. *Pay to Play: How Big Money Buys Access to the Texas Supreme Court* (Austin, Tex.: Texans for Public Justice, 2001), http://info.tpj.org/docs/2001/04/reports/paytoplay/paytoplay.pdf.

66. *Caperton v. Massey Coal Co.* 556 U.S. 868 (2009).

67. U.S. Census Bureau, "2012 Census of Governments: The Many Layers of Government," accessed January 25, 2016, http://www census.gov/govs/go/index.html.

68. U.S. Senate elections are staggered according to Article I, Section 3, of the Constitution, resulting in a third of U.S. Senate seats up for election in any federal election.

69. Recall that Nebraska has a unicameral legislature, resulting in a total of ninety-nine legislative chambers in the fifty states. See also National Conference of State Legislatures, http://www.ncsl.org/research/elections-and-campaigns/2014-state-legislative-seats-up.aspx, accessed January 27, 2016.

70. The New American Leaders Project, "States of Inclusion," accessed January 24, 2016, http://www.newamericanleaders.org/states_of_inclusion_2016_report.html.

71. Frank M. Bryan, *Real Democracy: The New England Town Meeting and How It Works* (Chicago: University of Chicago Press, 2003), 65–79.

72. See http://www.washingtonpost.com/blogs/the-fix/post/arizona-recall-why-russell-pearce-lost/2011/11/09/gIQALj6a5M_blog.html.

73. National Conference of State Legislatures, "Initiative, Referendum, and Recall," NCSL.org, http://www.ncsl.org/legislatures-elections/elections/initiative-referendum-and-recall-overview.aspx.

74. *Hollingsworth v. Perry*, 133 S. Ct. 2652 (2013).

75. http://www.iandrinstitute.org/BW%202015-2%20Results%20(v1).pdf, accessed January 25, 2016.

76. http://www.iandrinstitute.org/BW%202014-2%20Election%20results%20(v1)%202014-11-04.pdf, and http://www.iandrinstitute.org/BW%202014-1%20Preview%20(v1)%202014-10-15.pdf, accessed November 5, 2014; and http://www.wcvb.com/news/massachusetts-minimum-wage-set-to-increase-in-2016/37147868, accessed February 8, 2016.

77. Colorado Marijuana-Legalization Amendment Spending Tops $3 Million," *Denver Post*, accessed April 6, 2014, http://www.denverpost.com/ci_21820068/colorado-marijuana-legalization-amendment-spending-tops-3-million.

78. National Institute for Money in State Politics, http://www.followthemoney.org/media-room/news-releases/show/275, accessed January 25, 2016.

Chapter 4

1. Brutus, "*Antifederalist* 2," U.S. Constitution Online, accessed May 9, 2012, http://www.constitution.org/afp/brutus02.htm.

2. *West Virginia Board of Education v. Barnette*, 319 U.S. 624 (1943).

3. Annals of Congress, H439 (June 8, 1789), American Memory, Library of Congress, accessed May 18, 2012, http://memory.loc.gov/cgi-bin/ampage?collId=llac&fileName=001/llac001.db&recNum=221.

4. *Schenck v. United States,* 249 U.S. 47 (1919).

5. *Barron v. Baltimore*, 32 U.S. 243 (1833); Zechariah Chafee Jr., *Free Speech in the United States* (Cambridge, Mass.: Harvard University Press, 1967); *Gilbert v. Minnesota*, 254 U.S. 325 (1920).

6. *Ex Parte Starr*, 263 F. 145 (1920).

7. Judith A. Baer, *Equality Under the Constitution* (Ithaca, N.Y.: Cornell University Press, 1983).

8. *Chicago B & Q Railway Company v. Chicago*, 166 U.S. 226 (1897).

9. *Gitlow v. New York*, 268 U.S. 652 (1925).

10. *Palko v. Connecticut*, 302 U.S. 319 (1937).

11. Abraham Lincoln, "July 4th Message to Congress (July 4, 1861)," Miller Center, University of Virginia, accessed May 18, 2012, http://millercenter.org/president/speeches/detail/3508.

12. *Ex parte Milligan*, 71 U.S. 2 (1866).

13. *Ex parte McCardle,* 74 U.S. 506 (1868).

14. *Schenck v. United States,* 249 U.S. 47 (1919); *Debs v. United States,* 249 U.S. 211 (1919).

15. *Abrams v. United States,* 250 U.S. 616 (1919).

16. David Cole, "Enemy Aliens," *Stanford Law Review* 54 (2002): 953.

17. Bernard A. Weisberger, "Terrorism Revisited," *American Heritage* 44 (November 1993), accessed June 4, 2014, http://www.americanheritage.com/content/terrorism-revisited.

18. John Earl Haynes and Harvey Klehr, *Venona: Decoding Soviet Espionage in America* (New Haven, Conn.: Yale University Press, 1999).

19. *Watkins v. United States*, 354 U.S. 178 (1957).

20. *Barenblatt v. United States*, 360 U.S. 109 (1959).

21. Ellen Schrecker, *Many Are the Crimes: McCarthyism in America* (Boston: Little, Brown, 1998), xiii.

22. Select Committee to Study Governmental Operations, *Intelligence Activities and the Rights of Americans,* Book II, accessed May 18, 2012, http://www.intelligence.senate.gov/pdfs94th/94755_II.pdf, p. 213.

23. Zachary Fagenson, "U.S. Judge Re-sentences Jose Padilla to 21 Years on Terrorism Charges," *Reuters,* September 9, 2014, accessed February 7, 2016, http://www.reuters.com/article/us-usa-florida-padilla-idUSKBN0H41TW20140909.

24. *Hirota v. MacArthur*, 338 U.S. 197 (1948).

25. *Hamdan v. Rumsfeld,* 548 U.S. 557 (2006).

26. Charlie Savage, "U.S. Law May Allow Killings, Holder Says," *New York Times,* March 5, 2012.

27. See http://www.foxnews.com/politics/2014/04/21/federal-court-obama-administration-must-release-targeted-killings-memo/.

28. *Brandenburg v. Ohio*, 395 U.S. 444 (1969).

29. *Chaplinsky v. New Hampshire*, 315 U.S. 568 (1942).

30. David L. Hudson Jr., "Hate Speech and Campus Speech Codes," First Amendment Center, September 13, 2002, accessed May 9, 2012, http://www.firstamendmentcenter.org/hate-speech-campus-speech-codes.

31. *UWM Post v. Board of Regents of the University of Wisconsin,* 774 F. Supp. 1163 (1991).

32. Foundation for Individual Rights in Education (FIRE), "Speech Codes: Alive and Well, 10 Years Later," accessed June 4, 2014, http://www.thefire.org/speech-codes-alive-and-well-10-years-later/.

33. Alan Charles Kors and Harvey Silvergate, *The Shadow University: The Betrayal of Liberty on America's Campuses* (New York: Free Press, 1998).

34. *John Doe. v. University of Michigan*, 721 F. Supp. 852 (1989).

35. Ibid.

36. *UWM Post v. Board of Regents of the University of Wisconsin,* 774 F. Supp. 1163 (1991).

37. "Warning: College Students, This Editorial May Upset You," *Los Angeles Times,* March 31, 2014, http://www.latimes.com/opinion/editorials/la-ed-trigger-warnings-20140331,0,6700908.story#ixzz2yaSoYsXi.

38. See http://chronicle.com/blogs/conversation/2014/03/10/trigger-warnings-trigger-me.

39. Anemona Hartocollis, "Yale Lecturer Resigns After Email on Halloween Costumes," *New York Times*, December 7, 2015, A21.

40. Jonathan H. Adler, "Suzanne Venker is Unwelcome at Williams College," *Washington Post*, October 28, 2015, accessed February 16, 2016, https://www.washingtonpost.com/news/volokh-conspiracy/wp/2015/10/22/suzanne-venker-is-unwelcome-at-williams-college/.

41. *Virginia v. Black*, 538 U.S. 343 (2003).

42. See http://www.fas.org/irp/agency/doj/fisa/#rept.

43. Robin Toner and Neil A. Lewis, "A Nation Challenged: Congress; House Passes Terrorism Bill Much Like Senate's, but With 5-Year Limit," *New York Times,* October 12, 2011, accessed April 27, 2014, http://www.nytimes.com/2001/10/13/us/nation-challenged-congress-house-passes-terrorism-bill-much-like-senate-s-but.html.

44. Robert McMillan, "Obama Administration Defends Bush Wiretapping," *PC World,* July 15, 2009, http://www.pcworld.com/article/168502/obama_administration_defends_bush_wiretapping.html.

45. *Al Haramain Islamic Foundation v. Obama*, 690 F.3d 1089 (2012), accessed April 28, 2014, http://cdn.ca9.uscourts.gov/datastore/opinions/2012/08/07/11-15468.pdf.

46. *Smith v. Maryland*, 442 U.S. 735 (1979).

47. See http://www.nytimes.com/2013/06/08/us/mining-of-data-is-called-crucial-to-fight-terror.html?nl=todaysheadlines&emc=edit_th_20130608&_r=0.

48. Charlie Savage, "Judge Questions Legality of N.S.A. Phone Records," *New York Times*, December 16, 2013, accessed February 7, 2016, http://www.nytimes.com/2013/12/17/us/politics/federal-judge-rules-against-nsa-phone-data-program.html.

49. See http://www.nytimes.com/2014/03/25/us/obama-to-seek-nsa-curb-on-call-data.html.

50. Charlie Savage, "Judge Deals a Blow to N.S.A. Data Collection Program," *New York Times*, November 9, 2015, accessed February 7, 2016, http://www.nytimes.com/2015/11/10/us/politics/judge-deals-a-blow-to-nsa-phone-surveillance-program.html.

51. See http://epic.org/privacy/wiretap/stats/fisa_stats.html.

52. See http://afgeneralcounsel.dodlive.mil/2014/01/14/u-s-judiciary-weighs-in-on-special-advocates-before-fisa-court/.

53. See http://www.opencongress.org/bill/s990-112/show.

54. See http://www.nytimes.com/interactive/2015/06/01/us/elections/presidential-candidates-on-nsa-and-patriot-act.html?_r=0.

55. *Tinker v. Des Moines School District,* 393 U.S. 503 (1969). The quotation in the caption on page 117 is from this decision, at 506.

56. *Bland et al. v. Roberts,* E.D. Va. (Apr. 24, 2012).

57. *United States v. O'Brien*, 391 U.S. 367 (1968).

58. *Hill v. Colorado*, 530 U.S. 703 (2000).

59. *McCullen v. Coakley,* 134 S. Ct. 2518 (2014)

60. *West Virginia Board of Education v. Barnette*, 319 U.S. 624 (1943).

61. *Texas v. Johnson*, 491 U.S. 397 (1989).

62. *Morse v. Frederick,* 551 U.S. 393 (2007).

63. *Walker v. Sons of Confederate Veterans,* 135 S. Ct. 2239 (2015).

64. *ACLU of N.C. v. Conti,* 912 F. Supp. 2d 262 (2012)

65. *Grayned v. City of Rockford*, 408 U.S. 104 (1972).

66. *National Socialist Party of America v. Village of Skokie*, 432 U.S. 43 (1977).

67. William Blackstone, *Commentaries on the Laws of England*, 1769 (Chicago: University of Chicago Press, 2002), 4: 151–53.

68. *New York Times v. United States,* 403 U.S. 713 (1971).

69. *United States v. Progressive*, 467 F. Supp. 990 (1979).

70. See http://www.wikileaks.org.

71. Adam Liptak and Brad Stone, "Judge Shuts Down Web Site Specializing in Leaks," *New York Times*, February 20, 2008.

72. *Hustler Magazine v. Falwell*, 485 U.S. 46 (1988).

73. Anna Badkhen, "Web Can Ruin Reputation with Stroke of a Key," *San Francisco Chronicle*, May 6, 2007.

74. *Miller v. California*, 413 U.S. 15 (1973).

75. *Jenkins v. Georgia*, 418 U.S. 153 (1974).

76. *New York v. Ferber*, 458 U.S. 747 (1982).

77. *Ashcroft v. Free Speech Coalition*, 535 U.S. 234 (2002).

78. *Reno v. American Civil Liberties Union*, 521 U.S. 844 (1997).

79. *Brown v. Entertainment Merchants Association*, 131 S. Ct. 2729 (2011).

80. *United States v. Stevens*, 559 U.S. 460 (2010).

81. *Roberts v. United States Jaycees*, 468 U.S. 609 (1984).

82. *Boy Scouts v. Dale*, 530 U.S. 640 (2000).

83. Todd Leopold, "Boy Scouts Change Policy on Gay Leaders," *CNN*, July 28, 2015, accessed February 17, 2016, http://www.cnn.com/2015/07/27/us/boy-scouts-gay-leaders-feat/.

84. Edward Hart, "Remonstrance of the Inhabitants of the Town of Flushing to Governor Stuyvesant," December 27, 1657, Flushing Monthly Meeting of the Religious Society of Friends, accessed May 10, 2012, http://www.nyym.org/flushing/remons.html.

85. Henry J. Abraham and Barbara A. Perry, *Freedom and the Court*, 6th ed. (New York: Oxford University Press, 1994), 223.

86. Ontario Consultants on Religious Tolerance, "Religious Laws," ReligiousTolerance.org, accessed May 9, 2012, http://www.religioustolerance.org/lawmenu.htm.

87. *Rosenberger v. University of Virginia*, 515 U.S. 819 (1995).

88. *Church of Lakumi Babalu Aye v. City of Hialeah*, 508 U.S. 520 (1993).

89. *Reynolds v. United States*, 98 U.S. 145 (1878).

90. Bill Mears, "Judge Strikes Down Part of Utah Polygamy Law in 'Sister Wives' Case," *CNN*, December 16, 2013, http://www.cnn.com/2013/12/14/justice/utah-polygamy-law/.

91. Dustin Gardiner, "Phoenix Council Favors Silence Over Satanists—For Now," *Arizona Republic*, February 18, 2016, accessed February 25, 2016, http://www.azcentral.com/story/news/local/phoenix/2016/02/17/phoenix-council-favors-silence-over-satanists--now/80430980/.

92. *Clay, aka Ali, v. United States*, 403 U.S. 698 (1971).

93. *Employment Division v. Smith*, 494 U.S. 872 (1990).

94. *City of Boerne v. Flores*, 521 U.S. 507 (1997), at 536.

95. *Hosanna-Tabor Evangelical Lutheran Church and School v. Equal Employment Opportunity Commission*, 132 S. Ct. 694 (2012).

96. "Rethinking the Incorporation of the Establishment Clause: A Federalist View," *Harvard Law Review* 105 (1992): 1700.

97. *Everson v. Board of Education*, 330 U.S. 1 (1947).

98. *Lemon v. Kurtzman*, 403 U.S. 602 (1971).

99. *Engel v. Vitale*, 370 U.S. 421 (1962) (prayer); *Abington School District v. Schempp*, 374 U.S. 203 (1963) (Bible reading).

100. *Epperson v. Arkansas*, 393 U.S. 97 (1968).

101. *Edwards v. Aguillard*, 482 U.S. 578 (1987).

102. *Kitzmiller v. Dover Area School District*, 400 F. Supp. 2d 707 (2005).

103. See http://www.slate.com/articles/health_and_science/science/2014/01/creationism_in_public_schools_mapped_where_tax_money_supports_alternatives.html.

104. *Lee v. Weisman*, 505 U.S. 577 (1992).

105. *Santa Fe Independent School District v. Doe*, 530 U.S. 290 (2000).

106. *Board of Education v. Allen*, 392 U.S. 236 (1968).

107. *Meek v. Pittenger*, 421 U.S. 349 (1975).

108. *District of Columbia v. Heller*, 554 U.S. 570 (2008).

109. *McDonald v. Chicago*, 561 U.S. 3025 (2010).

110. See http://www.scribd.com/doc/133630146/NRA-s-National-School-Shield-Report.

111. See http://smartgunlaws.org/summary-of-enacted-laws-since-newtown.

112. See http://www.nytimes.com/2014/01/01/nyregion/federal-judge-upholds-majority-of-new-york-gun-law.html.

113. See http://www.cnn.com/2014/04/23/us/georgia-governor-signs-gun-bill/.

114. Manny Fernandez and Dave Montgomery, "Texas Lawmakers Pass a Bill Allowing Guns at Colleges," *New York Times*, June 2, 2015, A11.

115. *Florence v. County of Burlington*, 10-945 (2012).

116. *Riley v. California*, 134 S. Ct. 999 (2014).

117. *Schneckloth v. Bustamonte*, 412 U.S. 218 (1973).

118. *Missouri v. McNeely* 133 S. Ct. 1552 (2013).

119. *Maryland v. King*, 133 S. Ct. 1958 (2013).

120. Jeffrey A. Segal, "Predicting Supreme Court Decisions Probabilistically: The Search and Seizure Cases, 1962–1981," *American Political Science Review* 78 (1984): 801.

121. *California v. Ciraolo*, 476 U.S. 207 (1986).

122. *Florida v. Jardines*, 133 S. Ct. 1409 (2013).

123. *Kyllo v. United States*, 533 U.S. 27 (2001).

124. *Virginia v. Moore*, 553 U.S. 164 (2008).

125. *Prado Navarette v. California*, accessed April 28, 2014. http://www.supremecourt.gov/opinions/13pdf/12-9490_3fb4.pdf.

126. *United States v. Jones*, 132 S. Ct. 945 (2012).

127. *Vernonia School District 47J v. Acton*, 515 U.S. 646 (1995); *National Treasury Union v. Von Raab*, 489 U.S. 656 (1989); *Chandler v. Miller*, 520 U.S. 305 (1997).

128. *Mapp v. Ohio*, 367 U.S. 643 (1961).

129. Priscilla H. Machado Zotti, *Injustice for All: Mapp v. Ohio and the Fourth Amendment* (New York: Peter Lang, 2005).

130. *United States v. Leon*, 468 U.S. 897 (1984).

131. *Nix v. Williams*, 467 U.S. 431 (1984).

132. *Miranda v. Arizona*, 384 U.S. 436 (1966).

133. *Dickerson v. United States*, 530 U.S. 428 (2000).

134. *Powell v. Alabama*, 287 U.S. 45 (1932).

135. *Gideon v. Wainwright*, 372 U.S. 335 (1963).

136. *Argersinger v. Hamlin*, 407 U.S. 25 (1972).

137. *Williams v. Florida*, 399 U.S. 78 (1970); *Johnson v. Louisiana*, 406 U.S. 356 (1972).

138. *Georgia v. McCollum*, 505 U.S. 42 (1992); *J. E. B. v. Alabama*, 511 U.S. 127 (1994).

139. See http://www.justice.gov/opa/pr/federal-officials-close-investigation-death-trayvon-martin.

140. Matt Apuzzo, "Dylann Roof, Charleston Shooting Suspect, Is Indicted on Federal Hate Crime Charges," *New York Times*, July 22, 2015, A12.

141. Akhil Amar, *The Bill of Rights* (New Haven, Conn.: Yale University Press, 1998), 82.

142. *Rummel v. Estelle*, 445 U.S. 263 (1980).

143. *Furman v. Georgia*, 408 U.S. 238 (1972).

144. *Gregg v. Georgia*, 428 U.S. 153 (1976).

145. *District Attorney's Office v. Osborne*, 557 U.S. 52 (2009).

146. *Herrera v. Collins*, 506 U.S. 390 (1993).

147. *Griswold v. Connecticut*, 381 U.S. 479 (1965).

148. *Eisenstadt v. Baird*, 405 U.S. 438 (1972).

149. Gerald Rosenberg, *The Hollow Hope* (Chicago: University of Chicago Press, 1991), 262.

150. *Roe v. Wade*, 410 U.S. 113 (1973).

151. *Planned Parenthood of Southeastern Pennsylvania v. Casey*, 505 U.S. 833 (1992).

152. *Stenberg v. Carhart*, 530 U.S. 914 (2000).

153. *Gonzalez v. Carhart*, 550 U.S. 124 (2007).

154. *Whole Woman's Health et al. v. Hellerstedt* (2016). See http://www.guttmacher.org/statecenter/updates/2015/statetrends42015.html.

155. Guttmacher Institute, "State Policy Updates: Major Developments in Sexual & Reproductive Health." https://www.guttmacher.org/state-policy/explore/overview-abortion-laws.%20Accessed%20November%2010,%202016 (accessed November 10, 2016).

156. Lori A. Ringhand and Paul M. Collins Jr., "May It Please the Senate: An Empirical Analysis of the Senate Judiciary Committee Hearings of Supreme Court Nominees, 1939–2009" (University of Georgia School of Law Research Paper Series, Paper No. 10-12, 2010).

157. *Bowers v. Hardwick*, 478 U.S. 186 (1986).

158. National Opinion Research Center, General Social Survey, University of Chicago.

159. *Lawrence v. Texas*, 539 U.S. 558 (2003).

160. *Cruzan v. Director, Missouri Department of Health*, 497 U.S. 261 (1990), at 278.

161. *Washington v. Glucksberg*, 521 U.S. 702; *Vacco* v. *Quill*, 521 U.S. 793 (1997).

162. *Village of Belle Terre v. Boraas*, 416 U.S. 1 (1974).

163. *West Virginia State Board of Education v. Barnette*, 319 U.S. 624 (1943).

164. Robert Dahl, "Decision-Making in a Democracy: The Supreme Court as a National Policy-Maker," *Journal of Public Law* 6 (1957): 279–95.

165. Anthony Lewis, *Freedom for the Thought That We Hate: A Biography of the First Amendment* (New York: Basic Books, 2007).

166. John L. Sullivan, James Pierson, and George Marcus, *Political Tolerance and American Democracy* (Chicago: University of Chicago Press, 1973); James L. Gibson, "Enigmas of Intolerance: Fifty Years After Stouffer's *Communism, Conformity, and Civil Liberties*," *Perspectives on Politics* 4 (March 2006): 22.

167. August 2007 Freedom Forum Survey, retrieved May 13, 2012, from the iPOLL Databank, The Roper Center for Public Opinion Research, University of Connecticut.

Chapter 5

1. Information for this vignette came from Anna Fifield, "Tough Talk over Illegal Immigrants Leaves 'Dreamers' Disillusioned," *Financial Times*, February 27, 2012, accessed April 29, 2014 via LexisNexis Academic Universe; Lawrence Downes, "Questions for a Young Immigration-Rights Activist," *New York Times,* April 10, 2013, http://www.nytimes.com/2013/04/11/opinion/questions-for-a-young-immigration-rights-activist.html?_r=0; http://www.youtube.com/watch?v=FVZKfoXsMxk; http://freedomfromfearaward.com/celebrate/erikaandiola;http://www.facebook.com/erika.andiola; http://unitedwedream.org/press-releases/dream-youth-and-supporters-denounce-home-raid-and-detention-of-erika-andiolas-family-by-ice/; Julia Preston, "Report Finds Deportation Focus on Criminal Records, *New York Times,* April 29, 2014, p. A16, http://www.nytimes.com/2014/04/30/us/report-finds-deportations-focus-on-criminal-records.html?_r=0; "Erika Andiola Slams Obama over Deportations," accessed April 30, 2014, http://video.foxnews.com/v/3430812515001/erika-andiola-slams-obama-over-deportations/#sp=show-clips.

2. Paulina Firozi, "Listen To 4 Interviews From NPR's March 8 Live Special," NPR, March 9, 2016, accessed March 15, 2016, http://www.npr.org/2016/03/09/469566893/listen-to-4-interviews-from-nprs-march-8-live-special.

3. See Alexander Keyssar, *The Right to Vote* (New York: Basic Books, 2000), 17 (women) and 164 (Indians).

4. Senator Lyman Trumbull, quoted in Judith Baer, *Equality under the Constitution* (Ithaca, N.Y.: Cornell University Press, 1983), 96.

5. Quoted in Steven M. Gillon and Cathy D. Matson, *The American Experiment,* 2nd ed. (Boston: Houghton Mifflin, 2006), 61.

6. *Dred Scott v. Sandford*, 60 U.S. 393 (1857).

7. Peter H. Schuck and Rogers M. Smith, *Citizenship Without Consent* (New Haven, Conn.: Yale University Press, 1985), 1–2.

8. *Johnson v. M'Intosh*, 21 U.S. 543 (1823), at 569.

9. *Elk v. Wilkins*, 112 U.S. 94 (1884).

10. Institute for Texan Cultures, *The Tejanos*, accessed June 3, 2014, http://www.texancultures.com/assets/1/15/Texans_One_and_All%20-%20The%20Tejanos.pdf.

11. Kevin R. Johnson, "The Forgotten Repatriation of Persons of Mexican Ancestry and Lessons for the War on Terror," *Pace Law Review* 26, 1 (2005): 104.

12. Texas State Historical Association, *Operation Wetback,* accessed June 3, 2014, http://www.tshaonline.org/handbook/online/articles/pqo01.

13. Johnson, 111.

14. Johnson, 110.

15. California Alien Land Law (1913).

16. *Korematsu v. United States,* 323 U.S. 214 (1944).

17. Anne McDermott, "Orphans Tell of World War II Internment," March 24, 1997, CNN, http://www.cnn.com/US/9703/24/interned.orphans.

18. Immigration Act of 1907, 43 Statutes at Large 153.

19. Rogers M. Smith, *Civic Ideals* (New Haven, Conn.: Yale University Press, 1997), 16; Siobhan B. Sommerville, "Queer Alienage: The Racial and Sexual Logic of the 1952 U.S. Immigration and Nationality Act," Working Paper Series on Historical Systems, Peoples and Cultures (No. 12), 2002, 8, accessed June 6, 2014, http://www2.bgsu.edu/downloads/cas/file46880.pdf.

20. "Immigration Restriction," eHistory @ The Ohio State University, accessed May 12, 2012, http://ehistory.osu.edu/osu/mmh/clash/Imm_KKK/Immigration%20Pages/Immigration-page1.htm.

21. Smith, *Civic Ideals,* 17.

22. Immigration Act of 1924, 43 Statutes at Large 153.

23. *United States v. Cruikshank*, 92 U.S. 542 (1876).

24. Ronald Walters, "'The Association Is for the Direct Attack': The Militant Context of the NAACP Challenge to *Plessy,*" *Washburn Law Journal* 43 (Winter 2004): 329.

25. *Plessy v. Ferguson,* 163 U.S. 537 (1896).

26. Vicki L. Ruiz, "South by Southwest: Mexican Americans and Segregated Schooling, 1900–1950," *OAH Magazine of History* 15 (Winter 2001): 23–27.

27. *Westminster School District v. Mendez*, 161 F.2d 774 (1947).

28. Ruiz, "South by Southwest."

29. Quoted in Renata Fengler, "Abigail and John Adams Discuss Women and Republican Government: 1776," part of the "Documenting American History" project, University of Wisconsin–Green Bay, last modified July 29, 2009, accessed April 25, 2012, http://www.historytools.org/sources/Abigail-John-Letters.pdf.

30. Keyssar, *Right to Vote.*

31. *Minor v. Happersett*, 88 U.S. 162 (1874).

32. Justice Bradley, concurring in *Bradwell v. Illinois*, 83 U.S. 130 (1872), at 142.

33. Judith A. Baer, *The Chains of Protection* (Westport, Conn.: Greenwood Press, 1978), 6–10.

34. E. Susan Barber, comp., "One Hundred Years Toward Suffrage: An Overview," Library of Congress, National American Woman Suffrage

Association Collection, accessed May 14, 2012, http://memory.loc.gov/ammem/naw/nawstime.html.

35. Survey conducted by the Office of Public Opinion Research, July 1945, retrieved May 14, 2012, from the iPOLL Databank, The Roper Center for Public Opinion Research, University of Connecticut.

36. "The Law: Up from Coverture," *Time Magazine,* March 20, 1972, http://www.time.com/time/magazine/article/0,9171,942533,00.html.

37. *Kirchberg v. Feenstra*, 450 U.S. 455 (1981), at 456.

38. Richard Kluger, *Simple Justice* (New York: Knopf, 1975), 376.

39. See Laurence H. Tribe, *American Constitutional Law* (Mineola, N.Y.: Foundation Press, 1988), 1561–65.

40. Ibid.

41. Baer, *Chains of Protection,* 111–21.

42. *Hoyt v. Florida*, 368 U.S. 57 (1961).

43. See http://www.census.gov/quickfacts/table/PST045215/00,19,33,32.

44. Ibid.

45. See http://www.cnn.com/election/primaries/polls/nv/Dem.

46. Philip Bump, "Did Bernie Sanders Really Just Win the Hispanic Vote in Nevada?," *Washington Post*, February 22, 2016, accessed March 15, 2016, https://www.washingtonpost.com/news/the-fix/wp/2016/02/22/did-bernie-sanders-really-just-win-the-hispanic-vote-in-nevada/.

47. Maureen Michaels, "Super Tuesday Exit Poll: Black Voters Play Decisive Role in Clinton's Victories," *NBC News,* accessed March 4, 2016, http://www.nbcnews.com/politics/2016-election/super-tuesday-exit-poll-black-voters-play-decisive-role-clinon-n530021.

48. Abigail Abrams, "Black Votes Matter: In South Carolina, Clinton Outperforms Obama," *International Business Times*, February 27, 2016, accessed March 15, 2016, http://www.ibtimes.com/black-votes-matter-south-carolina-hillary-clinton-outperforms-obama-2326319.

49. See http://www.cnn.com/election/primaries/polls/mi/Dem.

50. Nicole Brown, "Here's Everyone Donald Trump's Insulted in November," *MSNBC*, November 30, 2015, accessed March 15, 2016, http://www.msnbc.com/msnbc/heres-everyone-donald-trump-has-insulted-november.

51. Janell Ross, "Donald Trump Apparently Won the Latino Vote in Nevada. It Doesn't Mean Latinos Suddenly Love Him," *Washington Post,* February 24, 2016, accessed March 15, 2016, https://www.washingtonpost.com/news/the-fix/wp/2016/02/24/donald-trump-apparently-won-the-latino-vote-in-nevada-it-doesnt-mean-latinos-suddenly-love-him/.

52. See http://www.washingtonpost.com/wp-srv/special/politics/2012-exit-polls/table.html.

53. Nick Corasaniti, "Univision Aims to Make Hispanic Voting Bloc Even More Formidable," *New York Times*, February 22, 2016, accessed March 15, 2016, http://www.nytimes.com/2016/02/23/us/politics/univision-hispanic-voting.html.

54. *Civil Rights Cases*, 109 U.S. 3 (1883); *Shelley v. Kraemer*, 334 U.S. 1 (1948).

55. *Missouri ex rel. Gaines v. Canada*, 305 U.S. 337 (1938); *Sipuel v. Board of Regents of University of Oklahoma,* 332 U.S. 631 (1948); *Sweatt v. Painter*, 339 U.S. 629 (1950).

56. *Bolling v. Sharpe*, 347 U.S. 497 (1954).

57. *Brown v. Board of Education*, 349 U.S. 294 (1955).

58. *Cooper v. Aaron*, 358 U.S. 1 (1958).

59. Gerald N. Rosenberg, *The Hollow Hope: Can Courts Bring About Social Change* (Chicago: University of Chicago Press, 1991), 46–54.

60. *Alexander v. Holmes County Board of Education*, 396 U.S. 1218 (1969).

61. *Browder v. Gayle*, 352 U.S. 903 (1956).

62. *Jackson v. Alabama*, 348 U.S. 888 (1954).

63. Quoted in Walter F. Murphy, *Elements of Judicial Strategy* (Chicago: University of Chicago Press, 1964), 193.

64. *Loving v. Virginia*, 388 U.S. 1 (1967).

65. David Fankhauser, "Freedom Rides: Recollections by David Fankhauser," last modified May 13, 2011, accessed April 25, 2012, http://biology.clc.uc.edu/fankhauser/society/freedom_rides/freedom_ride_dbf.htm.

66. Martin Luther King Jr., "Letter from Birmingham Jail," April 16, 1963, The King Center, accessed April 25, 2012, http://www.thekingcenter.org/archive/document/letter-birmingham-city-jail-0.

67. Martin Luther King Jr., "The I Have a Dream Speech," August 28, 1963, U.S. Constitution Online, accessed April 25, 2012, http://www.usconstitution.net/dream.html.

68. *Heart of Atlanta Motel v. United States*, 379 U.S. 241 (1964); *Katzenbach v. McClung*, 379 U.S. 294 (1964).

69. *Griggs v. Duke Power Co.*, 401 U.S. 424 (1971).

70. *Wards Cove Packing Co. v. Antonio*, 490 U.S. 642 (1989).

71. *Ricci v. DeStefano,* 557 U.S. 557 (2009).

72. *Guinn v. United States*, 238 U.S. 347 (1915); *Smith v. Allwright*, 321 U.S 649 (1944).

73. Martin Luther King Jr., "Civil Right No. 1: The Right to Vote," *New York Times Magazine*, March 14, 1965, 26.

74. Pew Hispanic Center, "Dissecting the 2008 Electorate: Most Diverse in U.S. History," Pew Research Center, April 30, 2009, accessed April 25, 2012,http://www.pewhispanic.org/2009/04/30/dissecting-the-2008-electorate-most-diverse-in-us-history/.

75. *Northwest Austin Municipal Utility District No. One v. Holder*, 557 U.S. 193 (2009).

76. Rachel Weiner, "Black Voters Turned Out at Higher Rate Than White Voters in 2012 and 2008," *Washington Post,* April 29, 2013, http://www.washingtonpost.com/blogs/the-fix/wp/2013/04/29/black-turnout-was-higher-than-white-turnout-in-2012-and-2008.

77. *Shelby County v. Holder,* 133 S. Ct. 2612 (2013).

78. Adam Liptak, "Supreme Court Invalidates Key Part of Voting Rights," *New York Times*, June 25, 2013, http://www.nytimes.com/2013/06/26/us/supreme-court-ruling.html ?pagewanted=all&_r=0›.

79. See blacklivesmatter.com/about.

80. Eugene Scott, "Black Lives Matter Protestors Confront Clinton at Fundraiser," *CNN,* February 25, 2016, accessed February 26, 2016, http://www.cnn.com/2016/02/25/politics/hilary-clinton-black-lives-matter-whichhillary/.

81. Dan Merica, "Black Lives Matter Protestors Shut Down Sanders Event in Seattle," *CNN,* August 8, 2015, accessed February 26, 2016, http://www.cnn.com/2015/08/08/politics/bernie-sanders-black-lives-matter-protesters/.

82. Polly Mosendz, "Donald Trump Rally Turns Chaotic; Supporters Threaten 'Black Lives Matter' Protestors," *Newsweek*, December 15, 2015, accessed February 26, 2016, http://www.newsweek.com/altercation-erupts-donald-trump-rally-405380.

83. Conor Friedersdorf, "'It's Time for Good Cops to Do Something About Bad Cops'," *The Atlantic*, June 27, 2015, accessed March 15, 2016, http://www.theatlantic.com/politics/archive/2015/06/its-time-for-good-cops-to-do-something-about-bad-cops/396890/.

84. J. David Goodman, "New York City Is Set to Adopt New Approach on Policing Minor Offenses," January 20, 2016, accessed March 15, 2016, http://www.nytimes.com/2016/01/21/nyregion/new-york-council-to-consider-bills-altering-how-police-handle-minor-offenses.html.

85. Ralph Ellis, Holly Yan, and Pat St. Claire, "After Fatal Shootings by Police, Chicago Mayor Calls for Changes in Officer Training," *CNN*, December 27, 2015, accessed March 15, 2016, http://www.cnn.com/2015/12/27/us/chicago-police-shooting/.
86. *Hernandez v. Texas*, 347 U.S. 475 (1954).
87. *Cisneros v. Corpus Christi Independent School District*, 404 U.S. 1211 (1970).
88. Reynaldo Contreras and Leonard A. Valverde, "The Impact of *Brown* on the Education of Latinos," *Journal of Negro Education* 63 (1994): 471–72.
89. *Plyler v. Doe*, 457 U.S. 202 (1982).
90. *San Antonio Independent School District v. Rodriguez*, 411 U.S. 1 (1973).
91. *Edgewood Independent School District v. Kirby*, 777 S.W.2d 391, 392 (Tex. 1989).
92. Library of Congress. *Hispanic Americans in Congress, 1822–1995*, http://www.loc.gov/rr/hispanic/congress/gonzalez.html; Molly Ivins, November 30, 2000, http://www.creators.com/opinion/molly-ivins/molly-ivins-november-30-2000-11-30.html.
93. *Katzenbach v. Morgan*, 384 U.S. 641 (1966); *Cardona v. Power*, 384 U.S. 672 (1966).
94. 42 USC sec. 203 (1975)
95. *White v. Regester*, 412 U.S. 755 (1973). See also *Graves v. Barnes*, 405 U.S. 1201 (1972).
96. Charles L. Cotrell and R. Michael Stevens, "The 1975 Voting Rights Act and San Antonio, Texas: Toward a Federal Guarantee of a Republican Form of Government," *Publius* (1977): 79–99; United States Commission on Civil Rights, "Using the Voting Rights Act" (Washington, D.C.: U.S. Government Printing Office, 1975).
97. Cotrell and Stevens, 87.
98. Guadalupe San Miguel, Jr., *"Let All of Them Take Heed": Mexican Americans and the Campaign for Educational Equality in Texas, 1910–1981* (Austin: University of Texas Press, 1987).
99. See http://svrep.org/.
100. *Johnson v. DeGrandy,* 512 U.S. 997 (1994).
101. National Conference of State Legislatures, January 4, 2016, *Voter Identification Requirements, Voter Laws*, http://www.ncsl.org/research/elections-and-campaigns/voter-id.aspx.
102. United Farm Workers, "Successes Through the Years," http://www.ufw.org/_page.php?menu=research&inc=history/02.html.
103. Steven Yaccino and Lizette Alvarez, "New G.O.P. Bid to Limit Voting in Swing States," *New York Times*, March 29, 2014, http://www.nytimes.com/2014/03/30/us/new-gop-bid-to-limit-voting-in-swing-states.html?hp&_r=1&assetType=nyt_now.
104. Cesar Chavez, *1984 Commonwealth Club Address*, http://www.ufw.org/_page.php?menu=research&inc=history/12.html.
105. Juilana Barrera, "Immigration Activist Erika Andiola Joins Bernie Sanders Campaign," *Latin Times*, November 3, 2015, accessed March 15, 2016, http://www.latintimes.com/immigration-activist-erika-andiola-joins-bernie-sanders-campaign-351134.
106. U.S. Bureau of Labor Statistics, *Highlights of Women's Earnings in 2014* (Washington, D.C., November 2015), Table 1, accessed March 3, 2016, http://www.bls.gov/opub/reports/cps/highlights-of-womens-earnings-in-2014.pdf.
107. Ibid.
108. *Burlington Northern and Santa Fe Railway Co. v. White,* 548 U.S. 53 (2006).
109. *Ledbetter v. Goodyear Tire and Rubber Co.,* 550 U.S. 618 (2007).
110. Ibid., at 645.
111. Lilly Ledbetter Fair Pay Act of 2009, Pub. L. No. 111-2, 42 USC 2000e-5 (2009), http://www.gpo.gov/fdsys/pkg/PLAW-111publ2/html/PLAW-111publ2.htm.
112. ABA Section of Labor & Employment Law, *Survey of Recent Cases Under the Lily Ledbetter Fair Pay Act,* March 2011, accessed May 23, 2012, http://www2.americanbar.org/calendar/ll0322-2011-midwinter-meeting/Documents/08_complexlitigation.pdf (on new cases), and U.S. Bureau of Labor Statistics, *Highlights of Women's Earnings*, on continuing pay disparity.
113. See http://beta.congress.gov/bill/113th-congress/senate-bill/84, accessed April 29, 2014.
114. Wesley Lowery, "Senate Falls Six Votes Short of Passing Paycheck Fairness Act," *Washington Post,* April 9, 2014, http://www.washingtonpost.com/blogs/post-politics/wp/2014/04/09/senate-falls-six-votes-short-of-passing-paycheck-fairness-act/.
115. Juliet Eilpern, "Obama to Sign Two Executive Orders Aimed at Narrowing Gender Gap in Wages," *Washington Post,* April 7, 2014, http://www.washingtonpost.com/politics/obama-to-sign-two-executive-orders-aimed-at-narrowing-gender-gap-in-wages/2014/04/07/3f0ce4a8-be74-11e3-bcec-b71ee10e9bc3_story.html.
116. See https://www.congress.gov/bill/114th-congress/house-bill/1619
117. *Bowers v. Hardwick*, 478 U.S. 186 (1986).
118. *Romer v. Evans*, 517 U.S. 620 (1996).
119. *Lawrence v. Texas,* 539 U.S. 558 (2003).
120. See http://www.gallup.com/poll/183332/majority-say-gays-lesbians-born-not-made.aspx.
121. See http://www.apd.army.mil/pdffiles/ad2013_24.pdf.
122. Steven Beardsley, "Overseas Benefits Elusive for Same-Sex Military Couples," February 6, 2015, accessed March 15, 2016, http://www.stripes.com/news/overseas-benefits-elusive-for-same-sex-military-couples-1.328129.
123. 135 S. Ct. 2584
124. A September 2015 Quinnipiac University poll found by a 55–38 margin that Americans support allowing same-sex couples to get married; data accessed February 22, 2016, from http://www.pollingreport.com/civil.htm.
125. U.S. Equal Employment Opportunity Commission, *The Americans with Disabilities Act: A Primer for Small Business,* last modified February 4, 2004, accessed May 15, 2012, http://www.eeoc.gov/eeoc/publications/adahandbook.cfm.
126. See http://www.charlotteobserver.com/news/politics-government/article68401147.html, accessed May 21, 2016.
127. See http://www.esquire.com/news-politics/news/a43931/north-carolina-anti-lgbt-law-boycott/, accessed May 21, 2016.
128. See http://www.eeoc.gov/eeoc/publications/fs-bathroom-access-transgender.cfm, accessed May 23, 2016.
129. See http://www.nytimes.com/2016/05/14/us/transgender-students-and-new-rules-in-public-schools.html, accessed May 21, 2016.
130. U.S. Equal Employment Opportunity Commission, *The Americans with Disabilities Act: A Primer for Small Business,* last modified February 4, 2004, accessed May 15, 2012, http://www.eeoc.gov/eeoc/publications/adahandbook.cfm.
131. "Employers Say OFCCP Disabilities Proposal Would Be Overly Burdensome," *Bloomberg BNA*, April 16, 2012, accessed May 14, 2012, http://www.bna.com/employers-say-ofccp-n12884908933.
132. David A. Harris, "Driving While Black: Racial Profiling on Our Nation's Highways," June 7, 1999, American Civil Liberties Union, accessed April 25, 2012, http://www.aclu.org/racial-justice/driving-while-black-racial-profiling-our-nations-highways.

133. *United States v. Travis,* 837 F. Supp. 1386 (1993); *Derricott v. State of Maryland* 611 A.2d 592 (1992).

134. "6 Men of Iraqi Descent Sue Over Detention," *Chicago Tribune,* November 2, 2007.

135. See http://www.nytimes.com/2014/04/16/nyregion/police-unit-that-spied-on-muslims-is-disbanded.html.

136. Krishnadev Calamur, "NYPD Settles Pair of Lawsuits Over Muslim Surveillance," *The Atlantic,* January 7, 2016, accessed February 22, 2016, http://www.theatlantic.com/national/archive/2016/01/nypd-surveillance-muslims-settlement/423174/.

137. "State Felon Voting Laws," Procon.org, last modified February 9, 2016, accessed February 22, 2016, http://felonvoting.procon.org/view.resource.php?resourceID=000286#washington.

138. Christopher Uggen, Sarah Shannon, and Jeff Manza, "State-Level Estimates for Felon Disenfranchisement in the United States, 2010," *The Sentencing Project,* July 2012, accessed April 5, 2014, http://www.sentencingproject.org/doc/publications/fd_State_Level_Estimates_of_Felon_Disen_2010.pdf.

139. Jeff Manza and Christopher Uggen, "Punishment and Democracy: Disenfranchisement of Nonincarcerated Felons in the United States," *Perspectives on Politics* 2 (2004): 491–505.

140. See http://www.richmond.com/news/virginia/government-politics/article_771db279-34d6-5a3d-9557-a417a8afb212.html, accessed May 23, 2016.

141. Gustave Valdes, "Undocumented Immigrant Population on the Rise in the U.S," *CNN,* September 25, 2013, accessed April 15, 2014, http://www.cnn.com/2013/09/24/us/undocumented-immigrants-population.

142. *United States v. Texas* U.S. LEXIS 4057 (2016).

143. MSNBC/Telemundo/Marist Poll, August 2015. USMARIST.091415MT.R01. Marist College Institute for Public Opinion. Storrs, CT.: Roper Center for Public Opinion Research, iPOLL [distributor], accessed February 26, 2016.

144. Robert Farley, "Trump Challenges Birthright Citizenship," FactCheck, accessed March 16, 2016, http://www.factcheck.org/2015/11/trump-challenges-birthright-citizenship/

145. *Plyler v. Doe,* 457 U.S. 202 (1982).

146. King, "Civil Right No. 1."

147. See https://www.census.gov/quickfacts/table/PST045215/48.

148. M. V. Hood, Quentin Kidd, and Irwin L. Morris, "The Key Issue: Constituency Effects and Southern Senators' Roll-Call Voting on Civil Rights," *Legislative Studies Quarterly* 26 (2001): 599–621.

149. Royce Carroll, Jeff Lewis, James Lo, Nolan McCarty, Keith Poole, and Howard Rosenthal, "'Common Space' DW-NOMINATE Scores with Bootstrapped Standard Errors (Joint House and Senate Scaling)," Voteview.com, last modified January 22, 2011, accessed May 14, 2012, http://www.voteview.com/dwnomjoint.asp.

150. Wallace Witkowski, "Nike Drops Pacquiao Endorsement Deal After Anti-gay Comments," *Morningstar,* February 17, 2016, accessed March 15, 2016, http://www.morningstar.com/news/market-watch/TDJNMW_20160217498/nike-drops-pacquiao-endorsement-deal-after-antigay-comments.html.

Chapter 6

1. "2011 Women Business Owner of the Year—J. Ann Selzer," *Business Record,* July 29, 2011, http://www.businessrecord.com/Content/OUR-EVENTS/Upcoming-Business-Record-Events/Article/2011-Women-Business-Owner-of-the-Year-J-Ann-Selzer/153/758/53853.

2. Ibid.

3. Ibid.

4. Ibid.

5. Molly Ball, "Friday Interview: The Polling Guru of the Iowa Caucuses," *The Atlantic,* November 25, 2011, http://www.theatlantic.com/politics/archive/2011/11/friday-interview-the-polling-guru-of-the-iowa-caucuses/249036/.

6. Ibid.

7. "2011 Women Business Owner of the Year," *Business Record.*

8. Austin Cannon, "Polling Power: J. Ann Selzer and the Iowa Poll," Iowa Caucus Project, October 25, 2015, http://iowacaucusproject.org/2015/10/polling-power-j-ann-selzer-and-the-iowa-poll/.

9. Steven Shepard, "Ann Selzer's Secret Sauce," *Politico,* December 12, 2015, http://www.politico.com/story/2015/12/ann-selzer-iowa-pollster-216151.

10. Cannon, "Polling Power."

11. Quoted in Harry Jaffa, *The Crisis of the House Divided,* 2nd ed. (Chicago: University of Chicago Press, 1959), 10.

12. James Bryce, *The American Commonwealth* (New York: Macmillan, 1895), 239.

13. The first scholar to discuss how the public rallies to support the president in time of trouble was John Mueller, *War, Presidents, and Public Opinion* (New York: Wiley, 1970).

14. Survey conducted by Quinnipiac University Polling Institute, January 15–19, 2014, retrieved April 7, 2014, from the iPOLL Databank, the Roper Center for Public Opinion Research, University of Connecticut.

15. See http://www.people-press.org/2015/11/23/public-trust-in-government-1958-2015/. See 2012 American National Election Studies, http://electionstudies.org/.

16. Barack Obama, Inaugural Address, January 20, 2009, http://www.whitehouse.gov/blog/inaugural-address.

17. Survey for Pew Research Center for the People & the Press, conducted by Princeton Survey Research Associates International, February 14–23, 2014, retrieved April 7, 2014, through the Roper Center for Public Opinion Research, University of Connecticut.

18. Art Swift, "Smaller Majority 'Extremely Proud' to Be an American," Gallup. July 2, 2015, http://www.gallup.com/poll/183911/smaller-majority-extremely-proud-american.aspx.

19. It is hard to know the exact share of people who would support overthrowing the American government because pollsters almost never ask that question. In our search of questions asked over the past seventy-five years, we have not found one such question. A database at the Roper Center at the University of Connecticut contains nearly five hundred thousand questions, allowing a detailed search.

20. Quoted in Francis B. Carpenter, *Six Months at the White House: The Story of a Picture* (New York: Hurd and Houghton, 1866), 218. See also Mario Cuomo, *Lincoln on Democracy* (New York: Harper, 1990).

21. Robert Hilderbrand, *Power and the People* (Chapel Hill: University of North Carolina Press, 1981).

22. Eli Saslow, *Ten Letters: The Stories Americans Tell Their President* (New York: Doubleday, 2011).

23. Quoted in John Geer, *From Tea Leaves to Opinion Polls* (New York: Columbia University Press, 1996), 50–51.

24. Benjamin Ginsberg, *The Captive Public* (New York: Basic Books, 1986).

25. Robert Erikson and Kent Tedin, *American Public Opinion,* 6th ed. (New York: Longman, 2003), 7.

26. V. O. Key, *Public Opinion and American Democracy* (New York: Knopf, 1961), 536.

27. George Gallup, *The Pulse of Democracy* (New York: Simon and Schuster, 1940).

28. Seymour Sudman and Norman M. Bradburn, "The Organizational Growth of Public Opinion Research in the United States," *Public Opinion Quarterly* 51, pt. 2, Supplement: 50th Anniversary Issue (1987): S67–S78.

29. Franklin Roosevelt made occasional use of polls. Truman had no use for polls, but Eisenhower's advisers clearly paid attention to them. For the best scholarly account of the presidential use of polls, see Robert Eisinger, *The Evolution of Presidential Polling* (New York: Cambridge University Press, 2003).

30. Ali Elkin, "Poll: Caitlyn Jenner's Transition Did Not Change Many Minds," Bloomberg Politics, June 24, 2015, http://www.bloomberg.com/politics/articles/2015-06-24/poll-caitlyn-jenner-s-transition-did-not-change-many-minds.

31. Erikson and Tedin, *American Public Opinion,* 8th ed. 26–33.

32. Joshua D. Clinton and Steven Rogers, "Robo-Polls: Taking Cues from Traditional Sources?" *PS: Political Science & Politics* 46, 2 (2013): 333–37.

33. "People & Events: The Swimsuit Competition and the Century of Svelte," *Miss America,* televised by PBS on *American Experience,* January 27, 2002, accessed April 27, 2012, http://www.pbs.org/wgbh/amex/missamerica/peopleevents/e_body.html.

34. Alicia C. Shepard, "How They Blew It," *American Journalism Review* (January/February 2001).

35. Nick Gass and Burgess Everett, "Cruz Denies Trump Accusations Over 'Push Polls,'" *Politico*, February 11, 2016, http://www.politico.com/story/2016/02/donald-trump-ted-cruz-south-carolina-push-polls-219158.

36. These data come from 2003 polls retrieved April 15, 2012, from the iPOLL Databank, the Roper Center for Public Opinion Research, University of Connecticut.

37. Philip E. Converse, "Nonattitudes and American Public Opinion: Comment: The Status of Nonattitudes," *American Political Science Review* 68 (June 1974): 650–60.

38. Pew Research Center for People & the Press, "Cell Phones and the 2008 Vote: An Update," Pew Research Center, July 17, 2008, accessed April 27, 2012, http://pewresearch.org/pubs/901/cell-phones-polling-election-2008.

39. Erikson and Tedin, *American Public Opinion,* 6th ed. 121.

40. M. Kent Jennings, Laura Stoker, and Jake Bowers, "Politics Across Generations," *Journal of Politics* 71 (July 2009): 782–99.

41. John Alford and John Hibbing, "Biology and Rational Choice," *Political Economy Newsletter,* Fall 2005.

42. Amy Lavoie, "The Genes in Your Congeniality: Researchers Identify Genetic Influence in Social Networks," *Harvard Science: Culture + Society,* January 26, 2009.

43. Peter Hatemi, Nathan A. Gillespie, Lindon J. Eaves, Brion S. Maher, Sarah E. Medland, David C. Smyth, Harry N. Beeby, Scott D. Gordon, Grant W. Montgomery, Ghu Zhu, Enda M. Byrne, Bradley T. Webb, Andrew C. Heath, and Nicholas G. Martin, "A Genome-Wide Analysis of Liberal and Conservative Political Attitudes," *Journal of Politics* 73 (2011): 1–15.

44. John R. Alford, John Hibbing, and Carolyn L. Funk, "Twin Studies, Molecular Genetics, Politics, and Tolerance," *Perspectives on Politics* 6 (December 2008); John Hibbing, John R. Alford, and Carolyn L. Funk, "Beyond Liberals and Conservatives to Political Genotypes and Phenotypes," *Perspectives on Politics* 6 (June 2008): 321–28.

45. Pew Research Center for the People & the Press, "Young Voters in the 2008 Election," Pew Research Center, November 12, 2008, accessed April 27, 2012, http://pewresearch.org/pubs/1031/young-voters-in-the-2008-election.

46. See http://www.huffingtonpost.com/2012/11/07/youth-vote-2012-turnout-exit-polls_n_2086092.html.

47. Tyler Kingkade. "Youth Vote 2012 Turnout: Exit Polls Show Greater Share of Electorate Than In 2008," *The Huffington Post,* November, 7, 2012, http://www.huffingtonpost.com/2012/11/07/youth-vote-2012-turnout-exit-polls_n_2086092.html; *New York Times*, "Election 2016: Exit Polls," http://www.nytimes.com/interactive/2016/11/08/us/politics/election-exit-polls.html?_r=0 (accessed November 12, 2016).

48. Pew Internet & American Life Project, "Millennials Will Benefit and Suffer Due to Their Interconnected Lives," Pew Research Center, February 29, 2012, accessed April 27, 2012, http://www.pewinternet.org/Reports/2012/Hyperconnected-lives.aspx?src=prc-headline.

49. Robert Erikson and Kent Tedin, *American Public Opinion,* 8th ed. (New York: Longman, 2010).

50. This theory comes out of the work of John Zaller, *Nature of Mass Beliefs* (New York: Cambridge University Press, 1992).

51. Federico A. Subervi-Velez, Richard Herrera, and Michael Begay, "Toward an Understanding of the Role of the Mass Media in Latino Political Life," *Social Science Quarterly* 68 (1987): 185–96.

52. Mark Hugo Lopez, Jens Manuel Krogstad, Eileen Patten, and Ana Gonzalez-Barrera, Pew Research Center, "Latinos' Views on Selected 2014 Ballot Measure Issues," October 16, 2014, accessed March 28, 2016, http://www.pewhispanic.org/2014/10/16/chapter-2-latinos-views-on-selected-2014-ballot-measure-issues.

53. Poll conducted by NBC News/*Wall Street Journal*, October 25–28, 1997, and January 17–20, 2007, retrieved April 15, 2012, from the iPOLL Databank, the Roper Center for Public Opinion Research, University of Connecticut.

54. Jocelyn Kiley, "Ideological Divide Over Global Warming as Wide as Ever," Pew Research Center, June 16, 2016, http://www.pewresearch.org/fact-tank/2015/06/16/ideological-divide-over-global-warming-as-wide-as-ever/. Roper iPoll Database, Fox News Polls, from June 2015 and June 2016.

55. The classic book that lays out the argument about party identification is Angus Campbell, Philip Converse, Warren Miller, and Donald Stokes, *The American Voter* (New York: Wiley, 1960).

56. Lydia Saad, "Obama Rated Best in Hawaii in 2015, Worst in West Virginia," Pew Research Center, February 3, 2016, http://www.gallup.com/poll/189002/obama-rated-best-hawaii-2015-worst-west-virginia.aspx?g_source=presidential%20approval&g_medium=search&g_campaign=tiles; Gallup, Presidential Job Approval Center, http://www.gallup.com/poll/124922/presidential-job-approval-center.aspx (accessed November 10, 2016).

57. See American National Election Studies, "Party Identification 7-Point Scale 1952–2008," *ANES Guide to Public Opinion and Electoral Behavior*, last modified August 5, 2010, accessed April 27, 2012, http://www.electionstudies.org/nesguide/toptable/tab2a_1.htm.

58. David Brooks, "What Independents Want," *New York Times*, November 5, 2009, A31.

59. John Sides, "Three Myths About Political Independents," *The Monkey Cage* (blog), December 17, 2009, http://www.themonkeycage.org/blog/2009/12/17/three_myths_about_political_in/.

60. Lydia Saad, "Conservatives Hang On to Ideology Lead by a Thread," *Gallup,* January 11, 2016, http://www.gallup.com/poll/188129/conservatives-hang-ideology-lead-thread.aspx?g_source=liberal%20conservative&g_medium=search&g_campaign=tiles.

61. This way of thinking about the public comes from Philip Converse, "Nature of Belief Systems in Mass Publics," in *Ideology and Discontent*, ed. David Apter (New York: Free Press, 1964).

62. The exact percentage of the public that was literate at the time of the founding is unclear. This percentage reflects the best guess of some historians.

63. *CIA World Factbook,* https://www.cia.gov/library/publications/the-world-factbook/geos/us.html.

64. Paul Lazarsfeld, Bernard Berelson, and Helen Gaudet, *The People's Choice* (New York: Duell, Sloane, Pearce, 1944).

65. Bernard Berelson, Paul F. Lazarsfeld, and William N. McPhee, *Voting: A Study of Opinion Formation in a Presidential Campaign* (Chicago: University of Chicago Press, 1954).

66. Converse, "Nature of Belief Systems in Mass Publics."

67. These data all come from Erikson and Tedin, *American Public Opinion*, 8th ed., 61.

68. John Zaller, "Monica Lewinsky and the Mainsprings of American Politics," in *Mediated Politics: Communication in the Future of Democracy*, ed. W. Lance Bennett and Robert M. Entman (Cambridge, U.K.: Cambridge University Press, 2001).

69. Stanley Kelley, *Interpreting Elections* (Princeton, N.J.: Princeton University Press, 1983).

70. Christopher Achen, "Mass Political Attitudes and the Survey Response," *American Political Science Review* 69 (1975): 1218–31.

71. Jennifer Hochschild, *What's Fair* (New Haven, CT.: Yale University Press, 1980).

72. Sam Popkin developed this concept in his book *The Reasoning Voter* (Chicago: University of Chicago Press, 1991).

73. "The Polarization of the Congressional Parties," Voteview.com, last modified March 6, 2012, accessed April 27, 2012, http://voteview.com/political_polarization.asp.

74. For a comprehensive account of these data, see Alan Abramowitz and Kyle Saunders, "Is Polarization a Myth?," *Journal of Politics* 70 (2008): 542–55.

75. "The Polarization of the Congressional Parties."

76. Pew Research Center, "Beyond Distrust: How Americans View Their Government," November 23, 2015, http://www.people-press.org/2015/11/23/beyond-distrust-how-americans-view-their-government/.

77. Alan Abramowitz, *The Disappearing Center* (New Haven, CT.: Yale University Press, 2010).

78. "The Abu Ghraib Files," *Salon*, March 14, 2006, http://www.salon.com/2006/03/14/introduction_2/.

79. Sarah Mendelson, "The Guantanamo Countdown," *Foreign Affairs*, October 1, 2009.

80. Survey by Pew Global Attitudes Project. Methodology: Conducted by Princeton Survey Research Associates International, April 13–May 3, 2015 and based on 1,003 telephone interviews, retrieved March 13, 2016, from the iPOLL Databank, the Roper Center for Public Opinion Research, Cornell University.

81. Survey conducted by Quinnipiac University Polling Institute, January 4–7, 2014, retrieved May 4, 2014, from the iPOLL Databank, the Roper Center for Public Opinion Research, University of Connecticut.

82. Surveys conducted by AP-NORC Center, August 12–29, 2013, and Associated Press/National Opinion Research Center, December 10–13, 2015, retrieved March 17, 2016, from the iPOLL Databank, the Roper Center for Public Opinion Research, University of Connecticut.

83. Survey conducted by Quinnipiac University Polling Institute, January 4–7, 2014, retrieved May 4, 2014, from the iPOLL Databank, the Roper Center for Public Opinion Research, University of Connecticut.

84. The data from 2000 are from the CBS/*New York Times* polls conducted during the presidential campaigns and available through the iPOLL Databank, the Roper Center for Public Opinion Research, University of Connecticut.

85. CBS News/*New York Times* Poll, Nov. 2016 [survey question]. USCBSNYT.110716.R01. CBS News/*New York Times* [producer]. Cornell University, Ithaca, NY: Roper Center for Public Opinion Research, iPOLL [distributor], accessed November 12, 2016.

86. Erikson and Tedin, *American Public Opinion,* 8th ed., 193.

87. Peter Moore, "Most Americans Support Marijuana Legalization," *YouGov:Politics*, January 15, 2016, https://today.yougov.com/news/2016/01/15/most-americans-support-marijuana-legalization/.

88. Survey conducted for CBS News/*New York Times*, February 19–23, 2014, retrieved April 7, 2014, from the iPOLL Databank, the Roper Center for Public Opinion Research, University of Connecticut.

89. Pew Research Center, "Muslim Americans: Middle Class and Mostly Mainstream," Pew Research Center, May 22, 2007, accessed April 27, 2012, http://pewresearch.org/pubs/483/muslim-americans.

90. Erikson and Tedin, *American Public Opinion,* 6th ed., 215.

91. *New York Times*, "Election 2016: Exit Polls," http://www.nytimes.com/interactive/2016/11/08/us/politics/election-exit-polls.html?_r=0 (accessed November 12, 2016).

92. Center for American Women and Politics, Eagleton Institute of Politics, Rutgers University, "The Gender Gap: Voting Choices in Presidential Elections," December 2008, accessed May 23, 2012, http://www.cawp.rutgers.edu/fast_facts/voters/documents/GGPresVote.pdf.

93. Survey for United Technologies, National Journal, conducted by Princeton Survey Research Associates International, October 3–6, 2013, retrieved April 8, 2014, from the iPOLL Databank, the Roper Center for Public Opinion Research, University of Connecticut.

94. Survey conducted for CNN by ORC International, May 17–18, 2013, retrieved April 8, 2014, from the iPOLL Databank, the Roper Center for Public Opinion Research, University of Connecticut.

95. Data from American National Election Studies, "Aid to Blacks/Minorities 1970–2008," *ANES Guide to Public Opinion and Electoral Behavior,* last modified August 5, 2010, accessed May 12, 2012, http://www.electionstudies.org/nesguide/2ndtable/t4b_4_1.htm.

96. Rebecca Riffkin, "Higher Support for Gender Affirmative Action Than Race," *Gallup,* August 26, 2015, http://www.gallup.com.proxy.library.vanderbilt.edu/poll/184772/higher-support-gender-affirmative-action-race.aspx.

97. Jens Manuel Krogstad, "After Decades of GOP Support, Cubans Shifting Toward the Democratic Party," *Pew Research Center*, June 24, 2016, http://www.pewresearch.org/fact-tank/2014/06/24/after-decades-of-gop-support-cubans-shifting-toward-the-democratic-party; Pew Research Center, "Latino Support for Democrats Falls, but Democratic Advantage Remains: Immigration Not a Deal-Breaker Issue for Half of Latino Voters," October 29, 2014, http://www.pewhispanic.org/files/2014/10/2014-10-29_NSL-latino-politics.pdf.

98. Rodolfo De la Garza, Louis DeSipio, F. Chris Garcia, John Garcia, and Angelo Falcon, *Latino Voices: Mexican, Puerto Rican, and Cuban Perspectives on American Politics* (Boulder, CO.: Westview Press, 1992).

99. David L. Leal, "Latino Public Opinion," Texas A&M University, Department of Political Science: Project for Equity, Representation, and Justice, accessed April 27, 2012, http://perg.tamu.edu/lpc/Leal.pdf; http://www.latinodecisions.com/blog/2016/11/09/the-rundown-on-latino-voter-election-eve-polling-and-latino-exit-polls (accessed November 12, 2016).

100. Alexander Kuo, Neil Malhotra, and Cecilia Hyunjung Mo, "Why Do Asian Americans Identify as Democrats? Testing Theories of Social Exclusion and Intergroup Solidarity," working paper, Vanderbilt University, February 25, 2014; http://www.nytimes.com/interactive/2016/11/08/us/politics/election-exit-polls.html?_r=0 (accessed November 12, 2016).

101. That figure combines Democratic identifiers with "leaners."

102. Pew Research Hispanic Trends Project, December 28, 2011, http://www.pewhispanic.org/2011/12/28/vii-views-of-the-political-parties-and-party-identification.

103. Efrén O. Pérez, 2015, "Xenophobic Rhetoric and Its Political Effects on Immigrants and Their Co-Ethnics," *American Journal of Political Science* 59(3): 549–564.

104. Pew Research Center for the People & the Press, "Where the Public Stands on Immigration Reform," Pew Research Center, November 23, 2009, accessed April 27, 2012, http://pewtrusts.org/our-work-report-detail.aspx?id=56203.

105. Norman H. Nie, Jane Junn, and Kenneth Stehlik-Barry, *Education and Democratic Citizenship in America* (Chicago: University of Chicago Press, 1996).

106. V. O. Key, *The Responsible Electorate* (Cambridge, MA.: Harvard University Press, 1966), 1.

107. Robert S. Erikson, Michael B. MacKuen, and James A. Stimson, *The Macro Polity* (Cambridge, U.K.: Cambridge University Press, 2002).

108. See Key, *Public Opinion and American Democracy*, and Douglas Arnold, *Logic of Congressional Action* (New Haven, CT.: Yale University Press, 1991).

Chapter 7

1. Chad Livengood, "Armed with His Delaware-Based 'Anonymous Shell Corporation,' Colbert Seeks 'Massive' Donations," *Dialogue Delaware*, last modified October 7, 2011, accessed April 14, 2014, http://blogs.delawareonline.com/dialoguedelaware/2011/10/07/armed-with-his-anonymous-delaware-shell-corporation-colbert-seeks-massive-donations/.

2. Cynthia Littleton, "Stephen Colbert's Rise: From South Carolina to Second City to Pop Culture Player," *Variety*, April 10, 2014, accessed April 14, 2014, http://variety.com/2014/tv/news/stephen-colberts-rise-from-south-carolina-to-second-city-to-pop-culture-player-1201155535/.

3. See http://www.hsc.edu/About-H-SC.html.

4. Littleton, "Stephen Colbert's Rise"; Ken Plume, "An Interview with Stephen Colbert," *IGN*, August 11, 2003, accessed April 14, 2014, http://www.ign.com/articles/2003/08/11/an-interview-with-stephen-colbert?page=1.

5. Ken Plume, "An Interview with Stephen Colbert"; Littleton, "Stephen Colbert's Rise."

6. "Truthiness," *Wikipedia*, last modified April 9, 2014, accessed April 14, 2014, https://en.wikipedia.org/wiki/Truthiness.

7. See http://www.merriam-webster.com/info/06words.htm.

8. James H. Fowler, "The Colbert Bump in Campaign Donations: More Truthful Than Truthy," *PS: Political Science & Politics* 41, 3 (2008): 533–39, http://jhfowler.ucsd.edu/colbert_bump.pdf.

9. "Stephen Colbert: 2010 Congressional Testimony," *Wikipedia*, last modified April 13, 2014, accessed April 14, 2014, https://en.wikipedia.org/wiki/Stephen_Colbert#2010_Congressional_testimony.

10. KrayolaTop, "Stephen Colbert to Congress 'Migrant Workers Suffer and Have No Rights,'" *YouTube*, uploaded September 24, 2010, accessed April 14, 2014, https://www.youtube.com/watch?v=nxelO4pW05s&noredirect=1.

11. Herbert Gans, *Democracy and the News* (New York: Oxford University Press, 2003), 1.

12. Thomas Jefferson to Edward Carrington, "Volume 5, Amendment I (Speech and Press), Document 8," January 16, 1787, *The Founders' Constitution*, ed. Philip B. Kurland and Ralph Lerner (Chicago: University of Chicago Press, 1986), accessed May 27, 2012, http://press-pubs.uchicago.edu/founders/documents/amendI_speechs8.html.

13. Pew Research Center's Project for Excellence in Journalism, "A Year in the News," *The State of the News Media 2009: An Annual Report on American Journalism*, accessed May 27, 2012, http://stateofthemedia.org/2009/a-year-in-the-news. See especially the section titled "The Economy Finally Emerges as a Major Story."

14. Bob Woodward and Carl Bernstein, *All the President's Men* (New York: Simon and Schuster, 1994).

15. Thomas E. Patterson, *Out of Order* (New York: Knopf, 1993), 82.

16. Joe Flint, "MSNBC's Reboot: More News, Less Leaning," *Wall Street Journal*, August 11, 2015, http://www.wsj.com/articles/msnbcs-reboot-more-news-less-leaning-1439337035.

17. *Near v. Minnesota*, 283 U.S. 697 (1931).

18. *New York Times Co. v. United States*, 403 U.S. 713 (1971).

19. *Obsidian Finance Group, LLC and Kevin D. Padrick v. Crystal Cox* (2014).

20. "Clear Channel Media + Entertainment," Clear Channel, accessed June 25, 2014, http://clearchannel.com/CCME/Pages/default.aspx.

21. Associated Press, "Gannett Co. Acquires Midwest South Newspapers for $280 M," *GazetteXtra*, October 8, 2015, http://www.gazettextra.com/20151008/gannett_co_acquires_midwest_south_newspapers_for_280m.

22. Jeremy D. Mayer, *American Media Politics in Transition* (New York: McGraw-Hill, 2007), 76.

23. *Federal Communications Commission v. Pacifica Foundation*, 438 U.S. 726 (1978).

24. *FCC v. Fox Television Stations*, 173 L. Ed. 2d 738 (2009).

25. Emma Llansó and Mark Stanley, "Communications Decency Act," Center for Democracy & Technology, September 21, 2011, accessed June 25, 2014, https://cdt.org/blog/shielding-the-messengers-section-230-and-free-speech-online/.

26. Liberty Counsel, "Legislative History of COPA," LC.org, accessed June 4, 2012, http://www.lc.org/profamily/copa.pdf.

27. Federal Trade Commission, "Facts for Consumers," 2007. See http://ftc.gov/for all available information collected by the FTC for consumers.

28. Library of Congress, "An Act to Prevent Child Abduction and the Sexual Exploitation of Children," see http://thomas.loc.gov/.

29. Federal Trade Commission, "Computers and the Internet: Privacy and Security." See http://www.ftc.gov for information on this issue and others.

30. Benjamin Franklin, "An Apology for Printers," *Pennsylvania Gazette*, May 27, 1731, reprinted as *An Apology for Printers* (Washington, D.C.: Acropolis Books, 1973).

31. Mayer, *American Media Politics in Transition*, 81.

32. Michael Schudson and Susan Tifft, "American Journalism in Historical Perspective," in *The Press*, ed. Geneva Overholser and Kathleen Hall Jamieson (New York: Oxford University Press, 2005), 19.

33. Michael Schudson, *Discovering the News: A Social History of American Newspapers* (New York: Basic Books, 1978).

34. William Riker, *The Strategy of Rhetoric: Campaigning for the American Constitution* (New Haven, CT.: Yale University Press, 1996).

35. David McCullough, *John Adams* (New York: Simon and Schuster, 2001).

36. Sedition Act, July 14, 1798, U.S. Constitution Online, accessed June 4, 2012, http://www.constitution.org/rf/sedition_1798.htm.

37. John Geer, *In Defense of Negativity: Attack Ads in Presidential Campaigns* (Chicago: University of Chicago Press, 2006).

38. Michael Schudson, *The Sociology of News* (New York: W. W. Norton, 2003), 75.

39. Melvin Laracey, "Who Listened? Political Media Communications by 'Pre-Modern' Presidents" (paper presented at the annual meeting of the Midwest Political Science Association, Chicago, IL., 2004).

40. James Hamilton, *All the News That's Fit to Sell: How the Market Transforms Information into News* (Princeton, N.J.: Princeton University Press, 2006).

41. Ibid., 53.

42. See Great Projects Film Company, "Yellow Journalism," Public Broadcast System (PBS), 1999, accessed May 15, 2012, http://www.pbs.org/crucible/journalism.html.
43. As quoted by Matt Drudge in "Anyone with a Modem Can Report on the World" (address before the National Press Club, June 2, 1998).
44. Jon Blackwell, "1906: Rumble over 'The Jungle,'" *Trentonian*, http://www.capitalcentury.com/1906.html.
45. Schudson and Tifft, "American Journalism in Historical Perspective," 17–46.
46. Rose McDermott, *Presidential Leadership, Illness, and Decision Making* (New York: Cambridge University Press, 2007).
47. Iyengar, *Media Politics*; American National Election Studies, *ANES Guide to Public Opinion and Electoral Behavior*, http://www.electionstudies.org/nesguide/nesguide.htm.
48. Brian Stelter, "Lester Holt Gets Anchor Chair in Moment for Black Journalists," *CNN Money*, June 18, 2015, http://money.cnn.com/2015/06/18/media/lester-holt-nbc-promotion.
49. Data retrieved May 1, 2012, from the iPOLL Databank, the Roper Center for Public Opinion Research, University of Connecticut.
50. Theodore H. White, *The Making of the President, 1960* (New York: Atheneum Publishers, 1961).
51. Sidney Krause, *The Great Debates: Kennedy v. Nixon, 1960* (Bloomington: Indiana University Press, 1977). The quotation is from Kennedy's telegram to the NBC board chair, accepting the invitation to debate, quoted in the *Tri City Herald*, July 28, 1960.
52. Schudson and Tifft, "American Journalism in Historical Perspective," 26.
53. Susannah Fox and Lee Rainie, "About This Report," *Pew Research Center, Internet, Science and Technology: The Web at 25 in the U.S.*, February 27, 2014, accessed April 20, 2014, http://www.pewinternet.org/2014/02/27/summary-of-findings-3/.
54. Charlie Sorrel, "Apple's iPad Sales Accelerate: Three Million Sold in 80 Days," *Gadget Lab* (blog), Wired, June 23, 2010, http://www.wired.com/gadgetlab/2010/06/apples-ipad-sales-accelerate-three-million-sold-in-80-days.
55. See http://expandedramblings.com/index.php/march-2013-by-the-numbers-a-few-amazing-twitter-stats/, accessed March 27, 2016.
56. Shea Bennett, "How Many Millennials, Gen-Xers and Baby Boomers Use Facebook, Twitter and Instagram," *Ad Week: Social Times*, June 3, 2014, accessed March 27, 2016, http://www.adweek.com/socialtimes/millennials-gen-x-baby-boomers-social-media/499110.
57. Data available at "Report: Community Journalism in the United States," Bill Lane Center for the American West, Stanford University, last modified August 7, 2011, accessed May 27, 2012, http://www.stanford.edu/group/ruralwest/cgi-bin/drupal/projects/newspapers.
58. For data on news consumption, see *The State of the News Media 2014* report available from the Pew Research Center's Project for Excellence in Journalism at http://www.journalism.org/packages/state-of-the-news-media-2014/.
59. Alex Jones, *Losing the News* (New York: Oxford University Press, 2009).
60. The data come from a study conducted for the Newspaper Association of America. See "Study: Newspapers Attract 102.8 million U.S. Internet Users," *SFN Blog*, World Association of Newspapers and News Publishers, http://www.sfnblog.com/2010/10/14/study-newspapers-attract-1028-million-us-internet-users.
61. Geoffrey Cowan, "Leading the Way to Better News" (Discussion Paper Series, Joan Shorenstein Center on the Press, Politics, and Public Policy, Harvard University, 2008), 7.
62. Ibid.
63. Michael Barthel, "Newspaper: Fact Sheet," *State of the News Media 2015*, Pew Research Center, April 29, 2015, accessed March 23, 2016, http://www.journalism.org/2015/04/29/newspapers-fact-sheet.
64. Ibid.
65. Nancy Vogt, "Audio: Fact Sheet," *State of the News Media 2015*, Pew Research Center, April 29, 2015, http://www.journalism.org/2015/04/29/audio-fact-sheet.
66. David Barker, *Rushed to Judgment* (New York: Columbia University Press, 2002).
67. Pew Research Center's Project for Excellence in Journalism, "Talk Radio," *The State of the News Media 2012*, Pew Research Center, accessed May 28, 2012, http://stateofthemedia.org/2012/audio-how-far-will-digital-go/#talk-radio.
68. No one has studied reasons why liberal talk radio has failed, but we offer some hypotheses here. Thank you to Markus Prior of Princeton University for brainstorming with us on this topic.
69. See http://www.journalism.org/media-indicators/evening-network-news-share-over-time/, accessed April 20, 2014.
70. See http://tvbythenumbers.zap2it.com/2016/01/14/late-night-ratings-jan-4-8-2016-daily-show-and-nightly-show-start-2016-on-upswing/.
71. See http://www.hollywoodreporter.com/news/john-olivers-talk-show-ratings-735187.
72. eBizMBA's ranking of the top fifteen blogs is available at http://www.ebizmba.com/articles/blogs. The rankings shown here were retrieved in April 2016.
73. Eric Lawrence, John Sides, and Henry Farrell, "Self-Segregation or Deliberation? Blog Readership, Participation, and Polarization in American Politics," *Perspectives on Politics* 8, 1 (2010): 146.
74. See http://www.drudgereport.com and http://www.rushlimbaugh.com/.
75. Dylan Tweney, "Controlled Chaos: An Interview with Kos," *Epicenter* (blog), Wired, May 8, 2007, http://blog.wired.com/business/2007/05/controlled_chao.html.
76. See https://www.facebook.com/facebook/info, accessed June 25, 2014.
77. Michael Barthel, Elisa Shearer, Jeffrey Gottfried, and Amy Mitchell, "The Evolving Role of News on Twitter and Facebook," Pew Research Center, July 14, 2015, http://www.journalism.org/2015/07/14/the-evolving-role-of-news-on-twitter-and-facebook.
78. Chris O'Brien, "CEO Mark Zuckerberg Predicts 5 Billion Facebook Users by 2030," *Vulture Beat*, July 4, 2016, http://venturebeat.com/2016/02/04/ceo-mark-zuckerberg-predicts-5b-facebook-users-by-2030.
79. See http://www.omnicoreagency.com/snapchat-statistics, accessed April 3, 2016.
80. See https://twitter.com/realDonaldTrump.
81. See http://tvbythenumbers.zap2it.com/2013/05/22/telemundo-delivers-best-season-ever-up-9-vs-2011-2012-season/183980 and http://www.deadline.com/2013/05/cbs-wins-season-abc-tops-adults-18-49-in-seasons-final-week.
82. Nick Corasaniti, "Univision Aims to Make Hispanic Voting Bloc Even More Formidable," *New York Times*, February 22, 2016, http://www.nytimes.com/2016/02/23/us/politics/univision-hispanic-voting.html?smprod=nytcore-iphone&smid=nytcore-iphone-share&_r=0; https://www.washingtonpost.com/news/monkey-cage/wp/2016/11/11/in-record-numbers-latinos-voted-overwhelmingly-against-trump-we-did-the-research (accessed November 12, 2016).
83. Thomas E. Patterson, *Young People and News* (Cambridge, MA: Joan Shorenstein Center on the Press, Politics, and Public Policy, Harvard University, July 2007).
84. Morley Winograd and Michael D. Hais, *Millennial Makeover: MySpace, YouTube and the Future of American Politics* (New Brunswick, N.J.: Rutgers University Press, 2008).

85. Jaime Fuller, "Iowa Dem Senate Hopeful Dismisses Grassley as 'Farmer from Iowa Who Never Went to Law School,'" *Washington Post*, March 25, 2014, accessed July 28, 2014.

86. Paul Lazarsfeld, Bernard Berelson, and Hazel Gaudet, *The People's Choice* (New York: Columbia University Press, 1944). It is worth noting that the 1940 campaign was probably the worst campaign in which to look for possible media effects. It was the only presidential election in U.S. history in which a sitting president, Franklin Roosevelt, was running for a third term. The stability of preference surely reflected the fact that people had opinions about Roosevelt and that not much would change them one way or the other. In contrast, Senator Obama was not a well-known figure in the 2008 presidential campaign.

87. Angus Campbell, Philip Converse, Warren Miller, and Donald Stokes, *The American Voter* (New York: Wiley, 1960).

88. Andrew Dugan, "Despite Enrollment Success, Healthcare Law Still Unpopular," *Gallup*, May 29, 2014, http://www.gallup.com/poll/170750/despite-enrollment-success-healthcare-law-remains-unpopular.aspx.

89. Bernard Cohen, *The Press and Foreign Policy* (Princeton, N.J.: Princeton University Press, 1963), 13.

90. Darrell M. West, Grover J. Whitehurst, and E. J. Dionne Jr., "Invisible: 1.4 Percent Coverage for Education Is Not Enough," Brookings.edu, December 2, 2009, accessed May 28, 2012, http://www.brookings.edu/research/reports/2009/12/02-education-news-west.

91. Shanto Iyengar and Jennifer A. McGrady, *Media Politics: A Citizen's Guide* (New York: W.W. Norton, 2007), 216.

92. These scholars have reshaped how we think about framing. In fact, Kahneman won a Nobel Prize for this work in 2003. See http://psych.hanover.edu/classes/cognition/papers/tversky81.pdf.

93. W. Lance Bennett, Regina C. Lawrence, and Steven Livingston, *When the Press Fails: Political Power and the News Media from Iraq to Katrina* (Chicago: University of Chicago Press, 2007).

94. Jonathan Ladd, *Why Americans Hate the Media* (Princeton, N.J.: Princeton University Press, 2012).

95. Ibid. Ladd also kindly provided us updated figures for this trend line.

96. Schudson, *The Sociology of News*, 33.

97. Paola Chavez and Veronica Stracqualursi, "The History of the Donald Trump–Megyn Kelly Feud," ABC News, March 3, 2016, http://abcnews.go.com/Politics/history-donald-trump-megyn-kelly-feud/story?id=36526503.

98. See the Accuracy in Media website at http://www.aim.org.

99. Conducted by Gallup Organization, September 4–September 7, 2014 and based on 1,017 telephone interviews. Sample: National adult. Interviews were conducted with respondents on landline telephones and cellular phones. The sample includes 50 percent landline and 50 percent cell phone respondents.

100. Thomas Patterson, "Political Roles of the Journalist," in *The Politics of the News*, ed. Doris Graber, Denis McQuail, and Pippa Norris (Washington, D.C.: CQ Press, 2000), 3.

101. For a thoughtful discussion of soft news, see Matthew Baum, *Soft News Goes to War: Public Opinion and American Foreign Policy in the New Media Age* (Princeton, N.J.: Princeton University Press, 2003), 6–7.

102. Schudson and Tifft, "American Journalism in Historical Perspective," 28.

103. Douglas Craig, *Fireside Politics* (Baltimore, MD.: Johns Hopkins University Press, 2000).

104. Gary Bunker, *From Rail-Splitter to Icon: Lincoln's Image in Illustrated Periodicals, 1860–1865* (Kent, OH.: Kent State University Press, 2001).

105. CB Presidential Research Services, "Presidential Campaign Slogans," PresidentsUSA.net, accessed May 28, 2012, http://www.presidentsusa.net/campaignslogans.html.

106. Pew Research Center for the People & the Press, "Public Knowledge of Current Affairs Little Changed by News and Information Revolutions," Pew Research Center, April 15, 2007, accessed May 28, 2012, http://www.people-press.org/2007/04/15/public-knowledge-of-current-affairs-little-changed-by-news-and-information-revolutions/.

107. Jacob Poushter, "Smartphone Ownership Rates Skyrocket in Many Emerging Economics, but Digital Divide Remains," Pew Research Center, February 22, 2016, http://www.pewglobal.org/2016/02/22/smartphone-ownership-rates-skyrocket-in-many-emerging-economies-but-digital-divide-remains.

108. Andrew Perrin and Maeve Duggan, "American's Internet Access: 2000–2015," Pew Research Center, June 26, 2015, accessed April 3, 2016, http://www.pewinternet.org/2015/06/26/americans-internet-access-2000-2015.

109. Pew Research Center, "Cell Phone and Smartphone Ownership Demographics," accessed April 21, 2014, http://www.pewinternet.org/data-trend/mobile/cell-phone-and-smartphone-ownership-demographics.

110. The argument presented over the next few paragraphs is inspired by the work of Markus Prior, *Post Broadcast Democracy* (New York: Cambridge University Press, 2007).

111. Ibid.

Chapter 8

1. Compiled from information on Common Sense Action's website, http://www.commonsenseaction.org; Andrew Kaplan and Sam Gilman, "Repairing Politics the Millennial Way," *Switch and Shift*, March 1, 2014, http://switchandshift.com/repairing-politics-the-millennial-way; an in-person interview with Andrew Kaplan and Sam Gilman, April 9, 2014, conducted for this text, which is the source of Gilman's quotation; and a follow-up e-mail interview with Sam Gilman in February 2016.

2. Alexis de Tocqueville, *Democracy in America*, ed. J. P. Mayer, trans. George Lawrence (New York: Doubleday & Company, 1969), 193.

3. William C. DiGiacomantonio, "Petitioners and Their Grievances," in *The House and Senate in the 1790s: Petitioning, Lobbying, and Institutional Development*, ed. Kenneth R. Bowling and Donald R. Kennon (Columbus: Ohio University Press, 2002), 29–56.

4. Interest groups at the state level have even been involved in elections for state judges. See Clive S. Thomas, Michael L. Boyer, and Ronald J. Hrebenar, "Interest Groups and State Court Elections: A New Era and Its Challenges," *Judicature* 87 (2003): 135–49.

5. Elizabeth Cady Stanton, Susan B. Anthony, and Matilda J. Gage, eds., *History of Woman Suffrage* (Rochester, N.Y.: Charles Mann Publishers, 1887), 1:70.

6. "141 Men and Girls Die in Waist Factory Fire; Trapped High Up in Washington Place Building; Street Strewn with Bodies; Piles of Dead Inside," *New York Times*, March 26, 1911, 1.

7. Office of the Secretary, United States Department of Labor, "Our Mission," accessed May 23, 2012, http://www.dol.gov/opa/aboutdol/mission.htm.

8. National Labor Relations Act, 29 U.S.C. §§ 151–169 (1935), http://www.nlrb.gov/national-labor-relations-act.

9. Beth L. Leech, Frank R. Baumgartner, Timothy M. La Pira, and Nicholas A. Semanko, "Drawing Lobbyists to Washington: Government Activity and the Demand for Advocacy," *Political Research Quarterly* 58, no. 1 (2005): 19–30.

10. Erik Schelzig, "UAW Adds to Unfair Labor Practices Allegations at Volkswagen," February 9, 2016, accessed February 13, 2016, http://abcnews.go.com/International/wireStory/uaw-adds-unfair-labor-practices-allegations-volkswagen-36819420.

11. Rachel Weiner, "Issue 2 Falls, Ohio Collective Bargaining Law Repealed," *The Fix* (blog), *Washington Post*, November 8, 2011, http://www.washingtonpost.com/blogs/the-fix/post/issue-2-falls-ohio

-collective-bargaining-law-repealed/2011/11/08/gIQAyZ0U3M_blog.html.

12. John Helton and Tom Cohen, "Walker's Wisconsin Win Big Blow to Unions, Smaller One to Obama," CNN, June 6, 2012, http://www.cnn.com/2012/06/05/politics/wisconsin-recall-vote/index.html?hpt=hp_t1.

13. United Automobile, Aerospace and Agricultural Implement Workers of America, accessed February 17, 2016, uaw.org/about.

14. Brent Snavely, "UAW Membership Tops 400,000 for First Time Since '08," *Detroit Free Press*, March 31, 2015, accessed February 13, 2016, www.usatoday.com/story/money/cars/2015/03/31/uaw-membership-tops-first-time-since/70753012.

15. National Right to Work Legal Defense Foundation, Inc., "Right to Work States," accessed August 20, 2014, http://www.nrtw.org/rtws.htm.

16. U.S. Bureau of Labor Statistics, "Union Members Summary," January 28, 2016, accessed February 8, 2016, http://www.bls.gov/news.release/union2.nr0.htm.

17. MoveOn.org, http://front.moveon.org/.

18. American Israel Public Affairs Committee, accessed June 4, 2014, http://www.aipac.org/.

19. Mark R. Amstutz, "Faith-Based NGOs and U.S. Foreign Policy," in *The Influence of Faith: Religious Groups and Foreign Policy,* ed. by Elliot Abrams (Lanham, Md.: Rowman and Littlefield Publishers, 2001), 175–87; National Council of the Churches of Christ in the USA, http://www.ncccusa.org.

20. http://www.amnestyusa.org/our-work/countries/middle-east-and-north-africa/syria; Human Rights Watch, accessed February 8, 2016, https://www.hrw.org.

21. http://www.rescue.org/crisis-syria.

22. Coral Davenport, "Citing Climate Change, Obama Rejects Construction of Keystone XL Oil Pipeline, *New York Times*, November 6, 2015, http://www.nytimes.com/2015/11/07/us/obama-expected-to-reject-construction-of-keystone-xl-oil-pipeline.html?R=0; Sierra Club, accessed February 8, 2016, http://content.sierraclub.org/press-releases/2015/11/how-sierra-club-and-its-allies-beat-keystone-xl-pipeline.

23. Kay Brilliant, "NEA's Response to Race to the Top," National Education Association, August 21, 2008, accessed May 23, 2012, http://www.nea.org/home/35447.htm.

24. League of United Latin American Citizens, accessed February 8, 2016, http://lulac.org/about/history/milestones.

25. For more information on general lobbying, see Anthony J. Nownes, *Total Lobbying* (New York: Cambridge University Press, 2006).

26. Center for Responsive Politics, "Lobbying Database," OpenSecrets.org, accessed January 24, 2016, http://www.opensecrets.org/lobby/.

27. Ibid.

28. Bureau of the Census, "NAIS 2011—Oil and Gas Extraction," http://thedataweb.rm.census.gov/TheDataWeb_HotReport2/econsnapshot/snapshot.hrml?NAICS=211&IND=%3DCOMP%28C2%2FC3*1000 %29&STATE=ALL&COUNTY=ALL.

29. Environmental Protection Agency, "EPA's Study of Hydraulic Fracturing and Its Potential Impact on Drinking Water Resources," accessed June 4, 2014, http://www2.epa.gov/hfstudy.

30. Environmental Protection Agency, "EPA's Draft Assessment of the Potential Impacts of Hydraulic Fracturing for Oil and Gas on Drinking Water Resources," accessed January 24, 2016, http://www.epa.gov/sites/production/files/2015-06/documents/draft_hf_assessment_fs_6_3_15_508_km_0.pdf.

31. ANGA, "About Us," http://anga.us/about-us#.UycJCfldWCk; NRDC "Consolidated Financial Statements," June 30, 2013, http://www.nrdc.org/about/NRDC_auditedfinancialstatements_FY2013.pdf.

32. ANGA, "Washington County Pennsylvania Retrospective Case Study Characterization Report," February 2013, http://anga.us/media/content/F7BDA298-DFF6-686B-2DF23939F9838B75/files/13%20Feb%2022%20FinalWashingtonCountyReport_clean%2021.pdf.

33. Natural Resources Defense Council, "Fracking: Community Defense," http://www.nrdc.org/land/fracking-community-defense/.

34. Ibid.

35. Natural Resources Defense Council, accessed January 24, 2016, http://switch-board.nrdc.org/blogs/bmordick/independent_expert_scientists.html.

36. Bart Jansen, "Legislative Summary: Congressional Affairs: Lobbying Practices and Disclosures," *CQ Weekly Online,* January 7, 2008, 39.

37. Citizens for Responsibility and Ethics in Washington, "About CREW," accessed March 14, 2014, http://www.citizensforethics.org/pages/about; http://www.citizensforethics.org/pages/under-investigation/.

38. Citizens for Responsibility and Ethics in Washington, "Scandals & Scoundrels," accessed January 24, 2016, http://www.citizens-foreethics.org/scandals-and-scoundrels.

39. U.S. Internal Revenue Service, "Exemption Requirements—Section 501(c)(3) Organizations," accessed June 4, 2014, http://www.irs.gov/Charities-&-Non-Profits/Charitable-Organizations/Exemption-Requirements-Section-501(c)(3)-Organizations.

40. James Oliphant, "Remember the IRS Tea-Party Scandal? Get Ready for Round Two," *National Journal*, February 5, 2014, accessed March 14, 2014, http://www.nationaljournal.com/white-house/remember-the-irs-tea-party-scandal-get-ready-for-round-two-20140205.

41. *Buckley v. Valeo,* 424 U.S. 1 (1976).

42. See www.thelibreinitiative.com/about/us, accessed February 8, 2016.

43. Mark Hugo Lopez and Ana Gonzalez-Barrera. "Inside the 2012 Latino Electorate," Pew Research Center, www.pewhispanic.org/2013/06/03/inside-the-2012-latino-electorate/.

44. www.thelibreinitiative.com/faqs; http://latino.foxnews.com/latino/politics/2015/09/29/conservative-group-libre-quietly-but-diligently-making-inroads-into-latino/, accessed February 8, 2016.

45. *New York Times* Staff, "Election 2016: Exit Polls," www.nytimes.com, accessed November 9, 2016, at http://www.nytimes.com/interactive/2016/11/08/us/politics/election-exit-polls.html.

46. See John R. Wright, *Interest Groups and Congress: Lobbying, Contributions, and Influence* (Boston: Allyn & Bacon, 1995, reprinted in Longman Classics Series, 2009); Michelle L. Chin, Jon R. Bond, and Nehemia Geva, "A Foot in the Door: An Experimental Study of PAC and Constituency Effects on Access," *Journal of Politics* 62 (2000): 534–49.

47. *Federal Election Commission v. Wisconsin Right to Life, Inc.,* 551 U.S. 449 (2007).

48. *McCutcheon et al. v. Federal Election Commission,* decided April 2, 2014, http://www.supremecourt.gov/opinions/13pdf/12-536_e1pf.pdf.

49. Tocqueville, *Democracy in America*, 514.

50. David Truman, *The Governmental Process: Political Interests and Public Opinion* (New York: Alfred Knopf, 1971).

51. Mancur Olson, *The Logic of Collective Action* (Cambridge, Mass.: Harvard University Press, 1971).

52. Robert Dahl, *A Preface to Democratic Theory* (Chicago: University of Chicago Press, 1956). Also see Robert Dahl, *Who Governs?,* 2nd ed. (New Haven, Conn.: Yale University Press, 2005).

53. C. Wright Mills, *The Power Elite* (New York: Oxford University Press, 1956).

54. Theodore J. Lowi, *The End of Liberalism: Ideology, Policy, and the End of Public Authority* (New York: Norton, 1969).

55. Larry M. Bartels, *Unequal Democracy*, 2nd ed. (Princeton, N.J.: Princeton University Press, 2016); Martin Gilens, *Affluence and Influence* (Princeton, N.J.: Princeton University Press, 2012).

56. E. E. Schattschneider, *The Semi-Sovereign People* (New York: Holt, Rinehart, and Winston, 1960). Also see E. E. Schattschneider, *Politics, Pressures, and the Tariff* (New York: Prentice-Hall, 1935).

57. National Highway Traffic Safety Administration, accessed January 24, 2016, http:/www.nhtsa.gov/fuel-economy.

58. Center for Climate and Energy Solutions, "Federal Vehicle Standards," accessed March 16, 2014, http://www.c2es.org/federal/executive/vehicle-standards#timeline.

59. Dwight D. Eisenhower, "Farewell Radio and Television Address to the American People," January 17, 1961; Gerhard Peters and John T. Woolley, The American Presidency Project, accessed May 23, 2012, http://www.presidency.ucsb.edu/ws/index.php?pid=12086&st=&st1=#axzz1uPYslFQG.

60. Thom Shankar and Helene Cooper, "Pentagon Plans to Shrink Army to Pre-World War II Level," *New York Times*, February 23, 2014, http://www.nytimes.com/2014/02/24/us/politics/pentagon-plans-to-shrink-army-to-pre-world-war-ii-level.html.

61. Hugh Heclo, "Issue Networks and the Executive Establishment," in *The New American Political System*, ed. Anthony King (Washington, D.C.: American Enterprise Institute, 1978), 87–124.

62. Shane Goldmacher, "The Long Arm (and Hidden Hand) of Jim DeMint," *National Journal*, October 1, 2013, accessed March 15, 2014, http://www.nationaljournal.com/politics/the-long-arm-and-hidden-hand-of-jim-demint-20131001.

63. Lauren French, Anna Palmer, Jake Sherman. "GOP Lawmakers Confront DeMint Over Ratings," *Politico.com*, January 28, 2015, accessed January 24, 2016, http://www.politico.com/story/2015/01/gop-lawmakers-jim-demint-heritage-foundation-ratings-114672.

64. Americans for Tax Reform, "About Americans for Tax Reform," accessed May 23, 2012, http://www.atr.org/about.

65. Robert H. Salisbury, "An Exchange Theory of Interest Groups," *Midwest Journal of Political Science* 13 (1969): 1–32.

66. In *Logic of Collective Action*, Olson labels these *selective incentives* (p. 51).

67. Ibid, pp. 50–51.

68. AARP, "2015 AARP Year in Review," accessed August 17, 2016, www.aarp.org/.../aarp/...aarp/annual_reports/.../2015-Year-in-Review-AARP.pdf.

69. AARP, "Consolidated Financial Statements Together with Report of Independent Certified Public Accountants." December 31, 2015 and 2014." Accessed September 12, 2016 at http://www.aarp.org/about-aarp/company/annual-reports/

70. James Hohmann, "Club for Growth Plots Role as 2016 Kingmaker, But Will It Find 'the One'," *Politico.com*, March 3, 2015, accessed February 8, 2016, http://www.politico.com/story/2015/03/club-for-growth-2016-candidate-115633.

Chapter 9

1. Compiled from Mia Love, "The America I Love," *The Daily Caller*, August 28, 2012, accessed February 19, 2016, http://dailycaller.com/2012/08/28/the-america-i-know/; Justin Wm. Moyer, "Meet Mia Love. You'll Be Seeing a Lot More of the Republicans' First Black Congresswoman," *Washington Post*, November 5, 2014, accessed February 18, 2016, https://www.washingtonpost.com/news/morning-mix/wp/2014/11/05/meet-mia-love-youll-be-seeing-a-lot-more-of-the-republicans-first-black-congresswoman/; Robert Gehrke and Matt Canham, "Mia Love: From Dreams of Broadway to Capitol Hill," *Salt Lake Tribune*, October 9, 2012, accessed February 17, 2016, http://archive.sltrib.com/story.php?ref=/sltrib/politics/55031749-90/love-mia-bourdeau-family.html.csp; "Rising GOP Star Mia Love Glides into the Spotlight at Convention," FoxNews.com, August 28, 2012, accessed February 16, 2016, http://www.foxnews.com/politics/2012/08/28/republican-convention-to-feature-rising-star-mia-love.html; Mia Love, "Mia Love Delivers 'State of the 4th District," February 2, 2016, accessed February 19, 2016, http://love.house.gov; Congress.gov, Mia Love, accessed February 20, 2016, https://www.congress.gov/member/mia-love/L000584?q=%7B%22sponsorship%22%3A%22cosponsored%22%7D.

2. V. O. Key Jr., *Politics, Parties, and Pressure Groups*, 5th ed. (New York: Thomas Y. Crowell Company, 1964).

3. Center for Responsive Politics, "Political Parties," accessed November 9, 2016, https://www.opensecrets.org/parties.

4. Ibid.

5. For more information on the informal networking that occurs among party activists, see Gregory Koger, Seth Masket, and Hans Noel, "Partisan Webs: Information Exchange and Party Networks," *British Journal of Political Science* 39 (2009): 633–53.

6. Marjorie Hershey, *Party Politics in America*, 12th ed. (New York: Pearson-Longman, 2007), 159.

7. Byron E. Shafer, *Quiet Revolution: The Struggle for the Democratic Party & The Shaping of Post-Reform Politics* (New York: Russell Sage Foundation, 1983), 172.

8. In the 2016 Democratic nomination contest between former Secretary of State Hillary Clinton and Senator Bernie Sanders (D-VT), superdelegates played a very important role, as they had in the 2008 contest between the Senator Barack Obama (D-IL) and then-Senator Hilary Clinton (D-NY). Almost from the start of the 2016 presidential nomination phase of the process, Secretary Clinton led Senator Sanders among superdelegates by large margins. Heading into the Democratic national party convention, Clinton had secured the pledges of 572 superdelegates out of a total of 713, or 80%. (David Chalian, "How CNN's count puts Clinton over the top," CNN Politics, June 6, 2016, http://www.cnn.com/2016/06/06/politics/superdelegates-hillary-clinton-nomination).

9. Republican National Committee, "New Timing Rules for 2012 Republican Presidential Nominating Schedule," as cited by Josh Putnam; "An Update on the 2012 Republican Delegate Selection Rules," *FrontloadingHQ* (blog), February 27, 2011, http://frontloading.blogspot.com/2011/02/update-on-2012-republican-delegate.html.

10. Peter Hamby, "GOP Adopts Changes to 2016 Presidential Primary Process," CNN.com, January 24, 2014, accessed April 3, 2014. http://politicalticker.blogs.cnn.com/2014/01/24/gop-adopts-changes-to-2016-presidential-primary-process/. Election Central, 2016 Primary Election Schedule. http://www.uspresidentialelectionnews.com/2016-presidential-primary-schedule-calendar; Jake Miller, "How Many GOP presidential debates is too many?" CBS News, January 16, 2015. http://www.cbsnews.com/news/how-many-gop-presidential-debates-is-too-many/; https://www.gop.com/2016-gophq/event_schedule/?schedule_type=debate.

11. George Washington, "Washington's Farewell Address," reprinted in Randall E. Adkins, *The Evolution of Political Parties, Campaigns, and Elections* (Washington, D.C.: CQ Press, 2008), 47–50.

12. John F. Bibby and Brian F. Schaffner, *Politics, Parties and Elections in America,* 6th ed. (Boston: Thomson-Wadsworth, 2008), 24.

13. U.S. Senate, Office of the Historian, *Biographical Directory of the United States Congress,* http://bioguide.congress.gov.

14. U.S. Senate, Office of the Historian, *Senate History,* http://www.senate.gov/artandhistory/history/minute/Nominating_presidents.htm.

15. Martin Van Buren, "Letter to Thomas Ritchie," 1827, reprinted in *The Evolution of Political Parties, Campaigns, and Elections: Landmark Documents, 1787–2007,* ed. Randall E. Adkins (Washington, D.C.: CQ Press, 2008), 65–69.

16. U.S. Census Bureau, "1990 Population and Housing Unit Counts: United States," Table 2, in *1990 Census of Population and Housing,* accessed May 31, 2012, http://www.census.gov/population/www/censusdata/files/table-2.pdf.

17. Quoted in James L. Sundquist, *Dynamics of the Party System* (Washington, D.C.: Brookings Institution Press, 1973), 65.
18. Sean M. Theriault, *The Power of the People* (Columbus: Ohio State University Press, 2005), Chapter 3.
19. Douglas W. Jones, "The Australian Paper Ballot," in "A Brief Illustrated History of Voting," University of Iowa, Department of Computer Science, 2003, accessed May 31, 2012, http://www.divms.uiowa.edu/~jones/voting/pictures/.
20. Erik J. Engstrom and Samuel Kernell, "Manufactured Responsiveness: The Impact of State Electoral Laws on Unified Party Control of the Presidency and the House of Representatives, 1840–1940," *American Journal of Political Science* 49 (July 2005): 531–49, see 535.
21. Anthony Downs, *An Economic Theory of Democracy* (New York: Harper, 1957).
22. Stuart Elaine Macdonald and George Rabinowitz, "Solving the Paradox of Nonconvergence: Valence, Position, and Direction in Democratic Politics," *Electoral Studies* 17, no. 3 (1998): 281–300.
23. Maurice Duverger, "Public Opinion and Political Parties in France," *American Political Science Review* 46, no. 4 (1952): 1069–78, especially 1071.
24. James R. Whitson, "President Elect: The Unofficial Homepage of the Electoral College," PresidentElect.org, accessed February 18, 2016, http://presidentelect.org/e1892.html.
25. See https://www.lp.org/candidates/elected-officials, accessed February 6, 2016.
26. Texas State Historical Association, *Raza Unida Party*, http://www.tshaonline.org/handbook/online/articles/war01.
27. Kate Zernike, Kitty Bennett, Ford Fessenden, Kevin Quealy, Amy Schoenfeld, Archie Tse, and Derek Willis, "Where Tea Party Candidates Are Running," *New York Times*, October 14, 2010, accessed April 4, 2014, http://www.nytimes.com/interactive/2010/10/15/us/politics/tea-party-graphic.html.
28. For an expanded analysis of the Tea Party, see Theda Skocpol and Vanessa Williams, *The Tea Party and the Remaking of Republican Conservatism* (New York: Oxford University Press, 2013).
29. John Terbush, "How the Tea Party Lost the 2014 Election," *The Week*, November 5, 2016, accessed February 18, 2016, http://www.nytimes.com/interactive/2010/10/15/us/politics/tea-party-graphic.html.
30. Jonathan Martin, "For Many Republican Incumbents, Challenge from Right Fizzles," *New York Times*, April 4, 2014, http://www.nytimes.com/2014/04/05/us/politics/tea-party-challenge-to-republican-incumbents-fizzles.html.
31. For a detailed discussion of how interest groups interact with parties in campaigning, see Matthew J. Burbank, Ronald J. Hrebenar, and Robert C. Benedict, *Parties, Interest Groups, and Political Campaigns* (Boulder, Colo.: Paradigm Publishers, 2008).
32. "Opinions on Gun Policy and 2016 Campaign," Pew Research Center, August 26, 2016. http://www.people-press.org/2016/08/26/opinions-on-gun-policy-and-the-2016-campaign.
33. Ibid.
34. Democratic National Committee, "The 2016 Democratic Party Platform," https://www.democrats.org/party-platform#gun-violence.
35. Republican National Committee, "The 2016 Republican Party Platform," https://prod-static-ngop-pbl.s3.amazonaws.com/media/documents/DRAFT_12_FINAL[1]-ben_1468872234.pdf.
36. Center for Responsive Politics, "Political Action Committees," accessed February 18, 2016, http://www.opensecrets.org/pacs/
37. Cornell Belcher and Donna Brazile, "The Black and Hispanic Vote in 2006," *Democratic Strategist*, March 29, 2007, http://www.thedemocraticstrategist.org/ac/2007/03/the_black_and_hispanic_vote_in.php.
38. "Election Results 2008," *New York Times*, December 9, 2008, http://elections.nytimes.com/2008/results/president/map.html.
39. The Roper Center, "US Elections: How Groups Voted in 2012," http://www.ropercenter.uconn.edu/elections/how_groups_voted/voted_12.html.
40. Becca Stanek, "3 Charts Show How American Voted in the Midterm Election," November 4, 2014, accessed February 6, 2016, http://mic.com/articles/103422/3-charts-show-how-america-voted-in-this-year-s-midterm-elections#.qVc99SKQ6.
41. Alec Tyson and Shiva Maniam, "Behind Trump's victory: Divisions by race, gender, education," Pew Research Center, November 9, 2016. http://www.pewresearch.org/fact-tank/2016/11/09/behind-trumps-victory-divisions-by-race-gender-education; Jon Huang, Samuel Jacoby, K. K., Rebecca Lai, and Michael Strickland, "Election 2016: Exit Polls," New York Times, November 8, 2016. http://www.nytimes.com/interactive/2016/11/08/us/politics/election-exit-polls.html.
42. David Damore and Matt Barreto, "The Latino Threshold to Win in 2016," July 17, 2015, accessed February 19, 2016, http://www.latinodecisions.com/blog/2015/07/17/the-latino-threshold-in-2016-to-win/.
43. Alec Tyson and Shiva Maniam, "Behind Trump's victory: Divisions by race, gender, education," Pew Research Center, November 9, 2016. http://www.pewresearch.org/fact-tank/2016/11/09/behind-trumps-victory-divisions-by-race-gender-education/; Jon Huang, Samuel Jacoby, K. K., Rebecca Lai, and Michael Strickland, "Election 2016: Exit Polls," New York Times, November 8, 2016. http://www.nytimes.com/interactive/2016/11/08/us/politics/election-exit-polls.html; "The Rundown on Latino Voter Election Eve Polling and Latino Exit Polls," Latino Decisions, November 9, 2016. http://www.latinodecisions.com/blog/2016/11/09/the-rundown-on-latino-voter-election-eve-polling-and-latino-exit-polls.
44. Jens Manuel Krogstag, Mark Hugo Lopez, Gustavo Lopez, Jeffrey S. Passel, and Eileen Patten, "Millennials Make Up Almost Half of Latino Eligible Voters In 2016," January 19, 2016, Pew Research Center, http://www.pewhispanic.org/2016/01/19/millennials-make-up-almost-half-of-latino-eligible-voters-in-2016/.
45. "Donald Trump Doubles Down on Mexico 'Rapists' Comments Despite Outrage," *Guardian*, July 2, 2015, accessed March 1, 2016, http://www.theguardian.com/us-news/2015/jul/02/donald-trump-racist-claims-mexico-rapes; Albert R. Hunt, "Republicans Risk Repeating Mistake on Hispanic Vote," *New York Times*, January 24, 2016, accessed March 1, 2016, http://www.nytimes.com/2016/01/25/us/politics/republicans-risk-repeating-mistake-on-hispanic-vote.html?ref=politics&_r=0.
46. Krogstag et al., "Millennials Make Up Almost Half of Latino Eligible Voters in 2016."
47. *Engel v. Vitale*, 370 U.S. 421 (1962).
48. For a broad discussion of the resurgence of Republican conservatives, see Mark A. Smith, *The Right Talk: How Conservatives Transformed the Great Society into the Economic Society* (Princeton, N.J.: Princeton University Press, 2007).
49. Scholar Tasha Philpot pointed to underlying shifts as early as 2004. See Tasha S. Philpot, "A Party of a Different Color? Race, Campaign Communication, and Party Politics," *Political Behavior* 26 (2004): 249–70.
50. Greg Giroux, "Final Tally Shows Obama First Since '56 to Win 51% Twice," Bloomberg News, accessed April 4, 2014, http://www.bloomberg.com/news/2013-01-03/final-tally-shows-obama-first-since-56-to-win-51-twice.html; Roper Center, accessed April 28, 2014, http://www.ropercenter.uconn.edu/elections/how_groups_voted/voted_12.html.
51. "Party Affiliation," Gallup.com, accessed February 7, 2016, http://www.gallup.com/poll/15370/party-affiliation.aspx.

Chapter 10

1. See Michael Barone and Chuck McCutcheon, "Arizona," in *The Almanac of American Politics 2014* (Chicago: University of Chicago Press, 2013). Also, "Kyrsten Sinema's Biography," *Project Vote Smart*, accessed April 20, 2014, http://votesmart.org/candidate/biography/28338/kyrsten-sinema#.U1SPgscmCZw.
2. Manuel Roig-Franzia, "Kyrsten Sinema: A Success Story Like Nobody Else's," *Washington Post*, January 2, 2013, accessed May 16, 2014, http://www.washingtonpost.com/lifestyle/style/kyrsten-sinema-a-success-story-like-nobody-elses/2013/01/02/d31fadaa-5382-11e2-a613-ec8d394535c6_story.html.
3. Ibid.
4. Barone and McCutcheon, "Arizona."
5. "Sinema: A Record of Accomplishment," http://kyrstensinema.com/record/, accessed May 15, 2014.
6. Quoted in Jeff Broadwater, *George Mason, Forgotten Founder* (Chapel Hill: University of North Carolina Press, 2006), 178.
7. *Presidential Elections, 1789–2004* (Washington, D.C.: CQ Press, 2005), 179.
8. For more on the differences between indirect and direct elections of U.S. senators, see Wendy J. Schiller and Charles Stewart III, *Electing the Senate: Indirect Democracy before the 17th Amendment* (Princeton, N.J.: Princeton University Press, 2014).
9. For a longer discussion of redistricting, see Bernard Grofman, Lisa Handley, and Richard G. Niemi, *Minority Representation and the Quest for Voting Equality* (New York: Cambridge University Press, 1992).
10. 478 U.S. 30 (1986).
11. 548 U.S. 399 (2006).
12. Stephen Nicholson, *Voting by Agenda* (Princeton, N.J.: Princeton University Press, 2005).
13. See http://www.americanbar.org/content/dam/aba/migrated/leadership/fact_sheet.authcheckdam.pdf, accessed May 4, 2014.
14. Susan Hyde and Nikolay Marinov, "National Elections Across Democracy and Autocracy: Which Elections Can Be Lost?" (manuscript, Yale University, 2010), accessed June 1, 2012, http://hyde.research.yale.edu/nelda.
15. Robert A. Dahl, "What Political Institutions Does Large-Scale Democracy Require?," *Political Science Quarterly* 120 (2005): 187–98.
16. Pew Research Center, "Election 2016: 2016 Campaign: Strong Interest, Widespread Dissatisfaction. http://www.people-press.org/2016/07/07/1-campaign-engagement-and-interest" (accessed November 2, 2016).
17. Michael McGerr, *The Decline of Popular Politics* (New York: Oxford University Press, 1986).
18. Nathan Martin and Maggie Haberman, "Ted Cruz Hopes Early Campaign Entry Will Focus Voters' Attention," *New York Times*, March 22, 2015.
19. Sidney Blumenthal, *The Permanent Campaign* (New York: Simon and Schuster, 1982).
20. Marty Cohen, David Karol, Hans Noel, and John Zaller, *The Party Decides: Presidential Nominations Before and After Reform* (Chicago: University of Chicago Press, 2008).
21. Aaron Bycoffe, "The Endorsement Primary. FiveThirtyEight. http://projects.fivethirtyeight.com/2016-endorsement-primary (accessed November 2, 2016)."
22. Cynthia Littleton and Oriana Schwindt, "Final Ratings for Third Donald Trump-Hillary Clinton Debate: 71.6 Million," Variety, October 20, 2016. http://variety.com/2016/tv/news/tv-ratings-donald-trump-hillary-clinton-final-debate-1201895174 (accessed November 2, 2016).
23. Sidney Krause, *The Great Debates: Kennedy v. Nixon 1960* (Bloomington: Indiana University Press, 1977).
24. Federal Election Commission, "The FEC and Federal Campaign Finance Law: Historical Background," February 2004, accessed June 4, 2012, http://www.fec.gov/pages/brochures/fecfeca.shtml.
25. "Contribution Limits for 2015–2016 Federal Elections," http://www.fec.gov/info/contriblimitschart1516.pdf.
26. Federal Election Commission, "*McCutcheon, et al. v. FEC Case Summary*," FEC.gov, accessed May 1, 2014, http://www.fec.gov/law/litigation/McCutcheon.shtml.
27. "Bernie Sanders Candidate Summary, 2016 Cycle," https://www.opensecrets.org/pres16/candidate.php?id=N00000528.
28. "Ted Cruz Candidate Summary, 2016 Cycle," https://www.opensecrets.org/pres16/candidate.php?id=N00033085.
29. Clare Foran, "Bernie Sanders's Big Money," *The Atlantic*, March 1, 2016, http://www.theatlantic.com/politics/archive/2016/03/bernie-sanders-fundraising/471648/.
30. Center for Responsive Politics, "2016 Presidential Race," https://www.opensecrets.org/pres16 (accessed November 10, 2016).
31. Richard Briffault, "Super PACs" (Working Paper 12-298, Columbia Law School, April 16, 2012).
32. Matea Gold and Anu Narayanswamy, "41% of All Super PAC Money Comes From Donors," *Boston Globe*, April 17, 2016, https://www.bostonglobe.com/news/nation/2016/04/16/all-super-pac-money-comes-from-donors/5TJLQ5gxHMRclXlhAVVK2H/story.html.
33. Center for Responsive Politics, "2016 Presidential Race," https://www.opensecrets.org/pres16 (accessed November 10, 2016).
34. Ibid.
35. Steven J. Rosenstone and John Mark Hansen, *Mobilization, Participation, and Democracy in America* (New York: Macmillan, 1993).
36. "2016 Outside Spending, by Super PAC," OpenSecrets.org. https://www.opensecrets.org/outsidespending/summ.php?chrt=V&type=S (accessed November 2, 2016).
37. Nate Silver, "Election Update: Where Are the Undecided Voters?" FiveThirtyEight, http://fivethirtyeight.com/features/election-update-where-are-the-undecided-voters (accessed November 10, 2016).
38. "2016 Election Toss-Up States," http://www.270towin.com/maps/2016-election-toss-up-states.
39. Daron R. Shaw, *The Race to 270: The Electoral College and the Campaign Strategies of 2000 and 2004* (Chicago: University of Chicago Press, 2006); figures for 2008 provided by Daron R. Shaw.
40. The Battleground States Project, politico.com. http://www.politico.com/2016-election/swing-states (accessed November 2, 2016).
41. Mark J. Penn with E. Kinney Zalesne, *Microtrends: The Small Forces Behind Tomorrow's Big Changes* (New York: Twelve, Hatchett Book Group USA, 2007), xiii.
42. Thomas B. Edsall, "Let the Nanotargeting Begin," *Campaign Stops* (blog), *New York Times*, April 15, 2012, http://campaignstops.blogs.nytimes.com/2012/04/15/let-the-nanotargeting-begin/.
43. See http://www.thevictorylab.com/for an account of the revolution in campaigns that is often called "microtargeting."
44. Darren Samuelsohn, "Inside Clinton's Plan to Win Over Millennials," Politico, http://www.politico.com/story/2016/06/hillary-clinton-millennials-young-voters-224507 (accessed November 12, 2016).

45. Katie Kuehner-Hebert, "Cover Story: The Direct Marketing Election," *Target Marketing*, November 1, 2012, http://www.targetmarketingmag.com/article/election-2012-barack-obama-mitt-romney-microtargeting-retargeting-mobile-marketing-social-media-voter-databases/1, accessed May 2, 2014.

46. See http://www.nbcnews.com/news/other/remembering-kennedys-micro-targeting-1960-election-f2D11641336, accessed May 2, 2014.

47. John G. Geer, *In Defense of Negativity* (Chicago: University of Chicago Press, 2006), 59–60.

48. Lynn Vavreck, *The Message Matters* (Princeton, N.J.: Princeton University Press, 2009).

49. Meg Anderson, "From the Economy to Race, See Where the Candidates Stand on the Big Issues," NPR, http://www.npr.org/2016/10/18/496926243/from-the-economy-to-race-see-where-the-candidates-stand-on-the-big-issues (accessed November 12, 2016).

50. Donald Stokes, "Spatial Models of Party Competition," *American Political Science Review* 57 (1963): 368–77.

51. Geer, *In Defense of Negativity*, 105.

52. Sunshine Hillygus and Todd Shields, *The Persuadable Voter* (Princeton, N.J.: Princeton University Press, 2008), 36.

53. Emily Cadei, "How Donald Trump Made Race the Wedge Issue of 2016," *Newsweek*, http://www.newsweek.com/trump-race-wedge-issue-494601 (accessed November 12, 2016).

54. Kathleen Jamieson, *Dirty Politics* (New York: Oxford University Press, 1992).

55. Erika Franklin Fowler and Travis N. Ridout, "Negative, Angry and Ubiquitous: Political Advertising in 2012," *The Forum, A Journal of Applied Research in Contemporary Politics* 10, no. 4 (2012): 51–61.

56. Wesleyan Media Project, "Advertising Analysis," http://mediaproject.wesleyan.edu (accessed November 10, 2016).

57. Geer, *In Defense of Negativity*.

58. Zachary Karabell, *The Last Campaign* (New York: Vintage, 2001).

59. Geer, *In Defense of Negativity*, 9–10.

60. *The Fiscal Times*, "Most Forecasters Predict a Win for Clinton, Except for Two," http://www.thefiscaltimes.com/2016/09/04/Most-Forecasters-Predict-Win-Clinton-Except-Two(accessedNovember12, 2016).

61. Ibid.

62. Morris Fiorina, *Retrospective Voting* (New Haven, Conn.: Yale University Press, 1980).

63. Anthony Downs, *An Economic Theory of Democracy* (New York: Harper, 1957).

64. Mark C. Westlye, *Senate Elections and Campaign Intensity* (Baltimore, Md.: Johns Hopkins University Press, 1991).

65. Federal Election Commission, *Federal Election Campaign Laws* (Washington, D.C.: Federal Election Commission, April 2008), 56–60, http://www.fec.gov. Note that the contribution levels have been increased slightly to adjust for inflation.

66. https://www.opensecrets.org/races (accessed November 12, 2016).

67. Albert Cover, "One Good Term Deserves Another: The Advantage of Incumbency in Congressional Elections," *American Journal of Political Science* 21, no. 3 (1977): 523–41.

68. Gary C. Jacobson, *The Politics of Congressional Elections*, 8th ed. (Upper Saddle River, N.J.: Prentice Hall, 2012).

69. Richard F. Fenno Jr., *Home Style: Home Members in Their Districts* (Boston: Little, Brown, 1978).

70. Jacobson, *The Politics of Congressional Elections*.

71. ABC News Poll, Nov. 2016 [survey question]. USABC.110616.R05. ABC News [producer]. Cornell University, Ithaca, NY: Roper Center for Public Opinion Research, iPOLL [distributor], accessed November 12, 2016.

72. Morris Fiorina, *Congress: Keystone to the Washington Establishment* (New Haven, Conn.: Yale University Press, 1977).

73. John Zaller, "Politicians as Prize Fighters," in *Politicians and Party Politics*, ed. John G. Geer (Baltimore, Md.: Johns Hopkins University Press, 1998), 128–85.

74. Bruce Oppenheimer, "Deep Red and Blue Congressional Districts: The Causes and Consequences of Declining Party Competitiveness," in *Congress Reconsidered*, 8th ed., ed. Lawrence Dodd and Bruce Oppenheimer (Washington, D.C.: CQ Press, 2005), 135–58.

75. Jacobson, *The Politics of Congressional Elections*.

76. Tracy Sulkin, "Promises Made and Promises Kept," in *Congress Reconsidered*, ed. Lawrence Dodd and Bruce Oppenheimer (Washington, D.C.: CQ Press, 2009), 119–40.

77. Tracy Sulkin and Nathaniel Swigger, "Is There Truth in Advertising?" *Journal of Politics* 70 (2008): 232–44.

78. Gary C. Jacobson and Samuel Kernell, *Strategy and Choice in Congressional Elections* (New Haven, Conn.: Yale University Press, 1983).

79. Jacobson, *The Politics of Congressional Elections*.

80. Gerald M. Pomper, *Elections in America* (New York: Longman, 1980), 161.

81. Poll conducted by The Roper Center for Public Opinion Research, February 9–23, 1980, retrieved June 9, 2012, from the iPOLL Databank, The Roper Center for Public Opinion Research, University of Connecticut.

82. Poll conducted by Penn and Schoen Associates, October 10–12, 1984, retrieved June 9, 2012, from the iPOLL Databank, The Roper Center for Public Opinion Research, University of Connecticut.

83. Poll conducted by Greenberg Quinlan Rosner Research, October 30–November 2, 2008, retrieved June 9, 2012, from the iPOLL Databank, The Roper Center for Public Opinion Research, University of Connecticut.

84. NBC News/*Wall Street Journal* Poll, Nov. 2016 [survey question]. USNBCWSJ.110616.R04A. Hart Research Associates/Public Opinion Strategies [producer]. Cornell University, Ithaca, NY: Roper Center for Public Opinion Research, iPOLL [distributor], accessed November 12, 2016.

85. V. O. Key, *The Responsible Electorate* (Cambridge, Mass.: Harvard University Press, 1966).

Chapter 11

1. Ta-Nehisi Coates, "There is No Post-Racial America," *The Atlantic*, July/August 2015, http://www.theatlantic.com/magazine/archive/2015/07/post-racial-society-distant-dream/395255/.

2. This story has been compiled from the following sources: Benjamin Wallace-Wells, "The Hard Truths of Ta-Nehisi Coates." July 12, 2015, *New York Magazine*, http://nymag.com/daily/intelligencer/2015/07/ta-nehisi-coates-between-the-world-and-me.html; NPR, "Ta-Nehisi Coates on His Work and the Painful Process of Getting Conscious," November 21, 2015, http://www.npr.org/2015/11/21/456879598/ta-nehisi-coates-on-his-work-and-the-painful-process-of-getting-conscious; Ta-Nehisi Coates, "The Case for Reparations," June 2014, *The Atlantic*; Michelle Alexander, "Ta-Nehisi Coates's 'Between the World and Me,'" August 17, 2015, *New York Times*, http://www.nytimes.com/2015/08/17/books/review/ta-nehisi-coates-between-the-world-and-me.html?_r=0; Ta-Nehisi Coates, *Between the World and Me* (New York: Spiegel & Grau, 2015).

3. "Ta-Nehisi Coates on His Work and the Painful Process of Getting Conscious," NPR interview, *All Things Considered*, November 21, 2015, http://www.npr.org/2015/11/21/456879598/ta-nehisi-coates-on-his-work-and-the-painful-process-of-getting-conscious.
4. Wallace-Wells, "The Hard Truths of Ta-Nehisi Coates."
5. Alexander, "Ta-Nehisi Coates's 'Between the World and Me.'"
6. "Ta-Nehisi Coates on His Work and the Painful Process of Getting Conscious," NPR interview.
7. Kevin Corder and Christina Wolbrecht, "Political Context and the Turnout of New Women Voters After Suffrage," *Journal of Politics* 68 (2006): 34–49.
8. Samuel Huntington, "The United States," in *The Crisis of Democracy*, ed. Michael Crozier, Samuel Huntington, and Joji Watanuki (New York: NYU Press, 1975), 59–115.
9. Steven E. Finkel "Reciprocal Effects of Participation and Political Efficacy: A Panel Analysis," *American Journal of Political Science* 29, no. 4 (1985): 891–913; Steven E. Finkel, "The Effects of Participation on Political Efficacy and Political Support: Evidence from a West German Panel," *Journal of Politics* 49, no. 2 (1987): 441–64. These articles provide empirical evidence that supports the arguments of Carol Pateman, *Participation and Democratic Theory* (New York: Cambridge University Press, 1970).
10. This section draws heavily on Alexander Keyssar, *The Right to Vote: The Contested History of Democracy in the United States* (New York: Basic Books, 2001).
11. Washington actually won 132 of the 135 Electoral College votes in 1792. Three electors—one from Vermont and two from Maryland—did not cast ballots.
12. Keyssar, *The Right to Vote*, 10–21.
13. For detailed data on the 1824 presidential election, see John T. Woolley and Gerhard Peters, "Election of 1824," The American Presidency Project, accessed June 7, 2012, http://www.presidency.ucsb.edu/showelection.php?year=1824.
14. Some now question the claims of a "corrupt bargain." See Jeffrey A. Jenkins and Brian R. Sala, "The Spatial Theory of Voting and the Presidential Election of 1824," *American Journal of Political Science* 42, no. 4 (1998): 1157–79.
15. Elisabeth Griffith, *In Her Own Right: The Life of Elizabeth Cady Stanton* (New York: Oxford University Press, 1984), 153–54. See also Doug Linder, "The Trial of Susan B. Anthony for Illegal Voting," 2001, accessed June 7, 2012, http://www.law.umkc.edu/faculty/projects/ftrials/anthony/sbaaccount.html.
16. Harold Gosnell, *Getting Out the Vote* (Chicago: University of Chicago Press, 1927).
17. Corder and Wolbrecht, "Political Context," 46.
18. Ibid.
19. Measuring turnout can be done a number of different ways, and each way can yield different estimates. If you ask people if they voted, many will say yes even if they did not. "Self-reports" inflate turnout numbers. The numbers used in the paragraph are simply the reported vote in the election divided by the number of people eligible to vote—or what is called voting-age population (VAP).
20. Harold W. Stanley and Richard Niemi, *Vital Statistics on American Politics 2013–2014* (Thousand Oaks, CA: CQ Press, 2013).
21. Ronald L. F. Davis, "Creating Jim Crow: In-Depth Essay," The History of Jim Crow, http://www.jimcrowhistory.org/history/creating2.htm.
22. This figure underestimates the true cost of the poll tax in today's dollars. We divided $2 by $86 to arrive at 2.3 percent. We then multiplied the 2.3 percent by $43,000, the median income in the United States in 2000. The precise dollar estimate is $989. But the average income of blacks in the South was surely less than $86, and that ignores the issue that African Americans would rarely have that much cash available to them.
23. J. Morgan Kousser, "Poll Tax," in *The International Encyclopedia of Elections* (Washington, D.C.: CQ Press, 1999), 208–09.
24. *Smith v. Allwright*, 321 U.S. 649 (1944).
25. Sarah A. Binder and Steven S. Smith, *Political or Principle: Filibustering in the United States Senate* (Washington, D.C.: Brookings Institution Press, 1996).
26. The term *negroes* was commonly used at the time. Poll conducted by Opinion Research Corporation, October 15–November 15, 1963, retrieved June 21, 2012, from the iPOLL Databank, The Roper Center for Public Opinion Research, University of Connecticut.
27. Stanley and Niemi, *Vital Statistics on American Politics 2013–2014*.
28. Thomas Rochon and Ikuo Kabashima, "Movement and Aftermath," in *Politicians and Party Politics*, ed. John G. Geer (Baltimore, Md.: Johns Hopkins University Press, 1998), 102–21.
29. Paul Taylor and Mark Hugo Lopez, "Six take-aways from the Census Bureau's voting report," Pew Research Center, May 8, 2013. http://www.pewresearch.org/fact-tank/2013/05/08/six-take-aways-from-the-census-bureaus-voting-report/; Tami Luhby, "How Hillary Clinton Lost," CNN Politics. November 9, 2016. http://www.cnn.com/2016/11/09/politics/clinton-votes-african-americans-latinos-women-white-voters/index.html?curator=MediaREDEF.
30. Even as of 2013, the U.S. Census estimated that over 25 percent of Americans aged 5 and over speak a language other than English at home. U.S. Census, "Detailed Languages Spoken at Home and Ability to Speak English for the Population 5 Years and Over: 2009–2013," October 2015, http://www.census.gov/data/tables/2013/demo/2009-2013-lang-tables.html. In 2009, among Latinos, the average across all groups was 76 percent. Tallese D. Johnson, Merarys Rios, Malcolm P. Drewery, Sharon R. Ennis, and Myoung Ouk Kim, U.S. Department of Commerce, U.S. Bureau of the Census, "People Who Spoke a Language Other than English at Home by Ethnic Origin and Race: 2009," 2010.
31. *Katzenbach v. Morgan*, 384 U.S. 641 (1966).
32. 42 USC 203 §1973 to 1973bb.
33. Voting Rights Act Language Assistance Amendments of 1992: Hearings on S. 2236 before the Subcomm. on the Constitution of the Senate Comm. on the Judiciary [1992 hearings], 102d Cong., 2d Sess., S. Hrg. 102-1066, at 134 (1992).
34. Jens Manuel Krogstag, "2016 Electorate Will Be the Most Diverse in U.S. History," Pew Research Center, February 3, 2016, http://www.pewresearch.org/fact-tank/2016/02/03/2016-electorate-will-be-the-most-diverse-in-u-s-history/.
35. Marisa Abrajano and Michael Alvarez, *New Faces, New Voices: The Hispanic Electorate in America* (Princeton, N.J.: Princeton University Press, 2010); Matt A. Barreto, Gary M. Segura, and Nathan D. Woods, "The Mobilizing Effect of Majority-Minority Districts on Latino Turnout," *American Political Science Review* 98, no. 1 (2004): 65–75; Matt A. Barreto, Loren Collingwood, and Sylvia Manzano, "A New Measure of Group Influence in Presidential Elections: Assessing Latino Influence in 2008," *Political Research Quarterly* 63 (2010): 908–21.
36. National Conference of State Legislatures, January 4, 2016, *Voter Identification Requirements, Voter Laws*, http://www.ncsl.org/research/elections-and-campaigns/voter-id.aspx.
37. *Crawford v. Marion County Election Board*, 553 U.S. 181 (2008). See also Bill Mears, "High Court Upholds Indiana's Voter ID Law," CNN, April 28, 2008, http://articles.cnn.com/2008-04-28/politics/scotus.voter.id_1_voter-impersonation-voter-id-laws-voter-fraud?_s=PM:POLITICS; Linda Greenhouse, "In a 6-to-3 Vote, Justices Uphold a Voter ID Law," *New York Times*, April 29, 2008.

38. American Civil Liberties Union, "*Applewhite et al. v. Commonwealth of Pennsylvania*, et al.," accessed May 19, 2012, http://www.aclupa.org/our-work/legal/legaldocket/applewhite-et-al-v-commonwealth-pennsylvania-et-al/; Rick Lyman, "Pennsylvania Voter ID Law Struck Down as Judge Cites Burden on Citizens," *New York Times*, January 17, 2014, http://www.nytimes.com/2014/01/18/us/politics/pennsylvania-voter-id-law-struck-down.html.

39. Wade Goodwin, "Texas Voter ID Law Creates a Problem for Some Women," October 20, 2013, http://www.npr.org/2013/10/30/241891800/texas-voter-id-law-creates-a-problem-for-some-women.

40. Matt A. Barreto and Gabriel R. Sanchez, "Accepted Photo Identification and Different Subgroups in the Eligible Voter Population, State of Texas," Expert Report Submitted on Behalf of Plaintiffs in *Veasey v. Perry*, Case 2:13-cv-00193, June 27, 2014, http://www.latinodecisions.com/blog/wp-content/uploads/2014/10/Texas-Voter-ID-Expert-Report_Barreto_Sanchez.pdf.

41. 42 USC 203 §1973 to 1973bb.

42. There were four exceptions: the voting age was 18 in Georgia and Kentucky, 19 in Alaska, and 20 in Hawaii.

43. See http://elections.gmu.edu/Turnout_2012G.html, accessed June 3, 2014.

44. Michael P. McDonald, "2016 Presidential Nomination Contest Turnout Rates," U.S. Elections Project, accessed April 2, 2016, http://www.electproject.org/2016P.

45. Jan Leighley, "Attitudes, Opportunities, and Incentives," *Political Research Quarterly* 48 (1995): 184.

46. Stanley and Niemi, *Vital Statistics on American Politics 2013–2014*.

47. See http://www.pewresearch.org/fact-tank/2013/05/08/six-take-aways-from-the-census-bureaus-voting-report/, accessed June 3, 2014.

48. Jan E. Leighley and Jonathan Nagler, *Who Votes Now?* (Princeton, N.J.: Princeton University Press, 2014).

49. See http://www.pewresearch.org/fact-tank/2013/05/08/six-take-aways-from-the-census-bureaus-voting-report/, accessed June 3, 2014; U.S. Census. *Voting and Registration in the Election of 2012*, https://www.census.gov/hhes/www/socdemo/voting/publications/p20/2012/tables.html.

50. Mark Hugo Lopez and Paul Taylor, "Latino Voters in the 2012 Election," Pew Research Center, November 7, 2012, http://www.pewhispanic.org/2012/11/07/latino-voters-in-the-2012-election/; Jens Manuel Krogstag and Mark Hugo Lopez, "Hilary Clinton wins Latino vote, but falls below 2012 support for Obama," Pew Research Center. November 9, 2016. http://www.pewresearch.org/fact-tank/2016/11/09/hillary-clinton-wins-latino-vote-but-falls-below-2012-support-for-obama/, accessed November 10, 2016.

51. See, for instance, Raymond Wolfinger and Steven Rosenstone, *Who Votes?* (New Haven, Conn.: Yale University Press, 1980). There has been much research since the publication of this book, but it remains a leading source on this topic.

52. U.S. Census, *Voting and Registration in the Election of 2012*, https://www.census.gov/hhes/www/socdemo/voting/publications/p20/2012/tables.html.

53. Cindy D. Kam and Carl L. Palmer, "Reconsidering the Effects of Education on Political Participation," *Journal of Politics* 70, no. 3 (2008): 612–31; Rachel Milstein Sondheimer and Donald Green, "Using Experiments to Estimate the Effects of Education on Voter Turnout," *American Journal of Political Science* 54, no. 1 (2010): 174–89.

54. Anthony Downs, *An Economic Theory of Democracy* (New York: Harper, 1957).

55. Howard Gillman, *The Votes That Counted* (Chicago: University of Chicago Press, 2001), 77.

56. William Riker and Peter Ordeshook, "A Theory of the Calculus of Voting," *American Political Science Review* 62 (1968): 25–42.

57. For other efforts to solve this problem, see John H. Aldrich, "Rational Choice and Turnout," *American Journal of Political Science* 37, no. 1 (1993): 246–78; Robert Grafstein, "An Evidential Decision Theory of Turnout," *American Journal of Political Science* 35 (1991): 989–1010.

58. These data are from a survey by Pew Research Center for the People & the Press, conducted by Princeton Survey Research Associates International, April 4–April 15, 2012, retrieved June 3, 2014, from the iPOLL Databank, The Roper Center for Public Opinion Research, University of Connecticut.

59. Allyson Holbrook and Jon Krosnick, "Vote Over-Reporting: Testing the Social Desirability Hypothesis in Telephone and Internet Surveys" (paper presented at the annual meeting of the American Association for Public Opinion Research, Miami Beach, Florida, 2009).

60. David Campbell, *Why We Vote* (Princeton, N.J.: Princeton University Press, 2006).

61. Kids Voting USA, http://www.kidsvotingusa.org/. The information in the caption for Image 11.4 is drawn from this website.

62. G. Bingham Powell Jr., "American Voter Turnout in Comparative Perspective," *American Political Science Review* 80 (1986): 17–43; Henry Brady, Sidney Verba, and Kay Schlozman, "Beyond SES: A Resource Model of Political Participation," *American Political Science Review* 89 (1995): 271–94.

63. John Zipp, "Perceived Representativeness and Voting: An Assessment of the Impact of 'Choices' vs. 'Echoes,'" *American Political Science Review* 79 (1985): 50–61.

64. Alan Gerber, Donald Green, and David Nickerson, "Getting Out the Vote in Local Elections: Results from Six Door-to-Door Canvassing Experiments," *Journal of Politics* 65 (2003): 4.

65. Allison Dale and Aaron Strauss, "Don't Forget to Vote: Text Message Reminders as a Mobilization Tool," *American Journal of Political Science* 53 (2009): 787–804.

66. Steven J. Rosenstone and John Mark Hansen, *Mobilization, Participation, and Democracy in America* (New York: Macmillan, 1993).

67. James H. Fowler, Laura A. Baker, and Christopher T. Dawes, "Genetic Variation in Political Participation," *American Political Science Review* 102, no. 2 (2008): 233–48.

68. James H. Fowler and Christopher T. Dawes, "Two Genes Predict Voter Turnout," *Journal of Politics* 70 (2008): 579–94.

69. Evan Charney and William English, "Candidate Genes and Political Behavior," *American Political Science Review* 106 (2012): 1–34.

70. Brad T. Gomez, Thomas G. Hansford, and George A. Krause, "The Republicans Should Pray for Rain: Weather, Turnout, and Voting in U.S. Presidential Elections," *Journal of Politics* 69 (2007): 649–63.

71. Frances Fox Piven and Richard A. Cloward, *Why Americans Still Don't Vote: And Why Politicians Want It That Way* (Boston: Beacon Press, 2000); Martin P. Wattenberg, *Where Have All the Voters Gone?* (Boston: Harvard University Press, 2002); Thomas E. Patterson, *The Vanishing Voter: Public Involvement in an Age of Uncertainty* (New York: Alfred A. Knopf, 2003).

72. "2016 November General Election Turnout Rates," United States Election Project, http://www.electproject.org/2016g (accessed November 15, 2016).

73. "2016 November General Election Turnout Rates," United States Election Project, http://www.electproject.org/2016g (accessed November 15, 2016); "National General Election VEP Turnout Rates, 1789–Present," United States Election Project, http://www.electproject.org/national-1789-present (accessed November 15, 2016).

74. Powell, "American Voter Turnout in Comparative Perspective," 17–37.

75. This "puzzle of participation" was first discussed by Richard Brody in *The New American Political System,* ed. Anthony King (Washington, DC: American Enterprise Institute for Public Policy Research, 1978).

76. Warren Miller, "Puzzle Transformed," *Political Behavior* 14 (1992): 1–43.

77. Rosenstone and Hansen, *Mobilization, Participation, and Democracy in America.*

78. Ibid.

79. Keena Lipsitz, Christine Trost, Matthew Grossman, and John Sides, "What Voters Want from Campaign Communication," *Political Communication* 22 (2005): 337–54.

80. Steven Ansolabehere and Shanto Iyengar, *Going Negative* (New York: Free Press, 1995).

81. John G. Geer, *In Defense of Negativity* (Chicago: University of Chicago Press, 2006).

82. See, for example, Joshua Clinton and John Lapinski, "'Targeted' Advertising and Voter Turnout: An Experimental Study of the 2000 Presidential Election," *Journal of Politics* 66 (2004): 69–96.

83. Richard R. Lau, Lee Sigelman, and Ivy Brown Rovner, "A New Meta-Analysis," *Journal of Politics* 69 (2007): 1176–209.

84. Jens Manuel Krogstag and Jeffrey S. Passel, "5 Facts About Illegal Immigration in the U.S.," Pew Research Center. November 19, 2015, http://www.pewresearch.org/fact-tank/2015/11/19/5-facts-about-illegal-immigration-in-the-u-s/.

85. Ann E. Carson, Bureau of Justice Statistics, "Prisoners in 2014," September 17, 2015, http://www.bjs.gov/index.cfm?ty=pbdetail&iid=5387; Pew Safety Performance Project, *One in 100: Behind Bars in America 2008* (Washington, DC: Pew Center on the States, February 2008), http://www.pewtrusts.org/en/research-and-analysis/reports/0001/01/01/one-in-100.

86. Michael P. McDonald and Samuel L. Popkin, "The Myth of the Vanishing Voter," *American Political Science Review* 95 (2001): 963–74.

87. *Evenwel v. Abbott*, 578 U.S. (2016).

88. Larry Bartels, *Unequal Democracy* (Princeton, NJ: Princeton University Press, 2008).

89. Task Force on American Inequality, "American Democracy in an Age of Rising Inequality," American Political Science Association, 2004.

90. Bartels, *Unequal Democracy.*

91. See http://www.slate.com/blogs/weigel/2014/04/24/gilens_and_page_find_that_rich_americans_rule_politics_but_despair_the_fact.html, accessed June 3, 2014.

92. See Dayton McKean, *The Boss: The Hague Machine in Action* (New York: Russell and Russell Publishers, 1967), for an account of the corrupt practices of machine politicians.

93. See James Bryce, *The American Commonwealth* (New York: Macmillan, 1895).

94. For the best account of the importance and impact of registration, see Benjamin Highton, "Voter Registration and Turnout in the United States," *Perspectives on Politics* 2 (2004): 507–15.

95. National Conference of State Legislatures, *Same-Day Voter Registration*, June 2, 2015, http://www.ncsl.org/research/elections-and-campaigns/same-day-registration.aspx. The states are Colorado, Connecticut, Idaho, Illinois, Iowa, Maine, Minnesota, Montana, New Hampshire, Wisconsin, and Wyoming.

96. Karyn Rotker, "State History and Immigrant Voting," *Milwaukee Journal Sentinel*, October 29, 2006.

97. Highton, "Voter Registration and Turnout."

98. Read about the National Voter Registration Act of 1993 at http://www.justice.gov/crt/about/vot/nvra/activ_nvra.php.

99. Texas Secretary of State Carlos H. Cascos' official website, http://www.sos.state.tx.us/ and http://www.votetexas.gov/.

100. See http://www.oregonlive.com/mapes/index.ssf/2013/03/in_last_presidential_election.html, accessed June 3, 2014.

101. See https://www.sos.state.co.us/pubs/rule_making/written_comments/2009/111009_commoncause_votebymailproject.pdf, accessed June 30, 2014.

102. National Conference of State Legislatures, *Absentee and Early Voting*, March 24, 2016, http://www.ncsl.org/research/elections-and-campaigns/absentee-and-early-voting.aspx.

103. Paul Gronke, Eva Galanes-Rosenbaum, and Peter A. Miller, "Early Voting and Turnout," *PS: Political Science and Politics* (October 2003): 639–45.

104. Steven Yaccino and Lizette Alvarez, "New G.O.P. Bid to Limit Voting in Swing States," *New York Times*, March 29, 2014.

105. Jeffrey Gottfried, "When Discussing Politics, Family Plays Larger Role for Women than for Men," Pew Research Center, August 5, 2015, http://www.pewresearch.org/fact-tank/2015/08/05/when-discussing-politics-family-plays-larger-role-for-women-than-for-men/.

106. Vietnam War Protests, http://www.history.com/topics/vietnam-war/vietnam-war-protests, accessed April 4, 2016.

107. See some of the following literature on social movements and protest behavior: David S. Meyer and Sidney Tarrow, eds., *The Social Movement Society: Contentious Politics for a New Century* (Lanham, MD: Rowman & Littlefield, 1998); Sidney Tarrow, *Power in Movement: Social Movements, Collective Action and Politics* (Cambridge, U.K.: Cambridge University Press, 1994); Russell J. Dalton, *Citizen Politics: Public Opinion and Political Parties in Advanced Industrial Democracies*, 6th ed. (Washington, DC: CQ Press, 2013); M. Kent Jennings, "Residues of a Movement: The Aging of the American Protest Generation," *American Political Science Review* 81 (1987): 367–82; Neal Caren, Andrew Raj Ghoshal, and Vanesa Ribas, "A Social Movement Generation: Cohort and Period Trends in Protest Attendance and Petition Signing," *American Sociological Review*, 76 (2011): 125–51.

108. Kevin Eagan, Ellen Bara Stolzenberg, Abigail K. Bates, Melissa C. Aragon, Maria Ramirez Suchard, and Cecilia Rios-Aguilar, *The American Freshman: National Norms Fall 2015*, Cooperative Institutional Research Program, Higher Education Research Institute, University of California, Los Angeles.

109. John Eligon and Richard Perez-Pena, "University of Missouri Protests Spur Day of Change," *New York Times*, November 9, 2015, http://www.nytimes.com/2015/11/10/us/university-of-missouri-system-president-resigns.html.

110. Ibid.

111. Theda Skocpol and Vanessa Williamson, *The Tea Party and Remaking of Republican Conservativism* (New York: Oxford University Press, 2012).

112. In a poll conducted by Vanderbilt University in May 2012, Tea Party identifiers were less likely to approve of Mitt Romney than Republicans generally. See http://www.vanderbilt.edu/csdi.

113. "The Sad Tale of the Bonus Marchers," Doughboy Center, accessed June 7, 2012, http://www.worldwar1.com/dbc/bonusm.htm.

114. 530 U.S. 703 (2000).

115. 134 S. Ct. 2518 (2014).

116. "Going Too Far: The American Public's Attitudes Toward Protest Movements," The Roper Center for Public Opinion Research, http://ropercenter.cornell.edu/going-too-far-the-american-publics-attitudes-toward-protest-movements/. Figures based on a 2013 poll conducted by AP/Gfk Knowledge Networks, accessed April 24, 2016.

117. Alia Wong and Adrienne Green, "Campus Politics: A Cheat Sheet," *The Atlantic*, April 4, 2016, accessed April 24, 2016, http://www.theatlantic.com/education/archive/2016/04/campus-protest-roundup/417570/.

118. Dennis Johnson, "Communicating with Congress," in *Congress and the Internet*, ed. James A. Thurber and Colton C. Campbell (New York: Prentice Hall, 2003).

119. Congressional Management Foundation. "Communicating with Congress: How Capitol Hill is Coping with the Surge in Citizen Advocacy," accessed April 2, 2016, http://www.congressfoundation.org/component/content/article/68. Data derived from the Office of Chief Administrative Office of the House of Representatives and the U.S. Senate Sergeant at Arms.

120. For one example, see Congressman Jim Cooper's official website at http://www.cooper.house.gov/.

121. Anna Staver, "Sen. Jeff Merkley Decisively Defeats Monica Wehby" *Statesman Journal*, November 4, 2014, accessed November 5, 2014, http://www.statesmanjournal.com/story/news/politics/elections/2014/11/04/sen-jeff-merkley-decisively-defeats-monica-wehby/18509023/.

122. Survey from Harvard Institute of Politics conducted by GfK Knowledge Networks, March 22–April 4, 2014, retrieved June 3, 2014, from the iPoll Databank, The Roper Center for Public Opinion Research, University of Connecticut.

123. See http://swampland.time.com/2012/11/15/exclusive-obamas-2012-digital-fundraising-outperformed-2008, accessed June 3, 2014.

124. Paul Blumenthal, "Election 2012: Fundraising Year-End Totals Reveal Obama Record, GOP Disparity, Rich Super PACs," *Huffington Post*, February 1, 2012, http://www.huffingtonpost.com/2012/02/01/election-2012/02/01/election-2012-fundraising-obama-romney-super-pacs_n_1247228.html; Paul Blumenthal and Aaron Bycoffe, "Here Are the Top Super PAC Mega-Donors in 2014 Elections," *Huffington Post*, November 3, 2014, accessed November 5, 2014.

125. Anu Narayanswamy, Aaron Williams, and Matea Gold, "Meet the wealthy donors who are pouring millions in the 2016 elections," *Washington Post*, November 2, 2016. https://www.washingtonpost.com/graphics/politics/superpac-donors-2016/; "Election 2016: Money Raised as of Oct. 19," *Washington Post*, https://www.washingtonpost.com/graphics/politics/superpac-donors-2016/, accessed November 11, 2016."

126. Jeff Manza and Christopher Ugge, *Locked Out: Felon Disenfranchisement and American Democracy* (Oxford, U.K.: Oxford University Press, 2007).

Chapter 12

1. This story was compiled from information on Representative Joaquín Castro's congressional website, http://castro.house.gov/; Georgia Park, "Castro Highlights Importance of Public Service Work, Leadership," *The Chronicle*, April 2, 2014, http://www.dukechronicle.com/articles/2014/04/02/castro-highlights-importance-public-service-work-leadership; "Interview with Representative Joaquin Castro," *The Situation Room*, CNN, January 4, 2013, http://www.realclearpolitics.com/articles/2013/01/04/interview_with_representative_joaquin_castro_116607.html#ixzz2yDth5yUN; Office of the Secretary of State of Texas, "Race Summary Report, 2012 General Election," November 6, 2012, http://elections.sos.state.tx.us; "Congressman Castro Visits Afghanistan," KSAT-San Antonio, April 7, 2014, http://www.ksat.com/news/Congressman-Castro-visits-Afghanistan/25370616; https://castro.house.gov/media-center/press-releases/castro-coffman-denham-introduce-bipartisan-legislation-supporting-women, accessed February 17, 2016; mysanantonio.com Staff, "2016 Election Winners in Bexar County and Texas," accessed November 9, 2016, at http://www.mysanantonio.com/news/local/politics/electionresults/us_house_by_texas_county.

2. Totals do not include House Delegates or the Resident Commissioner; see Jennifer E. Manning, *Membership of the 114th Congress: A Profile*, CRS Report for Congress, R43869 (Washington, D.C.: Congressional Research Service, October 31, 2015, accessed February 17, 2016, http://www.fas.org/sgp/crs/misc/R3869.pdf); Census.gov, "Annual Estimates of the Resident Population for Selected Age Groups by Sex for the United States, States, Counties, and Puerto Rico Commonwealth and Municipios: April 1, 2010 to July 1, 2014," accessed February 17, 2016, http://factfinder.census.gov/faces/tableservices/jsf/pages/productview.xhtml?src=bkmk.

3. Manning, *Membership*.

4. Ibid. For a broader discussion of the careers of women legislators in the House, see Jennifer Lawless and Sean Theriault, "Will She Stay or Will She Go? Career Ceilings and Women's Retirement from the U.S. Congress," *Legislative Studies Quarterly* 30 (2005): 581–96.

5. Letter from a Federal Farmer to a Republican, October 9, 1787; John DeWitt III, Boston, *American Herald*, November 5, 1787; Brutus III, *New York Journal*, November 15, 1787, http://csac.history.wisc.edu/house_of_representatives.htm.

6. See Wendy J. Schiller and Charles Stewart III, *Electing the Senate: Indirect Democracy Before the Seventeenth Amendment* (Princeton, N.J.: Princeton University Press, 2015), and Lana R. Slack, *Senate Manual: Standing Rules, Orders, Laws, and Resolutions Affecting the Business of the United States Senate* (Washington, D.C.: U.S. Government Printing Office, 1988), 684–85.

7. U.S. Senate, "Senate Classes," Senate.gov, accessed June 21, 2012, http://www.senate.gov/artandhistory/history/common/briefing/Constitution_Senate.htm#3.

8. In rare cases in which a senator dies or resigns, an interim replacement is typically chosen by the governor of the state until an election is held to fill the seat.

9. U.S. Census Bureau, Kristen D. Burnett, "Congressional Apportionment," November 2011, accessed February 17, 2016, http://www.census.gov/prod/cen2010/briefs/c2010br-08.pdf; Census.gov, "Annual Population Estimates," http://www.census.gov/popclock/.

10. After the first census of the new federal government under the Constitution, Congress grew to 105 members in 1792. See Brian Frederick, *Congressional Representation and Constituents: The Case for Increasing the Size of the U.S. House of Representatives* (New York: Routledge, 2010), 23–24.

11. U.S. House of Representatives, "Historical Highlights: The Permanent Apportionment Act of 1929," June 11, 1929, accessed June 21, 2012, http://artandhistory.house.gov/highlights.aspx?action=view&intID=200.

12. For a discussion of representation by Latino members, see Jason P. Casellas, "The Institutional and Demographic Determinants of Latino Representation," *Legislative Studies Quarterly* 34, no. 3 (2009): 399–426; see also David Leal and Frederick M. Hess, "Who Chooses Experience? Examining the Use of Veteran Staff by House Freshmen," *Polity* 36 (2004): 651–64.

13. U.S. Bureau of the Census, "Fast Facts for Congress," My Congressional District (the American Community Survey), accessed February 17, 2016, http://www.census.gov/fastfacts/.

14. See *Shaw v. Reno*, 509 U.S. 630 (1993); *Miller v. Johnson*, 515 U.S. 900 (1995); and *Easley v. Cromartie*, 532 U.S. 234 (2001). *Thornburg v. Gingles*, 478 U.S. 30 (1986), provides plaintiffs with a right to force a state to create a majority-minority district if the minority community is large and concentrated enough to form a potential voting majority in the district, the minority community votes cohesively, but the white voting prevents the minority community from electing its preferred candidate. For a longer discussion of redistricting, see Bernard Grofman, Lisa Handley, and Richard G. Niemi, *Minority Representation and the Quest for Voting Equality* (New York: Cambridge University Press, 1992).

15. Frances E. Lee and Bruce I. Oppenheimer, *Sizing up the Senate: The Unequal Consequences of Equal Representation* (Chicago: University of Chicago Press, 1999).

16. Two prominent works on this point are Richard F. Fenno Jr., *The Power of the Purse: Appropriations Politics in Congress* (Boston: Little, Brown, 1966), and Aaron B. Wildavsky, *The New Politics of the Budgetary Process* (Boston: Addison-Wesley Educational, 1992).

17. Fiona McGillivray, "Trading Free and Opening Markets," in *International Trade and Political Institutions,* ed. Fiona McGillivray, Iain McLean, Robert Pahre, and Cheryl Schonhardt-Bailey (Cheltenham, U.K.: Edward Elgar, 2001), 80–98.
18. *Wickard v. Filburn*, 317 U.S. 111 (1942).
19. U.S. Courts: Federal Courts, http://www.uscourts.gov/FederalCourts.aspx.
20. Sarah A. Binder and Forrest Maltzman, "Senatorial Delay in Confirming Federal Judges, 1947–1998," *American Journal of Political Science* 46, no. 1 (2002): 190–99.
21. Sarah A. Binder, *Majority Rights, Minority Rule* (New York: Cambridge University Press, 1997); Eric Schickler, *Disjointed Pluralism: Institutional Innovation and the Development of the U.S. Congress* (Princeton, N.J.: Princeton University Press, 2001).
22. Sean Gailmard and Jeffery A. Jenkins, "Minority-Party Power in the Senate and the House of Representatives," in *Why Not Parties? Party Effects in the United States Senate*, ed. Nathan W. Monroe, Jason M. Roberts, and David W. Rohde (Chicago: University of Chicago Press, 2008), 181–97.
23. Randall Strahan, *Leading Representatives: The Agency of Leaders in the Politics of the U.S. House* (Baltimore: Johns Hopkins University Press, 2007).
24. Ibid., 79–126.
25. David W. Rohde, *Parties and Leaders in the Postreform House* (Chicago: University of Chicago Press, 1991).
26. Gary W. Cox and Mathew D. McCubbins, *Legislative Leviathan: Party Government in the House* (Berkeley: University of California Press, 1993).
27. Jennifer Steinhauer, "John Boehner, House Speaker, Will Resign from Congress," *New York Times*, September 25, 2015, accessed February 17, 2016, http://www.nytimes.com/2015/09/26/us/john-boehner-to-resign-from-congress.html?_r=0; Mike DeBonis, "Paul Ryan Elected House Speaker," *Washington Post*, October 29, 2015, accessed February 17, 2016, https://www.washingtonpost.com/news/powerpost/wp/2015/10/29/paul-ryan-set-to-be-elected-62nd-house-speaker/.
28. Gallup.com, "Congressional Job Approval at 12% in February," accessed April 16, 2014, http://www.gallup.com/poll/167375/congressional-job-approval-february.aspx.
29. Gallup.com, "Anti-Incumbent Mood Toward Congress Still Going Strong," February 12, 2016, accessed February 17, 2016, http://www.gallup.com/poll/189215/anti-incumbent-mood-toward-congress-going-strong.aspx?g_source=POLITICS&g_medium=topic&g_campaign=tiles.
30. Barry C. Burden and Tammy M. Frisbee, "Preferences, Partisanship, and Whip Activity in the U.S. House of Representatives," *Legislative Studies Quarterly* 29 (2004): 569–90.
31. Ralph Huitt, "Democratic Party Leadership in the Senate," *American Political Science Review* 55 (1961): 333–44.
32. E. Scott Adler and John Wilkerson, "Intended Consequences: Jurisdictional Reform and Issue Control in the U.S. House of Representatives," *Legislative Studies Quarterly* 33, no. 1 (2008): 85–112.
33. David W. Rohde, "Committee Reform in the House of Representatives and the Subcommittee Bill of Rights," *Annals of the American Academy of Political and Social Science* 411, no. 1 (1974): 39–47.
34. For a list of current caucuses, see Committee on House Administration, "112th Congress Congressional Member Organizations (CMO)," updated April 11, 2012, accessed June 21, 2012, http://cha.house.gov/sites/republicans.cha.house.gov/files/documents/cmo_cso_docs/cmo_112th_congress.pdf.
35. Daily Digest, "Resume of Congressional Activity, First Session of the One Hundred Thirteenth Congress," *Congressional Record D195,* February 27, 2014; Daily Digest, "Resume of Congressional Activity, Second Session of the One Hundred Thirteenth Congress," *Congressional Record D224,* March 4, 2015, http://thomas.loc.gov.
36. For an extended discussion of the right of recognition and the powers it affords senators, see Floyd Riddick, *Senate Procedure,* ed. Alan Frumin (Washington D.C.: U.S. Government Printing Office, 1992), 1091–99.
37. Sarah A. Binder and Steven S. Smith, *Politics or Principle: Filibustering in the U.S. Senate* (Washington, D.C.: Brookings Institution Press, 1997). For a discussion of the use of the filibuster by retiring senators, see Martin Overby, L. Overby, and Lauren Bell, "Rational Behavior or the Norm of Cooperation? Filibustering Among Retiring Senators," *Journal of Politics* 66 (2004): 906–24.
38. For more details on the cloture rules and other changes, see Valerie Heitshusen, Congressional Research Service, "Majority Cloture for Nominations: Implications and the 'Nuclear' Proceedings," December 6, 2013, R43331, accessed April 16, 2014, http://www.fas.org/sgp/crs/misc/R43331.pdf.
39. David Stout, Carl Hulse, and Sheryl Gay Stolberg, "Senate Backs Disputed Judicial Nomination," *New York Times*, October 27, 2007, A21; Robert Barnes, "Scalia's Death Plunges Court, National Politics into Turmoil," *Washington Post*, February 13, 2016 accessed February 17, 2016, https://www.washingtonpost.com/national/scalias-death-plunges-court-national-politics-into-turmoil/2016/02/13/136c0590-d2a4-11e5-b2bc-988409ee911b_story.html.
40. Wendy J. Schiller, "Resolved the Filibuster Should Be Abolished—Con," in *Debating Reform*, 3rd ed., ed. Richard J. Ellis and Michael Nelson (Washington, D.C.: CQ Press, 2016).
41. Wendy J. Schiller, "Senators as Political Entrepreneurs: Using Bill Sponsorship to Shape Legislative Agendas," *American Journal of Political Science* 1 (1995): 186–203.
42. Glen Krutz, *Hitching a Ride: Omnibus Legislating in the U.S. Congress* (Columbus: Ohio State University Press, 2001).
43. For a general discussion on committees, see Keith R. Krehbiel, *Information and Legislative Organization* (Ann Arbor: University of Michigan Press, 1991).
44. For a few examples of this work, see Aage Clausen, *How Congressmen Decide* (New York: St. Martin's Press, 1973); John Kingdon, *Congressmen's Voting Decisions* (New York: Harper & Row, 1989); David W. Brady, *Critical Elections and Congressional Policy Making* (Stanford, Calif.: Stanford University Press, 1988); Stanley Bach and Steven S. Smith, *Managing Uncertainty in the U.S. House of Representatives* (Washington, D.C.: Brookings Institution Press, 1989). For examples of the ideological examination of roll call voting, see Keith T. Poole and Howard Rosenthal, *Ideology and Congress* (New Brunswick, N.J.: Transaction Publishers, 2009).
45. Donald R. Wolfensberger, Bipartisan Policy Center, "Information on the 114th Congress," accessed February 17, 2016, http://bipartisanpolicy.org/wp-content/uploads/2015/05/BPC-Profile-114th-Congress.pdf; David Hawkings, "Lessons for This Year in Voting Patterns of Last Year," Rollcall.com, March 16, 2015, accessed February 17, 2016, http://blogs.rollcall.com/hawkings/cq-vote-studies-2014/; Keith Poole and Howard Rosenthal, Voteview.com, "Party Unity Scores by Chamber for All Two-Party Systems," May 31, 2015, accessed February 17, 2016, http://voteview.com/Party_Unity.htm.
46. C. Lawrence Evans and Walter J. Oleszek, "Message Politics and Senate Procedure," in *The Contentious Senate: Partisanship, Ideology and the Myth of Cool Judgment,* ed. Colton C. Campbell and Nicol C. Rae (Lanham, Md.: Rowman and Littlefield, 2000).
47. Barbara Sinclair, *Unorthodox Lawmaking: New Legislative Processes in the U.S. Congress,* 4th ed. (Washington, D.C.: CQ Press, 2011).
48. Bureau of Labor Statistics, "Labor Force Statistics from the Current Population Survey," http://data.bls.gov/timeseries/LNS14000000.
49. Department of Labor, "Unemployment Insurance 75th Anniversary," accessed April 17, 2014, http://www.dol.gov/ocia/pdf/75th-Anniversary-Summary-FINAL.pdf.
50. Staff, Department of Labor, "Chronology of Federal Unemployment Compensation Laws, February 2014," accessed April 17, 2014, http://workforcesecurity.doleta.gov/unemploy/pdf/chronfedlaws.pdf.

51. Congressional Budget and Impoundment Control Act of 1974 (Public Law 93-344). For additional background on budget history, see the Senate Budget Committee's website, http://www.budget.senate.gov/democratic/public/index.cfm/history-of-the-budget-committee.

52. Balanced Budget and Emergency Deficit Control Act of 1985 (Public Law 99-177). For historical tables on the U.S. federal budget, see Congressional Budget Office, "The Budget and Economic Outlook Fiscal Years 2012 to 2022," January 31, 2012, accessed June 21, 2012, http://www.cbo.gov/publication/42905. The Fiscal 1985 budget deficit number is taken from Table F-1, http://www.cbo.gov/publication/42911.

53. Walter J. Oleszek, *Congressional Procedures and the Policy Process,* 6th ed. (Washington, D.C: CQ Press, 2004), especially 63–69. For a more comprehensive look at the history of budget politics and deficits, see Jasmine Farrier, *Passing the Buck: Congress, Budgets, and Deficits* (Lexington: University of Kentucky Press, 2004).

54. Kathleen Hunter, "GOP Readies Procedural Salvo Against Reconciliation Play," *CQ Weekly Online,* March 8, 2010, 568.

55. Charles M. Cameron, *Veto Bargaining: Presidents and the Politics of Negative Power* (New York: Cambridge University Press, 2000).

56. Albert D. Cover and Bruce S. Brumberg, "Baby Books and Ballots: The Impact of Congressional Mail on Constituent Opinion," *American Political Science Review* 76 (1982): 347–59.

57. Richard L. Hall, *Participation in Congress* (New Haven, Conn.: Yale University Press, 1998).

58. Tracy Sulkin, *Issue Politics in Congress* (New York: Cambridge University Press, 2005).

59. Daily Digest, "Resume of Congressional Activity, First Session of the One Hundred Thirteenth Congress," *Congressional Record D195*, February 27, 2014; Daily Digest, "Resume of Congressional Activity, Second Session of the One Hundred Thirteenth Congress," *Congressional Record D224*, March 4, 2015, http://thomas.loc.gov.

60. For a comprehensive look at this congressional activity, see Diana Evans, *Greasing the Wheels: Using Pork Barrel Projects to Build Majority Coalitions in Congress* (New York: Cambridge University Press, 2004).

61. Jennifer A. Dlouhy, "Alaska 'Bridge to Nowhere' Funding Gets Nowhere; Lawmakers Delete Project After Critics Bestow Derisive Moniker," *San Francisco Chronicle*, November 17, 2005, A7.

62. Citizens Against Taxpayer Waste, "2010 Pig Book Summary," accessed June 21, 2012, http://www.cagw.org/content/2010-pig-book-summary.

63. Richard F. Fenno Jr., *Home Style: House Members in Their Districts* (Boston: Little, Brown, 1978).

64. David R. Mayhew, *Congress: The Electoral Connection* (New Haven, Conn.: Yale University Press, 1974).

65. For an extended discussion of how senators from the same state interact, see Schiller, *Partners and Rivals.*

66. Center for Responsive Politics, "Reelection Rates Over the Years," opensecrets.com, accessed February 17, 2016, https://www.opensecrets.org/bigpicture/reelect.php.

67. Michael McDonald, United States Elections Project, "2016 November General Election Turnout Rates," accessed November 14, 2016, at http://www.electproject.org/2016g; Joseph P. Williams, "Clinton Made Her Case to Black Voters. Why Didn't They Hear Her?," U.S. News.com, accessed November 10, 2016, at http://www.usnews.com/news/politics/articles/2016-11-09/clinton-made-her-case-to-black-voters-why-didnt-they-hear-her; Jens Manual Krogstad, Mark Hugo Lopez, Gustavo Lopez, Jeffrey S. Passel, and Eileen Patten, "Millennials Make Up Almost Half of Latino Eligible Voters in 2016," Pew Research Center Hispanic Trends, accessed November 10, 2016, at http://www.pewhispanic.org/2016/01/19/millennials-make-up-almost-half-of-latino-eligible-voters-in-2016."

Chapter 13

1. Sylvia Mathews Burwell, "Testimony before the Senate Health, Education, Labor, and Pensions Committee," May 8, 2014, accessed May 15, 2014, http://www.help.senate.gov/imo/media/doc/Burwell.pdf.

2. This story was compiled from the Office of Management and Budget's website, http://www.whitehouse.gov/omb; President Barack Obama, transcript of "Remarks by the President in Nominating Sylvia Mathews Burwell as Secretary of Health and Human Services," October 9, 2013, http://www.whitehouse.gov; Dylan Matthews, "Sylvia Mathews Burwell: Six Things to Know about the New White House Budget Director," Wonkblog, *Washington Post*, March 3, 2013; "Q&A: Sylvia Mathews, President of the Gates Foundation Global Development Program," *Seattle Times*, March 17, 2007; Jennifer Haberkorn, "Sylvia Mathews Burwell's Hurdles," *Politico*, April 11, 2014; Sarah Plummer, "Obama Taps Hinton Native for Budget Chief," *The Register-Herald*, March 5, 2013.

3. Hedrick Smith, "Bush Says He Sought to Avoid Acting Like Surrogate President," *New York Times*, April 12, 1981, A1, http://www.nytimes.com/1981/04/12/us/bush-says-he-sought-to-avoid-acting-like-surrogate-president.html.

4. Bruce G. Peabody and Scott E. Grant, "The Twice and Future President: Constitutional Interstices and the Twenty-Second Amendment," *Minnesota Law Review* 83 (1999): 565–94.

5. "The Presidents," The White House, accessed June 22, 2012, http://www.whitehouse.gov/about/presidents.

6. Arthur Schlesinger Jr., *The Imperial Presidency* (New York: Mariner Books, 2004; first published 1973).

7. U.S. Department of Justice, Office of the Pardon Attorney, "Clemency Statistics," accessed September 12, 2016, http://www.justice.gov/pardon/statistics.htm.

8. Neil A. Lewis, "Delay Denied, Libby Is Seen as Weeks From Prison," *New York Times*, June 15, 2007, www.nytimes.com/2007/06/15/washington/15libby.html.

9. Robert Wielaard, "Kosovo Recognition Irritates Russia and China," *Herald-Tribune*, February 19, 2008, A11, http://www.heraldtribune.com/article/20080219/NEWS/802190626.

10. Charles M. Cameron, *Veto Bargaining: Presidents and the Politics of Negative Power* (New York: Cambridge University Press, 2000).

11. Glenn S. Krutz, *Hitching a Ride: Omnibus Legislating in the U.S. Congress* (Columbus: Ohio State University Press, 2001). Also see Cameron, *Veto Bargaining*.

12. William W. Lammers and Michael A. Genovese, *The Presidency and Domestic Policy* (Washington, D.C.: CQ Press, 2000), 315–24.

13. Wilson delivered the speech on December 2, 1913. See John T. Woolley and Gerhard Peters, "Length of State of the Union Messages and Addresses (in words), Washington–Obama," The American Presidency Project, accessed June 22, 2012, http://www.presidency.ucsb.edu/sou_words.php#axzz1yaTY1UIo.

14. Jeff Cummins, "State of the Union Addresses and the President's Legislative Success," *Congress and the Presidency* 37 (2010): 176–99.

15. The chronology that follows is taken from the *Washington Post*'s history of Watergate, available online at http://www.washingtonpost.com/wp-srv/onpolitics/watergate/chronology.htm.

16. Ibid.

17. William G. Howell, *Power Without Persuasion: The Politics of Direct Presidential Action* (Princeton, N.J.: Princeton University Press, 2003).

18. Harold C. Relyea, *Presidential Directives: Background and Overview,* CRS Report for Congress, 98-611 (Washington, D.C.: Congressional Research Service, 2007).

19. Kenneth R. Mayer, "Executive Orders and Presidential Power," *Journal of Politics* 61 (1999): 445–66, especially 448.

20. Ibid.

21. Harry S. Truman, "Memo 'Concerning the Interpretation of the President's Order . . . ,'" Harry S. Truman Library & Museum, ca. 1948, accessed June 22, 2012, http://www.trumanlibrary.org/whistlestop/study_collections/desegregation/large/documents/index.php?documentdate=1948-00-00&documentid=5-20&studycollectionid=&pagenumber=1&sortorder=.

22. "Executive Order 10730, Providing Assistance for the Removal of an Obstruction of Justice within the State of Arkansas," news release, September 24, 1957, Dwight D. Eisenhower Presidential Library & Museum, http://www.eisenhower.archives.gov/research/online_documents/civil_rights_little_rock/Press_Release_EO_10730.pdf.

23. Christopher S. Kelley and Bryan W. Marshall, "The Last Word: Presidential Power and the Role of Signing Statements," *Presidential Studies Quarterly* 38 (2008): 248–67; Michael J. Berry, "Controversially Executing the Law: George W. Bush and the Constitutional Signing Statement," *Congress and the Presidency* 36 (2009): 244–71.

24. The White House, "Memorandum for the Heads of Executive Departments and Agencies: Subject: Presidential Signing Statements," news release, March 9, 2009, http://www.whitehouse.gov/the-press-office/memorandum-presidential-signing-statements.

25. Gerhard Peters, "Executive Orders Washington–Obama," The American Presidency Project, ed. John T. Woolley and Gerhard Peters, accessed November 7, 2016, http://www.presidency.ucsb.edu/data/orders.php; John T. Woolley, "Presidential Signing Statements, Hoover–Obama," The American Presidency Project, ed. John T. Woolley and Gerhard Peters, accessed November 7, 2016, http://www.presidency.ucsb.edu/signingstatements.php?year=2016&Submit=DISPLAY.

26. Joseph A. Pika and John Anthony Maltese, *The Politics of the Presidency*, 8th ed. (Washington, D.C.: CQ Press, 2012), 14–16.

27. "Bully Pulpit," C-SPAN Congressional Glossary, accessed June 22, 2012, http://legacy.c-span.org/guide/congress/glossary/alphalist.htm.

28. George C. Edwards III, *On Deaf Ears: The Limits of the Bully Pulpit* (New Haven, Conn.: Yale University Press, 2006).

29. John T. Woolley and Gerhard Peters, "Presidential News Conferences, Hoover–Obama," The American Presidency Project, accessed November 7, 2016, http://www.presidency.ucsb.edu/news_conferences.php.

30. Zachary A. Goldfarb and Juliet Eilperin, "White House Looking for New Ways to Penetrate Polarized Media," *Washington Post*, May 6, 2014, accessed online May 7, 2014, http://www.washingtonpost.com/politics/white-house-looking-for-new-ways-to-penetrate-polarized-media/2014/05/06/ebd39b6c-d532-11e3-aae8-c2d44bd79778_story.html; Melvin C. Laracey, *Presidents and People: The Partisan Story of Going Public* (College Station: Texas A&M University Press, 2002); Reed L. Welch, "Presidential Success in Communicating with the Public Through Televised Addresses," *Presidential Studies Quarterly* 33 (2003): 347–65; Samuel Kernell and Laurie L. Rice, "Cable and the Partisan Polarization of the President's Audience," *Presidency Studies Quarterly* 41, no. 4 (2011): 693–711.

31. Richard E. Neustadt, *Presidential Power and the Modern Presidents* (New York: Free Press, 1990).

32. Jon R. Bond, Richard Fleisher, and B. Dan Wood, "The Marginal and Time Varying Effect of Public Approval on Presidential Success in Congress," *Journal of Politics* 65 (2003): 92–110.

33. Andrew Barrett and Matthew Eshbaugh-Soha, "Presidential Success on the Substance of Legislation," *Political Research Quarterly* 60 (2007): 100–12.

34. Emily Jane Charnock, James A. McCann, and Kathryn D. Tenpas, "Presidential Travel from Eisenhower to George W. Bush: An Electoral College Strategy," *Political Science Quarterly* 124 (2009): 323–39.

35. Joint Resolution of Congress, House Joint Resolution 1145, August 7, 1964, *Department of State Bulletin,* August 24, 1964, reprinted in Henry Steele Commager and Milton Cantor, eds., *Documents of American History,* 10th ed. (Englewood Cliffs, N.J.: Prentice Hall, 1988), 2: 690.

36. Louis Fisher, *Presidential War Power,* 2nd ed. (Lawrence: University Press of Kansas, 2004), 128–33.

37. Ibid., 144–51.

38. For a longer discussion of this struggle for power over the conduct of war, see William G. Howell and Jon C. Pevenhouse, *Congressional Checks on Presidential War Powers* (Princeton, N.J.: Princeton University Press, 2007).

39. For more on presidential decisions to engage in military conflicts, see James Meernick, "Domestic Politics and the Political Use of Military Force by the United States," *Political Research Quarterly* 54 (2001): 889–904.

40. U.S. House of Representatives, House Joint Resolution, 114 Section 3(a)1, Library of Congress, http://thomas.loc.gov.

41. John J. Kruzel, "Afghanistan Troop Level to Eclipse Iraq by Midyear," United States Army, March 25, 2010, http://www.army.mil/article/36297/.

42. Afghanistan International Security Assistance Force, ISAF, NATO, accessed August 23, 2016, http://www.isaf.nato.int/troop-numbers-and-contributions/index.php.

43. This paragraph is based on "Libya", *New York Times,* updated June 7, 2016, http://www.nytimes.com/topic/destination/libya.

44. This section is based on "Syria," *New York Times,* updated June 7, 2016, http://www.nytimes.com/topic/destination/syria.

45. Shibley Telhami, "American Public Attitudes Towards ISIS and Syria," Brookings Institution, January 8, 2015, accessed March 4, 2016, http://www.brookings.edu/research/reports/2015/01/08-american-opinion-poll-isis-syria-telhami.

46. *Hamdi v. Rumsfeld,* 542 U.S. 507 (2004).

47. *Rasul v. Bush*, 542 U.S. 466 (2004).

48. *Hamdan v. Rumsfeld*, 548 U.S. 557 (2006).

49. Scott Shane and Thom Shanker, "Yemen Strike Reflects U.S. Shift to Drones as Cheaper War Tool," October 2, 2011, *New York Times*, accessed May 6, 2014, http://www.nytimes.com/2011/10/02/world/awlaki-strike-shows-us-shift-to-drones-in-terror-fight.html?_r=0.

50. Craig Whitlock, "U.S. Airstrike that Killed American Teen in Yemen Raises Legal, Ethical Questions," *Washington Post*, October 22, 2011, accessed May 6, 2014, http://www.washingtonpost.com/world/national-security/us-airstrike-that-killed-american-teen-in-yemen-raises-legal-ethical-questions/2011/10/20/gIQAdvUY7L_story.html.

51. White House, Office of the Press Secretary, "Remarks by the President at the National Defense University, May 23, 2013," http://www.whitehouse.gov/the-press-office/2013/05/23/remarks-president-national-defense-university.

52. Staff, "Public Continues to Back U.S. Drone Attacks" Pew Research Center, May 28, 2015, accessed March 4, 2016, http://www.people-press.org/2015/05/28/public-continues-to-back-u-s-drone-attacks/

53. *Boumediene v. Bush*, 553 U.S. 723 (2008)

54. James P. Pfiffner, *The Modern Presidency,* 6th ed. (Boston: Wadsworth Cengage Learning, 2011), 99; White House, "The Executive Branch: Executive Office of the President," accessed May 15, 2014, http://www.whitehouse.gov/our-government/executive-branch#eop.

55. Fred I. Greenstein, *Presidential Difference,* 3rd ed. (Princeton, N.J.: Princeton University Press, 2009).

56. Mondale wrote a detailed memorandum to President Carter outlining his views of the office of vice president. For a broader discussion of Mondale's vice presidential tenure, see Richard Moe, "The Making of the Modern Vice Presidency: A Personal Reflection," *Minnesota History* 60 (2006): 88–99.

57. Joel K. Goldstein, "The Rising Power of the Modern Vice Presidency," *Presidential Studies Quarterly* 38, no. 3 (2008): 389.

58. For background on the story of Marian Anderson, see Raymond Arsenault, *Sound of Freedom: Marian Anderson, the Lincoln Memorial, and the Concert That Awakened America* (New York: Bloomsbury Press, 2009).

59. Stephen Skowronek, *The Politics Presidents Make: Leadership from John Adams to Bill Clinton* (Cambridge, Mass.: Harvard University Press, 1997). Also see Stephen Skowronek, *Presidential Leadership in Political Time: Reprise and Reappraisal* (Lawrence: University Press of Kansas, 2008).

60. Aaron Wildavsky, "The Two Presidencies" in *The Presidency,* ed. Aaron Wildavsky (Boston: Little, Brown, 1969), 231–43.

61. For a test of this theory, see Brandes Canes-Wrone, William G. Howell, and David E. Lewis, "Toward a Broader Understanding of Presidential Power: A Reevaluation of the Two Presidencies Thesis," *Journal of Politics* 69 (2007): 1–16.

62. Lammers and Genovese, *Presidency and Domestic Policy.* See also Neustadt, *Presidential Power and the Modern Presidents.*

63. Samuel Kernell, *Going Public: New Strategies of Presidential Leadership*, 4th ed. (Washington, D.C.: CQ Press, 2007), 131.

64. Ibid., 87–88.

65. Lammers and Genovese, *Presidency and Domestic Policy.*

66. Robert A. Caro, *The Years of Lyndon Johnson: The Passage of Power* (New York: Alfred A. Knopf, 2012), 487. Also see Lyndon Johnson's commencement address at Howard University, "To Fulfill These Rights," June 4, 1965, accessed June 22, 2012, http://www.lbjlib.utexas.edu/johnson/archives.hom/speeches.hom/650604.asp.

67. Lynn Rosellini, "'Honey, I Forgot to Duck,' Injured Reagan Tells Wife," *New York Times*, March 21, 1981, http://www.nytimes.com/1981/03/31/us/honey-i-forgot-to-duck-injured-reagan-tells-wife.html.

68. American Rhetoric, "Top 100 Speeches," accessed June 22, 2012, http://www.americanrhetoric.com/newtop100speeches.htm.

69. Hank C. Jenkins-Smith, Carol L. Silva, and Richard W. Waterman, "Micro- and Macro-level Models of the Presidential Expectations Gap," *Journal of Politics* 67 (2005): 690–715.

Chapter 14

1. Mike M. Ahlers, "Fired Air Marshal Loses Battle in Job Fight," *CNN.com*, August 5, 2011, http://www.cnn.com/2011/US/08/05/air.marshal.fired/index.html.

2. *Department of Homeland Security v. MacLean* (Supreme Court case), http://www.supremecourt.gov/opinions/14pdf/13-894_e2qg.pdf. 135 S. Ct. 913 (2015).

3. This story was compiled from the Transportation Security Administration website, http://www.tsa.gov/careers/; Jacob Gershman, "U.S. Takes Whistleblower Case against Air Marshal to Supreme Court," *Wall Street Journal*, January 28, 2014, http://blogs.wsj.com/law/2014/01/28/u-s-takes-whistleblower-case-against-air-marshal-to-supreme-court/; Peter Van Buren, "The Next Battleground in the War on Whistleblowers," *The Nation*, March 4, 2014; Dan Weikel, "Air Marshal Whistle-blower Fired in 2006 Claims Big Win in Court," *Los Angeles Times*, May 25, 2013; Government Accountability Project, "Robert MacLean, Air Marshal Whistleblower," http://www.whistleblower.org/robert-maclean-air-marshal-whistleblower; Laurence Hurley, "Supreme Court Agrees to Hear Air Marshal Whistleblower Case," Reuters News Service, printed in *Chicago Tribune*, May 19, 2014, http://www.chicagotribune.com/news/nationworld/la-na-nn-air-marshal-whistleblower-20140519,0,6366235.story; 135 S. Ct. 913 (2015) accessed April 2, 2016, at http://www.supremecourt.gov/opinions/14pdf/13-894_e2qg.pdf

4. Max Weber, *Economy and Society,* ed. Guenther Roth and Claus Wittich (Berkeley: University of California Press, 1978).

5. The White House, Office of Management and Budget, *Fiscal Year 2017 Analytical Perspectives, Budget of the U.S. Government* (Washington, D.C.: U.S. Government Printing Office, 2016), Table 8-3, Total Federal Employment, p. 83, accessed March 29, 2016, http://www.whitehouse.gov/sites/default/files/omb/budget/fy2017/assets/spec.pdf.

6. "President Jefferson in the White House," Eyewitness to History, 2006, accessed June 27, 2012, http://www.eyewitnesstohistory.com/jeffersonwhitehouse.htm.

7. "The Cabinet," The White House, accessed April 2, 2016, http://www.whitehouse.gov/administration/cabinet.

8. The White House, Office of Management and Budget, *Fiscal Year 2017 Analytical Perspectives, Budget*, Table 8.2, p. 82; Table 25-11, "Budget Authority by Agency in the Adjusted Baseline," p. 379, accessed March 29, 2016, http://www.whitehouse.gov/sites/default/files/omb/budget/fy2017/assets/spec.pdf.

9. Department of Health and Human Services, "HHS Programs and Services," accessed March 29, 2016, http://www.hhs.gov/about/programs/index.html.

10. The White House, Office of Management and Budget, *Fiscal Year 2017 Analytical Perspectives, Budget,* Table 8.2.

11. U.S. Department of Health and Human Services, "About HHS," http://www.hhs.gov/about/.

12. James Q. Wilson, *Bureaucracy* (New York: Basic Books, 1989), 91.

13. Donald F. Kettl, *System Under Stress: Homeland Security and American Politics,* 2nd ed. (Washington, D.C.: CQ Press, 2007), 37–39.

14. Matt Egan, "BP, Oil Plaintiffs Hammer Out Settlement," FOXBusiness, April 18, 2012, http://www.foxbusiness.com/industries/2012/04/18/bp-oil-spill-plaintiffs-hammer-out-settlement/.

15. Ian Urbina, "U.S. Said to Allow Drilling Without Needed Permits," *New York Times*, May 13, 2010, http://www.nytimes.com/2010/05/14/us/14agency.html?pagewanted=all.

16. NPR staff, "White House Lifts Ban on Offshore Drilling," NPR, October 12, 2010, http://www.npr.org/templates/story/story.php?storyId=130512541.

17. Egan, "BP, Oil Plaintiffs Hammer Out Settlement"; Jennifer Larina, "BP Oil Spill: Claims Payments Reach $5.6 Billion," *Times-Picayune*, September 3, 2015, accessed March 29, 2016, http://www.nola.com/business/index.ssf/2015/09/bp_oil_spill_claims_56_billion.html.

18. Michael Austin, "Everything You Need to Know About the GM Ignition Switch Recall," *Popular Mechanics,* February 26, 2014, accessed May 8, 2014, http://www.popularmechanics.com/cars/news/industry/everything-you-need-to-know-about-the-gm-ignition-switch-recall-16536509; Michael Frank, "The GM Recall Scandal: Who Knew What, and When?" *Popular Mechanics,* March 12, 2014, accessed May 8, 2014, http://www.popularmechanics.com/cars/news/industry/the-gm-recall-scandal-who-knew-what-and-when-16585901; Newsmax, "NTSB Fines GM Record $35M over Faulty Ignitions," May 16, 2014, accessed May 19, 2014, http://www.newsmax.com/Newsfront/gm-fined-millions-cobalt/2014/05/16/id/571748.

19. David Shepardson and Melissa Burden, "GM to Pay $900M to Resolve Ignition Switch Probe," *Detroit News*, September 16, 2015, accessed March 29, 2016, http://www.detroitnews.com/story/business/autos/general-motors/2015/09/16/gm-billion-fine-resolve-ignition-switch-probe/32526023/.

20. Benjamin Zhang, "There's No Way Volkswagen Will Pay the US $18 Billion in Fines for Cheating on Emissions Tests," *Business*

Insider, September 21, 2015, accessed April 4, 2016, http://www.businessinsider.com/theres-no-way-volkswagen-is-going-to-pay-the-us-18-billion-in-fines-for-cheating-on-emissions-tests-2015-9; Russell Hotten, "Volkswagen: The Scandal Explained," BBC News, December 10, 2015, accessed April 4, 2016, http://www.bbc.com/news/business-34324772; Staff, "FTC Sues Volkswagen over 'Clean Diesel' Claims; VW Could Face Billions in Fines," *Chicago Tribune* News Services, March 30, 2016, accessed April 4, 2016, http://www.chicagotribune.com/business/ct-ftc-sues-vw-emissions-20160329-story.html; US Environmental Protection Agency, "Volkswagen Clean Air Act Partial Settlement," June 28, 2016 accessed at https://www.epa.gov/enforcement/volkswagen-clean-air-act-partial-settlement

21. Wilson, *Bureaucracy*, 69–70.
22. Daniel P. Carpenter, *The Forging of Bureaucratic Autonomy: Reputations, Networks, and Policy Innovation in Executive Agencies, 1862–1928* (Princeton, N.J.: Princeton University Press, 2001).
23. U.S. Postal Service, Office of the Postmaster, *The United States Postal Service: An American History, 1775–2006* (Washington, D.C.: Government Relations, U.S. Postal Service, 2007), 6–7, http://about.usps.com/publications/pub100.pdf.
24. Davis Polk, "Dodd-Frank Progress Report," July 19, 2016, accessed August 23, 2016, https://www.davispolk.com/dodd-frank/
25. Michael Moss, "*E. coli* Path Shows Flaws in Beef Inspection," *New York Times*, October 3, 2009, A1; Michael Moss, "*E. coli* Outbreak Traced to Company That Halted Testing of Ground Beef Trimmings," *New York Times*, November 12, 2009, A16; Bill Tomson, "Tuna Blamed in Salmonella Outbreak Is Recalled," *Wall Street Journal*, April 17, 2012, A3.
26. U.S. Consumer Product Safety Commission, http://www.cpsc.gov.
27. "The Consumer Financial Protection Bureau," The White House, September 17, 2010, http://www.whitehouse.gov/photos-and-video/video/2010/09/17/consumer-financial-protection-bureau.
28. Lewis, *Politics of Presidential Appointments*, 12–13.
29. Theda Skocpol, *Protecting Soldiers and Mothers* (Cambridge, Mass.: Harvard University Press, 1992).
30. Sean M. Theriault, *The Power of the People* (Columbus: Ohio State University Press, 2005), Chapter 3.
31. Lewis, *Politics of Presidential Appointments*, 19–20, especially Figure 2.1.
32. U.S. Office of Personnel Management, "Federal Employment Statistics: Federal Civilian Employment," September 2013, accessed April 1, 2016, http://www.opm.gov/feddata/html/geoagy10.asp.
33. Department of Labor, Bureau of Labor Statistics, accessed April 1, 2016, http://www.bls.gov/ooh/about/ooh-faqs.htm.
34. For more on political appointees, see Jeff Gill and Richard Waterman, "Solidary and Functional Costs: Explaining the Presidential Appointment Contradiction," *Journal of Public Administration Research and Theory* 14 (2004): 547–69.
35. Lewis, *Politics of Presidential Appointments*, 11.
36. Ibid., 100, Figure 4.3.
37. Office of Personnel Management, "Diversity and Inclusion: Federal Workforce at a Glance," accessed April 2, 2016, http://www.opm.gov/policy-data-oversight/diversity-and-inclusion/federal-workforce-at-a-glance/.
38. Juliet Eilperin, "Obama Cabinet Picks Add Diversity, But Still Frustrate White House Allies," *Washington Post*, March 4, 2013, http://www.washingtonpost.com/national/health-science/obama-cabinet-picks-add-diversity-but-still-frustrate-white-house-allies/2013/03/04/7e2030a6-84fe-11e2-98a3-b3db6b9ac586_story.html.
39. For an in-depth example of private contracting in Medicaid in New York State, see Nina Bernstein, "Medicaid Shift Sees Rush for Profitable Clients," *New York Times*, May 8, 2014, http://www.nytimes.com/2014/05/09/nyregion/medicaid-shift-fuels-rush-for-profitable-clients.html.
40. U.S. Office of Special Counsel, "Hatch Act," updated October 6, 2011, http://www.osc.gov/hatchact.htm, and "Political Activity and the Federal Employee," http://www.osc.gov/documents/hatchact/ha_fed.pdf, both accessed June 27, 2012.
41. For more on the relationships among bureaucrats, members of Congress, and interest groups, see Anthony M. Bertelli and Christian R. Grose, "Secretaries of Pork? A New Theory of Distributive Public Policy," *Journal of Politics* 71 (2009): 926–45; and Sanford C. Gordon and Catherine Hafer, "Corporate Influence and the Regulatory Mandate," *Journal of Politics* 69 (2007): 300–19.
42. For in-depth studies of congressional oversight, see Charles R. Shipan, "Regulatory Regimes, Agency Actions, and the Conditional Nature of Congressional Influence," *American Political Science Review* 9 (2004): 467–80; Keith W. Smith, "Congressional Use of Authorization and Oversight," *Congress and the Presidency* 37 (2010): 45–63.
43. Richard A. Serrano, "Benghazi Suspect Was Captured While Planning Attacks, Prosecutors Say," *Los Angeles Times*, July 1, 2014, http://www.latimes.com/nation/nationnow/la-na-nn-benghazi-suspect-20140701-story.html.
44. See http://public.tableausoftware.com/views/Veterans_VA_mobile/VeteransAffairs?amp%3B:embed=y&:display_count=no&:showVizHome=no#, accessed May 25, 2014.
45. Scott Bronstein and Drew Griffin, "A Fatal Wait: Veterans Languish and Die on a VA Hospital's Secret List," CNN, April 30, 2014, accessed May 19, 2014, http://www.cnn.com/2014/04/23/health/veterans-dying-health-care-delays/index.html?iid=article_sidebar.
46. Chelsea J. Carter, Greg Seaby, and Greg Botelho, "Rights Group Calls VA Official 'Scapegoat' in Scandal over Wait Times, Care," CNN, May 16, 2014, accessed May 19, 2014, http://www.cnn.com/2014/05/16/politics/va-scandal/.
47. Daniel P. Carpenter, "Groups, the Media, Agency Waiting Costs, and FDA Drug Approval," *American Journal of Political Science* 46, no. 3 (2002): 490–505. Also see Susan L. Moffitt, "Promoting Agency Reputation Through Public Advice: Advisory Committee Use in the FDA," *Journal of Politics* 72, no. 3 (2010): 1–14. For a longer discussion of the history and effectiveness of the FDA, see Daniel P. Carpenter, *Reputation and Power: Organizational Image and Pharmaceutical Regulation at the FDA* (Princeton, N.J.: Princeton University Press, 2010).
48. U.S. Food and Drug Administration, "FDA Safety Communication: Shasta Technologies GenStrip Blood Glucose Test Strips May Report False Results," issued April 29, 2014, accessed May 8, 2014, http://www.fda.gov/MedicalDevices/Safety/AlertsandNotices/ucm395180.htm.
49. L. Paige Whitaker, "The Whistleblower Protection Act: An Overview," CRS Report for Congress, RL33918 (Washington, D.C.: Congressional Research Service, March 12, 2007).
50. Jeffrey M. Jones, "Federal Government Now Worst Rated," Gallup.com, August 24, 2015, accessed April 11, 2016, http://www.gallup.com/poll/184784/americans-views-oil-gas-industry-improvng.aspx?g_source=federal%20government&g_medium=search&g_campaign=tiles.

Chapter 15

1. Material for this vignette taken from Justice Sotomayor's memoir, *My Beloved World* (2013); the Supreme Court case *Schuette v. Coalition to Defend Affirmative Action*, 134 S.Ct. 1623 (2014), http://www.supremecourt.gov/opinions/13pdf/12-682_j4ek.pdf; and an interview on National Public Radio (http://www.npr.org/2013/01/14/167699633/a-justice-deliberates-sotomayor-on-love-health-and-family).
2. "Federal Judgeships," Administrative Office of the United States Courts, accessed May 12, 2014, http://www.uscourts.gov/JudgesAndJudgeships/FederalJudgeships.aspx.
3. Federal litigation data can be found at "Federal Judicial Caseload Statistics 2015," Administrative Office of the U.S. Courts, accessed June 6, 2016, http://www.uscourts.gov/statistics-reports/analysis-reports/federal-judicial-caseload-statistics.
4. *Steelworkers v. Weber*, 443 U.S. 193 (1979).
5. *Firefighters Local Union No. 1784 v. Stotts,* 467 U.S. 561 (1984).
6. *Johnson v. Transportation Agency*, 480 U.S. 616 (1987).
7. *Fullilove v. Klutznick*, 448 U.S. 448 (1980).
8. *Richmond v. J. A. Croson Co.*, 488 U.S. 469 (1989).
9. *Metro Broadcasting, Inc. v. FCC,* 497 U.S. 547 (1990); *Adarand Constructors, Inc. v. Pena,* 515 U.S. 200 (1995).
10. *Regents v. Bakke,* 438 U.S. 265 (1978).
11. *Hopwood v. Texas*, 78 F.3d 932 (1996).
12. See http://www.nbcnews.com/news/latino/more-latinos-whites-admitted-university-california-n85511, accessed June 5, 2014.
13. *Schuette v. BAMN*, 134 S.Ct. 1623 (2014).
14. *Fisher v. University of Texas at Austin*, 133 S. Ct. 2411 (2013).
15. *Fisher v. University of Texas*, 136 S. Ct. 2198 (2016).
16. Federal litigation data, Adminstrative Office of the U.S. Courts.
17. Paul M. Collins Jr., "Friends of the Court: Examining the Influence of *Amicus Curiae* Participation in U.S. Supreme Court Litigation," *Law and Society Review* 38 (2004): 807–32.
18. Rebecca Salokar, *The Solicitor General: The Politics of Law* (Philadelphia: Temple University Press, 1992).
19. Lisa Solowiej and Paul Collins Jr., "Counteractive Lobbying in the U.S. Supreme Court," *American Politics Research* 37 (2009): 670–99.
20. *Regents of the University of California v. Bakke,* 438 U.S. 265 (1978).
21. Federal Bureau of Investigation, *Crime in the United States 2014,* Fall 2015, accessed March 4, 2016, http://www.fbi.gov/about-us/cjis/ucr/crime-in-the-u.s/2014/crime-in-the-u.s.-2014/offenses-known-to-law-enforcement/clearances/main.
22. Mark Motivans, "Federal Justice Statistics 2010," U.S. Department of Justice, Office of Justice Programs, Bureau of Justice Statistics, accessed May 7, 2014, http://www.bjs.gov/content/pub/pdf/fjs10.pdf.
23. Gregory Caldeira and John R. Wright, "Organized Interests and Agenda Setting in the U.S. Supreme Court," *American Political Science Review* 82 (1988): 1109–28.
24. *Hopwood v. Texas*, 78 F.3d 932 (1996).
25. *Obergefell v. Hodges*, 135 S. Ct. 2071 (2015)
26. Nina Totenberg, "Record Number Of Amicus Briefs Filed In Same-Sex-Marriage Cases," *NPR*, April 28, 2015, accessed March 4, 2016, http://www.npr.org/sections/itsallpolitics/2015/04/28/402628280/record-number-of-amicus-briefs-filed-in-same-sex-marriage-cases.
27. Timothy Johnson, Paul Wahlbeck, and James Spriggs, "The Influence of Oral Arguments on the U.S. Supreme Court," *American Political Science Review* 100 (2006): 99–113.
28. Greg Stohr, *A Black and White Case* (Princeton, N.J.: Bloomberg Press, 2006), 277.
29. Timothy Johnson, Paul Wahlbeck, and James Spriggs, "The Influence of Oral Arguments on the U.S. Supreme Court," *American Political Science Review* 100 (2006): 99–113.
30. Alexander Bickel, *The Least Dangerous Branch: The Supreme Court at the Bar of Politics* (Indianapolis: Bobbs-Merrill, 1963).
31. Harold J. Spaeth, Sara Benesh, Lee Epstein, Andrew D. Martin, Jeffrey A. Segal, and Theodore J. Ruger, Supreme Court Database, Version 2015, Release 02, accessed April 6, 2016, http://supremecourtdatabase.org.
32. *Gonzalez v. Raich,* 545 U.S. 1 (2005).
33. Jeffrey A. Segal and Harold J. Spaeth, *The Supreme Court and the Attitudinal Model Revisited* (New York: Cambridge University Press, 2002).
34. Ibid.
35. Lee Epstein and Jack Knight, *The Choices Justices Make* (Washington, D.C.: CQ Press, 1998); Forrest Maltzman, James F. Spriggs II, and Paul J. Wahlbeck, *Crafting Law on the Supreme Court: The Collegial Game* (New York: Cambridge University Press, 2000).
36. Jan Crawford, "Roberts Switched Views to Uphold Health Care Law," *Face the Nation,* CBS News, July 1, 2012, http://www.cbsnews.com/8301-3460_162-57464549/roberts-switched-views-to-uphold-health-care-law/.
37. See Lawrence Baum, *The Puzzle of Judicial Behavior* (Ann Arbor: University of Michigan Press, 1997).
38. Jeffrey A. Segal and Robert M. Howard, "How Supreme Court Justices Respond to Litigant Requests to Overturn Precedent," *Judicature* 85 (2001): 148–57.
39. Jeffrey A. Segal and Robert M. Howard, "A Preference for Deference? The Supreme Court and Judicial Review," *Political Research Quarterly* 57 (2004): 131–43. See also Lori Ringhand, "The Changing Face of Judicial Activism: An Empirical Examination of Voting Behavior on the Rehnquist Natural Court," *Constitutional Commentary* 24 (2007): 43.
40. Gerald Rosenberg, *The Hollow Hope* (Chicago: University of Chicago Press, 1991).
41. *United States v. Nixon,* 418 U.S. 683 (1974).
42. *Reynolds v. Sims*, 377 U.S. 533 (1964).
43. *Roe v. Wade,* 410 U.S. 113 (1973).
44. "Samuel Chase—The Samuel Chase Impeachment Trial," Law Library, accessed May 10, 2012, http://law.jrank.org/pages/5151/Chase-Samuel-Chase-Impeachment-Trial.htm.
45. Lee Epstein and Jeffrey A. Segal, *Advice and Consent: The Politics of Judicial Appointments* (New York: Oxford University Press, 2006).
46. Denis Steven Rutkus and Mitchel A. Sollenberger, *Judicial Nomination Statistics: U.S. District and Circuit Courts, 1977–2003,* CRS Report for Congress, RL31635 (Washington, D.C.: Congressional Research Service, February 23, 2004), Table 2(b), accessed July 1, 2014, http://www.senate.gov/reference/resources/pdf/RL31635.pdf.
47. Russell Wheeler, "Judicial Nominations and Confirmations: Fact and Fiction." *Brookings*, accessed May 7, 2014, http://www.brookings.edu/blogs/fixgov/posts/2013/12/30-staffing-federal-judiciary-2013-no-breakthrough-year.

48. Carrie Severino, "Democrats Obscuring Judicial Facts," *USA Today*, June 7, 2013, http://www.judicialnetwork.com/democrats-obscuring-judicial-facts/.

49. Denis Steven Rutkus and Mitchel A. Sollenberger, *Judicial Nomination Statistics: U.S. District and Circuit Courts, 1977–2003,* CRS Report for Congress, RL31635 (Washington, D.C.: Congressional Research Service, February 23, 2004), Table 2(b), accessed July 1, 2014, http://www.senate.gov/reference/resources/pdf/RL31635.pdf.

50. "Florence E. Allen Named Federal Judge; First Woman to Get Place on Circuit Bench," *New York Times*, March 7, 1934, p. 9.

51. See http://www.blackpast.org/aah/hastie-william-henry-1904-1976, accessed March 4, 2016.

52. See http://www.jtb.org/index.php?src=directory&view=biographies&srctype=detail&refno=98&category=Hispanic%20Judges, accessed March 4, 2016.

53. All data here are from Barry J. McMillion, "U.S. Circuit and District Court Judges: Profile of Select Characteristics," Congressional Research Service, March 19, 2014, accessed March 28, 2016, https://www.fas.org/sgp/crs/misc/R43426.pdf.

54. Christina L. Boyd, Lee Epstein, and Andrew D. Martin, "The Causal Effects of Sex on Judging," *American Journal of Political Science* 54 (2010): 389–411.

55. Adam N. Glynn and Maya Sen, "Identifying Judicial Empathy: Does Having Daughters Cause Judges to Rule for Women's Issues," *American Journal of Political Science* 59 (2015): 37–54.

56. Ibid., 38.

57. Kenneth L. Manning, "¿Como Decide?: Decision-Making by Latino Judges in the Federal Courts," accessed March 4, 2016, http://citation.allacademic.com/meta/p_mla_apa_research_citation/0/8/3/3/9/pages83393/p83393-1.php.

58. Susan B. Haire and Laura P. Moyer, *Diversity Matters: Judicial Policy Making in the U.S. Courts of Appeals* (Charlottesville: University of Virginia Press, 2015).

59. Richard Nixon, "Transcript of President's Announcement," *New York Times*, October 22, 1971.

60. David Yalof, *Pursuit of Justices: Presidential Politics and the Pursuit of Supreme Court Nominees* (Chicago: University of Chicago Press, 1999).

61. Information is from Democratic strategy memos obtained and quoted in part by *USA Today. See* Severino, "Democrats Obscuring Judicial Facts."

62. Lee Epstein, Jeffrey A. Segal, Harold J. Spaeth, and Thomas G. Walker, *The Supreme Court Compendium*, 6th ed. (Washington D.C.: CQ Press, 2015).

63. Jonathan P. Kastellec, Jeffrey R. Lax, and Justin H. Phillips, "Public Opinion and Senate Confirmation of Supreme Court Nominees," *Journal of Politics* 72 (2010): 767–84.

64. *District of Columbia v. Heller*, 554 U.S. 570 (2008).

65. *McDonald v. Chicago*, 561 U.S. 742 (2010).

66. *Citizens United v. FEC*, 558 U.S. 310 (2010).

67. *Printz v. United States*, 521 U.S. 898 (1997).

68. *Friedrichs v. California Teachers Association*, 136 S.Ct. 1083 (2016).

69. Charlie Savage, "A Judge's View of Judging Is on the Record," *New York Times,* May 14, 2009, p. A21, http://www.nytimes.com/2009/05/15/us/15judge.html.

70. Charles M. Cameron, Albert D. Cover, and Jeffrey A. Segal, "Senate Voting on Supreme Court Nominees: A Neoinstitutional Model," *American Political Science Review* 84 (1990): 525–34.

71. Christina Boyd, Lee Epstein, and Andrew D. Martin, "Untangling the Causal Effects of Sex on Judging," *American Journal of Political Science* 54 (2010): 389–411.

72. See, e.g., Karen O'Connor and Jeffrey A. Segal, "Justice Sandra Day O'Connor and the Supreme Court's Reaction to Its First Female Member," *Women and Politics* 10 (1990): 95–104.

73. John J. Szmer, Tammy A. Sarver, and Erin B. Kaheny, "Have We Come a Long Way, Baby? The Influence of Attorney Gender on Supreme Court Decision Making," *Politics and Gender* 6 (2010): 1–36.

74. *McCulloch v. Maryland,* 4 Wheaton 316 (1819); *Gibbons v. Ogden,* 9 Wheaton 1 (1824); and *Cohens v. Virginia,* 6 Wheaton 264 (1821).

75. 60 U.S. 393 (1857).

76. *Slaughterhouse Cases,* 83 U.S. 36 (1873).

77. *United States v. Cruikshank,* 92 U.S. 542 (1876).

78. *Civil Rights Cases,* 109 U.S. 3 (1883).

79. *Brandenburg v. Ohio,* 395 U.S. 444 (1969) (speech rights); *New York Times v. Sullivan,* 376 U.S. 254 (1964) (press rights); *Memoirs v. Massachusetts,* 383 U.S. 413 (1966) (obscenity); and *Engel v. Vitale,* 370 U.S. 421 (1962); *Abington Township School District v. Schempp,* 374 U.S. 203 (1963) (prayer and Bible reading).

80. *Brown v. Board of Education*, 347 U.S. 483 (1954); *Wesberry v. Sanders*, 376 U.S. 1 (1964); *Reynolds v. Sims*, 377 U.S. 533 (1964).

81. *Griswold v. Connecticut*, 381 U.S. 479 (1965) (birth control); *Roe v. Wade,* 410 U.S. 113 (1973).

82. *Mapp v. Ohio*, 367 U.S. 643 (1961); *Miranda v. Arizona*, 384 U.S. 436 (1966).

83. *Swann v. Charlotte-Mecklenburg Board of Education*, 402 U.S. 1 (1971) (busing); *Roe v. Wade*, 410 U.S. 113 (1973) (abortion); *Furman v. Georgia*, 408 U.S. 238 (1972) (death penalty); *Reed v. Reed*, 404 U.S. 71 (1971) (sex discrimination); and *Regents of the University of California v. Bakke,* 438 U.S. 265 (1978) (affirmative action).

84. *San Antonio Independent School District v. Rodriguez*, 411 U.S. 1 (1973) (school funding); *United States v. Leon*, 468 U.S. 897 (1984) (limiting the exclusionary rule); and *New York v. Quarles*, 467 U.S. 649 (1984) (limiting *Miranda*).

85. *Lawrence v. Texas,* 539 U.S. 558 (2003).

86. *Planned Parenthood v. Casey,* 505 U.S. 833 (1992); *United States v. Lopez*, 514 U.S. 549 (1995); *Gratz v. Bollinger*, 539 U.S. 244 (2003); and *Grutter v. Bollinger*, 539 U.S. 306 (2003).

87. *Bush v. Gore*, 531 U.S. 98 (2000).

88. Adam Liptak, "Justices Offer Receptive Ear to Business Interests," *New York Times,* December 19, 2010, p. A1.

89. *Wal-mart Stores v. Dukes*, 131 S. Ct. 2541 (2011).

90. *Citizens United v. Federal Election Commission,* 558 U.S. 310 (2010).

91. *National Federation of Independent Business et al. v. Sebelius*, 132 S. Ct. 2566 (2012).

92. *Obergefell v. Hodges,* 135 S. Ct. 2584 (2015).

93. *Schuette v. Coalition to Defend Affirmative Action*, 133 S. Ct. 1653 (2014).

94. Robert Dahl, "Decision Making in a Democracy: The Supreme Court as a National Policy-Maker," *Journal of Public Law* 6 (1957): 179–295.

95. Herbert M. Kritzer, "Federal Judges and Their Political Environments: The Influence of Public Opinion," *American Journal of Political Science* 23 (1979): 194–207.

96. *West Virginia State Board of Education v. Barnette*, 319 U.S. 624 (1943), 638.

Chapter 16

1. This vignette has been compiled from a series of news items: City of Los Angeles, "Miguel A. Santana Biography," http://cao.lacity.org/SantanaBio.htm; Jon Regardie, "Money, Homelessness and Miguel Santana: The City's Top Budget Cruncher Branches Out in Unexpected Ways," October 13, 2015, Ladowntownnews.com, http://www.ladowntownnews.com/news/money-homelessness-and-miguel-santana/article_08be4c60-6edc-11e5-916a-4394e06dab0e.html; Steve Lopez, "L.A. Official Understands Homelessness as Policymaker, Concerned Citizen," *Los Angeles Times*, November 25, 2015, http://www.latimes.com/local/california/la-me-1125-lopez-santana-20151125-column.html; David Zahniser, "The Man Behind L.A. City Council's Job Cuts Vote," February 22, 2010, *Los Angeles Times*, http://articles.latimes.com/2010/feb/22/local/la-me-santana22-2010feb22.

2. Bryan D. Jones and Frank M. Baumgartner, *The Politics of Attention* (Chicago: University of Chicago Press, 2005).

3. Kate Sheppard, "North Carolina Coal Ash Spill Renews Push For Long-Delayed Federal Regulations" HuffPost.com, February 5, 2014, accessed May 24, 2014, http://www.huffingtonpost.com/2014/02/05/coal-ash-spill-north-carolina_n_4733164.html; U.S. Government Printing Office, July 2, 2015, *Federal Register*, https://www.gpo.gov/fdsys/pkg/FR-2015-07-02/pdf/2015-15913.pdf.

4. *New State Ice Co. v. Liebmann*, 285 U.S. 262 (1932) at 311. See Andrew Karch, *Democratic Laboratories: Policy Diffusion Among the American States* (Ann Arbor: University of Michigan Press, 2007).

5. Craig Volden, "States as Policy Laboratories: Emulating Success in the Children's Health Insurance Program," *American Journal of Political Science* 50 (2006): 294–312.

6. Chris Koski, "Greening America's Skylines: The Diffusion of Low-Salience Policies," *Policy Studies Journal* 38 (2010): 93–117.

7. Michael Mintron and Sandra Vergari, "Policy Networks and Innovations Diffusion: The Case of State Education Reforms," *Journal of Politics* 60 (1998): 126–48.

8. Christopher Stream, "Health Reform in the States: A Model of State Small Group Health Insurance Market Reforms," *Political Research Quarterly* 52 (1999): 499–525.

9. Frederick J. Boehmke and Richard Witmer, "Disentangling Diffusion: The Effects of Social Learning and Economic Competition on State Policy Innovation and Expansion," *Political Research Quarterly* 57 (2004): 39–51.

10. Charles R. Shipan and Craig Volden, "Bottom-Up Federalism: The Diffusion of Antismoking Policies from U.S. Cities to States," *American Journal of Political Science* 50 (2006): 825–43.

11. Robert R. Preuhs, "State Policy Components of Interstate Migration in the United States," *Political Research Quarterly* 52 (1999): 527–47.

12. David M. Konisky, "Regulatory Competition and Environmental Enforcement: Is There a Race to the Bottom?," *American Journal of Political Science* 51 (2003): 853.

13. *Shapiro v. Thompson*, 394 U.S. 618 (1969); *Saenz v. Roe*, 526 U.S. 489 (1999).

14. Craig Volden, "The Politics of Competitive Federalism: A Race to the Bottom in Welfare Benefits?," *American Journal of Political Science* 46 (2006): 352–63.

15. Department of Housing and Urban Development, "HUD Historical Background," http://portal.hud.gov/hudportal/HUD.

16. For details on these programs, see the U.S. Department of Health and Human Services, Centers for Medicare and Medicaid Services (CMS), http://www.cms.hhs.gov.

17. See http://portal.hud.gov/hudportal/documents/huddoc?id=HUDPrograms2016.pdf; also see Center on Budget and Policy Priorities, "Policy Basics: Section 8 Project-Based Rental Assistance," accessed March 22, 2014, http://www.cbpp.org/cms/?fa=view&id=3891.

18. Staff, "Policy Basics: Where Do Our Federal Tax Dollars Go?" Center on Budget and Policy Priorities, March 4, 2016, accessed April 20, 2016, http://www.cbpp.org/research/federal-budget/policy-basics-where-do-our-federal-tax-dollars-go.

19. Centers for Disease Control and Prevention, "Early Release of Selected Estimates Based on Data from the 2010 National Health Interview Survey," CDC.gov, updated and accessed June 14, 2016, http://www.cdc.gov/nchs/nhis/released201106.htm#1.

20. Sabrina Tavernise and Robert Gebeloff, "Immigrants, the Poor and Minorities Gain Sharply Under Affordable Care Act," April 17, 2016, *New York Times*, accessed April 20, 2016, http://www.nytimes.com/2016/04/18/health/immigrants-the-poor-and-minorities-gain-sharply-under-health-act.html?smprod=nytcore-iphone&smid=nytcore-iphone-share&_r=0.

21. Henry J. Kaiser Family Foundation, "Summary of Coverage Provisions in the Patient Protection and Affordable Care Act," *Focus on Health Reform,* updated April 14, 2011, accessed June 21, 2012, http://kff.org/health-costs/issue-brief/summary-of-coverage-provisions-in-the-patient/.

22. Mary Agnes Carey, "Burwell Says 'Beat Goes On' As HHS Seeks To Expand Health Law's Influence" February 5, 2016, Kaiser Health News, accessed April 20, 2016, http://khn.org/news/burwell-says-beat-goes-on-as-hhs-seeks-to-expand-health-laws-influence/.

23. Ibid.

24. Centers for Medicare and Medicaid Services, "Affordable Care Act," http://www.medicaid.gov/AffordableCareAct/Affordable-Care-Act.html.

25. Department of Health and Human Services, "The Affordable Care Act and Latinos," accessed March 10, 2014, http://www.hhs.gov/healthcare/facts/factsheets/2012/04/aca-and-latinos04102012a.html; Tamara Keith, "Obama Pitches Health Care Law to Latinos in a Bid to Boost Enrollment," National Public Radio, March 6, 2014, http://www.npr.org/blogs/codeswitch/2014/03/06/286859961/obama-pitches-health-care-law-to-latinos-in-bid-to-boost-enrollment.

26. Bryan Baker and Nancy Rytina, "Estimates of the Lawful Permanent Resident Population in the United States January 2013," Office of Immigration Statistics, Department of Homeland Security, September 2014, https://www.dhs.gov/sites/default/files/publications/ois_lpr_pe_2013.pdf.

27. U.S. Citizenship and Immigration Services, "About Us," accessed May 31, 2012, http://www.uscis.gov/aboutus.

28. Nadwa Mossaad, *Annual Flow Report: U.S. Lawful Permanent Residents: 2014* (Washington, D.C.: Office of Immigration Statistics, Department of Homeland Security, April 2016), 1. https://www.dhs.gov/sites/default/files/publications/LPR%20Flow%20Report%202014_508.pdf.

29. Ibid., 2. https://www.dhs.gov/sites/default/files/publications/LPR%20Flow%20Report%202014_508.pdf.

30. U.S. Citizenship and Immigration Services, "Statement from Secretary of Homeland Security Janet Napolitano on July 1, 2013," accessed June 13, 2014, http://www.uscis.gov/family/same-sex-marriages.

31. U.S. Citizenship and Immigration Services, "A Guide to Naturalization," http://www.uscis.gov/us-citizenship/citizenship-through-naturalization/guide-naturalization.

32. Bryan Baker and Nancy Rytina, "Estimates of the Unauthorized Immigrant Population Residing in the United States: January 2012," Office of Immigration Statistics Department of Homeland Security, March 2013, https://www.dhs.gov/sites/default/files/publications/ois_ill_pe_2012_2.pdf.

33. U.S. Immigration Support, "Your Online Guide to U.S. Visas, Green Cards and Citizenship," http://www.usimmigrationsupport.org.

34. Luis Miranda, "Get the Facts on the DREAM Act," *White House Blog*, December 1, 2010, http://www.whitehouse.gov/blog/2010/12/01/get-facts-dream-act.

35. The White House, Office of the Press Secretary, "Remarks by the President on Immigration," last modified on June 15, 2012, accessed July 2, 2012, http://www.whitehouse.gov/the-press-office/2012/06/15/remarks-president-immigration.

36. Adam Liptak and Michael D. Shear, "Obama Immigration Plan Seems to Divide Supreme Court," *New York Times*, April 18, 2016, accessed April 20, 2016, http://www.nytimes.com/2016/04/19/us/politics/supreme-court-immigration.html.

37. Randal C. Archibold, "Arizona Enacts Stringent Law on Immigration," *New York Times*, April 23, 2010, A1.

38. Alan Gomez, "In Wake of Immigration Law, Some Migrants Return to Alabama," *USA Today*, February 20, 2012, http://www.usatoday.com/news/nation/story/2012-02-21/alabama-immigration-hispanic/53180746/1.

39. Jack Lewis, "The Birth of the EPA," *EPA Journal* (Washington, D.C.: U.S. Environmental Protection Agency, 1985), http://www.epa.gov.

40. Bruce Jones, "Despite Growing Energy Independence, U.S. Cannot Escape Global Risks," Brookings Institution, May 27, 2014, accessed July 2, 2014, http://www.brookings.edu/blogs/planetpolicy/posts/2014/05/27-energy-independence-us-global-risks-jones.

41. U.S. Energy Information Administration, "International Energy Outlook 2016," May 11, 2016, http://www.eia.gov/forecasts/ieo/.

42. U.S. Census Bureau, "Quick Facts: Flint City, Michigan," accessed April 26, 2016, http://www.census.gov/quickfacts/table/PST045215/2629000.

43. Much of this paragraph and the next one is based on the timeline reported by Merritt Kennedy in "Lead-Laced Water in Flint: A Step-By-Step Look at the Makings of a Crisis," www.npr.com, April 20, 2016, accessed April 21, 2016, http://www.npr.org/sections/thetwo-way/2016/04/20/465545378/lead-laced-water-in-flint-a-step-by-step-look-at-the-makings-of-a-crisis. Also see Staff, "6 Michigan employees indicted in Flint water crisis: report," Jurist, July 29, 2016. Accessed August 29, 2016 at http://www.jurist.org/paperchase/2016/07/6-michigan-employees-indicted-in-flint-water-crisis.php

44. Lachlan Markay and Jay Lucas, "Timeline: Keystone's Three Years in Limbo," *The Foundry* (blog), January 19, 2012, http://blog.heritage.org/2012/01/19/timeline-keystones-three-years-in-limbo/.

45. "Keystone XL Pipeline Project," TransCanada, accessed May 22, 2012, http://www.transcanada.com/keystone.html.

46. House Energy and Commerce Committee, "Keystone XL Review=Anything But Ordinary," accessed June 14, 2016, https://energycommerce.house.gov/news-center/news/keystone-xl-review-anything-ordinary

47. Pierre Bertrand, "Keystone Pipeline: 5 Things You Need to Know," *International Business Times*, January 19, 2012, http://www.ibtimes.com/keystone-pipeline-5-things-you-need-know-397928.

48. John M. Broder, "TransCanada Renewing Request to Build Keystone Pipeline," *New York Times*, February 27, 2012, http://www.nytimes.com/2012/02/28/science/earth/keystone-pipeline-permit-request-to-be-renewed.html?_r=2&hp.

49. President Barack Obama, "Statement by the President on the Keystone XL Pipeline," November 6, 2015, accessed April 21, 2016, https://www.whitehouse.gov/the-press-office/2015/11/06/statement-president-keystone-xl-pipeline.

50. D. Andrew Austin, *The Debt Limit: History and Recent Increases*, CRS Report for Congress, RL31967 (Washington, D.C.: Congressional Research Service, October 1, 2015), http://www.fas.org/sgp/crs/misc/RL31967.pdf.

51. The White House, Office of Management and Budget, Historical Tables, Table 1.1—Summary of Receipts, Outlays, and Surpluses or Deficits (–): 1789–2017; The White House, Office of Management and Budget, Historical Tables, Table 7.1—Federal Debt at the End of Year:—2017. Both tables are available at http://www.whitehouse.gov/omb/budget/Historicals/.

52. Staff, "House Passes Budget Deal to Raise Debt Ceiling—Here Are the 79 Republicans Who Voted for It," TheBlaze.com, October 28, 2015, accessed April 21, 2016, http://www.theblaze.com/stories/2015/10/28/house-passes-budget-deal-to-raise-debt-ceiling-here-are-the-79-republicans-who-voted-for-it/.

53. U.S. Census Bureau, "Trade in Goods with China," accessed April 21, 2016, https://www.census.gov/foreign-trade/balance/c5700.html#2016.

54. Information in this paragraph is from World Trade Organization, http://www.wto.org.

55. "World Trade Organization Adopts Report Ruling in Favor of the United States in Chicken Products Trade Dispute with China," September 25, 2013, https://ustr.gov/about-us/policy-offices/press-office/press-releases/2013/september/WTO-ruling-favor-US-chicken-China.

56. Europa: Gateway to the European Union, http://europa.eu/.

57. Washington's Farewell Address, 1796, Yale Law School Avalon Project, http://avalon.law.yale.edu.

58. Woodrow Wilson, "Address to Congress Requesting a Declaration of War against Germany," April 2, 1917, http://www.millercenter.org.

59. Ellen C. Collier, "Instances of Use of United States Forces Abroad, 1798–1993," Congressional Research Service, October 7, 1993, http://fas.org/man/crs/crs_931007.htm. Also see Naval Historical Center, last modified September 12, 1997, accessed May 12, 2012, http://www.history.navy.mil.

60. John Mueller, *War, Presidents, and Public Opinion* (New York: Wiley, 1970).

61. Presidential Approval Ratings, Gallup Historical Statistics, accessed May 12, 2012, http://www.gallup.com/poll/124922/presidential-approval-center.aspx.

62. "Presidential Approval Ratings," George W. Bush, Gallup.com, accessed May 12, 2012, http://www.gallup.com/poll/124922/presidential-approval-center.aspx.

63. United Nations Office for Disarmament Affairs (UNODA), Treaty on the Non-Proliferation of Nuclear Weapons (NPT), http://www.un.org.

64. Staff, *The Washington Post*, "Full Text of the Iran Nuclear Deal," accessed April 21, 2016, http://apps.washingtonpost.com/g/documents/world/full-text-of-the-iran-nuclear-deal/1651/.

65. President Barack Obama, "Implementation Day," accessed April 21, 2016, https://www.whitehouse.gov/issues/foreign-policy/iran-deal.

66. United States Agency for International Development, http://www.usaid.gov.

67. FY 2016 Congressional Budget Justification , Department of State, Foreign Operations, and Related Programs, accessed April 21, 2016, https://www.usaid.gov/sites/default/files/documents/9276/FY16CBJStateFORP.pdf.

68. World Bank, http://www.worldbank.org.

69. Michael W. Doyle, "Liberalism and World Politics," *American Political Science Review* 80 (1986): 1151–69.

70. World Bank, Archives, http://www.worldbank.org.

71. World Bank, Projects and Operations, http://www.worldbank.org/projects.

72. Information in this and the next paragraphs from International Monetary Fund, http://www.imf.org.

73. "Total IMF Credit Outstanding for All Members from 1984–2016," http://www.imf.org/external/np/fin/tad/extcred1.aspx, and "IMF Members' Quotas and Voting Power, and IMF Board of Governors," http://www.imf.org/external/np/sec/memdir/members.aspx.

74. Bureau of Labor Statistics, "Labor Force Participation Rates from the Current Population Survey," March 2016, accessed April 21, 2016, http://www.bls.gov/web/empsit/cpseea10.htm.

75. Information in this and subsequent paragraphs is from Peace Corps, http://www.peacecorps.gov.

76. FY 2015 budget number taken from the U.S. State Department, https://www.usaid.gov/sites/default/files/documents/9276/FY16CBJStateFORP.pdf.

Index

Note: Page numbers followed by an "f" indicate figures or images. Page numbers followed by a "t" indicate tables.

A

AARP, 253, 279
Abolitionists, 77, 252, 252f, 297, 387
Abortion
  antiabortion protests, 112–13, 113f, 391
  interest groups on, 257–58
  party ideology on, 313
  public opinion on, 187, 192, 192f, 203, 203t, 204
  right to privacy and, 127–29
  Roe v. Wade on, 44, 128–29, 313, 537
Abrams, Jacob, 103
Abu Ghraib facility, 200
Action for America (AFA), 249
Actual malice, 216–17
Adams, Abigail, 144–45
Adams, John, 6–7, 7f, 34f, 44, 74, 102, 222, 296, 324, 452
Adams, John Quincy, 296, 361, 361f
Adams, Samuel, 29
Adams, Sherman, 468
Administrative Procedures Act, 558
Adversary process, 516
Advocacy caucuses, 418–19
Affirmative action, 204, 515, 519–23, 525, 527–29, 531–34. *See also Gratz* and *Grutter* cases
Affordable Care Act (ACA). *See also* Health care
  birth control and, 126–27, 560
  health insurance costs and, 564–65
  implementation of, 485, 565
  interest groups on, 274
  mandate for insurance, 407, 564, 565
  Medicaid expansion and, 407, 565
  passage through Congress, 428
  Supreme Court ruling on, 407, 565
Afghanistan War, 441–42, 456, 458, 462, 463, 580, 588
African Americans
  Black Lives Matter movement, 23f, 156, 271, 389, 389f, 391
  in bureaucracies, 499, 499f
  campaign targeting to, 340
  civil rights movement and, 150–56, 360, 365–66
  in Congress, 399, 400, 400f, 419
  Congressional Black Caucus and, 419
  discrimination against, 137. *See also* Racial segregation and discrimination
  health care for, 564
  Jim Crow laws and, 143, 363, 363f
  in judiciary, 539–40, 539t, 540f, 541, 544
  in news media, 225, 225f
  political opinion and political affiliation, 15, 309, 310–12
  population of, in U.S., 15, 16f
  in presidency, 442
  public opinion among, 204
  racial profiling of, 169–70
  redistricting among, 328–29, 329f, 404
  voting rights, 142–43, 155–56, 359, 360, 362–66
    denial of, 16, 142–43, 359, 362–65
  voting turnout, 148, 366, 367, 369f, 372
Age
  generational effects, 189–90
  generational replacement, 380
  of Millennials, 19, 190, 194f, 214, 235–36, 249, 372, 500–1, 500f
  news media sources by, 235f, 243
  public opinion influenced by, 189–90, 202
  voter turnout and, 315f, 371f, 372
  votes for president by, 315f, 371f
  voting age, 360, 370, 379–80, 380f, 381
Agenda setting
  by news media, 237–38
  by president, 459–60
  in Senate, 421–23
Agnew, Spiro, 441
Aiken, Clay, 347
Air travel
  air traffic controllers' strike, 475
  federal air marshals, 481
  NTSB and, 487–88, 488f
  TSA and, 481
Alabama, immigration actions of, 568
Alcohol use. *See* Drug and alcohol use
Ali, Muhammad, 118
Alito, Samuel, 109, 128, 534, 543, 544, 569
Allen, Florence, 539
al-Qaeda, 463, 466. *See also* bin Laden, Osama
Amendments (to the Constitution)
  amendment process, 43, 43f, 45
  Bill of Rights (First through Tenth Amendments), 39, 50–52, 54f, 68–69, 98, 99–102, 101t, 117, 120–21, 123t, 610–11
  on civil liberties, 52, 98, 99–102, 100f
  on civil rights, 53, 138, 139f, 162–63, 163f
  Civil War Amendments (Thirteenth through Fifteenth), 52–53, 77–78, 137
  on elections, 324, 324f, 328
  Equal Rights Amendment, 162–63, 163f
  to expand public participation, 53, 54f
  on federalism, 67f, 72, 77–79
  First, 52, 106–19, 267
  future amendments, 53, 55
  incorporated provisions of, 99–102, 101t, 117, 120–21, 123
  overturning Supreme Court decisions, 535, 535t
  on presidency, 440–41, 442f
  Second, 52, 120–21
  summary of, 54f
  text of, 610–16
  on voting, 53, 54f, 55, 359–60, 360f, 362, 370
American Anti-Slavery Society, 297
American Association of Automobile Manufacturers, 271
American Bar Association, 538, 540, 541
American Civil Liberties Union (ACLU), 111, 113, 162, 162f, 220, 368, 467
American Civil Rights Institute, 521
American G.I. Forum, 144t, 157
American Independent Party, 303
American Israel Public Affairs Committee (AIPAC), 258
American National Elections Studies, 194
American Nazi Party, 113–14
American Recovery and Reinvestment Act of 2009, 71, 426
American Revolution, 28–31, 30t
Americans for Tax Reform, 276
Americans with Disabilities Act (ADA), 168
America's Natural Gas Alliance (ANGA), 262–63
AmeriCorps, 593
Amicus curiae, 252, 524, 526, 527
Amnesty International, 258
Amtrak, 488
Anarchy, 99
Anderson, John, 303
Anderson, Marian, 469
Andiola, Erika, 135, 162, 321
Annapolis Convention, 33
Anthony, Susan B., 145, 361, 362f
Antifederalists, 48–50, 83, 84, 84f, 295–296, 295t
Anti-nuclear proliferation measures, 588–89, 588f
Appeals, 126, 516, 524–29
Appeals courts, 516, 517, 524–25, 524f, 538–39, 541
Appointments
  Congress and, 41, 406
  judicial, 15, 41, 316, 408f, 421, 422, 442, 450, 537–45
  political appointees, 449–50, 497–99, 502–3
  by president, 15, 44, 316, 408f, 421–22, 442, 449–50, 484, 537–45
  recess appointments, 450
  Schedule C, 498
  Senate approval of, 41, 406, 409, 421–22, 449–50, 537–45
Appropriation, 405

Approval rating, 178–79, 179f, 238, 459, 587
Arab Spring, 463–64
Arizona, immigration actions of, 568–69
Arizona v. United States, 568, 569
Arpaio, Joe, 69f, 321
Arthur, Chester A., 496
Article 1 courts, 517, 517t
Articles of Confederation, 32–33, 37f, 40t
Asian Americans, 16f, 137, 140–41, 143, 205, 369f, 372, 499f
Assange, Julian, 114
Assault weapons ban, 121, 306–7
Association, right of, 52, 116, 250–52
Australia, compulsory voting in, 379
Australian ballot, 299, 300f, 383
Authorize, 405
Autocracy, 14
Automobiles
  bailout for auto industry, 575
  emission standards, 491–92
  fuel efficiency standards, 81, 271–72, 272f
  GM ignition switches, 491
  safety regulations, 491
  unions in auto industry, 254, 255, 256, 278
Awlaki, Anwar al, 106, 466, 467

B

Bakke case, 520, 523, 525, 527, 529, 531, 532
Ballot, 290
  Australian, 299, 300f, 383
Ballot reform, 299, 300f
Banks
  bailout of, 575
  Federal Reserve system, 494, 575, 577–78, 578t, 579f
  National Bank, 70, 75, 76
  regulation of, 494
  World Bank, 589, 591
Barron v. Baltimore, 100
Bartels, Larry, 270
Barton, Joe, 418
Battleground states, 339
Bench trial, 522
Benghazi, Libya, attacks in (2012), 409, 504–5
Bernstein, Carl, 215, 215f, 453
Bicameral Congress, 40–41, 398
Biden, Joseph, 213, 333, 469, 543
Bill of Rights. *See also* Amendments
  civil liberties protection in, 52, 98, 99–102
  importance of, 51–52
  incorporation of provisions to states, 99–102, 101t, 117, 120–21, 123
  limits on power via, 68–69
  not included in original Constitution, 39, 50–51
  summary of, 54f
  text of, 610–11
Bills of attainder, 47, 68–69, 99
bin Laden, Osama, 178, 178f, 463
Birth control, 126–27, 127f, 560
Black Caucus, 419
Black codes, 142
Black Lives Matter movement, 23f, 156, 271, 389, 389f, 391
Bland, Sandra, 156
Blanket primary, 290, 291
Blogs, 218, 231–32, 392, 457–58
Blue slips, 538, 538f
Boehner, John, 412–13, 580–81
Boko Haram, 588
Bork, Robert, 131, 453, 541
Boston Marathon bombing, 56, 466, 474
Boston Massacre, 6, 7f, 29, 30t
Boston Tea Party, 30, 30t
Bowers v. Hardwick, 181
Boy Scouts, 116
Brady Campaign, 307
Branches of government, 10, 11f. *See also* Executive branch; Judicial branch; Legislative branch
Brandeis, Louis, 544, 560
Brat, Dave, 389
Brennan, William, 540
Brewer, Jan, 568
Breyer, Stephen, 529, 533, 534, 543
Bridge to nowhere (Alaska), 431
British Constitution, 28
British Petroleum (BP), 490–91, 491f
Brown, Kate, 63, 87
Brown, Michael, 156, 271
Brown v. Board of Education, 27, 44, 70, 79, 151–52, 153, 455, 534–35
Bryan, William Jennings, 302, 331f
Buchanan, James, 443f
Buckley v. Valeo, 265
Budget, federal
  concurrent budget resolution, 427–28
  continuing resolution, 427–28
  economic opportunity and, 21–22
  federal deficit and national debt, 4, 21, 425, 427, 580–82, 581f
  OMB role in, 439, 468, 476, 486, 559
  reconciliation process, 428
Budget, state, 86
Bully pulpit, 457, 457f
Bundy, Ammon, 84
Bunning, Jim, 423
Bureaucracy, 480–512
  accountability/responsiveness of, 503–9
    bureaucratic failure, 490, 508
    efficiency and transparency, 505–7
    judicial branch and, 505, 506
    legislative branch and, 503, 504–5
    whistleblowing and, 481, 508
  cabinet, 483, 498, 499
  cabinet departments, 484–85, 485t, 486f, 492–93
  cabinet secretaries, 483, 484
  civil service, 299, 497, 502–3
  civil service reforms, 299, 502–3
  components of, 488–92
    bureaucratic culture, 490–92, 491f
    decision-making process, 489
    expertise, 489
    mission, 489
  constitutional foundations, 483–84
  defined, 482–83
  democracy and, 15, 510
  diversity in, 499–501, 499f, 500f
  efficiency and transparency, 505–7
  executive departments, 484–85, 485t, 486f, 492–93
  federal organizations, other, 486–88, 487t, 488f, 495
  federal workforce statistics, 483, 497f
  functions of, 482–83, 482f
  historical evolution of, 492–503
    bureaucrats and politics, 502–3
    career civil servants, 497, 503
    civil service, 299, 497, 502–3
    diversity, 499–501, 499f, 500f
    expansion of executive branch departments, 492–93
    growth of agencies, 493, 495
    patronage system, 299, 495–97
    political appointees, 497–99, 502–3
    private-sector contract workers, 501–2, 501f
  independent agencies and commissions, 487
  interest groups lobbying, 252, 260, 273, 274f, 503
  merit system, 497, 503
  organizational charts, 486f
  oversight and, 409–10, 495, 504–5
  political appointees, 497–99, 502–3
  politics and, 502–3
  private-sector contract workers, 501–2, 503f
  public opinion on, 509
  reform of, 299, 502–3
  regulations and, 481, 483, 484, 559
  regulatory agencies and commissions, 487, 493, 495
  regulatory process, 558–59, 559f
  slowness of, 482, 505–7

structure of, 484–88
whistleblowing and, 481, 508
Burger Court, 181, 548, 549t
Burr, Aaron, 324
Burwell, Sylvia Mathews, 439, 468
Bush, Barbara, 470
Bush, George H. W.
approval ratings, 587
campaign promises of, 351
pardons of, 447
presidential debate, 336
"Read my lips, no new taxes," 351
third party impact on, 303
vice presidency of, 441
Bush, George W.
on affirmative action, 527
Afghanistan War and, 456, 458, 463, 588
antiterrorism measures, 200–1
approval ratings, 178, 238, 587
Bush v. Gore, 326
Cheney, Dick, and, 469
congressional elections and popularity of, 352
election to presidency (2000) and, 185–6, 314, 326, 327, 327f, 627
election to presidency (2004) and, 205, 311, 627
voting demographics, 311
federalism under, 81
foreign nation recognition by, 449
on fuel efficiency standards, 272
immigration stance, 141, 567
Iraq War and, 456, 462–63, 501–2, 587–88
judicial appointments, 539, 539t, 540f, 541
news coverage of, 238, 457
No Child Left Behind Act, 71, 81
pardons of, 447
presidential schedule of, 448, 448f
press conferences by, 457
private contractors and, 501–2
unemployment insurance and, 426
USA PATRIOT Act and, 105, 110
War on Terror and, 105, 456, 465, 467
warrantless wiretapping, 105, 110, 200
Bush, Jeb, 23, 331
Bush, Laura, 470
Bush v. Gore, 326
Byrd rule, 428

C

Cabinet, 485, 498, 499
Cabinet departments, 484–85, 485t, 486f, 492–93
Cabinet secretaries, 483, 484
CAFE (fuel efficiency) standards, 271–72
Calhoun, John C., 75, 77
California Democratic Party v. Jones, 290, 291
Campaign finance
Bipartisan Campaign Reform Act (McCain-Feingold), 267, 268–69, 278
congressional campaigns, 288–89, 346–47
Federal Election Campaign Act, 337
Federal Election Commission, 265, 337, 502
fundraising for, 288–89, 336–38, 337f, 346–47, 392
Internet fundraising, 337, 392
limits on, 268–69, 337–38
matching funds, 339
PACs and, 265–68, 268t, 306, 338
presidential campaigns, 288, 336–38, 337t
Super PACs and, 213, 265, 266, 338, 392
Supreme Court rulings on, 267, 268–69, 279, 337, 338
Campaign issues
congressional campaigns, 346–52
economy, 340–41, 343, 351, 352
fundraising and money, 336–38, 337f, 346–47
microtargeting, 339–40, 340f
negativity, 341–42, 341f–342f, 381
polls and prediction models on, 342–43
position issues, 340–41
presidential campaigns, 336–43
swing states, 338–39
valence issues, 340–41
wedge issues, 341
Campaign promises, 350–51, 350f
Campaigns, 320–54. *See also* Campaign finance; Campaign issues; Elections
battleground states, 339
bureaucratic separation from, 502
campaign promises, 350–51, 350f
citizen involvement in, 386–87, 386t
congressional, 343–52
decision to run and primaries, 343, 345
fall campaign, 345–46
fundraising for, 288–89, 346–47
incumbency advantage, 347–48, 347f, 432–34, 434f
issues in, 346–52
lack of interest and, 349, 351–52
democracy and, 352–53
incumbency advantage, 332–33, 347–48, 347f, 432–34, 434f
interest groups in, 265–69, 265f, 266t, 338
judicial, 87–89
microtargeting and, 339–40, 340f
negativity in, 341–42, 341f–342f, 381
news media and, 232, 234–35, 240, 242
party platform and, 350–51
permanent, 331
polls and prediction models, 186, 342–43
presidential, 330–43
caucuses and primaries, 289, 290–91, 292, 293–94, 299, 333, 333f, 371
debates, 225–26, 225f, 293f, 333f, 335–36, 336f
decision to run, 331–33
endorsements in, 334
evolution of modern, 330–31, 331f
fundraising for, 288, 336–38, 337f
insider-outsider dynamic, 334
invisible primary, 332
issues in, 336–43
national conventions, 292, 335
nomination process, 292–94, 292f–294f, 305
timetable for, 332t
swing states/voters, 338–39
Canada Free Trade Agreement, 582
Cantor, Eric, 389, 433
Capitalism, 12
Capital punishment, 56–57, 56f, 125, 126, 204, 524
Capitol, U.S., 401f
Cardona v. Power, 158
Career civil servants, 497, 503
Cars. *See* Automobiles
Carson, Ben, 331, 340f
Carson, Rachel, *Silent Spring,* 570
Carswell, G. Harrold, 544
Carter, Jimmy, 203, 313, 332, 336, 443, 469, 498, 502, 539
Carter, Rosalynn, 470
Castro, Joaquín, 304, 328, 397, 404, 418, 429, 431f
Castro, Julián, 162, 304, 397, 498, 499
Castro, Rosie, 304
Caucuses, 292, 333, 333f
advocacy, 418–19
party caucus, 288
Cell phones, 122
Censorship, 114–16, 220–21
Center for Constitutional Rights, 467
Center for Responsive Politics, 274
Central Intelligence Agency (CIA), 105, 489, 587
Certiorari, writ of, 518, 526–27
Chaffetz, Jason, 418f
Chamber of Commerce, 253, 254, 308
Chase, Samuel, 537
Chavez, Cesar, 144t, 161
Checks and balances, 10, 45, 46, 47f
Cheney, Richard (Dick), 469
Chevron U.S.A. v. Natural Resources Defense Council, 505, 506
Chief of staff, 468
Child, Lydia Maria, 252f
Child Online Privacy Protection Act (COPPA), 221
Child Online Protection Act (COPA), 221

Christakis, Erika, 108
Christie, Chris, 333, 334
Church, Frank, 104
Cicilline, David N., 306
Cisneros v. Corpus Christi, 70, 144t, 157
Citizen involvement, 4, 89, 264, 359, 386–87, 386t, 516. *See also* Interest groups; Participation; Public opinion; Voting
Citizens for Responsibility and Ethics in Washington (CREW), 264, 264f
Citizens' groups, 257, 264
Citizenship
citizenship clause, 612
defined, 139
demands/responsibilities of, 17, 19–23, 136. *See also* Civil rights
naturalization, 42, 139, 566, 567f
restrictions on, 139–42
undocumented immigrants and, 18, 171, 566
Citizens United v. Federal Election Commission, 54, 213, 267, 269, 338, 392, 543
Civic duty, 375–76
Civic interest, 10, 19, 376
Civil liberties, 96–133
American values and, 106
balancing liberty and order, 99
Bill of Rights and states and, 52, 99–102, 101t
vs. civil rights, 98, 98f, 99, 116, 136
compelling interest test, 101–2, 128
constitutional rights, 99
criminal procedure, 52, 121–26
double jeopardy, 52, 124–25
interrogations, 123, 124f
investigations, 121–23
searches and seizures, 52, 121–23
sentencing, 125
trial procedures, 123–24
verdict, punishment, and appeal, 124–26
defined, 98
democracy and, 129–31
First Amendment, 106–19
freedom of speech, 52, 106–14, 130, 130f
freedom of the press, 52, 114–16
religious freedom, 52, 116–19
right of association, 52, 116
national security and, 105–6, 110–11, 110f, 111f
political tolerance for, 130, 130f, 131
right to privacy, 126–29, 127f
birth control and abortion, 126–29, 127f
homosexual behavior, 129
right to die, 129
student housing, 129
Second Amendment (right to bear arms), 52, 120–21
in times of crisis, 102–06
Cold War and Vietnam, 104–5
Revolution to Civil War, 102–3
War on Terror, 105–06
the World Wars, 103
Civil rights, 134–75. *See also* Discrimination; Racial segregation and discrimination
citizenship restrictions, 139–42
vs. civil liberties, 98, 98f, 99, 116, 136
civil rights movement, 150–71, 360, 365–66
Constitution and, 16, 27, 53, 136–37, 138, 139f, 162–63, 163f
defined, 136
democracy and, 16, 172–73
Democratic party and, 141, 148, 310–13
equality of opportunity and outcome, 137
equal protection, 149–50, 155
ethnicity, discrimination based on, 137, 143, 144t, 150t
dismantling of, 157–62
federalism and, 77–78, 79, 80
felons, voting rights for, 170–71, 170f
frontiers in, 165–71
disability rights, 168–69, 169f
felon voting rights, 170–71, 170f
racial and religious profiling, 169–70
sexual orientation and same-sex marriage, 166–68, 167f, 168f
undocumented immigrants, 171
gender discrimination, 137, 144–47, 150t
dismantling of, 162–65
judicial review, 149–50, 150t
legal restrictions on, 137–68
citizenship restrictions, 139–42
end of, 150–65
ethnic segregation and discrimination, 137, 143, 144t, 150t
gender discrimination, 137, 144–47, 150t
immigration limits, 140, 141–42
racial segregation and discrimination, 137, 142–43, 150t
slavery, 137, 138, 138f
women's suffrage, 144–46, 146f, 147f
private discrimination, 136, 142–43, 149–50, 152, 154–55, 161–62
public discrimination, 136, 142–43, 149–50, 151–52
racial segregation and discrimination, 137, 142–43, 150–56, 150t
dismantling of, 151–56, 360, 365–66
racial voting barriers, dismantling of, 155–56, 360, 365–66
slavery and, 137, 138, 138f
state action, 149
women's suffrage, 144–46, 146f, 147f
workplace equality, 162, 164–65
Civil Rights Act (1866), 142
Civil Rights Act (1875), 78
Civil Rights Act (1964), 80, 154–55, 162, 164–65, 170, 310, 365, 472, 472f
Civil Rights Cases (1883), 78, 169, 547
Civil rights movement, 150–71, 360, 365–66
Civil service
career civil servants, 497, 505
Civil Service Commission, 497
Civil Service Reform Act, 502–3
private-sector contractors and, 501–2, 501f
reforms to, 299, 502–3
Civil society, 15
Civil suits (lawsuits), 516, 522–23
Civil War
Amendments to Constitution, 52–53, 77–78, 137
Emancipation Proclamation during, 77, 138
political parties following, 308–9
Reconstruction after, 142, 363
suspension of *habeas corpus* during, 102–3
Class action lawsuits, 521–22
Clay, Henry, 296, 297, 361
Clean Air Act, 571
Clean Water Act, 571
Clear and present danger test, 107
Climate change, 191, 193, 259, 447, 571
Clinton, Hillary
Benghazi, Libya, attacks and, 504
election for presidency (2008), 3, 163, 442
election for presidency (2016), 17, 22, 147, 148, 294f, 311, 312, 323, 332, 333, 334, 335, 339, 341, 342, 442, 474–75, 509, 592, 626
campaign, 332, 333, 334, 339, 341, 342
debates, 335
Electoral College votes, 323
electoral map, 626
Obama legacy and, 474–75, 509
policy stances, 592
presidential nomination process, 294f
voting demographics, 311, 312
First Lady role of, 470
interest groups on, 267
Clinton, William Jefferson (Bill)
bureaucracy reduction by, 501
campaigns of, 339
congressional elections and popularity of, 351–52
congressional relations with, 451–52
Defense of Marriage Act (DOMA), 73, 167
"don't ask, don't tell" policy, 166
federalism under, 81
impeachment of, 257, 452
judicial appointments, 540f
national health insurance plan, 81
pardons of, 447
party alignment and ideology of, 314
press conferences by, 457
third party impact on, 303
voter turnout for, 370

Cloture, 421, 422f
Club for Growth, 266, 279–80
Coates, Ta-Nehisi, 357, 388
Coercive Acts, 30, 30t
Cohens v. Virginia, 546
COINTELPRO, 104–5
Colbert, Stephen, 213, 231
Cold War, 104–1, 586
College education. *See* Education
Commander in chief, 41–42, 446–47
Commerce, regulation of, 35, 53, 75, 79, 406, 604
Commerce clause, 53, 72, 79, 604
Commission on Presidential Debates, 335
Committees, congressional, 415–18, 417t
  committee chairs, 417–18, 418f
  conference committee, 425
  House Rules Committee, 419–21
  lawmaking action of, 423–24
  legislative responsibility and, 430
  markup and, 417, 424
  ranking member, 418
  standing committees, 415–16, 417t
  subcommittees, 418
Common Cause, 274, 278–79
Common law, 516
Common Sense (Paine), 30–31, 222
Common Sense Action (CSA), 249
Communications Decency Act, 220
Communism
  fears of, 103, 104, 104f, 105f
  foreign policy and, 585, 586
  Vietnam War and, 461
Communities Organized for Public Service (COPS), 159
Compelling interest test, 101–2, 128, 150, 267
Compromise of 1846, 138
Compulsory voting, 379
Comstock, Anthony, 126
Concurrent budget resolution, 427–28
Concurrent powers, 68, 68f
Confederal system, 65, 766f
Conference committees, 425
Confidence interval, 186
Conformity costs, 93
Congress, 396–437. *See also* House of Representatives; Lawmaking; Senate
  Article 1 courts and, 517, 517t
  Articles of Confederation on power of, 32
  bicameralism of, 40–41, 398
  budget and reconciliation, 425, 427–28
  buildings for (U.S. Capitol), 401f
  bureaucratic interaction with, 503, 504–5
  committees in, 415–18, 417t, 419–21, 423–24, 425, 430
  Continental, 30, 30t, 31
  democracy and, 434–35
  demographics of 114th, 399, 400, 400f, 401
  differences between House and Senate, 35, 41, 399–404
    constituencies, 402–3, 403f
    mode of election, 35, 41, 401–2
    qualifications for office, 399, 399t, 401
    redistricting (House), 404
    terms of office, 402
  elections for, 288–89, 432–34
    campaigns, 343–52
    constitutional requirements for, 35, 37, 39, 41, 327–29, 401–2
    fundraising, 288–89, 346–47
    gerrymandering, 328–29, 329f
    incumbency advantage, 347–48, 347f, 432–34, 434f
    midterm, 345, 349, 349f, 351–52, 370–71
    next election, looking towards, 432–34, 434f
    primary, 345
    redistricting, 328–29, 329f, 404
  filibuster and cloture, 421–22, 422f, 539
  House of Representatives. *See* House of Representatives
  lawmaking process, 41, 49–50, 408, 417, 419–29, 430–31, 451, 557
  legislative authority, scope of, 446t, 49–50
  as legislative branch, 10, 11f, 36t, 40–41, 40t, 398–404, 446t, 504–5
  member at work, 429–34
    bill sponsorship, 423–24, 430
    committee work, 430
    communication with constituents, 431–32, 431f
    federal funds/earmarks, 431
    legislative responsibilities, 430–31
    office and staff, 429
    roll call votes, 424–25, 430–31
  omnibus bills, 451
  organization of, 410–19
    advocacy caucuses, 418–19
    committee system, 415–18, 417t
    in House of Representatives, 411–14, 411f–413f, 416f
    party leaders, 413–14, 415, 416f
    political parties and, 410–11
    in Senate, 413–14, 416f
  polarization in, 199f
  policy enactment in, 557. *See also* Policy/policies
  powers of, 405–10, 446t
    appointments and treaties, 41, 406
    authorization of courts, 408–9
    commerce regulation, 35, 53, 406
    enumerated powers, 35, 39, 41, 50–51, 53, 67
    impeachment/removal from office, 41, 406, 408, 452–54
    implied powers, 50, 72, 76
    lawmaking, 41, 49–50, 408
    legislative authority, 49–50, 446t
    override of veto, 41, 428–29, 450–51
    oversight, 409–10, 495, 504–5
    power of the purse, 405
    taxation and appropriation, 35, 41, 49, 53, 78, 79, 405, 407, 505, 580–82
    war powers, 35, 405–6, 446–47, 461–62
  power struggles with president, 461–65
  procedural rules, 419–23
  representation in, 35, 328–29, 398
  Senate. *See* Senate
  terms of office, 347–48, 402
Congressional Budget and Impoundment Control Act (1974), 427, 428
Congress of Racial Equality (CORE), 154
Connecticut Compromise, 35
Connerly, Ward, 521
Conservatives, 11–12, 12f, 195–196, 229, 229t, 231, 233, 233f, 241, 390, 390f. *See also* Republican Party; Tea Party movement
Constitution, 26–60. *See also* Amendments; Bill of Rights
  amendment process, 43, 43f, 45
  Articles of Confederation and, 32–33, 37f, 40t
  balance of freedom and order in, 37f
  British Constitution, 28
  bureaucratic constitutional foundations, 483–84
  capital punishment and, 56–57, 56f
  civil liberties and, 99. *See also* Bill of Rights
  civil rights and, 16, 27, 53, 136–37, 138, 139f, 162–63, 163f
  defined, 28
  democracy and, 6–11, 16, 18, 58
  electoral constitutional requirements, 35, 37, 39, 41, 322–30, 358
  executive authority under, 49, 446t
  executive branch in, 10, 11f, 35, 36t, 40t, 41–42, 446t. *See also* Presidency
  federal authority, 48–49
  federal system and, 10, 45, 46, 65–73, 66f, 76
  Framers of, 7, 9–10, 34f, 65–66, 398, 401f, 610
  as gatekeeper, 7–13
  government before, 28–33, 37f, 40t
  government under, 40–47
  implied powers, 50, 72, 76
  institutional changes, 55, 57
  interpretation of, 27, 53, 409
  judicial branch in, 10, 11f, 35, 36t, 40t, 42–43, 517–18. *See also* Judiciary
  legislative authority under, 49–50, 446t
  legislative branch in, 10, 11f, 36t, 40–41, 40t, 398–404, 446t. *See also* Congress
  partition of power, 45–47, 47f
  presidency eligibility under, 440–42
  public policy and, 556–61
  ratification debates, 48–51
  ratification process, 39
  responsiveness of, 51–57
  state constitutions, 31

Constitution (*continued*)
text of, 39f, 602–9
voting and, 16, 358
Constitutional Convention, 33–40
Bill of Rights not included, 39
Connecticut Compromise, 35
delegates, 33–34
fugitive slave clause, 37
large *vs.* small states, 34–35
nation *vs.* state, 35
New Jersey Plan, 35, 36t
North *vs.* South (slavery issues), 36–37, 38–39, 38f
popular influence limitations, 37, 39
three-fifths compromise, 36, 38–39, 38f
Virginia Plan, 34–35, 36, 36t
Constitutional system, 6–11
Consumer Financial Protection Bureau, 494–95
Consumer Product Safety Commission, 495
Containment, policy of, 586
Content-neutral justification, 112–13, 114f
Continental Congresses, 30, 30t, 31
Continuing resolution, 427–28
Contract with America, 81, 314, 412
Cook, Timothy, 111
Cooperative federalism, 78–80, 78f
Cooper v. Aaron, 455, 536
Cordray, Richard, 450, 494
Cornyn, John, 304
Corporations, 55, 254, 267, 338
Corporations, federal, 488
"Corrupt bargain" election, 361
Council of Economic Advisors, 468, 575
Countermajoritarian difficulty, 528
Court-packing plan, 79, 130, 471, 547
Courts. *See* Judiciary; Supreme Court
Coverture laws, 145, 146
Cox, Archibald, 453
Criminal case, 516, 523–24
Criminal procedure
amendments on, 52, 54f
civil liberties and, 52, 121–26
death penalty, 56–57, 56f, 125, 126, 204, 524
district courts', 523–24
double jeopardy, 52, 124–25, 523–24, 611
interrogations, 123, 124f
investigations, 121–23
plea bargains, 523
reserve powers in, 67–68, 611
searches and seizures, 52, 121–23
sentencing, 125, 524
trial procedures, 123–24, 523–24. *See also* Trial by jury
verdict, punishment, and appeal, 120–26
Cronkite, Walter, 225
Crosby, David, 526f
Cruel and unusual punishment, 52, 56, 125, 611
Cruz, Ted, 23, 42, 42f, 148, 162, 186, 198f, 268, 304, 331, 337, 389

D

Dahl, Robert, 13, 270
"Daisy spot" ad, 341–42, 342f
D'Amato, Alfonse, 538
Day, Benjamin, 223
Dean, Howard, 392
de Anda, James, 157
Death, right to die, 129
Death penalty, 56–57, 56f, 125, 126, 204, 524
Debates, presidential, 225–26, 225f, 293f, 333f, 335–36, 336f
Debs, Eugene V., 103
Debt, national. *See* National debt
Debt ceiling, 580–82
Declaration of Independence
on equality, 15–16, 17
signers of, 601
text of, 598–600
writing and adoption of, 31–32, 31f
Declaration of Sentiments, 145
Deepwater Horizon oil spill, 490–91, 491f
Defense of Marriage Act (DOMA), 73, 167
Delgado, Minerva, 27
DeMint, James, 274, 276
Democracy
alternative models of government, 14
bureaucracy and, 15, 510
civil liberties and, 129–31
civil rights and, 16, 172–73
Congress and, 434–35
constitutional system and, 6–11, 16, 18, 58
defined, 6
demands/responsibilities of, 17, 19–23
direct, 9, 69, 91, 92f
elections, campaigns, and, 15, 352–53
European, 16–17
evaluating, 4–5, 13–17
federalism and, 92–93
interest groups and, 10, 11, 15, 19, 280
judiciary and, 549–50
news, social media, and, 15, 244–45
political parties and, 316–17
presidency and, 476–77
promotion of, 589, 590–91
public opinion and, 15, 208
public policy and, 593–94
pure, 10
representative, 9, 13, 15
responsiveness and equality in, 13–17, 18
successes and problems of, 4–5
voting, participation, and, 10, 16, 19, 22–23, 392–93
Democracy in America (de Tocqueville), 13, 250
Democratic Party. *See also* Political parties
African American affiliation with, 310–12
blanket primaries, 290, 291
civil rights and, 141, 148, 310–13
congressional elections and, 433
emergence of, 297
federalism stance of, 74
Great Society program and, 80, 312
gun control and, 306–7
immigration stance of, 141, 567
interest groups supporting, 266t
Latino affiliation with, 311, 311f, 312
lawmaking by, 424–25
microtargeting strategy, 340
modern partisan landscape for, 314–16, 315f
national conventions of, 335
New Deal and, 79, 309–10, 309f
PACs supporting, 266t
party identification with, 194–95, 194f
party platform, 286
patronage system in, 298–99, 298f
polarization of, 198–99, 198f
presidential nomination process, 292–93
public opinion and ties to, 194–95, 194f, 198–99, 198f, 202, 203–4, 205, 206, 206t
realignment of, 310
Solid South and, 365
superdelegates, 293
tax policy, 574–75
Democratic-Republicans, 74–75, 102, 296–97
Department of Agriculture, 493
Department of Commerce, 493
Department of Defense (DOD), 200, 493, 584, 587, 588
Department of Education, 20, 70, 168, 493
Department of Energy, 492, 493, 571
Department of Health and Human Services (HHS), 70, 439, 485, 486f, 489, 493, 564
Department of Homeland Security (DHS), 481, 490, 493, 566, 568, 584, 588
Department of Homeland Security v. MacLean, 481
Department of Housing and Urban Development Act (1965), 310, 397, 493
Department of the Interior, 490, 493, 571

Department of Justice (DOJ), 164, 168, 200, 365, 493, 522, 566, 588
Department of Labor (DOL), 169, 253, 493
Department of State, 459, 492, 504, 566, 573, 576–77, 584, 589
Department of Transportation (DOT), 493
Department of the Treasury, 492, 574
Department of Veterans Affairs, 397, 493, 504f, 505
Desegregation, 151–52, 153, 157, 455, 534–35, 536
Diplomacy, 589, 591, 593
Direct democracy, 9, 69, 91, 92f
Directives, presidential, 455–56
Disability rights, 168–69, 169f
Discrimination
affirmative action and, 204, 515, 519–23, 525, 527–29, 531–34
ethnic, 137, 143, 144t, 150t, 157–62
gender-based, 116, 137, 144–47, 150t, 162–65
private, 136, 142–43, 149–50, 152, 154–55, 161–62
public, 136, 142–43, 149–50, 151–52
racial. *See* Racial segregation and discrimination
religious, 150t
District courts, 517, 519–24, 524f, 537–38
District of Columbia, voting rights in, 53, 54, 55f, 324, 360
District of Columbia v. Heller, 543
Divided government, 409
Dixiecrats, 303
Dodd-Frank Wall Street Reform Act, 494, 495
Dole, Robert, 370
Domestic policy, 561–74, 576–77. *See also* Economic policy
energy, environmental policy, and climate change, 570–74, 576–77
entitlement programs, income security, and health care, 562–65. *See also* Affordable Care Act; Medicaid; Medicare; Social Security
immigration, 566–70
layers in, 573
major federal programs, 562t
presidency and, 460, 470–74, 471f
Donovan, Shaun, 498
"Don't ask, don't tell," 166
Double jeopardy, 52, 124–25, 523–24, 611
Douglass, Frederick, 297
DREAM Act, 135, 144t, 321, 568
Dreams from My Father: A Story of Race and Inheritance (Obama), 3
Dred Scott v. Sandford, 77, 138, 546
Drinking age, 79, 81, 82, 146
Drones, 464, 466–67, 466t
Drug and alcohol use
criminal procedures related to, 122–23
disability rights related to, 168
drinking age, 79, 81, 82, 146
drunk driving, 122, 123
freedom of speech and, 113, 114f
marijuana legalization, 81–82, 91, 93, 531
religious freedom and, 118
Drunk driving, 122, 123
Dual federalism, 78, 78f
Due process of law, 52, 69, 124, 611, 612
Dust Bowl, 79f

E

Earmarks, 431
Economic interest groups, 255–56, 255f, 256f, 257t
Economic model of voting, 374–75
Economic opportunity, 21–22, 21f
Economic policy, 574–75, 577–83
elections and stances on, 592
Federal Reserve system and, 494, 575, 577–78, 578t, 579f
fiscal policy, 575, 577, 578t
interest rates, 578
international economic organizations and, 583
International Monetary Fund (IMF), 589, 591
monetary policy, 577–78, 578t
overview on intervention, 574–75
stakeholders in, 574–75, 575f
stimulus bill, 426, 575
taxation in. *See* Taxation
trade policy, 447, 548–49, 582–83
Economy
as campaign issue, 340–41, 343, 351, 352
capitalist, 12
Council of Economic Advisors on, 468, 575
debt ceiling, 580–82
Dodd-Frank Act, 494, 495
federal deficit, 425, 580–82
interest groups impacted by, 277
national debt, 4, 21, 425, 427, 580–82
National Economic Council on, 574
recession, 575
regulation of, 471, 494–95, 547
Education. *See also* Schools
affirmative action in, 515, 520–23, 522f, 525, 527–29, 531–34
cost of college, 20, 20f, 557
economic opportunity links to, 21, 21f
federalism and responsibility for, 70–71, 81
freedom of speech and, 107–9, 108f
No Child Left Behind Act, 71, 81
opportunity for, 18, 19–21, 70
public, as gateway to participation, 18, 157
public opinion and, 207–8, 207f
Race to the Top, 60, 71
separate-but-equal system, 143, 153, 157
student housing for, 129
student protests, 388–89, 388f, 391
undocumented immigrants', 18, 157, 171, 568, 570
voter turnout and, 373–74, 374t, 380
Efficacy, 180, 376
Egalitarianism, 12–13, 17
Eisenhower, Dwight D., 151, 273, 455, 461, 468, 469, 498, 541
Elections, 320–54. *See also* Campaigns; Voting
ballot reform, 299, 300f
battleground states, 339
campaign financing for. *See* Campaign finance
caucuses, 292, 333, 333f
congressional
campaigns for, 288–89, 343–52, 432–34
constitutional requirements for, 35, 37, 39, 41, 327–29, 401–2
gerrymandering and, 328–29, 329f
next, looking towards, 432–34, 434f
presidential coattails and, 349
presidential popularity and, 351–52
redistricting and, 328–29, 329f, 404
turnout in, 371–72
constitutional requirements for, 35, 37, 39, 41, 322–30, 358
democracy and, 15, 352–53
demographics of, 15–16, 16f, 22, 23f
Electoral College and, 37, 41, 322–27, 323f, 358, 360–61, 626–27
Federal Election Commission, 265, 337, 502
general, 289
incumbency advantage, 332–33, 347–48, 347f, 432–34, 434f
midterm, 345, 349, 349f, 351–52, 370–71
other, 329–30
party platform in, 350–51
polls and, 185–86, 342–43
presidential
of 2000, 185–86, 314, 326, 327, 327f, 627
campaign for, 225–26, 288–89, 290–91, 292–94, 299, 305, 330–43
campaign issues, 336–43
caucuses and primaries, 289, 290–91, 292, 293–94, 299, 333, 333f, 371
constitutional requirements for, 37, 322–27, 358
"corrupt bargain," 361
debates in, 225–26, 225f, 293f, 333f, 335–36, 336f
elected without popular majority, 37, 41, 324, 325, 325f, 360–61, 361f
Electoral College and, 37, 41, 322–27, 323f, 358, 360–61, 361f, 626–27
electoral maps, 626–27
eligibility requirements, 42, 440–42
incumbent advantage, 332–33
insider-outsider dynamic, 334
national conventions, 292, 335
news media and, 232, 234–35, 240, 242, 244, 245
nomination process, 292–94, 292f–294f, 305
policy stances in, 592
popular vote and, 325, 360–61, 361f

presidential (*continued*)
timetable for, 332t
turnout in, 361, 365, 367, 369f, 370–82, 371f, 373f, 373t–374t, 380f
primary, 289, 290–91, 292, 293–94, 299, 333, 345, 371
in Russia, 327
state, 90, 90f
swing states, 338–39
voting in. *See* Voting
Electoral College
advantages of, 325
constitutional requirements for, 37, 322–27, 323f, 358
electoral maps, 626–27
electors, 322–25, 323f, 362
presidents elected without popular majority, 37, 41, 324, 325, 325f, 360–61, 361f
problems with, 324–25
reform of, 325, 327
as winner-take-all system, 323–24
Elementary and Secondary Education Act, 71, 428, 472
Elites, 13, 191, 193
Emancipation Proclamation, 77, 138
Emanuel, Rahm, 156
Embargo Act (1807), 75
En banc review, 525
Enemy combatants, 465, 467
Energy and energy policy, 570–74, 570f, 576–77, 576f. *See also* Oil
England. *See* United Kingdom
English language literacy tests, 158, 366, 367
Entitlement programs, 428, 451–52, 562–65. *See also* Medicaid; Medicare; Social Security
Enumerated powers, 35, 39, 41, 50–51, 53, 67
Environmental policy
Clean Air Act, 571
Clean Water Act, 571
climate change and, 191, 193, 259, 447, 571
domestic policies as, 570–74, 576–77
Flint, Michigan water quality issues and, 572, 573–74
fracking, 262–63, 262f, 265f, 560f
Keystone XL Pipeline, 259, 576–77, 576f
lead exposure and, 572–73, 572f
Environmental Protection Agency
coal ash disposal regulations, 559
on emission standards, 491–92, 506
on fracking, 262–63, 560f
on fuel efficiency standards, 272
on Keystone XL Pipeline, 576–77
structure and function of, 487, 571
Supreme Court decision on, 505, 506
E-participation, 391–92
Equal Employment Opportunity Commission (EEOC), 164–65, 168
Equality
amendments concerning, 54f
civil rights supporting. *See* Civil rights
Constitution on, 16, 18, 27, 69, 142
in Declaration of Independence, 15–16, 17
of democracy, 13–17, 18
equal protection under the law, 69, 149–50, 155
of opportunity, 16, 137
of outcome, 16, 137
political, 15–16
political culture and, 12–13
racial, 17
voter turnout and inequality, 381–82
in workplace, 162, 164–65
Equal Pay Act, 162, 164
Equal protection, expansion of, 69, 149–50, 155
Equal protection clause, 142, 149, 612
Equal Rights Amendment (ERA), 162–63, 163f
Ernst, Joni, 236, 236f
Espionage Act of 1917, 103
Establishment clause, 118–19, 610
Estrada, Miguel, 539f, 541
Ethnicity. *See also specific ethnic groups*
bureaucratic demographics by, 499, 499f
ethnic profiling, 169–70
political attitudes and, 15
public opinion and, 204–6, 205f, 206t
segregation and discrimination based on, 137, 143, 144t, 150t
dismantling of, 157–62
voter ID laws and, 160–61
voter turnout and, 148, 158–59, 369f, 372
votes for president by, 315f, 369f
voting barriers based on, dismantling of, 158–59, 366–67
European Union (EU)
democracy in, 16–17
trade in, 583
Evolution, teaching of, 119
Exclusionary rule, 123
Executive authority, 49, 446t
Executive branch. *See also* Presidency
checks and balances, 10
Constitution on, 10, 11f, 35, 36t, 40t, 41–42, 446t
interest groups lobbying, 252, 260
in states, 85–87, 85f, 86f
Executive departments, 484–85, 485t, 486f, 492–93
Executive orders, 455–56
Executive power, 454–60
Executive privilege, 453–54
Exit polls, 185–86
Expectation of privacy test, 122–23
Ex post facto laws, 47, 68, 69, 99

F

Facebook, 214, 232, 232f, 259, 390, 390f, 457
Factions, 10, 11, 251, 269, 295–96
Fair Housing Act (1966), 310, 472
Fair Labor Standards Act, 8
Fair trade, 579
Fallin, Mary, 87
Falwell, Jerry, 115
Fannie Mae Corporation, 563
Farook, Syed Rizwan, 111f
Faubus, Orval, 536
FCC v. Fox Television Stations, 220
FCC v. Pacifica Foundation, 220
Federal Bureau of Investigation (FBI), 104–5, 200, 489
Federal Communications Commission (FCC), 218, 220
Federal corporations, 488
Federal deficit, 425, 580–82. *See also* National debt
Federal Election Campaign Act (FECA), 337
Federal Election Commission (FEC), 265, 337, 502
Federal Election Commission v. Wisconsin Right to Life, Inc., 269
Federal government. *See* Government, U.S.
Federalism, 62–95
across the world, 66
changing nature of, 73–83
vs. confederal and unitary systems, 65, 66f, 93
constitutional amendments on, 67f, 72, 77–79
constitutional framework for, 10, 45, 46, 66–73, 76
cooperative, 78–80, 78f
defined, 65
democracy and, 92–93
direct democracy and, 69
dual, 78, 78f
Framers and, 65–66
local governments and, 83, 89, 91, 91f
New Federalism, 80–83
nullification and, 75
partition of power in, 45–47, 47f
reasons for, 64–66
relationships under, 69, 71–73
revolt against national authority, 75, 77–78
self-government and, 65–66
state-centered, 74, 79, 81–82
state governments and, 10, 45, 46, 64–93
unification, reasons for, 64
Federalist Papers, 48, 49, 50, 222, 222f, 251
text of, 618–25
Federalist Party, 48, 74, 295–96
Federalists, 48–50, 74, 222, 295–96, 295t

Federal Register, 484, 559
Federal regulatory commission, 487
Federal Reserve/Federal Reserve Board, 494, 575, 577–78, 578t, 579f
Federal Trade Commission (FTC), 221, 495
Feinstein, Dianne, 306
Felons, voting rights for, 170–71, 170f
Feminine Mystique, The (Friedan), 162
Ferraro, Geraldine, 442
Fighting words doctrine, 107–9
Filibuster, 421–22, 539
Financial protection, consumer, 494–95
Fiorina, Carly, 331
First Amendment, 52, 106–19, 267
First Lady, Office of, 469–70, 469f
Fiscal policy, 575, 577, 578t
Fisher, Abigail, 521, 522f
501(c)(3) organizations, 265
501(c)(4) organizations, 265, 266, 268
Flag burning, 112, 113
Flint, Michigan, water quality issues, 572, 573–74
Food and Drug Administration (FDA), 495, 507, 508f
Food stamps, 472, 563
Ford, Betty, 472
Ford, Gerald R., 197, 335–36, 441, 454
Foreign Assistance Act, 589
Foreign Intelligence Surveillance Act (FISA), 110, 110f
Foreign policy, 584–93
  anti-nuclear proliferation measures, 588-89, 588f
  antiterrorism measures, 200–1, 588
  diplomacy and humanitarian assistance, 258–59, 258f, 589, 591, 593
  elections and stances on, 592
  globalization and, 584
  interest groups focus on, 258–59, 258f
  international relations and goals of, 584–87
  isolationism as, 584, 585
  military action and, 586, 587–88. *See also* War(s)
  multipolar world system, 586
  origins of U.S., 585–87
  presidency and, 447, 449, 459–60, 460f, 470, 473f, 474, 584–93
  promotion of democracy and, 589, 590–91
  Reagan stance on, 313, 473f, 475
  treaties in. *See* Treaties
Founders, 7, 34f
Fracking, 262–63, 262f, 265f, 560f
Framers, 7, 9–10, 34f, 65–66, 398, 401f, 60
Framing, 238–39
Franchise (suffrage), 358, 360
Franklin, Benjamin, 30, 34f, 64, 64f, 219, 221
Frederick, Joseph, 114f
Freedom, worldwide (Freedom House assessments), 590, 590f
Freedom of Information Act, 507
Freedom of religion. *See* Religious freedom
Freedom of speech
  advocacy of unlawful activities, 107
  clear and present danger test, 107
  college speech codes, 107–9, 108f
  content-neutral justification, 112–13, 114f
  fighting words and hate speech, 107–9
  First Amendment on, 52, 106–14, 130, 130f
  symbolic speech, 111–13, 113f, 114f
  time, place, and manner regulations, 113–14
  tolerance for, 130, 130f
  university speech zones, 107–9, 108f
Freedom of the press
  censorship *vs.*, 114–16, 220–21
  First Amendment on, 52, 114–16
  law and, 216–19
  prior restraint and, 114–15
  subsequent punishment and, 115–16
Free enterprise, 13, 268
Free exercise clause, 117–18, 610
Free rider problem, 277
Free Soil Party, 298, 302
Free trade, 579, 582–83
Friedan, Betty, 162
Friedrichs v. California Teachers Association, 255, 543
Fuel efficiency standards, 81, 271–72, 272f
Fugitive slave clause, 37, 77, 608
Fugitive Slave Law (1793), 77
Full faith and credit clause, 73, 608
Fundraising. *See* Campaign finance

G

Gallup polls, 183–84, 183f, 509
Garcia, Gus, 27
Garfield, James A., 496
Garland, Merrick, 316, 442, 450, 521, 541, 543, 544, 545
Garner, Eric, 156, 271
Garrison, William Lloyd, 297
Garza, Daniel, 268
Garza, Reynoldo, 539
Gatekeeper, Constitution as, 7–13
Gates, Robert, 483
Gateways to democracy, 3, 4, 23
GATT (General Agreement of Tariffs and Trade), 583
Gay Liberation Front, 166. *See also* GLBT issues
Gender. *See also* Women
  bureaucratic demographics by, 499, 499f
  discrimination, 116, 137, 144–47, 150t
    affirmative action and, 204, 515, 519–23, 525, 527–29, 531–34
    dismantling of, 162–65
  Equal Pay Act, 162, 164
  gender gap, 203–4
  public opinion and, 203–4, 204f
  transgender individuals, 167–68, 184
  voter turnout and, 371–72
  votes for president by, 315f
  workplace equality and, 162, 164–65
General election, 289
General Motors, 491, 522
General welfare clause, 49–50, 53, 604
Generational effects, 189–90
Generational replacement, 380
Genes, and voting, 377–78
Geneva Convention, 200
Gerry, Elbridge, 329f
Gerrymandering, 328–29, 329f
Gibbons v. Ogden, 75, 546
Gideon v. Wainwright, 124
Giffords, Gabby, 306
Gilens, Martin, 270
Gilman, Sam, 249
Gingrich, Newt, 294, 314, 412
Ginsburg, Douglas, 544
Ginsburg, Ruth Bader, 162, 162f, 165, 527, 534, 543, 544
GLBT issues. *See* Homosexual behavior; Same-sex marriage; Sexual orientation; Transgender individuals
Globalization, 584
Global Solidarity Network, 258
global warming/climate change, 191, 193, 259, 447, 571
Goldwater, Barry, 42, 313, 341–42, 342f
Gonzales, Henry B., 157–58
Good, R. Stephanie, 97, 121
Gore, Albert, Jr., 185–86, 326, 327, 447, 627
Government, U.S. *See also* Federalism; National debt
  branches of, 10, 11f. *See also* Executive branch; Judicial branch; Legislative branch
  divided government, 409
  powers of. *See* Power(s)
  public support of, 180
  relationship with states, 35, 71–72
  shut down of, 266, 413, 451–52, 581
Government in the Sunshine Act, 507
Gowdy, Trey, 409
Grandfather clauses, 142–43, 365
Grand jury, 124, 523
Grant, Oscar, 156
Grant, Ulysses S., 324f
Grassroots movements, 253, 257, 264
Gratz and *Grutter* cases, 515, 519, 520–23, 525, 527–29, 529f, 531–34

Graveyard voting, 383
Gray, Freddie, 156, 389f
Great Depression
  Dust Bowl during, 79f
  New Deal and, 79, 309–10, 309f, 470–72, 471f, 547, 563
  protest politics during, 389, 391
Great Society program, 80, 312, 472, 563
Green card, 566, 567f
Green Party, 303
Griswold v. Connecticut, 126, 127f
Grutter, Barbara. *See Gratz* and *Grutter* cases
Guantánamo Bay facility, 200, 458, 465
Guarantee clause, 69, 609
Guns
  assault weapons ban, 121, 306–7
  Giffords, Gabby, 306
  gun control, 121, 306–7
  right to bear arms, 52, 120–21
  Sandy Hook elementary school, 121
  Stand Your Ground laws, 125

H

Habeas corpus, writ of
  civil liberties protection, 99
  for enemy combatants, 465, 467
  suspension of, 47, 68, 102–3, 465, 467
Habitat for Humanity, 5f
Haley, Nikki, 87
Hamdi v. Rumsfeld, 200, 465, 467
Hamilton, Alexander, 34f, 55, 74, 296
  Federalist Papers of, 48, 49, 50, 222f
  Hamiltonian model of participation, 358–59, 359f
Harding, Warren G., 103
Hard news, 227, 241
Harrison, William Henry, 440, 443f
Hassan, Maggie, 87
Hastert, Dennis, 412
Hastie, William, 539
Hatch, Orin, 367
Hatch Act, 502
Hate speech, 107–9
Hayes, Rutherford B., 142, 325f, 363
Head of state, 459–60, 460f
Head Start, 70, 472
Health care
  Affordable Care Act, 126–27, 274, 407, 428, 485, 560, 564–65
    mandate for insurance, 407, 564, 565
  cost of insurance, 564–65
  federalism and, 81, 82
  health maintenance organizations, 502
  Obama and, 126–27, 407, 485
  undocumented immigrants', 171
  veterans', 504f, 505
Hearst, William Randolph, 218, 223, 223f
Heclo, High, 273
Henry, Patrick, 28, 48, 50
Heritage Foundation, 274, 276
Hernandez v. Texas, 27, 144t, 153, 157, 260
Higher Education Act, 71
Highway Act (1956), 493
Hill, Anita, 544, 544f
Hill v. Colorado, 391
Hispanic Caucus, 418
Hobbes, Thomas, 7
Hold, 423, 539
Holder, Eric, 106, 125
Holmes, Oliver Wendell, 99, 103
Holt, Lester, 225, 225f
Homelessness, 5f, 397, 555
Home style, 432
Homosexual behavior. *See also* Same-sex marriage
  Boy Scouts and, 116
  civil rights for, 166–68, 167f, 168f
  decriminalization of, 166
  public opinion on, 191, 203
  right to privacy, 129
  Supreme Court decisions, 166, 181
Hoover, Herbert, 391, 443
House of Representatives. *See also* Congress; Lawmaking
  Capitol housing, 401f
  composition and election of, 35, 41, 328–29, 346, 347–48, 347f, 349, 349f, 351–52, 399, 400, 400f, 401–2
  differences from Senate, 35, 41, 399–4
  impeachment power of, 406, 408, 452
  lawmaking process and, 419–21, 420f, 425
  majority/minority leader, 413–14, 416f
  party leaders in, 413–14, 416f
  polarization in, 199f
  political parties and, 410–11
  powers and function of, 41, 405–10
  presidential election role of, 324, 361
  redistricting and, 328–29, 329f, 404
  Reed's Rules and, 411
  Rules Committee, 419–21
  Speaker of the House, 411–13, 411f–413f
    presidential succession and, 440
Housing, 129, 563, 564
Huckabee, Mike, 331
Huerta, Dolores, 144t, 161
Hughes, Charles Evan, 547
Humanitarian assistance, 258–59, 258f, 589, 589f, 591, 593
Human rights, 258–59
Human Rights Watch, 258
Hussein, Saddam, 462

I

Ideological interest groups, 252, 257–58
Ideology. *See* Political ideology
Immigration
  children born in the United States, 18, 171, 566
  domestic policy on, 566–70
  DREAM Act, 135, 140t, 321, 568
  green card, 566, 567f
  Immigration Acts, 141
  Immigration and Nationality Act (1990), 566
  Immigration Reform and Control Act (1986), 567
  immigration status, queries about, 568–69
  legal immigration process, 566
  limits on, as citizenship restriction, 140, 141–42
  naturalized citizens, 42, 139, 566, 567f
  political parties and immigrants, 299
  protests related to, 387f
  quotas for, 566
  state actions on, 69f, 72, 568–70
  unauthorized immigration, 567–70
    Alabama law and, 568
    amnesty and, 567
    Arizona law and, 568–69
    local and federal action on, 568–70
  undocumented immigrants, 18, 135, 157, 171, 566, 567–70
    children of, 18, 171, 566, 568
    road to citizenship, 18, 171, 566
    state responses to, 568–70
Impeachment
  congressional power of, 41, 406, 408, 452–54
  judicial, 130, 406, 537
  presidential, 41, 257, 406, 408, 452–54
Imperial presidency, 445
Implied powers, 50, 72, 76
Income
  equal pay, 162, 164–65
  income security, 562–63. *See also* Social Security
  minimum wage, 8–9, 8t, 91
  unemployment insurance as, 426–27, 563
  voting and, 372–73, 373t
Incorporation, 99–102, 101t, 117, 120–21, 123
  selective, 101, 123
Incumbency advantage, 332–33, 347–48, 347f, 432–34, 434f
Independent agency, 487

Independents, 188, 194–95, 194f, 305, 307
Indian Appropriations Act (1851), 139
Indian Citizenship Act (1924), 139
Indian Removal Act (1830), 139
Individualism, 12, 17
Individuals with Disabilities Education Act (IDEA), 70, 168
Information, 214, 241–42, 259–60
Informed public, 198–200, 198f
Infotainment, 231
Initiative, 91, 92f
Innocence Project, The, 57
Inside strategy, 263–64
Instagram, 214, 259
Institutional model of voting, 376–77
Interest groups, 248–82
  campaign finance laws and, 267, 268–69, 278–79
  challenges to political parties, 307–08
  characteristics of successful, 276–80
    financial stability, 279
    influence in public sphere, 279–80
    leadership accountability, 276–77
    membership stability, 277–79, 278f
  defined, 250
  democracy and, 10, 11, 15, 19, 280
  economic and political change affecting, 277–79
  factions, 10, 11, 251, 269, 295–96
  501(c)(3) organizations, 265
  501(c)(4) organizations, 265, 266, 268
  free rider problem, 277
  functions of, 259–69
    campaign activities, 265–69, 265f, 266t, 338
    informing, 259–60
    lobbying, 251–52, 251f, 259, 260–64, 267–68
  grassroots movements, 253, 257, 264
  history of, 252–53
  impact of, 269–76
    natural balance or disproportionate power, 269–71
    open or closed routes of influence, 273–76
    self-service or public service, 271–73
  iron triangle and, 273, 274f, 503
  issue networks and, 273–74, 503
  lobbying by, 251–52, 251f, 259, 260–64, 267–68
  nongovernmental organizations, 259
  political action committees (PACs), 265–68, 276t, 306, 338
  public policy stances, 259–60, 262–63, 265, 272–73, 306–7, 560, 564f, 576–77
  revolving door, 274, 276
  right to assemble and petition, 250–52
  selective benefits, 277
  special interests, 270–71
  on Supreme Court appointments, 541–42
  top, national, 275, 275f
  types of, 254–59
    citizens' groups, 257, 264
    corporations, 254, 267, 338
    economic, 254–65, 255f, 256f, 257t
    foreign policy and international, 258–59, 258f
    ideological/issue-oriented, 252, 257–58
    single-issue, 257, 272
    trade/professional associations, 252, 254
    unions, 252–53, 254–56, 255f, 256f, 257t, 267, 338
    watchdog groups, 15, 264, 264f, 274
Interest rates, 578
Internal Revenue Service, targeting by, 265, 496
International aid groups, 258–59, 258f
International Atomic Energy Agency (IAEA), 588–89, 588f
International Ladies' Garment Workers' Union (ILGWU), 253
International Monetary Fund (IMF), 589, 591
International Organization for Migration (IOM), 258f
International relations. *See* Foreign policy
International Rescue Committee, 259
International trade agreements, 579, 582–83
Internet. *See also* Blogs; Social networking/Social media
  Child Online Privacy Protection Act, 221
  Child Online Protection Act, 221
  e-participation via, 391–92
  freedom of the press and, 114, 115, 220–21
  fundraising through, 337, 392
  interest groups using, 259, 264
  news on, 214, 218, 226, 227f, 230f, 231–32, 232f, 234, 235–36, 236f, 243, 245, 457–58
  polls via, 185
  voting via, 384–85
  Wikileaks, 114
Interposition resolutions, 79
Interrogations, 123, 124f
  harsh interrogation techniques, 200
Interstate commerce, 72, 75, 79, 2
Investigations, criminal, 121–23
Investigative journalism, 215–16, 224
Invisible primary, 332
Iran, nuclear facilities in, 588–89, 588f
Iran-contra scandal, 409–10, 476
Iraq War, 456, 462–63, 501–2, 587–88, 591
Iron law of oligarchy, 277
Iron triangle, 273, 274f, 503
ISIS, 464, 465, 588
Isolationism, 584, 585
Issue networks, 273–74, 503

J

Jackson, Andrew, 75, 183, 242, 296–97, 296f, 360–61, 361f
  patronage system and, 298, 496
Jackson, Jesse, 293
Jackson, Robert, 98, 129
Japanese-Americans, WWII internment camps, 140–41
Jay, John, 34f, 48, 222f, 546
Jaycees, 116
Jefferson, Thomas
  Articles of Confederation response, 32–33
  cabinet of, 483
  Declaration of Independence and, 31
  Democratic-Republicans and, 74–75, 102, 296
  federalism *vs.* states' rights stance of, 74–75, 296
  as Founder and Framer, 7, 34f
  freedom of the press support, 114, 214
  Jeffersonian model of participation, 358–59, 359f
  new media and criticism of, 222
  political party of, 55, 74–75, 102, 296
  presidency of, 324
  religious freedom support, 117, 119
  vice presidency of, 324
Jenner, Caitlyn (formerly Bruce), 184
Jim Crow laws, 143, 363, 363f
Job Corps, 472
Johnson, Andrew, 77, 450, 452
Johnson, Lady Bird, 470
Johnson, Lyndon Baines
  background and experience of, 443
  civil rights stance, 154, 155, 310, 472, 472f
  "Daisy spot" ad and, 341–42, 342f
  election of, 332
  federalism under, 80
  greatness of, 472–73, 472f
  Great Society program, 80, 312, 472, 563
  legislative achievements, 472–73. *See also* Great Society program
  political appointees of, 498
  press conferences by, 457
  public opinion, polls and, 184
  Vietnam War and, 461, 473
Johnson v. DeGrandy, 144t, 159
"Join or Die" cartoon, 64, 64f
Journalism. *See* News media
Judicial activism and restraint, 530–34
Judicial branch, 10, 11f, 35, 36t, 40t, 42–43, 87–89, 517–18. *See also* Judiciary; Supreme Court
Judicial independence, 537
Judicial review, 43, 44, 53, 149–50, 150t, 518, 529
Judiciary, 514–52. *See also* Judicial branch; Judicial review; Supreme Court
  adversary process, 516
  amicus curiae, 252, 522, 526, 527

Judiciary (*continued*)
appeals, 126, 516, 524–29
courts of appeals, 516, 517, 524–25, 524f, 538–39, 541
en banc, 525
Supreme Court and, 516, 525–29
appointment process, 537–45
congressional approval of, 41, 421
courts of appeal, 538–39, 541
district courts, 537–38
presidential nominations in, 450, 537–45
Supreme Court, 15, 316, 408f, 422, 442, 450, 541–42, 544
Article I (legislative) courts, 517, 517t
bench trial, 522
bureaucracy accountability and, 505, 506
Certiorari, writ of, in, 518, 526–27
common law, 516
congressional authorization of courts, 408–9
constitutional grants of power, 517–18
countermajoritarian difficulty, 528
decision making, 528–29, 529–37
democracy and, 549–50
district courts, 517, 519–24, 524f, 537–38
appointment process, 537–38
blue slips, 538, 538f
civil procedure, 522–23
criminal procedure, 523–24. *See also* Criminal procedure
diversity in, 539–41, 539f, 539t, 540f, 544–45
en banc review, 525
English legal traditions, 516–17
full faith and credit clause recognizing decisions by, 73, 608
Habeas corpus, writ of, in, 47, 68, 99, 102–3, 465, 467
impeachment from, 130, 406, 537
independence of, 537
judicial activism and restraint, 530–34
judicial branch of government, 10, 11f, 35, 36t, 40t, 42–43, 517–18
judicial review, 43, 44, 53, 149–50, 150t, 528, 529
jurisdiction, 517–18
lawsuits in
class action lawsuits, 521–22
criminal cases *vs.* civil suits, 516, 522–24. *See also* Criminal procedure
interest groups filing, 252, 560
as "least dangerous branch," 545
majority opinion, 525
organization in the United States, 518–25, 519f, 524f
power struggles with president, 465, 467
precedents, 516–17
responsiveness of, 550
role and powers of, 516–18
state courts, 89, 518, 519f
state judicial branches, 87–89, 88f
Supreme Court. *See* Supreme Court
trial by jury, 52, 123–24, 516, 523
Judiciary Act (1789), 44, 408, 517, 519
The Jungle (Sinclair), 224
Jurisdiction, 517–18

K

Kagan, Elena, 521, 543, 544, 569
Kahneman, Daniel, 238
Kaine, Tim, 294f
Kansas-Nebraska Act (1854), 138
Kaplan, Andrew, 249
Kasich, John, 331
Katzenbach v. Morgan, 144t, 158, 366
Katzmann, Robert, 538f
Kelly, Megyn, 186, 240
Kennedy, Anthony, 543, 569
Kennedy, John F.
background and experience of, 442
civil rights stance, 151, 154, 162
debate with Nixon, 225, 225f, 335
foreign policy, 589
judicial nominees, 539
microtargeting strategy, 340
political appointees of, 498
press conferences of, 459f
public opinion, polls and, 184
Vietnam War and, 461
voter support for, 365
Kerry, John, 205, 311, 315, 588, 627
Keystone XL Pipeline, 259, 576–77, 576f
Kids Voting USA, 376f
King, Marcus, 307
King, Martin Luther, Jr.
civil rights movement, 152, 154, 155, 172, 173, 388, 472f
"I Have a Dream" speech of, 154
on voting, 155, 172
King v. Burwell, 407
Koch brothers, 279–80
Kolbo, Kirk, 527–28
Korean War, 455, 458
Korematsu v. United States, 141
Kosovo, recognition of, 449
Ku Klux Klan, 116, 141, 142, 155
Kyoto Protocol, 447

L

Labor unions. *See* Unions
Lame duck, 441
La Raza Unida Party (LRUP), 304
Latinos
in bureaucracies, 499, 499f
campaign targeting to, 268, 339
citizenship of, 139–40
civil rights and, 27, 139–40, 143, 144t, 157–62
in Congress, 399, 400, 400f
discrimination against, 27, 143, 144t
dismantling of, 157–62
diversity of term, 204, 206
elected officials, 157–59, 162, 344–45, 344f
electorate, 205f
English language literacy tests and, 158, 366, 367
health care for, 564, 565
Hispanic Caucus, 418
in judiciary, 144t, 408, 515, 539, 539t, 540f, 541, 544
La Raza Unida Party (LRUP), 304
Libre Initiative, 268
LULAC, 27, 144t, 150, 157, 253, 260, 329
MALDEF, 144t, 157, 159, 252
migrant, 79f, 161
news media and, 234–35, 234f
political party affiliation, 206, 206t, 311, 311f, 312
population of, in U.S., 16f
public opinion among, 204–06, 205f, 206t
redistricting among, 328–29, 404
social issues stance, 192–95, 192f
Supreme Court Justice (Sotomayor), 144t, 260, 408f, 515, 541, 544
voting by, 148, 158–59, 161, 205, 205f, 328, 366–67, 369f, 372
Lawmaking, 419–29
agenda-setting in Senate, 421–23
bill sponsorship, 423–24, 430
budget process and reconciliation, 425, 427–28
cloture, 421, 422f
committee action, 423–24
conference committee, 425
congressional power of, 41, 49–50, 408
congressmember at work, 430–31
filibuster, 421–22
floor action and vote, 424–25
hold, 423
House and, 419–21, 420f, 425
legislative proposals, 423
markup, 417, 424
omnibus bills, 451
policy enactment and, 557. *See also* Policy/policies
presidential directives and signing statements *vs.*, 455–57
presidential signature or veto, and override, 41, 428–29, 450–52, 451t
procedural rules and, 419–23
roll call vote, 424–25, 430–31

Senate and, 420f, 421–23, 422f, 425
filibuster, 421–22
unanimous consent agreements, 423
Lawrence v. Texas, 129, 166, 181
Lawsuits. *See also* Judiciary; Supreme Court Cases
civil *vs.* criminal, 516, 522–24. *See also* Criminal procedure
class action, 521–22
interest groups filing, 252, 560
standing in, 517
Lazarsfeld, Paul, 237
Lead exposure, 572–73, 572f
League of Nations, 585
Ledbetter v. Goodyear Tire and Rubber Co., 164–65
Legislative authority, scope of, 49–50, 446t
Legislative branch. *See also* Congress; Lawmaking
bureaucracy and, 504–5
checks and balances, 10
Constitution on, 10, 11f, 36t, 40–41, 40t, 398–404, 446t
in states, 87, 90, 90f
Lemon test, 119
Levels of conceptualization, 195
Lew, Jacob, 468
LGBT issues. *See* Homosexual behavior; Same-sex marriage; Sexual orientation; Transgender individuals
Libby, I. Lewis, 447
Libel, 115, 216–17
seditious, 115, 219
Liberals, 11–12, 12f, 195–96, 195f, 231, 233, 233f, 241, 390, 390f. *See also* Democratic Party
Libertarian Party, 303–4
Libertarians, 12
Liberty. *See also* Civil liberties
balancing with order, 6–7, 37f, 99
"give me liberty, or give me death," 28, 50
Liberty Party, 298, 302
Libre Initiative, 268
Lilly Ledbetter Fair Pay Act, 165
Limbaugh, Rush, 229, 229t
Lincoln, Abraham
campaign image of, 242, 242f, 443f
campaign negativity of, 341f
Emancipation Proclamation, 77, 138
federalism stance of, 77
office seekers and, 496f
public opinion and, 178, 182
Republican support for, 298
suspension of habeas corpus by, 102–3
Literacy tests
English language, 158, 366, 367
for voting rights, 142–43, 158, 363–64, 364f, 365, 366, 367
Little Rock, Arkansas, school integration in, 455, 536
Lobbying
by interest groups, 251–52, 251f, 259, 260–64, 267–68
lobbyists, 260–61, 261f, 263
spending on, 261, 261t
strategies, 263–64
inside strategy, 263–64
Local governments
election to, 330
function and design of, 10, 83, 89, 91, 91f
lobbying by, 260
policy diffusion by, 561
political parties, 289, 289f
Locke, John, 7, 31
Love, Ludmya "Mia," 285, 288
Loving v. Virginia, 152
Lowi, Theodore, 270
LULAC (League of United Latin American Citizens), 27, 144t, 150, 157, 253, 260
LULAC v. Perry, 329

M

MacArthur, Douglas, 391
MacLean, Robert, 481, 508
Madison, James
Articles of Confederation response, 32–33
Democratic-Republicans and, 296
on factions, 10, 11, 251, 269, 295
Federalist Papers of, 48, 49, 222f, 251, 295, 398, 618–25
as Founder and Framer, 7, 9–10, 34, 34f, 398
on knowledge, 23, 196
on nullification, 75
on partition of power, 45, 46
political party of, 55, 296
religious freedom support, 119
on representative democracy, 9, 13
on republican government, 69
on spirit of locality, 37
Magna Carta, 28, 516
Mahoney, Maureen, 527–28
Majoritarian policy-making, 13
Majority opinion, 525
Majority rule, 6, 10, 251
Majority vote, 301
Malheur National Wildlife Refuge occupation, 4
Malice, actual, 216–17
Mapp v. Ohio, 123
Maps, electoral, 626–27
Marbury v. Madison, 43, 44, 408–9, 518, 546
Marijuana, legalized/legalization, 81–82, 91, 93, 531
Marketplace of ideas, 103, 130
Markup, 417, 424
Marriage
Defense of Marriage Act (DOMA), 73, 167
interracial, 152
legal immigration and, 566
polygamous, 117
same-sex. *See* Same-sex marriage
Marshall, John, 44, 75, 76, 546
Marshall, Thurgood, 27, 151, 153, 540, 544
Marshall Court, 44, 75, 76, 546, 549t
Martin, Trayvon, 125, 156, 169
Martinez, Susana, 86f, 87, 162, 345
Mass media, 214. *See also* News media
Mayo, Heath, 249
McAuliffe, Terry, 171, 288
McCain, John, 42, 141
election of 2008 and, 3, 337, 340, 627
McCain-Feingold Bipartisan Campaign Reform Act (2002), 267, 268–69, 278
McCardle decision, 103
McCarthy, Carolyn, 306
McCarthy, Joseph, 104, 105f, 241
McConnell, Mitch, 304, 542
McCullen v. Coakley, 391
McCulloch v. Maryland, 75, 76, 546
McCutcheon, et al., v. FEC, 269, 337
McDonald, Laquan, 156
McDonald v. Chicago, 120f, 543
McIntosh, Dave, 279
McKinley, William, 182, 242, 330, 331f
Meat Inspection Act, 224
Media. *See* News media
Median voter theorem, 301, 346
Medicaid, 80, 82, 171, 428, 472–73, 485, 502, 565
Affordable Care Act and, 407, 565
Medicare, 80, 81, 204, 428, 472–75, 485, 502, 563, 564f
Merit system, 497, 503
Merit Systems Protection Board (MSPB), 503
Mexican American Legal Defense and Education Fund (MALDEF), 144t, 157, 159, 252
Microtargeting, 339–40, 340f
Midterm elections, 345, 349, 349f, 351–52, 370–73
Miers, Harriet, 541
Mikulski, Barbara, 402f
Military
commander in chief of, 41–42, 446–47
"don't ask, don't tell" policy in, 166
integration of, 455

Military (*continued*)
military action, 586, 587–88. *See also* War(s)
military-industrial complex, 273
Millennials, 19, 190, 194f, 214, 235–36, 249, 372, 500–1, 500f
Miller test, 115–16
Milligan decision, 103
Mills, C. Wright, 13, 270
Minerals Management Service, 490
Minimal effects model, 237
Minimum wage, 8–9, 8t, 91
Minor, Virginia, 145, 362f
Minorities, minority rights, 6, 82. *See also* Ethnicity; Race; *specific minorities*
Miranda v. Arizona, 123, 124f, 548
Missouri Compromise, 138
Missouri Plan, 87, 88f
Mob rule, 6
Moderates, 12, 195
Monarchy, 14
Mondale, Walter, 204, 442, 469
Monetary policy, 577–78, 578t
Monopolies, 13, 30, 218, 236, 387, 406, 457f, 574
Monroe, James, 49, 296, 443
Moore, Roy, 537f
Mortgage crisis, 494
MoveOn.org, 257, 264, 271f
Moynihan, Daniel Patrick, 538, 538f
Muckraking, 224
Multipolar world system, 586
Murdoch, Rupert, 241
Murrow, Edward R., 104

N

NAACP, 150, 151, 152, 153, 155, 252, 368, 536
Nader, Ralph, 303
NAFTA (North American Free Trade Agreement), 582
Nash, Diane, 154
National Association for the Reform of Abortion Laws (NARAL), 128, 257
National Bank of the United States, 74, 75, 76
National committees, 288, 289f
National Constitution Center, 52f
National convention, 292, 335
National Council of the Churches of Christ, 258
National debt
in 2016, 4, 21, 581f
congressional budget process and, 425, 427
debt ceiling, 580–82
federal deficit and, 425, 580–82
National Defense Education Act, 71
National Economic Council, 574
National Education Association (NEA), 257t, 260
National endowment, 488
National Federation of Independent Businesses et al. v. Sebelius, 407
National Firearms Act (1934), 120
National Governors Association, 260
National Highway Transportation Safety Administration (NHTSA), 491
National Labor Relations Act, 253, 471
National Labor Relations Board v. Noel Canning, 450
National Minimum Drinking Age Act, 81
National Ocean and Atmospheric Administration, 490
National Organization for Women (NOW), 162
National power. *See also* Federalism
expansion of, 35, 74–75, 76, 78–80, 546, 547–48
limitation of, 82, 83, 546–47
public opinion on, 83
revolt against, 75, 77–78
shared powers, 68, 68f
Supreme Court rulings impacting, 545–48, 549t
National Railroad Passenger Corporation, 488
National Republicans, 297
National Rifle Association (NRA), 121, 253, 265, 277, 278f, 279, 306, 308
National Security Agency (NSA), 110–11, 490, 584
National Security Council (NSC), 468, 588
National Transportation Safety Board (NTSB), 487–88, 488f
National Unity Party, 303
National Voter Registration Act, 383–84
National Women's Suffrage Association (NWSA), 145, 361
Native Americans, 118, 137, 139, 143, 499f
Naturalization, 42, 139, 566, 567f
Natural Resources Defense Council (NRDC), 262–63
Natural (unalienable) rights, 7, 31, 98
Nazi Germany/Nazi Party, 585
Near v. Minnesota, 216
Necessary and proper clause, 49–50, 67, 76, 605
New Deal, 79, 309–10, 309f, 470–72, 471f, 547, 563
New England town meeting, 89, 91, 91f
New Federalism, 80–83
New Jersey Plan, 35, 36t
News media, 212–46
24-7 news cycle, 240
bias and, 224, 239–41
blogs, 218, 231–32, 457–58
cable news, 220, 226, 227f, 230–31
censorship and, 114–16, 220–21
obscene content, 115–16, 220–21
changing media environment, 226, 227f
concentration of ownership of, 218–19
defined, 214
democracy and, 15, 244–45
elections and, 232, 234–35, 240, 242, 244, 245
era of media choice, 243–44
evaluating, 239–44
FCC and, 218, 220
freedom of the press, 52, 114–16, 216–21
functions of, 214–16
information, 214, 241–42
interpretation, 216
investigation, 215–16, 224
hard news, 227, 241
history of the American press, 219–36
Colonial Era, 219, 221
Founding Era, 221–22
Partisan Era, 222–23
Professional Era, 223–24
Television Era, 224–26, 225f
Twenty-First Century, 226–36
image and, 242
impact of, 236–39
agenda setting, 237–38
framing, 238–39
minimal effects model, 237
not-so-minimal effects model, 237–39, 238f
priming, 238
propaganda model, 236–37
infotainment, 231
Internet, 243, 245. *See also online subentry*
Latino voters and, 234–35, 234f
law and free press, 216–19
mass media, 214
Millennials and, 214, 235–36
muckraking, 224
newspapers, decline of, 227–28, 228, 230f
online, 214, 218, 226, 227f, 230f, 231–32, 232f, 234, 235–36, 236f, 243, 245, 457–58
penny press, 223
political ideology and, 229, 229t, 231, 233, 233f, 241
political news, 214–16
president's relationship with, 457–58, 459f, 471, 473
priming and, 238
public faith in, 239, 240f
public opinion, impact on, 182f, 236–39
quality of information, 241–42
radio, 218, 220, 226, 227f, 228–30, 229f, 229t, 230f, 241–42, 242f
selective exposure/perception and, 237
soft news, 231, 241
sound bites, 242
sources, by age group, 235f
sources, variety of, 226, 227f, 230f, 243–44
television, 218, 220, 224–26, 225f, 226, 227f, 230–31, 230f, 231f
watchdog role of, 214, 215–16, 218
yellow journalism, 223, 223f
New York Times v. Sullivan, 216–17

New York Times v. United States, 114
New Zealand, voting in, 379
Ninan, Reena, 231f
Nixon, Richard M.
debate with Kennedy, 225, 225f, 335
federalism under, 74, 80
impeachment threat and, 215f, 408, 453–54, 454f
pardon of, 454
party alignment and ideology of, 313
Pentagon Papers and, 218
political appointees of, 498
public opinion, polls and, 184
resignation of, 215, 215f, 408, 454, 454f
Supreme Court appointees, 544
as vice president, 469
Vietnam War and, 461–62
voting rights support of, 370
Watergate scandal and, 453–54, 537
No Child Left Behind Act (2002), 71, 81
Nomination process, 289–94, 305
Nominations, presidential, 292–94, 292f–294f, 305
Nonattitudes, 187
Nongovernmental organizations (NGOs), 259
Nonstate actors, 587–88
Norquist, Grover, 276
Northwest Ordinance, 37
Norton, Eleanor Holmes, 55f
Not-so-minimal effects model, 237–39
NSA. *See* National Security Agency
Nuclear anti-proliferation, 588–89, 588f
Nuclear Regulatory Commission, 489
Nullification, 75

O

Obama, Barack
Affordable Care Act and, 126–27, 407, 485
Afghanistan War and, 441–42, 463
antiterrorism measure, 200
approval ratings, 178–79, 179f, 194
background and experience of, 442
Biden, Joe and, 469
cabinet of, 483, 498, 499
campaign promises of, 350–51, 350f
on change, 3
on college education, 20
in Congressional Black Caucus, 419
congressional elections and popularity of, 352
DREAM Act, 135, 568
drones, use of, 464, 466–67, 466t
economic policies, 494–95, 575, 580–82, 592
educational platforms, 60, 71
election to presidency (2008), 3, 17, 352–53
campaign for, 159, 334, 337, 340, 392
Electoral College votes, 324
electoral map, 627
polls on, 343
voting demographics, 190, 204, 205, 311, 315, 315f
election to presidency (2012)
campaign issues, 338
debates with Romney, 336, 336f
electoral map, 627
microtargeting strategy, 339
polls on, 186, 343
voting demographics and turnout, 190, 311, 316, 372, 380–81
Equal/Fair Pay Acts, 165
federal budget, 428, 580–82
federalism under, 81–82
foreign policy, 460f, 588–89, 591
on fuel efficiency standards, 272
gateways to democracy for, 3
on gun control, 121
immigration policies, 135, 171, 567
Iraq, involvement in, 463, 591
judicial appointments, 316, 408f, 442, 450, 539, 539t, 540f, 541–44
on Keystone XL Pipeline, 259, 576–77, 576f
legacy of, 474–75, 509
Libya airstrikes and, 464
national debt and federal deficit response, 580–82
on national security surveillance, 110–11
news media relationship with, 457–58
on offshore drilling, 490–91
organization of White House under, 468
pardons of, 447
political appointees of, 498
presidential schedule of, 448, 449f
press conferences of, 457
Race to the Top, 60, 71
recess appointments of, 450
on sexual orientation and same-sex marriage, 73, 166
signing statements and executive orders of, 456
stimulus package and, 426
Supreme Court appointees, 316, 408f, 442, 450, 541–44
Syrian conflict and, 464, 465
treaties of, 447
warrantless wiretapping and, 105–6, 110
Obama, Michelle, 3, 460f, 469f, 470
Obergefell v. Hodges, 44, 73, 91, 152f, 167, 181
Obscenity/obscene content, 115–16, 220–21
Occupy movement, 391
Ochs, Adolph, 224
O'Connor, Sandra Day, 128, 521, 527, 529–30, 533, 540, 541, 544
Office of the Attorney General, 492, 493
Office of Information and Regulatory Affairs, 559
Office of Inspector General, 508
Office of Legislative Counsel, 423
Office of Management and Budget (OMB), 439, 468, 476, 486, 559
Office of Personnel Management (OPM), 502–3
Office of the Solicitor General, 522, 527
Oil
energy use and policy on, 570–74, 570f, 576–77, 576f
fracking, 262–63, 262f, 265f, 560f
Gulf of Mexico spill (Deepwater Horizon), 490–91, 491f
Keystone XL Pipeline, 259, 576–77, 576f
offshore drilling regulations, 490–91
Oligarchy, 14. *See also* Iron law of oligarchy
Olson, Mancur, 269–70
Olson, Theodore, 527
O'Malley, Martin, 333
Omnibus bills, 451
"Operation Wetback," 140
Opinion. *See* Public opinion
Order, balancing with liberty, 6–7, 27f, 99
Override, 41, 428–29, 450–51
Oversight, 409–10, 495, 504–5

P

Pacquiao, Manny, 173
PACs. *See* Political action committees
Padilla, Jose, 105
Paine, Thomas, 30–31, 222
Palin, Sarah, 163
Palmer, A. Mitchell, 103
Panetta, Leon, 463
Pardons, presidential, 41, 49, 447, 454
Parks, Rosa, 152
Parliamentary systems, 409, 460, 463
Participation
Amendments expanding, 53, 54f
beyond voting, 386–92
campaign involvement, 386–87, 386t
competing view of, 358–59
democracy and, 22–23, 392–93
e-participation/Internet, 391–92
examples of. *See* first pages of each chapter
Hamiltonian and Jeffersonian models of, 358–59, 359f
opportunity for, 22–23
protest politics, 387–89, 387f–389f, 391
voting as. *See* Voting

Partisanship, 11, 194–95, 194f, 301, 308–16, 376. *See also* Political parties
  press and, 222–23
Party/parties. *See* Political parties
Patient Protection and Affordable Care Act. *See* Affordable Care Act
Patrick, Dan, 168
PATRIOT Act. *See* USA PATRIOT Act
Patriotism, 180
Patronage system, 298–99, 298f, 495–97
Paul, Rand, 304, 331, 387, 423
Paycheck Fairness Act, 165, 397
Peace Corps, 593
Pearce, Russell, 91
Pelosi, Nancy, 168, 411, 412, 412f
Pence, Mike, 294f
Pendleton Act, 299, 496–97
Penny press, 222
Pentagon Papers case, 114, 217–18
Permanent campaign, 331
Perot, Ross, 303
Perry, Katy, 377f
Perry, Rick, 172
Persuasion, power of, 457–59, 457f
Petition, right of, 251–52
Petition for a writ of *certiorari,* 518, 526–27
Peyote use, 118
Plea bargains, 523
Plessy v. Ferguson, 143, 153
Pluralism, 13, 270
Plurality vote, 301
Plyer v. Doe, 18, 53, 144t, 157
Pocket veto, 428, 450
Polarization, 198–99, 198f, 199f, 201, 301
Police powers, 67–68
Policy/policies, 554–97
  blocking implementation of, 560
  competing interests in, 15, 556
  constitutional system and, 556–61
  containment, 586
  democracy and, 593–94
  domestic policy, 460, 470–74, 471f, 561–74, 576–77
  economic policy, 426, 447, 494, 574–75, 577–83, 589, 591, 592
  elections and stances on, 592
  foreign policy, 200–1, 258–59, 313, 447, 449, 459–60, 460f, 470, 473f, 474, 584–93. *See also* Treaties
  interest groups on, 259–60, 262–63, 265, 265f, 272–73, 306–7, 560, 564f, 576–77
  policy agenda, 557
  policy diffusion, 560–61
  policy enactment, 557
  policy evaluation, 557
  policy formulation, 557
  policy implementation, 557
  policy making process, 5, 13, 556–57, 557f, 558f
  problem identification, 557
  public opinion on, 559, 560f, 576–77
  race to the bottom, 561
  regulatory process, 558–59, 559f
  stakeholders in, 557, 557f
  state governments and, 560–61
  Supreme Court policy making role, 533–34
Political action committees (PACs)
  as interest groups, 265–68, 266t, 306, 338
  news media awareness of, 213
  Super PACs, 213, 265, 266, 338, 392
Political appointees, 449–50, 497–99, 502–3
Political culture, 11–13
Political equality, 15–16
Political ideology, 11–13, 12f, 195–196, 195f, 229, 229t, 231, 233, 233f, 241, 309–10
  Supreme Court and, 529f, 532, 532f, 533f, 544
Political machines, 198–99, 380, 382–83
Political parties, 285–319. *See also* Democratic Party; Republican Party; Tea Party movement
  alignment and ideology, 308–16
    after Civil War, 308–09
    civil rights, Great Society, and southern strategy, 310–13
    modern partisan landscape, 314–16
    New Deal and, 309–10, 309f
    Reagan and conservative politics, 313–14
    realignment of, 310
  ballots and ballot reform, 290, 299, 300f
  Congress, role in, 288, 410–11
  Constitution and, 11, 55, 57
  defined, 11, 55, 286–87
  delegates, 292–94
    bonus delegates, 294
    superdelegates, 293
  democracy and, 316–17
  development of, 295–300, 303f
    American Independent Party, 303
    antislavery movement and, 297–98
    Democratic Party, 297
    Democratic-Republicans, 296–97
    Dixiecrats, 303
    Federalist *vs.* Antifederalist factions, 295–296
    Free Soil Party, 298, 302
    Green Party, 303
    La Raza Unida Party (LRUP), 304
    Libertarian Party, 303–4
    Liberty Party, 298, 302
    National Republicans, 297
    National Unity Party, 303
    patronage system and, 298–99, 298f
    Populist Party, 302
    Progressive Party, 299, 302–3
    reform and erosion of party control, 299, 300f
    Republican Party, 298, 302
    third parties, 297–98, 302–4, 302f, 303f
    United We Stand, 303
    Whig Party, 297
  functions of, 286–89
  fundraising by, 288–89, 347
  insider-outsider dynamic, 334
  national committees, 288, 289f
  national conventions, 292, 335
  nomination process, 289–94, 290f, 292f–294f, 305
  party alignment, 308–16
  party cartel system, 412
  party caucuses, 288
  party competition, 433
  party identification, 11, 194–95, 194f, 287
  party in government, 287, 288
  party in the electorate, 286, 287–88
  party machines, 298–99, 380, 382–83
  party organization, 287, 288–89, 289f, 334
  party platform, 286, 350–51
  polarization of, 198–99, 198f, 199f, 201, 301
  presidential nomination and, 292–94, 292f–294f, 305
  primary elections and, 289, 290–91, 299, 333
  public policy stances, 306–07
  responsible, 315–16
  role of, 286–94
  socialization into, 188, 189f
  state and local, 289, 289f, 290f
  two-party system, 300–8
    interest group challenges to, 307–8
    limited choice and, 300–1
    obstacles to third parties/independents, 305, 307
    presidential nomination control, 305
    structural limits, 301
    Tea Party, 304–5
    third parties and, 302–4, 302f, 303f
  voter registration and get-out-the vote, 287, 380–81
Political tolerance, 130, 130f, 131
Political trust, 180
Politics, defined, 11, 15
Polk, James, 223
Polls, 180, 182–88
  call-in or write-in, 185
  confidence interval, 186
  error in, 186–87
  exit polls, 185–86

future of, 187–88
Gallup poll, 183–84, 183f, 509
in-person, 184, 185f
nonattitudes, 187
prediction models and, 342–43
push polls, 186
random sample, 183
scientific polling, 183–84, 183f
telephone, 184–85
tracking polls, 185
types of, 184–86
Poll taxes, 53, 142, 158, 364f, 365, 366
Polygamy, 117
Popular vote, 325, 360–61, 361f
Populist Party, 302
Populists, 12
Pornography, 115–16
Position issues, 340–41
Post Office, 493
poverty, 5f, 8–9
Powell v. Alabama, 124
Power elite, 13
Power(s)
Articles of Confederation and, 32
checks and balances on, 10, 45, 46, 47f
concurrent, 68, 68f
of Congress, 35, 39, 41, 49–51, 53, 67, 72, 76, 78, 79, 405–10, 428–29, 446–47, 446t, 450–51, 452–54, 461–62, 495, 504–5, 580–82
Constitution and, 10, 35, 39, 41, 45–49, 47f, 49, 50–51, 53, 67–69
enumerated, 35, 39, 41, 50–51, 53, 67
implied, 50, 72, 76
of interest groups, 269–76
of judiciary, 517–18
limits on, 46–47, 68–69
national. *See* Federalism; National power
partition of, 45–47, 47f
police, 67–68
of president, 15, 41–42, 44, 49, 316, 408f, 421–22, 428–29, 442, 445–67, 484, 537–45
of public opinion, 178–81
of the purse, 405
reserve, 67–68, 611
separation of, 10, 45, 46
shared, 68, 68f
of states, 35, 46–47, 67–68, 69
war powers, 35, 405–6, 446–47, 461–62
Precedents, 516–17
Preemption, 72
Presidency, 438–79. *See also specific presidents*
agenda setting, 459–60
authority of, scope of, 49
cabinet and cabinet departments under, 482, 484–85, 485t, 486f, 492–93, 498, 499
campaigns for. *See* Campaigns, presidential
constitutional amendments on, 440–41, 442f
daily schedule of, 448, 448f–449f
democracy and, 476–77
directives and signing statements, 455–57
domestic policy and, 460, 470–74, 471f
economic policy and, 574–75, 580–82
elections for. *See* Elections, presidential
election without popular majority, 37, 41
executive authority, 49, 446t
as executive branch, 10, 11f, 35, 36t, 40t, 41–42, 252, 260, 446t
executive orders, 455–56
executive privilege and, 453–54
expansion of, 443, 445
foreign policy and, 447, 449, 459–60, 460f, 470, 473f, 474, 584–93
greatness in (examples), 470–76
growth of executive influence, 454–60
head of state, 459–60, 460f
impeachment and, 41, 257, 406, 408, 452–54
imperial presidency, 445
lame duck, 441
list of presidents, 444t–445t
news media, relationship with, 457–58, 459f, 471, 473
nomination process for, 292–94, 292f–294f, 305
organization of White House, 467–70
chief of staff, 468
Executive Office of President, 468
Office of the First Lady, 469–70, 469f
Office of Vice President, 468–69
policy enactment and, 557. *See also* Policy/policies
powers of, 445–67, 484
appointments/nominations, 15, 44, 316, 408f, 421–22, 442, 449–50, 484, 537–45
checks on, 445–46, 452–54
commander in chief, 41–42, 446–47
executive authority, 49
executive power, 454–60
other, 452
pardon, 41, 49, 447, 454
persuasion, 457–59, 457f
treaties/recognition of nations, 447, 449
veto, 41, 428–29, 450–52, 451t
in wartime, 455–56, 458, 461–67
press conferences, 457, 459f, 471
public approval of, 178–79, 179f, 238, 459, 587
qualifications for, 440–43
background/experience, 442–43
constitutional eligibility, 440–42
staff for, 468
State of the Union address, 452
succession, line of, 440–41, 441t
temporary transfer of power, 441
term limit for, 347–48, 441
"two presidencies" concept, 470
in wartime, 461–67
power struggles with Congress, 461–65
power struggles with judiciary, 465, 467
Steel Seizure case, 455–56, 458
Presidential coattails, 349
Presidential directives, 455–56
Presidential elections. *See* Elections, presidential
Presidential Succession Act (1792), 440
President pro tempore (Senate), 414–15, 440
Press. *See also* News media
freedom of, 52, 114–16, 216–21
history of, 219–36
penny press, 223
press conferences, 457, 459f, 471
watchdog role of, 214, 215–16, 218
Primary elections
blanket, 290, 291
congressional, 345
invisible primary, 332
presidential nomination and, 289, 290–91, 333
reform of, 299
turnout in, 371
white primary, 365
winner-take-all *vs.* proportional representation, 292, 293–94
Priming, 238
Printz v. United States, 543
Prior restraint, 114–15
Privacy
Child Online Privacy Protection Act, 221
expectation of, 122–23
NSA and, 110–11
right to, 126–29, 127f, 531, 548
Private discrimination, 136, 142–43, 149–50, 152, 154–55, 161–62
Private goods, 15
Private-sector contractors, 501–2, 501f
Privileges and immunities clause, 73, 608, 612
Problem identification, 557
Profiling, 169–70
Progressive Party, 299, 302–3
Prohibition, 253f
Propaganda model, 236–37
Proportional representation, 35, 293–94
Protectionism, 579, 582–83
Protest politics, 387–89, 387f–389f, 391
Psychological model of voting, 375–76
Public debt. *See* National debt
Public discrimination, 136, 142–43, 149–50, 151–52

Public goods, 14–15, 277
Public opinion, 176–210
on abortion, 186, 192, 192f, 205, 205t, 204
on antiterrorism measures, 200–1
approval ratings for president, 178–79, 179f, 238, 459, 587
on bureaucracy, 509
defined, 179–80
democracy and, 15, 208
drivers of, 188–93
elites, 191, 193
generational effects, 189–90
self-interest and rationality, 190–91
social and political environment, 188–89, 189f
efficacy, 180
on federalism, 83
group differences in, 202–08
age, 202
education, 207–8, 207f
gender, 203–4, 204f
race and ethnicity, 204–6, 205f, 206t
religion, 203, 203t
socioeconomic status, 202
ideology and, 195–96, 195f
microtargeting and, 339–40, 340f
news media and, 182f, 236–39
partisanship and, 194–95, 194f
polarization of public, 198–99, 198f, 199f, 201, 301
policy response, 559, 560f, 576–77
political trust, 180
polls, 180, 182–88, 509
error in, 186–87
future of, 187–88
Gallup poll, 183–84, 183f, 509
gauging opinion in the past, 182–83
scientific polling and surveys, 183–84, 183f
types of, 184–86
power of, 178–81
public's knowledge/information, 196–98, 198f
on same-sex marriage, 167, 168f, 190, 190f, 192, 192f, 203
shape of, 193–201
support of government, 180
Public policy, 554–597. *See also* Policy/policies
competing interests in, 15, 556
constitutional system and, 556–61
defined, 5, 556
democracy and, 593–94
domestic policy, 460, 470–74, 471f, 561–74, 576–77
economic policy, 426, 447, 494, 574–575, 577–83, 589, 591, 592
elections and stances on, 592
foreign policy, 200–1, 258–59, 313, 447, 449, 459–60, 460f, 470, 473f, 474, 584–93. *See also* Treaties
interest groups on, 259–640, 262–63, 265, 265f, 272–73, 306–7, 560, 564f, 576–77
political ideology on, 11–13
political parties on, 306–7
public policy process, 5, 13, 556–57, 557f, 558f
state governments and, 560–61
Puerto Rico, 158f
Pulitzer, Joseph, 223–24, 223f
Punishments
capital, 56–57, 56f, 125, 126, 204, 524
criminal procedure verdict, punishment, and appeal, 124–26
cruel and unusual, 52, 56, 125, 611
subsequent, 115–18
Pure Food and Drug Act, 224
Push polls, 186

Q

Quartering Acts, 30, 30t

R

Race. *See also* Racial segregation and discrimination
bureaucratic demographics by, 499, 499f
political attitudes and, 15
public opinion and, 204–6, 205f, 206t
racial equality, 17
racial profiling, 169–70
redistricting in relation to, 32829
voter ID laws and, 160–61, 160f
voter turnout and, 148, 155–56, 372, 373f
votes for president by, 315f, 373f
Race to the bottom, 561
Race to the Top, 60, 71
Racial segregation and discrimination
affirmative action addressing, 204, 515, 519–23, 525, 527–29, 531–34
black codes, 142
capital punishment and, 56–57
civil liberties issues with, 116
civil rights and, 137, 142–43, 150–56, 150t
desegregation, 151–52, 153, 157, 455, 534–35, 536
dismantling of, 151–56, 360, 365–66, 455
Jim Crow laws, 143, 363, 363f
military integration, 455
private discrimination, 136, 142–43, 152, 154–55
public discrimination, 136, 142–43, 151–52
school segregation, 27, 44, 70, 70f, 79, 143, 151–52, 153, 157, 455, 534–35, 536
separate-but-equal doctrine, 143, 153, 157
states' rights arguments on, 93
voting barriers
dismantling of, 155–56, 360, 365–66
history of voting and use of, 16, 142–44, 359, 362–65
literacy tests, 142–43, 363–64, 364f, 365
poll taxes, 53, 142, 364f, 365
Radio, 218, 220, 226, 227f, 228–30, 229f, 229t, 230f, 241–42, 242f
Raimondo, Gina, 87
Rainey, Joseph, 363
Rally-around-the-flag effect, 587
Ramos, Jorge, 234–35
Random sample, 183
Rankin, Jeannette, 146
Ranking member, 418
Raphaelson, Sheri A., 88
Rationality, 190–91
low information, 197
rational voting, 375
Reagan, Nancy, 470
Reagan, Ronald
assassination attempt on, 441, 475
background and experience of, 442
campaigns and election of, 334, 335, 352
federalism of, 82–81, 82
foreign policy of, 313, 473f, 475
gender gap in votes for, 203–4
as "Great Communicator," 475
greatness of, 473, 475–76
immigration policy, 567
Iran-contra scandal, 409–10, 476
party alignment and ideology of, 313–14
press conferences by, 457
Supreme Court appointees, 82, 541, 544
taxes and, 473, 475
Reagan Democrats, 313
Realignment, 310
Recall, 91, 92f
Recess appointments, 450
Recession, 575
Reconciliation (budget), 428
Reconstruction, 142, 363
Redistricting, 328–29, 329f, 404
Red Scare, 103, 104f
Reduce Homelessness for Female Veterans Act, 397
Reed, Thomas Bracket, 411, 411f
Reed's Rules, 411
Referendum, 91, 92f
Regulation(s), 481, 483, 484, 559
Regulatory agencies/commissions, 487, 493, 495
Regulatory process, 558–59, 559f
blocking implementation, 560
policy diffusion, 560–61

race to the bottom, 561
state governments and, 560–61
Rehabilitation Act (1973), 168
Rehnquist, William, 82, 528–29, 533
Rehnquist Court, 548, 549t
Reid, Harry, 421
Religion
discrimination, 150t
faith-based interest groups, 258
judicial appointments and, 544–45
news media on issues in, 215
party alignment and ideology related to, 313
political opinions and, 203, 203t
religious profiling, 169–70
same-sex marriage objections and, 537f
separation of church and state, 119
votes for president by, 315f
Religious freedom
establishment of religion, 52, 118–19
First Amendment on, 52, 116–19
free exercise, 117–18
Lemon test for, 119
Religious Freedom Restoration Act on, 118
Supreme Court on, 117–19
valid secular purpose, 117–18
Representation
British view of, 29
in Congress, 35, 328–29, 398
proportional, 35, 293–94
taxation without, 29–30
Representative democracy, 9, 13, 15
Republic, 9–10, 69
Republican form of government, 47, 69, 83
Republican Party. *See also* Political parties
bonus delegates, 294
civil rights and, 141
congressional elections and, 433
Contract with America, 81, 314, 412
debt ceiling stance, 580–82
federalism stance of, 74, 81
formation of, 298, 302
gun control and, 306–7
immigration stance of, 141, 567
interest groups supporting, 266t
Latino affiliation with, 311, 311f, 312
lawmaking by, 424–25
microtargeting strategy, 340
modern partisan landscape for, 314–16, 315f
national conventions of, 335
PACs supporting, 266t
party identification with, 194, 194f
party platform, 286
polarization of, 198–99, 198f
presidential nominating process, 292, 293–94, 305
public opinion and ties to, 194, 194f, 198–99, 198f, 202, 203–4, 205, 206, 206t
Reagan revolution in, 313–14
realignment of, 310
southern strategy, 313
tax policy, 310, 574–75, 580
Tea Party movement and, 23, 304–5, 387, 389, 580
Reserve powers, 67–68, 611
Responsible parties, 315–16
Retrospective voting, 343
Revolving door, 274, 276
Rice, Tamir, 156
Rich, Marc, 447
Richardson, Elliot, 453
Rights
of association, 52, 116, 250–52
to bear arms, 52, 120–21
civil. *See* Civil rights
constitutional. *See* Bill of Rights; Constitution
criminal. *See* Criminal procedure
to die, 129
natural (unalienable), 7, 31, 98
of petition, 251–52
of privacy, 126–29, 127f, 531, 548
states', 74, 93
Right to Life organization, 257
Roberts, John, 82, 407, 515, 533, 543
confirmation vote on, 539, 542, 542f, 544
Roberts, Owen, 547
Roberts Court, 82, 407, 515, 533, 543, 548, 549t
Robinson, Jackie, 150
Roe v. Wade, 44, 128–29, 313, 537
Roll call vote, 424–25, 430–31
Romney, Mitt
campaign issues, 338, 339
debates with Obama, 336, 336f
election (2012) and, 186, 294, 312, 336, 336f, 338, 339, 389, 627
immigration stance, 141
nominating process (2012), 294
public opinion and, 197
Super PACS and fundraising, 338
Tea Party movement and, 389
Roof, Dylann, 125
Roosevelt, Eleanor, 469
Roosevelt, Franklin Delano
Court-packing plan of, 79, 130, 471, 547
economic policy, 575
federalism under, 74, 78–79
fireside chats of, 241–42, 242f, 471
foreign nation recognition by, 449
greatness of, 470–72, 471f
judicial appointments by, 539, 541. *See also* Court-packing plan
legislation and programs of, 8, 547. *See also* New Deal
New Deal of, 79, 309–10, 309f, 470–72, 471f, 547, 563
organization of White House under, 468
polio of, 224
political appointees of, 498
political ideology of, 309–10
press conferences by, 457, 471
public opinion and, 182, 182f, 183
Social Security program and, 426–27
terms in presidency, 441
voter support for, 365
wartime internment of Japanese-Americans, 140–41
Roosevelt, Theodore "Teddy," 224, 302–3, 331, 457, 457f, 574
Rove, Karl, 186
Rubio, Marco, 23, 45, 148, 162, 268, 304, 331
Rule, 419–20
House Rules Committee, 419–21
Rule of four, 527
Rule of law, 6–7
Rush, Bobby, 3
Russia
Communism in, 585, 586
economic sanctions on, 587
elections in, 327
Syrian conflict and, 464, 464f
Ukrainian rebels and, 464–65
Ryan, Jack, 3, 413
Ryan, Paul, 389, 411, 413f, 581–82

S

Safari Club International, 306–7
Safe seats, 347
Same-sex marriage
civil rights and, 166–68, 167f, 168f
legal immigration and, 566
public opinion on, 167, 168f, 190, 190f, 192, 192f, 203
state stances on, 73, 91, 166–67, 181
Supreme Court on, 17, 44, 73, 73f, 91, 152f, 167, 181, 537f
Sample/sampling, 183
San Antonio Independent School District v. Rodriguez, 157
Sanders, Bernie, 20, 24, 135, 148, 307, 333, 334, 337, 389, 509
Sandy Hook elementary school, 121
Santana, Miguel, 555
Santorum, Rick, 294
SA READS, 397

Scalia, Antonin, 120, 121, 291, 316, 422, 515, 521, 531, 541, 542, 543, 569
Schattschneider, E. E., 270
Schedule C appointees, 498
Schenck, Charles, 103
Schlafly, Phyllis, 163
Schools. *See also* Education
  desegregation of, 151–52, 153, 157, 455, 534–35, 536
  disability rights in, 168
  evolution *vs.* creationism taught in, 119
  expectations of privacy in, 122
  freedom of speech at, 107–9, 108f
  religion or prayers in, 119, 313
  school lunch program, 472
  segregation of, 27, 44, 70, 70f, 79, 143, 151–52, 153, 157, 455, 534–35, 536
  transgender rights in, 168
  undocumented people and, 18, 157, 171, 568, 570
Schuette v. Coalition to Defend Affirmative Action, 515, 521
Scott, Walter, 156
Searches and seizures, 52, 121–23
Secession, 75, 77
Second Amendment, 52, 120–21
Section 8 program, 564
Securities and Exchange Commission (SEC), 471, 487, 494
Sedition Acts, 74, 102, 103, 222
Seditious libel, 115, 219
Segregation. *See* Racial segregation and discrimination
Selective benefits, 277
Selective exposure, 237
Selective incorporation, 101, 123
Selective perception, 237
Self-government, 6, 65–66
Self-incrimination, right against, 52, 123, 124, 611
Self-interest, 17, 19, 190–91, 374–75
Selzer, J. Ann, 177, 186
Senate. *See also* Congress; Lawmaking
  agenda-setting tools in, 421–23
  approval of presidential appointees, 41, 406, 409, 421–22, 449–50, 537–45
  Capitol housing, 401f
  cloture motions in, 421, 422f
  composition and election of, 35, 37, 39, 41, 327–28, 346, 347f, 348, 352, 399, 400, 400f, 401–2, 433
  differences from House, 35, 41, 399–4
  filibusters in, 421–22, 539
  holds in, 423, 539
  impeachment role of, 406, 408, 452
  lawmaking process and, 420f, 421–23, 422f, 425
  majority/minority leader, 415, 416f
  party leaders in, 415, 416f
  polarization in, 199f
  political parties and, 411, 433
  powers and functions of, 41, 405–10
  president pro tempore, 414–15, 440
Senior Executive Service (SES), 498–99
Sentencing, 125, 524
Separate-but-equal doctrine, 143, 153, 157
Separation of powers, 10, 45, 46
September 11, 2001, attacks. *See under* Terrorism
Service Employees International Union (SEIU), 255, 257t, 308
Sex. *See* Gender
Sexual orientation. *See also* Homosexual behavior; Same-sex marriage
  bisexual, 63, 166, 321
  civil liberties and, 116, 129
  civil rights and, 166–68, 167f, 168f
  public opinion on, 191, 203
  transgender individuals, 167–68, 184
Shay's Rebellion, 33, 33f
Shelby County v. Holder, 144t, 156, 161, 369
Shinseki, Eric, 504f, 505
Sierra Club, 253, 259, 265, 277, 278f, 308
Signing statements, 456–57
Silver, Nate, 343
Sinclair, Upton, 224
Sinema, Krysten, 135, 285, 321, 345
Single-issue groups, 257, 272
Single-member plurality system, 301
Slaughterhouse Cases, 546
Slavery
  abolitionist movement, 77, 252, 252f, 297
  civil rights and, 137, 138, 138f
  constitutional amendments concerning, 52–53, 77, 137, 138
  Constitution and, 16, 36–37, 38–39, 39f
  Dred Scott decision, 77, 138, 546
  Emancipation Proclamation, 77, 138
  fugitive slave clause, 37, 77, 608
  Missouri Compromise and, 138
  Northwest Ordinance, 37
  three-fifths compromise, 36, 38–39, 38f
  Underground Railroad escaping, 77f
Smith v. Allwright, 365
Smith v. Maryland, 110
Snapchat, 259
Snowden, Edward, 110, 114, 201
Snyder v. Phelps, 109
Social contract, 7
Socialism, 12
Socialization, 188–89, 374, 375–76
Social networking/Social media
  e-participation via, 392
  interest groups using, 259
  news via, 214, 226, 227f, 232, 232f, 234, 457–58
  political discussions via, 390, 390f
  presidential use of, 457–58
Social Security, 146, 426–27, 428, 471, 562–64, 564f
Social Security Disability Insurance, 563
Socioeconomic status, 202, 243, 372–73
Soft news, 231, 241
Solicitor General, 522, 27
Solid South, 365
Sotomayor, Sonia
  confirmation to Supreme Court, 260, 408f, 541–42, 542f, 544
  district court nomination of, 538
  as female, Latina Justice, 144t, 260, 408f, 515, 541, 544
  qualifications of, 543
Souter, David, 368, 527
Southern Manifesto, 151
Southwest Voter Registration and Education Project (SVREP), 144t, 159
Sovereign immunity, doctrine of, 72
Spanish-American War, 585
Speaker of the House, 411–13, 411f–413f, 440
Special interests, 270–71. *See also* Interest groups
Specter, Arlen, 198
Speech, freedom of. *See* Freedom of speech
Spoils system. *See* Patronage system
Stamp Act (1765), 28, 29f, 30t
Stanton, Elizabeth Cady, 145
State action, 149
State courts, 89, 518, 519f
State of the Union address, 452
States
  Articles of Confederation adoption by, 32
  battleground states, 339
  Bill of Rights, incorporation to, 99–102, 101t, 117, 120–21, 123
  budgets of, 86
  capital punishment in, 56–57
  caucuses in, 292, 333
  congressional representatives from. *See* Congress
  constitutional amendment ratification by, 43, 43f, 45, 163, 163f
  constitutional ratification by, 39
  constitutions of, 31
  direct democracy in, 91, 92f
  domestic policies and, 565
  Electoral College representing, 37, 41, 322–27, 323f, 358, 360–61, 626–27
  executive branches, 85–87, 85f, 86f
  federal aid to, 80, 80f, 82–83
  federalism and, 10, 45, 46, 65–93
  governors' authority and term limits, 85–87, 85f
  immigration actions, 69f, 72, 568–70
  interstate commerce, 72, 75, 79, 82
  judicial branches, 87–89, 88f
  judicial selection and campaigns, 87–89, 88f

laws
abortion, 128–29
preemption of, 72
sexual orientation and same-sex marriage, 166–67, 181
supremacy of national law over, 71–72
voting-related, 160–61, 160f, 358, 362, 363–66, 368–69
legislative branches, 87, 90, 90f
lobbying by, 260
nullification and, 75
policy diffusion, 560–61
political parties, 289, 289f, 290f
powers of
limits on, 35, 46–47, 69
reserve powers, 67–68
shared or concurrent, 68, 68f
primary elections in, 289, 290–91, 292, 293–94, 299, 333, 345, 371
race to the bottom, 561
relationships among, 72–73
relationship to national government, 35, 71–72
republican form of government, 47, 69, 83
secession of, 75, 77
state-centered federalism, 74, 79, 81–82
swing states, 338–39
vetoes in, 85–86
women's rights in, 145–47, 147f
States' rights, 74, 93
States' Rights Democratic Party, 79
Steel Seizure case, 455–56, 458
Steelworkers v. Weber, 520
Sterling, Donald, 173
Stevens, Christopher, 409, 504
Stevens, John Paul, 368, 528
Stevens, Theodore (Ted), 431
Stimulus package, 426, 575
Stockman, Steve, 304
Stonewall riots, 166
Strategic politician hypothesis, 352
Student Aid Expansion Act (2013), 397
Student housing, 129
Student Nonviolent Coordinating Committee (SNCC), 154
Student protests, 388–89, 388f, 391
Students for a Democratic Society, 388
Subsequent punishment, 115–16
Substance use. *See* Drug and alcohol use
Suffrage, 358, 360. *See also* Voting
Sugar Act (1764), 28, 30t
Sunshine Act, 509
Super PACs, 213, 265, 266, 338, 391
Supplemental Nutrition Assistance Program, 563
Supplemental Security Insurance, 563
Supremacy clause, 71, 76, 569, 609
Supreme Court
on affirmative action, 515, 520–21, 525, 527–29, 529f, 531–34
appellate jurisdiction of, 516, 525–29
appointment process, 15, 408f, 422, 442, 450, 541–42, 544
partisanship and, 316
Burger Court, 181, 548, 549t
on capital punishment, 56–57
on civil liberties, 100–2, 103, 104, 105, 106–7, 109, 110, 112–13, 114–16, 117–19, 120–21, 121–26, 126–31, 547–48
on civil rights, 137, 138, 139, 141–43, 144t, 145, 147, 149–50, 150t, 151–71, 547–48
constitutional interpretation by, 27, 53, 409
Court-packing plan, 79, 130, 471, 547
decisions, 528–37
decisions overturned by constitutional amendments, 535, 535t
diversity on, 540, 541, 544–45
on elections, 326, 329
federal laws declared unconstitutional by, 408–9, 530, 530f
on federal *vs.* state authority, 75, 76, 77–79, 82
granting review, 526–27, 526f
historical trends in rulings, 545–48, 549t
national power, expansion of, 546
national power, limits on, 546–47
national power, strengthened, 547–48
impact of decisions, 534–37
impeachment from, 130
on interest groups, 255, 265, 267, 268–69
judicial activism and restraint, 530–34
judicial review, 43, 44, 53, 149–50, 150t, 518, 529
jurisdiction, 517–18
Justices
diversity among, 540, 541, 544–45
ideology of, 529f, 532, 532f, 533f, 544
preferences of, 532
votes of, 528–29, 529f, 532, 533f
women, 162f, 408f, 515, 521, 540, 544
Marshall Court, 44, 75, 76, 546, 549t
on news media, 216–18, 220–21
Opinion of the Court, 528
concurring and dissenting opinions, 528
oral arguments, 527–28
procedures of, 525–29
public opinion alignment with, 181
Rehnquist Court, 82, 528–29, 533, 548, 549t
responsiveness and, 550
Roberts Court, 82, 407, 515, 533, 543, 548, 549t
rule of four, 527
on same-sex marriage, 17, 44, 73, 73f, 91, 152f, 167, 181, 537f
on slavery, 77, 138, 546
on state power limits, 69, 72
Taney Court, 138, 549t
Warren Court, 121, 548, 549t
Supreme Court Cases
Arizona v. United States, 568, 569
Bakke case, 520, 523, 525, 527, 529, 531, 532
Barron v. Baltimore, 100
Bowers v. Hardwick, 181
Brown v. Board of Education, 27, 44, 70, 79, 151–52, 153, 455, 534–35
Buckley v. Valeo, 265
Bush v. Gore, 326
California Democratic Party v. Jones, 290, 291
Cardona v. Power, 158
Chevron U.S.A. v. Natural Resources Defense Council, 505, 506
Cisneros v. Corpus Christi, 70, 144t, 157
Citizens United v. Federal Election Commission, 55, 213, 267, 269, 338, 392, 543
Civil Rights Cases, 78, 149, 547
Cohens v. Virginia, 546
Cooper v. Aaron, 455, 536
Department of Homeland Security v. MacLean, 481
District of Columbia v. Heller, 543
Dred Scott v. Sandford, 77, 138, 546
FCC v. Fox Television Stations, 220
FCC v. Pacifica Foundation, 220
Federal Election Commission v. Wisconsin Right to Life, Inc., 269
Friedrichs v. California Teachers Association, 255, 543
Gibbons v. Ogden, 75, 546
Gideon v. Wainwright, 124
Gratz v. Bolinger, 515, 520–21, 522, 525, 527, 531–34
Griswold v. Connecticut, 126, 127f
Grutter v. Bolinger, 515, 520–21, 522, 525, 527, 531–34
Hamdi v. Rumsfeld, 200, 465, 467
Hernandez v. Texas, 27, 144t, 153, 157, 260
Hill v. Colorado, 391
Johnson v. DeGrandy, 144t, 159
Katzenbach v. Morgan, 144t, 158, 366
King v. Burwell, 407
Korematsu v. United States, 141
Lawrence v. Texas, 129, 166, 181
Ledbetter v. Goodyear Tire and Rubber Co., 164–65
Loving v. Virginia, 152
LULAC v. Perry, 329
Mapp v. Ohio, 123
Marbury v. Madison, 43, 44, 409–9, 518, 546
McCardle decision, 103
McCullen v. Coakley, 391
McCulloch v. Maryland, 75, 76, 546
McCutcheon, et al., v. FEC, 269, 337
McDonald v. Chicago, 120f, 543
Milligan decision, 103
Miranda v. Arizona, 123, 124f, 548
National Federation of Independent Businesses et al. v. Sebelius, 407
National Labor Relations Board v. Noel Canning, 450

Supreme Court Cases (*continued*)
Near v. Minnesota, 216
New York Times v. Sullivan, 216–17
New York Times v. United States, 114
Obergefell v. Hodges, 44, 73, 91, 152f, 167, 181
Pentagon Papers case, 114, 217–18
Plessy v. Ferguson, 143, 153
Plyer v. Doe, 14, 53, 144t, 157
Powell v. Alabama, 124
Printz v. United States, 543
Roe v. Wade, 44, 128–29, 313, 537
San Antonio Independent School District v. Rodriguez, 157
Schuette v. Coalition to Defend Affirmative Action, 515, 521
Shelby County v. Holder, 144t, 156, 161, 369
Slaughterhouse Cases, 546
Smith v. Allwright, 365
Smith v. Maryland, 110
Snyder v. Phelps, 109
Steelworkers v. Weber, 520
Thornburg v. Gingles, 329
United States v. Cruikshank, 546
United States v. Nixon, 454
United States v. Texas, 567
United States v. Windsor, 167
White v. Regester, 140t, 158–59
Youngstown Sheet and Tube Co. v. Sawyer, 455–56, 458
Zubik v. Burwell, 560
Surveillance, 110–11
Survey research, 184. *See also* Polls
Swing states/voters, 338–39
Symbolic speech, 111–13, 113f, 114f
Syrian conflict, 464, 464f, 465

T

Take care clause, 607
Takings clause, 611
Taliban, 463, 587
Taney Court, 138, 549t
Tariffs, 574, 583
Tasarnaev, Dzhokhar, 56
Taxation
campaign promises on, 351
Democratic Party and, 574–75
economic policy and, 574–75
entitlement programs funded by, 563
interest groups on, 266, 276, 279–80
IRS and, 265, 496
poll taxes, 53, 142, 158, 364f, 365, 366
power of Congress, 35, 41, 49, 53, 78, 79, 405, 407, 505, 580–82
public goods support via, 15
Reagan and, 473, 475
Republican Party and, 310, 574–75, 580
state, 69, 72, 76, 561
tariffs, 574, 583
tax-exempt interest groups, 265
unemployment insurance funding via, 426
without representation, 29–30
Teach for America, 593
Tea Party movement, 22–23, 22f, 194, 198–99, 265, 304–5, 387, 389, 580
Teen2hot4u, 97, 121
Telecommunications Act (1996), 218
Television, 218, 220, 224–26, 225f, 226, 227f, 230–31, 230f, 231f
Temporary Aid to Needy Families, 473, 563
Term limits
congressional, 347–48, 402
congressional committee chair, 418
gubernatorial, 85–87
presidential, 347–48, 441
Terrorism
al-Qaeda and, 463, 466. *See also* bin Laden, Osama
antiterrorism measures, 200–1, 588
Benghazi, Libya, attacks in (2012), 409, 504–5
Boston Marathon bombing, 56, 466, 474
bureaucratic role in response to, 481
drones in flight against, 466–67, 466t
national security surveillance and, 110–11
nonstate actors, 587–88
September 11, 2001, attacks
bureaucratic failures and, 490
civil liberties issues following, 105–6, 110–11
federalism impacts of, 81, 81f
news coverage and, 238
presidential approval ratings after, 178, 587
racial and religious profiling following, 169–70
USA PATRIOT Act and, 81f, 105, 110
War on Terror, 105–6, 456, 465, 467, 587–88
Third parties, 297–98, 302–4, 302f, 303f
obstacles to, 305, 307
Thomas, Clarence, 515, 531, 534, 541, 543, 544, 544f, 569
Thomas, Kelly, 125f
Thornburg v. Gingles, 329
Three-fifths compromise, 36, 38–39, 38f
Thurmond, Strom, 79, 303
Tilden, Samuel, 142, 363
Tinker, Mary Beth and John, 111, 113f
Tocqueville, Alexis de, 13, 250, 269
Tolerance, political, 130, 130f, 131
Torture, 200
Townshend Acts, 28–30, 30t
Tracking polls, 185
Trade
balance of, U.S., 582, 582f
commerce clause on, 53, 72, 79, 604
international economic organizations and, 583
interstate commerce, 72, 75, 79, 82
trade associations and organizations, 252, 254
World Trade Organization on, 583
Trade policy, 578–79, 582–83
European Union, 583
fair trade, 579
international agreements, 579, 582–83
NAFTA, 582
protectionism *vs.* free trade, 579, 582–83
Trans-Pacific Partnership, 447, 582–83
Trade Representative, U.S., 459, 579
Trailerblazers College Tour, 397
TransCanada, 576–77
Transgender individuals, 167–68, 184
Trans-Pacific Partnership, 447, 582–83
Transportation Security Administration (TSA), 481, 487
Treaties, 41, 42, 69, 406, 447, 449. *See also* International trade agreements
Trial by jury, 52, 123–24, 516, 523
Trial procedures, 123–24, 523–24. *See also* District courts
Trudeau, Justin, 460f
Truman, David, 269, 270
Truman, Harry S., 79, 141, 186f, 342, 442, 455, 458, 539, 586
Truman Doctrine, 586
Trump, Donald
election for presidency (2016), 14f, 22, 23, 24, 42, 141, 148, 186, 187, 200, 205, 206, 232, 234–35, 240, 245, 294f, 304, 305f, 312, 323, 331, 332, 333f, 334, 335, 338–39, 341, 342, 509, 592, 626
antiterrorism stance, 200
campaign, 332, 333f, 334, 338–39, 341, 342
debates, 335
Electoral College votes, 323
electoral map, 626
immigration stance, 141, 205, 206, 312
news media and, 232, 234–35, 240, 245
policy stances, generally, 592
presidential nomination process, 294f, 305
public opinion, polls and, 186, 187
Tea Party support for, 304
Tumblr, 214
Turnout. *See under* Voting
Tversky, Amos, 238
Tweed, William Marcy "Boss," 298f
Twitter, 214, 226, 232, 232f, 259, 384–85, 392, 457
Two-party system, 300–8
Tyler, John, 440
Tyranny, 99

U

Unalienable rights, 7, 31, 98
Unanimous consent agreements, 423
Underground Railroad, 77f
Undocumented immigrants, 18, 135, 157, 171, 566, 567–70. *See also* Immigration
Unemployment insurance, 426–27, 563
Unification, reasons for, 64
Unions
  defined, 252
  as interest groups, 252–53, 254–56, 255f, 256f, 257t, 267, 338
  membership numbers, 255–56, 256f, 257t
Unitary system, 65, 66f, 93
United Auto Workers (UAW), 254, 255, 256, 278
United Farm Workers, 144t, 159, 161
United Kingdom (U.K.)
  British Constitution, 28
  exit from EU (Brexit), 585
  legal traditions from, 516–17
United Nations
  anti-nuclear proliferation measures of, 588–89, 588f
  founding of, 586
  interest groups and, 258f
  uprising response by, 463–64
United States Code, 423
United States Conference of Mayors, 260
United States v. Cruikshank, 546
United States v. Nixon, 454
United States v. Texas, 567
United States v. Windsor, 167
United Steelworkers, 455, 458, 520
United We Stand (Party), 303
Unlawful activities, advocacy of, 107
Uprisings in foreign lands, 463–65
Upton, Fred, 418
USAID (U.S. Agency for International Development), 589, 589f
USA PATRIOT Act, 81f, 105, 110
U.S. Citizenship and Immigration Services (USCIS), 566

V

Valence issues, 340–41
Valid secular purpose, 117–18
Van Buren, Martin, 296–97
Vanishing marginals, 347
Verdict, 124–25
Vesting clause, 606
Veterans
  bureaucracy and health care for, 504f, 505
  Reduce Homelessness for Female Veterans Act, 397
  veterans' protest (1932), 389, 391
Veto
  defined, 41
  "Frankenstein" veto, 86
  gubernatorial, 85–86
  line-item, 85
  override of, 41, 428–29, 450–51
  pocket, 428, 450
  presidential, 41, 428–29, 450–52, 451t
Vice president
  campaigns and election of, 324, 324f, 335, 440
  Office of, 468–69
  presidential succession and, 440–41
  as president of Senate, 414
  replacement of, 440–41
Vietnam War
  civil liberties and, 104–5, 111–12, 113f
  Johnson and, 461, 473
  Kennedy and, 461
  Nixon and, 461–62
  Pentagon Papers and, 114, 217–18
  presidential-congressional struggles over, 461–62
  protest politics and, 388
Vine, 259
Violence Against Women Act, 82
Virginia and Kentucky Resolutions, 75
Virginia Plan, 34–35, 36, 36t
Voice of America, 590
Volkswagen, 491–92
Voting, 356–95. *See also* Elections; Electoral College
  absentee voting, 385f
  anger of voters, 24, 24f
  Australian (secret) ballot, 299, 300f, 383
  civic duty/civic interest and, 10, 19, 375–76
  compulsory (in Australia), 379
  constitutional amendments on, 53, 54f, 55, 359–60, 360f, 362, 370
  Constitution and, 16, 358
  democracy and, 10, 16, 19, 392–93
  discussion of politics influencing, 390, 390f
  early voting, 384, 385f
  efficacy and, 376
  equality and rights for, 16
  ethnicity and, 148, 158–59, 161, 315f, 366–67, 369f, 372
  felons, voting rights for, 170–71, 170f
  franchise (suffrage), 358, 360
  generational replacement and, 380
  genes and, 377–78
  grandfather clauses and, 142–43, 365
  graveyard voting, 383
  history in America, 359–70
    1790s to 1870s expansion, 360–61
    African American suffrage, 142–43, 155–56, 359, 360, 362–66
    civil rights movement, 142–46, 148, 155–56, 158–59, 161, 172, 360, 365–66
    expansion of voting, 359–62, 365–70
    Jim Crow laws, 143, 363, 363f
    Latino vote, 148, 158–59, 161, 366–67, 369f
    vote for 18-year-olds, 360, 370
    voting restrictions, 359, 362–69
    women's suffrage, 144–46, 146f, 147f, 252, 358, 361–62, 362f
  Internet voting, 384–85
  Kids Voting USA, 376f
  laws and regulations, 382–85
    National Voter Registration Act, 383–84
    new forms of voting under, 384–85
    reforms in 1890s, 382–83
    voter ID, 160–61, 160f, 368–69, 368f
    voter registration, 291, 365, 383–84
    Voting Rights Act (VRA), 80, 155–56, 158, 170, 310, 328, 365, 367, 404, 472
  literacy tests, 142–43, 158, 363–64, 364f, 365, 366, 367
  median voter theorem, 301, 346
  models of
    economic, 374–75
    institutional, 376–77
    psychological, 375–76
  new forms of, 384–85
  participation beyond, 386–92
  plurality *vs.* majority vote, 301
  political machines and, 380, 382–83
  poll taxes and, 53, 142, 158, 364f, 365, 366
  popular vote, 325, 360–61, 361f
  practice and theory of, 358–59
  public opinion expression via, 179–80, 509
  racial barriers, dismantling of, 155–56, 360, 365–66
  rational, 375
  reasons for, 374–78
  retrospective, 343
  socialization and, 374, 375–76
  suffrage, 358, 360. *See also under specific groups*
  turnout, 362, 370–74, 378–82
    age and, 315f, 371f, 372
    assessment of, 378–82
    demographics of, 148, 315f, 365, 369f, 371–74, 371f
    education and, 373–74, 374t, 380
    income/socioeconomic status and, 372–73, 373t
    inequality and, 381–82
    level in United States, *vs.* other democracies, 379
    measuring, new ways for, 381
    in presidential elections, 361, 365, 367, 369f, 370–82, 371f, 373f, 373t–374t, 380f
    race/ethnicity and, 148, 155–56, 158–59, 369f, 372, 373f
    sex/gender and, 371–72

Voting (*continued*)
trends in, 379–81, 380f
VAP and, 379–80, 380f, 381
VEP and, 380f, 381
women's suffrage and, 362
vote-by-mail (VBM) system, 384, 385f
voter apathy, 365, 381
voter ID laws, 160–61, 160f, 368–69, 368f
voter registration, 287, 365, 383–84
voting-age population (VAP), 379–80, 380f, 381
voting-eligible population (VEP), 380f, 381
weather and, 378
white primary and, 365
women's rights, 16, 53, 137, 144–46, 146f, 147f, 252, 358, 361–62, 362f

W

Walker, Scott, 91, 255
Wallace, George, 80, 151, 303
Walmart, 254, 548
Walters, Barbara, 225
War on Terror, 105–6, 456, 465, 467, 587–88
War powers, 35, 405–6, 446–47, 461–62
War Powers Act, 462
Warrantless searches, 122–23
Warrantless wiretapping, 105–6, 110–11, 200
Warren, Elizabeth, 204f
Warren Court, 121, 548, 549t
War(s)
Afghanistan, 441–42, 456, 458, 462, 463, 588
Cold War, 104–5, 586
drones, use of, 464, 466–67, 466t
enemy combatants, 465, 467
Iraq, 456, 462–63, 501–2, 587–88, 591
Korean, 455, 458
military actions and, 586, 587–88
nonstate actors, 587–88
presidential powers in, 455–56, 458, 461–67
restrictions on civil liberties and rights during, 102–6
Spanish-American War, 585
uprisings in foreign lands, 463–65
Vietnam, 104–5, 111–12, 113f, 114, 217–18, 388, 461–62, 473
World War I and II, 103, 140–41, 585
Washington, George
American Revolution role of, 30
campaign and election of, 330, 360
federalism under, 74
on foreign entanglements, 584
as Founder and Framer, 34f
government of, 295–96
news media and criticism of, 222
presidency shaped for, 440, 442f, 443
public opinion and, 182
State of the Union address, 452
Supreme Court appointments, 541
voting for, 362
Watchdog groups, 15, 264, 264f, 274
Watchdog role of press, 214, 215–16, 218
Watergate scandal, 453–54, 537
Weather, and voting, 378
Weaver, James, 302
Webster, Daniel, 75, 76
Wedge issues, 341
Wehby, Monica, 392
Welfare system/benefits, 81, 561
Whig Party, 297
Whistleblowers, 481, 508
White House Office/staff, 468
White primary, 365
White v. Regester, 144t, 158–59
Wikileaks, 114
Williams, Roger, 117
Wilson, Henry, 324f
Wilson, James, 39f
Wilson, Woodrow, 365, 447, 452, 585
Winner-take-all system, 292, 293–94, 323–24
Wiretapping, 105–6, 110–11, 200
Women
in bureaucracies, 499, 499f
in Congress, 399, 400, 400f
discrimination against, 116, 137, 144–47, 150t
dismantling of, 162–65. *See also* Affirmative action
equality in workplace, 162, 164–65
equal pay for, 162, 164–65
Equal Rights Amendment, 162–63, 163f
First Lady, role of, 469–70, 469f
interest group participation by, 251f, 253
in judiciary, 162f, 408f, 515, 521, 539–40, 539t, 541, 544
Latina, as elected officials, 344–45, 344f
National Organization for Women (NOW), 162
in news media, 225, 231f
in presidency, 442
as state leaders, 63, 86–87, 86f, 90f
Supreme Court Justices, 162f, 408f, 515, 521, 540, 544
Violence Against Women Act, 82
voter turnout among, 315f, 362, 371–72
voting rights for, 16, 53, 137, 144–46, 146f, 147f, 252, 358, 361–62, 362f
Women's Rights Project, 162
Women's suffrage movement, 144–46, 146f, 147f, 252, 361–62, 362f
Woodhull, Victoria Claflin, 362f
Woodward, Bob, 215, 215f, 453
Workplace equality, 162, 164–65
World Bank, 589, 591
World Trade Organization (WTO), 583
World Wars, 103, 140–41, 585
Writ of *habeas corpus. See Habeas corpus*, writ of

Y

Yellen, Janet, 578, 579f
Yellow journalism, 223, 223f
Youngstown Sheet and Tube Co. v. Sawyer, 455–56, 458

Z

Zenger, John Peter, 115, 219
Zimmerman, George, 125, 156
Zubik v. Burwell, 560
Zuckerberg, Mark, 232

ă ĕ ĭ ŏ ŭ

căt ĕlf pĭg ŏtter dŭck

ay the name of each picture below. Write the **short vowel** ou hear on the lines.

______ ______ ______ ______ ______

______ ______ ______ ______ ______

Help the monsters fly through the clouds. Complete the words below by writing **a**, **i**, **o** or **u** on the lines.

Look at the vowel sign each monster is holding. Then, look at the snake beside the monster. Read the words on it. Color only the parts of the snake that have words with the matching vowel sound.

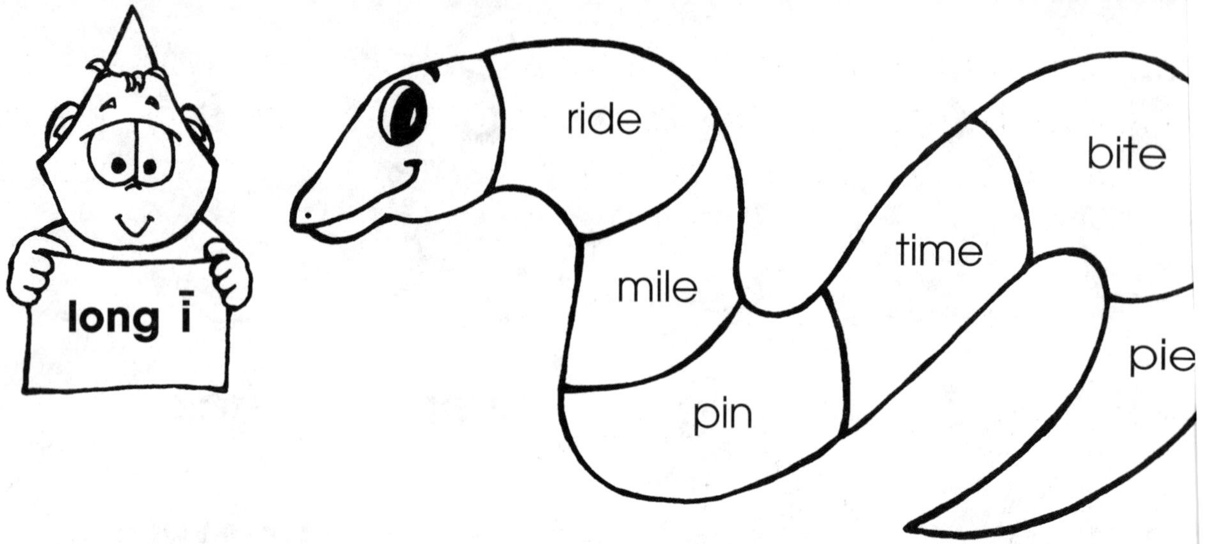

long ī
ride
mile
pin
time
bite
pie

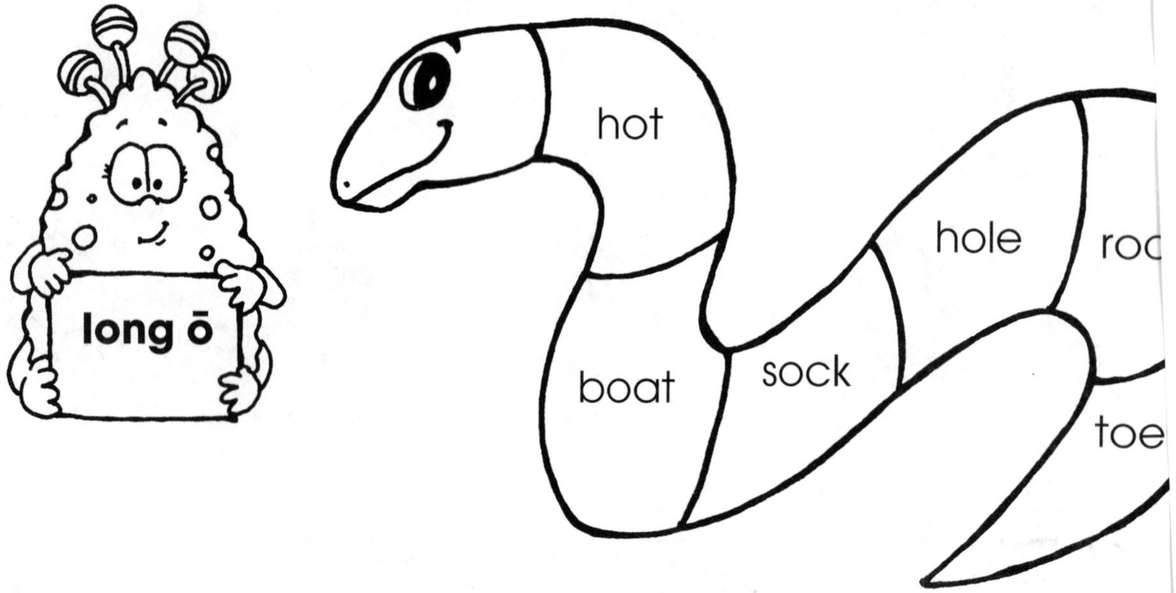

long ō
hot
boat
sock
hole
roc
toe

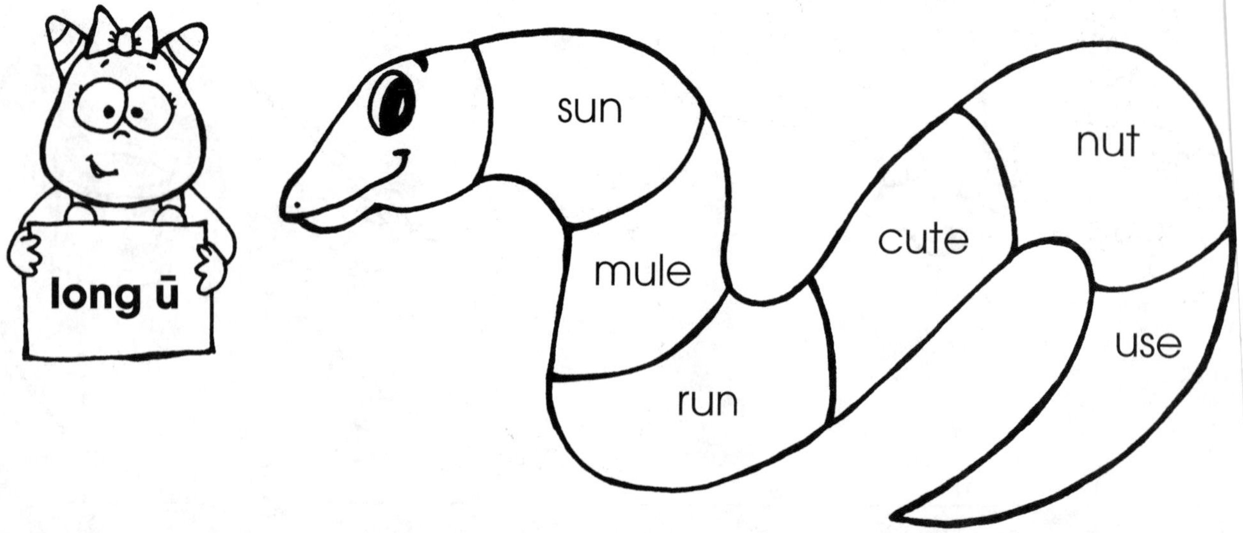

long ū
sun
mule
run
cute
nut
use

Pam likes hamburgers! You can make words that rhyme with **am**. Pick a letter from the box and write it in the lines.

y	**P**
c	**j**
r	**h**
l	**st**

Dan prefers sandwiches. Pick a letter from the box to fill in the sandwiches to make words that rhyme with **an**.

f	**D**
c	**m**
r	**st**
h	**s**

Short ă

Matt is a rat, and he lives in a saggy bag. Look at the **at** and **ag** words below and say the ones with pictures. Then, fill in the blanks with letters from the box. Do all the **at** words rhyme? Do all the **ag** words rhyme?

Use the box below to help you catch these **short ĕ** words. Then, fill in the letters on the lines.

Pet

Net

___et

___et

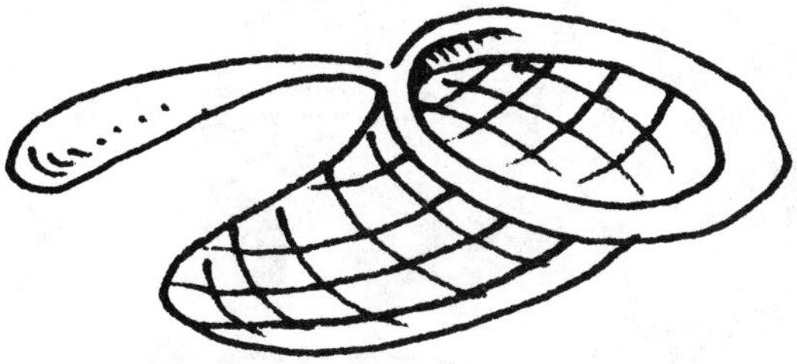

___et

___et

___et

___et

___et

___et

___et

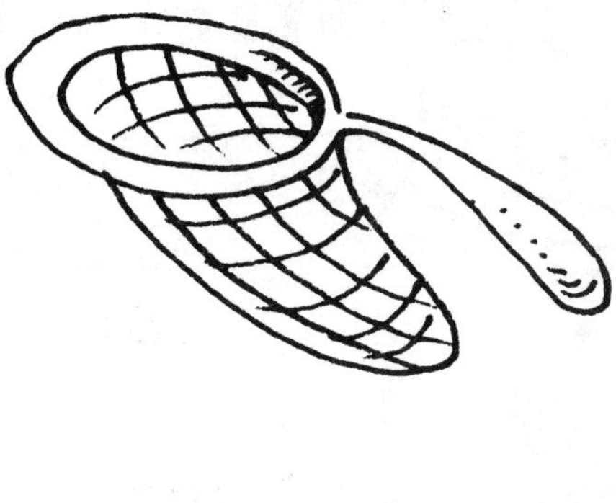

___et

___et

b	j
g	l
m	n
p	s
v	w
y	

Short ĕ

Circle **yes** under each picture that has a **short ĕ** sound. If the picture does not have a **short ĕ** sound, circle **no**.

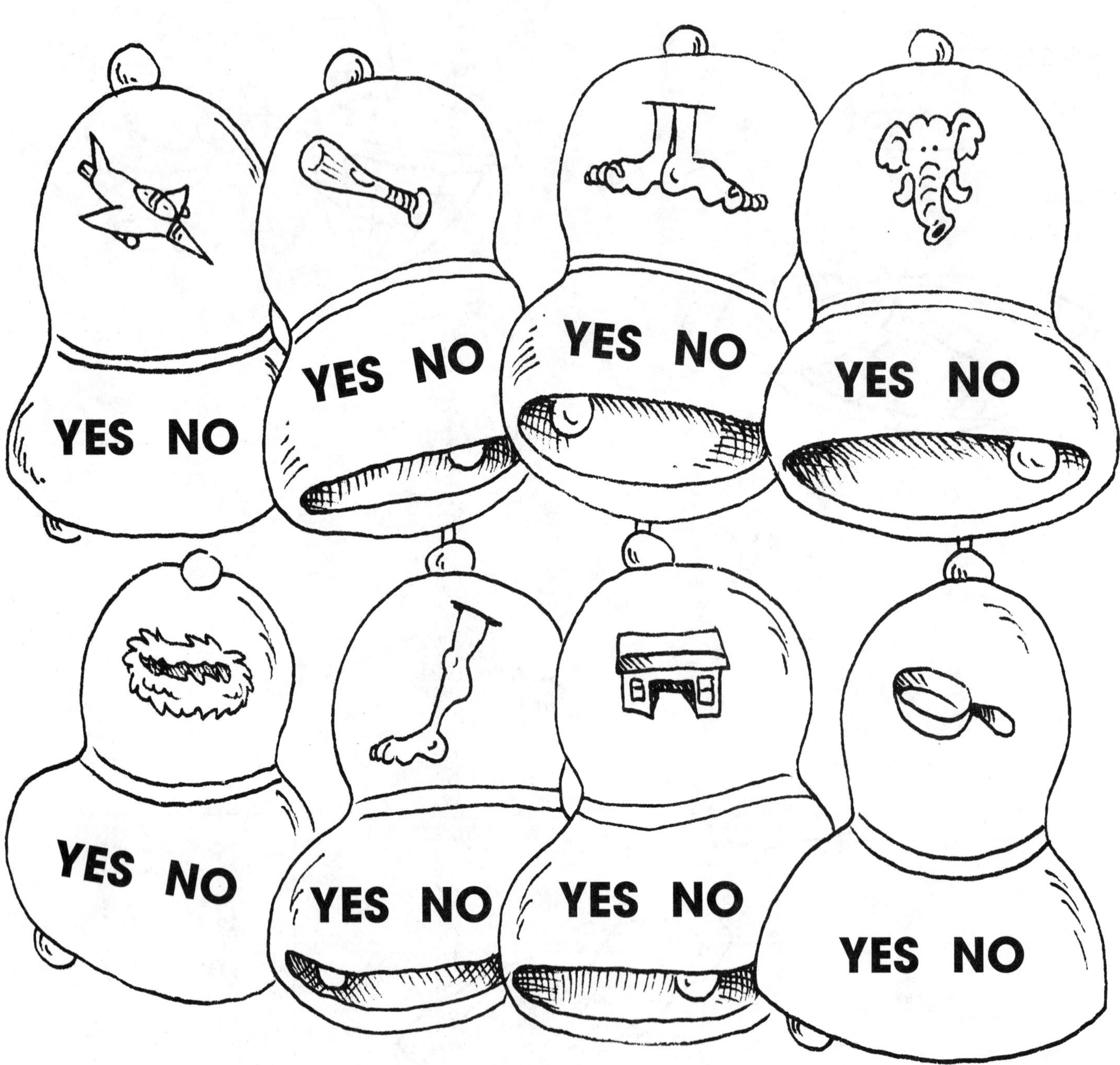

Jenny the Hen is building a nest for her many eggs. You can fill her eggs for her with **short ĕ** words from the box. The polka dot eggs each get an **en** word. The striped eggs get an **est** word.

best test hen
rest pen ten
west zest den
nest men Ben
pest vest

Short ă and ĕ

Tic-tac-toe can help you review the **short ă** and **short ĕ** vowel sounds. Draw a line through any three matching vowel sounds in a row. Remember that a line can be diagonal (↗↘).

Vinnie is a fish. So is Minnie. Their names both have the **short ĭ** sound. Vinnie and Minnie are swimming with lots of **short ĭ** words below. Say each word pair out loud and cross out the ones that do not rhyme.

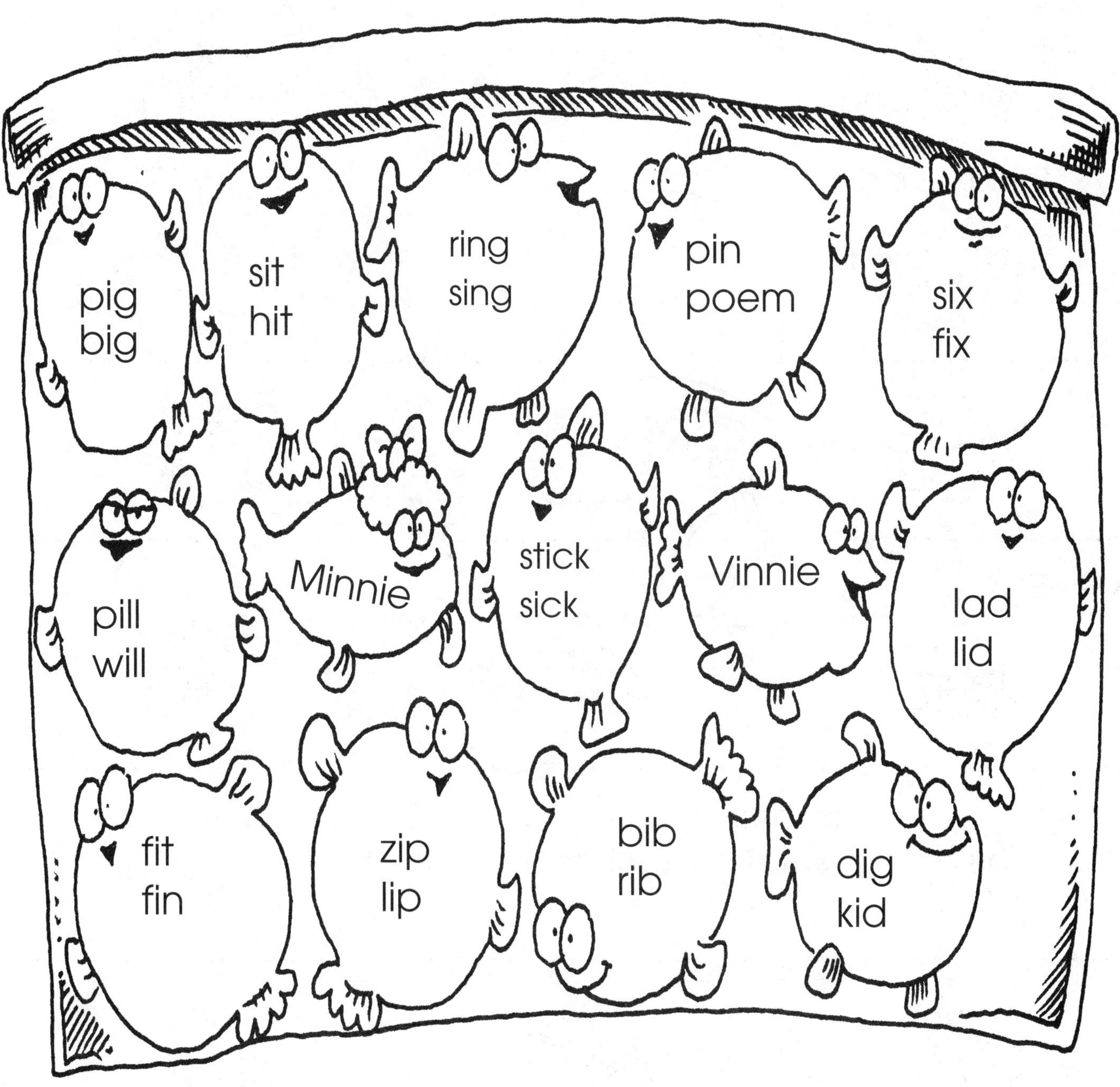

Short ĭ

The king is singing words that rhyme with **ing**! Help him sing out this rhyming set of words.

The king is up to something!
Write the missing **short ĭ** vowels to find out what he is doing.

He ______s br______ng______ng a r______ng to

the s______ng______ng queen!

Use the box to fill in the missing consonants to make whole **it** words. Then, write your own **it** words on the baseballs.

Short ĭ

Billy and Millie love to wiggle as they dance the jig. Circle the words below which rhyme with **ig** or **ill**. Then, cross out the words that do not rhyme.

Ollie the Octopus is juggling boxes again! Ollie's name has a **short ŏ** in it, and more **short ŏ** words are in Ollie's boxes. In each box, circle the word that goes with the picture and write it on the line.

Short ŏ

You can help Ollie add to his collection of **short ŏ** words. Circle the word in each row that names the picture in the box. Cross out the word in each row that contains a long vowel.

pop hop mop rope top cop

block rock sock soak lock clock

log jog dog go fog frog

dot hot note pot lot got

Fill in the missing consonants below. Then, write other **op** words on the lines.

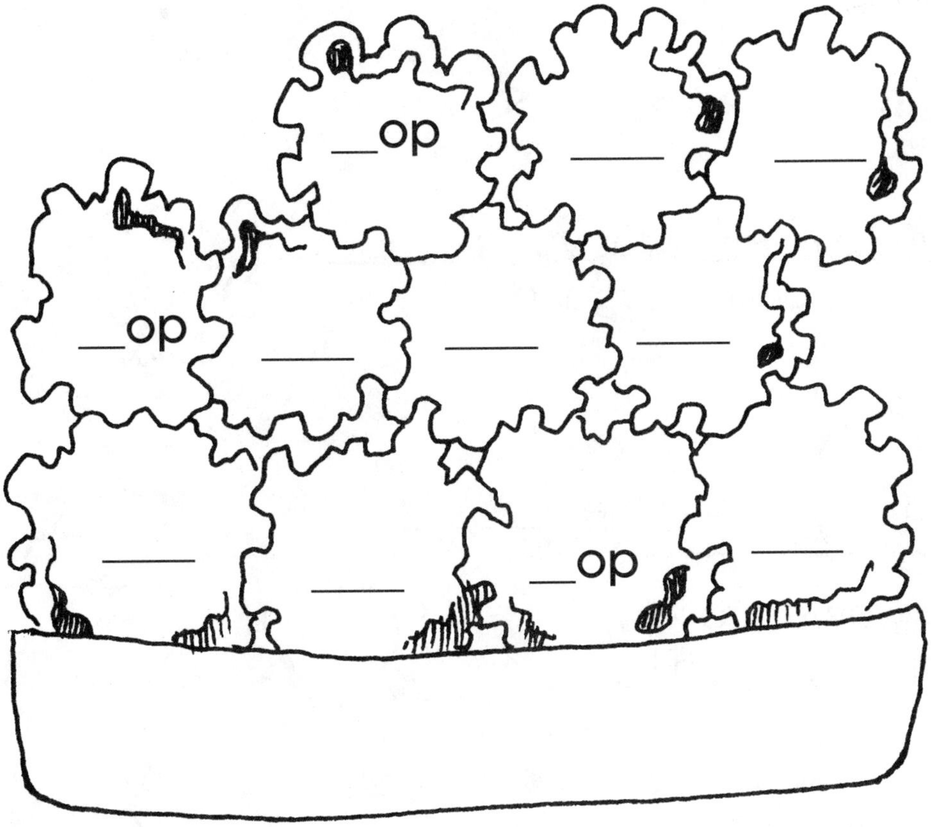

__op ____ ____

__op ____ ____ ____

____ ____ __op ____

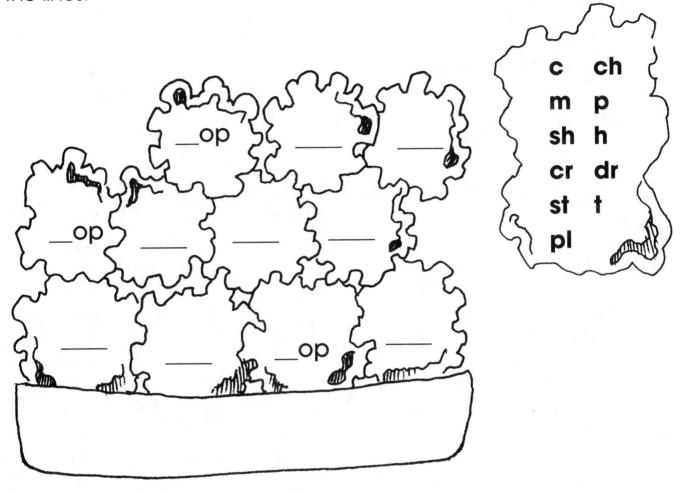

c ch
m p
sh h
cr dr
st t
pl

Now, fill in the lines to make **ock** words to go with the pictures. What words did you make?

1. s__ __ __ 2. cl__ __ __ 3. l__ __ __ 4. r__ __ __

Short ŏ

It's silly rhyme time! Fill in the lines with the **short ŏ** endings shown. If you need help, look at the picture clues.

Short ŏ endings	**Rhymes**
ot	Lucy's p___ ___ was very h___ ___. She was cooking sugar d___ ___s!
og	The d___ ___ and the h___ ___ Jumped off the l___ ___. They wanted to join The fr___ ___ in a j___ ___!
op	The m___ ___ from the sh___ ___ Fell in love with the t___ ___.
ock	"I'm so cold!" cried the cl___ ___ ___, "So on both hands I'll wear a s___ ___ ___!"

Hurry and get under the umbrella, because it's raining **short ŭ** words! Color the raindrops that have the **short ŭ** vowel sound.

Short ŭ

Look carefully in the rug—there are lots of snug little bugs! Use the consonants to the left to make **ug** words. The first one is done for you.

dug

Draw a line through any row down (↓) or across (→) that has the same **short vowel** sound.

Which short vowel sounds made a row? ___________

Which short vowel sounds made a row? ___________

Short Vowels

In each flower petal, write a word with the correct short vowel sound. Use all the words in the box below.

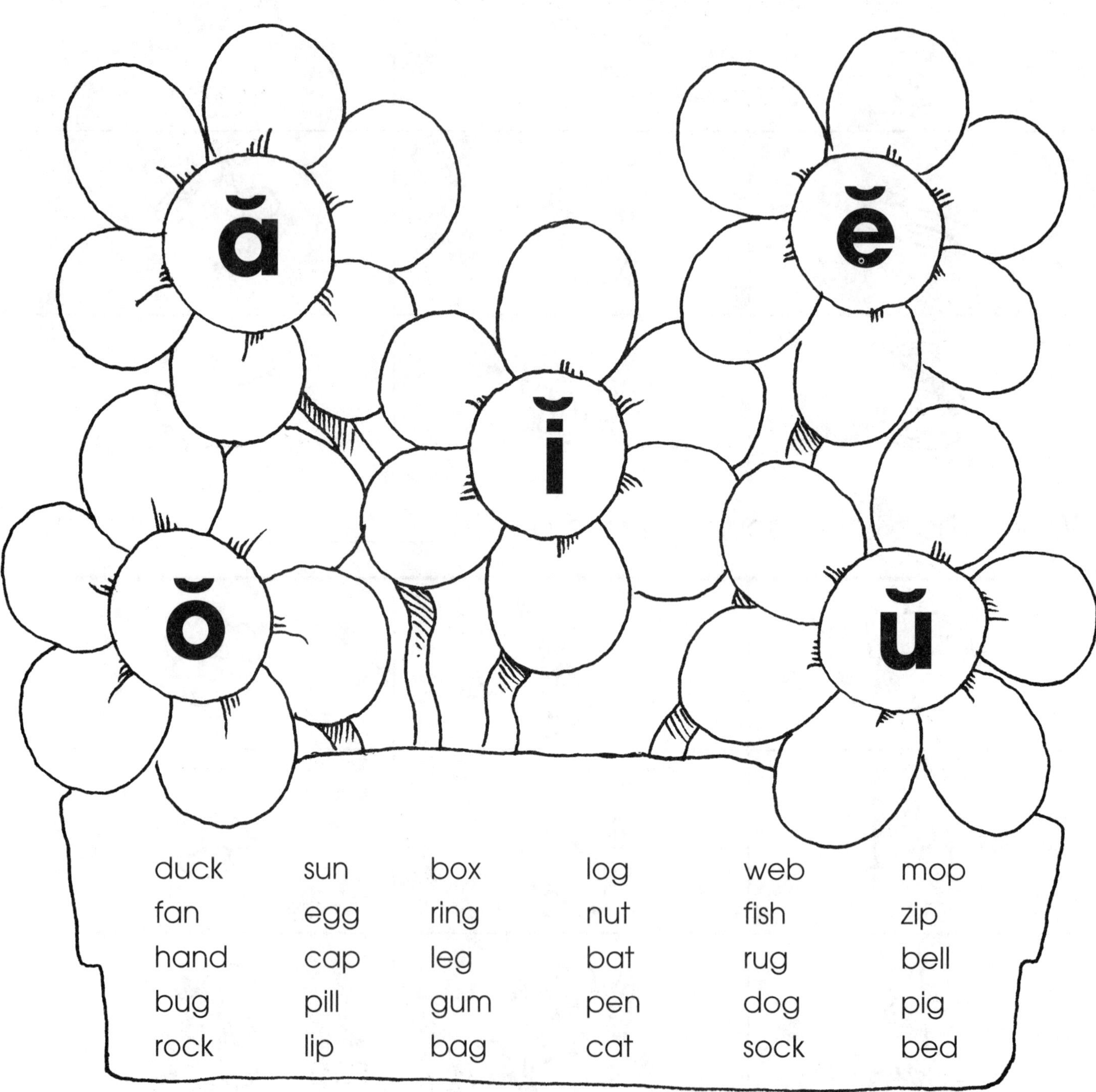

Read each word below. Color the rocket red if the word has a long vowel. Then, write which long vowel you hear (**ā**, **ē**, **ī**, **ō** or **ū**). If the vowel sound is short, color the rocket blue, and write which short vowel you hear (**ă**, **ĕ**, **ĭ**, **ŏ** or **ŭ**).

	vowel sound		**vowel sound**
lid	_____	rain	_____
boot	_____	duck	_____
fish	_____	rock	_____
bell	_____	pie	_____
rake	_____	bag	_____
key	_____	toe	_____

r Consonant Blends

What a mess! Drake the Dragon has dropped a lot of **r blends** on his cave floor. R blends are consonants combined with an **r** to make a special sound.

Help Drake clean up by circling the **br** words, drawing a box around the **cr** words and drawing a line under the **dr** words.
WORDS
BRUSH
DRINK
DRAGON
CRAB
DRUM
BRICK
BREAD
CRAYON
BRACELET
CRUTCHES

Follow the frog's trail, and say the name of each picture. Then, on the line, write the **r blend** you hear—**fr**, **gr**, **pr** or **tr**.

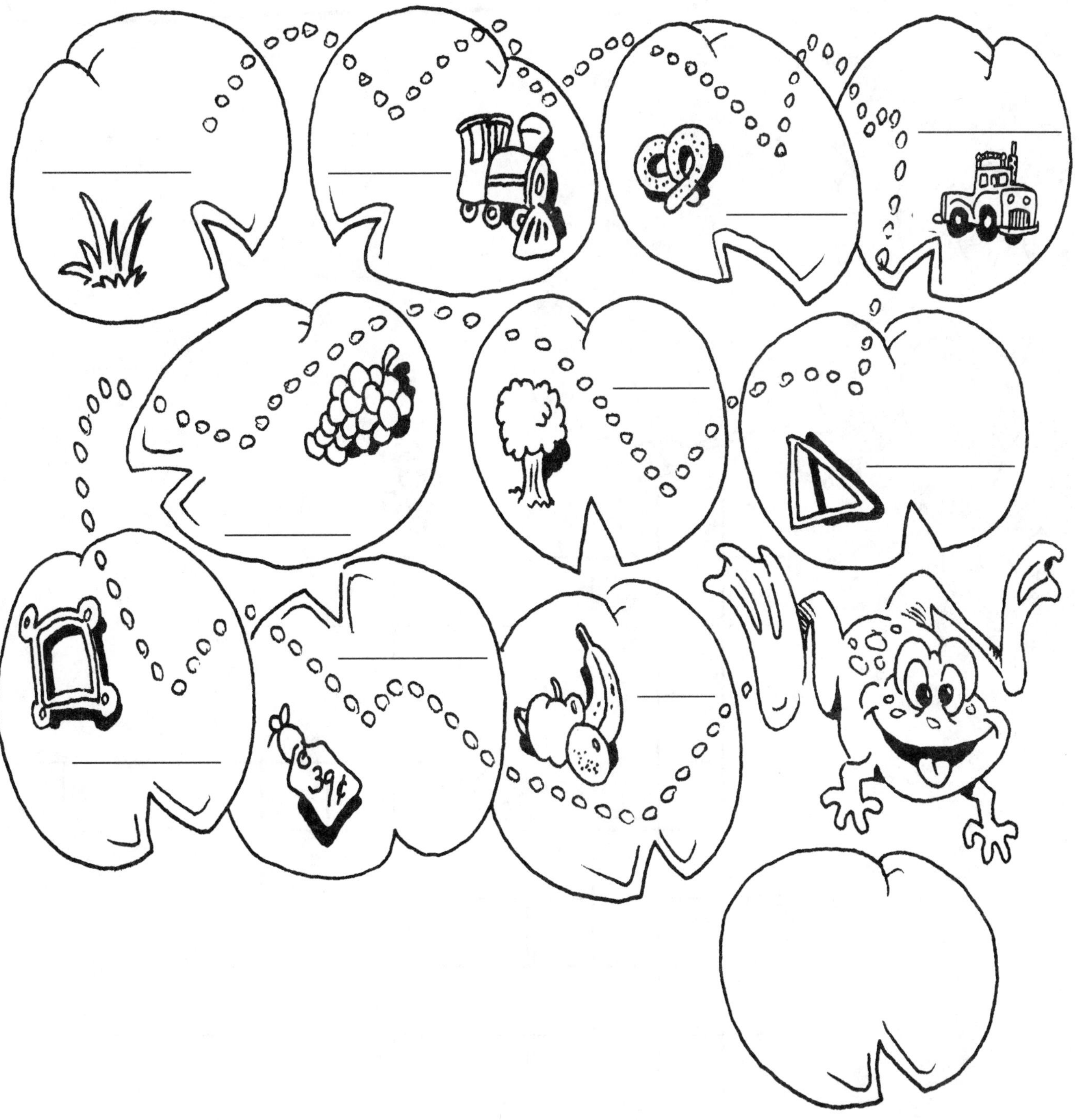

r Consonant Blends

Fill in the crossword puzzle with **r blend** words. Use the pictures at the start of each word as clues.

Look at these **l blends** below and on page 52. **L blends** combine a consonant with an **l** to make a special sound. Mark the different blends you see as follows:

bl blends ☆

cl blends ✗

fl blends ●

gl blends ○

pl blends ✓

sl blends ⚲

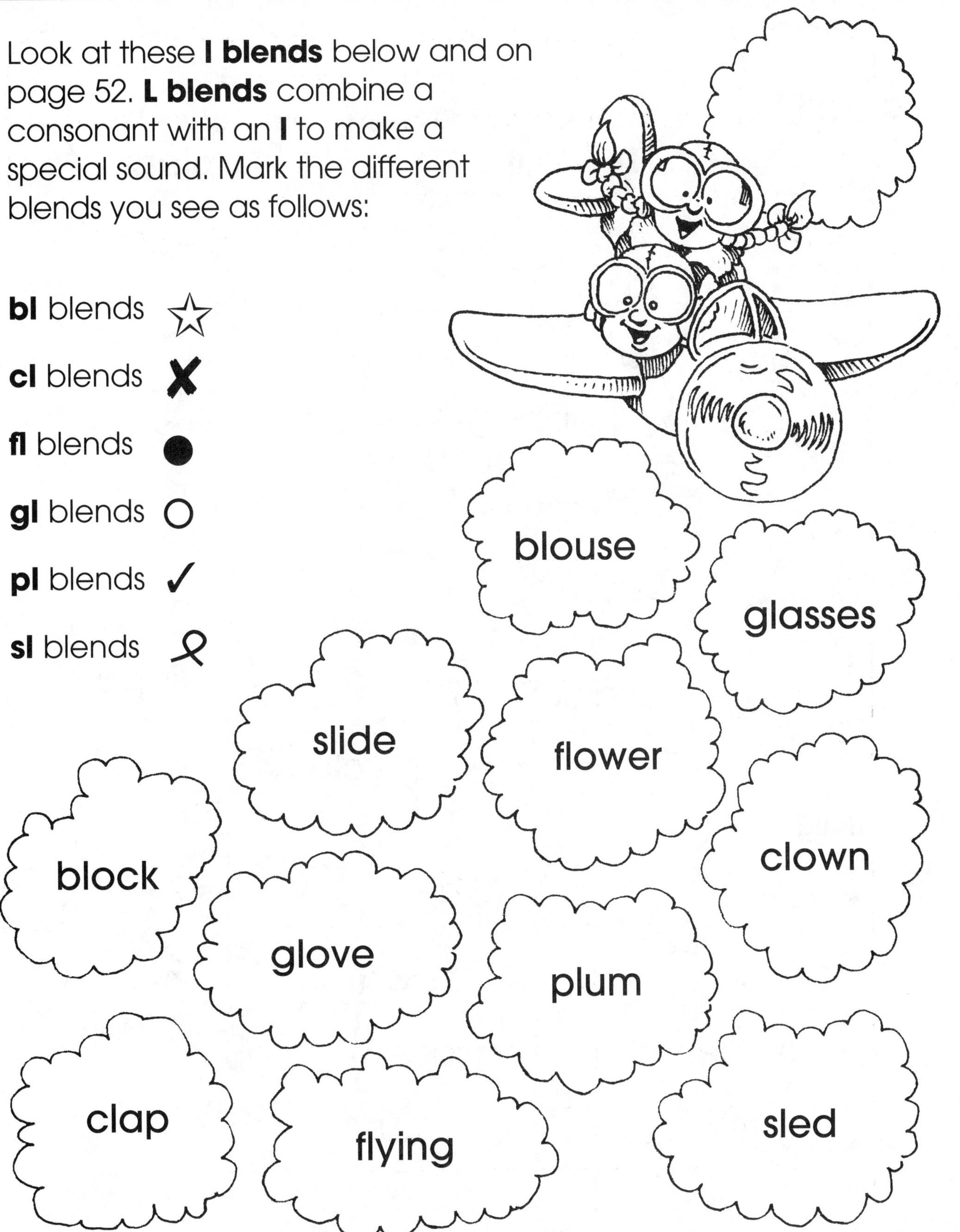

l Consonant Blends

Say the name of each **l blend** picture. Then, write the blend on the line in each flag.

s Consonant Blends

Each step below has a picture of a word with an **s blend**. Fill in the box with the **s blend** that goes with the picture. The first one is done for you.

Look who is racing down the stairs—the snail and the spider! Who do you think will win? Each step below has a picture of word with an **s blend**. Fill in the box with the **s blend** that goes with the picture.

s Consonant Blends

Fill in the missing **s blends** below.

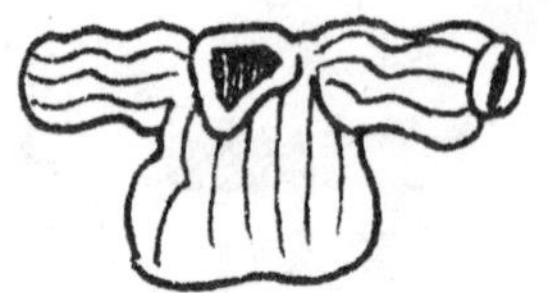

____eater

____ing

____an

____im

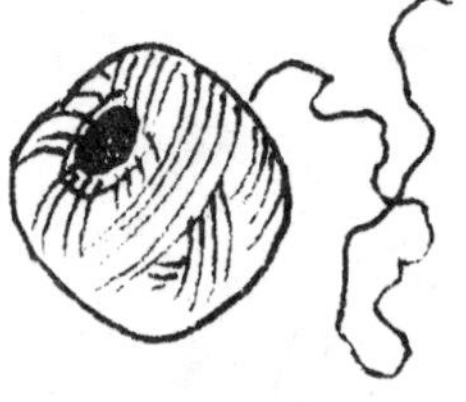

____ing

____inkler

____ash

____raw

____ray

____ong

These special stamps each contain an **s blend** picture. Write the **s blend** you hear on the line in each stamp.

Consonant Blends

Circle the correct **blend** below each picture.

gr pr tr

pl gl sl

sh sw sn

gr cr dr

sl st sk

pl gl bl

sw sh st

sk sp sl

pr tr gr

sn sw sc

sl sc sp

tr fr cr

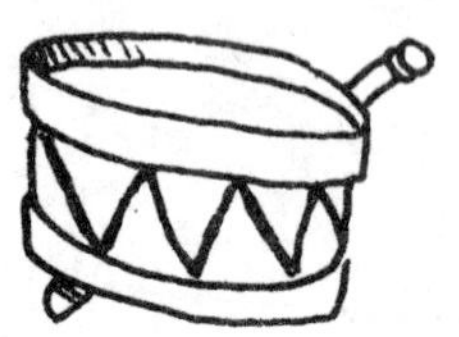

dr br tr

pr br dr

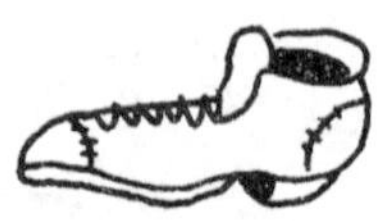

sk sw sh

pl cl fl

A **digraph** is a combination of a consonant with the letter **h** to make a special sound.

Here are four digraphs:

Now, match the **digraph** word on the left to its picture on the right. Draw a line to connect them.

church

wheelbarrow

thorn

Digraphs

To complete each of these silly sentences, fill in the correct digraph—**ch**, **sh**, **th** or **wh**.

The ____ ____icken munched on a ____ ____eeseburger.

The ____ ____oe told the bru____ ____, "I need a poli____ ____, please."

The ____ ____erries and ____ ____ips sat together on the ____ ____air.

  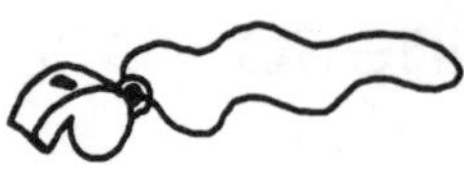

The ____ ____ark wore a ____ ____irt, and a ____ ____istle, too.

The ____ ____ale did ma____ ____ while in his ba____ ____.

READING
GAMES AND
PUZZLES

Upper- and Lowercase Letters

The noodles in this bowl of soup are shaped like the letters of the alphabet. Some letters of the alphabet are missing. Say the alphabet out loud. Circle each letter in the soup as you say it. When you come to a missing letter, write it in the bowl. Be sure to make all the letters **uppercase**, or **capitals**.

On the last page, all the letters in the soup were uppercase. Now, it is your turn to make a bowl of "lowercase-letter soup." Inside the bowl, write the whole alphabet in **lowercase**, or **small** letters. If you need help writing your letters, look at the letters on the tablecloth.

Upper- and Lowercase Letters

Darrel needs to put all the **uppercase** letters in one barrel and all the **lowercase** letters in the other barrel. Help him by drawing a line from each letter on his sign below to the barrel in which that letter belongs.

In the puzzle below, color each square that contains a **lowercase** letter.

Row 1	l	o	Y	N	M	w	e	r
Row 2	M	c	a	B	D	s	e	Z
Row 3	N	E	R	I	C	U	G	F
Row 4	C	Y	F	l	e	H	D	M
Row 5	J	P	S	t	t	R	V	K
Row 6	W	O	I	D	B	T	X	A
Row 7	e	r	s	P	S	a	r	e
Row 8	c	o	F	A	W	Y	o	l

Upper- and Lowercase Letters

Circle all the **uppercase** letters on the envelope below.

Miss Susan Small
12345 Alphabet Lane
Capital City, Kansas 00000

How many did you circle? ______________

Amanda is having a block party, and she is inviting you to come. The consonant blocks are all piled up below, but some of the consonants are missing. Help Amanda by writing in the missing letters on the blank blocks. Be sure to use **uppercase** letters.

Vowels and Consonants

On this page, Amanda has piled up her vowel blocks. Write one vowel on each block. Be sure to put the **vowels** in alphabetical order, but this time use **lowercase** letters.

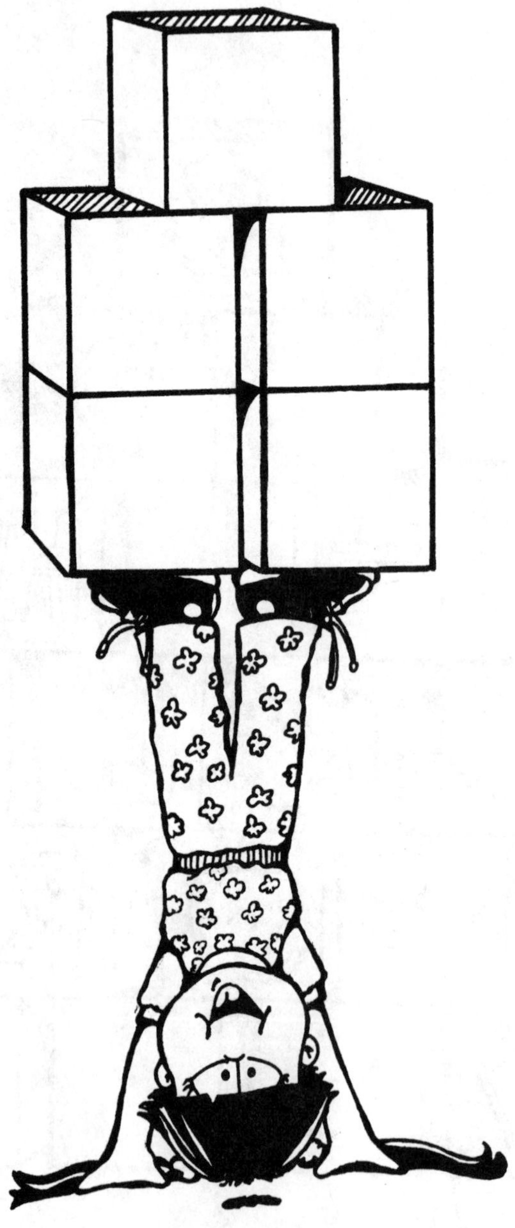

Each word below is missing a vowel. Complete the puzzle by filling in the missing **vowels**. Use each **vowel** only once. Some words go across (⟶) the puzzle. Other words go down (↓). The pictures will help you.

Vowels and Consonants

The puzzle box below has seven rows of squares that contain vowels and consonants. Go from left to right (⟶), saying the name of each letter in the row. When you come to a **consonant**, color in that square with your favorite color crayon.

Row 1	B	V	X	L	C	N	P
Row 2	A	O	I	R	E	U	O
Row 3	E	I	U	D	A	I	E
Row 4	O	E	A	G	O	E	U
Row 5	I	A	O	K	I	O	A
Row 6	E	U	I	Z	E	A	I
Row 7	U	O	E	C	A	I	O

Read each animal's name on the pages below. If the first letter of the name is a **vowel**, draw a square around that letter. If the first letter is a **consonant**, draw a triangle around it.

Long ā

Long vowels always sound like their names. Say the letter **a**. That is the **long ā** sound. Draw a line from each **long ā** word with the picture that shows what it means.

Circle each **long ā** word in the trail below.

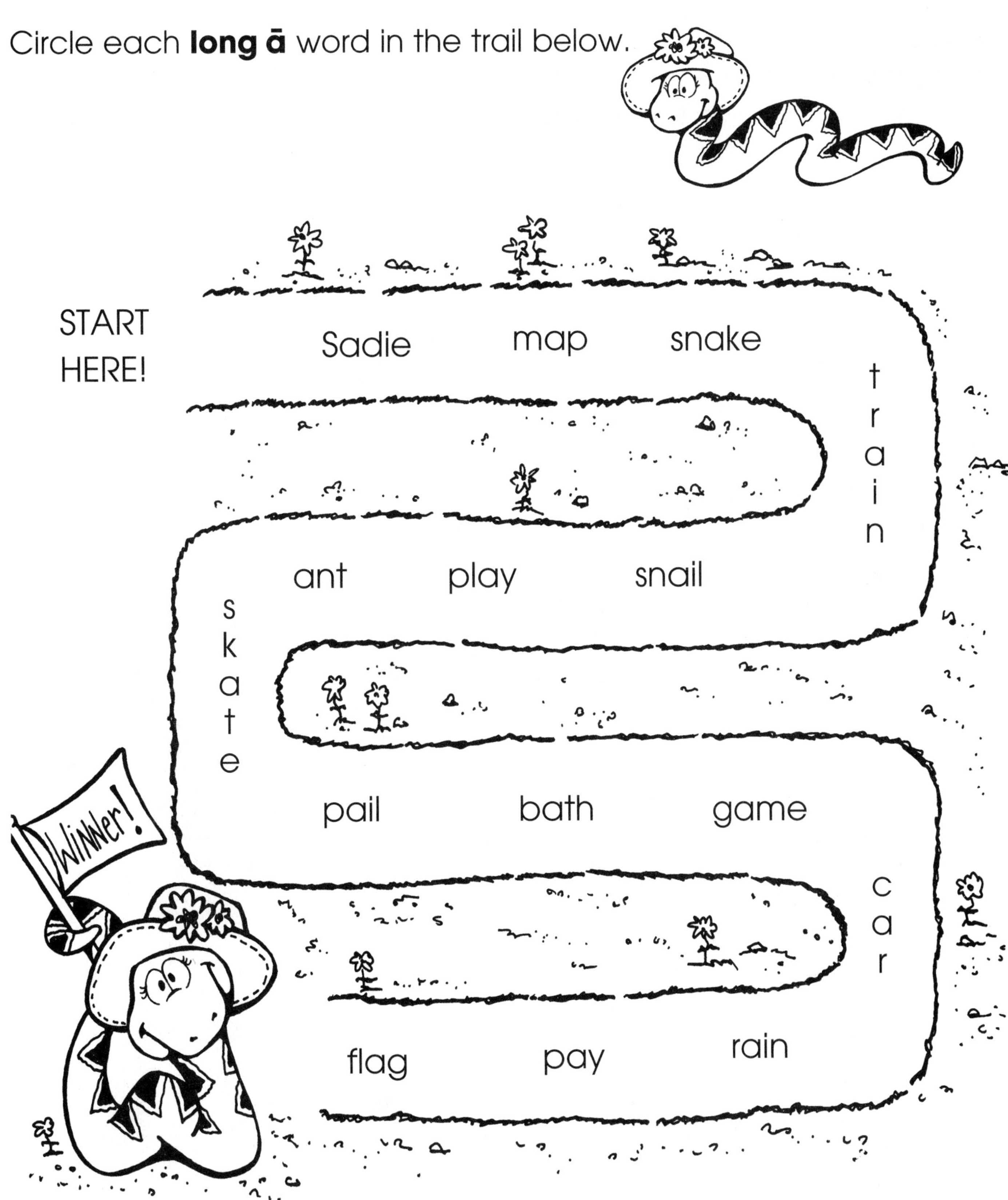

Long ē

All the animals that live on **Long Ē** Street have names with the **long ē** sound. Draw an **X** on the pictures of the animals whose names do not have the **long ē** sound.

Now, use crayons to color the **long ē** animals any way you like.

Long ī

Ride the **long ī** spiral from the inside out. Fill in the letter **i** to make the **long ī** sound in each word. Say each word out loud as you go.

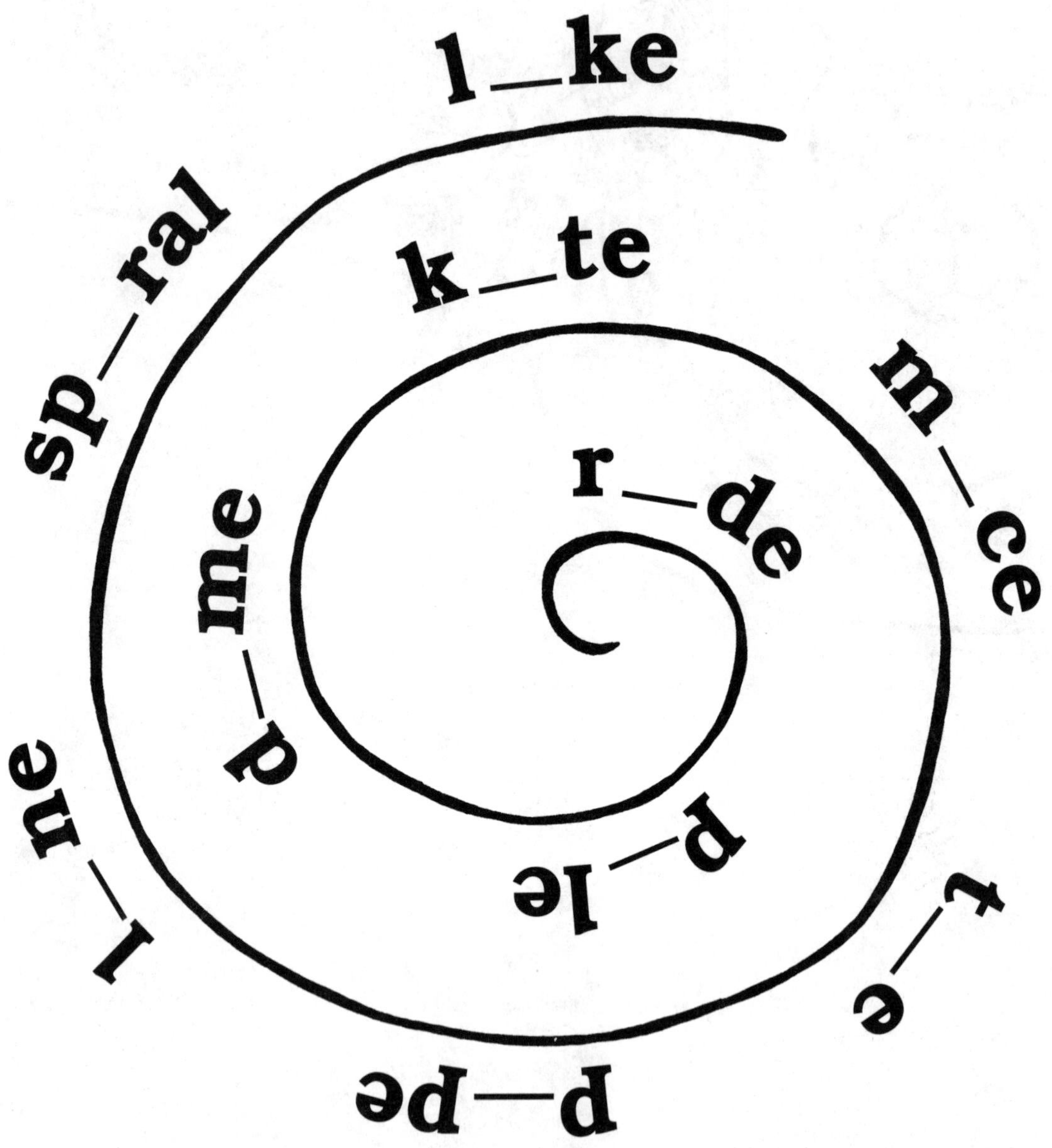

I is a very short word that has the **long ī** sound. This game is called "What am I?" To play, read each clue written in the center of the page. Then, find the picture that answers the question "What am I?" Draw a line from each clue to the picture that it describes.

I shine.

I fry.

I slide.

I dry.

I bite.

I buy.

I fly.

I cry.

Long ō

Climb the **long ō** pole. As you go up, circle each word that has the **long ō** sound.

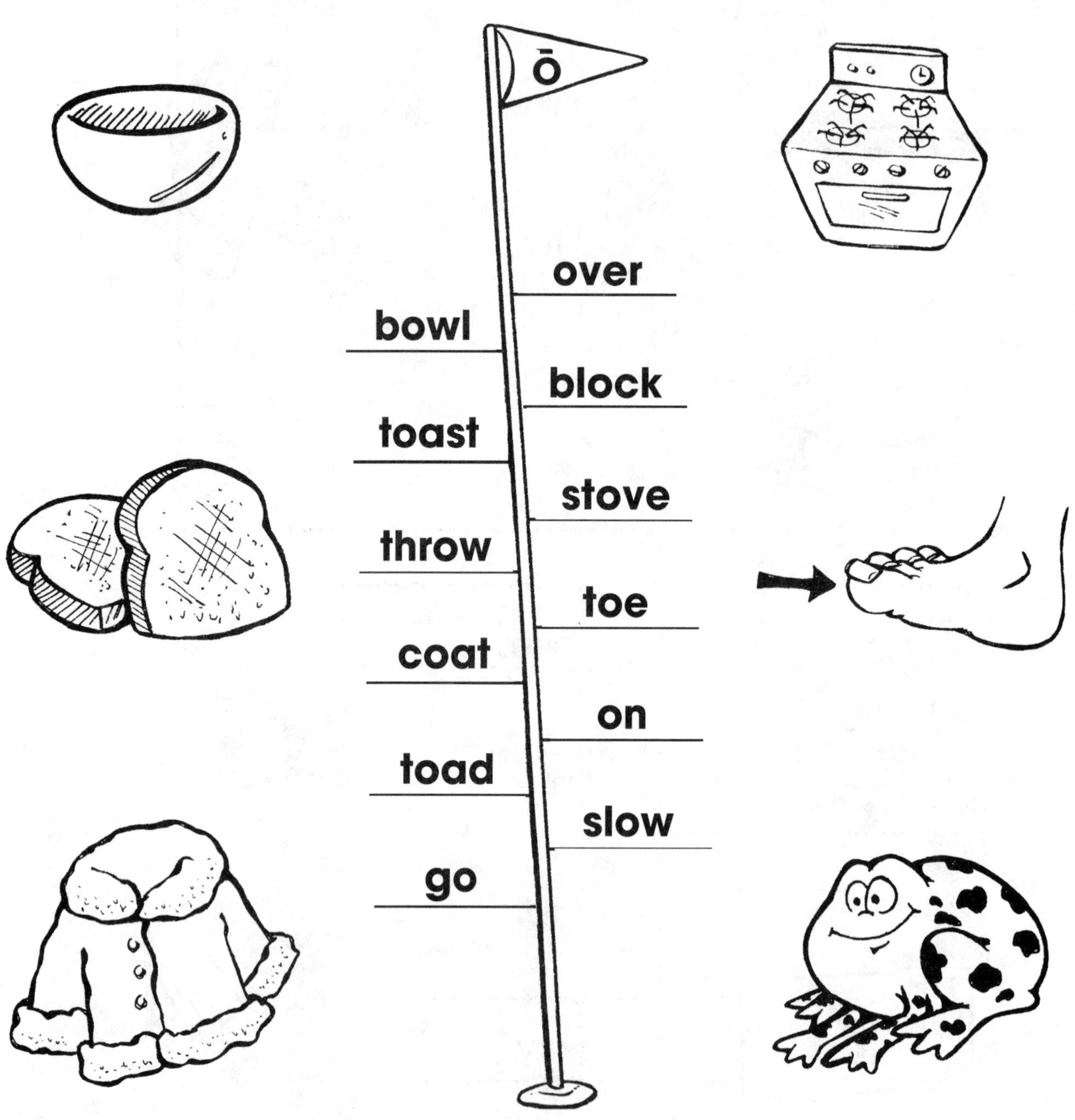

Use the pictures in the box below to help you fill in the words in this **long ō** puzzle. The first one is done for you.

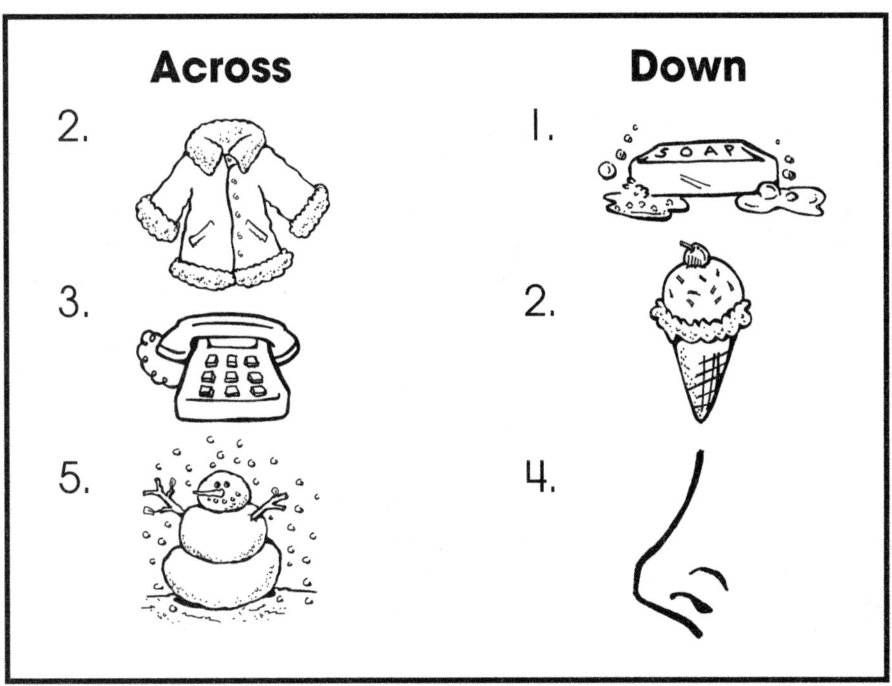

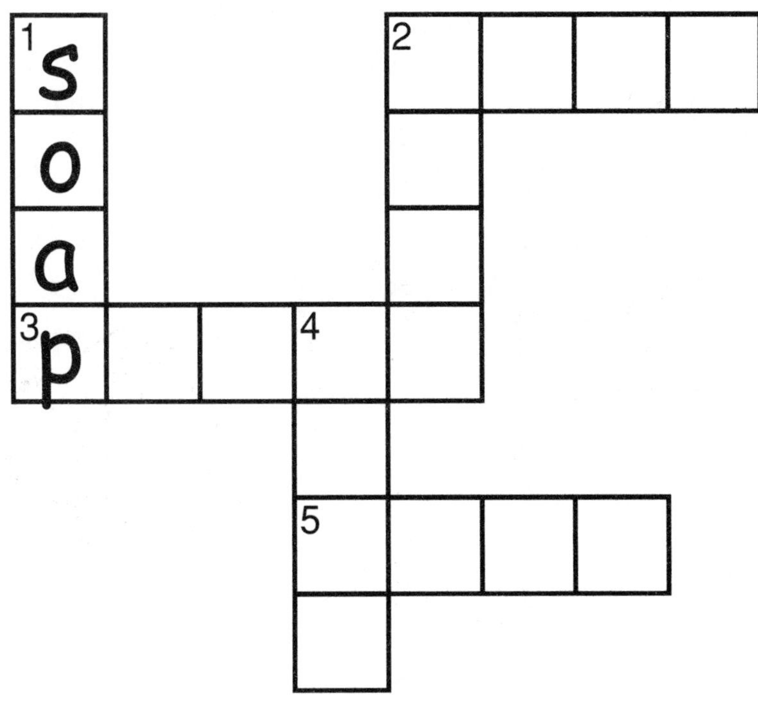

Long ū

Some of the musical instruments on this page have names with the **long ū** sound. Say the name of each instrument. Listen for the **long ū** sound. When you hear a different sound, draw an **X** over the picture.

Now, use your crayons to color the **long ū** instruments.

Look at the list of body parts below. Say each word out loud. Then, write its long vowel sound on the line next to it: **ā**, **ē**, **ī**, **ō** or **ū**. Draw a line from each word to that body part on the man. The first one is done for you.

face ā
ear ______
nose ______
tooth ______
throat ______
shoulder ______
waist ______
nails ______
thigh ______
knee ______
elbow ______
heel ______
toes ______

Long Vowel Review

In Mrs. Powell's long vowel store, she only sells clothes with names that have long vowels. Look at the clothes below. Say their names. Then, color the clothes that have **long vowel** names any way you like.

Short ă has the sound of the **a** in the name **Ann** and the words **hat** and **tap**. Look at the words and pictures. Say each word. Color each **short ă** picture. When you come to a word that has a different vowel sound, draw an **X** on that word and its picture.

rake

tray

cab

bath

lamp

braid

map

gas

flag

Short ă

Look at the parade of animals marching around this page. Circle each animal whose name has the **short ă** sound. Then, find and circle the names of the animals in the puzzle below. Names can go across (⟶) or down (↓).

O	K	B	A	O	B
H	I	C	R	B	A
E	C	M	A	H	A
A	A	A	M	O	X
P	T	E	E	N	Z
Q	N	L	A	M	B
E	G	Q	J	P	A
R	A	B	B	I	T

Short ĕ has the sound of the **e** in the words **yes**, **less** and **guess**. **Yes**, **less** and **guess** are also rhyming words because they end with the same sound. Look at each pair of **short ĕ** pictures below. If the names of the pictures rhyme, put a check mark (✓) on the line next to the pair.

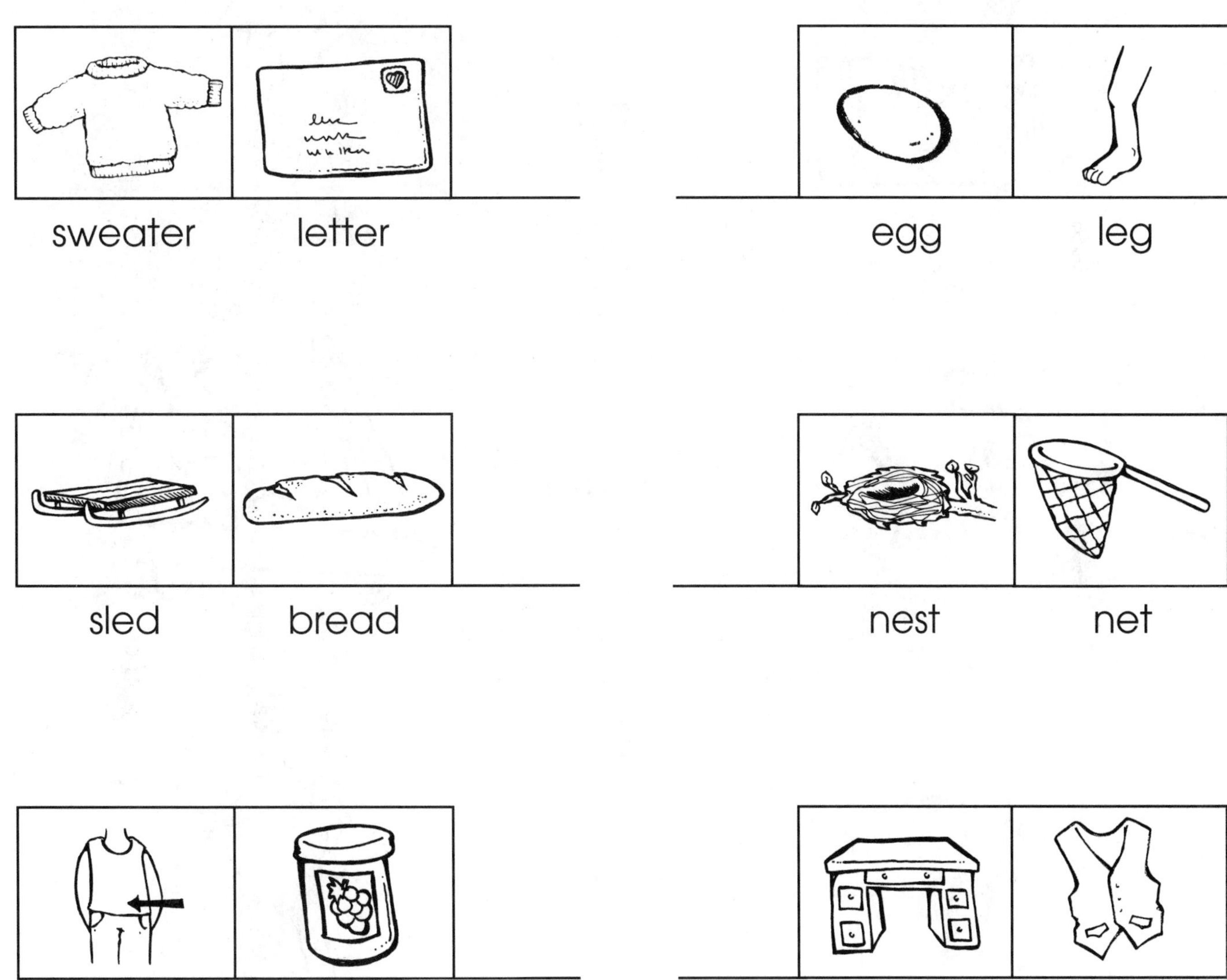

Short ĕ

Some words have more than one meaning. Say each **short ĕ** word below. Then, find the two pictures that show what that word means. Draw lines from both pictures to the **short ĕ** word.

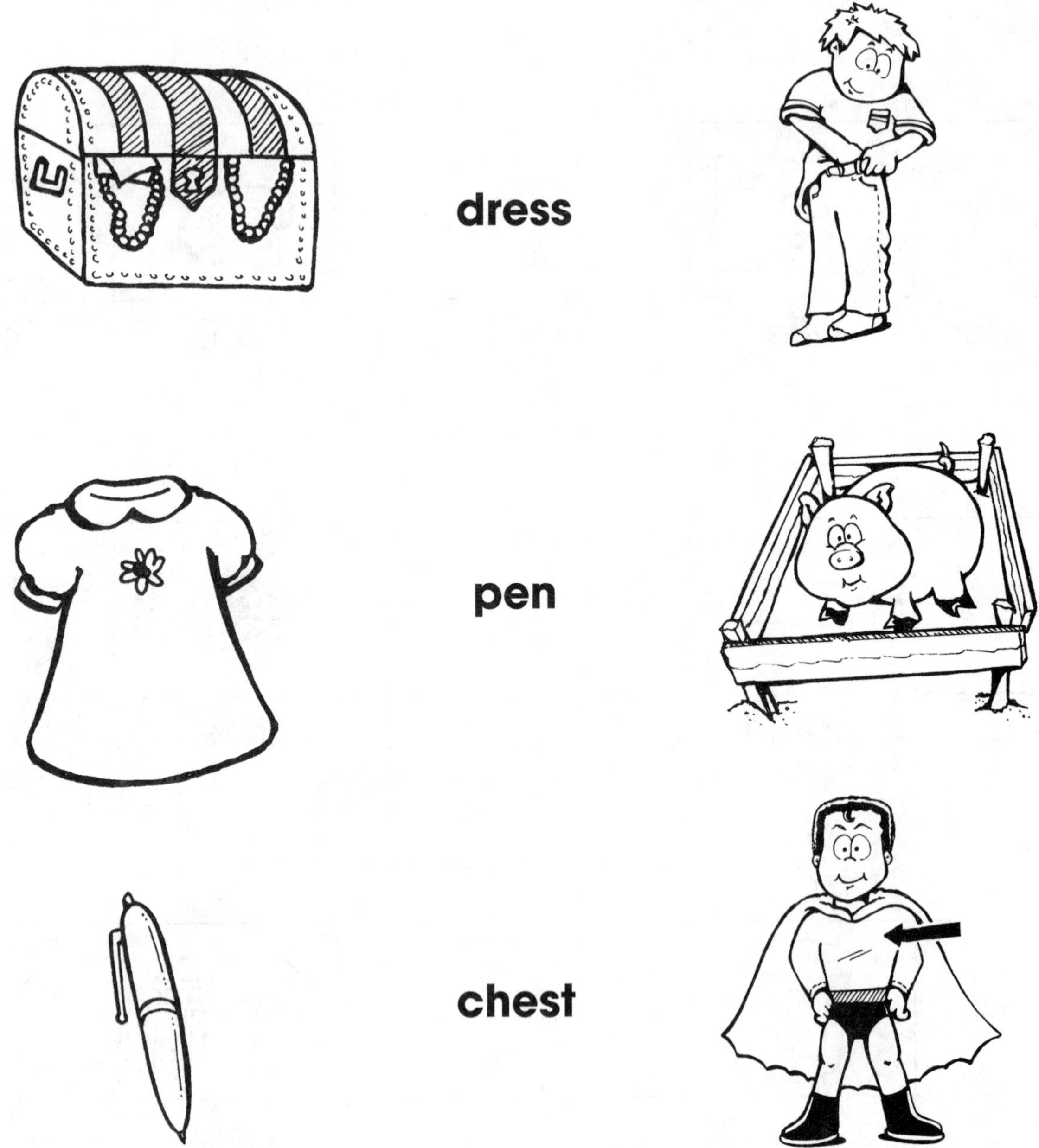

The crossword puzzle on this page has **short ĕ** words. Use the numbered clues to complete the puzzle. The first one is done for you.

Across

2. something a spider builds
5. a spotted cat
6. more than one man

Down

1. a tool for writing
3. they cover a bird's body
4. a place to sleep

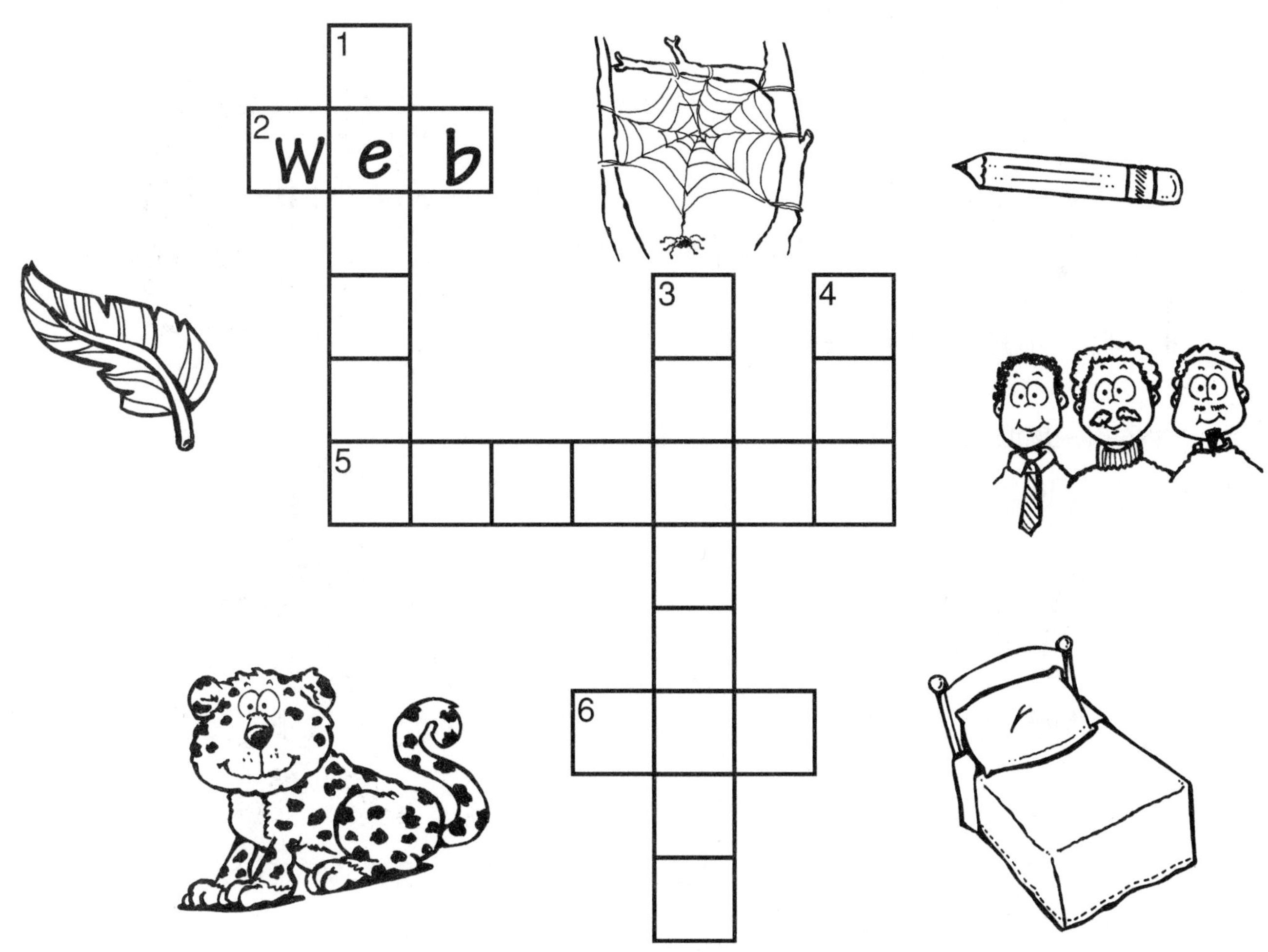

Short ĭ Bingo

Short ĭ has the sound of the i in the words **bingo** and **win**. Ask an adult to help you play a game of **short ĭ** bingo. Here is what you will need to make the game. Get everything together before you begin to play.

Now, follow these directions in order.

1. With a pair of scissors, cut out nine small squares of paper.
2. Write one word on each square. Use these words: **nickel**, **pig**, **ring**, **hill**, **zip**, **mitt**, **milk**, **dig**, and **pickle**.
3. Put the squares of paper inside a paper bag.
4. Have your adult friend pull one square at a time from the bag and read the word on it to you.
5. Find the picture that shows what the word means on the bingo card on the next page. Put a coin over that picture.
6. Continue this way until one row has three coins on it. Rows on your bingo card can either go across (⟶) or down (↓).
7. When you have a row with three coins, yell the word BINGO! You have won the game.

BINGO CARD

After you have won, you can use your bingo card to play again and again!

Short ĭ

The **Short ĭ** Bridge is for animals whose names make the **short ĭ** sound. Which animals do not belong on this bridge? Draw an **X** on any animal whose name has a different vowel sound.

Now, color all the animals that have **short ĭ** names.

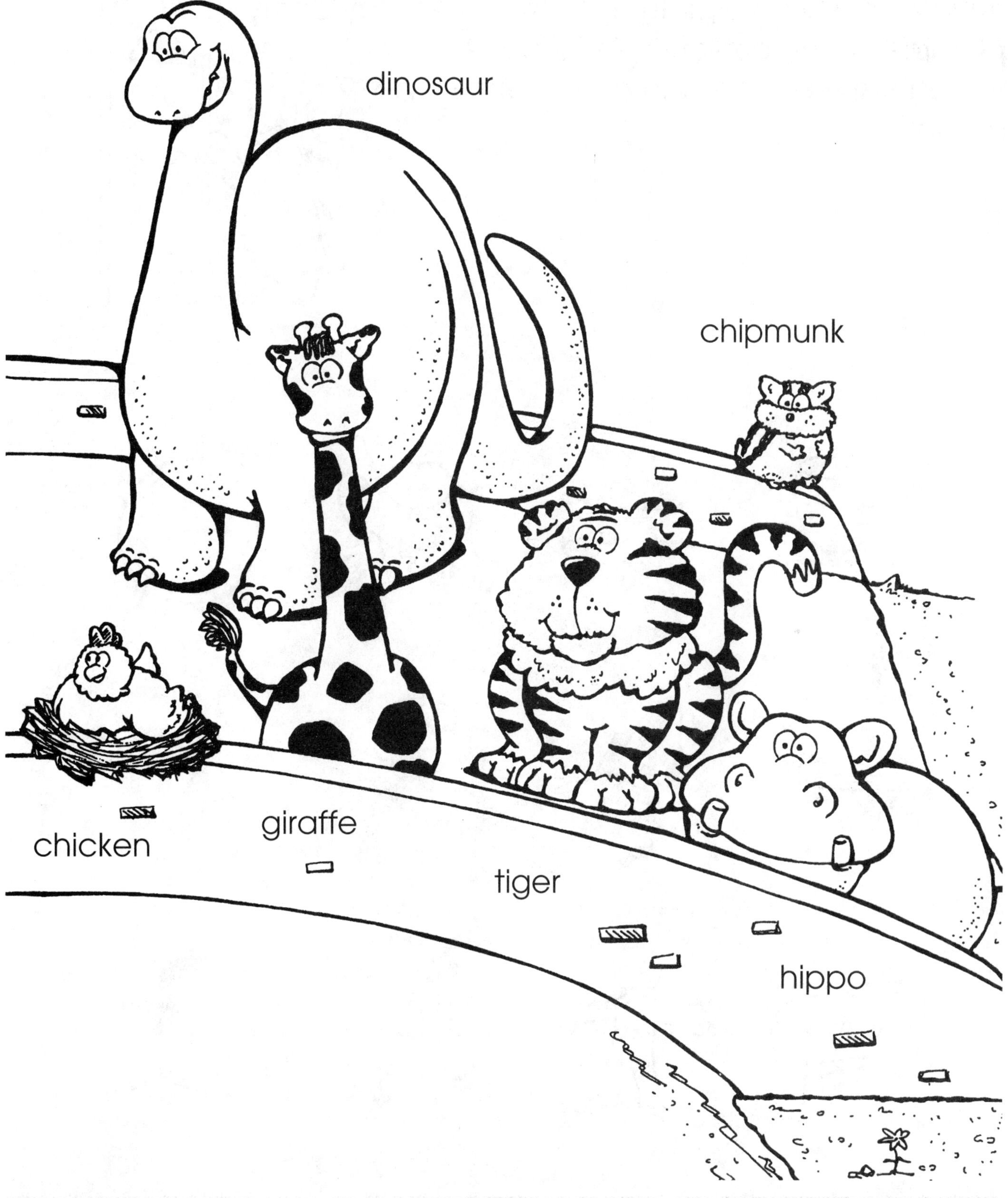

Short ŏ

Short ŏ has the sound of the **o** in the words **dog** and **knock**. Look at the pictures below. Then, say each picture's name out loud. Draw a line through any picture with a different vowel sound.

Oscar is filling a box with things whose names have the **short ŏ** sound. Help him decide which ones to put in the box. Draw a square around each **short ŏ** picture. Circle each picture whose name has a different sound.

Short ŭ

Short ŭ has the sound of the **u** in the name **Rusty** and the word **puzzle**. Rusty the juggler is juggling balls with **short ŭ** words on them! Find and circle the words in the puzzle. Words can go either across (→) or down (↓).

drum
number
gum
brush
bus
puzzle
buzz
pump
truck
fun

P	U	Z	Z	L	E	X
U	A	B	R	U	S	H
M	E	O	F	A	B	S
P	T	D	U	G	U	M
K	A	R	N	E	Z	Q
A	B	U	L	Y	Z	M
N	U	M	B	E	R	F
I	S	T	R	U	C	K

Use the code box below to help you read the **short ŭ** story. First, look at the number under each line below. Then, find the letter that goes with that number in the code box. Write that letter on the line. Fill in all the letters to complete the story. When you are finished, read the story out loud.

CODE

1 = A	4 = D	7 = I	10 = R
2 = B	5 = E	8 = K	11 = S
3 = C	6 = H	9 = N	12 = U
	13 = T		

___ ___ ___ ___ ___ ___ ___ ___ ___
13 6 5 3 12 2 1 9 4

___ ___ ___ ___ ___ ___ ___ ___ ___ ___ ___
13 6 5 11 8 12 9 8 3 12 13

___ ___ ___ ___ ___ ___ ___ ___
2 12 13 13 5 10 7 9

___ ___ ___ ___ ___ ___.
13 6 5 11 12 9

Short Vowel Review

Jack is going on a trip. He is packing only short vowel clothes. Help Jack figure out what to pack. Use crayons to color all the clothes that have **short vowel** names.

Fancy Nancy is a short vowel robot. The names of the parts it took to put her together are listed below. Say the name of each part. Then, write the **short vowel** sound you hear next to each part.

head ____________

lips ____________

chin ____________

neck ____________

chest ____________

tummy ____________

wrist ____________

hand ____________

thumb ____________

hip ____________

leg ____________

calf ____________

finger ____________

Short and Long Vowel Review

The animals need to board the ark in pairs. A **pair** is two things that go together. Put the animals in pairs by their vowel sounds: **short ă** with **long ā**, **short ĕ** with **long ē**, **short ĭ** with **long ī**, and so on. Draw lines to connect the animals in each pair.

The name of a color is written on each crayon below. Say each color's name and listen for the vowel sounds. Some of the colors may have more than one vowel sound. On the line under each crayon, write all the **vowel sounds** you hear. Then, use your crayons to color each crayon picture its correct color.

______

______

______

______

______

______

______

______

______

______

Short and Long Vowel Review

Around the outside of the circle below are numbers. Inside the circle are vowel sounds. Say each number out loud. Then, find the vowel sound of the number's name inside the circle. Draw a line from the number to the vowel sound.

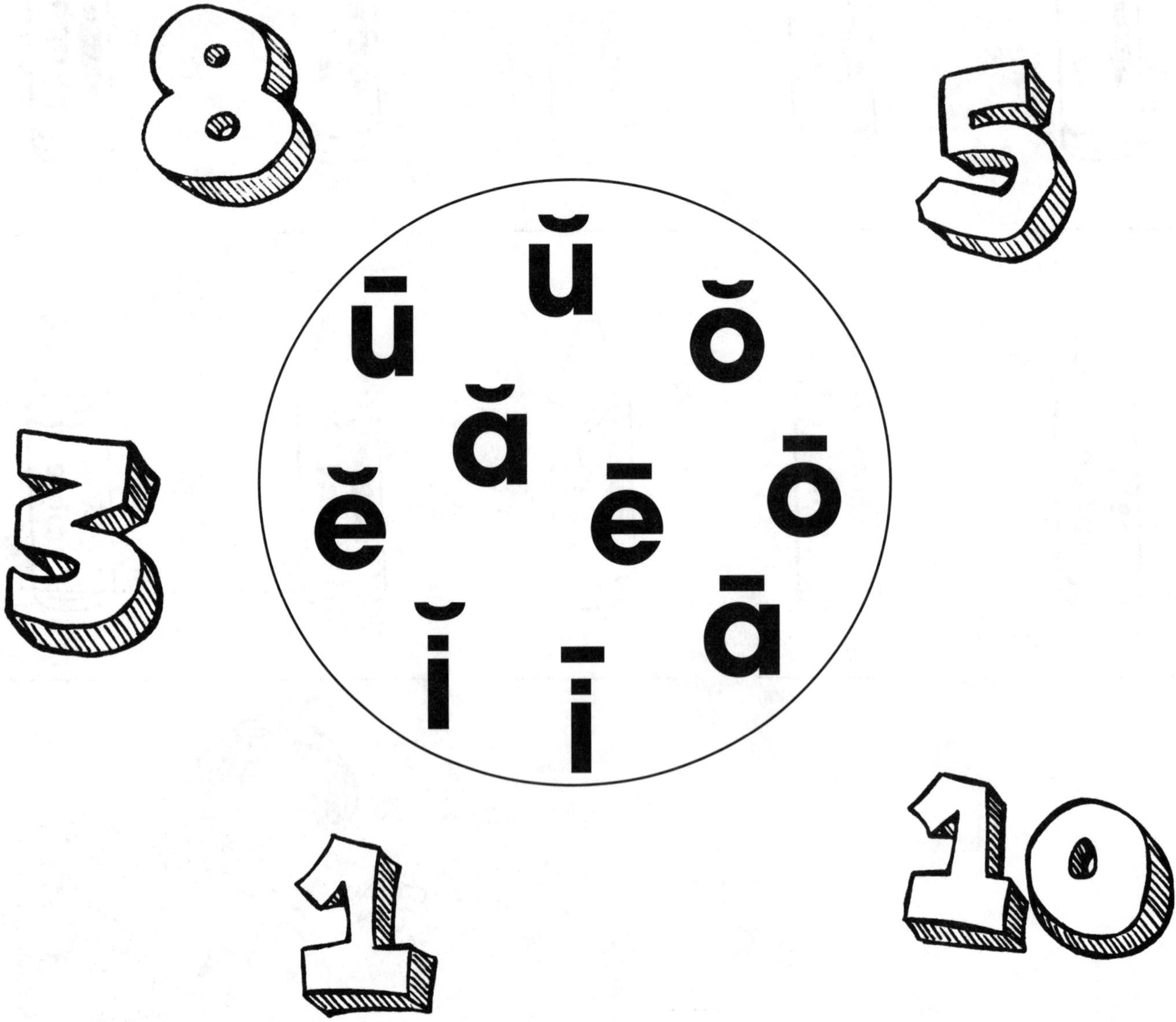

8

5

ŭ

ū ŏ

ă

ĕ ē ō

ā

ĭ ī

3

1

10

An **r blend** is a sound made by adding **r** after another consonant. Combine each set of consonants below, then write the **r blend** you make in the box. Then, draw a line connecting each **r blend** with the picture with that sound.

b + r = br

c + r =

d + r =

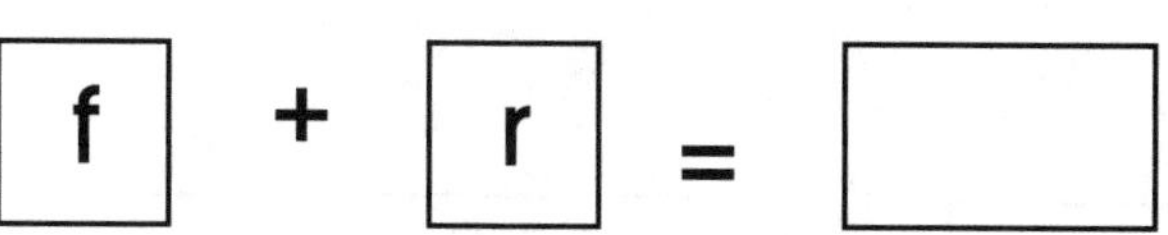

f + r =

g + r =

p + r =

t + r =

r Consonant Blends

Drew is using his crayons to draw **r blend** words. Look at his pictures below and say each word. Circle the **r blend** in it. Then, use your crayons to color each picture that Drew drew.

crayons

bridge

pretzel

crab

train

growl

Look at each word inside the block below. Draw a line under the **l** and the letter before it. Now, look at all the words again. Find a row of words that has the same **l blend**. Use a crayon to color in that row. The row can go across (→), down (↓) or diagonally (↗↘).

flag	climb	blimp	globe
plate	flame	sleep	glad
plus	clap	floor	black
plant	blue	fly	flip

l Consonant Blends

Flo is cleaning out her **l blend** closet. Help her by drawing an **X** on any picture whose name does not contain an **l blend**. Then, say the names of the rest of the pictures. Write each two-letter blend on one of the lines on the closet door.

Use the code box below to complete the **s blend** words. Look at the number under each line. Then, write the corresponding **s blend** on the line. When you are done, read each word out loud.

CODE	
1 = sk	**5 = sp**
2 = sl	**6 = st**
3 = sm	**7 = sw**
4 = sn	

____ i 1	____ in 5	____ op 6
____ ow 4	____ ed 2	____ ing 7
____ ide 2	____ ar 6	____ ile 3
____ im 7	____ in 1	____ ap 4

s Consonant Blends

Some **s blends** contain three letters instead of two. Circle the **s blend** in each word in the box. Then, find and circle the words in the puzzle below. Words can go across (→) or down (↓).

scream	stretch	splash	sprout
strike	spray	scrub	splits

Riley the Rhyming Rabbit loves to make up rhymes. Help him change the blend in each word on the left to make a different word that rhymes. First, read the word on the left. Then, look at the three choices of blends on the right. Draw a box around each blend that would make a word that rhymes. Say each new word real loud.

fry	**sk**	**sw**	**fl**
slow	**sn**	**gr**	**cr**
stop	**dr**	**bl**	**cr**
play	**cl**	**st**	**spr**
dream	**scr**	**str**	**gr**
swing	**spr**	**str**	**br**
splash	**tr**	**sn**	**cr**
drip	**fl**	**tr**	**sl**

Digraphs

The **th digraph** sounds like the **th** in the words **thunder** and **thorn**. Say the names of all the numbers in the box below. Whenever you say a number word that has a **th digraph**, use your favorite color crayon to color in that square.

14	26	3
50	33	10
9	66	13
30	37	44

An **h digraph** is a sound made by adding the letter **h** after another consonant. Say **wish**. The sound at the end of the word is the **sh digraph** sound. Now, say **cheese**. The sound at the beginning is the **ch digraph** sound. To play this game, look for the **h digraphs** in the picture below. Circle each picture which has an **sh** sound. Draw a box around each picture which has a **ch** sound.

Blends and Digraphs Review

MENU
cheese
grapes
bread
fish
chicken
strawberries
peaches
pretzels

Today's menu is filled with foods whose names have consonant blends and digraphs. Look at the words on the menu the chef is holding. Then, circle those words in the puzzle. Words can go across (→) or down (↓).

C	H	I	C	K	E	N	R	S
A	X	D	H	M	V	F	M	T
R	T	G	E	W	I	X	S	R
K	B	R	E	A	D	C	Q	A
N	I	A	S	T	P	O	F	W
O	B	P	E	R	J	S	I	B
P	R	E	T	Z	E	L	S	E
Y	I	S	Q	E	R	J	H	R
Q	P	E	A	C	H	E	S	R
E	Z	N	X	E	W	E	R	I
D	C	H	E	R	R	I	S	E
R	O	K	H	C	L	Z	Y	S

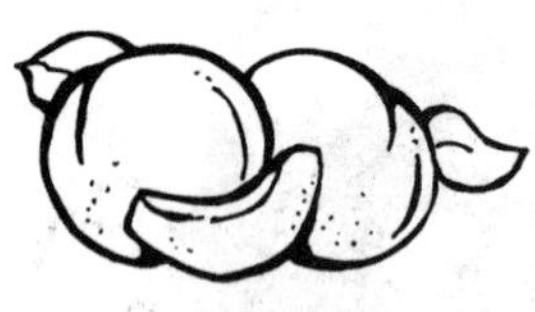

LANGUAGE

Sentence Sense

Sentences tell you about someone or something. Read the sentences below. Then, look at the pictures. Draw a line from each picture to the sentence that describes it.

The cat is on the rug.

The dog has a slipper.

It is raining.

A boat is in the water.

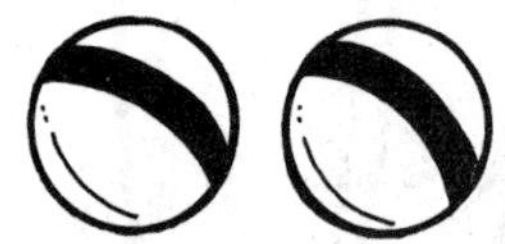

A bird is flying.

A cup is on the table.

The bike is broken.

The two balls are alike.

Read the two sentences below.

Mary chased the cat.

The cat chased Mary.

The order of words affects the meaning of a sentence. In the first sentence, Mary does the chasing. In the second sentence, the cat does the chasing!

Circle the sentences below that describe the pictures.

The book is on the table.

The table is on the book.

A dog is behind a tree.

A tree is behind a dog.

A bird sees a worm.

A worm sees a bird.

The bug is on the mat.

The mat is on the bug.

Sentence Sense

Help Stanley finish the sentences so they make sense. Use the words in the word box.

two hot dogs	a funny book
barked loudly	a big truck
flew up high	a new pencil

Jan read ______________________________.

The dog ______________________________.

Pat ate ______________________________.

I wrote with ______________________________.

The man drove ______________________________.

A little bird ______________________________.

The words in the sentences below are all mixed up. Write the words in the correct order on the lines.

went Jack the to zoo.

____

some saw He monkeys.

____

a in They tree. were

____

playing. They were

____

to Jack waved them.

____

Capital Letters—First Word in a Sentence

When writing sentences, don't forget Elmer Elephant's rule.

Every sentence begins with a capital letter.

Read the sentences. Circle each word that needs a capital letter. Write the words correctly on the lines.

colorful flags waved in the air. ____________________

inside a tent sat many people. ____________________

red balloons bobbed up and down. ____________________

clowns did funny tricks. ____________________

up on a chair jumped a monkey. ____________________

six horses trotted in a circle. ____________________

Where does Elmer work? To find out, write each capital letter in order on the lines below.

Elmer works at a __ __ __ __ __ __.

People's names begin with capital letters. Read the sentences below. Write the names correctly on the lines.

Hello!
My name is brad.
Hello!
My name is carla.
Hello!
My name is meg.
Hello!
My name is dave.
Hello!
My name is kirk.
Hello!
My name is lisa.

Capital Letters—Days of the Week

The names of the days of the week begin with capital letters. Read the sentences below. Circle the names of the days. Write them correctly on the lines.

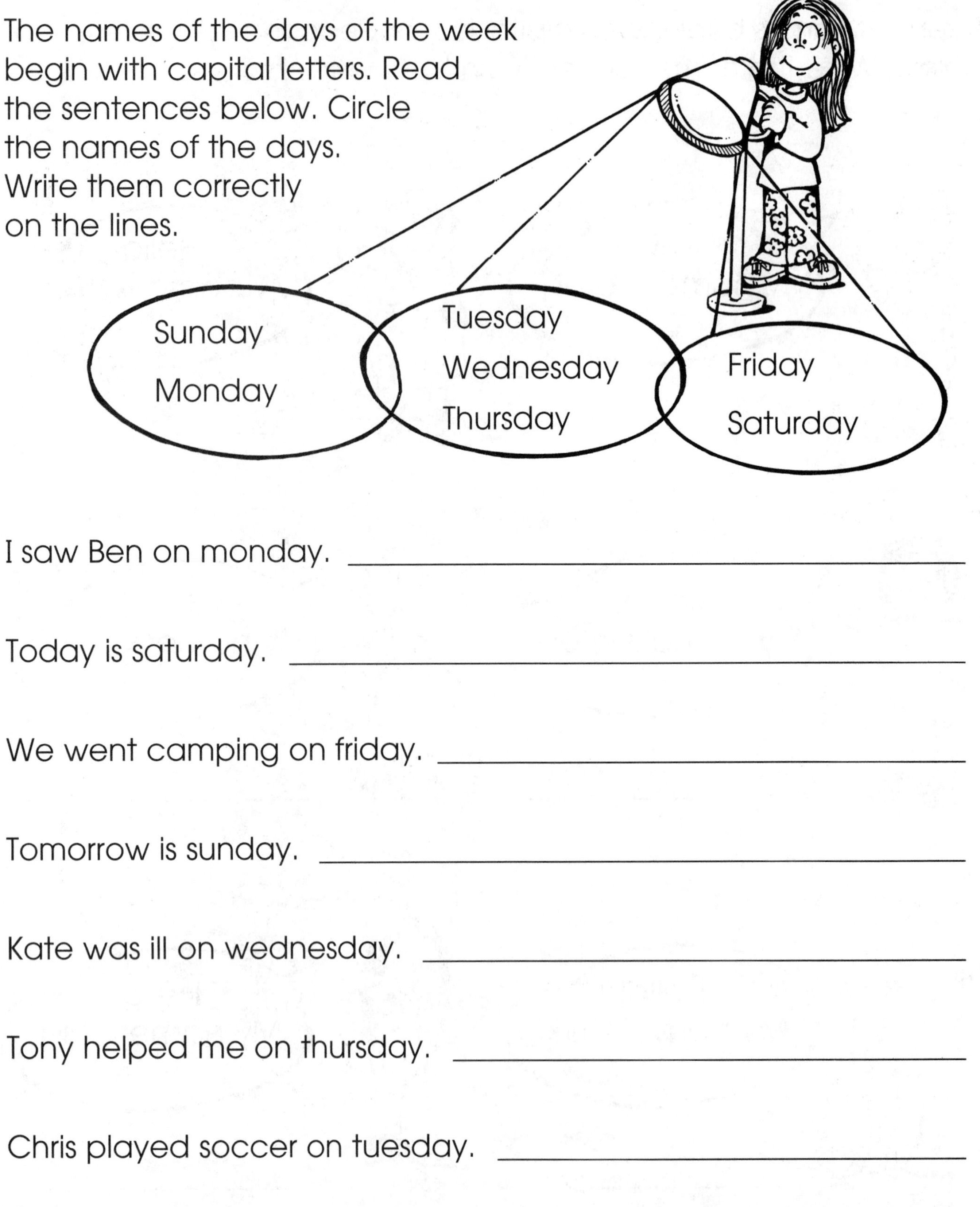

I saw Ben on monday. ____________________

Today is saturday. ____________________

We went camping on friday. ____________________

Tomorrow is sunday. ____________________

Kate was ill on wednesday. ____________________

Tony helped me on thursday. ____________________

Chris played soccer on tuesday. ____________________

The months of the year begin with capital letters.

January	May	September
February	June	October
March	July	November
April	August	December

Write the missing letters to complete the names of the months below. Use the letters on the balloons. Cross out each letter as you use it.

___ebruary	___ctober
___uly	___pril
___ay	___anuary
___ecember	___eptember
___ugust	___une
___arch	___ovember

Capital Letters—Holidays

The names of holidays begin with capital letters. Here are the names of some holidays.

Valentine's Day	Fourth of July	Thanksgiving
Easter	Halloween	Christmas

Write the names of the holidays beside the matching pictures. Don't forget to use capital letters!

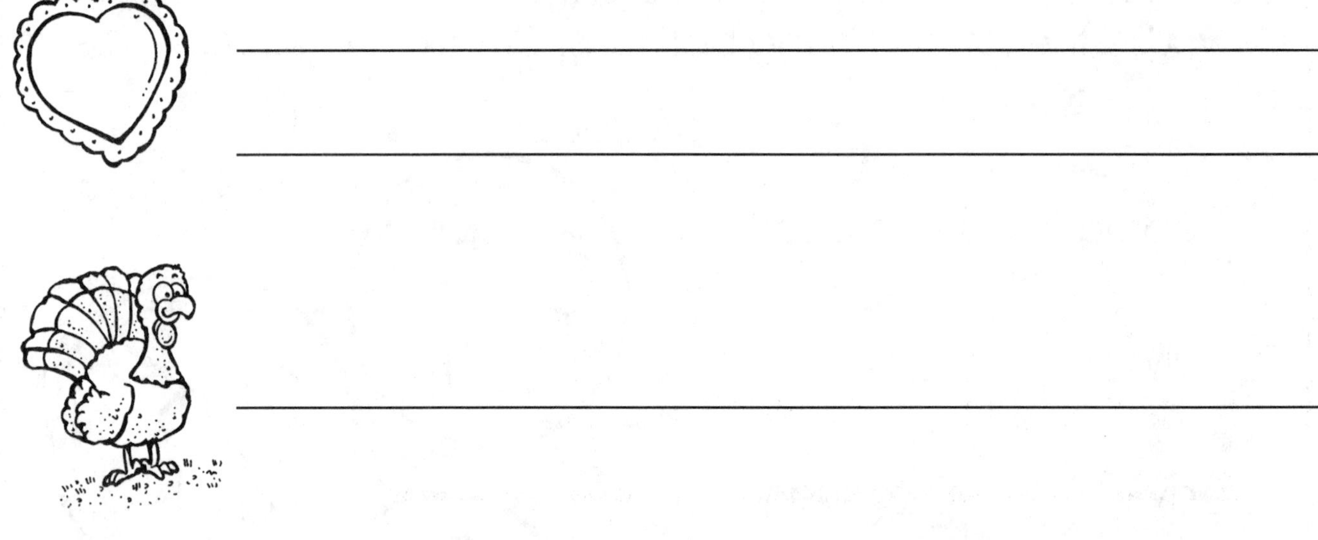

Who is in the picture? To find out, use brown to color the spaces that have words needing capital letters.

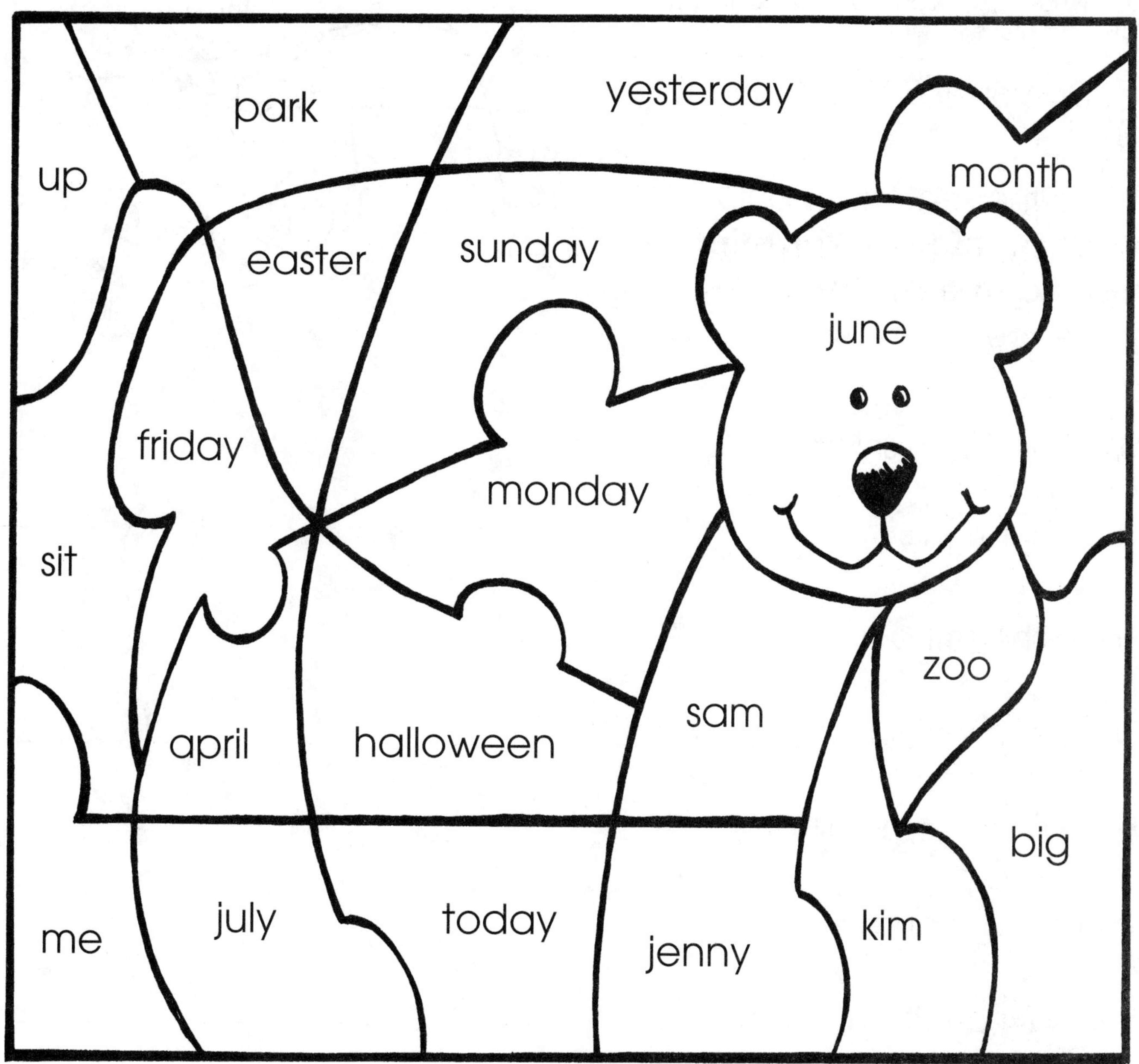

Periods and Question Marks

Sentences that tell something end with a **period** (**.**). Sentences that ask something end with a **question mark** (**?**). Look at these two examples.

Wendy likes to go fishing.

Do you like to go fishing?

Read the sentences below. Put a **period** or a **question mark** at the end of each sentence.

Wendy went fishing

She sat by the water

Soon she felt a tug

Do you know what Wendy did

She pulled and pulled

What did Wendy see

She saw a fish on her line

Later, she took the fish home

Read each sentence below. Add a **period** at the end if the sentence tells something. Add a **question mark** if the sentence asks something.

Farmer Bill is outside

What is he doing

He is feeding the animals

He gives the chicks some corn

Are the horses hungry

The horses want to eat some hay

What will Farmer Bill do next

He will go to the store

Do you think Farmer Bill is busy

Are you as busy as Farmer Bill

Punctuation Review

Can you help Terry Turtle with his work? Write each sentence correctly. Use **capital letters**. Put in **periods** and **question marks**.

today is friday

____

do you know why

____

my friend bert is coming

____

we are going to the pond

____

where do you like to go

____

Some words name only one person or thing (**ball**). Other words name more than one (**balls**).

Words that name more than one person or thing are called **plurals**. You often make plurals by adding **s** to the end of a word.

Change the words below to **plurals**.

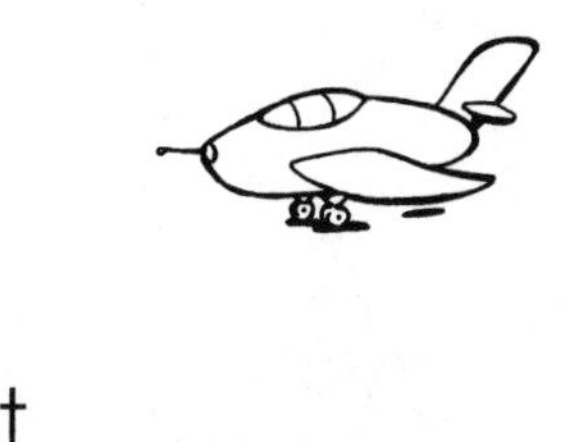

jet ____________________

duck ____________________

doll ____________________

drum ____________________

car ____________________

top ____________________

game ____________________

horn ____________________

Plurals: s

Circle the word that describes each picture.

frog

frogs

turtle

turtles

owl

owls

ant

ants

snake

snakes

tree

trees

pond

ponds

bear

bears

A **plural** is a word that means more than one person or thing. You can add **s** or **es** to the end of a word to make a plural.

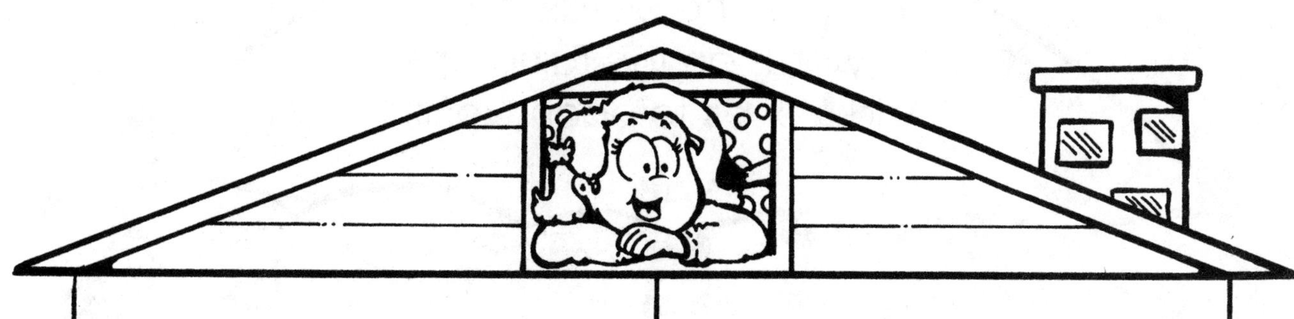

Add **s** to these words.

cup — cups

sink — sinks

stove — stoves

table — tables

Add **es** to words that end in **s**, **x**, **sh** or **ch**.

glass — glasses

box — boxes

dish — dishes

bench — benches

Write the **plurals** of these words.

house ____________________ bus ____________________

bush ____________________ fox ____________________

dress ____________________ rug ____________________

lamp ____________________ peach ____________________

Plurals Review

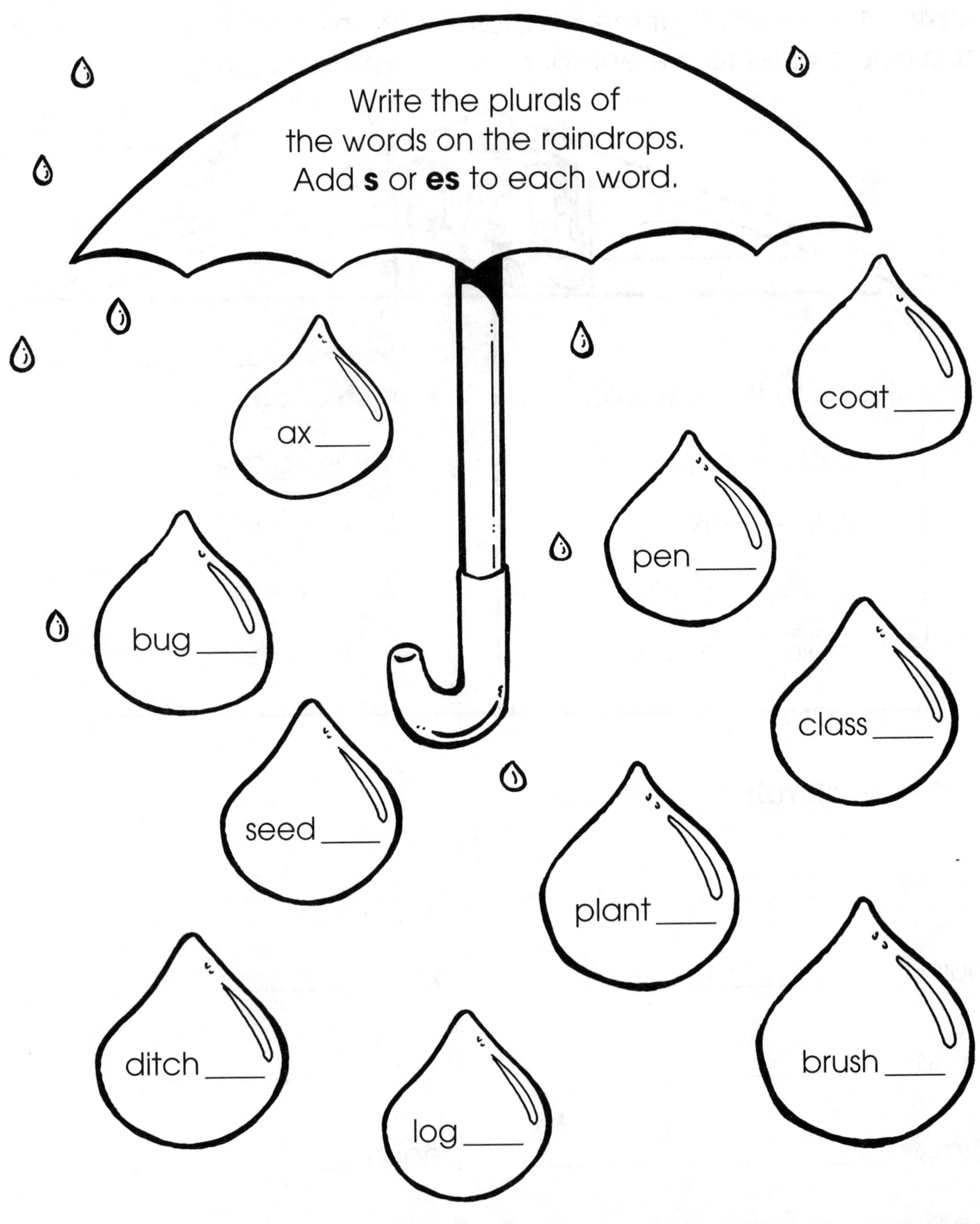

Contractions are words that are made from two words with one or more letters left out. A mark called an **apostrophe** (') is used in place of the missing letters.

Find the contraction for the word pair in each boat. Draw a line from the boat to the correct fish.

are not

aren't

did not

wasn't

didn't

was not

does not

doesn't

can't

cannot

have not

haven't

Contractions

Write the **contraction** for the words on each ice-cream cone. Use the words that are on the carton.

he is

it is

you are

we are

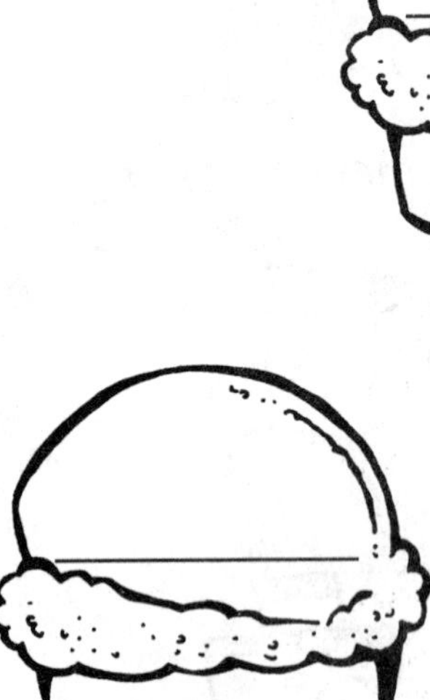

Read each sentence. Write the **contraction** for the two words that are below each line. Use the words that are on the kite.

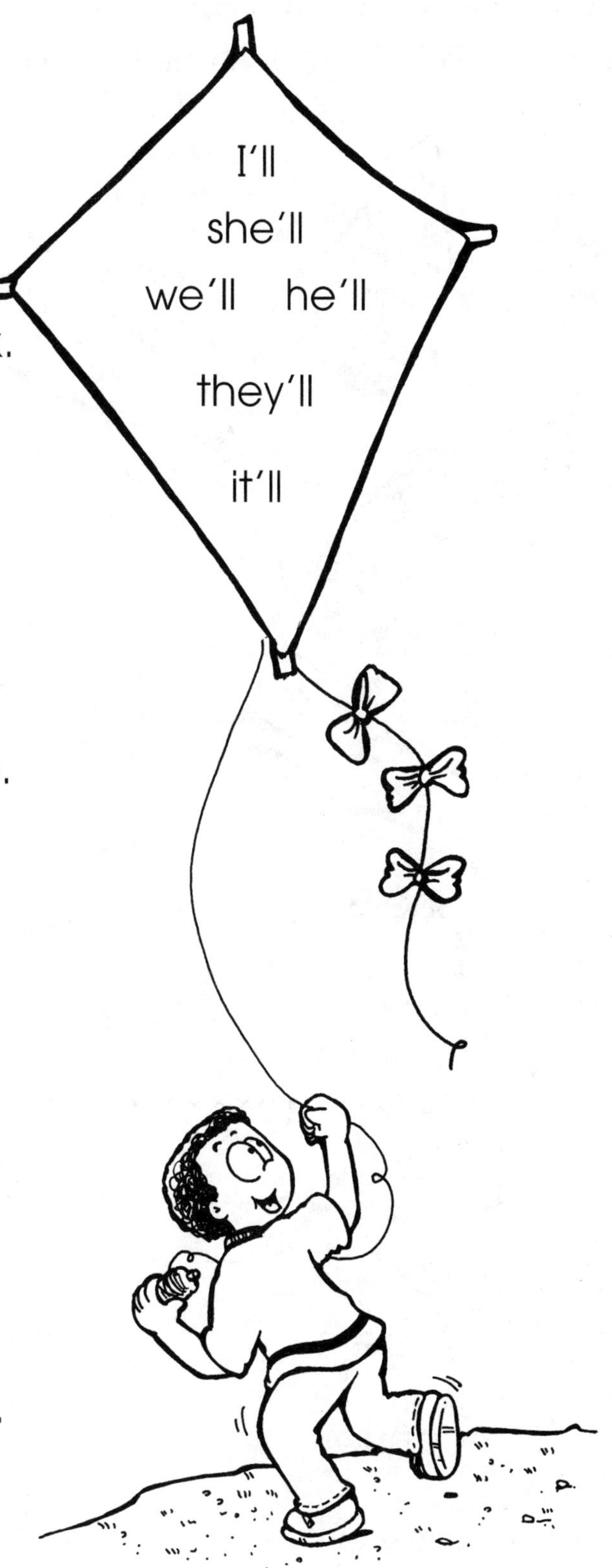

I'll
she'll
we'll he'll
they'll
it'll

____________ meet Paul at the park.
I will

I hope ____________ be windy.
it will

Paul said ____________ bring his kite.
he will

His mom said ____________ help us.
she will

I think ____________ be there soon.
they will

Later, ____________ go get a snack.
we will

Contractions

Write the **contraction** for each pair of words. Use the words on the stars to help you.

isn't
don't
can't
I'm
he's
we're
you're
they're
she'll
they'll

do not ________________

is not ________________

you are ________________

she will ________________

they will ________________

we are ________________

I am ________________

he is ________________

cannot ________________

they are ________________

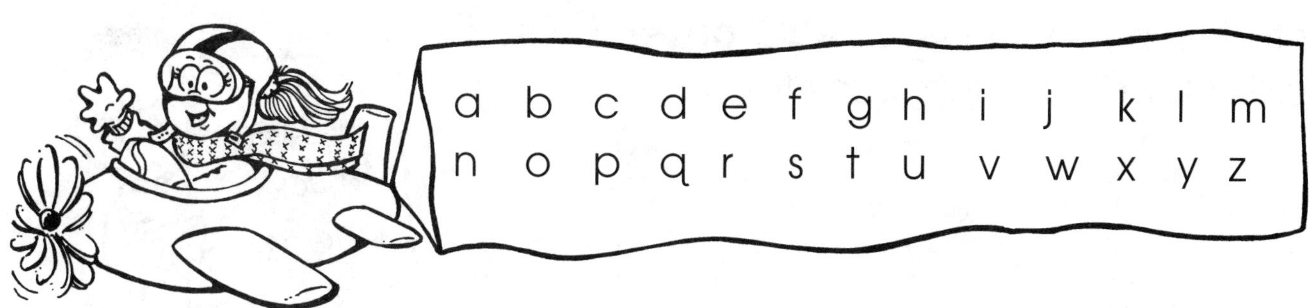

a b c d e f g h i j k l m
n o p q r s t u v w x y z

Write the letter that comes **after** each letter.

a, ______ g, ______ j, ______ m, ______ p, ______

d, ______ s, ______ o, ______ w, ______ e, ______

Write the letter that comes **before** each letter.

______, m ______, x ______, c ______, o ______, k

______, v ______, z ______, f ______, y ______, s

Try to solve this riddle!

What bird is always sad?

To find the answer, write the letter that comes **after** each letter shown below.

s g d   a k t d a h q c

ABC Order

Write each grocery list in **ABC order**. Look at the first letter of each word for help.

milk
eggs
butter

____
____
____

ham
grapes
peas

____
____
____

pie
juice
corn

____
____
____

beans
soup
fish

____
____
____

A **compound word** is a word that is made up of two smaller words. Look at the words below the pictures. Put the words together to make **compound words**. Write the new words on the lines.

sail + boat = sailboat 

sun + glasses = ______________ 

bird + house = ______________ 

rain + coat = ______________ 

Compound Words

Can you find the two words that make up each animal's name? Write them on the lines.

butterfly

____________________ ____________________

grasshopper

____________________ ____________________

bluebird

____________________ ____________________

Write the **compound word** that matches each description. Use the words in the box.

This fruit is red. ________________________________

This grows inside a shell. ________________________________

This snack is made from corn. ________________________________

This drink is sweet and cool. ________________________________

This is a small candy. ________________________________

This is baked in an oven. ________________________________

Compound Words Review

Find the hidden picture. Color each space that has a compound word **orange**. Color the other spaces **blue**.

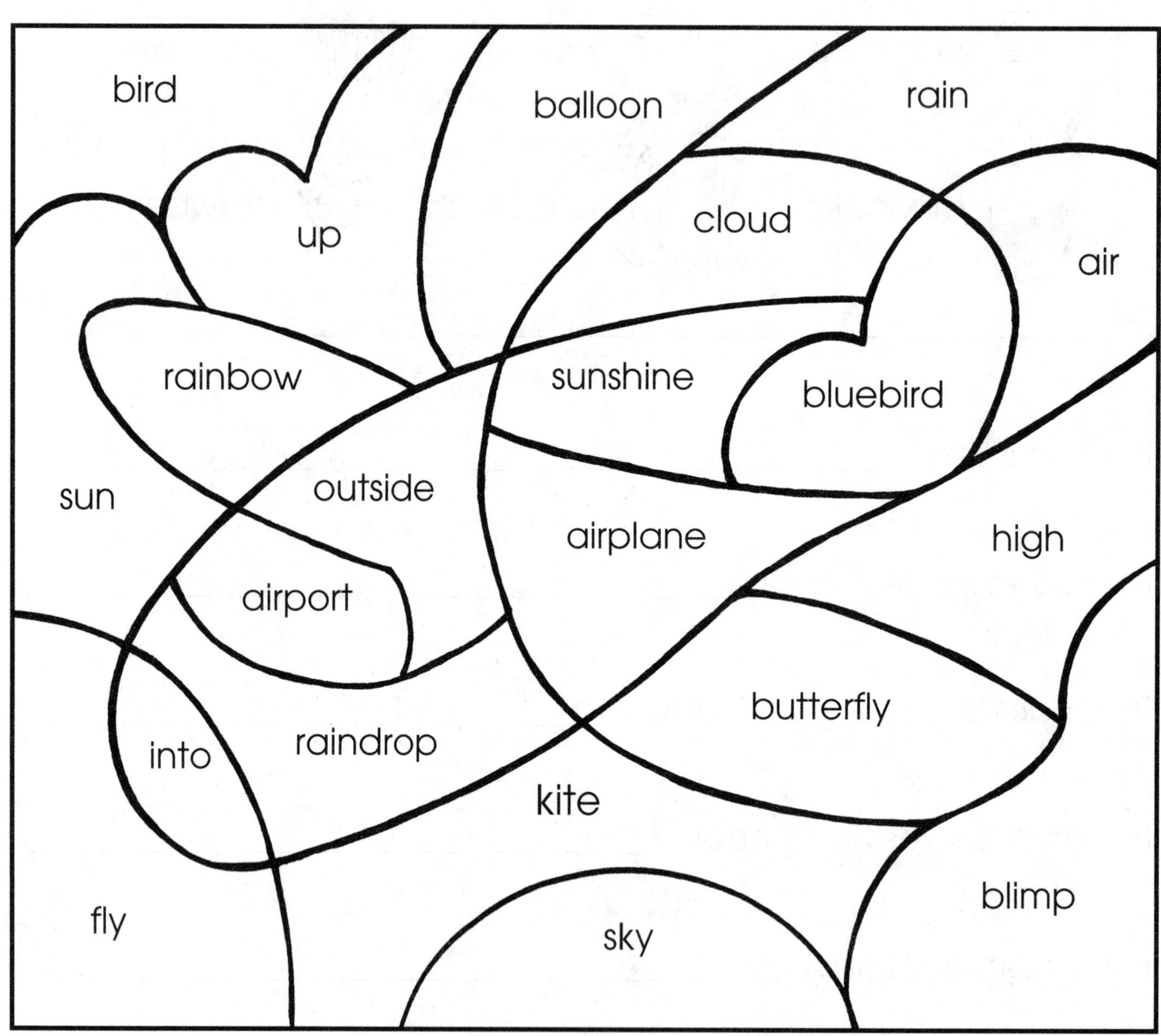

Action words tell what a person or a thing can do.

Examples:

The frog **hops**. The frogs **hop**.

An action word usually ends in **s** when it tells about only one person or thing. An action word usually does not end in **s** when it tells about more than one person or thing.

Circle the correct **action word** for each sentence.

The boy **read**, **reads**.

The girl **eat**, **eats**.

The lion **roar**, **roars**.

The whale **swim**, **swims**.

The baby **play**, **plays**.

The phone **ring**, **rings**.

The books **fall**, **falls**.

Verb Forms

Some **action words** tell about something that has already happened.

Example: Yesterday I **painted** a picture.

You add **ed** to most action words to tell about something that has happened in the past.

Add **ed** to these words.

jump ___________ plant ___________ wash ___________

walk ___________ cook ___________ bark ___________

Use your new words to complete these sentences.

Last night, our dog ______________________________ loudly.

Yesterday, I ______________________________ to school.

My mom ______________________________ flowers on Sunday.

A cat ______________________________ down from the fence.

My dad ______________________________ dinner two days ago.

We ______________________________ the dishes this morning.

Some **action words** tell about something that is happening now. These words usually have **ing** at the end.

Examples: My family is **eating**.

We are **enjoying** a picnic.

Add **ing** to these words.

play__________ watch__________ buy__________

talk__________ open__________ read__________

Use your new words to complete these sentences.

The teacher is ______________________________ a story.

Sandy is ______________________________ the piano quietly.

We are ______________________________ a new house.

The boy is ______________________________ his gift.

The children are ______________________________ a movie.

I am ______________________________ to my new friend.

Word Usage

When you talk about one person or thing, use **is**. When you talk about more than one person or thing, use **are**.

Examples:

The boat **is** in the water.

The boats **are** in the water.

Write **is** or **are** on the blank lines.

The boy and girl __________ on a boat.

The boat __________ big and safe.

The children __________ with their friend.

A whale __________ in the water.

The children __________ excited.

The girl __________ waving hello.

Which flowers have the words that complete the sentences correctly? Color them.

Scott is ____ some flowers.

Bev ____ her bike every day.

We ____ baseball last week.

The girls are ____ for bugs.

They are ____ to the park.

The boys ____ on the bars.

Synonyms

Synonyms are words that have the same, or almost the same, meaning. For example, **big** and **large** are synonyms. You can replace a word in a sentence with its synonym.

Choose **synonyms** to replace the words in bold. Look at the pieces of paper for clues. Write the words on the lines.

closed

unhappy

stone

yelled

leap

lovely

The boy is **sad**. ______________________________

The door is **shut**. _________________________

An ant is **little**. ______________________________

The flowers are **pretty**. ___________________

This **rock** is smooth. _________________________

Kangaroos can **jump** in the air. _________________

Leslie **shouted** across the room. _________________

Antonyms are words that have opposite meanings. For example, the words **up** and **down** are antonyms.

Write the **antonyms** of the words in bold in the sentences below. Use the words in the box to help you.

dry	last	low	tall
cold	slowly	small	hard

We have a **big** garden. ______________________

It is a **hot** day. ______________________

This plant is **short**. ______________________

The grass is **wet**. ______________________

The ground is **soft**. ______________________

Some bugs move **quickly**. ______________________

The birds are flying **high**. ______________________

Let's pick these flowers **first**. ______________________

Homophones

Homophones are words that sound the same but have different meanings.

Examples: I ate a **pear**.

I have a **pair** of shoes.

Pear and **pair** are homophones.

Match the **homophones**. Write the words from the tree on the lines below.

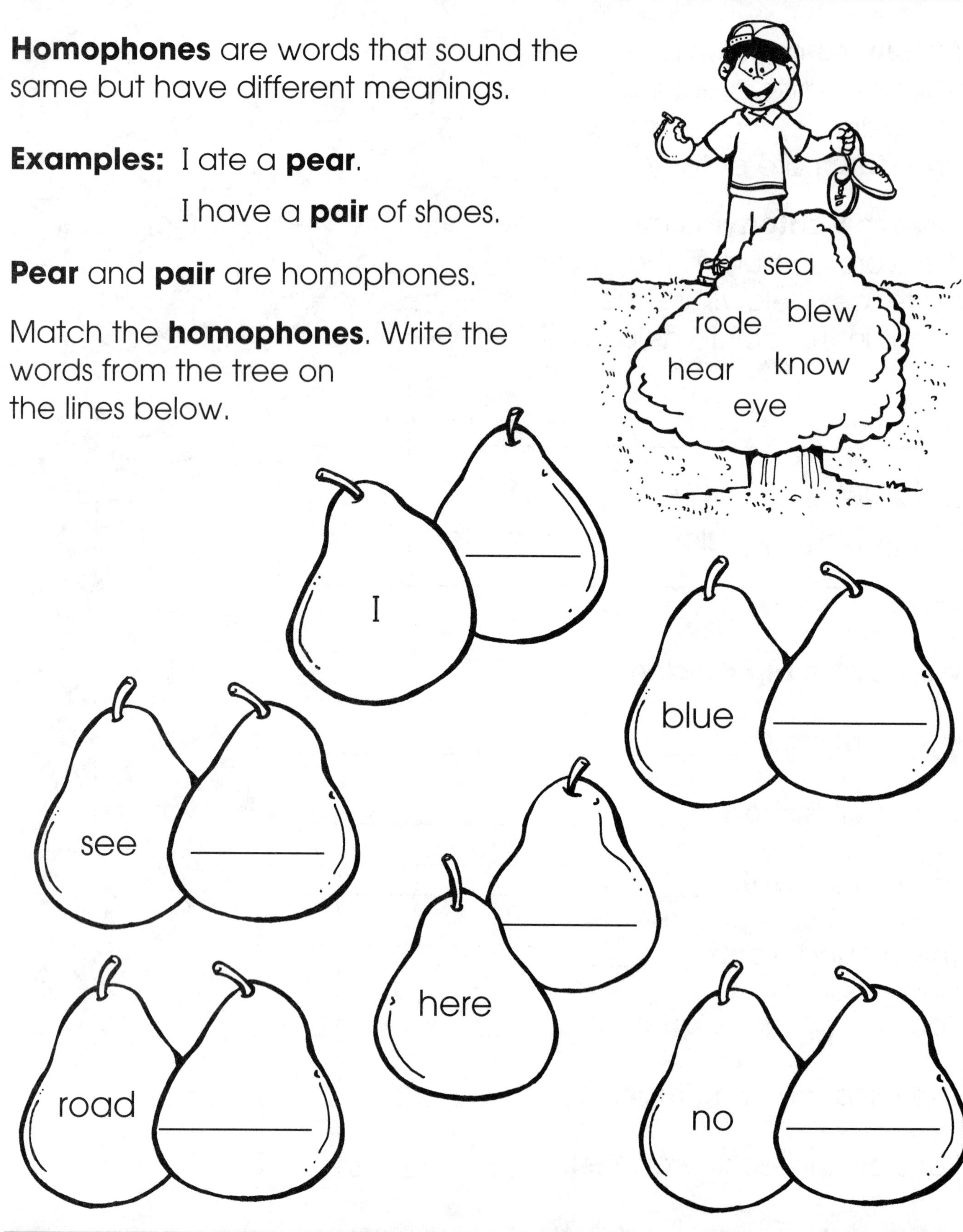

Try to solve these puzzles. Read the clues and use the words in the box. The words go down (↓) then across (⟶).

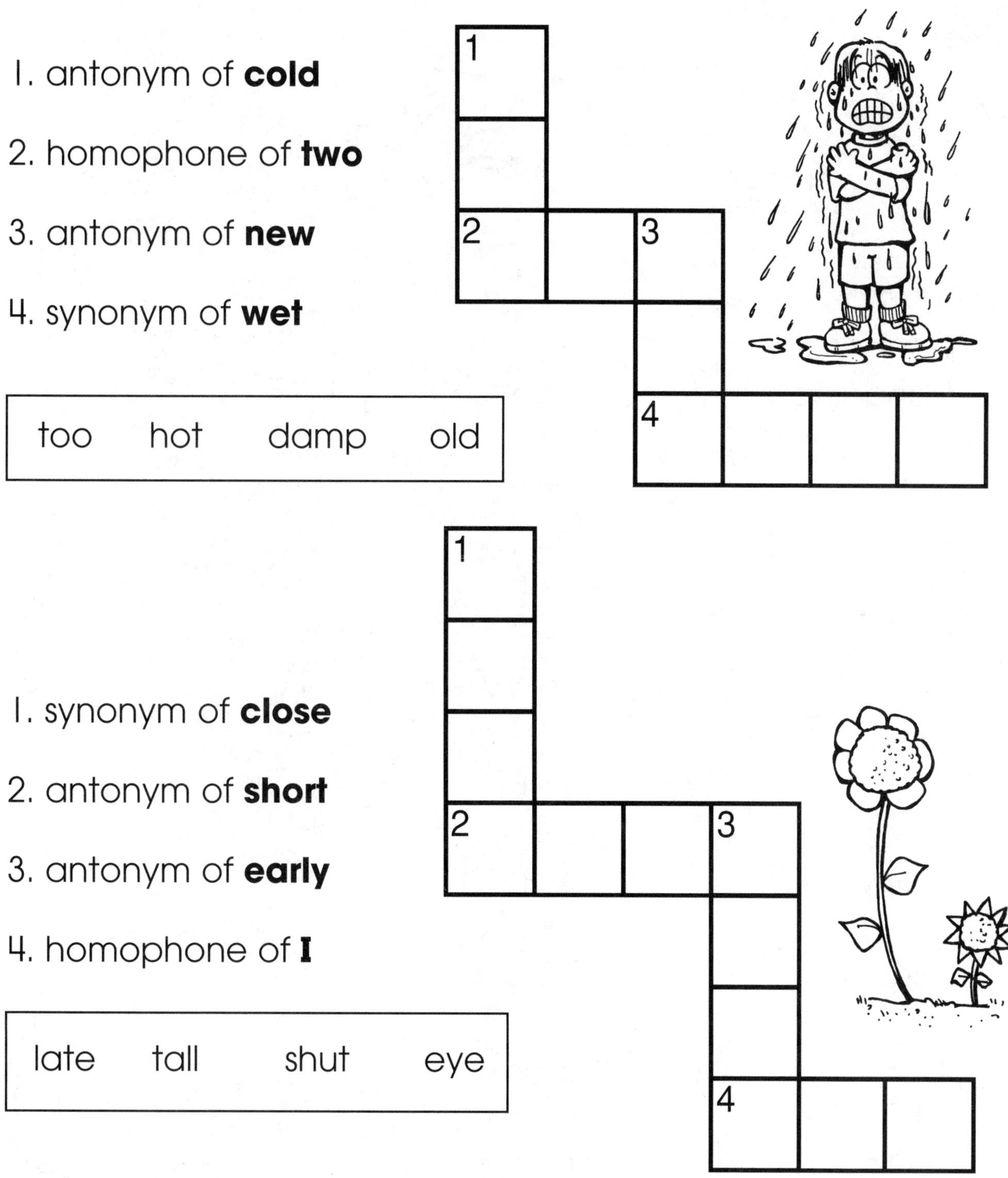

1. antonym of **cold**
2. homophone of **two**
3. antonym of **new**
4. synonym of **wet**
too hot damp old
1
2
3
4
1. synonym of **close**
2. antonym of **short**
3. antonym of **early**
4. homophone of **I**
late tall shut eye
1
2
3
4

Word Usage

When you talk about a person or a thing, use **a** if the next word begins with a consonant sound. Use **an** if the next word begins with a vowel sound.

Examples:

Kevin saw **a** turtle.

Marsha saw **an** owl.

Write **a** or **an** beside each word.

________ kangaroo	________ tiger
________ ostrich	________ cat
________ frog	________ ant
________ goat	________ zebra
________ lion	________ pig
________ elephant	________ dog
________ snail	________ whale
________ bat	________ skunk

Describing words can tell how a person, a place or a thing looks.

Example:

Emma found a coin.

Emma found a **shiny** coin.

The word **shiny** describes how the coin looks.

Circle the **describing word** in each sentence. Then, draw a line from the word to the correct picture.

The baby has a striped ball.

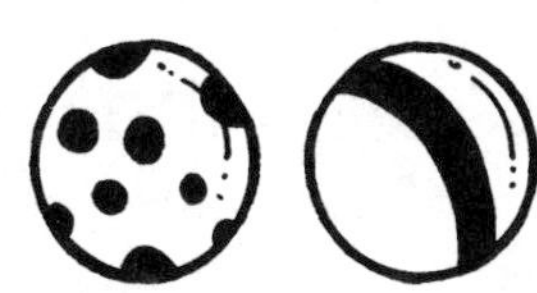

The clown has a pointed hat.

Vic found a long rope.

A thick book is on the table.

Describing Words

Describing words can also tell about an action.

Examples:

The turtle moved **slowly**.

The rabbit moved **quickly**.

The word **slowly** describes how the turtle moved. The word **quickly** describes how the rabbit moved.

Write a word to describe each action below. Choose a word from the box, or use a word of your own.

Sidney played the piano ______________________.

The child sang ______________________.

The horse ran ______________________.

The snow fell ______________________.

The man drove ______________________.

The teacher talked ______________________.

loudly
softly
quickly
slowly
sadly
happily

Describing words can also help make sentences more interesting.

Example:

The bear is climbing the tree.

The **huge** bear is climbing the tree **carefully**.

The words **huge** and **carefully** help "paint a picture" in your mind about what is happening.

Make the sentences below more interesting by adding **describing words**.

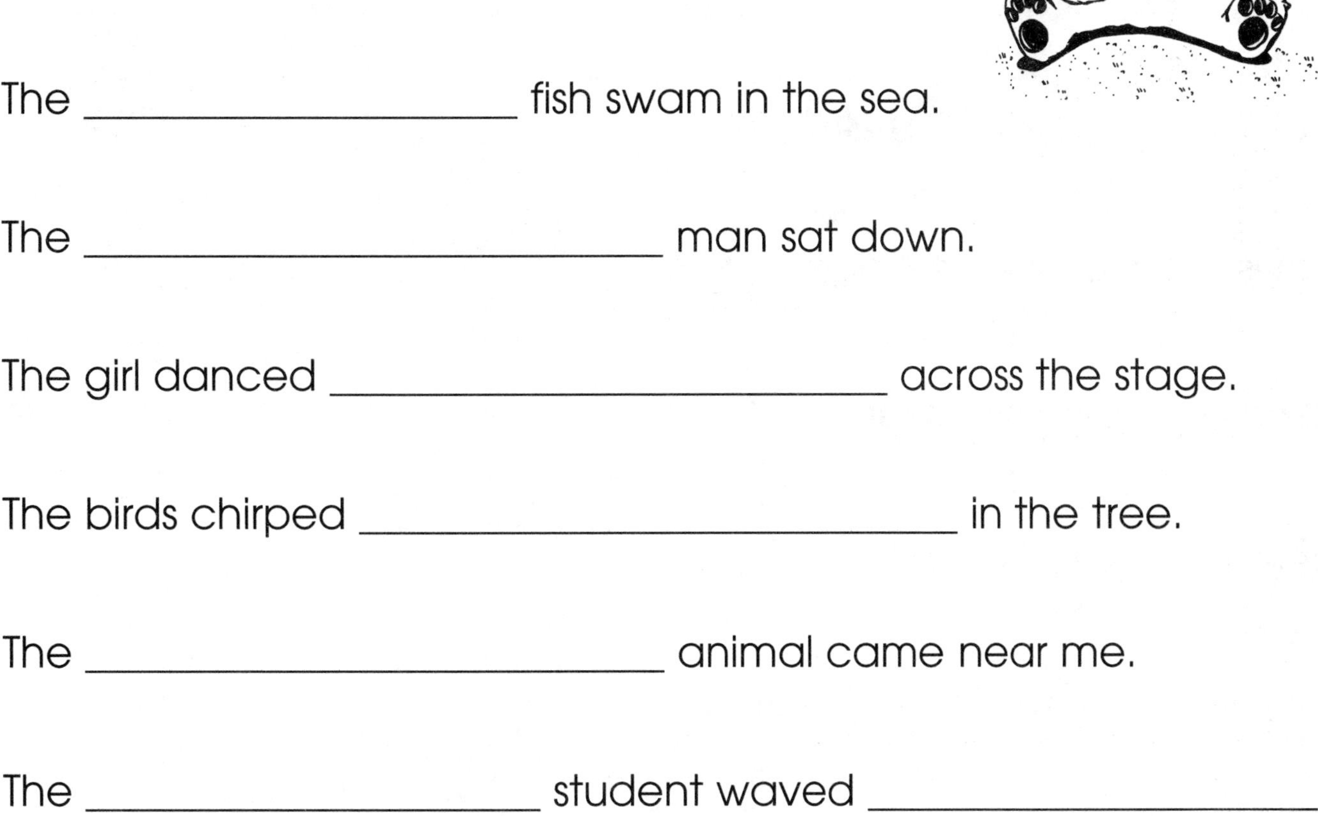

The ______________________ fish swam in the sea.

The ______________________________ man sat down.

The girl danced _____________________________ across the stage.

The birds chirped _______________________________ in the tree.

The ______________________________ animal came near me.

The _______________________ student waved _______________________.

Word Usage

Here's Sue. She is a **good** skater. She skates **well**.

When you describe a person, a place or a thing, use **good**. When you describe how something is done, use **well**.

Circle **good** or **well** in each sentence.

Andrew is a **good**, **well** singer.

Wanda dances **good**, **well**.

Antonio writes stories **good**, **well**.

Tim is a **good**, **well** reader.

Carmen is a **good**, **well** cook.

Helen paints **good**, **well**.

Doug adds numbers **good**, **well**.

Help the coach get to the castle. Complete each sentence on the path with the correct word.

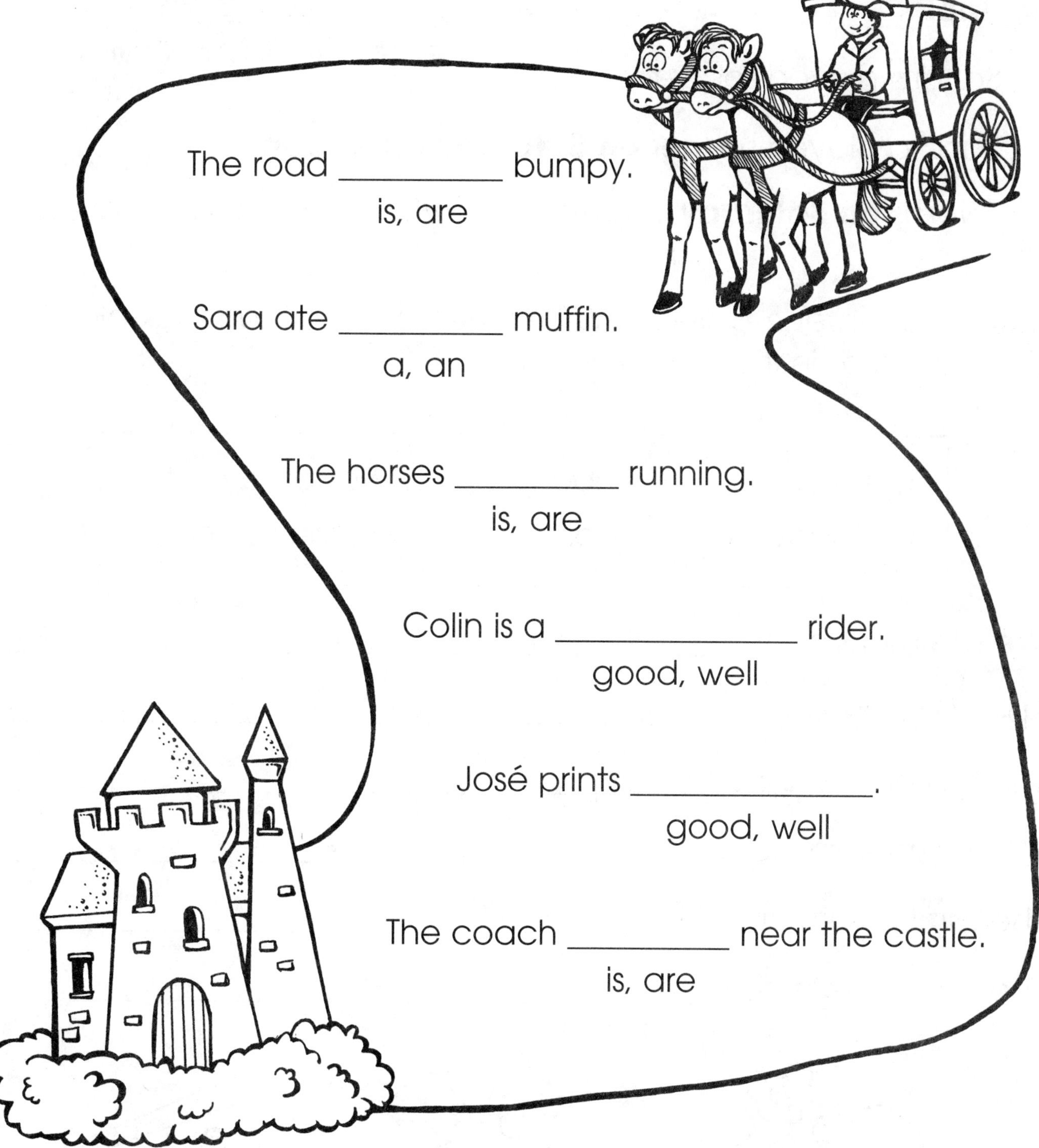

The road __________ bumpy.
is, are
Sara ate __________ muffin.
a, an
The horses __________ running.
is, are
Colin is a ______________ rider.
good, well
José prints ______________.
good, well
The coach __________ near the castle.
is, are

Expanding Sentences

You can make sentences more interesting by telling **when** something happened.

Example:

Sandra played soccer.

Sandra played soccer **on Saturday afternoon**.

The words **on Saturday afternoon** tell you when Sandra played soccer.

Read the sentences below. Write when each action took place. Use the words in the box to help you.

last week	at noon	yesterday
on Friday	in April	in the morning

We ate muffins ____________________.

I played baseball ____________________.

The bus picked up Emilio ____________________.

Nikki painted a picture ____________________.

The family went on a trip ____________________.

The kittens were born ____________________.

You can make sentences more interesting by using **colorful words**.

Example:

Fred walked into the room.

Fred **tiptoed** into the room.

The second sentence gives you a better idea of how Fred went into the room. The word **tiptoed** "paints a picture" in your mind.

Read the sentences below. Write a **colorful word** for each bold word. Choose words from the box.

sipped	soared	wailed
gobbled	whispered	crawled

The girl **drank** the milk. ______________________

Some ants **moved** along the wall. ______________________

The wolf **ate** the food. ______________________

The baby **cried** at the store. ______________________

A bird **flew** above me. ______________________

The boy **talked** to his friend. ______________________

Language Review

Read the sentences below. For each sentence, circle the word that describes a person, a place or a thing.

The scared kitten hid.

We went into a dark cave.

The new park has a slide.

A shiny button is on the floor.

Read the sentences below. For each sentence, circle the word that describes an action.

Clara printed neatly.

A car was honking loudly.

Marco read quietly.

The children ran quickly.

Write a sentence to describe each picture. Here are some questions that can help you decide what to write. Who is in the picture? What is happening? Where is it happening? When is it happening? You may use the words below to help you.

bee

bear

running

car

clown

riding

Sentence Order

When you write a story, put the sentences in **order** so the story makes sense.

Example: Eve got out the paints.

She painted a picture.

Eve hung the picture on the wall.

Read the sentences below. Write them in **order** so that they tell a story.

Sam ate the peas.

Sam washed the peas.

He cooked the peas.

The seeds grew into plants.

Jasmine dug a hole.

She put seeds in the hole.

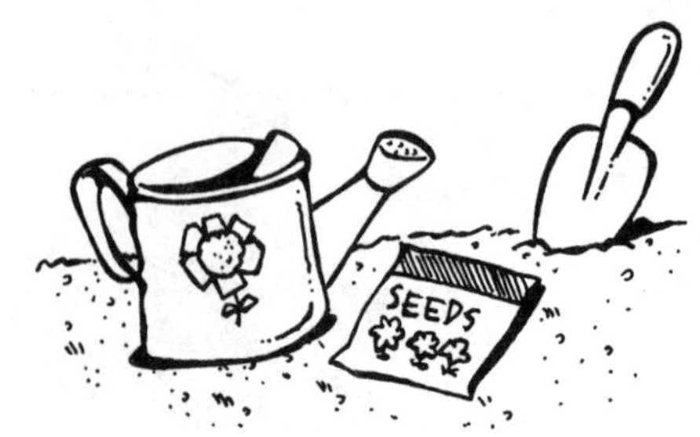

Did you know that you are a very special person? There is no one who is just like you! Draw a picture of yourself in the frame. Then, write at least three sentences about yourself on the lines below.

Writing a Story

Write a story about three things you did today. Write what you did first. Then, write what you did next. Finally, write what you did last.

#9005

MATH

Size and Shape Comparisons

When you **compare** objects, you look to see how they are the same or how they are different.

Pug and Gogg are the same size.

Stump and James are not the same size. Stump is **smaller**, and James is **bigger**.

Pug Gogg

Stump James

In each box, two monsters are the **same** size. Circle them.

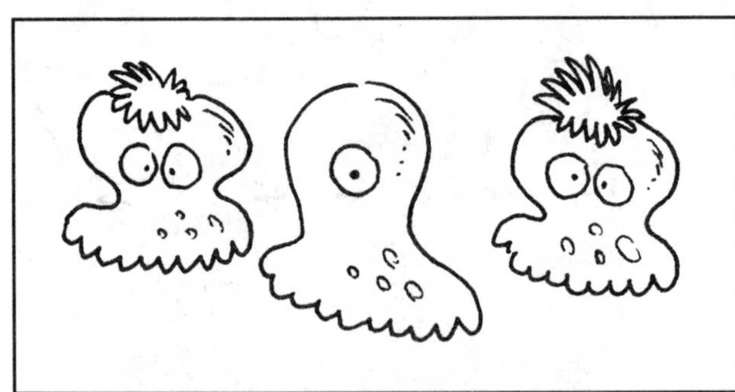

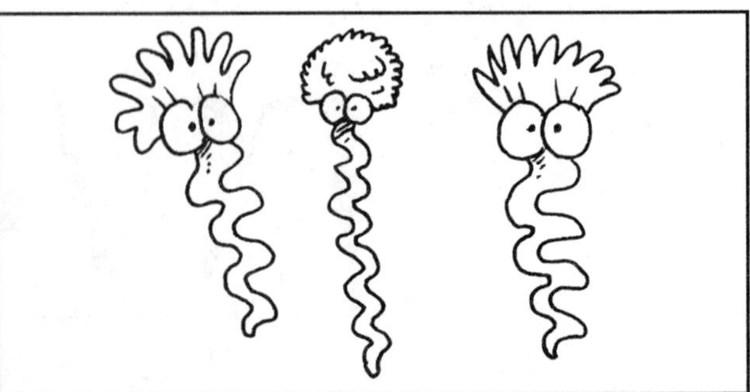

Two pictures in each box are the **same** size and shape.
Draw a circle around the ones that are the same.

These prints have the **same** shape.

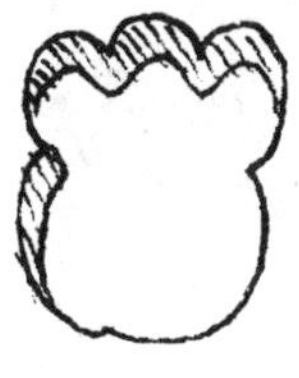

These have a **different** shape.

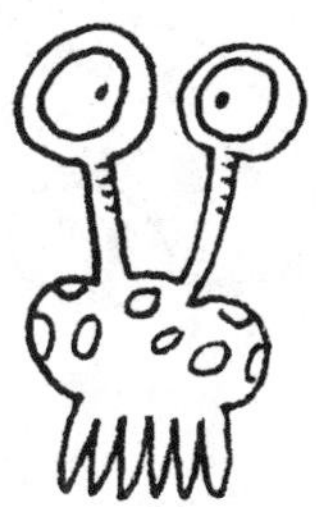
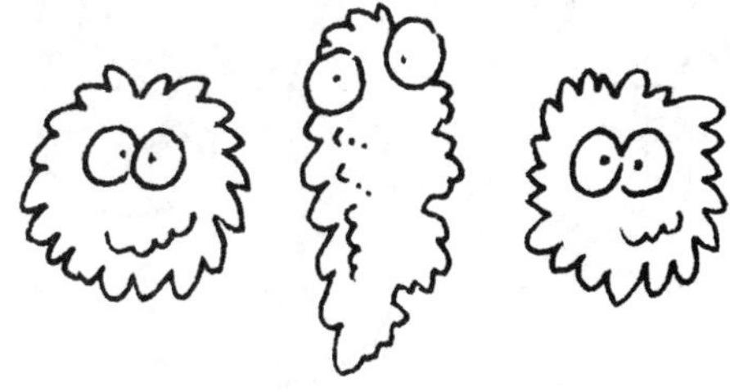
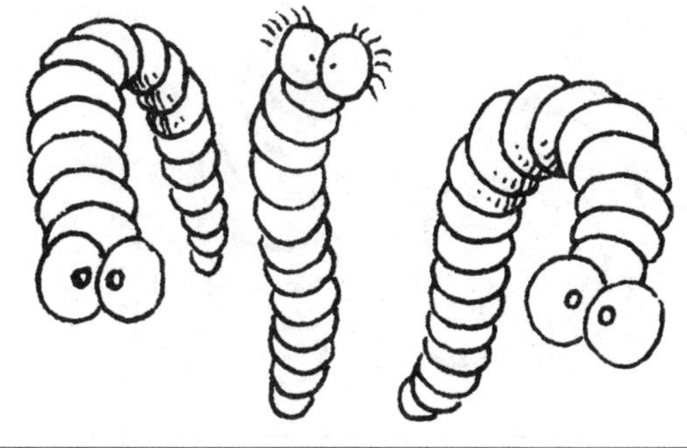

Size and Shape Comparisons

Circle the **biggest** picture in each box.

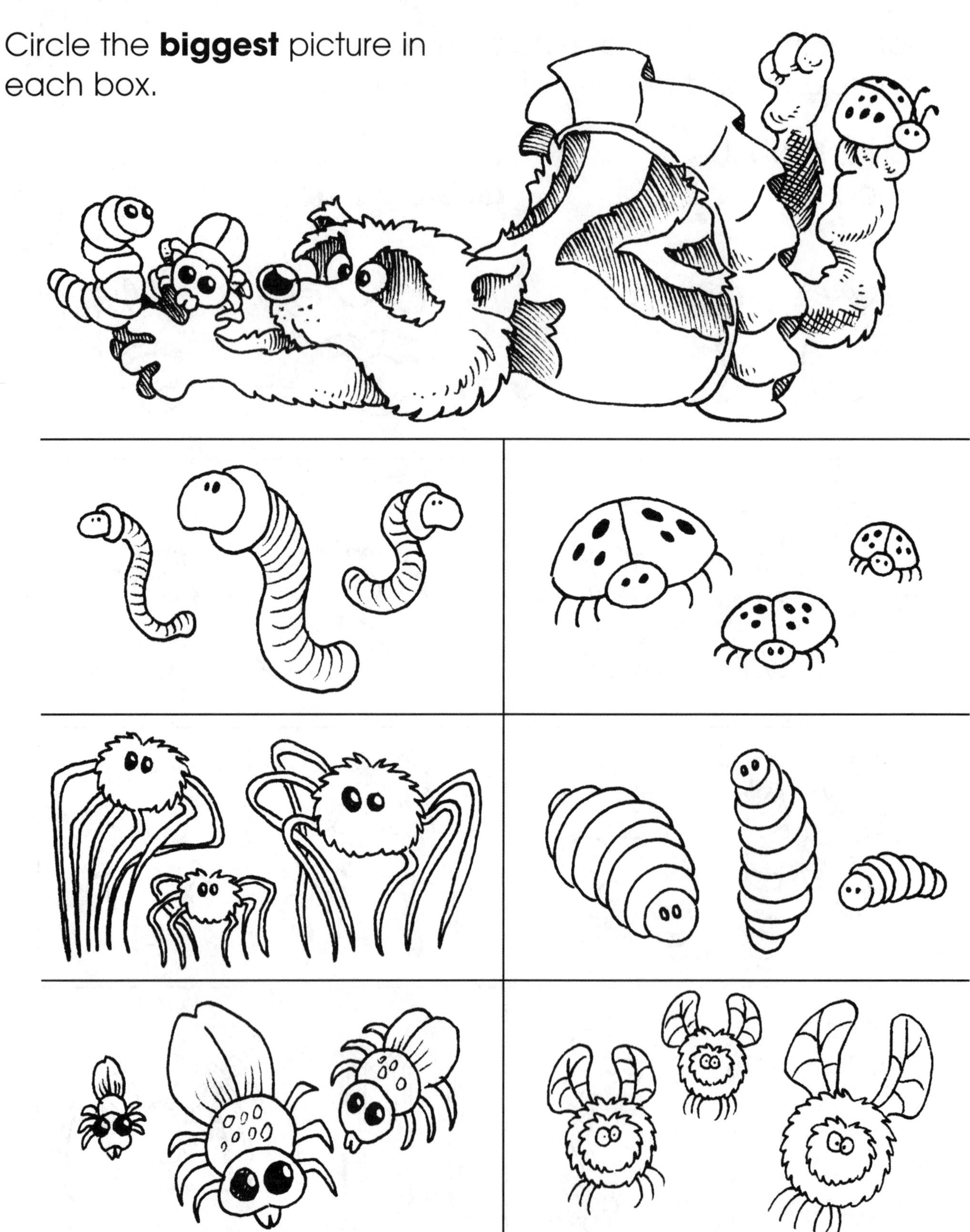

Trace the smallest picture in the boxes below. Then, draw the other two sizes on your own. The first one is done for you.

Counting 1 to 10

Help the monsters below line up in the correct order. The first monster is 1. The last monster is 10. Fill in each pumpkin with the correct number, so the other monsters know where to stand in line.

Categorizing and Counting

The monsters are having a good time! They love Halloween parties.

How many monsters have caramel apples? ____________________

How many monsters are playing "Pin the Tail on the Black Cat"? ____________________

Draw a circle around each monster with a trick-or-treat bag. ____________________

How many monsters are at the party? ____________________

Matching Like Objects

Monsters love to dance! Everyone is wearing special dancing shoes.

Help the monsters on the left find their partners on the right. Draw a line to connect the partners who are wearing the same kinds of shoes.

How many pairs of partners are at the dance? _____

Draw a circle around the monster without a partner.

Mr. Masher, who wears glasses, is looking for his child. His child has:

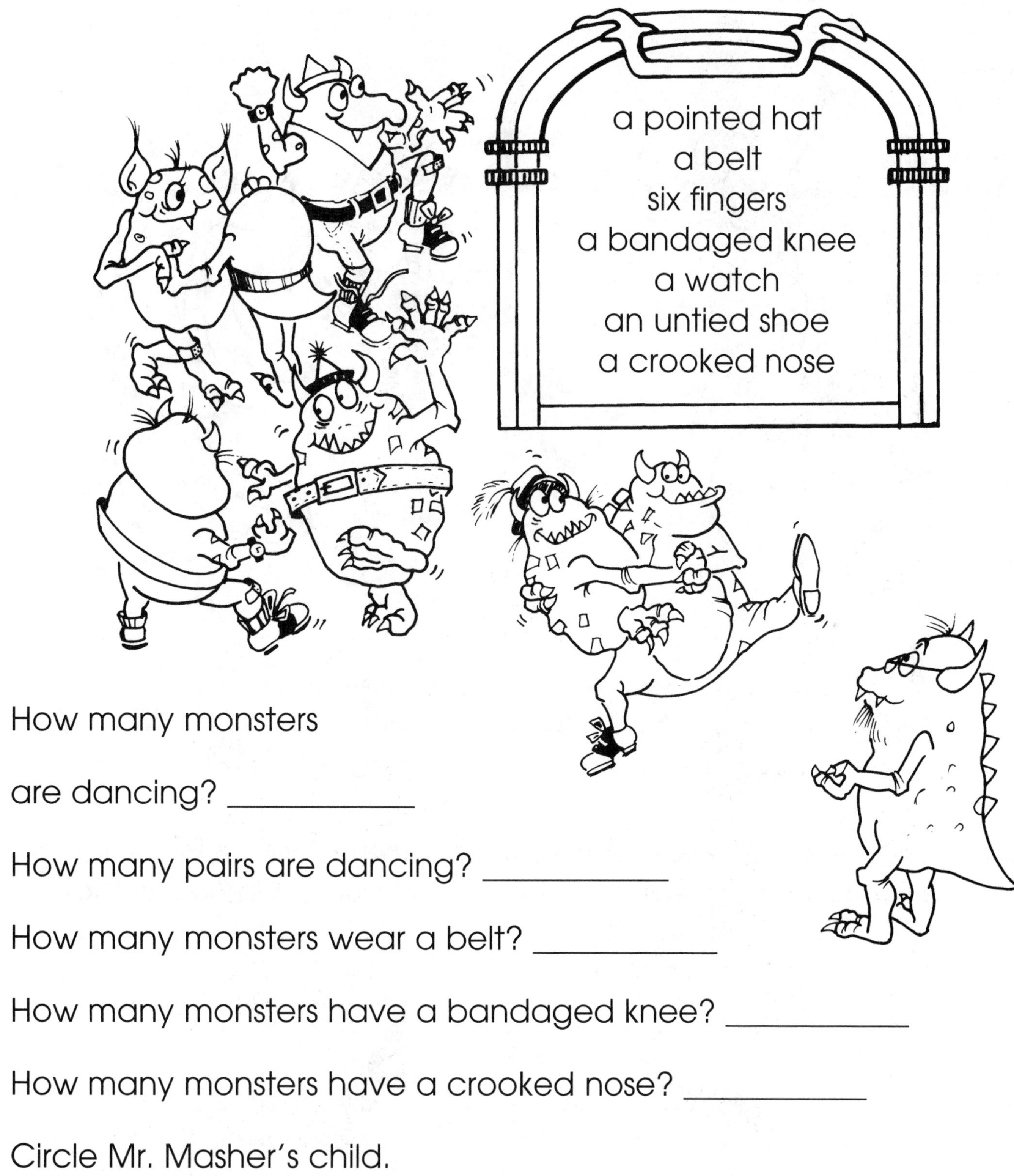

How many monsters

are dancing? ___________

How many pairs are dancing? ___________

How many monsters wear a belt? ___________

How many monsters have a bandaged knee? ___________

How many monsters have a crooked nose? ___________

Circle Mr. Masher's child.

More Than

Help Monty decide which branch has more bananas on it. One has 7 bananas on it. The other has 5.

7 is **more than** **5**

Sometimes, we write **more than** with a **symbol** that looks like this: **>**. On the line below, trace the math symbol that means **more than**.

7 ___>___ **5**

Monty and his friend Manuel have eaten a lot of bananas! Count the banana peels. Then, write the numbers on the lines below.

Who has eaten **more** bananas? ________________

__________ is **more than** __________

Write in the missing math symbol on the line.

7 __________ **4**

Less Than

Henrietta Hen has fewer eggs in one basket than in another. Point to the basket that holds **less**.

6 is **less than** **7**

Sometimes, we write **less than** using the symbol: **<**.
On the line below, write the math symbol that means **less than**.

6 ________ **7**

Now, count the decorated eggs. Then, fill in the numbers and math symbol to the right!

________ is **less than** ________
(number) (number)

________ ________ ________
(number) (symbol) (number)

Blue Sky, a Navajo girl, is watching some number clouds in the sky! For each pair of numbers, draw a circle around the number that is **more**.

Blue Sky's brother, Falling Star, is watching the number clouds, too. In each pair, circle the number that is **less**.

More/Less/Equal

Look at each tray of chocolate chip cookies. Count the number of chocolate chips each cookie on the trays has. Then, circle the cookie next to each tray that has the same number of chocolate chips as the ones on the tray.

Color the cookie which has the **most** chocolate chips **green**.
Color the cookie which has the **fewest** chocolate chips **blue**.

Circle the row in the rug that has **more** feathers in it.
How many **more** feathers does this row have? ______

Now, cross out the row that has **fewer**. How many **fewer** does it have? ______

How many feathers would you need to add to this row to make it **equal to** (the same as) the other row? ______

When you put numbers and symbols together to figure out a problem, you are writing an equation. Finish the equation.

More/Less

The monsters are waiting for their band instruments to arrive. There are tubas, flutes, trumpets and bells. Can you figure out how many monsters play each of the instruments? Use the clues below to answer each question.

- More than 5 but less than 7 monsters play the trumpet.
  How many play the trumpet? _____
- Less than 4 but more than 2 monsters play the flute.
  How many play the flute? _____
- More than 1 but less than 3 monsters play the tuba.
  How many play the tuba? _____
- More than 3 but less than 5 monsters play the bells.
  How many play the bells? _____

Circle the instrument that is played by **more** monsters. Cross out the instrument that is played by **fewer** monsters.

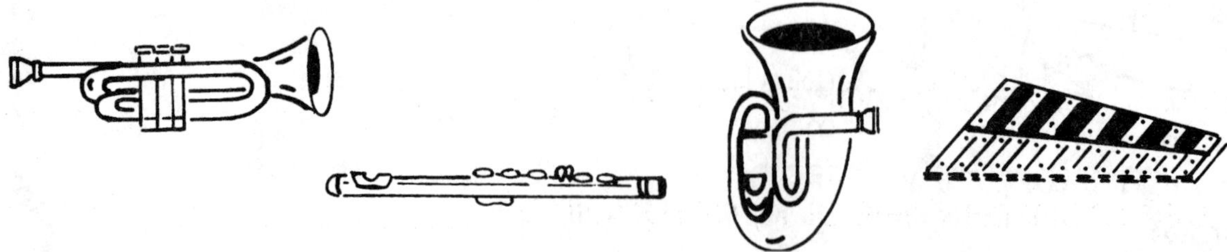

The bus is rolling back toward Slimepit Elementary. What are the monster children doing to pass the time as they travel?

Are **more** monsters reading or listening to music? ____________________

Are **fewer** monsters sleeping or reading? ____________________

Counting to 20

The monster boys and girls from Slimepit Elementary School have been on a field trip to the Green Swamp. Now, it is time to go home. Gus, the bus driver, needs to count all 20 passengers. He is marking off 1 square on his chart for each passenger as he or she boards the bus. Help Gus by filling in the missing numbers on his chart. Then, count the monsters in line. Is everybody there?

Mikey Monster is making a calendar for the month of May. He wants to make sure that he remembers to celebrate his birthday! Help him fill in the missing numbers on his calendar. Use these clues to figure out the date of Mikey's birthday.

Use these clues to figure out the date of Mikey's birthday.

- It is a number greater than 5.
- It ends with a zero.
- It does not fall on a Saturday.
- It is a number less than 24.

Draw a star on the calendar to mark Mikey's birthday.

Counting by 2's

All these monsters have come to the tennis court to play in a tournament. How many are there?

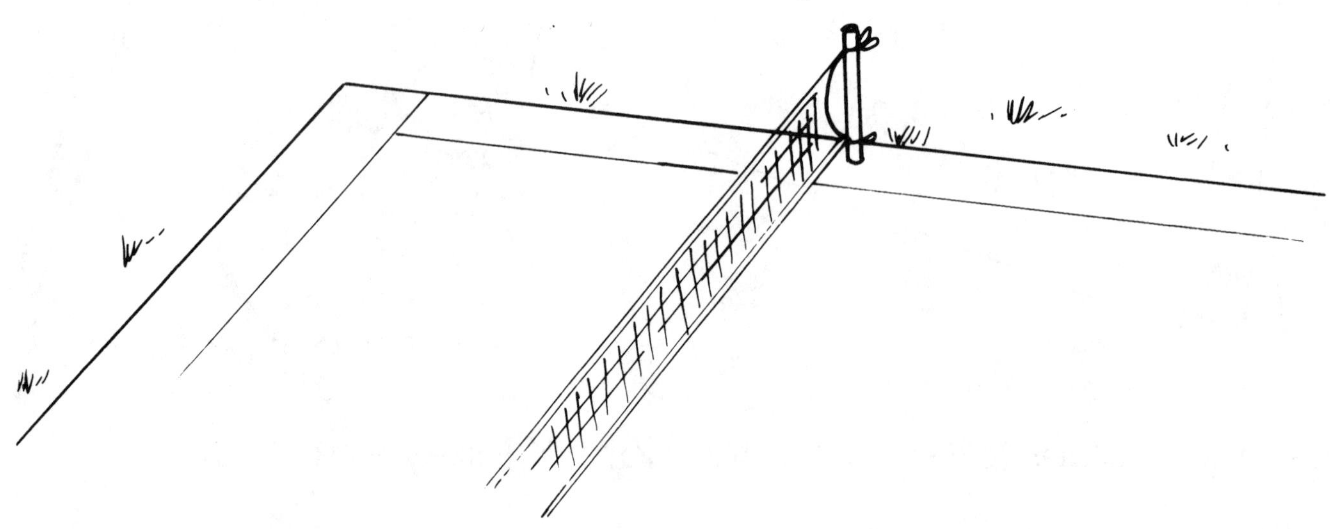

Instead of counting the monsters in the usual way, count by 2's. There are 2 monsters in the first pair, so put a 2 on the line beneath them. 2 more monsters make 4. Now, fill in the rest of the blanks.

The Frundell family is a very unusual monster family. They are known as the "Fearsome Frundells" because each member of the family has 5 frightening horns growing out of his or her head. How many horns do the Fearsome Frundells have altogether?

We don't have to count the horns one by one to find out! We can count by 5's.

5 ____ 10 ____ ____ ____ ____

Each monster has 5 horns, so we can begin with the number 5. 5 plus 5 more is 10, so put a 10 on the next line. 10 and 5 more equal what number? Write it under the third monster. Finish the rest of the row.

Addition

Putting numbers together is called **addition**. When you **add** two numbers together, you get a **total**, or **sum**. The symbol used for addition is called a **plus sign (+)**. The symbol used for a total is an **equal sign (=)**.

Follow the instructions below to create and solve the addition problems.

I pony is eating hay.	Draw I more pony in this box.	Write the total number of ponies.
+		= ______

I lamb is jumping.	Draw 2 more lambs in this box.	Write the total number of lambs.
+		= ______

Addition

The Barton family is having a picnic. But the ants have carried away their food. Use an addition equation to find out how many ants took food. The first one is done for you.

How many ants carried away fruit? 1 + 2 = 3
(one plus two equals three)

How many ants carried away vegetables?

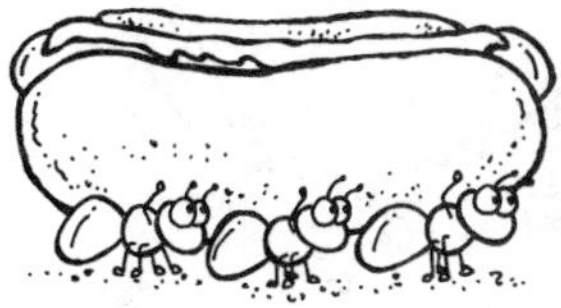
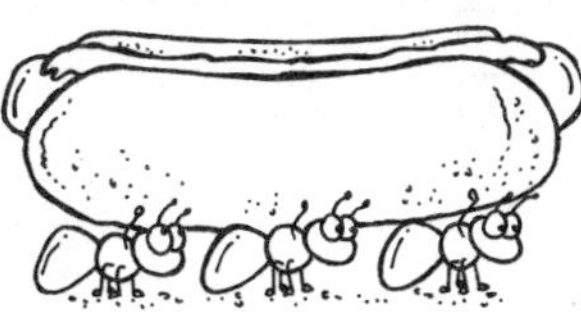

How many ants carried away hot dogs?

How many ants carried away bread? ______ + ______ = ______

Addition

Add up the dots on the domino pieces below. Write the total on the line below each piece.

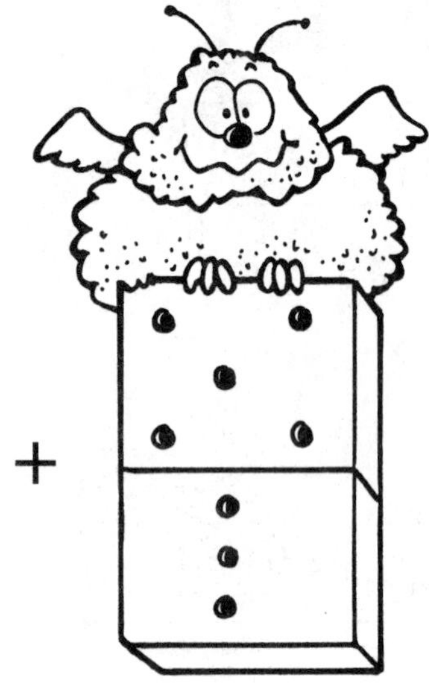

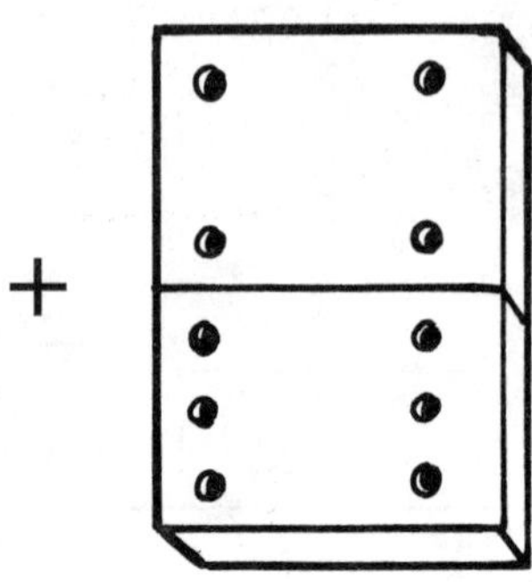

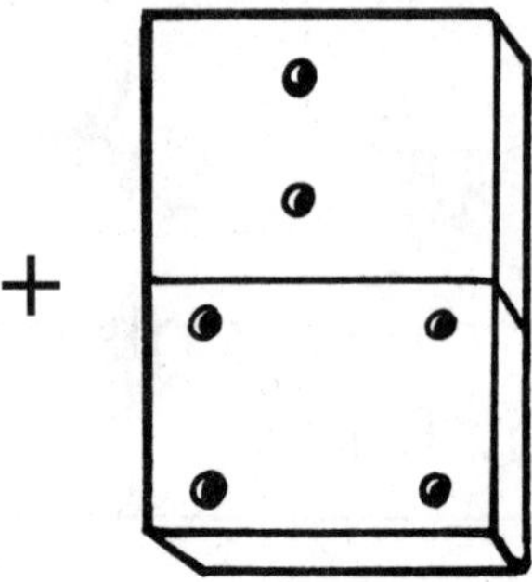

Now, draw the missing dots on each domino. Make sure the total number of dots adds up to the total on the line beneath each domino.

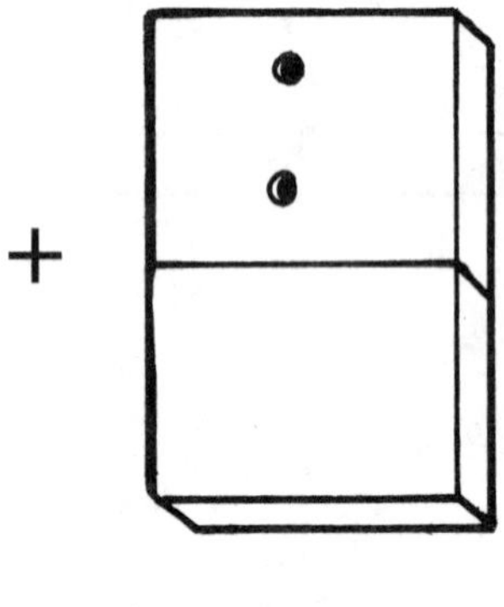

7

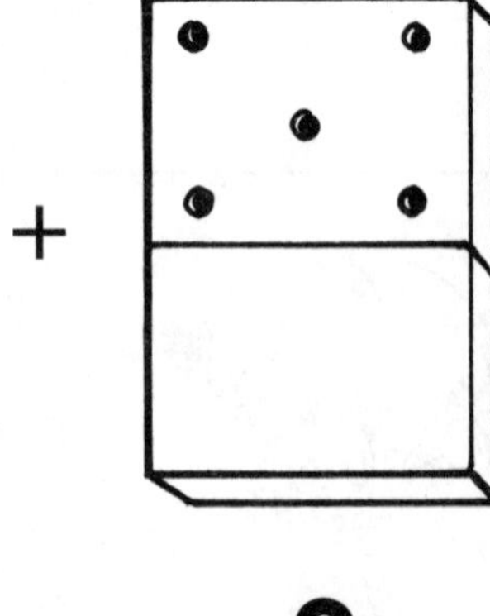

9

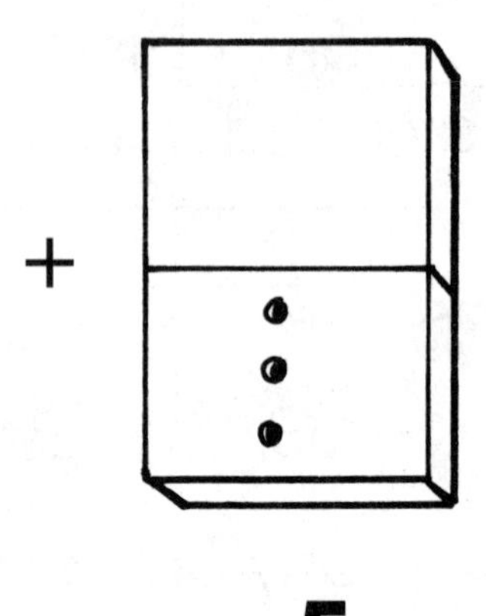

5

The geese are taking a stroll in the park. Use crayons to color 2 geese red, 3 geese green, 4 geese blue and 5 geese yellow.

Complete the addition equations to show how many geese of each color there are.

Green Geese	1 + ______ = 2	Red Geese	1 + ______ 2
Blue Geese	2 + 2 = ______	Yellow Geese	1 + ______ 5

Addition

Mrs. Murky asked 3 monster girls and 2 monster boys to come to the front of the class. She said, "If I have 3 monster girls and I add 2 monster boys, how many monster children do I have all together?"

Now, do the same problem on the board, but count the 2 boys first.

Does it matter which group is counted first? ______________

Look at each row of monster children. Write two number problems that describe each row.

_____ + _____ = _____

_____ + _____ = _____

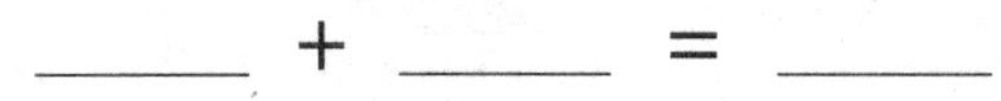

_____ + _____ = _____

_____ + _____ = _____

Adding and Subtracting

Taking numbers away is called **subtraction**. The symbol used for subtraction is a **minus sign (-)**. Look at the pictures below.

6 silly green frogs were sitting on six lily pads.

A big bird flew by and two jumped off into the water.

How many frogs were sitting on the lily pads? ______

How many frogs jumped off? ______

How many frogs were left? ______

Four hungry cats went on a picnic.

Two cats spotted some mice and took off to catch them!

How many cats went on the picnic? _____

How many cats ran after the mice? _____

How many cats were left? _____

Now, write the missing numbers in this subtraction problem.

4 - _____ = _____

You would say:

"Four minus ________ equals ________."

Adding and Subtracting

Benjamin Bunny likes to hop across the numbers. Help him fill in the missing numbers.

Adding 1's:

0 1 2 3 4 5 ____ ____ ____ ____ ____

Adding 2's:

0 2 4 6 8 10 ____ ____ ____ ____ ____

Now, help Benjamin fill in the blanks by subtracting.

Subtracting 1's:

10 9 8 7 6 5 ____ ____ ____ ____ ____

Subtracting 2's:

20 18 16 14 12 10 ____ ____ ____ ____ ____

You and Oliver Opossum have 25¢ to buy some of these toys.

When you buy a toy, cross it out. Then, write it in the table. The first toy is crossed out for you. Each time you buy a toy, subtract it until you have **no more money** to spend.

25¢	**-**	**4¢**	**=**	**21¢**
21¢	**-**	______**¢**	**=**	______**¢**
______**¢**	**-**	______**¢**	**=**	______**¢**
______**¢**	**-**	______**¢**	**=**	______**¢**
______**¢**	**-**	______**¢**	**=**	______**¢**
______**¢**	**-**	______**¢**	**=**	______**¢**

Even Numbers

Carla, Mark and Jack have saved their pennies. Help them figure out who has an even number of pennies. An **even number** is a number that can be split into two parts that are the same. Write the number of pennies each child has on the lines. Then, use a red crayon to circle the groups of pennies that have an even number. **Hint:** Try to separate each group into two equal parts.

____

____

____

After lunch, Mrs. Murky wanted to divide her class into 2 groups. Mrs. Murky lined up the boys and girls and told them to count off. The monsters had to shout out their numbers, in order, all the way down the line. Fill in the numbers they shouted.

"Now," said Mrs. Murky, "the **even** numbers will read and the **odd** numbers will do math problems!"

Draw a line from each student to the area where he or she should go to work.

Which group has more? ______________________________

Even and Odd Numbers

The two teams have just arrived at the playing field. Before they start their game, count the monsters on this page and the next to make sure everyone is here.

How many players are wearing **odd** numbers? _______

How many players are wearing **even** numbers? _______

How many coaches are here? _______

Draw a circle around the character who is not a part of the team.

Put the monsters into two teams. All the monsters wearing **odd** numbers are on Team #1. All the monsters wearing **even** numbers are on Team #2. Write their numbers on the team clipboards below.

Find out which team wins! If the answer is an **odd** number, Team #1 wins. If the answer is an **even** number, Team #2 wins.

4 + 2 = ______

Circle all the players who are on the winning team.!

Two-Digit Numbers

Some numbers have **two digits**. The number 15 has **two digits**—the **digit** 1 and the **digit** 5. Look at the pictures below. Hunt for **two-digit** numbers. Draw a circle around each **two-digit** number you find.

Draw a line from each **two-digit** number to its matching word.

16	**fourteen**
15	**nineteen**
14	**seventeen**
19	**eighteen**
17	**fifteen**
18	**sixteen**

Write the missing **two-digit** number in each group. Then, spell that number in the space below. The first one is done for you.

13, 14, 15

fourteen

9, 10, ____

12, ___, 14

11, ____, 13

Addition

Draw a circle around the groups of 10 bugs in each box. Write the number of tens before the word **tens**. Then, count the bugs that are left. Write the number of ones before the word **ones**. Then, write the sum of the equation. The first one is done for you.

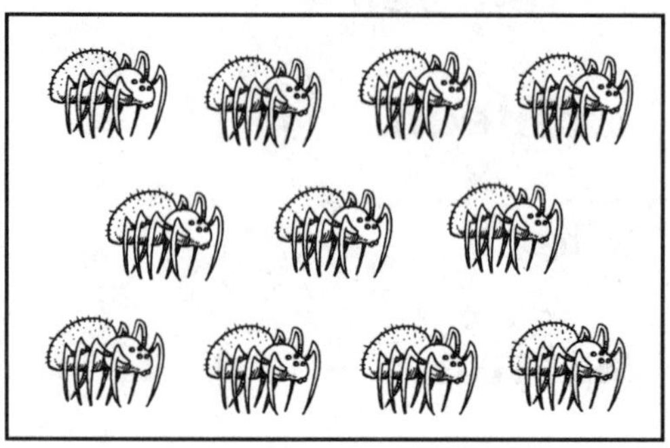

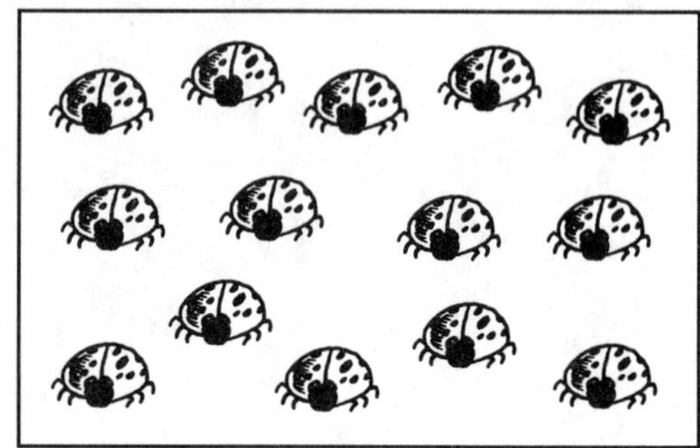

__1__ **ten +** __1__ **one =** __11__

_____ **tens +** _____ **ones =** _____

_____ **tens +** _____ **ones =** _____

_____ **tens +** _____ **ones =** _____

Millie and Milo are playing pick-up sticks. Help them count their sticks. Draw a circle around each group of 10 sticks.

How many groups of 10 does Millie have? __________

How many are left over? __________

How many groups of 10 does Milo have? __________

How many are left over? __________

What is Millie's score? __________

What is Milo's score? __________

Who won? __________

Counting to 20

Make the number of shapes in each row below add up to 20 by drawing the correct number of shapes in the empty squares.

Row 1:

△△ + [ ] + △△ = 20

Row 2:

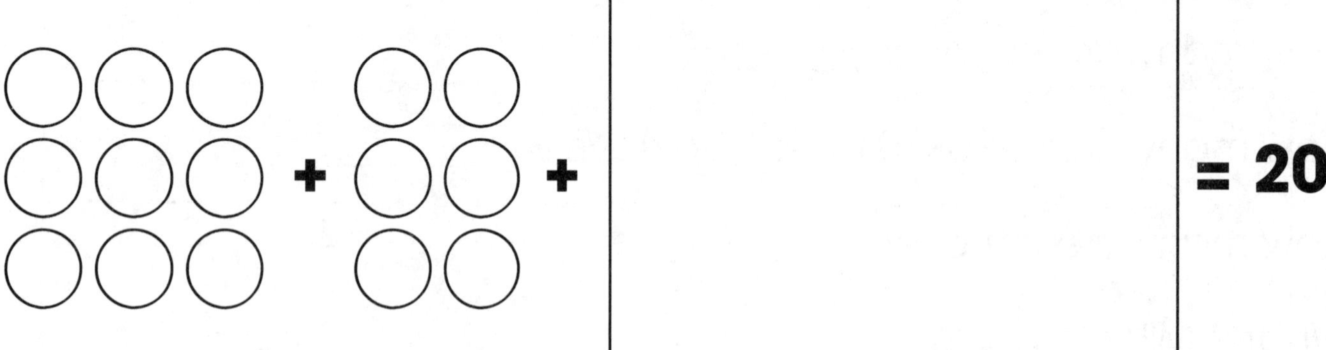

How many equations can you write using the number 20? It can be part of an addition problem or a subtraction problem.

Hint: You may want to use pennies, buttons or lima beans to help you create different equations. Two have been done for you.

10 + 10 = 20 ____________________

20 - 10 = 10 ____________________

____________________ ____________________

____________________ ____________________

____________________ ____________________

____________________ ____________________

____________________ ____________________

____________________ ____________________

____________________ ____________________

Estimation

How many are there of each sea creature in the aquarium? Before you count, guess the number of each creature. This kind of guess is called an **estimate**. Write your **estimates** in the chart below. Then, fill in the rest of the columns in the chart.

	Guess how many. Write your estimate.	Count how many. Write the number.	Did you guess more or less than the real number?

Look at the stars on this page. **Estimate** how many there are.

Write your estimate here: _______

Draw a circle around each group of 10.

How many groups of 10 are there? _______

How many stars are left outside the circle? _______

How many stars are there altogether? _______

Estimation

One hot summer day, Thor decided to take a nap in the shade. He couldn't get to sleep because of all the flies buzzing around his head. He tried to count them, but that made him dizzy! Estimate how many flies are bothering Thor. Write your **estimate** here. ______

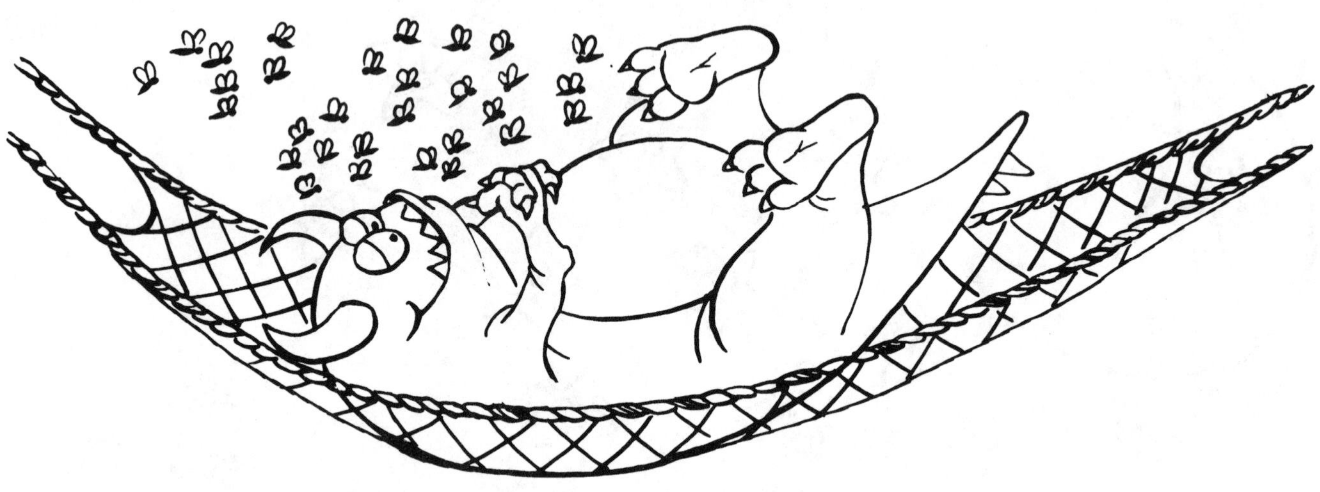

Check your **estimate** by counting the flies in groups of 10. Draw a circle around each group of 10.

How many groups of 10 flies are there? ______

How many flies are left over? ______

How many flies are there altogether? ______

Belinda Beastly wants to package buttons in bags of 10, but she is not sure how many bags she will need. She estimates that she will need 5.

What is your estimate? ________

Count the buttons in groups of 10 and draw a "bag" around each group.

How many groups of 10 did you count? _______

How many bags does Belinda need? _______

Pennies

Hector and Hugh, Gerta and Gussie, and Mug and Lug are getting ready to go to the store. They are counting their pennies. Each penny is worth 1 cent.

How much money does Hector have? _______ cents

How much money does Hugh have? _______ cents

How much do Hector and Hugh have? _______ cents

How much do Gerta and Gussie have? _______ cents

How much do Mug and Lug have? _______ cents

Cross out the pair who have the **most** money.

Circle the pair who have the **least** amount of money.

The monsters have counted their money. They are going to buy things at the store. Look at each item on sale. Then, answer each question by drawing an **X** on the pair who have enough money to buy the item.

Who can buy the toothbrush?

_______ Hector and Hugh

_______ Gerta and Gussie

_______ Mug and Lug

Who can buy the grapes?

_______ Hector and Hugh

_______ Gerta and Gussie

_______ Mug and Lug

Who can buy the apple?

_______ Hector and Hugh

_______ Gerta and Gussie

_______ Mug and Lug

Who can buy the doll?

_______ Hector and Hugh

_______ Gerta and Gussie

_______ Mug and Lug

Money

These monsters want to go to the pizza parlor. But they can't go until they know how much they have to spend. Count how much money each monster has. Then, fill in the blanks below.

How much money does Bob have? _______ cents

How much money does Babs have? _______ cents

How much money does Dot have? _______ cents

How much do they have altogether? _______ cents

The monsters are waiting to order. Look at page 208 to find out how much money they have. Then, answer the question below.

MENU	
All-You-Can-Eat Pizza	$2.50
Soup	$1.25
Lemonade	$ .25

What can each of the monsters buy with the money

they have? ____________________

Making Change

Rimsley's mom gave him $1.00 to buy stamps that cost 72¢. What will his change be? ______

Draw pictures to show the coins he could receive as change.

Rimsley might receive these coins in change:

Or he could receive these coins:

Milo needs 1 dollar to buy his favorite lunch at the Slimepit Elementary School cafeteria. He wants a salamander salami sandwich. His mother gave him 10 coins that add up to 1 dollar, and Milo put them in his pocket. His coins include at least 1 quarter, as well as some dimes and nickels. He has no pennies. What coins will Milo use to pay for his lunch? Draw them in the space below.

Dot has learned that she can earn money by recycling. She is saving her money so she can go to the movies. Count the money she earned in January and February by recycling cans, bottles and newspapers. Then, fill in the totals and answer the questions below.

GARBAGE →	(can)	(bottle)	(newspaper)
JANUARY	20¢	50¢	35¢
FEBRUARY	50¢	10¢	22¢
TOTAL			

How much money does she have altogether? _______ cents

Before she went to the movies, she spent:

- 10¢ on candy.
- 20¢ on a balloon.
- 30¢ on a comic book.

How much does she have left? _______ cents

It will cost $1.50 (or 150 cents) to go to the movies. Does she have enough? **YES** **NO**

Ursula ran into her room after school and flung her bookbag onto her desk. Unfortunately, she knocked over her piggy bank and it broke, spilling all the coins. Can you help her count the coins to see if she has found them all? She knows she had exactly $3.15.

Did Ursula find all of her coins? If not, what is missing? ____________

Addition

The monsters are planting a vegetable garden. They're going to do all the work themselves!

How many monsters have a shovel? _______

How many monsters have a hoe? _______

How many tools do you see? _______

- Joot has 2 packets of carrot seeds.
- Moot has 3 packets of pea seeds.
- Hoot has 1 packet of bean seeds.

Find out how many seed packets the monsters have by adding up the numbers below, then fill in the blank.

2 + 3 + 1 = ________

This chart shows the number of plants each monster is growing. Add up how many of each kind of vegetable they have planted. Fill in the totals at the bottom of the chart. Then, answer the questions below.

Vegetables →			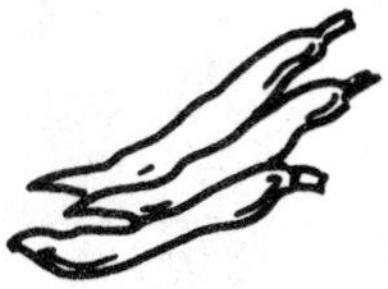
 JOOT	5	1	2
 MOOT	1	6	1
 HOOT	2	1	4
TOTAL			

How many carrots are the monsters growing? ________

How many peas are the monsters growing? ________

How many beans are the monsters growing? ________

How many plants are growing altogether? ________

Using a Table

Veronica, Ursula and Millie all play on the Slimepit Sluggers softball team. The table below shows how well the girls hit in last week's games.

Use the information in the table to answer these questions.

Which girl had the most hits? ___________

How many did she have? ___________

What is the total number of hits made by the girls on Monday? _______ On Wednesday? _______

On Saturday? _______

On which day did the girls perform best as a group? _____________

	Veronica	Ursula	Millie
Monday	4 hits	2 hits	0 hits
Wednesday	3 hits	1 hit	5 hits
Saturday	3 hits	3 hits	3 hits

Geoffrey and Georgia Giraffe love to make graphs.

A **graph** has **rows** of squares. A row goes **across**.

A graph has **columns** of squares, too. A column goes **up** and **down**.

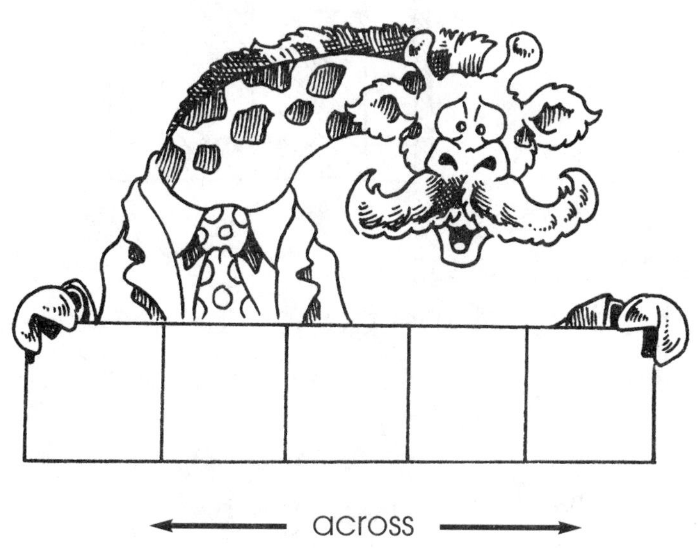

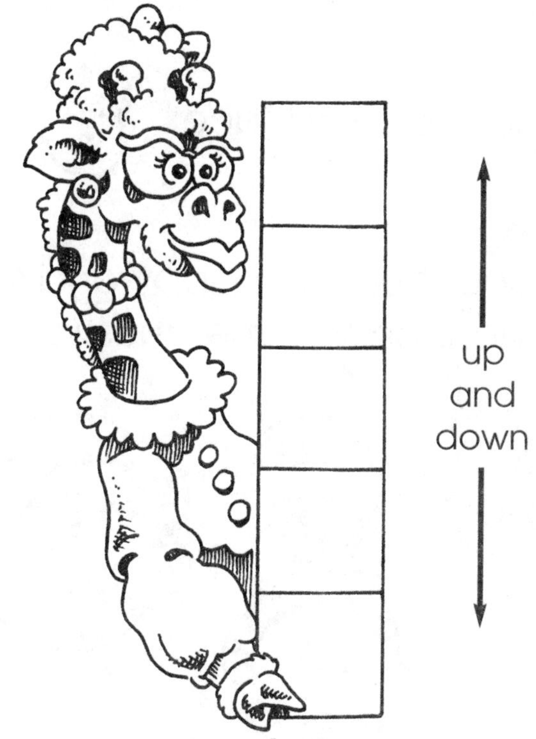

Together, the rows and columns make a graph that looks like this:

	Column 1	Column 2	Column 3	Column 4
Row 4				
Row 3				
Row 2				
Row 1				

Graphing

Make your own graph.

Here is a happy face: 

Here is a sad face: 

Count up the happy and sad faces you see below.
Then, answer the questions at the bottom of the page.

How many happy faces did you count? __________

How many sad faces did you count? __________

How many faces are there in all? __________

Now, make a graph of the happy and sad faces you counted on page 218. The first row has been done for you. A happy face and a sad face have been drawn in. Fill in the other rows to complete the graph.

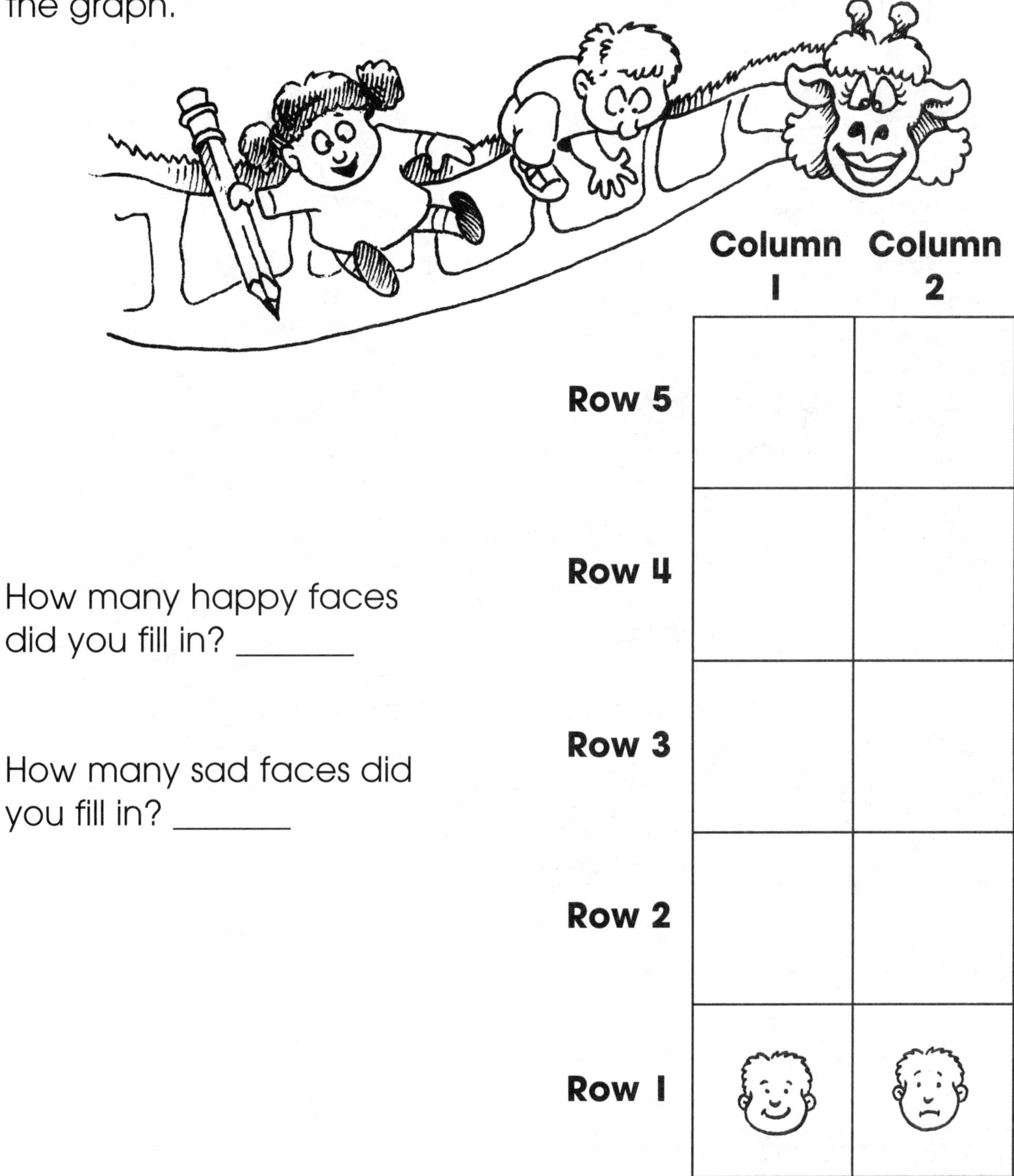

How many happy faces did you fill in? _______

How many sad faces did you fill in? _______

Graphing

It's a birthday party! There are lots of good foods to eat.

How many different kinds of food are there? _____
Count up all the foods you see!

How many egg rolls are there above? _______

How many pizzas did you count? _______

How many cakes did you see? _______

How many tacos are there in all? _______

Make a graph of the birthday party foods. Use the number of each food you counted to fill in your graph. Draw the pictures in the correct columns. The first row has been done for you.

	Column 1	Column 2	Column 3	Column 4
Row 6				
Row 5				
Row 4				
Row 3				
Row 2				
Row 1				

Which column has more? Circle one:  

Which column has less? Circle one:  

Estimation/Counting

The cookies below are in the shape of four different animals. Before you count them, estimate how many animals there are

in all: ______

Now, count the animal cookies!

How many giraffes did you count? _____

How many lions are there in all? _____

How many turtles are there? _____

How many dogs do you see? _____

Complete the graph below. Use the number of each animal you counted to fill in the rows with the missing pictures of turtles and dogs. The giraffes and lions have been filled in for you.

Which animal cookie is there the most of? ______________________

Which animal cookie is there the fewest of? ____________________

Two kinds of cookies have the same number.

How many are there? ______

Graphing

Ursula grew a great deal the past year! Help her make a graph that shows how much she grew each month. On page 225, color in one box for each inch she grew.

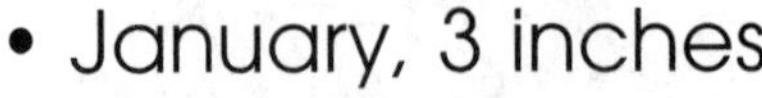

- January, 3 inches
- February, 0 inches
- March, 1 inch
- April, 2 inches
- May, 2 inches
- June, 0 inches
- July, 1 inch
- August, 0 inches
- September, 4 inches
- October, 1 inch
- November, 1 inch
- December, 2 inches

Inches Grown

January				
February				
March				
April				
May				
June				
July				
August				
September				
October				
November				
December				

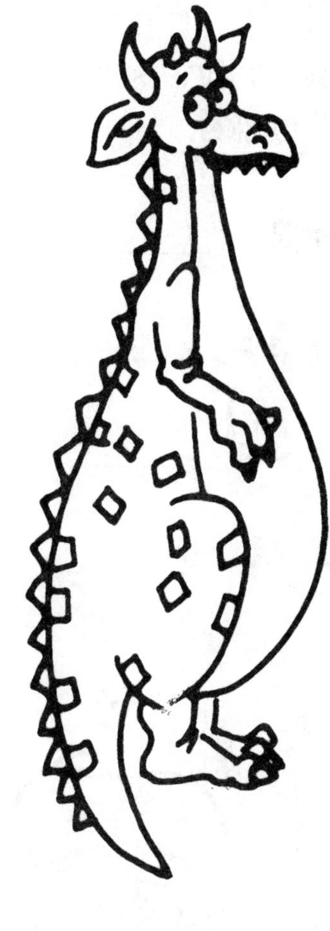

How many inches did Ursula grow altogether? _______

Did Ursula grow more in the first half of the year or in the last half of the year? _______

Addition

The monsters love to bake sweet things. Their favorites are snail tarts, slime cookies and thorny cream puffs. Simon and Stella are planning what they are each going to bake.

Fill in the blanks below to find out how many sweet things Simon will bake.

3 + 2 = ______ 

6 + 3 = ______ 

4 + 3 = ______ 

TOTAL ______

Fill in the blanks below to find out how many sweet things Stella will bake.

3 + 4 = ______ 

3 + 6 = ______ 

2 + 5 = ______ 

TOTAL ______

While Simon and Stella were in the back washing dishes. Simon's twin nephews came to visit. The nephews gobbled down some treats. They knocked over some bowls. They even sat on some pastries!

Simon made a list of all the sweets he and Stella lost. Can you help him add up the ruined sweets, then put the totals in the boxes below?

Sweets →					
STELLA	**6**	**4**	**9**	**5**	**7**
SIMON	**6**	**3**	**1**	**2**	**2**
TOTAL					

Once upon a time, 2 very hungry monsters named Zort and Zerta went looking for tasty things to put in their soup. Zort found 5 snails asleep under a bush.

"Mmm, delicious!" he said. He put the snails into his pockets. Zerta found 3 rotten apples in the dirt by a fence.

"Terrific!" she snorted, stuffing the apples into her basket.

They headed home to their kitchen, but on the way, 1 tricky snail slowly crawled out of Zort's pocket and escaped.

How many things can the monsters put in their soup? Complete the number sentences below.

What a feast! Eight monsters are eating a delicious dinner at the Monster Cafe. The chef has cooked his favorite meal of snails, worms and dirt sandwiches!

Everything was going fine, until . . .

Twister left to answer the telephone.
Toot went home because she forgot her money.
Buster left to pick up his sister at the bus stop.

How many monsters had to leave the table? _______

After Twister, Toot and Buster left, how many chairs were

empty? _______

How many monsters were left at the table? _______

Subtraction

Moot, the cook at the Monster Cafe, is working very hard. He has many orders to fill. Look on the menu to see what the most popular dishes are.

Count all the orders below. How many orders does Moot have to fill? __________

menu

Snail Soup

Worm Pasta

Dirt Sandwich

Moot worked very fast and filled:

1 soup order, 2 pasta orders and 3 sandwich orders

How many orders does Moot have left to fill?

_______ more soup order(s)

_______ more pasta order(s)

_______ more sandwich order(s)

The monster parade is about to begin. But only 6 monsters are ready to march! Read what happened to the missing marchers. Then, answer the questions at the bottom of the page.

- 1 monster broke her toe.
- 2 monsters lost their music.
- 1 monster caught a cold.
- 2 monsters were too big to fit into their uniforms.

How many monsters went home? _______

How many monsters would be in the parade if all the marchers came? _______

Addition/Subtraction

Monsters love parades! There are so many monsters, nobody can see what they look like—except for Fred. Fred took his binoculars up in a tree to see how many monsters were at the parade.

Add or subtract the numbers to find out what Fred counted.

2 + 3 + 1 = ______ have chalk on their noses.

6 + 2 - 2 = ______ have pencils behind their ears.

5 - 1 - 2 = ______ have holes in their socks.

4 - 1 - 1 = ______ have dinosaur backpacks.

4 + 3 + 2 = ______ have have skinned knees.

Add the totals above the find out how many

monsters Fred spotted altogether. ______

Try to figure out the following problem as you read it. Do the adding and subtracting in your head. Use a pencil and paper only if you get stuck!

Mary and Marvin asked all their friends to come to the park to play baseball. Mary, Marvin and 10 other monsters arrived at the park at 10 o'clock. 3 more monsters arrived at 11:00. At 12:00, 4 monsters had to go home for lunch, and 1 had to leave for a dentist appointment. At 1:00, the McGuire twins arrived, along with Marvin's cousin Milton.

How many monsters were at the park at 11:00? ______

How many monsters were at the park at 12:00? ______

How many monsters were at the park at 1:00? ______

Subtraction

Mibby the monster wins every card game she plays! It's the start of a new game. Look at all the cards in her hand.

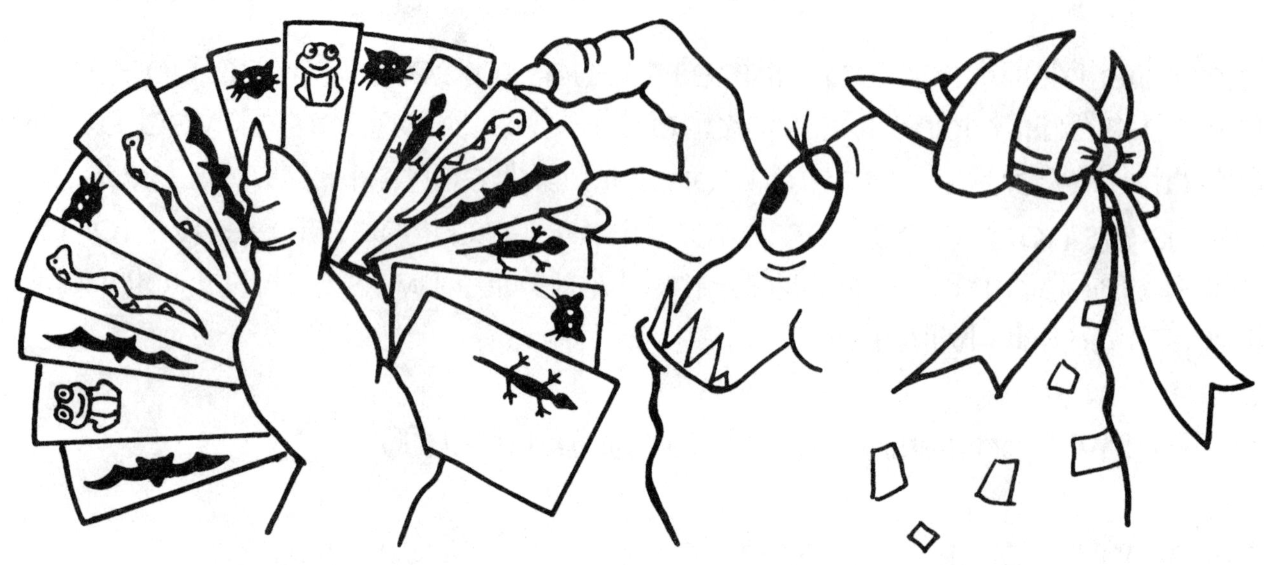

How many cards does she have? _______

Before the game is over, she has to give:

- 3 black cat cards to May.
- 2 snake cards to Jud.
- 3 bat cards to Wooster.
- 1 frog card to Mitsy.

How many cards does Mibby have left? _______

Rodney is sad because it is raining and he can't go out to play. He is sitting by the window, counting the raindrops as they land on the glass.

16 raindrops are on the window as Rodney begins to count. 4 of the raindrops slide away and soon disappear. 5 new drops hit the window. How many raindrops are on the window now? _______

8 of the raindrops slide away, but 2 new raindrops hit the window. Now, how many raindrops can Rodney see on the glass? _______

9 of these raindrops slide away. How many are left? _______

2 raindrops race each other to the bottom of the window pane. Now, how many raindrops does Rodney see? _______

Addition

Play this baseball game to test yourself on time and addition!

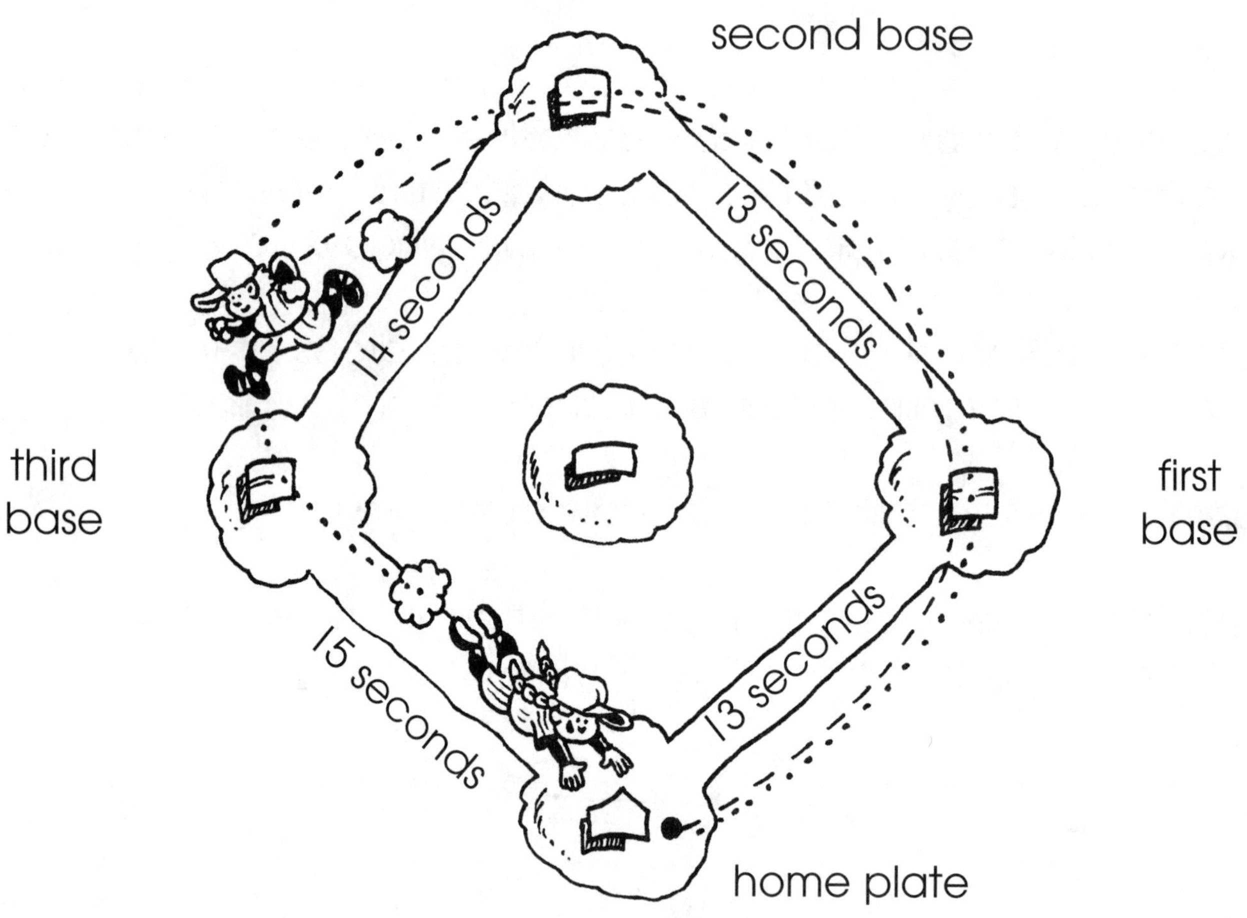

1. Samuel hits the ball and makes it all the way to third base! How long does it take him to get there? (**Note:** seconds = sec.)

_______ sec. + _______ sec. + _______ sec. = _______ sec.
(to first base) (to second base) (to third base)

2. Jenny hits a home run! How long does it take her to touch all the bases and reach home plate?

____ sec. + ____ sec. + ____ sec. = ____ sec. = ____ sec.
(to first base) (to second base) (to third base) (to home plate)

Some of the monster children went to the zoo on Sunday. They took pictures of their favorite animals.

- Millie took pictures of 4 elephants, 16 penguins and 11 wallabies.
- Milo took pictures of 18 wallabies, 9 monkeys and 3 tigers.
- Jed took pictures of 21 penguins, 7 giraffes and 4 monkeys.

Which monster took the most pictures? ____________________

Which monster took the fewest pictures? ____________________

How many different kinds of animals were

photographed? __________

Subtraction

Once there was a monster named Miles, who spent every day playing marbles. He kept his 20 favorite marbles in a beautiful marble bag. One day, he grabbed his marbles and went to play with his friends.

At Wilbur's house, he lost 10 marbles. How many marbles did he have left?

Fill in the blank and carry down the total to the next blank. **20 - 10 = ______**

At Rosie's house, he lost 2 more! Carry down the total to the next blank. ______ **- 2 =** ______

At Fuddy's house, he lost 3 more! ______ **- 3 =** ______

At Matilda's house, he lost 4 more! ______ **- 4 =** ______

What a sad day for Miles!

How many marbles did he have left? ______

Wilbur put the marbles he won from Miles into a bag. 5 of the marbles are white and 5 of them are black. Wilbur wants to give his brother Warren 2 of the marbles, but Warren wants the marbles to be the same color. If Wilbur reaches into his bag without looking, how many marbles will he have to pull out to make sure that he gets 2 of the same color?

The first marble Wilbur pulls out of the bag is black. Next, he pulls out a white marble. The third marble is sure to match one of the first 2.

Why?

____

Is it possible that Wilbur could pull out matching marbles in 2 tries? Why or why not? ______________________________

____

Probability

Jag has a penny. He is playing heads or tails. He would like you to play, too.

Find a penny around your house and flip it into the air. Let it land on a table. Look to see if it landed "heads up" or "tails up." Make a mark in the correct column on the tally chart. Do this 10 times. Does your tally chart look the same as Jag's? Keep flipping the penny and making marks.

How do you think your chart will look if you flip the penny 50 times? Why? Try it to see if your prediction is correct.

Jag's tally chart

heads	tails
𝍸	𝍷𝍷𝍷

your tally chart

heads	tails

Mit has 4 kinds of shoes and 3 kinds of socks. She has made this chart to help her see what the socks and shoes will look like together.

How many different sock-and-shoe combinations can

she make? _______

(**Hint:** It will help to draw each sock-and-shoe combination in the squares provided.)

Time

The **little hand** on a clock points to the **hour**. The **big hand** points to the **minutes**. When the big hand reaches 12, a new hour begins. Look at all the things Juan is doing today. Write the number that tells the time of each activity. The first one is done for you.

It is ___6___ o'clock.

It is ______ o'clock.

It is ______ o'clock.

It is ______ o'clock.

It is ______ o'clock.

It is ______ o'clock.

When the big hand is on the 6, it is on the **half hour**. A half hour is 30 minutes, or halfway between one hour and the next. You write it as **:30**. For example, 7:30 is halfway between 7 o'clock and 8 o'clock.

Alice is always half an hour late. Complete each clock to show what time she does each activity described below. Then, write the time on the lines below the clocks. The first one is done for you.

Alice's piano lesson is at 2 o'clock.
What time does she arrive?

2 : 30
(hour) (half hour)

Alice has a baseball game at 4 o'clock. What time does she arrive?

_____ : _____

Alice should go to bed at 9 o'clock.
What time does she go to bed?

_____ : _____

When something happens between 12:00 midnight and 12:00 noon, we say it is **A.M.**

When something happens between 12:00 noon and 12:00 midnight, it is **P.M.**

midnight noon

12:00 A.M.

noon midnight

12:00 P.M.

Billy says good-bye to his mom and dad at the airport. It is 9:00 A.M.

Billy flies away to see his grandma. It takes 4 hours.

What time is it when Billy sees his grandma? Fill in the clock hands.

 + 4 hours = 

9:00 A.M. + 4 hours = ______ ____.____.

Bobbie is going to visit his grandma, too. Show what time he completes each part of his trip by adding the correct number of hours to the times below. Write your answer on the lines. Then, draw that time on the clock. Include A.M. or P.M. in your answer. The first one is done for you.

Bobbie leaves his house at 7 o'clock in the morning. It takes 2 hours for his dad to drive him to the airport. What time does he arrive at the airport?

7:00 A.M. + ___2___ hours = 9:00 A.M.

Bobbie's plane leaves the airport at 10 o'clock in the morning. It arrives 4 hours later. What time does his plane land?

10:00 A.M. + ________ hours = ________

Then, Bobbie takes a bus at 3:00 in the afternoon. He arrives at his grandma's house 1 hour later. What time does he arrive?

3:00 P.M. + ________ hour = ________

Time

Millie and Maggie have decided to meet for dinner at the Disgusting Diner at 6:00.

If it takes Millie 20 minutes to paint her toenails and 2 minutes to walk to the diner, what time should she start getting ready?

____

If it takes Maggie 15 minutes to brush her fangs and 3 minutes to walk to the diner, what time should she start getting ready?

____

Maggie wants to go to Millie's house for a visit after dinner. How long will it take her to walk back to her home from Millie's house?

____

If she leaves at 8:20, what time will she arrive home?

____

Time

Ursula began to make 3 bracelets at 6 o'clock. It takes 15 minutes to make each bracelet. If Ursula does not take a break, at what time will she finish the 3 bracelets? Fill in the clock face below to show that time.

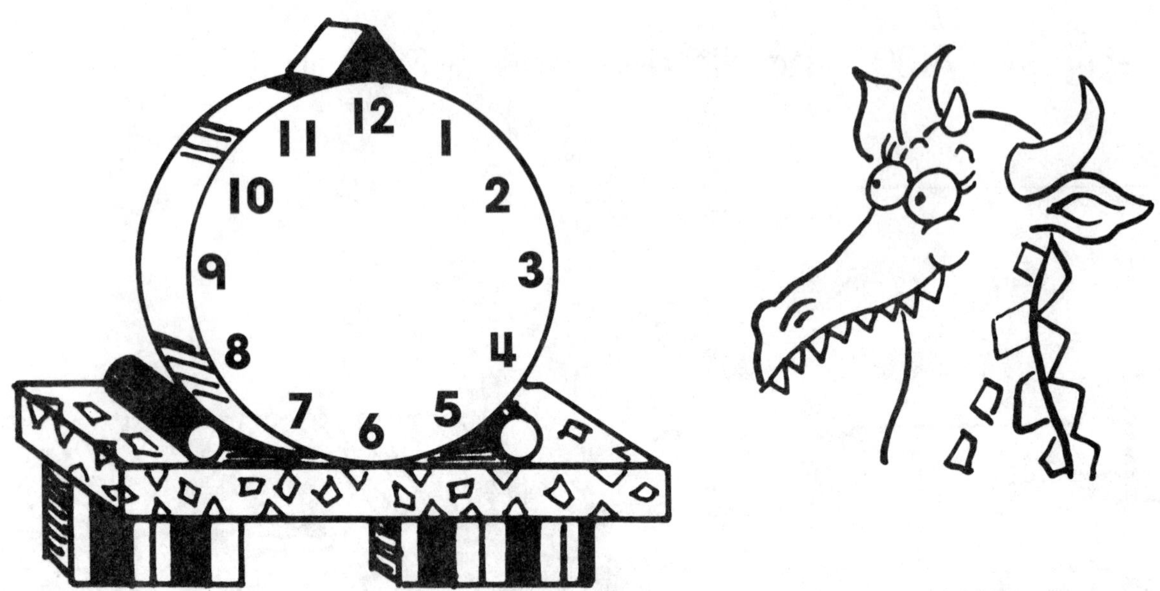

If Ursula takes a 5-minute break after completing each bracelet, at what time will she be finished with all 3? Fill in the clock face below to show that time.

Becky had a busy day. Look at her activities. What did she do first? What did she do second? What did she do third? Draw a line form the correct word to the picture.

first

second

third

Ordinal Numbers/Logic

Maggie, Fred and Gus went to a birthday party. They each brought flowers and a gift. Use the clues to find out the order in which they arrived at the party and what each one brought. Fill in the chart on page 251.

- Maggie did not arrive last.
- The monster who brought mugwort arrived first.
- The monster who brought dandelions arrived before the monster who brought some stinky cheese.
- Gus arrived after Fred.

Arrived	First	Second	Third
Maggie			
Fred			
Gus			
Gifts	Dandelions	Mugwort	Stinky Cheese
Maggie			
Fred			
Gus			

Ordinal Numbers

Nancy is learning her **ordinal numbers**. Help her by drawing the correct shapes in the boxes below. Follow the instructions above each box.

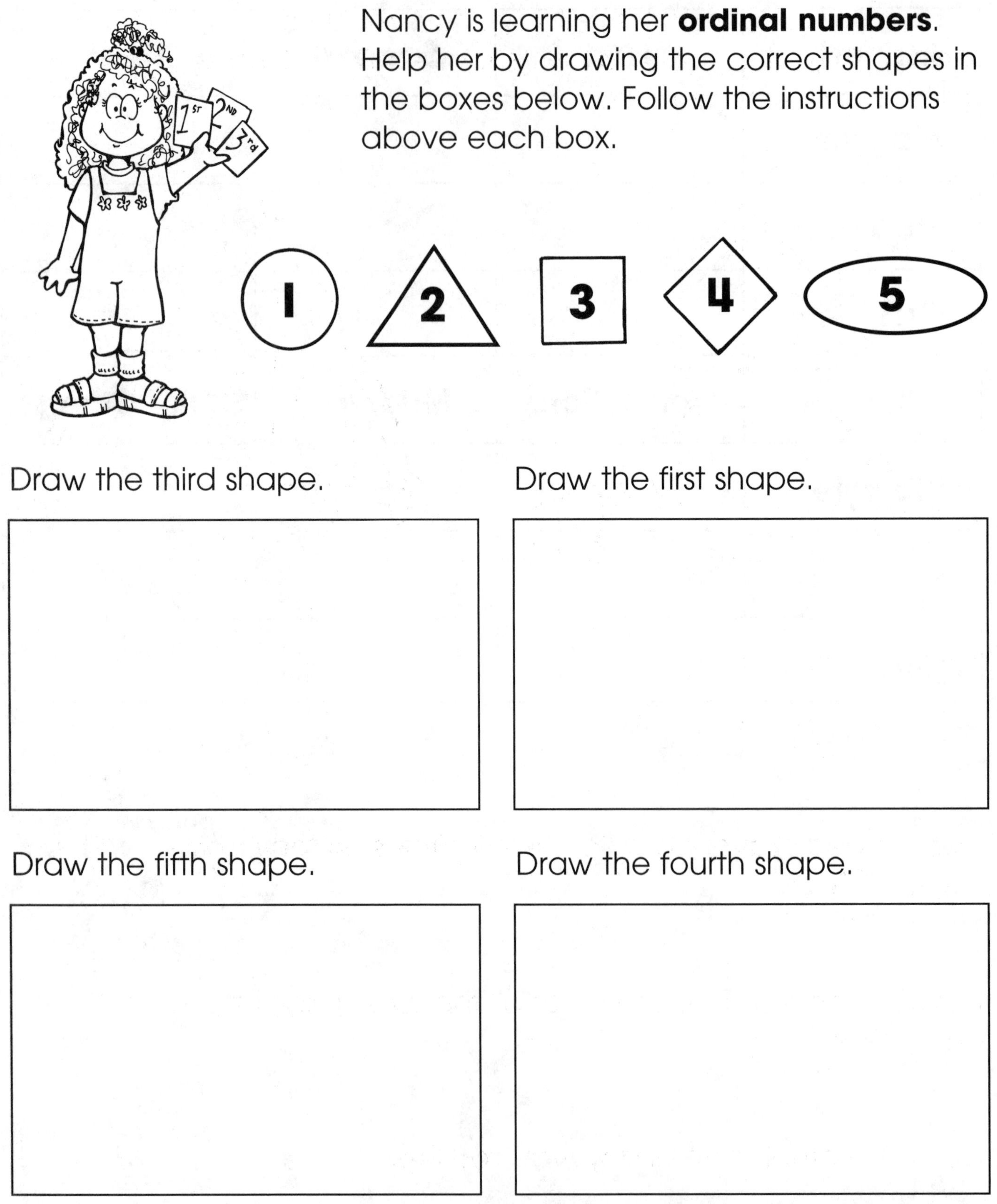

Draw the third shape.

Draw the first shape.

Draw the fifth shape.

Draw the fourth shape.

Robbie the robot and his pal Roger are made of many different-shaped objects. Look at all the shapes on their bodies. Then, follow the directions below.

Use a green crayon to color all the circles on their bodies. This is a circle: ◯ .

Use an orange crayon to color all the ovals on their bodies. This is an oval: ⬭ .

Color the other shapes any way you like.

Shapes

Some shapes have sides. How many sides does each shape below have? Write the number of sides inside each shape.

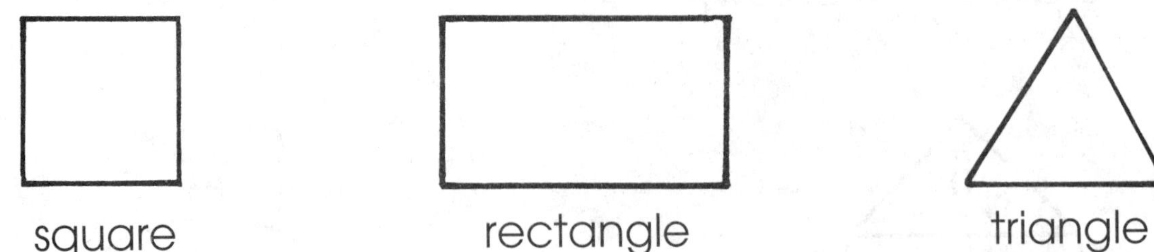

Help Robbie get to his space car by tracing the path that has only squares, rectangles and triangles.

Hint: You may want to draw an **X** on all the other shapes. This will help you see the path more clearly.

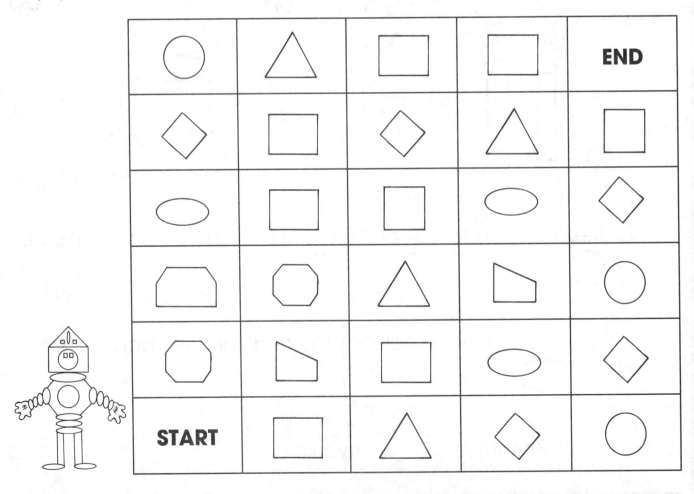

END

START

Look at the grid below. All the shapes have straight sides, like a square.

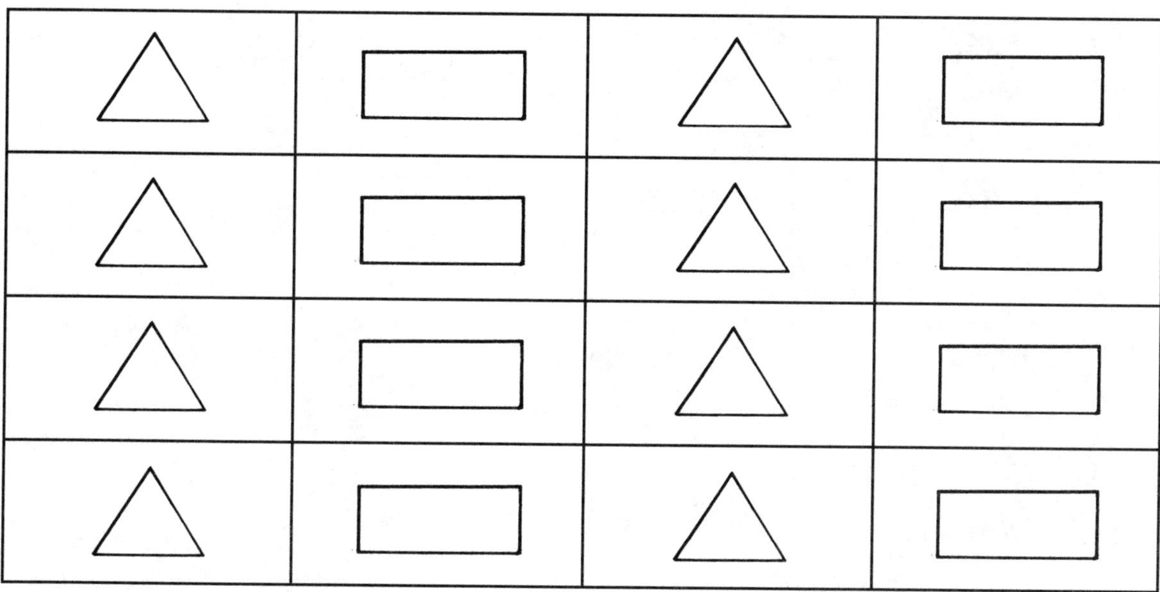

Now, make your own pattern grid. Use only shapes with straight sides like the grid above. The grid has been started for you.

□	△		

Shapes

Geometrus is a monster made of many different shapes. Look carefully to discover how many of each shape Geometrus has.

□ There are _______ squares.

△ There are _______ triangles.

▭ There are _______ rectangles.

⬠ There are _______ pentagons.

⯃ There are _______ octagons.

○ There are _______ circles.

⬭ There are _______ ovals.

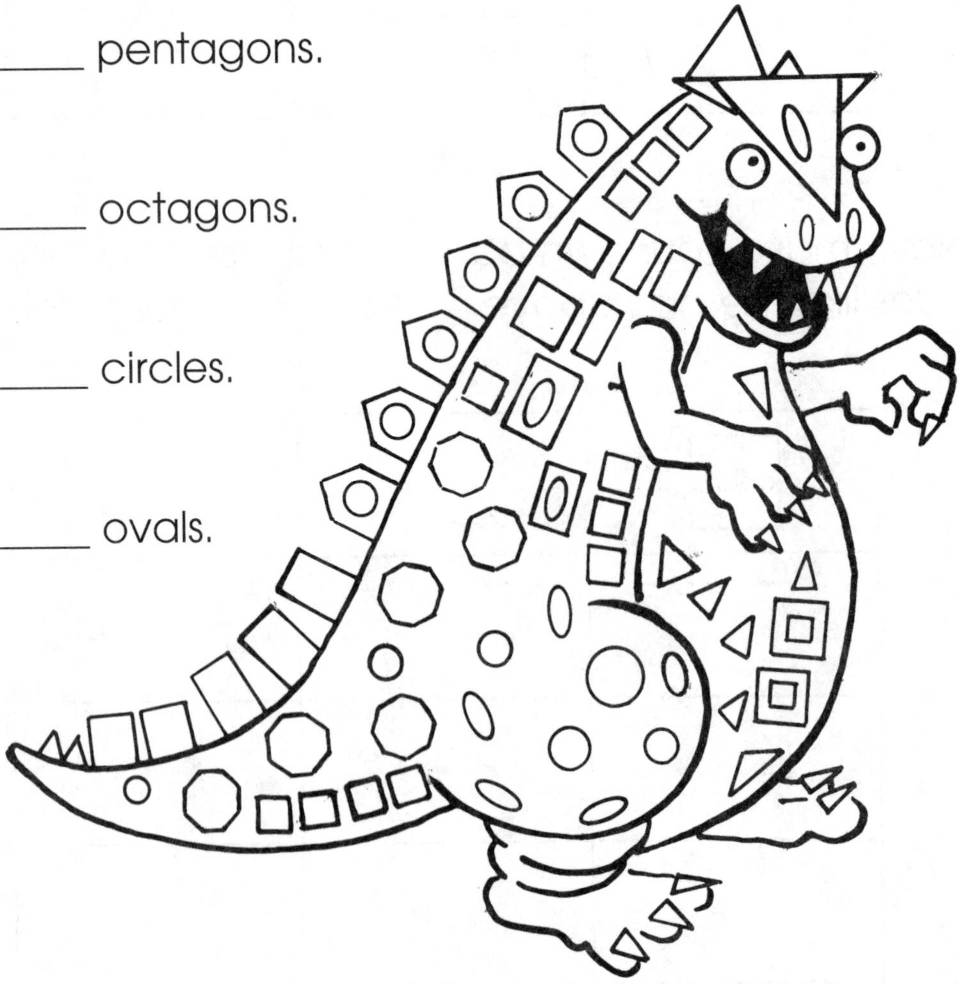

Mrs. Murky has asked each of the children to design a doghouse for a Monster Mutt. Can you help them? The house must contain at least 3 of the shapes you found on page 256. Draw your design in the space below.

Counting to 100

Mrs. Murky has asked the monster boys and girls to fill in the number chart on page 259 from 1 to 100. Then, use these clues to help the monsters find a secret number!

- The number is even.
- It is greater than 17.
- It is less than 80.
- When the number is separated into groups of 10, there are 2 left over.
- The numeral in the tens place is 1 greater than the numeral in the ones place.

1		3		5		7		9	
	12		14		16		18		20
21		23		25		27		29	
	32		34		36		38		40
41		43		45		47		49	
	52		54		56		58		60
61		63		65		67		69	
	72		74		76		78		80
81		83		85		87		89	
	92		94		96		98		100

Multiplication

The monster babies are having fun at their play group. They like to play with blocks the best. Look at all the tall towers they have built!

Use multiplication to find out how many blocks are in each monster's tall towers.

_______ x _______ = _______

number of towers | blocks in each tower | total number of blocks

_______ x _______ = _______

number of towers | blocks in each tower | total number of blocks

_______ x _______ = _______

number of towers | blocks in each tower | total number of blocks

Look at the monsters on this page. Use multiplication to find out how many fingers each monster has.

______ hands x ______ fingers = ______ total number of fingers

______ hands x ______ fingers = ______ total number of fingers

______ hands x ______ fingers = ______ total number of fingers

______ hands x ______ fingers = ______ total number of fingers

Multiplication

Ursula is busy making 3 bracelets for her friends. If she puts 3 beads on each bracelet, how many beads will she need?

________ x ________ = ________

number of bracelets | number of beads in each bracelet | total number of beads

If she puts 4 beads on each bracelet, how many beads will she need?

________ x ________ = ________

number of bracelets | number of beads in each bracelet | total number of beads

If she puts 5 beads on each bracelet, how many beads will she need?

________ x ________ = ________

number of bracelets | number of beads in each bracelet | total number of beads

If she puts 6 beads on each bracelet, how many beads will she need?

________	x	________	=	________
number of bracelets		number of beads in each bracelet		total number of beads

If she puts 7 beads on each bracelet, how many beads will she need?

________	x	________	=	________
number of bracelets		number of beads in each bracelet		total number of beads

If she puts 8 beads on each bracelet, how many beads will she need?

________	x	________	=	________
number of bracelets		number of beads in each bracelet		total number of beads

If she puts 9 beads on each bracelet, how many beads will she need?

________	x	________	=	________
number of bracelets		number of beads in each bracelet		total number of beads

Multiplication

Ursula's friends loved the bracelets she made. They want her to make them some necklaces to match. She has gone to the store to buy more beads. Help her choose the beads for the necklaces.

Ursula wants to put 4 beads on each necklace. How much will each necklace cost if she chooses:

- the 4¢ beads? ________
- the 5¢ beads? ________
- the 6¢ beads? ________
- the 7¢ beads? ________
- the 8¢ beads? ________
- the 9¢ beads? ________

Jag is counting his nickels. Help him find out how much money he has in each stack of nickels. Do the multiplication by following the examples below. Remember that each nickel is worth 5 cents!

1 x 5 = 5

2 x 5 = ______

______ x ______ = ______

______ x ______ = ______

______ x ______ = ______

______ x ______ = ______

______ x ______ = ______

______ x ______ = ______

______ x ______ = ______

Multiplication

The trolls came during the night. They left a secret number combination in the square rocks. Solve the math problems below to help the monsters unlock the door to Troll Mountain. (**Hint:** It will help you to count the boxes in each problem.)

4 x 2 = ______

4 x 3 = ______

3 x ______ **=** ______

4 x ______ **=** ______

Add up the 4 final answers to the problems the trolls left on the previous page to open the mountain door. If the total of the 4 answers is correct (the answer is upside down, below), the door will unlock. Write the answer on the combination lock below.

(The secret number combination is 42.)

Multiplication/Addition

Datto decided it was time to clean his closet. But, after he got to work, Datto found little monster bugs everywhere! Fill in the blanks below to help him find out how many bugs are in his closet.

Datto has 4 ties and on every tie there are 2 bugs. _______ bugs are on his ties.

Datto has 3 sweaters and on every sweater there is 1 bug.

_______ bugs are on his sweaters.

Datto has 2 hats and on every hat there are 5 bugs. _______ bugs are on his hats.

Datto has 6 shirts and on every shirt there are 2 bugs. _______ bugs are on his shirts.

How many monsters bugs did Datto find altogether in his

closet? _______

Rimsley is helping out at his mom's office. She has asked him to mail some letters.

Rimsley needs to buy 2 stamps for each envelope. If there are 9 envelopes, how many stamps will he need? _______

Each stamp costs 4 cents. How much will Rimsley have to spend on stamps to mail all the letters? _______

Multiplication

One Saturday, Cosmos went shopping in the city with his mother. He tried to count the windows in the tall buildings, but it made him dizzy. Explain to Cosmos how he could use multiplication to figure out how many windows there are on each building.

____

____

____

Read each problem. Then, write a number sentence and draw apples in the basket to show your answer.

If the farmer picks 1 apple off each tree, how many apples will he have?

__________ x __________ = __________

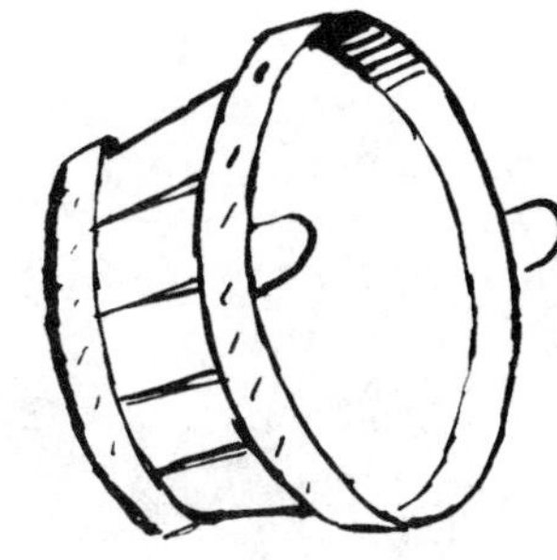

If the farmer picks 3 apples off each tree, how many apples will he have?

__________ x __________ = __________

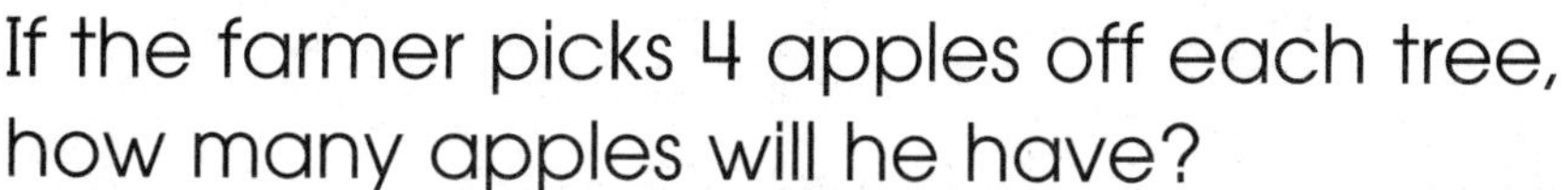

If the farmer picks 4 apples off each tree, how many apples will he have?

__________ x __________ = __________

Multiplication

The monsters are having a wonderful time at the farm! Everybody has a special job to do. Solve the problems below to find out how many monsters are needed for each job.

There are 4 cows to be milked. Each cow needs 3 monsters to milk it. How many monsters get to milk the cows?

__________ monsters are needed to milk the cows.

There are 7 horses on the farm. Each horse can carry 2 monsters at the same time. How many monsters can ride the horses at one time?

__________ monsters can ride at the same time.

This monster farmer is going to pick some apples off his trees. He has 3 trees. If he picks 2 apples off each tree, how many apples will he have in his basket?

Draw the apples in the basket. Below it, write a number sentence that explains your answer.

______	x	______	=	______
apples from each tree		trees		total apples

Division

10 monsters want to play on the monkey bars, but only 3 monsters are allowed on a bar at the same time.

Are there enough bars for all the monsters to play? __________

Explain your answer.

____

____

These 6 monsters are hungry! Their picnic lunch is ready! Look at the picture and count each of the food items. Then, divide the food equally to find out what each monster will eat. Write the answers on the lines.

_______ lollipops _______ cupcakes _______ apples

_______ carrots _______ drinks

Division

Mrs. Murky wants to give flowers to the 6 best spellers in her class. She wants to put at least 5 flowers in each bouquet.

Does she have enough flowers in her garden? __________

Could she put more flowers in each bouquet? Explain your answer.

____

____

The monsters are saving their money to go to the amusement park next week.

Look at the chart to see how much money they earn each day for each chore. Then, answer the questions below to find out how much money the monsters will have for the amusement park.

They swept floors on 3 different days.
How much did they earn? _______ cents

The monsters dusted on 4 different days.
How much did they earn? _______ cents

They mopped the floors on the same days they swept the floors. How much did they earn for mopping? _______ cents

They washed dishes on 6 different days.
How much did they earn? _______ cents

How much money did the monsters earn for the whole week? _______ cents

Chores	Money
(broom)	10¢
(duster)	20¢
(mop)	40¢
(dishes)	50¢

Multiplication

The monsters, with their money in their pockets, ran all the way to the amusement park. They want to buy tickets to go on the rides.

TICKETS
Ferris wheel 20¢
Merry-go-round 10¢
Pony ride 50¢
Bumper car 15¢

Look on page 277 to find out how much they earned: _______ cents

How much money would they spend on each ride if all 3 monsters go on every ride once?

Fill in the blanks below.

Ferris wheel tickets _______ cents

Merry-go-round tickets _______ cents

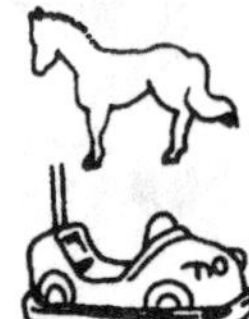

Pony ride tickets _______ cents

Bumper car tickets _______ cents

On Saturday, the Slimepit Elementary School basketball team played against the team from Grubwater Street School. Use the information found in this chart to answer the questions below.

	Slimepit attempted	Made	Grubwater attempted	Made
1-point shots (free throws)	12	8	10	6
2-point shots	28	17	33	18
3-point shots	7	4	4	3

Which team won the game? ______________________________

By how many points? __________

If both teams had made every free throw, which team would

have won? ______________________________

By how many points? __________

Fractions

The monsters are getting in shape Look below and on page 281 to see the different ways they are working out. Then, answer the questions on page 281.

Answer the questions and fill in the blanks below. The first one is done for you.

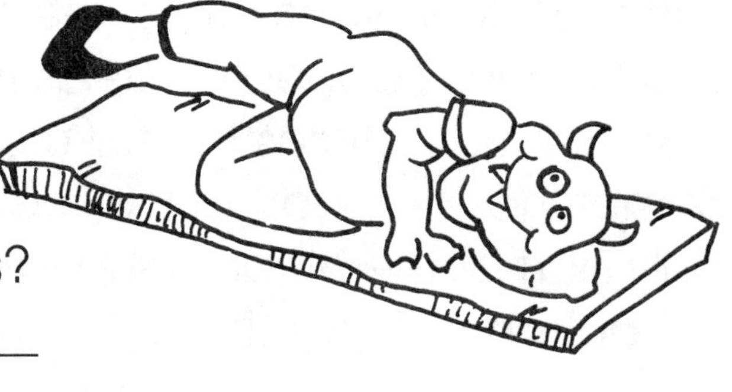

How many monsters touch their toes?

1 out of 10 monsters, or $\frac{1}{10}$ of the monsters.

How many monsters hang upside down?

_______ out of 10 monsters, or $\frac{\_\_\_}{10}$ of the monsters.

How many monsters run on the treadmill?

_______ out of 10 monsters, or $\frac{\_\_\_}{10}$ of the monsters.

How many monsters lift weights?

_______ out of 10 monsters, or $\frac{\_\_\_}{10}$ of the monsters.

How many monsters do leg lifts?

_______ out of 10 monsters, or $\frac{\_\_\_}{10}$ of the monsters.

Fractions

The monsters are studying the Moon. It changes its appearance as the month goes by. Sometimes the full moon is seen. Sometimes only part of it is seen. When only part of the Moon is showing, it is a **fraction** of its full size.

Help the monsters learn fractions by filling in the blanks below.

Pretend the Moon is divided into 2 equal parts.

$\frac{2}{2}$  The Moon is full. The monsters see both of its 2 parts.

$\frac{1}{2}$  This is a half moon. The monsters see only ______ of its 2 parts.

What if you divided the Moon into 4 equal parts?

$\frac{4}{4}$  The Moon is full. The monsters can see all 4 of its ______ parts.

$\frac{3}{4}$  The Moon is almost full. The monsters can see ______ of the 4 parts.

$\frac{\_\_\_}{4}$  The Moon is half full. The monsters can see ______ of the 4 parts.

$\frac{\_\_\_}{4}$  The Moon is almost gone. Only ______ part is left.

The monsters are on their way to the farthest part of the galaxy. Answer the questions below.

How many objects do they see out the window? ________

How many rockets do they see? ________

How many comets do they see? ________

How many planets to they see? ________

How many stars do they see? ________

Look at the picture above. Then, fill in the blanks below.

$\frac{\_\_\_}{4}$ of the objects are rockets.

$\frac{\_\_\_}{4}$ of the objects are comets.

$\frac{\_\_\_}{4}$ of the objects are planets.

$\frac{\_\_\_}{4}$ of the objects are stars.

Fractions

One day, the monsters went to the pizza stand for a snack.

- Mug ate $\frac{1}{2}$ of a pizza.
- Lug ate $\frac{2}{4}$ of a pizza.
- Gug ate $\frac{3}{6}$ of a pizza.

Color the portion of pizza that each monster ate.

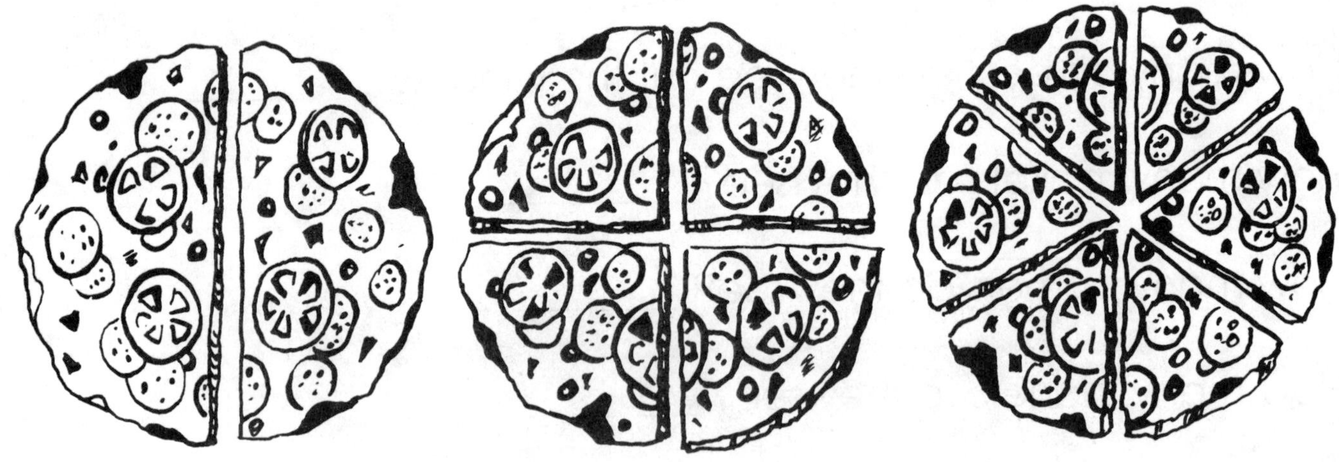

Which monster ate the most pizza?

Explain your answer.

____

____

____

____

One morning, Mrs. Murky asks her class:

"Which would you rather have, $\frac{1}{2}$ of a candy bar or $\frac{2}{4}$ of a candy bar?"

Which would you rather have? Explain your answer.

____

____

____

Fractions

Help the monsters use the candy bars below to answer the questions on page 287.

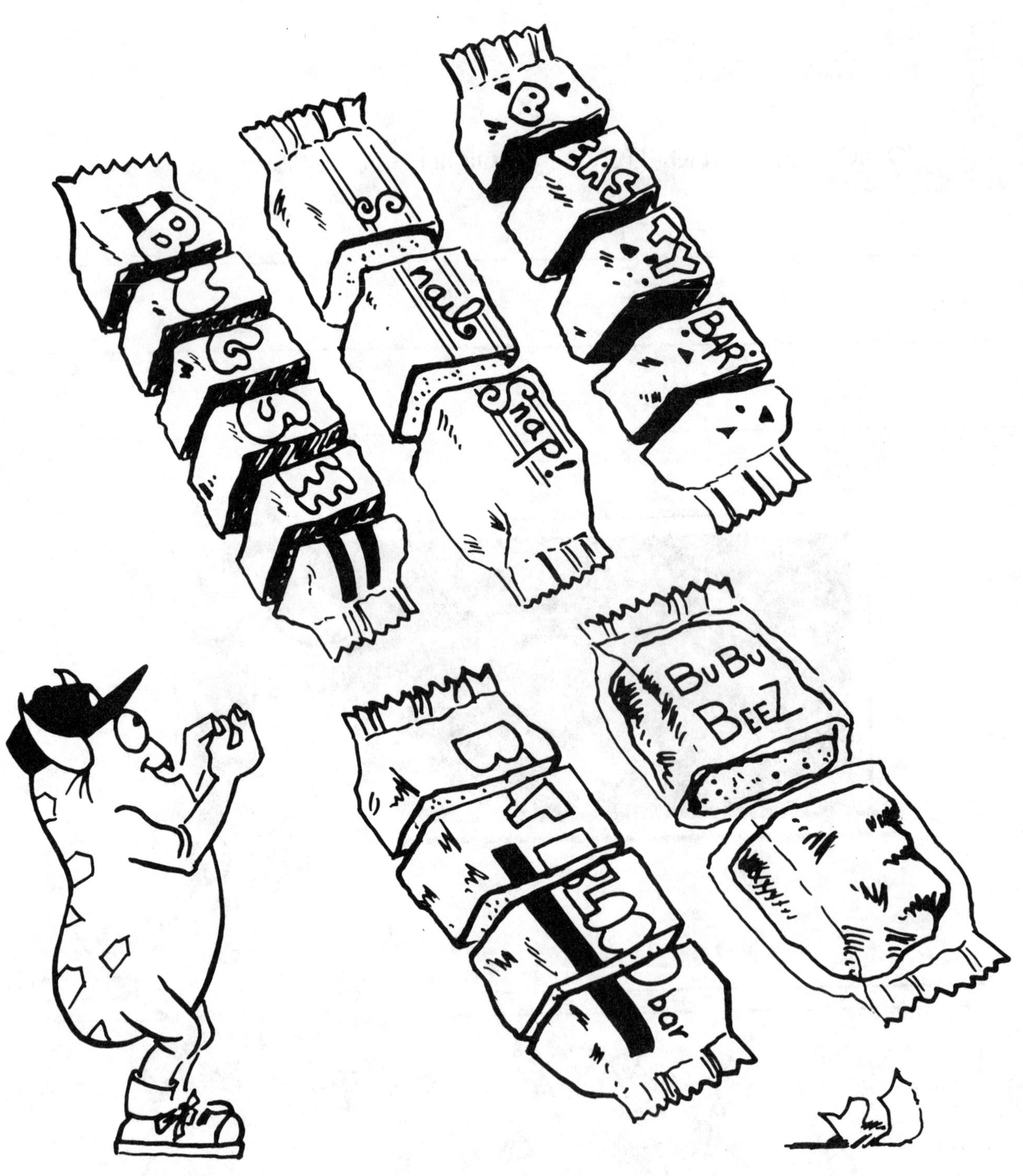

Which is more, $\frac{2}{3}$ or $\frac{3}{4}$? ________

Which is more, $\frac{2}{4}$ or $\frac{3}{6}$? ________

Which is more, $\frac{1}{2}$ or $\frac{3}{5}$? ________

Which is more, $\frac{2}{6}$ or $\frac{1}{3}$? ________

Which is more, $\frac{3}{4}$ or $\frac{4}{5}$? ________

Which is more, $\frac{4}{6}$ or $\frac{2}{3}$? ________

Fractions

Suji and Samantha had Millie and Milo over to play after school. Their mother gave them a plate of cookies to share. If they divide the cookies equally, how many cookies will there be for each monster? Draw the cookies on the plates to show how many each monster gets.

Rodney, Jed and Ursula had a pizza party. They ordered 1 large fish-eye pizza and 1 large toadstool pizza. Draw lines through the pizzas to divide them equally into slices. Color the pizza slices in 3 colors, 1 for each monster, to show how many slices each monster gets.

How many slices will each monster get? ____________________

Mrs. Murky shows the students a map of the Slimepit Elementary School play yard. Each box shows 1 square meter. Two half-boxes show 1 square meter.

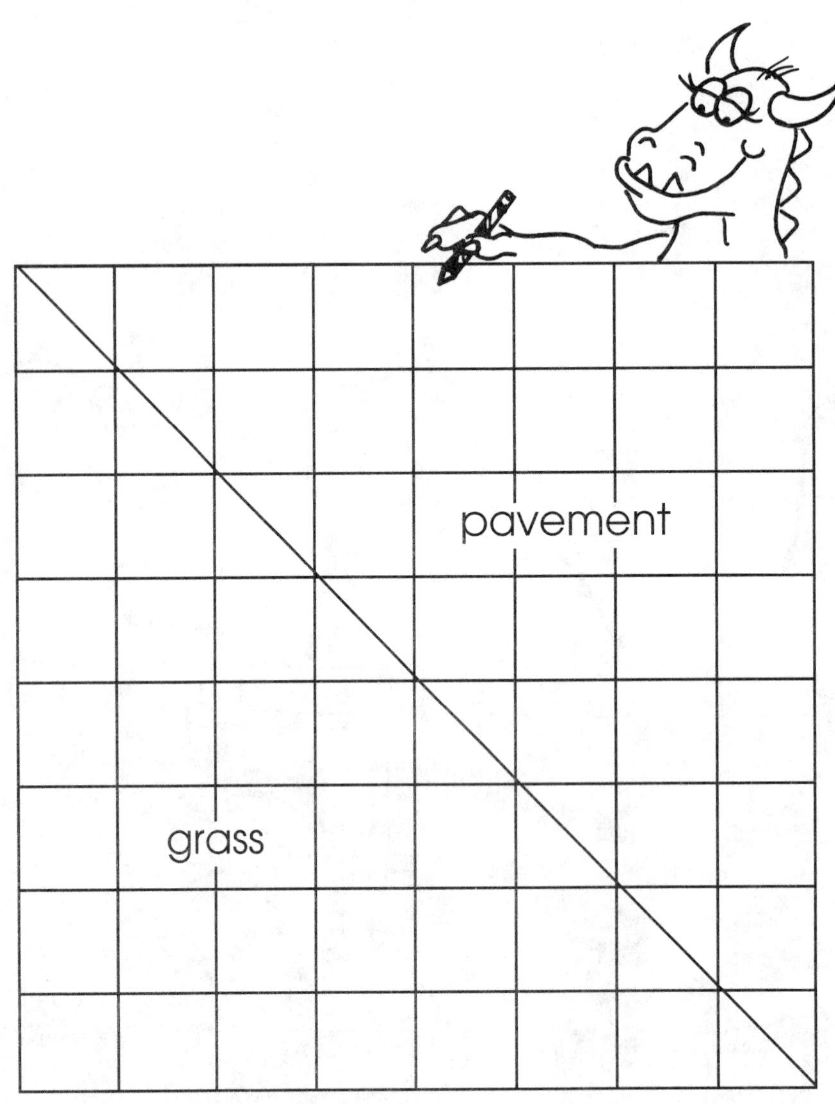

She asks them these questions:

How many square meters of the play yard are pavement? _______

How many square meters of the play yard are grass? _______

MATH GAMES AND PUZZLES

Addition

John and Emily are playing tic-tac-toe. John is **O** and Emily is **X**. Follow the instructions below to find out who wins the game. The winner is the player who gets 3 **X**'s or 3 **O**'s in any row—down (↓), across (⟶) or diagonally (↗↘).

- John puts an **O** on the sum of 5 + 2.
- Emily puts an **X** on the sum of 3 + 2.
- John puts an **O** on the sum of 1 + 0.
- Emily puts an **X** on the sum of 2 + 2.
- John puts an **O** on the sum of 2 + 1.
- Emily puts an **X** on the sum of 1 + 1.
- John puts an **O** on the sum of 2 + 4.
- Emily puts an **X** on the sum of 4 + 4.
- John puts an **O** on the sum of 7 + 2.

3	8	7
2	9	5
1	6	4

Who won the game? ______________________________

Spike the dog and Mookie the cat are playing tic-tac-toe. Spike is **O**. Mookie is **X**. Find out who wins the game by following the directions below.

- Spike puts an **O** on the sum of 10 + 2.
- Mookie puts an **X** on the sum of 13 + 4.
- Spike puts an **O** on the sum of 10 + 10.
- Mookie puts an **X** on the sum of 5 + 8.
- Spike puts an **O** on the sum of 9 + 6.
- Mookie puts an **X** on the sum of 13 + 5.
- Spike puts an **O** on the sum of 9 + 10.
- Mookie puts an **X** on the sum of 8 + 2.
- Spike puts an **O** on the sum of 3 + 11.

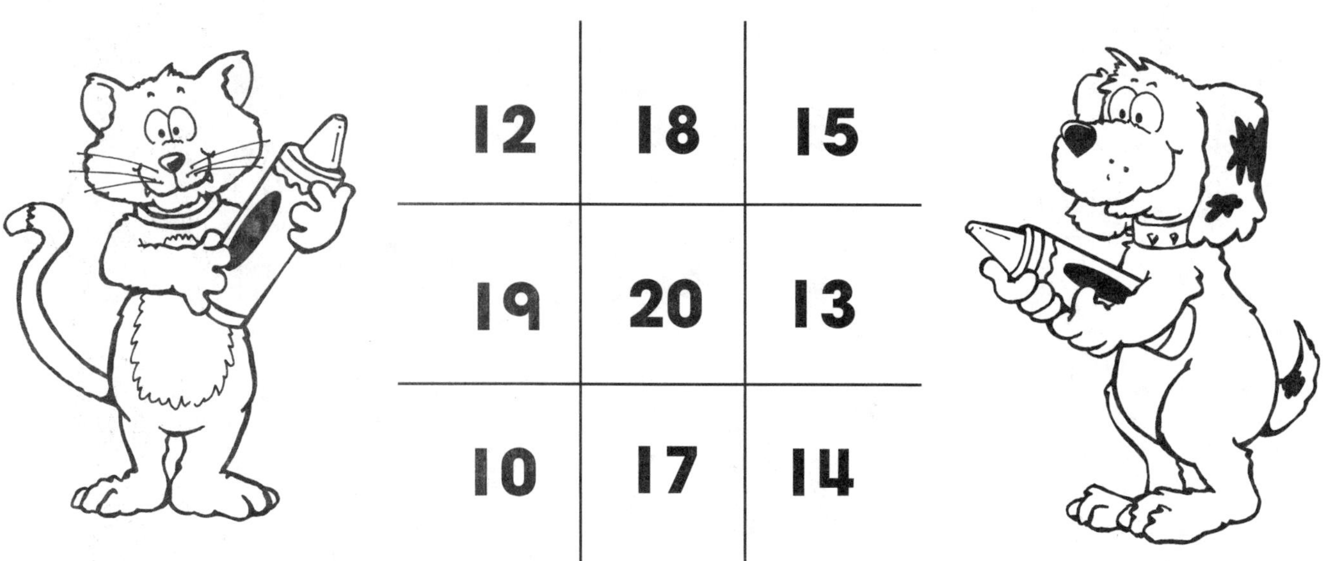

Who won the game? ______________________________

Multiplication

Bugsy and Bonnie are playing tic-tac-toe. Bugsy is **X** and Bonnie is **O**. Solve these problems to see who wins! Remember that a product is the answer to a multiplication problem.

- Put an **X** on the product of 3 x 2.
- Put an **O** on the product of 4 x 3.
- Put an **X** on the product of 5 x 1.
- Put an **O** on the product of 2 x 4.
- Put an **X** on the product of 5 x 3.
- Put an **O** on the product of 5 x 4.
- Put an **X** on the product of 3 x 3.
- Put an **O** on the product of 4 x 4.

Who won the game? ______________________________

Multiplication

Veronica and Jed are playing tic-tac-toe. Veronica is **X** and Jed is **O**. Solve these problems to see who wins! Remember that a product is the answer to a multiplication problem.

- Put an **X** on the product of 6 x 3.
- Put an **O** on the product of 6 x 4.
- Put an **X** on the product of 6 x 5.
- Put an **O** on the product of 6 x 6.
- Put an **X** on the product of 6 x 7.
- Put an **O** on the product of 6 x 8.
- Put an **X** on the product of 6 x 9.
- Put an **O** on the product of 6 x 2.

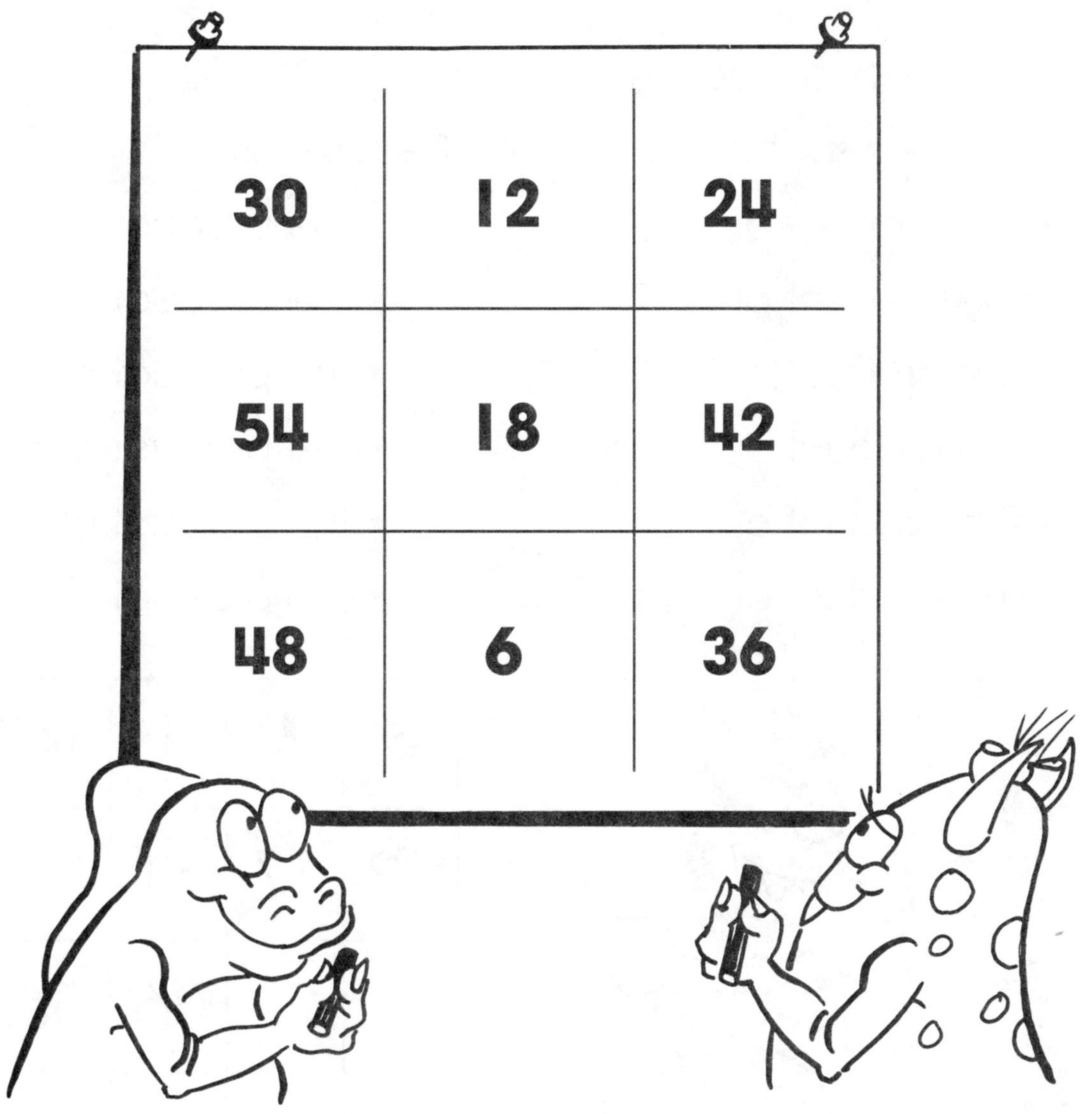

Who won the game? ______________________________

Multiplication

Rimsley and Maggie are playing SLIMO. Mark an **X** on each spot that is called to see who will get "SLIMO" first! The winner must get 5 **X**'s across a row.

Mark an **X** on these spaces:

- the **free** spot in the middle of each card
- the product of 7 x 4
- the product of 7 x 7
- the product of 8 x 9
- the product of 5 x 3
- the product of 7 x 5
- the product of 8 x 1
- the product of 8 x 7
- the product of 8 x 8
- the product of 8 x 4
- the product of 6 x 7
- the product of 9 x 4
- the product of 7 x 3

S	L	I	M	O
12	17	31	44	72
4	22	36	56	67
14	19	FREE	47	64
8	28	42	45	75
5	23	34	42	63

S	L	I	M	O
7	18	35	48	66
15	21	32	49	72
13	24	FREE	45	70
11	20	33	56	63
6	25	41	60	68

Who won the game? ______________________________

Multiplication

Samantha and Rodney are playing tic-tac-toe. Rodney is **X** and Samantha is **O**. Solve these problems to see who wins! Remember that a **product** is the answer to a multiplication problem.

- Put an **X** on the product of 9 x 2.
- Put an **O** on the product of 9 x 3.
- Put an **X** on the product of 9 x 4.
- Put an **O** on the product of 9 x 5.
- Put an **X** on the product of 9 x 6.
- Put an **O** on the product of 9 x 7.
- Put an **X** on the product of 9 x 8.
- Put an **O** on the product of 9 x 9.

Who won the game? ______________________________

Addition and Subtraction

Mark wants to play tic-tac-toe with you. Write the answers to all the equations. Then, color the three boxes in each game that have the same answers. One math problem has been done for you.

5 - 2 3	9 + 11	14 - 4
12 - 5	20 - 17	8 + 4
3 + 12	8 - 4	1 + 2

9 - 4	2 + 6	10 + 5
20 - 6	15 - 9	9 + 8
16 - 4	7 + 5	20 - 8

What is the message on the billboard? Complete the addition and subtraction equations below to find out. Write the letter under each equation on the line (or lines) on the billboard that matches the answer to that math problem.

$5 + 2 =$ ______
S

$11 + 9 =$ ______
A

$16 -$ ______ $= 11$
H

$10 -$ ______ $= 1$
T

$16 - 2 =$ ______
E

$2 +$ ______ $= 6$
Y

$11 - 1 =$ ______
M

$7 -$ ______ $= 4$
I

The monsters love to break secret codes. They also love movies! In fact, they think they know everything about every movie ever made. But they're not as smart as they think!

They have to discover the name of a famous movie song, and you can help them by breaking the secret code below. In the code, every letter stands for a number. Solve the problems on the next page to find out which letter goes in each blank. If all your answers are correct, you'll soon discover the mystery song title!

SECRET CODE KEY
A-5
B-8
C-2
D-0
E-6
F-10
G-12
H-7
I-9
J-1
K-3
L-11
M-4
N-20
O-25
P-28
Q-30
R-70
S-22
T-40
U-75
V-80
W-50
X-100
Y-90
Z-60
POPCORN

Here are 24 problems. Solve each of them and write down the sums. Then, find the letter in the secret code key that corresponds to each sum. The first one is done for you.

1. 5 + 5 + 5 − 5 =	10	F		13. 20 + 20 + 10 =	_____	_____
2. 6 + 6 − 4 =	_____	_____		14. 18 − 6 − 6 =	_____	_____
3. 3 + 2 + 10 − 4 =	_____	_____		15. 70 + 30 − 50 =	_____	_____
4. 70 − 30 =	_____	_____		16. 10 + 5 + 10 =	_____	_____
5. 20 + 30 − 41 =	_____	_____		17. 20 + 20 + 30 =	_____	_____
6. 3 + 2 + 6 =	_____	_____		18. 20 + 10 − 5 =	_____	_____
7. 3 + 3 + 6 − 1 =	_____	_____		19. 18 + 4 − 20 =	_____	_____
8. 15 + 15 + 40 =	_____	_____		20. 6 + 5 + 10 − 10 =	_____	_____
9. 10 + 5 + 10 =	_____	_____		21. 12 + 8 − 10 − 3 =	_____	_____
10. 11 − 6 =	_____	_____		22. 10 + 10 + 5 =	_____	_____
11. 70 − 60 − 4 =	_____	_____		23. 40 + 50 =	_____	_____
12. 20 + 4 − 21 =	_____	_____		24. 16 + 4 + 50 − 70 =	_____	_____

Write a letter in each blank below. There is one blank for each of the 24 problems. The first one is done for you.

___ ___ ___ ___ ___ ___   ___ ___ ___
1   16   3   7   18   13   4   21   14

___ ___ ___ ___ ___ ___
23   11   20   6   9   15

___ ___ ___ ___ ___   ___ ___ ___ ___
2   17   5   19   12   8   22   10   24

Ordinal Numbers

Follow the directions below to discover the mystery word. The puzzle begins on the left with the letter **A**.

- Cross out the ninth letter.
- Cross out the tenth letter.
- Cross out the fifth letter.
- Cross out the second letter.
- Cross out the seventh letter.
- Cross out the sixth letter.

A S H T O D Y M C R

Write the four letters that are left over:

_____ _____ _____ _____

Unscramble the four letters to spell the mystery word:

_____ _____ _____ _____

Two frogs are racing to the pond. Color one frog green. Color the other frog orange. The race begins behind rock #1. The green frog jumps over 1 rock at a time. The orange frog jumps over 2 rocks at a time. Draw a green **X** on each rock the green frog lands on. Draw an orange **X** on each rock the orange frog lands on.

Which frog reaches the pond first? ______________________

Even and Odd Numbers

Numbers that are not even are called **odd numbers**. **Odd numbers** cannot be divided into two groups that are exactly the same. Use a blue crayon to color the boxes that contain an **odd number**.

Hint: Use pennies or other small objects to help you count the odd numbers.

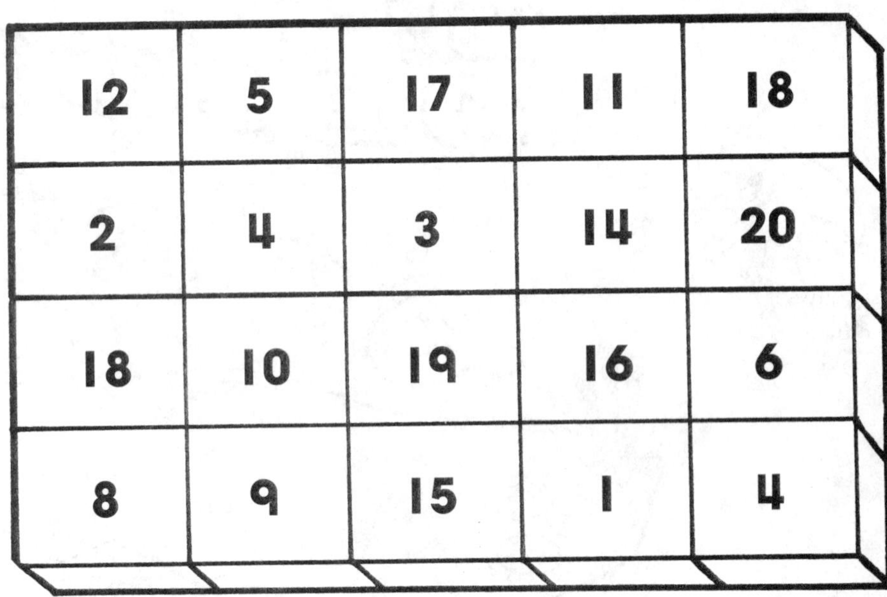

12	5	17	11	18
2	4	3	14	20
18	10	19	16	6
8	9	15	1	4

What letter did all the blue boxes form? __________

For an extra challenge, circle all the numbers that are odd.

1	2	3	4	5	6	7	8	9	10
11	12	13	14	15	16	17	18	19	20

Rosie is trying to open the safe. But she doesn't know the numbers that will open the lock. You can help her.

Fill in the answers to the mystery math problems. Then, draw an **X** in the **Even** column if the answer is even or in the **Odd** column if it's odd.

Number	Even	Odd
7 + 3 + 4 = ______		
8 − 5 + 3 = ______		
2 + 2 + 3 = ______		
9 − 3 + 2 = ______		
6 + 2 − 2 = ______		

If there are more than 2 odd numbers and fewer than 4 even numbers, then frogs are in the safe.

If there are more than 3 even numbers and fewer than 2 odd numbers, then gold is in the safe.

Circle the treasure Rosie found in the safe.

Addition

Play a game of tic-tac-toe with a friend. You and your friend should each use different-colored crayons. Instead of **X**'s and **O**'s, take turns writing numbers on the squares. The winner is the player who can make three numbers in any row add up to 20. Rows can go down (↓), across (⟶) or diagonally (↗↘). Numbers can be used more than once in a game.

Help the monster complete the problems in the grid below. Color them according to the chart.

If the answer is 3, color the space blue.
If the answer is 4, color the space green.
If the answer is 5, color the space purple.

19 - 8 4 + 9 19 - 3 15 - 12	13 - 5 16 + 1 5 + 2 8 - 5	4 + 4 10 + 6 11 - 2 16 - 3	9 + 2 10 - 10 7 + 7 12 + 1	11 - 5 6 + 6 12 + 2 13 - 10	9 + 1 8 + 8 5 + 5 11 - 8
3 + 1	9 - 5	12 + 9	14 + 3	23 - 19	20 - 16
2 + 2	8 - 4 11 - 6 13 - 9 1 + 3	16 - 12	25 - 21	3 + 2 7 - 3 12 - 8 17 - 13	15 - 11
5 - 1	6 - 2	19 - 15 13 - 8	16 - 11 14 - 10	18 - 14	14 - 10

Addition/Subtraction

Begin at the sign that says START. Move from a number to a plus or minus sign, then to another number as shown. You can only move to a square that touches the square you are in. Find a path that leads to the answer, which is marked EXIT.

One Monster Maze has been done for you. Help the monsters solve the other one!

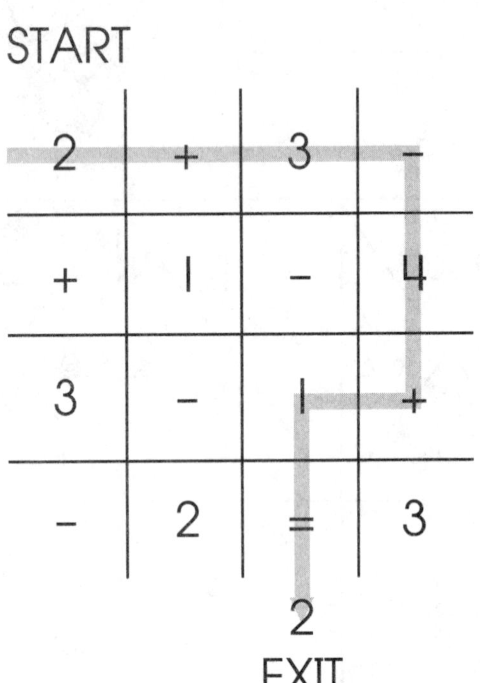

START

4	–	2	+
–	1	+	3
4	+	2	–
3	–	=	1

4
EXIT

Begin at the sign that says START. Find a path that leads to the answer.

START

6	+	6	–
+	1	–	3
2	–	4	+
–	5	=	1

5
EXIT

START

8	–	4	+
–	3	+	2
5	+	1	–
–	7	=	4

6
EXIT

Addition/Subtraction

Vinnie and Vivian lost their house keys. They know they left the keys at a place they visited today. They've been to the Monster Cafe, the Witch's House, the Elf Cave and the Troll Tree House. Use the clues in the box below and the map on the next page to help them get to the place where they left their keys.

1. Go to the number that is less than 20 and made with two 1's.
2. Then, subtract 4 from that number, and add 7.
3. Next, add 2 six times to that number.
4. Then, go to the number that is a reversal of the number you are on.
5. Now, subtract 10 six times from that number.
6. Next, add 7 to that number, and subtract 8.
7. After that, add 20 to that number.
8. Then, subtract 6 three times from that number.
9. Finally, add 7 to that number, then add a 0 to the end.

Put a marker in the START square. Solve each problem in the clue box, and move your marker to the number box that matches each answer. You may go in any direction.

If you answer all the clues correctly, you will land on the place where Vinnie and Vivian left their keys.

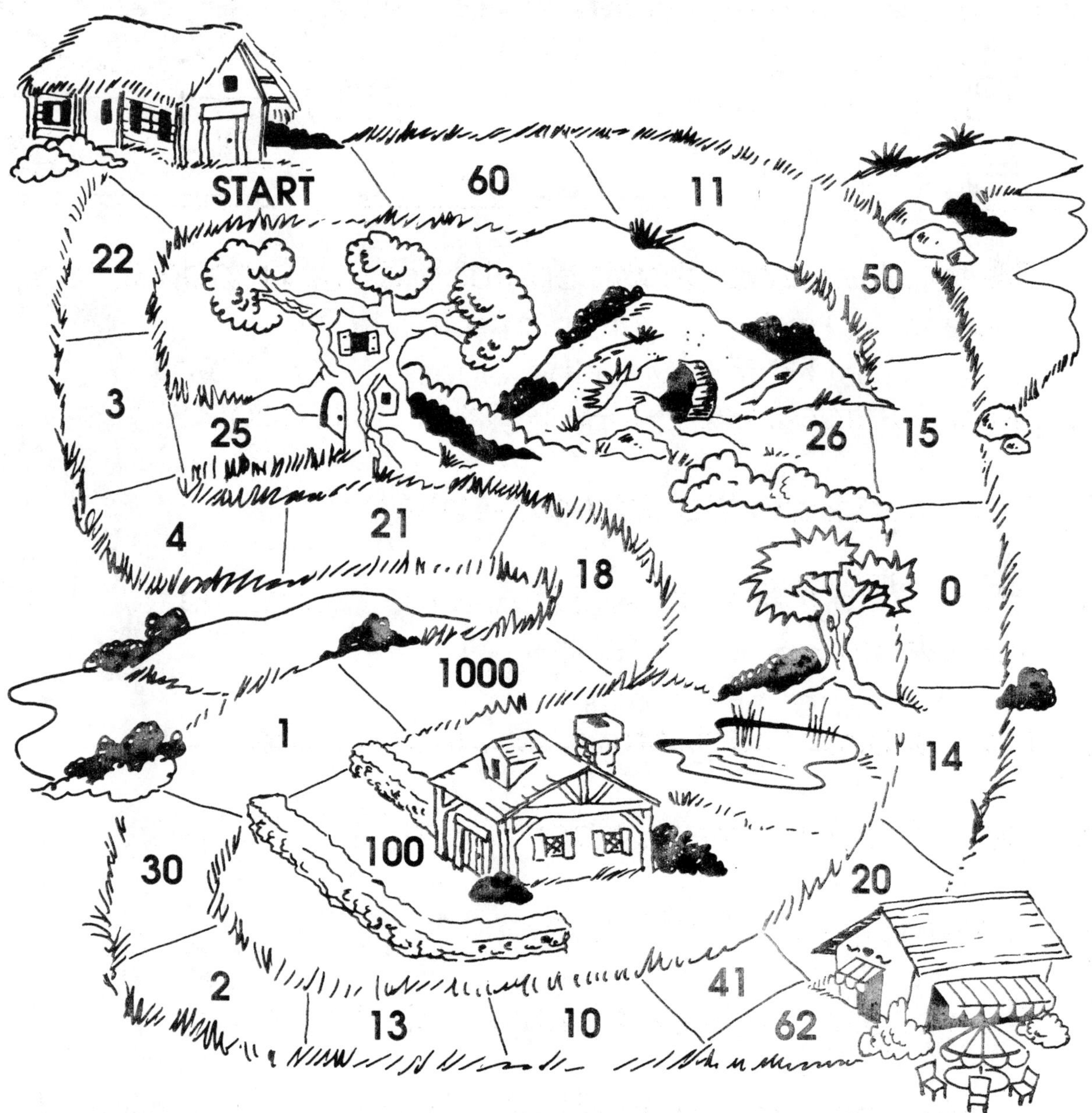

Where did the monsters leave their keys? ______________________________

Size /Even/Odd

Look at the two trains below. They are named Casey and Clank.

CLANK

Which train is shorter? ______________________________

Which train is longer? ______________________________

Cory the conductor needs to construct a brand-new train. He is going to name this train Chuck. Help Cory by following the clues below and drawing his new train in the box.

- Chuck is longer than Casey.
- Chuck is shorter than Clank.
- Chuck has an engine pulling an even number of rail cars.

When you compare the **height** of objects, you tell how **tall** or how **short** they are. Look at Timmy's action figures. Then, circle the answers to the questions.

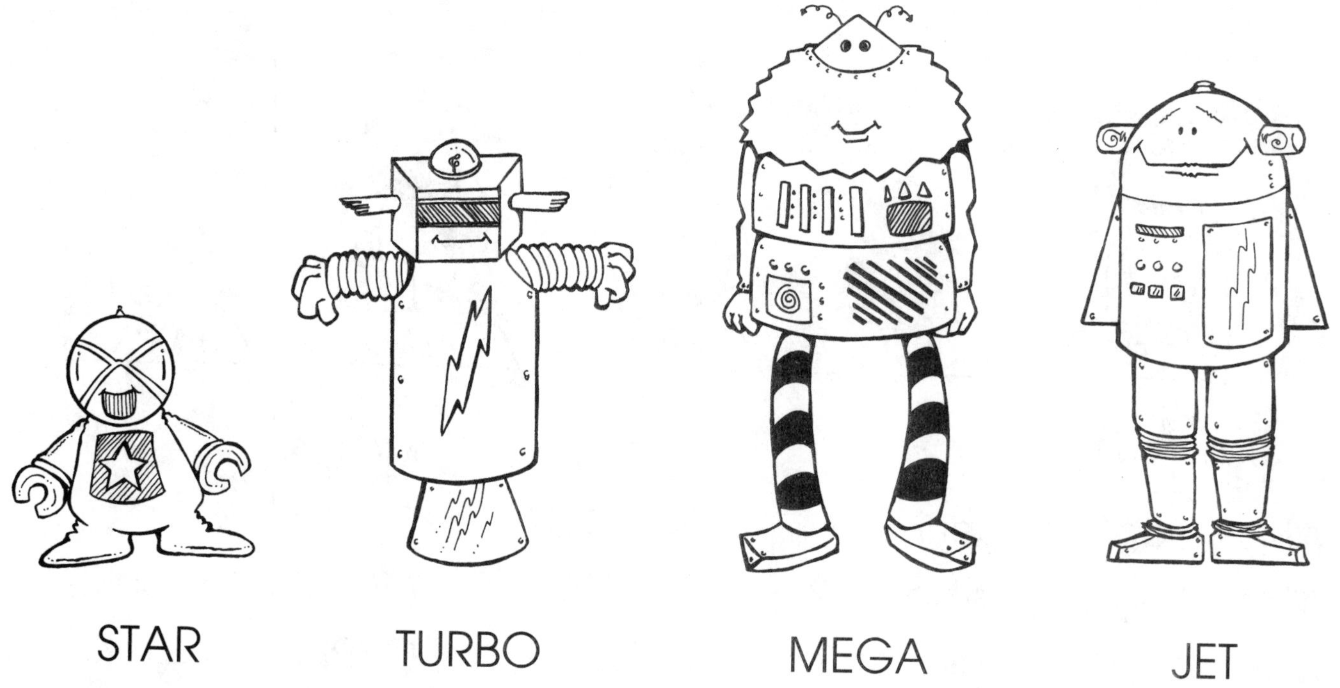

Which toy is shorter? STAR MEGA

Which toy is taller? TURBO JET

Which action figure is Timmy's newest one? Use these clues to find out.

- It is not the tallest or the shortest action figure.
- It is the action figure that is the taller of the remaining two toys.

Write its name: ________________________________

Size/Logic

Look at all the dogs who entered the dog show. Some dogs are big. Some dogs are small. Compare the sizes of the dogs. Then, circle the correct answers below. When you **compare** things, you look at how they are the same or different.

Which dog is smaller?	FRITZ	MONA	
Which dog is bigger?	FIDO	CURLY	
Which dog is the smallest?	FRITZ	MONA	CURLY
Which dog is the biggest?	FIDO	CURLY	DUKE
Which dogs are the same size?	DUKE	FRITZ	FIDO

Now, use these clues to find out which dog won first prize in the dog show.

Hint: Put an **X** on each dog that did not win.

- The winner is not the biggest dog.
- Neither of the two dogs that are the same size is the winner.
- The winner is not the smallest dog.

The first prizewinner is: ______________________

Karen lives in an apartment building that has 10 floors. Find out which floor Karen lives on by following the clues below.

Hint: Put an **X** on each floor that she does not live on.

- Karen does not live on the bottom floor.
- She does not live on the top floor.
- She lives somewhere between the 2nd floor and the 8th floor.
- She does not live on the 4th floor.
- She does not live on the floor above the 4th floor.
- She does not live on the 7th floor.
- There are two floors left. Karen lives on the floor with the higher number.

Karen lives on the ________ floor. (Write the ordinal number as a numeral.)